ISBN 978-0-266-03119-2
PIBN 10958193

1 MONTH OF
FREE
READING

at
www.ForgottenBooks.com

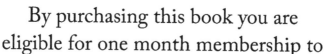

By purchasing this book you are
eligible for one month membership to
ForgottenBooks.com, giving you
unlimited access to our entire
collection of over 1,000,000 titles via
our web site and mobile apps.

To claim your free month visit:
www.forgottenbooks.com/free958193

English
Français
Deutsche
Italiano
Español
Português

www.forgottenbooks.com

Mythology Photography **Fiction**
Fishing Christianity **Art** Cooking
Essays Buddhism Freemasonry
Medicine **Biology** Music **Ancient**
Egypt Evolution Carpentry Physics
Dance Geology **Mathematics** Fitness
Shakespeare **Folklore** Yoga Marketing
Confidence Immortality Biographies
Poetry **Psychology** Witchcraft
Electronics Chemistry History **Law**
Accounting **Philosophy** Anthropology
Alchemy Drama Quantum Mechanics
Atheism Sexual Health **Ancient History**
Entrepreneurship Languages Sport
Paleontology Needlework Islam
Metaphysics Investment Archaeology
Parenting Statistics Criminology
Motivational

ANNUAL CALENDAR

OF

McGILL COLLEGE

AND

UNIVERSITY,

MONTREAL.

FOUNDED UNDER BEQUEST OF THE HON. JAMES McGILL,
ERECTED INTO A UNIVERSITY BY ROYAL CHARTER
IN 1821, AND RE-ORGANIZED BY AN
AMENDED CHARTER IN 1852.

SESSION 1898-99.

Montreal :
PRINTED FOR THE UNIVERSITY BY JOHN LOVELL & SON.

1898.

CONTENTS.

8/99

GENERAL ANNOUNCEMENTS :—

Governing Body ....
Committees ....
Officers of Instruction .... } iii to xxiv
General Statement...............................
Calendar..

FACULTY OF ARTS.. 1
DONALDA SPECIAL COURSE FOR WOMEN 81
FACULTY OF APPLIED SCIENCE................................. 87
FACULTY OF LAW... 157
FACULTY OF MEDICINE.. 180
FACULTY OF COMPARATIVE MEDICINE AND VETERINARY SCIENCE..... 236
McGILL NORMAL SCHOOL....................................... 253
UNIVERSITY SCHOOL EXAMINATIONS :—
For Associate in Arts.................................. 270
PASSED THE UNIVERSITY EXAMINATIONS......................... 285
SCHOLARSHIPS AND EXHIBITIONS............................... 291
PRIZES, HONOURS AND STANDING............................... 292
LIST OF STUDENTS OF THE UNIVERSITY........................ 330
OBSERVATORY... 346
GYMNASIUM... 347
REGULATIONS CONCERNING COLLEGE GROUNDS AND ATHLETICS........ 347
UNIVERSITY SOCIETIES...................................... 349
BENEFACTIONS.. 357

The *List of Graduates* corrected to April, 1897, and the *Examination Papers* (price 75 cents) for each Session, are published separately, and may be obtained on application to the Secretary.

ADDENDA.

THE JUNE ENTRANCE EXAMINATIONS for 1899 will begin on MONDAY, MAY 29th, and be continued through the first week of June.

THE SIR J. WILLIAM DAWSON EXHIBITION of $60, the gift of the New York Graduates' Society, will be open for competition to Candidates for Entrance in the Faculty of Arts (men or women) in September, 1898.

Governing Body of the University.

PRINCIPAL.

WILLIAM PETERSON, M.A., LL.D., Vice-Chancellor.

(The Principal has, under the Statutes, the general superintendence of all affairs of the College and University, under such regulations as may be in force.)

FELLOWS:

SIR WILLIAM DAWSON, M.A., LL.D., F.R.S., C.M.G., Governors' Fellow.

ALEXANDER JOHNSON, M.A., LL.D., D.C.L., F.R.S.C.,Vice-Principal, and Dean of the Faculty of Arts.

REV. D. H. MACVICAR, D.D., LL.D., Representative Fellow, Presbyterian College, Montreal, Principal of the College.

JOHN REDPATH DOUGALL, M.A., Representative Fellow in Arts.

REV. J. CLARK MURRAY, LL.D., F.R.S.C., Elective Fellow, Faculty of Arts.

HENRY T. BOVEY, M.A., D.C.L., LL.D., F.R.S.C., M.Inst.C.E., Dean of the Faculty of Applied Science.

BERNARD J. HARRINGTON, M.A., Ph.D., F.G.S., F.R.S.C., Elective Fellow, Faculty of Applied Science.

REV. E. I. REXFORD, B.A., Governors' Fellow.

VERY REV. R. W. NORMAN, M.A., D.C.L., Governors' Fellow.

S. P. ROBINS, M.A., LL.D., Principal of McGill Normal School.

FREDERICK W. KELLEY, B.A., Ph. D , Representative Fellow in Arts.

REV. JAMES BARCLAY, M.A., D.D., Governors' Fellow.

ROBERT CRAIK, M.D., LL.D., Dean of the Faculty of Medicine.

T. WESLEY MILLS, M.A., M.D., F.R.S.C., Representative Fellow in Medicine.

DUNCAN McEACHRAN, D.V.S., Dean of the Faculty of Comparative Medicine and Veterinary Science.

MALCOLM C. BAKER, D.V.S., Elective Fellow, Faculty of Comparative Medicine and Veterinary Science.

ALEXANDER FALCONER, B.A., B.C.L., Representative Fellow in Law.

CHAS. E. MOYSE, B.A., Elective Fellow, Faculty of Arts.

JOHN COX, M.A., Elective Fellow, Faculty of Arts.

R. F. RUTTAN, B.A., M.D., F.R.S.C., Elective Fellow, Faculty of Medicine.

WM. McLENNAN, B.C.L., Representative Fellow in Law.

C. H. McLEOD, Ma.E., F.R.S.C., Representative Fellow in Applied Science.

REV. C. R. FLANDERS, B.A., D.D., Representative Fellow, Stanstead Wesleyan College, Stanstead, Que., Principal of the College.

C. H. GOULD, B.A., Governors' Fellow.

REV. W. I. SHAW, M.A., LL.D., Representative Fellow, Montreal Wesleyan Theological College, Principal of the College.

FRANK D. ADAMS, M.A.Sc., Ph.D., Representative Fellow in Applied Science.

JOHN A. DRESSER, M.A., Representative Fellow, St. Francis College, Richmond, Q., Principal of the College.

D. P. PENHALLOW, B.Sc., M.A.Sc., Elective Fellow, Faculty of Arts.

Hon. JOHN S. HALL, B.A., B.C.L., Governors' Fellow.

Rev. DONALD MACRAE, D.D., Representative Fellow, Morrin College, Quebec, Q., Principal of the College.

Rev. FREDERICK J. STEEN, M.A., Representative Fellow, Montreal Diocesan Theological College.

Rev. J. HENRY GEORGE, D.D., Ph.D., Representative Fellow, Congregational College of Canada, Principal of the College.

F. P. WALTON, B.A., LL.B., Dean of the Faculty of Law.

C. W. WILSON, M.D, Representative Fellow in Medicine.

A. E. C. MOORE, D.V.S., Representative Fellow in Comparative Medicine and Veterinary Science.

(The Governors, Principal and Fellows constitute, under the Charter, the Corporation of the University, which has the power, under the Statutes, to frame regulations touching the Course of Study, Matriculation, Graduation and other Educational matters, and to grant Degrees.)

SECRETARY, REGISTRAR AND BURSAR :—

[And Secretary of the Royal Institution.]

W. VAUGHAN, OFFICE, EAST WING, McGILL COLLEGE.

Office Hours : 9 TO 5.

JAMES W. BRAKENRIDGE, B.C.L.
SAMUEL R. BURRELL, Clerk.

THE ACADEMIC BOARD.

CHAIRMAN—THE PRINCIPAL.

The Principal, the Deans of the several Faculties, the Professors and Associate Professors, and other members, not exceeding ten in number, of the teaching staff of the University, have been constituted, under the statutes, the Academic Board of the University, with the duty of considering such matters as pertain to the interests of the University as a whole and making recommendations concerning the same.

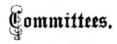Committees.

FINANCE COMMITTEE OF THE GOVERNORS.

(Meeting on the second Thursday of each month at 3 p.m.)

HUGH McLENNAN, Esq.
E. B. GREENSHIELDS, Esq.
GEORGE HAGUE, Esq.,

SAMUEL FINLEY, Esq.
C. J. FLEET, Esq.
R. B. ANGUS, Esq.

PETER REDPATH MUSEUM COMMITTEE.

(Meeting on the Monday before the Quarterly Meeting of Corporation, at 4 p.m.)

PRINCIPAL PETERSON, Chairman.
GEORGE HAGUE, Esq.
C. J. FLEET, Esq.
SIR WILLIAM DAWSON.

J. R. DOUGALL, Esq.
DR. B. J. HARRINGTON.
PROF. D. P. PENHALLOW.
DR. F. D. ADAMS.

PROF. ERNEST W. MacBRIDE.

UNIVERSITY LIBRARY COMMITTEE.

(Meeting on the Monday before the Quarterly Meeting of Corporation at 5 p.m.)

PRINCIPAL PETERSON, Chairman.
HUGH McLENNAN, Esq.
C. J. FLEET, Esq.
J. R. DOUGALL, Esq.
DR. ALEX. JOHNSON.

REV. DR. J. CLARK MURRAY.
DR. H. T. BOVEY.
DR. B. J. HARRINGTON.
PROF. C. E. MOYSE.
C. H. GOULD, Esq.

PROF. D. P. PENHALLOW.

COMMITTEE OF MANAGEMENT OF THE McDONALD PHYSICS BUILDING.

(Meeting on the Thursday before the Quarterly Meeting of Corporation at 5 p.m.)

PRINCIPAL PETERSON, Chairman.
W. C. McDONALD, Esq.
CHAS. S. CAMPBELL, Esq.

DR. ALEX. JOHNSON.
DR. H. T. BOVEY.
PROF. JOHN COX.

COMMITTEE OF MANAGEMENT OF THE ENGINEERING BUILDING.

(Meeting on the third Monday of each month at 4 p.m.)

PRINCIPAL PETERSON.
W. C. McDONALD, Esq.

C. J. FLEET, Esq.
DR. H. T. BOVEY.

PROF. C. H. McLEOD.

COMMITTEE OF MANAGEMENT OF THE McDONALD CHEMISTRY AND MINING BUILDING.

(Meeting on the third Monday of each month at 5 p.m.)

PRINCIPAL PETERSON.
W. C. McDONALD, Esq.
C. J. FLEET, Esq.

DR. H. T. BOVEY.
DR. B. J. HARRINGTON.
DR. J. B. PORTER.

COMMITTEE OF MANAGEMENT OF THE COLLEGE GROUNDS.

(Meeting on the second Tuesday of each month at 5 p.m.)

PRINCIPAL PETERSON.
C. J. FLEET, Esq.
PROF. A. McGOUN.

DR. F. D. ADAMS.
DR. C. McEACHRAN.
PROF. C. H. McLEOD (Sec. of Com.)

DR. R. F. RUTTAN.

And Representatives of the Graduates and the University Athletic Clubs.

Principal and Professors Emeriti,

[Retaining their Rank and Titles, but retired from active work.]

SIR WM. DAWSON, LL.D., F.R.S., C.M.G.
Emeritus Principal, and Emeritus Professor in the Faculty of Arts.

HENRY ASPINWALL HOWE, LL.D,
Emeritus Professor in the Faculty of Arts.

WM. WRIGHT, M.D.
Emeritus Professor in the Faculty of Medicine.

D. C. MacCALLUM, M.D.
Emeritus Professor in the Faculty of Medicine.

MATTHEW HUTCHINSON, D.C.L.
Emeritus Professor in the Faculty of Law.

Hon. J. EMERY ROBIDOUX, D.C.L.
Emeritus Professor in the Faculty of Law.

Hon. J. S. C. WURTELE, J.Q.B., D.C.L., (Officier d'Instruction Publique),
Emeritus Professor in the Faculty of Law

Officers of Instruction.

PROFESSORS.

WM. PETERSON, M.A. (Oxon), LL.D. (St. Andrews and Princeton).
   Principal and Professor of Classics.   889 Sherbrooke Street.

ALEXANDER JOHNSON, M.A., LL.D. (Dublin), D.C.L. (Bishops), F.R.S.C.
   Senior Moderator (Math. and Phys.), and late Classical Scholar Trin. Coll., Dub.
   Vice-Principal and Dean of the Faculty of Arts, and
   Peter Redpath Professor of Pure Mathematics.   895 Sherbrooke Street.

ROBERT CRAIK, M.D., LL.D.
   Dean of the Faculty of Medicine, and Professor of Hygiene
      and Public Health.   887 Sherbrooke Street.

GILBERT P. GIRDWOOD, M.D., F.R.S.C.
   Professor of Chemistry, Faculty of Medicine.   82 University Street.

Rev. J. CLARK MURRAY, LL.D. (Glasgow), F.R.S.C.
   Professor of Logic, and John Frothingham Professor of Mental
      and Moral Philosophy.   340 Wood Av., Westmount.

BERNARD J. HARRINGTON, M.A., Ph.D., (Yale), F.G.S. F.R.S.C.
   David J. Greenshields Professor of Chemistry and Mineralogy,
      Lecturer in Assaying, and Director of Chemistry and
      Mining Building.   295 University Street.

THOMAS G. RODDICK, M.D.
   Professor of Surgery.   80 Union Avenue.

WILLIAM GARDNER, M.D.
   Professor of Gynæcology.   899 Sherbrooke Street.

HENRY T. BOVEY, M.A. (Cantab.), M. Inst. C.E., LL.D., D.C.L. (Bishops), F.R.S.C.,
   late Fellow Queen's College, Cambridge.
   Dean of the Faculty of Applied Science, and William Scott
      Professor of Civil Engineering and Applied Mechanics.
                                                    Sunnandene, Ontario Avenue.

CHARLES E. MOYSE, B.A. (London).
   Molson Professor of English Language and Literature.   802 Sherbrooke Street.

C. H. McLEOD, Ma.E., F.R.S.C.
   Professor of Surveying and Geodesy, and Lecturer on Descriptive Geometry,
      Supt. of Meteorological Observatory.   Observatory, McGill College

FRANCIS J. SHEPHERD, M.D.
   Professor of Anatomy.   •   152 Mansfield Street.

FRANK BULLER, M.D.
   Professor of Ophthalmology and Otology.   123 Stanley Street.

JAMES STEWART, M.D.
   Professor of Medicine and Clinical Medicine.   285 Mountain Street.

GEORGE WILKINS, M.D.
   Professor of Medical Jurisprudence and Lecturer in Histology.   898 Dorchester St.

D. P. PENHALLOW, B.Sc. (Boston Univ.), M.A.Sc., F.R.S.C., F.R.M.S.
   Professor of Botany.   McGill College.

G. H. CHANDLER, M.A.
Professor of Applied Mathematics. 32 Lorne Avenue.

T. WESLEY MILLS, M.A , M.D., F.R.S.C.
Professor of Physiology. McGill College.

J. CHALMERS CAMERON, M.D.
Professor of Midwifery and Diseases of Infancy. 941 Dorchester Street.

Rev. DANIEL COUSSIRAT, B.A., B.D. (Université de France), D.D. (Queen's),
Officier d'Académie,
Professor of Hebrew and Oriental Literature. 171 Hutchison Street.

A. JUDSON EATON, M.A. (Harvard), Ph.D. (Leipsic).
Associate Professor of Classics. 34 Arlington Ave., Westmount.

ARCHIBALD McGOUN, M.A., B.C.L.
Professor of Civil Law. Dunavon, Westmount, and 181 St. James Street.

DUNCAN McEACHRAN, F.R.C.V.S , D.V.S.
*Dean of Faculty of Comparative Medicine and Veterinary Science, and
Professor of Veterinary Medicine and Surgery.* 6 Union Avenue.

MALCOLM C. BAKER, D.V.S.
Professor of Veterinary Anatomy. 6 Union Avenue.

CHARLES McEACHRAN, D.V.S.
Professor of Veterinary Obstetrics and Diseases of Cattle. 6 Union Avenue.

JOHN COX, M.A. (Cantab), late Fellow Trin. Coll., Cambridge.
*William C. McDonald Professor of Physics, and Director of
Physics Building.* McGill College.

Hon. CHRISTOPHER A. GEOFFRION, Q.C., D.C.L., P.C.
Professor of Civil Law. 97 St James Street.

THOMAS FORTIN, D.C.L., LL.L. (Laval),
Professor of Civil Law. 97 St James Street.

W. DeM. MARLER, B.A., D.C.L.
Professor of Civil Law. 157 St James Street.

Hon. CHARLES J. DOHERTY, D.C.L.
Professor of Civil Law. 232 Stanley Street.

EUGENE LAFLEUR, B.A., B.C.L.
Professor of International Law. N.Y. Life Building, Place d'Armes.

ALEX. D. BLACKADER, B.A., M.D.
*Professor of Pharmacology and Therapeutics, and Lecturer
on Diseases of Children.* 236 Mountain Street,

JOHN T. NICOLSON, B.Sc. (Edin.).
*Thomas Workman Professor of Mechanical Engineering,
Lecturer on Thermodynamics.* 260 University Street.

R. F, RUTTAN, B.A. (Toronto), M.D., F.R.S.Can.
Professor of Practical Chemistry, and Registrar Medical Faculty. McGill College.

JAMES BELL, M D.
Professor Clinical Surgery. 873 Dorchester Street.

J. GEORGE ADAMI, M.A., M.D. (Cantab.), F.R.S.E., late Fellow of Jesus
College, Cambridge.
Professor of Pathology and Director of Medical Museum. 331 Peel Street.

FRANK D. ADAMS, M.A. Sc., Ph.D. (Heidelberg) F.G.S.A , F.R.S.Can.
Logan Professor of Geology and Palæontology. 343 Mountain Street.

H. S. BIRKETT, M.D.
Professor of Laryngology. 123 Stanley Street.

C. W. COLBY, M.A. and Ph.D. (Harvard).
Professor of History. McGill College.

FRANK CARTER, M.A. (Oxon).
Professor of Classics.   McGill College.

F. G. FINLEY, M.B. (London), M.D.
Assistant Professor of Medicine and Associate Professor of
Clinical Medicine.   1013 Dorchester Street.

H. A. LAFLEUR, B.A., M.D.
Assistant Professor of Medicine and Associate Professor of
Clinical Medicine.   58 University Street.

GEO. E. ARMSTRONG, M.D.
Associate Professor of Clinical Surgery.   320 Mountain Street.

S. HENBEST CAPPER, M.A. (Edin.), A.R.I.B.A., A.R.C.A.,
William C. McDonald Professor of Architecture.   McGill College.

J. BONSALL PORTER, E.M., A.M., Ph.D. (Col. Univ., N.Y.), M. Can.
Soc. C.E.
William C. McDonald Professor of Mining and Metallurgy.   33 McTavish St.

F. P. WALTON, B.A. (Oxon), LL.B. (Edin).
Dean of the Faculty of Law and Gale Professor of Roman Law.   McGill College.

ERNEST WILLIAM MacBRIDE, M.A. (Cantab.), B. Sc. (Lond.), Fellow
of St. John's College, Cambridge.
Professor of Zoology.   McGill College.

Hon. CHARLES PEERS DAVIDSON, M.A., D C.L.
Professor of Criminal Law.   74 McGill College Ave.

DONALD MACMASTER, Q.C., D.C.L.
Professor of Commercial Law.   185 St. James Street.

....
William C. McDonald Professor of Electrical Engineering.   McGill College.

....
William C. McDonald Professor of Physics.   McGill College

....
William C. McDonald Professor of Chemistry.   McGill College.

RICHARD S. LEA, MA.E.
Assistant Professor of Civil Engineering and Lecturer in Mathematics.
                                                    59 Metcalfe Street.

HENRY F. ARMSTRONG,
Assistant Professor of Freehand Drawing and Descriptive
Geometry.   12 Park Ave.

R. J. DURLEY, B.Sc. (London), Ma.E., A.M.I.C.E.
Assistant Professor of Mechanical Engineering.   McGill College.

WYATT G. JOHNSTON, M.D
Assistant Professor in Public Health and Preventive Medicine.   71 Shuter Street.

....
Assistant Professor in Civil Engineering and Descriptive Geometry. McGill College.

LECTURERS, &c.

PAUL T. LAFLEUR, M.A.
Lecturer in Logic and English.   58 University Street.

LEIGH R. GREGOR, B.A., Ph.D. (Heidelberg).
Lecturer in German Language and Literature.   23 University Street.

T. J. W. BURGESS, M.D., F.R.S.C.,
Lecturer on Mental Diseases.   Drawer 2381, Montreal.

PERCY C. RYAN, B.C.L.
Lecturer on Civil Procedure.   Canada Life Building, St. James Street.

NEVIL NORTON EVANS, M.A.Sc.
Lecturer in Chemistry   217 Milton Street.

W. S. MORROW, M.D.
    Lecturer in Physiology.   96 Park Av.
J. G. G. KERRY, Ma.E., A.M. Can. Soc. C.E.
    Lecturer in Surveying and Descriptive Geometry.   149 Durocher Street.
MAXIME INGRES,
    Lecturer in French Language and Literature.   128 Crescent Street.
H. M. TORY, M.A.
    Lecturer in Mathematics and Demonstrator in Physics.   31 Park Ave.
CARRIE M. DERICK, M.A.
    Lecturer in Botany and Demonstrator in the Botanical Laboratory. McGill College.
JOHN M. ELDER, B.A., M.D.   *i*
    Lecturer in Medical and Surgical Anatomy and Demonstrator of Surgery
        4201 Sherbrooke Street, Westmount.
C. F. MARTIN, M.D.
    Lecturer in Medicine Faculty of Medicine, and Faculty of Comp.
        Med. and Vet. Sc., Demonstrator of Clinical Medicine.   46 Park Avenue.
LOUIS HERDT, Ma E., E.E. (Elect. Inst. Montefiore, Belgium).
    Lecturer in Electrical Engineering.   62 Laval Av.
J. J. GARDNER, M.D.
    Lecturer in Ophthalmology.   211 Peel Street.
J. A. SPRINGLE, B.A., M.D.
    Lecturer in Anatomy.   1237 Dorchester Street.
N. D. GUNN, M.D.   *'*
    Demonstrator of Histology Faculty of Medicine, and Lecturer on
        Materia Medica in the Faculty of Compar. Med. and
        Vet. Sc.   47 Union Avenue.
Rev. J. L. MORIN, M.A.
    Sessional Lecturer in French.   65 Hutchison Street.
S. B. SLACK, M.A. (Oxon).
    Lecturer in Classics.   McGill College.
AIMÉ GEOFFRION, B.C.L.
    Lecturer on Obligations.   20 Bayle Street.
GORDON W. MacDOUGALL, B.A., B.C.L.
    Lecturer on Civil Procedure.   N.Y. Life Building, Place d'Armes.
F. A. L. LOCKHART, M.B. (Edin.)
    Lecturer in Gynæcology.   38 Bishop Street.
J. C. WEBSTER, B.A.& M.D. (Edin.), F.R.C.P. (Edin.)
    Lecturer in Gynæcology.   287 Mountain Street.
R. TAIT McKENZIE., B.A., M.D.
    Medical Examiner and Instructor in Physical Culture, and
        Demonstrator of Anatomy.   59 Metcalfe Street.
JOHN P. STEPHEN,
    Instructor in Elocution.   875 Dorchester Street.
J. G. McCARTHY, M.D.
    Senior Demonstrator of Anatomy.   61 Drummond Street.
D. J. EVANS, M.D.
    Demonstrator of Obstetrics.   939 Dorchester Street.
G. GORDON CAMPBELL, B.Sc. (Dalhousie), M.D.
    Demonstrator of Clinical Medicine.   117 Metcalfe Street.
W. F. HAMILTON, M.D.
    Demonstrator of Clinical Medicine.   287 Mountain Street.
J. A. HENDERSON, M.D.
    Demonstrator of Anatomy.   191 Bleury Street.
J. W. SCANE, M.D.
    Demonstrator of Physiology,   4469 St Catherine Street.
KENNETH CAMERON, B.A., M.D.
    Demonstrator of Clinical Surgery   903 Dorchester Street.

C. G. L. WOLF, B.A. (Man), M.D.
Demonstrator of Practical Chemistry. McGill Medical College.

FRANK H. PITCHER, M.A. Sc.
Demonstrator of Physics. McGill College.

HOWARD T. BARNES, M.A.Sc.
Demonstrator of Physics. 14 Lorne Av.

W. I. BRADLEY, B A. (Toronto), M.D. .
Demonstrator of Pathology and Anatomy. 2812 St. Catherine Street.

A. E. GARROW, M.D.
Demonstrator of Surgery and Clinical Surgery. 2726 St Catherine Street.

ALEXANDER BRODIE. M.A.Sc.
Demonstrator of Practical Chemistry. McGill College.

JOHN W. BELL, B.A.Sc.
Demonstrator of Mining. McGill College.

HOMER M. JAQUAYS, B.A., B.A.Sc.
Demonstrator of Mechanical Engineering. McGill College.

R. A. KERRY, M.D.
Assistant Demonstrator of Pharmacy. 149 Durocher Street.

J. J. ROSS, B.A., M.D.
Demonstrator of Anatomy. 679 Wellington Street.

A. E. ORR, M.D.
Demonstrator of Anatomy. 900 Dorchester Street.

A. G. NICHOLLS, M.A., M.D.
Demonstrator of Pathology. 267 Mountain Street.

H. B. YATES, B.A. (Cantab), M.D.
Demonstrator of Bacteriology. 257 Peel Street.

A. A. ROBERTSON, B.A., M.D.
Demonstrator of Physiology. 79 St. Matthew Street.

J. ALEX. HUTCHISON, M.D.
Demonstrator of Surgery. 70 Mackay Street.

J. D. CAMERON, M.D.
Demonstrator of Gynæcology. 2068 St Catherine Street

E. J. SEMPLE, B.A. (St. Mary's College), M.D.
Curator. 2437 Notre Dame Street..

D. D. McTAGGART, B.A.Sc., M.D.
Assistant Demonstrator of Pathology. Montreal General Hospital.

S. RIDLEY MACKENZIE. M,D.
Assistant Demonstrator of Medicine. 144 Peel Street.

D. P. ANDERSON, B.A., M D.
Assistant Domonstrator of Pathology. 493E St. Urbain Street.

T. P. SHAW, M.D.
Assistant Demonstrator of Obstetrics. 1260 Dorchester Street.

JAMES BARCLAY, M.D.
Assistant Demonstrator of Obstetrics. McGill Medical College.

MISS HELEN S. GAIRDNER.
Lady Superintendent Donalda Ladies' Classes. 47 Victoria Street.

MISS HELEN O. BARNJUM.
Instructress in Physical Education, Donalda Ladies' Classes. 9 Drummond Street.

LIBRARY.

CHAS. H. GOULD, B.A.
University Librarian. 963 Dorchester Street.

H MOTT.
Assistant Librarian. 47 St. Famille Street

General Statement.

The Sixty-sixth Session of the University, being the Forty-sixth under the amended Charter, will commence in the autumn of 1898.

By Virtue of the Royal Charter, granted in 1821 and amended in 1852, the Governors, Principal and Fellows of McGill College constitute the Corporation of the University; and, under the Statutes framed by the Board of Governors with the approval of the Visitor, have the power of granting Degrees in all the Arts and Faculties in McGill College and Colleges affiliated thereto.

The Statutes and Regulations of the University have been framed on the most liberal principles, with the view of affording to all classes of persons the greatest possible facilities for the attainment of mental culture and professional training. In its religious character the University is Protestant, but not denominational, and while all possible attention will be given to the character and conduct of Students, no interference with their individual views will be sanctioned.

The educational work of the University is carried on in McGill College, Montreal, and in the Affiliated Colleges and Schools.

I. McGILL COLLEGE.

THE FACULTY OF ARTS.—The complete course of study extends over four Sessions of eight months each; and includes Classics and Mathematics, Experimental Physics, English Literature, Logic, Mental and Moral Science, Natural Science, and one Modern Language or Hebrew. The course of study is, with few exceptions, the same for all Students in the first two years; but in the third and fourth years extensive options are allowed, more especially in favour of the Honour Courses in Classics, Mathematics, Mental and Moral Science, Natural Science, English Literature, Modern and Semitic Languages. Certain exemptions are also allowed to professional students. The course of study leads to the Degrees of B.A., M.A. and LL.D.

The Degree of B.A. from this University admits the holder to the study of the learned professions without preliminary examination, in the Provinces of Quebec and Ontario, and in Great Britain and Ireland, etc.

In the Session 1894-5, special regulations were sanctioned by the Corporation, by which the degree of B.A. can be obtained along with the degree in the Faculty of Medicine or of Applied Science in six years. This is effected by avoiding the duplication of courses in the same subjects or in those which give the same educational training, and by a proper adaptation of the time tables. A certificate of Literate in Arts will be given along with the degree in either Faculty to candidates who have completed two years in Arts before entering the Professional Faculty.

The Degree of B.A. can be obtained along with the degree in the Faculty of Law also in six years.

THE DONALDA SPECIAL COURSE IN ARTS provides for the education of women, in separate classes, with course of study, exemptions, degrees and honours similar to those for men.

THE FACULTY OF APPLIED SCIENCE provides a thorough professional training, extending over four years, in Civil Engineering, Mechanical Engineering, Mining Engineering and Assaying, Electrical Engineering, and Practical Chemistry, leading to the Degrees of Bachelor of Applied Science, Master of Engineering, and Master of Applied Science.

THE FACULTY OF LAW.—.The complete course of law extends over three Sessions of eight months each, and leads to the Degrees of B.C.L. and D.C.L.

THE FACULTY OF MEDICINE.—The complete course of study in Medicine extends over four Sessions of nine months each, and leads to the Degree of M.D., C.M.

THE FACULTY OF COMPARATIVE MEDICINE AND VETERINARY SCIENCE.—The complete course extends over three Sessions of six months each, and leads to the Degree of D.V.S.

II. AFFILIATED COLLEGES.

Students of Affiliated Colleges are matriculated in the University, and may pursue their course of study in the Affiliated College, or in part in the Affiliated College and in part in McGill College, as the case may be, and may come up to the University Examinations on the same terms as the students of McGill College.

MORRIN COLLEGE, QUEBEC.—Is affiliated in so far as regards Degrees in Arts and Law. [Detailed information may be obtained from the REV. DONALD MACRAE D.D., Principal.]

ST. FRANCIS COLLEGE, RICHMOND, P.Q.—Is affiliated in so far as regards the Intermediate Examinations in Arts. [Detailed information may be obtained from J. A. DRES-ER, B A., Principal.]

THE STANSTEAD WESLEYAN COLLEGE, STANSTEAD, P.Q.—Is affiliated in so far as regards the Intermediate Examination in Arts. [Detailed information may be obtained from the Rev. C. R. FLANDERS, B.A., Principal.]

III. AFFILIATED THEOLOGICAL COLLEGES.

Affiliated Theological Colleges have the right of obtaining for their students the advantage, in whole or in part, of the course of study in Arts, with such facilities in regard to exemptions as may be agreed on.

THE CONGREGATIONAL COLLEGE OF CANADA, MONTREAL. Principal, REV. J. HENRY GEORGE, D.D., PH.D, 58 McTavish St.

THE PRESBYTERIAN COLLEGE, MONTREAL, in connection with the Presbyterian Church in Canada. Principal, REV. D. H. MACVICAR, D.D., LL.D., 69 McTavish St.

THE DIOCESAN COLLEGE OF MONTREAL. Principal, ——, 201 University St.

THE WESLEYAN COLLEGE OF MONTREAL. Principal, REV. W. I. SHAW, M.A., LL.D., 228 University St.

(Calendars of the above Colleges and all necessary information may be obtained on application to their Principals.]

IV. McGILL NORMAL SCHOOL.

THE McGILL NORMAL SCHOOL provides the training requisite for Teachers of Elementary and Model Schools and Academies. Teachers trained in this School are entitled to Provincial Diplomas, and may, on conditions stated in the announcement of the School, enter the classes in the Faculty of Arts for Academy Diplomas and for the Degree of B.A. Principal, S. P. ROBINS, LL.D., 32 Belmont St., Montreal.

V. AFFILIATED HIGH SCHOOLS, ETC.

The Trafalgar Institute for the higher education of women, Simpson St., Montreal, Principal, Miss Grace Fairley. The High School of Montreal, and The Girls' High School of Montreal, Metcalfe St., Principal, Rev. Elson I. Rexford, B.A.

Schools which have prepared successful candidates for A.A. or for matriculation (June, 1898).

Abingdon School, Montreal; Montreal Coll. Inst.; St. John the Evangelist School, Montreal; Miss Symmers' and Miss Smith's School, Montreal; Westmount Academy; Almonte High School; Aylmer Acad.; Bedford Acad.; Brantford Coll. Inst.; Chicoutimi Protestant School; Clarenceville Model School; Coaticook Acad.; Compton Ladies' Coll.; Cookshire Acad. : Cowansville Acad.; Danville Acad.; Dufferin Grammar School; Dunham Ladies' Coll.; Enfield School; Feller Inst.; Gananoque High School; Granby Acad ; Huntingdon Acad.; Knowlton Acad.; Lachute Acad.; Lennoxville Model School ; Magog Model School ; Orangeville High School; Ormstown Acad.; Ottawa Coll. Inst.; Pembroke High School; Portage du Fort Model School ; Girls' High School, Quebec ; Renfrew High School ; Church School for Boys, Rothesay, N.B.; Shelburne Acad. N.S.; Sherbrooke Acad. ; Stanstead Wesleyan Coll. ; Sutton Acad. ; St. Francis Coll. School ; St. Johns' High School ; Bishop Field Coll., St. John, Nfld., Three Rivers Acad. ; Buckland Coll., Vancouver, B.C. ; Waterloo Acad. ; Williamstown High School.

SEPTEMBER, 1898.

1	Thursday	Normal School opens.
2	Friday	
3	Saturday	Meeting of Medical Faculty.
4	**SUNDAY**	
5	Monday	Meeting of Faculty of Applied Science.
6	Tuesday	Matriculation in Law Lectures in Law begin
7	Wednesday	Normal School Committee.
8	Thursday	Finance Committee.
9	Friday	
10	Saturday	
11	**SUNDAY**	
12	Monday	
13	Tuesday	Register opens for students in Medicine. College Grounds Committee.
14	Wednesday	Meeting of Faculty of Arts.
15	Thursday	Matriculation and Supplemental Examinations (Classics). [For Exhibition and Scholarship Examinations see page xvi.]
16	Friday	Examinations continued (Mathematics).
17	Saturday	Matriculation in Veterinary Science.
18	**SUNDAY**	
19	Monday	Examinations continued (English, Logic, Mental Philosophy and Chemistry). Engineering Building Committee . Chemistry and Mining Building Committee.
20	Tuesday	Examinations continued (Modern Language sand Natural Science). Introductory Lecture in Medicine.
21	Wednesday	Lectures in Arts, Medicine and Veterinary Science begin. Meetings of Faculty of Arts and of Applied Science.
22	Thursday	
23	Friday	Lectures in Applied Science begin. Meeting of Faculty of Arts.
24	Saturday	Meeting of Governors.
25	**SUNDAY**	
26	Monday	
27	Tuesday	
28	Wednesday	
29	Thursday	
30	Friday	

OCTOBER, 1898.

1	Saturday	Summer Essays in Applied Science. Meeting of Medical Faculty.
2	**SUNDAY**	
3	Monday	Meeting of Faculty of Applied Science.
4	Tuesday	
5	Wednesday	Founder's Birthday. Normal School Committee.
6	Thursday	The William Molson Hall opened, 1862.
7	Friday	Meeting of Faculty of Arts.
8	Saturday	Supplemental Examinations, Applied Science.
9	**SUNDAY**	
10	Monday	
11	Tuesday	College Grounds Committee.
12	Wednesday	
13	Thursday	Finance Committee.
14	Friday	
15	Saturday	
16	**SUNDAY**	
17	Monday	Engineering Building Committee · Chemistry and Mining Building Committee
18	Tuesday	
19	Wednesday	
20	Thursday	Physics Building Committee.
21	Friday	University Athletic Sports. Meeting of Faculty of Arts.
22	Saturday	Meeting of Governors. Register closes for Students in Medicine.
23	**SUNDAY**	
24	Monday	Museum Committee . Library Committee.
25	Tuesday	
26	Wednesday	Regular Meeting of Corporation. Reports of Scholarships and Exhibitions. Accounts audited.
27	Thursday	
28	Friday	
29	Saturday	
30	**SUNDAY**	
31	Monday	New Library opened, 1893

Note.—Meetings of the Faculty of Arts are held at 4.30 P M. unless otherwise specified.

1 Tuesday	
2 Wednesday	Normal School Committee.
3 Thursday	
4 Friday	Meeting of Faculty of Arts.
5 Saturday	Meeting of Medical Faculty.
6 SUNDAY	
7 Monday	Meeting of Faculty of Applied Science.
8 Tuesday	College Grounds Committee.
9 Wednesday	
10 Thursday	Finance Committee.
11 Friday	
12 Saturday	
13 SUNDAY	
14 Monday	
15 Tuesday	
16 Wednesday	
17 Thursday	
18 Friday	Meeting of Faculty of Arts.
19 Saturday	
20 SUNDAY	
21 Monday	Engineering Building Committee : Chemistry and Mining Building Committee.
22 Tuesday	
23 Wednesday	
24 Thursday	
25 Friday	
26 Saturday	Meeting of Governors.
27 SUNDAY	
28 Monday	
29 Tuesday	
30 Wednesday	.

DECEMBER, 1898.

1 Thursday	
2 Friday	Meeting of Faculty of Arts.
3 Saturday	Meeting of Medical Faculty.
4 SUNDAY	
5 Monday	Meeting of Faculty of Applied Science.
6 Tuesday	
7 Wednesday	Normal School Committee.
8 Thursday	Finance Committee.
9 Friday	
10 Saturday	
11 SUNDAY	
12 Monday	
13 Tuesday	College Grounds Committee.
14 Wednesday	Lectures in Arts end.
15 Thursday	Christmas Examinations in Arts begin.
16 Friday	Autumn term of Faculty of Medicine ends. Lectures in Law end.
17 Saturday	Meeting of Governors.
18 SUNDAY	
19 Monday	Engineering Building Committee : Chemistry and Mining Building Committee.
20 Tuesday	
21 Wednesday	
22 Thursday	Christmas Vacation begins.
23 Friday	
24 Saturday	
25 SUNDAY	Christmas-Day.
26 Monday	
27 Tuesday	
28 Wednesday	
29 Thursday	

1 SUNDAY

2 Monday — Meeting of Faculty of Applied Science.
3 Tuesday
4 Wednesday — Christmas Vacation ends. Winter term Faculty of Medicine begins. Normal School Committee.
5 Thursday — Lectures in Arts and Applied Science resumed.
6 Friday — Meeting of Faculty of Arts.
7 Saturday — Meeting of Medical Faculty.

8 SUNDAY

9 Monday — Lectures in Law resumed.
10 Tuesday — College Grounds Committee.
11 Wednesday
12 Thursday — Finance Committee.
13 Friday — Meeting of Faculty of Arts.
14 Saturday

15 SUNDAY

16 Monday — Engineering Building Committee : Chemistry and Mining Building Committee.
17 Tuesday
18 Wednesday
19 Thursday — Physics Building Committee.
20 Friday
21 Saturday — Meeting of Governors.

22 SUNDAY

23 Monday — Museum Committee : Library Committee.
24 Tuesday
25 Wednesday — Regular Meeting of Corporation. Examiners appointed. Annual Report to Visitor.
26 Thursday
27 Friday — Meeting of Faculty of Arts.
28 Saturday

29 SUNDAY

30 Monday
31 Tuesday — Theses for M.A. and LL.D. to be sent in.

FEBRUARY, 1899.

1 Wednesday — Normal School Committee.
2 Thursday
3 Friday
4 Saturday — Meeting of Medical Faculty.

5 SUNDAY

6 Monday — Meeting of Faculty of Applied Science.
7 Tuesday
8 Wednesday
9 Thursday — Finance Committee.
10 Friday — Meeting of Faculty of Arts.
11 Saturday

12 SUNDAY

13 Monday
14 Tuesday — College Grounds Committee.
15 Wednesday — No Lectures.
16 Thursday
17 Friday
18 Saturday

19 SUNDAY

20 Monday — Engineering Building Committee : Chemistry and Mining Building Committee.
21 Tuesday
22 Wednesday
23 Thursday
24 Friday — Meeting of Faculty of Arts.
25 Saturday — Physics and Engineering Buildings opened, 1893. Meeting of Governors.

26 SUNDAY

27 Monday
28 Tuesday

1 Wednesday	Normal School Committee.
2 Thursday	
3 Friday	
4 Saturday	Meeting of Medical Faculty.
5 SUNDAY	
6 Monday	Meeting of Faculty of Applied Science.
7 Tuesday	
8 Wednesday	
9 Thursday	Finance Committee.
10 Friday	Meeting of Faculty of Arts.
11 Saturday	
12 SUNDAY	
13 Monday	
14 Tuesday	College Grounds Committee.
15 Wednesday	
16 Thursday	
17 Friday	
18 Saturday	
19 SUNDAY	
20 Monday	Engineering Building Committee: Chemistry and Mining Building Committee.
21 Tuesday	
22 Wednesday	
23 Thursday	
24 Friday	Meeting of Faculty of Arts. Reports of Attendance on Lectures. Winter term ends Faculty of Medicine.
25 Saturday	Meeting of Governors.
26 SUNDAY	
27 Monday	
28 Tuesday	
29 Wednesday	Lectures in Arts and Applied Science end.
30 Thursday	Convocation for Degrees in Veterinary Science. Lectures in Law end. Examinations in Arts, see p. xxiii.
31 Friday	Good Friday. Easter Vacation begins.

APRIL, 1899.

1 Saturday	Meeting of Medical Faculty.
2 SUNDAY	Easter Sunday.
3 Monday	Meeting of Faculty of Applied Science.
4 Tuesday	Easter Vacation ends.
5 Wednesday	Normal School Committee.
6 Thursday	
7 Friday	
8 Saturday	
9 SUNDAY	
10 Monday	
11 Tuesday	Spring term begins Faculty of Medicine. College Grounds Committee.
12 Wednesday	
13 Thursday	Finance Committee.
14 Friday	
15 Saturday	
16 SUNDAY	
17 Monday	Engineering Building Committee: Chemistry and Mining Building Committee.
18 Tuesday	
19 Wednesday	
20 Thursday	Physics Building Committee.
21 Friday	
22 Saturday	Meeting of Governors.
23 SUNDAY	
24 Monday	Museum Committee: Library Committee.
25 Tuesday	
26 Wednesday	Regular meeting of Corporation.
27 Thursday	
28 Friday	Convocation for Degrees in Arts, Law and Applied Science.
29 Saturday	Meeting of Examiners for School Examinations.
30 SUNDAY	

1 Monday	
2 Tuesday	
3 Wednesday	Normal School Committee.
4 Thursday	
5 Friday	
6 Saturday	Meeting of Medical Faculty.
7 SUNDAY	
8 Monday	Examinations in Normal School begin.
9 Tuesday	College Grounds Committee.
10 Wednesday	
11 Thursday	Finance Committee.
12 Friday	
13 Saturday	
14 SUNDAY	
15 Monday	Engineering Building Committee : Chemistry and Mining Building Committee.
16 Tuesday	
17 Wednesday	
18 Thursday	
19 Friday	
20 Saturday	
21 SUNDAY	Whit Sunday.
22 Monday	
23 Tuesday	
24 Wednesday	Queen's Birthday.
25 Thursday	
26 Friday	Lectures end Faculty of Medicine.
27 Saturday	Meeting of Governors.
28 SUNDAY	Trinity Sunday.
29 Monday	Examinations begin Faculty of Medicine, and for Matriculation and Associate in Arts.
30 Tuesday	
31 Wednesday	Normal School closes for Summer Vacation.

JUNE, 1899.

1 Thursday	
2 Friday	
3 Saturday	Meeting of Medical Faculty.
4 SUNDAY	
5 Monday	
6 Tuesday	
7 Wednesday	Normal School Committee.
8 Thursday	Finance Committee.
9 Friday	
10 Saturday	
11 SUNDAY	
12 Monday	
13 Tuesday	College Grounds Committee.
14 Wednesday	
15 Thursday	Physics Building Committee
16 Friday	Convocation for degrees in Medicine.
17 Saturday	
18 SUNDAY	
19 Monday	Engineering Building Committee : Chemistry and Mining Building Committee.
20 Tuesday	
21 Wednesday	
22 Thursday	
23 Friday	
24 Saturday	Meeting of Governors.
25 SUNDAY	
26 Monday	Museum Committee : Library Committee.
27 Tuesday	
28 Wednesday.	Regular Meeting of Corporation. Report of Normal School.
29 Thursday	
30 Friday	

JULY, 1899.

1 Saturday   Meeting of Medical Faculty.

2 SUNDAY

3 Monday
4 Tuesday
5 Wednesday
6 Thursday
7 Friday
8 Saturday

9 SUNDAY

10 Monday
11 Tuesday
12 Wednesday
13 Thursday
14 Friday
15 Saturday

16 SUNDAY

17 Monday
18 Tuesday
19 Wednesday
20 Thursday
21 Friday
22 Saturday

23 SUNDAY

24 Monday
25 Tuesday
26 Wednesday
27 Thursday
28 Friday
29 Saturday

30 SUNDAY

31 Monday

AUGUST, 1899.

1 Tuesday
2 Wednesday
3 Thursday
4 Friday
5 Saturday

6 SUNDAY

7 Monday
8 Tuesday
9 Wednesday
10 Thursday
11 Friday
12 Saturday

13 SUNDAY

14 Monday
15 Tuesday
16 Wednesday
17 Thursday
18 Friday
19 Saturday

20 SUNDAY

21 Monday
22 Tuesday
23 Wednesday
24 Thursday   Peter Redpath Museum opened 1882.
25 Friday
26 Saturday

27 SUNDAY

FACULTY OF ARTS.

ENTRANCE, EXHIBITION, SCHOLARSHIP, &c., EXAMINATIONS,
SEPTEMBER, 1898.

Day.	Date	First Year	Second Year.	Third Year.	Hour.
Thursday.	15	Latin.	Greek.	Greek.	9 to 12
"	15	Greek.	Latin.	Latin Prose Comp.	2 to 5
"	15			Mathematics.	9 to 12
Friday.	16	Geometry.	Mathematics.	Latin.	9 to 12
"	16			Mathematics.	9 to 12
"	16			Botany.	9 to 12
"	16	Algebra, Arithmetic and Trigonometry.	Mathematics.	Ancient History.	2 to 5
"	16			Botany.	2 to 5
Monday.	19	English.	English.	English.	9 to 12
"	19			Logic.	9 to 12
"	19	English.		English.	2 to
"	19		Chemistry	Chemistry.	2 to 5
Tuesday	20			Mathematics.	9 to 12
"	20			Botany.	9 to 12
"	20	French.	French.	French.	9 to
"	20	Grammar and Comp. (Classics for Exhib.)	General Paper. (Classics.)	English Composition	2 to 5
"	20	German.			2 to 5
Wednesday.	21	Physics and Nat. Sc.	Mathematics.	Mathematics.	9 to 12
		Physics and Nat. Sc.	English.	German.	2 to 5
			German.		

FACULTY OF ARTS.

CHRISTMAS EXAMINATIONS, DECEMBER, 1898.

Day.	Date	First Year.	Second Year.	Third Year.	Fourth Year.
Thursday.	15	Latin.	Latin	Mechanics.	Astronomy.
''	15		M'matics, P.M.		
Friday	16	Greek.	Greek.	Greek.	Greek.
''	16			Zoology, P.M.	Latin, P.M.
Monday.	19	Mathematics.	Psychology.	Latin.	Moral Philosophy.
''	19	French, P.M.	French, P.M.	Ment. Phil., P.M.	Geology, P.M.
Tuesday.	20	Physics.	Botany.		
''	20	German, P.M.	German, P.M.		
''	20	Hebrew, P.M.	Hebrew, P.M.		
Wednesday.	21	English.	History.		

FACULTY OF ARTS.

SESSIONAL AND HONOUR EXAMINATIONS, 1899.

Date.	First Year.		Second Year.		Third Year.		Fourth Year.	
	A.M.	P.M.	A.M.	P.M.	A.M.	P.M.	A.M.	P.M.
30 March	Hebrew		Hebrew.......		Hebrew....		Hebrew and B.A. Honours.	
April								
5 Wed.	Greek.........Greek.		Greek........Greek.		Mechanics.........		Ethics.	Ethics.
6 Thurs.	Latin..........Latin.		Latin........ . Latin.		Latin........Latin.		Latin.	Latin.
7 Fri.	English......English.		Mod. Hist		Ex. Phy- English.		Ex. Phy- English.	
10 Mon.	....		....		sics............ Botany....,.......		sics, Botany,	
11 Tues.	Geometry and Arithmetic....		Mathematics......		Greek. .....Greek.		Mechanics and B.A. Honours.	
12 Wed.	Trigonometry and Algebra.......		Mathematics...		Astronomy and .... Optics.........		Astr'y. and Optics. B.A. Honours.	
13 Thurs.	French. German.		French. German.		Metaphysics.......		Geology. Geology	
14 Fri.	Chemistry		Logic............		Zoology........ ...		Greek. Greek.	
17 Mon.	....		Botany.............		French.. .German.		French. German B.A. Honours.	
19 Wed.	Advanced Section Examinations.		Honour Examinations		Honour Exam'tions		B.A. Honours.	
20 Thurs.	....		....		....			
21 Fri.	Advanced Section Examinations.		Honour Examinations		Honour Exam'tions		B. A. Honours.	
22 Sat.	Meeting of Examin	ers and Faculty at	9.30 A.M.					
23 Sun.	....		....		....			
24 Mon.	Meeting of Examiner	s and Faculty at 9.30	A.M. Declaration	of results.				
25 Tues.	....		....		....		....,....	
26 Wed.	Regular Meeting of C	orporation.........		....		....	
27 Thurs.	....		.. ..		....		....	
28 Fri.	Convocation for Degr	ees in Arts.						

The Examinations begin at 9 A.M. and 2 P.M. when not specified otherwise.

FACULTY OF APPLIED SCIENCE.

SESSIONAL EXAMINATIONS, APRIL, 1899.

DATE.	FIRST YEAR.	SECOND YEAR.	THIRD YEAR.	FOURTH YEAR.
APRIL.				
1 Sat.	....	Building Const. a.m.	Testing Lab. a.m.	Geology.
2 Sun.	Easter Sunday.	....	....	....
3 Mon.	Desc. Geom., a.m.	Desc. Geom.	Theory of Structures	{ Chemistry. Theory of Struct.
4 Tues.	Mathematics.	Chemistry.	{ Chemistry. Elect. Eng.	{ Assaying. Dyn. of Machin'y
5 Wed.	....	Chemistry.	Theory of Structures	{ Chemistry. Elect. Engin. Theory of Struct.
6 Thurs.	Math. Lab.	Surveying.	{ Desc. Geom. Muncip. Eng, p.m. (Sanitary).	Geology (Adv.). Muncp. Eng. p.m. (Sanitary).
7 Fri.	....	Exp. Physics.	Exp. Physics.	{ Elect. Engin. Geodesy. Mechl. Eng.
8 Sat.	....	....	....	....
9 Sun.	....	....	....	....
10 Mon.	Pract. Chem. (1)	Kinematics.	Surveying.	Mechl. Engin. Lab.
11 Tues.	Mathematics.	Mathematics.	{ Machine Design. Org. Chemistry.	{ Hydraulics, a.m. and p.m. Org. Chemistry.
12 Wed.	Desc. Mechanism.	{ Mining. Elem. of Archt. p.m.	Elem. of Archt. p.m.	Elect. Eng.
13 Thurs.	Pract. Chem. (2)	Hist. of Archt. a.m. and p.m.	{ Hist. of Archt. a.m. and p.m. Dyn. of Mach.	{ Elect. Eng. Geology. Machine Design. Theory of Struct.
14 Fri.	Chemistry.	{ Mechl. Drawing. Zoology.	{ Mechl. Drawing. Geology. Phys.Lab.Wk.p.m	Phys. Lab. Wk. p.m.
15 Sat.	Pract. Chem. (3)	....	{ Mining. Thermodynamics.	Thermodynamics.
16 Sun.	....	....	....	....
17 Mon.	Mathematics.	Botany.	Railway Engin.	{ Railway Eng. Geology.
18 Tues.	....	Mathematics.	Mathematics.	{ Municipal Engin. Mechl. Designing.
19 Wed.	....	....	Mineralogy(Adv.).	Geology.
20 Thurs.	....	....	... .	Metallurgy.
21 Fri.	....	....	Mineralogy (Adv.).	....
22 Sat.	....	....	....	....
23 Sun.	....	....	....	....
24 Mon.	....	....	....	....
25 Tues.	....	....	....	....
26 Wed.	....	....	....	....
27 Thurs	....	....	....	....
28 Fri.	Convocation.	....	....	....

N.B.—The Examinations begin at 9.00 a.m. and 2.00p.m. when not specified otherwise.

FACULTY OF ARTS.

TABLE OF CONTENTS.

PART FIRST.

PAGE

I.—OFFICERS OF INSTRUCTION.................................... 3

II.—COURSES OF LECTURES, ETC......................................

    Greek.. 4
    Latin.. 7
    English.. 9
    French.. 12
    German.. 15
    Semitic Languages... 16
    History.. 17
    Mental and Moral Philosophy..................................... 19
    Mathematics and Astronomy....................................... 21
    Mathematics and Physics... 22
    Natural Philosophy.. 23
    Chemistry... 26
    Mineralogy.. 27
    Botany.. 28
    Zoology... 29
    Geology... 29
    Meteorology... 31
    Pedagogy.. 31
    Elocution... 31
    Physical Culture.. 32
    Time Table.. 32-3
        APPENDIX.. 34

III.—UNIVERSITY EQUIPMENT.

    Library... 35
    Museum.. 36
    Physics Building.. 37
    Chemical Laboratories... 40
    Botanical Laboratories.. 40
    Botanic Garden.. 41
    Zoological Laboratory... 41
    Petrographical Laboratory....................................... 42
    Observatory... 42

2

PART SECOND.

	PAGE
I.—REGULATIONS FOR ENTRANCE	44
II.—REGULATIONS FOR DEGREES IN ARTS	51
1. Ordinary Course for B.A.	52
2. Honour Courses and Exemptions	55
3. M.A.	58
4. LL.D.	60
5. Examinations.	60
6. Exemptions for Students in Professional Faculties	64
7. Medals, Prizes, Classing, and Certificates	66
8. Partial Students	70
9. Attendance and Conduct	71
III.—FEES	72
IV.—SCHOLARSHIPS, EXHIBITIONS, AND BURSARIES	74
V.—GENERAL INFORMATION FOR STUDENTS	80
VI.—SPECIAL COURSE FOR WOMEN	81
Time Table	85

Part First.

SIR J. W. DAWSON, LL.D., Emeritus Principal, and Emeritus Professor in the Faculty of Arts.

I. OFFICERS OF INSTRUCTION.

PROFESSORS.

W. PETERSON, M.A., LL.D., Principal, and Professor of Classics.

ALEXANDER JOHNSON, M.A., LL.D., D.C.L., Vice-Principal, Dean of the Faculty of Arts, and Professor of Mathematics.

REV. J. CLARK MURRAY, LL.D., Professor of Mental and Moral Philosophy.

BERNARD J. HARRINGTON, M.A., Ph.D., Professor of Chemistry and Mineralogy.

CHARLES E. MOYSE, B.A., Professor of the English Language and Literature.

D. P. PENHALLOW, B.Sc., M.A.Sc., Professor of Botany.

REV. DANIEL COUSSIRAT, B.A., D.D., O.A., Professor of Hebrew and Oriental Literature.

JOHN COX, M.A., Professor of Physics.

A. JUDSON EATON, M.A., Ph.D., Associate Professor of Classics.

FRANK D. ADAMS, M.A.Sc., Ph.D., Professor of Geology and Palæontology.

———, Professor of Physics.

C. W. COLBY, M.A., Ph.D., Professor of History.

FRANK CARTER, M.A., Professor of Classics.

ERNEST WILLIAM MACBRIDE, M.A., B.Sc., Professor of Zoology.

———, Professor of Chemistry.

LECTURERS.

PAUL T. LAFLEUR, M.A., Lecturer in Logic and English.

LEIGH R. GREGOR, B.A., Ph.D., Lecturer in the German Language and Literature.

MAXIME INGRES, Lecturer in French.

(The above Professors and Lecturers constitute the Faculty.)

OTHER OFFICERS OF INSTRUCTION.

C. H. MCLEOD, Ma.E., Superintendent of the Observatory.

NEVIL NORTON EVANS, M.A.Sc., Lecturer in Chemistry.

REV. H. M. TORY, M.A., Lecturer in Mathematics, and Demonstrator in Physics.

C. M. DERICK, M.A., Lecturer in Botany.

REV. J. L. MORIN, M.A., Sessional Lecturer in French.

S. B. SLACK, M.A., Lecturer in Classics.

F. H. PITCHER, B.A.Sc., Demonstrator in Physics.

ALEX. BRODIE, B.A.Sc., Demonstrator in Chemistry.

HOWARD T. BARNES, M.A.Sc., Demonstrator in Physics.

J. P. STEPHEN, Instructor in Elocution.

R. TAIT MCKENZIE, B.A., M.D., Instructor in Physical Culture.

II. COURSES OF LECTURES.

Classical Literature and History.

Professors :—W. Peterson, M.A., LL.D.
Frank Carter, M.A.

Associate Professor :—A. J. Eaton, M.A., Ph.D.
Lecturer :—S. B. Slack, M.A.

In this department, the work of the first two years is divided mainly between exercise in Grammar and Composition and the reading of selected authors. The attention of the student is at the same time directed to the collateral subjects of History, Literature, Antiquities, and Geography, in connection with which various text-books are recommended, as specified below.

In the Third and Fourth Years (as also in the Honour Courses) the instruction takes more of the lecture form, and an attempt is made to give a connected view of the leading branches of ancient literature and the most important phases of ancient life and thought.

Students may be examined on the whole of the work prescribed for each class, even though it may not have been overtaken in lecture.

Subjects are suggested for Summer Readings in the various branches of class work. Students are strongly recommended to undertake these subjects during their long vacation, and credit will be given for them at an examination held in the course of the Session.

———

Greek.

Ordinary First Year. 1. In this class, besides a review of grammatical principles (Rutherford's Greek Grammar, Accidence), portions of some Greek authors—*e. g.*, XENOPHON, HOMER, HERODOTUS, LUCIAN and EURIPIDES —are read and explained.

For 1898-99 the work will be Demosthenes, Olynthiacs I-III (Glover, Pitt Press); Homer, Odyssey IX (Mayor, Macmillan); Euripides, Alcestis, 1-746 (Hadley, Pitt Press). *History*—from B. C. 560 to 479, Cox's Greeks and Persians (Longmans' Epoch Series). For *Composition*, the manual used will be Abbott's Arnold's Greek Prose Composition (Longmans); for *Translation at Sight*, written and oral, Turner's Latin and Greek Passages (Longmans).

Second Year. 2. The work of the Second Year will be selected mainly from the Greek Dramatists, and from THUCYDIDES, PLATO or DEMOSTHENES.

Subjects for 1898-99:—

SUMMER READINGS. — Luciani Vera Historia (Jerram, Clarendon Press). *History* —The Athenian Supremacy; Cox's "Athenian Empire" (Longmans' Epoch Series) with Abbott's Pericles (Putnam). *Literature.*—Outlines as contained in Jebb's Primer of Greek Literature, pp. 1-100. Students are also recommended to work through some portion of Burnet's Greek Rudiments (Longmans).

SESSIONAL LECTURES.—Thucydides, The Seige of Plataea (Sing, Rivingtons); and the Retreat from Syracuse (Rouse, Rivingtons); Sophocles, Ajax (Jebb, Rivingtons, or Campbell & Abbott, Clarendon Press). The practice of *Composition* and *Translation at Sight* will be continued as before ; Sidgwick's First Greek Writer and Jerram's Anglice Reddenda (First Series).

The following books are recommended for general use during the first two years of the course :—Jebb's Introduction to Homer (Maclehose) ; Jebb's Primer of Greek Literature, supplemented by readings in Murray, Jevons or Mahaffv ; Gow's Companion to School Classics (in part); Oman's History of Greece (Longmans); Mahaffy's Primer of Greek Antiquities; and Tozer's Primer of Classical Geography (Macmillan). Rutherford's Greek Grammar (Accidence and Syntax); or Sonnenschein's (Parallel Grammar Series), or Burnet's Greek Rudiments.

Students should provide themselves also with Kiepert's Atlas Antiquus.

Subjects for 1898-99:—

3. SUMMER READINGS. — Sophocles, Antigone (Jebb, Pitt Press, or Campbell & Abbott, Clarendon Press). *History.*—The Peloponnesian War and Outlines to the Battle of Chaeronea (Oman's History, with Sankey's Spartan and Theban Supremacies, Longmans). *Literature.*—The origin and growth of the Drama. The Historians and Orators (Murray's Ancient Greek Literature, Heinemann). **Third Year .**

SESSIONAL LECTURES.—Isocrates, Panegyricus (Sandys, Longmans): Euripides, Iphigenia at Aulis (Headlam, Pitt Press). For practice in *Composition*, Sidgwick's Introduction to Greek Prose Composition will be used; for *Translation at Sight* Fowler's Sportella (Longmans).

4. Subjects for 1898-99.—

SUMMER READINGS.—Merriam's "The Phaeacians of Homer" (Harper's); The Constitutional History of Athens, with a general study of Greek Antiquities and Literature. **Fourth Year.**

SESSIONAL LECTURES.— Plato, Republic, I. and X. (Adam, Cambridge University Press); Aeschylus, Eumenides (Sidgwick, Clarendon Press). *Composition* and *Translation at Sight* as in the Third Year.

The following books are recommended for general use : Gow's Companion to School Classics (Macmillan) ; Jebb's Growth and Influence of Classical Greek Poetry (Macmillan); Campbell's Guide to Greek Tragedy (Percival); Abbott's Pericles (Putnam); Jevon's or Mahaffy's or Murray's History of Greek Literature; Kiepert's Manual of Ancient Geography (Macmillan); Greenidge's Constitutional History. King & Cookson's Comparative Grammar (Clarendon Press).

Honours.

Third and Fourth Years. 5. The work of the Honours Classes in Greek has been so arranged as to admit of separate courses of lectures being given, with illustrative readings, along certain main lines of literary study, in addition to supplementary work as provided for below. In 1898-99, the Lecture Courses will be as under, the books selected for class reading being specified under each separate head :—

A. Greek Lyric Poetry : PINDAR, Seymour's Selected Odes (Ginn).

B. Greek Oratory : DEMOSTHENES, de Corona (Drake, Macmillan).

C. Greek Drama : EURIPIDES, Hercules Furens (Gray & Hutchinson, Pitt Press).

Translation at Sight.—Fox & Bromley's Models and Exercises (Clarendon Press).

Prose Composition —Sidgwick, and from Dictation.

Seminary Work —Essays and lectures on History, Literature, Comparative Philology and Ancient Philosophy.

Third Year. *Private Reading.*—Homer, Iliad XVI-XVIII (Leaf, Macmillan); Plato, Phaedo (Archer Hind, Macmillan) ; Thucydides, VI (Marchant, Macmillan); Sophocles, Antigone (Jebb, Pitt Press ; or Campbell & Abbott, Clarendon Press).

In *History* the examination will be directed to testing a general knowledge of the course of Greek History to the death of Alexander, and a more minute knowledge of the development of the Athenian Constitution and the period of Athenian Supremacy. In *Literature*, a general knowledge will be expected of the course of Greek literature, and a more minute knowledge of the lives and writings of the authors prescribed.

Fourth Year. 6. *Private Reading.*—HOMER, Iliad, XVI-XVIII (Leaf, Macmillan) ; SOPHOCLES, Trachiniae (Jebb) ; HERODOTUS, Book VII (Butler, Macmillan) ; THUCYDIDES, VII (Marchant, Macmillan), ARISTOPHANES, Wasps (Starkie, Macmillan); Attic Orators (Jebb's Selections, Macmillan); ARISTOTLE, Poetics, omitting XX and XXV (Butcher, Macmillan); Ethics I, II, and X (Bywater, Oxford); THEOCRITUS, I-XV (Snow, Clarendon Press); PLATO, Gorgias (Lodge, Ginn).

History, Literature and Antiquities.—Oman, Symonds, Murray ; Jebb's Growth and Influence of Classical Greek Poetry; Leaf's Companion to the Iliad; Butcher's Aspects of the Greek Genius; Mahaffy's Social Life in Greece; Jebb's Attic Orators.

Grammar and Philology.—Goodwin's Greek Moods and Tenses, and Giles's Short Manual of Philology (Macmillan); Monro's Homeric Grammar (Clarendon Press).

Latin.

Ordinary First Year.

1. In this class, besides a general review of grammatical principles (Sonnenschein's Latin Grammar; Parallel Grammar Series)—portions of some Latin author, such as OVID, TIBULLUS, LIVY, SALLUST, VIRGIL, HORACE or CICERO—are read and explained.

For 1898-99, the subjects will be OVID, Metamorphoses XIII, 1-622 (Keene, Bell & Sons; Simmons, Macmillan) : CICERO, De Senectute (Howson, Longmans) ; VIRGIL, Georgics IV (Sidgwick, Pitt Press.) For practice in *Composition*, both written and oral, the text-book in use during the first two years will be Heatley's Latin Exercises (Longmans), with selected Passages for continuous Prose; and for *Translation at Sight*, Turner's Latin and Greek Passages (Longmans). *History.*—Carthaginian Wars, B. C., 263-146; Shuckburgh's History of Rome, or Rome and Carthage (Longmans' Epoch Series).

2. For 1898-99, the subjects will be :—

Second Year.

SUMMER READINGS. — Livy XXI (Capes & Melhuish, Macmillan). *History.*—The last Century of the Republic, B. C., 133-31 ; The Roman Triumvirates (Merivale, Longmans' Epoch Series); Beesly's The Gracchi, Marius and Sulla (Longmans' Epoch Series). Students are also recommended to work through some portion of Ramsay's Manual of Latin Prose Composition (Vol. I).

SESSIONAL LECTURES.—CICERO, The Fourth Verrine Action (Hall, Macmillan); HORACE, (Wickham's Selected Odes, Clarendon Press); QUINTILIAN X, ch. I, sections 37-131, being Quintilian's Review of Ancient Literature (Peterson, Clarendon Press, smaller edition). *Composition* and *Translation at Sight,* Ramsay's Manual of Latin Prose Composition, Vol. I. (Clarendon Press); and Jerram's Anglice Reddenda (First Series).

The following books are recommended for general use during the first two years of the course: Shuckburgh's History of Rome (Macmillan) ; Strachan-Davidson's CICERO, and Warde-Fowler's CAESAR (Putnam); Wilkins's Primer of Roman Literature, Wilkins's Primer of Roman Antiquities; Latin Grammar, Gildersleeve and Lodge.

Students should provide themselves also with Kiepert's Atlas Antiquus.

Third Year.

3. Subjects for 1898-99.

SUMMER READINGS. — VIRGIL Aeneid VI. (Sidgwick, Pitt Press). *History.*—The Making of Rome (to 390 B. C.), Ihne's Early Rome (Epoch Series), and Shuckburgh's History. *Literature.*—Mackail's Primer of Roman Literature.

SESSIONAL LECTURES. —Pliny's Letters—Books i-ii (Cowan, Macmillan); TERENCE, Phormio (Sloman, Clarendon Press); Martial, Selections.

The text-book for *Composition* will be Sargent's Easy Latin Prose Exercises (Clarendon Press); and for *Translation at Sight*, Fowler's Sportella (Longmans).

Fourth Year.

4. Subjects for 1898-99.

SUMMER READINGS. — TACITUS, Annals IV (Furneaux, Clarendon Press). *History.*—Capes's Early Roman Empire (Longmans' Epoch Series); or Bury's History (John Murray), down to Domitian.

SESSIONAL LECTURES.— LIVY, V (in part), (Whibley, Pitt Press); JUVENAL, Selected Satires (Strong, Clarendon Press); TIBULLUS Selections). *Composition* and *Translation at Sight*, as in the Third Year.

NOTE —The following books are recommended for general use : Gow's Companion to School Classics (Macmillan) ; Mackail's Latin Literature (Murray); How & Leigh's History of Rome (Longmans); Pelham's Outlines of Roman History (Percival) ; Cape's Early Roman Empire (Longmans' Epoch Series) ; Kiepert's Manual of Ancient Geography (Macmillan).

Honours.

Third and Fourth Years.

5. As in Greek, the work of the Honours Classes in Latin has been so arranged as to admit of separate courses of lectures being given, with illustrative readings, along certain main lines of literary study, in addition to supplementary work as provided for below. In 1898-99, the Lecture Courses will be as under, the books selected for class reading being specified under each separate head —

A. Latin Comedy and Satire : PLAUTUS, Captivi (Hallidie, Macmillan), and HORACE, Satires, Book I (Palmer, Macmillan).

B. Latin Oratory : CICERO, Pro Milone (Reid, Cambridge Press), with TACITUS Dialogus de Oratoribus.

C. Latin Poetry : LUCRETIUS, V (Duff, Pitt Press), and MARTIAL Selections (Paley and Stone, Bell).

Translation at Sight.—Fox & Bromley's Models and Exercises (Clarendon Press). *Prose Composition.*—Nixon's Prose Extracts ; and Selected Passages.

Seminary Work.—Essays and Lectures on History, Literature, Comparative Philology and Ancient Philosophy.

Private Reading. HORACE, Epistles I (Wilkins, Macmillan) ; CICERO, Pro Roscio Amerino (Donkin, Macmillan); VIRGIL, Aeneid VI (Sidgwick, Pitt Press); SALLUST. Catiline (Capes, Clarendon Press); Cicero, Select Letters (Pritchard & Bernard, Clarendon Press). **Third Year.**

History.—A general knowledge of Roman History to the end of the First Century A. D., and more minute knowledge of the period from B. C. 146 to the Death of Augustus.

Literature.—A general knowledge will be expected of the course of Roman Literature, and a more minute knowledge of the lives and writings of the authors prescribed.

6. *Private Reading.*—PLAUTUS, Trinummus (Gray, Pitt Press); CICERO, de Officiis (Holden, Pitt Press); HORACE, Odes I and II (Gow, Pitt Press); VIRGIL, Aeneid X. (Sidgwick, Clarendon Press); TACITUS, Annals I. (Furneaux, Clarendon Press) ; Dialogus de Oratoribus (Peterson, Clarendon Press) ; PERSIUS (Conington, Clarendon Press). **Fourth Year.**

History, Literature, and Antiquities.—How & Leigh's History of Rome (Longmans); Tyrrell's Latin Poetry; Students' Companion to Latin Authors (Middleton & Mills, Macmillan).

Grammar and Philology.—Lindsay's Short Historical Latin Grammar (Clarendon Press) and Giles's Short Manual of Philology (Macmillan); Lindsay's Textual Emendation (Macmillan).

English Language and Literature.

Professor :—Chas. E. Moyse, B.A.

Lecturer in Rhetoric and English :—P. T. Lafleur, M.A.

1. A. ENGLISH LITERATURE AND COMPOSITION—A course of lectures chiefly synthetical, on the principles of English composition, with special reference to the use of words and the construction of sentences and paragraphs. Regular essays are required of all students. One hour a week. **Ordinary First Year.**

Studies of authors and masterpieces of English literature in a course of about twenty-five lectures. For 1898-9 the subject will be the leading prose Essayists of England from Bacon to Goldsmith. The treatment is critical rather than biographical, the intention being to explain the origin and growth of essay-writing as a characteristic form of modern literary expression, together with the causes which have assisted in permanently establishing its popularity. Incidentally, this course proves ancillary to (A) through the opportunity which it offers of discussing analytically the style of the authors under examination. One hour a week.

B. EUROPEAN HISTORY, (DR. COLBY)—Twenty-five lectures will be given on the outlines of Classical, Mediæval and Modern History, including

Colonial expansion since the 15th century. The design of this course is less to present a mass of facts than to illustrate the chief features of racial, political and social progress. Short historical papers will be required at regular intervals from each student. One hour a week.

Third Year. 2. A course on MIDDLE ENGLISH. CHAUCER'S, Prologue to the Canterbury Tales (Morris and Skeat, Clarendon Press) will be read in class, and used to illustrate the leading features of the development of the English Language. The life and thought of Chaucer's day will be touched on, and the social aspects of England illustrated by lantern slides. (To be taken with 3.) One hour a week.

Third Year. 3. A course on RHETORIC. Text-Book : GENUNG, Rhetoric. (To be taken with 2.) One hour a week.

Fourth Year. 4. A course on the LEADING POETS OF THE NINETEENTH CENTURY. The chief aspects of the French Revolution will be considered, and Republican feeling in England illustrated, chiefly from the works of WORDSWORTH, COLERIDGE and SOUTHEY. The indirect revolutionary poets BYRON and SHELLEY will then be considered, and their typical poems, together with those of the poets already mentioned, critically examined. The remainder of the course will be given to SCOTT, KEATS, TENNYSON, BROWNING and SWINBURNE— *In the course for 1898-99, special attention will be given to Tennyson and Browning.* One hour a week.

Private reading will also be required of the student, and the time to be given to this part of the subject may be regarded as equivalent to that required to obtain a good knowledge of the matter of the lectures.

Honours.
Fourth Year. 5. MŒSO-GOTHIC. The course on Moeso-Gothic is intended to open the way to the comparative study of allied Teutonic languages. Particular attention will be given to the phonological relations of Moeso-Gothic and Anglo-Saxon. *Text-book :* The Gospel of St. Mark (Skeat, Clarendon Press). One hour a week.

Third Year. 6. ANGLO-SAXON. An elementary course on Anglo-Saxon. The object of the course is to make the student familiar with the grammar of the language and to enable him to read easy passages at sight. Leading features of Teutonic philology will be noticed when the text calls for them. Exercises in Anglo-Saxon scansion will form a part of the regular work of the class. *Text-Books :* SWEET, Anglo-Saxon Primer and Anglo-Saxon Reader, Extt. IV.-VIII., and the pieces in verse. Two hours a week.

7. ANGLO-SAXON, BEOWULF. The text will be read in class and illustrated by notes on origins, philology, and verbal emendations. *Text-Book:* Harrison and Sharp (Ginn). One hour a week. Fourth Year.

8. EARLY AND MIDDLE ENGLISH. The course is intended to give a knowledge of dialectal English, and to illustrate the changes which the language has undergone. *Text-books :* MORRIS and SKEAT'S Specimens, Part II., Extt. I.-IX. CHAUCER, Parlement of Foules. (Skeat, Minor poems of Chaucer, Clarendon Press.) One hour a week. Third Year.

9. EARLY ENGLISH. The course is a continuation of 8. *Text-book :* MORRIS and SKEAT'S Specimens, Part II., Extt. X. -XX. One hour a week. Fourth Year.

10. ELIZABETHAN AND EARLY STUART PERIODS The general influences visible in the literature of the periods will be noticed by way of introduction to a critical examination of the following works which have been selected for private study : SPENSER, Shepheards Calender (Herford, Macmillan); Faerie Queene, Bk. I. (Percival, Macmillan); SIDNEY, An Apology for Poetry (Cook) ; MILTON, Shorter English Poems (Browne, Clarendon Press) ; and Areopagitica (Hales). One hour a week. Third Year.

11. SHAKSPERE. The social and literary conditions of Elizabethan England will be noticed, and the characteristics of the pre-Shaksperian drama specially illustrated. The following plays have been selected for special criticism and private study : Love's Labour Lost (Rolfe) ; A Midsummer Night's Dream (Deighton, Macmillan); Hamlet (Deighton, Macmillan) ; and the Tempest (Deighton, Macmillan). One hour a week. Fourth Year.

12. LATER STUART PERIOD. The method of 10 will be followed. The works selected for private study are : DRYDEN, Annus Mirabilis, Absolom and Achitophel, Part I., the Preface to the " Fables " (Globe Edition, or for Absolom and Achitophel, Dryden's Satires, ed. Collins, Macmillan). ADDISON, Essays on Paradise Lost and on the Imagination (Spectator, ed. Henry Morley, Routledge). One hour a week. Third Year.

13. LATER STUART PERIOD. An introductory sketch of the critical and philosophical essayists in verse, leading up to a more minute examination of the following works of POPE, which have been selected for private study : Essay on Criticism (Churton Collins, Macmillan) ; Essay on Man (Morris, Macmillan). One hour a week. Fourth Year.

Third Year.
14. PERIOD OF POPULAR INFLUENCE. Influence of the French Revolution. The influence of the French Revolution on contemporary English Literature will be discussed. The following poems have been selected for special criticism and private study ; WORDSWORTH, Prelude (Moxon's edition or Deut's), and CAMPBELL, Pleasures of Hope. One hour a week.

Fourth Year.
15. MODERN POETS. An interpretation in detail of TENNYSON'S In Memoriam and a comparative criticism of other famous English poems of the same class. An outline of the growth of the Arthur Saga and a special examination of TENNYSON'S Idylls of the King. BROWNING, Christmas Eve and Easter Day.

In addition to the poems just mentioned, MILTON'S Lycidas, SHELLEY'S Adonais, and MATTHEW ARNOLD'S Thyrsis have been selected for private study. One hour a week.

Note.—**Honour** students of the Third Year will privately study the following works, and write an essay on some topic arising from them: BURKE. Reflections on the French Revolution; LESLIE STEPHEN, English Thought in the Eighteenth Century, Vol. II., chap. X., secs. V. to X. inclusive. The Essay will count in the awarding of honours.

Honour students of the Fourth Year will, in like manner, take the following : MORE, Utopia ; MATTHEW ARNOLD, Essays in Criticism (the Second Series).

Readings from authors who do not find a place in the above courses will be given by Prof. Moyse on Saturdays, at noon. The selections will be taken for the most part from writers of the present century. Attendance is voluntary.

French.

Lecturer in French :—M. Ingres, B-ès-Lettres.
Sessional Lecturer :—J. L. Morin, M.A.

The earlier courses of instruction in French have been framed with the view of enabling the student to speak and write the language with facility and correctness. In the later courses, particular attention will be given to the style and substance of leading French writers, both in prose and verse, and also to the historical development of the French language and literature. Instruction will be given according to the natural method, the French language being exclusively used.

Ordinary First Year.
1. The following outline will indicate the character of the course:
(a) The oral reproduction of stories by French writers of the present century, so selected as to bring out the national aspects of French life.

In connection with this part of the work, words will be referred to groups and their formation noticed. (b) Biographical sketches of the leading writers of the present century, illustrated by typical selections from their works, which will be read by the class, and committed to memory. Points of grammar will be treated incidentally, and the elements of French prosody taught. (c) Private Reading, the amount and character of which will be determined by the requirements of the individual student. The following works may be taken as specimens of the literature chosen for the class : Pages choisies d'ANATOLE FRANCE (G. Lanson), ed. Colin ; Pages choisies d'ALEXANDRE DUMAS (H. Parigot), ed. Colin; A. DE VIGNY, Servitude et Grandeur militaire; BALZAC, Eugénie Grandet. In the examination of the students of affiliated colleges the extracts given for translation from French into English will be taken, in part, from the four works mentioned above.

There will be regular written exercises—dictation and composition. Students are recommended to use Le Dictionnaire Larousse (Paris edition.) Four hours a week.

2. The method of the course is the same as that of 1, but the more advanced points of grammar will be treated, and in literature particular attention will be directed to characteristics of style. **Second Year.**

The following works may be taken as specimens of the literature chosen for the class : Pages choisies de G. FLAUBERT (G. Lanson), ed. Colin ; Pages choisies de TH. GAUTIER (P. Sirven), ed. Colin ; VICTOR HUGO, Notre · Dame de Paris; G. SAND, Le Marquis de Villemer.

In the examination of the students of affiliated colleges the extracts given for translation from French into English will be taken, in part, from the four works mentioned above.

There will be regular written exercises—dictation and composition. Students are recommended to use Le Dictionnaire Larousse.

Three hours a week.

3. A continuation of 2. The form and origin of words will be treated more fully than in previous courses, and an outline of philology given. In the literary portion of the course the leading characteristics of the Classic, Romantic, Realistic, Impressionist and other schools will be described. Biographical sketches of writers who belong to the XVII. and XVIII. centuries will be given, and illustrated by typical selections from their works, which will be read in class and committed to memory. The following works, or portions thereof, of the same period have been chosen for private reading previous to their consideration by the class : B. DE ST. PIERRE, Paul et Virginie; VOLTAIRE. Siècle de Louis XIV.; ROUSSEAU, Emile, Le **Third Year.**

Contrat Social; CORNEILLE, Le Cid, Horace, Cinna; RACINE, Athalie,
Phèdre, Andromaque; MOLIÈRE, Tartuffe, Le Misanthrope, Le Bourgeois Gentilhomme; MME DE SEVIGNÉ, Lettres; BOSSUET, Discours
sur l'Histoire universelle; Oraisons funèbres; PASCAL, Lettres pro-
vinciales.

There will be regular written exercises in composition.

Two hours a week.

Fourth Year.

4. Important historical changes of various kinds in the vocabulary
of French will be noticed, and sentences presenting peculiar difficulties ·
explained. The origin of the French language will be more fully
treated, and French literature previous to Corneille read. Biographical sketches of leading writers of that period will be given, and
typical selections from their works committed to memory. The following works or portions thereof, have been chosen for private reading previous to their consideration by the class: MONTAIGNE, Essais, La Satire
Ménippée ; DESCARTES, Discours de la méthode; AMYOT, Traduction
de Plutarque ; CALVIN, L'Institution chrétienne ; RABELAIS, Gargan-
tua, Pantagruel ; COMMINES, Louis XI.; JOINVILLE, Vie de saint
Louis; FROISSART, Chroniques ; VILLEHARDOUIN, Chroniques.

There will be regular written exercises in composition.

Two hours a week.

Honours. Third Year.

5. *Grammar.*—A course on French grammar treated historically.
Students are recommended to consult the following works: BRACHET,
Grammaire Historique de la Langue Française, Dictionnaire Etymo-
logique ; BRUNOT, Grammaire historique de la Langue française ;
CLÉDAT, Grammaire de la vieille langue française; LITTRÉ, Histoire
de la Langue française ; F. BRUNETIÈRE, Études critiques ; G. PARIS,
La Littérature française au moyen age.

Literature.—The student is expected to undertake a thorough study
of the following works, portions of which will be read in class : LE
ROMAN DE LA ROSE ; LE ROMAN DE RENART ; J. BÉDIER, Les Fabliaux;
PETIT DE JULLEVILLE, Les Mystères.

Two hours a week.

Fourth Year.

6. A course in Old French. The student will be guided in a comparative study of the Romance languages, and will use the following
works of reference : E. RENAN, Essaie sur la Poésie des Races cel-
tiques; EGGER, l'Hellénisme en France ; ROQUEFORT, Glossaire de la
Langue romane ; CUSGNY, Grammaire de la Langue d'Oil ; BRÉAL,
Grammaire comparée ; F. DIEZ Grammaire des Langues romanes ;
MEYER-LUBKE, Grammaire des Langues romanes.

The literary biography and history of the period will be treated, and in connections therewith the following works will be read:

JEAN BODEL, Le Jeu de saint Nicolas ; WACE, Le Roman de Rou, Le Roman de Brut, LA CHANSON DE ROLAND ; LA VIE DE SAINT ALEXIS, LA VIE DE SAINT LEGER.
Two hours a week.

German Language and Literature.

Lecturer :—L. R. Gregor, B.A., Ph.D.

The ordinary Courses mainly keep practical ends in view. As far as possible they place the student at the German standpoint, so that he may study the language from within. Some time is devoted to colloquial exercises in the First and Second Courses ; special attention is given to Literature in the Third and Fourth. The German Language is employed to a considerable extent in the Third and Fourth Courses. Importance is attached to correct and expressive reading. Classic texts are carefully studied, from the aesthetic and critical, as well as from the historical and linguistic points of view. A considerable amount of translation is done in class, and English-German exercises are supplemented by the "retranslation" of texts.

1. THE JOYNES-MEISSNER German Grammar (Heath & Co.) ; **First Year.** FREYTAG, Die Journalisten ; UHLAND, Ballads and Romances (Macmillan) ; BAUMBACH, Der Schwiegersohn (Heath & Co.) ; SCHILLER, Maria Stuart; prominence is given to written exercises.
Four hours a week.

2. THE JOYNES-MEISSNER German Grammar ; SCHILLER, Die **Second** Jungfrau von Orleans ; STORM, Immensee (Heath & Co.); HEINE, **Year.** Die Harzreise; Dictation; prominence is given to written exercises.
Two hours a week.

3. BENEDIX, Die Hochzeitsreise ; GOETHE, Iphigenie ; LESSING, **Third** Nathan der Weise ; German Grammar ; Translations from English **Year.** into German; History of German Literature.
Two hours a week.

4. SCHILLER, Die Braut von Messina ; GOETHE, Egmont ; HEINE, **Fourth** Prose Selections ; German Grammar ; History of German Literature. **Year.**
Two hours a week.

Lectures in this Course are given entirely in the German Language. **Honours.** They reproduce and extend the main elements of the Ordinary Courses. In addition to this class of studies an account is given of the development of the German Language. Students are encouraged to undertake independent work, to write German compositions on literary subjects of especial interest to themselves. In order to obtain First or Second Rank honours, candidates must also be capable of speaking German.

Two hours a week.

Honour Students of the Third and Fourth Years take lectures together. The order in which the following text-books are taken up is subject to re-arrangement :—

Third Year.

5a A special study of GOETHE's Faust (Part I.) ; GOETHE. Leiden des jungen Werther ; Selections from HERDER'S Volkslieder ; Macmillan's German Composition.

N.B.—The above constitutes the Additional course. See p. 57.

5b. GOETHE, Egmont ; LESSING, Emilia Galotti ; Extracts from FREYTAG'S Bilder aus der deutschen Vergangenheit; SCHILLER Don Carlos ; History of German Literature (KLUGE) ; Historical Grammar.

Fourth Year.

6a. LESSING, Laokoon ; BEHAGHEL, Deutsche Sprache ; GRILLPARZER, Sappho ; SCHILLER, Die Braut von Messina ; Macmillan's German Prose Composition.

N.B.—The above constitutes the Additional Course. See p. 57.

6b. GOETHE, Sessenheim (Heath & Co.) ; KLOPSTOCK, Messias. (one canto); WIELAND, Oberon (Selections); SUDERMANN, Die Ehre ; SCHEFFEL, Trompeter von Säkkingen, Selections from HEINE's Lyrical Poems ; HARTMANN VON AUE, Gregorius auf dem Steine; ZARNCKE, Das Nibelungenlied. History of German Literature (KLUGE) ; Original Compositions in German.

Semitic Languages.

Professor :—D. Coussirat, B.A., B.D., D.D., Officier d'Académie.

The course comprises lectures on the above languages and their literature, their genius and peculiarities. Comparative philology, affinity of roots, etc., also receive due attention, while the portions selected for translation will be illustrated and explained by reference to Oriental manners, customs, history, etc.

1. Hebrew grammar and translation continued. English rendered into Hebrew. Masoretic notes explained. The Hebrew text compared with the .Septuagint and Vulgate Versions. Two hours a week. Ordinary Second Year.

2. Hebrew Syntax. Translation of difficult passages of the Old Testament. Notes on the MASSORA and the TALMUD (Mishna and Gemara). Two hours a week. Third Year.

3. Translation continued.` Characteristics of the Semitic Languages, particularly of ARAMAIC, SYRIAC, SAMARITAN, RABBINIC, ARABIC, ASSYRIAN, SEMITIC INSCRIPTIONS. Two hours a week. Fourth Year.

Honours

4a. HEBREW. Genesis. Isaiah, 40-66. Ecclesiastes. *Literature.*—F. LENORMANT, The beginnings of History. Third Year.

4b. ARAMAIC,—Daniel. Ezra. Selections from the Targums. *Literature.*—SAYCE, Lectures on the Origin and Growth of Religion. Two hours a week.

5a. HEBREW.—Malachi, Psalms, 1-72 ; Job, 26-42. *Literature.*— RENAN. A general History of the Semitic Languages. Fourth Year.

5b. SYRIAC.—Selections from the Peshito, and from the CHRONICLES OF BAR HEBRÆUS. *Literature.*—W. WRIGHT, Comparative Grammar of the Semitic Languages. Two hours a week.

4b and 5b. (*Literature excepted*) are the Additional Courses.

History.

Professor :—Charles W. Colby, M.A., Ph.D.

Ordinary First Year.

1. THE MAIN EPOCHS OF EUROPEAN HISTORY.

Twenty-five lectures will be given on the outlines of Classical, Mediaeval and Modern History, including colonial expansion since the 15th century. The design of this course is less to present a mass of facts than to illustrate the chief features of racial, political and social progress. At the Sessional Examination the results will be taken account of under the head of English. Short historical papers will be required at regular intervals from each student. (*Vide* English. I. pp. 9 and 10.) One hour a week.

Second
Year.

2. THE POLITICAL HISTORY OF EUROPE FROM 1789 TO 1878.

The method of instruction followed in this course is topical rather than chronological. The lectures seek to present leading movements and tendencies in relief with a view to explaining the course of modern international relations. The most important subjects to be examined are the French Revolution, the growth of Democracy and Nationality, the Eastern Question, and the actual political state of the British Empire.

Two hours a week.

Honours.

Th rd and
Fourth
Year.

3. THE GERMAN INROADS AND THE MIDDLE AGES.

These lectures extend from the recognition of Christianity as a state religion to the death of Dante. Among the subjects with which they deal may be reckoned the character and organization of the Early Church; the laws, political institutions, and conquests of the German nations; the Empire of Charlemagne ; the Holy Roman Empire in its relations with the Papacy; Feudalism; Monasticism; the Crusades; Romanesque and Gothic Architecture; the Schoolmen; and Dante. An attempt will be made to present mediaeval civilization in its positive aspects.

Three hours a week.

4. STUDIES IN THE HISTORY OF DEMOCRATIC INSTITUTIONS DURING THE MIDDLE AGES.

Two hours a week.
(Omitted in 1898-99.)

5. THE RENASCENCE AND THE REFORMATION.

Three hours a week.
(Omitted in 1898-99.)

6. THE FRENCH REVOLUTION, 1789-95.

Three hours a week.
(Omitted in 1898-99.)

SUMMER READINGS.

Students who are devoting special attention to the literary branches of the University course are advised to read, during the long vacation, either the first or the second set of the subjoined selections.

I. HERODOTUS, VI-VIII, Macaulay's trans.; THUCYDIDES, I., II., 1-65, VI., VII., Jowett's trans : PLATO, the Republic, Jowett's trans : PLUTARCH, the Lives of Aristides, Themistocles, Pericles, and Timoleon, Clough's trans : POLYBIUS, I., II., V., Shuckburgh's trans ; LIVY, XXI.-XXII., Church and Brodribb's trans : TACITUS, Annals II., Germania, Vita Agricolae, Church and Brodribb's trans.

II. CLARENDON, History of the Rebellion, Book XI.; GIBBON, Decline and Fall, Chaps. XLIV., L., LI., LXVI.; BURKE, Reflections on the French Revolution ; HALLAM, Middle Ages, Chap. III.; MACAULAY, History of England, Chap. III.; BAGEHOT, The English Constitution ; STUBBS, Select Charters, Introduction ; BRYCE, The Holy Roman Empire, Chaps. I.-XV.; LORD ACTON, German Schools of History, English Historical Review, Vol. I.; MATTHEW ARNOLD, Pagan and Mediaeval Religious Sentiment, in Essays in Criticism (First Series).

Mental and Moral Philosophy.

Professor :—J. Clark Murray, LL.D.

Lecturer :—P. T. Lafleur, M.A.

Ordinary Second Year.

1. This course takes up in the first term the elements of Psychology, in the second the elements of Logic. Students are referred, among other works, to MURRAY, Handbook of Psychology, Book I., and to JEVONS, Elementary Lessons on Logic.

Three hours a week.

Third Year.

2. In the first term the course takes up the Logic of Induction. Students are referred specially to MILL, System of Logic, Book III.

Two hours a week.

In the second term the course takes up the most interesting problems in the Psychology of Cognition, tracing, as far as possible, the principal stages in the evolution of intelligence. The general problem, also, of the nature of knowledge is discussed, in view of the light which it throws on the ultimate nature of reality. Students are referred, among other works, to MURRAY, Handbook of Psychology, Book II., Part I. Students are also required to write an essay on some philosophical subject.

Two hours a week.

Fourth Year.

3. This course is devoted entirely to Moral Philosophy, and follows, in its general outline, the subjects discussed in MURRAY's Introduction to Ethics. Students are also required to write essays on ethical questions.

Three hours a week.

Honours. Third Year.

4. This course is devoted mainly to the history of Greek Philosophy. It begins with the colonial period, during which philosophical activity was most energetic among the colonies of the Greeks in Asia Minor and Italy. It then passes on to the Athenian period,

beginning about the middle of the fifth century, B.C., when Philosophy found a home in the greatest centre of intellectual life in the
ancient world. A third period is then described, during which Philosophy extends its culture over ancient life by the spread of the great
schools, especially the Stoical and the Epicurean, which arose towards
the end of the fourth century, B. C. Finally, some account is given
of the movement, of which Alexandria was the centre, and by which
Greek Philosophy was brought into contact with Oriental thought.
The history is carried down to the closing of the Pagan Schools in
Athens by the Emperor Justinian. Occasional lectures are also given
on the other special studies of the Third Year Honour Course.
Students are expected to make an independent study of the fragments
of one of the early philosophers, and to write an essay embodying
the results of their study.

Two hours a week.

The subjects of examination will be, in addition to the lectures,
the following :—

Part I.—Schwegler's History of Philosophy, Chapters 1-21 inclusive;
Mill's System of Logic, Books IV. and V. ; James' Principles
of Psychology, Chapters 10-16 inclusive ; selected portions
from Thomson's Outline of the Laws of Thought, from
Jevons' Principles of Science, and from Venn's Empirical
Logic. Any two of these subjects, along with the Honour
Lectures, may be taken as the Additional Course.

Part II.—Plato's Theatetus (by S. W. Dyde) ; Fraser's Selections
from Berkeley.

**Fourth
Year.**

5. The lectures of this Year form two courses. One is devoted
to the ·earlier period· of· Modern Philosophy.· After 'sketching the
transition from Mediaeval to Modern thought, the course gives some
account of the Empirical movement started in England by Bacon and
Hobbes, and developed by Locke and his school. The Idealistic
tendency of speculation during this period is sketched mainly in three
movements :—that which began in England with the Cambridge
Platonists. and culminated in Berkeley; the German movement originated by Leibnitz, and formulated by Wolf ; the Cartesian movement
which culminated in Spinoza. The course closes with a lengthy
exposition of KANT's three Critiques.

First term, two hours a week ; second term, one hour a week.

6. The other course is on the History of English Philosophy from
Hartley to Herbert Spencer. The lectures discuss the chief characteristics of English thought during the last one hundred and fifty

years, more particularly as shewn in the works of English psychologists and political writers during that time. The writers to whom special attention is given are : in Psychology—PRIESTLEY, HARTLEY ERASMUS DARWIN. the two MILLS, BAIN, and HERBERT SPENCER ; in Political and Social Science—BURKE, PAINE, GODWIN, PALEY, BENTHAM, MALTHUS. References are also made to minor writers, whose work may be deemed to be of sufficient importance in the general movement and development of philosophy. No text-book is specially recommended; but the student is expected to read appointed selections from the writers under discussion, as well as to consult LESLIE STEPHEN's History of English Thought in the Eighteenth Century, and a few chapters in LEWES' History of Philosophy. The principal points emphasized in the lectures are the empirical character of the English school in psychology and metaphysics, and the practical, utilitarian view of English political writers.

Second term; one hour a week.

Students are expected to write an essay exhibiting an independent study of one of the modern philosophers.

The subjects of examination, in addition to the lectures, will be the following :—

Part I.—Erdmann's History of Philosophy, Vol. II. (Engl. Transl.); James' Principles of Psychology, Vol. II. ; Spencer's First Principles ; Watson's Comte, Mill and Spencer, an Outline of Philosophy ; Mill's System of Logic, Book VI. Any two of these subjects along with the Honour Lectures may be taken as the Additional Course.

Part II.—Aristotle's Nicomachean Ethics ; Zeller's Stoics, Epicureans and Sceptics ; Spinoza's Ethics ; Watson's Selections from Kant ; Maine's Ancient Law.

Mathematics and Astronomy.

Professor :—Alexander Johnson, M.A., LL.D.
Lecturer :—Rev. H. M. Tory, M.A.

1. MATHEMATICS—Arithmetic.—Euclid, Books, 1, 2, 3, 4, 6 (omitting propositions 27, 28, 29), with definitions of Book 5, TODHUNTER's edition, or HALL AND STEVENS'; the latter is recommended to Students in Advanced Sections especially. COLENSO's Algebra (Part I.) to end of Quadratic Equations. — GALBRAITH AND HAUGHTON, Plane Trigonometry. Nature and use of Logarithms.

Ordinary First Year

Four hours a week.

Advanced*
Section. 2. MATHEMATICS.—HALL and STEVENS, Euclid; CASEY, Sequel to Euclid ; HALL and KNIGHT, Advanced Algebra ; TODHUNTER or BURNSIDE and PANTON, Theory of Equations (selected course). Two or three hours each week.

Second. 3. MATHEMATICS.—Arithmetic, Euclid, Algebra and Trigonometry as
Year. before.—Nature and use of Logarithms.—Numerical solution of triangles and practical applications.
One hour a week.

Third Year 4. (*Optional, but open to those only who have studied Mathematical Physics*).—ASTRONOMY—LOCKYER, Elementary Astronomy, English edition ; first five chapters, viz. : The Stars and Nebulae ; The Sun ; The Solar System ; Apparent movements; Time. Students are recommended to use with this an " Easy Guide to the Constellations," by GALL. This subject is taken with Optics.
Hours to be arranged.

Fourth 5. ASTRONOMY.—(*Optional*.) GALBRAITH and HAUGHTON'S Astronomy
Year. or Brinkley by Stubbs and Brunnow.—This subject is taken with Optics as one course. The lectures will be given before Christmas.
First term ; two hours a week.

Mathematics and Physics.

Professors (Mathematics) :—A. Johnson, M.A., LL.D.
     "   (Physics) :—John Cox, M.A.
     "   "

Lecturer (Mathematics, First Year):—Rev. H. M. Tory, M.A.
Demonstrators in Physics:—Rev. H. M. Tory, M.A., and F. H. Pitcher, B.A.Sc.

Honours. 6. MATHEMATICS.—LOCK, Higher Trigonometry, with McCLELLAND
Second. and PRESTON, Spherical Trigonometry, Part I. ; SALMON,
Year. Conic Sections, chapters 1, 2, 3, 5, 6, 7, and 10 to 13 inclusive ; WILLIAMSON, Differential and Integral Calculus (selected course).
Three hours a week.

Third 7. MATHEMATICAL PHYSICS.—MINCHIN, Statics, Vol. I. (selected
Year. chapters) ; WILLIAMSON and TARLETON, Dynamics, Chaps. 1 to 8 inclusive ; BESANT Vol. I., Hydro-Mechanics, Part I., chaps. 1, 2, 3, 7 ; PARKINSON, Optics.
Two hours a week.

* *Honours may be awarded in the Advanced Section (see page* 52.)

8. MATHEMATICS.—WILLIAMSON, Differential and Integral Calculus and BOOLE or FORSYTH, Differential Equations, or Salmon, Geometry of Three Dimensions, (alternate years).

ASTRONOMY.—GODFRAY.

Two hours a week.

EXPERIMENTAL PHYSICS.— Courses 5 and 7.

9. MATHEMATICS.—WILLIAMSON, Differential and Integral Calculus ; **Fourth** SALMON, Conic Sections ; SALMON, Geometry of Three **Year.** Dimensions (course selected in text-book) ; BOOLE or FORSYTH, Differential Equations (selected course).

10. PHYSICAL ASTRONOMY.—GODFRAY, Lunar Theory ; or CHEYNE, Planetary Theory ; or the Theory of the Tides ; NEWTON, Principia, Lib. I., secs. 9 and 11, with the necessary preliminary propositions.

11. MATHEMATICAL PHYSICS.—MINCHIN, Statics, Vol. II., selected chapters ; WILLIAMSON and TARLETON, Dynamics ; ROUTH, Dynamics of a Rigid Body (for reference) ; BESANT, Hydro-Mechanics ; PRESTON, Theory of Light ; CUMMING, Theory of Electricity.

EXPERIMENTAL PHYSICS.—Courses 6 and 8.

The ANNE MOLSON MATHEMATICAL PRIZE ($64) will be offered for competition in September in a part of the above courses.

Natural Philosophy.

Professors :— John Cox, M.A.

Demonstrators :— Rev. H. M. Tory, M.A.
F. H. Pitcher, B.A.Sc.
Howard T. Barnes, M.A.Sc.

I. Physics.

1. PHYSICS.—This course has two objects:—(1) to give the minim- **Ordinary** um acquaintance with Physical Science requisite for a liberal edu- **First Year.** cation to those whose studies will be mainly literary; (2) to be introductory to the courses in Chemistry and other branches of Natural Science, and to the more detailed courses in Physics in the Third and Fourth Years. Only the most important principles in each branch of the subject will be treated, as far as possible with reference to their historical development and mutual relations; and they will

receive concrete illustration in the study of the principal instruments in daily use in the laboratory. Two illustrated lectures will be given per week. During the session each student will be required to attend in the laboratory eight times, and make measurements involving the use of the following instruments;—*Balance, Pendulum, Barometer, Thermometer, Sonometer, Spherical Mirror or Lens, Tangent Galvanometer, Wheatstone's Bridge.*

Outline of Syllabus. The scope and method of Science. Primary Phenomena ("States and Properties of Matter") Motion, Velocity, Acceleration. Laws of Motion, Momentum, Energy, Work. The Parallelogram Law for Velocities and Forces. Equilibrium and the Simple Machines. Uniform circular motion, Vibration, the Pendulum. Fluid Pressure, the Barometer, Specific Gravity. Summary of *Mechanics*, indicating the Principle of the Conservation of Energy.

The missing Energy traced in (1) *Sound*. Nature of wave Motion. Intensity, Pitch, and Quality of Musical notes. The stretched String and Organ Pipe. Resonance.

(2) *Heat.* Temperature and the Thermometer. The Calorimeter, Fusion and Vaporisation. Laws of Boyle and Gay-Lussac. The Mechanical Equivalent. Application of Conduction, Connection and Radiation to common problems of Climate, Ventilation, etc.

(3). *Light.* Reflection, Refraction, the Spherical Mirror, Prism, Lens, Microscope, Telescope, Spectroscope, Polariscope. Principle of Interference and sketch of the Undulatory Theory.

(4). *Electricity and Magnetism.* The Electrophorus, the Modern Induction Machine, the Condenser. Coulomb's Law of Force. The idea of Potential. The Quadrant Electrometer. Atmospheric Electricity, Magnetic Pole, Moment, Field, and Law of Force. The Compass and Terrestrial Magnetism. Effects of Current. The Voltameter and Storage Cell. The Galvanometer. Heating effects. Simple Batteries. Ohm's Law. Units and Measurement of Current, Resistance, Electromotive Force. Mutual Mechanical Effects of Conductors and Magnetic Fields. Principle of the Electric Motor. The Electro-magnet. Induction of Currents, and Principle of the Dynamo. Applications to Telegraph, Telephone, Lighting, and supply of Power.

Conclusion.—Restatement of Principle of Conservation of Energy in complete form. Description of Energy.

Two hours a week.

Ordinary   **II. Mathematical Physics.**

Second   2. ELEMENTARY MECHANICS. One hour a week up to February.
Year. An introductory course, without a Text-book, developing the fundamental principles of Mechanics.

One hour a week.

MECHANICS AND HYDROSTATICS ; *Text-book*, LONEY, Mechanics and Hydrostatics for Beginners.
Two hours a week till January.

Third Year.

4. OPTICS; *Text-book*, GALBRAITH and HAUGHTON.
Two hours a week, from January to end of Session.

Third Year.

III. Experimental Physics.

5. LAWS OF ENERGY, SOUND, LIGHT AND HEAT. *Text-book*, GANOT or JONES, Physics. Lectures fully illustrated.
Two hours a week.

Third Year.

6. ELECTRICITY AND MAGNETISM. *Text-Book*, GANOT or S. P. THOMPSON, Physics. Lectures fully illustrated.
Two hours a week.

Fourth Year.

IV. Laboratory Courses.

In Experimental Physics, requiring three hours per week to be spent in practical measurements in the Macdonald Physical Laboratory, during the Third and Fourth Years, in conjunction with the Lecture Courses 4 and 5.

7. (*a*) SOUND —Velocity of Sound ; Determination of rates of vibration of Tuning Forks ; Resonance ; Laws of vibration of strings.

Third Year.

(*b*) LIGHT—Photometry ; Laws of Reflection and Refraction ; Indices of Refraction ; Focal Lengths and Magnifying Powers of Mirrors, Lenses, Telescopes and Microscopes; the Sextant, Spectroscope, Spectrometer, Diffraction Grating, Optical Bench, and Polariscopes.

(*c*) HEAT—Construction and Calibration of Thermometers ; Melting and Boiling Points ; Air Thermometer ; Expansion of solids, liquids, and gases ; Calorimetry.

8. MAGNETISM.—Measurements of Pole Strength and Moment of a Magnet ; the Magnetic Field ; Methods of Deflection and Oscillations ; comparison of moments and determination of elements of Earth's magnetism. Frictional Electricity. Current Electricity.—Complete course of measurements of Current Strength, Resistance and Electromotive Force : Calibration of Galvanometers ; the

Fourth Year.

Electrometer ; comparison of Condensers ; Electromagnetic Induction.

Text-book.— GLAZEBROOK and SHAW, Practical Physics.

N.B.—For Advanced Courses intended for Electrical Engineering Students and Graduates pursuing the study of Physics, see Calendar, Faculty of Applied Science.

Chemistry.

Professors :—B. J. Harrington, M.A., Ph. D.

Lecturer :—Nevil Norton Evans, M.A.Sc.
Demonstrator :—Alexander Brodie, B.A.Sc.

1*a.* GENERAL CHEMISTRY.—A course of lectures on elementary chemical theory, and on the principal elements and their compounds. The lectures are fully illustrated by means of experiments, and are supplementedby tutorial classes. *This course, given in the Faculty of Applied Science, is open to Partial Students in Arts.*

Three hours a week.

Text-book.— REMSEN'S Introduction to the Study of Chemistry.

1*b.* ELEMENTARY PRACTICAL CHEMISTRY.— Experiments in connection with the above course of lectures performed by the students, and Elementary Qualitative Analysis. (*Open to Partial Students in Arts.*

Ordinary One afternoon a week.

Second Year. 2. INORGANIC CHEMISTRY (*Advanced and Optional*).—The Chemistry of the principal electro-positive elements and their compounds. (Arrangements may be made for this Course for Session 1898-99.)

Third Year 3. ORGANIC CHEMISTRY.— Lectures, with occasional demonstrations, on the analysis of organic bodies, calculation of formulæ. determination of molecular weights, polymerism, isomerism, etc., followed by a discussion of some of the more important Methane derivatives and their constitution. Students intending to enter the Medical Faculty, would find courses 3 and 4 and the laboratory work connected therewith of great advantage.

Fourth Year. 4. ORGANIC CHEMISTRY.—Lectures in continuation of those in Course 3, discussing some of the principal Benzene and Pyridine derivatives. Students should have previously taken Course 3.

5. ANALYTICAL CHEMISTRY (QUALITATIVE).—A systematic study of the **Third Year**
more important bases and acids, including their detection and
separation. The laboratory work is accompanied by explanatory lectures.

Text-book.—Qualitative Chemical Analysis, by ARTHUR A
NOYES.
Six hours a week.

6. ANALYTICAL CHEMISTRY (QUANTITATIVE).—Laboratory practice in **Fourth**
methods of gravimetric, volumetric and electrolytic Quantita- **Year.**
tive Analysis. The course is open to those who have taken
No. 5.
Text-book.—CLOWES & COLEMAN'S Quantitative Analysis.
Six hours a week.

7. PHYSICAL CHEMISTRY *(Optional)*.—A course of lectures on **Third Year**
Stoechiometry and Chemical Affinity. Special attention is
directed to those parts of the subject which have a direct bearing on the processes of practical chemistry, such as the modern
theories of solution and electrolytic dissociation.
One hour a week.

Mineralogy.

Professor:—B. J. Harrington, M.A., Ph.D.

8. MINERALOGY.—Lectures and demonstrations illustrated by models **Honours. Third Year**
and specimens in the Peter Redpath Museum. Among the
subjects discussed are : Crystallography ; physical properties
of minerals dependent upon light, electricity, state of aggre-
gation, etc. ; chemical composition, calculation of mineral
formulae, quantivalent ratios, etc. ; principles of classification,
description of species.
First term, one hour a week; second term, two hours a week.

9. MINERALOGY **(In** continuation of No. 8.).—Description of **Fourth**
species, particular attention being paid to those which are **Year.**
important as rock constituents and to the economic minerals
of Canada.
First term, two hours a week.

10. ⊃ DETERMINATIVE MINERALOGY.—Laboratory practice in blowpipe **Third Year**
analysis and its application to the determination of mineral
species.
Thursday, 2 to 5 p.m.

Botany.

Professor :—D. P. Penhallow, B.Sc., M. A.Sc.
Lecturer :—C. M. Derick, M.A.

Ordinary Second Year. 1. GENERAL MORPHOLOGY. This course is designed to give a thorough general knowledge of the principles of General Morphology and Classification. It comprises :

(*a*) A practical course embracing the determination of species from both fresh and dry material, and type studies of Spermatophytes, Pteridophytes, Bryophytes and Thallophytes, with reference to their life histories. Gray's Manual, Penhallow's Outlines of Classification, and Botanical 'Collector's Guide.
First term, three hours a week.

(*b*) A course of lectures dealing with General Morphology and Classification, Elements of Histology, and Physiology ; Biological relations of plants ; Geographical Botany.
Second term, two hours a week.

Third Year 2. ADVANCED BOTANY. This course, open only to students who have taken Botany 1, is designed to give an extended knowledge of vegetable anatomy and special morphology. It comprises :—
(*a*) Optics and construction of the microscope ; determination of amplifications ; micrometry ; drawings ; section cutting ; preparation of microscopic objects ; micro-chemical reactions; study of cell contents and tissues; comparative studies of type forms of angiosperms and gymnosperms.
Botanical Microtechnique (Zimmermann, trans. by Humphrey).
Six hours a week.

Honours Fourth Year. (*b*) A course in Special Morphology, forming a part of the Honours Course in Biology, and open to students who have satisfactorily completed Botany 1 and 2*a*, of which latter it is a continuation. It includes critical studies of the structure and development of the Thallophyta, Bryophyta and Pteridophyta, together with special readings on Biological problems. The following types will be studied:—A Myxomycete, Bacteria, Chroococcus, Nostoc, Rivularia, Spirogyra Pleurococcus, Oedogonium, Vaucheria, Fucus, Nemalion, Rhizopus, Penicillium, Puccinia, Agaricus, Pellia, Polytrichum, Pteris, Equisetum, Lycopodium, Selaginella. Comparisons with other forms in each group will also be made.
This course, when taken separately, ranks as an ordinary subject.
Six hours a week.

The fee for the Session in each of the above courses, viz. 2 (*a*) and 2 (*b*) is $10. Students are required to supply their own slides and cover glasses.

Zoology.

Professor :—Ernest William MacBride, M. A., B.Sc.
Demonstrator:—

1. ELEMENTARY ZOOLOGY.—This course is designed to make the student thoroughly acquainted with the main types of structure met with in the animal kingdom, and with the principles on which the modern science of Zoology is founded. It comprises a study both theoretical and practical of the following types, viz·: Amoeba, Vorticella, Hydra, Craspedote Medusa, Alcyonium, Lumbricus, Nereis, Cambarus, Cyclops, Limulus, Periplaneta, Asterias, Echinus, Unio, Buccinum. Amphioxus, Mustelus, Rana and Lepus·
Six hours a week.

Ordinary Third Year.

2. ADVANCED ZOOLOGY.—This course, open only to students who have acquitted themselves creditably in the Third Year Examination in Zoology, forms part of the course for Honours in Biology. It comprises a study, theoretical and practical, of a number of additional types; a comparative study of the principal forms of development met with in the animal kingdom, and a special knowledge of vertebrate embryology. Attention will also be given to the general problems of philosophical zoology, especially such as are engaging the attention of zoologists at the present time.

Honours.

This course, when taken separately, ranks as an ordinary subject.
Six hours a week.

N.B.—Both these courses include two formal lectures. and two periods of laboratory instruction in the week. Under no circumstances will a student be allowed to attend the lectures without taking practical work.

The fee for the Session in each of the above courses is $10.

Geology and Palæontology.

Professor :—Frank D. Adams, M.A.Sc., Ph. D.
Demonstrator :—

1. GENERAL GEOLOGY.—The lectures will embrace a general survey of the whole field of Geology, and will be introduced by a

Ordinary Fourth Year.

short course on Mineralogy.   Especial attention will be devoted to Dynamical Geology and to Historical Geology, including a description of the fauna and flora of the earth during
the successive periods of its past history.

The lectures will be illustrated by the extensive collections in
the Peter Redpath Museum, as well as by models, maps, sections
and lantern views. There will be an excursion every Saturday
until the snow falls, after which the excursion will be replaced
by a demonstration in the Museum.

Text-book.—DAWSON, Hand-book of Geology.*Books of Reference.*—DANA, Manual of Geology; BONNEY, Story of our Planet.

Three hours a week throughout the year, with additional excursions and demonstrations as above stated.

Honours.
**Fourth
Year.**

2. PETROGRAPHY.—The modern methods of study employed in Petrography are first described, and the classification and description
of rocks is then taken up.

One lecture a week during the second term. One afternoon
a week during the second term will be devoted to special
microscopical work in the Petrographical Laboratory.

Books of Reference.—ROSENBUSCH, Mikroskopische Physio-
graphie, and RUTLEY, Rock-forming Minerals

**Fourth
Year.**

3. PALÆONTOLOGY.— An extension of the Palaeontology of Course
I, with special studies of some of the more important groups
of fossils.

One lecture a week during the second term and one demonstration a week, with special studies in the Peter Redpath
Museum.

Books of Reference.— NICHOLSON and LYDEKKER, Manual of
Palaeontology; ZITTEL, Text-Book of Palaeontology.

**Fourth
Year.**

4. PRACTICAL AND APPLIED GEOLOGY.—A description of the methods
employed in observing and recording geological facts, concluding with a general treatment of the nature and mode of
occurrence of Ore Deposits.

One lecture and one demonstration a week during first term.

Text-book.—GEIKIE, Outlines of Field Geology ; KEMP,
Ore Deposits of the United States. PHILLIPS and LOUIS, A.
Treatise on Ore Deposits.

**Fourth
Year.**

5. CANADIAN GEOLOGY.—A general description of the Geology and
Mineral Resources of the Dominion.

One lecture a week during the second term.

Text-book.—DAWSON, Hand-book of Geology.

Books of Reference.—The Reports of the Geological Survey of Canada.

6. GEOLOGICAL COLLOQUIUM.—A discussion each week of some Geological topic, references to the literature of which have been given by the Professor in the week preceding. The course is intended to give students some acquaintance with Geological literature, as well as a wider knowledge of the great principles which underlie the Science. **Fourth Year.**

One hour a week in second term.

Additional private reading will also be required of Candidates for Honours.

Students taking any of these courses are entitled to tickets of admission to the Museum of the Natural History Society of Montreal.

Meteorology.

Superintendent of Observatory :—C. H. McLeod, Ma.E.

Instruction in Meteorological Observations will be given in the Observatory at hours to suit the convenience of the senior students.

Certificates will be granted to those students who pass a satisfactory examination on the construction and use of Meteorological instruments and on the general facts of Meteorolgy.

Pedagogy.

Principal of the Normal School:—S. P. Robins, M.A., LL.D.

Lectures on this subject will be given in the Normal School to undergraduates of the Third and Fourth Years who wish to obtain the Provincial Academy Diploma.

Lecture hours to be arranged.

Elocution.

Instructor :—J. P. Stephen.

Instruction is given in this subject at hours that may be settled at the beginning of the session.

Physical Culture

Medical Examiner and Instructor :—R. Tait McKenzie, B.A., M.D.
The classes will meet at the University Gymnasium, at hours to be announced at the commencement of the Session. The Wicksteed Silver and Bronze Medals (the gift of Dr. R. J. Wicksteed) are offered for competition to students of the Graduating Class and to students who have had instruction in the Gymnasium for two sessions,—the silver medal to the former, the bronze medal to the latter. (See Regulations appended.)

LECTURES IN THE UNDERGRADUATE COURSE IN THE FACULTY OF ARTS.

Session 1898-99.

YEARS	HOURS.	MONDAY.	TUESDAY.	WEDNESDAY.	THURSDAY.	FRIDAY.
FIRST YEAR.	9	Mathematics.	Mathematics.	Mathematics.	Greek.	Mathematics.
	10	Latin.	Greek.	Latin.	French.	Greek.
	11	French.	German.	German.	German.	English.
	12	Physics.	French.	English.	Latin.	Physics.
	2	Greek.	English.	French.		Latin.
	3		.			German.
SECOND YEAR.	9	French. German.	Logic.	French.	German. Hebrew.	French.
	10	Greek.	Hebrew.	Logic.	Logic.	†Mathematics.
	11	Mathematics.	Latin.	Botany. †Mathematics.	Latin.	Greek.
	12	Botany. †Mathematics.	Greek.	Latin.	Mod. History.	Mod. History.
	2	Math. Phys.				
	3					
	4					

THIRD YEAR.

9	English.	Greek Phys. Hebrew			German.
10	Chaldee.	French.	Math. Physics. Chaldee.	French. Chemistry.	Rhetoric.
11	Metaphysics. I	Zoology.	Metaphysics.	Zoology.	Math.Physics
12	Latin.	Exp. Physics.	Greek.	Exp. Physics, Hebrew.	Latin.
2	Pract. Chem.	Botany.	Pract. Chem. Pract Zool.		Botany.
3		German ?	Pract Zool.		
4					†History.

FOURTH YEAR.

9	Exp. Physics.	Astronomy (a)	Geology. Syriac.	Exp. Physics.	Latin. German.
10	Geology. Syriac.	French. Latin.	Latin.	English Lit.	Geology.
11	Greek.	Moral Phil.	Greek.	Moral Phil.	French.
12	Moral Phil.	Organic Chem	Miner. Demons.	Hebrew. Astronomy,(a)	
2	Pract. Chem. Zoology.	Botany.	Pract. Chem. Zoology.	Pract. Chem.	Botany.
3		German ?			
4					

Advanced Sections will be formed in all subjects in the first two years, so far as practicable and in these Honours may be awarded. In Mathematics there is an Advanced Section in the First Year, 2 hours a week.

† For Candidates for Honours. (a) During First Term.

Honour Courses (Third and Fourth Years) will be given in the following subjects, the precise hours for which will be arranged to suit the convenience of the classes :—

CLASSICS : Third and Fourth Years, 6 hours a week.
ENGLISH : Third Year, 6 hours a week ; Fourth Year, 6 hours a week.
FRENCH : Third Year, 2 hours a week ; Fourth Year, 2 hours a week.
GERMAN : Third Year, 2 hours a week ; Fourth Year, 2 hours a week.
SEMITIC LANGUAGES : Third Year, 2 hours a week ; Fourth Year, 2 hours a week.
HISTORY : Third and Fourth Years, 5 hours a week.
MENTAL AND MORAL PHILOSOPHY : Third Year, 2 hours a week ; Fourth Year, 2 hours a week.
MATHEMATICS, MATHEMATICAL PHYSICS AND ASTRONOMY : Third Year, 4 hours a week ; Fourth Year, 4 hours a week.
GEOLOGY AND MINERALOGY : Third Year, 4 hours a week (First Term) ; 5 hours a week (Second Term) ; Fourth Year, 7 hours a week.
BIOLOGY : 4 hours a week and 4 periods of Practical Work.

The CHEMICAL LABORATORIES are open every day (except Saturday) from 9 a.m. to 5 p.m. The Lectures on Chemistry and Laboratory classes are all open to Arts Students.

PRACTICAL PHYSICS : Third Year, Monday, 10 a.m. to 1 p.m., or Friday, 2.30 p.m. to 5.30 p.m. ; Fourth Year, Wednesday, 2.30 p.m. to 5.30 p.m.

The BOTANICAL LABORATORIES are open daily from 9 a.m. to 5 p.m. Saturday Classes in General Morphology (2nd Year), 11 a.m. to 1 p.m.

GEOLOGY : Demonstrations and Excursions on Saturday. The Petrographical Laboratory is open every day throughout the Second Term.

The ZOOLOGICAL LABORATORY is open daily from 9 a.m. to 1 p.m. and from 2 p.m. to 5 p.m. Practical Work under the supervision of the Professor and Demonstrator, Monday and Wednesday, 2 to 4 p.m., and Saturday, 9 to 12 a.m. The time for Practical Work in the Fourth Year will be arranged.

N.B.—*The hours in this table are subject to alteration during the session.*

C

Appendix.

A revision of the curriculum is in progress.

In the Third and Fourth Years the various subjects of study will be arranged in groups, as under, and students will be permitted to select *not more than six*, under certain conditions, to be afterwards specified in detail.*

Language and Literature.—English, Latin, Greek, *Sanskrit*, French, German, *Italian*, *Spanish*, Hebrew, Chaldee and Syriac.

Philosophy.—Logic and Metaphysics, Moral Philosophy, *Political Science*, *Economics*, Education, History of Philosophy.

Science.—Mathematics, Physics, Astronomy, Chemistry, Zoology, Botany, Geology, Physiology, Human Anatomy.

History and Law.—History, Art and Archaeology, Constitutional Law and History, Roman Law, Public Law, History of Philosophy, *History of Political Science*.

Honour Courses, which shall not commence before the Third Year, are or will be established in the following subjects:—

1. Classics (*i.e.*, Latin and Greek, with optional subjects, such as Comparative Philology, Ancient Philosophy and Classical Archaeology).
2. English Language and Literature.
3. Modern Languages and Literature.
4. Semitic Languages and Literature.
5. History.
6. Mental Philosophy.
7. Mathematics; Physics; Chemistry (as may be arranged).
8. Biology: (*a*) Botany. (*b*) Zoology.
9. Geology (including Mineralogy and Palaeontology).

---

*The subjects printed in italics are those for which no instruction is as yet provided by the University.

III. UNIVERSITY BUILDINGS, Etc.

The University Library.

The various libraries of the University now contain about 67,000 bound volumes, besides many valuable pamphlets.

The books have been selected with a view to illustrating the various courses of University study. They are, therefore, to a considerable extent, general in character ; and the Committee endeavours to provide for the symmetrical growth of the entire library.

There are, however, several large special collections, besides the departmental libraries. The late Mr. Peter Redpath was, for years before his death, engaged in forming the REDPATH HISTORICAL COLLECTION, which is now of great value, and affords unusual opportunities for the study of English History. An important feature of this collection is a series of 3,500 political and religious tracts, which date from 1601 to about the middle of the present reign.

Abundant materials, bearing upon the History of Canada, have been gathered together. Of these the nucleus is formed by the entire library of the late Mr. Frederick Griffin, whose choice books were, some years ago, bequeathed to the University. This branch of the library is being steadily augmented.

The Medical Library, directly controlled by the Faculty of Medicine, is the largest of the departmental libraries, and is one of the most complete collections of its kind in the Dominion.

About 175 current periodicals, literary and scientific, are subscribed for through the various departments of the University. Besides these, the library regularly receives many Secials, Transactions and Proceedings of Societies. The list of both periodicals and serials is being extended yearly.

A new Card Catalogue of the entire library has been for some time in hand, but is not as yet complete.

In the autumn of 1893, the general library was moved to the noble building erected by the late Mr. Peter Redpath. The building affords ample accommodation for two hundred readers, the reading room being exceptionally spacious and convenient. The reading room is open in the evening, and contains a reference library, and leading English and Foreign periodicals.

Although the library is maintained primarily for members of the University, the Corporation has recently provided for the admission, upon certain conditions, of such persons as may be approved by the Library Committee. It is the desire of the Committee to make the library as useful to the entire community as is consistent with the safety of the books and the general interests of the University.

EXTRACT FROM THE LIBRARY REGULATIONS.

1. During the College Session the Library is open daily (except Sundays and general public holidays), from 9 a.m. till 5 p.m. ; and the Reading Room from 9 a.m. till 6 p.m., and also from 8 till 10 p.m. On Saturdays, both Library and Reading Rooms close at 5 p.m. During vacations, both Library and Reading Rooms close at 5 p.m., and on Saturdays at 1 p.m.

2. Students in the Faculty of Arts, of Law, or of Applied Science may borrow books on depositing the sum of $5 with the Bursar, which deposit, after the deduction of any fines due, will be repaid at the end of the Session on the certificate of the Librarian that the books have been returned uninjured.

3. Students in the Faculties of Medicine, or Comparative Medicine, who have paid the Library fee to the Bursar, may read in the Library, and on depositing the sum of $5 with the Bursar, may borrow books on the same conditions as Students in Arts. They are required to present their Matriculation Tickets to the Bursar and to the Librarian.

4. Graduates in any of the Faculties, on making a deposit of $5, are entitled to the use of the Library, subject to the same rules and conditions as Students, but they are not required to pay the annual Library fee.

5. Books may be taken from the Library only after they have been charged at the Delivery Desk; borrowers who cannot attend personally must sign and date an order, giving the titles of the books desired.

6. Books in the Reference Library must not be taken from the Reading Room ; and, after they have been used, they must be returned promptly by readers to their proper places upon the shelves.

7. Before leaving the Library, readers must return the books they have obtained, to the attendant at the Delivery Desk.

8. All persons using books remain responsible for them, so long as they are charged to them, and borrowers returning books, must see that their receipt for them is properly cancelled. Damage to, or loss of books shall be made good to the satisfaction of the Librarian and of the Library Committee. Writing or making any mark upon any book belonging to the Library is unconditionally forbidden. Any person found guilty of wilfully damaging any book

in any way shall be excluded from the Library, and shall be debarred from the use thereof for such time as the Library Committee may determine.

9. Should any borrower fail to return a book upon the date when its return is due, he may be notified by postal card of his default, and be requested to return the book. If the loan is not renewed, or the book returned, after a further delay of at least three days, it may be sent for by special messenger, at the borrower's expense.

10. Before the close of the session, Students in their final year shall return uninjured; or replace to the satisfaction of the Librarian, all books which they have borrowed.

11. Silence must be strictly observed in the Library.

The Peter Redpath Museum.

This building was erected in 1882 by the liberal benefactor whose name it bears. It occupies a commanding position at the upper end of the campus, and besides its central hall and other rooms devoted to the collections, contains a large lecture theatre, class-rooms and work-rooms.

The general arrangement of the collections is as follows:—

1. The Botanical Room on the ground floor contains the Herbarium, consisting of 30,000 specimens of Canadian and exotic plants, and collections illustrating structural and economic botany.

2. On the first floor is a room over the entrance hall, in which are cases containing archaeological and ethnological objects, with large slabs of fossil foot-prints on the walls.

3. This room opens into the great Museum Hall, on either side of which are alcoves with upright and table cases containing the collections in Palaeontology, arranged primarily to illustrate the successive geological systems, and subordinately to this, in the order of zoological and botanical classification, so as to enable the student to see the general order of life in successive periods, and to trace any particular group through its geological history.

4. At the extreme end of the Hall are placed the collections of minerals and rocks, arranged in such manner as to facilitate their systematic study. In the centre of the Hall are economic collections and large casts and models.

5. In the upper story or gallery of the great Hall are placed the zoological collections—the invertebrate animals in table cases in regular series, beginning with the lower forms, the vertebrate animals in upright cases, in similar order. The PHILIP CARPENTER COLLEC-

TION of shells is especially noteworthy for its arrangement and completeness.

Details as to the several departments of the Museum are given in the " Museum Guide," and papers or memoirs relating to type specimens in the collections can be obtained from the Museum Assistant. Tickets are issued to students by the Professors in charge of the several departments, and classes of pupils from schools can be admitted on certain days, under regulations which may be learned from the Professors or from the Secretary of the University.

The Macdonald Physics Building.

The Macdonald Physical Laboratory contains five storeys, each of 8,000 square feet area. Besides a lecture theatre and its apparatus rooms, the Building includes an elementary laboratory nearly 60 feet square; large special laboratories arranged for higher work by advanced students in Heat and Electricity; a range of rooms for optical work and photography ; separate rooms for private thesis work by Students; and two large laboratories arranged for research, provided with solid piers and the usual standard instruments. There are also a lecture room, with apparatus room attached, for Mathematical Physics, a special physical library, and convenient workshops. The equipment is on a corresponding scale, and comprises: (1) apparatus for illustrating lectures; (2) simple forms of the principal instruments for use by the Students in practical work; (3) the most recent types of all important instruments for exact measurement, to be used in connection with special work and research.

The following extract made from the report for the year 1894-95 of the Physics Building Committee will indicate the general nature and extent of the equipment.

Resistance Standards.—There are thirty standard resistance coils of various patterns, including the B.A., the Board of Trade and the German, with a few others, ranging in value from 1,000 ohms to one ten-thousandth, and adapted for various purposes. These have been tested and compared, and their values are found to agree as closely as could be expected with the Cambridge certificates, and those of the Reichsanstalt and the makers. The temperature coefficients of a few have also been determined. The comparisons have been made chiefly with Nalder's pattern of the Carey-Foster Bridge.

There is also a duplicate of the Fleming Bridge used at Cambridge, presented by the Duke of Devonshire.

Resistance Boxes.—The collection of resistance boxes includes almost all the best types. There is a Thomson-Varley slide-box by

Nalder, which has proved extremely useful and accurate. Among the other boxes, may be mentioned : two megohm boxes and four 100,000 ohm boxes of different patterns; a four dial and a six dial P. O. box; and a bar-dial box of Professor Anthony's pattern; also a compensated resistance box with mercury contacts, reading from o to 50 ohms continuously by the Carey-Foster method ; this is extremely useful for the accurate determination of resistances which cannot be made up of any simple combination of standards, and has been accurately calibrated throughout.

For the comparison and determination of small resistances, there is a Kelvin conductivity bridge and a Lorenz apparatus, with the improvements made by Prof. V. Jones, which is now being completed under his supervision.

Current Standards.—There is a Kelvin composite balance, which can also be used as a voltmeter, and wattmeter, and two Siemens dynamometers. The constants of these have been determined by the voltametric method, and found to be accurate to one-half of one per cent. They have been used for calibrating common types of alternate current instruments. There is also a set of 4 large storage cells with convenient commutators and resistances for furnishing large steady currents for the testing of ammeters and low resistances and for other purposes. This equipment is similar to that in use at the Board of Trade in England and in the laboratories of some leading instrument makers.

As an absolute current standard there is a duplicate of the Weber electro-dynamometer made by Latimer Clark for the Committee of the British Association, the coils of which were wound by Clerk Maxwell, and used by Lord Rayleigh in his standard experiments. The coils of this instrument have been rewound and measured, and it is proposed to use it for an absolute determination of the E. M. F. of a Clark Cell.

Insulation and Capacity Tests.—For these and other tests there is a suitable collection of delicate reflecting galvanometers of the astatic, ballistic, differential and D'Arsonval types. The most delicate of these has a resistance of 110,000 ohms, and a figure of merit of upwards of 60,000 megohms with a 20 second swing.

There are eight quadrant electrometers of different types, the chief of which have been set up and used for various insulation and other tests. There is also one Kelvin absolute electrometer, and smaller portable electrometers and gauges on the same principle.

As a standard of capacity there is a cylindrical air condenser of the B. A. pattern.

Its capacity has not yet been determined absolutely. By comparison with our certificated mica standards, it was found to be nearly one two-hundredth of a microfarad, the value intended by the maker.

The mica-standards and subdivided boxes have been carefully compared with each other and tested for insulation and absorption. They are above the average in quality and accuracy.

For the purpose of studying the behaviour of insulators under the influence of long continued and intense electric stress, a subject which is now becoming of importance in connection with the transmission of power at very high voltage, there is in preparation a transformer capable of working up to 100,000 volts and of sufficient power to give useful practical results.

Magnetic Tests.—Determinations of the dip and horizontal intensity have been made with the Kew instruments in different parts of the laboratory, and of the horizontal intensity with two other types of magnetometer. The values obtained showed a very satisfactory agreement, and were in all cases verified by the local and bifilar variometers. A preliminary magnetic survey with the portable variometers has been made of all the laboratories in which experiments affected by the horizontal intensity are carried on. The results have been of great utility, and show that the precautions taken in erecting parts of the building with copper pipes and heating apparatus were by no means unnecessary, and might even have been extended with advantage to the elementary laboratories. It was also found that the disposition of the motors and machinery at the other end of the building was such as to produce a magnetic disturbance scarcely appreciable for most purposes in the portions devoted to delicate work.

A complete set of apparatus for testing the magnetic quality of iron and steel by various methods has also been provided. These experiments are mainly carried on in the Engineering Building, but some tests have been made by the magnetometric method for which the Physics Building is more suitable.

Considerable progress has also been made with the equipment for advanced work in Optics, Acoustics, and Heat, but little work has as yet been done by the students in these branches owing to the arrangement of the present course of study. The collection of apparatus is on a corresponding scale to the electrical equipment, and includes several fine and valuable instruments, such as a set of Ewing Seismographs on which records of two earthquakes have already been obtained ; a Rieffler standard clock ; a set of direct-reading electrical thermometers reading to .01 Fahr., which are now being used for determining soil temperatures ; a six inch Rowland grating with mountings and accessories by Brashear ; a complete set of spectrum and Crooke's tubes by Geissler ; mechanical models and apparatus from the Engineering Laboratory and the Instrument Company at Cambridge.

It is expected that in the course of the summer vacation, a complete catalogue of the apparatus will be made and published, which may be of use to outside students and experimentalists who may wish to know what facilities the laboratory may offer for any particular line of research.

The Macdonald Chemistry and Mining Building.

In September next the Chemical work will be transferred to the new building, where admirable facilities will be provided for study and research in the various departments of Chemistry. In addition to three large general laboratories, accommodating nearly 200 students at a time, the building contains a number of smaller laboratories and rooms for special purposes, including research work in inorganic and organic Chemistry and in Mineralogy. Among the special laboratories may be mentioned those for organic chemistry, physical chemistry, electrolytic analysis, gas analysis, iron and steel analysis, water analysis, photography, determinative mineralogy, etc.

The chemical lecture theatre, extending through two floors, is entered at the ground level; and is arranged to seat about 250 students. On the second floor there is a library and also a museum for chemical products. As far as possible the rooms for allied purposes have been grouped together on the same floor, and a lift will run from the basement to the top storey. The building is practically fire-proof, and is lighted throughout by electricity.

Botanical Laboratories.

The Botanical Laboratories occupy the upper floor of the central Arts building.

The laboratory for general Morphology provides table accommodation for fifty students, and is equipped with all the necessary appliances for the practical study of plants, either fresh or dry.

In connection with this laboratory, a large collection of dried plants is maintained, from which material is drawn for practical work.

Each student is supplied with a dissecting microscope, which he is required to return in good order at the close of the session.

The laboratory for Histology at present affords accommodation for twenty-four students. Each table is provided with a complete outfit of instruments and reagents. Provision is also made for accurate micrometric work, and for the production of accurate drawings by means of the camera lucida and Leitz's drawing instrument. More special instruments, including polariscope, spectroscope and photographic apparatus, afford opportunities for detailed studies in these several directions.

Ample provision for material of all kinds is found in the resources of the Botanic Garden, and in a large supply of stock preparations.

An investigator's table held by the University at the Biological Laboratory, Wood's Holl, Massachusetts, is available for such students as may successfully complete the advanced course of the third and fourth years.

Botanic Garden.

The Botanic Garden occupies a commanding situation at the summit of the Cote des Neiges Hill, distant from the College about one and one-half miles, and comprises an area of about nine acres.

The conservatories embrace a continuous series of houses having a total ground area of 4,600 square feet. They include a camellia house, 20 x 60 feet; a mixed stove, 20 x 80 feet ; a greenhouse, 20 x 60 feet ; and an Australian house, 20 x 30 feet.

The collection comprises an important and somewhat extensive representation of Australasian plants, and type-forms of vegetation from various parts of the world.

During the winter, material for practical study is provided in large quantity to meet the requirements of the College, and of such of the City schools as may have acquired special privileges in this respect.

Students are admitted to the garden and allowed the use of material for practical study, under special conditions. For this purpose, students' tickets are issued at the opening of the session to all those taking the course in Botany.

The public are admitted to the garden without charge, every day, except Sunday.

Zoological Laboratory.

The Zoological Laboratory is situated in the uppermost floor of the Law Building (East Wing of McGill College).

Accommodation is provided for a class of 40 students.

Dissecting trays, simple and compound microscopes, reasonable quantities of the ordinary reagents and of glass, are provided by the Laboratory.

The Laboratory is provided with several large tanks, in which the commonest species of the local fauna can be studied in the living condition, and so far as possible practical work is done on fresh specimens of species inhabiting the vicinity of Montreal.

For advanced work a rocking microtome of the most improved model and a thermostat have been purchased from the Cambridge Scientific Instrument Company.

Petrographical Laboratory.

The Petrographical Laboratory, containing the chief rock collections of the University, is situated in the McDonald Chemistry and Mining Building, and is arranged for the use of Honour and Graduate students. It is provided with a number of petrographical microscopes by Seibert and Crouch, as well as with models, sets of thin sections, electro-magnets, heavy solutions, etc., for petrographical work.

For purposes of study and comparison, in connection with advanced work and petrographical investigation, Dr. Adams' extensive private collection of rocks and thin sections is available.

Observatory.

Latitude, N. 45° 30′ 17″. Longitude, 4 54^m 18.67.

Height above sea level 187 ft.

Meteorological Observations are made every fourth hour, beginning at 3 h. 0 m. Eastern standard time; also at 8 h. 0m.; 20 h. 0m, independent series of bi-hourly temperature observations are also made. The principal instruments employed are two standard mercurial barometers ; one Kew standard thermometer ; two Pastorelli thermometers; one maximum thermometer; one minimum thermometer; one set of six self-recording thermometers, with controlling clock, battery, etc.; two anemometers; one wind vane (windmill pattern); one anemograph with battery, etc.; one sunshine recorder; one rain-band spectroscope and one rain gauge.

The Anemometer and Vane are on the summit of Mount Royal, at a point about three-quarters of a mile northwest of the Observatory. They are 57 feet above the surface of the ground and 810 feet above sea level.

Soil temperatures are observed, in co-operation with the Physical Laboratory, by means of platinum thermometers at depths ranging from one inch to nine feet.

The astronomical equipment consist of:——The Blackman Telescope (6¼ in.) ; a photoheliograph (4½ in.) ; a 3¼ in. transit with striding level, etc. ; a prismatic (8 cm.) transit instrument also arranged as a zenith telescope, a 2 in. transit in the prime vertical ;

two collimating telescopes; one sidereal clock; one mean time clock; one sidereal chronometer; one mean time chronometer; one chronograph; batteries, telegraph lines, and sundry minor instruments.

Observations for clock errors are made on nearly every clear night. Time exchanges are regularly made with the Toronto Observatory. Time signals are distributed throughout the city by means of the noon time-ball, continuous clock-signals, and the fire-alarm bells; and to the country, through the telegraph lines.

The longitude of the Observatory was determined in 1892 by direct telegraphic connection with Greenwich, with exchange of observers and instruments. The position is believed to be the most accurately determined in America.

Part Second.

The next session of this Faculty will begin on September 15th, 1898, and will extend to April 29th, 1899.

I. REGULATIONS FOR ENTRANCE.

Students in the Faculty of Arts are classified as Undergraduates or Partial Students.

Undergraduates.

Undergraduates alone can proceed to the degree of B.A. Candidates for admission to the First Year, as Undergraduates, are required to pass the First Year Entrance Examination. Two examinations for entrance are held in each year, as follows :

(1) In the first week of June, concurrently with the examinations for Associate in Arts.

Note to Heads of Schools.—Candidates for entrance may present themselves in June at McGill College ; or papers may be sent to schools at a distance, if the following conditions are complied with:—
(a) The names of Deputy Examiners must be submitted for approval, to the Secretary of the University, on or before May 1st ; and (b) the application must be accompanied by a list of candidates.

(2) At the opening of the session, on September 15th, and following days, in McGill College alone.

The following regulations with regard to the First Year Entrance Examination are in force :—

Except in special cases, no candidate will be admitted to the First Year Entrance Examination unless he is at least sixteen years of age, and produces a certificate to this effect, if deemed necessary.

No. candidate can become an Undergraduate of the First Year except by passing the June or September Entrance Examination of the First Year.

These examinations are held only on the days in June and September appointed in the Calendar. Special arrangements can be made for the examination of candidates who are prevented from complying with the above regulation by severe illness or domestic affliction.

June Candidates Candidates who, at the examinations for Associate in Arts, have passed in the subjects of the Entrance Examination are admitted as Undergraduates.

Candidates who fail in one or more subjects at the June examination, or who have taken part only of the examination and present themselves again in the following September, will be exempted from examination in those subjects in which the Examiners may have reported them as specially qualified.

September Candidates Any candidate who fails in one and not more than one subject at the September Entrance Examination. may pass an equivalent examination at Christmas, or at the following Sessional Examinations, in the precise part of the subject in which he failed. In this regulation, Classics, Mathematics, and English are each regarded as a single subject.

Ontario Candidates At the June examination, candidates from Ontario may present an equivalent amount from the books prescribed for the Junior Matriculation Examination of the University of Toronto.

The Matriculation or Junior Leaving Examination accepted by the Universities of Ontario is accepted by the Faculty, in so far as the subjects of their programme satisfy the Examiners of the Faculty, *i.e.*, when the subjects taken are the same as, or equivalent to, those required in McGill University.

In the case of Candidates from Ontario, Second Class non-professional certificates will be accepted *pro tanto* in the Examination.

Normal School Candidates For qualifications required of Normal School Students, see Normal School Regulations.

Note.—As the examination is intended as a test of qualification for admission to the classes of the University, certificates of passing are granted to those only who subsently atte nd lectures, ex: ept in special cases and for cause shown. Candidates who have passed the examination are not matriculated until they have paid all the prescribed fees for the session and complied with the other University regulations. (See the Directions given, p. 51.)

First Year Entrance Examination.

Examinations begin on May 30th in McGill College and local centres; on September 15th in McGill College only.

The subjects of the Entrance Examination are :—

1. English (including History).
2. Latin or Greek.
3. Geometry, Arithmetic, Algebra.
4. Greek or Latin (if not already taken).
   or two Modern Languages or one Modern Language with the Additional Mathematics of the First Year Exhibition Examination.
5. Elementary Natural or Physical Science, viz.:
   one of the following : (a) Physiography ; (b) Botany ; (c) Chemistry; (d) Physics ;
   Or alternatively a Language not previously taken.

Exhibitions are offered for competition (see page 76), to candidates who take the prescribed examination in Greek, Latin, Mathematics, English, one Modern Language, together with an additional amount specified below.

Greek.—XENOPHON, Anabasis, Book I. ; Greek Grammar.

Latin.—CÆSAR, Bell. Gall., Books I. and II. ; and VIRGIL, Aeneid, Book I. ; Latin Grammar.

In both Greek and Latin, Translation at Sight and Prose Composition (sentences or easy narrative, based upon the prescribed prose text), will be required.

At the September, but not at the June, examination, other works in Greek or Latin equivalent to those specified may be accepted, if application be made to the Professors of Classics at least a fortnight before the day of examination,

Mathematics. —*Arithmetic*, Elementary rules, Vulgar and Decimal Fractions, Proportion, Percentage, Simple Interest, etc., Square-root, and a knowledge of the Metric System. *Algebra*, Elementary rules, Fractions, Factors, Equations of the First Degree, Simultaneous Equations of the First Degree, Indices, Surds and easy Quadratics; Problems leading to equations, Binomial Theorem. *Euclid*, Elements, Books I., II., III., with easy deductions.

English.—Writing from Dictation. *Grammar.*—A paper on English grammar, including Analysis. The candidate will be expected to show a good knowledge of Accidence, as treated in any grammar prepared for the higher forms of schools. A similar statement applies to grammatical Analysis, in which the nomenclature used by MASON will be preferred. West's Elements of English Grammar (Pitt Press series) is recommended as a text-book. Analysis must be presented in tabular form, as on pages 208-211 of West. *English History.*—Candidates will be required to give the chief details of leading events. While any text-book written for the upper forms of schools may be used in preparation for the examination, GARDINER'S Outline of English History (Longmans) is recommended. *Composition.*—Candidates will write a short essay on a subject given at the time of the examination. *Literature.*— SHAKSPERE'S Richard II., ed. Deighton (Macmillan), and SCOTT'S Lady of the Lake, ed. Stuart (Macmillan).

[Note.—*Candidates* may take Arithmetic, and all the English subjects except Literature, at the June Examination of one year, and the remainder at the Entrance Examination of the following year.]

French.—Grammar including Syntax. An easy translation from French into English; and from English into French; Dictation or similar exercise. Candidates are expected to be able to write French without gross mistakes in spelling or grammar; special credit will be given for evidence of familiarity with the spoken language.

German.—The whole of JOYNES' German Reader (or equivalent amount) together with German accidence and translation into German as in the First Part of VANDERSMISSEN'S German Grammar (or equivalent amount.)

Note.—Students of Theological Colleges who propose to take Hebrew are exempt from examination in Modern Languages.

Physiography.—Requirements as under **Physical Geography** in Optional Course for A. A. Examinations.

Botany.—As in Groom's Elementary Botany, Penhallow's Guide to the Collection of Plants and Blanks for Plant Description.

Credit will be given for plant collections.

Note.—Teachers may substitute any plant of the same family for any one of those specified in part II. of Groom's Elementary Botany, according to requirements of the locality.

Chemistry.—Elementary Inorganic Chemistry, comprising the preparation and properties of the chief non-metallic elements and their more important compounds, the laws of chemical action, combining weights, etc. (The ground is simply and effectively covered by Remsen's "Elements of Chemistry," pp. 1 to 160.)

Additional Mathematics.—The additional requirements referred to above in the Mathematical subjects for Exhibitions are as follows:—
Euclid :—Bks. 4 and 6, with Defs. of Bk. V. and easy deductions.
Algebra :—The three Progressions : Ratio, Proportion and Variation ; Permutations and Combinations; Scales of Notation ; Logarithms ; Interest and Annuities.
Trigonometry :—To the beginning of the solution of oblique angled triangles, as in Galbraith & Haughton, with deductions.

Additional for Exhibitions.

Greek.—Homer, Iliad, Bk. IV. or VI.; Homer, Odyssey, Bk. VII. or XIII.

Latin.—Virgil, Aeneid, Bk. III. may be substituted for Book I.; Cicero, In Catilinam, Orat. I. and II.; *or* Horace, Odes I.; Caesar, Bell. Gall., Bks. II. and III. may be substituted for Bks. I. and II.
A paper on Greek and Latin Grammar. Translation at sight from the easier Greek and Latin authors. Easy Latin and Greek Prose Composition.
Candidates who do not offer the books prescribed above will have the option of an additional paper in Composition and Translation at sight.
Text-Books.—Sonnenschein's or Rutherford's Greek Grammar or Burnet's Greek Rudiments; Abbott's Arnold's Greek Prose Composition; Sonnenschein's Latin Grammar, or Allen and Greenough's; Arnold's Latin Prose Composition by Bradley, or Collar's Latin Composition, Pts. III. and IV.

Mathematics.—Euclid, Bks. I., II., III., IV., with easy deductions; Algebra to end of Harmonical Progression (Colenso); Arithmetic.

English.—*Grammar*.—An advanced knowledge of this subject will be required, and, in addition, some acquaintance with the historical development of English, as illustrated in common and important words. The candidate is recommended to read Mason's English Grammar, and will be expected to supplement Mason by using Morris's Historical Outlines of English Accidence (Macmillan), as a book of reference. *English Literature*.—The works to be read are those selected for the First Year Examination for Passing, viz., Shakspere's Richard II, Ed. Deighton (Macmillan), and Scott's Lady of

D

the Lake, Ed. Stuart (Macmillan), with the addition of Milton's L'Allegro and other short poems, ed. Bell (Macmillan). *Composition* —The candidate will be required to write an essay on some subject connected with the literature prescribed. *History*—A paper bearing on the chief landmarks in European History will be set. Attention should be given to great movements of thought, and to the courses and results of important wars. Lavisse's General View of the Political History of Europe (Longmans) will serve to indicate the character of the knowledge required.

French.—*Grammar.*—Syntax, in addition to the grammar of the Entrance Course. Easy translation from French into English, and English into French. Labiche, Le Voyage de M. Perrichon. J. Macé, Histoire d'une Bouchée de Pain. Oral examinations.

Or, instead of French :

German—Grammar (an amount equal to Vandersmissen, Accidence and Syntax, including exercises in translation); Joynes' German Reader; Baumbach, Der Schwiegersohn (Heath & Co.) ; Benedix, Plautus und Terenz, and Die Sonntagsjäger (Heath & Co.).

The First Year Exhibitions will not be awarded unless an adequate standard of merit has been reached ; but in awarding the Exhibitions of higher value to the successful candidates, the results of an examination in the following subjects will also be taken into account :—

1. Higher Composition and Translation at Sight (Latin and Greek).

2. Euclid, Book VI (omitting Props. 27, 28, 29), with Defs. of Book V. and easy deductions.

Algebra.—The three Progressions; Ratio, Proportion and Variation; Permutations and Combinations; Scales of Notation; Logarithms; Interest and Annuities.

Trigonometry.—To the beginning of the solution of oblique-angled triangles, as in Galbraith & Haughton, with deductions.

3. English.—Henry Morley's First Sketch of English Literature, chaps. VII and VIII.

Second Year.

There will be no specified examination as heretofore for immediate admission to the Second Year, as an Undergraduate; but in certain cases, to be dealt with by a Standing Committee appointed for the purpose, the Faculty may admit to the Second Year candidates who shall be deemed qualified. Candidates for Second Year Exhibitions may be admitted, by the Committee, to the Second Year.

Except in special cases, no one will be admitted to the Second Year unless he is at least seventeen years of age, and produces a certificate to this effect if deemed necessary.

Medical Students.—Partial Students.—Students of other Universities.

Medical Students and Candidates for entrance into the first year of the Faculty of Medicine may present themselves for the First Year entrance examinations.

Partial Students. — Candidates for admission as Partial Students may attend any class, without previous examination, provided they give the Professor satisfactory evidence of their ability to proceed with the work of the course.

No one will be admitted as a Partial Student unless he is at least sixteen years of age, and produces a certificate to this effect if deemed necessary.

Students of other Universities. — Any student of another University desirous to be admitted to this University with equivalent standing is requested to send with his application:—

1st.—A Calendar of the University in which he has studied, giving a full statement of the courses of study.

2nd.—A complete statement of the course he has followed.

3rd.—A certificate of the standing gained, and of conduct.

These will be submitted to the Faculty.

The Faculty, if otherwise satisfied, will decide what examination, if any, or what conditions, may be necessary before admitting the candidate.

General Regulations.

Every student is expected to state at entrance the name of the religious denomination to which he belongs, and of the Minister under whose care he desires to be placed.

Lists of the students belonging to the several denominations with the information thus given, shall be sent, at the beginning of each session as soon as the classes are fully formed, to the Secretary's office, where they will be available for reference.

Every student is required to sign the following

Declaration.

" I hereby declare that I will faithfully observe the statutes, rules, and ordinances of this University of McGill College, to the best of my ability."

Directions to Candidates for Matriculation or Admission.

Candidates are required:—

(a) To present themselves to the Dean at the beginning of the session, and fill up a form of application for matriculation or admission.

(b) To pass or to have passed the required examinations (p. 44). Candidates claiming exemption, according to the regulations above given, from examination in any subject on the ground of examinations previously passed, must present certificates of standing in the latter. Candidates must pay a fee of $5 before admission to the entrance examination in September. (See Fees. p. 72)

(c) To procure tickets from the Registrar (p. 73), and to sign the declaration above given.

(d) To present their tickets to the Dean. (Fine, etc., for delay stated on p. 73).

(e) To provide themselves with the Academic dress (p. 72).

II. REGULATIONS FOR DEGREES IN ARTS.

REGULATIONS FOR THE DEGREE OF B.A.

After passing the First Year Matriculation Examination, an Undergraduate, in order to obtain the Degree of B.A., is required to attend regularly the appointed courses of lectures for four years, and to pass the required Examinations in each year. A student cannot proceed with his course un-

!ess he has passed each Examination in its assigned order. If he fails at any one of these Examinations, he must pass it before being allowed to proceed with his course. Under-graduates are arranged in Years, from First to Fourth, ac-cording to their academic standing.

1. Ordinary Course for the Degree of B.A.

N. B. The Roman numerals used in the following conspectus have no reference to any other parts of the Calendar—whereas the Arabic numerals refer to the numbering of the courses on pp. 4-31 for example, Greek, 2. refers to the second course given under the head of Classical Literature and History, p. 4.

First Year.

 I. GREEK, 1, or LATIN 1.
 II. ENGLISH I WITH HISTORY I.
 III. MATHEMATICS, I.
 IV. LATIN I, OR GREEK I, OR FRENCH I, OR GERMAN I.
 V. PHYSICS, I.

With a view to the encouragement of higher work, advanced sec-tions will be formed in all subjects as far as practicable, and in these Honours may be awarded.

Students taking the work of advanced sections may be excused from the work of the corresponding ordinary sections on the recommenda-tion of the professor. No exemptions from other subjects will be granted to students in advanced sections.

Second Year.

 VI. GREEK, 2.
 VII. LATIN, 2.
 VIII. FRENCH, 2.
 IX. GERMAN, 2. (Optional—instead of VIII.)
 X. HEBREW, 2. (Optional—instead of VIII.)
 XI. HISTORY, 2.
 XII. MENTAL AND MORAL PHILOSOPHY, I
 XIII. MATHEMATICS, 2.
 XIV. MATHEMATICAL PHYSICS, 2. (Medical students may substitute the second half of the Chemistry course of the Faculty for XII and XIV.)
 XV. BOTANY, I. (Medical students may substitute the Botany course of their Faculty.)

Third Year.

XVI. GREEK, 3.
XVII. LATIN, 3. (Optional—instead of XVI.)
XVIII. MATHEMATICAL PHYSICS, 3.
*(In addition to the above, the student will take one subject from Div. (a)
a second from Div. (b), and a third from either.)*

(Div. a.)

XIX. GREEK, 3. (If XVII has been taken.)
XX. LATIN, 3. (If XVI has been taken.)
XXI. ENGLISH AND RHETORIC, 3.
XXII. MENTAL PHILOSOPHY, 2.
XXIII. FRENCH, 3. (If the subject has been taken in 1st. or 2nd. Year.)
XXIV. GERMAN, 3. (If the subject has been taken in 1st. or 2nd. Year.)
XXV. HEBREW, 3.

(Div. b).

XXVI. OPTICS, 4. AND DESCRIPTIVE ASTRONOMY, 3. (Open to students
who have taken XVIII.)
XXVII. EXPERIMENTAL PHYSICS, 5. (Open to students who have taken
XVIII.)
XXVIII. LABORATORY COURSE IN PHYSICS, 7.
XXIX. BOTANY, 2a.
XXX. ZOOLOGY, 1. Physiology and Histology, or Anatomy and Practical
Anatomy, may, by Medical students only, be substituted
for two courses of this Division.

Fourth Year.

XXXI. GREEK, 4.
XXXII. LATIN, (Optional—instead of XXXI.)
XXXIII. MORAL PHILOSOPHY, 3.
XXXIV. MATHEMATICAL PHYSICS, 3. (Optional instead of XLI.)
*(In addition to the above, the student will take one subject from Div. (t)
a second from Div. (b), and a third from either.)*

Div. (a).

XXXV. GREEK, 4. (If XXXII has been taken.)
XXXVI. LATIN, 4. (If XXXI has been taken.)
XXXVII. ENGLISH LITERATURE, 4.
XXXVIII. FRENCH, 4. (If XXIII has been taken.)
XXXIX. GERMAN, 4. (If XXIV has been taken.)
XL. HEBREW, 4.

Div. (b.)

XLI. ASTRONOMY, 4, AND OPTICS, 4. (If XVIII has been taken.)
XLII. EXPERIMENTAL PHYSICS, 6.
XLIII. LABORATORY COURSE IN PHYSICS, 8.
XLIV. BOTANY, 2b.
XLV. ZOOLOGY, 2.
XLVI. MINERALOGY AND GEOLOGY, 1.

N.B.—Students claiming exemptions cannot count XLI and XLII, as subjects for the B.A. Examinations, unless they have taken XVIII.

For details of each subject, see Courses of Lectures, pp. 4.

A Candidate who seeks to obtain an Ordinary B.A. Degree of the First Class must fulfil the following conditions. He must not only obtain the required aggregate of marks (viz., three-fourths of the maximum), but he must also obtain First Class standing in three of the departments, and not less than Second Class in the remainder.

Declaration.

Every Candidate for the Degree of B.A. is required to make and sign the following declaration :

" Ego———polliceor sancteque recipio me pro meis viribus studiosum fore communis hujus Universitatis boni, et operam daturum ut ejus decus et dignitatem promoveam."

Notes on the Ordinary Course for B.A.

Third and Fourth Year Students are not restricted to the choice **Additional Courses.** of two distinct subjects in one of the above divisions. They may select one subject only, together with an Additional Course in the same subject, or in any other of the subjects which they have chosen, in which such Additional Course may be provided by the Faculty; the above rules, however, must be complied with, and Students must have been placed in the First Class in the corresponding subject at the preceding Sessional Examination, viz. :—Intermediate or Third Year, according to standing.

The Additional Course is intended to be more than equivalent, in the amount of work involved, to any of the other subjects in the Division.

(For details of Additional Courses provided, see pp. 56-57).

French and German. **Hebrew.** Students may take Hebrew instead of French or German.

Professional Students. For arrangements enabling Students in Medicine or Applied Science to take the course in Arts also, and obtain B. A., with B. A. Sc. or M.D., in six years, see p. 64 and 65.

Partial Students. Undergraduates who have previously been Partial Students, and have in this capacity attended a particular Course or Courses of Lectures, may, at the discretion of the Faculty, be exempted from further attendance at these Lectures; but no distinction shall in consequence be made between the Examination of undergraduates and of those regularly attending Lectures.

2. Honour Courses.

Honours of First, Second, or Third Rank will be awarded to successful candidates in any Honour Course established by the Faculty, provided they have passed creditably the ordinary Examinations in all the subjects proper to their year.

No Undergraduate is permitted to attend the Honour lectures unless (a) he has been placed in the First Class in the subject at the preceding Sessional Examination, if there be one ; (b) has satisfied the Professor that he is otherwise qualified; and (c) while attending lectures makes progress satisfactory to the Professor. In case his progress is not satisfactory, he may be notified by the Faculty to discontinue attendance.

The Honour lectures of the Third and Fourth Years are open to all Partial Students who can satisfy the Professor of their fitness to proceed with the work of the course. Such Students will not be ranked with Undergraduates in the Examination lists.

Candidates for Honours in the Second Year.

Honour Exemptions. A Candidate for Honours in the Second Year, who has obtained Honours in the First Year, may claim exemption from the lectures and examinations in Modern Languages, or Hebrew, or Botany. He must, however, inform the Dean at the beginning of the Session that he intends to claim exemption from a particular course.

Candidates for Honours in the Third Year.

A Candidate for Honours in the Third Year, in order to obtain exemptions, must in the Examinations of the Second Year have taken First or Second Rank Honours, if Honours be offered in the subjects, or if not, First Class at the Ordinary Sessional Examinations in the subject in which he proposes to compete for Honours ; must stand higher than Third Class in not less than half of the remaining subjects, and have no failure in any subject. Such Candidate shall be entitled in the Third Year to exemption from lectures and examinations in any one of the subjects of the Year (see p ˁ3), except that in which he is a Candidate for Honours. A Candidate for Honours in the Third Year who has failed to obtain Honours shall be required to take the same examinations for B.A. as the ordinary Undergraduate.

Candidates for B. A. Honours.

A Student who has taken First or Second Rank Honours in the Third Year, and desires to be a Candidate for B.A. Honours, shall be required to attend two only of the courses of lectures given in the ordinary departments, and to pass the two corresponding examinations only, at the ordinary B.A. Examination. A Candidate, however, who at the B.A. Examinations obtains Third Rank Honours, will not be allowed credit for these exemptions at the end of the Session, unless the Examiners certify that his knowledge of the whole Honour Course is sufficient to justify it.

Note.—For subjects ˑf Ordinary Course see pp. 52-53.

Honour and Additional Courses.

(N.B.—The numbers which stand after the Academic years refer to the corresponding numbers of the Courses given on pp.4·3ˡ.)

1. Classical Literature and History.

THIRD YEAR HONOURS.   Greek, 5.
                      Latin, 5.
FOURTH YEAR HONOURS. Greek, 6.
                      Latin, 6.

2. English Language and Literature.

THIRD YEAR HONOURS, 6, 8, 10, 12, 14.
THIRD YEAR ADDITIONAL, 6 or 10.
FOURTH YEAR HONOURS. 5, 7. 9, 11, 13, 15.
FOURTH YEAR ADDITIONAL, 7 or 11 or 15.

3. French·

THIRD YEAR HONOURS, 5.
FOURTH YEAR HONOURS, 5.

4. German.

THIRD YEAR HONOURS, 5*a* and 6*b*.
THIRD YEAR ADDITIONAL, 5*a*.
FOURTH YEAR HONOURS, 6*a* and 6*b*.
FOURTH YEAR ADDITIONAL, 6*a*.

5. Semitic Languages.

THIRD YEAR HONOURS, 4*a* and 4*b*.
THIRD YEAR ADDITIONAL, 4*b* without Literature.
FOURTH YEAR HONOURS, 5*a* and 5*b*.
FOURTH YEAR ADDITIONAL, 5*b* without Literature.

6. History.

THIRD AND FOURTH YEAR HONOURS, 3.

7. Mental and Moral Philosophy.

THIRD YEAR HONOURS, 4.
FOURTH YEAR HONOURS, 5, 6,

8. Mathematics and Physics.

FIRST YEAR, ADVANCED SECTION, 2.
SECOND YEAR HONOURS, 6.
THIRD YEAR HONOURS, 7, 8.
FOURTH YEAR HONOURS, 9, 10, 11.

9 Mineralogy.

THIRD YEAR HONOURS, 8, 10.
FOURTH YEAR HONOURS, 9.

10. Chemistry.

THIRD YEAR ADDITIONAL, 3, 5.
FOURTH YEAR ADDITIONAL, 4, 6.
Courses 2 (*Second Year*) *and* 7 (*Fourth Year*) *are optional.*

11. Biology.

FOURTH YEAR HONOURS, { Botany, 2*b*. Zoology, 2.

12. Geology.

FOURTH YEAR HONOURS, 2, 3, 4, 5, 6.

NOTE.—By an order of the Lieutenant-Governor of Ontario in Council, Honours in this University confer the same privileges in Ontario as Honours in the Universities of that Province as regards certificates of eligibility for the duties of Public School Inspectors, and as regards exemption from the non-professional Examination of Teachers for first-class Certificates for Grades "A. and B."

3. Regulations for the Degree of M A.

1. A Candidate must be a Bachelor of Arts of at least three years' standing.

Thesis.

2. He is required to prepare and submit to the Faculty a thesis on some literary or scientific subject, under the following rules :—

(a) The subject of the thesis must be submitted to the Faculty before the thesis is presented.

(b) A paper read previously to any association, or published in any way, cannot be accepted as a thesis.

(c) The thesis submitted becomes the property of the University, and cannot be published without the consent of the Faculty of Arts.

(d) The thesis must be submitted before some date to be fixed annually by the Faculty, which date must not be less than two months before the Candidate proceeds to the Degree.

N.B.—The last day in the session of 1898-99 *for sending in Theses for M.A., will be Jan.* 31st, 1899.

Examinations.

3. All Candidates, except those who have taken First or Second Rank B.A. Honours, or have passed First Class in the Ordinary Examinations for the Degree of B.A., are required to pass an examination also, either in Literature or in Science, as each Candidate may select.

(a) The subjects of the Examination in *Literature* are divided into two groups as follows:—

Group A.—LATIN, GREEK, HEBREW.

Group B.—FRENCH, GERMAN, ENGLISH.

(b) The subjects of the Examination in *Science* are divided into three groups :—

Group A.—PURE MATHEMATICS (advanced or Ordinary), MECHANICS (including Hydrostatics), ASTRONOMY, OPTICS.

Group B.—Geology and Mineralogy, Botany, Zoology, Chemistry.

Group C—Mental Philosophy, Moral Philosophy, Logic, History of Philosophy.

(c) Every candidate in Literature is required to select for Examination two subjects out of one group in the *Literature* section, and one out of the other group in the same section. Every Candidate in Science is required to select two out of the three groups in the *Science* section; and in one of the groups so chosen to select for Examination two subjects, and in the other group one subject.

(d) One of the subjects selected as above will be considered the principal subject (being so denoted by the candidate at the time of application), and the other two as subordinate subjects.

(e) The whole examination may be taken in one year, or distributed over two or three years, provided the examination in any one subject be not divided.

For further details of the examination, application must be made to the Faculty before the above date. For fees see p. (In case of failure, the candidate may present himself in a subsequent year without further payment of fees.) The examination will be held in April in McGill College only.

Note.—*Candidates who obtained the degree of B.A. before 1884, may proceed to the degree of M.A. under the regulations in force previous to* 1884.

Lectures to Bachelors of Arts.

Lectures are open to Bachelors of Arts who are candidates for M.A., the sessional examinations corresponding to these lectures being reckoned as parts of the M.A. examination. The subjects are Greek, Latin, English, French, German, History, Mental and Moral Philosophy, Chemistry, Botany, Geology and Mineralogy.

4. Regulations for the Degree of LL.D.

This degree is intended as a recognition of special study by Masters of Arts in some branch of Literature or Science. The thesis or short printed treatise referred to below is regarded as the chief test of the candidate's mastery of the subject he has chosen. A very wide range of choice is allowed in order to suit individual tastes.

The following are the regulations :—

1.   Candidates must be Masters of Arts of at least twelve years' standing. Every candidate for the Degree of LL.D. in Course is required to prepare and submit to the Faculty of Arts, not less than three months before proceeding to the degree, twenty-five printed copies of a thesis on some Literary or Scientific subject which has been *previously approved by the Faculty.* The thesis must exhibit such a degree of literary or scientific merit, and give evidence of such originality of thought or extent of research as shall, in the opinion of the Faculty, justify recommendation for the degree.

N.B.—The subject should be submitted before the Thesis is written.

2.   Every Candidate for the Degree of LL.D. in Course is required to submit to the Faculty of Arts, with his thesis, a list of books treating of some one branch of Literature or of Science, satisfactory to the Faculty, in which he is prepared to submit to examination, and in which he shall be examined, unless otherwise ordered by vote of the Faculty. For fees, see p. 74.

---

5. Examinations.

(A) College Examinations.

For Students of McGill College only.

1.   There are two examinations in each year, viz., at Christmas and April. Successful students are arranged in three classes at the April examinations.

Christmas Examinations will be held in all the subjects of the First and Second Years. There shall be no Supplemental Examination in case of failure. Candidates who fail in

courses of the First and Second Years, terminating at Christ.
mas, will be required to pass at the Sessional Examinations
on an extra paper in the subject in which they have failed.

Christmas Examinations in the Third or Fourth Years,
may be held at the option of the Professors.

In the Fourth Year only, there is no Sessional Examination; the University Examination for B.A. takes its place.

2. Undergraduates who fail in one subject at the Sessional Examinations of the First or of the Second Year are required to pass a Supplemental Examination therein in the
following September. Should they fail in this Examination,
they must in the following Session attend the Lectures and
pass the Examination in the same subject, in addition to the
regular course, or pass the Examination only, without attending Lectures, at the discretion of the Faculty.

3. Failure in two or more subjects at the Sessional Examinations of the First or of the Second Year, or in one
subject at the Third Year Sessional Examinations, involves
the loss of the Session. The Faculty may permit the student
to recover his standing by passing a Supplemental Examination at the beginning of the following Session.

4. Examinations Supplemental to the Sessional Examinations will be held in September, simultaneously with the Entrance Examinations, and at no other time.

5 A list of those to whom the Faculty may grant Supplemental Examinations in the following September will be published after the Sessional examination. The time for the
Supplemental Examination will be fixed by the Faculty; the
examination will not be granted at any other time, except by
special permission of the Faculty, and on payment of a fee
of $5.

(B) University Examinations.

For Students of McGill College and of Colleges affiliated in Arts.

I. For the Degree of B.A.

There are three University Examinations : The Matriculation
at entrance; the Intermediate, at the end of the Second Year; and
the Final, at the end of the Fourth Year.

1. The subjects of the Matriculation Examination are stated on pp. 46-48.

2. In the Intermediate Examination, the subjects are Classics, Pure Mathematics, Logic, and Modern History with one Modern Language, or Botany. Students are allowed to take Hebrew instead of a Modern Language. The subjects of the examination in 1899 are as follows :—

Intermediate.

Greek.—THUCYDIDES The Siege of Plataea (Sing, Rivingtons); and The Retreat from Syracuse (Rouse, Rivingtons); SOPHOCLES, Ajax. Prose Composition and Translation at sight of Greek (easy narrative) into English. General questions will also be set,—in History, on the Period of Athenian Supremacy Cox's Athenian Empire, (Longmans' Epochs of Ancient History), with Abbott's Pericles (Putnams), and in Literature on the outlines as contained in Jebb's Primer of Greek Literature (pp. 1 to 100), (Macmillan).

A paper will also be set in the course of the Session on Luciani Vera Historia (Jerram, Clarendon Press.)

(SUMMER READINGS, see p. 5.)

Latin.—Cicero, The Fourth Verrine Action (Hall, Macmillan); Quintilian X, Sections 37-131 (Peterson, Clarendon Press, smaller edition); Horace (Wickham's Selected Odes, Clarendon Press); Latin Prose Composition and Translation at sight of Latin into English; History, from the Tribunate of Gaius Gracchus to the Battle of Actium (Shuckburgh's History of Rome, Macmillan); Literature: Wilkins Primer (Macmillan).

A paper will also be set in the course of the Session on Livy Book xxi (SUMMER READINGS, see p. 7.)

Mathematics.—Arithmetic.
　　　　Euclid, Books I., II., III., IV., VI., and defs. of Book V. Algebra, to Quadratic Equations inclusive (as in Colenso).
　　　　Trigonometry, including use of Logarithms.

Logic.—Jevons' Elementary Lessons in Logic.

English.—(For affiliated colleges.)—SPALDING's History of English Literature; LODGE's History of Modern Europe, 1789-1878. Essay on a subject to be given at the time of the Examination.

European History.—(For McGill College Students) as on p. 18.

With one of the following:—

Botany.—(For McGill College Students.) See p. 28.

French.—V. HUGO, Notre Dame de Paris ; Th. GAUTHIER, Le Roman de la Momie ; MME DE STAEL, Corinne. Translations into French :—Rasselas ; Grammatical questions.

German.—The JOYNES-MEISSNER German Grammar ; SCHILLER, Die Jungfrau von Orleans ; Storm, Immensee (Heath & Co.); Heine, Die Harzreise ; Translation at Sight ; Dictation ; Colloquial exercises.

Hebrew.—Genesis, chap. IV. to VIII ; Exodus, XX.; Judges, V. Exercises : Hebrew into English, and English into Hebrew. Syntax. Reading of the MASORETIC notes, the Septuagint version and the Vulgate.

3. For the Final or B.A. Ordinary Examination the subjects appointed are the obligatory subjects of the Third and Fourth Years, viz., Latin or Greek; Mathematical Physics (Mechanics and Hydrostatics, or Astronomy and Optics) ; Moral Philosophy; and those three subjects which the Candidate has selected in the Third and Fourth Years. (See p. 53.)

Final.

Greek.—PLATO, Republic I. and X; AESCHYLUS, Eumenides; Composition and Translation at Sight; paper on the Constitutional History of Athens, Greek Literature and Antiquities. A Paper will also be set in the course of the Session on Merriam's "The Phaeacians of Homer" (Harpers),—SUMMER READINGS, see p. 5.

Latin.—LIVY, Book V (in part); JUVENAL, Selected Satires; TIBULLUS Selections. Composition and Translation at Sight. History of the Roman Empire to the reign of Domitian. A Paper will also be set in the course of the Session on Tacitus, Annals IV,—SUMMER READINGS, see p. 8.

64

Mathematical Physics.—Mechanics and Hydrostatics, as in LONEY'S Mechanics and Hydrostatics ; or Optics and Astronomy, as in GALBRAITH and HAUGHTON or BRINKLEY.

Mental and Moral Philosophy.—MURRAY'S Introduction to Ethics.

Natural Science—(a) Mineralogy and Geology, or (b) Botany. Practical Geology and Palaeontology (Additional); or Practical Chemistry (Additional).

Experimental Physics.—Electricity and Magnetism. (See courses of Lectures, p. 25.)

History.—(For affiliated Colleges.) MYERS Mediaeval and Modern History; Bryce, Holy Roman Empire (omit Chaps. 6, 8, 9, 13, and Supplementary Chapter).

English Literature—(For McGill College.) The Course on English Literature for the Fourth Year, p. 11.

French.—The Course on French for the Fourth Year, p. 14.

German.—The Course on German for the Fourth Year, p. 16.

Hebrew.—Job, I., II., III., IV., XIV., XIX., XXIX.; Ecclesiastes, I., II., III., XII.; PSALMS, LVI. to LXV.; GESENIUS, Grammar ; HARPER, Elements of Syntax ; Reading of the Masoretic notes, the Septuagint Version and the Vulgate. Translation at Sight.

N. B.—For Additional Courses on above subjects see pp. 56-57.

6. Exemptions for Students in Professional Faculties.

General Regulations.—Students of the Third and Fourth Years, matriculated in the Faculties of Law, or Medicine, or Applied Science, or in any affiliated Theological College, are entitled to exemption from any one of the Ordinary Subjects required in the Third and Fourth Years. (For rule concerning Special Certificates, see p. 67.)

To be allowed these privileges in either Year, they must give notice, at the commencement of the session, to the Dean of the Faculty of Arts, of their intention to claim exemptions as Professional Students, and must produce, at the end of the session, certificates of attendance on a full course of Professional Lectures during the Year for which the exemption is claimed.

E

Medicine. Students registered in the Faculty of Medicine are allowed the following privileges :—

In the First and Second Years in Arts, they may substitute certain equivalents for parts of the Ordinary Course.

In the Third Year in Arts, they may, if following the full course of the First Year in Medicine, take Physiology and Histology with practical work therein, or Anatomy and Practical Anatomy, as two of the courses under the heading of Science in the Ordinary Course.

Medical Students who have completed the Third Year in Arts and First Year in Medicine are required in the Fourth Year in Arts to take two only of the subjects of the Ordinary Course (or one subject with the Additional Course therein). Medical Students are recommended to continue in the Third and Fourth Years of the Arts Course subjects they have taken in the First and Second Years.

To secure these privileges, certificates of registration in the Medical Faculty must be presented at the beginning of each year to the Dean of the Faculty of Arts; and at the end of each session in the first two years, certificates of attendance on lectures and of passing the corresponding examinations must also be presented. At the end of the Third and Fourth Years, certificates must be presented to show that the full curriculum of the Medical Faculty for the year has been completed.

Applied Science. Students in the Faculty of Applied Science, who have passed the first two years in Arts, are allowed, while pursuing the course in Applied Science, to substitute certain courses in Applied Science for the corresponding courses in Arts, and to distribute the work of the Third and Fourth Years in Arts over three years, so that they may be enabled to take the B.A. Degree at the end of the Fifth Year from entrance. For the details, application may be made to the Dean of the Faculty of Arts. Certificates of attendance, etc·, in Applied Science will be required.

The above arrangements will enable candidates for the M.D. or B.A. Sc degrees to pursue the course in Arts also, leading to the B. A. degree, and complete both courses in six years.

Literate in Arts.—A certificate of "LITERATE IN ARTS" will be given along with the professional degree in Medicine or Applied Science, to those who have completed two years' study in the Faculty of Arts, and have pased the prescribed examinations.

Students of the University attending affiliated Theological Colleges.

Theological Colleges. 1. These students are subject to the regulations of the Faculty of Arts in the same manner as other students.

: . The Faculty will make formal reports to the governing body of the Theological College which any such student may attend, as to :—(1) their conduct and attendance on the classes of the Faculty; and (2) their standing in the several examinations ; such reports to be furnished after the Examinations, if called for.

3. Undergraduates are allowed no exemptions in the course for the Degree of B.A. until they have passed the Intermediate Examination; but they may take Hebrew in the First or Second Years, instead of French or German.

4. In the Third and Fourth Years they are allowed exemptions, as stated above.

*Any student who, under any of the above rules, desires to take Experimental Physics is required to take Mechanics and Hydrostatics also, in the Third Year.

7. Medals, Prizes, Classing and Certificates.

1. **Gold Medals** will be awarded in the B.A. Honour Examinations to Students who take the highest Honours of the First Rank in the subjects stated below, and who shall have passed creditably the Ordinary Examinations for the Degree of B.A., provided they have been recommended therefor to the Corporation by the Faculty on the report of the Examiners :—

The **Henry Chapman Gold Medal** for Classical Languages and Literature.

The **Prince of Wales Gold Medal** for Mental and Moral Philosophy.

The **Anne Molson Gold Medal** for Mathematics and Natural Philosophy.

The **Shakspere Gold Medal** for the English Language, Literature and European History.

The **Logan Gold Medal** for Geology, Mineralogy and Palaeontology.

The **Major Hiram Mills Gold Medal** for a subject to be chosen by the Faculty from year to year.

If there be no candidate for any Medal, or if none of the Candidates fulfil the required conditions, the Medal will be withheld. and the proceeds of its endowment for the year may be devoted to prizes in the subject for which the Medal was intended. For details, see announcements of the several subjects below.

2. Special Certificates will be given to those Candidates for B.A. who have been placed in the First Class at the ordin-ary B.A. Examination ; have obtained three-fourths of the maximum marks in the aggregate of the studies proper to their year ; are in the First Class in not less than half the subjects, and have no Third Class. At this examination, no Candidate who has taken exemptions (see p. 64), can be placed in the First Class unless he has obtained First Class in four of the departments in which he has been examined, and has no Third Class.

3. Certificates of High General Standing will be granted to those Undergraduates of the first two years who have ob-tained three-fourths of the maximum marks in the aggregate of the studies proper to their year, are in the First Class in not less than half the subjects, and have not more than one Third Class. In the Third Year the conditions are the same as for the Special Certificate for B.A.

4. Prizes or Certificates will be given to those Under-graduates who have distinguished themselves in the studies of a particular class, and have attended all the other classes proper to their year.

5. His Excellency the Earl of Aberdeen has been pleased to offer annually during his term of office a **Gold Medal** for the study of Modern Languages and Literature, with European History, or for First Rank General Standing, as may be announced.

(a) The Regulations for the former are as follows :—

(1) The subjects for competition shall be French and German, together with a portion of the History prescribed for the Honour Course for the Shakspere Medal. Information concerning the History may be obtained from the Professor of History.

(2) The Course of Study shall extend over two years, viz., the Third and Fourth Years.

(3) The successful Candidate must be capable of speaking and writing both languages correctly.

(4) There shall be examinations in the subjects of the course in both the Third and Fourth Years, at which Honours may be awarded to deserving Candidates.

(5) The general conditions of competition and the privileges as regards exemptions shall be the same as for the other Gold Medals in the Faculty of Arts.

(6) Students from other Faculties shall be allowed to compete, provided they pass the examinations of the Third and Fourth Years in the above subjects.

(7) Candidates desiring to enter the Third Year of the Course, who have not obtained first-class standing at the Intermediate or Sessional Examinations of the Second Year in Arts, are required to pass an examination in the work of the first two years of the Course in Modern Languages, if called on to do so by the Professors.

(8) The subjects of Examination shall be those of the Honour Course in Modern Languages.

(b) The Regulations for the Gold Medal, if awarded for First Rank General Standing, are as follows :—

(1) The successful Candidate must take no exemptions or substitutions of any kind, whether Professional or Honour, in the Ordinary B.A. Examinations.

(2) He shall be examined in the following subjects :—

(a) CLASSICS (both languages) ; (b) MECHANICS, HYDROSTATICS, OPTICS, ASTRONOMY; (c) MORAL PHILOSOPHY ; and any two of the following subjects, or any one of them with its Additional Course ; (d) GEOLOGY, etc. ; (e) EXPERIMENTAL PHYSICS ; (f) ENGLISH ; (g) GERMAN.

(3) His answering must satisfy special conditions laid down by the Faculty.

(4) The same Candidate cannot obtain the Gold Medal for First Rank General Standing and also a Gold Medal for First Rank Honours.

6. The Neil Stewart Prize of $18 is open to all Undergraduates and Graduates of this University, and also to Graduates of any other University, who are students of Theology in some College affiliated to this University. The rules which govern the award of this prize are as follows :—

(1) The Candidate must pass, in the First Class, a thorough examination upon the following subjects: Hebrew Grammar; reading and translation at sight from the Pentateuch, and from such poetic portions of the Scriptures as may be determined.

(2) In case competitors should fail to attain the above standard, the prize will be withheld, and a prize of $36 will be offered in the following year for the same.

(Course for the present year : Hebrew Grammar (Gesenius) ; Translation and analysis of Exodus; Isaiah XL. to the end of the book.)

(3) There will be two Examinations of three hours each—one in Grammar and the other in Translation and Analysis .

This Prize founded by the late Rev. C. C. Stewart, M.A., and terminated by his death, was re-established by the liberality of the late Neil Stewart, Esq., of Vankleek Hill.

7. Early English Text Society's Prize.—This prize, the annual gift of the Early English Text Society, will be awarded for proficiency in (1) Anglo-Saxon, (2) Early English before Chaucer.

The subjects of Examination will be :—

(1) The Lectures of the Third and Fourth Years on Anglo-Saxon.

(2) Specimens of Early English, Clarendon Press Series, ed. Morris and Skeat, Part II., A. D. 1298—A. D. 1393. The Lay of Havelok the Dane (Early English Text Society, ed. Skeat).

8. New Shakspere Society's Prize.—This Prize, the anual gift of the New Shakspere Society, open to Graduates and Undergraduates, will be awarded for a critical knowledge of the following plays of Shakspere :—

Hamlet; Macbeth; Othello; King Lear.

9. Charles G. Coster Memorial Prize.—This Prize, intended as a tribute to the memory of the late Rev. Chas. G. Coster, M.A., Ph.D., Principal of the Grammar School, St. John, N.B., is offered by Colin H. Livingstone, B.A., to Undergraduates (men or women) from the Maritime Provinces, Nova Scotia, New Brunswick and Prince Edward Island. In April, 1899, it will be awarded to that Undergraduate of the First, Second or Third Year, from the above Provinces, who, in the opinion of the Faculty, has passed the most satisfactory Sessional Examinations, under certain conditions laid down by the donor. .

10. **Vancouver Society's Prize.**—The Vancouver (B.C.) Society of McGill Graduates, offers a prize of $10, which will be awarded in 1898-99 for proficiency in History.

11. **Science Scholarships Granted by Her Majesty's Commission for the Exhibition of 1851.**—These scholarships of the value of £150 a year are tenable for two or, in rare instances, three years. They are limited, according to the Report of the Commission, "to those branches of Science (such as Physics, Mechanics and Chemistry) the extension of which is specially important.for our national industries." Their object is not to facilitate ordinary collegiate studies, but "to enable students to continue the prosecution of science with the view of aiding in its advance or in its application to the industries of the country."

Three nominations to these scholarships have already been placed by the Commissioners in 1891 and 1893 at the disposal of McGill University, and have been awarded.

. When nominations are offered, they are open to Students of not less than three years standing in the Faculty of Arts or of Applied Science, and are tenable at any University or at any other Institution approved by the Commission.

12. The names of those who have taken Honours, Certificates or Prizes will be published in order of merit, with mention, in the case of Students of the First and Second Years, of the schools in which their preliminary education has been received.

8. Partial Students.

As will be seen from the announcement in Part First, the courses of lectures to which Partial Students are admitted are such as are likely to prove attractive to those who have limited time at their disposal, and wish to enjoy the advantages of that higher instruction which the University offers to all qualified persons.

For conditions of Entrance see p. 50.

9. Attendance and Conduct.

All students shall be subject to the following regulations:—

1. A Class-book shall be kept by each Professor or Lecturer, in which the presence or absence of Students shall be carefully noted; and the said Class-book shall be submitted to the Faculty at all their ordinary meetings during the Session.

2. Each Professor shall call the roll at the beginning of the lecture. Credit for attendance on any lecture may be refused on the grounds of lateness, inattention, neglect of study, or disorderly conduct in the class-room. In the case last mentioned, the student may, at the discretion of the Professor, be required to leave the class-room. Persistence in any of the above offences against discipline shall, after admonition by the Professor, be reported to the Dean of Faculty. The Dean may, at his discretion, reprimand the student, or refer the matter to the Faculty at its next meeting, and may in the interval suspend from Classes.

3. Absence from lectures can only be excused by necessity or duty, of which proof must be given, when called for, to the Faculty. The number of times of absence, from necessity or duty, that shall disqualify from the keeping of a session shall in each case be determined by the Faculty.

4. While in College, or going to or from it, Students are expected to conduct themselves in the same orderly manner as in the class-rooms. Any Professor observing improper conduct in the College buildings or grounds may admonish the student, and, if necessary, report him to the Dean. Without as well as within the walls of the College, every student is required to maintain a good moral character.

5. When students are brought before the Faculty under the above rules, the Faculty may reprimand, report to parents or guardians, impose fines, disqualify from competing for prizes or honours, suspend from classes, or report to the Corporation for expulsion.

6. Any student who does not report his residence on or before November 1st in each year is liable to a fine of one dollar.

7. Any student injuring the furniture or buildings will be required to repair the same at his own expense, and will, in addition, be subject to such other penalty as the Faculty may see fit to inflict.

8. All cases of discipline involving the interests of more than one Faculty, or of the University in general, shall be immediately reported to the Principal, or, in his absence, to the Vice-Principal.

(N.B.—All students are required to appear in Academic dress while in or about the College buildings.

At a meeting of the Corporation in April, 1895, it was agreed to request all members of the University to appear in Academic dress at University Receptions, Conversaziones, etc.

Students are requested to take notice that petitions to the Faculty on any subject cannot, in general, be taken into consideration, except at the regular meetings appointed in the Calendar.)

III. FEES.

All fees and fines are payable to the Bursar.

The fees must be paid to the Bursar, and the receipts shown to the Dean within a fortnight after the commencement of attendance in each session. In case of default, the student's name will be removed from the College books, and can be replaced thereon only by permission of the Faculty, and on payment of a fine of $2.

Undergraduates matriculated before May, 1898, and Partial Students who have entered the affiliated Theological Colleges before May, 1898, and are pursuing the curricula of such Colleges, are subject to the old scale of fees.

1. **Undergraduates.**—$60 per session. This will include the fees for Laboratory work, Library, Gymnasium and Grounds, and Graduation. In the Third and Fourth Years, it will cover the normal amount of practical instruction given in each subject having a Laboratory Course.

Every candidate for the September Matriculation Examination in any Faculty must pay a fee of $5 *before admission to the examination.* This will be reckoned as part of the regular fees if he pass, but will not be returned in case of failure.

Matriculation fee for entrance into the Second Year, $10, in addition to the sessional fee.

2. **Partial Students.**—(First and Second Years.)—$16 per session for one course of lectures, including the use of the Library; $12 per session for each additional course.

3. **Partial Students.**—(Third and Fourth Years.)—$25 per session for one course of lectures, including the use of the Library; $20 per session for each additional course.

N.B.—The lectures in one subject in any one of the four College years constitute a "Course."

Partial Students are also required to pay $2 yearly for "Athletics and the care of the College grounds," unless they state in writing to the Dean their intention not to use the grounds.

Partial Students taking the full curriculum in any one year pay the same fees as Undergraduates in that year.

N.B.—Every student is required to deposit with the Bursar the sum of $3 as caution money for damage done to furniture, apparatus or books, etc.

Special Fees.

ELOCUTION (optional)..	$5 00
GYMNASIUM (for partial students), optional....................	2 50
SUPPLEMENTAL EXAMINATION, at the regular date fixed by the Faculty..	2 00
SUPPLEMENTAL EXAMINATION, when granted at any other time than the regular date fixed by the Faculty........................	5 00
FEE FOR A CERTIFICATE OF STANDING, if granted to a student on application..	1 00
FEE FOR A CERTIFICATE OF STANDING, if accompanied by a statement of classification in the several subjects of examination.....	2 00
EXAMINATION FEE for candidate intending to enter the Medical Faculty..	5 00

(Note.—The special laboratory fees for the Second, Third and Fourth Years will be found in the Calendar of 1897-98.)

All applications for certificates must be addressed to the Secretary of the University, accompanied by the required fee.

No certificates are given for attendance on lectures unless the corresponding examinations have been passed.

Special fees are additional to the regular fees paid by Undergraduates or Partial Students, but are payable only for the optional classes or objects named above.

All fees for Supplemental Examinations must be paid to the Bursar, and the receipts shown to the Dean before the examination.

(All fines are applied to the purchase of books for the Library.)

Graduates in Arts of this University are allowed, on payment of one-half of the usual fees, to attend all lectures. except those for which a special fee is exigible.

FEE FOR THE DEGREE OF M.A.... .... $16 00
"   "   " :. LL.D.... .... 80 00

If the Degree of M.A. be granted, with permission to the Candidate, on special grounds, to be absent from Convocation, the fee is $25.

The M.A. or LL.D. fee must be sent with the thesis to the Secretary of the University. This is a condition essential to the reception of the application. The Secretary will then forward the thesis to the Dean of the Faculty.

Extract from the Regulations of the Board of Governors for Election of Fellows under Chap. V. of the Statutes of the University.

" From and after the graduation of 1888, all new Graduates " shall pay a Registration Fee of $2.50 at the time of their " graduation, in addition to the Graduation Fee; and shall " be entered in the University list as privileged to vote, and " shall have voting-papers mailed to them by the Secretary."

IV. SCHOLARSHIPS AND EXHIBITIONS.
General Regulations.

1. A Scholarship is tenable for *two* years; an Exhibition for *one* year.

2. Scholarships are open for competition to Students who have **Scholar-** passed the University Intermediate Examination, provided that not more than three sessions have elapsed since their Matriculation; and also to Candidates who have obtained what the Faculty may deem equivalent standing in some other University, provided that application be made before the end of the Session preceding the examination.

3. Scholarships are divided into two classes :—(1) **Science Scholarships;** (2) **Classical and Modern Language Scholarships**. The subjects of examination for each are as follows :—

Science Scholarships.—MATHEMATICS—Differential and Integral Calculus; Analytic Geometry; Plane and Spherical Trigonometry; Higher Algebra and Theory of Equations. NATURAL SCIENCE—Botany; Chemistry; Logic. (For subdivision, see below.)

Classical and Modern Language Scholarships.—Greek, Latin, English Composition; English Language and Literature; French or German.

Exhibitions.   4. Exhibitions are assigned to the First and Second Years.

First Year Exhibitions are open for competition to candidates for entrance into the First Year.

Second Year Exhibitions are open for competition to Students who have passed the First Year Sessional Examinations, provided that not more than two sessions have elapsed since their Matriculation; and also to candidates for entrance into the Second Year.

The subjects of examination are as follows:—

First Year Exhibitions. — CLASSICS, MATHEMATICS, ENGLISH, FRENCH.

Second Year Exhibitions.—CLASSICS, MATHEMATICS, ENGLISH LANGUAGE AND LITERATURE, FRENCH OR GERMAN.

5. The First and Second Year Exhibition Examinations will, for Candidates who have not previously entered the University, be regarded as Matriculation Examinations.

6. No student can hold more than one Exhibition or Scholarship at the same time.

7. Exhibitions and Scholarships will not necessarily be awarded to the candidates who have obtained the highest marks. An adequate standard of merit will be required.

8. If in any College Year there be not a sufficient number of candidates showing adequate merit, any one or more of the Exhibitions or Scholarships offered for competition may be given to more deserving candidates in another year.

9. A successful candidate must, in order to retain his Scholarship or Exhibition, proceed regularly with his College Course to the satisfaction of the Faculty.

10. The annual income of the Scholarships or Exhibitions will be paid in four instalments, viz. :—In October, December, February and April, about the 20th day of each month.

11. The Examinations will be held at the beginning of every Session.

For the session 1898-99 there are thirty-four Scholarships and Exhibitions including the following :—

The Jane Redpath Exhibition, founded by Mrs. Redpath, of Terrance Bank, Montreal:—value, about $90 yearly, open to both men and women.

The McDonald Scholarships and Exhibitions, founded by W. C. McDonald, Esq., Montreal :—value, $125 each, yearly.

The Charles Alexander Scholarship, founded by Charles Alexander, Esq., Montreal, for the encouragement of the study of Classics and other subjects:—value, $90 yearly.

The George Hague Exhibition, given by George Hague, Esq., Montreal, for the encouragement of the study of Classics :— value, $125 yearly.

The Major H. Mills Scholarship, founded by bequest of the late Major Hiram Mills :—value, $100 yearly.

The Barbara Scott Scholarship, founded by the late Miss Barbara Scott, Montreal, for the encouragement of the study of the Classical languages and literature :—value, $100 to $120 yearly.

Two Donalda Exhibitions, open to women in the Donalda Department :—value, $100 and $120 yearly.

One Donalda Scholarship.— value, $125 yearly.

Ottawa Valley Graduates' Society Exhibition, awarded on results of June Examination.

Exhibitions and Scholarships Offered for Competition at the Opening of the Session, Sept. 15th, 1898.

Through the liberality of private donors, the University is enabled to offer a number of additional Exhibitions (tenable for one year) to students entering the First Year.

The following is a complete list:—

Two Exhibitions of $200 each.

Two	"	"	125	"	(Open to men only)
One	"	"	120	"	
One	"	"	120	"	(Open to women only)
One	"	"	100	"	(Open to women only) *
One	"	"	90	"	
Twelve	"	"	60 each.		

*Open also to the Second Year. A modern language may be substituted for Greek (see announcement for Donalda Department p. 81.)

The twelve Exhibitions of sixty dollars each shall be open for competition to residents in any part of Canada *except the Island of Montreal.* All the other Exhibitions shall be open to general competition without such limitation.

The Examination will be held at McGill College, Montreal ; and also at any of the following centres, provided that application in writing be made to the Secretary of McGill University by intending candidates, not later than September 1st.

In the Province of Ontario, at Toronto, Kingston and Ottawa.

In the Province of Nova Scotia, at Halifax.

In the Province of New Brunswick, at St. John.

In the Province of Prince Edward Island, at Charlottetown.

In the Province of Manitoba, at Winnipeg.

In the Province of British Columbia, at Victoria and Vancouver.

In the Island of Newfoundland, at St. John's.

No application received after September 1st will be considered.

All the other Entrance, Exhibition and Scholarship Examinations of September, 1898, will be held at McGill University only.

For subjects of Examination see under pp. 46-49.

To Students entering the Second Year, three Exhibitions of $125, and one of $100.

Subjects of Examination.

Greek.—Xenophon, Luciani Vera Historia (Jerram) ; Demosthenes, Olynthiacs, I. and II.; Euripides, Alcestis.

Latin.—Virgil, Georgics, Bk. I.; Horace, Odes, Bk. IV.; Livy, Bk. XXI.

Greek and Latin Prose Composition, and Translation at sight.

A paper on Grammar and History.

Text Books.—Myers' Ancient History; Abbott's Arnold's Greek Prose Composition, or Sidgwick's First Greek Writer; Ramsay's Latin Prose, Vol. I.

Mathematics.— Euclid (six books) ; Casey's Sequel to Euclid ; Algebra (HALL AND KNIGHT'S Advanced); Theory of Equations (in part); Trigonometry (first six chapters, GALBRAITH AND HAUGHTON with deductions).

English and Modern History.—*Language.*—TRENCH, Study of Words. *Literature.*—SPENCER, Faerie Queene, Bk. I., ed. Percival (Macmillan); TENNYSON, Selections from Tennyson, ed. Rowe and Webb (Macmillan). *History.*—CHURCH, The Beginning of the Middle Ages (Epochs of Modern History, Longmans'). *English Composition.*—The candidate will be required to write an essay on some subject connected with the literature or history prescribed.

French.—French Grammar including Syntax.—PAUL BOURGET, Un Saint; F. COPPÉE, La Grève des Forgerons; V. HUGO, Le roi s'amuse. Oral Examinations.

Or, instead of French :—

German.— German Grammar (an amount equal to VANDERSMISSEN, Accidence and Syntax, including exercises in Translation); GRIMM, Kinder-und Hausmaerchen (Vandersmissen's edition); SCHILLER, Der Neffe als Onkel, Der Gang nach dem Eisenhammer; GOETHE, Hermann und Dorothea; Translation from English into German.

No Candidate who has been placed in the Third Class in more than one subject can be awarded a Second Year Exhibition.

To Students Entering the Third Year, three Scholarships of $125, one of $100, and one of $90, tenable for two years.

Two of these are offered in **Mathematics and Logic,** one of the two being for the Donalda Department only, and one in **Natural Science and Logic** as follows:—

Mathematics. — Differential Calculus (WILLIAMSON, Chaps. 1, 2, 3, 4, 7, 9; Chap. 12, Arts. 168-183 inclusive; Chap. 17, Arts. 225-242 inclusive). Integral Calculus (WILLIAMSON,) Chaps. 1, 2, 3, 4, 5; Chap 7, Arts. 126-140 inclusive; Chap. 8, Arts. 150-156 inclusive; Chap. 9, Arts. 168-176 inclusive). Analytic Geometry (SALMON, Conic Sections, subjects of chaps. 1-13 (omitting Chap. 8), with part of Chap. 14). Lock, Higher Trigonometry; McLELLAND and PRESTON, Spherical Trigonometry, Part I. SALMON, Modern Higher Algebra (first four chapters). TODHUNTER or BURNSIDE and PANTON, Theory of Equations (selected course).

Logic as in Jevons' Elementary Lessons in Logic.

2. Natural Science.—BOTANY, as in course I, including a practical acquaintance with Canadian species of Spermatophytes and Pteridophytes. Text-book of Botany, by Strasburger, Noll, Schenck and Schimper (trans. by Porter), Parts II and III., and Sachs' History of Botany. CHEMISTRY as in Roscoe's Lessons in Elementary Chemistry. LOGIC, as in Jevons' Elementary Lessons in Logic.

The remaining two Scholarships [viz., the Barbara Scott, $100 and the Charles Alexander, $90] are offered in Classics and Modern Languages, as follows :—

Subjects of Examina- tion.

Greek.—PLATO, Phaedo; THUCYDIDES, Book VI.; SOPHOCLES, Antigone.

Latin.—HORACE, Epistles, Book I.; CICERO Pro Roscio Amerino ; VIRGIL, Aeneid, Book VI.; SALLUST, Catiline; CICERO, Select letters (Pritchard and Bernard, Clarendon Press Series).

Greek and Latin Prose Composition, and Translation at Sight.

Ancient History.— Text-Books.—SMITH, Student's Greece; MOMMSEN, Rome (abridged).

English and History.— Literature. — SHAKSPERE, Tempest, ed. Deighton (Macmillan); MILTON, Paradise Lost, Bks. I. and II. (Macmillan); LAMB, Essays of Elia, ed. Hallward and Hill (Macmillan). History.—MYERS, Mediaeval and Modern History (Ginn), Part I. English Composition.—The candidate will be required to write an essay on some subject connected with the literature or history prescribed.

English Composition—High marks will be given for this subject.

French.—RACINE, Britannicus ; MOLIERE, Les Femmes Savantes. French Grammar. BOUNEFON, Les Ecrivains célèbres de la France. Oral examination; Dictation.

For September, 1899. RACINE, Britannicus ; MOLIERE, Le Misanthrope ; A. DE MUSSET, Les Nuits; A. DE VIGNY, Cinq Mars. Grammar, LANSON, Literature Francaise. Oral Examination.

Or, instead of French:—

German.— SCHILLER — Egmont's Leben und Tod (Buchheim), die Kraniche des Ibycus, Das Lied von der Glocke, der Kampf mit dem Drachen ; IMMERMANN, Der Oberhof (Wagner, Pitt Press) ; GOETHE, Egmont ; German Grammar and Composition ; Translation from English into German ; Dictation.

Changes for September, 1899.

In the Exhibition Examinations, September, 1899, the following will be substituted for the corresponding books in the Calendar for 1897-98.

FIRST YEAR.—Greek.—Xenophon, Anabasis II or I.; Homer, Odyssey XIII.; Euripides, Sidgwick's Scenes from Hecuba, or Iliad VI.

FIRST YEAR.—Latin—Caesar B. G., V. VI.; Virgil, Aeneid, V. or I.; Cicero, Catiline Orations III., IV.

FIRST YEAR.—French—A. Dumas, La question d'Argent; About L'homme à l'oreille cassée; Labiche, Moi.

FIRST YEAR.—English—In place of *History* the following Essays of Macaulay :—Ranke's History of the Popes; Frederick The Great; Dumont's Recollections of Mirabeau.

SECOND YEAR.—French—Balzac, Le Cousin Pons ; Victor Hugo, Ruy Blas; De Vigny, Le Cor; Barbier, l'Idole.

SECOND YEAR.—German.—*Add* to texts already prescribed Baumback, Die Nonna (Heath & Co.).

V. GENERAL INFORMATION FOR STUDENTS.

Boarding Houses.

Board and Rooms can be obtained at a cost of from $15 to $25 per month; Rooms only, from $4 to $10 per month; Board only, from $12 to $18 per month.

Students can obtain a list of Boarding Houses on application to the Secretary.

Special Course for Women*

IN THE FACULTY OF ARTS.

Donalda Endowment.

Professors and Lecturers (as on page 3). Lady Superintendent, Miss Helen Gairdner.

The classes for women under this endowment are wholly separate, except those for Candidates for Honours (including most of the additional courses in the Third and Fourth Years). The examinations are identical with those for men. Women will have the same privileges with reference to Classing, Honours, Prizes and Medals as men.

Regulations for Examinations, Exemptions, Boarding-Houses, Attendance, Conduct, Library and Museum are the same as for men. Undergraduates wear the Academic Dress; others do not.

In September, 1898, a Scholarship, value $125 yearly (tenable for two years), will be offered for competition in Mathematics to Students of the Third Year. The course is the same as for the Mathematical Scholarship open to men.

The Jane Redpath Exhibition is open for competition, at the beginning of the First or Second Year, to both men and women.

For September, 1898, there are fifteen Exhibitions open to the First Year only, both men and women. (See pp. 76-77),

Two other Exhibitions (one of the value of $120, the other $100) are open for competition in the First or Second Year to Students of the Donalda Department only. For Subjects see pp. 46-49. Candidates for these Exhibitions are allowed, according to the general rule of the Donalda Department, to substitute an additional modern language for Greek in the examination. In this case while the regulation concern-

Subject to re-arrangement on the opening of the Royal Victoria College.

ing one modern language will, for Entrance only, be as on p. 46, the course in that which is to be substituted for Greek in the Exhibition Examination will be:—

For First Year :—

French.—See pages 46-49.

> or German.—German Grammar and Composition ; THEODOR STORM, Immensee (Heath & Co.); VON HILLERN, Höher als die Kirche (Heath & Co.); SCHILLER Der Gang nach dem Eisenhammer, Das Lied von der Glocke : STIFTER, Haidedorf (Heath & Co.); GOETHE, Götz von Berlichingen. Translation at Sight. Translation from English into German.

For Second Year :—

French.—See page 7S.

> or German.—SCHILLER, Der Neffe als Onkel, Egmont's Leben und Tod, Der Geisterseher, Die Kraniche des Ibykus ; Goethe, Torquato Tasso. Translation at Sight; German Grammar and Composition ; Translation of French and English into German.

The income of the Hannah Willard Lyman Memorial Fund will be given in prizes.

I. MATRICULATION AND ADMISSION.

The same Examination as for men.

II. ORDINARY COURSE OF STUDY FOR THE DEGREE OF B.A.

(In separate Classes.)

For all Subjects (except German) in all the Years, see pp. 4-34

The Second Year course in **German** is as follows :—

THOMAS' German Grammar; LESSING, Minna von Barnhelm ; GOETHE, Hermann und Dorothea; BAUMBACH, Der Schwiegersohn (Heath & Co.).

Two hours a week.

Physical Education.

A class will be conducted by Miss Barnjum, which will be optional and open to Partial Students.

Elocution.

Instruction in this subject will be given to those who desire it, by arrangement with Mr. J. P. Stephen.

Honour and Additional Courses.

(*In Mixed Classes.*)

Undergraduates desiring to take one of the Honour Courses in CLASSICS, MATHEMATICS, MATHEMATICAL PHYSICS, MENTAL AND MORAL PHILOSOPHY, ENGLISH LANGUAGE AND LITERATURE, HISTORY, THE NATURAL SCIENCES, MODERN LANGUAGES or such portions of the Honour Courses as constitute the Additional Courses, may in the Third and Fourth Years obtain exemptions to the same extent as men, and must take the lectures with men.

Details will be found on pp. 56 &c.

III. DEGREES.

Students are admissible to the degrees of B.A., M.A., and LL.D., conferred in the usual way, on the usual conditions ; and will be entitled to all the privileges of these degrees, except that of being elected as Fellows.

IV. FEES.

The fees, which are the same as for men (see pp. 72-73), are to be paid to the Registrar of the University, from whom tickets for the Library and copies of the Library Rules may be obtained.

V. LODGINGS, &c.

Women not resident in Montreal, proposing to attend classes, and desiring to have information as to suitable lodgings, are requested to intimate their wishes in this respect to the Registrar of the University, at least two weeks before the opening of the session. Students desiring information as to the above or other matters are referred to the Lady Superintendent, who will be found in her office in the rooms of the Donalda Department, every day during the session, except Saturday.

Lectures Open to Partial Students, Session 1898-99.

Botany :—*Prof. Penhallow.*
Zoology :—*Prof. MacBride.*
Geology :—*Dr. Adams.*
Experimental Physics :—*Prof. Cox and* —— ——
Psychology and Logic :— *Rev. Dr. Murray and Mr. Lafleur.*
·Mental Philosophy :— *Rev. Dr. Murray and Mr. Lafleur.*
Moral Philosophy :—*Rev. Dr. Murray.*

Rhetoric :—*Mr. Lafleur.*
English :—*Prof. Moyse.*
History :—*Dr. Colby.*
*Latin and Greek.
*French.
*German.
*Mathematics and
*Mathematical Physics.

Those Courses in which two lectures weekly are delivered will each amount to about 45 lectures, and the others in proportion.

* The lectures on these subjects extend over all the Years of the Course.

DONALDA DEPARTMENT.
TIME TABLE, SESSION 1898-9.

YEARS	HOURS.	MONDAY.	TUESDAY.	WEDNESDAY.	THURSDAY.	FRIDAY.
FIRST YEAR.	9	Greek.	Physics.	French.	Greek.	Greek.
	10	English.	English.	Greek.		Mathematics.
	11	German.	Mathematics.	Latin.	English.	French.
	12	Latin.	Latin.	Mathematics.	German.	Latin.
	2	Mathematics.	French.	German.	French.	German.
	3				Physics.	
SECOND YEAR.	9		Greek.	Latin.	French.	
	10	Mathematics.	†Mathematics.	French.	Greek.	Latin.
	11	Botany.	Math. Phys.	Greek.	† Mathematics.	German.
	12	Logic.	Latin.	Botany.		†Mathematics.
	2			Logic.		Logic.
	3	German.		Mod. History.	French.	Mod. History
	4					

THIRD YEAR	9	Latin.	German.	German. Greek.		
	10		Exp. Physics.		Greek. Exp. Physics.	French.
	11	French.	Rhetoric.		Math. Phys.	Latin.
	12	English.	Zoology.		Zoology.	Math. Phys.
	2		Botany.	Pract. Zool.		Botany.
	3	Metaphysics.		Metaphysics. Pract. Zool.		
	4	German.				
FOURTH YEAR	9	Astronomy (a)	German.	German.	Moral Phil.	Geology.
	10	French.	Exp. Physics. Greek.	Geology.	Exp. Physics.	French.
	11		Latin.	English Lit.	Math. Phys.	Latin. Astronomy(a)
	12	Geology.	Moral Phil.	Mineralogy (a) Moral Phil.	Greek.	Math. Phys.
	2	Zoology.	Botany.		Zoology.	Botany.
	3					
	4				German.	

Advanced Sections will be formed in all subjects in the first two years so far as practicable and in these Honours may be awarded. In Mathematics there is an Advanced Section in the First Year. 2 hours a week.

† For Candidates for Honours   (a) During First Term.

Honour Courses (Third and Fourth Years) will be given in the following subjects, the precise hours for which will be arranged to suit the convenience of the classes.

CLASSICS : Third and Fourth Years, 6 hours a week.

ENGLISH · Third Year, 6 hours a week ; Fourth Year, 6 hours a week.

FRENCH : Third Year, 2 hours a week ; Fourth Year, 2 hours a week.

GERMAN : Third Year, 2 hours a week ; Fourth Year, 2 hours a week.

HISTORY : Third and Fourth Years, 5 hours a week.

MENTAL AND MORAL PHILOSOPHY : Third Year, 2 hours a week ; Fourth Year, 2 hours a week.

MATHEMATICS, MATHEMATICAL PHYSICS AND ASTRONOMY : Third Year, 4 hours a week ; Fourth Year, 4 hours a week.

GEOLOGY AND MINERALOGY : Third Year, 4 hours a week (First Term) ; 5 hours a week ; (Second Term) ; Fourth Year, 7 hours a week.

BIOLOGY : 4 hours a week and 4 periods of Practical Work.

THE CHEMICAL LABORATORIES are open every day (except Saturday) from 9 a.m. to 5 p.m. PRACTICAL PHYSICS : Third Year, Monday, 10 a.m. to 1 p.m., or Friday, 2.30 p.m. to 5.30 p.m.; Fourth Year, Wednesday, 2.30 p.m. to 5.30 p.m.

THE BOTANICAL LABORATORIES are open daily from 9 a.m. to 5 p.m. Saturday Classes in General Morphology (2nd Year), 11 a.m. to 1 p.m.

GEOLOGY : Demonstrations and Excursions on Saturday. The Petrographical Laboratory is open every day throughout the Second Term.

THE ZOOLOGICAL LABORATORY is open daily from 9 a.m. to 1 p.m. and from 2 p.m. to 5 p.m. Practical Work under the supervision of the Professor and Demonstrator, Wednesday, 2 p.m. to 4 p.m., and Saturday, 9 to 12 a.m. The time for Practical Work in the Fourth Year will be arranged.

N. B.— *The hours in this table are subject to alteration during the Session.*

FACULTY OF APPLIED SCIENCE.

CONTENTS.

	PAGE
Officers of Instruction, etc	88
General Statement	90
Conspectus of Subjects	91
Matriculation and Admission	92
Examinations	94
Graduate Course	96
Attendance and Conduct	98
Library	98
Museum	99
Fees	100
Medals, Exhibitions, etc	101
Special Provisions	104
Special Lectures	105
Courses of Lectures :—	
Architecture	106
Civil Engineering and Applied Mechanics	108
Hydraulics	111
Surveying and Geodesy	113
Descriptive Geometry	115
Freehand and Engineering Drawing	115
Electrical Engineering	116
Mechanical Engineering	119
Mining and Metallurgy	121
Chemistry and Assaying	125
Thermodynamics	126
Geology and Mineralogy	126
Zoology	127
Botany	127
Experimental Physics	128
Mathematics and Mathematical Physics	130
English Language and Literature	131
Meteorology	131
Laboratories	131
Museums	149
Workshops	150
Board and Lodging	151
Societies	152
Research Work, 1897-98	154
Time Table	156

Faculty of Applied Science.

William Peterson, M.A., LL.D., Principal.
Henry T. Bovey, M.A., D.C.L., LL.D., M. Inst. C.E., F.R.S.C., Dean of the Faculty.

PROFESSORS.

B. J. Harrington, M.A., Ph.D., F.R.S.C., Greenshields Professor of 'Chemistry and Mineralogy.
Henry T. Bovey, M.A., D.C.L., Scott Professor of Civil Engineering and Applied Mechanics.
C. H. McLeod, Ma.E., F.R.S.C., M.Can.Soc.C.E., Professor of Surveying and Geodesy, Lecturer in Descriptive Geometry, and Superintendent of the Observatory.
G. H. Chandler, M.A., Professor of Applied Mathematics.
John Cox, M.A., McDonald Professor of Physics.
J. T. Nicolson, B.Sc., M.Can.Soc.C.E., Workman Professor of Mechanical Engineering, and Lecturer in Thermodynamics.
Stewart Henbest Capper, M.A., A.R.I.B.A., R.C.A., McDonald Professor of Architecture.
J. B. Porter, E.M., Ph.D., M.Can.Soc.C.E., McDonald Professor of Mining.
.. .. McDonald Professor of Chemistry.
.. .. McDonald Professor of Physics.
.. .. McDonald Professor of Electrical Engineering.

(The above Professors constitute the Faculty.)

ASSISTANT PROFESSORS AND LECTURERS.

R. S. LEA, Ma.E., Asso.M.Can.Soc.C.E., Assistant Professor of Civil Engineering, and Lecturer in Mathematics.

HENRY F. ARMSTRONG, Assistant Professor of Descriptive Geometry and Freehand Drawing.

R. J. DURLEY, B.Sc., A.M.Inst.C.E., Assistant Professor of Mechanical Engineering.

. . . . Assistant Professor of Civil Engineering.

NEVIL NORTON EVANS, M.A.Sc., Lecturer in Chemistry.

J. G. G. KERRY, Ma.E., Asso.M.Can.Soc.C.E., Lecturer in Surveying and Descriptive Geometry.

L. HERDT, Ma.E., E.E., Lecturer in Electrical Engineering.

DEMONSTRATORS.

H. M. TORY, M.A., in Physics.

F. H. PITCHER, M.A.Sc., in Physics.

ALEXANDER BRODIE, M.A.Sc., in Practical Chemistry.

H. T. BARNES, M.A.Sc., in Physics.

H. M. JAQUAYS, B.A., B.A.Sc., in Mechanical Engineering.

JOHN W. BELL, B.A.Sc., in Mining.

With the foregoing are associated the following PROFESSORS and LECTURERS of the Faculty of Arts:—

CHARLES E. MOYSE, B.A., Molson Professor of English Language and Literature.

D. P. PENHALLOW, B.Sc., M.A.Sc., F.R.S.C., Professor of Botany.

FRANK D. ADAMS, M.A.Sc., Ph.D., F.G.S., Logan Professor of Geology.

C. W. COLBY, B.A., Ph.D., Professor of History.

E. W. MACBRIDE, M.A., B.Sc., Professor of Zoology.

FACULTY OF APPLIED SCIENCE.

§ I. GENERAL STATEMENT.

The Instruction in this Faculty is designed to afford a complete preliminary training, of a practical as well as theoretical nature, to Students who desire to pursue the profession of Architecture, or who are preparing to enter any of the various branches of the professions of Engineering and Surveying, or are destined to be engaged in Assaying, Practical Chemistry, and the higher forms of Manufacturing Art.

The Degrees conferred by the University upon such undergraduates of the Faculty as shall fulfill the conditions and pass the Examinations hereinafter stated will be, in the first instance, "Bachelor of Applied Science," mention being made in the Diploma of the particular Department of study pursued ; and, subsequently, the degree of "Master of Engineering" or "Master of Applied Science." (§ IV.)

§ II. SUBJECTS OF INSTRUCTION.

The table on the following page shows the subjects of instruction and the hours per week devoted to each subject in the several Courses, viz:—

 I.—ARCHITECTURE.

 II.—CIVIL ENGINEERING AND SURVEYING.

 III.—ELECTRICAL ENGINEERING.

 IV.—MECHANICAL ENGINEERING.

 V.—MINING ENGINEERING.

 VI.—PRACTICAL CHEMISTRY.

	SUBJECTS:		I	II	III	IV	V	VI
FIRST YEAR	Chemistry....	¿ XIII., 9	2	2	2	2	2	2
	Descriptive Geometry....	" 4	6(a),3(b)	6(a),3(b)	6(a),3(b)	6(a),3(b)	6(a),3(b)	2
	English........	" 16	2	2	2	2	2	10
	Mathematics................	" 15	10	10	10	10	10	1
	Mechanism....................	" 7	1	1	1	1	1	3
	Freehand Drawing..........	" 5	3	3	3	3	3	3
	Chemical Laboratory..........	¿ XIV. 2	3	3	3	3	3	3(b)
	Mathematical Laboratory.....	" 9	3 (b)	3 (b)	3 (b	3 (b)	3 (P)	
	Shopwork................	§ XVI.	7	7	7	7	7	7
SECOND YEAR	Architecture, Theory of........	§ XIII., 1	1	—	—	—	—	—
	Architectural History.........	"	2	2	—	—	—	—
	Botany....................	" 13	—	—	—	—	—.	2
	Building Construction..........	" 2	1	1	1	1	1	—
	Chemistry..................	" 9	—	—	—	—	7	14
	Descriptive Geometry.........	" 4	3	3	3	3	3	—
	Freehand Drawing...........	" 5	3					
	Kinematics of Machinery......	" 7	—	1 (b)	1		
	Mathematics.............	" 15	6	6	6	6	6	—
	Mining	" 8						
	Metallurgy...............	" 8						
	Modelling	" 2						
	Physics.....................	" 14	2	2	2	2	2	2
	Surveying*...................	" 3	3	3	-	—	3	—
	Zoology*..., ...	" 13		3	3	—	3	—
	Drawing................	" 5	10	6	3	3	3	—
	Physical Laboratory..........	¿ XIV. 16	3	3	3	3	3	3
	Shopwork..	§ XVI. 3	3	3	6	6	3	—
THIRD YEAR	Architecture & Arch. History.	¿ XIII., 1	4					
	Chemistry......	" 9	—	—	—	—	6	16
	Decoration, Ornament, etc.....	" 1	1					
	Descriptive Geometry	" 4	2	2	—	—	—	—
	Determinative Mineralogy.....	" 11	—	—	—	3	3
	Dynamics of Machinery..	" 7		—	2	2	—	—
	Electrical Engineering........	" 6	—	1	—	—	—
	Freehand Drawing (Figure, etc).	" 1	4					
	Geology and Mineralogy ** ...	" 11	—	3	—		4 to 5	4 to 5
	Mathematics................	" 15	3	3	3	3	3	—
	Machine Design and Exercises.	" 7	—	—	2	5	—
	Metallurgy............	" 8						
	Modelling	" 1	3					
	Municipal Engineering........	" 2						
	Physics.....................	" 14		2	2	2	2	2
	Railroad Engineering.	" 2		1	—	—	Opt.	—
	Surveying.	" 3	3	3	—	—	3	—
	Theory of Structures	" 2		5 (a)	5 (a)	5 (a)	5 (a)	—
	Zoology *....................	" 12		—	—	—	—	3
	Drawing and Designing	" 1	11	9	3	3	3	—
	Electrical Engineering Lab....	§ XIV. 6	9	—	3 (b)	—	—	
	Mining and Metallurgical Lab...	" 13						
	Physical Laboratory..........	" 16		3	3,6 (d,h)	3	3	3
	Testing Laboratory......	" 2		7(b)	4 (b)	4 (b)	4 (b)	—
	Shopwork.	¿ XVI.		—	6	6	6	—
FOURTH YEAR	Architecture & Arch. History..	§ XIII. 1	2					
	Art, History of..	" 1	2					
	Assaying.......................	" 9	—	—	—	—	9	
	Chemistry.....	" 9	—	—	—	—	—	24
	Decoration, Ornament,etc	" 1	6					
	Dynamics of Machinery	" 7	—	1(a),2(b)	1(a),2(b)	—	—
	Electrodynamics	" 6	—	2	—	—	—
	Electrical Engineering........	" 6	—	1	1(b) opt.	—	—
	Geodesy......................	" 3	2	—	—	—	—
	Geology and Mineralogy ** ...	" 11	—	—	—	3	3
	Heating and Sanitation.........	" 1						
	Hydraulics....................	" 2	2	2	2	2	2	—
	Machine Design	" 7	—	1	1	—	—
	Modelling	" 3						
	Municipal Engineering	" 2	1	—	—	1	—
	Metallurgy...................	" 8	—	—	—	2	2
	Mining	" 8	—	—		Opt.	—
	Railroad Engineering..........	" 2	4	1	—	—	—
	Theory of Structures....	" 2		4	—	—	—
	Thermodynamics..............	" 10		2	2	2	2	—
	Drawing and Designing.... ...		10	8	3	9	8	—
	Electrical Engineering Lab....	¿ XIV. 6	—	12	—	—	—
	Geodetic Laboratory	" 7		3	—	—	—
	Hydraulic Laboratory.	" 8		3	—	3	3	—
	Mechanical Laboratory	" 10						

§ III. MATRICULATION AND ADMISSION.

All Students are recommended to take one or two years
of the Arts Course. They are then admitted into the Faculty
of Applied Science without examination. (See § IV. iv.)

Students and Graduates in Arts will be admitted to such
standing in the Faculty of Applied Science as their previous
studies will warrant, but are recommended to take the drawing and shop work during their Arts Course.

Candidates for examination must present themselves on the
first day of examination, and all Students, excepting those
engaged in surveying field work, must attend punctually at
9 a.m. on Friday, September 23rd, when the lectures will begin.

Examinations for entrance will be held in 1898 (1) on May
30th, and following days, in McGill College and at local
centres, and (2) on Thursday, September 15, and following
days, in McGill College only.

Any Head Master or other person desiring a local examination in June must, before May 10th, submit the name of
some suitable person, preferably a University graduate, who
is willing to act as Deputy Examiner, *i.e.*, receive the questions, hold the examinations, and forward the answers to
Montreal. Further particulars relating to this examination
will be given on application to the Secretary of the University.

SUBJECTS OF EXAMINATION.

Mathematics—*Arithmetic.*—All the ordinary rules, including square
root and a knowledge of the Metric System. *Algebra*—Elementary
rules, involution, evolution, fractions, indices, surds, simple and
quadratic equations of one or more unknown quantities. *Geometry*
—Euclid, Bks. I. II., III., IV. and VI., with definitions of Bk. V.,
and easy deductions. *Trigonometry*—As in Hamblin Smith, pp. 1-
100, omitting Ch. XI.

English.—Writing from Dictation. *Grammar*—A paper on English Grammar, including Analysis. The candidate will be expected
to show a good knowledge of Accidence, as treated in any grammar
prepared for the higher forms of schools. A similar statement

applies to grammatical Analysis in which the nomenclature used by Mason will be preferred. West's Elements of English Grammar (Pitt Press series), is recommended as a text-book. Analysis must be presented in tabular form, as on pages 208-211 of West.. *English History.*—Candidates will be required to give the chief details of leading events. While any text-book written for the upper forms of schools may be used in preparation for the examination, Gardiner's Outline of English History (Longmans) is recommended. *Composition.*—Candidates will write a short essay on a subject given at the time of the examination. *Literature.*—SHAKSPERE's Richard II., ed. Deighton (Macmillan), and Scott's Lady of the Lake, ed. Stuart (Macmillan).

[Note.—Candidates may take Arithmetic, and all the English subjects except Literature, at the June Examination of one year, and the remainder at the Entrance Examination of the following year.]

Any one of the following Languages.

French.—Grammar including syntax. An easy translation from French into English and from English into French; Dictation or similar exercise. Candidates are expected to be able to write French without gross mistakes in spelling or grammar. Special credit will be given for evidence of familiarity with the spoken language.

German.—The whole of JOYNES' German Reader (or equivalent amount) together with German Accidence and translation into German as in the First part of Vandersmissen's German Grammar (or equivalent amount).

Greek.—XENOPHON, Anabasis, Book I.; Greek Grammar.

Latin.—CÆSAR, Bell. Gall., Books I. and II.; and Virgil, Aeneid, Book I.; Latin Grammar.

In both Greek and Latin, Translation at sight and Prose Composition (sentences or easy narrative, based upon the prescribed prose text), will be required.

At the September, but not at the June, examination, other works in Greek or Latin equivalent to those specified may be accepted, if application be made to the Professors of Classics at least a fortnight before the day of examination.

Candidates, who at the examination for Associate in Arts have passed in the above subjects, are admitted as Undergraduates.

Candidates who have passed Academy Grade II. of the Province of Quebec, or the Preliminary Subjects of the Associate in Arts, will, on entrance, be exempt from examination in English Grammar, Dictation, English History and Arithmetic.

Candidates who fail in one or more subjects at the June examination, or who have taken part only of the examination and present themselves again in the following September, will be exempted from examination in those subjects only in which the Examiners may have reported them as specially qualified.

At the June examination, candidates from Ontario may present an equivalent amount from the books prescribed for the Junior Matriculation Examination of the University of Toronto.

The Matriculation or Junior Leaving Examination accepted by the Universities of Ontario is accepted by the Faculty, in so far as the subjects of their programme satisfy the Examiners of the Faculty, *i. e.*, when the subjects taken are the same as, or equivalent to, those required in McGill University.

In the case of Candidates from Ontario, Second Class non-professional certificates will be accepted *pro tanto* in this Examination.

Candidates who pass an examination at entrance in Freehand Drawing, equivalent to the First Year examination, may, on the recommendation of the examiner, be exempted from this subject in the First Year.

Candidates who produce certificates of having already completed a portion of a course in some recognized School of Applied Science may be admitted to an equivalent standing.

PARTIAL STUDENTS.—Students may be allowed to take one or more courses of instruction, upon showing, by examination or otherwise, that they are qualified to do so.

---

§ IV. EXAMINATIONS.

I. FOR THE DEGREE OF BACHELOR OF APPLIED SCIENCE.

1. FACULTY EXAMINATIONS.

There will be a Christmas examination for Students of the First Year in all the subjects, and for Students of the other years in such subjects as shall be determined by the Faculty. A sessional examination in all the subjects will be held at the end of the First and Second Years.

2. UNIVERSITY EXAMINATIONS.

(a) There will be a Primary examination at the end of the Third Year in all the subjects of that year. Candidates must pass this Examination before entering the Final Year.

(*b*) There will be a Final examination for the degree of Bachelor of Applied Science at the end of the Fourth Year in all the subjects of that year.

Successful Students will be arranged in order of merit.

II. FOR THE DEGREE OF MASTER OF ENGINEERING.

Candidates must be Bachelors of Applied Science of at least three years' standing, and must produce satisfactory certificates of having been engaged during that time upon *bona fide* work in either the Civil, Electrical, Mechanical or Mining Branch of Engineering.

They must pass with credit an examination extending over the general theory and practice of Engineering, in which papers will be set having special reference to that particular branch upon which they have been engaged during the three preceding years.

Candidates must present applications for examinations, together with the necessary certificates and fees. The Faculty will notify the candidates whether their certificates are satisfactory, and also of the date of the examination. (See also § V.)

III. FOR THE DEGREE OF MASTER OF APPLIED SCIENCE.

Candidates must be Bachelors of Applied Science of at least three years' standing, must present certificates of having been employed during that time in some branch of scientific work, and must pass with credit an examination on the theory and practice of those branches of scientific work in which they may have been engaged. The other conditions as under the last heading. (See also § V.)

IV. SPECIAL PROVISIONS FOR OBTAINING THE TWO DEGREES OF BACHELOR OF ARTS AND BACHELOR OF APPLIED SCIENCE IN SIX YEARS.

The Regulations heretofore in force have been modified so as to enable Students to take the two degrees of B.A. and B.A.Sc. in six years, as follows :—

1. Students who have passed the Intermediate in Arts may enter the First Year of the Applied Science Course, and will be exempted from the modern languages which they have already taken in Arts.

2. The remaining subjects required for the B.A. degree may be spread over three years instead of two.

3. The Faculty of Arts will accept the Mathematical Physics of the Applied Science Course in lieu of the Mathematical Physics of the Arts Course.

4. The Faculty of Arts will accept the Laboratory Work in Physics in lieu of the Natural Science of the Arts Course.

A certificate of Licentiate in Arts will be given along with the professional degree in Applied Science to those who, previous to entrance upon their professional studies proper, have completed two years in the Faculty of Arts, and have duly passed the prescribed examinations therein, but who do not wish to proceed to the degree of B.A.

§ V. GRADUATE COURSES.

Students who take the Bachelor's degree in one of the courses provided by the Faculty of Applied Science may graduate in any of the remaining courses by attending one or more subsequent sessions.

Graduates may also take an advanced course in the branch in which they have received their degree. On passing an examination at the end of such advanced course, the Master's degree will be conferred without further examination, on presentation at the end of one additional year of a satisfactory thesis on approved work.

Students are strongly recommended to take a Graduate Course, and special arrangements will be made for advanced and research work in the following :—

In Architecture—Advanced study in design. (See § XIII, 1.)

In Chemistry and Mineralogy. (See § XIII., 8, 9 and 11, and § XIV., 4.)

In the determination and comparison of the errors and the co-efficients of standards of length. (See § XIII., 3, and §XIV., 7.)

In the determination of gravity. (See § XIV., 7.)

The elasticity and strength of materials. (See § XIII., 2, and § XIV., 17.)

In Mining and Metallurgy—Advanced study in metallurgy and ore dressing can be carried on with great advantage in the new laboratories. (See § XIII., 8, and XIV., 9, 10 and 13.)

The efficiency of pumps and hydraulic motors. (See § XIII., 2, and § XIV., 8.)

The efficiency of power transmission by air, water, gas, steam and electricity. (See § XIII., 2, 6, 7.)

The efficiency of steam, gas, oil and hot-air engines and of refrigerators. (See § XIII., 7 and 10.)

The efficiency of machines and machine tools, and the power absorbed by the several processes of mechanical work, (See § XIII., 7.)

The efficiency of dynamometers, belting and shafting, including investigations into the relative merits of the several unguents. (See § XIII., 7.)

The efficiency of the several types of boilers, including investigations on the heat-producing power of the several fuels. (See § XIII., 10.)

On the efficiency of dynamos and electric motors.

The flow of water through orifices and pipes, and over weirs. (See § XIII., 2, and § XIV., 8.)

In geodesy and practical astronomy. (See § XIV., 7.)

In Street Railway design and theory, and in alternating apparatus.

In Physics.—The McDonald Physics' Building has been equipped and arranged with special reference to Graduate Courses and original research work in various branches of pure Physics. Every facility will be afforded in the workshops for the construction of special apparatus required for such investigations. (See § XIV., 16.)

IN MATHEMATICS.—Students taking Graduate Courses will receive guidance in any advanced Mathematics required in connection with their work.

---

§ VI. ATTENDANCE AND CONDUCT.

1. Absence from any number of lectures can only be excused by necessity or duty, of which proof must be given, when called for, to the Faculty. The number of times of absence, from necessity or duty, that shall disqualify for the keeping of a session, shall in each case be determined by the Faculty. The Professor may, at his discretion, refuse credit for attendance, on the ground of lateness, inattention or disorderly conduct.

2. Any student who does not report his residence on or before November 1st in each year is liable to a fine of one dollar. All subsequent changes of address must be immediately reported to the Dean.

3. Every Student is required to deposit with the Secretary of the University the sum of $5.00 as caution money for damage done to the furniture, machinery or other apparatus. In the case of improper or disorderly conduct in the University buildings or grounds, the Faculty may impose such penalty as may be deemed advisable, and may also inflict fines, to be deducted, if the Faculty thinks fit, from the caution money.

If individual responsibility for damage cannot be traced, a *pro rata* assessment will be made over all the Students more directly concerned.

---

§ VII. LIBRARY.

Librarian:—C. H. GOULD, B.A.

Assistant Librarian:—H. MOTT.

1. During the College Session the University Library is open daily (except on Sundays and general public holidays, from 9 a.m. till 5 p.m.; and the Reading Rooms from 9 am. till 6 p.m., and also from 8 till 10 p.m. On Saturdays, both Library and Reading Rooms close at 5 p.m. During vacations, both Library and Reading Rooms close at 5 p.m., and on Saturdays at 1 p.m.

2. Students in the Faculty of Applied Science may borrow books

on depositing the sum of $5 with the Bursar, which deposit, after the deduction of any fines due, will be repaid at the end of the session on the certificate of the Librarian that the books have been returned uninjured.

3. Graduates in any of the Faculties, on making a deposit of $5, are entitled to the use of the Library, subject to the same rules and conditions as Students; but they are not required to pay the annual Library fee.

4. No borrower other than a Professor or Lecturer may keep any book belonging to the Library longer than two weeks, on penalty of a fine of 5cts a volume for each day of detention, but any borrower may renew the loan of a book for fitting reasons. A borrower incurring fines beyond the sum total of $1 shall be debarred from the use of the Library until they have been paid.

5. Before leaving the Library, readers must return the books they have obtained, to the attendant at the Delivery Desk.

All persons using books remain responsible for them, so long as the books are charged to them, and borrowers returning books must see that their receipt for them is properly cancelled. Damage to, or loss of books shall be made good to the satisfaction of the Librarian and of the Library Committee. Writing or making any mark upon any book belonging to the Library is unconditionally forbidden. Any persons found guilty of wilfully damaging any book in any way shall be excluded from the Library, and shall be debarred from the use thereof for such time as the Library Committee may determine.

6. Silence must be strictly observed in the Library.

§ VIII. PETER REDPATH MUSEUM.

1. The Museum will open every lawful day from 9 a.m. till 5 p.m., except when closed for any special reason by order of the Principal or Committee.

2. Students can obtain tickets of admission from the Principal on application.

3. Students are to enter by the front door only, except when going to the lectures.

4. Any student wilfully defacing or injuring specimens, or removing the same, will be excluded from access to the Museum for the session.

§ IX. FEES.

The total fees for Undergraduates are $155.00 per annum, and this amount includes the fees for Tuition, Library, Matriculation, Graduation, Laboratories, Workshops, Gymnasium, Grounds, wear and tear of Apparatus, etc., etc.

The Matriculation fee of $5.00 (included in the $155.00 fee) must be paid to the University Secretary previous to the examination.

Deposit for caution money (see § VI.), $5.00.

Partial Students will be admitted to the Professional Classes in any year on payment of the ordinary fees for that year; or they may attend the lectures on any subject on payment of a special fee, which, unless otherwise specified, is $12.50 for each term, or $25.00 for the whole session.

SPECIAL LABORATORY FEES.—Partial Students desirous of taking Courses in any of the several Laboratories will be required to pay a fee of $25.00 for each Course.

' SPECIAL WORKSHOP FEES.—Partial Students desirous of taking the workshop courses will be required to pay the following fees, which include cost of materials and use of all tools:—

I day, or 7 hours per week for the whole Session from
September to April : $25 00
2 days, or 14   "   "   "   "   45 00
3 days, or 21   "   "   60 00
4 days, or 28   "   "   ..   "   70 00
Fee for Supplemental Examination, at date fixed by
Faculty   2 00
   "   "   if for any special reason granted
at any other date than that fixed by the Faculty   5 00
Fee for a certificate of standing   2 00

The fees must be paid to the Secretary, and the receipts shown to the Dean, within fourteen days after the commencement of attendance in each Session. In case of default, the Student's name will be removed from the College books, and can be replaced thereon only by permission of the Faculty, and on payment of a fine of $2.

The fee for a Graduate Course is $150.00. Graduates of this Faculty will be required to pay only one-half of this amount.

Fee for the Degree of MASTER OF ENGINEERING or MASTER OF APPLIED SCIENCE, $10.00.

If for any special reason the Master or Bachelor degree be granted *in absentiâ*, the fee will be $25.00.

§ X. MEDALS, EXHIBITIONS, PRIZES AND HONOURS.

1. THE BRITISH ASSOCIATION MEDALS AND EXHIBITION, founded by the British Association for the Advancement of Science, in commemoration of the meeting held in Montreal in the year 1884.

A BRITISH ASSOCIATION MEDAL AND PRIZE IN BOOKS are open for competition to students of the Graduating Class in each of the six Departments of the Faculty, and, if recommended by the examiners, will be awarded to the student taking the highest position in the final examinations.

2. THE GOVERNOR GENERAL'S SILVER MEDAL (the gift of His Excellency The Right Honourable the Earl of Aberdeen.)

The Medal will be awarded in the Graduating Class. The conditions will be specified at the opening of the Session.

3. SUMMER WORK. (See § XI., 1.) The following prizes are offered for the best summer Theses:—

To the students of the Civil Engineering Course a British Association prize of $25.

To the students of the Electrical Engineering Course a prize of $25 presented by E. B. Greenshields, Esq., B.A.

To the students of the Mechanical Engineering Course a prize of $25 presented by H. Paton, Esq.

Two Prizes of $35 and $15 offered by the General Mining Association of the Province of Quebec will be open for competition to students from McGill University, Toronto University and Queen's University, and will be awarded to the two students presenting the best Summer Theses on some subject connected with mining. Preference will be given to those Theses which show decided originality.

To the students of the Architectural Course a prize of $25 presented by A. T. Taylor, Esq., F.R.I.B.A., R.C.A., President of Quebec Architects' Association.

The following Exhibitions and Prizes will be open for competition at the beginning of the Session. *Students are required to notify the Dean of their intention to compete, at least one week before the commencement of the examination.*

4· A Scott Exhibition of $50.00 and a British Association prize of $25.00 to the Students entering the Fourth Year, the subjects of examination being the Mathematics and Theory of Structures of the Ordinary Course.

5. Two prizes of $25.00 and $15.00, to Students entering the Third Year, the subjects of Examination being:—The Mathematics of the Second Year Course.

6. A Scott Exhibition of $50.00, founded by the Caledonian Society of Montreal, in commemoration of the Centenary of Sir Walter Scott, and two prizes of $25.00 and $15.00 to Students entering the Second Year, the subjects of Examination being:—

(a) An Essay, in the form of a character sketch, on Brunel, or Davy or Maisonneuve. On the day of the Examination, the candidates will be required to write an essay on one of these characters, three hours being allowed for this. (b) Mathematics of the First Year Course. (c) Descriptive Geometry of First Year Course.

7. A Prize of $10.00, presented by the McGill University Graduates' Society of British Columbia, to Students entering the Third Year, the subject of Examination being the Descriptive Geometry of the Second Year Course.

8. Two Prizes, each of $10.00, presented by J. M. McCarthy, Esq., B.A.Sc., to Students entering the Third Year, for proficiency in Levelling or Transit Work.

9. Two Prizes, one of $100, the other of $50, presented by W. A. Carlyle, Esq., Ma.E., may be awarded to students of the Mining Course taking the highest positions in the degree examinations of 1899.

10. Three prizes, of $12.00, $8.00 and $5.00, presented by A. C. Hutchison, Esq., R.C.A., will be awarded to the three undergraduates taking the highest standing in the Freehand Drawing of the First Year.

11. A scholarship of the value of $100, for proficiency in Practical Chemistry, on the endowment of the late Dr. T. Sterry Hunt, to students entering the Second Year of the Chemical Course. For further conditions apply to the Dean.

12. Prizes or certificates of merit are given to such Students as take the highest place in the Sessional and Degree Examinations.

13. Honours.—On graduation, Honours will be awarded for advanced work in Professional subjects.

14. SCIENCE SCHOLARSHIPS GRANTED BY HER MAJESTY'S COMMISSION FOR THE EXHIBITION OF 1851.—The Scholarships of £150 sterling a year in value are tenable for two or, in rare instances, three years. They are limited, according to the Report of the Commission, "to those branches of Science (such as Physics, Mechanics and Chemistry) the extension of which is specially important for our national industries." Their object is, not to facilitate ordinary collegiate studies, but "to enable Students to continue the prosecution of Science with the view of aiding in its advance or in its application to the industries of the country."

A nomination to one of these scholarships for the year 1897 was placed by the Commission at the disposal of McGill University, and another may be granted in 1899.

It is open to Students of not less than three years' standing in the Faculties of Arts or Applied Science, and is tenable at any University or at any other Institution approved by the Commission.

This Exhibition has been awarded as follows :—

Evans, P., 1891.   Macphail, J. A., 1893.   King, R. O., 1895.
                       Gill, J. L. W., 1897.

15. The Mason prize of $50.00 in Electrical Engineering, given by Dr. A. F. Mason for original investigation in the practical application of Electricity.

16. WORKSHOP PRIZES.—A prize of $20.00, presented by C. J. Fleet, B.A., B.C.L., for bench and lathe work in the woodworking department, open to Students of not more than two terms' standing in workshop practice.

17. A prize of $20, in books, presented by H. W. Umney, Esq., will be awarded to the student, of the Graduating Class, who obtains the highest standing in the subject of Hydraulics (theoretical and practical).

------

§ XI. SPECIAL PROVISIONS.

1. SUMMER WORK.—During the summer vacation following the close of each year, all students entering the Third and Fourth Years are required to prepare a thesis on a subject specified by the Faculty. Any student may substitute for the specified subject, a report on some practical work in course of construction. The marks given for these theses will be added to the results of the sessional examinations. The theses must be handed in to the Dean on or before the 1st October.

2. All Students in the Architectural, Civil and Mining Engineering Courses entering the Second and Third Years, and Students in the Civil Engineering Course entering the Fourth Year, are required to be in attendance at the University on the 1st September, when the Field-work in Surveying will commence. (See § XIII., 3.)

3. Partial Students may be admitted to the professional classes upon payment of special fees. (§ IX.)

4. Students in Applied Science may, by permission of the Faculty, take the Honour Classes in the Faculty of Arts.

5. Undergraduates in Arts of the Second and Third Years, or Graduates of any University, entering the Faculty of Applied Science, may, at the discretion of the Professors, be exempted from such lectures in that Faculty as they have previously attended as Students in Arts.

6. Students who have failed in a subject in the Christmas or Sessional Examinations may regain their standing by passing a supplemental examination at a time appointed by the Faculty. Unless such supplemental examination is passed, Students will not be allowed to proceed to any subsequent examination in the subject. A second supplemental examination will not be granted unless under exceptional circumstances, to be investigated in each case by the Faculty.

7. Students may be required to answer satisfactorily a weekly paper on such subjects of the course as the Faculty may determine.

8. Credit will be given in the Sessional Examinations for work done during the session in certain of the subjects which will be specified at the commencement of the first term.

9. Students who fail to obtain their Session, and who in consequence repeat a Year, will not be exempted from examination in any of those subjects in which they may have previously passed, except by the express permission of the Faculty. Application for such exemption must be made at the commencement of the Session.

10. Partial Students are not eligible for prizes.

11. Certificates may be given to Students who have passed through any of the special courses attached to the curriculum.

12. The headquarters of the Canadian Society of Civil Engineers are located in Montreal. The Society holds fortnightly meetings, at which papers upon practical current engineering subjects are read and discussed. Undergraduates joining the Society as Students may take part in these meetings, and acquire knowledge of the utmost importance in relation to the practical part of the profession.

13. Caps and gowns, also the overalls for the workshops, may be obtained from the janitor of the Engineering Building.

§ XII. SPECIAL LECTURES.

In addition to the ordinary work of the Faculty, the following courses of special lectures were delivered during session 1897-98 :—

J. A. L. WADDELL, Ma.E., M. Am. Soc. C.E., a series of lectures on " Bridge Designing."

IRA G. HEDRICK, B. A. Sc., M. Am. Soc. C.E., a series of lectures on " Bridge Calculations."

H. IRWIN, B.Sc., M. Can. Soc. C.E., lectures on " The Land Systems of the Province of Quebec."

Under the auspices of the Applied Science Graduates' Society:—

G. H. FROST, C.E., on " Sewage Disposal and Purification."

ROBT. BELL, M.D., F.R.S., on " Hudson Bay."

H. T. BARNES, Ma.E., on " Formation of Frasil Ice."

Also, under the auspices of the McGill Mining Society:—

J. E. HARDMAN, B.Sc., on " The Duties of the Young Mining Engineer."

PEERS DAVIDSON, M.A., B.C.L., two lectures on " Mining Law."

---

§ XIII. COURSES OF LECTURES.

N.B.—The following courses are subject to such modifications during the year as the Faculty may deem advisable.

I. ARCHITECTURE.

Professor :—S. HENBEST CAPPER, M.A.
Lecturer :—H. F. ARMSTRONG.

The professional work of the Architectural Course begins in the Second Year, for which the First or preliminary year is preparatory, especially in the departments of Mathematics and Drawing (Freehand, Lettering, and Projections).

The work of the Second Year is of a general character, and is planned to combine to some extent the work of the Architectural and of the Civil Engineering Students, for whom the lectures on the History of Architecture and on Building Construction are compulsory.

The Third and Fourth Years are devoted to more specialized architectural study in various branches, and a Fifth or Graduate Year will be organized for advanced study, especially in design.

In the Second Year the Historical Course embraces a rapid resumé of Architectural History from ancient Egyptian to modern times. The great eras of European civilization are successively dealt with and the evolution of styles is traced in their constructional and ornamental forms and methods. The course embraces Ancient Egypt, Ancient Greece, Rome and Byzantium, Early Christian and Romanesque Architecture, Gothic, the Renaissance and Revived Classic.

In the Third and Fourth Years the historical lectures are arranged in continuation and extension of this general course, Renaissance and Modern Architecture being studied in the Third Year and detailed courses being delivered in the Fourth Year upon Ecclesiastical, Domestic and Public Architecture, with the object of preparing the Student for the problems and requirements of modern work in the light of the various solutions worked out for similar problems in the past and with the help derived from familiarity with historic evolution in architecture.

The constructive side of architecture is dealt with in the Architectural Engineering Courses.

In the Second Year a general course, common to all Architectural and Engineering Students, is given upon Building Construction and Materials, which is supplemented and continued in the Testing Laboratories, where practical experiments are conducted.

The Theory of Structures is dealt with, as also Municipal Engineering and Sanitation and Hygiene; special courses on Heating and Ventilation, and on Electrical Installation are also included.

Specifications, including Working Drawings and Architectural Practice, are dealt with in the Third and Fourth Years.

For the scientific requirements of the profession the courses in Mathematics are very fully developed and include Descriptive Geometry, Shades and Shadows and Perspective. Surveying is also studied in the Second and Third Years.

In Drawing full instruction is given during all four years, freehand drawing (figure and ornament) from the cast and architectural draughtmanship occupying much of the students' time during the three years of the professional course. Modelling in clay is included in the Third Year (§ XIV, 14).

Problems in Architectural Design form the basis of work in the Architectural Drawing Class from the earliest practical period, and are combined with the study of the Classical Orders and with the Elements of Architecture (doors, windows, arches and arcades, cornices, mouldings, etc.), upon which, as well as upon historical ornament, courses of lectures are given.

In the Fourth Year a course of lectures is included upon General Art History, so as to place the architectural student in touch not only with the decorative details of the different architectural styles, but also with the contemporary forms in other branches of art, especially the decorative arts employed in building.

Architectural Equipment.

The architectural equipment consists of a representative collection of casts of architectural detail and ornament and sculpture; of photographs and illustrations; an arc-light electric lantern; a large collection of slides, diagrams and models; and a library for architectural study. (See § XV).

Women Students.

The Architectural and Modelling Classes are open to Women Students. Information as to admission may be obtained on application to the Dean of the Faculty or to the Professor of Architecture.

---

2. CIVIL ENGINEERING AND APPLIED MECHANICS.

Professor:— HENRY T. BOVEY, M. INST. C. E. (Scott Professor of Civil Engineering and Applied Mechanics).

Assistant Professors :— $\begin{cases} \text{R. S. LEA, MA.E.} \\ \text{————   ———— To be appointed.} \end{cases}$

THEORY OF STRUCTURES.

The lectures on this subject embrace :—

(a) The analytical and graphical determination of the stresses in the several members of framed structures,' both simple and complex, as, e.g., cranes, roof and bridge trusses, piers, etc.

(b) The methods of ascertaining and representing the shearing forces and bending moments to which the members of a structure are subjected.

(c) A study of the strength, stiffness and resistance of materials, including a statement of the principles relating to work, inertia, energy and entropy, together with a discussion of the nature and effect of the different kinds of stress and the resistance offered by a material to deformation and to blows.

(d) The design and proper proportioning of beams, pillars, shafts, roofs, bridge piers and trusses, arches, arched ribs, masonry dams, foundations, earth works and retaining walls.

Graphics.—A complete course of instruction is given in the graphical analysis of arches and of bridge, roof and other trusses, and in the graphical solution of mechanical problems. It is therefore possible for the student to apply both the analytical and graphical methods of treatment, and thus to verify the accuracy of his calculations.

TEXT-BOOK.—Bovey's Theory of Structures and Strength of Materials.

The Laboratory Work (see also § XIV.) is as follows :—

FOURTH YEAR.—During the Fourth Year, students are expected to engage in a research upon the physical properties of a material of construction, with special reference to the form and position of such material in the structure.

THIRD YEAR.—During the Third Year the Laboratory work will include the following :—

(*a*) *The testing of Timber.*—Transverse Tests on Hard and Soft Timber. Compressive Tests on specimens of various lengths cut out of the same timbers. Bearing Tests on specimens from same timbers. Tensile Tests on specimens from same timbers. Shearing Tests on specimens from same timbers·

(*b*) *The testing of Iron and Steel.*—Tensile Tests of Wrought Iron, Mild Steel, Cast Steel and Cast Iron. Compressive tests of ditto. Transverse Tests of ditto.

(*c*) *The testing of Brick and Stone.*

(*d*) *The testing of Concrete and Cement.*—A complete course in the testing of cements according to the Standard Methods of the Canadian Society of Civil Engineers.

Materials of Construction.

(*a*) Timber.—Growth, characteristics, diseases, enemies, preservatives, life, strength, tests, etc.

(*b*) Iron and Steel.—Manufacture, characteristics, strength, special uses, tests, etc.

(*c*) Brick, Terra Cotta.—Manufacture, chemistry of clays, uses, strength, tests, etc.

(*d*) Stone, Slate, etc.—Characteristics, weathering qualities, strength, hardness, uses, tests, etc.

(*e*) Cement, Lime, Mortars, Concretes, etc.—Chemistry of cements, manufacture, uses, strength, tests, etc.

Elements of Building Construction.

(*a*) Foundations on Land.—Bearing power of soils, safe loads, testing, drainage, etc.

(1) Piling, bearing power, formulae and data, cost.

(2) Pedestals and footings of concrete and steel, timber grillages. etc.

(3) Methods of timbering and excavation in sinking, pumping, Poehle, air lift, etc.

(*b*) Foundations in Water or Deep Foundations.—Preparing foundations by piling, dredging, etc., coffer dams, open caissons, pneumatic caissons and piles, open dredging, Poetsch freezing process, hydraulic shields, blasting, explosives.

(*c*) Foundation Courses.—Monolithic concrete, concrete and steel, stone, timber, broken stone, drainage, equal distribution of loads to prevent unequal settlement.

(*d*) Walls and Buildings.—(1) Brick.—masonry, mortar, joints, arches, centering, strength, specifications, cost.

(2) Stone.—Bonding, laying, classes of masonry, mortar, joints, methods and nomenclature of cutting, tooling, strength, specifications, cost.

(3) Concrete Artificial stone, terra cotta, enamelled brick.

(4) Timber.—Simple joints, framing for buildings and structures.

(5) Steel Columns.—Girders, flooring, rivetting, fire-proofing of walls and ceilings.

(*e*) Retaining Walls.—Abutments, arches, culverts, engine foundations of brick, stone, concrete.

Lectures to be illustrated by wall diagrams, lantern slides, models and museum specimens.

HYDRAULICS. (For Laboratory Work, see § XIV.)

The lectures deal with this subject both theoretically and with reference to its practical application.

The Student is instructed in the fundamental laws governing the equilibrium of fluids, and in the laws of flow through orifices, mouth-pieces, submerged (partially or wholly) openings, over weirs, through pipes and in open channels and rivers. The impulsive action of a free jet of water upon vanes, both straight and curved, is carefully discussed, and is followed by an investigation of the power and efficiency of the several hydraulic motors, as, *e.g.*, Reaction Wheels, Pressure Engines, Vertical Water Wheels, Turbines, Pumps, etc.

Text-Book.—Bovey's Hydraulics.

The laboratory work (see also § XIV.) will include the follow-ing :—

(a) *Flow through orifices.*—The determination of the coefficients of discharge, velocity, etc.

(b) *Flow over weirs.*—The determination of the coefficient of dis-charge with and without side contraction. Also the measure-ment of the section of the stream.

(c) *Flow through pipes.*—The determination of the effect upon the flow, of angles, bends and sudden changes in section.

(d) *Impact.*—The determination of the coefficient of impact.

(e) *Motors, etc.*—The determination of the efficiency of Pelton and other wheels, of vortex and other turbines, of centrifugal and other pumps, etc.

Hydraulic Machinery.

The lectures in this Course are of a descriptive character, including the details of construction of Vertical and Horizontal Water Wheels, Three Cylinder Engines, Pumps, Accumulators and Presses, Workshop Tools and Appliances, Dock and Harbour Ma-chinery, and the Transmission of Power.

Transportation.

On Common Roads, Railways and Canals.

The lectures will embrace :—

(a) A brief historical review of the inception and carrying out of the great Canadian systems of transportation.

(*b*) A resumé of the laws regarding transportation and of the effect of government influences upon such projects.

(*c*) Common roads.—Provision made for them in settling up land; methods and costs of construction and maintenance; the traffic for which they are suited, and the cost of hauling it over different surfaces.

(*d*) Canals and rivers.—The Canadian canal system, the methods and costs of construction and maintenance, the traffic it is designed to carry, and the cost of transportation.

(*e*) Steam railroads.—The reasons for building of various Canadian roads, the position of the Government with regard to them, the traffic they serve and the cost of handling it, the details of location and the influence of physical features and trade possibilities upon it, the cost and design of construction, the duties of the engineer upon such work, the appliances at present in use for safe and speedy handling of trains.

(*f*) Electric roads.—The traffic which they now carry, their location and construction, the reasons for their rapid extention, and their probable future.

(*g*) Street pavements and sidewalks.—The materials used in their construction, and the merits of each system, their cost and their benefit to the community.

The questions of the development and applying of motive power and the various appliances, mechanical and electrical, now in use for these special purposes are taken up in special descriptive lectures in the mechanical and electrical departments.

MUNICIPAL ENGINEERING.

The lectures on this subject will embrace :—

(*a*) *Water Supply.*—The quantity and quality of water ; systems and sources of supply ; rainfall and evaporation ; storage as related to the supplying capacity of water-sheds ; natural and artificial purification ; distribution, including the location of mains, hydrants, stop-valves, etc., combined or separate fire and domestic systems ; details of construction, including dams, reservoirs, pumps, etc., preliminary surveys, estimates of cost, statistics, etc.

(*b*) *Sewerage of Cities and Towns.*—The various systems for the

removal of sewage; special methods in use for its treatment and ultim.
ate disposal ; the proportioning and construction of main branch
and intercepting sewers ; manholes, flush-tanks, catch-basins, etc.;
materials used in construction ; estimates of cost.

---

3. SURVEYING AND GEODESY.

Professor :—C. H. McLeod, Ma.E.
Lecturer :—J. G. G. Kerry, Ma.E.

This course is designed to give the student a theoretical and
practical training in the methods of land and Geodetic Surveying, in
the field work of engineering operations and in Practical Astronomy.
The course is divided as follows :—

Second Year.—Chain and angular surveying ; the construction,
adjustment, use and limitations of the various instruments. Underground surveying. Topography, levelling, contour surveying.

Third Year.—Construction surveying, including the location of
roads, simple and transition curves, setting out work and calculation
of quantities. Geodetic, trigonometric and barometric levelling. Descriptions for deeds. General land systems of the Dominion and Provinces. Topographic and photographic surveying. Hydrographic
surveying. Introduction to Practical Astronomy. Graphical determination of spherical triangles, spherical projections, construction of
maps.

In the field the students of the Second and Third Years are required to carry out the following :—(1) A chain survey. (2) A chain
and compass survey. (3) A pacing survey. (4) A contour survey.
(5) A plane table survey. (6) A survey and location of a line of road
with determination of topography and contours and subsequent
staking out for construction. (7) A hydrographic survey of a river
channel, including measurement of discharge. (8) A survey at night
illustrating underground methods.

All students are required to keep complete field notes, and from
them prepare maps, sections and estimates of the work.

The large drawing rooms are furnished with fixed mountings for
the various instruments, in order to permit of their use and investigation during the winter months.

Fourth Year.—Practical Astronomy :—the determination of time,
latitude, longtitude and azimuth. Geodesy :—figure of the earth ;

H

measurements of base lines and triangulation systems ; adjustments and reductions of observations.

The field work of the Fourth Year consists in the measurement of a base-line, in triangulations and precision levelling.

The practical work in Astronomy (for equipment of observatory see XIV, Art. 7) comprises : (1) Comparisons of clocks and chrono-meters. (2) Determination of meridian by solar attachment. (3) Meridian, latitude and time by solar and stellar observations with the Engineer's transit. (4) Latitude and time by sextant. (5) Time by astronomical transit. (6) Latitude by zenith telescope. (7) Latitude by transit in prime vertical. Field work required of all students of the Second and Third Years in the courses of Architecture, Civil and Mining, and of the Fourth Year in the Civil course. The work will begin on the first of September and continue through the entire month. The surveys will be made in a place some distance from Montreal. Suitable provision for board and lodging will be arranged for at the place selected.

Exercises in the Geodetic laboratory (for equipment see § XIV, Art. 7) carried out in this year include the following:—(1) Measure-ment of magnifying power. (2) Determination of vernier errors. (3) Errors of graduation. (4) Measurement of eccentricity of circles. (5) Determination of errors of run of theodolite microscopes. (6) Investigation of the errors of a standard bar. (7) Graduating scales with the dividing engine, and comparison thereof on the comparator. (8) Investigation of the errors of circles on the circular comparator. (9) Determination of the constants of steel tapes. (10) Investigation of the graduation errors of steel tapes on the fifty-foot comparator. (11) Investigation of the errors of aneroid barometers. (12) Investi-gation of the errors of level tubes, and determination of their scale values. (13) Measurement of the force of gravity with a reversible pendulum. (14) Measurements of magnetic dip, declination and horizontal force.

The equipment of the surveying department comprises the follow-ing, in addition to the apparatus of the Observatory and Geodetic Laboratory:—Eleven transit theodolites by various makers, with solar and mining attachments. A photo-theodolite. 8-in. aet-azimuth. Seven dumpy and three wye levels. Hand levels and clinometers. Two precision levels. Five surveyors' compasses. Three prismatic compasses. Pocket compasses. One solar compass. Three marine sextants. Artificial horizons. Four box sextants. Two reflecting circles. Two large plane tables. Four traverse plane tables. Four current meters. Rochon micrometer. Double image micrometer. Field-glasses. Two heliotropes. Several barometers. 300 ft. and

500 ft. steel tapes suitable for base measurements. Steel chains and steel bands. Linen and metallic tapes. Sounding lines. Pickets. Levelling rods. Micrometer targets. Slope rods. Pedometers. Station pointer, pantographs, planimeter, slide rules and minor appliances.

Examinations for Land Surveyors:—Any graduate in the Faculty of Applied Science in the Department of Civil Engineering and Land Surveying may have his term of apprenticeship shortened to one year for the profession of Land Surveyor in Quebec or Ontario, or for the profession of Dominion Land Surveyor.

TEXT BOOKS :—Gillespie's Surveying, Johnson's Theory and Practice of Surveying, Shortland's Nautical Surveying, Green's Practical and Spherical Astronomy, Nautical Almanac, Baker's Engineers' Surveying Instruments.

4. DESCRIPTIVE GEOMETRY.

Lecturers :—   C. H. McLEOD, Ma.E.
H. F. ARMSTRONG.

This course deals with the methods of representing objects on one plane, so that their true dimensions may be accurately scaled. It discusses the methods employed in the graphical solution of the various problems arising in engineering design, and deals generally with the principles underlying all constructive drawing. The methods taught are in all cases illustrated by applications to practical problems. It is the aim of the work to develop the imagination in respect to the power of mentally picturing unseen objects, and incidentally precision in the use of the drawing instruments is attained.

FIRST YEAR.—Geometrical drawing, orthographic projections, including penetrations, developments, sections, etc. Isometric projection.

SECOND YEAR.—Problems on straight line and plane. Projections of plane and solid figures. Curved surfaces and tangent planes. Intersections of curved surfaces. Axometric projections. Shades and shadows. Mathematical perspective and the perspective of shades and shadows.

5. FREEHAND DRAWING, LETTERING, ETC.

Assistant Professor :—H. F. ARMSTRONG.

In the *Freehand Course*, the object is to train the hand and eye, so that students may readily make sketches from parts of machin ery, etc., either as perspective drawing in light and shade or as preparatory dimensioned sketches from which to make scale drawings.

In the *Lettering Course*, plain block alphabets, round writing, and titles will be chiefly dealt with. In this course, also, tinting, tracing, blue printing and simple map drawing will be included.

---

6. ELECTRICAL ENGINEERING.

Professor:— —— —— —— (McDonald Professor of Electrical Engineering).

Lecturer:—L. HERDT, Ma.E., E.E.

The object of this course is to introduce the Student to the principles underlying the practice of Electrical Engineering. But little time is devoted to the consideration of strictly technical details, which the student can far better study in the factory, where he is strongly recommended to go after his college course. The methods and the instruments are, in almost every case, those that the Student will have eventually to use in practice. The object of the lectures is not to go over ground already covered by the text-books, but rather to direct the reading of the Students and to discuss problems arising out of the Laboratory work.

The work in the Electrical Engineering laboratories is not commenced until the Third Year. By that time the Students will have gained a fair general acquaintance with Electricity in the Physical Laboratory. They will then begin a series of experiments on Electricity and Magnetism on a practical scale, using methods and instruments in ordinary practical use, confining their attention more to the principles than to their application. This term's work is preparatory to that of the Fourth Year, when the Students will, in the Dynamo Room, study the practical application of these principles.

Here they will make experiments on electrical machinery of all kinds : series, shunt, and compound dynamos ; motors, motor-generators, alternators, etc. They will carry out tests of dynamos, transformers and motors under practical working conditions, not only on the apparatus in the dynamo room but also throughout the building, where there are several motors driving lathes, fans, etc. besides an electric elevator and an electric drill. In addition to these advantages, the Faculty possesses a typical lighting station of more than three thousand lights at work, in which the students may become familiar with the best practice and design of engines, dynamos, switchboard, and wiring.

The following is the general plan of work in this Department:—

THIRD YEAR.—Commencing in November. (a) 3 hours weekly, Electrical Laboratory. Practical use of the Instruments commonly employed in Electrical Engineering, such as ammeters and voltmeters. The Students will be instructed in the management of currents and how to use the instruments, make connections, etc. (b) 1 hour lecture, 2 hours demonstration, weekly, in the Magnetic Laboratory. Practical magnetic measurements. Commercial tests of iron. Magnetic principles, underlying dynamo design, illustrated by examples worked out numerically in class from data obtained by experiment.

Some changes may be made in this part of the Electrical Course.

FOURTH YEAR.—(c) 2 hours weekly, Electro-Dynamics, lectures.

(d) 1 hour demonstration weekly, in the dynamo room, methods and principles referred to in lecture illustrated by practical experiments before the whole class. (e) 3 hours weekly, same experiment as in (d) worked out by the students in groups of four or five in the dynamo room. (f) 3 hours weekly, problem paper, examples bearing on the lectures worked out by each student independently in class. (g) 3 hours weekly, graphic solution of practical problems in the draughting room. (h) 3 hours weekly, dynamo design, whole class in the draughting room. (j) 1 hour weekly, lecture, descriptive electrical engineering, general description of apparatus from the engineering point of view, e.g., laying out of electric roads, design of power stations, etc. (k) 1 hour weekly during March, lecture, advanced electro-dynamics. (l) 1 hour weekly during February, lecture, practical testing of electrical systems for faults and insulation. (m) 3 hours weekly, examining and sketching electrical apparatus in the city, lighting and power plants, elevators, etc.

The course of lectures in Electro-Dynamics will treat of the following subjects:—

Motors.

The Induction Factor: physical meaning of; general equation for, in terms of given data; variation of, due to series winding and reactions; its influence on design.

Elementary Conditions of Displacement: direction of rotation;

general equations for speed and current; relation between torque and induction factor; power diagrams.

Experimental Proof of equation for torque ; corrections for friction and hysteresis; practical methods of finding ¡the induction factor.

Motors with Constant Induction Factor: curves of torque, speed and power; parallel running of two or more motors; effect of unequal induction factors ; application to testing ; Kapp's method; Hopkinson's method; graphic solutions; speed regulation.

Motors with Variable Induction Factor : curves of torque, speed and power; parallel running; graphic solutions; effect of unequal induction factors; effect of residual magnetisation.

Armature Reaction : theorétical considerations ; experimental results ; the reactions of the slotted armature; influence on design; sparking.

Acceleration: analytical and graphical solutions; braking action.

Motor Control: different types of controllers discussed; the series-parallel controller; practical results, with figures showing the speed curves obtained on various electric roads; discussion of the advantages of the different controllers under special circumstances, grades, etc.

Frictional Resistance: experimental determination of ; case of elevators with worm and spur gearing; tests of standard street car equipments.

Alternating Currents.

Self Induction. Helmholtz's Law. Solution of general current equation. Measurements ˌof current and electromotive force and self-induction. Inductive Drop. Calculation of losses for given circuits. Graphic solutions. Power measurements. Theory of the watt-meter. Errors of watt-meters. Theory of the Transförmer, hysteresis, leakage, drop. Efficiency. Methods of testing. Transformer design.

DESCRIPTIVE ELECTRICAL ENGINEERING.

A special course of lectures in Descriptive Electrical Engineering is given by Mr. Herdt to the Fourth Year Students. ˈ

The lectures on this subject embrace:—

(a) Dynamo electric machines ; construction of dynamos ; coupling of dynamos. Alternators of different types ; construction of alternators. (b) Different systems for the distribution of electrical energy ; sectional area of conductors; aerial lines and underground conduits. (c) Central stations; their emplacement; selection of machinery; feeders and regulators; switchboards. (d) Electric railways; different systems; overhead construction. (e) Storage batteries.

Graduate Course.

A special course in Electrical Engineering will be arranged for the session 1898-99. This course will be open to graduates in Mechanical Engineering or others who can show by examination or certificate that they are sufficiently qualified.

---

7. MECHANICAL ENGINEERING.

Professor :—J. T. Nicolson, B.Sc., M.Can.Soc. C.E. (Workman Professor of Mechanical Engineering).

Assistant Professor:—R. J. Durley, B.Sc., Ma.E., A.M.Inst. C.E.
Demonstrator :—H. M. Jaquays, B.A., B.A.Sc.

This course embraces four subjects of study, as follows :—

I. Descriptive Mechanism and Kinematics of Machinery.

A course of lectures, illustrated by the lantern, is given in the First Year, introducing the subject of mechanism in general to the Student. Beginning with elementary contrivances and common forms, the functions and principles of all kinds of ordinary mechanisms are explained; and the course concludes with detailed descriptions of prime movers, machine tools, locomotives, and other machinery.

In the Second Year the science of Kinematics applied to machinery is taken up. Reuleaux's principles and classifications are followed, and illustrated by the fine and unique collection of models in the Museum. The synopsis of the course includes the following subjects: Definition of a machine. Lower Pairs. Kinematic chains and trains. Centrodes. Restraint. Higher Pairs. Force and chain closure. Dead points. Notation Analysis of the quadric crank chain, the slider-crank chain, the double-slider crank chain. Chamber crank and wheel trains. Kinematic synthesis.

II. Dynamics of Machinery.

While motion without regard to force was considered in the kinematic course, the action of external forces so as to compel rest or prevent change of motion, or so as to produce or to change motion in the links of mechanisms, is now considered in a series of lectures extending over two years.

The Third Year course embraces the following:—

Friction. Laws based on recent experiments, applied to journals and pivots. Railway brakes. Resistance to rolling. Friction in mechanisms treated graphically. Dynamics of belt and rope drives. Friction clutches. Elementary parts of dynamics of the steam engine, curves of crank effort for single and multiple cranks. Fluctuation of energy and of speed. Fly-wheels. Indicators. Absorption and transmission dynamometers.

FOURTH YEAR:—Balancing of double and single acting engines and of the locomotive. Rigid dynamics applied to the connecting rod, the oscillating engine, the governor, and gyrostatic action in machinery. The inter-relation between fly-wheel and governor. Dynamics of machine tools, of pumping and of forging machines. Graphic treatment of the dynamics of complicated machines. Knocking of steam engines.

III. MACHINE DESIGN.

In the above courses the parts of the machines considered have been supposed perfectly rigid; their real state in this respect is considered in two courses of lectures extending over the Third and Fourth Years.

In the Third Year the principles of the strength of materials are applied to the elements of machines; e.g.,:—bolts and nuts, keys and cotters, rivets and riveted joints; journals, pivots, axles, shafts and their couplings.

In the Fourth Year the first term is devoted to the more complicated parts of machines, as : bearings, pulleys, toothed wheels, pistons and their rods, connecting rods, cranks and their shafts, fly-wheels, valves, pipes and cylinders. The second term is taken up with the discussion of the theoretical principles involved in the special machine which is being designed in the drawing office. In successive years, a marine engine, a slotting machine, an overhead traveling crane, an experimental pump, an air pump and other machinery have been taken up.

IV. MECHANICAL DRAWING.

This course extends over three years :—

SECOND YEAR.—Elementary principles of mechanical drawing.

Simple machine details.   Sketching of machinery.   Dimensioning, Tracing and conventional coloring.

THIRD YEAR.—Making of working drawings.   Simple designing. Engine designing.

FOURTH YEAR.—Practical machine design.   The complete design of a machine, such as a steam engine, a pump, a crane, a turbine, a machine tool, or an air pump and condenser.

Graduate Course.

A graduate course in Mechanical Engineering has now been arranged for, and will consist of part or all of the following work :

Experimental researches on steam engines and boilers, hot air and gas engines, compressed air plant for power transmission, refrigerating machines; on superheated steam, cylinder condensation, and feed heating; and on the value of fuels.

Experiments on the relative value and properties of lubricants, on transmission and absorption dynamometers, on the efficiency of transmission machinery, and of machine tools.

Researches on the tempering and welding of various materials; and on the properties of alloys.

----

8. MINING AND METALLURGICAL ENGINEERING.

Professor :—JOHN BONSALL PORTER, E.M., Ph.D. (McDonald Professor of Mining and Metallurgy).

Demonstrator :—JOHN W. BELL, B.A.Sc.

The undergraduate work of this department extends over the latter three Years of the course, and consists of lectures, classes in designing and drawing metallurgical and mining machinery, in the specification of appliances and establishments; and in laboratory work in Ore-Dressing, Assaying, and Metallurgy.

I. A course of lectures is given to the Second Year students, in which both Mining and Metallurgy are treated in a general and descriptive way.   These lectures are illustrated by means of lantern slides, photographs, drawings and specimens from the department Museum, and are intended to give the student a thorough grounding in the subjects, in order that he may be prepared to appreciate the mining or metallurgical establishments which he is expected to visit during his vacation, and to enter properly into the advanced and detailed work of the Third and Fourth Years.

In this Year, the student is expected to spend one afternoon per week in the drawing room, working on the mechanical drawing of machinery.

II. In the Third Year, a detailed course of lectures is given in Metallurgy, the headings being as below:—

GENERAL CONSIDERATIONS.—The properties of metals; alloys; typical processes, etc., etc.

FUELS.—The principles of combustion; calorific power; calorific intensity, etc. Natural fuels; wood, peat, coal, oil, and natural gas. Artificial fuels: coke, compressed fuels, water-gas, producer-gas.

ORES.—The ores of the various metals.

REFRACTORY MATERIALS, ETC.—Sand, clay, fire-brick, etc., etc.

FURNACES.—The general types of furnaces and the characteristics of each.

IRON AND STEEL.—The blast-furnace and its accessory machinery; pig iron, cast iron, etc. The conversion of pig iron into wrought iron and steel by means of puddling, blister, Bessemer, open-hearth, and other methods. The rolling mill; methods and machinery for making structural iron and steel rails, special shapes, heavy forgings, armour, etc., etc. General design and location of iron and steel plants.

COPPER.—Sampling and mixing of ores; calcination and roasting; mechanical calciners ; smelting in reverberatory and shaft-furnaces; matte fusions ; Bessemerizing, refining, etc. Wet methods for copper; electro metallurgy; copper rolling mill and manufacture.

LEAD.—Sampling and mixing of ores; calcination and roasting; mechanical roasters; smelting in shaft and reverberatory-furnaces; softening and refining.

GOLD AND SILVER.—Extraction of precious metals from free milling ores; stamp mill amalgamation, amalgamating pan and barrels, patio process, etc. Extraction from refractory ores : roasting chlorination, cyanide process, special methods, etc. Extraction from base metals; desilverization of lead, Pattinson, Parkes, etc. Cupellation, parting, wet methods, electro-metallurgy, etc.

OTHER METALS.—Zinc, tin, mercury, nickel, cobalt, aluminium, etc. The elements of the metallurgy of the less important metals are discussed briefly.

In addition to the lectures on Metallurgy, which are thoroughly illustrated, the Third Year students are required to spend a certain number of hours weekly in the drawing room, working on the designing of metallurgical apparatus, and in the metallurgical laboratory where actual work is carried on.

III. In the Fourth Year, a detailed course of lectures is given in Mining, Ore-Dressing and Fire Assaying, the headings being as below:—

MINING.—Prospecting and hydraulic mining; diamond drills, etc.; artesian wells. Excavation and quarrying; rock drills, channelling machines, and coal cutters; explosive materials and blasting. Shaft sinking, tunneling. Getting out material by stoping, chambering, long-wall system, etc.; supporting excavation by timbering, masonry, etc., etc. Mine-pumping and ventilation; underground haulage and hoisting. Mine accidents and their prevention. General arrangement of mining plant; administration, miners' stores and dwellings. Law relative to mining claims and patents.

ORE DRESSING.—Theoretical consideration. Treatment of ores underground and at the surface; hand picking, crushing, screening and sizing; jigs and other concentrators; spitzkasten, spitzlütten, vanners, buddles; tables, magnetic separators, etc. Ore and coal-washing machinery; storage and delivery of ores and coal for transportation.

FIRE ASSAYING.—Sampling; preparing ores for assay; furnaces, crucibles, re-agents, etc. During the second term of the Fourth Year the students are given a thorough course of practical work in the Assay Laboratory on ores of gold, silver, copper and lead.

IV.—Special courses in advanced work are offered in both Mining and Metallurgy, and these courses, owing to the unequalled equipment of the new laboratories, as detailed below, can be made exceedingly valuable both theoreticaly and practically.

V. ILLUSTRATIONS, MUSEUMS, SOCIETIES, ETC.—The department already owns a collection of one thousand photographs, eight hundred of which are kept in series in duplicate, and loaned to students for the session; and arrangements are being made to furnish sets of these, at cost price, to such students as wish to retain them. This collection is rapidly being enlarged.

The Museum of the new building will contain suites of ores, fuels, and metallurgical materials, models of mines and furnaces, and specimens of finished products.

The McGill University Mining Society meets fortnightly to read and discuss papers by graduate and student members, and from time to time to hear lectures given by outsiders eminent in the profession.

VI. Excursions are made by the classes, from time to time, to such metallurgical works and mining establishments as are within reach, and a short summer session in the coal and gold region of Nova Scotia is arranged for this Year, and open to the students of the Third Year. This work occupies about one month of the vacation between the Third and Fourth Years.

VII. LABORATORIES.—The unequalled laboratories of the University are of peculiar advantage to students in the Mining Course, and enable them not only to become acquainted with the theory of their subject, but to personally investigate its methods on a large scale.

During the first three years of the course, the students do systematic work in the several workshops and laboratories. During the last part of the Third and the chief part of the Fourth Year, they spend a large proportion of their time in the working laboratories for Ore Dressing and Metallurgy. (See § XIV.) In these latter, the general method is to assign to each student certain methods and pieces of apparatus which he must use and study out in detail, and upon which he must make a written report. In this work he is guided by the professor and demonstrator and assisted by the other students, each of whom he must in turn assist in his special work. In this way every student must acquire detailed knowledge of certain typical operations and a fair general experience of all of the other important methods in use.

VIII. SUMMER SCHOOL.—The summer vacation class in Mining proposed in last year's issue of the Announcement is now being carried on. A party of about twenty of the students of the Mining Department—accompanied by the Professor of Mining and his Assistant—are at present in Nova Scotia. The class will spend about six weeks at work, during which time both the coal and gold regions of Nova Scotia and Cape Breton will be visited, and the students given every opportunity to study the actual work of mining and milling, and also to do some mine surveying and geologising.

Thanks to the courtesy of the managers of the several mines visited, and to the assistance of others interested in the work, the school promises to be very successful, and it is hoped that it may be made a regular part of the course in the future.

___

9. CHEMISTRY AND ASSAYING.

Professors:— } B. J. HARRINGTON, M.A., Ph.D.

Lecturer:—NEVIL NORTON EVANS, M.A.Sc.

Demonstrator:—ALEXANDER BRODIE, M.A.Sc.

This course includes lectures and laboratory work. In the First Year, Students of all Departments attend a course of lectures in the laws of Chemical Combination, Chemical Formulæ and Equations, the preparation and properties of the more important Elements and their Compounds, etc. They also devote one afternoon a week throughout the session to practical work in the Laboratory, where they learn the construction and use of ordinary apparatus, perform a series of experiments designed to cultivate the powers of observation and deduction, and begin Qualitative Analysis.

In the Second and Third Years, Students in the Department of Practical Chemistry attend lectures on the Chemistry of the Metals or on Organic Chemistry, and receive instruction in Qualitative and Quantitative Analysis, including gravimetric and volumetric methods and the application of electrolytic methods to the estimation of copper, nickel, etc. Blowpipe Analysis and Determinative Mineralogy also constitute part of the work of the Third Year.

In the Fourth Year, special attention is devoted to such subjects as Mineral Analysis and Assaying, and the Analysis of Iron and Steel; but considerable latitude is allowed to Students in the choice of subjects, and Organic work may be taken up if desired.

Students of the Mining Course take Qualitative and Quantitative Analysis during the Second and Third Years, and devote considerable attention in the Fourth Year to Mineral Analysis and Assaying of various ores, fuels, etc. They also attend the class in Blowpipe Analysis and Determinative Mineralogy in the Third Year.

The Chemical Laboratories (see § XIV) are open daily (Saturdays excepted) from 9 a.m. to 5 p.m.

10. THERMODYNAMICS.

Lecturer:—J. T. Nicolson, B.Sc., M. Can. Soc. C.E.

Demonstrator:—H. M. Jaquays, B.A., B.A.Sc.

Fundamental laws and equations of thermodynamics. Application to perfect gases and to steam saturated and superheated. Efficiency of perfect heat engines. Efficiency of actual air, gas, petroleum, and steam engines.

A study of the steam engine, including wire-drawing, cylinder condensation and jacketing, and the most efficient and most economical point of cut-off. Sizes and proportions of cylinders in single, double and triple expansion engines to develop a given power. Expected indicator diagrams. Sizes and proportions of the principal types of steam generators. Comparison of practical suitability of steam and caloric engines. Theory of engine and boiler testing.

Text-Book.—Ewing's Steam Engine.
Peabody's Tables of Properties of Steam.

---

11. GEOLOGY AND MINERALOGY.

Professors :—{ B. J. Harrington, Ph.D.
Frank D. Adams, M.A.Sc., Ph.D.

Second Year.—A preliminary course in Zoology, with special reference to Fossil Animals.

Third Year.—Mineralogy (Ordinary and Honour), Petrography, Physical and Chronological Geology and Paleontology, Geology of Canada, Methods of Geological Exploration.

Fourth Year.—Special studies in Ore Deposits, Mineralogy and Petrography; Advanced Course in General Geology and Palæontology; Geology of Canada; Practical Geology and Field-work.

For further details see Announcement of the Faculty of Arts.

Note.—Students of the Mining and Chemistry courses take the Honour Mineralogy of the Third Year in Arts. Mining Students take the whole Honour Course of the Fourth Year. Chemistry Students take, in addition to the ordinary Course in Geology, the Honour Mineralogy of the Fourth Year.

The Petrographical Laboratory, (See § XIV) is open to Fourth Year Mining Students during the second term.

12. ZOOLOGY.

Professor :—E. W. MacBride, M.A., B.Sc.

1. ELEMENTARY ZOOLOGY.—This course is designed to make the student acquainted with the principal types of structure met with in the animal kingdom.

The following types are studied both theoretically and practically:— Amoeba, Vorticella, Hydra, Tubularia, Craspedote Medusa, Aurelia, Alcyonium, Lumbricus, Nereis, Cambarus, Cyclops, Limulus, Periplaneta, Unio, Buccinum, Asterias, Echinus, Amphioxus, Mustelus, Rana.

Two hours of formal lectures a week, and two laboratory demonstrations a week.

No student is permitted to attend the lectures without also taking the practical work.

---

13. BOTANY.

Professor :—D. P. PENHALLOW, B.Sc., M.A.Sc.

Lecturer :—C. M. DERICK, M.A.

1. GENERAL MORPHOLOGY.—This course is designed to give a thorough general knowledge of the principles of General Morphology and Classification. In comprises :—

(a) A practical course embracing the determination of species from both fresh and dry material, and type studies of Spermatophytes, Pteridophytes, Bryophytes and Thallophytes, with reference to their life histories.

Gray's Manual, Penhallow's Outlines of Classification and Botanical Collector's Guide.

FIRST TERM, three hours a week.

(b) A course of lectures dealing with General Morphology and Classification, elements of Histology and Physiology; Biological relations of plants; Geographical Botany.

SECOND TERM, two hours a week.

2. ADVANCED BOTANY.—This course, open only to students who have taken Botany 1, is designed to give an extended knowledge of vegetable anatomy and special morphology. It comprises:—

(a) Optics and construction of the microscope; determination of amplifications; micrometry; drawings; section cutting; preparation of microscope objects; micro-chemical reactions; study of cell contents and tissues; comparative studies of type forms of angiosperms and gymnosperms.

Botanical Microtechnique. (Zimmermann, trans. by Humphrey.)

(*b*) A course in Special Morphology, forming a part of the Honours Course in Biology and open to students who have satisfactorily completed Botany 1 and 2, of which latter it is a continuation. It includes critical studies of the structure and development of the Thallophytes, Bryophytes and Pteridophytes, together with special readings on Biological problems. The following types will be studied:— A Myxomycete, Bacteria, Chroococcus, Nostoc, Rivularia, Spirogyra, Pleurococcus, Oedogonium, Yaucheria, Fucus, Nemalion, Rhizopus, Penicillium, Puccinia, Agaricus, Pellia, Polytrichum, Pteris, Equisetum, Lycopodium, Selaginella. Comparisons with other forms in each group will also be made.

Student taking 2*a* and *b* will be required to supply their own slides and cover glasses.

Fee for the courses 2*a* and 2*b*, $10.00.

---

14. EXPERIMENTAL PHYSICS.

Professors:— { JOHN COX, M.A. (McDonald Professor of Physics).
—— —— —— (McDonald Professor of Physics.

The instruction includes a fully illustrated course of Experimental Lectures on the general Principles of Physics (embracing, in the Second Year—*The Laws of Energy—Heat, Light and Sound* ; in the Third Year—*Electricity and Magnetism*), accompanied by courses of practical work in the Laboratory, in which the Students will perform for themselves experiments, chiefly quantitative, illustrating the subjects treated in the lectures. Opportunity will be given to acquire experience with all the principal instruments used in exact physical and practical measurements. Students of Electrical Engineering will continue their work in the Laboratory in the Fourth Year, when they will undertake, under the guidance of the Professors, advanced measurements and special investigations bearing on their technical studies.

FOURTH YEAR ELECTRICAL STUDENTS.—Students of Electrical Engineering will continue their work in the Physical Laboratory in the Fourth Year. The following is a brief outline of the Course:

Magnetic elements and measurements. Use of Variometers. Testing magnetic qualities of iron.

Theory and practice of absolute electrical measurements.

Comparison and use of electrical standards, of resistance, E.M.F., self-induction, and capacity.

Principles of construction of electrical instruments.

Testing and calibration of ammeters, voltmeters and wattmeters.

Insulation and capacity tests. Electrometers and Ballistic methods.

Construction and treatment of storage cells. Testing for capacity and rate of discharge.

Electric light photometry.

An additional course on telegraph and telephone work is under consideration.

The following are some of the sections in which special provisions have been made for advanced physical work:—

Heat.—Thermometry. Comparison and verification of delicate thermometers. Air thermometry. Measurement of high temperatures. Electrical resistance thermometers and pyrometers. Thermoelectric pyrometers. Absolute expansion of mercury.

Calorimetry. Mechanical Equivalent of Heat. Variation of specific heat with temperature. Latent heat of fusion and vaporisation. Heat of solution and combustion. Electrical methods.

Radiation and conduction of heat with special methods and apparatus. Dynamical theory of gases.

Viscosity. Surface Tension. Variation of properties with temperature.

Light.—Photometric standards. Spectro-photometry. Theory of colour vision. Spectroscopy and spectrum photography. Compound prism spectrometers. Six inch and 2½ inch Rowland Gratings. Study of spectra of gases. Fluorescense and anomalous dispersion. Polarimetry. Landolt and other polar-meters. Form of wave surface.

Sound.—Velocity in gases and various media. Absolute determinations of period. Harmonic analysis of sounds. Effects of resonance and interference.

Electricity and Magnetism.—Magnetic properties. Influence of stress and torsion. Influence of temperature. Effects of hysteresis. Magneto-optics. Other effects of Magnetisation. Diamagnetism.

Electrical standards and absolute measurements. Calibration of electrical instruments.

Insulation and capacity testing. Electrometer and Ballastic methods. Temperature variation of resistance and E.M.F. Thermoelectric effects. Electrolysis. Chemistry of primary and secondary batteries. Resistance of Electrolytes, Polarisation.

Electric discharge in gases and high vacua. Dielectric strength.

Behaviour of insulators under electric stress. Specific inductive capacity. Electric oscillations. Electro-magnetic optics. Alternating currents of high frequency and voltage.

N.B.—Students taking a Graduate Course will receive guidance in any advanced Mathematics required in connection with their work.

---

15. MATHEMATICS AND MATHEMATICAL PHYSICS.

Professor :—G. H. CHANDLER, M.A
Lecturer :—R. S. LEA, Ma.E.

The work in this department is conducted from the outset with special reference to the needs of Students of Applied Science. Much time is given to practice in the use of Mathematical Tables, particular attention being paid to the solution of triangles, the tracing of curves, graphical representation of functions, reduction of observations, etc. Areas, volumes, masses, centres of gravity, moments of inertia, etc., are determined both by calculation and by observation or experiment, and each method is made to supplement or illustrate the other. In this connection, use will be made, in actual laboratory practice, of a large amount of apparatus, such as balances, Atwood's machines, inclined planes, chronographs, rotation apparatus of various kinds, etc. The different methods of approximation, the reduction of results of experiments and observations by least squares, etc., will also receive due attention.

The lectures will embrace the following subjects :—

FIRST YEAR.—Euclid, to the end of Book VI., with exercises on Loci, Transversals, etc., Algebra, including the Binomial Theorem. Elements of Solid Geometry and of Geometrical Conic Sections. Plane and Spherical Trigonometry. Elementary Kinematics and Dynamics.

SECOND YEAR.—Analytic Geometry. Differential and Integral Calculus. Dynamics of Solids and Fluids.

THIRD YEAR.—Continuation of Analytic Geometry, Calculus and Dynamics.

Classes may also be held for advanced (optional) work in these or other subjects.

N.B.—Students taking Graduate Courses will receive guidance in any advanced Mathematics required in connection with their work.

Text-Books (Partial list).—Todhunter's or Mackay's Euclid, Hall

& Knight's Elementary Algebra, Wilson's Solid Geometry and Conic Sections, Wentworth's Analytic Geometry, Chandler's Calculus. Blakie's Dynamics, Wright's Mechanics, Bottomley's Mathematical Tables, Chambers' Mathematical Tables.

16. ENGLISH LANGUAGE AND LITERATURE.

Professor :—C. E. MOYSE, B.A. (Molson Professor of English Language and Literature).

Lecturer :—C. W. COLBY, Ph.D.

FIRST YEAR.—A special course in English Composition.

17. METEOROLOGY.

Instruction in Meteorological Observations will be given in the Observatory at hours to suit the convenience of the Senior Students. Certificates will be granted to those Students who pass a satisfactory examination on the construction and use of Meteorological Instruments and on the general facts of Meteorology.

§ XIV. LABORATORIES.

In the Laboratories the Student will be instructed in the art of conducting experiments, a sound knowledge of which is daily becoming of increasing importance in professional work.

1. ASSAYING LABORATORY. See MINING and METALLURGICAL LABORATORIES.

2. ASTRONOMICAL OBSERVATORY. See GEODETIC LABORATORY.

3. CEMENT LABORATORY. See TESTING LABORATORIES.

4. CHEMICAL LABORATORIES.—The Chemistry and Mining Building which, with his wonted liberality for the University, Mr. W. C. McDonald has erected, will be ready for occupation in September, 1898. The building, in addition to three large general laboratories accommodating about 200 students at a time,

will have a number of smaller laboratories and rooms for special purposes and for research work in inorganic and organic chemistry. Among the special rooms may be mentioned those for physical chemistry, organic chemistry, iron and steel analysis, water-analysis, gas-analysis, electrolytic-analysis, photography, etc. Provision is also made for practical work in mineralogy and petrography, subjects which have come to be essentially departments of chemistry and physics, and which are at the same time intimately related to mining and metallurgy.

The Chemistry lecture-room, extending through two floors, is entered at the ground level, but each of the higher floors will also have its class-room. On the second there is a library, and also a museum for chemical products. The rooms for allied purposes have, as far as possible, been grouped together on the same floor, and there is a hydraulic lift running from the basement to the top storey. The building is practically fire-proof, and lighted throughout by electricity.

5. DYNAMICS, LABORATORY OF. See MATHEMATICS and DYNAMICS, LABORATORY OF.

6. ELECTRICAL LABORATORIES.—These consist of:—

(a) *The Electrical Laboratory proper*, where the standard instruments are kept and experiments made in the electrical course. The instruments comprise amongst others two of Lord Kelvin's electric balances, a Thomson galvanometer, four d'Arsonval galvanometers, two Siemens' dynamometers, two Kelvin electrostatic voltmeters, a complete set of Weston ammeters and voltmeters, besides resistance coils, etc.

Current is supplied to all parts of the room from one of the lighting dynamos direct and from the accumulator room.

During the past session a new standard speed indicator has been set up in the Electrical Laboratory for the purpose of measuring the frequency of alternating currents by comparison with a standard tuning fork. Several measurements have already been made with this instrument on the self-induction of coils of different sizes and shapes.

(b) *The Magnetic Laboratory.*—Here are set up a ballistic galvanometer, Ewing's curve tracer, and a variety of apparatus made in the College for magnetic tests of various kinds.

(c) *The Dynamo Room.*—The apparatus here consists of a 25 KW Edison dynamo, two 12 KW Edison dynamos, a 12 KW Mordey alternator made specially for this laboratory (the coils on the armature can be moved round through any angle, and two or three currents of any phase difference obtained), a 7 KW Victoria dynamo, a 7 KW Fort Wayne dynamo, a 6 KW Thomson-Houston arc-light dynamo, a 15 KW Thomson-Houston incandescent dynamo, and a 5 KW Brush arc-light dynamo. All these are driven off magnetic clutch pulleys by an 88 horse power MacIntosh & Seymour engine. There are also here several different transformers, motors, arc lamps, etc., and a 3 KW motor generator.

A Standard Street Railway motor presented by the Canadian General Electric Co. has been set up during the past winter and is fitted with brakes and other apparatus for experimental work. Arrangements are also being made to instal a complete street railway testing department.

(d) During the past year the lighting station has undergone extensive enlargement and alterations.—A room 34 × 36 ft. in the basement floor of the Workman Building, has been set apart for this purpose.

The equipment now comprises a 30 KW Edison-Hopkinson dynamo, and a 30 KW Siemens' dynamo, each driven by a Willans' engine, and a 75 KW Multipolar Canadian General Electric Generator, driven by a Goldie and McCulloch horizontal engine. The switchboard, panel in form, is made of highly polished enameled slate. It is so arranged that the different buildings—containing 3,000 lights—can be lighted by two dynamos in series, or, if the load is light, by one running on the two wire system, or by accumulators. The power service is independent of the light, and derives its current from the 75 KW Generator. Electric motors, ranging in size from 1 H.P. to 25 H.P., and with total of 135 H.P., are already in operation.

Space has been reserved in the dynamo room for enlarging the plant to double its capacity.

The batteries are charged from a 7 KW. motor-generator, call a booster, of the Tindell type.

The whole is in every respect typical of the latest and best English and American practice.

(*e*) *The Accumulator Room.*—Containing Crompton-Howell storage cells of a united capacity of eight hundred ampere hours.

During the past year the advanced students in the Electrical Engineering Course have carried out an extensive series of experiments on different subjects of interest.

Tests of efficiency were made on transformers submitted by the makers by a new method.

The photometer has been used for testing the candle-power and efficiency of a large number of incandescent lamps of different types.

Several samples of iron have been sent in for magnetic experiments, and have served a useful purpose in the students' work.

The efficiency of the magnetic clutches used in the dynamo room, which were designed at the College, was determined by a series of tests ; these clutches have been running for three years, and have proved perfectly satisfactory.

An extended series of experiments has been made on armature reaction on some of the dynamos in the laboratory; these are now being completed, and will, it is hoped, give valuable results.

A series of experiments have been made on a Street Railway motor to ascertain its conditions of speed and acceleration.

7. MATHEMATICS AND DYNAMICS, LABORATORY OF.—The equipment of this Laboratory includes instruments for the measurement of distance (scales, micrometers, cathetometer), of area (planimeters), of volume (flasks, graduated vessels, etc.), of time (clocks, chronographs), of mass (beam and spring balances) ; it is also provided with a mechanical integrator, specific gravity balances, Atwood and Morin machines for experiments on the Laws of Motion, inclined planes, a variety of rotation apparatus (gyroscope, Maxwell's dynam-

ical top, torsion balance, pendulums, etc.), air-pumps, thermometers, barometers, etc.

The Mathematical Laboratory is used chiefly in connection with
the course in Dynamics. Lectures are given on the fundamental and
derived units of the Science, as well as on the Laws of Motion, and
deductions from the same. When the students have in this way been
made acquainted with some of the ideas of the subject, they are admitted to the laboratory, where experiments of a progressive character are assigned to them. These experiments are in all cases quantitative, and embrace the measurement of mass by means of accurate
physical balances, of intervals of time by clock and chronograph, and
of distance by means of scales, screw micrometers, etc. They then
proceed to the measurements of areas, volumes, velocities, accelerations, forces, specific gravities, friction, and also to pendulum experiments, etc. The equipment of the laboratory for this work is very
complete, embracing as it does the ordinary instruments for the
purpose to be found in most physical laboratories, together with a
variety of apparatus specially constructed for this laboratory. Particular attention is given in the lectures to the principles of observing, in general, the sources of error, etc.; the whole course having
reference to the subsequent work of the student in the Physical and
Engineering Laboratories.

8. MECHANICAL LABORATORY.—In this Laboratory experiments are carried out on the efficiency of belts, shafting, and
machine tools. Governors are tested with the chronograph.
Lubricants by journal friction-testing machine. Sliding and
rolling friction and the stiffness of ropes also form subjects
for experiment.

Much valuable apparatus has been added to this laboratory since
the opening of the Buildings, all of which has been made in the
mechanical workshops, and mainly by students. The Thurston oil
tester and the *Bunte's* viscosimeter,which formed the original equipment, have been supplemented by a hydraulic dynamometer for testing the efficiency of machines, a rotary transmission dynamometer
on a new principle, with recording attachment, a pneumatic gauge
for measuring delicate pressures down to the 3000th of a lb. per
square inch, two other draft gauges, a belt transmission dynamometer
and a belt-testing apparatus.

With these instruments, and with the machines and other appliances in the workshops, experiments are carried on during the

winter session, and students sometimes carry out researches during the summer months.

Many visits have also been paid to engineering works and manufactories of importance.

9. METALLURGICAL LABORATORY. See MINING and METALLURGICAL LABORATORIES.

10. MILLING ROOM. See MINING and METALLURGICAL LABORATORIES.

11. GEODETIC LABORATORY.—The equipment of this laboratory consists of:—

(*1*) Linear instruments.
  (*a*) A Rogers' comparator and standard bar for investigating standards of length.
  (*b*) A fifty-foot standard and comparator for standardizing steel bands, chains, tapes, rods, etc.
  (*c*) A Whitworth end-measuring machine and set of standards.
  (*d*) A Munro-Rogers linear dividing engine.

(*2*) Circular instruments.
  (*a*) A Rogers' circular comparator and dividing engine.
  (*b*) Two level triers.

(*3*) Time.
  (*a*) An astronomical clock and clock circuit in connection with the observatory clocks.
  (*b*) Chronometers running on mean and sidereal time.
  (*c*) Chronograph.

(*4*) Gravity.—A portable Bessel's reversible pendulum apparatus, with special pendulum clock and telescopic apparatus for observing coincidences of beats.

(*5*) A water gauge apparatus for testing aneroid barometers.

(*6*) Magnetic instruments:
  (*a*) A Kew dip circle.
  (*b*) A Kew filar magnetometer.

The laboratory is constructed with double walls and enclosed air spaces, and has a special heating apparatus, so that the temperature within may be brought to, and held at, any desired degree.

The ordinary course of instruction in this laboratory is described in § XIII., Art. 3.

ASTRONOMICAL OBSERVATORY.—The observatory equipment for the purpose of instruction in practical astronomy consists of:—

(a) A Bamberg prismatic transit with zenith attachment.
(b) Two astronomical transits for meridian observations. Collimating telescopes.
(c) A Troughton & Simms' zenith telescope.
(d) An astronomical transit in the prime vertical.
(e) Sidereal and mean time clocks and chronometers.
(f) Chronograph and electrical circuits by which observations and clock comparisons within or without the observatory may be made.

12. HYDRAULIC LABORATORY.—Here the student will study practically the flow of water through orifices of various forms and sizes, through submerged openings, over weirs, through pipes, mouth-pieces, etc.

The equipment of this laboratory includes:—

(a) A large Experimental Tank, 30 ft. in height and 25 sq. ft. in sectional area. With this tank experiments are conducted on the flow of water through orifices either free or submerged. By a simple arrangement the orifices can be rapidly interchanged without lowering the head, and with the loss of only about one pint of water. The indicating and measuring arrangements connected with the tank are exceedingly delicate and accurate, all times being automatically recorded by an electric chronograph ; and valuable results have already been obtained. By means of a special connection with the city water-supply, the available head of water may be increased up to 280 ft.

(b) An Impact Machine, which renders it possible to measure the force with which water flowing through an orifice, nozzle, or pipe, strikes any given surface, and also the impulsive effect of the water entering the buckets of hydraulic motors.

(*c*) A Rife's Hydraulic Ram.

(*d*) A Jet Measurer specially designed for investigating the dimensions of the jet produced in the phenomena known as "the inversion of the vein." With this apparatus it is possible to determine, within .001 inch, the dimensions of a jet in any plane and at any point of the path.

(*e*) Numerous orifices, nozzles, and mouth-pieces.

(*f*) A specially designed stand-pipe, with all the necessary connections for pipes of various sizes for investigations on frictional resistance. The pressures are measured by recording gauges, etc.

(*g*) A flume about 35 feet in length, by 5 ft. in width by 3 ft. 6 ins. in depth.

(*h*) Weirs up to 5 ft. in width, and with a depth of water over the sill varying from nil to 8 inches. A weir-depthing machine, with three adjustable heads, gives the surface depth of the stream at any three points in a transverse section. The velocity of the stream is also determined by means of a double Pitôt tube.

(*i*) Numerous hydraulic pressure-gauges.

(*j*) A mercury column 60 feet in height.

(*k*) Gauge-testing apparatus.

(*l*) Various rotary, and piston meters, and a Venturi meter.

(*m*) Apparatus for illustrating vortex motion.

(*n*) Apparatus for illustrating vortex ring motion, and for determining the critical velocity of water flowing through pipes.

(*o*) Five specially built gauging tanks with suitable indicators, each having a capacity of 800 cubic feet. Also other portable tanks.

(*p*) Transmission and absorption dynamometers·

(*q*) An experimental centrifugal pump, which can be tested with varying heights of suction and discharge.

(*r*) An inward-flow turbine, a new American turbine, a Pelton, and other motors and turbines.

(*s*) Standard gallon and litre measures with glass strikes,

This Laboratory is also provided with a set of pumps, specially designed for experimental work and research. They are adapted to work under all pressures up to 120 lbs. per sq. in., and at all speeds up to the highest found practicable. The set is composed of three vertical single acting plunger pumps of 7 in. diam., 18 in. stroke, driven by one shaft. They have two interchangeable valve chests, and it is arranged that both the valves and their seats may be removed and replaced by others. The pumps are also provided with a double set of continuous triple recording indicators designed in the laboratory and having electrical connections. With these, an accurate record of the history of the suction and discharge valves may be obtained at any given time, all fluctuations of time, speed, pressure, etc., being automatically recorded.

In the Hydraulic Laboratory, investigations are being carried out on the flow of water through orifices of different sizes and forms, on the effect of viscosity upon the flow, and for the purpose of determining the co-efficients of discharge through conical nozzles.

Similar experiments and also experiments on the flow of water over weirs have been directly conducted by the students, who are thus able to obtain experience in the scientific treatment of hydraulic problems, which will certainly be of the utmost value to them in their future career. ·

13. MINING AND METALLURGICAL LABORATORIES.—The McDonald Chemistry and Mining Building is now completed, and the Mining and Metallurgical Laboratories, to be situated in the lower part of the structure, are fully equipped.

These laboratories, with the lecture rooms and library, the professor's office, and rooms for apparatus, supplies and fuel, are very conveniently arranged individually and with regard to one another, and occupy the lower part of the main building and the whole of both wings. The total floor space covered is approximately 12,500 square feet, divided as follows :—

Mining and Ore-Dressing Laboratory, or Milling Room, 3,500 square feet ; Metallurgical Laboratory, or Furnace Room, 2,500 square feet; Assay Laboratory, 2,000 square feet : Wet Assaying Rooms, 500 square feet; Technical Lecture Room, 600 square feet; Library and Drawing Room, 500 square feet; Offices, Stores and so forth, 3,000 square feet.

The two rooms first mentioned are of great size, and are the chief laboratories of the department. In these it is possible to take any ores of gold, silver, copper or lead in the condition in which they come from the mines, and to treat them from beginning to end precisely as they are treated in the ore-dressing works and smelting plants of the West. They may therefore be considered a small commercial plant for the actual production of metals. They differ from commercial plants, however, in that an ordinary ore-dressing establishment or smelter is designed to treat the ores of only one district and sometimes of only one part of a district. The University Laboratories must of course be adapted to all ores now found or likely to be found in the Dominion, and therefore contain a greater number of pieces of apparatus than are to be found in any one commercial establishment, although probably no case will come up when all of these machines will be used for any one test.

THE MILLING-ROOM is equipped with a complete working plant, capable of treating, if necessary, 10 to 20 tons of ore per day, the chief pieces of apparatus being :—Rock Crushers of three kinds ("Blake," "Dodge" and "Gates"), to break the large pieces of ore to small size. Stamp mills of 500, and 950 lbs., respectively, for the fine crushing and amalgamating of gold ores. Huntingdon mill, for crushing and amalgamating. Rolls, both coarse and fine, to reduce ores to powder when necessary. Trommels and sieves, for sizing the crushed ores. Hartz and Collom jigs for concentrating minerals by gravity. Revolving, bumping, and belt tables, for separating valuable minerals contained in fine sands and crushed rock. Plates and pans for amalgamating gold and silver ores. Spitzkasten, Spitzlütten, magnetic separators and various other special pieces of ore-dressing apparatus.

The machinery above mentioned is not in miniature; it is of full size, such as the graduates will afterwards find in use in commercial establishments, and is provided with belt and bucket elevators—on hand trucks, etc., etc. It is, however, so arranged that each piece can be worked by itself, taken apart and cleaned up; and such of the larger pieces as cannot be used for small quantities of material are duplicated in miniature. The laboratory, while thus adapted to illustrate continuous work on a comparatively large scale, is even more perfectly designed for experimental work on as small a scale as is compatible with accuracy of result.

THE METALLURGICAL LABORATORY is fitted with a water-jacket blast-furnace, 24 ins. inside diameter, for smelting lead and copper,

and with the necessary blast apparatus; also with reverberatory furnaces, a Bruckner-cylinder furnace, a reverberatory roasting-furnace,
an English cupellation-furnace, and several crucible furnaces.

It has also a complete set of apparatus for the chlorination and
leaching of silver and other ores, and a cyanide extraction-plant for
gold ores, these being the new methods which are revolutionizing
the gold metallurgy of the world and producing such extraordinary
yields in the mines of South Africa and Australia.

These two laboratories are very large and well lighted, and are
each 20 ft. high in the clear. Close to them are the rooms for storage of ores, fuel, etc., etc., from which lines of tracks lead to
the elevator and connect with the crushers and furnaces. There is
also an overhead system of tramways, with travelling hoists and
buckets. Material can therefore be moved from one point to another
with the greatest ease, and pieces of apparatus can be readily taken
apart, and, if necessary, moved by the same means.

It is not the purpose of the University to use these laboratories
for commercial work, although they are quite large enough for such
service. They are to be used solely for educational work and for
investigation; but, owing to their thoroughly practical nature, instruction given in them will be of immensely greater value to the
students than could be the case if the work were done in miniature;
and, at the same time, the investigations made by means of such
apparatus will be of great use to the mining and metallurgical community, as they can be carried out in all respects under working conditions, and will, therefore, be free from the disturbing causes likely
to interfere with attempts to reproduce commercial processes on a
small scale.

THE ASSAYING LABORATORY is equipped with a complete set of
muffle and crucible furnaces, some of each being arranged for gas and
oil and others for coke and charcoal, as in some parts of the West
one of these fuels must be used, while in other parts another is found
more desirable. Connected with this laboratory are rooms with pulp-
and assay-balances, and others equipped for wet analysis of ores.

14. MODELLING LABORATORY.—A Laboratory for modelling
in clay, as part of the work in the Architectural Department,
is arranged in connection with the Cement-testing Laboratory. Third Year Architectural Students follow a regular
course in Modelling under the instruction of the Assistant
Professor of Freehand Drawing. The Laboratory is fully

equipped for the work, including the making of plaster casts from the executed clay models.

15. PETROGRAPHICAL LABORATORY.—The Petrographical Laboratory, containing the chief rock collections of the University, is situated in the east wing of the Arts building, but is about to be transferred to the new Chemistry and Mining building. It is arranged for the use of Students in the Mining Course as well as for those desiring to take advanced work, and is provided with a number of petrographical microscopes by Seibert and Crouch, as well as with models, sets of thin sections, electro-magnets, heavy solutions, etc., for petrographical work.

For advanced work and petrographical investigation Dr. Adams's extensive private collection of rocks and thin sections is available for purposes of study and comparison.

16. PHYSICAL LABORATORY.—The McDonald Physical Laboratory contains five storeys, each of 8,000 square feet area. Besides a lecture theatre and its apparatus rooms, the building includes an elementary laboratory nearly 60 feet square ; large special laboratories arranged for higher work by advanced students in heat and electricity, a range of rooms for optical work and photography ; separate rooms for private thesis work by students; and two large laboratories arranged for research, provided with solid piers and the usual standard instruments. There are also a lecture room, with apparatus room attached, for mathematical physics, a special physical library, and convenient workshops. The equipment is on a corresponding scale, and comprises : (1) apparatus for illustrating lectures; (2) simple forms of the principal instruments for use by the students in practical work; (3) the most recent types of all the important instruments for exact measurement, to be used in connection with special work and research.

The basement contains the cellars, furnaces, and janitor's department at the west end of the building. The machine room—containing a small gas engine and dynamo, which are fitted for testing, but can also be used for light and power, a motor-alternator and a motor-dynamo—is situated at the extreme western corner of the basement, so as to be as far removed as possible from the delicate magnetic and electrical instruments. Here is also the switch-board for controlling the various circuits for supplying direct or alternating current to different parts of the building. The Accumulator Room contains a few large storage cells, charged by the motor-dynamo, which are fitted with a suitable series-parallel arrangement, and with rheostats for obtaining and controlling large currents up to 4,000 amperes for testing ammeters and low resistances, etc.

The Magnetic Laboratory contains magnetic instruments and variometers of different patterns, and also a duplicate of the B. A. Electro-dynamometer, which has been completely remodelled and set up with great care for absolute measurements of current. The Gravitation Laboratory, on the opposite side of the basement, contains a very fine Lorenz apparatus for the absolute measurement of resistance, constructed under the supervision of Prof. Viriamu Jones. It also contains a set of Ewing Seismographs and a pair of Darwin Recording Mirrors for measuring small movements of the soil. It is intended to add a special form of Kater Pendulum and a Cavendish apparatus for further researches.

There is a Constant Temperature Room, surrounded by double walls, which contains a Standard Rieffler Clock, and is fitted for comparator work. The addition of a standard Barometer of special construction is also in contemplation.

The Ground Floor contains at the western corner a small machine shop, fitted with a milling machine and suitable lathes and tools, driven by electric motors, and such appliances as are required for the making and repairing of the instruments, for which the services of a mechanical assistant are retained. There is also a store room for glass, chemicals and cleaning materials, and extensive lockers and lavatories for the use of the students.

The Main Electrical Laboratory is a room 60 feet by 40, and is fitted with a number of brick piers which come up through the floor, and rest on independent foundations, in addition to the usual slate shelves round the walls. This room contains a large number of electrometers, galvanometers, potentiometers and other testing instruments of various patterns, and adapted for different uses. It connects with a smaller room at the side, in which are kept the resistance boxes and standards, and also the capacity standards. A small research laboratory, adjoining the electrical laboratory, is fitted up for the study of the viscosity of gases and of the electrical discharge in high vacua.

The First Floor contains the Main Lecture Theatre, with seats for about 250 students. The lecture table is supported on separate piers, which are independent of the floor. Complete arrangements are provided for optical projection and illustration. The Preparation Room in the rear contains many of the larger pieces of lecture apparatus, but the majority of the instruments, when not in use, are kept in suitable cases in the adjoining apparatus room. On the same floor there is the Heat Laboratory, devoted to advanced work in Thermometry, Pyrometry and Calorimetry, and also to such electrical work as involves the use of thermostats and the measurement of the effects of temperature. There are also two smaller rooms for Professors and Demonstrators.

The Second Floor is partly occupied by the upper half of the Lecture Theatre. There is also an Examination Room for paper work, a Mathematical Lecture Room, with a special apparatus room devoted to apparatus for illustrating Mathematical Physics, and a special Physical Library chiefly devoted to reference books and periodicals relating to Physics. A store room, lavatories and Professors' room occupy the remainder of the flat.

The Third Floor contains the Elementary Laboratory, a room 60 feet square, devoted to elementary practical work in Heat, Sound and Electricity and Magnetism. There is a Demonstrator's room adjoining, and an optical annex devoted to experiments with lenses, galvanometers, etc., which require a darkened room. On the other side of the building there is a spectroscopic room containing a six-inch Rowland grating, with mountings by Brashear, and other large spectrometers and polarimeters. Also a series of smaller optical rooms, including a photometric room, specially fitted for Arc photometry, and a dark room for photographic work. Above are spacious and well-lighted attics, which are at present used for storing wood and other materials, but may in the future be applied to other purposes. Communication between the different flats is facilitated by means of a hydraulic elevator. The building is lighted throughout by electricity, and heated by hot water. The walls are of pressed brick, and the floors of hard maple. There is a ventilating system, consisting of Tobin tubes and suitable exit flues, assisted by a fan in the roof.

17. TESTING LABORATORIES.—The principal experiments carried out in these will relate to the elasticity and strength

of materials, friction, the theory of structures, the accuracy of springs, gauges, dynamometers, etc. The equipment of this laboratory includes :—

(*a*) A Wicksteed 100-ton and an Emery 75-ton machine for testing the tensile, compressive and transverse strength of the several materials of construction. To the former has been added a specially designed arrangement, by which the transverse strength of girders and beams up to 26 ft. in length can be determined. These machines are provided with the holders required for the various kinds of tests, and new holders have also been specially designed and made in the laboratory for investigating the tensile and shearing strength of timber for wire rope and belt tests, etc. Numerous attachments have also been made to the machines, which have already increased their efficiency. The most recent addition is a double-bearing support for transverse testing.

(*b*) An Impact Machine, with a drop of 30 ft., and with gearing which will enable specimens to be rotated at any required speed, and the blows to be repeated at any required intervals. By means of a revolving drum, a continuous and accurate record of the deflections of the specimens under the blows can be obtained.

(*c*) An Unwin Torsion Machine with a specially designed angle-measurer, by which the amount of the torsion can be measured with extreme accuracy.

(*d*) An Accumulator, furnishing a pressure of 3,600 lbs. per square inch, which is transmitted to the several testing machines, and ensures a perfectly steady application of stress, which is impossible when any form of pump is substituted for an Accumulator.

(*e*) A Blake and a Worthington Steam Pump, designed to work against a pressure of 3,600 lbs. per square inch. The Accumulator may be actuated by either of the pumps, and, if at any time it is desirable to do so, either of the pumps may be employed to actuate the testing machine direct. When in operation the work of the pump and the accumulator is automatic.

(*f*) Extensometers of the Unwin, Martens, Marshall and other types. The extensometer equipment has recently been enriched by seven sets of improved extensometer apparatus designed and made in the laboratory.

(*g*) Portable cathetometers, and also a large cathetometer specially designed and constructed for the determination of the extensions, compressions and deflections of the specimens under stress in the testing machines.

(*h*) An automatic electric motor pump for actuating the Accumulator ; also various electric motors for working the several machines.

(*i*) A drying oven for beams up to 26 ft. in length. The hot air in this oven is kept in circulation by means of a fan driven by an electric motor.

(*j*) Numerous gauges, amongst which may be specially noticed an Emery Pressure Gauge, graduated in single lbs. up to 2,500 lbs. per square inch. The whole of the testing machines are on the same pressure circuit, and are connected with the Emery gauge and also other standard gauges, including recording gauges. This arrangement provides a practically perfect means of checking the accuracy of the testing.

(*k*) Special apparatus and recording gauge for the testing of hose, etc.

(*l*) Dynamometers for measuring the strength of textile fabrics, the holding power of nails, etc.

(*m*) Apparatus for determining the elasticity of long wires.

(*n*) Apparatus for determining the hardness of materials of construction.

(*o*) Zeiss and other Microscopes.

(*p*) Delicate chemical and other Balances. A very important part of the equipment is the Oertling Balance, capable of indicating with extreme accuracy weights of from .00001 lb. up to 125 lbs.

(*q*) Micrometers of all kinds.

18. CEMENT LABORATORY.—The importance of tests of

the strength of mortars and cements is very great. The equipment of the Laboratory for the purpose is on a complete plan, including:—

(*a*) Three one-ton tensile testing machines, representing the best English and American practice.

(*b*) One 50-ton hydraulic compressive testing machine.

(*c*) Volumenometers for determining specific gravity and for determining the carbonic acid in the raw material.

(*d*) Faija steaming apparatus for blowing tests.

(*c*) Mechanical hand and power mixers.

(*f*) Apparatus for determining standard consistency.

(*g*) Vicats' and Gilmore's needles for determining set.

(*h*) Weighing hopper, spring and other balances·

(*i*) Gun metal moulds for tension, compression and transverse test pieces, and special moulds for placing mortar into the moulds under a uniform pressure, which, together with the mechanical mixers, enable the personal error to be eliminated.

(*j*) Sieves of 20, 30, 40, 50, 60, 70, 80, 100, 120 and 180 meshes per lineal inch for determining the fineness.

The laboratory is also fitted with copper-lined cisterns, in which the briquettes may be submerged for any required time, and with capacious slated operating tables, bins and tin boxes for keeping the cement dry for any period.

In the Cement Testing Laboratory, researches have been made on the strength of mortars set under pressure, the effect of frost on natural and Portland cements, the effect of sugar on lime and cement mortars, the strength of lime and cement mortars and of the bricks in brick piers, the effect of fine grinding on the adhesive strength of cements, of using hot water in mixing mortars. Continued tests on the strength of concrete blocks in series are made by Fourth Year Students.

In addition to these researches, a large amount of work is done each year by the Third Year students, in investigating the specific gravity, fineness, setting properties, constancy of volume, and the tensile, compressive and transverse strengths of cement, both neat and with the sand. A special investigation is now being carried on on the new material called "Sand-Cement" which is being introduced on the Canadian market.

19. THERMODYNAMIC LABORATORY.—The Thermodynamic Laboratory is furnished with an experimental steam engine of 100 I.H.P., specially designed for the investigation of the behaviour of steam under various conditions; there are four cylinders, which can be connected so as to allow of single, compound, triple or quadruple expansion, condensing or non-condensing, with or without jackets. The measurements of heat are made by large tanks, which receive the condensing water and the condensed steam. There are two hydraulic absorption brakes for measuring the mechanical power developed, and an alternative friction brake for the same purpose, Besides this large steam engine, a high speed automatic cut-off by Robb-Armstrong of Amherst, N.S., an Atkinson Cycle, and an Otto gas engine, a Stirling hot air engine by Woodbury Merrill of Ticonderoga, are provided and completely fitted for purposes of measurement and research. Many smaller instruments are provided or are in course of construction for illustrating the general principles of thermodynamics, such as calorimeters, delicate thermometers and gauges, a mercury column apparatus for investigating the properties of superheated steam and other working fluids, draft gauges, pyrometers, fuel testers, indicators, planimeters and a Moscrop recorder.

A 40 horse power two-stage air compressor of modern design for a central station is under construction in the workshops of the College, and will, it is hoped, be added to the Laboratory during next session.

During the past session two new boilers have been added to the equipment by the munificence of Mr. W. C. McDonald. They are of 130 horse-power each; one being of locomotive type, the other an internally fired tubulous boiler, with return flues, by the Robb Engineering Company, of Amherst, N.S. These, together with the new 100 horse-power Goldie-McCulloch engine and the Willans' engine in the Dynamo Room, are now completely fitted for testing and available for experimental work. In this way there are available for research five distinct types of steam boilers, and eight steam engines.

The last session was distinguished by a series of trials carried out by the Fourth Year Mechanical Students on the 3,000 horse-power compound steam engine, by the Laurie Engine Company, at the Montreal Street Railway's William Street Power Station. From these important scientific results are expected, as the tests were carried out in a very complete manner, including the drilling of holes in the cylinder covers and the insertion of electrical thermometers in the walls.

A small engine of the Root type, called "the Dake" has been presented to the Laboratory, in return for a series of tests reported thereon, by the Jenckes Engineering Company. A mass of apparatus for testing the dryness of steam (including separating, throttling and super-heating calorimeters), a steam orifice, a Penberthy injector and a fuel calorimeter have been permanently fitted up, and form, together with numerous pyrometers, indicators and springs, the subjects of the preliminary part of the course.

§ XV. MUSEUMS.

The Peter Redpath Museum contains large and valuable collections in Botany, Zoology, Mineralogy and Geology, arranged in such a manner as to facilitate the work in these departments. Students have access to this Museum, in connection with their attendance on the classes in Arts in the subjects above named, and also by tickets which can be obtained on application. Students will also have the use of a Technical Museum, occupying the whole of the third storey of the Engineering Building. Amongst other apparatus, the Museum contains the Reuleaux collection of kinematic models, presented by W. C. McDonald, Esq., and pronounced by Professor Reuleaux to be the finest and most complete collection in America.

ARCHITECTURAL EQUIPMENT.—The Architectural Department has been endowed by Mr. McDonald, the founder, with a very thorough equipment for practical purposes of instruction; this is at present in course of provision and completion. In the Museum of the Engineering Building is included a large collection of casts both of architectural detail and ornament (fully illustrative of the historical develop-

ment of the various styles) and of architectural and figure
sculpture. The freehand-drawing classes for architectural
students, as also the classes of architectural drawing and design, are conducted in this portion of the building.

A special architectural department has been added to the
Faculty Library for the use of students, and numerous important works have been added to the University Library.
A collection of architectural photographs is being formed
in addition to diagrams and a very complete series of lantern
slides in illustration of the historical courses. Diagrams, models and specimens of materials and fittings are also included
for use in the courses on building construction and materials,
sanitation, etc.

§ XVI. WORKSHOPS.

The workshops, erected on the Thomas Workman Endowment, have a floor area of more than 25,000 sq. ft.

The practical instruction in the workshops is designed to
give the Student some knowledge of the nature of the materials of construction, to familiarize him with the more important hand and machine tools, and to give him some manual
skill in the use of the same. For this purpose, the Student,
during a specified number of hours per week, will work in the
shops under the superintendence of the Professor of Mechanical Engineering, aided by skilled mechanics. The courses
commence with graded exercises, and gradually lead up to
the making of joints, members of structures, frames, etc., finally concluding in the iron-working department with the
manufacture of tools, parts of machines, and, if possible, with
the building of complete machines.

The equipment includes the following:

IN THE CARPENTER, WOOD-TURNING AND PATTERN-
MAKING DEPARTMENTS.—Carpenters' and pattern-makers'
benches, wood-lathes, a large pattern-maker's lathe, circular-

saw benches, jig and band saws, buzz-planer, wood-borer, universal wood-worker, etc.

IN THE MACHINE SHOP.—The most improved engine lathes, a 36-in. modern upright drill, with compound table, universal milling machine, with vertical milling attachment, hand lathes, planer, universal grinding machine, universal cutter and reamer grinder, buffing machine, a 16-in. patent shaper, vise-benches, etc.

IN THE SMITH SHOP.—Forges, hand drill, and a power hammer.

IN THE FOUNDRY.—A cupola for melting iron, core oven, brass furnace, moulders' benches, etc.

The machinery in the shops is driven by a 50 I.H.P. compound engine and a 10 I.H.P. high speed engine.

In the workshops, a 40 H. P. air compressor has formed the staple object upon which energy has been spent. This, it is hoped, will be completed and added to the Thermodynamic Laboratory during the present year. A large boring bar, with automatic feed and double heads, an Emery brass buffing machine, an overhead travelling crane of one ton capacity, with two transverse motions, in the foundry; and two electric arc lamps and projecting lanterns complete for class demonstration have been the principal results of steady application in the workshops.

———

BOARDING HOUSES, ETC.

Good board and lodging may be obtained at $18 per month ; or separately, board at $12 to $14, and rooms $5 to $10 per month. The cost of drawing instruments for the whole course may be placed at from $15 to $30. Gown and overalls, $7 to $10. Books per session $10 to $30.

Estimated necessary cost per session of 7½ months, including fees, but exclusive of clothing and travelling expenses, $270 to $320.

Students can obtain a list of boarding houses on application to the secretary.

The Applied Science Graduates' Society.

This Society has been recently established with a view to promote a closer relationship between the Faculty and the Graduates, and also between the Graduates themselves. The Society has issued a number of important bulletins relating to the work in the different departments, and giving an account of the development of the Faculty. The membership already includes more than one-third of the whole number of Graduates, and it is hoped that before long all of the Graduates will have joined the Society.

All information respecting the objects of the Society may be obtained on application to the Secretary.

Honorary President, Dr. H. T. Bovey.

President, J. M. McCarthy.

Vice-President, Prof. F. D. Adams.

Sec.-Treas., J. G. G. Kerry, Engineering Building, McGill University.

Resident Committee.—W. F. Angus, J. W. Bell, A. L. Mudge, R. O. King, R. H. Jamieson.

Non-resident Committee.—R. B. Rogers, Peterboro, O.; A. A. Cole, Rossland, B.C.; W. P. Laurie, Quebec, Q.; W. G. Smart, Sherbrooke, Q.; J. K. Scammell, Fairville, N.B.; H. M. McKay, Pictou, N.S.; W. J. Bulman, Charlottetown, P.E.I.; O. S. Whiteside, Anthracite, N.W.T.; J. M. McGregor, Rossland, B.C.; E. H. Hamilton, Pueblo, Col., U.S.A.; P. N. Evans, Lafayette, Ind., U.S.A.; G. H. Frost, New York, U.S.A.; L. L. Street, Marlboro, Mass., U.S.A.

The McGill Mining Society.

This Society was organized in 1891-2 by the Undergraduates of the Mining Department, but its scope has since been enlarged, and now any graduate or undergraduate interested in mining and allied work is eligible for membership. Meetings are held fortnightly for reading and discussion of papers on subjects of interest to the Society, and frequent lectures are given by outside professional men.

The primary object of the Society is of course to give the Undergraduates an opportunity to meet one another and to become acquainted with the older members of the Society, but an almost equal part of its work consists in keeping the graduates of the department in touch with the work of the University.

The officers for the year 1898-99 are :—

Honorary President, Dr. B. J. Harrington.
President, J. E. Preston, Sc., '99·
Sec.-Treasurer, R. H. Gillean, Sc., '00·

The Committee consists of the officers and of two members from each year, who are elected at the beginning of the session.

———

APPLIED SCIENCE SOCIETY.

During the last session this Society has been organized with the object of reading papers of technical and scientific interest.

The following are the officers:—

Hon. President, Prof. H. T. Bovey.
President, W. W. Colpitts, representing Civil Engineering and Architecture.
1st Vice-President, S. F. Kirkpatrick, representing Mining Engineering and Chemistry.
2nd Vice-President, R. M. Wilson, representing Electrical Engineering.
3rd Vice-President, J. S. Whyte, representing Mechanical Engineering.
Secretary, J. G. Glassco.
Treasurer, R. H. Gillean.
Second Year Representatives, B. S. McKenzie, P. Ogilvie.

RESEARCH WORK IN THE LABORATORIES, 1897-98.

The following papers have been read before the Royal Societies
of England and Canada, the British Association for the Advancement
of Science, the Inst. of C.E. (England), the Can. Soc. C. E., and
other learned Societies :—

" Report on observations of soil temperatures with electrical thermometers."

" Report on Canadian earthquakes, with a reproduction of the
trace of the first automatic record taken in Canada at the McDonald
Physics Building, March 27th, 1897."

"The Hydraulic Laboratory, McGill University, with results of experiments on the values of hydraulic coefficients."

" Some experiments on the flow of rocks."

" On the variation of the electromotive force of different forms
of the Clarke Standard Cell, with temperature and with strength of
solution, including determinations of the solubility of zinc sulphate,
and of the density of its solution."

" A new electrical method of determining the specific heat of a
liquid, with preliminary results of its application to the cases of
water and mercury."

" On the behaviour of argon in X-Ray tubes."

" A research in thermo-electricity by means of the platinum resistance pyrometer."

" A simple modification of the Board of Trade form of the Clark
Cell, with application to the Cadmium Cell."

" A new form of Hysteresis Tester."

" On the effect of temperature on the magnetic properties of iron."

" On the absolute measurement of the Thomson effect in copper."

" On the variation of the viscosity of gases with temperature."

" On the variation of the specific heat of water."

" An electrical method of measuring the temperature of a surface
on which steam is condensing."

" On the law of condensation of steam, deduced from measurements of temperature cycles of the walls and steam, in the cylinder
of a steam engine, including determinations of the electrical and
thermal properties of cast iron."

" A new apparatus or studying the rate of condensation of steam
on a metal surface at different temperatures and pressures."

" On the strength of Canadian timbers, Douglas fir, red pine,
white pine and hemlock."

FACULTY OF APPLIED SCIENCE—TIME TABLE.

YEARS	HOURS	MONDAY.	TUESDAY.	WEDNESDAY.	THURSDAY.	FRIDAY.	SATURDAY.
FIRST YEAR.	9	Mathematics.	Mathematics.	Mathematics.	Mathematics.	Mathematics.	Shopwork.
	10	Mathematics.	Mathematics.	Mathematics.	Mathematics.	Mathematics.	Do
	11	Desc. Mechanics.	English.	Drawing.	Drawing.	English.	Do
	12	Chemistry.	English.	Chemistry.	Drawing.	Chemistry.	Do
	2 to 5	Practical Chem.stry. Geom. Drawing. (9).	Pract. Chemistry. Shopwork.	Geom. Drawing(a). Mathematical Lab. (b).	Freehand Drawing.	Pract. Chemistry. Workshop.	
SECOND YEAR.	9	Mathematics.	Mathematics.	Architecture, 1.	Mathematics.	Mining, (a). Metallurgy, (b). Freeband Drawing, 1.	Drawing, 1, 5.
	10	Physical Laboratory, 2, 5, 6. Freehand Drawing, 1.	Drawing, 1.	Mathematics.	Chemistry, 6. Kinematics, 3, 4. Surveying, 1, 2, 5.	Freehand Drawing, 1.	Do
	11	Do	Drawing, 1.	Botany, 6. Mathematics.	Kinematics, 3, 4. Zoology, 5.	Mathematics.	Do
	12	Theory of Architecture. Botany, 6.	Exp. Physics, 1, 2, 3, 4, 5. Chemistry, 6.	Surveying, 1, 2, 5. Kinematics, 3, 4.	Experimental Physics.	Chemistry, 5, 6. Architecture, 1.	Do
	2 to 5	*Chemical Lab, 5, 6. Mapping, (a) 1, 2. Shopwork, 3, 4. Drawing (b), 1.	Desc. Geometry, (c) (b) 1, 2, 3, 4, 5, 6.	*Chemical Lab, 5, 6. Mechl. Drawing, 3, 4. Shopwork, 1, 2.	Chemical Lab, 6. Drawing, 1. Mapping, 2, 5. Shopwork, 3, 4.	Physical Laboratory, 3-4. Shopwork, 1, 5.	

(a) First Term. (b) Second Term. (c) After Nov. 1st. *The Chemical Laboratories are open to Second, Third and Fourth Year classes daily (Saturday excepted) from 9 a.m. to 5 p.m. 1. Architectural Students. 2. Civil Engineering Students. 3. Electrical Engineering Students. 4. Mechanical Engineering Students. 5. Mining Engineering Sudents. 6. Practical Chemistry Students.

FACULTY OF APPLIED SCIENCE.—TIME TABLE—*Continued.*

YEARS.	HOURS.	MONDAY.	TUESDAY.	WEDNESDAY.	THURSDAY.	FRIDAY.	SATURDAY.
THIRD YEAR.	9	Experimental Physics., 1, 2, 3, 4, 5, 6.	Metallurgy (a) 4, 5, 6. Elect. Eng. 3. Mineralogy (b), 5, 6. Architecture, 1.	Dyn. of Mach., 3, 4. Geology, 2, 5, 6.	Experimental Physics. 1, 2, 3, 4, 5, 6.	Mach. Design (b), 4. Mineralogy (b), 5, 6. Freehand Drawing, 1.	Elect. Eng. Lab, (a), 3. Geology (c), 5. Metal. Lab. (d), 5. Testing Lab. (b), 2, 3, 4, 5. Archt. Drawing, 1.
	10	Dyn. of Mach., 3, 4. Geology, 2, 5, 6. Freehand Drawing, 1.	Thermodynamics (b), 4. Surveying, 1, 2, 5.	Surveying, 1, 2, 5. Shopwork, 3, 4.	Chemistry, 6. Machine Design, 3, 4. Railroad Eng., 2, 5. Architecture, 1.	Geology, 2, 5, 6. Mach. Design, 4. Freehand Drawing, 1.	Do
	11	Freehand Drawing, 1. Machine Design, 3, 4. Surveying, 2, 5.	Theory of Structures, 2, 3, 4. Zoology, 6.	Metallurgy, 5, 6. Desc. Geom., 2. Shopwork, 3, 4.	Mathematics, 1, 2, 3, 4, 5. Zoology, 6.	Graphics (a), 1, 2, 3, 4, 5. Metallurgy (b), 5, 6.	Do
	12	Mathematics, 1, 2, 3, 4, 5.	Theory of Structures, 2, 3, 4, 5. Theory of Architecture, 1.	Metallurgy, 5, 6. Municipal Eng., 1, 2. Shopwork, 3, 4.	Theory of Structures, 2, 3, 4.	Mathematics, 1, 2, 3, 4, 5.	Do
	2 to 5	Chemistry, 5, 6. Drawing, 4, (b) 1. Mapping, (a) 1, 2 Physical Lab, 3.	Chemistry, 6. Drawing, 1, 2. Elect. Lab., 3. Mapping (a), 5. Metall.r. Lab. (b), 5.	Chemistry, 5, 6. Physical Lab., 1, 2, 3, 4.	Det. Mineralogy, 5, 6. Drawing, 1, 3, 4. Mapping, 2.	Chemistry, 6. Desc. Geo. (d), 1, 2. Graphics (b), 2. Phys. Lab., 5. Shopwork, 3, 4. Modelling (b), 1.	
FOURTH YEAR.	9	Thermodynamics, 2, 3, 4, 5.	Dyn. of Mach 3, 4. Mineralogy (a), 5, 6. Pa'eontology (b), 5.	Designing, 1, 2, 4, (b). 5. Electrodynamics, 3. Geology, 6. Mining (a), 5. Museum Work.	Thermodynamics, 2, 3, 4, 5. Mining, 5.	Electrodynamics, 3. Metall. Lab. (b) 5. Mining Lab. 'a) 5. Municipal Eng. 1, 2.	Designing, 1. Electrical Erg. Lab., 3. Geodetic Lab., 2. Mining Lab. 5. Shopwork, 4.
	10	Hydraulics, 1, 2, 3, 4, 5. Mining Thesis (b) 5.	Canadian Geology, (b) 5. Mechanical Lab., 4. Ore Deposits (a) 5. Physical Lab. 3	Designing, 1, 2, 4, Elec. Eng. Lib., 3. Mech. Lib., 3. Mineral. (a) 5, 6. Min. Thesis, (b) 5.	Hyd. Mach. (Motors, etc.) 1, 2, 3, 4, (a) 5. Mining Thesis, (b) 5.	Elect. Eng. Lab., 3. Geodesy, 2. Mining Lab. (a) 5. Metall. Lab. (b) 5. Thermo. Lab., 4.	Do
	11	*Geodesy, 2. Geology (a) 5. Petrography (b) 5.	Designing, 5. Mechanical Lab., 4. Physical Lab., 3. Theory of Structures, 1, 2.	Advanced Geology (b) 5. Designing, 1, 2, 4. Electrical Eng. Lab., 3. Mineralogy, (a) 5, 6.	Dyn. of Mach., 3, 4. Railroad Eng., 2, 5.	Elect. Eng. Lab., 3. Min. Lab. (a), 5. Metall. Lab. (b), 5. Th. of Structures, 1, 2. Thermo. Lab. 4.	Do
	12	Machine Design, 3, (a) 4 Metallurgy, 5, 6.	Designing, 5. Mech. Lab., 4. Physical Lab., 3.	Designing, 4. Electrical Eng. Lab., 3. Municipal Eng., 1, 2, 5.	Desc. Elect. Eng. 1, 2, 3, 4, 5.	Elect. Eng. Lab., 3. Min. Lab (a) 5. Metall. Lab. (b), 5. Th. of Structures, 1, 2. Thermo. Lab. 4.	Do
	2 to 5	Chemical Lab., 5, 6. Designing, 1, 2, 3, 4.	Chem Lab, 6. Mech. Lab. 4. Mining Lab. (a), 5. Petrog. Lab. (b), 5. Physical Lab., 3. Testing Lab., 1, 2.	Chemical Lab, (a) 5, 6. Electrical Eng. Lab. . 3 Fire Assay Lab., (b) 5. Hydraulic Lab. (b), 1, 2, 4.	Cement Lab., 1, 2, Chemistry, 6. Designing, 4. Hyd. Lab. (a) 5. Testing Lab., 1, 2. 3.	Chemical Lab., 6. Elect. Lab. (a), 3. Graphics, 1, 2. Metall. Lab. (b), 5. Min. Lab. (a), 5. Phys. Lab. (b), 3. Thermo. Lab., 4.	

(a) First Term. (b) Second Term. (c) First half of first Term. (d) Second half of first Term. 1. Architectural Students. 2. Civil Engineering Students. 3. Electrical Engineering Students. 4. Mechanical Engineering Students. 5. Mining Engineering Students. 6. Practical Chemistry Students.

Faculty of Law.

THE PRINCIPAL : Ex Officio.

PROFESSORS EMERITI.

MATTHEW HUTCHINSON, D.C.L.
HON. J. EMERY ROBIDOUX, D.C.L.
HON. MR. JUSTICE WÜRTELE, D.C.L.

PROFESSORS.

F. P. WALTON, B.A. (Oxon.), LL.B. (Edin.), Gale Professor of Roman Law, and Dean of the Faculty.
HON. C. A. GEOFFRION, Q. C., D.C.L., P.C. ⎫
A. McGOUN, M.A., B.C.L. ⎪
T. FORTIN, LL.L., D.C.L. ⎬ Professors of Civil Law.
HON. MR. JUSTICE DOHERTY, D.C.L. ⎪
W. DE M. MARLER, B.A., D.C.L. ⎭
E. LAFLEUR, B.A., B.C.L., Professor of International Law.
HON. MR. JUSTICE DAVIDSON, D.C.L., Professor of Criminal Law.
D. MACMASTER, Q.C., D.C.L., Professor of Commercial Law.
The above constitute the Faculty.

LECTURERS.

P. C. RYAN, B.C.L.
AIME GEOFFRION, B.C.L.
GORDON W. MACDOUGALL, B.C.L.

The Curriculum extends over three years. It includes courses of lectures upon all the branches of the Law of the Province of Quebec, and also upon Roman Law, Legal History, and the Constitutional Law of the Empire and of the Dominion. Its primary design is to afford a comprehensive legal education for Students who intend to practise at the Bar of Lower Canada. In all the courses the attention of Students will be directed to the sources of the Law, and to its historical development. During their first year the students will attend a course of one hundred lectures on Roman Law, from which the Law of the Province is in great part derived. In the lectures on Legal History the relations of our Law with the Law of France and its History since the Cession will be explained. First Year Students will also attend courses on the Law of Persons; the Law of Real Estate; the Law of Obligations; the Law of Successions, Ab-intestate and Testamentary; and the Elementary rules of Procedure. The remaining branches of the law, civil, commercial and criminal, will be dealt with in the Second and Third Years. During the three years' course the civil code, the criminal code and the code of civil procedure will be covered and lectures will also be given upon subjects such as Bills of Exchange, Merchant Shipping, and Banking, which are regulated mainly by special statutes.

Students have the free use of the Law Library of the Faculty. This includes the law libraries of the late F. Griffin, Esq., Q.C., Mr. Chancellor Day, Mr. Justice MacKay and Mr. Justice Torrance. Many new books have been added, and the principal reports and legal periodicals are taken. A special room for Law Students is provided in the Redpath Library. This room is open during the day and in the evenings from eight to ten o'clock.

The lectures are delivered in the rooms furnished for the Faculty in the East Wing of McGill College by its munificent benefactor, W. C. McDonald, Esq. The Faculty desire to impress upon English students the great importance of obtaining a familiar knowledge of French. In the practice of the profession in this Province it is almost indispensable that a lawyer shall be able to write and speak French, and to understand it when it is spoken. Gentlemen who intend to become students of law are urged to pay special attention to this subject. The courses of lectures in the Faculty by Professor Fortin and Mr. Aimé Geoffrion, will be delivered in the French language.

Those students who are able to take the B.A. course before entering upon their legal studies are strongly recommended to do so. Those for whom this is impossible are advised to attend the courses in the Faculty of Arts for two years.

The requirements for Matriculation in the Faculty will be found below in the Faculty Regulations.

SCHOLARSHIPS AND PRIZES.

Various scholarships and prizes will be awarded to the students of each year who obtain the highest distinction at the Examinations in April, 1899.

No scholarship or prize shall, however, be awarded to any student unless in the estimation of the Faculty, a sufficiently high standing be attained to merit it.

CLASSIFICATION OF STUDENTS.

Matriculated Students who do not take the whole course are classed as Partial Students, and are not entitled to proceed to the Degree of B.C.L.

Occasional Students will be admitted for attendance on any particular series of Lectures without matriculation.

Students who have completed their course of three years, and have passed a satisfactory examination, will be entitled, upon the certificate and recommendation of the Faculty, to the Degree of Bachelor of Civil Law.

FACULTY REGULATIONS.

1. Any person desirous of becoming a Matriculated Student may apply to the Secretary of the University for examination and entry in the Register of Matriculation, and may procure a ticket of Matriculation and tickets of admission to the Lectures for each Session of the Course.

2. The Degree of B.A. obtained from any Canadian or other British University; or a certificate of having passed the examination before the Bar for admission to study Law in the Province of Quebec; or

160

the intermediate Examination in the Faculty of Arts in McGill University, will be accepted in lieu of examination for Matriculation in this Faculty. For other candidates the Matriculation Examination this year will be in the following subjects :—

Latin.—Virgil, Aeneid, Book I.; Cicero, Orations I. and II. against Catiline, Latin Grammar.

Candidates will be expected to be able to translate a simple passage at sight.

French.—De Fivas' "Grammaire des Grammaires ;" *Moliere, "Le Bourgeois Gentilhomme"; †Translation into French of Macaulay's Essay on Frederick the Great.

Candidates must be able to translate French easily, and must have some familiarity with the spoken language.

Exercises in Composition and Grammatical Analysis, in English and French.

Mathematics.—Arithmetic; Algebra to the end of Simple Equations; Euclid, Books I., II., III.

History.—White's Outline of Universal History (or any equivalent manual); *Green's Short History of the English People ; Miles' School History of Canada; †Duruy, Histoire de France.

Literature.—*Collier's Biographical History of English Literature ; †Laharpe Course de Littérature ; †Lefranc, Course de Littérature.

Rhetoric.—Whately's Rhetoric ; Blair's Lectures (small edition).

Philosophy.—Whately's Logic; †Logique de Port Royal ; †Cousin. Histoire de la Philosophie ; * Stewart's Outline of Moral Philosophy.

N.B.—The works mentioned above preceded by an asterisk are for English Students only. Those preceded by a cross are for French Students only. The remainder are for both English and French.

The Examination will be held on the first day of the Session at 10 a.m.

3. Students of Law shall be known as of the First, Second and Third Years, and shall be so graded by the Faculty. In each year, Students shall take the studies fixed for that year, and those only, unless by special permission of the Faculty.

4. The register of Matriculation shall be closed on the 1st October in each year, and return thereof shall be immediately made by the Dean to the Registrar of the University. Candidates applying thereafter may be admitted on a special examination to be determined by the Faculty; and, if admitted, their names shall be returned in a supplementary list to the Registrar.

5. Persons desirous of entering as Partial Students shall apply to the Dean of the Faculty for admission as such Students, and shall obtain a ticket or tickets for the class or classes they desire to attend.

6. Students who have attended collegiate courses of legal study in other Universities for a number of terms or sessions may be admitted, on the production of certificates, to a like standing in this University.

7. All students shall be subject to the following regulations for attendance and conduct :—

(a) Gowns must be worn during attendance at lectures and when in the College building.

(b) A class-book shall be kept by each Professor and Lecturer, in which the presence or absence of Students shall be carefully noted, and the Faculty shall, after examination of such class-book, decide which Students shall be deemed to have been sufficiently regular in their attendance to entitle them to proceed to the examination in the respective classes.

(c) Punctual attendance on all the classes proper to his year is required of each student. Professors will note the attendance immediately on the commencement of their lectures, and will omit the names of Students entering thereafter, unless satisfactory reasons are assigned. Absence or tardiness, without sufficient excuse, or inattention or disorder in the Class-room, if persisted in after admonition by the Professor, will be reported to the Dean of the Faculty, who may reprimand the Student or report to the Faculty as he may decide. While in the building, or going to and from it, Students are expected to conduct themselves in the same orderly manner as in the Class-rooms. Any Professor observing improper conduct in the Class-rooms, or elsewhere in the building, will admonish the Student, and, if necessary, report him to the Dean.

(d) When Students are reported to the Faculty under the above rules, the Faculty may reprimand, report to parents or guardians, disqualify from competing for prizes or honours, suspend from classes, or report to the Corporation for expulsion.

(e) Any Student injuring the furniture or building will be required to repair the same at his own expense, and will, in addition, be subject to such penalty as the Faculty may see fit to impose.

(f) The number of times of absence, from necessity or duty, that shall disqualify for the keeping of a Session, shall in each case be determined by the Faculty.

(*g*) All cases of discipline involving the interests of more than one Faculty, or of the University generally, shall be reported to the Principal, or, in his absence, to the Vice-Principal.

8. The College year shall be divided into two terms, the first extending to the Christmas vacation, and the second from the expiration of the Christmas vacation to the end of April following.

The lectures will be delivered between the hours of half-past eight and half-past nine in the morning, and between four and half-past six in the afternoon; and special lectures in the evening, at such hours and in such order as shall be determined by the Faculty. Professors shall have the right to substitute an examination for any such lecture.

9. At the end of each College year there shall be a general examination of all the classes, under the superintendence of the Professors, and of such other examiners as may be appointed by the Corporation. The examination shall be conducted by means of printed questions, answered by the Students in writing in the presence of the Examiners. The result shall be reported as early as possible to the Faculty.

After the examinations, the Faculty shall decide the general standing of the Students.

10. At the end of the third College year there shall be a Final Examination of those students who have completed the Curriculum. This Examination shall be conducted partly by written papers and partly orally. It shall cover all the subjects upon which lectures have been delivered during the three years' course. Those Students who satisfy the examiners shall be entitled, after making the necessary declaration and payment of the Graduation Fee, to proceed to the Degree of B.C.L. The Elizabeth Torrance Gold Medal shall be awarded to the Student who shall obtain the highest marks in the Examination, providing his answers shall, in the estimation of the Faculty, be of sufficient merit to entitle him to this distinction. There shall be no Sessional Examination of Students who are candidates in the Final Examination.

11. No Student shall be considered as having kept a Session unless he shall have attended regularly all the courses of Lectures, and shall have passed the Sessional Examinations to the satisfaction of the Faculty in the classes of his year.

12. The Faculty shall have the power, upon special and sufficient cause shown, to grant a dispensation to any Student from attendance on any particular Course or Courses of Lectures, but no distinction shall in consequence be made between the Examinations of such Students and those of the Students regularly attending Lectures.

13. Every Candidate, before receiving the Degree of B.C.L., shall make the following declaration :—

Ego A.B. polliceor sancteque recipio, me, pro meis viribus, studiosum fore communis hujus Universitatis boni, et operam daturum ut ejus decus et dignitatem promoveam, et officiis omnibus ad Baccalaureatus in Jure Civili gradum pertinentibus fungar.

14. The fees in the Faculty will be as follows for Students matriculating after Nov., 1897:—

Matriculation or Registration Fee...........................$ 5 00
Sessional Fee by Ordinary Students (including Grounds Fee).. 52 00
Grounds Fee, payable by Partial Students................... 2 00
Graduation Fee, including registration as voter in election of
   fellows.............. .... 12 50
Fee for each supplemental examination..................... 5 00
Sessional Fee by Partial Students, for the course of Roman
   Law, $20; for each of the courses on Successions, Criminal
   Law, and Civil Procedure, $15; and for each one of the shorter
   courses............... .... 10 00
Students matriculated before Nov., 1897, will continue to pay a
   Sessional fee of............... .... 36 00

Matriculation and Sessional Fees must be paid on or before Oct. 1st; and, if not so paid, the Student in default shall incur a fine of $3; his name shall be removed from the books; and his attendance at lectures shall not be credited until his fees and the said fine have been paid. Students already on the books of the University shall not be required to pay any Matriculation Fee.

15. Partial Students may be admitted into class on such terms as shall be arranged by the Faculty.

16. The requirements and conditions for obtaining the Degree of D.C.L. in course can be ascertained upon application to the Dean.

SYLLABUS.

Tuesday, 6th September, 1898, Matriculation, Ordinary Lectures begin.

Friday, 9th December. Last day for notice to be sent to Secretary of Section of the Bar by candidates at the January Examinations for admission to study or to practice Law in the Province of Quebec.

Monday, 9th January, 1898. Lectures, Second Term, begin.

Tuesday, 10th January. Bar Examinations take place at Montreal.

Friday, 28th April. Convocation for Degrees in Law.

Saturday, 3rd June. Last day for notice to be sent to Secretàry of Section of the Bar by Candidates at the July Examination for admission to study or to practice Law in the Province of Quebec.
Tuesday, 4th July. Bar Examinations take place at Quebec.

EXAMINATIONS.

The date of the several Examinations will be announced during the session.

APPENDIX.

The attention of intending Students is called to the following provisions of the Revised Statutes of Quebec and amendments, as bearing on the requirements for the study and practice of Law in the Province.

Article 3544 R.S.Q.—Examinations for admission to study and to practice law in the Province of Quebec are held at the time and place determined by the General Council.

The places and dates as at present fixed are :

MONTREAL......Tuesday, 10th Jan., 1899.
QUEBEC..........Tuesday, 4th July, 1899.

and alternately in Montreal and Quebec every six months, namely— at Montreal on the second Tuesday of each January, and at Quebec on the first Tuesday of each July.

All information concerning these examinations can be obtained from the General Secretary's Office. The present General Secretary is Arthur Globensky, Esq., Montreal.

Article 3546.—Candidates must give notice as prescribed by this article at least one month before the time fixed for the examination to the Secretary of the Section in which he resides, or in which he has resided for the last six months.

The present Secretary of the Montreal Section is L. E. Bernard, Esq., New York Life Building, Montreal.

Article 3503a.—Added by Statute of Quebec, 53 Victoria (1890), Cap. 45, provides that Candidates holding the diploma of Bachelor of Arts, Bachelier-es-Lettres, or Bachelier-es-Science from a Canadian or other British University are dispensed from the examination for admission to study. Such Candidates are required to give the notice mentioned above.

Article 3548 R.S.Q. (as altered by by-law of the General Council). On giving the notice prescribed by Article 3546, the Candidate pays the Secretary a fee of $2, and makes a deposit of $30 for admission to study, or of $70 for admission to practice, which deposit, less $10, is returned in case of his not being admitted.

Article 3552 (amended 1894, Q. 57 Vic., c. 35).—To be admitted to practice, the Student must be a British subject, and must have studied regularly and without interruption during ordinary office hours, under indentures before a Notary as Clerk, or Student with a practicing Advocate, during Four Years, *dating from the registration of the certificate of admission to study.* This term is reduced to Three Years in the case of a student who has followed a regular law course in a University or College in this Province and taken a degree in law therein.

The By-Laws passed by the General Council of the Bar of the Province of Quebec, 16th Sept., 1886, and amended 10th Feb., 1892, provide as follows:—

PROGRAMME FOR UNIVERSITY COURSE OF LECTURES ON LAW.

Art. 42.—A course of lectures on law given and followed at a University or College in this Province, and a diploma or degree conferred on students by such university or college, shall be held to be such as contemplated in art. 3552, R.S.Q., only when the university or college conferring the degree and the student who receives it shall have efficiently followed the programme herein set forth. This article and article 44 shall apply to students already admitted only as regards lectures to be given after the 1st of January, 1887.

2. The subjects on which lectures shall be given, and the number of lectures required on each subject for a regular course of lectures on law in a university or college shall be as follows —:

ROMAN LAW:—103 Lectures.

This subject shall include an introduction to the study of Law and the explanation of and comments on the Institutes of Justinian and the principal jurisconsults of Rome.

CIVIL, COMMERCIAL AND MARITIME LAW:—413 Lectures.

Lectures on these subjects shall cover at least three years. They consist of the history of French and Canadian law, the explanation of and comments on the Civil Code of the Province of Quebec and the Statutes relating to Commerce and Merchant Shipping.   '

CIVIL PROCEDURE:—103 Lectures.

Lectures on this subject shall extend over at least two years. It shall consist of the explanation of and comments on the Code of Civil Procedure and the Statutes amending it, the organisation of the Civil Courts of this Province and the history of the different judicial systems of the country; also, the special modes of procedure provided by statutes and laws of general application.

INTERNATIONAL LAW, Private and Public:—21 Lectures.

CRIMINAL LAW:—69 Lectures.

This subject includes the history of criminal law in Canada, the constitution of criminal courts, criminal procedure, comments on statutes relating to criminal law, the relation of criminal law in Canada to the criminal law of England. The lectures shall extend over two years.

ADMINISTRATIVE AND CONSTITUTIONAL LAW:—41 Lectures.

These subjects include an inquiry into the different political institutions and the public institutions of the country, the powers, organisation and procedure of the Federal Parliament and of the Local Legislature, the laws on Education and the Municipal Code.

Art. 43.—Candidates for practice who hold a degree in law from a university or college in this Province, shall produce, with their notices, a certificate from the principal or Rector of such university or college to the effect that they followed a course of lectures on law in the same, during at least three years, in conformity with the by-laws of the Bar; and such certificate shall further specify the number of public lectures

at which they shall have attended on each subject mentioned
in the foregoing programme, during each of the said three
years. The last part of this certificate shall only be required
for courses of lectures given after the 1st of January, 1897.

Art. 44.—The examiners shall not consider a university degree in law valid for the purposes of admission to the Bar, if
they find that the candidate has not in fact followed the programme above.

REQUIREMENTS FOR DEGREE OF DOCTOR OF CIVIL LAW.

ADOPTED OCTOBER, 1891.

Every Candidate for the degree of D.C.L. in Course must be a Bachelor of Civil Law of twelve years' standing, and must pass such examination for the Degree of D.C.L. as shall be prescribed by the Faculty of Law. He shall also, at least two months before proceeding to the Degree, deliver to the Faculty twenty-five printed copies of a Thesis or Treatise of his own composition on some subject, selected or approved by the Faculty, such Thesis to contain not less than fifty octavo pages of printed matter, and to possess such degree of merit as shall, in the opinion of the Faculty, justify them in recommending him for the degree.

The candidate shall also pay to the Secretary of the Faculty, annually during the period of twelve years, for the retention of his name on the books of the Faculty, a fee of two dollars, to form part of the Library Fund of the Faculty. Upon cause shown, however, and with the consent of the Faculty, such fees may be paid at one time before the granting of the degree.

The Examination for the Degree of D.C.L. in Course, which shall be open to all who have taken the degree of B.C.L. of this University in the past, as well as to such as may take the degree in future, shall, until changed, be on the following subjects and authors, with the requirement of special proficiency in some one of the groups below indicated. In the groups other than the one selected by the Candidate for special proficiency, a thorough acquaintance with two works of each group shall be sufficient, including in all cases the work first mentioned in each group and the first two works in group third.

1. INTERNATIONAL LAW.

Phillimore, International Law.
Hall,   "   "
Wharton, Conflict of Laws.
Savigny's International Law, by Guthrie.
Foelix, Droit International Privé.
Brocher, Droit International Privé.
Dicey on Domicile.
Story, Conflict of Laws.
Maine, Lectures on International Law.

2. ROMAN LAW.

Ortolan's Institutes.
Mommsen's History of Rome.
Roby's Introduction to the Digest.
Muirhead's Roman Law.
Mackenzie's Roman Law.
Savigny's Roman Law in the Middle Agès.
Bryce's Holy Roman Empire.
Institutes of Gaius.
Fustel de Coulanges, La Cité Antique.

3. CONSTITUTIONAL HISTORY AND LAW.

Dicey's Law of the Constitution.
Stubbs, Constitutional History of England.
Hearn, Government of England.
Bagehot, English Constitution.
Franqueville, Gouvernement et Parlement Britanniques.
Gneist, Constitution of England.
Hallam, Constitutional History of England.
May,   "   "   "
Gardiner,   "   "   "
May, Democracy in Europe.
Freeman, Growth of the English Constitution.
Mill, Representative Government.
Bentham, Fragment on Government.
Maine, Popular Government.

4. CONSTITUTION OF CANADA AND WORKS
RELEVANT THERETO.

Todd, Parliament Government in the British Colonies.
Bourinot, Federal Government in Canada.
Doutre, Constitution of Canada.
Cartwright, Cases under the British North America Act.
Lord Durham's Report on British North America.
Lareau, Histoire du Droit Canadian.
Houston's Constitutional Documents of Canada.
Volume O., Statutes of Lower Canada.
Masères' Collection of Quebec Commissions.
Laferrière, Essai sur l'Histoire du Droit Français.
Dilke, Problems of Greater Britain.
Matthews (Jehu), A Colonist on the Colonial Question.
Bryce, American Commonwealth.
Curtis, History of the Constitutional of the United States.
Cooley, Principles of Constitutional Law.

5. CRIMINAL LAW, JURISPRUDENCE, AND POLITICAL SCIENCE.

Stephens, History of the Criminal Law.
Blackstone, Vol. IV.
Harris, Principles of Criminal Law.
Pike, History of Crime.
Holland, Elements of Jurisprudence.
Austin, Lectures, omitting chapters on Utilitarianism.
Lorimer's Institutes.
Amos, Science of Law.
Woolsey, Political Ethics.
Lieber, Political Ethics.
Freeman, Comparative Politics.
Aristotle's Politics, by Jowett.

COURSES IN THE FACULTY OF LAW FOR 1898-99.

ROMAN LAW.

Professor Walton.

The course will consist of about one hundred lectures. During the first part the external history of the law from the early period to the codification of Justinian, will be dealt with. The sources of the law will be described, and the gradual evolution explained, by which the law of the city of Rome became fitted to be the law of the civilized world. A brief sketch will be given of the legal institutions of Rome in the first period and of the early constitutional history.

In the doctrinal part of the course matters mainly of antiquarian interest will be touched only slightly. Those portions of the Roman Law which have been followed most closely in the existing law of the Province, e. g. Things, Servitudes, Pignus and Hypothec, Contracts, Obligations, will be treated in detail, and the modifications made by the modern law will be noticed. Class-examinations will be held from time to time, and a first and second prize of books will be given to the two students who obtain the highest marks in these examinations.

Text-book, Moyle's or Sandar's Institutes of Justinian.
Books of Reference.
Maine's Ancient Law.
Muirhead's Historical Introduction to Roman Law.
Muirhead's Institutes of Gaius.
Maynz, Cours de Droit Romain.
Puchta, Institutionen.

CONSTITUTIONAL LAW.

Professor Walton.

This subject will be divided into two courses of about twenty lectures each.

Part I. will consist of a sketch of the Constitutional Law of the British Empire. The subject will be considered in the following order: (1) the executive power; (2) the legislative power; (3) the rights and liberties of the subject. Under (1) the power of the sovereign, of the Privy Council, of the great officers of state, and of Parliament, will be discussed. Under (2) the process of legislation in the Imperial Parliament will be explained. Under (3) will fall the right to trial by jury, Habeas Corpus, and the constitutional limitations of the power of the Crown. Afterwards the following topics among others will be dealt with. Liability, Civil and Criminal, of Governors of Colonies, Naval and Military officers, and of Judges for their official conduct.

After treating of the actual law of the constitution the "conventions of the constitution" will be taken up. Under this head will fall a description of the history and functions of the Cabinet, of the means of adjusting differences between the Sovereign and the two Houses, and between the two Houses themselves, and of the kind of circumstances, under which it is usual for ministers to resign. If time permits the course will conclude with a comparison of the British Constitution with the Constitution of the United States.

Part I. will be given to First Year Students. No text-book is prescribed, but students are recommended to refer to Dicey, Law of the Constitution; Anson, Law and Custom of the Constitution; and Bagehot, The English Constitution.

Part II. will not be delivered this year. It will consist of a sketch of the Constitution of Canada.

LEGAL HISTORY AND BIBLIOGRAPHY.

Professor McGoun.

This course comprises an outline of the history of the law in force in the Province of Quebec.

The main sources from which this law are derived are the Customary Law of France, as modified by the principles of Roman Law as embodied in several of the codes or collections of Roman Law before the time of Justinian. The Customs of France after being reduced to writing, were further modified by the influence of modern Roman Law, which prevailed throughout the larger part of France. The ordinances of the French kings and the commentaries of the great jurists from Cujas and Dumoulin down to Pothier brought the Civil Law of France into the systematic form into which it was introduced into this Province. The custom of Paris, one of the most important of those recognized in France, became formally the basis of the Civil Law in this country, and the ordinance of 1667 was the main authority for procedure.

Since the opening of the British régime the development of Lower Canadian Civil Law has proceeded independently of the Civil Law of France, where the Code Napoléon was passed early in the Century. In Lower Canada a code on the same lines was adopted shortly before the Confederation. Lower Canadian Law has been modified by English law in commercial matters, and also by statutes passed in the Province. Criminal Law, on the other hand, has been derived almost exclusively from the Criminal Law of England.

The leading authorities upon the main branches of the law with the reports of decisions of our courts, are brought under the attention of the students in this course.

LAW OF CORPORATIONS AND OF JOINT STOCK COMPANIES.

Professor McGoun.

This course is the sequel on the one hand, of the course on Agency and Partnership, with which it is closely connected, by reason of the facilities given in the Incorporation of Companies to the undertaking of important enterprises, by a species of partnership or association between individuals upon a larger scale than can be undertaken in a simple partnership. The doctrine of limited liability and the opportunity which it affords for carrying out enterprises of great importance, with combinations of capital derived from a large number of individuals, is treated of in this course. On the other hand, the growth of Corporations, both those established by long custom, and those created by Royal Charter, or by Parliamentary or Legislative authority, is also explained, and the relation between these corporations and the ordinary forms of joint stock companies. Corporations sole and Corporations aggregate are defined, and the principles of laws relating to Corporations and Companies explained, and the authors who treat of these principles, and who trace the limits of the powers and authority of such corporations, are brought under the notice of the students.

CRIMINAL LAW.

Professor Mr. Justice Davidson.

This course includes:—

A history of the Criminal Law and Criminal Procedure of England; and of their introduction into and development throughout Canada;

Discussion of the Criminal Code and other Statutes enacting criminal offences; of the rules of evidence in criminal cases, of the Fugitive Offenders Act; of extradition, and generally of the principal features belonging to the Criminal Law of the Dominion.

COMMERCIAL LAW.

Professor Macmaster.

The course on carriers will cover:

1. Carriers: contracts with:
   (a) Affreightment.
   (b) Merchant Shipping.
   (c) Bottomry and Respondentia.

The course on Insurance will cover:

2. Insurance contracts of:
   (a) Marine Insurance.
   (b) Fire Insurance.
   (c) Life Insurance.

CIVIL PROCEDURE.

Mr. Percy C. Ryan.

The advanced course for the Second and Third Years covers all matters of procedure not dealt with in the First Year Course, and includes Provisional Remedies, such as capias, attachment before judgment, injunction, etc., and special proceedings, such as proceedings relating to corporations and public offices, mandamus, etc., as well as the rules of pleading in the more complicated classes of action. It will be divided into two parts, one of which will be taken in each alternate year.

CIVIL PROCEDURE.

Mr. Gordon W. Macdougall.

This course to the students of the First Year is intended to form an introduction to the subject, to explain the simpler kinds of actions, the general rules of pleading, and the jurisdiction of the several courts.

The revised Code of Civil Procedure for the Province of Quebec is the text-book.

PRESCRIPTION AND LEASE.

Professor Fortin.

Two courses.

SUCCESSIONS.

Professor Mr. Justice Doherty.

The Law of Succession.

The course consists of a commentary and explanation of the whole of Title I., and the third Chapter of Title II.of the Third Book of the Civil Code. The order followed by the Code in dealing with the different matters, coming within the scope of this course, has however been departed from with a view to presenting to the Student the Law governing successions as one whole. The subject will be developed as nearly as possible in the following order :—

1. General notions, definitions and divisions of the subject. The Testamentary Succession. The Ab-Intestate Succession.

2. Rules of Law common to both Successions.

3. Rules peculiar to the Testamentary Succession.

4. Rules peculiar to the Ab-Intestate Succession.

5. Partition of the Succession (and of property held in undivided ownership generally), its incidents and effects.

OBLIGATIONS.

Mr. Aimé Geoffrion.

This course of lectures will consist of a commentary on the title on obligations in the Civil Code, less the chapter of proof articles 982 to 1,202 inclusive. Our law on the subject will be compared with the old French law and the modern French law; and its general principles will be explained and illustrated. In the second year course some of the more difficult parts of the subject will be taken up more minutely and lectures will be given on the law of evidence.

REAL RIGHTS REGISTRATION AND NOTARIAL LAW.

Professor Marler.

Two courses.

PUBLIC INTERNATIONAL LAW.

Professor Lafleur.

Sovereignty and equality of Independent States. Recognition of Belligerency and Independence. Justifiable grounds of intervention. Modes of territorial ac quisition. Territorial boundaries. Doctrine of Exterritoriality. Treaties and Arbitrations. Laws of War. Neutrality of States and of individuals. Laws of Blockade. Contraband. Confiscation. Prize-Courts and their jurisprudence.

N.B.—The students' attention will be specially directed to Treaties, Diplomatic Relations, and International Arbitrations, in which Canada is directly concerned.

PRIVATE INTERNATIONAL LAW.

Professor Lafleur.

Distinction between the *a priori* and positive methods. Sources of the positive law of Quebec on the subjects. Application and illustration of the rules for solving conflicts of law in regard to the different titles of the Civil Code. Comparisons between our jurisprudence and that of England, France, and Germany.

Note.—The Hon. Mr. Justice Hall has kindly consented to deliver a lecture in the Faculty, upon a day to be afterwards fixed in the early part of next session.

TIME TABLE.

FIRST YEAR STUDENTS, 1898-99.

TUESDAY, 6TH SEPT., TO FRIDAY, 4TH NOV., 9 WEEKS.

HOURS.	MONDAY	TUESDAY.	WEDNESDAY.	THURSDAY.	FRIDAY.
8.30	Succession. Prof. Mr. Justice Doherty.	Procedure. Mr. Gordon Macdougall.	Succ.	Procedure.	Succ.
4.00	Roman Law. The Dean.	Rom.	Rom.	Rom.	Rom.
5.00	Legal History. Prof. McGoun.	Persons. Prof. Lafleur.	Hist.	Persons.	Hist.

N.B.—The lectures on Successions will not commence till Mon. 19 Sept.

MONDAY, 7TH NOV., TO FRIDAY, 16TH DEC., 6 WEEKS.

HOURS.	MONDAY.	TUESDAY.	WEDNESDAY.	THURSDAY.	FRIDAY.
8.30	Succ.	Procedure.	Succ.	Proced.	Succ.
4.00	Rom.	Rom.	Rom.	Rom.	Rom.
5.00	Real Rights. Prof. Marler.	Persons. 2 wks. Obligations. 3 wks. Mr. A. Geoffrion	Real Rights.	Persons. 2 wks. Obligations. 3 wks.	Real Rights.

CHRISTMAS.

MONDAY, 9TH JAN., TO FRIDAY, 10TH MARCH, 9 WEEKS.

HOURS.	MONDAY.	TUESDAY.	WEDNESDAY.	THURSDAY.	FRIDAY.
8.30	Succ. 5 wks.	Const. The Dean.	Succ.	Const.	Succ.
4.00	Rom.	Rom.	Rom.	Rom.	Rom.
5.00	Obligations. 7 wks.		Obligations.		Obligations.

MONDAY, 13TH MARCH, TO FRIDAY, 31ST MARCH, 3 WEEKS.

HOURS.	MONDAY.	TUESDAY.	WEDNESDAY.	THURSDAY.	FRIDAY.
8.30					
4.00	Rom.	Const.	Rom.	Const.	Rom.
5 00	Criminal Law. Prof. Mr. Justice Davidson.	Crim.	Crim.		Crim.

Roman Law	100 lectures.	Procedure	25 lectures.	
Succession	50 "	Obligations	25 "	
Legal History	25 "	Criminal	10 "	
Persons	25 "			
Real Rights	25 "	Total	285	

TIME TABLE.

SECOND AND THIRD YEAR STUDENTS.

TUESDAY, 6TH SEPT., TO FRIDAY, 4TH NOV., 9 WEEKS.

HOURS.	MONDAY.	TUESDAY.	WEDNESDAY.	THURSDAY.	FRIDAY.
8.30	Obligations. Mr. A. Geoffrion		Obl.		Obl.
4.00	Prescription. Prof. Fortin.		Pres.		Pres.
5.00	Criminal Law. Prof. Mr. Justice Davidson.	Carriers. Prof. Macmaster	Crim.	Carr.	Crim.

MONDAY, 7TH NOV., TO FRIDAY, 16TH DEC., 6 WEEKS.

HOURS.	MONDAY.	TUESDAY.	WEDNESDAY.	THURSDAY.	FRIDAY.
8.30	Civ. Procedure Mr. RYan.		C. P.		C. P.
4.00	Lease. Prof. Fortin.		Lease.		Lease.
5.00	Criminal.	Carriers.	Crim.	Carr.	Crim.

MONDAY, 9TH JAN., TO FRIDAY, 10TH MARCH, 9 WEEKS.

HOURS.	MONDAY.	TUESDAY.	WEDNESDAY.	THURSDAY.	FRIDAY.
8.30	C. P.	Corporations. Prof. McGoun.	C. P.	Corp.	C. P.
4.00	Roman Law of Succession. Dean. 3 weeks. Real Rights and Registration. Prof. Marler. 6 weeks.	Rom.	Rom. R. R.	Rom.	Rom. R. R.
5.00	Pub. Internat. Law. Prof. Lafleur.	Insurance. Prof. Macmaster	P. I. L.	Ins.	P. I. L.

MONDAY, 13TH MARCH, TO FRIDAY, 31ST MARCH, 3 WEEKS.

HOURS.	MONDAY.	TUESDAY.	WEDNESDAY.	THURSDAY.	FRIDAY.
8.30	Corp.		Corp.		Corp.
4.00	R. R.		R. R.		R. R.
5.00	Insurance.		Ins.		Ins.

Corporations .... 25 lectures.
Real Rights .... 25 "
Prescription .... 25 "
Lease...................... 15 "
Criminal.................. 40 "
Carriers .... 25 "
Insurance................. 25 "

Obligations .... 25 lectures.
International .... 25 "
Precedure................. 40 "
Roman .... 15 "

Total............. 285

Faculty of Medicine.

THE PRINCIPAL (*ex-officio.*)

Professors.

WRIGHT,	STEWART,	ADAMI,
MACCALLUM,	WILKINS,	BIRKETT,
CRAIK,	PENHALLOW,	ALLOWAY,
GIRDWOOD,	MILLS,	FINLEY,
RODDICK,	CAMERON,	LAFLEUR,
GARDNER,	BLACKADER,	ARMSTRONG,
SHEPHERD,	RUTTAN,	JOHNSTON.
BULLER,	BELL,	

Dean.—R. CRAIK, M.D., LL.D.

Registrar.—R. F. RUTTAN, B.A., M.D., F.R.S.Can.

Librarian.—F. G. FINLEY, B.A., M.D.

Director of Museum.—J. G. ADAMI, M.A., M.D., F.R.S. (EDIN.)

The Sixty-sixth Session of this Faculty will be opened on Tuesday, September 20th, 1898, by an introductory lecture at 3 p.m. The regular lectures in all subjects will begin on September 21st, at the hours specified in the time-table, and will be continued until May, 26th, 1899, when the annual examinations will begin.

The Medical School of McGill University was founded in 1822 as the "Montreal Medical Institution," by Drs. W. Robertson, W. Caldwell, A. F. Holmes, J. Stephenson and H. P. Loedel—all of them at the time members of the staff of the Montreal General Hospital.

Although founded in 1822, yet no session of the "Medical Institution" was held until 1824, when it opened with 25 students; in 1844, the number of students in the Faculty was 50; in 1851, 64, with 15 graduates ; in 1872-73, 154, with 35 graduates ; in 1892-93, 315, with 46 graduates ; in 1894-95, 403, with 54 graduates ; in 1895-96, 419, with 90 graduates.

There were no sessions held during the political troubles from 1836 to 1839, and it is owing to this fact that the present is the 66th session of the Faculty. This is in reality the 69th session of the school, which is the direct continuation of the " Montreal Medical Institution."

In 1828, the " Medical Institution " was recognized by the Governors of the Royal Institution as the Medical Faculty of McGill University. At this time the lectures were given in a building on the site of the present Bank of Montreal. Later the school was removed to a brick building still standing near the corner of Craig and St. George streets.

In 1846, the lectures of the Faculty were given in the present central building of the University now occupied by the Faculty of Arts. On account of the inconvenience arising from the distance of the University buildings from the centre of the city, it was decided in 1850, to erect a Medical school building in Coté Street, provided with ample accommodation for Library and Museum, and furnished with a large dissecting-room and two lecture rooms ; this building was occupied for the first time during the session 1851-52, and sufficed for the wants of the Faculty until 1872-73, when the present main building was provided by the Governors of the University.

In 1885, the building in the University grounds, erected by the Governors for the use of this Faculty, was found inadequate. A new building was then added, which, at the time, afforded ample facilities for carrying out the great aim of the Faculty,—that of making the teaching of the primary branches thoroughly practical.

Owing to the larger classes and the necessity of thorough laboratory teaching, the Lecture Rooms and Laboratories added in 1885, soon became insufficient in size and equipment to meet the requirements of the Faculty.

The late Mr. John H. R. Molson, with timely generosity came to the aid of the Faculty and in 1893, purchased property adjoining the college grounds and enabled the Faculty to erect new buildings and extensively alter and improve those already in use.

These buildings were completed and officially opened by His Excellency, the Earl of Aberdeen, visitor of the University, January 8th, 1895.

As will be seen on reference to the architect's plans in the special Calendar of the Medical Faculty, the new buildings have been erected as an extension of the old ones, towards the northwest, partially facing Carlton road, and convenient to the Royal Victoria Hospital. They connect the Pathological building acquired in 1893, with the older buildings and comprise a large modern lecture room, capable of accommodating 450 students, with adjoining preparation-rooms and new suites of laboratories for Pathology, Physiology, Histology, Pharmacology and Sanitary Science. The laboratories, etc., in the older buildings, have been greatly enlarged and improved ; the whole of the second floor has been devoted to the department of anatomy, and consists of dissecting-room, anatomical museum and bone-room, preparation rooms, Professors' and Demonstrators' rooms, and a special Lecture Room.

On the ground floor the Library and Museum have been greatly enlarged; a room forming part of the Library has been furnished as a reading room for the use of students, where the extensive reference library of the Faculty may be consulted.

On this floor are situated also the Faculty room, the Registrar's office, the special museum for Obstetrics and Gynæcology, together with Professors' rooms, etc. The chemical laboratories have been increased by including the laboratories formerly used by the department of Physiology.

In the basement are placed the janitor's apartments, cloak rooms with numerous large lockers, the Lavatory, etc., recently furnished with the most modern sanitary fittings.

Through the great liberality of Lord Strathcona and Mount Royal in founding the "Leanchoil Endowment," and of the citizens of Montreal and Medical Graduates in subscribing to the " Campbell Memorial Fund," the Faculty has been enabled to conduct and maintain the teaching of the different branches in a high state of efficiency.

The Faculty is glad to be able to announce that, by the liberality of Lord Strathcona and Mount Royal in endowing the chairs of Pathology and Sanitary Science with one hundred thousand dollars, it is able to establish these departments on a footing fully commensurate with their importance and with the advances and requirements of modern medical science.

The attention of Practitioners is called to the Post Graduate and advanced courses established in 1896 in the hospitals and laboratories connected with the Faculty of Medicine. (See page 211.)

Lecture Rooms.

In the buildings now occupied by the Faculty, as will be seen by reference to the diagrams, in addition to the laboratories, dissecting room, etc., there are three large lecture rooms, two capable of comfortably seating about 300 students, and one for general lectures, examinations, etc., capable of seating 450 students. These theatres are well ventilated and lighted by electricity, as indeed is the entire building. The seats are numbered and a lecture room ticket securing a seat for the session is given each student on enregistering and paying the sessional fee.

Rooms for Students Use.

Three cloak rooms are provided in convenient portions of the building and in addition commodious lockers can be procured at a nominal rental. A large well lighted reading-room containing newspapers, magazines and the current medical journals, is provided in the new block, and is managed by the students themselves. The original library has been refitted as a reading-room for students desiring to avail themselves of the reference works in the library of the Faculty.

Dissecting Room.

The Dissecting Room, which is situated on the second floor, is L shaped, one arm of which is 76 feet in length and 31 feet in breadth and the other arm 45 by 32 feet. It is supplied with thirty dissecting tables and over 200 specially constructed lockers, and is well lighted for work during the day and night.

In connection with the dissecting room, there is a Bone room, and Anatomical Museum where students have an excellent opportunity of studying osteology, frozen sections, anatomical models and dry preparations. In connection with the bone room is a small but well arranged museum of comparative osteology. There are also rooms for the demonstrators of anatomy.

Physiological Laboratories.

The new Physiological Laboratories, which are situated on the upper floor of the new building, are supplied with the most modern apparatus for the practical teaching of this most important branch of the medical curriculum. They consist of one large room forty-five by thirty-five feet for undergraduate work and two smaller ones for more advanced work and private research. In addition there is a room set apart for a consulting library and for the special use of the Professor of this department. The Students' laboratory is arranged in such a way as to permit of students assisting at, and taking part in demonstrations.

Histological Laboratories.

The Histological Laboratory proper, is a large, well lighted room on the second floor of the new building. It is so arranged that over eighty students can be present at the microscopical demonstrations. It is supplied with 50 microscopes. Students are given special facilities for studying and making themselves thoroughly acquainted with the specimens that are the subjects of demonstration. In addition to the students' laboratory there is a smaller laboratory adjoining for the use of the professor and demonstrators and for special work.

Pharmacological Laboratory.

The Pharmacological Laboratory is a large room 45 by 35 feet, situated on the second floor of the new building and is now furnished with the necessary appliances for the practical teaching of pharmacology. In this room is placed a teaching museum of drugs and pharmaceutical preparations arranged according to their physiological action, and tables arranged for teaching dispensing and the preparation of medicines.

Chemical Laboratory.

The Chemical Laboratory is large, lofty, and lighted, from three sides. It can accommodate comfortably 124 men, but only a much smaller number are allowed to work at one time. Each student, when entering on this course, has a numbered table in the laboratory assigned to him for his use during the session. Each table has its own gas and water fixtures, and is provided with shelves for its corresponding set of reagent-bottles, as well as a drawer and locker containing set of chemical apparatus especially adapted for the work. This apparatus is provided by the Faculty, and supplied to each student without extra charge. The student is only required to pay for apparatus broken or destroyed.

The laboratory is ventilated by an electric fan and fully equipped for the various courses of study giving the student unsurpassed advantages for acquiring a sound and practical knowledge of medical chemistry.

Pathological Laboratories.

A large building of three stories, 47 by 40 feet, adjoining the College, recently acquired by the Faculty, thanks to the generosity of the late Mr. J. H. R. Molson, constitutes the Pathological Laboratory ; it has undergone extensive alterations to fit it for the purpose. The uppermost floor has been converted into a work-room for the osteologist and curator ; the second floor is one large laboratory for classwork in Practical Pathology and Bacteriology; upon the floor beneath, are two laboratories for research, a preparation room, professor's private room and library, and culture rooms ; while upon the ground floor are rooms for the attendant, for storage and for keeping animals.

I.

MATRICULATION.

I. Regulations of the Faculty of Medicine of McGill University.

Every Student before he can be enregistered as an undergraduate in Medicine, must present a certificate of having passed the Matriculation Examination of the Faculty of Medicine or Arts of this University, or of having passed some State or University examination accepted by this University.

Graduates in Arts of any recognized university and those who have passed the Entrance Examination of a Provincial Medical Council and thus become enregistered students in medicine of a province in Canada, are exempt from further preliminary examination.

Students from the United States who have passed a State or University examination fully equivalent to that required by this University, may at the discretion of the Faculty be admitted to study without further examination.

The Matriculation Examination of this University for Medicine is held twice each year, in May or June and September, at the same time as that for Arts and Science. The fee for this examination is five dollars payable on application to the Secretary of the University, W. Vaughan.

Papers for the spring examinations will be sent to local centres on application to the Acting Secretary. An additional fee of four dollars, to meet local expenses, will be charged for such examination.

The September examinations are held just before the lectures in Medicine begin. These are held in McGill College, Montreal, only, and at these examinations alternative books in Classics will be accepted.

The subjects for examination are Classics, Mathematics and English, and one of the optional subjects as below.

COMPULSORY SUBJECTS.

Examinations begin on May 29th, 1899, in McGill College and local centres; and on September 15th, 1898, in McGill College only.

Latin.—Cæsar, Bell. Gall. Books I. and II.; Virgil, Aeneid, Book I., and Latin Grammar.

In both Greek (when taken as an optional subject) and Latin, translation at sight and prose composition (sentences or easy narrative, based upon the prescribed prose text), will be required.

At the September examination, other works in Greek or Latin equivalent to those specified may be accepted, if application be made to the Secretary of the Examining board at least a fortnight before the day of examination.

Mathematics.—Arithmetic, Elementary rules, Vulgar and Decimal Fractions, Proportion, Percentage, Simple interest, etc. Square root, and a knowledge of the Metric System; Algebra, Elementary rules, Fractions, Factors, Equation of the First Degree, Indices, Surds and easy Quadratics ; Problems leading to equations; Euclid's Elements, Books I., II., III., with easy deductions.

English.—Writing from Dictation. Grammar—A paper on English Grammar, including Analysis. The candidate will be expected to show a good knowledge of accidence, as treated in any grammar prepared for the higher forms of schools. A similar statement applies to *grammatical* Analysis, in which the nomenclature used by Mason will be preferred. The complete English Grammar published in Sonnenschein's Parallel Grammar Series may be regarded as giving the minimum amount of information expected. English History—Candidates will be required to give the chief details of leading events. While any text-book written for the upper forms of schools may be used in preparation for the examination, Gardiner's Outline of English History (Longman's) is recommended. Composition—Candidates will write a short essay on a subject given at the time of the examination. Shakespeare's Richard II., ed· Deighton (Macmillan), and Scott's Lady of the Lake, ed. Stuart (Macmillan).

OPTIONAL SUBJECTS.

(One only of these subjects is required.)

1. *French.*—Grammar up to the beginning of Syntax. An easy translation from French into English, and from English into French ; Dictation or similar exercise. Candidates are expected to be able to write French without gross mistakes in spelling or grammar, special credit will be given for evidence of familiarity with the spoken language.

2. *German.*—The first eighty pages of Joynes' German reader (or equivalent amount) together with German accidence and translation into German as in the First Part of Vandersmissen's German Grammar (or equivalent amount).

3. *Greek.*—Xenophon, Anabasis, Book I.; Greek Grammar.

4. *Chemistry.*—(As in Remsen's Elements of Chemistry, pages 1 to 160) *and Physics* (Gage, Introduction to Physical Science).

Candidates who at the examination for Associate in Arts have passed in the above subjects are admitted as Undergraduates.

Candidates who fail in one or more subjects at the June examination, or who have taken part only of the examination and present themselves again in the following September, will be exempted from examination in those subjects only in which the Examiners may have reported them as specially qualified.

Ontario Candidates.—At the June examination as well as the September one, candidates from Ontario may present an equivalent amount from the books prescribed for the Junior Matriculation Examination of the University of Toronto.

The Junior Leaving Examination accepted by the Universities of Ontario is accepted by the Faculty of Arts for those who purpose taking the double course of Arts and Medicine, in so far as the subjects of their programme satisfy the Examiners of the Faculty, *i.e.*, when the subjects taken are the same as, or equivalent to, those required in McGill University.

A. *Matriculation Examination for those who wish to obtain a license to practice in England, India, or any other British Possession (Canada excepted.)*

The Matriculation Examination in Medicine of this University, as described above, is accepted by the General Medical Council of Great Britain and Ireland. Graduates of this University desiring to enregister in England are thus exempted from any examination in preliminary education on production of the McGill Matriculation certificate together with a certificate that all the subjects of this Examination were passed at one time. Certificates of this University for attendance on lectures are also accepted by the General Medical Council.

B. *Matriculation Examination for those who wish to obtain a license to practice in the Province of Quebec.*

No University Matriculation Examination is accepted by the College of Physicians and Surgeons of this Province. Graduates in Arts of any British or Canadian University are however exempted from examination, on presentation of their Diplomas.

Those who pass the Preliminary Examination described below, or Graduates in Arts who enregister as students in the C. P. & S., Quebec, *on beginning their studies in Medicine,*

obtain on graduating from McGill University, a license to
Practice in Quebec without further examination in any professional subject.

The requirements for this examination:

LATIN.—Cæsar's 'Commentaries, Bks. I., II., III., IV. and
V.—Virgil's Aeneid, Bks. I. and II.—The Odes of
Horace, Bk. I., with a sound knowledge of the
Grammar of the Language.

ENGLISH.—For *English-speaking* candidates.—A critical know-
ledge of one of Shakspere's plays, viz., Twelfth
Night, for 1898, with English Grammar, as in Dr.
Smith or Mason.

For *French-speaking* candidates.—Translation into
French of passages from the first eight Books of
Washington Irving's Life of Columbus, with questions of Grammar. Translation into English of
extracts from Fénélon's Télémaque.

FRENCH.—For *French-speaking* candidates.—A critical knowledge of Molière's Le Bourgeois Gentilhomme, Fénélon's Aventures de Télémaque and La Fontaine's
Fables, Books I., II., III., with questions of Grammar and Analysis.

For *English-speaking* candidates.—Translation into
English of passages from Fénélon's Télémaque, with
questions of Grammar. Translations into French of
easy English extracts.

BELLES LETTRES AND RHETORIC.—Principles of the subject as
in Haven's Rhetoric, or Boyd's Rhetoric and Literary Criticism. History of the Literature of the
age of Pericles in Greece, of Augustus in Rome, and
of the 17th and 18th centuries of England and France.

HISTORY.—Outlines of the History of Greece and Rome, with
particular knowledge of the History of Britain,
France and Canada.

GEOGRAPHY.—A general view, with particular knowledge of
Britain, France and North America.

ARITHMETIC.—Must include Vulgar and Decimal Fractions, Simple and Compound Proportion, Interest and Percentages, and Square Root.

ALGEBRA.—Must include Fractions and Simultaneous Equations of the First Degree.

GEOMETRY.—Euclid, Books I., II., III. and VI., or the portion of plane Geometry covered by those Books. Also the measurement of the lines, surfaces and volumes, of regular geometrical figures.

CHEMISTRY.—Outlines of the subject as in Remsen's Elements of Chemistry.

BOTANY.—Outlines as in Gray's "How plants grow."

PHYSICS.—Outlines as in Peck-Ganot's Physics.

PHILOSOPHY.—Elements of Logic as in Jevon's Logic ; Elements of Philosophy, as in Professor Murray's Hand-book.

The Examinations will be held in September, 1898, at Quebec, and in June, 1899, at Montreal. (See almanac at front of this Calendar for exact date of examinations.) Applications to be made to Dr. A. T. Brosseau, Montreal, or Dr. Belleau, Quebec, either of whom will furnish schedule giving text books and percentage of marks required to pass in each subject.

Examination Fee, twenty dollars. Should the candidate be unsuccessful, one half of the fee will be returned.

Of the four years' study *after* having passed the Matriculation Examination, three six months' sessions, at least, must be attended at a University, College, or Incorporated School of Medicine, recognized by the " Provincial Medical Board." The first session must be attended during the year immediately succeeding the Matriculation. Examination, and the final session must be in the fourth year.

C. *To obtain a license to Practice in Ontario.*

Every one desirous of being registered as a matriculated medical student in the register of this College, except as hereinafter provided, must present to the Registrar the official

certificate of having passed the " Departmental Pass Arts
Matriculation Examination," and in addition Physics and
Chemistry—whereupon he shall be entitled to be so registered upon the payment of twenty dollars and giving proof of
his identity.

Graduates in Arts, in any University in Her Majesty's
dominions, are not required to pass this examination, but
may register their names with the Registrar of the College,
upon giving satisfactory evidence of their qualifications, and
upon paying the fee of twenty dollars.

A certificate from the Registrar of any chartered University
conducting a full Arts course in Canada, that the holder
thereof matriculated prior to his enrolment in such University
and passed the examination in Arts prescribed for students
at the end of the first year, shall entitle such student to registration as medical student under *The Ontario Medical Act.*

Every medical student, after matriculating, shall be registered in the manner prescribed by the Council, and this
shall be held to be the beginning of his medical studies,
which shall date from that registration.

Full details may be obtained by application to Dr. R. A.
Pyne, Registrar, Cor. Bay and Richmond St., Toronto.

D. *To practice in the Maritime Provinces.*

The examination required by the Faculty of Medicine of
this University is accepted in the provinces of Nova Scotia,
New Brunswick, Prince Edward Island and Newfoundland,
subject to the following conditions:

The Nova Scotia Medical Board requires that 60 per cent.
of the required marks be taken, and that Physics be taken as
the optional subject.

The New Brunswick Medical Board accepts the McGill
Matriculation, as it is the same as that required for entrance
to the Faculty of Arts.

The Prince Edward Island Medical Board has requirements
identical with those of New Brunswick.

The Newfoundland Medical Board accepts the McGill Matriculation, as it is identical with the Arts Matriculation, but requires Physics in addition.

Students desiring ultimately to practice in any of these provinces should, when enregistered in the Faculty of Medicine, notify the Registrar of that province of the fact, and have their matriculation enregistered.

The Registrars are : For Nova Scotia, Dr. A. H. W. Lindsay, Halifax ; for Newfoundland, Dr. J. Sinclair Tait, St. Johns ; and for New Brunswick, Dr. G. H. Coburn, Fredericton, who will furnish all details of requirements, etc.

Special matriculation examinations are held annually in New Brunswick and Nova Scotia, at dates stated in the Almanac, at the beginning of this Calendar.

These examinations, as stated above, are accepted by this University as equivalent to its Matriculation Examination.

E. *To obtain license to practice in Manitoba.*

An examination accepted by the University of Manitoba as equivalent to their matriculation, is required on entrance, and to obtain License an examination in Professional subjects is required. Dr. J. S. Gray of Winnipeg, Manitoba, is the Provincial Registrar.

F. *To obtain license to practice in North-West Territories.*

No special matriculation standard is specified. Licensed practitioners of any of the other provinces are admitted to practice without examination.

Those not licensed to practice elsewhere in Canada are examined in professional subjects only. Dr. H. W. Bain, of Prince Albert, is Registrar of this Province.

G. *To practice in British Columbia.*

No special standard of matriculation is specified.

All desiring a license must be graduates of some recognized medical school, and pass an examination in professional subjects only. Dr. C. J. Fagan, of New Westminster, is the Provincial Registrar.

II.

ENREGISTRATION.

The following are the University Regulations:—

All Students desirous of attending the Medical Lectures shall, at the commencement of each Session, enrol their names and residences in the Register of the Medical Faculty.

The said Register shall be closed on the 22nd of October next, for the Session of 1898-99.

Fees are payable to the Registrar, and must be paid in advance at the time of enregistration.

The class tickets for the various courses are accepted as qualifying candidates for examination before the various Colleges and Licensing bodies of Grèat Britain and Ireland, and the College of Physicians and Surgeons of Ontario. The degree in Medicine of this University carries with it at the Licensing Boards of Great Britain the same exemptions in certain subjects as are granted to all colonial degrees.

To meet the circumstances of the General Practitioners in British North America, where there is no division of the profession into Physicians and Surgeons exclusively, the degree awarded upon graduation is that of " Doctor of Medicine and Master of Surgery," in accordance with the general nature and character of the curriculum, as fully specified hereafter. The degree is received by the College of Physicians and Surgeons of the Province of Quebec, provided the graduate from this university matriculated before the College of Physicians and Surgeons of Quebec, when entering on the study of medicine.

Any graduate therefore in medicine of this University, may obtain a license to practise in the Province of Quebec without further examination, if he has complied with the above regulations.

TIME TABLE FOR SESSION 1897-98.

Time Tables for the Session of 1898-99 will be issued to each student with his Lecture Room ticket on enregistration.

TIME TABLE OF FIRST YEAR LECTURES.

LECTURES.	Mon.	Tues.	Wed.	Thur.	Fri.	Sat.	Lecture Theatre.
Anatomy	9	9	9	9	9	....	Autumn & Winte Terms-No I.
Physiology........	4	4	......	4	......	......	No. I.
Chemistry...... {	......	3	......	3	3	....	Autumn Term No. IIL
	......	......	2	......	2	....	Winter and Spring Terms—No. III
Zoology	......	11	......	11	......	10	Autumn & Winter Terms.
Botany....	......	11	......	11	......	......	Spring Term.
LABORATORY WORK.							
Practical Anatomy	10–12½	10–12½	10–12½	10–12½	10–12½	9–12½	
*Prac. Physiology	......	.....	3–5	......	......	......	
*Prac. Histology ..	2–4	......	......	......	4–6	10–12	
*Prac. Chemistry .	9–11	9–11	9–11	9–11	......	......	Autumn Term.
*Prac. Botany.....	11–12	......	11–12	......	10–12	.....	Spring Term

*Class taken in division.

TIME TABLE OF SECOND YEAR LECTURES.

LECTURES.	Mon.	Tues.	Wed.	Thur.	Fri.	Sat.	Lecture Theatre.
Anatomy....... .	9	9	9	9	9	....	Autumn & Winter Terms ·No. I.
Physiology........	2	......	2	......	2	......	No. I.
Chemistry........	3	......	3	......	3	......	
Pharmacology and Therapeutics }	4	......	4	......	4	......	No. I.
LABORATORY WORK.							
Anatomy. ...... {	10	10	10	10	10	10	Autumn & Winter Terms.
	12.30	12.30	12.30	12.30	12.30	12.30	
† Prac. Chemistry..	9–11	9–11	9–11	9–11	9–11	9–11	Spring Terms.
†Prac. Physiology.	......	2–4	......	2–4	......	......	

†Half the class only.

NOTE—Students of the second year when not engaged in the laboratories are required to attend the Out Patients' Clinics (only) of M. G. H. or R. V. H. (11 a m. to 1 p m.); at-

TIME TABLE OF THIRD YEAR LECTURES.

LECTURES.	Mon.	Tues.	Wed.	Thur.	Fri.	Sat.	Lecture Theatre.
Gynæcology and Obstetrics	9	...	.....	9	....	....	II
Medicine	....	10	*11–12	10	.....	......	III
Surgery	10	.....	*12–1	......	10	.....	III
Jurisprudence and Mental Diseases	11	.....	.....	11	......	....	II
Pharmacology and Therapeutics	......	11	....	.....	11	......	III
Gen. Pathology and Bacteriology	5	......	9	......	......	......	III
Hygiene	......	9	......	....	9	*9–11	III
Morbid Anatomy	......	......	......	......	......	......	
Clinical Medicine	......	1 p.m. MGH	......	2 p.m RVH	......	......	
Clinical Surgery	2 p.m. RVH	......	......	......	1 p.m. MGA	......	
Practical Pathology	......	4–6	4–6	4–6	4–6	......	{ Path. Lab, Winter.
‡Clinical and Sanitary Chemistry.	......	4–6	4–6	4–6	4–6	......	Chem. Lab. Autumn
‡Bacteriology and Hygiene..	......	4–6	4–6	4–6	4–6	.....	Path. Lab. Autumn
‡†Clinical Microscopy	......	4–6	4–6	4–9	4–6	.....	Path. Lab. Spring
‡†Operative Surgery	......	4–6	4–6	4–6	4–6	.....	Anat. Lab. Spring

*Alternate weeks M.G.H. and R.V.H.   †Optional.   ‡Classes taken in groups.

TIME TABLE OF FOURTH YEAR LECTURES.

LECTURES.	Mon.	Tues.	Wed.	Thur.	Fri.	Sat.	Lecture Theatre.
Gynæcology	......	9	......	......	......	......	II
Obstetrics	......	......	9	......	11	......	II
Medicine	......	10	‡11–12	10	....	......	III
Surgery	10	......	‡12–1	......	10	......	III
Med. & Surg. Pathology	......	......	......	9	......	......	III
Ophthalmology	9	......	......	......	......	......	II
*Out Patients' Clinics	11-12 12-1	11-12 12-1	11-12 12-1	11-12 12-1	11-12 12 1	11-12	R.V.H. M.G.H.
Clinical Medicine	1	......	......	......	2	.....	R.V.H. M.G.H.
Clinical Surgery	......	1	......	2	......	......	M.G.H. R.V.H.
Gynæcological Operations	......	11	......	......	......	......	R.V.H.
*Clinical Ophthalmology	4	......	4	......	4	....	M.G.H. R.V.H.
†Gynæcological Clinics	11	4	4	4	......	......	M.G.H. R.V.H.
Morbid Anatomy	......	......	......	......	......	‡9–11	Maternity Hosp.
Clinical Obstetrics	......	......	......	......	......	1-2.30	nity Hosp.
*Dermatological Clinic	......	......	2	......	......	......	M.G.H.
Genito-Urinary Clinic	......	......	......	......	......	3	R.V.H.
*Diseases of Children Clinic	......	4	......	......	4	......	M.G.H.
*Laryngology	4	......	......	......	4	.....	M.G.H.
Medical and Surgical Anatomy	5	......	......	......	.....	.....	Autumn term.
Children's Diseases	5	......	......	......	.....	.....	Winter term.

*In groups of eight or ten.   †In groups of four.   ‡Alternate weeks M.G.H. and R.V.H.

III.

COURSES OF LECTURES.

The Corporation of the University, on the recommendation of the Faculty of Medicine, in 1894, consented to the extension of the courses of lectures in medicine over a period of about nine months instead of six.

By this means, (1) The students of the primary years have a more ample opportunity of becoming acquainted, by laboratory work, with those branches of study which form the scientific basis of their profession, and (2) the final students will be able to derive the greatest benefit from the abundance of clinical material provided in the two Hospitals.

By this arrangement while the actual number of didactic lectures per session will be decreased, there will be a corresponding increase in the amount of tutorial work and individual teaching in the laboratories for Chemistry, Physiology, Anatomy, Pathology and Hygiene as well as giving more time, during the last two years of the course, for the thorough study of disease in the wards of the Royal Victoria and Montreal General Hospitals.

The Faculty expects, by thus increasing the time that the different professors, lecturers and demonstrators devote to each student, to accomplish two very important ends: First, to do away with the injurious effects which result from attempting to condense the teaching of medicine and surgery into four or even five sessions of six months; Second, to give each student a sounder and more thoroughly practical knowledge of his profession than could be obtained by attending during even five sessions of six months each.

ANATOMY.

(DESCRIPTIVE AND PRACTICAL).

PROFESSOR, FRANCIS J. SHEPHERD.

J. M. ELDER and J. A. SPRINGLE, Lecturers ; J. G. Mc-
CARTHY, Senior Demonstrator ; R. TAIT McKEN-
ZIE, J. A. HENDERSON, W. I. BRADLEY, J. J. ROSS,
and A. E. ORR, Demonstrators.

Anatomy is taught in the most practical manner possible,
and its relation to Medicine and Surgery fully considered.
The lectures are illustrated by the fresh subject, moist and
dry preparations, sections, models and plates, and drawings
on the blackboard.

A course of practical demonstrations in Medical, Surgical
and Topographical Anatomy is also given in the final year of
the course.

The department of *Practical Anatomy* is under the direct
control and personal supervision of the Professor of Anatomy,
assisted by his staff of Demonstrators.

The methods of teaching are similar to those of the best
European schools, and Students are thoroughly grounded in
this branch.

Every Student must be examined *at least* three times on
each part dissected, and no certificate is given unless the examinations are satisfactory.

Special Demonstrations on the Brain, Thorax, Abdomen,
Bones, etc., are frequently given. Prizes are awarded at the
end of the Session for the best examination on the fresh
subject.

The Dissecting Room is open from 8 a.m. to 6 p.m. Abundance of material can be obtained, owing to the Anatomy Act
of the Province of Quebec.

CHEMISTRY.

PROFESSOR, GILBERT P. GIRDWOOD.

The course in this subject is carefully graded. Students of
the first year receive lectures on Chemical and Physiological

Physics and the general principles and theories of the science. In the second year the course on chemistry is extended to embrace its application to physiology and medicine, and includes a course in Organic Chemistry. The lectures are fully illustrated by experiments, for which the department is equipped with all modern Lecture-room apparatus.

PRACTICAL CHEMISTRY.

PROFESSOR, R. F. RUTTAN.
• *DEMONSTRATOR, C. G. L. WOLF.*
LABORATORY ASSISTANT, CHARLES STEVENSON.

Laboratory instruction in practical chemistry is given during each of the first three years of study thoughout one term.

The first year's course illustrates the general principles of chemical action and the properties of typical elements. During the second year the course will include methods of qualitative analysis and the detection of poisons. In the third year a course of clinical and sanitary chemistry will be given, in which the student will be made familiar with the application of chemistry to the diagnosis and prevention of disease. Special attention is directed to instructing the student in making accurate notes of his experiments and his conclusions. These notes are examined daily and criticised.

PHYSIOLOGY.

The JOSEPH MORLEY DRAKE, PROFESSOR, — WESLEY MILLS.
LECTURER, W. S. MORROW.
DEMONSTRATORS, J. W. SCANE and A. A. ROBERTSON.

The purpose of this Course is to make Students thoroughly acquainted, as far as time permits, with modern Physiology : its methods, its deductions, and the basis on which the latter rest. Accordingly a full course of lectures is given, in which the physical, the chemical and other aspects of the subject receive attention.

In addition to the use of diagrams, plates, models, etc., every department of the subject is experimentally illustrated.

The experiments are mostly free from elaborate *technique*, and many of them are of a kind susceptible of ready imitation by the Student.

Laboratory work for Senior Students:—

(1.) During a part of the Session there will be a course on Physiological Chemistry, in which the Student will, under direction, investigate food stuffs, digestive action, blood, and the more important secretions and excretions including urine. All the apparatus and material for this course will be provided.

(2.) The remainder of the Session will be devoted to the performance of experiments which are unsuitable for demonstration to a large class in the lecture room, or that require the use of elaborate methods, apparatus, etc., together with such as each individual of the class can himself conduct.

Laboratory work for Junior Students:—

This will be somewhat similar to the course for senior students, but simpler and anatomico-physiological rather than chemical; like the work for second year students its main object will be the illustration of important physiological principles.

HISTOLOGY.

PROFESSOR, GEO. WILKINS.
DEMONSTRATOR, N. D. GUNN.

The teaching of Histology and Microscopical methods is spread over two years.

During the latter half of the first year a course of ten demonstrations is given upon elementary Histology and systematic Histology up to, and including the digestive system. During the second year fifteen or twenty demonstrations will be given upon the whole of Histology. The practical instruction upon the preparation and mounting of specimens is given during the first year. Examinations both practical and written will be held at the end of both first and second years.

PHARMACOLOGY AND THERAPEUTICS.

PROFESSOR, A. D. BLACKADER.
DEMONSTRATOR, R. A. KERRY.

The lectures on this subject are graded in the following manner :

During the primary course, attention is directed chiefly to Pharmacology, including the important chemical and physical properties of the various drugs, and a brief consideration of their physiological action ; therapeutics is considered only in outline. A complete museum of Materia Medica affords the student opportunity for making himself acquainted with the drugs themselves. During the session, a course of demonstrations on Practical Materia Medica and Pharmacy is given.

During the final course, the physiological action of drugs is dwelt upon at length, and attention is given to the therapeutic application of all drugs and remedial measures. Prescription writing, and the various modes of administering drugs are explained and illustrated. During the course a series of lectures will be delivered in the theatres of the hospitals on special cases or groups of cases, illustrating important points in both general and special Therapeutics.

MEDICINE.

PROFESSOR, JAMES STEWART.
ASSISTANT PROFESSORS, { *F. G. FINLEY.*
{ *H. A. LAFLEUR.*
LECTURER, C. F. MARTIN.
DEMONSTRATORS, } *G. GORDON CAMPBELL.*
} *W. F. HAMILTON.*
ASSISTANT DEMONSTRATOR, S. RIDLEY MACKENZIE.

While the lectures on this subject are mainly devoted to Special Pathology and Therapeutics, no opportunity is lost of illustrating and explaining the general laws of disease. With the exception of certain affections seldom or never observed in this country, all the important internal diseases of the body, except those peculiar to women and children, are discussed, and their Pathological Anatomy illustrated by the large collection of morbid preparations in the University Museum, and by fresh specimens contributed by the Professor of Pathology.

The College possesses an extensive series of Anatomical plates and models illustrative of the Histological and Anatomical appearances of disease, and the wards of the General and Royal Victoria Hospitals afford the lecturer ample opportunities to refer to living examples of very many of the maladies he describes, and to demonstrate the results of treatment.

CLINICAL MEDICINE.

PROFESSOR, JAMES STEWART.
ASSOCIATE PROFESSORS, F. G. FINLEY and H. A. LAFLEUR.
LECTURER, C. F. MARTIN.

The instruction in Clinical Medicine is conducted in the theatres, wards, out-patient rooms and laboratories of the Royal Victoria and Montreal General Hospitals.

The courses include :—

I. The reporting of cases by every member of the Graduating Class, a certain number of beds being assigned to each student.

II. Bedside instruction for members of the Graduating Class.

III. Two Clinics weekly in each hospital.

IV. Tutorial instruction for the Junior Classes, in the wards and out-patient rooms of both hospitals.

V. Instruction in Clinical Chemistry and Bacteriology.

SURGERY.

PROFESSOR, THOMAS G. RODDICK.
DEMONSTRATORS, { *A. E. GARROW, J. M. ELDER* *J. ALEX. HUTCHISON.*

This course consists of the Principles and Practice of Surgery and Surgical Pathology, illustrated by a large collection of preparations from the Museum, as well as by specimens obtained from cases under observation at the Hospitals. The greater part of the course however is devoted to the Practice of Surgery, in which attention is constantly drawn to cases which have been observed by the class during the session. The various surgical appliances are exhibited, and their uses and application explained. Surgical Anatomy and Operative Surgery form special departments of this course.

CLINICAL SURGERY.

PROFESSOR, JAMES BELL.
ASSOCIATE " GEORGE E. ARMSTRONG.
DEMONSTRATORS, KENNETH CAMERON and A. E. GARROW.

The teaching in Clinical Surgery is conducted at the Montreal General and Royal Victoria Hospitals.

I. In the amphitheatre of each of these Hospitals, demonstrations are given and operations are performed before the senior and junior classes on alternate days.

II. Small ward classes of about 10 men in each are taken through the wards by the surgeon in attendance, and instruction given at the bedside concerning the nature and management of surgical cases, in each hospital, at least once per week.

III. Beds are assigned to students in rotation, and each student is required to carefully study and report cases and to assist in the surgical dressing of the same. Certificates of case reporting are given and are essential for graduation.

IV. In the Out-patient Department students have an exceptionally good opportunity to study a great variety of injuries, to witness operations in minor surgery, to come into personal contact with patients and to take part in the application of a variety of surgical dressings and appliances.

OBSTETRICS AND DISEASES OF INFANTS.

PROFESSOR, J. CHALMERS CAMERON.
DEMONSTRATOR, D. J. EVANS.
ASSISTANT DEMONSTRATORS, { *T. P. SHAW.* / *JAMES BARCLAY.* }

This course will embrace: 1. Lectures on the principles and practice of the obstetric art, illustrated by diagrams, fresh and preserved specimens, the artificial pelvis, complete sets of models illustrating deformities of the pelvis, wax preparations, bronze mechanical pelvis, &c. 2. Bedside instruction in the Montreal Maternity, including external palpation, pelvimetry, the management and after-treatment of cases. 3. A complete course on obstetric operations with the phantom and preserved fœtuses. 4. The diseases of Infancy.

5. A course of individual clinical instruction at the Montreal Maternity.

Arrangements have now been made for a graded course in Obstetrics, instruction being given separately to third year and final students.

Particular attention is given to Clinical instruction, and a Clinical examination in Midwifery similar to that held in Medicine and Surgery now forms part of the final examination.

A short course of lectures on diseases of infancy is given, supplemented by Clinical demonstration and ward work.

GYNÆCOLOGY.

PROFESSOR, WM. GARDNER.
LECTURERS, F. A. L. LOCKHART and J. C. WEBSTER.

The didactic course is graded and consists of from forty to forty-five lectures given at intervals alternating with the lectures on Obstetrics and extending throughout the session. The anatomy and physiology of the organs and parts concerned is first discussed. Then the various methods of examination are fully described, the necessary instruments exhibited, and their uses explained.

The diseases peculiar to women are considered as fully as time permits, somewhat in the following order:—Disorders of Menstruation ; Leucorrhœa ; Diseases of the External Genital Organs ; Inflammations, Lacerations and Displacements of the Uterus ; Pelvic Cellulitis and Peritonitis and Inflammations of the Ovaries and Fallopian Tubes ; Benign and Malignant growths of the Uterus; Tumours of the Ovary;

Diseases of the Bladder and Urethra. The lectures are illustrated as fully as possible by drawings and morbid specimens.

Clinical teaching, including out-patient and bed-side instruction, is given at both Royal Victoria and Montreal General hospitals by Professor Gardner and Doctors Lockhart and Webster. A large amount of Clinical material is thus available for practical instruction in this department of medicine. Numerous operations are done before the class, and made the subject of remarks. In addition to the ward-patients each hospital conducts a large out-patient Gynæcological Clinic to which advanced students are admitted in rotation and instructed in digital and bimanual examination and in the use of instruments for diagnosis.

Particular attention is thus given to Clinical instruction, and a Clinical examination in Gynæcology similar to that held in Medicine and Surgery now forms part of the final examination.

MEDICAL JURISPRUDENCE.

PROFESSOR, GEO. WILKINS,
LECTURER ON MENTAL DISEASES, T. J. W. BURGESS.
LECTURER ON MEDICO-LEGAL PATHOLOGY, WYATT JOHNSTON.

This course includes Insanity, the subject being treated of in its Medical as well as Medico-Legal aspects. Special attention is devoted to the subject of blood stains, the clinical microscopic and spectroscopic tests for which are fully described and shown to the class. The various spectra of blood in its different conditions are shown by the Microspectroscope, so well adapted for showing the reactions with exceedingly minute quantities of suspected material. Recent researches in the diagnosis of human from animal blood are alluded to. In addition to the other subjects usually included in a course of this kind, Toxicology is taken up. The modes of action of poisons, general evidence of poisoning and classification of poisons are first treated of, after which the more common poisons are described, with reference to symptoms, post-mortem appearances, and chemical tests. The post-mortem appearances are illustrated by plates, and the tests are shown to the class. A series of demonstrations and Clinics will be given by Prof. Johnston on the Medico-Legal cases, arising out of the coroner's court, as well as those in the Montreal General Hospital. In this way Students will have practical clinical instruction in methods of Medico-Legal investigation in civil as well as in criminal cases.

OPHTHALMOLOGY AND OTOLOGY.

PROFESSOR, F. BULLER.
LECTURER, J. J. GARDNER.

This will include a course of twenty-five lectures on diseases of the Eye and Ear, both didactic and clinical. In the former, the general principles of diagnosis and treatment will be dealt with ; including three lectures on the errors of refraction and faults of accommodation. At the clinical lectures given in the Hospitals cases illustrative of the typical forms of ordinary diseases of the Eye and Ear will be exhibited and explained to the class. In the out-patients' department of each Hospital students have excellent opportunities of gaining clinical experience.

BIOLOGY.

D. P. PENHALLOW, PROFESSOR BOTANY.
E. W. MACBRIDE,   "   ZOOLOGY.

This course will be given during the Autumn term of the first session, and will be almost entirely practical.

The course will consist of Zoology and Botany.

A. Zoology. This course will embrace a comparative study of the following forms Amœba, Vorticella, Hydra, Lumbricus, Cambarus (cray fish), Unio and Mustelus, as the last type is the most important an extra allowance of time will be devoted to it.

B. Botany. The following types will be studied:—A Myxomycete, Bacillus, Yeast, Pleurococcus, Fucus, Polytrichum, Pteris, Selaginella, with a comparison of allied forms. The course is especially arranged to be introductory to the study of human physiology and anatomy.

PATHOLOGY.

The SIR DONALD SMITH, PROFESSOR, — J. G. ADAMI.

DEMONSTRATORS. { *W. I. BRADLEY.*
{ *A. G. NICHOLS.*

ASSISTANT DEMONSTRATORS, } *D. D. MACTAGGART,*
} *D. P. ANDERSON.*

LABORATORY ASSISTANT, E. W. HAMMOND.

The following courses constitute the teaching on this subject :—

1. A course of General Pathology for Students of the Third Year (optional for those of the Fourth). Lectures are delivered twice weekly throughout the year.

2. A course of demonstrations in the performance of Autopsies, for Students of the Third Year. The demonstrations are held once a week, from October until Christmas.

3. Demonstrations upon the Autopsies of the week for Students of the two Final Years· These are given during the session by Dr. Adami at the Royal Victoria Hospital, and by Dr. Wyatt Johnston at the General Hospital.

Practical Courses.

4. The performance of autopsies· Each student is required to take an active part in at least six autopsies. The autopsies are conducted at the General and Royal Victoria Hospitals by the Pathologists of these Hospitals and their assistants. In addition to the actual performance of the *sectio cadaveris*, students are expected to attend the practical instruction given in connection with each autopsy, in the method of preparation and microscopic examination of the removed tissues, so as to become proficient in methods of preparation, staining and mounting.

208

5. A practical course in Morbid Histology for Students of the Third Year. This class is held once a week during the winter months. Six sections are as a rule distributed at each meeting of the class so that each student obtains a large and representative series of morbid tissues, and upon an average twenty minutes are devoted to the description and examination of each specimen. Laboratory fee to cover cost of slides, reagents, microscope, etc., $5.

6. A course of demonstrations upon Morbid Anatomy (Museum ·specimens) once weekly during the winter months, for students of the Fourth Year.

In addition to the above the staff of the department give instruction to the more advanced students who desire to undertake any special work in the laboratories. Classes in clinical pathology and microscopy are given from time to time, at the Pathological Laboratory and at the General and Royal Victoria Hospitals under the direction of the Professors of Clinical Medicine·

DEPARTMENT OF PUBLIC HEALTH AND PREVENTIVE MEDICINE.

The SIR DONALD SMITH, PROFESSOR, — ROBT. CRAIK.
SANITARY PHYSICS { PROF. ROBT. CRAIK.
AND CHEMISTRY. { PROF. R. F. RUTTAN.
BACTERIOLOGY AND { PROF. J. G. ADAMI.
PREVENTIVE MEDICINE { PROF. WYATT JOHNSTON.
{ DR. H. B. YATES.

The Department of Public Health and Preventive Medicine has, owing to its endowment by Sir Donald A. Smith, been made one of the most important subjects of the third year.

The instruction will consist of two lectures per week, for the whole session. A systematic course in Bacteriology and Preventive Medicine, including Serum Therapy, will be followed by courses on the sanitary relations of water, soil, food and air, the use and relative value of disinfectants, domestic sanitation, including plumbing, heating, ventilation, the construction of habitations, etc., and will be illustrated by models and special apparatus. Lectures will also be given on personal hygiene, including bathing, exercise, etc., and on climate and health resorts. In addition to the course of systematic lectures, laboratory courses will be given in the Pathological and Chemical laboratories on Bacteriology, clinical and sanitary Chemistry. The laboratory work will extend over a period of three months and will be given twice weekly.

A working museum and model room is being equipped with working models and apparatus to illustrate the application of hygienic principles. Demonstrations will be given in the hygienic museum from time to time as required. (See Museums.)

LARYNGOLOGY AND RHINOLOGY.

PROFESSOR, H. S. BIRKETT.

This course will consist of practical lessons in the use of the Laryngoscope and Rhinoscope. The instruction will be carried on with small classes so that individual attention may be insured. A limited number of clinical lectures bearing upon interesting cases attending the clinic will be delivered during the session. These lectures will be, however, of an eminently practical nature.

MENTAL DISEASES.

LECTURER, T. J. W. BURGESS.

This course will comprise a series of lectures at the University on Insanity in its various forms, from a medical as well as from a medico-legal standpoint. The various types of mental diseases will be illustrated by cases in the Verdun Asylum, where clinical instruction will be given to groups of senior students at intervals throughout the session.

DISEASES OF INFANTS AND CHILDREN.

PROFESSORS,   J. O. CAMERON.
A. D. BLACKADER.

Although this subject does not constitute a special chair in the University, systematic instruction is given (a) in connection with the chair of Obstetrics and Diseases of Infants, by Prof. Cameron ; (b) by a course of lectures, clinical and didactic by Prof. Blackader, and (c) through the Children's Clinic at the Montreal General Hospital and at the Infants' Home.

IV.

DOUBLE COURSES.

By special arrangement with the Faculty of Arts, it is now possible for students to obtain the double degree of B.A., and M.D., C.M·, after only six years of study.

It has been decided to allow the Primary subjects (Anatomy, Physiology and Chemistry) in medicine to count as Honor subjects of the third and fourth years in Arts. It follows then that at the end of four years study a student may obtain his B.A. degree and have two years of his medical course completed.

The remaining two years of study are devoted to the third and fourth year subjects in Medicine.

The special provisions for Medical Students in the Arts course are as follows :

In the Second Year.—The remaining half of the Course in Chemistry of the Medical Faculty may be substituted for the Psychology of the First Term and the Mathematical Physics of the Second Year. The Botany Course of the Medical Faculty may be substituted for the Botany in the Arts Course.

[NOTE.—The Faculty of Medicine advises Medical Students who are following the Courses in Arts prescribed for the double degree, to take the subject of Psychology if possible.]

Third Year·—Physiology and Histology with practical work therein, or Anatomy with Practical Anatomy, together with the regular examinations therein in the Faculty of Medicine, may be substituted for two courses under the heading of "Division b" in the curriculum of the Third Year in Arts.

[NOTE.—If a special course of Physics for Medical Students should be established, Natural Philosophy may not be compulsory.]

Fourth Year.—Students who have completed the Third Year in Arts and First Year in Medicine shall have the same privileges in the Fourth Year as Honour Students in this year, viz., they shall be required to attend two only of the courses of¹ lectures given in the ordinary departments (or one course with the additional course therein), and to pass the corresponding examinations only at the Ordinary B. A. Examination.

Students are recommended in the Third and Fourth Years to continue the study of subjects which they have already taken in the First and Second Years.

In order to obtain the above privileges, the student must give notice at the commencement of the Session to the Dean of the Faculty of Arts, of his intention to claim them, and present a certificate from the Registrar of the Medical Faculty that his name is entered on the books of that Faculty. He must produce at the end of the sessions in the first two years a certificate of attendance on the required lectures and of standing at the corresponding examinations. In the Third and Fourth Years, he must produce certificates that he has completed each year of the Medical curriculum.

A certificate of Licentiate in Arts will be given along with the professional degree in Medicine to those who, previous to entrance upon their professional studies proper, have completed two years in the Faculty of Arts, and have duly passed the prescribed examinations therein·

GRADUATE AND ADVANCED COURSES.

The Faculty of Medicine in 1896 established post-graduate and special courses in connection with the Montreal General and Royal Victoria Hospitals and the various laboratories in the University buildings. These courses will be continued in 1899.

There will be two distinct sets of courses, one a short practical and clinical course for medical men in general practice who desire to keep in touch with recent advances in Medicine, Surgery and Pathology, and who wish special clinical experience in Gynæcology, Ophthalmology, Laryngology, etc. This course will last about six weeks, beginning about the first of May.

A special detailed programme will be prepared and will be sent on application in February next. The fee, including hospital fees for both Hospitals, is fifty dollars.

The other courses will be for those who have just completed their regular course in Medicine, and desire special Laboratory or Clinical teaching before beginning practice.

Arrangements have also been made to accommodate a limited number of such graduates who desire advanced and research work.

Commodious laboratories for advanced work have been equipped in connection with the Pathological and Clinical departments of both the Royal Victoria and Montreal General Hospitals, and in connection with the general laboratories for Pathology, Physiology and Chemistry, recently altered and extended in the new buildings of the Faculty.

Recent graduates of recognized universities desiring to qualify for examinations by advanced laboratory course, or who wish to engage in special research, may enter at any time by giving a month's notice, stating the courses desired and the time at their disposal.

All the regular clinics and demonstrations of both hospitals will be open to such students on the same conditions as undergraduates in medicine of this University.

These laboratories have been open for graduates since May 1st, 1896.

Further details regarding courses, fees, etc., may be obtained on application to the Registrar.

THE GRADUATE COURSE OF 1898.

The Faculty of Medicine of McGill University has just completed its third Post-Graduate Course. This course of instruction which was given in the various departments of Medicine and Surgery is especially arranged to meet the requirements of the general practitioner who is unable to devote more than a few weeks to thè task of overtaking the more recent advances in his profession. The course began May 3rd, 1898 and closed June 12th.

A special time-table was issued each week stating the hour at which each clinic or demonstration is held, and the laboratory or hospital at which it is held. This time-table was subject to alterations to meet the special demands of those attending the course.

The following is an outline of the course:—

A.—A series of **Evening Lectures**, four evenings per week, at 8.30, illustrated by lantern slides, models, etc., as required, were given on the more recent advances in Medicine and Surgery, Pathology, etc. These included the following:—

PROF· WM. GARDNER.—Uterine displacements.

PROF. JAS. STEWART.—(1) "Diagnosis and treatment of Tabes Dorsalis." (2) "The cause, diagnosis and treament of Compression Myelitis.'

PROF. T. G. RODDICK.—"Diagnosis and treatment of Tuberculous Joints."

PROF· F. J. SHEPHERD.—"Hare Lip."

PROF. A. D. BLACKADER.—(1) "Diarrhœal disorders of Infancy." (2) "Digestion disorders of Infancy." (3) "Diseases of Nutrition."

PROF. G. E. ARMSTRONG.—(1) "Cancer of tongue, its diagnosis, and the extent and technique of removal." (2) "Appendicitis."

PROF· GEO. WILKINS.—"The duties of a Medical Examiner in Life Insurance" (two lectures).

PROF. JAS. BELL.—"Intestinal obstruction" (two lectures.")

PROF. WYATT JOHNSTON.—"The Medico-Legal Relation of Injuries."

Prof. J. G. Adami.—A course of lectures on the relation of one diseased organ to another and to the whole organism, also two lectures on Cirrhosis of the Liver.

Prof. F. G. Finley.—"Tuberculosis of the Pleura and Peritoneum" (two lectures).

B. **General Clinics.**—The afternoons of each day were devoted to Clinical Work in the Wards of the Montreal General and Royal Victoria Hospitals. Clinics in General Surgery were given by Professors Shepherd and Bell, and in General Medicine by Professors Jas. Stewart, Blackader, Lafleur and Finley.

These Clinics were given on four days of each week and were usually followed by a special Clinic.

The afternoons of the remaining two days, in addition to those which were given in the morning, were occupied entirely by one or more of the following Special Clinics:—

C. **Special Clinics.**—In Ophthalmology, including diseases of the Conjunctiva, Iris, Cornea, and Retina, at the Royal Victoria by Prof. Buller ; and at the Montreal General Hospital by Dr. J. J. Gardner. Special instruction in the use of the Ophthalmoscope was also given.

In Gynæcology, at the Royal Victoria Hospital, by Prof. Wm. Gardner, and at the Montreal General Hospital by Dr. Lockhart.

In Laryngology and the use of the Laryngoscope, at the Montreal General Hospital, by Prof. Birkett.

In external palpation and aseptic midwifery, at the Montreal Maternity Hospital, by Prof. J. C. Cameron.

In diseases of Children, at the Montreal General Hospital, by Prof. A. D. Blackader and Dr. G. G. Campbell.

In Dermatology, at the Montreal General Hospital, by Prof. Shepherd.

In diseases of the Genito-Urinary Organs, at the Royal Victoria Hospital, by Prof. J. Bell.

In Orthopœdics, at the Montreal General Hospital, by Dr. C. W. Wilson.

In the mornings, two or more of the following Special Demonstrations, Laboratory Courses or Laboratory Demonstrations, were given.

D. **Special Demonstrations.**— One or more as required, on modern treatment of Diphtheria, PROF. FINLEY ; Pelvimetry and Aseptic Midwifery (at Montreal Maternity Hospital), PROF. J. C. CAMERON ; Mental Diseases (at Verdun Asylum), DR· T. J. W. BURGESS ; Medico Legal Autopsy Methods, etc., DR. WYATT JOHNSTON; Clinical Application of the Roentgen Rays, PROF. GIRDWOOD, etc. Treatment of curved spine by exercise, DR. TAIT MACKENZIE.

E. **Laboratory Courses.**—For which a small extra fee was charged to cover the cost of material. These courses included:—Operative Surgery, PROF. ARMSTRONG ; Clinical Bacteriology, PROF. ADAMI; Clinical Microscopy of Dejecta and Blood, DR. C. F. MARTIN; Clinical Chemistry, PROF. RUTTAN; Post Mortem Methods, PROF. WYATT JOHNSTON, etc.

E. **Laboratory Demonstrations.**—Morbid Anatomy, PROF. ADAMI ; Medical and Surgical Anatomy, DR. J. M. ELDER and DR. McCARTHY; Microscopical Methods, DR. GUNN; Urinalysis, PROF. RUTTAN. Practical Methods in Legal Medicine and Hygiene, including Autopsy Methods; Examination of Blood Stains; Disinfection Methods; Employment of cultures and inoculation methods for diagnosis, including serum diagnosis of typhoid, etc., PROF. WYATT JOHNSTON.

Members of the Profession who purpose attending in 1899 are requested to communicate with the Registrar on or before May 1st next.

VI.
QUALIFICATIONS FOR THE DEGREE.*

1st. No one entering after September, 1894, will be admitted to the Degree of Doctor of Medicine and Master of Surgery, who shall not have attended Lectures for a period of four nine months' sessions in this University, or some other University, College or School of Medicine, approved of by this University.

2nd. Students of other Universities so approved and admitted, on production of certificate to a like standing in this University, shall be required to pass all Examinations in Primary and Final Subjects in the same manner as Students of this University.

3rd. Graduates in Arts who have taken two full courses in General Chemistry, including Laboratory work, two courses in Biology, including the subjects of Botany, Embryology, Elementary Physiology and dissection of one or more types of Vertebrata, may, at the discretion of the Faculty, be admitted as second-year Students, such courses being accepted as equivalent to the first-year in Medicine. Students so entering will however, not be allowed to present themselves for examination in Anatomy until they produce certificates of dissection for two sessions.

4th. Candidates for Final Examination shall furnish Testimonials of attendance on the following branches of Medical Education,† viz:

ANATOMY.
PRACTICAL ANATOMY.
PHYSIOLOGY.
CHEMISTRY.
PHARMACOLOGY AND THERAPEUTICS.
PRINCIPLES AND PRACTICE OF SUGERY.
OBSTETRICS AND DISEASES OF INFANTS.
GYNÆCOLOGY.
THEORY AND PRACTICE OF MEDICINE.
CLINICAL MEDICINE.
CLINICAL SURGERY.
} Of which Two full Courses will be required.

MEDICAL JURISPRUDENCE.
GENERAL PATHOLOGY.
HYGIENE AND PUBLIC HEALTH.
PRACTICAL CHEMISTY.
OPHTHALMOLOGY AND OTOLOGY.
} Of which One full Course will be required.‡

BIOLOGY.
HISTOLOGY.
PATHOLOGICAL ANATOMY.
BACTERIOLOGY.
MENTAL DISEASES.
PEDIATRICS.
MEDICAL AND SURGICAL ANATOMY.
} Of which One Course will be required.†

* It shall be understood that the programme and regulations regarding courses of study and examinations contained in this calendar hold good for this calendar year only, and that the Faculty of Medicine, while fully sensible of its obligations towards the students, does not hold itself bound to adhere absolutely, for the whole four years of a student's course, to the conditions now laid down.

† Students enregistered in the Province of Quebec are required to attend and pass examinations in Laryngology and Minor Surgery.

‡ Provided, however, that Testimonials equivalent to, though not precisely the same as those above stated, may be presented and accepted.

He must also produce Certificates of having assisted at six Autopsies, of having dispensed Medicine for a period of three months, and of having assisted at twenty Vaccinations.

5th. Courses of less length than the above will only be received for the time over which they have extended.

6th. No one will be permitted to become a Candidate for the degree who shall not have attended at least one full Session at this University.

7th. The Candidates must give proof of having attended during at least eighteen months the practice of the Montreal General Hospital or the Royal Victoria Hospital or of some other Hospital of not fewer than 100 beds, approved of by this University. Undergraduates are required to attend the Out-Patient departments of the Hospitals during their second year.

8th. He must give proof of having acted as Clinical Clerk for six months in Medicine and six months in Surgery in the wards of a general hospital recognized by the Faculty, of having reported at least 10 medical and 10 surgical cases.

9th. He must also give proof by ticket of having attended for at least nine months the practice of the Montreal Maternity or other lying-in-hospital approved of by the University, and of having attended at least six cases.

10th. Every candidate for the degree must, on or before the 15th day of May, present to the Registrar of the Medical Faculty testimonials of his qualifications, entitling him to an examination, and must at the same time deliver to the Registrar of the Faculty an affirmation or affidavit that he has attained the age of twenty-one years.

11th. The trials to be undergone by the Candidate shall be in the subjects mentioned in Section 4.

12th. The following oath of affirmation will be exacted from the Candidate before receiving his degree :

SPONSIO ACADEMICA.

In Facultate Medicinæ Universitatis.

Ego, A—— B——, Doctoratus in Arte Medica titulo jam donandus, sancto coram Deo cordium scrutatore, spondeo :—me in omnibus grati animi officiis erga hanc Universitatem ad extremum vitæ halitum perseveraturum ; tum poro artem medicam caute, caste, et probe exercitaturum ; et quoad in me est, omnia ad ægrotorum corporum salutem corducentia cum fide procuraturum ; quæ denique, inter medendum, visa vel audita silere conveniat, non sine gravi causa vulgaturum. Ita praesens mihi spondenti adsit Numen.

13th. The fee for the Degree of Doctor of Medicine and Master of Surgery shall be thirty dollars, to be paid by the successful candidate immediately after examination.

VII.

EXAMINATIONS.*

Frequent oral examinations are held to test the progress of the Student, and occasional written examinations are given throughout the Session.

The PASS AND HONOR examinations at the close of each Session are arranged as follows :—

First Year.

Examinations in BOTANY or ZOOLOGY, HISTOLOGY, PHYSIOLOGY, ANATOMY, CHEMISTRY Theoretical and Practical.

Students who have taken one or more university courses in Botany or Chemistry before entering may be exempted from attendance and examination· Students exempted in their first year subjects are allowed only a pass standing, but may present themselves for examination if they desire to attain an honor standing.

Second Year.

Examinations in ANATOMY, CHEMISTRY, PRACTICAL CHEMISTRY, PHYSIOLOGY, HISTOLOGY, PHARMACOLOGY and THERAPEUTICS.

Third Year.

Examinations in PHARMACOLOGY and THERAPEUTICS, MEDICAL JURISPRUDENCE, PUBLIC HEALTH and PREVENTIVE MEDICINE (including BACTERIOLOGY), GENERAL PATHOLOGY, MENTAL DISEASES, CLINICAL CHEMISTRY, OBSTETRICS. MEDICINE and SURGERY.

---

* See foot Note *, page 216.

Fourth Year.

Examinations in MEDICINE, SURGERY, OBSTETRICS, GYNÆ-
COLOGY, OPHTHALMOLOGY, CLINICAL MEDICINE, CLINICAL
SURGERY, CLINICAL OBSTETRICS, CLINICAL GYNÆCOLOGY,
CLINICAL OPHTHALMOLOGY and PRACTICAL PATHOLOGY.

By means of the above arrangement a certain definite
amount of work must be accomplished by the student in each
year, and an equitable division is made between the Primary
and Final branches.

A minimum of 50 *per cent. in each subject is required to Pass
and* 75 *per cent. for Honors.*

Candidates must pass in all the subjects of each year, those
who fail to pass in not more than two subjects of either the
first, second or third years may be granted a supplemental
examination at the beginning of the following session.

Supplemental examinations will not be granted, except by
special permission of the Medical Faculty, and on written application stating reasons, and accompanied by a fee of $5.00
for each subject.

No candidate will be permitted, without special permission
of the Faculty, to proceed with the work of the final year until he has passed all the subjects comprised in the Primary examination.

No student will be allowed to present himself for his final
examinations who has not certificates of having passed all
his Primary examinations in this University.

Candidates who fail to pass in a subject of which two courses
are required, may, at the discretion of the Faculty, be required to attend a third course, and furnish a certificate of attendance thereon· A course in Practical Anatomy will be
accepted as equivalent to a third course of lectures in General
and Descriptive Anatomy.

VIII.

MEDALS AND PRIZES.

1st. The "HOLMES GOLD MEDAL," founded by the Medical Faculty in the year 1865, as a memorial of the late Andrew Holmes, Esq., M.D., LL.D., late Dean of the Faculty of Medicine. It is awarded to the student of the graduating class who receives the highest aggregate number of marks in the different branches comprised in the Medical Curriculum.

The Student who gains the Holmes' Medal has the option of exchanging it for a Bronze Medal, and the money equivalent of the Gold Medal.

2nd. THE FINAL PRIZE.—A Prize in Books (or a Microscope of equivalent value) awarded for the best examination, written and oral, in the Final branches· The Holmes' medallist is not permitted to compete for this prize.

3rd. THE THIRD YEAR PRIZE.—A Prize in Books awarded for the best examination, written and oral, in the branches of the third year.

4th. THE SECOND YEAR PRIZE.—A prize in books for the best examination in all the branches of the second year in course.

5th. THE FIRST YEAR PRIZE. A prize in books for the best examination in all the branches of the first year in course.

6th. The "SUTHERLAND GOLD MEDAL," founded in 1878 by the late Mrs. Sutherland in memory of her late husband, Professor William Sutherland, M.D· It is awarded for the best examination in General and Medical Chemistry, together with creditable examination in the primary branches. The examination is held at the end of the third year.

7th. The "CLEMESHA PRIZE IN CLINICAL THERAPEUTICS," founded in 1889 by John W. Clemesha, M.D., of Port ·Hope, Ont. It is awarded to the student making the highest marks in a special clinical examination.

8th. The BRITISH COLUMBIA GRADUATES' SO-
CIETY'S PRIZE is awarded each year for the highest
standing in some third year practical subject. In 1897 it
was given for clinical surgery, in 1898 for clinical medicine·

IX·
FEES.

The total Faculty fees for the whole medical course of four
full sessions, including clinics, laboratory work, dissecting material and reagents, will be four hundred dollars, payable in
four annual instalments of $100 each.

For the convenience of the undergraduates the Hospital
fees will hereafter be payable in the Registrar's office at the
University. Ten dollars to be paid at the beginning of each
of the last three sessions, viz., the second, third and fourth
years. This will entitle each undergraduate to perpetual
tickets for both the Montreal General and Royal Victoria
Hospitals.

Partial students will be admitted to one or more courses
on payment of special fees. An annual University fee of two
dollars is charged students of all the faculties for the maintenance of college grounds and athletics.

Students repeating the course of study of any Academic
session are not required to pay full fees. A fee of twenty-
five dollars will be charged which will include Hospitals,
dissecting material, chemical reagents, etc. ·The same fee is
charged students entering from other colleges who have already paid elsewhere fees for the courses taken.

It is suggested to parents or guardians of students that the
fees be transmitted direct by cheque or P. O. Order, to the Re-
gistrar, who will furnish official receipts·

All fees are payable in advance to the Registrar, and except
by permission of the Faculty will not be received later than Octo-
ber 20th.

For Graduation Fees, see page 217.

For Hospital Fees, see pages 230 and 234.

X.

TEXT BOOKS.

ANATOMY.—Gray, Morris, Quain (Eng. Ed.).

PRACTICAL ANATOMY.—Cunningham's Practical Anatomy, Ellis' Demonstrations, Holden's Dissector and Landmarks.

PHYSICS.—Balfour Stewart.

INORGANIC CHEMISTRY.—Remsen, Wurtz's Elementary Chemistry.

ORGANIC CHEMISTRY.—Remsen.

PRACTICAL CHEMISTRY.—Odling.

PHARMACOLOGY and THERAPEUTICS.—Butler, White, Hare and Wood.

PHYSIOLOGY.—Foster and Shore's Physiology for Beginners, Mills' Textbook of Animal Physiology, Foster's Physiology, Mills' Class Laboratory Exercises.

PATHOLOGY.—Ziegler, Coats'.

PRACTICAL PATHOLOGY.—Mallory and Wright, Delafield & Prudden, Boyce.

BACTERIOLOGY.—Muir & Ritchie, Abbott.

HISTOLOGY.—Klein's Elements, Schäfer's Essentials of Histology.

SURGERY.—Holmes, Moullin, Walsham, Erichsen, Treves. American Text-book of Surgery, Da Costa.

PRACTICE OF MEDICINE.—Osler, Tyson, Wood and Fitz.

CLINICAL MEDICINE.—Musser's Medical Diagnosis ; Simon, Klemperer, Rainy and Hutchison.

MEDICAL JURISPRUDENCE.—Reese, Guy and Ferrier.

MENTAL DISEASES.—Insanity and its Treatment, Blandford, 4th Ed.

MIDWIFERY.—Lusk, and American Text Book.

DISEASES OF CHILDREN.—Holt, Rotch, Smith and Starr.

GYNÆCOLOGY.—Hart and Barbour, Garrigues, Webster.

HYGIENE.—Parks, Wilson, Rohe.

BOTANY.—Gray's. Text Book of Histology and Physiology.

ZOOLOGY.—Shipley (Invertebrata), Wiedersheim, (Vertebrata.
OPHTHALMOLOGY.—De Schweinitz, Nettleship and Swanzy.
OTOLOGY·—Pritchard, Dalby.
LARYNGOLOGY.—Watson Williams and Karl Seiler.
OPERATIVE SURGERY.—Jacobson, Treves, Kocher.
DERMATOLOGY.—Malcolm Morris, Hyde, Crocker, Unna.
MEDICAL DICTIONARY.—Gould, Dunglison, Hoblyn.

XI.

MUSEUMS.

The Faculty has during recent years devoted special attention to the development of its museums in the several departments in which objective teaching is of especial value in the education of the student·

There are now four museums in the Medical Building: (1) the Museum of Pathology, (2) the Anatomical Museum, (3) the Museum of Public Health and Preventive Medicine, (4) the Museum of Pharmacy.

Each collection is arranged and selected with the primary object of making it a teaching museum. These several collections are open to students and the public between 9 a.m. and 5 p.m.

PATHOLOGICAL MUSEUM.

PROF. J. G. ADAMI, DIRECTOR.
E. J. SEMPLE, CURATOR.
J. F. D. BAILLY, OFFICIER D'ACADEMIE, OSTEOLOGIST AND ARTICULATOR.

For the past fifty years, the rich Pathological Material furnished by the Montreal General Hospital has been collected here. The Faculty is also greatly indebted to many medical men throughout Canada and different parts of the world for important contributions to the Museum.

During the past few years, numerous and extremely important additions have been made to the Medical Museum.

It is particularly rich in specimens of Aneurisms. In addition to containing a large number of the more common varieties of these formations, there are specimens of such rare conditions as Aneurism of the Hepatic and Superior Mesenteric Arteries, Traumatic Aneurism of the Vertebral, together with several of the cerebral and pulmonary arteries. The most important collection probably in existence of hearts affected with "Malignant Endocarditis" is also found. The Faculty are indebted to Prof· Osler, late of this University, for this collection.

The Museum contains also a very large collection of different forms of calculi. The Faculty are mainly indebted to the late Prof. Fenwick for this collection. They have been mounted by Prof. Z. W. Hammond.

During the past six years, M. Bailly, osteologist and articulator (lately with Tramond of Paris), has been engaged in arranging and mounting the very large number of specimens of disease and injuries of bones which have been accumulating for years. In this collection are to be found examples of fractures and dislocations of the spine, osteoporosis, congenital dislocation of the hip, fracture of the astragalus, multiple exostoses, &c., &c.

The Pathological Museum has recently undergone complete alteration. All the old fixtures have been removed, a new gallery has been erected about both rooms, reached by a single staircase in a small intermediate room in which is placed the medico-legal collection.

The first room on entering contains the extensive bone collection and calculi. The second and larger room is reserved for the moist preparations, which are arranged so as to be of easy access for the student. Water color drawings made from the fresh specimens are mounted on swinging frames and also form a frieze at the ceiling· These serve to recall the fugitive colors of those preparations which become more or less altered on keeping.

Numerous specimens have been added to the museum during the past year. There were sent in from the Surgical and

medical wings of the Royal Victoria Hospital, and from the
different departments of the Montreal General Hospital.

MUSEUM OF PUBLIC HEALTH AND PREVENTIVE MEDICINE.

DIRECTOR, R. F. RUTTAN.
MUSEUM ASSISTANT, CHARLES STEVENSON.

This Museum has been established from the interest ac-
cruing through the endowment of the Chair of Hygiene by
Lord Strathcona and Mount Royal in 1893.

The museum at present is chiefly of interest on account of
the number and excellence of the working models, illustrating
the best modern methods of sterilisation, disinfection, filtra-
tion and ventilation, together with a very useful collection of
modern sanitary apparatus, illustrating the advantages and
disadventages of the water carriage system for the disposal
of refuse, etc.

The Director has much pleasure in acknowledging contributions of value from:

1. The Sanitary Construction Company of New York.
2. Richard King, King, Sprague & Co., New York.
3. Maigens Filtre Rapide Co., London, Eng.
4. L. Casella, London, Eng.
5. Messrs. Doulton & Co., Lambeth Pottery, London, E.C.
6. The Sanitary Institute, Parke's Museum, London.
7. The Hygienic Refe·endum, Hornsey, London, Eng.
8. Messrs. Newton & Co·, London.
9. The Expanded Metal Co., London._
10. A. B. Reck, Copenhagen, Denmark.
11. Fischer, Filter Plate ·Co.
12· J. W. Hughes, Montreal.
13. Wormser, Filterplatten-Werk, Worms, Germany.
14. The Laing Packing Company, Montreal.

The Department of Hygiene is also indebted to Mr. Fleming, Sanitary Engineer, for assistance and advice.

ANATOMICAL MUSEUM.

DIRECTOR, PROFESSOR F. J. SHEPHERD.
M. JULES BAILLY, OSTEOLOGIST AND ARTICULATOR.

This Museum occupies a large room on the same floor and adjoining the Anatomy Lecture Room and Dissecting Room. Smaller apartments in connection are used for private research, which is encouraged in every way by the Faculty.

The Museum is well furnished and comfortable, and students have every opportunity of studying Human, Comparative and Applied Anatomy.

This department has, during the past few years, added a very complete collection of plaster and papier maché models by Steger, after the well-known works of His and Braune, comprising:

(*a*) A complete set of Steger's brain sections.

(*b*) Models of the cerebro-spinal and sympathetic nervous systems.

(*c*) Professor Cunningham's well-known and beautiful casts of the head, showing the relation of the cerebral convolutions to the skull and its sutures.

A large collection of human brains, made by Professor Osler, formerly of this University, exhibiting the various types and extremes.

A large and rare collection of anomalies of the Renal vessels and ureter, and the aorta and its branches.

In Comparative Anatomy the student will find a fair amount of material, the study of which will greatly aid him in the elucidation of many points in Human Anatomy.

Many skeletons mounted by Mons. Jules Bailly, Articulator to the University, representing the various classes, orders, genera and species of the animal kingdom may be consulted.

A large collection, showing the pectoral girdle in birds, has been prepared under the supervision of the Professor of Anatomy.

Moist and dry preparations of dissections, a large collection of frozen cross sections of the human body, showing the normal relations of the viscera, etc., will be found convenient for study.

During the past year numerous valuable specimens have been presented to the Museum and its stores, which will be acknowledged in the next Calendar.

XII.

LIBRARY.

LIBRARIAN, FROF. F. G. FINDLEY.
ASSISTANT LIBRARIAN, Miss M. R. CHARLTON.

The Library of the Medical Faculty now comprises upwards of fifteen thousand volumes, the largest special library connected with a medical school on this continent.

The valuable libraries of the late Professors Robert Palmer Howard, George Ross, Richard L. MacDonnell and T. Johnston Alloway, have been donated to the Medical Faculty. They consist of several thousand volumes, including a very complete collection of works on Diseases of the Chest.

The standard text-books and works of reference, together with complete files of the leading periodicals, are on the shelves. Students may consult any work of reference in the library between 9 a.m. and 5 p.m. A library reading room for the use of students is provided.

XIII.

McGILL MEDICAL SOCIETY.

This Society, composed of enregistered Students of the Faculty, meets every alternate Saturday during the Autumn and Winter Terms, for the reading of papers, case reports and discussions on medical subjects. A prize competition has been established in senior and junior subjects, the senior being open to all to write upon, while only the 1st, 2nd and 3rd year students are allowed to compete in the junior subjects. The papers are examined by a board elected from the Professoriate, and a first and second prize in each division of subjects is awarded to the successful candidates.

Names of competitors and titles of papers shall be sent to the Chairman of the Programme Committee before September 1st, and all papers shall be subject to the call of the Committee on October 1st. All papers shall be handed in for examination on or before January 10th.

The Students' reading room has been placed under the control of this Society, in which the leading English and American Medical Journals are on file as well as the leading daily and weekly newspapers of the Dominion.

The annual meeting is held the first week of the Spring Term, when the following officers are elected : Hon. President, elected from the Faculty; President, Vice-President, Secretary, Assistant Secretary, Treasurer, Reporter, Pathologist, and three Councilmen (of whom two shall be elected from the Faculty.)

XIV.

COST OF LIVING, &c.

This will, of course, vary with the tastes and habits of the Student, but the necessary expenses need not exceed those in smaller towns. Good board may be obtained from $15 to $20 per month. A list of boarding-houses, which are inspected annually by a sanitary committee, is prepared by the Secretary of the University, and may be procured from the Janitor at the Medical College.

XV.

HOSPITALS.

The City of Montreal is celebrated for the number and importance of its public charities. Among these its public hospitals are the most prominent and widely known. Those in which medical students of McGill University will receive clinical instruction are: (1.) The Montreal General Hospital. (2.) The Royal Victoria Hospital. (3). Montreal Maternity Hospital.

The Montreal General Hospital has for many years been the most extensive clinical field in Canada. The old buildings, having proved inadequate to meet the increased demand for hospital accommodation, have recently been increased by the addition of two surgical pavilions ; the Campbell Memorial, and the Greenshields Memorial, and of a new surgical theatre. The interior of the older buildings now has been entirely reconstructed on the most approved modern plans.

The Royal Victoria Hospital at the head of University Street, which in structure and arrangements ranks among the finest modern hospitals of either continent, was opened for the reception of patients the first of January, 1894, and affords exceptional opportunities for clinical instruction and practical training.

Montreal General Hospital.

· This hospital has been for many years the most extensive clinical field in Canada.

It consists of a Surgical and Medical Department.

The Surgical Department has two large pavilions, containing four wards 135 feet long by 35 broad, with an intervening and connecting building in which is a large operating theatre of the most modern type, capable of seating over three hundred and fifty students. In connection with this are preparation, etherising, instruments, sterilising and surgeons' rooms, also smaller operating rooms. The Surgical pavilions which were built three years ago, accommodate over one hundred patients.

The old part of the hospital, consisting of the Reed, Richardson and Morland wings, has during the past year been completely rebuilt and remodelled and forms the Medical Department. This part contains four wards, 100 feet by 40 and is arranged for 150 beds. In this building there are wards for Gynæcological and Ophthalmogical patients, a number of private wards and laboratories for Clinical Chemistry. There is also a medical amphitheatre capable of seating 150 students and a gynæcological operating room fitted up in the most modern manner. The central part of the old building is for administration purposes.

A completely new and commodious out-door patient department has been provided on the ground floor of the Richardson wing, and there is ample accommodation for the various special departments as well as large rooms for general medical and surgical patients.

The Pathological Department is a completely new building in which are the post-mortem theatre and rooms for microscopical and bacteriological work, and also a mortuary and chapel. In this building students are offered every opportunity of perfecting their knowledge of morbid anatomy and pathological histology.

The old Fever Wards on the grounds of the Hospital, have been completely remodelled, and are now used as a laundry and kitchen.

A much larger number of patients receive treatment in the Montreal General Hospital than in any other Canadian Hospital. Last year's report shows that between two and three thousand Medical and Surgical cases were treated in the wards, and the great proportion of these were acute cases, as may be gathered from the fact that the average duration of residence was only 24.02 days. Upwards of thirty-two thousand patients are annually treated in the out-door department of this Hospital.

Annual tickets entitling students to admission to the Hospital must be taken out at the commencement of the session, price $5.00. These are obtained at the College. Perpetual tickets will be given on payment of the third annual fee.

The Royal Victoria Hospital.*

This Hospital is situated a short distance above the University Grounds on the side of the Mountain, and overlooks the city. It was founded in July, 1887, by the munificence of Lord Mount Stephen and Sir Donald Smith, who gave half a million dollars each for this purpose.

The buildings, which were opened for the reception of pa-

---

* Fees for this hospital are the same as those for the Montreal General Hospital, p. 74

tients on the first of January, 1894, were designed by Mr. Saxon Snell of London, England, to accommodate between 250 and 300 patients.

The Hospital is composed of three main buildings connected together by stone bridges; an Administration Block in the centre and a wing on the east side for medical patients, in immediate connection with which is the Pathological wing and mortuary, and a wing on the west side for surgical patients.

The Administration block contains ample accommodation for the resident medical staff, the nursing staff and domestics. The patients' entrance, the dispensary and admission rooms are also situated in this building.

The Medical wing contains three large wards, each 123 feet long by 26 feet 6 inches wide, one ward 40 feet by 26 feet 6 inches, and fifteen private and isolation wards averaging 16 feet by 12 feet, also a medical theatre with a seating capacity for 250, and three rooms adjacent to it for clinical chemistry and other purposes. North of this wing and in direct connection with it are the Pathological laboratories and mortuary.

In this wing are situated the mortuary proper, the chapel, a post mortem room capable of accommodating 200 students, and laboratories for the microscopic and bacteriological study of morbid tissues, some designed for the use of students and others for post graduation courses and special research. Special laboratories for Pathological chemistry, Experimental Pathology, Bacteriology and Photography are also provided.

The Surgical wing contains three large wards, each 123 feet long by 26 feet 6 inches wide, four wards each 40 feet by 32 feet, and seven private and isolation wards, averaging 16 feet by 12 feet; also a surgical theatre with a seating capacity for 250, with six rooms adjacent for preparation and after recovery purposes.

In this wing are also the wards for Gynæcology and Ophthalmology.

XVI.

CLINICAL INSTRUCTION.

During the Session of 1897-98, two Medical, two Surgical, one Gynæcological and one Ophthalmological clinic will be held weekly in both the Montreal General and Royal Victoria Hospitals.

In addition, tutorial instruction will be given in these different departments in the wards, out-patient rooms and laboratories. Special weekly clinics will be given in the Montreal General Hospital on Dermatology and Laryngology and and in the Royal Victoria Hospital on diseases of the Genito-Urinary system.

CLINICAL CLERKS in the medical and surgical wards of both Hospitals are appointed every three months, and each one during his term of service conducts, under the immediate directions of the Clinical Professors, the reporting of all cases in the ward allotted to him. Students entering on and after October 1893 will be required to show a certificate of having acted for six months as clinical clerk in medicine and six months in surgery, and are required to have reported at least ten cases in medicine and ten in surgery. The instruction obtained as clinical clerk is found to be of the greatest possible advantage to Students, as affording a true *practical* training for his future professional life.

DRESSERS are also appointed to the Out-door Departments. For these appointments, application is to be made to the Assistant Surgeons, or to the resident surgeon in charge of the out-patient department.

The large number of patients affected with diseases of the eye and ear, now attending the special clinics at both hospitals, will afford Students ample opportunity to become familiar with all the ordinary affections of those organs, and to make themselves proficient in the use of the ophthalmoscope, and it is hoped that every student will thus seek to gain a practical knowledge of this important branch of Medicine and Surgery. Operations are performed on the eye by the Ophthalmic Surgeon after the outdoor patients have been seen, and Students are invited to attend the same, and as far as practicable, to keep such cases under observation so long as they remain in the Hospital.

There are now special departments in both Hospitals. for Gynæcology, presided over by Specialists in the branches. Students are thus enabled to acquire special technical knowledge under skilled direction. The plan of teaching practical gynæcology for the past five years with marked success has been the limitation of the number of Students to two or three, who, in rotation, assist at the examinations, and receive instruction in the diagnosis and treatment of uterine diseases and the use of gynæcological instruments.

The Clinics at the Montreal General Hospital in Dermatology, and Laryngology are very large and afford a practical training in affections of the skin and throat rarely obtained by medical students.

A special clinic for diseases of the Genito-Urinary Organs has been established at the Royal Victoria Hospital.

Infectious diseases and Insanity will also be taught clinically, the former in the special wards for infectious diseases and the latter at the Verdun Hospital for the Insane.

The Montreal Maternity.

The Faculty has great pleasure in announcing that the Corporation of the Montreal Maternity has recently made very important additions to its building, and has still further improvements in contemplation. Students will therefore have greatly increased facilities for obtaining a practical knowledge of obstetrics and diseases of infancy. An improved Tarnier-Budin phantom is provided for the use of the students, and every facility afforded for acquiring a practical knowledge of the various obstetric manipuations. The institution is under the direct supervision of the Professor of Midwifery, who devotes much time and attention to individual instruction. Students who have attended the course on obstetrics during the autumn and winter terms of the third year will be furnished with cases in rotation, which they will be required to report and attend till convalescence. Clinical midwifery has been placed upon the same basis as Clinical Medicine and Surgery, and a final Clinical examination instituted. Regular courses of clinical lectures are given throughout the session. Special attention being paid to the important subject of infant feeding. The Walker Gordon process of modifying milk is explained and demonstrated. During the autumn and winter terms the Demonstrator of Obstetrics gives Clinical Demonstrations in the wards and instruction in operative work on the phantom. Students will find it very much to their advantage to pay special attention to their Clinical work during the spring term of the third year and the following summer. Two resident accoucheurs are appointed yearly from the graduating class to hold office for a period of six months each.

Fee for twelve months, $12.00, payable at the Maternity Hospital.

XVII.
STUDENTS' APPOINTMENTS.

Montreal General Hospital—Seven Resident Medical Officers.

The following were the candidates at the examination, successful for positions on the house staff of the Montreal General Hospital, for the year beginning May 1st, 1897:—A. R. Pennoyer, M.D.; E. M. Von Eberts, M.D.; F. R. Wainwright, M.D.; H. M. Robertson, M.D.; Charles C Gurd, M.D.; W. K. Brown, M.D., House Pathologist; E. S. Harding, M.D., Anæsthetist; H. Wolferstan Thomas, M.D., Extern Pathological assistant.

Royal Victoria Hospital—Six Resident Medical Officers.

The following graduates in 1897 were appointed to fill vacancies in the Royal Victoria Hospital.

In Medicine, J. G. MacDougall, M.D.; E. C. McCallum, M.D., and A. S. McElroy, M.D.

In Surgery, C. B. Keenan, M.D., and J. J. Roy, M.D.

In Ophthalmology, I. G. Campbell M.D., D.V.S.

University Maternity—Two Resident Medical Officers.

James Barclay, M.D., was appointed in 1897.
Clinical Clerk, Gynæcology.
    "   " Laryngology.
    "   " Diseases of Children.
    ʀ   " Dermatology.
    "   " Diseases of Nervous System.
Out-door Dressers.
Dressers in Eye and Ear Department.
Medical Clinical Clerks.
Post-mortem Clerks.
Student Demonstrators of Anatomy, 4 third-year Students.
Prosectors to Chair of Anatomy, 4.
Assistants in Practical Histology Course, 2.
Assistants in Practical Physiology Course, 4.
Assistants in Practical Chemistry, 6.

VIII.
RULES FOR STUDENTS.

1. In the case of disorderly conduct, any Student may, at the discretion of the Professor, be required to leave the class-room. Persistence in any offence against discipline, after admonition by the Professor, shall be reported to the Dean of the Faculty. The Dean may, at his discretion, reprimand the Student, or refer the matter to the Faculty at its next meeting, and may in the interval suspend from classes.

2. Absence from any number of lectures can only be excused by necessity or duty, of which proof must be given, when called for, to the Faculty. The number of times of absence, from necessity or duty, that shall disqualify for the keeping of a Session, shall in each case be determined by the Faculty.

3. While in the College, Students are expected to conduct themselves in the same orderly manner as in the Class-room.

4. When Students are brought before the Faculty under the above rules, the Faculty may reprimand, impose fines, disqualify from competing for prizes and honors, suspend from Classes, or report to the Corporation for expulsion.

Faculty of Comparative Medicine and Veterinary Science.

THE PRINCIPAL (*ex-officio*).

Professors:

D. McEACHRAN, F.R.C.V.S., V.S. Edin., D.V.S., Dean of the Faculty.
M. C. BAKER, D.V.S.
CHARLES McEACHRAN, D.V.S., Registrar of the Faculty.

Associate Professors:

G: P. GIRDWOOD, M.D.   WESLEY MILLS, M.A., M.D., D.V.S.
GEO. WILKINS, M.D.   J. G. ADAMI, M.A., M.D. (Cantab.).
D. P. PENHALLOW, B.Sc.

Lecturers:

N. D. GUNN, M.D.   C. F. MARTIN, B.A., M.D.

Examiners:

The Professors and Associate Professors, together with the following gentlemen nominated by the Provincial Government:

J. A. COUTURE, D.V.S., 49 Garden Street, Quebec.
A. McCORMICK, D.V.S., Ormstown, P.Q.
A. W. HARRIS, D.V.S., Ottawa, Ont.
JOHN M. PARKER, D.V.S., Haverhill, Mass.
FRANK MILLER, V.S., New York.
A. W. CLEMENT, D.V.S., Baltimore, Md., U.S.

Matriculation Examiner.—A. N. SHEWAN, M A., Lansdowne School, Montreal.

SESSION 1898-99.

The ninth Session of the Faculty (being the thirty-third of the Montreal Veterinary College) will be opened on Wednesday, 21st September, 1898, by an introductory lecture, at 8 p.m., in the lecture-room of the Faculty, No. 6 Union Avenue. The regular course of lectures will begin on the following day, at the hours named in the time table, and will continue till the end of March. The hours of lectures will be announced later, together with any alterations which may be necessary, the course as herein announced being subject to such changes as the Faculty may see fit to make.

The Montreal Veterinary College was inaugurated in 1866.

The complete course of study in this Faculty extends over three years. Graduates of recognized Medical Colleges are allowed to present themselves for examination after regular attendance on one full course; graduates of recognized Agricultural Colleges in which Veterinary Science constitutes a branch of study, after regular attendance for two full courses.

Allowances will be made to students of Human or Comparative Medicine, or others who can produce certified class tickets for attendance on any of the subjects embraced in the curriculum from any recognized college or university.

Graduates and students who avail themselves of the above privileges will nevertheless be required to pass an examination in the subjects comprised in the three years' course, unless, from satisfactory evidence otherwise produced, the examiners consider it to be unnecessary.

Graduates of recognized Veterinary Colleges desirous of taking the degree may do so by attendance on the final subjects for one full session, but will be required to pass the examinations on all the subjects embraced in the curriculum, botany excepted.

Occasional and agricultural students will be received without matriculation for attendance on any particular series of lectures. Such students will not be examined, nor will they be entitled to receive class certificates except as occasional students, nor will such attendance be accepted should the student subsequently wish to become a regular student of the Faculty.

MATRICULATION.

Every student, previous to his admission, must produce a certificate of educational requirements satisfactory to the Faculty, or submit himself to a matriculation examination in (1) writing, (2) reading aloud, (3) dictation, (4) English grammar and (5) composition, (6) outlines of geography, with special reference to North America, (7) arithmetic, including vulgar and decimal fractions.

NOTE.—It is contemplated to add the rudiments of Latin to the matriculation in the near future.

A. N. Shewan, M.A., will hold the matriculation examination on Saturday, 17th September, 9 a.m., at the College, 6 Union Avenue, when all those intending to enter the course should present themselves for examination. Candidates possessing certificates of education or of previous matriculation should produce them for the inspection and approval of the examiner. Graduates of any Faculty in a recognized University or Agricultural College are not required to matriculate.

No College is recognized unless its students are required to matriculate.

REGISTRATION AND PAYMENT OF FEES.

The following are the College regulations:—

All students desirous of attending the classes shall, at the commencement of each session, enrol their names and residences in the register of the Faculty, and procure from the Registrar a ticket of registration, for which each student shall pay a fee of $5.

The said register shall be closed on the last day of October in each year. The fees are payable to the Registrar, and all class tickets will be issued by him, *and must be paid in advance* at the time of registration; the Registrar will on no consideration issue tickets till the fees are paid. Intending students must govern themselves accordingly.*

All students must register, including those who receive free bursaries.

Fees for the whole course are $75 per session, and, in all cases, must be paid on entering. Matriculation fee, $5, which is to be paid prior to the examination; $5 for registration, and $5 for re-registration, payable at the beginning of each of the following two Sessions, and $20 on receiving the diploma. Students who are allowed time for previous study will be required to pay full fees, and $5 for registration each session. Payments must be made in all cases as above.

In addition to the above Faculty fees, every undergraduate must pay an annual fee of $2 for maintenance and use of college grounds.†

*Owing to losses incurred by non-payment of fees, the Registrar must refuse registration till the fees are paid, which may be returned if the applicant fails to matriculate.

†First Year. Fees ... $75	Second Year. Fees ... $75	Third Year. Fees.... $75
Matriculation " 5	Registration " ... 5	Registration " 5
Registration " ... 5	Grounds " 2	Grounds " 2
Grounds " ... 2		Diploma " 20
$87	$82	$102

STUDENTS OF THE PROVINCE OF QUEBEC.

In consideration of the annual grant, the Council of Agriculture has the privilege of sending thirteen pupils, free of expense, to the whole course ; such students, however, pay a fee of $5 for the course in Botany, $5 annually for registration, and $2 annual ground fees. These Bursaries may be obtained by young men resident in the Province of Quebec, by application made to the Dean of the Faculty in the handwriting of applicant, accompanied by a recommendation from the Agricultural Society of the district in which they reside, provided the Council considers them qualified by education and in other respects for entering the College.

In all cases, except when specially arranged, Bursars will be required to give a guarantee that they will attend three Sessions, and failing to do so, they shall be required to pay the fees for the Sessions which they have attended. These Bursaries are not intended for nor will they be given to such students as do not require such aid.

GENERAL REGULATIONS.

Students of this Faculty will be graded as of the first, the second, and the final year. In each year students will take the studies fixed for that year only, unless by special permission of the Faculty.

Persons desirous of entering as Occasional Students shall apply to the Dean of the Faculty for admission as such, and shall obtain a ticket or tickets for the class or classes they desire to attend.

All students shall be subject to the following regulations as regards attendance and conduct:—

A class-book shall be kept by each Professor and Lecturer, in which the presence or absence of Students shall be carefully noted; and the said class-book shall be submitted to the Faculty at a meeting to be held between the close of the lectures and the commencement of the examinations; and the Faculty shall, after examination of such class-book, decide which students shall be deemed to have been sufficiently regular in their attendance to entitle them to proceed to the examination in the respective classes.

Punctual attendance on all the classes proper to his year is required of each Student. Absence or tardiness, without sufficient excuse, or inattention or disorder in the Class-room, if persisted in after admonition by the Professor, will be reported to the Dean of the Faculty, who may reprimand the Student or report to the Faculty, as he may decide. While in the building, or going to or from it, Students are expected to conduct themselves in the same orderly manner as in the Class-rooms. Any Professor observing improper conduct in the Class-rooms, or elsewhere in the building, will admonish the Student, and, if necessary, report him to the Dean.

When Students are reported to the Faculty under the above rules, the Faculty may reprimand, report to parents or guardians, disqualify from competing for prizes or honors, suspend from classes, or report to the Corporation for expulsion.

Any Students injuring the furniture or building will be required to repair the same at his own expense, and will, in addition, be subject to such penalty as the Faculty may see fit to impose.

All cases of discipline involving the interest of more than one Faculty, or of the University generally, shall be reported to the Principal, or, in his absence, to the Vice-Principal.

The College year shall be divided into two terms, the first extending to the Christmas vacation, and the second from the expiration of the Christmas vacation to the 30th March following.

Each lecture shall be of one hour's duration, but the Professors shall have the right to substitute an examination for any such lecture.

At the end of each term there shall be a general examination of all the classes, under the superintendence of the Professors and such other examiners as may be appointed by the Corporation. The results shall be reported as early as possible, to the Faculty.

The students have all the privileges of the McGill Medical Faculty's Laboratories, which are thus described in their annual calendar:—

PHYSIOLOGICAL LABORATORY.

The Physiological Laboratory, which is situated on the ground floor, is supplied with the most modern apparatus for the practical teaching of this most important branch of the medical curriculum. It contains, amongst other valuable instruments: kymographs, various manometers, etc., for demonstrating blood pressure; myographs, rheocords, moist chambers, etc., and various electrical appliances for demonstrating experiments in connection with nerve and muscle; special apparatus for illustrating various points in respiration ; apparatus specially suitable for demonstrating the processes of digestion, as well as the chemical composition and nature of the secretions, and the chief constituents of the tissues and nutritive fluids. The laboratory is arranged in such a way as to permit of Students assisting at, and taking part in, these demonstrations. During the past session, important additions of apparatus have been made to the Physiological Laboratory.

CHEMISTRY.

The course in chemistry embraces Chemical Physics, in the first portion of the course, the theory of Chemistry, both inorganic and organic, in the latter part of the course. The Chemical Laboratory, which is available to the Students of Comparative Medicine, is large, lofty and well lighted, and can accommodate comfortably 76 men at one time. Each Student when entering on his course, has a numbered table in the laboratory assigned to him for his use during the session. Each table has its own gas and water fixtures, and is provided with shelves for its corresponding set of reagent bottles, as well as a drawer and locker containing a modern set of chemical apparatus especially adapted for the work. This apparatus is provided by the Professor of Chemistry, and supplied to each Student without extra charge. The Student is required to pay only for apparatus broken or destroyed.

The laboratory is furnished with a large draught closet for ventilation, sulphuretted hydrogen apparatus, gas and combustion furnaces, etc., giving to the student unsurpassed advantages for acquiring a sound and practical knowledge of medical chemistry.

PATHOLOGICAL LABORATORY.

In the Pathological Laboratory accommodation will be provided for Students or practioners who desire to carry on advanced study or private pathological research. The laboratory has been entirely re-built recently, and is well stocked with the usual apparatus for pathological and bacteriological work.

The demonstrations in Morbid Anatomy will be given in a small laboratory, specially arranged for the work. The classes in Pathological Histology will be held in the Pathological Laboratory.

Through the generosity of the late Mr. J. H. R. Molson, the large house previously occupied by Professor Harrington has been converted into a Pathological Laboratory, having on the upper floor the Class and Demonstration room, capable of holding practical classes of fifty students. This is fully fitted with microscopes and other apparatus for the purpose of Pathological Histology and Bacteriology. Upon the first floor are the Library and Professor's room, the Preparation and Research rooms, with a smaller Incubator room for Bacteriological use. On the ground floor are situated the animal and store rooms and the apartments of the assistant.

Accommodations will be provided for students or practitioners who desire to carry on advanced study or pathological research.

HISTOLOGICAL LABORATORY.

The Histological Laboratory is a large, well-lighted room on the second floor. It is so arranged that over eighty students can be present at the microscopical demonstrations. For this purpose it is supplied with thirty-five microscopes, all from the well-known makers, Zeiss, Hartnock and Leitz. From the large number of microscopes employed, students will have special facilities in studying and making themselves thoroughly acquainted with the specimens that are the subjects of demonstration.

PRACTICAL MICROSCOPY.

This is an entirely optional course, in charge of Prof. Wilkins, assisted by Dr. Gunn. It is intended especially for teaching the technique of Microscopy. Students will be shown how to examine blood, etc., also to cut, stain, and mount specimens. For this purpose, they will have furnished them normal structures, with which they will be able to secure a cabinet of at least 100 specimens, which will be of great benefit when in practice. Reagents and everything, except cover glasses and cabinet cases, provided. Fee, $8.

COURSES OF LECTURES.

BOTANY.

D. P. Penhallow, M.A.Sc.

The course in Botany is designed to give Students a thorough grounding in the general morphology of plants and ability to determine species. It includes a practical study of the Spermaphytes and Pteridophytes during the first half of the session, and after Christmas a Course of lectures on general Morphology, together with a special discussion of plants possessing poisonous properties, and therefore liable to produce injury to grazing animals.

The Morphological Laboratory is well equipped with efficient dissecting microscopes, while the Botanic Garden and Herbarium afford an ample supply of fresh and dried material.

ZOOLOGY.*

Ernest W. MacBride, M.A., B.Sc.

This course includes a systematic study of the classification of animals, illustrated by Canadian examples, and by the collections in the Peter Redpath Museum. It affords suitable preparation for

* Students may either take Botany or Zoology, but must intimate at the beginning of the Session their choice, and adhere to this, except by special permission of the Faculty. Students desiring to attend both subjects in one session may do so by permission of the Faculty.

collecting in any department of Canadian Zoology, or Palaeontology, and as an introduction to Comparative Physiology.

Students in Botany or Zoology will receive tickets to the Peter Redpath Museum, and to the Museum of the Natural History Society of Montreal.

It is optional with students to select either the course on Botany or on Zoology.

CHEMISTRY.

Gilbert P. Girdwood, M.D.

Inorganic Chemistry is fully treated ; a large portion of the course is devoted to Organic Chemistry and its relations to Medicine. The branches of Physics bearing upon or connected with Chemistry also engage the attention of the Class. For experimental illustration, abundant apparatus is possessed by the College.

The Chemical Laboratory will be open to members of the Class to repeat experiments performed during the course, under the superintendence of the Professor or his Assistant.

PHYSIOLOGY.

T. Wesley Mills, M.A., M.D., D.V.S.

The purpose of this Course is to make students thoroughly acquainted, so far as time permits, with modern Physiology, its methods, its deductions, and the basis on which the latter rest. Accordingly, a full course of lectures is given, in which both the Physical and the Chemical departments of the subject receive attention.

In addition to the use of diagrams, plates, models, etc., every department of the subject is experimentally illustrated. The experiments are free from elaborate *technique*, and many of them are of a kind susceptible of ready imitation by the student.

Laboratory work for Senior Students:—

(1) During a part of the Session there will be a course on Physiological Chemistry, in which the student will, under direction, investigate food-stuffs, digestive action, blood, and the more important secretions and excretions, including urine. All the apparatus and material for this course will be provided.

(2) The remainder of the Session will be devoted to the performance of such experiments as are unsuitable for demonstration to a large class in the lecture room and such as require the use of elaborate methods, apparatus, etc. The course for first year students is similar to that for senior students, though less advanced, and more attention will be given to the anatomico-physiological aspects of the subject than to the chemical.

HISTOLOGY.

Geo. Wilkins, M.D.

This will consist of a course of ten lectures and twenty-five weekly demonstrations with the microscope. As the demonstrations will be chiefly relied upon for teaching the Microscopic Anatomy of the various structures, the specimens under observation will then be minutely described. Plates and diagrams specially prepared for these lectures will be freely made use of.

COMPARATIVE PATHOLOGY.

J. G. Adami, M.D., Professor.

C. F. Martin, M.D., Lecturer.

The teaching in Pathology at McGill Medical College includes courses in general and special Pathology, in Bacteriology (held during the summer Session), and instruction in the performance of Autopsies. These courses—while directed especially towards giving to the Students a due knowledge of the causation and course of disease in man—are necessarily based largely upon the results of observations upon the lower animals, and the greater part of all these causes is applicable equally to conditions obtaining in the domestic animals. There is in addition a practical course of Pathological Histology for Students of Comparative Medicine, and instruction is given upon the performance of Autopsies upon the lower animals.*

MEDICINE AND SURGERY.

D. McEachran, F.R.C.V.S.

Students of all years must attend.

The course embraces the principles and practice of Veterinary Medicine, including the diseases of domestic animals, their nature, causes, symptoms, and treatment. It necessarily includes Pathology and Pathological Anatomy, with daily clinical demonstrations in the hospital and the yard practice of the College, as well as illustrations from plates, preserved specimens, and fresh material furnished by the Pathologist.

The course on Surgery embraces Surgical Anatomy and Practices of Surgery, and will be illustrated by a large collection of surgical appliances.

* Undergraduates in the second and third sessions are particularly recommended to take the practical course in Bacteriology during the summer session, if possible.

The large and varied practice of the College furnishes abundance of cases for demonstration purposes. Attendance and practical work in the Pharmacy and Hospital is compulsory during the entire course, in the order arranged at the beginning of each Session, and forms an important part of the qualifications for graduation.

ANATOMY.

M· C. BAKER, D.V.S.

In this course the Anatomy· of the horse is the subject of special study, while the structural differences of all the domestic animals are carefully explained and illustrated by fresh subjects. There is a very large collection of anatomical models by Dr. Auzoux, of Paris, natural injections and dissections, and a most complete collection of diagrams including Marshall's complete set, Mons. Achille Compte's Anatomical and Zoological series; also a large collection of drawings specially prepared for the school by Mr. Scott Leighton, artist, Boston, and Mr. Hawksett, Montreal.

The dissecting room is open at all hours, subjects are easily procured, and either the Professor or Demonstrator will be in attendance to superintend and direct students in practical dissection. The room is furnished with every convenience, is thoroughly lighted, and affords students all that can be reasonably desired.

Students are required to pay for the material necessary for practical anatomy.

Before a student can be allowed to present himself for his pass examination, he must produce tickets certified by the demonstrator that he has dissected two entire subjects,—that is, one each session.

MATERIA MEDICA AND THERAPEUTICS.

NEIL GUNN, M.D., Lecturer.

This course comprises a description of the physiological and therapeutic action of all the more important medicines used in Veterinary Practice, with a short reference to their general properties and principal preparations. It will also include a course in the practical work of compounding and administering medicines in the pharmacy and hospital. There will also be experimental demonstrations of the action of some of the more important drugs on animals.

CATTLE PATHOLOGY AND OBSTETRICS.

C. McEachran, D.V.S.

A special course on Cattle Diseases and Veterinary Obstetrics will be delivered, embracing the history of Cattle Plagues : their nature, symptoms, pathological anatomy, prophylactic and thera- peutic treatment ; breeding and general management of breeding animals, disease incident to gestation and parturition, etc.

SPECIAL COURSE ON DOGS.

Professor Wesley Mills will give a special course on Dogs, which will include :—

(1.) Lectures on the physical and psychic characteristics of all the leading varieties, illustrated by specimens from his own kennels and other sources, as well as by plates, etc.

(2.) The principles of training; the feeding and general manage- ment of dogs.

(3.) The principles of breeding ; the management of brood bitches and the rearing of puppies.

(4.) Bench show management and the public judging of dogs.

(5.) The rights and duties of dog owners.

In all the above courses the clinical and pathological aspects of the subjects will be considered, as well as the normal.

THE MUSEUM.

Contains a large collection of natural and artificial specimens, consisting of skeletons of almost all the domestic animals, numerous specimens of diseased bones, preparations by Dr. Auzoux of all the different organs in the body, natural dissections, colored models, diagrams, etc., etc., all of which are used, in illustrating the lectures, and to which the Students have frequent opportunities of referring. Students will also enjoy the privileges of the Museum of the Medical Faculty of McGill University, which is rich in pathological speci- mens.

THE PHARMACY.

All the medicines used in the practice of the College are com- pounded by the Students, under the direction of the Professors, from prescriptions for each particular case, and most of them are admin- istered or applied by them. For this purpose they are detailed for certain pharmaceutical duties alternately. By this means they become familiar with the physical properties, compatabilities, doses and uses of the medicines, and become expert in administering them to the different patients brought for treatment. Attendance and practical work in the Pharmacy are compulsory.

THE PRACTICE.

The Hospital and Daily Clinics, as well as a very extensive outdoor practice, including most of the largest stables in the city and numerous farms in the vicinity, afford excellent opportunities for clinical observation on horses of all breeds and ages. Owing to the numbers of cattle kept in the city, and the valuable thoroughbred herds in the neighborhood, advanced Students are enabled to see and do considerable cattle practice. The dog practice is the largest in Canada. All canine diseases can be studied clinically, owing to the large number of dogs brought to the College for medical or surgical treatment.

Senior Students will be appointed to act alternately as dressers in the Hospital, and first and second year men must assist in administering medicines and at operations.

*TEXT BOOKS.

The following text books are recommended:—

Anatomy.—Chauveau's Comparative Anatomy ; Strangeway's Veterinary Anatomy : McFadyean's Veterinary Anatomy ; Dissector's Manual, Clement.

Physiology.—Physiology for Beginners by Foster and Shore ; Prof. Mills' Text Book of Comparative Physiology ; Class Laboratory Exercises by the same author.

Histology.—Klein's Elements; Schafer's Essentials of Histology.

Botany.—Gray's Structural Botany: Bessey's Botany.

Zoology.—Dawson's.

Chemistry.—Wurtz's Elementary Chemistry; Armstrong ; Remsen's Organic Chemistry.

Medicine and Surgery.—Williams' Principles and Practice of Veterinary Medicine ; Fleming's Sanitary Science and Police ; Williams' Surgery ; Fleming's Operative Surgery ; Robertson's Equine Medicine : Liautard's Operative Veterinary Surgery: Zuill's Translation of Friedberger and Fröhner's Pathology, etc.

* Students are advised not to buy text books extensively till after consultation with the Professor who teaches the subject.

Materia Medica.—Dun's Veterinary Medicines; Walley's Veterinary Conspectus; Tuson's Pharmacy; Hoare's Therapeutics.

Cattle Diseases.—Steel's Bovine Pathology ; Clatter's Cattle Doctor (Armitage); Fleming's Veterinary Obstetrics.

Canine Diseases.—Prof. Mills' The Dog in Health and in Disease.

Diseases of the Dog.—Geo. Müller, tr. by A. Glass, V.S.

Entozoa.—Cobbold's Entozoa of Domestic Animals.

Pathology.—Payne's Pathology; Fraenkel's Bacteriology ; Clement on Post Mortems.

BOARD AND TRAVELLING EXPENSES.

Board can be obtained at from $15 to $20 per month.

By the kindness of the Railway Companies, certified students of the College will be granted return tickets from Montreal to any part of their lines at greatly reduced rates, the said tickets to hold good from the close of one session to the beginning of the next.

Return tickets will also be granted for the Christmas vacation.

VETERINARY MEDICAL ASSOCIATION.

This Association is for the mutual improvement of its members in all matters pertaining to the profession.

Graduates and students of Veterinary Medicine and graduates and students of Human Medicine are eligible to membership.

The meetings are held fortnightly, at which papers are read and discussed, cases reported, etc.

The advantages which students derive from these meetings are very great. Not only do they hear carefully prepared papers on subjects of professional importance, but an opportunity is afforded for practising public speaking, which in after life is often extremely useful. The fees of the Association are expended in the purchase of books for the Library, drugs for experimental purposes and the prizes awarded for papers read.

The Library is owned by the Association, and is under the control of officers who are elected annually. It contains nearly 600 volumes, embracing works of great antiquity, as well as the modern works on Veterinary Science and collateral subjects, in both the English and French languages, all of which are available for consultation and study by members.

Every student is expected to become a member. The entrance fee is $5, and the yearly subscription $2.50. A Diploma of Honorary Fellowship is conferred on all members who have complied with the regulations of the Association.

ASSOCIATION FOR THE STUDY OF COMPARATIVE PSYCHOLOGY.

This Society is similar in constitution to the Veterinary Medical Association, and has a special library of about 100 volumes. Its object is the study of the Psychic Phenomena (intelligence, etc.) of all classes of animals, and the diffusion of sounder views on this subject. Naturally, it is of great importance in the practice of medicine upon dumb animals as well as of peculiar scientific interest.

DONATIONS.

The late John Wesley Gadsden, M.R.C.V.S., of Philadelphia, Penn., U.S.A., generously donated to this Faculty his valuable library of nearly 400 volumes and the specimens of his private museum, many of which are of unusual value.

QUALIFICATIONS FOR THE DEGREE.

Candidates for the Final Examination shall furnish testimonials of attendance on lectures on the following subjects:—

Either Botany or Zoology—One course of six months, 1st year.

Histology,
Chemistry,
Physiology,
Anatomy.
} Two courses of six months, 1st and 2nd years.

General Pathology and Demonstrations, one course of six months.

Cattle Diseases and Obstetrics,
Practice of Medicine and Surgery,
Materia Medica and Therapeutics,
} Two courses, 2nd and 3rd years.

No one will be permitted to become a candidate for examination who shall not have attended at least one full course of lectures in this Faculty, including all the subjects embraced in the curriculum. Courses of less length than the above will be received only for the time over which they have extended.

Students, except by special permission of the Faculty, must pursue the subjects of Anatomy, Physiology, Chemistry, Histology and Botany or Zoology in their first session.

Candidates of the 1st and 2nd years, who fail to pass in not more than two subjects, may be granted a supplemental examination at the beginning of the following session. Supplemental examinations will not be granted, except by special permission of the Faculty and on written application stating reasons, and on payment of a fee of $2, which must be paid prior to examination.

Candidates who fail to pass in a subject of which two courses are required, may, at the discretion of the Faculty, be required to attend a third course, and furnish a certificate of attendance thereon.

In addition to the written and oral examinations, candidates must pass a practical clinical test, including examination of horses for soundness, written reports being required; the clinical reports to include diagnosis, prognosis, and treatment.

The following oath or affirmation will be exacted from the candidate before receiving the degree:—

DECLARATION OF GRADUATES IN COMPARATIVE MEDICINE AND VETERINARY SCIENCE.

I, —— ——, promise and solemnly declare that I will, with my best endeavors, be careful to maintain the interests of this University. and that, to the best of my ability, I will promote its honor and dignity.

EXAMINATIONS.

First Year.—Pass Examinations in Botany or Zoology, Histology (oral), 1st Chemistry, Anatomy, Physiology, and on all other subjects in the course of this year.

Second Year.—Pass examinations in Chemistry, Physiology, Histology (written) and Anatomy, in addition to sessional examinations in these and the other subjects of the year.

Third Year.—Pass Examinations in Practice of Medicine and Surgery, General and Special Pathology, Veterinary Obstetrics, Diseases of Cattle, and Materia Medica and Therapeutics.

N.B., Written and Oral Examinations will be held from time to time during the session, and attendance at these is compulsory. The standing attained at these examinations will be taken into account at pass examinations.

AGE FOR GRADUATION.

Students under seventeen will be received as apprentices. but cannot be entered as regular Students before attaining that age.

Minors may pass the Examinations, but cannot receive the Diploma until they are twenty-one years of age.

REGULATIONS GOVERNING THE CONFERRING OF THE DEGREE UPON FORMER GRADUATES OF THE MONTREAL VETERINARY COLLEGE.

The Degree of Doctor of Veterinary Science may be conferred on former graduates of Montreal Veterinary College at any Convocation of McGill University held for conferring degrees, subject to the following regulations, which were adopted at a meeting of the Corporation of McGill University, held on the 22nd January, 1890, governing the conferring of Degrees on former graduates :

1st.—That the candidate must be found to have conducted himself throughout his professional career with honor and integrity.

2nd.—That he has not been connected with the manufacture or sale of proprietary medicines.

3rd.—That he has been engaged in actual practice for at least one year since graduating, or that he has been engaged in professional study at some European school.

4th.—That he shall be required to satisfy the Board that he has made reasonable progress in professional knowledge and skill.

In estimating the fitness of a candidate for a degree, account will be taken specially of work done in professional teaching, original research, publication of books or contributions to the journals of the profession.

The fee for the Diploma shall be Twenty Dollars.

An affirmation shall be administered similar to that of other Faculties, and in English.

The Degree may be conferred on absentees.

The regulations relating to fees and affirmations shall apply to ordinary undergraduates on taking the degree.

Graduates intending to apply for the Degree of D.V.S. should notify the Registrar of the Faculty at their earliest convenience, and at the same time state the grounds explicitly on which they base their claims for the Degree.

HINTS TO STUDENTS

The Matriculation Examination which you have to undergo is by no means a severe one, and if you are not prepared to pass it you should begin at once to improve your education.

You had better not 'commence professional reading till you have become familiar with the fundamental subjects. Practice, unless under the guidance of a thoroughly educated practitioner, is more likely to mislead than aid you.

It is advisable that you should arrive in Montreal before the opening day, in order to procure suitable lodgings. Endeavor by all means to be present at the introductory lectures on all subjects; you cannot miss one lecture without thereby losing valuable preparatory information. Come prepared to procure at once the necessary text books and note books. Make your arrangements so as to enable you to devote your entire time and undivided attention to your studies, as the three sessions which the curriculum covers will be found none too long to accomplish the necessary proficiency in the various branches of study required of you. The McGill Y. M. C. A. is especially recommended to you.

NOTICE TO GRADUATES.

For the purpose of increasing pathological material for the classes, graduates are earnestly requested to send any interesting or obscure pathological specimens which may be met with in their practice, to the Pathological Laboratory, McGill Medical College. The specimens may be sent C.O.D. ·by express, and will in all cases be acknowledged. It is suggested that where reports are desired those reports can be satisfactory only when the material arrives in the freshest possible condition. It is urged, therefore, that when forwarded in bottles the tissues be placed immediately either in alcohol, fifty to seventy-five per cent., or in a mixture of equal parts of glycerine and water to which five per cent. of pure carbolic acid has been added. If dry carriage be preferred the method of surrounding the tissues with a cloth well moistened with one in one thousand corrosive sublimate solution, and wrapping this securely in oiled silk, is recommended. A report upon the nature of the specimen will be sent if desired, and the specimens, when of sufficient interest, will be preserved in the Museum with the names of the donors affixed.

STUDENTS' MEETINGS.

The use of the lecture room or other rooms of the College, for holding students' meetings, can be obtained by application to the Dean, stating the object of the meeting, and he may attend personally or appoint someone to represent the Faculty at said meeting. It is strictly forbidden to hold meetings for the discussion of any subject not approved by the Faculty, and students holding such meetings except as above will be dealt with by the Faculty as it may see fit.

McGill Normal School.

The McGill Normal School, in the city of Montreal, is established chiefly for the purpose of training teachers for the Protestant population, and for all religious denominations of the Province of Quebec, other than the Roman Catholic. The studies in this school are carried on chiefly in English, but French is also taught.

GOVERNMENT OF THE SCHOOL.

The Corporation of McGill University is associated with the Superintendent of Public Instruction in the direction of the McGill Normal School, under the regulations of the Protestant Committee of the Council of Public Instruction, and it is authorized to appoint a standing committee consisting of five members, called the "Normal School Committee," which shall have the general supervision of the affairs of the Normal School. The following members of the Corporation of the University constitute the committee of the Normal School for the Session of 1898-99:

NORMAL SCHOOL COMMITTEE.

PROF. W. PETERSON, M.A., LL.D., Principal of the University *Chairman.*
MR. SAMUEL FINLEY, Governor of McGill College.
REV. PRINCIPAL MACVICAR, D.D., LL.D., } Fellows of
J. R. DOUGALL, M.A., } McGill University.
REV. E. I. REXFORD, B.A., }
    J. W. BRAKENRIDGE, B.C.L., *Secretary.*

OFFICERS OF INSTRUCTION.

McGILL NORMAL SCHOOL.

SAMPSON PAUL ROBINS, M.A., LL.D., *Principal and Ordinary Professor of Mathematics, and Lecturer on Art of Teaching.*

ABNER W. KNEELAND, M.A., B.C.L., *Ordinary Professor of English Language and Literature.*

MADAME SOPHIE CORNU, *Professor of French.*

MISS GREEN, *Professor of Drawing.*

MR. R. J. FOWLER, *Instructor in Music.*

MISS LILIAN B. ROBINS, B.A., *Assistant to the Principal, and Instructor in Classics.*

MR. W. H. SMITH, *Instructor in Tonic Sol-Fa.*

MR. JNO. P. STEPHEN, *Instructor in Elocution.*

PROF. D. P. PENHALLOW, M.A.Sc., *Lecturer on Botany.*

T. D. REED, M.D., C.M., *Lecturer on Physiology and Hygiene.*

NEVIL N. EVANS, M.A.Sc., *Lecturer on Chemistry.*

MR. JAMES WALKER, *Instructor in Penmanship and Book-keeping.*

MISS LOUISE DERICK, *Instructor in Kindergarten Methods.*

MR. A. W. ARTHY, *Lecturer in the Theory of Kindergarten and Transition Work.*

— —

MODEL SCHOOLS OF THE McGILL NORMAL SCHOOL.

ORRIN REXFORD, B.A.Sc., *Head Master of Boys' School.*

MISS MARY I. PEEBLES, *Head Mistress of Girls' School.*

MISS SELINA F. SLOAN, *Head Mistress of Primary School.*

———

ANNOUNCEMENT FOR THE SESSION 1898-99.

This Institution is intended to give a thorough training to teachers, by instruction and training in the Normal School itself and by practice in the Model Schools; and the arrangements are of such a character as to afford the greatest possible facilities to students from all parts of the province. Hereafter the Protestant Central Board of Examiners for the Province of Quebec will grant diplomas only to teachers-in-training of this Institution and to graduates of British or Canadian Universities.

The forty-third Session of this School will commence on the first of September, 1898, and close on the thirty-first of May, 1899.* The students are graded as follows :

1.—*Elementary Class.*—Studying for the Elementary Diploma.
2.—*Advanced Elementary Class.*—Studying for the Advanced Elementary Diploma.
3.—*Model School Class.*—Studying for the Model School Diploma.
4.—*Kindergarten Class.*—Studying for the Kindergarten Diploma.
5.—*Class in Pedagogy.*—Preparing for the Academy Diploma.

All the following regulations and privileges apply to male and female students alike.

I. MODE OF ADMISSION TO THE NORMAL SCHOOL.

The Central Board of Examiners alone have the right to admit to the several courses of study in the McGill Normal School.

Elementary Classes.—Any British subject who produces a certificate of good moral character from the minister of the congregation to which he belongs, and evidence to show that at the time of his application he has entered upon the seventeenth year of his age, may be admitted to examination for entrance into the elementary class of the McGill Normal School.

Each candidate for admission to the elementary class shall notify the Secretary of the Central Board of Examiners, G. W. Parmelee, Esq., B.A., Department of Public Instruction, Quebec, in accordance with form No. 3, on or before the 15th of April next preceding the examination, of his intention to

* In the Elementary Class only, the session opens on January 4th, 1899, and closes April 28th, 1899.

present himself for examination.* Each candidate shall at the same time deposit with the Secretary of the Central Board, first a certificate of good moral character, according to the authorized form No. 1, signed by the minister of the congregation to which he belongs, and by at least two school commissioners or trustees or school visitors of the locality in which he has resided for six months during the preceding two years; second, an extract from a register of baptism or other sufficient proof, showing that he is of the requisite age.

Each candidate shall at the same time pay to the Secretary of the Central Board of Examiners the sum of two dollars. This fee shall be used in paying the expenses of the Central Board of Examiners. The fee shall not be returned to a candidate who has failed to enter the Normal School, but at the next examination such candidate may again present himself without extra payment.

On receiving the candidate's notification, certificates of moral character, satisfactory evidence of age and examination fee, the Secretary of the Central Board shall notify the candidate of the place and time of the examination, and shall also notify the deputy examiner or examiners at the centre of examination chosen, to admit the candidates to the examinations of the second grade academy, or to such of the examinations as may be indicated by the Central Board of Examiners.

The answers of all such candidates shall be written on paper of a special tint, shall be promptly read and valued with other answers to the same questions; then collected and sent with another copy of the questions submitted and a statement of the results to the Secretary, who shall submit the whole to the Central Board or to a sub committee of that Board. In view of the results and the answers submitted the Central Board of

---

* As it has not been possible to publish earlier notice of the time for application to be admitted to the McGill Normal School, the Central Board of Examiners order that, for this year only, an examination for admission on trial shall be held in the McGill Normal School beginning Sept. 1st, 1898, and that candidates may send form No. 3 to the Secretary of the Board of Examiners on or before August 15th, 1898.

Examiners or its sub-committee shall authorize the candidate to enter the Normal School for the four months' course or for the nine months' course in the elementary school class or shall refuse admission, as each case may warrant. But when a candidate is authorized to enter for the four months' course he may, if he choose, enter at the beginning of the session for the nine months' course.

Holders of elementary diplomas are exempt from examination for entrance to the elementary classes.

Model School Class.—Any British subject who produces a certificate of good moral character from the minister of the congregation to which he belongs, and evidence to show that at the time of his application he has entered upon the eighteenth year of his age, may be admitted to examination for entrance into the model school class of the McGill Normal School.

Each candidate for admission to the model school class shall at the same time* and in the same manner as candidates for admission to the Elementary school class give notification and deposit a certificate of good moral character and satisfactory evidence of age together with an examination fee of four dollars, which sum shall admit, in case of failure, without further payment to the examination of the year next ensuing.

Examinations for admission to the model school class shall be either the examinations in the Normal School for the advanced elementary diploma, or the A.A. examinations of the universities. On receipt of the notification, certificate of moral character, examination fee and satisfactory evidence of age, the Secretary of the Central Board shall notify the candidate of the place and time of the examination, and shall also notify the Principal of the Normal School or the Secretary of the University examiners, as the case may be, to admit the candidate to examination. If the examination chosen be that of the A.A. examiners, he shall remit the examination fee to their Secretary.

* See note on preceding page.

Persons who already hold elementary school diplomas are exempt from the examination fee and will be liable to examination only in algebra, geometry, Latin and French, with such additional subjects as in the judgment of the Central Board or its sub-committee may be deemed necessary in particular instances. But satisfactory evidence of having taught successfully for eight months shall give exemption from such examinations.

No evidence of standing at the A.A. examinations other than the certificates of the universities shall be taken. For admission to the model school class of the Normal School such certificate must show that the candidate has passed in Latin, French, arithmetic, algebra, geometry and the English Language, or English Literature. A candidate, who has failed to enter the model school class, may be admitted to the elementary school class.

Kindergarten Class.—Admission to the class for kindergartners shall be granted by the Central Board of Examiners or its sub-committee only to such persons as, holding advanced elementary school diplomas, notify the Secretary of the Central Board on or before the fifteenth day of April* in any year of their wish to enter this class, and are reported by the Principal of the Normal School to possess the necessary special fitness for kindergarten work.

All Classes.—Authorization to enter any class of the McGill Normal School holds good for two years from the date of the issue, but no longer, and is forfeited by failure to pass the semi-sessional examinations to the satisfaction of the Principal of the Normal School.

The Central Board of School Examiners may admit on trial to any class, in exceptional cases, persons whose qualifications may be insufficient for entrance. Such persons may be excluded from the school by the Principal whenever he may judge it best so to do ; but none shall be permitted to enter or to remain on trial after the semi-sessional examinations.

No candidate is admitted to the Normal School until the

---

*See note on preceding page.

provisions of the School laws respecting admission have been fulfilled. All necessary forms of application may be had from the Secretary of the Central Board.

II. CONDITIONS OF CONTINUANCE IN THE NORMAL SCHOOL.

Attendance.—Persons admitted to the Normal School must attend on the first day of the opening, and must thereafter attend punctually every day of the session, or give reasons satisfactory to the Principal of the School for their absence or tardiness.

Fees.—Each teacher-in-training who during attendance at the school resides at home with parents or guardians shall pay monthly in advance the sum of four dollars school fee. The Principal of the school is permitted to wait until the end of the fifth day of the month for payment, but no longer; if the amount be not then paid the teacher-in-training must withdraw from the school until the amount is paid, but if it be not paid within the next five days, that is, before the eleventh day of the month, the delinquent teacher-in-training shall be held to have withdrawn, and his name shall be removed from the books of the school.

Conduct.—In order to continuance in the Normal School teachers-in-training must maintain conduct and character suitable to their present position and their future calling.

Each professor, lecturer or teacher has the power of excluding from his lectures any student who may be inattentive to his studies, or guilty of any minor infraction of the regulations, until the matter can be reported to the Principal.

The Principal of the school has power to suspend from attendance any pupil, for improper conduct or neglect of duty, for a week, or when he deems it advisable to submit the case to the Normal School Committee, until the next meeting of that body.

The Normal School Committee is empowered, for any grave cause, to expel any teacher-in-training from any class.

Teachers-in-training must give their whole time and attention to the work of the school, and are not permitted to engage in any other course of study or business during the session of the school.

Examinations.—All teachers-in-training, in order to continue in the Normal School, must pass the Christmas semi-sessional examinations to the satisfaction of the Principal.

Retirement.—Teachers-in-training who leave the Normal School in the middle of a session are expected to assign to the Principal satisfactory reasons, accompanied, in case of failure of health, by a medical certificate. Neglect to comply with this regulation will be a bar to future admission to the Normal School.

III. ATTENDANCE ON RELIGIOUS INSTRUCTION.

Teachers-in-training will be required to state with what religious denomination they are connected; and a list of the students connected with each denomination shall be furnished to one of the ministers of such denomination resident in Montreal, with the request that he will meet weekly with that portion of the teachers-in-training, or otherwise provide for their religious instruction. Every Thursday after four o'clock will be assigned for this purpose.

In addition to punctual attendance at weekly religious instruction, each student will be required to attend public worship at his own church, at least once every Sunday.

IV. BOARDING HOUSES.

No boarding house is attached to the institution, but every care will be taken to ensure the comfort and good conduct of the students in private boarding houses approved by the Principal, who will furnish lists to applicants for admission. Board can be obtained at from $12 to $16 per month.

1. The teachers-in-training shall state the places of their residence, and those who cannot reside with their parents will

be,permitted to live in boarding houses, but in such only as shall be specially approved of. No boarding houses having permission to board male teachers-in-training, will be permitted to receive female teachers-in-training as boarders, and *vice versa*.

2. They are on no account to be absent from their lodgings after half-past nine o'clock in the evening.

3. They will be allowed to attend such lectures and public meetings only as may be considered by the Principal conducive to their moral and mental improvement.

4. A copy of the regulations shall be sent to all the keepers of lodging houses at the beginning of the session.

5. In case of lodgings being chosen by parents or guardians a written statement of the parent or guardian shall be presented to the Principal.

6. All intended changes of lodgings shall be made known beforehand to the Principal or to one of the Professors.

7. Boarding houses shall be visited monthly by a committe of professors.

8. Special visitations shall be made in case of sickness being reported, either by professors or by ladies connected with the school; and, if necessary, medical attendance shall be procured.

9. Students and lodging house keepers are required to report, as soon as possible, all cases of serious illness and all infractions of rules touching boarding houses.

V. PRIVILEGES OF TEACHERS-IN-TRAINING.

Diplomas.—All teachers-in-training who pass the semi-sessioual examinations in the Normal School with 60 per cent. of the total marks and who have not fallen below 50 per cent. in any one of the groups of subjects, English, Mathematics, French and Miscellaneous, nor in any one of the subjects required by the authorized course of study for schools of the grade which they aspire to teach, or make more than one mistake in spelling in one hundred words of dictation chosen from any authorized text book, shall be entitled to continue in their classes after Christmas. Except by the special permission of the Principal, none others shall be entitled to this privilege.

All teachers-in-training who attain the standards defined above at the final examinations in the Normal School shall be entitled to diplomas of the grade of the class to which they belong; and except with the concurrence of two-thirds of the members of the Central Board of Examiners who may be present at the discussion none others shall receive diplomas. But the Central Board of Examiners may grant an elementary diploma to a teacher-in-training who fails to pass the examinations in the Model School Class, or those for the advanced elementary diploma.

Bursaries.—Each holder of an advanced elementary diploma or of a model school or kindergarten diploma, on showing that he has taught successfully in some school of this province under the control of school commissioners or school trustees other than the Protestant Board of School Commissioners of Montreal, shall be paid by the Principal of the Normal School, out of its funds, the sum of two dollars for each month of successful teaching, not exceeding eight months in each year, during each of the two scholastic years immediately succeeding the award of his diploma. If in two years of consecutive attendance at the Normal School a teacher-in-training has taken an advanced elementary diploma and either a model school diploma or a kindergarten diploma the amount to be paid shall be four dollars for each month; if three sessions of the Normal School elapse between the admission of the teacher-in-training and the conferring of the second diploma the amount to be paid shall be three dollars for each month.

Successful teaching shall be shown by submitting at the annual meeting of the Central Board of Examiners a certificate of the form 5 signed by the chairman or by the secretary-treasurer of each board under which the teacher has taught and by each school inspector in whose district of inspection

he has taught.   But the signature of any school inspector
stating that he was unable to visit the school during the in-
cumbency of that teacher shall be accepted.

Travelling Expenses.—On being awarded an advanced elementary diploma, a model school diploma, or a kindergarten
diploma, each teacher-in-training at the McGill Normal School
shall be paid by the Principal of the Normal School, out of its
funds, the sum of three cents for each mile that his home, in
the Province of Quebec, is more than fifty miles distant from
the City of Montreal.

Prizes.—The J. C. Wilson prize of forty dollars and a book,
annually chosen by the donor, shall be given to that teacher-in-
training of the advanced elementary school class who passes
for a diploma, and takes the highest aggregate of marks at the
final examinations of the year.

The Prince of Wales' medal and prize shall be given to that
teacher-in-training of the model school class who passes for a
diploma, and takes the highest aggregate of marks at the final
examinations of the year.

The Superintendent of Public Instruction gives annually
a gold medal to the teacher-in-training of the model school
class, who passes for a diploma, and stands second at the
final examinations of the year. He also gives a prize in books
to the student in the model school year, who stands highest
in French.

The G. W. Parmelee prize of valuable books is given annually at the pleasure of the donor by G. W. Parmelee, Esq.,
Secretary of the Department of Public Instruction, to the
teacher-in-training who, passing for an advanced elementary
diploma, takes the second highest aggregate of marks at the
final examinations of the year.

His Excellency the Governor-General gives a bronze medal
to the student who passes the best final examination in the
Art of Teaching, whether in the elementary classes or the
model school class.

Exemption from matriculation examinations in McGill Univer-

sity.—Holders of model school diplomas of the McGill Normal School who are certified by the Principal of the Normal School to have taken 75 per cent. of the total marks at their final examinations, with not less than 60 per cent. of the marks in Mathematics, French, Latin and Greek, respectively, will be admitted without further examination to the first year in Arts of the McGill University ; but all such students must make good their standing at the Christmas examinations.

Academy diplomas without further professional courses or examinations.—All holders of model school diplomas that have been granted by the McGill Normal School or that shall hereafter be granted by the Central Board of Examiners shall be entitled to receive academy diplomas on graduating in Arts at some Canadian or other British university, provided that they pass in Mathematics, Latin, Greek and French at the degree examinations, or, failing this in any subject or subjects, pass examinations in such subject or subjects that are certified by the universities to have given to the graduate concerned a standing not lower than that of second class at the close of the second year in arts.

VI. ACADEMY DIPLOMAS TO GRADUATES.

To meet the requirements of graduates and undergraduates in Arts, who, not having previously taken a Normal School course, desire to receive Academy diplomas, and until the Universities themselves undertake the work, provision has been made for the delivery of a course of lectures on pedagogy in the Normal School and for practice in teaching in the McGill Model School for fifty half days, open to graduates in arts of any British or Canadian University, to undergraduates of the third year, and with the permission of the Faculty and the concurrence of the Principal of the Normal School, to those of the fourth year. An examination on this course of lectures is held annually on the 20th day of May, or on the school day next succeeding that date ; the hours are from 10 a.m. to 12 noon.

Undergraduates will be permitted to teach the fifty half days referred to above, at times extending over the sessions of the Model School, corresponding to the third and fourth years of their college course. Graduates will be permitted to teach in the Model Schools at such times as may be agreed on with the Principal.

Each person taking this course of study in the Normal School shall be held to be subject to the regulations of the said school and to be under the supervision of its Principal while in attendance thereat, and is required to furnish him with all necessary certificates of standing and of good character, as well as to pay to the Secretary of the Central Board of Examiners the fee of $4.00 before receiving an academy diploma.

VII. COURSE OF STUDY.

N.B.—The subjoined Course of Study has been designed, and all instruction in it is given with express reference to the work of teaching.

1. ELEMENTARY CLASS, STUDYING FOR THE ELEMENTARY DIPLOMA.

Teachers-in-training are admitted to this class after the Christmas vacation on the authority of the Central Board of School Examiners, who take full responsibility for the academic qualifications of those who enter.

Organization and Discipline.—A Course of Lectures.

Teaching.—Courses' of Lectures on teaching Elementary Subjects, including French.

Model Lessons.—Given by teachers of the Model School staff to be reported on in detail by teachers-in-training.

Practice teaching in the Model Schools.— Under supervision of the Model School staff and of certain members of the Normal School staff. These lectures are definitely reported by the supervisors.

Model Lessons.—Given by teachers-in-training to their fellow teachers, under the supervision of the Normal School staff.

The final examination leading to the Elementary School Diploma will consist of written and oral examinations on the lecture courses. and the reception of reports on actual school work done by teachers-in-training and observed by the staff of the Normal and Model-Schools.

Examination papers will be set only on the lectures given and on school work observed; but the staff of the Normal School will refuse to sign certificates necessary to receiving diplomas, if these examinations reveal marked literary deficiencies.

Attendance on some of the lectures given to the Advanced Class will be permitted, especially on those in elocution, chemistry, physiology and hygiene, and tonic sol-fa; but examinations in such subjects will not be compulsory.

2. ADVANCED ELEMENTARY CLASS STUDYING FOR THE ADVANCED ELEMENTARY DIPLOMA.

FIRST TERM, from September 2nd to December 23rd.

English.—The structure of sentences. Orthography and orthoëpy. The study of Milton's L'Allegro.

Geography.—General view of continents and oceans. Eléments de Géographie Moderne.

History.—Outline of ancient history. Histoire du Canada en Français.

Arithmetic.—Simple and compound rules.

Algebra.—The elementary rules.

Geometry.—Elementary notions, with Mensuration.

French.—Darey's Principes de Grammaire Française to page 50, with verbs of first conjugation. Méthode Naturelle. Curtis' Oral Lessons in French.

Latin.—Grammar; a Delectus of Cæsar.

Reading and Elocution.—General principles, practice and criticism.

Drawing.—Elements, simple outlines and map drawing.

Music.—Vocal music with part songs. Junior Certificate of Tonic Sol-Fa College.

Penmanship and Accounts.

SECOND TERM, January 6th to end of Session.

English.—Structure of words and sentences. Etymology, derivation and syntax. Study of Macaulay's Essay on Milton and of Goldsmith's Deserted Village.

Geography.—Typical lessons.

History.—Outline of ancient history. Sacred history. Histoire du Canada, continuée.

Arithmetic.—Fractions, Decimals, Proportion, Interest.

Book-keeping.—Single Entry and Penmanship.

Algebra.—Simple equations of one unknown quantity, with problems.

Geometry.—First book of Euclid, with deductions.

Art of Teaching.—Lectures on school organization, discipline and instruction.

French.—Principes de Grammaire Française, page 100, with verbs regular and irregular. Méthode naturelle.

Latin.—Grammar; Cæsar Gallic War, Book I.

Chemistry.—Lectures.

Physiology and Hygiene.—Lectures.

Reading and Elocution.—As before, with lectures on teaching the subject.

Drawing.—Freehand drawing from the solid, and elements of perspective.

Music.—Elements of vocal music and part songs. Elementary Certificate of Tonic Sol-Fa College.

Practice in teaching in the McGill Model Schools, as directed by the Principal.

Religious Instruction will be given throughout the session.

In addition to the text-books named above, each Student of the Advanced Elementary School Class must be provided with an Atlas of recent date, an Arithmetic, an Algebra and a Euclid.

3. MODEL SCHOOL CLASS, STUDYING FOR THE MODEL SCHOOL DIPLOMA.

Students entering the school in this second year must have passed satisfactory examination in the subjects of the elementary school class. The class will pursue its studies throughout the session, without division into terms.

English.—Principles of grammar and composition. Style. History of the English Language. Study of the course of the National Home Reading Union.

Geography.—Mathematical and physical. Use of the globes.

History.—England, Rome.

Art of Teaching.—Lectures on the principles of education, especially on those derived from the physical, mental and moral nature of the child.

Arithmetic.—Commercial arithmetic. Logarithms. Properties of numbers.

Book-keeping.—Double entry and penmanship.

Algebra.—Equations of more than one unknown quantity, and quadratics.

Geometry.—Second, third and fourth books of Euclid, with application to mensuration.

Botany.—High School Botany, Spotton.

Latin.—Grammar; Cæsar Bell. Gall., Book II; and Virgil, Aeneid, Book I.

French.—Translation from French into English, and from English into French. Darey's Principes de Grammaire. Eléments de littérature française, Lectures françaises, Méthode Berlitz, Histoire de France, Lavisse.

Agricultural Science.—Principles, especially chemical and botanical, and application to Canadian agriculture.

Elocution.—Special attention to methods of teaching.

Drawing.—Elements of perspective, drawing from the cast and map drawing.

Music.—Instrumental music, part songs and rudiments of harmony. Intermediate Certificate of Tonic Sol-Fa College.

Practice in Teaching.—In the McGill Model Schools, as directed by the Principal.

Religious Instruction throughout the session.

Students of exceptional ability may, with the consent of the Principal and the professors of the several subjects, choose one of the following courses of extra study:—

(*a*) Greek; Xenophon. Anabasis-book I, with special attention to Greek and Latin grammar.

(*b*) Mathematics: trigonometry.

(*c*) Old English.

(*d*) French: classiques français, composition et grammaire.

(*e*) Drawing: water-color.

(*f*) Music: violin.

In addition to the text-books named above, each Student of the Model School Class must be provided with an Arithmetic, an Algebra, a Euclid, and Dawson's Scientific Agriculture.

4. CLASS OF KINDERGARTNERS.

Persons who have taken the advanced elementary school diploma, and have the necessary qualifications, especially love of children, a good voice, musical ability and an engaging manner, may enter the training school for kindergartners, and receive kindergarten diplomas at the close of the second year of Normal School training.

Kindergartners will be employed in the practical work of the kindergarten during the forenoon of each school day, and will follow a selected course of practical and professional training every afternoon.

Among the subjects taken in the afternoons will be mother play, gifts, occupations, clay modelling, nature lessons, games and songs, drawing, music, French, psychology of the child, history of education and art of teaching.

Special attention will be paid to transition work, so that, it is hoped, those who take the training of this class will be specially fitted for the difficult task of training young children effectually in the rudi_ments of ordinary school work in succession to the work of the kindergarten, bridging over the chasm that too frequently separates the kindergarten from the primary class.

MODEL SCHOOLS OF THE McGILL NORMAL SCHOOL.

Boys' School.—Orrin Rexford, B.A.Sc., *Head Master.*
    Elizabeth Reid, } *Assistants.*
    Florence Tucker, }

Girls' School.—Mary I. Peebles, *Head Mistress.*
    Ethel Stuart,
    Gertrude Blackett, } *Assistants.*
    Gertrude W. Brandt,

Primary School.—Selina F. Sloan, *Head Mistress.*
    Annie L. Woodington, } *Assistants.*
    Clara L. Douglas, }

Kindergarten.—Louise Derick.

These Schools can accommodate about 400 pupils, are supplied with the best furniture and apparatus, and conducted on the most modern methods of teaching. They receive pupils from the age of four and upwards, and give a thorough English education. Fees:—Boys' and Girls' Model Schools, $1.00 to $1.50 per month; Primary School and Kindergarten, 75c.; payable monthly in advance.

University School Examinations,

1899.

FOR CERTIFICATES OF THE UNIVERSITIES AND THE TITLE OF ASSOCIATE IN ARTS.

HELD UNDER THE SUPERINTENDENCE OF McGILL UNIVERSITY, MONTREAL, AND THE UNIVERSITY OF BISHOP'S COLLEGE, LENNOXVILLE; AND RECOGNIZED BY THE PROTESTANT COMMITTEE OF THE COUNCIL OF PUBLIC INSTRUCTION.

These Examinations are held in Montreal and at Lennoxville; and local centres may be appointed elsewhere on application to the Principal of either University, accompanied with the names of satisfactory Deputy Examiners, and guarantee for the payment of necessary expenses.

The Examinations are open to Boys or Girls from any Canadian school.

PART I.—ORDINARY A.A.

SUBJECTS OF EXAMINATION.

I. PRELIMINARY SUBJECTS.

Writing.

English Dictation.

English Grammar, including Easy Analysis.

A Short Essay on a subject to be given at the time of the Examination.

Arithmetic (all the ordinary rules, including Square Root and a knowledge of the Metric System).

Geography (acquaintance with the maps of each of the four continents, and of British North America).

British History and *Canadian History.*

*New Testament History.** (Gospels and Acts, as in Maclear).

---

* Candidates will be exempted from examination in this subject only if their parents or guardians make written objection thereto. In such case Taylor's First Principles of Modern History will be required.

II. OPTIONAL SUBJECTS.

Section 1.—Languages.

Latin:

Cæsar.—Bell. Gall., Bks. I. and II.
Latin Grammar.
Virgil.—Aeneid, Bk. I.
Prose Composition, based on the prescribed prose } 200 marks.
text, and Easy Translation at Sight.

Greek:—

Xenophon.—Anabasis, Bk. I.
Greek Grammar.
Prose Composition, based on the prescribed prose } 200   do.
text, and Easy Translation at Sight.

French:—

French Grammar.
Easy translation, from English into French,
and from French into English. } 100   do
The reproduction in French of an easy narrative read in English.

German:—

Grammar.—Vandersmissen's Accidence and
Syntax, especially the Accidence, including
English German Exercises. An equivalent
amount of Grammar and English-German } 100   do
translation from any good manual will· be
accepted in place of Vandersmissen.
Joynes' German Reader.

Section 2.—Mathematics.

Arithmetic:—

As required for Model School Diploma. All
ordinary commercial rules, fractions of
greater complexity, circulating decimals, cube

root, the mensuration of rectangles, circles,
rectangular prisms, rectangular pyramids,
cylinders, cones, spheres, and all such figures
as can be resolved into or referred to these
elements. The use of six figure Loga-
rithms..   100   do

Geometry:—

Euclid, I., II., III., with easy Deductions.. ..   100   do

Algebra:—

Elementary Rules, Involution, Evolution, Fractions, Indices, Surds, Simple and Quadratic
Equations of one or more unknown quan-   } 100   do
tities.

Plane Trigonometry:—

(As in Hamblin Smith, pp. 1-100. omitting Ch.   100   do
XI.)

Section 3.—English.

The English Language:—
West's Elements of English Grammar (Cam-
  bridge University Press.)   } 100   do
Trench's Study of Words.

English Literature:—

Stopford Brooke's Primer of English Literature,
  (New Edition.)
Shakspere's Richard II.   } 100   do
Selections from Tennyson, Part 1., (Rowe and
  Webb. Macmillan.)

History.—(As in Primers of Greece and Rome, and
  Collier's Great Events)..   100   do

Physical Geography:—Hinman's Eclectic Physical
  Geography is recommended..   100   do

Section 4.--Natural and Physical Sciences, etc.

*Botany** (as in Groom's Elementary Botany, with
Penhallow's Guide to the Collection of
Plants, and Blanks for Plant Descriptions†).   100   do

: A collection of not more than 50 specimens properly mounted and named will be required of
each pupil.

Chemistry (as in Remsen's Elements of Chemistry,
pp. 1 to 160)..   100   do

Physiology and *Hygiene* (as in Cutter's Intermediate.)..   100   do

Physics (as in Gage Introduction to Physical Science,
(Chapters I., II., III., IV. and V.)..   100   do

Geometrical and Freehand Drawing..   100   do

Geometrical.—Vere Foster R1 and R2, also problems 119 to 129 of
R3, or McLeod's Geometrical Drawing.

Freehand.—Rules of Perspective, Drawing from the object (as in
the Dominion Freehand Drawing books, numbers 1 to 5, inclusive.)

The following subjects may be taken instead of *Geometrical
Drawing:*

(*a*) Freehand object drawing with shades and shadows.
(*b*) Drawing from the cast.
(*c*) Elementary water color drawing.

REGULATIONS.

1. To obtain the Certificate of Associate in Arts, Candidates
must pass in all the Preliminary subjects, and also in any six of the
Optional subjects, provided that the six include one subject at least
from each of the four Sections.

* The Head Teacher of each school will forward one specimen from each pupil's
collection, and also (on a furnished form) a detailed statement as to the collection
made.

† These blanks may be obtained from booksellers in Montreal or elsewhere.

S

2. In addition to the six Optional subjects selected for passing, Candidates may take other Optional subjects, but the total possible number of marks obtainable in all the Optional subjects chosen must not exceed 1000.

3. Candidates will not be considered as having passed in any subject, unless they have obtained at least 40 per cent. of the total number of marks obtainable in that subject.*

4. The total number of marks gained by every Candidate in the Optional subjects shall be added up, and the Candidates arranged in order of merit in a printed list at the close of the Examination, those who are over 18 years of age on the first day of June being in a separate list. The marks in any subject shall not be counted if the Candidate has obtained less than 40 per cent. in that subject.

5. Candidates who obtain at least 75 per cent. of the marks in any Optional subject shall be considered as having answered creditably in that subject, and special mention of the same will be made in the Associate in Arts Certificate.

6. Candidates who pass in the subjects of the University Matriculation Examinations may, without further examination, enter the Faculties of Arts and Applied Science. (See Note 2 *infra*.)

7. Candidates who fail, or who may be prevented by illness from completing their examination, may come up at the next examination without extra fee.

8. Candidates who pass in all the Preliminary subjects may, at any subsequent examination, take the Optional subjects only, and without extra fee.

9. The Head Master or Mistress of each school must certify to the character and ages of the pupils sent up for examination.

10. The examinations will begin on Monday, May 29th, at 9 a.m.

---

* When *two or more books or subjects are prescribed for one examination it is necessary to pass in each*. Candidates will not be allowed to pass in the Preliminary Grammar, unless they show a satisfactory knowledge of Syntax (Parsing, Analysis, and questions connected therewith). In Classics, at least one-third of the marks allotted to Grammar must be obtained.

11. Lists of the names, ages, and Optional subjects to be taken by the Candidates, together with a fee of $4 for each Candidate, must be transmitted to the Secretary, McGill University, Montreal, on or before April 30th. (Blank forms and copies of the regulations will be furnished on application.)

NOTE 1.—No fees will be exacted for the examination of pupils of Academies under the control of the Protestant Committee ; but in order to obtain the certificate from the Universities, the prescribed fee, viz., $4, must be paid to the Secretary of the University.

Candidates who pass Grade II of the Academy Course of Study will be exempted from the Preliminary Subjects of the A. A. Examination.

The answers must be written in the answer book, specially made for the purpose, under the direction of the Board of Examiners.

The complete regulations of the Protestant Committee of the Council of Public Instruction with reference to these examinations may be obtained on application to the English Secretary, Department of Public Instruction, Quebec.

NOTE 2.—MATRICULATION SUBJECTS REFERRED TO IN REG. 6.

In Arts.—(1) Latin or Greek; (2) Geometry ; (3) Algebra ; (4) Arithmetic ; (5) English Grammar ; (6) English Dictation ; (7) British History ; (8) English Literature ; (9) Greek or Latin (if not already taken), *or* two Modern Languages ; (10) Botany **or** Chemistry, Physical Geography, Physics, *or alternatively* a Language not previously taken.

In Applied Science.—Geometry (Euclid, Bks. I. to IV., VI., and definitions of Bk. V.), Algebra, Trigonometry, Arithmetic, English Dictation, Composition, English Grammar, British History, English Literature, and one Language, viz., Greek, Latin, French or German.

(Matriculation Examinations are also held at the opening of the University Session in September. See Calendars of the Universities.)

PART II.—ADVANCED A. A.

SUBJECTS OF EXAMINATION.

I. Preliminary Subjects.

As under Part I.

II. Optional Subjects.

Section 1.—Languages.

Latin:—

Virgil.—Aeneid, I.
Cicero.—In Catilinam, I. and II.
Grammar, Prose Composition (Collar's Practical Latin Composition, Parts III. and IV.), Translation at Sight.

Greek:—

Xenophon.—Anabasis, I. and II.
Homer.—Illiad, IV., and Odyssey, VII.
Translation at Sight.
Grammar and Prose Composition (Abbott's Arnold's Greek Prose Composition, Exercises 1 to 25).

French:—

Le Livre de mon Ami, by A. France.
Molière, Le Bourgeois Gentilhomme.
Translation at sight from French into English, and from English into French.
Grammar and Dictation.

German:—

Lessing, Emilia Galotti.
Schiller, Der Kampf mit dem Drachen.
Grammar and translation from English into German.

Section 2.—Mathematics.

Geometry:—

Euclid, Bks. I. to IV., Defins. of Bk. V., Bk. VI.

Algebra:—

To the end of Progressions.

Trigonometry:—

As in Hamblin Smith (the whole).

Section 3.—English.

The English Language:—

Lounsbury's History of the English Language.
Cook's First Book of Old English (Ginn, Boston), Extı. ᵪ
XIII inclusive, with grammatical question arising therefrom.
Chaucer's Prologue to the Canterbury tales, (Skeat, Clarendon
Press.)
A Composition.

English Literature:—

The Elizabethan Period (Morley's First Sketch, Herford's
Age of Wordsworth (Bell), Pope's Essay on Criticism (Churton, Collins, Macmillan), Milton's Paradise Lost, Bk. I.

History:—

Grecian History.—The Persian and Peloponnesian Wars.
Roman History.—From the Wars of Marius and Sulla to the
death of Tiberius.
English History.—The Reformation and Puritan England, as
in Green's Short History.

Section 4.—Natural and Physical Sciences, etc.

*Botany:—*Gray's Text-Book of Structural Botany.

General Morphology and Classification, Determination of
Canadian Species, exclusive of Thallophytes. Distribution of
Orders represented in Canada.
Credit will be given for collections of plants as under Part I.

*Chemistry:—*Inorganic, as in Remsen's Elements.

Also, an examination in Practical Work (to be held only in
Montreal and at Lennoxville.)

Physics:—As in Gage and Fessenden's High School Physics.

Also, an examination in Practical Work (to be held only in Montreal and Lennoxville.)

Drawing:—Orthographic Projection, including Simple **Penetrations**, Developments and Sections, as in Davidson's Orthographic Projection.

REGULATIONS.

The Regulations of Part I., with the following modifications and additions, will apply to the advanced subjects:—

1. Candidates who pass in six of the advanced subjects including one at least from each of the four Sections) will receive an Advanced A. A. certificate. The number of marks given to each subject will be the same as in Part I., and additional advanced subjects may be taken as in Reg. 2, Part I.

2. Candidates who fail in one or more of the subjects required for the advanced A. A. may, on the recommendation of the Examiners, be given an ordinary A. A. certificate.

3. The examinations in the advanced subjects will be held at the same time and in the same manner as those in the ordinary subjects. They will be open to all who have already passed in the preliminary subjects, whether they have taken the ordinary A. A. or not. The preliminary subjects must be taken either one or two years before the advanced subjects.

4. Candidates must, before April 30th, give notice of intention to present themselves for the examination, specifying the optional subjects in which they wish to be examined.

5. The ordinary fee of $4.00 must be paid before taking the preliminary subjects, and an additional fee of $10 at the time of making application for the advanced Examination† A Candidate who fails to pass the Advanced A. A. Examination shall be required to pay a fee of $5 for every subsequent Advanced A. A. Examination at which he may present himself.

---

† Candidates from Academies under the control of the Protestant Committee of the Council of Public Instruction are exempt from the former fee, but not from the latter.

LIST

OF

SUCCESSFUL CANDIDATES

RESULTS OF EXAMINATIONS, 1898.

No.   Marks

ADVANCED ASSOCIATES IN ARTS.

1 Sarah K. Crawford (Lennoxville Model School),   386

ASSOCIATES IN ARTS.

I. *Under* 18 *Years of Age.*

No.		Marks
44	James Stevenson (Danville Academy),	781
72	Eva Jackson Fraser (Lachute Academy),	760
92	Wm. E. C. Miller (Quebec High School),	757
59	John A. McDonald (Huntingdon Academy),	756
134	Jean Angus (Westmount Academy),	753
143	Kathleen Terrill (Westmount Academy),	740
93	Wm. Clement Munn (Quebec High School),	732
141	Winifred Nolan (Westmount Academy),	731
79	Henry D. Hunting (Lennoxville Model School)	727
94	Margaret O. Buchanan (Girls' High School, Quebec),	721
122	Janet Dunlop Douglas (Waterloo Academy),	715
111	Sherman Boright (Sutton Academy),	706
139	Gertrude Jarvis (Westmount Academy),	703
142	Mabel Robertson (Westmount Academy),	684
60	Francis H. McLaren (Huntingdon Academy),	679
114	Walter J. Healy (St. Francis College School),	677
130	Maggie Isabel Savage (Waterloo Academy), } equal	669
96	Emma M. Munn (Girls' H. School, Quebec),	
76	Eva A. Bown (Lennoxville Model School),	658
25	Robert Edey (Aylmer Academy),	558
140	Alice Nelson (Westmount Academy),	653
144	Florence Woodley (Westmount Academy),	650
58	Frederick R. Maxwell (Huntingdon Academy),	643
117	Gerald M. Smith (St. Johns High School),	639
124	Pearl W. Lawrence (Waterloo Academy),	632

No.		Marks.
40	Grace Wales (Cookshire Academy),	631
132	Maud Effie Whitehead (Waterloo Academy),	606
97	Florence M. C. Raymond (Girls' High School, Quebec),	605
136	Helena Brodie (Westmount Academy), } equal	601
138	Georgina Hood " "),	
71	Ermina Carpenter (Lachute Academy),	597
5	Rupert B. Buchanan (Abingdon School),	590
126	Annie C. Matheson (Waterloo Academy),	583
7	Guy L. Ogilvie (Abingdon School),	573
81	Ada F. Smiley (Lennoxville Model School),	541
88	Herbert Fraser (Portage du Fort Model School),	539
84	Grace E. Wallace, (Magog Model School),	537
66	Anita B. Bailey (Knowlton Academy),	536
16	Mary S. Greenleese (Miss Symmers' and Miss Smith's School),	526
145	Arthur Woodley (Westmount Academy),	522
498	Eva Morin,	493
123	Bertha L. Fessenden (Waterloo Academy),	487
52	Janie I. Norris Granby Academy),	485
125	Sylvia B. Lee (Waterloo Academy),	484
42	Della R. Barnard (Danville Academy), } equal	482
67	Harold MacGowan (Knowlton Academy),	
34	Carrie Trenholme (Coaticook Academy),	474
131	Esther M. Swett (Waterloo Academy),	468
41	Guy C. Boright (Cowansville Academy),	462
102	Sarah C. Foss (Sherbrooke Academy),	452
127	Gertrude E. Neill (Waterloo Academy),	437
39	Persis Coates (Cookshire Academy),	435
87	Constance Eason (Portage du Fort Model School),	428
33	George L. Doak (Coaticook Academy),	425
48	Fanny Robinson (Dunham Ladies' College),	418
35	Kate E. Hitchcock (Compton Ladies' College),	416
121	Florence M. Ogden (Three Rivers Academy),	409
89	George W. Findlay (Quebec High School),	402
28	George Batcheller (Bedford Academy),	381
116	Clement J. Wilcox (St. Francis College School),	371
120	Muriel Houliston (Three Rivers Academy),	358
73	Margaret E. Mackie (Lachute Academy),	356
83	Allen E. Smith (Magog Model School),	353
108	Edith A. Fee (Stanstead Wesleyan College),	346
77	John Burrill (Lennoxville Model School),	332
133	Wm. T. Anglin (Westmount Academy),	328

II. *Over 18 Years of Age.*

No.		Marks.
61	Kenneth C. Muir (Huntingdon Academy),	797
55	Ellen Brims (Huntingdon Academy),	793
14	Lillian Beatrice Evans (Miss Symmers' and Miss Smith's School),	705
135	Muriel Baillie (Westmount Academy),	614
26	Harold Watt (Aylmer Academy),	6c8
95	Theodora MacNaughton (Girls' High School, Quebec),	603
21	Frank H. Fox (Private Tuition),	570
18	Florence C. Prowse (Miss Symmers' and Miss Smith's School),	542
104	Jas. E. Waterhouse (Sherbrooke Academy),	497
146	Anson L. Raymond (Williamstown High School),	494
36	Grace H. W. Stevens (Compton Ladies' College),	489
46	Mina B. Filliter (Dunham Ladies' College),	484
62	Hartley M. Pearson (Huntingdon Academy),	453
56	Wilhelmina Cunningham (Huntingdon Academy),	446
57	Marion E. Gamble (Huntingdon Academy),	444
45	Herman K. Stockwell (Danville Academy),	426
75	Edith L. Strong (Lachute Academy),	418
149	Marion A. Blair (Chicoutimi English Protestant School),	401
30	Louise M. Miller (Clarenceville Model School),	398
27	John M. Montle (Bedford Academy),	395
32	Nellie M. Tasker (Clarenceville Model School),	392
50	Edith K. Wells (Dunham Ladies' College),	361
105	Edward J. Witty (Sherbrooke Academy),	303
53	Florence Runnells (Granby Academy),	298

PASSED IN 1897 AND AGAIN IN 1898.

70	Catherine C. Barron (Lachute Academy),	896
85	Gertrude McClenaghan, (Ormstown Academy),	665
43	Alfred Carson, (Danville Academy),	601

PASSED THE PRELIMINARY SUBJECTS.
(In order of numbers.)

8	10	11	12	13	15
17	19	20	23	80	90
162	153	154	155	157	159
174	164	168	169	170	173
182	175	177	179	180	181
188	183	184	185	186	187
196	189	190	191	193	194
210	198	200	202	207	208
221	216	217	218	219	220
231	222	223	224	227	229
243	234	235	237	238	241
251	244	245	248	249	250
260	2,2	253	254	255	258
269	261	264	266	267	268
	499	500			

McGILL UNIVERSITY, MONTREAL.

JUNE, 1898.

The following Candidates have passed the Examinations required for Entrance.

I. In Arts.

Angus, Jean,	Montreal	MacNaughton, Theodore I.,	Quebec
Baillie, Muriel,	Westmount, Q	Miller, Wm. E. C.,	Quebec
Barron, Catherine C.,	Lachute, Q	Munn, Wm. Clement,	Quebec
Brodie, Helena,	Westmonnt, Q	Muir, Kenneth C.,	Huntingdon, Q
Buchanan, Rupert B ,	Montreal	Munn, Emma M.,	Quebec
Carson, Herman A.,	Danville. Q	Nelson, Alice,	Westmount, Q
Cole, George E.,	Westmount, Q	Nolan, Winnifred,	Westmount, Q
Dickson, Ada D.,	Pembroke, O	Parker, Edward,	Toronto, O
Evans. Beatrice L.,	Montreal	Raymond, Florence M. C.,	Quebec
Fox, Frank H.,	Montreal	Robertson, Mabel,	Westmount, Q
Greenleese, Mary S.,	Montreal	Schrag, Astor R.,	Brantford, O
Healey, Walter J.,	Richmond, Q	Seamen, John C.,	Montreal
Heatlie, Fred. W.,	Enfield, O	Stevenson, James,	Danville, Q
Hood, Georgina,	Westmount, Q	Terrill, Kathleen,	Westmount, Q
Hunting, Henry D.,	Lennoxville, Q	Townsley, Robert,	Montreal
Jarvis, Gertrude,	Westmount, Q	Wales, Grace,	Cookshire, Q
Irwin, Wm. H.,	London, O	Warren, Anna B.,	Toronto, O
Jack, Milton,	Montreal	Warren, James D.,	Toronto, O
McDonald, John A.,	Huntingdon, Q	Woodley, Arthur,	Westmount, Q
McClemaghan, Gertrude,	Ormstown, Q	Woodley, Florence,	Westmount, Q
McAvity, Allan G.,	Rothsay, N.B.		

II. Medicine.

Byers, John R.,	Gananoque, O	Allum, A. W.	Renfrew, O

III. Applied Science.

Abraham, Leonard,	Montreal	Moore, Douglas J. E.,	Montreal
Baker, Percival C.,	Montreal	Murphy, Wm. E.,	Shelburne, N.S.
Barwick, Wm. S.,	Vancouver, B.C.	Newton, Samuel R.,	Brigham, Q
Bigger, Howell,	Ottawa, O	Ogilvie, Guy L.,	Montreal
Dunfield, John C. W.,	Newfoundland	Ralph, Claude E.,	Ottawa, O
Hartman, Clifford C. A.,	Montreal	Ramsey, Colin P.,	Brigham, Q
McBride, Wilbert G.,	Orangeville, O	Sugden, Oswald W.,	London, O
McLaren, Francis H.,	Huntingdon, Q	Warren, Guy E.,	Toronto, O

STANDING IN THE OPTIONAL SUBJECTS.

[The numbers correspond with those in the preceding lists. Candidates whose numbers are n parentheses are equal in standing. Those preceding a single asterisk have obtained at least three-fourths of the marks ; those preceding a double asterisk, at least one-half ; those following, at least forty per cent. The numbers of the Schools and Candidates are as follows : Lennoxville Model School, 1 and 76 to 81, inclusive ; Montreal Collegiate Institute, 2 and 3 ; Abingdon School, 4 to 10, inclusive ; Miss Symmers' and Miss Smith's, 11 to 20, inclusive ; Sabrevois College, 22 to 24, inclusive ; Aylmer Academy, 25 and 26 ; Bedford Academy, 27 to 29, inclusive ; Clarenceville Model School, 30 to 32, inclusive ; Coaticook Academy, 33 and 34, Compton Ladies' College, 35 and 36 ; Cookshire Academy, 37 to 40, inclusive ; Cowansville Academy, 41, Danville Academy, 42 to 45, inclusive ; Dunham Ladies' College, 46 to 50, inclusive ; Granby Academy, 51 to 54, inclusive ; Huntingdon Academy, 55 to 62, inclusive ; Inverness Academy, 63 to 65, inclusive ; Knowlton Academy, 66 and 67 ; Lachine Model School, 68, and 69 ; Lachute Academy, 70 to 75, inclusive ; Lennoxville Model School, 1 and 76 to 81, inclusive ; Magog Model School, 82 to 84, inclusive ; Ormstown Academy, 85 and 86 ; Portage du Fort Model School, 87 and 88 ; Quebec High School, 89 to 93, inclusive ; Girls' High School, Quebec, 94 to 97 and 266 to 268, inclusive ; Sawyerville Academy, 99 and 100 ; Sherbrooke Academy, 101 to 106, inclusive ; Stanstead Wesleyan College, 107 to 109 ; Sorel Model School, 110 ; Sutton Academy, 111 ; St. Francis College School, 112 to 116, inclusive ; High School, St. John's, Quebec, 117 ; St. Lambert Model School, 118 and 119 ; Three Rivers Academy, 120 and 121 ; Waterloo Academy, 122 to 132, inclusive ; Westmount Academy, 133 to 145, inclusive ; High School, Williamstown, Ont., 146 ; Chicoutimi Eng. Prot. School, 147 to 149, inclusive ; The Grammar School, Montreal, 150 ; Montreal High School, 151 to 219, inclusive ; Montreal High School, (Girls'), 220 to 265 ; Girls' H. S., St. John, N.B., 499 and 500.

Greek.—70, 44, 61, 141,* 114, 134, 24, 143, (2, 79, 92), 59, 14, (96, 139), 93, 85, 21, 144, 136, 145, 135, 97, 5,** (43, 84), 104, 62, 95, 18, 80, 83.

Optional History.—117, 27,* 134, 139, (41, 149), (7, 28), 36, 67, 498, 66, 98, 108,** (109, 121).
Advanced A.A—1.

French.—98, (92, 149), 94, (55, 59), (44, 61, 143), 18, (70, 111, 140), 134, 95, 79* 89, (26, 97), (14, 41, 52, 93, 101, 142), (25, 46, 96), 114, (33, 40, 45, 56, 57, 72, 85, 104, 112, 122, 136, 139), 2, (71, 144), 48, 60, (16, 39, 42, 53, 58, 77, 82, 135, 138), 120, 141, 34, (23, 100, 102), 29, (27, 28, 35, 76, 83, 88, 103, 113, 117, 124, 126),** 30, 81, (5, 43), (3, 50, 66, 87, 109, 119, 121, 130, 132, 145, 148), 67, (36, 73, 78, 116).
Advanced A.A.—1,**

Latin.—70, 44, 114,* (7, 40, 72), 61, 134, 92, 25, 59, 85, 2, 140, 88, (14, 93), 5, (96, 141), (95, 111, 113, 124), 26, 143, 94, (43, 117, 122), 97, 139, 144, (79, 130), 142, (36, 126), 87, 21, 120, (45, 123), 52, (127, 136),** (132, 145), 66, (16, 119), 112, (62, 81), 150, (35, 42, 108), 34, (76, 115, 125), 71, 121, (33, 104, 109), 67, 3, (4, 32, 39, 41, 75, 84, 100, 131, 135, 138, 146).

English Language.—14, 94, 18, 16, 30, 149, 32.

Optional Geography.—111,* 76, (77, 144), (67, 122, 141), (94, 126), (46, 55, 104, 125, 135, 142), 138, 38, (113, 25, 86, 498), 140, (5, 101, 124, 143), (95, 96, 127, 136), (39, 48, 51, 66, 97), 49, (24, 40, 131, 132, 145), (58, 110, 130), 114, 84, (2, 6, 21, 26, 47, 116), (60, 115), (30, 83, 105), 33,** (7, 146), 52, (34, 82, 102), 50, 123, 27, (32, 56, 118), (10, 112, 119), (53, 57, 106).

Optional Arithmetic.—70, 72, 130, 28, 117, 98, (94, 102), 122, 132, 55, 76, 124, 58,* 123, 88, 60, 111, (21, 127), (41, 77), 71, 25, (75, 125), 80, 68, 27, 56, 6, (42, 131), (87, 126, 150),** 38, 73, 57, 119, 69, (10, 105).

Geometry.—141,* (70, 134, 138), (136, 139), 18, (130, 143), 2, (59, 60, 117, 122), 102, (61, 88, 135, 144), (30, 55, 79, 132), 67, (4, 7, 142)*, (43, 56, 66, 147), 121, (6, 96), (25, 26, 44, 58, 92), (14, 72, 97, 125), 93, (50, 109, 124), 32, (5, 62, 95, 113), (16, 40, 86, 110) '111, (45, 140), (85, 114)'

(36, 145, 150), (10, 52), (35, 48, 126), (26, 33, 46, 51), (3, 21), (34, 57, 89, 94, 133), 146, (42, 71), (39, 123), 87,** (47, 80), (38, 84, 104), 77, 116, (41, 101), 120, (49, 53, 112, 115, 131).

Advanced A.A.—1,**

Physics.—146,* 5.

Chemistry.—133, 146, 142, 140, 5, 114,** (7, 115), (116, 138).

Trigonometry.—(76, 79), 81, 60, 93, (2. 89), (59, 61), (55, 92), 44, 4,* 43, 5, 6, 7, 58, 3, 10 42,** 85, (21, 116), 78, 62.

Advanced A.A.—1**.

Drawing.—(71, 72), 81, 26, (58, 117), (74, 75), 76, 60, 73, 55, 25.**

Physiology and Hygiene.—55, 61 (70, 93), 498, (60, 126), 46, (72, 94),* 132, 127, (43, 66), (59, 92), 104, (49, 122), (26, 42), 142, (41, 71, 88, 111), (44, 85, 108), 87, (57, 102, 121, 124), (45, 143) 40, (48, 53, 89, 135), (58, 95, 130), (50, 109, 125), (56, 97, 103, 123), (30, 81, 96, 136), (32, 38, 84, 105, 117), 75, (34, 35, 51, 77, 149)** (27, 106), (100, 131), (68, 69, 74, 82), (21, 120, 141), (25, 29, 67, 86, 138), (47, 101), 62, (39, 116), 28, 73.

English Literature.—45, 26, 55, 122, (131, 143), (70, 93), 125, (79, 94, 96), (14, 18, 59, 92, 97, 135, 142),* (57, 114, 127), 40, (124, 126), (46, 104), (84, 88, 130), 61, 82, 95), (149, 498), 85, (254 58, 60, 87, 89), (76, 109, 144), 110, (6, 7, 29, 43, 44, 56, 112, 139, 140), 141, (62, 133, 138), (5, 42, 66, 111), (39, 113), (16, 27, 52, 72, 117, 134), (2, 53, 73, 115), 36, 48, 49,** (120, 121), (68, 71), (35, 47, 100, 136), (10, 50, 145), (51, 81, 9°, 101, 123), (74, 75, 105, 108), 77, 34, (3, 4, 33, 67, 83, 99, 106, 107, 116, 119, 146).

Advanced A.A.—1.

Botany.—70, 142, (134, 139), 135, (72, 79, 111, 138), 141, 14, 140, 85, 76, (46, 143), 48,* 176, (16, 130), 122, (14, 55, 125), (71, 75, 105), 74, (60, 144, 498), 81, 131, 58, (36, 52, 145), (18, 110), 33, 50, (35, 132), (32, 124, 126, 133), 56, (30, 49), 47, (53, 73, 78, 84, 123),* (102, 103), 51, 57, 83.

Advanced A.A.—1.

Algebra.—(36, 70, 141), (55, 143), (44, 72), 40, 61, 139, 92, (25, 39, 52, 83, 93), 84, 111, (59, 71), (3, 144), (102, 150), (96, 122, 134), (58, 85, 88), (21, 146), 28, (81, 109, 130), (2, 38),* (4, 18, 33), (26, 79, 82), (41, 76, 98, 114), 34, (73, 149), (46, 66, 123, 124, 145), 127, (35, 43, 67, 86, 94, 142), 27, 14, (51, 57, 95, 132), (62, 74, 100, 135), (7, 60, 116, 498), (121, 138), (75, 120), (89, 136), 48, (69, 78), (10, 97), 42, (5, 30, 87, 117),** (50, 113), 131, 68, 6, (56, 133, 140), (16, 45), (107, 126), (49, 108), (29, 106).

Advanced A.A.—1.*

German.—109,* (40, 140), 138, (16, 108), 142,** 146, 133

𝔓assed the 𝔘niversity 𝔈xaminations.

SESSION 1897-98.

FACULTY OF LAW.

PASSED FOR THE DEGREE OF B.C.L.

(In order of merit.)

E. Edwin Howard, B.A.,Philipsburg, Q.
Samuel Clay, B.A. (Cantab.), Montreal.
Herbert M. Marler, Montreal.
Arthur Burnet, Farnham Centre, Q.
Charles Iles, Montreal.
Henry Johnson Elliott, Montreal.

James Claud Hickson, B.A., Montreal.
Charles Champoux, B.A. (Laval), Montreal.
John Keefer Kennedy, Montreal.
Reginald Heber Rogers, B.A , Alberton, P.E.I., *aegrotat.*

FACULTY OF MEDICINE.

PASSED FOR THE DEGREE OF M.D., C.M.

(Arranged alphabetically.)

Banfill, S. A.,	Magog, Que
Barlow, W. M., B.A ,	Montreal
Bayfield, G. E.,	Charlottetown, P.E.I
Bearman, G. P ,	Bell's Corners, Ont
Beattie, R. F.,	Economy, N.S
Bell, J.,	New Glasgow, N.S
Blackett, J. W., B.A.,	Ormstown, Que
Brears, C. F.,	Regina, N.W.T
Brown, C. H., B.A., Carleton Place, Ont
Corbet, G. G.,	St. John, N.B
Corcoran, J. A.,	Warden, Que
Covert, A. M.,	Grand Manan, N.B
Cushing, H. B., B.A.,	Montreal, Que
Dalpé, W. H., B.A.,	Montreal, Que
Darche, J. A.,	Sherbrooke, Que
Davidson, C.,	Montreal, Que
Deane, R. B ,	Montreal, Que
Dickson, S. M.,	Montreal, Que
Duncan, R. G.,	Bathurst, N.B
Duval, J. L.,	Grande Ligne, Que
Fagan, G. A., B.A., North Adams, Mass
Finnie, J. H.,	Montreal, Que
Forbes, A. M. T.,	Montreal, Que
Fox, A. C. L.,	Winnipeg, Man
Fraser, F. C., B.A.,	Montreal, Que
Gadbois, F. A.,	Sherbrooke, Que
Gillies, B. W. D.,	Teesewater, Ont

Gladman, E. A.,	Lindsay, Ont
Grace, N.,	Montreal, Que
Green, F. W ,	Victoria, B.C
Harvey, F. W., B.A.,	Abercorn, Que
Houston, J. C.,	New Glasgow, P.E.I
Hudson, H. P.,	Chelsea, Que
Hume, G. W. L.,	Leeds Village, Que
Jamieson, W. R.,	Ottawa, Ont
Lamb, J. A.,	Ottawa, Ont
Lang, A. A. J.,	Almonte, Ont
Long, C. B.,	Whitehall, N.Y
Lynch, W. W.,	Knowlton, Que
Macaulay, J. F.,	St. John, N.B
Macaulay, H. R.,	Montreal, Que
McAllister, D. H., B.A , Belle Isle, N.B
McCabe, J. A., B.A.,Windsor Mills, Que
MacLean, J. N.,	Sarnia, Ont
McLaren, R. W.,	St. Raphaels, Ont
McLean, J. R., B.A ,	Arnprior, Ont
McLennan, P. A.,	Lancaster, Ont
McLeod, J.,	Hartsville, P.E.I
McMurtry, A. L.,	Bowmanville, Ont
Mooney, M. J.,	Inverness, Que
Myers. D. A.,	Prentiss, Wis
Ogilvy, C., B.A.,	Montreal, Que
Oppenheimer, S. S.,	Vancouver, B.C
O'Saughnessy, L. J.,	Oldham, N.S

Outhouse, J. S., B.A.,	St. Andrews, N.B	Schwartz, H. J.,	Quebec City, Que
Patterson, F. P.,	St. Martins, N.B	Sibler, W. F.,	Simcoe, Ont
Patterson, R. U.,	Baltimore, Md	Smith, A. M., B.A.,	Petit Codiac, N.B
Peters, U. A.,	St. John's, Nfld	Stockwell, H. P.,	Danville, Que
Pigeon, W. H.,	Peterborough, Ont	Telford, R.,	Valens, Ont
Powers, M., B.A.,	Ottawa, Ont	Tiffany G. S.,	Alexandria, Ont
Robertson, D. McD.,	Pertn, Ont	Walker, P. McH.,	Grafton, N.D
Rose, W. O.,	Latteville, P.E.I	West, J.,	Montreal, Que
Scanlan, Harry,	Gloucester, Mass	Whitton, D. A.,	Ottawa, Ont

FACULTY OF ARTS.

PASSED FOR THE DEGREE OF B.A.

In Honours.

(Alphabetically arranged).

McGILL COLLEGE.

First Rank.—BATES, GEORGE E.
BISHOP, W. GORDON.
BOURKE-WRIGHT, KATHERINE.
BROOKS, HARRIET.
CAMERON, FRANCES M. T.
CAMPBELL, J. A. E.
CARR, MURIEL B.
DALGLEISH, ROBERT W
DUFF, ALEXANDER H
HEINE, M. CASEWELL.
MEYER, JOHN B.
MUNN, D. WALTER.
PATERSON, ROBERT C.
PLACE, EDSON G.
SEIFERT, ETHEL M.
SHIP, MOSES M.
THOMPSON, JAMES R.
WALKER, LAURA F. M.

Second Rank.—McGREGOR, JAMES ALBERT
MacLAREN, ARCHIBALD.
McLEOD, HENRY S.
SHAW, A. LOUISE.
TURNER, HENRY H.
VINEBERG, ABRAHAM.

Ordinary B.A.

(In order of merit)

McGILL COLLEGE.

Class   I.—PEARSON, KATIE C.

Class II.—GRACE, A. H.
PRUDHAM, W. W. } equal.
TURNER, W. D.
REYNOLDS, M. EDNA.
GARDNER, W. A.
LENEY, J. M. } equal.
TARLETON, B. B.
JORDAN, FLORENCE M. } equal.
TODD, J. L.
GILDAY, H. L. C.
ROSS, ARTHUR B.
Class III.—DOVER, MARY V.
STEEN, ALICE G.
COLBY, J. C.
WORTH, FULTON J.
STUART, JAS. A.
THOMAS, J. WOLFERSTAN.
MOORE, PERCY C.
Æger.—BLYTH, R. B.

PASSED IN SEPTEMBER, 1897.

CRACK, H. ARTHUR.
MOORE, WILLIAM.
WATSON, WILLIAM.

BACHELORS OF ARTS PROCEEDING TO THE DEGREE OF M. A. IN COURSE.

CROMBIE, WILLIAM T. B.
DEEKS, WILLIAM E.
GUSTIN, WILLIAM ALFRED.
HONEYMAN, HOWARD ARTHUR.
KEITH, NEIL DANIEL.
ROGERS, REGINALD HEBER.
WALLACE, JAMES MUIR.
YOUNG, HY.

ADMITTED TO THE DEGREE OF LL.D. *" Honoris causa."*

HUGH L. CALENDAR, M.A. (Cantab.), F.R.S.

INTERMEDIATE EXAMINATION.

McGILL COLLEGE.

Class I.—FERGUSON, COLIN C.,
NUTTER, J. APPLETON. } equal.
RADFORD E. ALAN.

DEY, M. HELENA.
WILLIS, SAMUEL J.
GARLICK, EDYTHE A.
BROOKS, ELIZABETH A.

Class II.—FORBES WILFRED M.

COCHRANE, DONALD. ⎫
COHEN, ABRAHAM. ⎪ equal.
DIXON, JAS. D. ⎬
MARCUSE, BELLA. ⎭

CROWELL, BOWMAN C ⎫ equal.
ELDER ROBERT. ⎬

HARDY, CHAS. A ⎫ equal.
JACKSON, E. GERTRUDE. ⎬

SMITH, LILLIAN A.

JOHNSON, J. GUY W. ⎫ equal.
WEINFELD, HENRY. ⎬

Class III.—RORKE, HELEN. ⎫ equal.
ROWELL, ARTHUR H. ⎬

ELLS, SYDNEY C. ⎫ equal.
SCOTT, HENRY E. ⎬

SCOTT, GEO. W., ⎫ equal.
SEVER, HANNAH D. ⎬

AINLEY, LAWRENCE. ⎫
DEWITT, JACOB, ⎬ equal.
WALKER, HORATIO. ⎭

COOKE, H. LESTER.

MACMILLAN, CYRUS J. ⎫ equal.
MACKINNON, CECIL G. ⎬

RITCHIE, CHAS. F.
NEWSON, WM. G.
GRIER, GEO. W. (*s*).
HOLMAN, CARRIE E. (*s*).
JENKINS, CHAS. E. (*s*).
LUTTRELL, HENRY P. (*s*).
MITCHELL, SYDNEY. (*s*).
REFORD LEWIS L. (*s*).
SANGSTER, LIZZIE. (*s* ·
· WOODLEY, EDWARD C. (*s*).

s. With supplemental in one subject (arranged alphabetically).

MORRIN COLLEGE.

Class II.—FYLES, FAITH.
Class III.—LAVERIE, J. H. (*s*).

STANSTEAD WESLEYAN COLLEGE.

Class II.—HILL, (O. W.) FLINT (MARY).
Class III.—FLINT, ROY.

FACULTY OF APPLIED SCIENCE.

PASSED FOR THE DEGREE OF BACHELOR OF APPLIED SCIENCE.

(In Order of Merit).

CIVIL ENGINEERING.

McCarthy, George Arnold, Moncton, N.B.
Macphail, William Matheson, Orwell, P.E.I.
Irving, Thomas Tweedy, Vernon River Bridge, P.E.I.
Anderson, William, Beaumont, Ottawa, Ont.
Matheson, Ernest George, Oyster Bed Bridge, P.E.I.
Bond, Frank Lorne Campbell, Montreal.
Benny, Walter Wilfrid, D'Aillebout, Que.

ELECTRICAL ENGINEERING.

Cape, Edmund Graves, Hamilton, Ont., }
Sheffield, Charles, Kingston, Ont.   } equal.
Eaves, Edmund, Montreal, Que.
Maclennan, Frank William, Cornwall, Ont.
Symmes, Howard Church, Aylmer, Que.
Archibald, Harry Patton, Antigonish, N.S.
Scott, James Henderson, Outremont, Que.

Simpson, Joseph Manley, Stratford, Ont., ægrotat.

MECHANICAL ENGINEERING.

Angel, Frederick William, St. John's, Newfoundland.
Laurie, Albert, Montreal.
Waterous, Charles Alexander, Brantford, Ont.
Patton, Walter Hugh, Huntingdon, Que.
McRae, John Bell, Ottawa, Ont.
Mackerras, John Dennistoun, Kingston, Ont.
Dean, Bertram Dodd, Hamilton, Ont.
Thomas, Leonard Edward Lawson, Melbourne, Que.
Bacon, Frederick Thomas Howard, Montreal.
Davidson, James Herbert, Montreal.
Beatty, David Herbert, Sarnia, Ont.

Reaves, Campbell, Montreal,   }
Mackie, James Douglas, Kingston, O.   } ægrotant.

MINING ENGINEERING.

Davis, Angus Ward, Montreal.
Butler, Percy, Montreal.
Young, George Albert, Kingston, Ont.
Atkinson, Donald Cameron Thomson, Etchemin, Que.

Ainley, Charles Newth, Almonte, Ont.
MacLean, Thomas Archibald, Charlottetown, P.E.I.
Atkinson, William Josiah, Glenboro, Man.
Hillary, George Michael, Whitby, Ont.

PRACTICAL CHEMISTRY.

Scott, Arthur Putnam, Montreal.
Drysdale, George Arrowsmith, Boston, Mass., U.S.A.

ADMITTED TO THE DEGREE OF BACHELOR OF APPLIED SCIENCE.

(Ad eundem.)

Durley, Richard John, B.Sc., University of London, England.
Hardman, John E., B.Sc., Mass. Inst. Tech., Boston, Mass., U.S.A.
Hedrick, Ira Grant, B.C E., University of Arkansas, U.S.A.
Strickland, Tom Percival, B.E., University of Sydney, N.S.W.
Australia.

ADMITTED TO THE DEGREE OF MASTER OF APPLIED SCIENCE.

(In Course.)

Brodie, Alexander, B.A.Sc., McGill University, Montreal.
Hersey, Milton L., B-A.Sc., Montreal.
King, Robert O., B.A.Sc., Toronto, Ont.

ADMITTED TO THE DEGREE OF MASTER OF ENGINEERING.

(In Course.)

Durley, Richard John, B.Sc., B.A.Sc., McGill University, Montreal.
Hardman, John E., B.Sc., B.A.Sc., Montreal.
Herdt, Louis, B.A.Sc., E.E., McGill University, Montreal.

FACULTY OF COMPARATIVE MEDICINE AND VETERINARY SCIENCE.

PASSED FOR THE DEGREE OF D.V.S.

Baldwin, B. K.	Cullen, D.	Paquin, L. A.
Bell, W. Lincoln,	Hart, J. B.	Pfersick, J. G.
Burke, G. II.	Hollingsworth, J. B.	Spanton, John P.
Cleaves, A. W.	Lambert, G. H.	Wallis, W. B.

Scholarships and Exhibitions.

FACULTY OF ARTS.

I. SCHOLARSHIPS (Tenable for two years).

Year of Award.	Names of Scholars.	Subjects of Examination.	Annual Value.	Founder or Donor.
1896	Gardner, Wm. A.	Mathematics.	$125	W. C. McDonald.
1896	Brooks, Harriet	Mathematics.	125	Lord Strathcona and Mt. Royal.
1896	Duff, Alex. H.	Nat. Science.	125	W. C. McDonald.
1896	Munn, D. Walter	Class.&Mod.Lang	120	Miss Barbara Scott
1896	Heine, M. C.	Class.&Mod.Lang	110	Chas. Alexander.
1897	McClung, Robt. K.	Mathematics.	125	W. C. McDonald.
1897	Henderson, ErnestH.	Nat. Science.	125	W. C. McDonald.
1897	Robertson, Lemuel	Class.&Mod.Lang	125	W. C. McDonald.
1897	Wainwright, Arnold	Class.&Mod.Lang	125	W. C. McDonald.

II. EXHIBITIONS (Tenable for one year.)

NAMES OF EXHIBITIONERS.	Academic Year.	Annual Value.	Founder or Donor.
Nutter, J. Appleton	Second	$125	W. C. McDonald.
Dey, M. Helena	"	120	Lord Strathcona and Mount Royal.
Radford, E. Alan	"	125	George Hague.
Brooks, Elizabeth A.	"	100	Lord Strathcona and Mount Royal.
McEwen, John R.	First	125	W. C. McDonald.
Copeman, Jos.Hodge	"	125	W. C. McDonald.
Sterns, H. Edgar	"	100	Major Hiram Mills.
MacNaughton, W.G	"	90	Mrs. Jane Redpath

At the Second Year Exhibition Examination a W. C. McDonald Bursary, value $62.50, was awarded to Donald Cochrane.

At the First Year Exhibition Examination a W. C. McDonald Bursary, value $62.50, was awarded to Edwin O. Brown, and two Sir William Dawson Bursaries given by the New York Graduates' Society, value $30 each, were awarded to Norval Dickson and Robert J. Harper.

Prizes, Honours and Standing.

SESSION 1897-1898.

FACULTY OF LAW.

RESULTS OF EXAMINATIONS.

THIRD YEAR.

Eratus Edwin Howard, B.A., Philipsburg, Q , First Rank Honours and Elizabeth Torrance Gold Medal.

Samuel Clay, B.A. (Cantab.), London, Eng., First Rank Honours and Prize of
Fifty Dollars.

Herbert Meredith Marler, Montreal, First Rank Honours and Prize of Twenty-five
Dollars.

Arthur Burnet, B.A., Farnham Centre, Q., First Rank Honours.

SECOND YEAR.

Frank C. Saunders, B.A., First Rank General Standing and Prize of Fifty Dollars.
Walter H. Lynch, First Rank General Standing and Prize of Twenty-Five Dollars.

PASSED THE SESSIONAL EXAMINATIONS.

Frank C. Saunders, B.A., Walter H. Lynch, Wm. Evander MacIver, Melbourne,
Q.; Edmond B. Drolet, William Carlos Ives, Joseph N. F. Décarie, Walter
E. G. Thorneloe, William Frederick Carter, Ernest E. Vipond, William S.
Ball, Edward P. F. McCabe.

FIRST YEAR.

A. W. G. Macalister, First Rank General Standing and Scholarship of $100.

Samuel G. Archibald, B.A., First Rank General Standing and Scholarship of
$100.

Henry N. Chauvin, First Rank General Standing, Prize of $25, and British Col-
umbia Graduates' Society Prize of $10.

Lawrence Macfarlane, B.A., First Rank General Standing.

PASSED THE SESSIONAL EXAMINATION.

A. W. G. Macalister, S. G. Archibald, B.A., H. N. Chauvin, L. Macfarlane, B.A.,
Thomas E. Walsh, G. H. Baker, Alfred Dobell, B.A., Harry Tribey, F. T.
Enright, J. C. Redpath, L. Margolese, Edmund A. Burke, W. F. Kav.

ROMAN LAW.

SPECIAL PRIZE LIST.

In this list the results of the four Class Examinations are added to those of
the final examination.

293

1. Archibald, S. G.
2. Clay, S.
Proxime accessit, Howard, E. E.

STANDING IN THE CLASSES.

THIRD YEAR.

ROMAN LAW—Dean WALTON.
Clay; Howard and Marler, equal; Burnet, Iles, Hickson, Elliott, Champoux, Kennedy.

HISTORY AND MUNICIPAL LAW—Professors McGoun and Fortin,

Howard, Burnet, Iles, Clay, Marler, Champoux, Hickson, Elliott, Kennedy.

CONSTITUTIONAL AND INTERNATIONAL LAW—Professors McGoun and LAFLEUR.

Howard, Clay, Marler, Iles, Kennedy, Burnet, Hickson, Champoux, Elliott.

COMMERCIAL LAW—Prof. McGoun.

Howard, Iles, Clay, Marler, Burnet, Champoux, Hickson, Elliott, Kennedy.

CIVIL LAW, No. 1—Professors Fortin and Lafleur.
Howard, Iles, Burnet, Marler, Elliott, Kennedy, Hickson, Champoux and Clay, equal.

CIVIL LAW No. 2—Professor DOHERTY.
Clay and Howard, equal; Burnet; Marler and Elliott, equal; Iles, Kennedy, Hickson, Champoux.

CIVIL LAW No. 3—Professor Fortin and Lecturer GEOFFRION.

Clay, Elliott, Burnet, Marler, Howard, Kennedy, Hickson, Iles, Champoux.

CRIMINAL LAW—Professor HON. C. P. DAVIDSON.

Clay, Burnet; Howard and Marler, equal; Elliott, Hickson, Iles, Kennedy, Champoux.

CIVIL PROCEDURE—Lecturer RYAN.

Iles, Clay, Elliott, Hickson, Champoux, Howard, Burnet, Marler, Kennedy.

SECOND YEAR.

ROMAN LAW.

Lynch, Saunders, Thorneloe, McIver, Drolet, Décarie, Ives, Vipond, Ball.

CIVIL PROCEDURE.
> Saunders, Lynch, Bercovitch, McIver, Décarie, Drolet, Carter, Thorneloe, Ives, McCabe, Barlow and Vipond, equal; Ball, Whelan and Baby, equal; Thomson.

SUCCESSIONS.
> Saunders, Lynch and Carter, equal; Décarie, Ives, McIver, Vipond, Thorneloe and Drolet, equal; Ball and Bercovitch, equal; Robertson, McCabe, Baby and Whelan, equal; Barlow.

LEGAL HISTORY.
> Saunders, Carter and Drolet, equal; Ives, McIver, Ball, Whelan and Décarie, equal; Lynch, McCabe and Barlow, equal; Thorneloe, Vipond, Baby, Bercovitch.

AGENCY AND PARTNERSHIP.
> Saunders, Carter, Lynch, Décarie, Ives, McIver, Ball, McCabe, Vipond, and Robertson, equal; Thorneloe, Thomson, Baby, Whelan.

CONSTITUTIONAL.
> Saunders, McIvor, Ball, Lynch and Thorneloe, equal; Carter and Robertson, equal; Whelan, Ives, Vipond, Décarie, Barlow, equal; Baby, Thomson, McCabe, Bercovitch.

PRIVATE INTERNATIONAL LAW.
> Saunders, Thorneloe, Lynch, Décarie and Vipond, equal; McIver, Ives, Carter and Drolet, equal; McCabe, Robertson, Barlow, Bercovitch, Ball.

MARRIAGE COVENANTS.
> Lynch, Thorneloe, Saunders, Vipond, Whelan, McIver, Ives, Baby, Carter, Drolet, Décarie, McCabe, Bercovitch, Barlow, Thomson, Robertson and Ball, equal.

CRIMINAL.
> Lynch, Saunders, Drolet and Ives, equal; Thorneloe, McIver, Décarie, Ball, Carter, Vipond.

FIRST YEAR.

SUCCESSIONS.
> Macalister; Archibald and Redpath, equal; Chauvin, Margolese; Baker; Macfarlane; Walsh and Tribey, equal; Kay; Enright; Garneau; Dobell; Burke.

PERSONS.
> Macalister; Chauvin; Archibald; Walsh; Macfarlane; Kay, Dobell; Tribey; Baker and Enright, equal; Redpath; Burke.

OBLIGATIONS.
> Macfarlane; Macalister; Chauvin and Archibald, equal; Redpath; Baker; Dobell; Enright; Burke and Mackay, equal; Margolese; Walsh; Garneau; Tribey, Kay, Sharswood.

CONSTITUTIONAL LAW.

Macalister ; Chauvin ; Macfarlane ; Archibald ; Baker; Dobell ; Garneau ; Margolese; Tribey ; Redpath and Walsh, equal ; Enright ; Reeve ; Mackay, Burke ; Kay.

ROMAN LAW.

Macalister ; Archibald ; Chauvin ; Macfarlane ; Walsh ; Redpath ; Enright ; Dobell.

HISTORY OF LAW.

Archibald ; Macalister ; Macfarlane ; Chauvin ; Walsh ; Kay ; Redpath ; Dobell ; Baker ; Tribey and Burke, equal ; Enright, Margolese.

REAL RIGHTS.

Archibald ; Macfarlane ; Chauvin ; Macalister ; Enright and Baker, equal ; Margolese and Tribey, equal ; Walsh ; Kay, Redpath and Dobell, equal ; Burke ; Mackay.

CIVIL PROCEDURE.

Archibald ; Chauvin ; Macalister and Macfarlane, equal ; Enright and Walsh, equal ; Tribey ; Baker ; Margolese ; Dobell and Burke, equal.

FACULTY OF MEDICINE.

MEDALS AND PRIZES.

The HOLMES GOLD MEDAL for highest aggregate in all subjects forming the Medical Curriculum, W. O. ROSE, of Lakeville. P.E.I.

The FINAL PRIZEMAN for highest aggregate in Fourth Year Subjects, R. F. BEATTIE, of Economy, N.S.

The CLEMESHA PRIZE for Clinical Therapeutics, C. A. PETERS of St. John's, N'f'd.

The McGILL MEDICAL SOCIETY PRIZES, 1st Prize W. L. BARLOW, B.A., of Montreal, 2nd Prize W. A. DALPÉ, B.A., of Montreal.

The THIRD YEAR PRIZEMAN, A. H. GORDON of St. John, N.B.

The SUTHERLAND MEDALLIST, J. R. O'BRIEN, B.A., of Ottawa, Ont.

The GRADUATES' SOCIETY OF BRITISH COLUMBIA PRIZE, was this year awarded to T. TURNBULL of Stratford, Ont. For best Examination in Clinical Medicine.

The SECOND YEAR PRIZEMAN, E. R. SECORD of Brantford, Ont.

The SENIOR ANATOMY PRIZE, E. R. SECORD of Brantford, Ont.

The FIRST YEAR PRIZEMAN, J. BRUCE, B.A , of Moncton, N.B.

The JUNIOR ANATOMY PRIZE, J. BRUCE, B.A., of Moncton, N.B.

FACULTY OF COMPARATIVE MEDICINE AND VETERINARY SCIENCE.

PRIZES.

Veterinary Medicine and Surgery—W. B. Wallis.
Cattle Pathology—W. B. Wallis.
Pathology—W. B. Wallis.
Materia Medica—W. B. Wallis and W. L. Bell, equal.
Anatomy—James McGregor.
Physiology—James McGregor.
Chemistry—James McGregor.
Botany—B. F. Humphries.

For the best general examination in all subjects, a silver medal, the gift of the Dean, won by W. B. Wallis.

Extra Prizes:—For the best essay read before the Veterinary Medical Association—1st—J. W. Symes. 2nd—W. Lincoln Bell. 3rd—W. B. Wallis.

For the best essay read before the Society for the study of Comparative Physiology—1st—J. B. Hart. 2nd—L. A. Paquin.

Junior Class—E. W. Hammond.

FACULTY OF ARTS.

GRADUATING CLASS.

B. A. Honours in Mathematics and Natural Philosophy.
BROOKS, HARRIET.—First Rank Honours and Anne Molson Gold Medal.

B. A. Honours in Classics.
CARR, MURIEL B.—First Rank Honours and Chapman Gold Medal.
MUNN, WALTER D.—First Rank Honours.

B. A. Honours in Geology, Mineralogy and Palæontology.
DALGLEISH, ROBERT W.—First Rank Honours.
McGREGOR, JAMES ALBERT.—Second Rank Honours.

B. A. Honours in Mental and Moral Philosophy.
PATERSON, ROBERT C.—First Rank Honours and Prince of Wales Gold Medal.
PLACE, EDSON J.—First Rank Honours.
BATES, GEORGE.—First Rank Honours.
SHIP, MOSES L.—First Rank Honours.
SEIFERT, ETHEL M.—First Rank Honours.
CAMPBELL, J. A. E.—First Rank Honours.
THOMPSON, JAMES R.—First Rank Honours.

DUFF, ALEXANDER H.—First Rank Honours.
VINEBERG, ABRAHAM.—Second Rank Honours.
TURNER, HENRY H.—Second Rank Honours.
SHAW, A. LOUISE.—Second Rank Honours.
MacLEOD, HENRY S.—Second Rank Honours.

B. A. Honours in English Language, Literature and History.

HEINE, M. CASEWELL.—First Rank Honours and Shakspere Gold Medal.
BOUKKE-WRIGHT, KATHERINE.—First Rank Honours.
WALKER, LAURA M.—First Rank Honours.
BISHOP, W. GORDON. —First Rank Honours.
MacLAREN, ARCHIBALD.—Second Rank Honours.

B. A. Honours in Modern Languages and History.

CAMERON, FRANCES.—First Rank Honours and Aberdeen Gold Medal.

B. A. Honours in Semitic Languages and Literature.

MEYER, J. B.—First Rank Honours.

THIRD YEAR.

McCLUNG, ROBERT K.—First Rank Honours and Prize in Mathematics and Natural Philosophy. First Rank General Standing.

ROBERTSON, LEMUEL.—First Rank Honours in Classics. First Rank General Standing.

HENDERSON, ERNEST.—First Rank Honours in Natural Science, Vancouver Graduates Society's Prize for Zoology.

HOLIDAY, ANNIE.—First Rank Honours in Natural Science. Prize in French.

ELLS, HUGH.—First Rank Honours in Natural Science.

SCRIMGER, ANNIE M.—First Rank Honours and Prize in Mental and Moral Philosophy. First Rank General Standing.

McLEOD, JOHN B.—First Rank Honours and Prize in Mental and Moral Philosophy.

WAINWRIGHT, ARNOLD.—First Rank Honours and Prize in Mental and Moral Philosophy.

POTTER, LUCY E.—First Rank Honours in Mental and Moral Philosophy.

BROWN, WALTER G.—First Rank Honours in Mental and Moral Philosophy.

THOMPSON, JAMES E.—First Rank Honours in Mental and Moral Philosophy.

KEITH, HENRY J.—First Rank Honours in Mental and Moral Philosophy. First Rank General Standing.

LAURIE, ERNEST.—First Rank Honours in Mental and Moral Philosophy. First Rank General Standing.

McGILL, WINNIFRED.—First Rank Honours in Mental and Moral Philosophy.

PATCH, FRANK S.—First Rank Honours and Prize in English Language, Literature and History.

FINLEY, KATHLEEN.—First Rank Honours in Modern Languages and History. Prize in French. Prize in German.

RICE, HORACE.—First Rank Honours in Semitic Languages and Literature. Prize in Hebrew.

REID, LENA McK.—Second Rank Honours in Natural Science.

RADFORD, JANET I.—Second Rank Honours in Natural Science.

McDOUGALL, LOUISE.—Second Rank Honours in English Language, Literature and History.

HARDISTY, RICHARD.—Second Rank Honours in English Language, Literature and History.

JOHNSON, HELENA.—Third Rank Honours in Mathematics and Natural Philosophy.

COTTON, CHARLES M.—First Rank General Standing.

BRUCE, GUY O. T.—First Rank General Standing.

THIRD YEAR.

PASSED THE SESSIONAL EXAMINATION.

McClung and Scrimger, equal; Cotton Bruce and Keith and Robertson, equal; Henderson and Laurie, equal; Brown and Holiday and McDonald and McLeod, equal; Ells and Thompson and Wainwright, equal; Johnson (H.); Cumming; Patch and Potter and Radford, equal; King; Mackay and Rice, equal; Finley; Brodie, McGill, Lundie, Holland and Reid, equal; Hardisty and McDougall, equal.

STUDENTS REGISTERED IN THE MEDICAL FACULTY.

Arranged alphabetically.

Dixon, Gardner, Goodall, Johnson, Larmonth, White.

SECOND YEAR.

FERGUSON, COLIN C.—(Prince of Wales College, P. E. I.). First Rank Honours and Prize in Mathematics; First Rank General Standing; Prize in Latin; Prize in Logic, Prize in German.

RADFORD, ALAN E.—(Abingdon School, Montreal). First Rank Honours and Prize in Mathematics.; First Rank General Standing; Prize in History.

DEY, MARY HELENA.—(Simcoe H. S.). Second Rank Honours in Mathematics; First Rank General Standing; Prize in French.

SCOTT, G. W.—(Montreal H. S.). Second Rank Honours in Mathematics.

JOHNSON, J. GUY W.—(Montreal Coll. Inst.). Second Rank Honours in Mathematics.

NUTTER, J. APPLETON.—(Montreal, H. S.). First Rank General Standing; Prize in Greek; Prize in French; Prize in Botany.

WILLIS, SAMUEL J.—(Prince of Wales College, P. E. I.), First Rank General Standing; Prize in Latin.

GARLICK, EDYTHE,—First Rank General Standing.

BROOKS, ELIZABETH A.—(McGill Normal School). First Rank General Standing.

MARCUSE, BELLA.—(Montreal G. H. S.). Prize in Botany; Prize in German.

COCHRANE, DONALD.—Prize in Chemistry.

FORBES, WILFRED.—Prize in German.

SECOND YEAR.

PASSED THE SESSIONAL EXAMINATION.

Class I.—Ferguson ; Nutter and Radford, equal ; Dey ; Willis, Garlick, Brooks.

Class II.—Forbes; Cochrane and Cohen and Dixon and Marcuse, equal; Crowell and Elder, equal ; Hardy and Jackson, equal ; Smith ; Johnson and Weinfeld, equal.

Class III.—Rorke and Rowell, equal ; Ells and Scott (H.), equal ; Scott (G.) and Sever, equal ; Ainley and DeWitt and Walker (H,), equal ; Cooke ; Macmillan and Mackinnon, equal; Ritchie, Newson, Grier (*s*), Holman (*s*), Jenkins (*s*), Luttrell (*s*), Mitchell (*s*), Reford (*s*), Sangster (*s*), Woodley (*s*).

----

s.—With supplemental examination in one subject (arranged alphabetically.)

FIRST YEAR.

STERNS, EDGAR H.—(Prince of Wales College, P.E.I.). First Rank Honours and Prize in Mathematics ; First Rank General Standing ; Prize in Greek ; Prize in Latin ; Prize in Chemistry; Prize in German. Coster Memorial Prize ; Special Professor's Prize in Greek Composition.

WILLIAMS, J. MANVILLE.—(Watford H. S.). First Rank Honours and Prize in Mathematics ; First Rank General Standing ; Prize in Hebrew.

McEWEN, JOHN R.—(Huntingdon Academy). First Rank Honours in Mathematics ; First Rank General Standing ; Prize in Latin ; Prize in French.

BROWN, EDWARD O.—(Prince of Wales College, P.E.I.).—First Rank Honours in Mathematics ; First Rank General Standing.

BARRINGTON, FREDERICK H.—(Waterloo Academy). First Rank Honours in Mathematics ; First Rank General Standing.

McNAUGHTON, WILLIAM J.—(Huntingdon Academy). First Rank Honours in Mathematics ; First Rank General Standing.

Lochead, A. W.—First Rank Honours in Mathematics.

Copeman, Joseph H.—(Quebec H. S.). First Rank General Standing; Prize in English.

Williams, Henry S.—(Montreal H. S.), First Rank General Standing; Prize in Latin; Prize in French.

Dickson, Norval.—(Huntingdon Academy). First Rank General Standing.

McLeod, Angus B.—(Prince of Wales College, P.E.I.). First Rank General Standing.

FIRST YEAR

PASSED THE SESSIONAL EXAMINATION.

Sterns, Williams (J. M.) and McEwen, equal; Williams (H. S.) and MacNaughton and Copeman, equal; Dickson; McLeod (A. B.) and Barrington, equal; Bennett and Lochead, equal; Tees and Strong, equal; Molson (Evelyn) and Cotton, equal; Harper; McDonald and Lindsay and Brown (A. D.), equal; Radford and Scott and McLean and Chipman, equal; Huxtable, Mitchell and McMurtry (S. O.), equal; Clogg and Neville and McMurtry (G. O.), equal; Anderson and Viner and Scrimger and McPherson, equal; Hickson; White (D. R.) and Molson (P.) and Moffatt, equal; Stephens, Noyes, Boulter, Ireland, Mowatt, Bourne (s), Brodie (s) Carruthers (s), Irving (s), Mount (s), Budden (E.) (s), Budden (J.) (s).

(s)—With supplemental examination in one subject (arranged alphabetically).

AWARD OF SCHOLARSHIPS, EXHIBITIONS AND CLASSING AT HIGHER ENTRANCE, SEPTEMBER, 1897.

I. Third Year.—Scholarships (tenable for two years.)

> Mathematical Scholarship.—(a) McClung (Robt. K.).
> Natural Science Scholarship.—(a) Henderson (Ernest H.).
> Classical and Modern Language Scholarship.—(a) Robertson (Lemuel) and (a) Wainwright (Arnold), equal.

II. Second Year.—Exhibitions, &c. (tenable for one year).

> (a) Nutter (J. Appleton), Montreal H. S.
> (e) Dey. (M Helena), Simcoe H. S.
> (d) Radford (E. Alan), Abingdon School, Montreal.
> (f) Brooks (Elizabeth A.), McGill Normal School.
> (g) Cochrane (Donala), Montreal H. S.

III. First Year.—Exhibitions, &c. (tenable for one year).

> (a) McEwen (Jno. R.), Huntingdon Academy.
> (a) Copeman (Joseph Hodge), Quebec H. S.
> (b) Sterns (H. Edgar), Prince of Wales College, P.E.I.

(c) MacNaughton (Wm. G.), Huntingdon Academy.
(g) Brown (Edwin O.), Prince of Wales College, P.E I.
(h) Dickson (Norval), Huntingdon Academy.
(i) Harper (Robt. J.), Montreal H.S.

FIRST YEAR.—*Higher Entrance Examination*

Class I.—MacEwen (Jno. R.), Copeman (Jos. H.), Sterns (H. Edgar), MacNaughton (W. Gilbert), Brown (Edwin O.), Dickson (Norval), Harper (Robt. J.), Tees (Fred. J.).

Class II.—Neville (James).

Passed.—Kemp (May D.), Brown (Albert V.), Evans (L. Thornton).

(a) Annual value $125—Founder, W. C. McDonald, Esq.
(b) "   " $100—Founder, Major Hiram Mills.
(c) "   " $ 90—Founder, Mrs. Jane Redpath.
(d) "   " $125—Donor, Geo. Hague, Esq.
(e) "   " $120—Donor, Lord Strathcona and Mount Royal.
(f) "   " $100—Donor, Lord Strathcona and Mount Royal.
(g) "   " $62.50—Bursary, W. C. McDonald, Esq.
(h) "   " $30—Sir Wm. Dawson Bursary } (given by New York
(i) "   " $30— "   "   "   " } Graduate Society)

SUPPLEMENTAL EXAMINATIONS.

PASSED.

September to Christmas, 1897.

(a) *Supplemental Sessional.*

B.A.—Crack (H. A.), Moore (Wm.), Watson (Wm.)
THIRD YEAR.—McLeod (Hy. S.), Moore (Percy T.)
SECOND YEAR.—Reid (Lena McK.)
FIRST YEAR.—Dickson (W. Howard), Mitchell (Sydney.)

(b) *Supplemental in one Subject.*

SECOND YEAR.—Holland, Munroe, Stewart (Donald), Reynolds (L. E. Maude), Armstrong (Cath rine).
FIRST YEAR.—Ainley, Horsfall, McCormick, Rowat, Walker (J. J.), Perley, Baker (G. P.), Charters.

SESSIONAL EXAMINATIONS, 1898.

McGILL COLLEGE.

GREEK.

B. A. ORDINARY.—*Class I.*—Munn, Carr, *Class II.*—Tarlton, Grace. *Class III.*—Worth, Gardner, Leney.

THIRD YEAR.—*Class I.*—Robertson, Cotton. *Class II.*—Bruce, McLeod. *Class, III.*—Rice, Holland, Hurst, Potter.

SECOND YEAR.—*Class I.*—Nutter (*Prize*), Ferguson, Willis, Radford (E.A.), Brooks, Forbes, Dixon (J. D.), Cochrane, Garlick, Crowell, Jackson and Woodley, equal. *Class II.*—Rowell, Hill (2), Smith (L. A.) ; Elder and Cohen, equal ; Scott (H. E.), Hardy, Sever, Ells ; Ainley and Newson, equal ; Mitchell (S.). *Class III.*—Walker (H.), Johnson (J. G. W.), Ritchie ; Cooke and Jeakins, equal ; Mackinnon, Flint (2) ; DeWitt and Holman, equal ; Weinfeld, Scott (G. W.), Lundie, Walker (J. J.), Sangster, Tatley, Grier, Reford, Macmillan, Laverie (1), MacRae (1).

(2) Stanstead College. (1) Morrin College.

FIRST YEAR.—*Class I.*—Sterns (*Prize*), McEwen, Dickson, Macnaughton, Copeman, Williams (H. S.), Barrington, Locnead, Brown (E. O.), Harper, Strong, Williams (J. M.). *Class II.*—Brown (A V.), McLeod (A. B.), Page (2), Cotton, McDonald, Clogg, Chipman, Scott, Lindsay, Viner, Mount, Neville, McLean, Tees. *Class III.*—Dobson (2), Hickson, McPherson, Mitchell, Radford (I), McMurtry (G. O.), Moffat ; Day and Carruthers, equal ; McMurtry (S. O.), Noyes ; Scrimger and White (D. R.), equal ; Mowatt, Bourne, Molson, Brodie,* Parker* ; Anderson and Fuller (3) and Irving and Ireland.

* Partial Students. (1) Morrin College. (2) Stanstead College Students. (3) St. Francis College.

LATIN.

B. A. ORDINARY.—*Class I.*—Carr, Munn, Pearson, Tarlton. *Class II.*—Steen, Leney, Worth. *Class III.*—Ross, Gardner, Jordan, Gilday, Reynolds, Colby, Dover and Todd, equal ; Stephens.

THIRD YEAR.—*Class I.*—Robertson, Bruce, Scrimger, Potter, Cotton. *Class II.*—Cumming, Goodall, Ells, Thompson. *Class III.*—McGill, Lundie, Dixon, Radford, King, Johnson (H.), Johnson (R. de L.), Hurst, Brodie, McDougall, Finley, Reid.

SECOND YEAR—*Class I.*—Ferguson (*Prize*) and Willis (*Prize*), equal ; Dey, Radford Nutter Forbes, Smith (L.), Garlick, Brooks, Cochrane, Jackson. *Class II.*—Marcuse, Dixon, Cohen, Scott (H. E.) ; Crowell and Elder, equal ; Mitchell (S.) and Woodley, equal ; Rorke and Weinfeld, equal. *Class III.*—MacRae (1), Fyles (1) ; Cooke, Ells and Hill (2) and Newson, equal ; DeWitt and Hardy and Rowell, equal ; Scott (G. W.), Walker (H.), Macmillan ; Holman and Mackinnon, equal ; Johnson, Ritchie, Sever, Luttrell, Sangster, Ainley, Laverie (1), Flint Roy (2), Flint Mary (2).

(1) Morrin College. (2) Stanstead College.

First Year.—*Class 1.*—McEwen (*Prize*), and Williams (H. S.) (*Prize*) and Sterns, (*Prize*), equal; Dickson; Barrington and Brown (E. O.), equal; Macnaughton, Copeman; Harper Lochead, McDonald, Williams (J. M.), Chipman. *Class II.*—Brown (A. V.) and Huxtable and Lindsay, equal; Bennet; Strong and Tees, equal; McPherson and Mitchell and McLean, equal; McLeod and Cotton, equal; Radford (I.); Budden (J. M.) and Mount, equal; Viner; Hickson and Stephens, equal; Scott, Molson (E.), Fuller (3), Clogg, Budden (E.M.) *Class III.*—Mowatt and White, equal; McMurtry (S. O.), Bourne, Dobson (2), Neville; Carruthers and Moffatt and Boulter, equal; Scrimger; Molson (P.) and Ascah and Fee (3), equal; Cole; Irving and Price. equal; Porter,* Day; McMurtry (G. O.) and Noyes, equal; Cross (3) Ireland; Anderson and Brodie.*

---

(2) Stanstead College. (3) St. Francis College. * Partial Students.

MENTAL AND MORAL PHILOSOPHY.

B.A. Ordinary (*Moral Philosophy*).—*Class 1.*—Grace; Paterson and Seifert and Ship, equal; Place, Bates, Reynolds, Pearson, Vineberg; Bourke-Wright and Gardner and Heine, equal; Duff and Prudham, equal; Blythe; Shaw and Turner (H. H.), equal; Campbell (J. A. E.) and Stephens and Thompson, equal; Ross, MacLeod, Tarlton. *Class II.*—Cairns, and Dover and Meyer and Stuart, equal; Gilday, Jordan, Moore, Steen, Turner (W. D.); Cameron (A. G.) and Runnells and Thomas, equal; Anderson and Todd, equal; Worth, Colby; Down and Leney, equal; Bishop and Walker, equal. *Class III.*—Halpenny, McGregor (G.), Mick, Bartlett, Williamson, Campbell (J. D.), Maclaren.

Third Year.—(*Mental Philosophy*).—*Class 1.*—Potter and Scrimger, equal; Cotton, Munroe, Bruce; Holiday and McClung, equal; Wainwright; Rice and Thompson, equal; Brown; Laurie and MacLeod, equal; Cairns and Holland and Reynolds, equal. *Class II.*—Keith and Lundie and McGill, equal; Brodie and McDonald, equal; White, Bartlett, McDougall. *Class III.*—Down and Reid, equal; Henderson; Angell and Heeney, equal; Armstrong, Cumming, Oke, Harding.

Prize for Honour Work.—McLeod and Scrimger and Wainwright, equal.

Second Year (*Logic*).—*Class I.*—Ferguson, Nutter, Willis, Sever Forbes, Marcuse, Cohen, Garlick, Elder, Dey, Jackson, Hardy. *Class II.*—Dewitt; Macmillan and McGregor, equal; Crowell, Masson, Cooke; Brooks and Davies and Radford, equal; Rorke, Scott (G. W.), Woodley, Rowell; Ainley and Scott (H. E.) and Secord, equal; Rowat; Cochrane and Crack and Dixon and Evans and Newson and Walker (H.), equal; Jeakins and Powell, equal. *Class III.*—Johnson (G.), Smith, Weinfeld, Sangster, Hicks; Ells and Holman and Morrow and Ritchie, equal; MacInnes, Grier; Lundie and Perley, equal; Mackinnon, Mitchell, Burke, Reford, Tippett, Charters; Greig and Horsfall, equal; Luttrell, Howden, Crabb, Wiggins; Ireland and McCormick and Mick, equal.

ENGLISH LITERATURE.

B.A. ORDINARY.—*Class 1.*—Thomas, Bourke-Wright, Heine, Todd, Pearson and Walker, equal. *Class 11.*—Gilday, Bishop, Jordan and Dalgleish and Prudham, equal ; Gardner, Brooks, Bates and Grace, equal ; Duff and Maclaren and Ross, equal. *Class III.*—Stephens, Leney and McLeod and Reynolds, equal; Worth, Tarlton, Stuart, McConnell, Steen, Moore.

ENGLISH LITERATURE AND RHETORIC.

THIRD YEAR.—*Class 1.*—Patch and Wainwright, equal. *Class II.*—Hurst and Keith, equal; Bruce, Holland, McDougall, McLeod, Ells and Munroe equal. *Class III.*—Duguid, Heeney, Hardisty ; *Harding, Reynolds.

MODERN HISTORY.

SECOND YEAR.—*Class 1.*—Radford (*Prize*); Dewitt and Marcuse and Nutter, equal; Forbes, Ferguson, Horsfall, Topley, Dey and Luttrell, equal; Mitchell and Woodley, equal; Rorke, Cohen, Macmillan. Reford; Ells and Weinfeld, equal; Hardy, Mackinnon. *Class II.*— Brooks and Johnson equal ; Lundie and Willis, equal; Dixon and MacInnes, equal; Cochrane and Jeakins, equal; Jackson, Garlick ; Scott (G.) and Secord, equal ; Crowell and Elder and Grier and Walker, equal; Ainley and Cooke and Ritchie, equal; Smith. *Class III.*— Charters, . Newson and Rowell and Sever, equal; Scott (H.), MacCormick, Rowat, Holman, Davies, Harding, McGregor ; Crack and Ireland, equal ; Burke, Greig, Howden, Johnston.

ENGLISH LITERATURE.

FIRST YEAR.—*Class 1.*—Copeman, Carruthers, Lochead, Sterns, Blythe, Munroe, Scott, Williams (J. M.), Lindsay, Williams (H. S.), MacLeod (A. B.) ; Chipman and MacNaughton, equal. *Class II.*—Edgar, McEwen ; Bennett and Moffatt, equal ; Ireland, Molson (P.) and Tees, equal; Brown (A. V.) and Day and Radford, equal ; Irving, Scrimger Molson (E.), Greenaway, Dickson, McDonald, Mount, Huxtable, Strong, McPherson, McMurtry (G. O.), White, Carden, Clogg, Budden (J. M.). *Class III.*—Mitchell, Mulholland, Harper, Cole, Viner, Hickson, Parker, Boulter, Barrington, McMurtry (S. O.), Noyes, McLean, Budden (E. M.), Anderson, Cotton, Mowat, Swinton, Kingsley, Stephens, Boyd, Ness, Neville, McLeod (M.), Penhallow, Mathieson, Mosgrove.

MECHANICS.

B. A. ORDINARY.—*Class 1.*—Turner (H. H.) ; Dover and Gardner and Reynolds and Tailton and Turner (W. D.), equal. *Class 11.*—Jordan and Leney and Prudham and Thomas and Todd, equal; Gilday and Grace and McGregor and Pearson and Steen, equal.—*Class III.*—Stuart; Colby and Moore, equal.

THIRD YEAR.— *Class 1.*—McClung ; Bruce and Cotton and Gardner and Keith and McLeod and Robertson and White, equal; MacDonald and Thompson, equal. *Class II* —Brown and Cumming and Henderson and Laurie and Wainwright, equal; Holiday and Johnson (H) and Johnson (R. de L.) and King and Patch, equal· *Class III.*—Armstrong and Hardisty and Mackay and Potter, equal; Brodie and Larmonth and Lundie, equal

ASTRONOMY AND OPTICS.

B. A. ORDINARY.—*Class I.*—Thompson. *Class II.*—Gardner; Turner (W. D.). *Class III.*—Leney and Pradham, equal; Stuart and Tarlton and Thomas, equal; Moore.

THIRD YEAR.—*Class I.*—Cumming and Keith and McClung, equal; Cotton and Johnson (H.), equal. *Class II.*—Armstrong and Bruce and Laurie and Lundie and Patch, equal; Brown and Thompson, equal. *Class III.*—Heeney and MacKay and Wainwright, equal; Hardisty; Duguid.

EXPERIMENTAL PHYSICS.

B. A. ORDINARY.—*Class I.*—Brooks, (H)

THIRD YEAR —*Class I.*—McClung. *Class II.*—McDonald and Mackay, equal. *Class III.*—Johnson (H.)

LABORATORY COURSE.

B. A. ORDINARY.—*Class. I.*—Brooks (H.)

THIRD YEAR.—*Class I.*—Johnson and McClung and McDonald, equal.

GEOMETRY AND ARITHMETIC.

SECOND YEAR.—*Class I.*—Crowell and Nutter, equal; Brooks and Elder and Ferguson and Hardy and Johnson and Radford, equal; Cohen and Dey and Dixon and Hol man and Smith (L.) and Willis, equal. *Class II.*—Ainley and Cochrane and Ells and Garlick and Grier and Rowell and Scott (H. E.) and Walker (H.), equal; Charters and Cook and Crack and Jackson and Mackinnon and Mitchell and Rorke and Rowatt and Scott (G. W.) and Weinfeld and Woodley, equal. *Class III.*—Davies and Ireland and McCormack and McGregor and Sangster and Sever, equal; Dewitt and Dorion and Forbes and Macmillan and Marcuse and Newson and Reford and Ritchie, equal ; Jeakins and Luttrell and Perley, equal.

FIRST YEAR.—*Class I.*—Sterns; McEwan and McLeod and Williams (J. M.), equal; Brown (E. O.) and Dickson and McMurtry (S. O.) and McNaughton and Molson (E.), Parker and Strong and Williams (H. S.) equal. *Class II.*—Anderson and Barrington and Bennett and Brown (A. V.) and Copeman and Cotton and McMurtry (G. O.) and Neville and Lochead and Price and Scrimger and Tees, equal; Carden and Harper and Hickson and Huxtable and Mathieson and McDonald and Molson (P.) and Scott, equal. *Class III.*—Ascah and Brodie and Clogg and McLean, Mitchell and Moffat and Radford, Viner and White, equal; Budden (E.), Chipman and Cole and Lindsay and McPherson and Noyes and Stephens, equal ; Boulter, Bourne, Carruthers, Ireland and Irving and McLeod and Mount and Mowatt and Penballow.

U

TRIGONOMETRY AND ALGEBRA.

SECOND YEAR.—*Class I.*—Ferguson and Radford, equal; Brooks and Johnson and Willis, equal. *Class II.*—Scott (G W.) and Smith (L.) and Weinfield, equal.; Dingley and Cochrane and Cohen and Crowell and Davies and Dey and Dixon and Elder and Garlick and Nutter and Rowell, equal. *Class III.*—Ells and Hardy and Holman and Jackson and Mackinnon and Lundie and Rorke and Sangster and Scott (H. E.) and Sever and Walker (H.), equal; Crack and Dewitt and Forbes and Grier and Macmillan and Reford and Ritchie and Rowat, equal; Cooke and Howden and Jeakins and Luttrell and MacGregor Marcuse and Newson and Perley, equal.

FIRST YEAR.—*Class I.*—Barrington and Sterns and Williams (J. M.), equal; Bennett and Copeman and Cotton and Dickson and McEwen, equal; Anderson and MacNaughton, equal. *Class II.*—Brown (E. O.) and McDonald and McLeod and McMurtry (G. O.) and Molson (E.) and Neville and Strong and Tees and Williams (H. S.), equal; Boulter and Clogg and Harper and Lochead and McLean and McMurtry (S. O.) and McPherson and Molson (P.), equal. *Class III.*—Ascab, Brodie and Chipman and Hickson and Huxtable and Ireland and Mathieson and Mitchell and Moffatt and Ness and Noyes and Price and Radford and Scrimger and Viner and White (R. D.), equal; Budden (J.) and Carden and Lindsay and Parker and Scott and Stephens, equal; Boyd and Brown (A. V.) and Mowat, equal.

HONOURS IN MATHEMATICS AND NATURAL PHILOSOPHY.

B. A. HONOURS.—Brooks (Harriet), *First Rank Honours* and Molson Gold Medal.

THIRD YEAR.—*First Rank Honours.*—McClung (*Prize*). *Third Rank Honours.* Johnson (H.).

SECOND YEAR.—*First Rank Honours.*—Ferguson and Radford (E. A.), equal, (*Prizes*). *Second Rank Honours.*—Dey, Scott (G. W., Johnson (J. G. W.)

FIRST YEAR.—*First Rank Honours.*—Sterns (*Prize*), Williams (*Prize*), Brown and McEwen, equal; Barrington, MacNaughton and Lochead.

FRENCH.

B.A. ORDINARY.—*Class I.*—Ship; Cameron and Place and Seifert, equal. *Class II.*—Leney; Pearson and Reynolds, and Shaw and Steen and Vineberg, equal. *Class III.*—Todd; Gilday and Jordan and McConnell and Dover, equal.

THIRD YEAR.—*Class I.*—Finley and Goodall and Holiday, equal. *Class II.*—Brodie and Duguid, equal. *Class III.*—Cumming and Dixon and Larmonth and Gardner and Hardisty, equal.

SECOND YEAR.—*Class I.*—Nutter ; Dey and Radford, equal. *Class II.*—Garlick and Marcuse and Mitchell and Ritchie and Weinfeld, equal ; Cohen and Dixon and Elder and Johnson and McCormick and Reford and Rowatt and Rowell and Scott (Geo.W.) and Sever and Willis, equal. *Class III.*— Brooks and Cochrane and Cooke and Crowell and DeWitt and Howden and Lundie and McMillan and McKinnon and Sangster and Scott (H) E.) and Walker (H. J.), equal ; Ainley and Davies and Grier and Jackson and Luttrell and Newson and Rorke and Smith (L. A.) and Tatley. equal ; Burke and Charters and Crack and McGregor and Perley, equal

FIRST YEAR.—*Class I.*—McEwen and Radford and Williams (H. S.), equal. *Class II.*—Bennet ; Copeman and Dickson and McMurtry (Sh. O.) and MacNaughton and Noyse and Tees, equal ; McMurtry (G.); Molson (Evelyn) and Stephens, equal. *Class III.*—Barrington and Budden (Jessie) and Cardin and Cole and Cotton and Harper and Neville and Scott (W. J.) and Scrimger and Strong, equal ; Budden (Ellen) ; Boulter and Chipman and Clogg and Huxtable and Ireland and MacDonald and McPherson and Moffat and Viner and White (D. R.), equal ; Archibald ; Brodie and Day and Hickson and McLeod and Molson (P.) and Mowatt and Ness and Parker and Penhallow, equal.

GERMAN.

B.A. ORDINARY.—*Class I.*—Cameron, Colby. *Class II.*—Grace.

THIRD YEAR.—*Class I.*—Finley (*Prize*), Scrimger. *Class II.*—Radford, McGill, Robertson, King. *Class III.*—Reid.

SECOND YEAR.—*Class I.*—Ferguson (*Prize*), Forbes (*Prize*). *Class II.*—Weinfield, Hardy.

SECOND YEAR.—*Donalda Dept.*—*Class I.*—Marcuse (*Prize*), Dey. *Class II.*— Rorke, Browne.* *Class III.*—de Courtenay.*

FIRST YEAR.—*Class I.*—Sterns (*Prize*); Mitchell, Brown. *Class II.*—Lochead. *Class III.*—Scott, Copeman, Edgar.

FIRST YEAR.—*Donalda Dept.* — *Class II.* — Bennett'; Molson and Huxtable, equal; Budden (J.), Radford. *Class III.*—Budden (E).

ARTS AND MEDICINE.

Class III.—Boulter, Stephens.

HEBREW.

B. A. ORDINARY. —*Class I.*—Meyer, Turner (W. D.) and Prudham, equal.

THIRD YEAR.—*Class I.*—Rice (*Prize*), Brown (W. G.), MacKay (H.)

SECOND YEAR.—*Class II.*—Williams (W. J.), Jeakins, Woodley, Anderson (T. J. *Class III.*—Halpenny (E. W.), Campbell (J. D.), Cameron, Williamson (A. W.), Ireland A.), Thom, Horsfall, Runnells.

First Year.—*Class I.*—Williams (J. M), (*Prize*), McLeod (A. B.), Greenaway, Munroe (Wm.), Tanner, Brown (A. V), Lindsay and Down, equal. *Class II.*—Lapointe, MacLean (K.), Mathieson, Cairns, Mount, Irving, Anderson (R. G.) *Class III.*—Greig (J. G.), Carruthers and Brown, equal; Ascah and Angell, equal.

GEOLOGY.

B A. Ordinary.—*Class I.*—Dalgleish, McGregor (J. A.), Leney. *Class II.*—Grace; Gardner and Gilday, equal; Colby; Stuart and Jordan, equal; Campbell (J. A. E.), Thomas; Dover and Williams (W. J.), equal; Todd and Reynolds, equal; Tarlton; Worth and Halpenny and Anderson, equal; Pearson, Turner (W. D.). *Class III.*—Campbell (J. D.), Steen, Ross (A. B.); Cameron and Moore (P.), equal; McGregor (G.) and Runnells, equal; Mick.

CLASS LIST IN ZOOLOGY.

Class I.—Henderson (Vancouver Graduates' Prize), Laurie, Monroe. *Class II.*—Brodie, Holiday; Radford and Reid, equal; Ells, King. *Class III.*—Rice, Patch, Lundie, Reynolds, McGill, Holland, Finley; and McDougal equal · Hurst.

BOTANY.

Second Year.—*Class II.*—Marcuse (*Prize*), Nutter (*Prize*) Reford, Jackson, Garlick, Woodley, Hardy, Lundie. *Class II.*—Elder, Sever, Forbes, Smith, DeWitt; Davies and *Secord, equal; Cohen and McGregor, equal; Rowell. *Class III.*—Brooks, Rorke; Willis and Topley*, equal; Ainley, Scott and Holman, equal; Mitchell; Jeakins and Newson, equal; Ells and Macmillan and Sangster, equal; Crack and Grier, equal; Mackinnon, Rowatt, Greig*; Cooke and Ireland, equal; Cochrane and Horsfall and Luttrell, equal.

Third Year.—*Class I.*—Scrimger, Henderson, Ells, King, Radford.

B.A. Ordinary.— *Class I.*—Paterson, *Going. *Class II.*—Radford, Dover, Colby.

CHEMISTRY.

First Year. (Optional.)—*Class I.*—Sterns. *Class II.*—None. *Class III.*—Angell and Halpenny, equal; Tees, Greenaway, Down.

Second Year. (Optional).—*Class I.*—Cochrane.

PHYSICAL CULTURE.

Blackett, J. W., B.A., (4th year Medicine), Wicksteed Silver Medal.

McLean, T. A., (4th year Applied Science), Hon. Mention.

Archibald, E. M., (3rd year Applied Science), Wicksteed Bronze Medal.

PHYSICAL CULTURE—DONALDA DEPARTMENT.

Louise Shaw, (4th year), Prize.

Winifred McGill, (3rd year), Prize.

MORRIN COLLEGE.

THIRD YEAR.

MECHANICS.—*Class I.*—Seifert. *Class III.*—Walters.

ASTRONOMY AND OPTICS.—*Class II.*—Seifert. *Class III.*—Jackson.

MENTAL PHILOSOPHY.—*Class II.*—Seifert. *Class III.*—Jackson.

INTERMEDIATE EXAMINATION.

GREEK.—*Class III.*—Laverie and MacRae, equal.

LATIN.—*Class III.*—Fyles and MacRae, equal ; Laverie.

TRIGONOMETRY AND ALGEBRA.—*Class II.*—Fyles ; Pidgeon and Rothney and Walters, equal. *Class III.*—MacRae and Ritchie, equal ; Laverie.

GEOMETRY AND ARITHMETIC.—*Class I.*—Rothney, Walters. *Class II.*—Fyles and Pidgeon and Ritchie, equal. *Class III.*—MacRae.

LOGIC.—*Class III.*—Fyles, Rothney, MacRae, Ritchie ; Laverie and Pidgeon, equal.

MODERN HISTORY.—*Class I.*—MacRae. *Class II.*—Pidgeon, Ritchie. *Class III.*—Laverie and Rothney. equal ; Fyles.

FRENCH.—*Class I.*—Webster. *Class II.*—Fyles ; Bignell and Ritchie and Rothney, equal.

GERMAN.—*Class I.*—Webster and Bonham, equal ; Fry, Fyles, Hunter, Meiklejohn, DuPlessis. *Class II.*—Walters.

HEBREW.—*Class I.*—Laverie. *Class II.* Pidgeon.

FIRST YEAR.

GEOMETRY AND ARITHMETIC.—*Class I.*—Reid. *Class II.*—Fraser and Nicholson and Smith, equal ; Fanjoy.

TRIGONOMETRY AND ALGEBRA.—*Class I.*—Reid. *Class II.*—Fanjoy and Fraser and Nicholson and Smith, equal.

STANSTEAD WESLEYAN COLLEGE.

INTERMEDIATE EXAMINATION.

GREEK.—*Class II.*—Hill. *Class III.*—Flint.

LATIN.—*Class III.*—Hill ; Flint (M.) and Flint, R.), equal.

TRIGONOMETRY AND ALGEBRA.—*Class II.*—Hill, Flint (M.). *Class III.*—Flint (R.)

GEOMETRY AND ARITHMETIC.—*Class I.*—Hill, Flint (M.) *Class II.*—Flint (R.)

Logic.—*Class II.*—Flint (M.) and Hill, equal. *Class III.*—Flint (R.)

Modern History.—*Class I.*—Hill. *Class II.*—Flint (M.), Flint (R.)

French.—*Class II.*—Flint (M.) and Hill, equal. *Class III.*—Flint (R.)

German.—*Class I.*—Flint.

PASSED THE INTERMEDIATE EXAMINATION.

Class II.—Hill, Flint (M.)

Class III.—Flint (R.)

FIRST YEAR.

Greek.—*Class II.*—Page, Dobson.

Latin.—*Class II.*—Page. *Class III.*—Dobson.

Geometry and Arithmetic.—*Class II.*—Page, Dobson.

Trigonometry and Algebra.—*Class I.*—Page. *Class II.*—Dobson.

English.—*Class II.*—Page, Dobson.

French.—*Class I.*—Page.

German.—*Class I.*—Page.

PASSED THE SESSIONAL EXAMINATION.

Class I.—Page.

ST. FRANCIS COLLEGE.

FIRST YEAR.

Latin.—*Class II.*—Fuller. *Class III.*—Fee, Cross.

Greek.—*Class III.*—Fuller.

Geometry and Arithmetic.—*Class I.*—Fuller. *Class III.*—Fee, Killock.

Trigonometry and Algebra.—*Class II.*—Killock. *Class III.*—Cross and Fuller, equal.

English.—*Class III.*—Fuller, Fee and Cross, equal ; Killock.

French.—Fee and Fuller, equal ; Killock.

PASSED THE SESSIONAL EXAMINATION.

Class III.—Fuller.

FACULTY OF APPLIED SCIENCE.

GRADUATING CLASS, 1897 98.

AINLEY, CHARLES NEWTH.—Honours in Assaying.

ANDERSON, WILLIAM BEAUMONT.—Honours in Hydraulic Laboratory, and Geodetic Laboratory.

ANGEL, FREDERICK WILLIAM.—British Association Medal and Prize in Books; Honours in Dynamics of Machinery, Machine Design, Mechanical Engineering, Designing, Mechanical Laboratory and Thermodynamics.

ATKINSON, DONALD CAMERON THOMSON.—Honours in Assaying.

BUTLER, PERCY.—Prize for Summer Work; Honours in Designing and Hydraulics.

CAPE, EDMUND GRAVES.—British Association Exhibition; Special Prize in Hydraulics; Honours in Experimental Physics, Hydraulics, Hydraulic Laboratory and Dynamics of Machinery.

DAVIS, ANGUS WARD.—Honours in Geology, Mineralogy, Metallurgy and Hydraulic Laboratory.

EAVES, EDMUND.—Honours in Electrical Laboratory and Experimental Physics.

IRVING, THOMAS TWEEDY.—Honours in Geodesy, Geodetic Laboratory and Hydraulic Laboratory.

LAURIE, ALBERT.—Prize for Summer Work; Honours in Machine Design, Designing, Thermodynamics and Mechanical Engineering.

MACLEAN, THOMAS ARCHIBALD.—Prize for Summer Work; Honours in Assaying and Hydraulic Laboratory, Hon. Mention in Wicksteed Competition.

MACLENNAN, FRANK WILLIAM.—Honours in Experimental Physics and Designing.

MACPHAIL, WILLIAM MATHESON.—Honours in Geodetic Laboratory and Hydraulic Laboratory.

MATHESON, ERNEST GEORGE.—Honours in Testing Laboratory Work.

McCARTHY, GEORGE ARNOLD.—British Association Medal and Prize; British Association Exhibition; Prize for Summer Work; Special Prize in Hydraulics; Honours in Geodesy, Geodetic Laboratory, Hydraulics, Hydraulic Laboratory, Theory of Structures and Designing.

McRAE, JOHN BELL.—Prize for Summer Work; Honours in Hydraulic Laboratory.

SCOTT, ARTHUR PUTNAM.—British Association Medal and Prize; Honour in Chemistry and Metallurgy.

SHEFFIELD, CHARLES.—Honours in Experimental Physics, Electrical Laboratory and Hydraulic Laboratory.

SYMMES, HOWARD CHURCH, B.A.Sc.—Honours in Experimental Physics.

THOMAS, LEONARD EDWARD LAWSON.—Honours in Designing.

WATEROUS, CHARLES ALEXANDER.—Honours in Mechanical Laboratory.

THIRD YEAR.

Archibald, Ernest M.—Prize for Summer Work ; Wicksteed Bronze Medal.

Colpitts, Walter W.—Prize for Summer Work ; 1st McCarthy Prize for Surveying Fieldwork ; Prizes for Theory of Structures, Mapping and Graphical Statics.

Grier, Arthur G.—Prizes for Mathematics and Machine Design.

Hutchinson, William S.—Prize for Organic Chemistry.

Kirkpatrick, Stafford F.—Prizes for Surveying, Metallurgy and Ore Dressing.

McLean, William B.—Scott Exhibition ; British Columbia McGill Graduate Society's Prize for Descriptive Geometry ; Prize for Dynamics of Machinery.

McLeod, Norman M.—2nd McCarthy Prize for Surveying Fieldwork.

Peden, Frank.—Prize for Summer Work.

Shaw, John A.—Prize for Physics.

Wilson, Robert M.—Prize for Summer Work.

Young, William M.—Prize for Mechanical Drawing.

Passed the Primary Examinations.

(In Order of Merit).

ARCHITECTURE.

Hyde, George T., Montreal.
McLeod, Norman M., Montreal
*Peden, Frank, Montreal

CIVIL ENGINEERING.

Colpitts, Walter W., Moncton, N.B.
Fraser, C. E., Montreal.
Gagnon, Louis F., Westmount, Que.
*Gough, Richard T., Halifax, N.S.
*Bachand, George A., Montreal.

ELECTRICAL ENGINEERING.

McLean, William B., Pictou, N.S.
Grier, Arthur G., Montreal.
Shaw, John A., Montreal.
Denis, Leopold, Montreal.
Archibald, E. M., Halifax, N.S.
Fraser, James W., Bridgeville, N.S.
Wilson, Robert M., Montreal.
Burgess, R. Earl, Wolfeville, N.S.
*Fetherstonhaugh, Edward P., Montreal.
Hyde, James C., Montreal.
*Bowman, Archibald A., New Glasgow, N.S.
*Cornwall, Clement A. K., Ashcroft, B.C.
*Pergau, Harry, Lyn, Ont.

* To pass Supplemental Examination.

*Hawker, James T., St. John, N.B
*Fraser, Harold, Brockville, Ont.

MECHANICAL ENGINEERING.

Young, William M., Renfrew, Ont.
*Whyte, John S., Osgood, Ont.
*Dargavel, James S., Elgin, Ont.
*Hickey, John V., Montreal.
*Davidson, William A., Peterboro, Ont.
*Wenger, Edgar I., Ayton, Ont.
*Ewan, Herbert M., Montreal.

MINING ENGINEERING.

Kirkpatrick, Stafford F., Kingston, Ont.
Yuile, Norman M., Montreal.
Morgan, Charles B., Hamilton, Ont.
*Pitcher, Norman C., Stanstead, Que.
Preston, John A., Toronto, Ont.
*Campbell, Norman M., Montreal.
*MacInnes, Henry W., Halifax, N.S.
*Stevens, Angus P., Dunham, Que.
*Waller, George W., Bartonville, Ont.
*Moore, William M., Ottawa, Ont.
*Henderson, Richard A., Chilliwack, B.C.

PRACTICAL CHEMISTRY.

Hutchinson, William S., Montreal.
McLaren, Archibald J, Montreal.

SECOND YEAR.

Black, Thompson T.—2nd Fleet Workshop Prize, Prize in Descriptive Geometry
Ewart, George R.—Prizes in Surveying and Experimental Physics.
Gillean, Robert H.—Prizes in Mapping and Surveying Fieldwork.
Shepherd, Harry L.—Prize in Kinematics.

Passed the Sessional Examinations.

(In Order of Merit).

ARCHITECTURE.

Byers, Archibald F., Gananoque, Ont.

CIVIL ENGINEERING.

Angl'n, James P., Kingston, Ont.
Ewart, George R., Kilauea, Kauai, Hawaiian Islands.
*Burgoyne, Stanley J., Halifax, N.S.

———
*To pass Supplemental Examination.

ELECTRICAL ENGINEERING

Shepherd, Harry L., Brockville, Ont.
Nelson, George J., Montreal.
Allen, Samuel J., Maitland, N.S.
Walker, Frank W., Montreal.
Black, Thompson T., Sackville, N.B.
Duncan, G. Rupert, Montreal.
Miller, Angus K., Bridgeburg, Ont. ⎫
Percy, Howard M., Montreal.   ⎬ equal.
Smith, George B , Stratford, Ont. ⎭
St. George, Harry L., Montreal.
*Montgomery, George, Morrisburg, Ont.
Glassco, Jack G., Hamilton, Ont.

MECHANICAL ENGINEERING.

Neville, Thomas P. J., Halifax, N.S.
*Hamilton, George M., Peterboro, Ont.
Macmaster, Arthur W., Montreal.
*Arkley, Lorne M., East Angus, Que.

MINING ENGINEERING.

Gillean, Robert H., Montreal.
Buffett, Aaron F., Grand Bank, Newfoundland.
Cowans, Frederick, Montreal.
Corriveau, Raoul de B., Iberville, Que.
Moore, Ernest V., Peterboro, Ont.
*Robertson, Philip W.'K., Mexico City, Mexico.

PRACTICAL CHEMISTRY.

Barber, Rene R., Georgetown, Ont.

FIRST YEAR.

Burson, Herbert A.—Hutchison Prize for Freehand Drawing; 2nd Fleet Work-shop Prize.
Clement, Sheldon B.—Prizes for Chemistry and Mathematics.
Egleson, James E. A.—Prizes for Chemistry and Descriptive Geometry.
Fry, David M.—1st Fleet Workshop Prize.
Gagnon, Edmund E.—Hutchison Prize for Lettering.
Lloyd, Herbert M.—Prize for Descriptive Mechanism, Hutchison Prize for Free-hand Drawing.
McKenzie, Bertram S.—Prize for Mathematics, Hutchison Prize for Lettering.
Taylor, Charles W.—Prizes for English and Practical Chemistry.
Ward, Percy W.—Hutchison Prize for Lettering.

*To pass Supplemental Examination.

Passed the Sessional Examinations.

(In Order of Merit).

Clement, Sheldon B., Clinton, Ont.
Burson, Herbert A., St. Catharines, Ont.
Egleson, James E. A., Ottawa, Ont.
Taylor, Charles W., Richmond, Ont.
Wilson, Thomas A., Halifax, N S.
Fry, David M., Bright, Ont.
Edwards, William M., Ottawa, Ont.
Fraser, Donald C., New Glasgow, N.S.
McLaren, John, Montreal.
McKenzie, Bertram S., London, Ont.
Ward, Percy W., Lachine, Que.
Paterson, Charles S , Montreal.
Higman, Ormond, Ottawa, Ont.
DeBlois, William H., Halifax, N.S.   ·
Schwitzer, Thomas H., Ottawa, Ont.
Lloyd, Herbert M., New Westminster, B.C.
*Glassco, Archie P. S., Hamilton, Ont.
Blue, Allen P., Eustis, Que.
Plant, Verner L., Montreal.
Fréchette, Howells, Ottawa, Ont.
*Hampson, E. Greville, Montreal.
Lowden, Warden K., Montreal.
Galbraith, Malcolm T., Montreal.
*Ogilvie Paul, Cumming's Bridge, Ont.
Coote, Sydney R., St. Albans, Vt., U.S.A.
Wakeling, Otty S., St. John, N.B.
*Scott, Henry M., Montreal.
Hearn, John F., St. John's, Newfoundland.
Gagnon, Edmund E.. Montreal, Que.
*McIntosh, John G., London, Ont.
*White, Gerald, V., Pembroke, Ont.
Askwith, Charles E., Ottawa, Ont.
*Tupper, Charles, Vancouver, B.C.
*Labatt, John S., London, Ont.
Cameron, Hugh D., Montreal.
*Flint, William G., Montreal.
*Ritchie, Joseph N., Halifax, N.S.
*Howard, Rupert F., Lachine, Que.
*Wells, Samuel S., Montreal.
Reynolds, Leo B., Waterford, Ont.
Burwell. Ernest V., London, Ont.
*Jamieson, George E. T., Montreal.

*To pass Supplemental Examination.

STANDING IN THE SEVERAL SUBJECTS.

ALTERNATING CURRENTS.

FOURTH YEAR.—*Class I.*—Symmes, Eaves. *Class II.*—Sheffield, Archibald (H. P.) ; Cape and Maclennan, equal. *Class III* —Scott (J. H.), McLea.

ARCHITECTURAL DRAWING.

THIRD YEAR.—*Class I.*—Hyde (G. T.) and Staveley, equal. *Class II.*—Peden, *Class III.*—McLeod (N. M.).

SECOND YEAR.—*Class I.*—None. *Class II.*—Coote, Byers. *Class III.*—Anglin and Toole, equal.

ARCHITECTURE, HISTORY OF.

THIRD YEAR.—*Class I.*—Staveley, Hyde (G. T.). *Class II.*—Peden. *Class III.* —McLeod (N. M.).

SECOND YEAR.—*Class I.*—Coote. *Class II.*—Anglin ; Byers and Toole, equal.

Optional.

SECOND YEAR.—*Class I.*—None. *Class II.*—Black, Ewart. *Class III.*— Burgoyne, Smith (G. B.), Shepherd.

ARCHITECTURE, THEORY OF.

SECOND AND THIRD YEARS.—*Class I.*—None. *Class II.*—Coote and Staveley, equal ; Hyde (G. T.), Anglin. *Class III.*—Toole ; McLeod (N. M.) and Peden, equal ; Byers.

ASSAYING.

FOURTH YEAR.—*Class I.*—Atkinson (D. C. T.), Ainley, MacLean. *Class II.*— Davis and Butler, equal ; Young (G. A.), Atkinson (W. J.), Hillary.

BUILDING CONSTRUCTION.

SECOND YEAR.—*Class I.*—Nelson, Shepherd, Byers, Miller (A. K.) ; Black and Macmaster and Walker, equal ; Corriveau and Staveley, equal ; Anglin and Allen and Burgoyne and Gillean, equal. *Class II.*—Buffett, Cary ; Coussirat and Duncan and Percy, equal ; Arkley ; Cowans (F.) and Ewart and Howard (L. O.) and Moore (E. V.), equal ; St. George ; Forman and Neville and Smith, equal ; Osborne and Robertson, equal ; Donaldson and Montgomery, equal ; Fraser (John W.). *Class III.*— Glassco (J. G.) and Ogilvie (N. C.), equal ; Sise, Millar (J. L.), Pyke.

CHEMISTRY.

SECOND YEAR.—(*Practical Chemistry Course*).—*Class I.*—None. *Class II.*— Barber.

FIRST YEAR.—*Class 1.*—Egleson. *Class II.*—Ritchie, Burson, Fry, Taylor, Edwards, Wakeling, Wilson (T. A), DeBlois ; Hampson and Higman and McLaren (J.), equal ; Lloyd, Plant, White (G. V.) ; Askwith and Glassco (A. P. S.), equal ; Ogilvie (P.). *Class III.*—Cowen (E. A. A.), Blue ; Fraser (D. C.) and Reynolds, equal ; Galbraith, Labatt, Gagnon (E. E.) ; Fréchette and Schwitzer, equal ; Coote ; Burwell and Lowden, equal ; Cameron, Wells, Ward (P. W.).

CHEMISTRY, INORGANIC.

FOURTH YEAR.—*Class 1.*—Scott (A. P.). *Class II.*—None. *Class III.*— Drysdale.

CHEMISTRY, ORGANIC.

FOURTH YEAR.—*Class 1.*—Scott (A. P.). *Class II.*—None. *Class III.*— Drysdale.

THIRD YEAR.—*Class I.*—Hutchinson. *Class II.*—McLaren (A. J.).

SECOND YEAR.—*Class I.*—Olds. *Class II.*—Barber. *Class III.*—Taylor.

DESCRIPTIVE GEOMETRY.

SECOND YEAR.—*Class I.*—Black, Anglin, Nelson, Paterson, Shepherd. *Class II.*— Gillean, Allen, Moore (E V.), Miller (A. K.), Smith (G. B.), Ewart, Buffett; *Class III.*—Cowans (F.), Hamilton (G. M.), Montgomery, Walker, Burgogne, Byers, Coote, Neville, Arkley, Sise, Glassco (J. G.), St. George Hearn, Percy, Duncan.

FIRST YEAR.—*Class I.*—Egleson, Fry, Clement, Ward (P.), Wilson (T. A.), McKenzie, Fréchette, McLaren (J.), Fraser (D. C.), McIntosh, Scott (H. M.), Burson, Higman, Lloyd, Flint, Galbraith. *Class II.*- DeBlois, Cameron, Gagnon (E. E.), Taylor, Glassco (A. P. S.), Edwards, Hampson, Schwitzer, Lowden, Labatt, Jamieson, Tupper, Askwith, Wells, Ogilvie (P.), Blue, Cowen (E. A. A.), Walsh, Wakeling, Plant, White (G. V.). *Class III.*—Farquharson, Brookfield, Reynolds, Ward (C. R.), Boyd, Burchell, Buchanan.

DESCRIPTIVE MECHANISM.

FIRST YEAR.—*Class I.*—Lloyd, Egleson ; McKenzie and Paterson, equal. *Class II.*—Wilson (T. A.), Wakeling, McLaren (J.), Clement ; Higman and Taylor, equal ; Burson and Fry, equal ; Gagnon (E. E.). *Class III.*— Fréchette and Plant and Ward (P. W.), equal ; Schwitzer, Lowden, Cowen (E. A. A.), Edwards ; Glassco (A. P. S.) and Ogilvie (P.) and Tupper, equal ; Blue and Burchell, equal ; Flint and Ward (C. R.), equal ; Askwith and Galbraith, equal ; Jamieson and DeBlois, equal ; Buchanan ; Fraser (D. C.) and Scott (H. M.), equal ; Boyd, Reynolds ; Cameron and McDonald (S.) and McIntosh, equal.

DESIGNING.

FOURTH YEAR.—(*Civil Engineering Course*). *Class 1.*—McCarthy, Macphail, Irving. *Class II.*—Bond, Matheson, Anderson, Benny. (*Electrical Engineering Course*). *Class 1.*—Maclennan. *Class II.*—Sheffield, Symmes; Eaves and Scott (J. H.), equal; Archibald (H. P.), Cape. *Class III.*—McLea. (*Mechanical Engineering Course*).— *Class 1.*—Angel, Thomas Laurie. *Class II.*—Waterous, Mackerras, Patton, McRae, Dean, *Class III.*—Bacon, Beatty, Davidson (J. H.). (*Mining Engineering Course*).—*Class 1.*—Butler, MacLean, Atkinson (D. C. T.). *Class II.*— Davis, Young (G. A.), Atkinson (W. J.), Ainley, Hillary.

DETERMINATIVE MINERALOGY.

THIRD YEAR.—*Class 1.*—Hutchinson; Pitcher and Stevens, equal. *Class II.*— Waller and Yuile, equal; McLaren (A. J.); Campbell and Kirkpatrick, equal; Morgan and Preston, equal; Moore (W. M.). *Class III.*— MacInnes, Macmillan.

DYNAMICS OF MACHINERY.

FOURTH YEAR.—(*Electrical Engineering Course*). *Class I.*—Cape. *Class II.*— Maclennan, Sheffield, Eaves. *Class III.*—Scott (J. H.) (*Mechanical Engineering Course*). *Class 1.*—Angel, Laurie. *Class II.*—Dean, Waterous, Thomas, Patton. *Class III.*—Yorston, Mackerras, McRae. Davidson (J. H.), Bacon, Beatty.

THIRD YEAR.—*Class I.*—McLean (W. B.), Grier. *Class II.*—Shaw, Hyde (J. C., Wilson (R. M.); Archibald (E. M.) and Fraser (J. W.), equal; Young (W. M.), Denis. *Class III.*—Bowman, Fetherstonhaugh; Burgess and Hickey, equal; Davidson (W. A.); Whyte (J. S.) and Pergau, equal; Wenger; Cornwall and Dargavel, equal; Ewan. .

DESCRIPTIVE ELECTRICAL ENGINEERING.

FOURTH YEAR.—*Class I.*—Maclennan, Archibald (H. P.); Cape and Sheffield and Waterous, equal; Eaves and McCarthy and Symmes, equal. *Class II.*— Mackerras; Angel and McLea and Scott (J. H.), equal; Irving, Anderson, Macphail, MacLean (T. A.); Laurie and McRae and Thomas, equal; Atkinson (D. C. T.) and Butler and Davidson (J. H.), equal. *Class III.*—Matheson and Young (G. A.), equal; Ainley; Hillary, Atkinson (W. J.) and Bacon, equal; Beatty and Davis and Dean and Patton, equal; Bond, Benny.

ELECTRICAL ENGINEERING.

FOURTH YEAR.—*Class I.*—Eaves. *Class II.*—Scott (J. H.), Cape, Sheffield, Symmes. *Class III.*—Maclennan, Archibald (H. P.).

THIRD YEAR.—*Class I.*—Denis; McLean (W. B.) and Shaw, equal. *Class II.*— Grier, Pergau. *Class III.*—Fraser (H.), Hyde (J. C.), Wilson (R. M.); Archibald (E. M.) and Burgess and Fraser (J. W.), equal.

ENGLISH.

FIRST YEAR.—*Class I.*—Taylor, Paterson, Brookfield, Plant, Burson; Buchanan and Fry and Ward (P.), equal; McIntosh; Clement and Fraser (D. C.) and Higman and Wilson (T. A.), equal. *Class II.*—Lloyd, Ogilvie (P.), Peck, Egleson, Scott (H. M.), Fréchette, Schwitzer, Wakeling; Farquharson and Labatt, equal; Tupper and White (G. V.), equal; Edwards and Hale, equal; Cowen (E.) and Gagnon (E. E.) and Jamieson and Walsh, equal; DeBlois and Slayter, equal; Ritchie and Ward (R.), equal; Reynolds, Cameron, McLaren (J.); Blue and Lowden, equal. *Class III.*—Burchell; Hampson and Wilkins, equal; Askwith and McKenna, equal; Galbraith and Glassco (A. P. S.), equal; Stevenson, Boyd, Flint, Mitchell, Wells, McDonald (S.), Meldrum.

FREEHAND DRAWING.

THIRD YEAR.—(*Architectural Course*). *Class I.*—Hyde (G. T.). *Class II.*—McLeod (N. M.), Peden. Staveley, Anglin, Byers, Slayter, Trenholme, Toole.

FIRST YEAR.—*Class I.*—Burson and Lloyd, equal; Ward (P.); Cameron and McKenzie, equal; Fry and Galbraith, equal; Peck, Gagnon(E. E.); Jamieson and McLaren (J.), equal; Clement; Taylor and White (G. V.), equal. *Class II.*—Egleson, Lowden; Fréchette and Scott (H. M.) and Wilson (R. C.), equal; Higman and Plant and Wilson (T. A.), equal; Blue, Edwards, Labatt; Schwitzer and Ward (R. C.), equal; Walsh; Flint and Wakeling, equal. *Class III.*—DeBlois and Fraser (D. C.); equal; McDonald (S.) and McIntosh and Wells, equal; Buchanan and Farquharson, equal; Burchell and Mitchell and Tupper, equal; Brookfield and Glassco (A. P. S.) and Ogilvie (P.), equal; Askwith and Hampson and Ritchie, equal.

GEODESY.

FOURTH YEAR.—*Class I.*—McCarthy, Irving. *Class II.*—Macphail, Anderson, Bond. *Class III.*—Matheson, Benny.

GEOLOGY.

THIRD YEAR.—*Class I.*—None. *Class II.*—Kirkpatrick, Pitcher, Hutchinson, Campbell (N. M.), McLaren (A. J.), Fraser (C. E.), Colpitts, Gagnon (L. F.), Yuile. *Class III.*—Moore (W. M.) and Corriveau, equal; Preston; MacInnes and Waller, equal; Morgan; Bachand and Van Horne, equal; Henderson.

GEOLOGY (ADVANCED).

FOURTH YEAR.—*Class I.*—Davis. *Class II.*—Young (G. A.), Atkinson (D. C. T.), Atkinson (W. J.), Ainley, Butler, Hillary. *Class III.*—MacLean (T. A.)

GRAPHICAL STATISTICS.

THIRD YEAR.— *Architectural and Civil Engineering Courses).— Class I.*—Colpitts. *Class II.*—Peden; Hyde (G. T.) and McLeod (N.M.), equal; Gough; Fraser (C. E.) and Gagnon (L. F.), equal. *Class III.*—Van Horne, Bachand, Parizeau, (*Electrical, Mechanical and Mining Engineering Courses. Class I.*—Shaw; Burgess and Gisborne, equal; Davidson (W. A.) and Hyde (J. C.), equal; Denis and Grier and McLean (W. B.), equal., *Class II.*—Archibald (E. M.) and Kirkpatrick, equal; Cornwall and Fetherstonhaugh and Fraser (J. W.), equal; Hickey and Whyte (J,S.), equal; Young (W. M.); Hawker; Corriveau and Pergau, equal; Preston and Wenger, equal; Morgan; Campbell and Wilson (R.M.), equal; Dargavel. and MacInnes, equal. *Class III*—Moore (W. M.) and Stevens, equal; Austin; Bowman and Yuile, equal; Fraser (H.); Ewan and Henderson and Nicholls and Waller, equal.

HYDRAULICS.

FOURTH YEAR.—*Class I*—Cape and McCarthy equal; Irving. *Class II.*— Butler, Anderson, Dean, Davis; Laurie and Eaves and Waterous, equal; Macphail, Angel, Sheffield. *Class III.*—Thomas, Bond, MacLean (T. A.), Young (C. A.), Ainley, Patton, Maclennan, Atkinson (W. J.), Benny; Atkinson (D. C. T.) and Davidson (J. H.) and Matheson, equal; Bacon, McRae, Archibald (H. P.) McLea, Mackerras.

KINEMATICS OF MACHINES.

SECOND YEAR.—*Class I.*—Nelson, Shepherd. *Class II.*—Percy, Walker, St. George; Miller (A. K.) and Smith (G. B.), equal; Black; Allen and Duncan, equal; Arkley.—*Class III.*—Macmaster, Neville; Coussirat and Glassco (J. G.), equal; Hamilton (G. M.), Forman, Osborne, Montgomery.

LABORATORY WORK.

FOURTH YEAR.—(*Chemical Laboratory).— Class I.*—Scott (A. P.). *Class II.*—Drysdale.

THIRD YEAR.—(*Chemical Laboratory, Mining Engineering Course).—Class I.*—Kirkpatrick, Yuile, Waller. *Class II.*—Stevens, Preston, Campbell, Morgan, MacMillan, MacInnes, Nicholls. *Class III.*—Henderson, Blaylock, Moore (W. M.). (*Chemistry Course).—Class I.*—Hutchinson. *Class II.*—Olds, MacLaren (A. J.). *Class III.*—Gamble.

SECOND YEAR.--*Chemical Laboratory.* (*Mining Engineering and Chemistry Courses.)—Class I.*—Howard (L. O.), Gillean, Taylor. *Class II.*—Cowans (F.) and Pitcher, equal; Buffett, Moore (E. V.), Barber, Corriveau, Donaldson, Cary. *Class III.*—Maclaren (G. M.), Robertson, Pyke.

First Year.—*Chemical Laboratory.*—*Class I.*—Taylor, Schwitzer; McKenzie and Wakeling, equal; Fraser (D. C.), Burson and Edwards, equal; Scott (H. E.), Higman; DeBlois and Lloyd, equal; Ritchie; Clément and Wilson (T. A.), equal; Egleson, Coote, Ward (P. W.); Scott (H. M.) and White (G. V.), equal; Fry. *Class II.*—Labatt; Blue and Glassco (A. P. S.), equal; Fréchette and McLaren (J.), equal; Farquharson; Cowen (E. A. A.) and F.int and Plant, equal; Hampson, Galbraith, Lowden, Tupper, Jamieson, Gagnon (E. E.), Wells; Jamieson and Ward (R.), equal. *Class III.*—Miner, Burwell, Walsh, Reynolds, Askwith, Burchell, Boyd, McKenna.

Fourth Year.—(*Electrical Laboratory*).—*Class I.*—Eaves. *Class II.*— Sheffield, Scott (J. H.); Symmes, Cape, Maclennan, Archibald(H. P.), *Class III.*—McLea.

Third Year.—(*Electrical Laboratory*).—*Class I.*—Wilson (R. M.), Fraser (H.). Shaw. *Class II.*—Bowman; Archibald (E. M.) and Denis and Fether, stonhaugh and Grier, equal. *Class III.*—Burgess and Cornwall, equal; Hawker and Hyde (J. C.), equal; McLean (W. B.); Fraser (J.W.) and Pergau, equal.

Fourth Year.—(*Geodetic Laboratory*).—*Class I.*—Anderson; Irving and McCarthy and Macphail, equal; Bond. *Class II.*—Matheson, Benny.

First Year.—(*Mathematical Laboratory*)—*Class I.*—Burson; Clement and DeBlois, equal; Fraser (D. C.); Fry and Wilson (T. A.), equal; Egleson and Higman, equal; McKenzie; Edwards and Taylor, equal; Burwell and Fréchette and Paterson and Schwitzer, equal; Lloyd and McLaren (J.) and McIntosh and Ward (P. W.) and White (G. V.), equal; Plant; Cameron and Flint, equal. *Class II.*—Blue and Galbraith and Glassco (A. P. S.) and Hampson and Reynolds and Scott (H. M.), equal; Askwith and Lowden and Wakeling and Wells, equal; Gagnon (E. E.) and McKenna and Ogilvie (P.), equal; Hearn and Labatt and Ritchie, equal; Boyd and Tupper, equal; Farquharson; Burchell and Coote and Jamieson, equal; Ward (R.).

Fourth Year.—(*Mechanical Engineering Laboratory*).—*Class I.*—Waterous. *Class II.*—Angel and Laurie, equal; Patton, Davidson (J. H.), McRae, Mackerras, Dean. *Class III.*—Bacon, Beatty, Thomas.

Fourth Year.—(*Physical Laboratory, Electrical Engineering Course*).— *Class I.*—Eaves and Sheffield, equal; Cape, Maclennan, Symmes.— *Class II.*—Archibald (H. P.). *Class III.*—McLea, Scott (J. H.).

Fourth Year.—(*Testing Laboratory*).—*Class I.*—McCarthy and Matheson, equal; Irving and Macphail, equal; Anderson. *Class II.*—Bond Benny.

Third Year.—(*Testing Laboratory*).—*Class I.*—Grier; Colpitts and Corriveau, equal; McLean (W. B.) and Shaw, equal. *Class II.*—Kirkpatrick and

Whyte (J. S.), equal; Archibald (E. M.), Ewan, Young (W. M.)
Fetherstonhaugh ; Denis and Wilson (R. M.), equal ; Bowman and Burgess
and Cornwall and Hyde (J. C.) and Wenger and Yuile, equal ; Morgan,
MacInnes, Hickey. *Class III.*—Campbell, Gisborne, Fraser, J. W.),
Dargavel and Davidson (W. A.), equal ; Fraser (C. E.), Fraser (H.) and
Gagnon (L. F.) and Gough, equal; Austin and Hawker and Preston,
equal ; Bachand ; Pergau and Waller equal ; Moore (W. M.); Henderson
and Stevens, equal ; Parizeau and Van Horne, equal.

FOURTH YEAR.—(*Thermodynamic Laboratory*).—*Class I.*—Angel, McRae,
Waterous. *Class II.*—Patton. *Class III.*—Dean, Laurie, Mackerras,
Beatty, Davidson (J. H.), Thomas, Bacon, Yorston.

LETTERING.

FIRST YEAR.—*Class I.*—Gagnon (E. E.) and McKenzie and Ward (P.) equal ;
Burson ; ylŭod ndaPaterson, equal; Cameron and White (G. V.), equal ;
Fry and Lowden, equal ; McLaren (J.) and Wilson (T. A.), equal ; Fraser
(D. C.) and Taylor, equal ; Jamieson ; Higman and Ward (R. C.), equal.
Class II.—Blue and Edwards, equal ; Peck ; Clement and Labatt
and Plant, equal; DeBlois and Mitchell, equal; Tupper, Fréchette ;
Buchanan and Galbraith and Egleson and Walsh, equal ; Schwitzer ;
Hampson and McIntosh and Ogilvie (P.) and Ritchie and Wakeling and
Wells, equal; Brookfield and Farquharson and Glassco (A. P. S.) and
McDonald (S.) and Slayter, equal. *Class III.*—Burchell and Scott
(H. M.), equal; Flint; Boyd and Cowen (E. A. A.), equal; Meldrum,
Askwith.

MACHINE DESIGN.

FOURTH YEAR.—(*Electrical Engineering Course.*)—*Class I.*—None. *Class II.*—
Cape and Sheffield, equal ; Archibald (H.P.), Maclenna n,
Simpson (J.M.). *Class III.*—Eaves, Scott (J.H.), McLea. (*Mechanical
Engineering Course*)—*Class I.*—Angel and Laurie, equal. *Class II.*—
Dean, Patton, Waterous, Mackerras, Thomas. *Class III.*—Beatty ;
Bacon and Davidson (J.H.), and McRae, equal.

THIRD YEAR.—(*Electrical and Mechanical Engineering Courses.*)—*Class I.*—Grier.
Class II.—McLean (W.B.) and Wilson (R.M.), equal ; Shaw, Hyde (J.C.),
Denis. *Class III.*—Archibald (E.M.), Young (W.M.), Whyte (J.S.) ;
Burgess and Wenger, equal; Hickey, Fetherstonhaugh, Bowman, Fraser,
(J.W.), Cornwall.

MAP CONSTRUCTION AND PERSPECTIVE.

THIRD YEAR.—(*Civil Engineering Course*)—*Class I.*—Colpitts, Fraser (C E.) *Class
II.*—Gagnon (L.F.) *Class III.*—Gough, Bachand.

MAPPING.

THIRD YEAR.—(*Architectural Course.*)—*Class I.*—Hyde (G.T.) and McLeod (N) and
Peden, equal. (*Civil Engineering Course*)—*Class I.*—Colpitts, Gagnon
(L F.), Fraser (C.E.), Gough. *Class II.*—Van Horne, Bachand.
Class III.—Parizeau.

Second Year.—*(Architectural and Mining Engineering Courses.)*—*Class I.*— Gillean. *Class II.*—Cowans (F.), Buffett, Moore (E.V.), Byers, Donaldson , Cary. *Class III.*—Robertson, Pyke *(Civil Engineering Course.) Class I.*— None. *Class II.*—Anglin, Burgoyne, Ewart.

MATHEMATICS.

Third Year.—*Class I.*—Grier, McLean, (W.B.) *Class II.*—Blaylock, Shaw, Kirkpatrick, Colpitts, Archibald (E M.), Fraser (J.W.), Hyde (G.T.), Burgess, Denis, Fetherstonhaugh, Stevens, Pergau, Young (W.M.), Fraser, (C.E.), Cornwall, Wilson (R.M.). *Class III.*—Dargavel, MacInnes ; Davidson (W.A.) and Gagnon (L.F.) and Preston, equal ; Peden ; Whyte (J.S.), and Yuile, equal ; Hawker, McLeod (N.), Hyde (J.C.), Waller ; Bachand and Bowman and Morgan, equal; Moore (W.M.), Gough, Henderson.

Second Year.—*Class I.*—None. *Class II.*—Gillean, Shepherd, Nelson, Allen. Neville, Walker, Buffett, Robertson, Duncan ; Cowans (F.) and Olds, equal ; Percy, Ewart, St. George, Macmaster, Miller, (A.K). *Class III.* —Anglin, Hamilton, G.M.), Corriveau, Maclaren (G.M.J..) ; Glassco (J.G.) and Moore (E.V.), equal ; Smith ; Black and Byers, equal ; *Montgomery.

First Year.—*Class I.*—McKenzie, Clement, Edwards, Wilson (T.A.), Egleson Taylor, Burson, Paterson, Fraser, (D.C.), McLaren (J.), Fry. *Class II.*— Glassco (A.P.S), Ogilvie (P.), Hampson, Ward (P.), DeBlois, Blue, Schwitzer, McIntosh, Higman, Askwith, Plant, Tupper, Scott (H.M.), Lowden ; Flint and Galbraith, equal. *Class III.*—Reynolds ; Frechette and Lloyd, equal ; Hearn, Ritchie, Labatt, †White (G.V.), Wakeling, Coote, Wells, Burwell, Cameron, Gagnon (E.E.), †Howard (R.F.), †McKenna, Boyd.

MECHANICAL DRAWING.

Third Year.—*(Electrical Engineering Course).*—*Class I.*—Burgess, Shaw, Archibald (E. M.), Fetherstonhaugh. *Class II.*— Bowman, Grier, Fraser (J. W.), Cornwall, Hawker. *Class III.*—Hyde (J. C.), Pergau, Fraser (H.), *(Mechanical Engineering Course)*—*Class I.*—Whyte (J. S.), Young (W. M.), McLean (W. B.), Denis and Gisborne, equal; Davidson (W. A.), Wilson (R. M.), Hickey. *Class II.*—Dargavel, Wenger, Garrett. *Class III.*—Austin, Ewan.

Second Year.—*Class I.*—Hamilton (G. M.), and Shepherd, equal ; Nelson and Percy, equal ; Smith (G. B.). *Class II.*—Walker, Black, Howard (R. T.), Miller (A. K.) and Montgomery and Duncan, equal ; Allen and Whiteway, equal ; Glassco (J. G.), Ogilvie (N. C.). *Class III.*— St. George, Macmaster ; Arkley and Sise, equal ; Hearn ; Kane and Osborne, equal ; Fraser (John W.), Neville, Forman.

---

* Supplemental in Calculus.
† Supplemental in Dynamics.

MATHEMATICAL PERSPECTIVE.

THIRD YEAR.—*Architectural Course.* — *Class I.*—Peden, McLeod (N. M.). *Class II.*—Hyde (G. T.)

MECHANICAL ENGINEERING.

FOURTH YEAR.—*Class I.*—Laurie, Angel. *Class II.*—Waterous, Dean, McRae, Patton. *Class III.*—Mackerras, Davidson (J. H.), Bacon, Yorston, Thomas, Beatty.

METALLURGY.

FOURTH YEAR.—*Class I.*—Scott (A. P.), Davis, Butler. *Class II.*—Atkinson, (D. C. T.), Ainley ; MacLean (T. A.) and Young (G. A.), equal ; Atkinson (W. J.), Hillary. *Class III.*—Drysdale.

THIRD YEAR.—*Class I.*—Kirkpatrick, Blaylock. *Class II.*—Yuile, Pitcher, Preston, Morgan, Olds, McLaren (A. J.), Moore (W. M.) Campbell, Gamble, Hutchinson, Nicholls, MacInnes. *Class III.*—Henderson, Stevens, Waller.

MINERALOGY (ADVANCED.)

FOURTH YEAR.—*Class I.*—Davis ; Butler and Young (G. A.), equal ; Ainley, *Class II.*—Atkinson (D. C. T.), Atkinson (W. J.), MacLean (T. A.) Hillary. *Class III.*—Drysdale.

THIRD YEAR.—*Class I.*—None. *Class II.*—Hutchinson and Kirkpatrick, equal ; McLaren (A. J.) *Class III.*—Yuile, Preston, Gamble, Campbell, Morgan.

MINING.

SECOND YEAR.—*Class I.*—Corriveau and Shepherd, equal ; Allen and Cary, equal ; Burgoyne, Gillean, Buffett. *Class II.*—Black, Ewart, Robertson, Cowans (F.), Smith ; Howard (L. O.) and Anglin, equal ; Duncan and Nelson, equal ; Arkley and Coussirat and Donaldson, equal ; Walker, Miller (A. K.), Forman ; Moore (E. V.) and Byers, equal ; Neville ; Osborne and Sise, equal ; Fraser (John W.), and Glassco (J. G.), and Percy, equal. *Class III.*—Montgomery ; Kane and Ogilvie (N. C.). equal ; Macmaster, St. George ; Maclaren (G. M.) and Hamilton (G. M.), equal ; Millar (J. L), Pyke.

MINING DRAWING.

THIRD YEAR.—*Class I.*—Morgan, Corriveau, Preston, Kirkpatrick. *Class II.*—Campbell, Henderson, Yuile, Nicholls, MacInnes. *Class III.*—Waller, Stevens, Olds.

SECOND YEAR.—*Class I.*—Cowans (F.), Gillean, Howard (L. O.). *Class II.*—Buffett, Burgoyne, Donaldson, Maclaren (G. M.) and Moore (E. V.), equal ; Robertson, Cary, Pyke.

MODELLING (CLAY).

Class I.—Hyde (G. T.), McLeod (N. M.), Peden. *Class II.*—Staveley, Trenholme. *Class III.*—Slayter.

MUNICIPAL ENGINEERING (ROADS AND PAVEMENTS).

FOURTH YEAR.—*Class I.*—McCartby, Irving, Macphail. *Class II.*—Anderson, Matheson, Benny. *Class III.*—Bond.

MUNICIPAL ENGINEERING (SANITATION).

FOURTH YEAR.—*(Civil Engineering Course)*—*Class I.*—Anderson, Macphail, Irving, McCarthy. *Class II.*—Bond, Penny, Matheson.

THIRD YEAR.—*(Architectural and Civil Engineering Courses).*—*Class I.*—Colpitts *Class II.*—Fraser (C. E.) and Hyde (G. T.) and Van Horne, equal; Mc⁻ Leod (N.), Gagnon (L. F.), Gough. *Class II.*—Peden, Bachand, Parizeau.

MUSEUM WORK IN MINERALOGY AND GEOLOGY.

FOURTH YEAR.—*Class I.*—Davis. *Class II.*—Atkinson (D. C. T.), Butler, Young (G. A.). Ainley and Atkinson (W. J.), equal; MacLean (T. A.) *Class III.*—Hillary.

ORE DRESSING.

FOURTH YEAR.—*Class I.*—Davis, Atkinson (D. C. T.), Butler. *Class II.*—Scott (A. P.), Atkinson (W. J.); MacLean and Young (G. A.), equal; Ainley, Hillary and Drysdale, equal.

THIRD YEAR.—*Class I.*—Kirkpatrick, Olds, Pitcher, Hutchinson. *Class II.*— Moore (W. M.); Henderson and McLaren (A. J.), equal; Campbell and Gamble, equal; Yuile, Morgan, Blaylock, Pitcher; MacInnes and Waller, equal; Nicholls. *Class III.*—Stevens.

PHYSICS (THEORETICAL AND PRACTICAL).

THIRD YEAR.—*Class I.*—Shaw, Grier, McLean (W. B.) *Class II*—Archibald (E. M.), Kirkpatrick, Denis, Wilson (R. M.); Fetherstonhaugh and MacInnes, equal; Fraser (H.) and Yuile, equal; Colpitts and Fraser (C. E.), equal; Fraser (J. W.), McLeod (N. M.). *Class III.*—Hyde, (J. C.); Burgess and Hyde (G. T.), equal; Young (W. M.), Whyte (J. S.) Corriveau and Wenger, equal; Bowman, Cornwall and Gagnon (L. F.), equal; Hutchinson and Peden, equal; Van Horne; Ewan and Moore (W. A.), and Morgan, equal; Bachand and Dargavel and Gisborne and Hawker and Hickey and Pergau and Preston, equal.

SECOND YEAR.—*Class I.*—Ewart; Anglin and Barber, equal; Shepherd, Allen, Walker, Burgoyne; Byers and Gillean, equal. *Class II.*—Hamilton (G. M.), Nelson; Duncan and Robertson, equal; Arkley and Neville and Montgomery, equal; Buffett; Ogilvie (N. C.) and Percy, equal; Glassco (J. G.), Cowans (F.), MacMaster; Hearn and Millar (J. L.) and Smith (G.

B.), equal. *Class III.*—St. George, Donaldson, Maclaren (G. M.) and Miller (A. K.), equal; Black and Cary, equal; Moore (E. V.), Osborne, Howard (R. F.); Forman and Fraser (John W.), equal; Sise.

RAILWAY WORK.

FOURTH YEAR.—*Class I.*—McCarthy; Irving and Macphail, equal. *Class II.*—Anderson, Matheson, Bond, Benny.

THIRD YEAR.—*Class I.*—Colpitts. *Class II.*—Fraser (C. E.), Gagnon L. F.), Gough; Bachand and Van Horne, equal.

SUMMER WORK.

FOURTH YEAR.—*Class. I.*—Butler (*Guggenheim Smelting Works at Perth-Amboy N. Y.*) and Laurie (*Lancashire Boiler*) and McCarthy (*Steel Roof Truss* and McRae (*Lancashire Boiler*), equal; MacLean (T. A.), (*Coal Mining*); Angel (*Lancashire Boiler*) and Cape (*Lancashire Boiler*) equal; Atkinson (D. C. T.). (A Nova Scotian Gold Mine and Chlorination Plant.) *Class II.*—Matheson (*Two Stress Diagrams*) and Patton (*Lancashire Boiler*) and Scott (A. P.), (*Steel*), equal; Archibald (H. T.), (*The Huntingdon Electric Light System*) and Mackerras (*Gold Mining as carried on at Goldenville, N. S.*), equal; Simpson (J. M.) (*One month of App'ied Electricity*), Macphail (*60 ft. Roof Truss*), Eaves (*Lancashire Boilers*); Mackie (*Petroleum and Natural Gas*) and Young (G.A.) (*Hudson Bay Survey Trip*), equal; Atkinson W. J. (*Some hints for Prospectors and Miners*) and Scott (J.H.) (*Lancashire Boiler*), equal; McLea (*Lancashire Boiler*) and Sheffield (*Lancashire Boiler*), equal; Ainley (*The Sudbury District and its Minerals*). *Class III.*—Beatty (*Lancashire Boiler*) and Maclennan (*Lancashire Boiler*), equal; Bacon (*Lancashire Boiler*); Bond (*Prospecting in Western Ontario*) and Davis (*Assaying and Drysdale (*Petroleum*), equal; Benny (*Design of Roof Truss with Stress Diagram*) and Irving (*Combination Roof Truss*), equal; Davidson (J. H.) (*Lancashire Boiler*), Waterous (*Lancashire Boiler*); Reaves (*Lancashire Boiler*, Dean (*Tank Locomotive*) and Hillary (*The Metallurgy of Copper*) and Thomas (*General View of Steam Shovel and Hoisting Friction*), equal; Yorston (*Hydraulic Press*).

THIRD YEAR.—*Class I.*—Archibald (E. M.) (*Engine and Boiler*); Denis (*Engine and Boiler*) and Ewan (*Engine and Boiler*), equal; Morgan (*Hamilton Blast Furnace Plant*); Bachand (*Plans and Survey*) and Colpitts (*Different Styles of Stair-case*) and Fraser (C. E.), (*Topographic Map of Brousse Park, N. Y.*) and Gagnon (*Plans and Survey*) and Gough (*Plans and Survey*) and Preston (*Eustis Copper Mines*), equal; Peden (*Porch of Engineering Building*); Whyte (J. S.) (*Steam Plant for Morgan Cement Works*); Blaylock (*Asbestos Mining and Milling at Danville*) and Hutchinson (*The Alums*) and Wilson (10,000 *volt two phase Power Transmission, Three Rivers*), equal. *Class III.*—Hyde (G. T.) (*Measured Work and Sketches*) and McLean (W.B.) (*Engine and Boiler*) and McLeod (N) (*Measured Work and Sketches*), equal; MacInnes (*People's Heat and*

Light Company, Halifax, N. S.), Young (W. M.) (Engine and Boiler of Electric Lighting Station, Renfrew) ; McLaren (A. J.) (The Alums) and Yuile (Methods of Blasting Manufacture and Use of Explosives), equal ; Bowman (Outline Plan of Electric Light Station, Madoc, O.) and Grier (Babcock and Wilcox Boiler), equal ; Burgess (Engine and Boiler) ; Fetherstonhaugh (Babcock and Wilcox Boiler) and Moore (W.M.) (Manufacture of Iron in a Blast Furnace) and Shaw (Babcock and Wilcox Boiler) and Van Horne (Location and Early Construction Crow's Nest Pass Railway), equal ; Campbell (Methods of Blasting and Manufacture of Explosives), Kirkpatrick (Explosives). Class III.—Hyde (J. C.), (Engine and Boiler), Waller (Blasting and Explosives), Hickey (Horizontal Tubular Boiler) ; Henderson (Methods of Blasting and Manufacture of Explosives) and Parizeau (Plans and Survey) and Stevens (The Manufacture of Iron in a Blast Furnace) and Wenger (Engine and Boiler), equal ; Austin (Drawing of an Engine) and Davidson (W. A.) (Corliss Engine) and Nicholls (The Lanark Mine), equal ; Cornwall (Steam Pump and Boiler, C.P.R. Station, Ashcroft, B.C.), and Dargavel (Steam Engine) and Fraser (H.) (Vertical Section of an Upright Engine) and Fraser (James W.) (High Speed Laurie Engine) and Hawker (Engine and Boiler at Maine Central R.R. Shops, Waterville, Maine), and Pergau (Plan of Horizontal Engine), equal ; Gisborne Shafting), Pitcher (Hydraulic Press).

SURVEYING.

THIRD YEAR.—(Architectural Course). Class I.—None. Class II.—McLeod (N.), Hyde (G. T.) (Civil and Mining Engineering Courses). Class I.—Kirkpatrick, Colpitts. Class II.—Stevens, Fraser (C. E.), Corriveau, Yuile, Pitcher ; Gagnon (L. F.) and Preston, equal. Class III.—Campbell, Waller, MacInnes, *Henderson ; *Gough and Moore (W. M.) and *Morgan, equal.

SECOND YEAR.—(Architectural, Civil and Mining Engineering Courses). Class I. —Ewart. Class II.—Cowans (F.), Buffett, Anglin, Robertson, Burgoyne, Gillean. Class III.—Byers ; Cary and Moore (E. V.), equal.

*Supplemental in Practical Astronomy.
    "   " Surveying.

SURVEYING FIELD WORK.

THIRD YEAR.—Class I.—Colpitts. Class II.—Gagnon (L. F.), Henderson, Preston, Corriveau, Kirkpatrick, Fraser (C. E.), *Pitcher ; Morgan and Stevens, equal ; MacInnes. Class III.—Yuile, Campbell, Gough, Waller, Moore (W. M.) ; Bachand and Parizeau, equal.

SECOND YEAR.—Class I.—Gillean ; Cowans (F) and Ewart, equal. Class II.— Byers, Anglin, Donaldson ; Burgoyne and Robertson, equal ; Cary, Pyke, Buffett. Class III.—Moore (E. V.), Howard (L. O.).

*Supplemental in Fieldwork.

THEORY OF STRUCTURES.

FOURTH YEAR.—*Class I.*—McCarthy. *Class II.*—Macphail, Anderson, Irving, Matheson. *Class III.*—Benny and Bond, equal.

THIRD YEAR.—*Class I.*—Colpitts, Grier, McLean (W. B.) *Class II.*—Kirkpatrick and Young (W. M.), equal; Archibald (E. M.), Shaw; Denis and Fraser (J. W.), equal; Ewan, Fetherstonhaugh; Cornwall and Dargavel and Hickey, equal; Fraser (C. E.) and Pergau, equal; Burgess; Davidson (W. A.) and Hyde (G. T.), equal; White (J. S.), Bowman. *Class III.*— Austin and *Gough and *Morgan and Peden and Yuile, equal; Hyde (J. C.) and McLeod (N.) and *Wenger, equal; Campbell; Preston and Wilson (R. M.), equal; Gagnon (L. F.); †MacInnes, *Van Horne, Nicholls, Parizeau; Fraser (H.) and *Henderson, equal; Bachand and Moore (W.M.), equal.

THERMODYNAMICS.

FOURTH YEAR.—(*Civil, Electrical and Mining Engineering Courses*). *Class I.*— McCarthy and Maclennan, equal; Cape and Macphail, equal. *Class II.* —Sheffield; Anderson, Young (G. A.), Ainley, Davis, Irving, Eaves, Butler. *Class III.*—MacLean (T. A.), Matheson, Scott (J. H.), Atkinson (D. C.T.), Archibald (H. P.); Atkinson (W. J.) and Hillary, equal; Bond Benny. (*Mechanical Engineering Course*) *Class I.*—Angel, Laurie; *Class II.*—Waterous, Dean, Patton; Bacon and McRae, equal. *Class III.*—Thomas, Beatty, Davidson (J. H.), Mackerras.

THIRD YEAR.—*Class I.*—None. *Class II.*—McLean (W. B.), Wilson (R. M.) Young (W. M.). *Class III.*—Denis, Dargavel.

WORKSHOPS.

FOURTH YEAR.—*Class I.*—Patton, McRae, Angel, Mackerras; Davidson (J. H.) and Waterous, equal. *Class II.*—Dean; Laurie and Mackie, equal; Bacon, Thomas, Reaves.

THIRD YEAR.—*Class I.*—Bowman, McLean (W. B.). *Class II.*—Fraser (J. W.) Young (W. M.), Wilson (R. M.), Fraser (H.), Hyde (J. C.), Shaw, Austin; Denis and Cornwall, equal; Pergau and Dargavel, equal. *Class III.*— Grier and Hawker, equal; Hickey and Archibald (E. M.), equal; Wenger, Burgess, Fetherstonhaugh, Davidson (W. A.).

SECOND YEAR.—(*Architectural, Civil and Mining Engineering Courses*).— *Class I.* —None. *Class II.*—Gillean, Buffett, Burgoyne; Ewart and Staveley, equal; Anglin and Byers and Cowans (F.) and Moore (E. V.), equal. *Class III.*—Robertson, Pyke, Cary, Coote, Howard (L. O.). (*Electrical and Mechanical Engineering Courses.*)—*Class I.*—Black, Fraser (John W.). *Class II.*—Arkley, Miller (A. K.); Scott (H. E.) and Smith (G.B.), equal; Shepherd and Walker, equal; Montgomery; Allen and Burwell and Hamilton (G. M.), equal; Paterson, Nelson, Howard (R. F.), Duncan; Forman and Neville and Percy and Scott (G. W.), equal; St. George, Whiteway. *Class III.*—Millar (J. L.), Osborne, Ogilvie (N. C.), Glassco (J. G.), Hearn.

---

† Suplemental in Paper I.
* " " II.

First Year.—*Class 1.*—None. *Class II.*—McLaren (J.), Fry, Fréchette; Burson, and Lowden and McIntosh, equal; Ward (P. W.), Galbraith, Taylor, Wiener, Fraser (D. C.), Peck, Scott (H. M.), Lloyd; Egleson and Gagnon (E. E.) and Schwitzer (T. H.), equal; Clement and DeBlois and Plant and Wells and Wilson (T. A.), equal; Buchanan and Higman and Rolland (L.), equal. *Class III.*—Edwards and Wakeling, equal; Burchell and Miner, equal; Askwith (C. E.) and Blue and Ogilvie (P.), equal; Ritchie and White (G. V.), equal; Cameron and Cowen (E A.A.) and McDonald (S.) and Mitchell, equal; Farquharson and Reynolds and Walsh, equal; Brookfield, Ward (R.); Jamieson and Tupper, equal; McKenna; Labatt and Meldrum, equal; Boyd, Flint; Hampson and Wilkins, equal.

ZOOLOGY.

Third Year.—*(Practical Chemistry Course.)*—*Class 1.*—None. *Class II.*—None. *Class III.*—Hutchinson, McLaren (A. J.).

Second Year.—*(Mining Engineering and Practical Chemistry Courses.)*—*Class 1.*—None. *Class II.*—None. *Class III.*—Buffett, Donaldson, Barber, Moore (E. V.).

Students of the University.

SESSION 1897-98.

McGILL COLLEGE.

FACULTY OF LAW.

FIRST YEAR.

Archibald, Sam. G., B.A., Montreal
Baker, George H., Sweetsburg, Q
Burke, Edmund A., Montreal
Chauvin, Henry A., Montreal
Dobell, Alfred, B.A., Quebec
Enright, Fred. T., Sherbrooke, Q
Garneau, Leon, Ottawa, O
Kay, Wm. F., Montreal
Macalister, A. W. G., Danville, Q
Macfarlane, L., B.A., Montreal
Mackay, Hugh, Montreal
Margolese, Louis, Montreal
Redpath, Joscelyn C., Montreal
Sharswood, Wm. F., Montreal
Tribey, Harry, Montreal
Walsh, Thos. E., Montreal

SECOND YEAR.

Baby, Henri, jun., B.A., Montreal
Ball, Wm. S., E. Bolton, Q
Barlow, Jos. C., Montreal
Bercovitch, Peter, Montreal
Carter, Wm. F., B.A.Sc., Cowansville, Q
Décarie, J. N. F., B.A., N.D. de Grace
Drolet, Edmond B., Montreal
Ives, Wm. C., Coaticook, Q
Lynch, Walter H., Mansonville, Q
McCabe, Ed. E. P. F., Windsor Mills, Q
McIver, Wm. E., Melbourne, Q
Robertson, Wm. G. M., B.A., Sherbrooke, Q
Saunders, Frank C., Montreal
Thomson, Arthur B., Montreal
Thorneloe, Walter E. G., B.A., Montreal
Vipond, Ernest E., Montreal
Whelan, Joseph, Montreal

THIRD YEAR.

Burnet, Arthur, B.A., Farnham Centre, Q
Champoux, Charles, B.A., Montreal
Clay, Samuel, B.A., Montreal
Elliott, Henry J., Montreal
Hickson, James Claude, B.A., Montreal
Honan, Cornelius, Montreal
Howard, E. Edwin, B.A., Philipsburg, Q
Iles, Charles, Montreal
Kennedy, John K., Montreal
Marler, Herbert M., Montreal
Rogers, Reginald H., B.A., Alberton, P.E.I.
Semple, G. Hugh, Montreal

PARTIAL STUDENTS.

Reeve, Sidney N., Chicago, Ill
Seath, Percival K., Montreal

FACULTY OF MEDICINE

FIRST YEAR.

Alexander, J. H., Westmount, Que
Bayfield, T. F., Charlottetown, P. E. I
Beatty, H. W., Sarnia, Ont
Belanger. E. R., Ottawa, Ont
Bell, A. J , Westmount, Que
Bishop, L. C., Marbleton, Que
Blake. J. J., Charlottetown, P. E I
Blaquiere, J., North Rustico, P. E. I
Borden, H. L., B A., Canning, N. S
*Boulter, J. H., Picton, Ont
*Boyd. R M., Belleville. Ont
Bradshaw, J. E., Montreal, Que
*Briggs, J A., New Westminster, B. C
Browne, J. G., B.A., Montreal, Que
Bruce, J , B.A., Moncton, N. B
Burrows. A. E Kingston. Ont
Burton. H. T., Short Hills, N. J., U. S. A
Butler. P. E., B.A., Milltown, N. B.
Callbec. K. D., Tryon, P. E. I
Campbell, R. P., B.A . Montreal, Que
Cantlie, F. P. L . Montreal, Que
Carlyle, D. A., Moorewood, Ont
Chamberlain, H. B., Perth, Ont
Chandler. E. C., Montreal, Que
Collison, H. McN., Dixon's Corners, Ont
Collison. J., Dixon's Corners, Ont
Crang. F. W., Toronto. Ont
Croly. E. H., Dunville, Ont
*Crowell, B. C., Yarmouth. N. S
Cullen, W. H., Montreal, Que
Dalton, C. H., Tignish, P. E. I
*Dickson, W. H., Pembroke, Ont
Donovan, J. B., Lewiston, Maine, U. S. A
Duncan, J. W., Montreal, Que
Ellis, R. L , Youghall N. B
Fearn. C. J., Montreal, Que
Featherston, H. C., Montreal, Que
Fleming, J. E , North Rustico. P. E. I
Fuller. A. T., B A., Truro, N. S
Fuller, H. T., Halifax, N. S
*Gardner, R. L , Sherbrooke, Que
George. J D., Redwood, N. Y
†Gouley, H A., Montreal, Que
Grant, W. W., Montreal, Que
Harley, R J. O., Montreal, Que
Harper, A. A , North Adams, Mass
Hope, J. T., Glen Robertson, Ont
Howard, A. C. P , B.A., Montreal, Que
Hughes, H. J., Charlottetown, P. E. I
Hunter. E. N. McL., Mirrimac. Mass
†Hutchison, L. W., Ottawa, Ont
Jackson, G. F., Brockville, Ont
*Johnson, R. DeL., Montreal, Que
Johnston, J. L , Martintown, Ont
Jones, J. H., Brockville, Ont
Kendall. A. L., Vancouver, B C
Ker, R. H., B A., Montreal, Que
Lamb, H. A., Portland, Maine
*Learmonth, G. E., Montreal, Que
Leggett, T. H., Ottawa, Ont
Lidstone, A. E., Brinston's Corners, Ont
Little, H. M., B.A., London, Ont
Lomas, A J., Montreal, Que
Lunney, T. H., St. John, N. B
MacCarthy, F. H., Ottawa, Ont

Mackay, M., B A., Montreal, Que
Mackenzie, S. D., Sarnia, Ont
McAleer, E. F., Bedford, Que
McDonald, C. A., Milltown, N. B
*McDonald, P. A., Dundee Centre, Que
*McEwen, J. R., Dewittsville, Que
McKay, D. S , Reserve Mines, C. B.
McNeil, J. W., Kensington, P. E. I
*McPherson, T., Stratford, Ont
Martin, E A., Kemptville, Ont
Meighen, W. A., Perth, Ont
Millar, S., South Durham, Que
Miller, G. H. S., Alexandria, Ont
*Mitchell, I. E., Sherbrooke, Que
Morgan A. D., Nanaimo, B. C
Moses, H. C., Caledonia, Ont
Mullally, E. J., Souris, P. E. I
Munroe, A. T., Moose Creek, Ont
Munro, J. A., Pugwash, N. S
*Ness, W., Howick, Que
Newcombe. W. E., Vancouver, B. C
Niven, K. S., London, Ont
Paquin, U., B A., St. Eustache, Que
Penner. E., B.A., Gretna, Man.
Pilot, F.W.H , St. John's, Newfoundland
Ramsay, W A., Westmount, Que
†Rawlings, W. T., Montreal, Que
Redon, L. H., B.A , Victoria, B. C
†Reeve, S N., Chicago, Ill , U. S. A
Richards, B A., Yarmouth, N. S
*Ritchie, C. F., Montreal, Que
Roberts, J., Woodburn, Ont
Robertson, C. G., Hawkesbury, Ont
Robertson, R. D., St. John, N. B
Robertson, W. G., Montreal, Que
Robidoux E , B A., Shediac, N. B
Rogers, H. B., Victoria, B. C
Ross, T. M., Bainsville, Ont
Russel, C. K., B. A., Montreal, Que
Rutherford. C. A., Waddington, N. Y
Ryan, W. T., B.A., Fredericton, N. B
Sanders, C. W., Kemptville, Ont
Saunders, W. E., Woodstock, N. B
Shearer, C., Montreal, Que
Shearer, R. L , Kelso, Que
Simpson, E. G.W., B.A., Lennoxville,Que
†Simpson, J. C., Montreal, Que
Simpson, S., Bay View, P. E. I
Stentaford, G. L., Heart's Content, Nfld
Stevenson, J., B.A., Montreal, Que
Stewart, C. J., Russell, Ont
Strong, N. W., Cambria, Que
Taylor, D. A., Havelock, N. B
Taylor, W. L., Waterloo, Que
Tobin, A. J., Cornwall, Ont
Ward, J. A., Lewiston, Maine
Warren, J G., Montreal, Que
*White, G. D., Trenton, Ont
Wiley, B. E., Fredericton, N B
Williams, F. T., Bosnto,. Mass
Williams, W., Rensen, N. Y
Wilson, J. J., Montreal, Que
Wyman, H. B., B.A., Chute à Bondeau, Ont

*Double Course.
†Partial,

SECOND YEAR.

†Ackerley. A. W. K., Montreal, Que
Almon, W. B., Halifax, N.S
Anton, D. L.S., Powerscourt Castle, Ireland
Armstrong, J. W., B.A , Bristol, Que
Paird, J. A., Brucefield
Ballantyne. C. T., Ottawa, Ont
Barry, F. A., Montreal, Que
Bishop, T. F.. Harvey, N.B
Boire, W., Manchester, N.H., U.S.A
Bonner, J. A., New York City, U S,A
Brown, E. L., Chesterville. Ont
Buffet. C.. B.A., Grand Bank, Nfld
Burnett, P , Montreal, Que
Campbell, O. E., Apohaqui, N.B
Carnwath, J.E M., Riverside, N.B
Cartwright. C., Kingston, Ont
Charlton, G. A., Montreal, Que
†Charron, A., Ottawa, Ont
Clemesha, W. F., Port Hope, Ont
Coates, H. W., Kingston, N.B
Coffin, J. D., Charlottetown, P.E.I
Cook, C. R.. Montreal, Que
Coristine, W. H , Montreal, Que
Costello, A. E., Montreal, Que
Cowperthwaite, W. M., Carbonear, Nfld
Cox, J. R., Hull, Que
Crozier, J. A., B A., Grand Valley, Ont
*Dixon, J. D., Montreal, Que
*Dixon, W. E., Montreal, Que
Donaldson, A. S., Montreal, Que
Donnelly, A. J., B A., Sturgeon, P.E.I
Doull, A E..Montreal, Que
†Dowler. O.. Billings' Bridge, Ont
Duffy, P. F., Charlottetown, P.E.I
Eagar, W. H., Dartmouth, N.S
Fairle. J. A.. Montreal, Que
Freeman, C H.F., B.A., Milton, N.S
Gibson, E. J., Campbellford. Ont
*Gilday, A.L.C , Montreal, Que
*Goodall. J. R., Ottawa, Ont
Gray, H. R D.. B.A., Montreal, Que
Hall, A. R., Washington, Ont
Hall, W. T., Montreal, Que
Harvie, S. K., B.A., Newport, N.S
Haszard, C. F. L., Charlottetown, P.E.I
Henry, C K P., Ottawa, Ont
Hiebert, G , Gretna, Man
Hill, W. H. P., Montreal, Que
Hughes, R. E., Ottawa, Ont
Igoe, O. A., Tarrytown, N.Y.. U.S.A
Jardine, J., Freetown, P.E.I
Johnston, A., Leeds. Que
Johnston, E. H., Washington, D.C
Jones, H. A., B.A., Moncton, N.B
Kannary, E. L., B. A., Northfield, Min ,
Keating, B. H., Montreal, Que

Keating, H. T., Montreal, Que
Lawlor, F. E , Dartmouth, N.S
Lester, C. W., S. Durham, Que
Littig, J V., Davenport, Iowa, U.S.A
Lynch, J. B., Fredericton, N.B
MacKinnon, J. W., Charlottetown, P.E.I
Macpherson, C., St. John's, Nfld
McAuley, A. G., Ventnor, Ont
*McConnell, R. E., Montreal, Que
McDiarmid, W. B., Maxville, Ont
McDonald, W. F., Westville, N.S
McKee, S. H., B.A., Fredericton, N.B
McSorley, H. S., Enderby, B.C
Martin, L.W , Warden, Que
May, L. W., Ottawa, Ont
Morrison, A. S., Montreal, Que
Morrison, G. D., Vankleek Hill, Ont
Morrow, J. J., Fergus, Ont
Murray, L. M., Truro, N. S
O'Reilly. E. P., B.A., Hamilton, Ont
O'Reilly, R. H.. Ottawa, Ont
O'Sullivan, M. T., Little Glace Bay, C. B
Paintin, A. C , Mansonville, Que
Paterson, W. F., B.A., Montreal, Que
Pattee, F. J., Vankleek Hill, Ont
Patton, J. W. T., Ponds, N.S
Payne, R. H., Kingston, Jamaica, B. W. I
Pittis, W. H., Plainfield, N.J.. U.S.A
Pope, E. L., B. A., Belleville, Ont
Porter, F. S., Powassan, Ont
Reynolds, F. L., St. John, N.B
Richard, F. A.. B.A., Richibucto, N B
Robb, G. W. A., Oxford, N.S
Ross, H , B.A., Montreal, Que
Rowley, W. E., B.A., Marysville, N.B
Russell, E. M., Springfield, Mass., U.S.
Rutherford, A E., Montreal, Que
Sayre, T. D.. Amherst, N.S
Scriver, E. F., Montreal, Que
Secord, E. R., Brantford, Ont
Shaughnessy, C. R., St. Stephen, N.B
Snetsinger, H. W., Moulinette, Ont
Stevenson, R. H., Danville, Que
Stewart, C A., Dunvegan, Ont
Symmes, C. R., Aylmer, Que
Tanner, C. A. H , Windsor Mills, Que
Todd, J. L.. Victoria, B. C
Townshend, C., Parrsboro, N.S
Turnbull, J. A., Bear River, N.S
Turner, W. G.. B. A., Quebec City, Que
*Walker, H., New York City, N.Y
Wheeler, F. C.. Richford, Vermont
*White, E. H., Montreal, Que
Wilmot, LeB. B., Oromocto, N.B
Wilson, W. A., Carleton Place, Ont

THIRD YEAR.

Alley, G. T.. Charlottetown, P.E.I
Aylmer, A. L., Montreal, Que
Beadie, W. D., Lachine, Que
Bowles, C T., Ottawa, Ont
Bradley, J. H., Charlottetown, P.E.I
Brannen, J. P., Montreal, Que
Brennan, F. A., St. Albans, Vt., U.S.A

Brown, W. F.. B A., Plattsburg, N.Y.,
Browning, W. E., Exeter, Ont.
Burnett, W. B , B A., Montreal, Que
Burnett. P , Montreal, Que
Burris, J. S., Halifax, N.S
Cameron, L G., Cascades, Que
Campbell, V. B.. Finch, Ont

* Double Course.
† Partial.

Casselman, P. C., Morrisburg, Ont
Conroy, R. J., Peterboro, Ont
Craig, J. E., North Gower, Ont
Cumming, W. A., Buckingham, Que
Cunningham, A. A., Huntingdon, Que
Cuzner, G., Ottawa, Ont
Darche, C. E., B. L. Danville, Que
Drier, N. E., Woodstock, N.B
Dyer, E. O., B.A., Sutton, Que
Fitzgerald, C. T., Harbor Breton, Nfld
Fourney, F. W., B.A., Montreal, Que
Fuller, G. F LeRoy, Sweetsburg, Que
Galbraith, W. S., Lethbridge, Alberta
Gillis, E. G., Indian River, P.E.I
Gordon, A. H , St. John, N.B
Gray, C. F. A., Montreal, Que
Greene, E., Leitrim, Ont.
Higgins, C. P., Victoria, B.C
Jones, D. C., Maitland, Ont
Law, R , Ottawa. Ont
Levy, A., B A., Montreal, Que
Lineham, D. M., Calgary, Alberta
Loeb, A. A., Montreal, Que
Logie, A. E., Charlottetown, P.E.I
Love, R. H., Carleton Place, Ont
Macdonald, J. S., Montreal, Que
MacKenzie, C. A., Toronto, Ont
McCombe, J., Iberville, Que
McDougall, A., Kippen, Ont
McIntyre, J. D., Clifton, P.E.I
McKay, J. G., Moorewood, Ont
McKechnie, W. C , Marquette, Man
McNally, D. A., Abram's Village, P.E.I
McNaughton, F.M.A., B.A., Huntingdon

McNiece, T. G., Carsonby, Ont
Mellon, P. B., Ottawa, Ont
Morris, T. E., St. John, N.B
Mousseau, E, A., Hall, Que
Murphy, E. F., St. John, N.B
Mussen, A. T., Montreal, Que
Nash, A C., Ogdensburg, N.Y., U.S.A
Nicholson, F. J., B.A., Victoria, B.C
Noble, E, C , Potsdam. N.Y., U.S.A
O'Brien, J. R., B.A., Ottawa, Ont
Paterson, A., B.A., Montreal, Que
Peake, E. P , B.A., Oshkosh, Wis., U.S.A
Peppers, H. W., B.A., Fredericton, N.B
Pittis, H., Plainfield, N. J., U.S.A
Ross, S. A., Hintonburg, Ont
Ross, W. J., Martintown, Ont
Ryan, G. H. W., Montreal, Que
Scott, J. F., D.V S., Montreal, Que
Shore, R. A. A., B.A., Toronto, Ont
Snyder, A. E. W., Coaticooke, Que
Sparrow, C. J , Alexandria, Ont
Sutherland, W. H., Sea View, P.E.I
Symmes, C. R., Aylmer, Que
Thompson, G. H., North Sydney, C.B
Tooke, F. T., B.A., Montreal, Que
Trites, D. , Petit Codiac, N.B.
Turnbull, T., Stratford, Ont
Whillans, H A., Hintonburg, Ont
Wilkins, F. F., Montreal, Que
Wilkins, W. A., Montreal, Que
Witherbee, W. D , Potsdam, N.Y , U.S.A
Wood, D. F., Faribault, Minn., U.S.A
Wood, J. H. M , Montreal, Que
Woodley, J. W., Rockland, Ont

FOURTH YEAR.

Banfill, S. A., Magog, Que
Barlow, W. L., B. A., Montreal, Que
Bartlett, G. W., Brigus, Nfld
Bayfield, G. E., Charlottetown, P.E I
Bearman, G. P., Bell's Corners, Ont
Beattie, R. F., Montreal, Que
Bell, J , New Glasgow, N.S
Blackett, J W., Ormstown, Que
Brears, C. F., Regina, Assa
Brown, C. H., B.A., Carleton Place, Ont
Corbet, G. G. St. John, N.B
Corcoran, J. A., Warden. Que
Covert, A. M., Grand Manan, N.B
Cushing, H. B., B.A., Montreal, Que
Dalpé, W. H., B.A., Montreal, Que
Darché, J. A., Sherbrooke. Que
Davidson, C., Montreal Que
Deane, R. B., Montreal, Que
Dickson, S. M., B.A., Montreal, Que
Duncan, R. G., Bathurst, N.B
Duval, J. L., Grand Ligne, Que
Fagan, G. A., B.A., North Adams, Mass
Fawcett, R. F. M , St. Andrew's, Jamaica, B.W.I
Finnie, J. H., Montreal, Que
Forbes, A. M. T., Montreal, Que
Fox, A. C. L., Winnipeg, Man
Francis, B., Sydney Mines, N. S
Fraser, F. C., B. A., Montreal, Que
Gadbois, F. A., Sherbrooke, Que
Gillies, B. W. D., Teeswater, Ont
Gladman, E. A., Lindsay, Ont
Grace, N., Montreal, Que
Green, F. W., Victoria, B. C

Harvey, F. W., B.A., Abercorn, Que
Houston, J. C., New Glasgow, P.E.I
Hudson, H. P., Chelsea, Que
Hume, G. W. L., Leeds, Que
Jackson, F. Slater, Montreal, Que
Jamieson, W. R., Ottawa, Ont
Jones, F. B., Montreal, Que
Lamb, J. A , Ottawa, Ont
Lang, A. A. J., Almonte, Ont
Long, C. B., Whitehall N.Y
Lynch, W. W., Knowlton, Que
Macaulay, J. F., St. John, N B
Macaulay, H. R., Montreal, Que
McCabe, J. A., B A., Windsor Mills, Ont
McAllister, D. H., B.A., Belleisle, N.B
McLaren, R. W., St. Raphael's, Ont
McLean, J. N., Sarnia, Ont
McLean, J. R., B.A , Arnprior, Ont
McLennan, P. A., Lancaster, Ont
McLeod, J., Hartsville, P E.I
McMurtry, A. L., Bowmanville, Ont
Mooney, M. J., Inverness, Que
Moss, J. N., Montreal, Que
Myers, D. A., Prentice, Wis., U.S.A
Ogilvy, C., B.A., Montreal, Que
Oppenheimer, S. S., Vancouver, B.C
O'Shaughnessy, L. J., Oldham, N. S
Outhouse, J. S , B.A , St. Andrews, N.B.
Patterson, F. P., St. Martins, N.B.
Patterson, R. U., Baltimore, Md., U.S.A.
Peters, C. A., St. John's, Nfld
Pigeon, W. H. Peterborough, Ont
Powers, M., B.A., Ottawa, Ont
Prodrick, W. S., Ottawa, Ont

Rajotte, E. C. F., Montreal, Que
Robertson, D. McD., Perth, Ont
Rose, W.O., Lakeville, P.E.I
Rutherford, R. M., Hawkesbury, Ont
Scanlan, Harry, Gloucester, Mass, U.S.A.
Schwartz, H. J., Quebec city, Que
Sibler, W. F., Simcoe, Ont

Smith, A. M., B.A., Petit Codiac, N.B.
Stockwell, H. P., Danville, Que
Telford, R., Valens, Ont
Tiffany G. S., Alexandria, Ont
Walker P. McH., Grafton, N. D., U.S.A
West J., Montreal, Que
Whitton, D. A., Ottawa, Ont

GRADUATES.

Anderson, D. P., B.A., M.D., Montreal, Que
Bazin, A. T., M.D., Montreal, Que
Burnett, J. U., M.D., Sussex, N. B
Boone, S. W., B.A., M.D., Presque Ile, Maine
Church, H. M., M.D., Montreal, Que
Foster, A. L., M.D., Ottawa, Ont
Finnimore, D. W., M D., Potsdam, N. Y
Fyfe, Mary, M. D., Montreal, Que
Gibson, T., M. B. C. M., Ottawa, Ont
Jakes, R. W. M.D., Greenwood, B.C
Mackenzie, W. D., M.D., Parrsboro, N.S
Macdonald, Helen, B.A., M.D., Montreal, Que

McElroy, A. S., M.D., Montreal, Que
Main, C. G., M.D., Edmundston, N. B
Mitchell, Wm, M. D., Quebec, Que
Moriarty, J. W., M.D., Churubusco, N.Y
O'Neill, J. W., M.D., Mooer's Forks, N.Y
Pater, H. K., M.D., Pittsfield, Mass
Pearson, J. E., M.D., Sylaconga, Ala
Rielly, W., M.D., Montreal, Que
Ranuey, E. O., M.D., Barton Landing, N.Y
Rodger, D. A., M.D., Montreal, Que
Sharp, J. C., M.D., Marysville, N.B
Sprague, W. E., M.D., Belleville, Ont
Williams,—, M. D., Montreal, Que
Yonker W., M. D., Belleville, Ont

FACULTY OF ARTS.

Undergraduates.

FIRST YEAR.

Name.	School.	Residence.
Anderson, Richard,	Albert College,	Kenlis, Assa
Ascah, Robt. G.,	Montreal Dioc. Theol. College,	Peninsula, Gaspé, Q
Barrington, Fred. H.,	Waterloo Academy,	Waterloo, Q
Boulter, J. Henry,	Picton H. S.,	Demorestville, O
Bourne, Jas.,	Dufferin Gram. S., Brigham, Q.,	Barbadoes, W. I
Brown, Albert V.,	Montreal H. S.,	Montreal
Brown, Edwin O.,	Prince of Wales College, P.E.I.,	Little York, P.E.I
Carruthers, Chris.,	Montreal Dioc. Theol. College,	Aylwin, Q
Chipman, Warwick F.,	Abingdon School, Montreal,	Montreal
Cole, G. Percy,	Montreal, H. S.,	Montreal
Copeman, Joseph Hodge,	Quebec H. S.,	Quebec
Cotton, Wm. U.,	Feller Inst., Grande Ligne, Q.,	Sweetsburg, Q
Dickson, Norval,	Huntingdon Academy,	Allan's Corners
Evans, L. Thornton,	Montreal Coll. Institute,	Montreal
Harper, Robt. J.,	Montreal H. S,	Montreal
Hickson, Robt. N.,	Abingdon School, Montreal,	Montreal
Ireland, F. Chas.,	Montreal Coll. Institute,	Westmount, Montreal
Irving, George,	Prince of Wales Coll., P.E.I.,	Vernon Bridge, P.E.I
Lindsay, J. Edwin,	Montreal Dioc. Theol. Col.,	Rawdon, Q
Lochead, Arthur W.,	Kemptville H.S.,	North Gower, O
McDonald, John,	Montreal H. S.,	Montreal
McEwan, John R.,	Huntingdon Academy,	Dewittville, Q
McLean, Kenneth,	Glencoe H. S,	Strathburn, Q
McLeod, Angus B.,	Prince of Wales Coll., P.E.I.,	Springton, P.E.I
McMurtry, Gordon O.,	Montreal H S.,	Montreal
McMurtry, Shirley O.,	Montreal H. S.,	Montreal

Name.	School.	Residence.
MacNaughton, Wm. G.,	Huntingdon Academy,	Huntingdon, Q
McPherson, Thos.,	Collegiate Inst. Stratford,	Stratf.rd, O
Mitchell, Isaiah Edward,	Private Tuition	Sherbrooke, Q
Moffatt, Chas.,	Montreal H. S.	Montreal
Molson, Percival,	Montreal H. S.,	Montreal
Mount, Hector,	Montreal Dioc. Theol. Coll.,	Montreal
Mowatt, Jos. A.,	Montreal H. S.,	Montreal
Ness, Wm. Huntingdon,	Huntingdon Academy,	Howick, Q
Neville, Jas , .	Huntingdon Academy,	Huntingdon, Q
Parker, Dan. T.,	Lachute Academy,	Cambria, Q
Scott, Wm. J.,	Montreal H. S.,	Montreal
Scrimger, Francis A. C.,	Montre l H. S.,	Montreal
Stephens, Laurence,	Clifton College, Eng.,	Montreal
Sterns, H. Edgar,	Prince of Wales Coll., P.E.I.,	Charlottetown, P.E.I
Strong, Norman W.,	Waterloo Academy,	Cambria, Q
Tees, Fred. J.,	Montreal H. S.,	Montreal
Viner, Norman,	Montreal H. S.,	Montreal
White, Geo. D.,	Jameson ave. Coll. Inst., Toronto,	Trenton, O
White, D. Roderick,	Huntingdon Academy,	Huntingdon Q
Williams, Hy. S.,	Montreal H. S.,	Knowlton, Q
Williams, J. Manville,	Watford H. S.,	Watford, Ont
Wilson, Thos. J.,	Montreal Dioc. Theol. Coll.,	Shawville, Q

SECOND YEAR.

Name.	School.	Residence.
Ainley, Laurence,	Almonte H. S.,	Almonte, O
Baker, George P.,	St. Paul's School, Concord, N.H.,	Yarmouth, N.S
Charters Herbert.	Montreal H. S.,	Montreal
Cochrane, Donald,	Montreal H. S.,	Montreal
Cohen, Abraham,	Montreal H. S.,	Montreal
Cooke, H. Lester,	Montreal Collegiate Institute,	Montreal
Crack, Isaac E.,	St. Francis Coll., Richmond,	Kingsbury, Q
Crowell, Bowman C.,	Milton H.S., Yarmouth, N.S.,	Yarmouth, N.S
DeWitt, Jacob,	Montreal Coll. Institute,	Montreal
Davies, Nelson C.,	McGill Normal School,	Bedford, Q
Dickson, W. Howard,	Pembroke H.S.,	Pembroke, O
Dixon, James D.,	St. John's School,	Montreal
Dorion, W. A.,	McGill Normal School,	Montreal
Elder Robert,	Huntingdon Academy,	Trout River, Q
Ells, Sydney C.,	Ottawa Collegiate I.stitute,	Ottawa, O
Ferguson, Colin C.,	Prince of Wales Coll., P.E.I.,	Marshfield, P.E.I
Forbes, Wilfrid,	Prince of Wales Coll., P.E.I.,	Vernon River Bridge, P.E.I
Goodhue, Harry,	Institute Feller,	Danville, Q
Grier, Geo. W.,	Montreal Collegiate Institute,	Montreal
Hardy, Charles, A.,	Prince of Wales College, P.E.I.,	Fortune Cove, P.E.I
Horsfall, Frank L.,	Montreal Collegiate Institute,	Montreal
Ireland, A. Austin,	Montreal Diocesan Theol. Coll.	Montreal
Jeakins, Charles E.,	Huntingdon Academy,	Huntingdon, Q
Johnson, J. Guy W.,	Montreal Collegiate Institute,	Montreal
Luttrell, Hy. P.,	Montreal H.S.,	Montreal
McCormick, Alex , S.,	Abingdon School,	Westmount, Montreal
Mackinnon, Cecil G.,	Bishop's College School,	Cowansville, Q
Macmillan, Cyrus J.,	Prince of Wales Coll., P.E.I.,	Charlottetown, P.E.I
Mathers, Wm. R.,	Grammar School, St. John, N.B.,	St. John, N.B
Mitchell, Sydney,	Montreal H.S.,	Montreal
Newson, Wm. V.,	Prince of Wales Coll., P.E.I.,	Charlottetown, P.E.I

Name.	School.	Residence.
Nutter, J. Appleton,	Montreal H.S.,	Montreal
Radford, E. Alan,	Abingdon School, Montreal.	Montreal
Reford, Lewis,	Montreal Collegiate Institute,	Montreal
Ritchie, Charles F.,	Montreal H.S.,	Montreal
Rowat, T. Alex.,	Huntingdon Academy,	Athelstan, Q
Rowell, Arthur H.,	McGill Normal School,	Montreal
Scott, George W.,	Montreal H S.,	Montreal
Scott, Harry E.,	Napanee Collegiate Institute,	Napanee, O
Smith, F. Napier,	Bishop's College School,	Montreal
Walker, Horatio,	Quebec H. S.,	L'ile d'Orléans, Q
Walker, John J.,	Huntingdon Academy,	Ormstown, Q
Weinfield, Henry,	Montreal H. S.	Montreal
Willis, Samuel J.,	Prince of Wales Coll , P.E.I.,	Kingston, P.E.I
Woodley, Edward C.,	Montreal H.S.,	Montreal

THIRD YEAR.

Name.	Residence.	Name.	Residence.
Brown, Walter G.,	Athelstan, Q	Laurie Ernest,	Montreal
Bruce, Guy O. T.,	Huntingdon, Q	Lundie, John Alex.,	Montreal
Cotton, Chas. M.,	Sweetsburg, Q	McClung, Robert K.,	Kingsbury, Q
Cumming, W. Gordon,	Montreal	McDonald, Paul A.,St. Agnes de Dundee	
Dixon, Wm. E.,	Montreal	MacKay, Hector,	Ripley, O
Duguid, Robert C.,	Montreal	McKenzie, Bertram S.,	London, O
Ells, Hugh,	Ottawa	McLeod, John B.,	Springton, P.E.I
Gardner, R. Lorne,	Brockville, O	Munro, Thos. A.,	Montreal
Goodall, James R.,	Ottawa	Patch, Frank S.,	Montreal
Hardisty, Richard,	Montreal	Rice, Horace G.,	New Durham, O
Heeney, Wm. Bertal	Danford Lake, Q	Robertson, Lemuel,	Marshfield, P.E.I
Henderson, Ernest H.,	Franklin Centre	Stewart, Donald,	Dunbar, O
Holland, Thos. B.,	London, Eng	Thompson, James E.,	Coaticook
Johnson, R. De Lancey,	Montreal	Wainwright, Arnold,	Montreal
Keith, Henry J..	Smith's Falls, O	White, E. Hamilton,	Montreal
Larmouth Geo. E.,	Montreal	Yule, George,	Scotland

FOURTH YEAR.

Name	Residence	Name	Residence
Bates, George E.,	Lanark, O	Moore, Percy T.,	Montreal
Bishop, W. Gordon,	Montreal	Munn, D. Walter,	Quebec
Blyth, R. B.,	Belwood, O	Paterson, Robert Childs,	Montreal
Campbell, J. Aug. Ewat,	Montreal	Place, Edson G.,	Millington, Q
Colby, John Child,	Stanstead, Q	Prudham, W. W.,	Waterdown, O
Dalgleish, R. Wallace,	Huntingdon, Q	Ross, Arthur B.,	Montreal
Duff, Alex. H.,	Montreal	Ship, Moses L.,	Montreal
Gardner, William A.,	Huntingdon, Q	Stephens, J. G.,	New Rocklands, Q
Gilday, Arch. L. C.,	Montreal	Stuart, James A.,	Montreal
Grace, Arch. H.,	Montreal	Tarlton, B. B.,	Montreal
Heine, M. Casewell,	New York City	Thomas, J. Wolferstan,	Montreal
Leney, John Muirhead,	Montreal	Thompson, Jas. R.,	Kinnear's Mills, Q
McConnell, Robert Ernest,	Montreal	Todd, J. L.,	Victoria, B. C
McGregor, Jas. Albert,	Huntingdon, Q	Turner Henry H.,	Appleton, O
MacLeod, Hy. S.,	Dunstaffuage, P.E.I	Turner, William D.,	Appleton O
Maclaren, A. Henderson,	Huntingdon, Q	Vineberg, Abraham,	Montreal
Meyer, John B.,	Montreal	Worth, Fulton J.,	Wellington, B.C

Partial Students.

A Student who is not an Undergraduate, or Graduate, is called a Partial Student.

The figure (1), (2), or (3), prefixed to a name, indicates that the Student takes a class in the corresponding year as well as in that where the name is found.

FIRST YEAR.

Name.	Residence.	Name.	Residence.
Allen, Ambrose,	Kemptville, O	Hosmer, Elwood B.,	Montreal
Anderson, Fred. J.,	Montreal	Lapointe, C.,	Montreal
Angell, Ernest E.,	Mooers, N.Y	Lough, Dan. A,	Ottawa, O
Bishop, Leslie C.,	Marbleton, Q	McLeod, Norman V.,	Granby, Q
Blythe, J. J.,	Montreal	McNaughton, Ernest A., Huntingdon,Q	
Boyd, Robert M.,	Belleville, O	Mathieson P.,	Forester's Falls, O
Bradford, W. G.,	Montreal	Mitchell, Walter G., Drummondville Q	
Briggs, John A.,	New Westminster	Mosgrove, E. J. W.,	Mosgrove, O
Brodie, Hugh H.,	Montreal	Munroe, William,	Woodstock, O
Brown, Asa I.,	Sombra, O	Ogilvie, Lorne C.,	Montreal
Cairns, Hugh G.,	Sawyerville, Q	Parkins, Edgar R.,	Montreal
Coulin, J. Edward,	Montreal	Penhallow, D. Pearce,	Montreal
Cruchon, Charles,	Montreal	Poston, —,	Montreal
Demole, John E.,	Montreal	Price, Joseph, Campbelltown, N.B	
Dempsay, William B.,	Calabogie, O	Purves, Reginald W., North Sydney,C.B	
Donnelly, William H.,		Reeve, Sydney N.,	Montreal
Down, George Wm.,	Newport, O	Rondeau, A. G.,	Hull City, Q
Dubois, Hy. J.,	St. Elizabeth, Q	Runnells, A. E.,	Egypt, Q
Edgar, John H.,	Montreal	Shepherd, Ernest G.,	Montreal
Ferguson, Arthur L.,		Swinton, James,	Rockton, O
Gilmour, C. R.,	Brockville, O	Tanner; Agenor H.,	Joliette, Q
Graham, Robert,		Taylor, Alf. M.,	Montreal, Q
Greenaway, Robt. Brandon, Hamilton, O		Tippett, Ernest H.,	North Bay, O
Graig, John G.,	Montreal	Watson, Hugh,	Montreal
Halpenny, E. Wesley,	Bear Brook, O	Webster, L. B. B.,	Kentville, N.S
Hopkin, Robert,	Montreal	Williamson, A. W.,	Shawbridge, Q

SECOND YEAR.

	Name	Residence		Name	Residence
(1)	Anderson, Fred J.,			Miller, John H.,	Cashel, O
	Barker, Arthur,	London, O		Milson, Walter E.,	Glanworth, O
(1)	Blythe, J. J.		(1)	Mitchell, Walter G.	
	Burke, Maurice N.,	Montreal		Morrow, Chas. W.,	Strathroy, O
	Cameron, Arch. G.,	Montreal	(1)	Munroe William,	
	Campbell, J. D.,	Leaksdale, O		Oke, Jno. J.,	Oka, Q
	Colborne, Jas. H.,	Hyndman, O	(1)	Parkins, Edgar R.	
	Crabb, Geo. J.,	Pembroke, O		Powell, Thomas,	Almonte, O
	Douglas, Fred C.,	Montreal	(1)	Reeve, Sydney N.	
	Evans, W.. G.,	Tiverton, O	(1)	Runnells, A. E.	
(1)	Greig, John G.			Secord, Albert,	New Durham, O
(1)	Halpenny, E. Wesley			Shaw, Leonard D., St. John, N.B	
	Harding, Albert E.,	London, O	(1)	Shepherd, Ernest G.	
	Hicks, Robert,	Exeter, O		Skinner, W. W.,	St. John, N.B
	Johnston, J. L.,	Toronto, O		Thom, Geo. W..	Appleton, O
(1)	Lough, Dan. A.			Trenholme, Harold W.,	Montreal
	McInnes, Finlay, S. Kinloss, Lucknow, O			Wiggins, M. E.,	Malakoff, O
	Masson, Wm. D., St. Catherines, O			Williams, Walter J.,	Montreal
	Mick, D.,	Mick-bug, O	(1)	Williamson, A. W.	

W

Name.	Residence.	Name.	Residence.
(1) Angell, Ernest E.		2) Millson, Walter E.	
Bartlett, L.)	South London, O	(2) Morrow, Charles W.	
(2) Blythe, J. J.		(2) Oke, John J.	
Bonin, Alex. L.,	Montreal	(2) Powell, Thomas	
(2) Crabb, George J.		(2) Shaw, Leonard D.	
(2) Douglas, Fred. C.		Stovel, R. W. (B.A.Sc), Minnea-	
(1) Down, George Wm.			polis, Minn., U.S.
(2) Harding, Albert E.		(1) Tippett, Ernest H.	
(2) McInnes, Finlay		(2) Wiggins, M. E.	
2) Miller, John H.		(2) Williamson, A. W.	

FOURTH YEAR.

(2) Anderson, Fred J.			McGregor, George,	Montreal
(3) Bartlett, L.		(2) Masson, William D.	
(3) Bonin, Alex.		(2) Mick, D.,	
(1) Bradford, W. G.		(3) Miller, John H.	
(1) Cairns, Hugh G.		(3) Millson, Walter E.	
(2) Cameron, Arch. G.		(3) Oke, Jno. J.	
(2) Campbell, J. D.		(3) Powell, Thos.	
(2) Colborne, Jas. H.		(2) Runnells, A. E.	
(3) Crabb, Geo. J.		(3) Tippett, Ernest H.	
(3) Dorion, George Wm.		(3) Wiggins, M. E.	
Farrell, Chas.,	Montreal	(2) Williams, Walter J.	
(2) Halpenny, E. Wesley		(3) Williamson A. W.	
(2) Lough, Dan. A.			

B. A.

Coburn, David N.,	Upper Melbourne, Q	Wallace, James M.,	North Gower, O
Macmillan, T. R.,	Newhaven, P.E.I	Willis, John J.,	Montreal
Keith, Neil D.,	Glencoe, Ont	Young, Henry,	Blakeney, O
Scrimger, J. Tudor,	Montreal		

DONALDA DEPARTMENT.

SPECIAL COURSE FOR WOMEN.

Undergraduates.

FIRST YEAR.

Name.	School.	Residence.
Bennett, C. Winifred,	Montreal G. H. S.,	Montreal
Budden, Jessie M.,	Montreal G. H. S.,	Montreal
Budden, Ellen M.,	Montreal G. H. S.,	Montreal
Carden, Matilda A.,	McGill Normal School,	Montreal
Clogg, Vivian E.,	Westmount Academy,	Westmount, Montreal
Day, Daisy W.,	Montreal G. H. S.,	Montreal Annex
Huxtable, Gertrude M.,	Perth Coll. Ins.,	Montreal
Kingsley, Alice M.,	Victoria School, St. John, N.B, &	
	Montreal G. H. S.,	Montreal
McLeod, May A.	Westmount Academy	Westmount, Montreal
Molson, Evelyn,	Montreal G. H. S.,	Montreal
Noyes, Emily M.,	Montreal Coll. Inst.,	Cowansville, Q
Radford, Isabel,	Misses Symmers & Smith Sch.,	Montreal

SECOND YEAR.

Name.	School.	Residence.
Bickerdike, May C.,	Montreal G. H. S.,	Lachine
Brooks, Elizabeth A.,	McGill Normal School	Montreal
Dey, Mary Helena,	Simcoe H S.,	Simcoe, O
Garlick, Edythe A.,	Montreal G. H. S.,	Montreal
Holman, Caroline E,	Prince of Wales Coll., P. E. I.,	Summerside, P.E.I.
Howden, Jennie E,	Stanstead Wesleyan Coll ,	Montreal
Jackson, E. Gertrude,	Montreal G. H. S.,	Montreal
Kerr, Grace I.,	Trafalgar Institute, Montreal	Montreal
Lundie, Jessie F.,	Montreal Collegiate Institute,	Montreal
McGregor, Claire R.,	Private Tuition,	Victoria, B. C
Marcuse, Bella,	Montreal G. H. S.	Danville, Q
Perley, Frances B.,	Girls' H. S. St. John, N.B.,	Upper Mangerville, Sunbury Co., N. B
Rorke, Helen,	St. Thomas H S.,	South Woodslee, O
Sangster, Elizabeth,	McGill Normal School, Montreal,	Sherbrooke, Q
Sever, Hannah D.,	McGill Normal School, Montreal,	St.Chrysostome Q
Smith, Lillian A.,	Morrisburg Collegiate Institute	Morrisburg

THIRD YEAR.

Name.	Residence.	Name.	Residence.
Armstrong, Catharine,	Bristol, Q	McDougall, Louise,	Montreal
Brodie, Margt.,	Montreal	McGill, I. Winifred,	Ottawa, O
Finley, Kathleen E.,	Montreal	Potter, Lucy E.,	Montreal
Holiday, Annie,	Rawdon, Q	Radford, Janet I.,	Montreal
Hurst, Isabel M.,	Montreal	Reid, Lena McK.,	Montreal
Johnson, Helena,	Montreal	Reynolds, Elizabeth E. M.,	Winchester, O
King, Christina C.,	Sarnia	Scrimger, Anna M.,	Montreal

FOURTH YEAR.

Bourke-Wright, K. M. H.,	Ireland	Pearson, Katie C.,	Montreal
Brooks, Harriet,	Sherbrooke, Q	Reynolds, M. Edna,	Winchester, O
Cameron, Frances M. T.,	Kingston, O	Seifert, Ethel M,	Quebec
Carr, Muriel B.,	St. John, N. B	Shaw, A. Louise,	Montreal
Dover, Mary V.,	Peterboro, O	Steen, Alice G.,	Farran's Point, Q
Jordan, Florence M.,	Montreal	Walker, Laura F. M.,	Montreal

Partial Students.

FIRST YEAR.

Archibald, Nancy C.,	Montreal	Mudge, F. Nora,	Montreal
Armstrong. Mabel C.,	Montreal	Mulholland, Minnie W.,	Montreal
Bond, Muriel C.,	Montreal	Plimsoll, Gladys,	Montreal
Borden, Elizabeth M,.	Canning. N. S	Ranken, Helen F.,	Montreal
Borden, J. Maude,	Canning, N. S	Reiffenstein, Margaret B.,	Montreal
Brice, Louise L.,	Montreal	Richardson, Mabel,	Montreal
Browne, Joanna H.,	Montreal	Robb, E. Winnifred,	Montreal
Carson, Lillian M.,	Montreal	Stewart Edith F.,	Montreal
Darling, Ethel,	Montreal	Thomas, Annie L,	Montreal
Fortier, Georgie H.,	Montreal	Topley, Helena, S. de C.,	Ottawa, O
Greenshields, E. Muriel,	Montreal	Vasey, Sarah E.,	Montreal
Holland, Estelle,	Montreal	Warrriner, J. Eva,	Montreal
Ker, Mary A.,	Montreal	Waud, Alice S.,	Montreal
Loud, Edith M.,	Montreal	Waud, Gertrude A.,	Montreal
McConnell, Adelaide V.,	Montreal	Whitcomb, H. Mildred,	Waterloo, Q
McDonald, Barbara,	Montreal	Wright, Elizabeth,	Montreal
McIntyre, Ethel R.,	Montreal		

SECOND YEAR.

Name.	Residence.	Name.	Residence.
Bannister, Mabelle A.,	Montreal	Luttrell, Maggie M.,	Montreal
(1) Bond, Muriel C.,	Montreal	(1) McDonald, Barbara.	Montreal
(1) Brice, Louise L.,	Montreal	(1) McIntyre, Ethel R.,	Montreal
(1) Browne Joanna H,	Montreal	Macfarlane, Hilda M..	Montreal
Buchanan, Bertha L. Q.,	Montreal	Meighen, Maggie F. S.,	Montreal
Burns, Margaret O.,	Montreal	Murphy, Louise I.,	Montreal
Clark, Nora M.	Montreal	(1) Plimsoll, Gladys,	Montreal
Craig, Mabel,	Montreal	(1) Richardson, Mabel,	Montreal
Durnford, Gwendolen,	Montreal	Taylor, Flora,	Montreal
(1) Fortier, Georgie H.,	Montreal	(1) Topley, Helena S. de C.,	Ottawa, O
(1) Greenshields, E. Muriel,	Montreal	Whittet, C. Maud,	Montreal
Lamb, Mary L., St. Andrews East, Q			

THIRD YEAR.

deCourtnay, Alice W.,	Montreal	Porter, Julia S. G.,	Montreal
Ferguson, Jennie A.,	Montreal	Reford, Katie F.,	Montreal
Going, E. Maud,	Montreal	(2) Taylor, Flora,	Montreal
Nowers, Winifred,	Montreal		

FOURTH YEAR.

(1) Armstrong, Mabel C.	Montreal	(2) Luttrell, Maggie M.,	Montreal
(2) Brice, Louise L.	Montreal	(2) McIntyre, Ethel R.	Montreal
(2) Clark, Nora M.,	Montreal	Maltby, Emma,	Montreal
(1) Darling, Ethel,	Montreal	Muir, Mary L. D.,	Montreal
Foley, Jean S,	Montreal	(1) Robb, E. Winnifred,	Montreal
(2) Fortier, Georgie H.,	Montreal	Seymour, Clara G.,	Montreal
(3) Going, E. Maud,	Montreal	White, Edith S.,	Montreal
Jackson, M. Lillian,	Montreal		

B. A.

Armstrong, L. Ethel,	Montreal	Palmer, Jane V.,	Montreal
Brown, Justine M.,	Montreal	Radford, Ethel S.,	Montreal
Craig, Margaret,	Montreal	Tatley, Eleanor,	Montreal
Jackson, Annie Louise	Montreal	Watson, Mona T.,	Montreal
Nicholls, Amy W.,	Montreal		

FACULTY OF APPLIED SCIENCE.

FIRST YEAR.

Askwith, Charles English,	Ottawa, O	Coote, Sydney R., St Albans,Vt., U.S.A
Blue, Allan Pollock,	Rustis, Q	*Cowen, Edwin Arthur Amos, Montreal
Buchanan, Dorlon T., Cote St.Mitchell,Q		DeBlois, William Howard, Halifax, N.S
Boyd, Hugh Harkness,	Montreal	Edwards, William M., Ottawa, O
Brookfield, John Waites, Halifax, N.S		Egleson, James Ernest Aiken, Ottawa,O
Burchell, George Bartlett, New Camp-		Farquharson, Cameron, Montreal
bellton, C.B		Flint, William George, Montreal
Burson, Herbert Arthur, St Catherines, O		Fournier, Raymond Camille, Montreal
Burwell, Ernest Victor, London, O		Fraser, Donald C., New Glasgow, N.S
Cameron, Hugh Donald, Montreal		Frechette, Howells, Ottawa, O
Clement, Sheldon Byrne, Clinton, O		Fry, David Merner, Bright, O

Gagnon, Edmund·Ernest, Westmount, Q
Galbraith, Malcolm Thomas, Montreal
Glassco, Archie P. S., Hamilton, O
Hale, Lorne, Pembroke, O
Hampson, Edward Greville, Montreal
Hearn, John F., St. Johns, Nfld
Higman, Ormond, Ottawa, O
Howard, Lawrence O., Lachine, Q
Howard, Rupert F., Lachine, Q
Jamieson, George Ernest T., Montreal
Labatt, John Sackville, London, O
Lloyd, Herbert M., New Westminster, B.C
Lowden, Warden King, Montreal
McDonald, Sidney, Montreal
McDonald, Rod. B., Glenaladale, P.E.I
McIntosh, John Gordon, London, O
McKenna, William Francis, Montreal
McKenzie, Bertram Stuart, London, O
McLaren, John, Montreal
Meldrum, Robert Hunter, Montreal
Mitchell, George Gooderham, Toronto, O
*Miner, William Haron, Granby, Q
Ogilvy, Paul, Cumming's Bridge, O
*Peck, Thomas Esmond, Montreal
Paterson, Charles Stiven, Montreal

Plant, Verner Lovelace, Montreal
Presner, Philip, Montreal
Reeves, James D, Grenville, Q
Reynolds, Leo Bowldy, Waterford, O
Ritchie, Joseph Norman, Halifax, N.S
*Rolland, Leon, Montreal
Schwitzer, Thomas Henry Ottawa, O
*Scott, Harry Evart, Napanee, O
Scott, Henry Maurice, Montreal
*Slayter, Charles Keeler L., Halifax, N.S
Stevenson, Herbert Richard, Montreal
Taylor, Charles W., Richmond, O
Tupper, Charles, Vancouver, B.C
Wakeling, Otty Sylvester, St John, N.B
Ward, Percy Walton, Lachine, O
Ward, Reginald C., Charing Cross, O
Walsh, William Nelson, Ormstown, O
*Watson, Hugh, Montreal
*Watson, Robert G., Montreal
Wells, Samuel Scott, Montreal
White, Gerald Verner, Pembroke, O
*Wiener, Abram, Montreal
Wilkins, George H., Montreal
*Wilson, Reginald C, Cumberland, O
Wilson, Thomas Albert, Waverley, N.S

SECOND YEAR.

Allen, Samuel J., Maitland, N.S
Anglin, James Penrose, Kingston, O
Arkley, Lorne M., East Angus, Que
Barber, René R., Georgetown, O
Black, Thompson Trueman, Sackville, N.B
Buffett, Aaron Forsey, Grand Bank, Nfld
Burgoyne, Stanley John, Halifax, N.S
Byers, Archibald F., Gananoque, O
Cary, George M., Goderich, O
Corriveau, Raoul de B., Iberville, Que
Coussirat, Henri A., Montreal
Cowans, Frederick, Montreal
Donaldson, Hugh W., Hamilton, Ont
Duncan, G Rupert, Montreal
Ewart, George R., Kilauea, Kanai, Hawaiian Islands
Fraser, John W., Charlottetown, P.E.I
Forman, Andrew S., Montreal
Gillean, Robert H., Montreal
Glassco, Jack G., Hamilton, O
Hamilton, George H., Peterboro', O
Hamilton, James, Peterboro', O
Kane, Roderick A. C., Montreal
Maclaren, George McG., Ottawa, O

MacMaster, Arthur F., Montreal
MacMillan, George P., Petrolia, O
Millar, James L., Pembroke, O
Miller, Angus K., Bridgeburg, O
Montgomery, George, Morrisburg, O
Moore, Ernest Vivian, Peterboro', O
Nelson, George J., Montreal
Neville, Thomas P. J., Halifax, N.S
Ogilvie, Norman C, Montreal
Osborne, J. Ewart, Toronto, O
Percy, Howard M., Montreal
Pyke, Gordon McT., Montreal
Robertson, Philip W. K., Mexico City, Mexico
Rolland, Jean, St. Jerome, Que
Scott, George W, Montreal
Shepherd, Harry L., Brockville, O
Sise, Paul F., Montreal
Smith, George B., Stratford, O
*Staveley, Edward B., Quebec, Q
St. George, Harry L, Montreal
*Toole, John L., Montreal
*Trenholme, Arthur, Montreal
Walker, Frank W., Montreal
Whiteway, William V. E., St. Johns, Nfld

THIRD YEAR.

Archibald, Ernest M, Halifax, N.S
Austin, Claude V. C., Ottawa, O
Bachand, George A., Montreal
Blaylock, Selwyn G., Danville, Q

Bowman, Arch'd A., New Glasgow, N.S
Burgess, R. Earl, Wolfville, N.S
Campbell, Norman M., Montreal
Colpitts, Walter W., Moncton, N.B

Cornwall, Clement A. K., Ashcroft, B.C
Dargavel, James S.,   Elgin, O
Davidson, William A.,   Peterboro, O
Denis, Leopold,   Montreal
Ewen, Herbert M.,   Montreal
Fetherstonhaugh. Ed. P.,   Montreal
Fraser, Charles E.,   Montreal
Fraser, Harold,   Brockville, O
Fraser, James W.,   Bridgeville, N.S
Gagnon, Louis F.,   Montreal
Gamble, William Paul, Cumberland, O
Gisborne, Lionel L.,   Ottawa, O
Gough, Richard T.,   Halifax, N. S
Grier, Arthur G.,   Montreal
Hawker, James T.,   St. John, N.B
Henderson, Richard A., Chilliwack,B.C
Hickey, John V.,   Montreal
Hutchinson, William S.,   Montreal
Hyde, George T.,   Montreal
Hyde, James C.,   Montreal
Kirkpatrick, Stafford F.,   Kingston, O
MacInnes, Henry W.   Halifax, N.S

McLaren, Archibald J ,   Montreal
McLean, William B ,   Pictou, N.S
McLeod, Norman M.,   Montreal
Moore, Wm. M. Agnew,   Ottawa, O
Moore, William A.,   Toronto, O
Morgan, Charles B.,   Hamilton, O
Nicholls, Harry G.,   Toronto O
Olds, William T.,   Simcoe, O
Parizeau, Henri D.,   Boucherville, Q
Peden, Frank,   Montreal
Pergau, Harry,   Lyn, O
Pitcher, Norman C.,   Montreal
Preston, John,   Toronto, O
Shaw, John A ,   Montreal
Stevens, Angus P.   Dunham, Q
Van Horne, Richard B.,   Montreal
Waller, George W.,   Bartonville, O
Wenger Edgar I.,   Ayton, O
Whyte, John S.,   Osgood, O
Wilson, Robert M.,   Montreal
Young, William M.,   Renfrew, O
Yuile, Norman M.,   Montreal

FOURTH YEAR.

Ainley, Charles N.,   Almonte, O
Anderson. Wm., Beaumont, Ottawa, O
Angel, Frederick W., St. John's, Nfld
Atchibald, Harry P., Antigonish, N. S
Atkinson, Donald C. T., Etchemin, Q
Atkinson, Wm. J.,   Glenboro, Man
Bacon, Frederick T. H.,   Montreal
Beatty, David H.,   Sarnia, O
Benny, Walter W.,   D'Aillebour, Q
Bond, Frank L. C..   Montreal
Butler, Percy,   Montreal
Cape, Edmund G.,   Hamilton, O
Davidson J. Herbert,   Montreal
Davis, Angus W.,   Montreal
Dean, Bertram D.,   Hamilton, O
Drysdale, Geo. A., Boston, Mass, U.S A
Eaves, Edmund,   Montreal
Hillary, Geo. M.,   Whitby, O
Irving, Thos. T., Vernon River Bridge, P.E.1
Laurie, Albert,   Montreal
Mackerras, John D.,   Kingston, O

Mackie, James D.,   Kingston, O
MacLean, Thomas A., Charlottetown. P.E I
Maclennan, Frank W.,   Cornwall, O
MacPhail, Wm. M.,   Orwell, P.E.I
Matheson, Ernest G., Oyster Bed Bridge, P E I
McCarthy, George A.,   Moncton, N.B
McLea, Ernest H.,   Montreal
McRae, John B.,   Ottawa, O
Patton, Walter H.,   Huntingdon, Q
Reaves, Campbell,   Montreal
Scott, Arthur P.,   Montreal
Scott, James H ,   Outremont, Q
Sheffield, Charles,   Kingston, O
Simpson, J. Manley,   Toronto, O
Summa, Vito M.,   Avigliano, Italy
Thomas, Leonard E L., Melbourne, Q
Waterous, Charles A.,   Brantford, O
Yorston, Louis,   Pictou, N.S
Young, George A.,   Kingston, O

GRADUATES.

Cole, Arthur A.,B.A.Sc., Rossland, B.C
Dougall, Ralph B.A.Sc.,   Montreal
Drinkwater, Chas. G., B.A.Sc., Montreal
Green. J. Raoul, B.A.Sc., Rossland, B.C
Gill, James L. W., B.A.Sc., Little York, P.E.I

King, Robert O , B.A.Sc., Toronto, O
Ross, John K. L., B.A.Sc.,   Montreal
Strickland, Tom P., B.E., Sydney, N.S.W., Australia
Stovel, Russell W., B.A.Sc., Toronto, O
Symmes, Howard C., B.A.Sc , Aylmer, Q

Partial Students.

Colby, Mrs. C. W.,   Montreal
Edgar, Miss,   Montreal
Hill, Miss,   Montreal
Hoffman, Auguste, Eberfeld, Rhineland, Germany

Molson, Mrs. M.,   Montreal
Powell, John P.,   Carbonear, Nfld
Redpath, Miss H.,   Montreal
Trotter, Miss,   Montreal

FACULTY OF COMPARATIVE MEDICINE AND VETERINARY SCIENCE.

FIRST YEAR.

Allen, Frank T.,   Springfield, Mass | Smith, W. C.,   Winnipeg, Man
Hayes, T.,   Waltham, Mass | Stanbridge, Geo W., Hubbardston, Mass
Humphreys, Bernard K.,   Boston, Mass

SECOND YEAR.

Gellatley, Geo.,   Huntingdon, Que | Kato, Y.,   Tokio, Japan
Groves, John W.,   Hamilton, O | McGregor, Jas.,   Aubrey, Que
Hammond, Geo. W.,   Montreal

THIRD YEAR.

Baldwin, B. K.,   Philadelphia, Pa | Lambert, G. H.,   Ashville, N.C
Bell, W. Lincoln,   Brooklyn, N.Y | Paquin, L. A.,   Northampton, Mass
Burke, R. H.,   Rock Island, Que | Pfersick, J. G.,   Shelburne Falls, Mass
Cleaves, A. H.,   Bar Harbour, Me | Spanton, J. P.,   Dover, England
Cullen, D.,   Boston, Mass | Symes, J. W.,   Leeds, Que
Fahey, John,   Mt. Carmel, Conn | Wallis, W. B.,   Colchester, England
Hart, J. B.,   Montreal

COLLEGES AFFILIATED IN ARTS.

MORRIN COLLEGE, QUEBEC

Undergraduates.

FIRST YEAR.

Fraser, Ella M., | Reid, Allan S.,
May, Fanjoy C., | Smith, Essie.
Nicholson, William,

SECOND YEAR.

Fyles, Faith, | Pidgeon, E. Leslie,
Laverie, James H., | Ritchie, Jessie R.,
MacRae, Donald N., | Rothney, William O.

THIRD YEAR.

Jackson, Emma, | Seifert, Fred W.,

Partial Students.

Beemer, N. E., | Cockburn, Mrs. F ,
Bignell, A. E., | Cook, M.,
Bonham, E., | Cook, Mrs. A. H.,
Boswell, M. L., | Dankerley, C. F.,
Clapham, M. B. S., | Duffete, G.,
Cleary, F. L. S., | Duggan, Mrs. F. M.,

Duplessis, L.,
Foote, M.,
Fry, E. M.,
Fry, Frances M.,'
Gilmour, H. M.
Graham, P. H.,
Grant, Jean,
Gwyn, E. P.,
Hamilton, M.,
Henderson, M.,
Hicks, M. E.,
Holloway, A.,
Holt, Mrs. J ,
Hunter, Louise L ,
King, Mrs.,
Laurie, Mrs. H.,
Lee, M.,
Le Vasseur, W.,
Macrae, C ,
Macrae, V.,
Macdonald E.,
MacNaughton, T. M.,
Meiklejohn, Harriet T.,
Miller, L. C.,
McCutcheon, O. F.,

McLeod, E ,
McLimont, A ,
Poston, Mrs. T. E.,
Reid, L.,
Ritchie, M. A.,
Ritchie, Mrs. John,
Rondeau, C. E.,
Ross, Mrs. A. D.,
Sewell, C. M.,
Simpson, May,
Smith, Mrs.,
Sparling, Wm.,
Stevenson, A.,
Tait, Donald,
Thomson, J. H.,
Tremaine, L. L.,
Von Iffland, K.,
Walters, A. E.,
Walton, Mrs. F. W.,
Webb, Mrs. E. E.,
Webster, M.,
Wheeler, James,
Winn, H. E.,
Wood, H. B.,

ST. FRANCIS COLLEGE, RICHMOND.

Undergraduates.

FIRST YEAR.

Cross, Ruby M.,
Fee, James E.,

Fuller, George D.,
Kellock, Jessie J.

Partial Student.

Ewing Wm. J.

STANSTEAD WESLEYAN COLLEGE.

Undergraduates.

FIRST YEAR.

Page, Harriet A.

SECOND YEAR

Flint, Mary,
Flint, Roy,

Hill, O. Wendell.

Partial Student.

Dobson, Perry A.

SUMMARY.

Students in Law, McGill College			47
" in Medicine, "			429
" in Arts:— "			

	Men	Graduates	7	
		Undergraduates	159	
		Partial	83	370
	Women	Graduates	9	
		Undergraduates	54	
		Partial	58	

Total in Arts including Students from other Faculties, about 650		
Students in Arts, Morrin College		74
" " " St. Francis College		5
" " " Stanstead Wesleyan College		5
" " Applied Science, McGill College :—		
Undergraduates, Partial and Graduates		226
" " Veterinary Science		23
		1179
McGill Normal School, Teachers-in-training		168
		1347
Deduct, repeated in different lists		24
Total		1323

Observatory.

Latitude, N. 45° 30′ 17″. Longitude, 4ʰ 54ᵐ 18ˢ. 67.

Height above sea level, 187 ft.

Superintendent—C. H. McLeod, Ma.E.

Assistant—George R. McLeod, B.A.Sc.

Meteorological Observations are made every fourth hour, beginning 3ʰ0ᵐ Eastern standard time; also at 8ʰ 0ᵐ and 20ⁿ 0ᵐ. Independent series of bi-hourly temperature observations are also made. The principal instruments employed are two standard mercurial barometers; one Kew standard thermometer; two Pastorelli thermometers; one maximum thermometer; one minimum thermometer; one set of six self-recording thermometers, with controlling clock, battery, etc.; two anemometers; one wind vane (wind-mill pattern); one anemograph, with battery, etc.; one sunshine recorder; one rain-band spectroscope; and one rain gauge.

The Anemometer and Vane are on the summit of Mount Royal at a point about three-quarters of a mile northwest of the Observatory. They are 57 feet above the surface of the ground and 810 feet above sea level.

Soil temperatures are observed, in co-operation with the Physical Laboratory, by means of platinum thermometers at depths ranging from one inch to nine feet.

The Astronomical Equipment consists of :—The Blackman Telescope (6¼ in.); a photoheliograph (4½ in.); a 3¼ in. transit, with striding level, etc.; a prismatic (8 c.m.) transit instrument also arranged as a zenith telescope, a 2 in. transit in the prime vertical ; two collimating telescopes; one sidereal clock; one meantime clock; one sidereal chronometer; one meantime chronometer; one chronograph; batteries, telegraph lines and sundry minor instruments.

Observations for clock errors are made on nearly every clear night. Time exchanges are regularly made with the Toronto Observatory. Time signals are distributed throughout the city by means of the noon time-ball, continuous clock signals, and the fire alarm bells; and to the country, through the telegraph lines.

The longitude of the Observatory was determined in 1892 by direct telegraphic connection with Greenwich and with exchange of observers and instruments. The position is believed to be the most accurately determined in America.

Courses of instruction are given in the use of the meteorological instruments, see page 31, and in astronomical work to the Fourth Year Students in the Civil Engineering Courses, see page 114.

University Gymnasium.

Medical Examiner and Instructor.—R. TAIT McKENZIE, B.A., M.D.

The classes, which are open to Students of all the Faculties, will meet at the University Gymnasium, at hours to suit, as far as possible, the convenience of Students, and which will be announced at the commencement of the Session.

The recent addition of some special apparatus enables the instructor to devote some attention to the application of exercise in treating special cases of weakness or deformity, which should be reported to him before the regular class work is undertaken.

THE WICKSTEED SILVER AND BRONZE MEDALS FOR PHYSICAL CULTURE (the gift of Dr. R. J. Wicksteed) are offered for competition to Students of the graduating class and to Students who have had instruction in the Gymnasium for two sessions: the silver medal to the former, the bronze medal to the latter.

The award of these medals is made by Judges, appointed by the Corporation of the University.

Every competitior for the silver medal is required to lodge with the Judges, before the examination, a certificate of good standing in the graduating class signed by the Dean or Secretary of the Faculty to which he belongs, and the medal will not be awarded to any Student who may fail in his examination for the degree.

Classes for the Students of the DONALDA SPECIAL COURSE FOR WOMEN will be conducted by MISS BARNJUM at hours found most suitable.

REGULATIONS.

CONCERNING THE MANAGEMENT OF

THE COLLEGE GROUNDS AND ATHLETICS.

All matters relating to the management of the College grounds and of Out-Door Athletics and Sports are under the control of a Committee consisting of :—

One Governor.
The Principal.
One Member of the Faculty of Arts.
One Member of the Faculty of Applied Science.
One Member of the Faculty of Law.
One Member of the Faculty of Medicine.
One Member of the Faculty of Comp. Medicine.
One Graduate.

One Undergraduate, member of the Football Club.
One Undergraduate, member of the Tennis Clubs.
One Undergraduate, member of the Cricket Club.
One Undergraduate, member of the Hockey Club.
The President of the Athletic Association.

The several Members of the Committee are elected annually by their respective bodies; and the Committee meets for organization on the first Saturday of February in each year. The Undergraduate Members of the Committee are entitled to vote only on matters relating to Athletics.

———

The following extracts are made from the rules and regulations of the Committee, for the guidance of Members of the University and the several Athletic Clubs and Associations which are from time to time permitted to use the grounds :

The University and McTavish Street gates shall be closed between 6 p.m. and 7 a.m. on week days and the whole day on Sunday.

The Sherbrooke Street gates shall be closed between 10 p.m. and 6 a.m.

Such persons as are entitled to use the Grounds shall be provided with tickets renewable each year.

Those entitled to tickets are the Members of the University and promient Benefactors, and the families of Governors and Professors.

The several Clubs shall be permitted to issue special tickets (without charge), entitling the holders to admission to the Grounds for the purpose of viewing matches, or for other special occasions of public interest.

All Students desirous of taking part in football matches, or otherwise engaging in violent athletic contests, must pass a medical examination, to be held under the direction of the Superintendent of the Gymnasium. A complete record of all such examinations shall be kept by the Superintendent or other officer appointed to this duty.

All Clubs must submit their Regulations, Rules and By-Laws, and any changes in the same, for the approval of the Committee. They must make application for the use of such portions of the Grounds as they require, and for any special privileges.

The Athletic Association must submit its programme for each year for the approval of the Committee.

All Undergraduates of the University are required to pay a fee of two dollars ($2.00) for the use of the Grounds. The amount so paid is handed over to the Committee, and is by it expended in the interest of College Athletics and in the permanent improvement of the Grounds.

University Societies.

GRADUATES' SOCIETY OF McGILL UNIVERSITY.

INCORPORATED 24TH JULY, 1880.

Officers 1898-99.

President—C. W. Colby, M.A., Ph.D.
Vice-Presidents—Miss H. R. Y. Reid, B.A.; Miss C. M. Derick, M.A.; Peers Davidson, M.A.
Secretary—Homer M. Jaquays, B.A., B.A.Sc.
Treasurer—Francis Topp, B.A., B.C.L.
Resident Councillors—F. D. Adams, M.A.Sc., Ph.D.; M. C. Baker, D.V.S.; Arch. MacArthur, B.A.; A. R. Holden, B.A., B.C.L.; A. R. Hall, B.A., B.C.L.; Chas. Wilson, M.D.
Non-Resident Councillors—Hon. W. W. Lynch, D.C.L., Knowlton, Que.; Rev. E. H. Krans, LL.D., New York; S. J. Tunstall, B.A., M.D., C.M., Vancouver, B.C.; W. W. White, M.A., M.D., St. John, N.B.; Robert H. Conroy, B.C.L., Aylmer, Que.; J. J. MacLaren, Q.C., LL.D., Toronto, Ont.

THE APPLIED SCIENCE GRADUATES' SOCIETY.

Honorary-President—Dr. H. T. Bovey.
President—J. M. McCarthy.
Vice-President—Prof. F. D. Adams.
Sec.-Treas.—J. G. G. Kerry, Engineering Building, McGill University.
Resident Committee—W. F. Angus, J. W. Bell, A. L. Mudge, R. O. King, R. H. Jamieson.
Non-resident Committee—R. B. Rogers, Peterboro, O.; A. A. Cole, Rossland, B.C.; W. P. Laurie, Quebec, Q.; W. G. Smart, Sherbrooke, Q.; J. K. Scammell, Fairville, N.B.; H. M. McKay, Pictou, N.S.; W. J. Bulman, Charlottetown, P.E.I.; O. S. Whiteside, Anthracite, N.W.T.; J. M. McGregor, Rossland, B.C.; E. H. Hamilton, Pueblo, Col., U.S.A.; P. N. Evans, Lafayette, Ind., U.S.A.; G. H. Frost, New York, U.S.A.; L. L. Street, Marlboro, Mass., U.S.A.

ALUMNÆ SOCIETY OF McGILL UNIVERSITY.

President—Georgina Hunter, B.A.
Vice-Presidents—Kate M. Campbell, B.A.; L. Ethel Armstrong, B.A.
Cor.-Secretary—Carrie M. Derick, M.A.

Assistant Cor.-Sec.—J. Ethel Hurst, B.A.
Rec.-Secretary—Elizabeth Hall, B.A.
Assistant Rec.-Sec.—Eleanor Tatley, B.A.
Tacasurer—H. Inez R. Botterell, B.A.
Additional Members of Committee of Management of Girls' Club—
Helen R. Y. Reid, B.A.; Alice Murray, B.A.; Rosalia F. Campbell,
B.A.

OTTAWA VALLEY GRADUATES' SOCIETY.

ORGANIZED 1890.

Honorary President—The Rt.-Hon. Sir Wilfrid Laurier. P.C.,
K.C.M.G., LL.D.
President—R. W. Ells, M.A., LL.D.
Vice-Presidents—W. C. Cousens, M.D., C.M.; G. C. Wright. B.A.,
B.C.L.; D. B. Dowling, B.A.Sc.
Treasurer—J. Herbert Larmonth, B.A.Sc.
Secretary—J. F. Warne, B.A. (106½ Sparks Street).
Committee—R. F. Conroy, B.C.L.; A. E. Barlow, M.A.; James Mc-
Evoy, B.A.Sc.; E. L. Quirk, M.D., C.M.; Henry M. Ami. M.A.,
D.Sc.

NEW YORK GRADUATES SOCIETY OF McGILL
UNIVERSITY.

ORGANIZED 1895.

President—Rev. Edward H. Krans, M.A., LL.D.
Vice-Presidents—Wolfred D. E. Nelson, M.D.; James A. Meek,
M.D.; Wm. de Courcy Harnett, B.C.L.
Secretary—W. Ferguson, M.D., 948 E. 166th St., New York.
Treasurer—Hiram N. Vineberg, M.D.
Executive Committee—Rev. J. J. Rowan Spong, M.A., B.C.L., LL.B.;
Geo. C. Becket, M.D.; James A. Stevenson, B.A.Sc.
Non-Resident Councillors—Right Rev. J. D. Morrison, M.A., D.D.,
Bishop of Duluth ; Rev. Charles Bancroft, M.A., New Hampshire ;
William Osler. M.D., Baltimore, Md.; Thomas Kelly, M.D., Omaha,
Neb. ; Rev. J. C. Bracq, Vassar College, N.Y. ; H. Holton Wood,
B.A., Derby, Conn.

McGILL GRADUATES SOCIETY OF TORONTO.

ORGANIZED 1896.

Hon.-President—E. A. Meredith, LL.D.
President—J. J. MacLaren, Q.C., LL.D.
1st Vice-President—H. A. Burritt, M.D.
2nd Vice-President—A. R. Lewis, B.A., Q.C.
Secretary—R. B. Henderson, B.A., 24 Adelaide street East.
Treasurer—A. H. U. Colquhoun, B.A.
Executive Committee—J. Algernon Temple, M.D. ; C. Swabey, B.A. ; P. E. Ritchie, B.A. ; Rev. Canon Sweeney, D.D. ; George Pringle, M.D.; Frank Pedley, B.A.

THE BRITISH COLUMBIAN SOCIETY OF GRADUATES OF McGILL UNIVERSITY.

ORGANIZED 1896.

Hon.-President—I. W. Powell, M.D. (Victoria).
President—E. B. C. Hannington, M.D. (Victoria).
Vice-Presidents—Wm. A. DeWolff-Smith, M.D. (New Westminster); J. M. McGregor, B.A.Sc. (Rossland); R. E. McKechnie, M.D., C.M. (Nanaimo); Rev. J. S. Gordon, B.A. (Vancouver).
Secretary—W. J. McGuigan, M.D., LL.B. (Vancouver).
Treasurer—Simon J. Tunstall, B.A., M.D. (Vancouver).
Executive Committee—W. A. Carlyle, B.A.Sc. (Victoria); D. B. Holden, B.A., M.D., (Victoria); Alfred Poole, M.D., (Vancouver); W. S. Johnson, B.A.Sc. (Slocan City); Rev. H. M. McIntosh, B.A. (New Westminster).

THE NEW BRUNSWICK GRADUATES' SOCIETY OF McGILL UNIVERSITY.

ORGANIZED 1896.

President—F. H. Wetmore, M.D. (Hampton, N.B.).
Vice-President—B. S. Price, M.D. (St. John, N.B.).
Secretary-Treasurer—J. H. Scammell, M.D. (76 Waterloo street, St. John, N.B.).
Executive Committee—J. H. King, M.D.; W. L. Ellis, M.D.

NOVA SCOTIA SOCIETY OF McGILL GRADUATES.

ORGANIZED 1896.

Hon.-President—Rev. Robert Laing, M.A. (Halifax).
President—John McMillan, M.D. (Pictou).
1st Vice-President—E. A. Kirkpatrick, M.D. (Halifax).
2nd Vice-President—Wm. Jakeman, D.V.S.

352

Secretary-Treasurer—W. H. Hattie, M.D. (11 Spring Garden Road, Halifax).
Executive Committee—A. A. Mackay, B.A.; N. Ayer, M.D.; F. S. Yorston, M.D.; James Ross, M.D.

McGILL GRADUATES' SOCIETY OF THE DISTRICT OF BEDFORD.

1898.

PROVISIONAL OFFICERS.

President—Hon. W. W. Lynch, D.C.L.
Vice-Presidents—R. C. McCorkill, M.D.; Rev. E. M. Taylor, M.A.; C. A. Nutting, B.C.L.
Sec.-Treasurer—Rev. Jas. A. Elliott, B.A.
Committee—J. C. McCorkill. B.C.L. ; Hon. H. T. Duffy, M.A., B.C.L.; Rev. W. T. Gunn, M.A.; H. Leroy Fuller, B.A., M.D.; Rev. Jas. A. Elliott, B.A.

UNDERGRADUATES' LITERARY SOCIETY.

CONSTITUTED 1880.

President—W. Gordon Bishop, Arts, '98.
1st Vice-Pres.—W. Ball, Law, '99.
2nd Vice-Pres.—E. V. M. Hunter, Med., '01.
Secretary—Lemuel Robertson, Arts, '99.
Assist.-Secretary—A. W. Lockhead, Arts, '01.
Treasurer—Robert C. Paterson, Arts, '98.
Committee—R. H. Rogers, B.A., Law '98 ; S. G. Archibald, B.A., Law, '00; A. H. Duff, Arts, '98; W. G. Brown, Arts, '99; F. S. Patch, Arts, '99.

DELTA SIGMA SOCIETY.

ESTABLISHED 1884

OFFICERS FOR 1898-99.

President—Kathleen Finley.
Vice-President—Helena Dey.
Sec.-Treasurer—Evelyn Molson.
Committee—Misses F. Botterell, B.A., L. MacDougall, I. Radford, J. Budden.

McGILL COLLEGE CLASSICAL CLUB.

For the purpose of fostering a greater interest in and promoting the further study of Classical Languages, Literature and Art.

Hon.-President—Principal Peterson.
Hon.-Treasurer—Prof. A. Judson Eaton, Ph.D.
President—D. W. Munn, Arts '99·
1st Vice-President—M. Carr, Arts, '98·
2nd Vice-President—L. Robertson, Arts, '99·
Secretary—C. C. Ferguson, Arts, '99·
Treasurer—F. S. Patch, Arts, '99·
Executive Committee—S. B. Slack, M.A.; Prof. C. Colby, M.A., Ph.D.; L. E. Potter, Arts, '99·

APPLIED SCIENCE SOCIETY.

ORGANIZED 1897.

Hon.-President—Prof. H. T. Bovey.
President—W. W. Colpitts, representing Civil Engineering and Architecture.
1st Vice-President—S. F. Kirkpatrick, representing Mining Engineering and Chemistry.
2nd Vice-President—R. M. Wilson, representing Electrical Engineering.
3rd Vice-President—J. S. Whyte, representing Mechanical Engineering.
Secretary—J. G. Glassco.
Treasurer—R. H. Gillean.
Second Year Representatives—B. S. McKenzie, P. Ogilvie.

THE McGILL MINING SOCIETY.

ORGANIZED 1891.

Honorary President—Dr. B. J. Harrington.
President—J. E. Preston, App. Sc., '99·
Sec.-Treasurer—R. H. Gillean, App. Sc., '00·

YOUNG MEN'S CHRISTIAN ASSOCIATION OF McGILL UNIVERSITY.

OBJECT.—To promote the piety of its members and the cause of Christianity in the University.

MEMBERSHIP.—The active Membership of the Association shall consist of Graduates and Students of the University who are members of some Protestant church. Any Graduate and Student of good moral character may become an associate member. A social reception is given to new students at the beginning of the session.

Officers for 1898.

Hon.-President—Sir J. W. Dawson.
President—A. H. Gordon, Med. '99·
1st Vice-President—R. C. Paterson, B.A., Med. '02·
2nd Vice-President—J. S. Whyte, App. Sc. '99·
Recording Secretary—W. H. De Blais, App. Sc. '01
Treasurer—W. S. Galbraith, Med. '99·
Asst.-Treasurer—G. W. Irving, Arts '01·
General Secretary—A. H. Grace, B.A.

CHAIRMEN OF COMMITTEES.

Religious Meeting—Prof. H. F. Armstrong.
Bible Study—C. E. Fraser, App. Sc. '99·
Social—R. C. Paterson, B.A., Med. '02·
Membership—A. H. Gordon, Med. '99·
Missionary—C. Macpherson, Med. '00·
Musical—H. M. Lloyd, App. Sc. '01·
Finance—W. S. Galbraith, Med. '99·
Work for New Students—A. H. Grace, B.A.
Building—A. H. Gordon, Med. '99·
Graduate—W. L. Hamilton, M.D.

YOUNG WOMEN'S CHRISTIAN ASSOCIATION.

ESTABLISHED 1887 (AS THEO DORA SOCIETY).

OBJECT.—The development of Christian character in the members, and the development of active Christian work, particularly among the young women of the University. Open for membership to students of the Donalda Special Course for Women.

SESSION 1898-99·

President—Christina King.
Vice-President—Edythe Garlick.
Cor.-Secretary—Margaret Brodie.
Rec.-Secretary—Winifred Bennett.
Treasurer—Alice Kingsley.

Devotional—Catherine Armstrong.
Theo Dora—Lillian Smith.
Membership—Anna Scrimger.
Relief—Helena Dey.

McGILL UNIVERSITY ATHLETIC ASSOCIATION.

ESTABLISHED 1884.

Hon.-President—Principal Peterson.
President—R. A. A. Shore, Med. '99·
Vice-President—J. W. Woodley, Arts '00·
Secretary—J. L. Todd, Arts, '98·
Treasurer—H. P. Hill, Med. '00·
Representatives: Arts—P. Molson, '01; Law—W. M. Robertson, '99; Medicine—Walter Wilkins, '99; Applied Science—Rupert Howard, '00; Comp. Medicine—Geo. Galletly, '99·

McGILL UNIVERSITY RUGBY CLUB.

Hon.-President—Principal Peterson.
Hon.-Treasurer—Dr. J. M. Elder.
President—R. O. King, B.A.Sc.
Vice-President—G. T. Alley, Med. '99.
Manager—C. P. Howard, B.A., Med. '00·
Hon.-Secretary—W. H. Sutherland, Med. '99·
Treasurer—S. A. Ross, Med. '99·
Captain 1st XV.—A. H. Grace, Arts '98·
Captain 2nd XV.—A. Glassco, App. Sci. '01·
Captain, 3rd XV.—J. Mowatt, Arts '01·
Committee.—Arts: Percy Molson, '01· L. Reford, '00; Medicine : W. H. P. Hill, '00· P. Duffy, '00; App. Science: W. M. Young, '99· N. Ogilvie, '00; Law: S. G. Archibald, B.A., '00· W. G. M. Robertson, '99; Vet. Science: E. W. Hammond, '99· Y. Kato, '99·

McGILL CRICKET CLUB.

President—Prof. C. E. Moyse, B.A.
Vice-President—A. B. Wood, B.A.
Acting Sec.-Treas.—W. W. Walker, (Box 514 P.O.)
Executive Committee—A. R. Oughtred, B.C.L.; J. F. Mackie, B.C.L.; E. McLea, Sc., '98: H. W. Wonham, H. C. Hill.

McGILL LAWN TENNIS CLUB.

Hon.-President—Prof. H. L. Callendar.
President—J. R. Kennedy, Law '98·
Vice-President—J. A. Fairie, Med. '99·
Secretary—F. T. H. Bacon, App. Sc. '98·
Treasurer—E. A. Grafton, M.D.
Committee—G. T. Hyde, App. Sc. '99; N. M. Burke, Arts '00 ;
A. C. P. Howard, Med. '01; E. Burke, Law '00; — Humphries,
Comp. Medicine.

McGILL UNIVERSITY SKATING CLUB.

President—A. W. Davis, App. Sc. '98·
Vice-President—R. H. Rogers, B.A.
Treasurer—E. W. Hammond.
Secretary—R. C. Paterson, Arts '98·
Committee.—Medicine: S. A. Ross, '99; J. L. Todd, '00; M. Hut-
chison, '01; Applied Science: A. W. Davis, '98; H. P. Archibald,
'98; W. W. Colpitts, '99; Arts: R. C. Paterson, '98; F. S. Patch, '99;
E. Shepherd, '00; Law: R. H. Rogers, B.A., '98; M. Robertson, '99;
Comp. Medicine: E. W. Hammond, '99; Y. Kato, '99·

McGILL HOCKEY CLUB.

President—W. G. Bishop, Arts '98·
Vice-President—Percy Butler, App. Sc. '98·
Sec.-Treasurer—Colin K. Russel, Med. '01·
Committee—Applied Science: N. M. Yuile, '99; L. O. Howard, '01;
Arts: P. Molson, '01; A. T. Rowell, '00; Medicine: Ross, '99; A. T.
Mussen, '98· Law: W. G. M. Robertson, '99; S. G. Archibald, '00.

McGILL GLEE, BANJO AND MANDOLIN CLUB.

OFFICERS FOR 1898-99.

Hon.-President—Prof. Capper.
President—W. W. Colpitts, App. Sc. '99·
Vice-President—R. E. McConnell, Arts '98, Med. '00·
Secretary—R. L. Gardner, Arts '99· Med. '01·
Business Manager—A. F. Byers, App. Sc. '00·
Asst. Business Manager—G. T. Hyde, App. Sc. '99·
Leader Glee Club—E. Burke, Law '00·
Asst. Leader Glee Club—(Unappointed.)
Leader Banjo Club—(Acting)—R. E. McConnell.
Asst. Leader Banjo Club—(Unappointed.)
Leader Mandolin Club—D. F. Wood, Med. '98·

𝕸𝖈𝕲𝖎𝖑𝖑 𝖀𝖓𝖎𝖛𝖊𝖗𝖘𝖎𝖙𝖞, 𝕸𝖔𝖓𝖙𝖗𝖊𝖆𝖑.

I. GENERAL ENDOWMENTS AND SUBSCRIPTIONS.

1. ORIGINAL ENDOWMENT, 1811.

THE HONORABLE JAMES McGILL, who was born at Glasgow 6th Oct. 1744, and died at Montreal, 19th Dec , 1813, by his last will and testament, under date 8th January, 1811, devised the estate of Burnside, situated near the city of Montreal, and containing forty-seven acres of land, with the Manor House and Buildings thereon erected, and also bequeathed the sum of ten thousand pounds in money unto the " Royal Institution for the Advancement of Learning," a Corporation constituted in virtue of an Act of Parliament passed in the Forty-first Year of the Reign of His Majesty, King George the Third, to erect and establish a University or College, for the purpose of Education and the advancement of learning, in the Province of Lower Canada, with a competent number of Professors and teachers to render such Establishment effectual and beneficial for the purposes intended ; requiring that one of the colleges to be comprised in the said University should be named and perpetually be known and distinguished by the appellation of " McGill College.' '
The value of the above mentioned property was estimated at the date of the bequest at.......... .... $120,000

2. UNIVERSITY BUILDINGS, ETC.

THE WILLIAM MOLSON HALL, being the west wing of McGill College buildings with the connecting Corridors and Class Rooms, was erected in 1861,through the munificent donation of the founder whose name it bears.

THE PETER REDPATH MUSEUM, the gift of the donor whose name it bears, was announced by him as a donation to the University in 1880, and formally opened August, 1882.

Lots for University buildings adjoining the College grounds confronting on McTavish St., presented by J. H. R. Molson, Esq.,—$42,500.

THE UNIVERSITY LIBRARY BUILDING, the gift of Peter Redpath, Esq., announced by him as a gift to the University in 1891, and formally opened Oct. 31st, 1893.

UNIVERSITY OFFICES, Rooms in East Wing remodeled and furnished for offices of Principal and Secretary and for a Board Room by W. C. McDonald, Esq., in 1895.

3. ENDOWED CHAIRS, ETC.

THE JOHN FROTHINGHAM PRINCIPAL FUND, to be invested for the endowment of the Principalship of the University; founded in 1889 by the Rev. Frederick Frothingham and Mrs. J. H. R. Molson,—$40,000.

THE WILLIAM C. McDONALD AUXILIARY FUND, founded in 1897, by W. C. McDonald, Esq., the interest to be used solely to maintain the income of certain of his endowments on a five per cent. per annum basis,—$227,500.

4. ENDOWMENTS AND DONATIONS OF MEDALS AND PRIZES.

In 1883, a Gold, a Silver and a Bronze Medal were given by R. J. Wicksteed, Esq , M.A., LL D., for competition in " Physical Culture," by Students in the Graduating Class and second year of any Faculty, who have attended the University Gymnasium. The Gold Medal was continued to 1889 and the Silver and Bronze have been continued to date.

Ottawa Valley Graduates' Society's Exhibition. For competition by candidates
from the Ottawa Valley at the June matriculation examinations of any
Faculty. Value, $50.00. Given annually since 1895.
A Prize given by the British Columbia Society of Graduates of McGill University
to be divided amongst the five Faculties. Annual value $50.00. Given an-
nually since 1896.

5. SUBSCRIPTIONS TO GENERAL ENDOWMENT.

1856.

John Frothingham, Esq	$2000	Forward	$19,200
John Torrance, Esq	2000	Moses E. David, Esq	600
James B. Greenshields, Esq	1200	Wm. Carter, Esq	600
Wm. Busby Lambe, Esq	1200	Thomas Patton, Esq	600
Sir George Simpson, Knight	1000	Wm. Workman, Esq	600
Henry Thomas, Esq	1000	Hon. Luther H. Holton	600
John Redpath, Esq	1000	Henry Lyman, Esq	600
James McDougall, Esq	1000	David Torrance, Esq	000
James Torrance, Esq	1000	Edwin Atwater, Esq	600
Hon. James Ferrier	1000	Theodore Hart, Esq	600
Harrison Stephens, Esq	800	Wm. Forsyth Grant, Esq	600
Henry Chapman, Esq	600	Robert Campbell, Esq	600
Hon. Peter McGill	600	Alfred Savage, Esq	600
John James Day, Esq	600	James Ferrier, jun., Esq	600
Thomas Brown Anderson, Esq	600	Wm. Stephen, Esq	600
Peter Redpath, Esq	600	N. S. Whitney, Esq	600
Thomas M. Taylor, Esq	600	William Dow, Esq	600
Joseph Mackay, Esq	600	William Watson, Esq	600
Donald Lorn McDougall, Esq	600	Edward and Alicia Major	600
Hon. Sir John Rose	600	Hon. Sir A. T. Galt	360
Charles Alexander, Esq	600	John R. Esdaile, Esq	200
Forward	$19,200	Total	$30,560

1871.

John Frothingham, Esq	$5150	Forward	$24,350
William Molson, Esq	5000	T. W. Ritchie, Esq	300
William C. McDonald, Esq	5000	Messrs. Sinclair, Jack & Co	250
Thomas Workman, Esq	5000	John Reddy, M.D	100
J. H. R. Molson, Esq	2000	Wm. Lunn, Esq	100
John McLennan, Esq	1000	Hon. F. W. Torrance	60
B. Gibb, Esq	600	Wm. Rose, Esq	50
Messrs. A. & W. Robertson	600		
Forward	$24,350	Total	$25,210

1881-82.

Hugh McLennan. Esq	$5000	Forward	$21,000
G. A. Drummond, Esq	4000	O. S. Wood, Esq	1000
George Hague, Esq	3000	J.B. Greenshields, Esq. (London)	1000
M. H. Gault, Esq	2000	Warden King, Esq	1000
Andrew Robertson, Esq	1000	W. P. Cumming, Esq	1000
Robertson Campbell, Esq	1000	Mrs. Hew Ramsay	500
Sir Jos. and Lady Hickson	1000	R. A. Ramsay, Esq	500
Mrs. Andrew Dow	1000	H. H. Wood, Esq	500
Alexander Murray, Esq	1000	James Burnett, Esq	500
Miss Orkney	1000	Charles Gibb, Esq	500
Hector McKenzie, Esq	1000	J. S. McLachlan, Esq	200
Forward	$21,000	Total	$27,700

1883-84.

Edward Mackay, Esq............................ ....$5,000

6. ENDOWMENT FUND FOR GENERAL PURPOSES.

1897.

Bequest of the late John H. R. Molson, Esq., $100,000.

7. SUBSCRIPTION FOR IMPROVEMENTS TO COLLEGE, 1856·

Hon. Charles Dewey Day......... .... $200

8. SUBSCRIPTIONS FOR CURRENT EXPENSES, 1881-82.

Principal Dawson..					$1000
J. H. R. Molson, Esq............	1000	per annum,	5 years,	being......	5000
George Stephen, Esq......................	1000	"	"	"	5000
Hon. Donald A. Smith..	1000	"	"	"	5000
David Morrice, Esq......................	200	·	"	"	1000
Messrs. Gault Brothers & Co	200	"	"	"	1000
Messrs. S. H. & A. S. Ewing........	200	"	"	"	1000
Hon. Robert MacKay....................	300	"	2	"	600
Jonathan Hodgson, Esq...................	100	::	5	"	500
Geo. M. Kinghorn, Esq	100	··	"	" ,......	500
David J. Greenshields, Esq...........	......				300
Thomas Craig, Esq	100	"	2	"	200
John Rankin, Esq...					200
John Duncan, Esq..					200
George Brush, Esq., $25 for five years, being					125
Robert Benny, Esq...					100
Miss E. A. Ramsay,...					100
Hugh Paton, Esq,, $50 for two years, being...					100
J. M. Douglas, Esq					50
James Court, Esq...					50

Total $22,025

1887-88.

John H. R. Molson, Esq	$1000	per annum,	3 years,	being......	$3000
W. C. McDonald, Esq......................	1000	"	"	"	3000
Peter Redpath, Esq	1000	"	"	"	3000
Hon. Sir D. A. Smith, K.C.M.G.....:	1000	"	"	· ..	3000
Hon. James Ferrier......-..........	500	"	"	..	1500
Sir Joseph Hickson	500	"	"	..	1500
Hugh McLennan, Esq....................	250	"	"	" , ..	750
E, B. Greenshields, Esq	250	"	"	" .	750
George Hague, Esq......	250	"	"	" ,	750
John Molson, Esq........................	250	"	"		750
Samuel Finley, Esq	250	"	"		750
Mrs. Mackay, $100 annually, 1889 to 1893.......................................					500

Total............... $19,250

9. SUBSCRIPTIONS FOR A BUILDING FOR THE CARPENTER COLLECTION OF SHELLS.

1868.

Peter Redpath, Esq. ....$	500	Forward......$ 1,600	
William Molson, Esq.	500	Geo. H. Frothingham, Esq.........	100
Harrison Stephens, Esq............	100	Wm Dow, Esq	100
Robert J. Reekie, Esq..........	100	Thomas Rimmer, Esq	100
John H. R. Molson, Esq	100	Andrew Robertson, Esq......	100
Sir Wm. E. Logan, F.R.S.........	100	Mrs. Redpath	100
John Molson, Esq......	100	Benaiah Gibb, Esq......	50
Thos. Workman, Esq., M.P......	100	Hon. John Rose.........	50
Forward......$ 1,600		Total......$ 2,200	

10. SUBSCRIPTIONS FOR THE ERECTION OF THE LODGE AND GATES.

William Molson, Esq...........$	100	Forward ......$ 1,100	
John H. R. Molson, Esq...........	100	John Frothingham, Esq......	100
William Workman, Esq	100	James A. Mathewson, Esq.	100
Joseph Tiffin, jun., Esq.........	100	Peter Redpath, Esq	100
Thos. J. Claxton, Esq......	100	G. H. Frothingham, Esq......	100
James Linton, Esq.........	100	G. D. Ferrier, Esq............	100
William McDougall, Esq............	100	John Smith, Esq.........	100
Charles J. Brydges, Esq............	100	Charles Alexander, Esq............	100
George A. Drummond, Esq......	100	J. Evans, Esq	100
Thomas Rimmer, Esq.........	100	Henry Lyman, Esq.........	50
William Dow, Esq......	100		
		Total. ......$ 1,950	
Total......$ 1,100			

11. LIBRARY AND MUSEUM.

Special Collections of Books presented to the Library.

1. The Peter Redpath Collection of Historical Books, presented by Peter Redpath, Esq., of Montreal, 3,500 Volumes, with subsequent additions.
2. The Robson Collection of works in Archæology and General Literature, presented by Dr. John Robson, of Warrington, England, 3,436 Volumes.
3. The Charles Alexander Collection of Classical Works, presented by C. Alexander, Esq., of Montreal, 231 Volumes.
4. Frederick Griffin, Esq., Q. C., Collection of Books, being the whole of his Library, bequeathed by his will, 2695 Volumes.
5. The Hon. Mr. Justice Mackay, Collection of Books, being the whole of his Library, 2007 Volumes.
6. The "T. D. King Shakespeare Collection," presented by the Hon. Sir Donald A. Smith and W. C. McDonald, Esq, of Montreal, being 214 Volumes.

Endowments for Library.

Wm. Molson, Esq., for Endowment of a Library Fund (1871)$4,000		Forward......$ 6,000	
Hon. F. W. Torrance for Endowment of Mental, Moral and Political Philosophy Book Fund (1876)............	1,000	A friend, by the Hon. F. W. Torrance, for Endowment of a Library Fund (1882).........	400
Mrs. Redpath, for the Endowment of the Wm. Wood Redpath Memorial Fund (1881)......	1,000	Hugh S. McLennan, Library Endowment, a gift from Estate late Hugh S. McLennan to the Library of McGill College, the income to be applied to binding (1892)	250
Forward $6,000		Total $6,650	

Subscriptions, etc., to Library.

John Thorburn, for purchase of Books ....$ 90
Andrew Drummond, do., for Applied Science............................... 25
The Graduates in Arts and Applied Science of 1885 for purchase of Books 31
    do   do   of 1886 28
The late R. A. Ramsay, Esq., Bequest for purchase of books (1887). 1,000
Andrew Drummond, Esq., to Library Fund of Faculty of Applied Science............... 25
Hon. Sir Donald A. Smith, for purchase of books from the R. W. Boodle Library........ 200
Ottawa Valley Graduates' Society, for binding books in the University Library..... 25

Forward................$ 1,424

Forward.. ....$ 1,424
Peter Redpath, Esq., in aid of the new catalogue of the Library (1892).. 500
Mrs. Peter Redpath for maintenance of Library, $5,000 per annum since 1894 20,000
Hon. Sir Donald A. Smith, donation for the purchase of books for the Library, particularly in the French Department (1897) 250
John H. R. Molson, donation for purchase of books for the Library (1897)......... 195
Hon. Treas. Redpath Memorial Fund, London, England. The balance remaining over of the above fund, to be used for purchase of books for the Library..... 47

Total..... • $22,416

Special Collections presented to the Museum.

1. The Holmes Herbarium, presented by the late Andrew F. Holmes, M.D.
2. The Carpenter Collection of Shells, presented by the late P. P. Carpenter, Ph.D.
3. The Collection of Casts of Ivory Carvings, issued by the Arundel Society, presented by Henry Chapman, Esq.
4. The McCulloch Collection of Birds and Mammals, collected by the late Dr. M. McCulloch of Montreal, and presented by his heirs.
5. The Logan Memorial Collections of Specimens in Geology and Natural History, presented by the heirs of the Late Sir W. E. Logan, LL.D., F.R.S.
6. The Dawson Collection in Geology and Palæontology, being the Private Collections of Principal Dawson, presented by him to the Museum.
7. The Bowles Collection of Lepidoptera, presented by W. C. McDonald, Esq., and J. H. Burland, Esq.
8. R. Morton Middleton, jr., London, Eng., Collection of Plants.
9. Collection of Butterflies, presented by the Members of the Board of Governors of the University.
(See also "List of Donations to the Library and Museum," printed in the Annual Report of the University and Report of the Museum.)

Endowment for the Museum.

Wm. Molson, Esq., for the Endowment of a Museum Fund (1873). $2,000

Subscriptions, etc., for the Museum.

T. J. Claxton, Esq., for purchase of Specimens for Museum......................................$ 250

Peter Redpath, Esq., for Museum expenses, $1,000 per annum from 1882 to 1893................... 12,000

Mrs. Peter Redpath, for Museum expenses, 1894 to 1897......... 5,500

Mrs. H. G. Frothingham, for the arrangement of Dr. Carpenter's Collection of Mazatlan shells.................................... 233

Peter Redpath, Esq., for improvements to Museum (1891). 1,000

Forward. $18,983

Forward $18,983

A Lady, for Museum Expenses from 1882 to 1894................. 7,000

A friend, for the purchase of specimens for the Museum......... 4,300

John H. R. Molson, for purchase of books on "Butterflies of Eastern U S. and Canada."... 50

Hon. Sir Donald A. Smith, for mounting skin and skeleton of Musk Ox...... 150

Total................$30,483

12. MISCELLANEOUS.

Chas. T. Blackman, Esq., of Montreal. the gift of a Telescope and Astronomical Instruments called after his name.

J. J. Arnton bequest to McGill University (1895)............................... $ 900

R. A. Ramsay, M. A., B. C. L., to defray the expenses of re-erecting the tomb of the late Hon. James McGill (1877)........................ 150

13. UNIVERSITY PORTRAITS AND BUSTS.

Portrait of the Founder, presented by the late Thomas Blackwood, Esq.

Portrait of William Molson, Esq., presented to the University.

Bust of William Molson, Esq., by Marshall Wood, presented by Graduates of the University.

Portrait of Peter Redpath, Esq , painted by Sydney Hodges, presented by Citizens of Montreal.

Portrait of Rev. Dr. Leach, by Wyatt Eaton, presented by Friends and Graduates of the University.

Portrait of Sir William Dawson, by Wyatt Eaton, presented by Friends and Graduates of the University.

Portrait of Hon. James Ferrier, by Robert Harris, presented by Friends and Graduates of the University.

Portrait of Peter McGill, presented (through Mr. A. T. Taylor), by Judge Parker, of Edinburgh.

Portrait of Dr. William Robertson, founder of the Medical Faculty, presented in loving remembrance by his family and descendants.

Bust of Peter Redpath, Esq., by Reynolds Stephens, presented by Mr. Redpath's personal friends in England.

Portrait of Peter Redpath, Esq., by Robert Harris, presented by Friends and Undergraduates of the University.

Portrait of Mrs. Peter Redpath, by Robert Harris, presented by the Governors of the University.

II. ENDOWMENTS AND SUBSCRIPTIONS FOR THE FACULTY OF ARTS.

1. BUILDINGS, CHAIRS, ETC.

Endowment Fund, 1856.

John Gordon McKenzie, Esq., $2,000
Ira Gould, Esq.,   2,300

Total, $4,300

THE MOLSON CHAIR OF ENGLISH LANGUAGE AND LITERATURE, in 1856, endowed by the Honorable John Molson, Thomas Molson, Esq., and William Molson, Esq.—$20,000; and supplemented in 1892 by John H. R. Molson, Esq., with a further sum of $20,000. Total, $40,000.

THE PETER REDPATH CHAIR OF PURE MATHEMATICS (founded as Chair of Natural Philosophy), in 1871, endowed by Peter Redpath, Esq.,—$20,000.

THE LOGAN CHAIR OF GEOLOGY, in 1871, endowed by Sir W. E. Logan, LL.D., F.R.S., and Hart Logan, Esq.,—$20,000.

THE JOHN FROTHINGHAM CHAIR OF MENTAL AND MORAL PHILOSOPHY, 1873, endowed by Miss Louisa Frothingham,—$20,000, and supplemented in 1891 with a further sum of $20,000. Total, $40,000.

THE MAJOR HIRAM MILLS CHAIR OF CLASSICS, in 1882, endowed by the last will of the late Major Hiram Mills, of Montreal,—$42,000.

THE DAVID J. GREENSHIELDS CHAIR OF CHEMISTRY AND MINERALOGY in the Faculties of Arts and Applied Science, in 1883, endowed by the last will of the late David J. Greenshields, Esq., of Montreal, with the sum of $40,000 half of which is devoted to the Faculty of Arts.

THE WILLIAM C. MCDONALD CHAIRS OF PHYSICS, in the Faculties of Arts and Applied Science, endowed by William C. McDonald, Esq., in 1890,—$50,000; in 1893,—$50,000. Total, $100,000.

THE CHARLES GIBB BOTANICAL ENDOWMENT, subscriptions received to date :
A Friend,— $8,000.
Mrs. Catherine Hill,—   200. Total $8,200.

THE WILLIAM C. MCDONALD Physics Building and Equipment, in the Faculties of Arts and Applied Science. The gift of William C. McDonald, Esq, announced by him as a gift to the University in 1890, and formally opened February, 1893.

THE W. C. MCDONALD PHYSICS BUILDING Maintenance Fund in the Faculties of Arts and Applied Science, endowed by W. C. McDonald, Esq.,—$150,000.

2. ENDOWMENT FOR PENSION FUND.

This endowment was given in 1894 to be invested and the revenue used exclusively for providing Pensions or Retiring Allowances for members of the teaching staff of the Faculties of Arts and Applied Science.

Hon. Sir Donald A. Smith, $50,000
John H. R. Molson, Esq.,   50,000
William C. McDonald, Esq.,   50,000

Total, $150,000

3. EXHIBITIONS AND SCHOLARSHIPS, ETC.

THE JANE REDPATH EXHIBITION, in the Faculty of Arts,—founded in 1868 by Mrs. Redpath, of Terrace Bank, Montreal, and endowed with the sum of $1,667.

THE MCDONALD SCHOLARSHIPS AND EXHIBITIONS, 10 in number, in the Faculty of Arts—founded in 1871, and endowed in 1882 with the sum of $25,000 by William C. McDonald, Esq.

THE CHARLES ALEXANDER SCHOLARSHIP, for Classics—founded in 1871 by Charles Alexander, Esq. Endowed in 1893 with the sum of $2,000.

THE BARBARA SCOTT SCHOLARSHIP FOR CLASSICAL LANGUAGE AND LITERATURE— founded in 1884 by the last will of the late Miss Barbara Scott of Montreal, in the sum of $2,000.

THE GEORGE HAGUE EXHIBITION—founded in 1881—Annual value $125.

THE MAJOR HIRAM MILLS MEDAL AND SCHOLARSHIP—founded by the will of the late Major Hiram Mills of Montreal, and endowed with the sum of $1,500.

T. M. THOMPSON, ESQ.—$250 for two Exhibitions in September, 1871 ; $200 for two Exhibitions in 1872,—$450.

REV. COLIN C. STUART—for the "Stuart Prize in Hebrew,"—$60.

THE TAYLOR SCHOLARSHIP—founded in 1871, by T. M. Taylor, Esq.—Annual value $100—terminated in 1878.

PROFESSOR ALEXANDER JOHNSON—for Scholarship for three Sessions, terminated 1886-87,—$350.

HER MAJESTY'S COMMISSION for the Exhibition of 1851—Nomination Scholarships for 1891, 1893, 1895 and 1897, value £150 annually, tenable for two years.

THE PHILIP CARPENTER FELLOWSHIP—founded by Mrs. Philip Carpenter, for the Maintenance of a Post-Graduation Teaching Fellowship or Scholarship in Natural Science or some branch thereof in the Faculty of Arts in McGill College, endowed in 1892 with the sum of $7,000.

A Lady, to provide four free tuitions in the Faculty of Arts for sessions 1892-93 and 1893-94.

THE NEW YORK GRADUATES SOCIETY EXHIBITION—a gift of $60 in 1897, for an Exhibition in the Faculty of Arts, to be associated with the name of Sir William Dawson.

To provide Bursaries in the Faculty of Arts 1898, subscriptions from.

W. W. Ogilvie,	$1,000
Hugh McLennan,	120

4. ENDOWMENTS AND DONATIONS OF MEDALS AND PRIZES.

In 1856 Henry Chapman, Esq., founded a gold medal, to be named the "Henry Chapman Gold Medal," to be given annually in the graduating class in Arts. This medal was endowed by Mr. Chapman in 1874 with the sum of $700.

In 1860 the sum of £200, presented to the College by H. R. H. the Prince of Wales, was applied to the foundation of a Gold Medal, to be called the "Prince of Wales Gold Medal," which is given in the graduating class for Honour Studies in Mental and Moral Philosophy.

In 1864 the "Anne Molson Gold Medal" was founded and endowed by Mrs John Molson of Belmont Hall, Montreal, for an Honour Course in Mathematics and Physics.

In the same year the "Shakespeare Gold Medal," for an Honour Course. to comprise and include the works of Shakespeare and the Literature of England from his time to the time of Addison. both inclusive, and such other accessory subjects as the Corporation may from time to time appoint, was founded and endowed by citizens of Montreal, on occasion of the three hundredth anniversary of the birth of Shakespeare.

In the same year the "Logan Gold Medal," for an Honour Course in Geology and Natural Science, was founded and endowed by Sir William Logan, LL.D., F.R.S , F.G.S , etc.

In 1874 a Gold and a Silver Medal were given by His Excellency the Earl of Dufferin, Governor-General of Canada, for competition in the Faculty of Arts, and continued till 1878.

In 1875 the "Neil Stuart prize in Hebrew" was endowed by Neil Stuart, Esq., of Vankleek Hill, in the sum of $340.

In 1880 a Gold and a Silver Medal were given by His Excellency the Marquis of Lorne, Governor-General of Canada, the former for competition in the Faculty of Arts, the latter for competition in the Faculty of Applied Science ; continued till 1883.

In 1884 a Gold and a Silver Medal were given by His Excellency the Marquis of Lansdowne, Governor-General of Canada, the former for competition in the Faculty of Arts, the latter for competition in the Faculty of Applied Science, continued till 1888.

In 1889 a Gold and a Silver Medal were given by His Excellency Lord Stanley, Governor-General of Canada, the former for competition in the Faculty of Arts, the latter for competition in the Faculty of Applied Science. Continued till 1893.

The "Charles G. Coster Memorial Prize" for general proficiency—given annually by Colin H. Livingstone, Esq., B.A.; founded in 1889.

In 1894 a Gold and a Silver Medal were given by His Excellency the Earl of Aberdeen, Governor-General of Canada, the former for competition in the Faculty of Arts, the latter for competition in the Faculty of Applied Science. Continued till 1898.

5. SUBSCRIPTIONS FOR THE SUPPORT OF THE CHAIR OF BOTANY,
1883-84.

Principal Dawson	$500	per annum, for 5 years, being...				$2,500
Hon. Sir D. A. Smith	250	"	"	"		1,250
J. H. R. Molson, Esq	100	"	"	"		500
Mrs. J. H. R. Molson	100	"	"	"		500
G. Hague, Esq	100	"	"	"		500
Mrs. Redpath	100	"	"	"		500
Hugh McKay, Esq	100	"	"	"		500
Robert Moat, Esq	100	"	"	"		500
W. C. McDonald, Esq	100	"	"	"		500
Charles Gibb, Esq	50	"	"	"		250
Miss Orkney	50	"	"	"		250
Robert Mackay, Esq	50	"	"	"		250
Mrs. Wm. Molson	50	"	"	"		250
Mrs. John Molson	50	"	"	"		250
John Stirling, Esq	50	"	"	"		250
Warden King, Esq	50	"	"	"		250
Miss Hall	50	"	"	"		250
Robert Angus, Esq	50	"	"	"		250
D. A. P. Watt, Esq	50	"	"	"		250
Hugh McLennan, Esq	25	"	"	"		125
Sir Joseph Hickson	10	"	"	"		50
Mrs. Phillips						20

$9,945

6. BOTANIC GARDEN, ETC.
Subscriptions, 1890-91.

Hugh McLennan, Esq	$100	Forward	$900
Gilman Cheney, Esq	100	Jonathan Hodgson, Esq	100
James Johnston, Esq	100	Robert Mackay, Esq	100
James Slessor, Esq	100	H. Shorey, Esq	50
A friend	100	J. S. Shearer, Esq	50
Hugh Graham, Esq	100	Geo. Sumner, Esq	25
A. F. Gault, Esq	100	A. Ramsay & Co	25
W. T. Costigan, Esq	100	Garth & Co	25
Jonathan Brown, Esq	100		
Forward	$900	Total	$1,275

To Erect Plant House in Botanic Garden.

Hon. Sir Donald A. Smith	$362 00
John H. R. Molson, Esq	361 51
William C. McDonald, Esq	361 02

Total..................$1,084 53

7. SUBSCRIPTIONS IN AID OF THE CHAIR OF HEBREW.

Warden King, Esq	in 1889	$50 per annum, 3 years, being			......	$150
Principal Sir William Dawson.....	"	50	"	"	"	. .....	150
Hon. Hugh Mackay	"	50	"	"	"	......	150
A. F. Gault, Esq	"	25	"	"	"	....	75
Geo. Hague, Esq	"	25	"	"	"		75
T. A. Dawes, Esq	"	25	"	"	"	......	75
S. Carsley, Esq............	"	25	"	"	"	......	75
S. Davis, Esq.............................	in 1892	....				20
Warden King, Esq.........	"	50 per annum for 3 years			....	150
A. F. Gault, Esq......	"	50	"	"	"	......	150
Robert Mackay, Esq......	"	50	"	"	"	......	150
Hugh McLennan, Esq...................	"	25	"	"	"	......	75
George Hague, Esq	"	25	"	"	"	......	75
T. A. Dawes, Esq	"	25	"	"	"	......	75
S. Carsley, Esq...............	"	....	....			25
J. Murphy, Esq.........	"	....				25

Total........ ....$1,495

8. SUBSCRIPTIONS TO PROVIDE SESSIONAL LECTURERS, ETC.

Hon. Sir Donald A. Smith, sessions 1891-92 to 1896-97.............................$23,500
Mrs. John H. R. Molson, sessions 1891-92 to 1897-98...... 6,300
W. C. McDonald, Esq., to provide for certain salaries in the Department of
    Physics, etc., sessions 1894-95 and 1895-96............ 2,627

Total........... $32,427

9. ENDOWMENTS FOR APPARATUS.

The Local Committee of the British Association for the Advancement of Science, to found the British Association Apparatus Fund in the Faculties of Arts and Applied Science, in commemoration of the meeting of the Association in Montreal in 1884 ... .$1,500

10. SUBSCRIPTIONS, ETC., FOR APPARATUS.

Philosophical Apparatus, 1867.

		Forward.	$4,292
William Molson, Esq	$500	W. C. McDonald, Esq., fittings	
John H. R. Molson, Esq	500	of Upper Chemical Laboratory	2,075
Peter Redpath, Esq..............	500	A. J. Lawson, a Dynamo.	
George Moffatt, Esq	250	Benjamin Dawson, 3 Micro-	
Andrew Robertson, Esq	100	scopes	
John Frothingham..	100	Botanical Apparatus, 1897.	
David Torrance, Esq..	100	W. C. McDonald, Esq............	420
Thos. J. Baron, B.A.............	50	Hugh McLennan, Esq............	111
J. H. R, Molson, Esq., Dyna-		Samuel Finley, Esq..............	111
mo, Gas Engine and fixtures	1,792	A. F. Gault, Esq...................	111
Mrs. Redpath, Storage battery ...	400		
		Total..............	$7,120
Forward......	$4,292		

11. MISCELLANEOUS.

Hugh McLennan, Esq., subscription towards expense of table at the Biological
   Station, Wood's Holl, Mass., for McGill Professor of Botany (1896) $250

III. SPECIAL COURSE FOR WOMEN IN THE FACULTY OF ARTS.

1. THE DONALDA ENDOWMENT FOR THE HIGHER EDUCATION OF WOMEN.

This endowment, given by the Honourable Sir Donald A. Smith of Montreal, is to provide for the education of women in the subjects of the Faculty of Arts, up to the standard of the examination for B.A. in classes wholly separate, to constitute a separate Special Course or College for Women, in 1884, $50,000 and in 1886—$70,000...Total...$120,000

2. MISCELLANEOUS SUBSCRIPTIONS.

Hon. Sir Donald A. Smith, for musical instruction in sessions 1889-90 and 1890-91...$400
Hon. Sir Donald A. Smith, for appliances in Zoology in the special interest of Donalda classes in 1895...$100

3. ENDOWMENT HELD IN TRUST BY THE BOARD OF ROYAL INSTITUTION.

The " Hannah Willard Lyman Memorial Fund," contributed by subscriptions of former pupils of Miss Lyman, and invested as a permanent endowment to furnish annually a Scholarship or Prizes in a " College for Women " affiliated to the University, or in classes for the Higher Education of Women, approved by the University. The amount of the fund is at present $1,100.

IV. ENDOWMENTS AND SUBSCRIPTIONS FOR THE FACULTY OF APPLIED SCIENCE.

1. BUILDINGS, CHAIRS, ETC.

THE WILLIAM SCOTT CHAIR OF CIVIL ENGINEERING, in 1884, endowed by the last will of the late Miss Barbara Scott, of Montreal.—$30,000.

THE DAVID J. GREENSHIELDS CHAIR OF CHEMISTRY AND MINERALOGY, in the Faculties of Arts and Applied Science, in 1883, endowed by the last will of the late David J. Greenshields, Esq., of Montreal, with the sum of $40,000, half of which is devoted to the Faculty of Applied Science.

THE THOMAS WORKMAN DEPARTMENT OF MECHANICAL ENGINEERING—founded in 1891 under the last will of the late Thomas Workman, Esq., who bequeathed the sum of $117,000—$60,000 for the maintenance of a Chair of Mechanical Engineering, with the assistance, shops, machinery and apparatus necessary thereto, $57,000 to be expended in provision of necessary buildings, machinery and apparatus.

WILLIAM C. McDONALD, ESQ, in 1890, towards erection of Thomas Workman Workshops, $20,000.

THE MACDONALD ENGINEERING BUILDING AND EQUIPMENT—announced by the donor as a gift to the University in 1890, and formally opened February, 1893.

THE MACDONALD PHYSICS BUILDING, AND EQUIPMENT in the Faculties of Arts and Applied Science, the gift of William C. McDonald, Esq., announced by him as a gift to the University in 1890, and formally opened February, 1893.

THE WILLIAM C. McDONALD CHAIRS OF PHYSICS, in the Faculties of Arts and Applied Science, endowed by William C. McDonald, Esq., in 1890—$50,000. in 1893, $50,000. Total, $100,000.

THE WILLIAM C. MCDONALD CHAIR OF ELECTRICAL ENGINEERING, endowed by
Wm. C. McDonald, Esq·. in 1891, with the sum of $40,000.

THE MACDONALD ENGINEERING BUILDING MAINTENANCE FUND, endowed by W. C.
McDonald, Esq., in 1892 and 1896.—$85,000.

THE MACDONALD PHYSICS BUILDING MAINTENANCE FUND in the Faculties of Arts and
Applied Science, endowed by W. C. McDonald, Esq., in 1892 and 1896—
$150,000.

THE MACDONALD CHEMISTRY AND MINING BUILDING AND EQUIPMENT, given to the
University by Wm, C. McDonald, Esq., in 1896.—$240,000.

THE MACDONALD CHEMISTRY AND MINING BUILDING MAINTENANCE FUND, endowed
by William C. McDonald, Esq., in 1896.—$135,000.

THE WILLIAM C. MCDONALD CHAIR OF MINING AND METALLURGY, endowed in
1896 by William C. McDonald, Esq., with the sum of $50,000.

THE WILLIAM C. MCDONALD CHAIR OF ARCHITECTURE, endowed in 1896. by Wm.
C. McDonald. Esq·, with the sum of $50,000.

THE WILLIAM C. MCDONALD CHAIR OF CHEMISTRY endowed in 1897 by William
C. McDonald, Esq·, with the sum of $50,000.

THE WILLIAM C. MCDONALD ARCHITECTURAL DEPARTMENT MAINTENANCE FUND,
endowed by William C. McDonald, Esq., in 1898.—$10,000.

2. ENDOWMENT FOR PENSION FUND.

This endowment was given in 1894 to be invested and the revenue used exclusively for providing Pensions or Retiring Allowances for members of the
teaching staff of the Faculties of Arts and Applied Science :

Hon. Sir Donald A. Smith,	$50,000
John H. R. Molson, Esq·,	50,000
Wm. C. McDonald, Esq·,	50,000

Total $150,000

3. EXHIBITIONS AND SCHOLARSHIPS.

THE SCOTT EXHIBITION.—founded by the Caledonian Society of Montreal, in commemoration of the Centenary of Sir Walter Scott, and endowed in 1872 with
the sum of $1,100 subscribed by members of the Society and other citizens of
Montreal. The Exhibition is given annually in the Faculty of Applied Science—Annual value $50.

THE BURLAND SCHOLARSHIP, founded 1882 by J. H. Burland, B.A., Sc., $100 for a
Scholarship in Applied Science for three years, being $300.

HER MAJESTY'S COMMISSION for the Exhibition of 1851—Nomination Scholarships
for 1891, 1893, 1895 and 1897, value £150 annually, each tenable for two
years.

THE DR. T. STERRY HUNT SCHOLARSHIP—Founded in 1894 by the will of the late
Dr. T. Sterry Hunt, and endowed with the sum of $2,082, the income to be
given and paid annually to a student or students of Chemistry.

4. MEDALS AND PRIZES.

In 1880, a Gold and a Silver Medal were given by His Excellency the Marquis of
Lorne, Governor-General of·Canada, the former for competition in the
Faculty of Arts, the latter for competition in the Faculty of Applied Science ;
continued till 1883.

In 1884 a Gold and a Silver Medal were given by His Excellency the Marquis of
Lansdowne, Governor-General of Canada, the former for competition in the
Faculty of Arts, the latter for competition in the Faculty of Applied Science ;
continued till 1888.

In 1885 the British Association Gold Medal for competition in the Graduating
class in the Faculty of Applied Science, was founded by subscription of members of the British Association for the Advancement of Science, and by gift
of the Council of the Association, in commemoration of its meeting in Montreal in the year 1884.

In 1889 a Gold and a Silver Medal were given by His Excellency Lord Stanley, Governor-General of Canada, the former for competition in the Faculty of Arts, the latter for competition in the Faculty of Applied Science. Continued till 1893.

In 1894 a Gold and a Silver Medal were given by His Excellency The Earl of Aberdeen, Governor-General of Canada, the former for competition in the Faculty of Arts, the latter for competition in the Faculty of Applied Science. Continued till 1898.

5. ENDOWMENTS AND SUBSCRIPTIONS FOR MAINTENANCE OF FACULTY.

Endowment Fund.

Daniel Torrance, Esq	$5000
Charles J. Brydges, Esq	1000
R. J. Reekie, Esq	100
Total	**$6,100**

Graduates' Endowment Fund.

Graduates' Endowment Fund—	
Class 1890, $70 a year for 5 years, $350 ; received to date... $	85

Annual Subscriptions, 1871-1879.

Hon. James Ferrier ($100 per annum for 10 years)	$1000
Peter Redpath, Esq. ($400 per annum for 10 years)	4000
John H. R. Molson, Esq. ($400 per annum for 10 years)	4000
George H. Frothingham, Esq., ($400 per annum for 7 years)	2800
T. James Claxton, Esq. ($100 per annum for 6 years)	600
Donald Ross, Esq. ($50 per annum for 5 years)	250
Miss Mary Frothingham (400 per annum for 3 years)	1200
Forward	$13,850

Forward	$13,850
H. McLennan, Esq. ($100 per annum for 5 years)	500
A. F. Gault, Esq. ($100 per annum for 5 years)	500
Gilbert Scott, Esq. ($100 for 2 years)	200
Joseph Hickson, Esq. ($100 for 2 years)	200
Principal Dawson ($300 for 2 years	600
His Excellency the Marquis of Lorne	500
Mrs. Redpath, (Terrace Bank)	100
Total	**$16,450**

Subscriptions towards Maintenance of Engineering Department.

W. C. McDonald, Esq., sessions 1891-92 to 1897-98		$56,341
do	for advertising	675
do	to cover certain salaries, session 1894-95 and 1897-98	1,920
do	to meet the expenses of the course of summer work for Mining Engineering Students (1898)	825
	Total	**$59,761**

Subscriptions to provide lectures in Mechanical and Sanitary Engineering.

E. B. Greenshields, Esq	$50
J. E. Bovey, Esq	50
Professor H. T. Bovey	61
Forward	$161

Forward	$161
Jeffrey H. Burland, B.A.Sc., $100 for 2 years	200
Smaller amounts	40
Total	**$401**

Subscriptions for Maintenance of Chair of Practical Chemistry, 1862.

Hon. C. Dunkin, M.P.	$1200
Principal Dawson	1200
Peter Redpath, Esq.	226
Total	**$2,626**

For Maintenance of Chair of Mining Engineering and Metallurgy, 1891.

R. B. Angus, Esq	$2000	Forward	$4000	$6200
Mrs. Dow	1000	E. K. Greene, Esq	750	
Hugh McLennan, Esq	1000	Dr. T. Brainerd	750	
Miss Benny	1000	A. F. Gault, Esq	750	
T. A Dawes, Esq	750	Messrs. H. & A. Allan	750	
A. A. Ayer, Esq	250	Hector Mackenzie, Esq	750	
G. W. Reid, Esq	100	Peter Lyall, Esq	750	
Evans Bros	100	James Ross, Esq	600	
	$6200	A. Robertson, Esq	300	
		John Duncan Esq	300	
Payable in Three Years.		Geo. Hague, Esq	300	
		Jonathan Hodgson, Esq	300	
Sir Wm. Dawson.	1000	James Moore, Esq	200	
Alex. Stuart, Esq. (London, Eng)	1500	Messrs. Ames & Holden	150	
R. G. Reid, Esq	1500	James Cooper, Esq	150	10,800
Forward	$4000 $6200	**Total**		**$17,000**

Remodelling East Wing for Class Rooms for Faculty of Applied Science, 1888.

John H. R. Molson, Esq	$3000	Total	$6000
W. C. McDonald, Esq	3000		

6. ENDOWMENTS FOR APPARATUS.

The Local Committee of the British Association for the Advancement of Science, to found the British Association Apparatus Fund in the Faculties of Arts and Applied Science, in commemoration of the meeting of the Association in Montreal in 1884 ....$1,500

7. SUBSCRIPTIONS, ETC., FOR APPARATUS.

A lady, for the purchase of Mining Models	$1000	Forward	$1175
Thos. McDougall, Esq., for the same	25	for the purchase of appliances for the department of Civil Engineering in Faculty of Applied Science	475
J. Livesey, Esq., through Dr. Harrington, for the same	50	Capt. Adams, Chemical Apparatus	10
Geo. Stephen, Esq., for the same.	50	J. H. Burland, B.A.Sc., Chemical Apparatus	25
Chas. Gibb, B.A., donation for Apparatus in Applied Science..	50	W. C. McDonald, Esq., for Surveying and Geodetic Apparatus in 1890	1500
The Local Committee for the reception (1881) of American Society of Civil Engineers			
Forward	$1175	**Total**	**$3,185**

8. LIST OF SUBSCRIBERS AND DONORS TO THE EQUIPMENT OF THE NEW ENGINEERING BUILDINGS OF McGILL UNIVERSITY, TO MAY, 1898.

Abbott, W ....Equipment
Adams, Capt. R. C...Mining Photographs
American Rail Joint Co. (Cleveland, Ohio)............ .....Specimens of Rail Joint
American Steam Gauge Co., (Boston) Indicator.
Archbald, H....... ....Books
Ashton Valve Co. (Boston) Sectional Valve
Bell Telephone Co...... ....A set of Telephone Apparatus
Bertram & Sons, J., (Dundas)............... 24 in. Planer
Birch & Co. J. (England)............ Hydraulic Tubes
Birks, Henry............ .... Clock
Bishop, George... ....Equipment
Blackwell, Kennet............... Equipment
Blake Mnfg. Co., The Geo. F.............. Blue Prints of Pump
Blake Pump Co., The Geo. (New York & Boston)............ ....Pump
Bovey, Prof H. T....................... Books
Bremner, A............... .... $50
British Columbian Mills, Timber and Trading Company, Timber Beams of large Scantling for Testing Laboratory
Brockhaus, Herr F. A...... ....Books
Brodie & Harvey........ .... $50
Brush, G............... ....Boiler
Cameron, General..... ....Rotary Drill
Campbell Tile Co. (England), per Jordan & Locker............Equipment
Campbell, Kenneth................... $50
Canadian General Electric Co............. (Toronto), per F. Nichols...Equipment
Canadian General Electric Co .... Electric Drill, Edison Generator Edison Street Railway Motor
Canadian Government............ ....
Collection of Canadian Timber
Canadian Pacific Railway Co..... .. .. Timber for Testing, Timber Beams of large Scantling for Testing Laboratory, Photographs
Canadian Rubber Co., Rubber Belting
Carsley, S............... .... $100
Carus-Wilson, Prof. C. A.....Equipment
Cary, A. A.......Photographs of Boilers
Chadwick, F...................Truss Models
Chanteloup, E...... .... $50
Claxton, T J......Timber Beams of large Scantling for Testing Laboratory
Consumers' Cordage Co., (Halifax, N.S.) Ropes of different sizes for Testing purposes

Costigan, J...... ....Equipment
Cowen, Amos............Samples of Bricks
Cowper, P. H....... .... Model of Steam Engine
Craig, Messrs. J. & M., (Kilmarnoch, Scotland)........Sanitary Sections (full size) and models
Crocker-Wheeler Electric Motor Co., The (New York).......... ....Motor
Crosby Steam Gauge and Valve Co., The (Boston).........Gauge and Valve, Indicator and Valves
Darling, Brown & Sharpe (Providence, R. I.) ....6 in. Rule
Date, John ....Equipment
Dawson, W. B...........Iron Rail showing effect of long immersion in water
Dominion Wire Manfg Co., per F. Fairman............ ....Shaper
Drysdale, D...................... .....Tools
Drysdale, W .... Tools
Earle, S R .... Air Injector
Edison General Electric Co......Two 450 light dynamos, Brake Shoe and Disc.
Egleston, Dr. (New York).........Framed Photograph of the Moon, Books, Photos, etc.
Electric Welding Company, (Boston) Equipment
"Engineering Magazine" (New York City)............Mining Illustrations and Photographs
Eureka Tempered Copper Co............... Equipment
Ewan, A........................ ....$100
Felton & Gilleaume...... .... Samples of Cable Wire, etc.
Forsyth, R ....Equipment
Frothingham & Workman...... . ...Tools
Furlong, G. W., B.A Sc............ ....Specimens of Pine and Wood bored by Teredos
Gardner & Son, R. W..... 16 in. Lathe
Gardner, R ....Equipment
Garth & Co $500
Garth Henry......... ....Equipment
Government of New South Wales......... Collection of Australian Timbers
Government of Queensland, Australia, Collection of Queensland Timbers
Gower, W. E...... ....
Graham. H...... ....$100
Grier, G. A...... .... Equipment
Gurney & Co., E. & C......... ..... $604
Hadfield, Messrs. (Sheffield).Equipment
Hamilton Bridge Works Co....... .... A Model of the Stoney Creek Arch

Hamilton Powder Co........... Electrical
Blasting Machine, and appliances,
etc., tor blasting.
Hearn & Harrison, per L. Harrison,
Barometer & Clock
Hersey, R $1200
Hodgson, Jonathan $200
Holden, A.................. ..... Equipment
Hosoki, Dr., of Tokio, Japan ....
Collection of Japanese Wood
Hughes & Stephenson...... ...Equipment
Hutton, W. H............. ....Equipment
Ingersoll Rock Drill Co....A. Rock Drill
Irwin & Hopper...............Equipment
Ives, H. R.......... .... Cupola
Joyce, Alfred $50
Jordau & Locker...... ....Equipmen;
Kennedy, John...... ....Equipment
Timber Beams of large Scantling for
Testing Laboratory
Kennedy, W. & Sons.American Turbine
Kennedy, W. (Owen Sound) ......Pump
Kerr, R. & W .... Tools
King & Son, Warden........ .... $534
Laughlin-Hough Drawing Table Co.,
Drawing Tables
Laurie & Bro. J ...... .Compound Engine
Lawson, A J............. ......Equipment
Lehigh Zinc & Iron Co .... .Franklin
Furnace, N. J, Mining Specimens &
Photographs
Lindsay & Co., C. F........... Equipment
Lovell & Son, John...... ....Books
Lyster, A. G.................Drawings and
Sketches of London and Liverpool
Docks
Macpherson, A...... ....Tools
Mason, Dr...... .... Equipment
Maxwell & Co., E. J .....Equipment
McCarthy, D. & J. (Sorel).. ....$300
McDougall, Mrs. J.....................$4000
McLachlin Bros. (Arnprior) ....
Timber for Testing
McLaren, D................'...............$100
McLaughlin Bros .... Timber
beams ot large Scantling for Testing
Laboratory
McNally & Co., W............. .. ..$100
McPherson Sand Box Co. (Troy, N.Y.)
Model of Sand Box
Miller Bros. & Sons..... ....Elevator
Mitchell, P .... Equipment ($300)
Mitchell & Co., R............Equipment
Naismith, P. L., B.A.Sc........... Speci-
mens of Cast-Iron showing effect of
mine water
Nalder Bros. & Co. (England) ....
Standard Cell
National Electric Mfg. Co...... ....
100 volt Transformer, Transformers

Nicholson, Peter $100
Norton, A. O. Boston, Mass............Two
Norton Ball-hearing Lifting-jacks
Norton Emery Whee'. Co. (Worcester,
U.S.)............... ....Equipment
Notman, Wm................. Photographs
Ogilvie, W..................................$500
Palmer, A......................Equipment
Parker, M...... .... Equipment
Paton, H...................... ...... Equipment
Peckham Motor Truck and Wheel Co.
(Kingston, N.Y.) ....;....
Model of Motor Truck
Pelton Water Wheel Co. (New York)
Two Motors
Pennsylvania Railroad Co... . ....Work-
ing Drawings ef Locomotives (32)
Phelps Engine Co , per A. R. Williams
& Co., A. Dake Steam Engine, 4
Horse Power Engine
Pillow, J. A...... ....$250
Pratt & Whitney (Hartford, Conn)......
Epicycloidal Gear Model
Prowse, G. R............. ..... Equipment
Queensland Government per Sir
Thomas McIlwraith...... ....
Collection of Timbers
Radiator Co. (Toronto) $500
Ramsay & Son, A...... ....$100
Rathbun, E. W..........Samples of Fire-
proof Construction...... .... $112
Reddaway & Co., F... . Belt (value $50)
Redpath, F. R............. ..... Equipment
Redpath, Mrs...................................$100
Reed, G. W...... .... $100
Reford, R $1000
Reid, R..........................Equipment
Reid, R. G...... .... $1000
Renouf, E. M...... .... Books
Rhode Island Locomotive Works... ......
Photos of Locomotives
Rife's Hydraulic Engine Mfg. Co.
(Roanoke, Va., U.S.A.) ....
Hydraulic Ram
Robb & Armstrong .
80 H. P. High Speed Engine
Robertson, J .... Equipment
Rogers, Professor (Waterville, Maine)
Equipment
Ross, James $500
Rodden, W........ .... Equipment
Royal Electric Co............ ....
12 Arc Light Dynamos
30 Light Stanley transformer
Rutherford, W........ ....Equipment
Sadler, G. (Robin & Sadler)... . ...
Belting ($400)
Seeley, John........ .... Insulators
Schaeffer & Budenbery (Brooklyn, N.Y.)
Double Indicator

Scholes, F..$100
Scovill Mfg. Co ....Equipment
Sharp, Stewart & Co. (Manchester,
   Eng).....................................Equipment
Shearer, James.................. .... $200
Sheppard, Chas...... .... $200
Siemens Bros. (London, Eng).. ....
                  Cable Samples
Smith, C. B ....
      Framed Photos of Bridges (2)
Smith, R .... Equipment
Spence, J. P., C.E...... ....Specifica-
   tions and Drawings showing con-
   struction of Sault Ste. Marie Canal
   Locks
Smith, R. Guilford ....Books
Steel Co. of Scotland, The.................
    Samples of Cable Wire, etc.
St. George, P. W ....Models
Stirling Co., The................... ....
    Sectional Blue Prints of Boilers

Sturtevant Co., The. B. F. (Boston) ....
               Blowers
Swan Lamp Mfg. Co...... ....Lamps-
Taylor, A. T...... .... $300
Tees & Co ....Equipment
Thomson-Houston Co. (Boston)...........
        Incandescent dynamos
Twyford & Co..... ....Equipment
Vail, Stephen...........Piece of first Tele-
         graph Wire Used
Walker & Co., James ....Tools
Wanklyn, F. L ....Equipment
Ward, Hon. J. K...... .... $50
Warrington Wire Co... .Cable Samples
Whittier Machine Co. (Boston) ....
        Electric Elevator
Wiley & Sons, John (New York)..Books
Yale & Towne Mfg. Co. (Stamford,
   Conn) .... Equipment
Yates & Thom ....
    Blue Prints of Machinery

The above representing a total of about $80,000.

9. FACULTY OF APPLIED SCIENCE LIBRARY ENDOWMENT, 1893.

Hugh Paton.......... ....$ 25
A. Joyce...... 25
R. Gardner...... ....:.. 50
H. Garth..... 100
Hughes & Stephenson...... 100
R. Mitchell 300

     Forward............ .... $600

Forward .... $ 600
W. Rodden 25
M. Parker........................ 25
Robin & Sadler...... 50
J. Robertson, Esq 50
Mrs. John McDougall (1895) 20

     Total.............. ....$ 770·

V. ENDOWMENTS AND SUBSCRIPTIONS IN AID OF THE FACULTY OF MEDICINE.

1. LEANCHOIL ENDOWMENT, 1884.

Hon. Sir Donald A. Smith, G.C.M.G........ ....$50,000

2. CAMPBELL MEMORIAL ENDOWMENT, 1884.

Established to commemorate the service rendered to the Faculty during 40 years by the late Dean, George W. Campbell, M.D., LL.D.

Mrs. G. W. Campbell .... $ 2000
H. A. Allan, Esq 1500
Hon. Sir D. A. Smith......... 1500
Sir George Stephen, Bart 1000
R. B. Angus, Esq........ 1000
George A. Drummond, Esq......... 1000

     Forward............ ....$8,000

Forward......... ....$8,000
Alex. Murray, Esq..................... 1000·
Robert Moat, Esq..................... 1000
W. C. McDonald, Esq...... 1000
A Friend............ .... 1000·
Duncan McIntyre, Esq 1000

     Forward .... $13,000·

Forward......... ....$13,000	Forward......... ....$46,300
A. F. Gault, Esq........................ 1000	Benj. Dawson, Esq............... 200
M. H. Gault, Esq 1000	R. Wolff, Esq.................... 150
G. W. Stephens, Esq.............. .. 1000	James Stuart, M.D.................. 150
James Benning, Esq...... 1000	A. T. Paterson, Esq................... 100
R. P. Howard, M.D 1000	H. W. Thornton, M.D. (New
G. B & J. H. Burland, Esqs 1000	Richmond, Q.)....................... 100
Miss Elizabeth C. Benny............. 1000	C. B. Harvey, M.D. (Yale, B.C.). . 100
J. C. Wilson, Esq..................... 1000	D. Cluness, M.D. (Nanaimo, B.C.) 100
Mrs. John Redpath......... 1000	W. Kinlock, Esq. 100
Hon. John Hamilton 1000	Hua. Richardson & Co...... 100
Miss Orkney............. 1000	Mrs. Cuthbert (N. Richmond, Q.). 100
Hugh Mackay, Esq 1000	J. M. Drake, M.D 100
Hector Mckenzie, Esq. 1000	Hugh Patton, Esq 100
Thomas Workman, Esq............. 1000	R. T. Godfrey, M.D 100
Hugh McLennan, Esq............. ... 1000	T A. Rodger, M.D................... 100
O. S. Wood, Esq...... 1000	W. A. Dyer, Esq.................. 100
Frank Buller, M.D....... 500	Geo. W. Wood, M.D. (Faribault,
James Burnett, Esq................. 500	Minn.) 100
Andrew Robertson, Esq...... 500	A. A. Browne. M D 100
Robert Mackay, Esq..... 500	Geo. Wilkins, M.D 100
John Hope, Esq 500	R. L. MacDonnell, M.D 100
Alex. Urquhart, Esq........ 500	Jos. Workman, M.D. (Toronto)... 50
R. A. Smith, Esq 500	Hon. Sir A. T. Galt 50
George Hague, Esq...................... 500	Henry Lunam, B A., M.D. (Camp-
J. K. Ward, Esq 500	bellton, N.B.) 50
Warden King, Esq 500	T. J. Alloway, M.D............. 30
John Stirling, Esq......... 500	R. J. B. Howard, M D 25
John Rankin, Esq..... 500	Louis T. Marceau, M.D. (Napier-
Robert Reford, Esq...... 500	ville, Q.)....... 25
Messrs. Cantlie, Ewan & Co 500	Griffith Evans, M.D. (Vet. Dept.
Messrs. J. & W. Ogilvie............... 500	Army) 26
Randolph Hersey, Esq.............. 500	J. J. Farley, M.D (Belleville)..... 25
John A. Pillow, Esq...... 500	Henry R. Gray, Esq..... 25
S. Carsley, Esq....................... 500	J. E. Brouse, M D. (Prescott)...... 20
D. C. MacCallum, M.D.............. 500	R. N Rinfret (Quebec) 20
Messrs. S. Greenshields, Son & Co. 500	Robert Howard, M.D. (St. Johns) 20
Jonathan Hodgson, Esq 500	Drs. J. & D. J. McIntosh (Vank-
George Ross, M.D..................... 500	leek Hill) 20
T. G. Roddick, M D 500	J. H. McBean, M.D............... 15
Wm Gardner, M.D 500	J. C Rattray, M.D. (Cobden, O.) 10
Messrs. Cochrane, Cassils & Co... 500	E. H Howard, M.D. (Lachine)..... 10
Sir Joseph Hickson.................... 500	J. W. Oliver, M.D (Clifton, O.)... 10
Allan Gilmour, Esq., Ottawa..... 500	D. A. McDougall, M.D. (Ottawa,
R. W. Shepherd, Esq............ 500	O.)...... 10
G. E. Fenwick, M.D.................. 300	A. Poussette, M.D. (Sarnia, O)... 10
Miles Williams, Esq 300	A. Rattan, M.D. (Napanee, O.) ... 10
G. P. Girdwood, M.D......... 250	James Gunn, M.D. (Durham, O.) 10
Charles F. Smithers, Esq 250	J. McDiarmid, M.D. (Hensall, O.) 5
John Kerry, Esq.................... 250	W. J. Derby, M.D. (Rockland, O.) 5
A. Baumgarten, Esq............. 250	J. Gillies, M.D. (Teeswater, O.) .. 5
R. W. Elmenhorst, Esq...... 250	J. B. Benson, M.D. (Chatham,
W. F. Lewis, Esq...... 250	N.B.)......... 5
George Armstrong, Esq 250	L. A. Fortier, M.D. (St. David
J. M. Douglas, Esq 250	Q.).......... 5
Messrs. H. Lyman, Sons & Co... .. 250	J. A. McArthur, M.D. (Fort
F. J Shepherd, M D........ 250	Elgin, O.)................. 5
Duncan McEachran, Esq., F. R.	John Campbell, M.D. (Seaforth,
C. V. S...... 200	O.).......................... 5
Forward.....................$46,300	Total................$48,906

3. ENDOWED CHAIRS, ETC.

Sir Donald A. Smith Chair of Pathology, endowed in 1893 by the Hon. Sir Donald A. Smith with the sum of..... .... $50,000·

Sir Donald A. Smith Endowment for the Department of Hygiene, endowed in 1893 with the sum of........... .... 50,000·

Mrs. Mary Dow Bequest—Bequest by the will of the late Mrs. Mary Dow for the Faculty of Medicine, 1893, $10,000, less Government Tax of 10 per cent...... .... 9,000·

John H. R. Molson Donation— in 1893, $25,000 for the purchase of land and $35,000 for additional building and equipment...... .... 60,000·

Walter Drake, Esq., for benefit of Chair of Physiology, an annual donation of $500 given 1891 to 1897....... .... 3,500·

Dr. Robert Craik Fund—

Mr. John McDougall, toward formation of above (1893-94). 1,000 }
Jane F. Learmout, bequest   do   do   (1894)......3,000 }

4,000

Joseph Morley Drake, Chair of Physiology, endowed in 1898 by Walter Drake, Esq·, with the sum of............ .... 10,000·

4. MEDALS AND SCHOLARSHIPS.

In 1865 the " Holmes Gold Medal " was founded by the Faculty of Medicine as a memorial of the late Andrew Holmes, Esq., M.D., LL.D·, late Dean of the Faculty of Medicine, to be given to the best student in the graduating class in Medicine, who should undergo a special examination in all the branches whether Primary or Final.

In 1878 the " Sutherland Gold Medal " was founded by Mrs. Sutherland of Montreal, in memory of her late husband, Prof.William Sutherland, M D., for competition in the classes of Theoretical and Practical Chemistry in the Faculty of Medicine, together with creditable standing in the Primary Examinations.

The David Morrice Scholarship—in the subject of Institutes of Medicine, in the Faculty of Medicine—founded in 1881—value $100. (Terminated in 1883.)

5. LIBRARY, MUSEUM AND APPARATUS.

For the fittings of the Library and Museum of the Faculty of Medicine, 1872.

G. W. Campbell, A.M., M.D.......$1200	Forward............. ....,......$2,000	
W. E Scott, M.D 200	Robert Craik, M.D 200	
Wm. Wright, M.D..... 200	Geo. E. Fenwick, M.D..... 200	
Robert P. Howard, M.D 200	Joseph M. Drake, M.D..... 200	
Duncan C. MacCallum, M.D....... 200	George Ross, M.A., M.D 50	
Forward...... ....$2,000	Total..... ....$2,650	

The Professors and Lecturers in the Summer Sessions of the Faculty of Medicine .... } Donation to Apparatus,- Museum Library, etc, of the Medical Faculty, 1887, $1,182; 1888, $1,023. } $2,205

For Physiological Laboratory of Faculty of Medicine, 1879.

Dr. Campbell............ .... $100	Forward............... ..... $700	
Dr. Howard..... 100	Dr. Ross .... 50·	
Dr. Craik 100	Dr. Roddick........ .... 50·	
Dr. MacCallum........ 100	Dr. Buller 50	
Dr. Drake 100	Dr. Gardner .... 50·	
Dr. Godfrey...... 100	Dr. Osler. 50	
Dr. McEachran, F.R.C.V.S......... 100		
Forward..................... $700	Total...... .... $950·	

Cameron Obstetrical Collections,

Dr. J. C. Cameron...$10,000

6. MISCELLANEOUS.

Anonymous Donor toward Expenses of Pathology for Session 1892-93...........$ 500

VI. ENDOWMENTS AND SUBSCRIPTIONS FOR THE FACULTY OF LAW

1. ENDOWED CHAIRS, ETC.

THE GALE CHAIR, in the Faculty of Law, endowed in 1884 by the late Mrs. Andrew Stuart (*née* Agnes Logan Gale) of Montreal. in memory of her father, the late Hon. Mr. Justice Gale.—$25,000

THE WILLIAM C. MCDONALD FACULTY OF LAW ENDOWMENT, founded by Wm. C. McDonald, Esq., in 1890—$150,000.Supplemented in 1897 by $50,000. Total $200,000.

W. C. MCDONALD, ESQ., remodelling part of East Wing in 1895 for Class Rooms, Lecture Rooms, etc., for Law Faculty.

2. MEDAL.

In 1865 the "Elizabeth Torrance Gold Medal" was founded and endowed by John Torrance, Esq., of St. Antoine Hall, Montreal, in memory of the late Mrs. John Torrance, for the best student in the graduating class in Law, and more especially for the highest proficiency in Roman Law.

VII. GRADUATES' FUNDS.

1. THE FUND FOR ENDOWMENT OF THE LIBRARY.

The Graduates' Society of the University, in 1876, passed the following Resolution :—

Resolved ;—" That the members and graduates be invited to subscribe to a fund "for the endowment of the Libraries of the University; said fund to be invested " and the proceeds applied under the supervision of the Council of the Society in " annual additions to the Libraries ; an equitable division of said proceeds to be " made by the Council between the University Library and those of the Profes-"sional Faculties."

In terms thereof subscriptions have been paid in to the Graduates's Society, amounting in all to $3,120 ; the interest on which is annually expended in the purchase of books for the several libraries under the direction of a special committee appointed for that purpose.

2. THE DAWSON FELLOWSHIP FOUNDATION.

The Graduates' Society of the University, in 1880, and in commemoration of the completion by Dr. Dawson of his twenty-fifth year as Principal, resolved to raise with the assistance of their friends, a fund towards the Endowment of the Fellowship, under the above name.

Details of the scheme can be had from the Treasurer, Francis Topp, B.A., B.C.L. The following subscriptions have been announced to date, May 1st, 1897 They are payable in one sum, in instalments, without interest or with interest till payment of capital, as subscribers have elected.

Alphabetically arranged.

Abbott, H., B.C.L ....$	60
Archibald, H., B.A.Sc..............	20
Bethune, M. B., M.A., B:C.L.....	50
Carter, C. B., B.C.L..................	100
Cruickshank, W. G., B.C.L	100
Dawson, W. B., M.A., Ma.E	50
Dougall, J. R., M.A................ .	250
Gibb, C., B.A......	100
Hall, Rev. Wm , M.A................	100
Hall, J.S., jun., B.A., B.C.L......	100
Harrington, B. J., B.A., Ph.D,...	50
Hutchinson, M., B.C.L.......	400
Kirby, J., LL.D., D.C.L	50
Krans, Rev. E. H., M.A., LL.D...	100
Leet, S. P., B C.L	100
Lighthall, W. D., M.A., B.C.L...	100

Forward $1,730

Forward............ ....$1,730	
Lyman, H. H., M.A................	100
Lyman, A. C., M.A., B.C.L.	50
McCormick, D., B.C.L	100
McGibbon, R. D., B.A., B.C L...	100
McGoun, A., jun. M.A., B.C.L .	50
McLennan, J. S., B.A..............	100
Ramsay, R. A., M.A., B.C L	50
Spencer, J. W., B.A.Sc., Ph D...	50
Stephen, C. H , B.C L............ ...	100
Stewart, D. A., B.A.Sc.....	20
Stewart, J., M.D............	60
Tait, M. M., B.C.L........	100
Taylor, A. D., B.A., B.C.L	100
Trenholme, N. W., M.A., D.C L.	400

Total to date $3,110

EXAMINATION PAPERS

OF THE

McGILL UNIVERSITY,

MONTREAL.

SESSION OF 1897-8.

Montreal:

PRINTED BY JOHN LOVELL & SON,

ST. NICHOLAS STREET.

1898.

ORDER OF EXAMINATION PAPERS.

1. FACULTY OF ARTS.

PAGE

ENTRANCE, EXHIBITION AND SCHOLARSHIP EXAMINATIONS, 1897............ 3

SESSIONAL EXAMINATIONS, 1898.

GREEK :—*Ordinary*....... 85
. " *Honour*........... 113
LATIN :—*Ordinary* 140
" *Honour*...... 160
MATHEMATICS AND NATURAL PHILOSOPHY :—*Ordinary*...................... 177
"   "   "   "   *Honour*...... 191
ENGLISH LANGUAGE AND LITERATURE :—*Ordinary*............... 211
"   "   "   *Honour*...... 220
MENTAL AND MORAL PHILOSOPHY :—*Ordinary*...................... 250
"   "   "   *Honour*...... 252
FRENCH :—*Ordinary*...................... 261
" *Honour*...... 264
GERMAN :—*Ordinary*....... 266
" *Honour*........... 281
HEBREW :—*Ordinary*........... 284
" *Honour* 289
NATURAL SCIENCE (Chemistry—Botany—Mineralogy—Geology and
Zoology):—
Ordinary....... 294
Honour...... 301

2. FACULTY OF APPLIED SCIENCE.

ENTRANCE EXAMINATIONS, ETC., 1897...... 77
PRACTICAL CHEMISTRY, MINING, ETC 313
MATHEMATICS, ETC............ 325
ELECTRICAL ENGINEERING............ 339
ARCHITECTURE............ 342
MACHINERY, ETC............ · 353
MODERN LANGUAGES, NATURAL AND PHYSICAL SCIENCE.—(*See Arts
Examinations.*)

3. FACULTY OF LAW..... 395

4. UNIVERSITY SCHOOL EXAMINATIONS.

ORDINARY A. A............ 415
ADVANCED A. A............ 443

McGILL UNIVERSITY,

MONTREAL.

ENTRANCE, EXHIBITION AND SCHOLARSHIP
EXAMINATIONS,

SEPTEMBER, 1897.

SEPTEMBER 15TH :—MORNING, 9 TO 12.

XENOPHON, ANABASIS I.

Translate with notes (including parsing) or notes and phrases underlined:

(1) ὁ δὲ Κῦρος ὑπολαβὼν τοὺς φεύγοντας συλλάξας στράτευμα ἐπολιόρκει Μίλητον καὶ κατὰ γῆν καὶ κατὰ θάλατταν καὶ ἐπειρᾶτο κατάγειν τοὺς ἐκπεπτωκότας. καὶ αὕτη αὖ ἄλλη πρόφασις ἦν αὐτῷ τοῦ ἀθροίζειν στράτευμα.

(2) Κῦρος δὲ ἐπεὶ εἰσήλασεν εἰς τὴν πόλιν, μετεπέμπετο τὸν Συέννεσιν πρὸς ἑαυτόν· ὁ δὲ οὔτε πρότερον οὐδενί πω κρείττονι ἑαυτοῦ εἰς χεῖρας ἐλθεῖν ἔφη οὔτε τότε Κύρῳ ἰέναι ἤθελε, πρὶν ἡ γυνὴ αὐτὸν ἔπεισε καὶ πίστεις ἔλαβε.

(3) ἐκ δὲ τούτου ἀνίσταντο οἱ μὲν ἐκ τοῦ αὐτομάτου, λέξοντες ἃ ἐγίγνωσκον, οἱ δὲ καὶ ὑπ᾽ ἐκείνου ἐγκέλευστοι, ἐπιδεικνύοντες οἷα εἴη ἡ ἀπορία ἄνευ τῆς Κύρου γνώμης καὶ μένειν καὶ ἀπιέναι.

(4) διρφθέρας ἃς εἶχον στεγάσματα ἐπίμπλασαν χόρτου κούφου, εἶτα συνῆγον καὶ συνέσπων, ὡς μὴ ἅπτεσθαι τῆς κάρφης τὸ ὕδωρ· ἐπὶ τούτων διέβαινον καὶ ἐλάμβανον τὰ ἐπιτήδεια, οἶνόν τε ἐκ τῆς βαλάνου πεποιημένον τῆς ἀπὸ τοῦ φοίνικος καὶ σῖτον μελίνης.

(5) μετὰ δὲ τὴν ἐξέτασιν. ἅμα τῇ ἐπιούσῃ ἡμέρᾳ ἥκον-
τες αὐτόμολοι παρὰ μεγάλου βασιλέως ἀπήγγελλον Κύρῳ
περὶ τῆς βασιλέως στρατιᾶς.

(6) ὁρῶν δὲ ὁ Κλέαρχος τὸ μέσον στῖφος καὶ ἀκούων
Κύρου ἔξω ὄντα τοῦ εὐωνύμου βαοιλέα — τοσοῦτον γὰρ
πλήθει περιῆν βασιλεὺς ὥστε μέσον τῶν ἑαυτοῦ ἔχων τοῦ
Κύρου εὐωνύμου ἔξω ἦν — ἀλλ᾽ ὅμως ὁ Κλέαδχος οὐκ
ἤθελεν ἀποσπάσαι ἀπὸ τοῦ ποταμοῦ τὸ δεξιὸν κέρας,
φοβούμενος μὴ κυκλωθείη ἑκατέρωθεν, τῷ δὲ Κύρῳ ἀπεκ-
ρίνατο ὅτι αὐτῷ μέλοι ὅπως καλῶς ἔχοι.

(7) ὡς δὲ εἶδον οἱ Ἕλληνες ἐγγύς τε ὄντας καὶ παρατε-
ταγμένους, αὖθις παιανίσαντες ἐπῆσαν πολὺ ἔτι προθυμό-
τερον ἢ τὸ πρόσθεν.

_____

FIRST YEAR ORDINARY ENTRANCE EXAMINATION

GREEK.

1. Translate into Greek :—

   (a) Cyrus loosed the men.

   (b) Clea1chus used to march many parasangs.

   (c) He remained there three days.

   (d) The inhabitants abandoned the city.

   (e) The general burnt the palace.

   (f) Cyrus gave each man three minae.

   (g) He ordered the hoplites to remain.

   (h) He calls them into his own tent.

2. Translate into English :—

Κυρῳ ἐδόκει εἰς τὴν πόλιν ἐλθεῖν. καὶ πάντες ἐπῄνουν
τοῦτον τὸν λόγον. ὁ δὲ στρατὸς προελθὼν ἐπορεύετο

πολλὰς ἡμέρας—αἱ δὲ πολέμιοι ἐν κώμῃ τινι οὐ μεγάλῃ ἔμενον. μαχῆς δὲ γενομένης οἱ Ἕλληνες ἐνίκησαν. πολλᾷ γὰρ προεῖχον τῇ τε ἀνδρείᾳ καὶ τῇ τέχνῃ οὐχ ἧσσον. καὶ πολλοὺς μὲν ἀποκτείναντες τοὺς δὲ ἄλλους πολὺν χρόνον διώξαντες τρόπαιον κατέστησαν ὧν ἔλαβον.

3. (*a*) Give accusative singular and dative plural of :—
θυγατήρ, λεώς, πόλις, ναῦς, οὗτος, οὔ, πολύς.

(*b*) Give future active, aorist active, perfect active and aorist passive of .—πίπτω, λαμβάνω, ἔχω, αἱρέω, ἵστημι ἔρχομαι, βαίνω.

(*c*) With what cases, and with what meanings, are the following prepositions used ;—ἐπί, μετά, κατά, πρός, ὡς.

(*d*) Give the comparative and superlative of :—ἀγαθός καλός, ταχός, φίλος, πολύς, κρατερός, δίκαιος.

FIRST YEAR ENTRANCE.

WEDNESDAY, SEPTEMBER 15TH :— AFTERNOON, 3.15 TO 5.

CAESAR AND VIRGIL.

1. Translate :—

(*a*) Interim cotidie Caesar Aeduos frumentum, quod essent publice polliciti, flagitare. Nam propter frigora, quod Gallia sub septentrionibus, ut ante dictum est, posita est, non modo frumenta in agris matura non erant, sed ne pabuli quidem satis magna copia suppetebat: eo autem frumento, quod flumine Arare navibus subvexerat, propterea minus uti poterat, quod iter ab Arare Helvetii averterant, a quibus discedere nolebat. Diem ex die ducere Aedui: conferri, comportari, adesse dicere.

Account for the mood and tense of *essent, flagitare, ducere, conferri, dicere:* for the case of *Aeduos, frumentum, flumine, navibus, diem, Aedui.*

(*b*) Dum paucos dies ad Vesontionem rei frumentariae com-
meatusque causa moratur, ex percontatione nostrorum voci-
busque Gallorum ac mercatorum, qui ingenti magnitudine
corporum Germanos, incredibili virtute atque exercitatione
in armis esse praedicabant (saepenumero sese cum his con-
gressos ne vultum quidem atque aciem oculorum dicebant
ferre potuisse), tantus subito timor omnem exercitum occu-
pavit, ut non mediocriter omnium mentes animosque pertur-
baret.

Where was *Vesontio* situated? What is the construction of
ingenti magnitudine?

(*c*) Ad haec Caesar respondit: Se magis consuetudine sua
quam merito eorum civitatem conservaturum, si prius, quam
murum aries attigisset, se dedidissent; sed deditionis nullam
esse conditionem, nisi armis traditis. Se id, quod in Nerviis
fecisset, facturum finitimisque imperaturum, ne quam dedi-
ticiis populi Romani iniuriam inferrent. Re nuntiata ad
suos, quae imperarentur, facere dixerunt. Armorum magna
multitudine de muro in fossam, quae erat ante oppidum, iacta,
sic ut prope summam muri aggerisque altitudinem acervi
armorum adaequarent, et tamen circiter parte tertia, ut
postea perspectum est, celata atque in oppido retenta, portis
patefactis, eo die pace sunt usi.

Describe the *aries.* Write out in direct narration the passage *Se magis . . . . iniuriam inferrent.*

2. Translate :—

(*a*) Inde lupae fulvo nutricis tegmine laetus
Moenia, Romanosque suo de nomine dicet.
Romulus excipiet gentem, et Mavortia condet
His ego nec metas rerum nec tempora pono;
Imperium sine fine dedi. Quin aspera Iuno,
Quae mare nunc terrasque metu caelumque fatigat,
Consilia in melius referet, mecumque fovebit
Romanos, rerum dominos, gentemque togatam.
Sic placitum. Veniet lustris labentibus aetas,
Cum domus Assaraci Phthiam clarasque Mycenas
Servitio premet, ac victis dominabitur Argis.
Nascetur pulchra Troianus origine Caesar,
Imperium oceano, famam qui terminet astris,
Iulius, a magno demissum nomen Iulo.

(*b*) Haec dum Dardánio Aeneae miranda videntur,
Dum stupet, obtutuque haeret defixus in uno;
Regina ad templum, forma pulcherrima Dido,
Incessit, magna iuvenum stipante caterva.
Qualis in Eurotae ripis, aut per iuga Cynthi
Exercet Diana choros, quam mille secutae
Hinc atque hinc glomerantur Oreades: illa pharetram
Fert humero, gradiensque deas supereminet omnes;
Latonae tacitum pertentant gaudia pectus;
Talis erat Dido, talem se laeta ferebat
Per medios, instans operi regnisque futuris.

Scan the first three lines of extract (*a*). Write brief notes on the following :—*Mavortia moenia; gentem togatam; Phthiam clarasque Mycenas; molem et montes ; nec vox hominem sonat ; non ignara mali.*

FIRST YEAR ENTRANCE.

LATIN GRAMMAR AND COMPOSITION.

Wednesday, September 15th :—Afternoon, 2 to 3 15.

1. Decline:—*dies, consul, idem* (in all gender). Decline together:—*totus orbis ; vetus istud vinum.*

2. Give the vocative of *Gains Julius Caesar;* the ablative plural of *aliquis ;* the genitive plural of *corpus, urbs, manus.*

3. Compare the adjectives *parvus, felix, idoneus;* the adverbs *bene, audacter.*

4. Give the Latin for eighteen, thirteenth, one apiece.

5. Inflect *eo* in the imperfect subjunctive ; *moneo* and *rego* in the future indicative, and present subjunctive active; *loquor,* in the imperfect indicative.

6. Write down the principal parts of :—*cado, caedo, fero, tollo, augeo.*

7. Account for the case of italicised words in the following:—contentio *honorum;* inde *loci;* damnare *capitis;* neque adsentior *eis ;* neque cernitur *ulli ;* cui *Africano* fuit cognomen; Belgae *Rhenum* traducti sunt.

8. Translate into Latin: (a) The force of custom is great. (b) From whence do you come? (c) Rome is our country. (d) Cicero wrote on friendship. (e) They run down with great swiftness. (f) He set out to attack the town. (g) After encouraging the soldiers, and giving the signal, he ordered the lieutenant to make a sudden attack upon the enemy.

MATRICULATION IN ARTS.

MATHEMATICS.

THURSDAY, SEPT. 16TH :—MORNING, 9 TO 12.

Examiners,........ .... $\begin{cases} \text{ALEXANDER JOHNSON, M.A., LL.D.} \\ \text{H. M. TORY, M.A.} \end{cases}$

1. The straight line drawn perpendicular to a tangent to a circle from the point of contact passes through the centre.

2. Divide a straight line into two parts, so that the rectangle under the whole line and one part shall be equal to the square on the other part.

3. If a straight line be divided into two equal and also into two unequal parts, the sum of the squares on the two unequal parts shall be equal to twice the square on half the line together with twice the square on the part of the line between the points of section.

4. The three angles of any triangle are together equal to two right angles.

(a) Trisect a right angle.

5. If the square on one side of a triangle be equal to the sum of the squares on the other two sides, then the angle contained by these two sides shall be a right angle.

6. Solve the equations :

(1) $x^2 - 14x = 120$.

(2) $\sqrt{5(x + 2)} = \sqrt{5x} + 2$

(3) $2x + 3y = 8,\ 7x - y = 5$

(4) $(2 + x)(a - 3) = -4 - 2ax$

(5) $\dfrac{x + 2}{x - 2} + \dfrac{x - 2}{x + 2} = \dfrac{13}{6}$.

7. Extract the square root of

$$x^4 + 2x^3 + 3x^2 + 2x + 1, \text{ and}$$

reduce to its lowest terms

$$\frac{x^3 - x^2 - 7x + 3}{x^4 + 2x^3 + 2x - 1}.$$

8. Simplify $2\sqrt[3]{4} + 5\sqrt[3]{32} - \sqrt[3]{108}$,
and rationalize the denomination of

$$\frac{2\sqrt{3} + 3\sqrt{2}}{3\sqrt{3} - 2\sqrt{5}}.$$

9. Simplify $\dfrac{1\frac{1}{3} + \frac{2}{5} - \frac{1}{6}}{\frac{4}{4} \text{ of } \frac{8}{9}}$. Reduce $.27\dot{6}\dot{5}$ to a vulgar fraction, proving your work.

10. Express a meter as the decimal of a mile.

11. Find the interest on $3456.53 for 4 months at $5\frac{1}{2}$ per cent.

12. Extract the square root of 3.14159

————

FACULTIES OF ARTS AND APPLIED SCIENCE.
ENTRANCE EXAMINATIONS.
ENGLISH GRAMMAR.
FRIDAY, SEPTEMBER 17TH :—9 TO 10.30 A.M.

(Questions 10 and 11 are compulsory.)

1. Explain the following terms : alliteration, diphthong, root, stem, hybrid, sonant, surd, rhythm, orthoepy. Illustrate the first five.

2. Enumerate and illustrate the various ways of indicating gender in English. Write two nouns which have a plural meaning without plural inflexion and two others which have a plural inflexion without plural meaning.

3. Tabulate the pronominal adverbs.

4. Define and illustrate : weak verb, auxiliary verb, defective verb, causal verb.

5. Write two noun suffixes which form diminutives, and two which form augmentatives. Illustrate the use of each. State the meaning of the following prefixes: a, for, with, vice, mono.

6. Illustrate the various ways in which the subject of a sentence is expanded. " The Saxons invaded England ;" write out the sentence with the predicate expanded by means of a prepositional phrase and again by means of an adverbial clause of time.

7. Show that the meaning of a sentence is affected by the position of the adverb.

8. Write sentences illustrating the use of *before* and *since* as prepositions, adverbs and conjunctions.

9. Analyse:

> *We* leave the well-beloved *place*
> Where *first* we gazed upon the sky ;
> The roofs that *heard our earliest* cry
> Will shelter *one* of *stranger* race.

10. Parse the words in italics.

FACULTIES OF ARTS AND APPLIED SCIENCE.

ENTRANCE EXAMINATIONS.

BRITISH HISTORY.

FRIDAY, SEPT. 17TH :—10.30 TO 12 P.M.

(First Year candidates will answer any five of the first 6 questions. Second Year candidates will answer questions 1, 2, 3, 7, 8.)

1. What sovereigns since the Norman Conquest have been deposed or have met violent deaths? Mention the circumstances in each case.

2. Name those five persons whose services to English political liberty between 1200 to 1700 seem to you most conspicuous. Justify your opinion.

3. Write a short essay on the feudal system in England.

4. Sketch the career of William of Orange.

5. Draw up a list of the occasions when England and France have been in direct antagonism since 1300.

6. Make brief notes on : St. Augustine, Dunstan, Anselm, Becket, ·Cardinal Pole.

7. Write what you know about points of contact between English and Spanish History.

8. Assign dates to the following events : Death of Cnut, Battle of Bouvines, Wat Tyler's Rebellion, Act of Supremacy, Indian Mutiny.

FACULTIES OF ARTS AND APPLIED SCIENCE.
ENTRANCE EXAMINATIONS.
DICTATION.
ꞏ Friday, Sept. 17th :—2.30 p.m·

My first thought was wonder where he could have been concealed so many years ; my second, a transport of joy to find him still alive ; my third, another transport to find myself in his company ; and my fourth, a resolution to accost him. I did so, and he received me with a complacence in which I saw equal sweetness and dignity. I spoke of his Paradise Lost, as every man must, who is worthy to speak of it at all, and told him a long story of the manner in which it affected me, when I first discovered it, being at that time a school-boy. He answered me by a smile and a gentle inclination of his head. He then grasped my hand affectionately, and, with a smile that charmed me, said, " Well, you for your part will do well also ; " at last recollecting his great age (for I understood him to be two hundred years old), I feared that I might fatigue him by much talking. I took my leave, and he took his, with an air of the most perfect good breeding. His person, his features, his manners, were all so perfectly characteristic, that I am persuaded an apparition of him cou'd not represent him more completely.

FIRST AND SECOND YEAR ENTRANCE EXAMINATIONS.
ENGLISH LITERATURE.
Friday, September 17th :—2 or 2½ Hrs.

(N.B. Candidates will observe the following conditions :—

(a) The paper for *Ordinary* Entrance into the First Year consists of the first *six* questions.

(b) The paper for *Higher* Entrance into the First Year consists ·of the first *eight* questions.

(c) The paper for Entrance into the Second Year consists of the first *six* questions, and questions 9 and 10).

1. Give in substance the events contained in any *one* act of King Richard the Second.

2. Explain the following Shaksperian words or phrases : doubly portcullis'd with my teeth and lips, the sepulchre in stubborn Jewry, change the complexion of her maid-pale peace to scarlet indignation, till they have *fretted* us a pair of graves, his Jack o'the clock.

3. State what you know concerning the date of production of the play of King Richard the Second.

4. Describe, in outline and in your own words, *either* (a) the combat between Fitz James and Roderick Dhu, *or* (b) the sports of the Scotsmen in Canto V of the Lady of the Lake.

5. Write *short* notes on : the Fiery Cross, Scottish customs of hospitality, mavis, shallop, Benvenue.

6. Quote at least ten lines from the Lady of the Lake, which possess distinct literary merit, and justify your selection.

7. Give some account of the nature of the contrast between l'Allegro and Il Penseroso.

8. Explain the following : buxom, blithe and debonair ; the cynosure of neighbouring eyes, Cynthia checks her dragon yoke, Faery Mab the junkets eat.

9. Discuss the character of Richard the Second in the play of the same name, and support your statements with quotations.

10. Make notes on two striking characteristics of the poetry of Scott as shown in the Lady of the Lake, and verify each point with a short illustrative quotation.

EXAMENS D'ENTRÉE.

LETTRES ET SCIENCES—1ere ANNÉE.

Lundi, 20 Septembre.

Examinateurs,. .... { M. Ingres.
{ J. L. Morin.

I. Répondre aux questions suivantes :

1. Pourquoi ne vous êtes-vous pas présenté en juin ?

2. Où et comment avez-vous passé juillet et août ?

3. Depuis quand étudiez-vous le français, et pourquoi l'apprenez-vous?

4. Quel est l'emploi des pronoms *en* et *y* ?

II. Faire des questions qui conviennent aux réponses suivantes :

1. Je suis arrivé à 9 heures.

2. Non, je suis venu à pied.

3. Pour subir mes examens d'entrée.

4. Généralement en ajoutant —ment— au féminin de l'adjectif.

III. Faire une description de la chambre où vous travaillez ordinairement (50 mots au moins).

IV. Dans le passage suivant remplacer les infinitifs par les formes que le sens exige.

SAGESSE D'UN PERSAN.

Un roi de Perse, qui *être surnommer* le Juste et qui *mériter* ce glorieux surnom, *vouloir*, un jour qu'il *être* à la chasse, *manger* du gibier qu'il *avoir tuer*. Comme il n'*avoir* point de sel, il *envoyer* un esclave pour en *chercher* au village voisin, et lui *recommander* de le *payer* très exactement. Les courtisans du prince *trouver* que leur maître *attacher* beaucoup d'importance à une bien petite chose. "Un roi, leur *répondre*-il, *devoir* ne *donner* que de bons exemples. Qu'il *prendre* un fruit dans un jardin, ses vizirs *vouloir arracher* l'arbre ; qu'il se *permettre* de *prendre* un œuf sans *payer*, ses soldats *tuer* toutes les poules."

V. Dans le passage suivant remplacer les tirets par des mots qui conviennent au sens.

GARE ! GARE !

Un habitant d'Athènes, qui —— une poutre, ayant heurté rudement Diogène avertit ensuite —— philosophe —— —— criant : gare ! Un peu étourdi —— coup, le célèbre cynique poursuivit -—— route —— —— dire. Mais —— jours après, ayant rencontré —— même homme, —— ——asséna un grand coup —— bâton —— —— tête, —— —— criant à son tour · gare ! gare !

VI. Traduire en anglais :

L'ANE ET LE CHARDON.

Un jour de l'automne dernier,
Un chardon tout en fleurs fut atteint par la foudre.
Survint un âne : "Encor, si c'était ce pommier
Dont les fruits de mon maître abreuvent le gosier,
Je rirais de le voir ainsi réduit en poudre;
Mais un chardon, quel meurtre !" Un passant l'entendit :

"Malpeste ! cria-t-il à la bête de somme,
Comme un grain d'égoïsme aux gens ouvre l'esprit !
Vous êtes, mon grison, moins âne qu'on ne dit,
Et vous raisonnez comme un homme."

FILLEUL DES GUERROTS.

VII. Dater en toutes lettres et motiver l'orthographe des adjectifs numéraux.

MATRICULATION EXAMINATION.

GERMAN.

MONDAY, SEPT. 20TH.—MORNING, 9 TO 12.

Examiner, ...L. R. GREGOR, B A., PH.D.

FOR MEN AND WOMEN.

1. Translate :—

(a) Nun hatte der Reiche, was er wollte, ritt heimwärts und
besann sich, was er sich wünschen sollte. Als er so nachdachte und
den Zügel fallen ließ, fing das Pferd an zu springen, so daß er
immerfort in seinen Gedanken gestört wurde und sie gar nicht
zusammenbringen konnte. Da ward er über das Pferd ungeduldig
und sprach: „So wollt' ich, daß du den Hals brächest!" Und als
er das Wort ausgesprochen hatte, plump! fiel er auf die Erde, und
das Pferd lag tot und regte sich nicht mehr; und nun war der erste
Wunsch erfüllt. Weil er aber geizig war, wollte er das Sattelzeug
nicht im Stiche lassen, schnitt's ab, hing's auf den Rücken, und
mußte nun zu Fuße nach Hause gehen. Doch tröstete er sich, daß
ihm noch zwei Wünsche übrig geblieben.

(b) Drei Worte nenn' ich euch, inhaltschwer,
    Sie gehen von Munde zu Munde;
Doch stammen sie nicht von außen her;
    Das Herz nur giebt davon Kunde.
Dem Menschen ist aller Wert geraubt,
Wenn er nicht mehr an die drei Worte glaubt.

Der Mensch ist frei geschaffen, ist frei,
  Und wär' er in Ketten geboren,
Laßt euch nicht irren des Pöbels Geschrei,
  Nicht den Mißbrauch rasender Thoren!
Vor dem Sklaven, wenn er die Kette bricht,
Vor dem freien Menschen erzittert nicht!
Und die Tugend, sie ist kein leerer Schall,
  Der Mensch kann sie üben im Leben,
Und sollt' er auch straucheln überall,
  Er kann nach dem Göttlichen streben;
Und was kein Verstand der Verständigen sieht,
Das übet in Einfalt ein kindlich Gemüt.

2. Translate into German :—

(a) The difference between my brother and me is not great.
(b) The city of Berlin is the capital of the Kingdom of Prussia.
(c) Buying is pleasant, but paying is very disagreeable. (d)
In winter I visit the university, but in summer I live with my
parents in the country. (e) The students to whom these books
belong do not study them diligently, which is a pity. (f) The
soldier had been wounded by a ball. (g) The general rode
across the bridge with his officers. (h) Do you remember
what I told you about the old castle? (i) One general commands
thousands of soldiers. (j) The coachman drove first to the post-
office and then to the bank. (k) It was a quarter past eight
when the concert began. (l) My father could have sold his
house last year, but now it is impossible. (m) I know one of
them, but I cannot remember his name. (n) By means of a microscope living animals can be seen in a drop of water.

3. Decline in singular and plural, (a) the relative pronoun
der, (b) the German for *my new house*, (c) any one possessive
pronoun, (d) *die Montrealer Zeitung*, (e) *dergleichen* used adjec-
tively, (f) *der Mann*, (g) *das Buch*, (h) *die Frau*, (i) *der
Schwager*, (j) *der König*.

4. Give the three principal parts of the strong verbs in
extracts (a) and (b) of Question I.

5. What do you know about (*a*) diminutive terminations, (*b*) the mood of the verb in dependent questions, (*c*) contractions of certain prepositions with the unemphasized definite article, (*d*) prepositions governing genitive case, (*e*) the order of the different classes of adverbs, (*f*) the pronouns of address ?

For Women Only.

6. Translate :—

Daß keine welche lebt, mit Deutschlands Sprache sich
In den zu kühnen Wettstreit wage !
Sie ist — damit ich's kurz, mit ihrer Kraft es sage —
An mannigfalt'ger Uranlage
Zu immer neuer und doch deutscher Wendung reich ;
Ist, was wir selbst in jenen grauen Jahren,
Da Tacitus uns forschte, waren :
Gesondert, ungemischt und nur sich selber gleich.

7. Mr. B. caught a cold some weeks ago and has not yet been allowed to leave his room. He is getting better slowly, but he will not be able to resume his occupations for a long time. His physician advises him to take a sea voyage. I have heard that his wife would like to pass the winter in the south of France, where the climate is so warm and delightful. It will not cost much more to live there than here. Of course, the travelling expenses must be included. Fortunately, they are not nearly so large as they used to be. I have been told that you can go from New York to Genoa, first-class, for one hundred dollars, or even less.

SECOND YEAR ENTRANCE.

GREEK AND LATIN GRAMMAR AND COMPOSITION.

Monday, September 20th :—Afternoon, 2 to 5.

1. Decline in full :—$\pi\alpha\tau\acute{\eta}\rho$, $\pi\acute{o}\lambda\iota\varsigma$, $\epsilon\hat{\iota}\varsigma$, $\mu o\hat{v}\sigma a$, $\tau\epsilon\hat{\iota}\chi o\varsigma$, $\acute{o}\rho o\varsigma$, $\nu o\mu o\delta\acute{\epsilon}\tau\eta\varsigma$, $\pi a\hat{\iota}\varsigma$, $\gamma\upsilon\nu\acute{\eta}$, $\kappa\hat{\eta}\rho\upsilon\xi$.

2. Give the meanings of and the cases governed by the following prepositions as well as their force in compounds :—περὶ, μετά, παρά, ὑπό, διά.

3. Write out in full the following parts of λύω :—1st Aor. Ind. Act., 1st Aor. Ind. Pass., Pres. Imper. Act. Perf. Part. Act·, 1st Aor. Inf. Pass., 1st Aor. Part. Mid., Fut. Opt. Mid. ; also the Aor. Act. of δίδωμι and the Pres. Subj. of τιμάω.

4. Give the principal parts in use of αἱρέω, ἐσθίω, ἔρχομαι, βάλλω, ἔχω, λέγω, σπείρω, λαμβάνω, πείθω, πάσχω, γίγνομαι, τρέφω, βαίνω.

5. State the constructions usual with τυγχάνω, χρῆσθαι, εἰ, ἐάν, ἔρασθαι, αἰσθάνομαι; illustrate by examples the force of the Middle Voice. Give with examples the different uses and meanings of ὡς, αὐτὸς, ἄν.

6. Translate into Greek :—

(a) Some of these things are private and some common.

(b) The king having died the city was taken (use ἁλίσκομαι).

(c) Alexander, the son of Philip, was called the Great.

(d) We must first say of what sort (use ποῖος) these people ought to be.

(e) He escaped without being noticed (use λανθάνω).

(f) If I had seen him I should have fled.

(g) The person who is to (use μέλλω) govern well ought first to be governed.

7. Give the principal parts of eo, refero, premo, accingo, figo, fundo, requiro.

8. (a) Express the following dates according to our notation; a.d. IV. Non. Sextiles, C. Terentio Varrone L. Aemilio

Paullo II. cos.; prid. Id. Jan. A.U.C., CCCCXL. (b) Write the following in Latin: June 20th, B.C. 207; November 8th, B.C. 64.

9. Translate and explain the grammatical construction of italicised words: (a) paro militum *capti* sunt. (b) regna, honores, divitiae *incerta* sunt. (c) ubinam *gentium* sumus. (d) *me sententiam* rogavit. (e) 2. Verrem *Romilla*, nihil *ignoveris*. (f) *maturato* opus est. (g) nisi tu amisisses, numquam *reccpissam*.

10. Translate into Latin :—

Thereupon, that faithful slave, having heard everything and perceived in what direction things were tending, fearing that his master might fall unawares into a trap, snatched the sword out of the hand of an armed Gaul who was standing sentinel near the King with such suddenness that he had not time even to make resistance.

SECOND YEAR ENTRANCE.

LATIN.

SEPTEMBER 15TH:—AFTERNOON, 2 TO 5.

1. Translate :—

Tum pater Anchises: "Animae, quibus altera fato
Corpora debentur, Lethaei ad fluminis undam
Securos latices et longa oblivia potant.
Has equidem memorare tibi atque ostendere coram,
Iampridem hanc prolem cupio enumerare meorum:
Quo magis Italia mecum laeterę reperta.
O pater, anne aliquas ad caelum hinc ire putandum est
Sublimes animas, iterumque in tarda reverti
Corpora? quae lucis miseris tam dira cupido?
Dicam equidem; nec te suspensum, nate, tenebo:"
Suscipit Anchises, atque ordine singula pandit.

Virgil, Aen. VI.

(1) Write out and divide into feet, marking the quantity of every syllable, and the position of the caesura, the first four lines. (2) Give the derivation and meaning of *ingens, comes, trames, nuntius, securus, alumnus.* (3) How are prohibitions expressed in Latin? Illustrate.

2. Translate —

I. Recognosce tandem mecum noctem illam superiorem; iam intelleges multo me vigilare acrius ad salutem quam *te* ad perniciem rei publicae. Dico te priore *nocte* venisse inter falcarios—non agam obscure—in M. Laecae domum; convenisse eodem compluris eiusdem amentiae scelerisque socios. Num negas? quid taces? convincam, si negas. Video enim esse hic in senatu quosdam, qui tecum una fuerunt.—Cicero In Catil., I. 4.

II. Cum ille, homo audacissimus, conscientia convictus, primo reticuisset, patefeci cetera: quid ea nocte *egisset*, quid in proximam constituisset, quem ad modum esset *ei* ratio totius belli descripta, edocui. Cum haesitaret cum teneretur, quaesivi quid dubitaret *proficisci* eo, quo iam pridem, *pararet*, cum arma, cum securis, cum fascis, cum aquilam illam argenteam cui etiam sacrarium *domi suae* fecerat, scirem esse praemissam.—In Catilinam, II. 13.

III. Quod si omnis impetus domesticorum hostium, depulsus a vobis, se in me unum convertit, *vobis* erit videndum, Quirites, qua *condicione* posthac eos esse *velitis*, qui se pro salute vestra obtulerint invidiae periculisque omnibus: mihi quidem ipsi, quid est quod iam ad vitae fructum *possit* adquiri, cum praesertim neque in honore vestro, neque in gloria virtutis, quicquam videam altius, quo mihi libeat ascendere?—Cicero In Catil., III. 12.

IV. Quam ob rem, sive hoc statueritis, dederitis mihi comitem ad contionem populo carum atque incundum: sive Silani sententiam sequi malueritis, facile me atque vos crudelitatis vituperatione exsolveritis, atque obtinebo eam multo teniorem fuisse. Quamquam, patres conscripti, quae potest esse in tanti sceleris immanitate punienda crudelitas? Ego enim de meo sensu iudico. Nam ita mihi *salva* re publica vobiscum perfrui liceat, ut ego, quod in hac causa vehementior sum, non atrocitate animi moveor—quis est enim me mitior?—sed singulari quadam humanitate et misericordia.—Cicero In Catil., IV. 11.

(a) Explain the Grammatical construction of the words printed in italics. (b) Comment on the meaning of the following words :— securis, fasces, aquilam argenteam, sacrarium, Quirites.

3. Translate :—Livy Bk. I.

EXAMENS D'ENTRÉE.

LETTRES—2me ANNÉE.

Lundi 20 Septembre.

Examinateurs...... .... { M. Ingres.
                                                               { J. L. Morin.

1. Donner quelques renseignements sur la vie et l'œuvre de deux écrivains français de notre siècle. (150 à 200 mots sur chacun).

2. Ecrire sous forme d'analyse eu de compte-rendu environ 500 mots sur un livre français au choix du candidat.

3. Remplacer dans le passage suivant les infinitifs par les formes qui conviennent au sens.

LE LION ET LE RENARD.

" Sire, *dire* un jour le renard au lion, je *vouloir* vous *faire* une confidence importante, mais je n'*oser*. — *Parler* en toute liberté, *répondre* le monarque. — En bien, sire, *croire*-vous que l'âne *avoir* l'audace de *parler* mal de Votre Majesté?...Que je *vanter* votre courage, ou que j'*exalter* votre générosité, quoique je *dire* enfin à votre louange, il *soutenir* aussitôt le contraire." *Avoir* ainsi *parler*, le renard s'*arrêter*. " *Continuer*-donc, lut *dire* le lion. — *C'être* tout, sire ! — Vraiment ? J'*espérar*, je te l'*avouer*, qu'il y *avoir* autre chose. Si tu n'*avoir* pas d'autre révélation à me *faire* renard, *garder* le silence ; car, que *vouloir*-tu que me *faire* les propos d'un âne.

4. Remplacer dans le passage suivant les tirets par des mots convenan au sens.

L'OFFRE TROMPEUSE.

Les mots suivants étaient —— sur la porte d'un beau jardin : " Je donne —— parterre —— quiconque —— content.". Voilà bien —— affaire ! dit tout bas —— passant ; je vas donc —— un terrain !" Là-dessus, —— court, —— de joie, s'adresser —— propriétaire —— jardin. " Que —— vous ? demande celui-ci —— —— voyant paraître. — Je désire —— jardin. Mon croit à m'y établir —— paraît incontestable, car je suis content —— mon sort. — Erreur ! mon —— ami : —— veut avoir —— —— n'a pas ne sautait être content. Reprenez —— chemin."

5. Indiquer l'emploi de l'imparfait, du passé défini et du passé indéfini

6. Remplacez le titre " Les Bons Livres " par "Les Mauvais Livres," et donnez le contraire des mots en italique.

LES BONS LIVRES.

La lecture peut être la *meilleure* des *distractions.* Aussi faut-il *aimer*
les *bons* livres et les *rechercher. Heureux* l'enfant qui en fait ses com-
pagnons ! ils placent sous ses yeux les plus *belles* pages de la vie des
hommes *vertueux,* les *glorieuses* actions des *bons* citoyens, et lui montrent
l'exemple *réjouissant* des *travailleurs,* esclaves de leurs *devoirs, triomphant*
au milieu des difficultés de la vie. Par ces *précieux* exemples, son carac-
tère s'*élève,* son cœur s'*anoblit,* ou bien sa mémoire emmagasine mille coni
naissances *utiles.* Il devient chaque jour plus *respertueux* et plus *obéis-*
sant envers sa famille, plus *attentif* à l'école, plus *agréable* aux autres et à
lui-même. Ses camarades l'*estiment, ses* parents le *bénissent.* — Les *bons*
livres sont des *amis* en compagnie desquels on *gagne* toujours.

7 Répondre par écrit l'anecdote suivante. Cette anecdote sera racontée par l'examinateur.

8. Dater en toutes lettres et motiver l'orthographe des adjectifs numéraux.

HIGHER ENTRANCE EXAMINATION.

SEPTEMBER 15TH :—MORNING, 9 TO 12.

Translate, with notes on words and phrases underlined,
A, B (1) or B (2), and C or C (2).

A. Xenophon, Anabasis I.

(*a*) ἐκάλεσε δὲ καὶ τοὺς Μίλητον πολιορκοῦντας, καὶ τοὺς
φυγάδας ἐκέλευσε σὺν αὐτῷ στρατεύεσθαι, ὑποσχόμενος
αὐτοῖς, εἰ καλῶς καταπράξειεν ἐφ᾽ ἃ ἐστρατεύετο, μὴ πρόσθεν παύσεσθαι πρὶν αὐτοὺς καταγάγοι οἴκαδε.

(*b*) καὶ οἱ μὲν ὄνοι, ἐπεί τις διώκοι, προδραμόντες ἕστασαν·
πολὺ γὰρ τῶν ἵππων ἔτρεχον θᾶττον· καὶ πάλιν, ἔπει
πλησιάζοιεν οἱ ἵπποι, ταὐτὸν ἐποίουν, καὶ οὐκ ἦν λαβεῖν,
εἰ μὴ διαστάντες οἱ ἱππεῖς θηρῷεν διαδεχόμενοι.

(*c*) ἢν δ᾽ ἡμεῖς νικήσωμεν, ἡμᾶς δεῖ τοὺς ἡμετέρους φίλους
τούτων ἐγκρατεῖς ποιῆσαι. ὥστε οὐ τοῦτο δέδοικα μὴ οὐκ
ἔχω ὅ, τι δῶ ἑκάστῳ τῶν φίλων, ἂν εὖ γένηται, ἀλλὰ μὴ
οὐκ ἔχω ἱκανοὺς οἷς δῶ.

(*d*) εἰ δὲ τινα ὁρῴη δεινὸν ὄντα οἰκονόμον ἐκ τοῦ δικαίου καὶ κατασκευάζοντά τε ἧς ἄρχοι χώρας καὶ προσόδους ποιοῦντα, οὐδένα ἂν πώποτε ἀφείλετο, ἀλλ᾽ ἀεὶ πλείω προσεδίδου.

B. (1) Homer, Iliad I.

(*a*) ἔκλαγξαν δ᾽ ἄρ᾽ ὀιστοὶ ἐπ᾽ ὤμων χωομένοιο,
αὐτοῦ κινηθέντος· ὁ δ᾽ ἤιε νυκτὶ ἐοικώς.
ἕζετ᾽ ἔπειτ᾽ ἀπάνευθε νεῶν, μετὰ δ᾽ ἰὸν ἔηκεν·
δεινὴ δὲ κλαγγὴ γένετ᾽ ἀργυρέοιο βιοῖο.
οὐρῆας μὲν πρῶτον ἐπῴχετο καὶ κύνας ἀργούς,
αὐτὰρ ἔπειτ᾽ αὐτοῖσι βέλος ἐχεπευκὲς ἐφιεὶς
βάλλ᾽ αἰεὶ δὲ πυραὶ νεκύων καίοντο θαμειαί.

(*b*) ἀλλ᾽ ἄγε, διογενὲς Πατρόκλεις, ἔξαγε κούρην
καί σφωιν δὸς ἄγειν. τὼ δ᾽ αὐτὼ μάρτυροι ἔστων
πρός τε θεῶν μακάρων πρός τε θνητῶν ἀνθρώπων
καὶ πρὸς τοῦ βασιλῆος ἀπηνέος, εἴ ποτε δὴ αὖτε
χρειὼ ἐμεῖο γένηται ἀεικέα λοιγὸν ἀμῦναι
τοῖς ἄλλοις.

(*c*) ἦ δὴ λοίγια ἔργα τάδ᾽ ἔσσεται οὐδ᾽ ἔτ᾽ ἀνεκτά,
εἰ δὴ σφὼ ἕνεκα θνητῶν ἐριδαίνετον ὧδε,
ἐν δὲ θεοῖσι κολῳὸν ἐλαύνετον· οὐδέ τι δαιτὸς
ἐσ θλῆς ἔσσεται ἦδος, ἐπεὶ τὰ χερείονα νικᾷ.
μητρὶ δ᾽ ἐγὼ παράφημι καὶ αὐτῇ περ νοεούσῃ,
πατρὶ φίλῳ ἐπὶ ἦρα φέρειν Διί, ὄφρα μὴ αὖτε
νεικείῃσι πατήρ, σὺν δ᾽ ἡμῖν δαῖτα ταράξῃ.

B. (2) Iliad IV.

(*a*) οὐ μέν πως ἅλιον πέλει ὅρκιον αἷμά τε ἀρνῶν
σπονδαί τ᾽ ἄκρητοι καὶ δεξιαί, ἧς ἐπέπιθμεν.
εἴ περ γάρ τε καὶ αὐτίκ᾽ Ὀλύμπιος οὐκ ἐτέλεσσεν,
ἔκ τε καὶ ὀψὲ τελεῖ, σύν τε μεγάλῳ ἀπέτισαν,
σὺν σφῇσιν κεφαλῇσι γυναιξί τε καὶ τεκέεσσιν.

(*b*) σφῶιν μέν τ' ἐπέοικε μετὰ πρώτοισιν ἐόντας
ἐστάμεν ἠδὲ μάχης καυστείρης ἀντιβολῆσαι·
πρώτω γὰρ καὶ δαιτὸς ἀκουάζεσθον ἐμεῖο,
ὁππότε δαῖτα γέρουσιν ἐφοπλίζωμεν Ἀχαιοί.
ἔνθα φίλ' ὀπταλέα κρέα ἔδμεναι ἠδὲ κύπελλα
οἴνου πινέμεναι μελιηδέος, ὄφρ' ἐθέλητον·
νῦν δὲ φίλως χ' ὁρόῳτε, καὶ εἰ δέκα πύργοι Ἀχαιῶν
ὑμείων προπάροιθε μαχοίατο νηλέι χαλκῷ.

(*c*) ἐνθ' Ἀμαρυγκεΐδην Διώρεα μοῖρα πέδησεν·
χερμαδίῳ γὰρ βλῆτο παρὰ σφυρὸν ὀκριόεντι
κνήμην δεξιτερήν· βάλε δὲ Θρηκῶν ἀγὸς ἀνδρῶν.
Πίροος Ἰμβρασίδης, ὃς ἄρ' Αἰνόθεν εἰληλούθειν·
ἀμφοτέρω δὲ τένοντε καὶ ὀστέα λᾶας ἀναιδὴς
ἄχρις ἀπηλοίησεν· ὁ δ' ὕπτιος ἐν κονίησιν
κάππεσεν, ἄμφω χεῖρε φίλοις ἑτάροισι πετάσσας
θυμὸν ἀποπνείων.

C. (1) Odyssey VII.

(*a*)   αὐτὰρ Ὀδυσσεὺς
Ἀλκινόου πρὸς δώματ' ἴε κλυτά· πολλὰ δὲ οἱ κῆρ
ὥρμαιν' ἱσταμένῳ, πρὶν χάλκεον οὐδὸν ἱκέσθαι.
ὥς τε γὰρ ἠελίου αἴγλη πέλεν ἠὲ σελήνης
δῶμα καθ' ὑψερεφὲς μεγαλήτορος Ἀλκινόοιο.
χάλκεοι μὲν γὰρ τοῖχοι ἐληλέδατ' ἔνθα καὶ ἔνθα,
ἐς μυχὸν ἐξ οὐδοῦ, περὶ δὲ θριγκὸς κυάνοιο.

(*b*) ἠῶθεν δὲ γέροντας ἐπὶ πλέονας καλέσαντες
ξεῖνον ἐνὶ μεγάροις ξεινίσσομεν ἠδὲ θεοῖσιν
ῥέξομεν ἱερὰ καλά, ἔπειτα δὲ καὶ περὶ πομπῆς
μνησόμεθ' ὥς χ' ὁ ξεῖνος ἄνευθε πόνου καὶ ἀνίης
πομπῇ ὑφ' ἡμετέρῃ ἣν πατρίδα γαῖαν ἵκηται
χαίρων καρπαλίμως, εἰ καὶ μάλα τηλόθεν ἐστίν,
μηδέ τι μεσσηγγώς γε κακὸν καὶ πῆμα πάθῃσιν,

πρίν γε τὸν ἧς γαίης ἐπιβήμεναι· ἔνθα δ᾽ ἔπειτα
πείσεται, ἅσσά οἱ αἶσα κατὰ κλῶθές τε βαρεῖαι
γιγνομένῳ νήσαντο λίνῳ, ὅτε μιν τέκε μήτηρ.

(c) αἲ γὰρ, Ζεῦ τε πάτερ καὶ ᾿Αθηναίη καὶ ῎Απολλον,
τοῖος ἐὼν οἷός ἐσσι, τά τε φρονέων ἅ τ᾽ ἐγώ περ,
παῖδα τ᾽ ἐμὴν ἐχέμεν καὶ ἐμὸς γαμβρὸς καλέεσθαι
αὖθι μένων· οἶκον δέ τ᾽ ἐγὼ καὶ κτήματα δοίην,
εἰ κ᾽ ἐθέλων γε μένοις· ἀέκοντα δέ σ᾽ οὐ τις ἐρύξει
Φαιήκων· μὴ τοῦτσ φίλον Διὶ πατρὶ γένοιτο.

C. (2) Odyssey XI.

(a)   οἰδέ οἱ εὐναὶ
δέμνια καὶ χλαῖναι καὶ ῥήγεα σιγαλόεντα,
ἀλλ᾽ ὅ γε χεῖμα μὲν εὕδει, ὅθι δμῶες ἐνὶ οἴκῳ,
ἐν κόνι ἄγχι πυρός, κακὰ δὲ χροΐ εἵματα εἶται·
αὐτὰρ ἐπὴν ἔλθῃσι θέρος τεθαλυῖά τ᾽ ὀπώρη,
πάντῃ οἱ κατὰ γουνὸι ἀλωῆς οἰνοπέδοιο
φύλλων κεκλιμένων χθαμαλαὶ βεβλήαται εὐναί.

(b) ἐννέωροι γὰρ τοί γε καὶ ἐννεαπήχεες ἦσαν
εὖρος, ἀτὰρ μῆκός γε γενέσθην ἐννεόργυιοι.
οἵ ῥα καὶ ἀθανάτοισιν ἀπειλήτην ἐν ᾿Ολύμπῳ
φυλόπιδα στήσειν πολυάικος πολέμοιο
῎Οσσαν ἐπ᾽ Οὐλύμπῳ μέμασαν θέμεν, αὐτὰρ ἐπ᾽ ῎Οσσῃ
Πήλιον εἰνοσίφυλλον, ἵν᾽ οὐρανὸς ἀμβατὸς εἴη.

(c) στεῦτο δὲ διψάων, πιέειν δ᾽ οὐκ εἶχεν ἐλέσθαι·
ὅσσακι γὰρ κύψει ὁ γέρων, πιέειν μενεαίνων,
τοσσάχ᾽ ὕδωρ ἀπολέσκετ᾽ ἀναβροχέν, ἀμφὶ δὲ ποσσὶν
γαῖα μέλαινα φάνεσκε, καταζήνασκε δὲ δαίμων.
δένδρεα δ᾽ ὑψιπέτηλα κατὰ κρῆθεν χέε καρπόν,
ὄγχναι καὶ ῥοιαὶ καὶ μηλέαι ἀγλαόκαρποι,
συκέαι τε γλυκεραὶ καὶ ἐλαῖαι τηλεθόωσαι·
τῶν ὁπότ᾽ ἰθύσει᾽ ὁ γέρων ἐπὶ χερσὶ μάσασθαι.
τὰς δ᾽ ἄνεμος ῥίπτασκε ποτὶ νέφεα σκιόεντα.

EXAMINATION FOR EXHIBITIONS AND HIGHER ENTRANCE.

SEPTEMBER.

1. Translate into Greek:—

(a) Cyrus gave five minae to each soldier.

(b) He said that Cyrus began his speech thus.

(c) He will do harm to our city.

(d) Cyrus commanding it, I killed him.

(e) Are we to march against the enemy?

(f) You say that it is no longer necessary to guard against this man.

(g) I will save Athens, as being the city of our friends.

(h) No one has yet seen your daughter either living or dead.

2. Translate into English :—

Ἐπεὶ δὲ εἰσῆλθον ἐπὶ τὸ δεῖπνον τῶν τε Θρᾳκῶν οἱ κράτιστοι τῶν παρόντων καὶ οἱ στρατηγοὶ καὶ οἱ λοχαγοι τῶν Ἑλλήνων, τὸ δεῖπνον μὲν ἦν καθημένοις κύκλῳ· ἔπειτα δὲ τρίποδες εἰσηνέχθησαν πᾶσιν, οὗτα δὲ ἦσαν κρεῶν μεστοί. κέρατα δὲ οἴνου περιέφερον, καὶ πάντες ἐδέχοντο· ὁ δὲ Ἀρύστας, ἐπεὶ πὰρ αὐτὸν φέρων τὸ κέρας ὁ δοῦλος ἧκεν, εἶπεν ἰδὼν τὸν Ξενοφῶντα οὐκέτι δειπνοῦντα, Ἐκείνῳ, ἔφη, δός.

3. (a) Give 10 examples, showing how the meaning of prepositions varies when they are used with different cases.

(b) What classes of verbs govern the genitive? Give examples.

(c) Give the chief tenses of λανθάνω, ἔρχομαι, ἐθέλω, αἱρέω, καθίστημι, καθέζομαι ; express in as many different ways as possible "I will say," " I said."

(d) What are the ways of expressing purpose and consequence in Greek?

FIRST YEAR EXHIBITIONS.

SATURDAY, SEPT. 18TH :—MORNING, 9 TO 12.

HIGHER GREEK COMPOSITION.

Padios once told this story about himself: "I was walking in the city and I met a certain man, who seemed to me to be my friend Malleios. And when he saw me, he came towards me in a friendly way, as though about to greet me. But when we were nearer each of us wondered greatly, for, by Zeus, it was neither of us."

walk βαδίζω,	greet ἀσπάζομαι,
meet περιτυγχάνω dat.,	near ἐγγύς,
in a friendly way φιλικῶς.	wonder θαυμάζω.

FIRST YEAR EXHIBITIONS AND HIGHER ENTRANCE.

LATIN GRAMMAR AND COMPOSITION.

1. Comment on the case of the words underlined in the following :—codex optimae *notae*, et *mea* et *tua* maxime interest, *sapientiae* parum, *institiaene* prius mirer?, nate *dea*, doctas iam nunc eat inquit *Athenas*, paucis ante *diebus*, dignum *laude* virum, quid mihi Celsus agit? ventum erat ad *Vestae*. Name six verbs governing a Dative.

2. What various ways are there of translating :—He sent messengers to ask for peace.

3. What is meant by (a) a subordinate sentence in Oratio Obliqua, (b) Indirect Question? Give an example of each in English and Latin.

4. State Grimm's Law, and give examples which illustrate it.

5. Write out the Pres. Subj. of nolo, the Fut. Indic. Act. of rego, and the Pres. Subj. of hortor.

6. Translate into Latin :—Towards evening Metellus was informed by one of his scouts that large masses of the enemy could be seen assembling upon the surrounding hills. The Roman army was encamped on a low-lying plain, which the recent rains had rendered marshy and treacherous to the feet. On their rear was a river that was impassable from the same cause; in front and on both flanks lay the slopes which the enemy had already occupied. As matters seemed so desperate, Metellus determined to summon a council of war—a thing which he had never previously done. He reminded his assembled captains that the danger was urgent, and asked what they advised.

FIRST YEAR EXHIBITIONS AND HIGHER ENTRANCE.
LATIN:—3 hours.

N.B.—In the first three Questions Candidates may answer either the portion marked A., or that marked B., but no Candidate will get credit for both portions.

1. (A) Translate :—

At pius Aeneas, per noctem plurima volvens,
Ut primum lux alma data est, exire locosque
Explorare novos, quas vento accesserit oras,
Qui teneant, nam inculta videt, hominesne feraene,
Quaerere constituit, sociisque exacta referre.
Classem in convexo nemorum sub rupe cavata
Arboribus clausam circum atque horrentibus umbris
Occulit; ipse uno graditur comitatus Achate,
Bina manu lato crispans hastilia ferro.
Cui mater media sese tulit obvia silva,
Virginis os habitumque gerens et virginis arma.
Spartanae, vel qualis equos Threissa fatigat
Harpalyce volucremque fuga praevertitur Hebrum.

Translate, adding a short note, *where necessary*:—

(a) Ni faciat, maria ac terras caelumque profundum

Quippe ferant rapidi secum verrantque per auras.
(b)   Mene Iliacis occumbere campis
Non potuisse tuaque animam hanc effundere dextra.
(c)   .   Tenet ille immania saxa
Vestras, Eure, domos.   ·
(d) Tum Cererem corruptam undis Crealiaque arma
Expediunt fessi rerum, frugesque receptas
Et torrere parant flammis et frangere saxo.
(e) Vos et Scyllaeam rabiem penitusque sonantes
Accestis scopulos.
(f) O fortunati quorum iam moenia surgunt.
(g) Ipse hostis Teucros insigni laude ferebat
Seque ortum antiqua Teucrorum ab stirpe volebat.
(h) Urit atrox Juno et sub noctem cura recursat.

(B) Translate :—
Vivite felices, quibus est fortuna peracta
Iam sua; nos alia ex aliis in fata vocamur.
Vobis parta quies; nullum maris aequor arandum,
Arva neque Ausoniae semper cedentia retro
Quaerenda. Effigiem Xanthi Troiamque videtis,
Quam vestrae fecere manus, melioribus, opto,
Auspiciis, et quae fuerit minus obvia Grais.
Si quando Thybrim vicinaque Thybridis arva
Intraro gentique meae data moenia cernam,
Cognatas urbes olim populosque propinquos,
Epiro, Hesperia, quibus idem Dardanus auctor
Atque idem casus, unam faciemus utramque
Troiam animis: maneat nostros ea cura nepotes.

Translate, adding a short note, *where necessary* :—
(a) Inruimus ferro, et divos ipsumque vocamus
In partem praedamque Iovem.
(b)   .   Tum litore funem
Deripere, excussosque iubet laxare rudentes.
(c) Quid puer Ascanius? superatne et vescitur aura
Quem tibi iam Troia—
(d) Aulai medio libabant pocula Bacchi,
Impositis auro dapibus, paterasque tenebant.
(e) Tum pater Anchises magnum cratera corona
Induit implevitque mero.
(f) Hinc sinus Herculei, si vera est fama, Tarenti
Cernitur; attollit se diva Lacinia contra,

Caulonisque arces et navifragum Scylaceum.
(g)   Dira inluvies immissaque barba
Consertum tegumen spinis.
(h) Argolici clipei aut Phoebeae lampadis instar.

2. (A) Translate :—

Hic ego vehemens ille consul, qui verbo cives in exsilium ejicio, quaesivi a Catilina in nocturno conventu apud M. Laecum fuisset necne. Quum ille, homo audacissimus, conscientia convictus, primo reticuisset, patefeci cetera; quid ea nocte egisset, ubi fuisset, quid in proximam constituisset, quemadmodum esset ei ratio totius belli descripta, edocui. Quum haesitaret, quum teneretur, quaesivi quid dubitaret proficisci eo quo iampridem pararet, quum arma, quum secures, quum fasces, quum tubas, quum signa militaria, quum aquilam illam argenteam, cui ille etiam sacrarium domi suae fecerat, scirem esse praemissam. In exsilium ejiciebam quem iam ingressum esse in bellum videbam? Etenim, credo, Manlius iste centurio, qui in agro Faesulano castra posuit, bellum populo Romano suo nomine indixit; et illa castra nunc non Catilinam ducem expectant, et ille ejectus in exsilium se Massiliam ut aiunt non in haec castra conferet.

(B) Translate :—

Albi, ne doleas plus nimio memor •
Immitis Glycerae, neu miserabiles
Decantes elegos, cur tibi iunior
Laesa praeniteat fide.
Insignem tenui fronte Lycorida
Cyri torret amor, Cyrus in asperam
Declinat Pholoen; sed prius Apulis
Iungentur capreae lupis,
Quam turpi Pholoe peccet adultero.
Sic visum Veneri, cui placet impares
Formas atque animos sub iuga aenea
Saevo mittere cum ioco.
Ipsum me, melior cum peteret Venus,
Grata detinuit compede Myrtale ·
Libertina, fretis acrior Hadriae
Curvantis Calabros sinus.

3. (A) Translate :—

Quod fratres a senatu Aeduos appellatos diceret, non se tam barbarum neque tam imperitum esse rerum, ut non sciret,

neque bello Allobrogum proximo Aeduos Romanis auxilium
tulisse neque ipsos in his contentionibus, quas Aedui secum
et cum Sequanis habuissent, auxilio populi Romani usos esse.
Debere se suspicari simulata Caesarem amicitia, quod.exerci-
tum in Gallia habeat, sui opprimendi causa habere. Qui
nisi decedat atque exercitum deducat ex his regionibus, sese
illum non pro amico, sed hoste habiturum.   Quodsi eum in-
terfecerit, multis sese nobilibus principibusque populi Romani gratum esse facturum; id se ab ipsis per eorum nuntios
compertum habere, quorum omnium gratiam atque amicitiam
eius morte redimere posset.   Quodsi discessisset et liberam
possessionem Galliae sibi tradidisset, magno se illum praemio
remuneraturum et quaecunque bella geri vellet, sine ullo eius
labore et periculo confecturum.

Explain the political position of Caesar, which is here alluded to by Ariovistus.

(B) Mittuntur etiam ad eas civitates legati, quae sunt ci-
terioris Hispaniae finitimae Aquitaniae; inde auxilia duces-
que arcessuntur. Quorum adventu magna cum auctoritate
et magna cum hominum multitudine bellum gerere conantur.
Duces vero ii deliguntur, qui una cum Q. Sertorio omnes
annos fuerant summamque scientiam rei militaris habere ex-
istimabantur. Hi consuetudine populi Romani loca capere,
castra munire, commeatibus nostros intercludere instituunt.
Quod ubi Crassus animadvertit, suas copias propter exigui-
tatem non facile diduci, hostem et vagari et vias obsidere et
castris satis praesidii relinquere, ob eam causam minus com-
mode frumentum commeatumque sibi supportari, in dies hostium numerum augeri non cunctandum existimavit quin
pugna decertaret. Hac re ad consilium delata ubi omnes
idem sentire intellexit, posterum diem pugnae constituit.

State briefly what you know of the Sertorius here mentioned.

4. Translate :—Horum adventu tauta rerum commutatio
est facta, ut nostri etiam qui vulneribus confecti procubuis-
sent, scutis innixi proelium redintegrarent; tum calones per-
territos hostes conspicati etiam inermes armatis occurrerunt,
equites vero, ut turpitudinem fugae virtute delerent, omnibus in locis pugnant, quo se legionariis militibus praeferrent.
At hostes etiam in extrema spe salutis tantam virtutem
praestiterunt ut, cum primi eorum cecidissent, proximi iacen-

tibus insisterent, atque ex eorum corporibus pugnarent; his
delectis et coacervatis cadaveribus, qui superessent, ut ex tu·
mulo tela in nostros conicerent et pila intercepta remitte-
rent; ut non nequiquam tantae virtutis homines iudicari de-
beret ausos esse transire latissimum flumen, ascendere altis-
simas ripas, subire iniquissimum locum; quae facilia ex
difficillimis animi magnitudo redegerat.

In what years did Caesar's Gallic campaign fall? State
briefly if you can, the events of each year.

    5. Translate :—

    Quorum post abitum princeps e vertice Peli
    Aduenit Chiron portans silvestria dona ;
    Nam quodcunque ferunt campi, quos Thessala magnis
    Montibus ora creat, quos propter fluminis undas
    Aura parit flores tepidi fecunda Favoni,
    Hos in distinctis plexos tulit ipse corollis,
    Quo permulsa domus iucundo risit odore.
    Confestim Peneus adest, viridantia Tempe,
    Tempe, quae silvae cingunt super impendentes,
    Minosim linquens Doris celebranda choreis,
    Non vacuus: namque ille tulit radicitus altas
    Fagos ac recto proceras stipite laurus
    Non sine nutanti platano lentaque sorore
    Flammati Phaethontis et aeria cupressu.
    Haec circum sedes late contexta locavit,
    Vestibulum ut molli velatum frondi vireret.
    Post hunc consequitur sollerti corde Prometheus,
    Extenuata gerens veteris vestigia poenae,
    Quam quondam silici restrictus membra catena
    Persolvit pendens e verticibus praeruptis.

FIRST YEAR EXHIBITION.

ALGEBRA—ARITHMETIC.

Thursday, September 16th:—Afternoon, 2 to 5.

Examiner..................................ALEXANDER JOHNSON, M.D., LL.D.
Assistant Examiner....................H. M. Tory, M.D.

    1. Find three numbers in geometrical progression such that the
sum of the first and second shall exceed the third by 1 ; and three
times the second shall be equal to twice the third.

2. Find the limit to the sum of the series

$$1 - \frac{2}{5} + \frac{4}{25} - ac$$

3. Find the arithmetical, geometrical and harmonic means between 2 and 3.

4. Find the harmonic means between a and b.

5. Prove that the product of two dissimilar surds cannot be rational.

6. Solve the equations

(a) $\dfrac{10x + 17}{18} - \dfrac{12x + 2}{11x - 8} = \dfrac{5x - 4}{9}$

(b) $x - \dfrac{y \mp 2}{7} = 5$; $4z - \frac{1}{3}(x + 10) = 3$

(c) $a + x + \sqrt{a^2 + bx + x^2} = b$

(d) $\dfrac{a}{x} + \dfrac{b}{y} = \dfrac{1}{r}$; $\dfrac{a}{x} + \dfrac{c}{z} = \dfrac{1}{q}$; $\dfrac{6}{y} + \dfrac{c}{z} = \dfrac{1}{p}$

(e) $\dfrac{.3x - 2}{.5x - .4} = \dfrac{.5 + 1.2x}{2x - .1}$.

7. Two rectangles contain the same area, viz., 480 square yards. The difference of their lengths is 10 yards, and of their breadths 4 yards; find their sides.

8. Extract the square root of .03567.

9. Find fourth proportional to 3.81, .085 and .0023.

10. The differences between the hypotenuse and the two sides of a right angled-triangle are 3 and 6, respectively; find the sides.

FIRST YEAR EXHIBITIONS.

GEOMETRY.

THURSDAY, SEPT. 16TH:—MORNING, 9 TO 12.

Examiners,...... .... | A. JOHNSON, LL.D.
                                              | H. M. TORY, M.A.

1. Describe a parallelogram which shall be equal to given triangle and have one of its angles equal to a given angle.

2. If a straight line be divided into any two parts, the square on the whole line is equal to the sum of the squares on the two parts together with twice the rectangle contained by the two parts.

3. In a right angled triangle, if a perpendicular be let fall from the right angle upon the hypothenuse, the square on the perpendicular shall be equal to the rectangle contained by the segments of the hypothenuse.

4. Describe a circle which shall pass through two given points and have its radius equal to a given line. When will this be impossible?

5. If two chords in a circle cut one another, the rectangle contained by the segments of the one shall be equal to the rectangle contained by the segments of the other.

6. Describe an isosceles triangle such that each of the base angles shall be double the vertical angle.

*7. Find a third proportional to two given straight lines.

*8. Two triangles, which are equal in area and have an angle in the one equal to an angle in the other, have the sides about the equal angles reciprocally proportional.

*9. On a given straight line, describe a rectilineal figure similar to a given rectilineal figure.

FIRST YEAR EXHIBITIONS AND HIGHER ENTRANCE EXAMINATIONS.
ENGLISH GRAMMAR.

FRIDAY, SEPT. 17TH :—3 AND 1½HRS.

A. (Candidates for Higher Entrance will answer questions 1, 2, 3, 4, 5, 6, 9, 10 of the Ordinary entrance examination and also the following set.)

B. (Candidates for Second Year Entrance will answer questions 1, 2, 9, 10 of the Ordinary Entrance Examination and questions 11, 12 and 13 of the following set.)

11. Classify mute consonants as labials, dentals and gutturals, and also as thin, middle and aspirate. Write two words which contain a surd spirant and a sonant spirant respectively, and underline the letters in question.

12. Give an historical account of the introduction of the Latin element into the English language.

13. Write etymological notes on the following words: palsy, alms, thunder, newt, pagan, alchemy, bask, Monday, island.

*Extra questions.

3

14. When is the nominative case used in English? Define and illus.
trate Subjective and Objective genitive.

15. Trace as fully as you can the history of the inflections of the third
personal pronoun.

BOURSES ET PRIX.

1ʀᴇ ANNÉE—LETTRES.

Lundi, 20 Septembre.

Examinateurs,........ ....:..... .... { M. Ingres.
{ J. L. Morin.

Reproduire par écrit l'anecdote suivante. Cette anecdote sera racontée par l'examinateur.

I. Répondre aux questions suivantes :

1. Pourquoi ne vous êtes-vous pas présenté en juin ?

2. Où et comment avez-vous passé juillet et août ?

3. Depuis quand étudiez-vous le français, et pourquoi l'apprenez-vous ?

4. Quel est l'emploi des pronoms *en* et *y* ?

II. Faire des questions qui conviennent aux réponses suivantes :

1. Je suis arrivé à 9 heures.

2. Non, je suis venu à pied.

3. Pour subir mes examens d'entrée.

4. Généralement en ajoutant — ment — au féminin de l'adjectif.

III. Faire une description de la chambre où vous travaillez ordinairement (50 mots au moins).

IV. Dans le passage suivant remplacer les infinitifs par les formes que
le sens exige.

SAGESSE D'UN PERSAN.

Un roi de Perse, qui *être surnommer* le Juste et qui *mériter* ce glorieux surnom, *vouloir*, un jour qu'il *être* à la chasse, *manger* du gibier qu'il
avoir tuer. Comme il n'*avoir* point de sel, il *envoyer* un esclave pour en
chercher au village voisin, et lui *recommander* de le *payer* très exactement.
Les courtisans du prince *trouver* que leur maître *attacher* beaucoup d'importance à une bien petite chose. Un roi, leur *répondre*-il, *devoir* ne
donner que de bons exemples. Qu'il *prendre* un fruit dans un jardin, ses
vizirs *vouloir arracher* l'arbre ; Qu'il se *permettre* de *prendre* un œuf sans
payer, ses soldats *tuer* toutes les poules."

V. Dans le passage suivant remplacer les tirets par des mots qui conviennent au sens.

GARE ! GAR !

Un habitant d'Athènes, qui —— une poutre, ayant heurté rudement Diogène avertit ensuite —— philosophe —— —— criant: gare ! Un peu étourdi —— coup, le célèbre cynique poursuivit —— route —— —— dire. Mais —— jours après, ayant rencontré —— même homme, —— —— asséna un grand coup —— bâton —— —— tête, —— —— criant à son tour : gare ! gare !

VI. Dater en toutes lettres et motiver l'orthographe des adjectifs numéraux.

HIGHER ENTRANCE EXAMINATIONS.

FIRST YEAR. OUTLINES OF EUROPEAN HISTORY.

SATURDAY, SEPT. 18TH :—2½ HRS.

1. Point out the leading historical effects which are due to Charlemagne's restoration of the Empire.

2. (a) By what steps was France formed ?

(b) What was the process of French expansion ?

3. What do you consider to be the general characteristics of modern times ?

4. Give some account of Russia's political development.

5. Define the spirit of modern nationality.

6. Enumerate the main causes of war and peace under existing social conditions.

FIRST YEAR EXHIBITIONS.

ENGLISH LITERATURE.

MORLEY : *First Sketch*, chaps. VII. and VIII.

TUESDAY, SEPT. 21ST :—2.30 TO 5 P.M.

1. Give an outline of Knox's *First Blast of the Trumpet*, OR of Marlowe's *Faustus*.

2. Assign a work to each of the following authors, and state its character *very briefly :* Sackville, Lyly, Gascoigne, Gosson, Hakluyt, Chettle. State in what works the following characters are found : Captain Tucca, Sacrapant, Philautus, Videna, and name the authors concerned.

3. Sketch the life of Ben Jonson.

4. Write on Bacon's Instauratio Magna.

5. Notice religious pamphleteering in the reigns of Elizabeth and Charles I.

SECOND YEAR EXHIBITIONS.

SEPTEMBER.

1. Translate :—

εἰ δὲ προησόμεθα, ὦ ἄνδρες Ἀθηναῖοι, καὶ τούτους τοὺς ἀνθρώπους, εἶτ' Ὄλυνθον ἐκεῖνος καταστρέψεται φρασάτω τις ἐμοί, τί τὸ κωλῦοι ἔτ' αὐτὸν ἔσται βαδίζειν ὅποι βούλεται; ἀρά γε λογίζεταί τις ὑμῶν, ὦ ἄνδρες Ἀθηναῖοι, καὶ θεωρεῖ τὸν τρόπον δι' ὃν μέγας γέγονεν ἀσθενὴς ὢν τὸ κατ' ἀρχὰς Φίλιππος; τὸ πρῶτον Ἀμφίπολιν λαβών, μετὰ ταῦτα Πύδναν, πάλιν Ποτίδαιαν, Μεθώνην αὖθις, εἶτα Θετταλίας ἐπέβη· μετὰ ταῦτα, Φεράς, Παγασάς, Μαγνησίαν, πάνθ' ὃν ἐβούλετο εὐτρεπίσας τρόπον, ᾤχετ' ἐς Θρᾴκην· εἶτ' ἐκεῖ τοὺς μὲν ἐκβαλών, τοὺς δὲ καταστήσας τῶν βασιλέων ἠσθένησε· πάλιν ῥαΐσας οὐκ ἐπὶ τὸ ῥαθυμεῖν ἀπέκλινεν, ἀλλ' εὐθὺς Ὀλυνθίοις ἐπεχείρησεν. τὰς δ' ἐπ' Ἰλλυριοὺς καὶ Παίονας αὐτοῦ, καὶ πρὸς Ἀρύμβαν, καὶ ὅποι τις ἂν εἴποι, παραλείπω στρατείας.

2. Translate :—

βροτοῖς ἅπασι κατθανεῖν ὀφείλεται,
κοὐκ ἔστι θνητῶν ὅς τις ἐξεπίσταται
τὴν αὔριον μέλλουσαν εἰ βιώσεται·
τὸ τῆς τύχης γὰρ ἀφανὲς οἷ προβήσεται,   785
κἄστ' οὐ διδακτόν, οὐδ' ἁλίσκεται τέχνῃ.
ταῦτ' οὖν ἀκούσας καὶ μαθὼν ἐμοῦ πάρα,
εὔφραινε σαυτόν, πῖνε, τὸν καθ' ἡμέραν
βίον λογίζου σόν, τὰ δ' ἄλλα τῆς τύχης.
τίμα δὲ καὶ τὴν πλεῖστον ἡδίστην θεῶν   790
Κύπριν βροτοῖσιν· εὐμενὴς γὰρ ἡ θεός.
τὰ δ' ἄλλ' ἔασον ταῦτα, καὶ πείθου λόγοις
ἐμοῖσιν, εἴπερ ὀρθά σοι δοκῶ λέγειν·
οἶμαι μέν. οὔκουν τὴν ἄγαν λύπην ἀφεὶς
πίει μεθ' ἡμῶν τάσδ' ὑπερβαλὼν πύλας,   795

στεφάνοις πυκασθείς ; καὶ σάφ' οἶδ' ὁθούνεκα
τοῦ νῦν σκυθρωποῦ καὶ ξυνεστῶτος φρενῶν
μεθορμιεῖ σε πίτυλος ἐμπεσων σκύφου.
ὄντας δὲ θνητοὺς θνητὰ καὶ φρονεῖν χρεών,
ὡς τοῖς γε σεμνοῖς καὶ ξυνωφρυωμένοις,   800
ἅπασίν ἐστιν, ὥς γ' ἐμοὶ χρῆσθαι κριτῇ,
οὐ βίος ἀληθῶς ὁ βίος, ἀλλὰ συμφορά. '

3. Translate :—

Οἱ δὲ βάρβαροι προς-ῄεσαν σιγῇ καὶ βραδέως. καὶ ἐν
τούτῳ Κῦρος, παρ-ελαύνων σὺν τῷ ἑρμηνεῖ καὶ ἄλλοις
τρισὶν ἢ τέτταρσιν, ἐκέλευε τὸν Κλέαρχον ἄγειν τὸ
στράτευμα κατὰ τὸ μέσον τῶν πολεμίων, ὅτι βασιλεὺς
εἴη ἐκεῖ· "Ἐὰν γὰρ τοῦτο," ἔφη, " νικῶμεν, πάντα
πεποιήκαμεν." ὁ δὲ Κλέαρχος οὐκ ἤθελεν ἀπο-σπάσαι
τὸ δεξιὸν κέρας ἀπὸ τοῦ ποταμοῦ, φοβούμενος μὴ κυκλωθείη ἑκατέρωθεν· ἀπ-εκρίνατο δὲ τῷ Κύρῳ, " Ἐμοὶ," ὦ
Κῦρε, " μελήσει ὅπως ταῦτα καλῶς ἔχῃ." καὶ ἐνταῦθα ὁ
Κῦρος ἔτι παρ-ελαύνων κατ-εθεᾶτο τὸ στράτευμα, ἀπο-
βλέπων εἴς τε τοὺς πολεμίους καὶ εἰς τοὺς φίλους.

4. For Greek Prose :—

And having decided thus they send Antalcidas to Tiribazas, having instructed him to inform him of these things
and to endeavour to make peace between the city and the
King. And hearing this the Athenians send a counter-
embassy along with Konon, namely Hermogenes and Dion
and Kallisthenes. And they invited also ambassadors
from the allies ; and there came ambassadors from the
Borotians and from Korinth and from Argos. And when
they were there Antalcidas told Tiribazas that he had come
seeking peace between the city and the King, and that
such a peace as the King desired.

5. Translate :—

Οὐδενὸς δὲ τολμήσαντος ἄλλο τι εἰπεῖν ἢ τοῖς οἴκοι πείθεσθαι ποιεῖν τε ἐφ᾽ ἃ ἥκει, ἐλθὼν παρὰ Κῦρον ᾔτει μισθὸν τοῖς ναύταις· ὁ δὲ αὐτῷ εἶπε δύο ἡμέρας ἐπισχεῖν. Καλλικρατίδας δὲ ἀχθεσθεὶς τῇ ἀναβολῇ καὶ ταῖς ἐπὶ τὰς θύρας φοιτήσεσιν, ὀργισθεὶς καὶ εἰπὼν ἀθλιωτάτους εἶναι τοὺς Ἕλληνας, ὅτι βαρβάρους κολακεύουσιν ἕνεκα ἀργυρίου, φάσκων τε, ἢν σωθῇ οἴκαδε, κατά γε τὸ αὐτοῦ δυνατὸν διαλλάξειν Ἀθηναίους καὶ Λακεδαιμονίους, ἀπέπλευσεν εἰς Μίλητον· κἀκεῖθεν πέμψας τριήρεις εἰς Λακεδαίμονα ἐπὶ χρήματα, ἐκκλησίαν ἀθροίσας τῶν Μιλησίων τάδε εἶπεν.

SECOND YEAR EXHIBITIONS.

GENERAL PAPER.

MONDAY, SEPTMEBER 20TH :—AFTERNOON, 2 TO 5.

1. State briefly what you know of Spurius Maclius, Hamilcar Barca, Seianus, Antony, Sextus Pompeius.

2. When were the following peoples or countries brought under the Dominion of Rome :—the Latins, Sicily, Macedonia, Egypt ?

3. Show how the Laws of the Twelve Tables originated, and in what the political significance of this code lay.

4. Sketch the history of Sulla.

5. (a) Explain the forms *ausust, vin,' sultis, hodie.* (b) Derive the words *fashion, chivalry, chimney.* (c) Name some English words cognate with the following Latin :—*genus, genu, veho, fores, iugum.*

6. How are the reciprocals *one another* and *each other* expressed in Latin ? Illustrate.

7. Inflect *edo* (I eat) in the present Indicative and Imperative Active.

8. Translate and explain the grammatical construction of the following sentences :—

(*a*) labor voluptasque societate quadam inter se naturali sunt *iuncta*.

(*b*) *longior quans latior* acies erat. ·

(*c*) *nostri* melior pars animus est.

(*d*) *Thebae ipsae, quod* Boeotiae caput est.

(*e*) Antipbo me excruciat *animi*.

(*f*) bona *mihi* abstulisti.

(*g*) Si *pereo* hominum manibus periisse *iuvabit*.

9. Translate into Latin :

"For it frequently happens," he said, " that Antony, after having ordered his supper, enters into conversation with some one and forgets that he has ordered it. The order must, of course, be obeyed ; but if, after finishing his conversation, he were to find his supper cold, he would perhaps order the cook to be put to death. Only last night " he added, "I thought that he would have died of passion because his supper was served up one minute later than he had expected."

LATIN.

SECOND YEAR EXHIBITIONS,

WEDNESDAY, SEPT. 15 :—AFTERNOON, 2 to 5.

1. Translate with brief notes :—

(*a*) Humida solstitia atque hiemes orate serenas,
Agricolae; hiberno laetissima pulvere farra,
Laetus ager; nullo tantum se Mysia cultu
lactat, et ipsa suas mirantur Gargara messes.
Quid dicam, iacto qui semine cominus arva
Insequitur cumulosque ruit male pinguis arenae?
Deinde satis fluvium inducit rivosque sequentes,
Et, cum exustus ager morientibus aéstuat herbis,
Ecce supercilio clivosi tramitis undam
Elicit? illa cadens raucum per levia murmur
Saxa ciet, scatebrisque arentia temperat arva.
Quid, qui, ne gravidis procumbat culmus aristis,
Luxuriem segetum tenera depascit in herba,
Cum primum sulcos aequant sata? quique paludis

Collectum humorem bibula deducit arena?
Praesertim incertis si mensibus amnis abundans
Exit, et obducto late tenet omnia limo,
Unde cavae tepido sudant humore lacunae.

                                    Virgil, Georgics, I.

(*b*) Sic te diva potens Cypri,
    Sic fratres Helenae, lucida sidera,
Ventorumque regat pater,
    Obstrictis aliis, praeter Iapyga,
Navis, quae tibi creditum
    Debes Virgilium finibus Atticis.
Reddas incolumem, precor,
    Et serves animae dimidium meae.
Illi robur et aes triplex
    Circa pectus erat, qui fragilem truci
Commisit pelago ratem
    Primus, nec timuit praecipitem Africum
Decertantem Aquilonibus,
    Nec tristes Hyadas, nec rabiem Noti
Quo non arbiter Hadriae
    Maior, tollere seu ponere vult freta—Ode III.

(*c*) Parcus deorum cultor et infrequens,
    Insanientis dum sapientiae
Consultus erro, nunc retrorsum
    Vela dare atque iterare cursus

Cogor relictos: namque Diespiter,
Igni corusco nubila dividens
    Plerumque, per purum tonantes
    Egit equos volucremque currum;

Quo bruta tellus, et vaga flumina,
Quo Styx et invisi horrida Taenari
    Sedes Atlanteusque finis
    Concutitur.—Ode XXXIV.

                                    Horace, Odes, Bk. I.

(*d*) Ibi infit Albanus: Iniurias et non redditas res ex
foedere quae repetitae sint, et ego regem nostrum Cluilium,
causam huiusce esse belli, audisse videor: nec te dubito, Tulle,
eadem prae te ferre. Sed si vera potuis quam dictu speciosa
dicenda sunt, cupido imperii duos cognatos vicinosque po-

pulos ad arma stimulat. Neque recte, an perperam, inter-
pretor: fuerit ista eius deliberatio, qui bellum suscepit. me
Albani gerendo bello ducem cre avere. Illud te, Tulle, moni-
tum velim. Etrusca res quanta circa nos teque maxime sit,
quo propriores vos, hoc magis scis, multum illi terra, pluri-
mum mari pollent. Memor esto, iam cum signum pugnae
dabis, has duas acies spectaculo fore; ut fessos confectosque
simul victorem ac victum aggrediantur. Itaque, si nos dii
amant quoniam non contenti libertate certa. in dubiam imperii servitiique aleam imus; ineamus aliquam viam, qua utri
utris imperent, sine magna clade, sine multo sanguine utriusque populi, decerni possit. Haud displicet res Tullo, quamquam tum indole animi, tum spe victoriae feracior erat. Quae-
rentibus utrimque ratio initur, cui et fortuna ipsa praebuit
materiam.

Livy. Bk. I.

2. Comment on the following expressions :—

(a) *Eleusinae matris* ; (b) Ergo inter sese paribus concurrere telis Romanas acies iterum videre Philippi. (c) Fratres Helenae. (d) Maeonii carminis aliti. (e) Saevam Pel-
opis domum. (f) dies nefasti. (g) Sacrificium lustrate.

3. Translate (at sight):—

(a) Est in Africa Hipponensis colonia, mari proxima: ad-
iacet navigabile stagnum: ex hoc in modum fluminis aestu-
arium emergit, quod vice alterna, prout aestus aut repressit
aut inpulit, nunc infertur mari nunc redditur stagno. Omnis
hic aetas piscandi, navigandi, atque etiam natandi studio
tenetur, maxime pueri, quos otium lususque sollicitat. His
gloria et virtus altissime provehi: victor ille qui longissime
ut litus ita simul natantes reliquit. Hoc certamine puer
quidam audentior ceteris in ulteriora tendebat. Delphinus
occurrit, et nunc praecedere puerum, nunc sequi, nunc cir-
cumire, postremo subire, deponere, iterum subire, trepidan-
temque perferre primum in altum, mox flectit ad litus reddit-
que terrae et aequalibus. Serpit per coloniam fama: concurrere
omnes, ipsum puerum tamquam miraculum aspicere, inter-
rogare, audire, narrare. Postero die obsident litus, prospec-
tant mare et si quid est mari simile. Natant pueri: inter
hos ille, sed cautius. Delphinus rursus ad tempus, rursus

ad puerum venit. Fugit ille cum ceteris. Delphinus, quasi invitet et revocet, exilit, mergitur variosque orbes inplicitat expeditque. Hoc altero die, hoc tertio, hoc pluribus, donec homines innutritos mari subiret timendi pudor. Accedunt et adludunt et appellant, tangunt etiam pertrectantque praebentem. Crescit audacia experimento. Maxime puer qui primus expertus est adnatantis insilit tergo, fertur referturque, agnosci se, amari putat, amat ipse: neuter timet, neuter timetur: huius fiducia, mansuetudo illius augetur.

(b)

Rectius vives, Licini, neque altum
Semper urgendo, neque dum procellas
Cautus horrescis, nimium premendo
    Litus iniquum.

Auream quisquis mediocritatem
Diligit, tutus caret obsoleti
Sordibus tecti, caret invidenda
    Sobrius aula.

Saepius ventis agitatur ingens
Pinus, et celsae graviore casu
Decidunt turres, feriuntque summos
    Fulmina montes.

Sperat infestis, metuit secundis
Alteram sortem bene praeparatum
Pectus. Informes hiemes reducit
    Iuppiter, idem

Summovet. Non, si male nunc, et olim
Sic erit. Quondam cithara tacentem
Suscitat Musam, neque semper arcum
    Tendit Apollo.

Rebus angustis animosus atque
Fortis appare: sapienter idem
Contrahes vento nimium secundo
    Turgida vela.

SECOND YEAR EXHIBITIONS.

EUCLID—ALGEBRA—TRIGONOMETRY.

THURSDAY, SEPT. 16TH :—MORNING, 9 to 12.

Examiners,........................ { G. H. CHANDLER, M.A.
{ H. M. TORY, M.A.

Write answer to parts A and B in separate books.

A

1. In a right-angled triangle, any rectilineal figure described on the hypothenuse is equal to the sum of the similar and similarly described figures on the sides containing the right angle.

2. Similar triangles are to one another in the duplicate of their homologous sides.

3. Inscribe a regular pentagon in a circle.

4. If two chords in a circle cut one another, the rectangle contained by the segments of the one shall be equal to the rectangle contained by the segments of the other.

5. Solve the equations :—

(1) $\dfrac{x}{a} + \dfrac{y}{b} = 1, \quad \dfrac{x}{b} + \dfrac{y}{a} = 1$

(2) $x + \dfrac{1}{x - 3} = 5$

(3) $x + y = 5, \ x^3 + y^3 = 65.$

6. Simplify :—

(1) $\dfrac{1}{x^4 - x^2 - 2x - 1} + \dfrac{1}{x^2 + x + 1} + \dfrac{1}{x^2 - x - 1}$

(2) $\sqrt{2} \times \sqrt[3]{54} \times \sqrt[4]{10}.$

B

7. Find two numbers, one of which is $\frac{3}{5}$th of the other, so that the difference of their squares may be 16.

8. Two persons, A and B, have the same income. A lays by one fifth of his, but B, by spending $60 per annum more than A, finds himself at the end of three years $100 in debt. What is the income of each?

9. Prove the following relations —

(1) $\dfrac{\sec\theta - 1}{\sec\theta}$ = versin θ

(2) $\tan^2\theta - \sin^2\theta = \sin^4\theta \sec^2\theta$

(3) $\cos(30 - \theta) - \cos(30 + \theta) = \sin\theta$.

10. Prove the following :—

(1) $\tan(A \pm B) = \dfrac{\tan A \pm \tan B}{1 \mp \tan A + \tan B}$

(2) $\cos 2A = 2\cos^2 A - 1 = 1 - 2\sin^2 A$

(3) $\dfrac{1 - \cos A}{1 + \cos A} = \tan^2\dfrac{A}{2}$.

11. Trace the changes in sign of the tangent of an angle as the angle increases from 0° to 360°.

12. (1) Find the sine of 18°

(2) Find the sine of 1″

———

SECOND YEAR EXHIBITIONS.

GEOMETRY.

THURSDAY, SEPT. 16TH :—AFTERNOON, 2 TO 5.

Examiners,............ .... $\left\{\begin{array}{l}\text{G. H. Chandler, M.A.}\\ \text{H. M. Tory, M.A.}\end{array}\right.$

Write answers to parts A and in B separate books.

1. Bisect a triangle by a straight line drawn from a given point in one of its sides.

2. One vertex of a triangle given in species turns round a fixed point, and another vertex moves along a fixed straight line ; find the locus of the remaining vertex.

3. Describe a circle touching a given circle and a given straight line at a given point.

4. If any transversal cut a pencil of four rays, the ratio of the rectangle under the whole transversal and its middle segment to the rectangle under its extreme segments is constant.

5. If two triangles be co-polar they shall also be co-axial.

6. If two tangents be drawn to a circle, any third tangent will be cut harmonically by its point of contact with the two former tangents and the chord of contact.

B

7. If a straight line be drawn from the vertex of an isosceles triangle to the base or the base produced, the difference between its square and the square on a side of the triangle is equal to the rectangle under the segment of the base.

8. The perpendiculars from the middle point of the base of a triangle on the bisectors of the internal and external vertical angles cut off from the two sides portions equal to half the sum or half the difference of the sides.

9. Draw a common tangent to two given circles.

10. The reciprocals of lines in harmonical progression are in arithmetical progression, and conversely, the reciprocals of lines in arithmetical progression are in harmonical progression.

11. The anharmonic ratio of four fixed points on a circle is constant.

12. Given a triangle, to describe the circle with respect to which the triangle is self-conjugate.

SECOND YEAR EXHIBITIONS.

Tuesday, Sept. 21st:—Morning, 9 to 12.

Examiners,........................ $\left\{\begin{array}{l}\text{G. H. Chandler, M.A.}\\\text{H. M. Tory, M.A.}\end{array}\right.$

A.

1. Find the equation whose roots are the roots of the equation
$x^5 + 4x^3 - x^2 + 3 = 0$, each diminished by 3.

2. Solve the equation $x^5 - 1 = 0$.

3. In any equation $x^n + P_1 x^{n-1} + P_2 x^{n-2} + P_n = 0$. If the first negative term be $- P_r x^{n-r}$, and if the greatest negative coefficient $b - P_k$, then $\sqrt[r]{P_k} + 1$ is a superior limit to the positive roots.

4. Find the positive root of the equation
$4x^3 - 13x^2 - 31x - 275 = 0$ by Horner's method.

5. Find the number of triangles that can be formed by joining the angular points of a quindecagon.

6. Find the first three terms in the expansion of

$$(1 + 3x)^{\frac{1}{2}} (1 - 2x)^{-\frac{1}{2}}.$$

B.

7. Solve the equation

$$x^4 + 2x^3 - 5x^2 + 6x + 2 = 0,$$

which has a root $- 2 + \sqrt{3}$.

8. State and prove Descartes' rule of signs.
Find the value of roots of the equation

$$x^4 + 15x^2 + 7x - 11.$$

9. Solve the equation $x^3 - 9x^2 + 14x + 24 = 0$, two of whose roots are in the ratio of 3 to 2.

10. If the roots of the equation, $f(x) = 0$, be $a \; \beta \; \gamma \; \delta$, etc.,
Show that

$$f^1(x) = \frac{fx}{x - a} + \frac{f(x)}{x - \beta} + \frac{f(x)}{x - \gamma} + 0.$$

11. Resolve into partial fractions

$$\frac{6x^3 + 5x^2 - 7}{3x^2 - 2x - 1}.$$

12. Investigate a formula for finding the present worth of an annuity to continue for a given number of years, allowing compound interest.

BOURSES ET PRIX.

2ᴹᴱ ANNÉÉ.—LETTRES.

Lundi, 20 Septembre.

Examinateurs,... { M. Ingres.
                                                     { J. L. Morin.

Equisser un portrait de Triboulet (le Roi s'amuse), de dom Gabriele Griffi et de Philippe Dubois (Un Saint)—100 à 150 mots sur chacun.

Rendre en prose et sous forme de narration la Grève des Forgerons. Abrégé.

Questions orales.

1. Donner quelques renseignements sur la vie et l'œuvre de deux écrivains français de notre siècle. (150 à 200 mots sur chacun).

2. Ecrire sous forme d'analyse ou de compte-rendu environ 500 mots sur un livre français au choix du candidat.

3. Remplacer dans le passage suivant les tirets par des mots convenant au sens.

L'OFFRE TROMPEUSE.

Les mots suivants étaient —— sur la porte d'un beau jardin : "Je donne —— parterre —— quiconque —— content." Voilà bien —— affaire ! dit tout bas —— passant ; je vais donc —— un terrain !" Là-dessus, —— court, —— de joie, s'adresser —— propriétaire —— jardin. "Que —— vous? demande celui-ci —— —— voyant paraître. — Je désire —— jardin. Mon droit à m'y établir ——, paraît incontestable, car je suis content —— mon sort. — Erreur ! mon —— ami : —— veut avoir —— —— —— n'a pas ne saurait être content. Reprenez —— chemin."

4. Indiquer l'emploi de l'imparfait, du passé défini et du passé indéfini.

5. Réproduire par écrit l'anecdote suivante. Cette anecdote sera racontée par l'examinateur.

6. Dater en toutes lettres et motiver l'orthographe des adjectifs numéraux

---

SECOND YEAR EXHIBITIONS, 1897.

ENGLISH COMPOSITION.

FRIDAY, SEPTEMBER 17TH :— 12 TO 1 P.M.

Write an essay of not less than *two* pages on one of the following subjects —

(a) The character of the Red Cross Knight.

(b) The influence of the monks on the early mediæval world.

(c) The place of Tennyson in English Poetry.

FACULTY OF ARTS.

SECOND YEAR EXHIBITIONS.

ENGLISH LITERATURE.

SPENSER AND TENNYSON.

FRIDAY, SEPTEMBER 17TH :—MORNING, 9 TO 12.

(*Write the answers to sets A and B in different books.*)

A.

1. Give some idea of the general purpose of Spenser in writing the Faerie Queene.

2. Give some account of Duessa, Sir Trevisan, Una.

3. What are the principal literary qualities of Spenser's poetry ?

4. Contrast the English of Spenser with that of Tennyson.

B.

1. Refer the following extracts to the poems in which they occur, and give, as precisely as you can, the connection of each. Write explanatory notes, when necessary.

        (*a*) Pavilion of the Caliphat.

        (*b*) The mirror crack'd from side to side.

        (*c*) I am the daughter of a River-God.

        (*d*) Death is the end of life ; ah, why

           Should life all labour be ?

        (*e*) God accept him, Christ receive him.

        (*f*) Dry clash'd his harness in the icy caves.

2. Write on the characteristics of Tennyson's poetry, and illustrate them from the "Selections."

3. Mention the sources of the Lotos-Eaters, Dora, Ulysses, the Revenge, Morte d'Arthur, the Ballad of the Revenge. Give an outline of the Dream of Fair Women and of the Ballad of the Revenge.

4. Compare the characters of Dora and Mary.

5. Explain the following words and phrases, and state the connection in which they occur : bulbul, Gargarus, white samite, moving isles of winter, three Queens, the casque of men, the Prussian trumpet blow.

6. Quote or give the substance, in prose, of about ten consecutive lines in Arthur's last speech to Bedivere.

SECOND YEAR EXHIBITION EXAMINATIONS.

ENGLISH LANGUAGE AND EUROPEAN HISTORY.

TUESDAY, SEPTEMBER 21ST :—AFTERNOON, 2 TO 5.30 P.M.

(*Write the answers to sets A and B in different books.*)

A.

1. State the points which Trench illustrates by means of the following words Nirvana, Gaunt, capricious, Drepanum, Ah!, St. Nicholas' clerks, castle, delf, affiance, isothermal.

2. Distinguish between *illegible* and *unreadable*; *foresight* and *providence*; *interference* and *interposition*; *arrogant* and *presumptuous* and *insolent*; *hate* and *loathe* and *detest* and *abhor*. State briefly how synonyms arise.

3. Write on the following matters:

    (*a*) The Arabic element in English,

    (*b*) The origins of the monastic system are to be sought in the Greek branch of the Church.

    (*c*) Words derived from the names of gods and men.

4. Illustrate Trench's position in regard to phonetic spelling from the words savage, fancy, analize. What idea is common to all the senses of *post* and *stock*? Account etymologically for the different meanings of *page, host, mosaic, quire, seal.*

B.

1. What main influences affected the Teutonic settlers in the Roman Empire?

2. Trace the rise of Mohammedan power.

3. Follow out the fortunes of the Gothic race in its East and West branches.

4. What do you know about the conversion of the English and the character of the Anglo-Saxon Church?

5. Make brief notes on: Alboin Austrasia; " False Decretals "; Bede; Hugh Capet; Peace of Wedmore.

SECOND YEAR EXHIBITIONS.
DONALDA DEPARTMENT.
GERMAN.

WEDNESDAY, SEPT. 22ND:—MORNING, 9 TO 12.

Examiner,.................... ....L. R. GREGOR, B.A., PH.D.

1. Translate *Der Neffe als Onkel*, Act. II., Scene 15.

2. Translate in Schiller's *Geisterseher* the paragraph beginning with the words *Einige kräftige.*

3. Translate the first two paragraphs of Goethe's *Torquato Tasso*, Act. II, Scene 1.

4. Translate in *Egmont's Leben und Tod* the first paragraph of Chapter IV.

5. Translation at sight.

Der deutsche Kaiser Heinrich VI. war im Jahre 1197 ohne Erben gestorben, und hatte auch niemand zu einem Nachfolger bestimmt, daher wurde von der Hohenstaufischen Partei Philipp von Schwaben zum Kaiser gewählt, während die Guelfen Otto von Braunschweig, einen Neffen des Königs Johann von England zum Gegenkandidaten aufstellten. Obgleich die Gegner zu verschiedenen politischen Parteien gehörten, achteten sie sich doch als Menschen. Nach dem Kampfe um die Krone, in welchem Otto Sieger war, fand die Versöhnung zwischen beiden statt. Als Philipp gefangen vor Otto geführt wurde, rief letzterer aus: "Von jetzt ab betrachte ich dich als meinen Freund, nicht als meinen Gefangenen!" Was Philipp betrifft, so hielt er Otto für einen Ehrenmann und echten Ritter. Die beiden Freunde lebten in engster Gemeinschaft, schliefen in einem Bett und tranken aus einem Becher, Otto nannte Philipp nicht nur seinen Freund, sondern ernannte ihn sogar zu seinem Mitregenten. So stellt die Geschichte beide Gegner als edle Menschen dar.

6. Translation at sight into German :—

It is reported that a burglar once came to the house of the famous savant Molières, who was in the habit of retiring early. When the burglar entered the bedroom he found the learned man studying in bed, as he very often did when tired.

" Who are you, and what do you want here ? " asked Molières calmly.

" Never mind my name, I want your money," answered the burglar threateningly.

" All I have, and that's very little, is in the right drawer of that table. Open it and take the money, but on no account disturb my papers."

After the chief had pocketed all the money, he left the room in such a hurry that he did not shut the door.

"You didn't disturb my papers, did you? " Molières called after him.

" No, of course not," was the thief's anwer.

" Well, then, please be good enough to close the door, for there is a frightful dranght here and I don't want to catch cold."

7. To what extent are Goethe's own experiences at the court of Weimar symbolised in his Tasso?

8. What part did William the Silent play in the revolt of the Netherlands? Mention Schiller's chief historical works.

9. Give detailed statement of the rules which govern the order of words in a German sentence.

10. Give as full a statement as possible of the differences between separable and inseparable verbs.

11. State as fully as you can in what situations the definite article is employed in German but not in English.

SECOND YEAR EXHIBITIONS.
GERMAN.

WEDNESDAY, SEPT. 22ND :—MORNING, 9 TO 12.

Examiner,................ ....L. R. GREGOR, B.A., PH.D.

1. Translate *Der Neffe als Onkel*, Act II, Scene 3.

2. Translate the first twenty lines of *Klio, Hermann und Dorothea.*

3. Translate the first paragraph of *Sneewittchen*.

4. Translate into German :—

(*a*) The boat leaves Montreal at seven o'clock in the evening, or as soon after seven as possible. It waits for the Toronto boat, you know. You will arrive in Quebec the following morning. If you are fortunate enough to have fine weather, you will have one of the finest views in North America. The Hudson cannot be compared to the St. Lawrence.

(*b*) Have you ever been in Europe ? No, I should like very much to take the trip next summer. My health is not very good and my physician has advised me to travel for a year. He proposes a summer in Norway and a winter in the south of France.

(*e*) Schiller and Schumann were Germans, the latter was a great musician, the former a great poet. The names of both are mentioned with love and respect wherever the German language is spoken.

5. Translate the following sentences, etc. (*a*) Kann ich dafür? (*b*) Die Gesichter, die der ehrliche Onkel schneiden wird. (*c*) Dabei bleibt's. (*d*) Es hätte doch Händel zwischen ihnen setzen können. (*e*) Wer kann für die Ähnlichkeit. (*f*) Es fällt mir gar nicht ein. (*g*) Lassen Sie Sich nichts weiß machen. (*h*) Auf dem Herweg. (*i*) Euer Gnaden begreifen, daß, u. s. w.

6. What is the name of the French original of *Der Neffe als Onkel ?* Mention comedies of Plautus, Shakspeare and Regnard which turn on confusing resemblances of principal characters.

7. (*a*) Give as full a statement as possible of the differences between separable and inseparable verbs. (*b*) What do you know about the order of words in a German sentence?

8. Translation at sight.

Als ich vor mehreren Jahren im Schwarzwald lebte, hatte ich einen alten Bauer zum Nachbar. Er war ein Mann von geringer Bildung, aber von kindlich frommem Glauben und eisernem Willen. Er war ein Kind des Forstes, sein Vater war Kohlenbrenner gewesen, und seine Vorfahren trieben dieselbe Beschäftigung. Mein Nachbar war aber als junger Mann zu einem seiner Vettern gegangen, der ein Gut besaß, und nachdem er ihm zwanzig Jahre treu gedient, hatte er diesem Vetter sein kleines Gut abgekauft. Der Mann war ein echter Schwarzwälder von hohem kräftigem Wuchs, hatte ein starkknochiges Gesicht, und ein treues Herz blickte aus den blauen Augen. Seine Kleidung war einfach, denn er trug stets eine kurze Jacke und hohe Stiefel, jedoch im Hause meistens Holzpantoffeln. Er war das Muster eines treuen Unterthans.

CLASSICAL SCHOLARSHIPS.

GREEK.

Translate with notes :—

A. Plato, Crito.

(1) ἔπειτα οὐχ ὁρᾶς τούτους τοὺς συκοφάντας ὡς εὐτελεῖς, καὶ οὐδὲν ἂν δέοι ἐπ' αὐτοὺς πολλοῦ ἀργυρίου ; σοὶ δὲ ὑπάρχει μὲν τὰ ἐμὰ χρήματα, ὡς ἐγὼ οἶμαι, ἱκανά· ἔπειτα καὶ εἴ τι ἐμοῦ κηδόμενος οὐκ οἴει δεῖν ἀναλίσκειν τἀμά, ξένοι οὗτοι ἐνθάδε ἕτοιμοι ἀναλίσκειν· εἷς δὲ καὶ κεκόμικεν ἐπ' αὐτὸ τοῦτο ἀργύριον ἱκανόν, Σιμμίας ὁ Θηβαῖος· ἕτοιμος δὲ καὶ Κέβης καὶ ἄλλοι πολλοὶ πάνυ.

(2) Οὐκ ἄρα, ὦ βέλτιστε, πάνυ ἡμῖν οὕτω φροντιστέον, τί ἐροῦσιν οἱ πολλοὶ ἡμᾶς, ἀλλ' ὅ τι ὁ ἐπαΐων περὶ τῶν δικαίων καὶ ἀδίκων, ὁ εἷς, καὶ αὐτὴ ἡ ἀλήθεια. ὥστε πρῶτον μὲν ταύτῃ οὐκ ὀρθῶς εἰσηγεῖ, εἰσηγούμενος τῆς τῶν

πολλῶν δόξης δεῖν ἡμᾶς φροντίζειν περὶ τῶν δικαίων καὶ καλῶν καὶ ἀγαθῶν καὶ τῶν ἐναντίων. ἀλλὰ μὲν δή, φαίη γ᾽ ἄν τις, οἷοί τέ εἰσιν ἡμᾶς οἱ πολλοὶ ἀποκτιννύναι.

(3) φαῖεν γὰρ ἂν ὅτι ʻ ὦ Σώκρατες, μεγάλα ἡμῖν τούτων τεκμήριά ἐστιν, ὅτι σοί καὶ ἡμεῖς ἠρέσκομεν καὶ ἡ πόλις.

B. Plato, Apology.

(1) τῆς γὰρ ἐμῆς, εἰ δή τίς ἐστι σοφία καὶ οἵα, μάρτυρα ὑμῖν παρέξομαι τὸν θεὸν τὸν ἐν Δελφοῖς. Χαιρεφῶντα γὰρ ἴστε που. οὗτος ἐμός τε ἑταῖρος ἦν ἐκ νέου, καὶ ὑμῶν τῷ πλήθει ἑταῖρός τε καὶ ξυνέφυγε τὴν φυγὴν ταύτην καὶ μεθ᾽ ὑμῶν κατῆλθε· καὶ ἴστε δὴ οἷος ἦν Χαιρεφῶν, ὡς σφοδρὸς ἐφ᾽ ὅ τι ὁρμήσειεν. καὶ δή ποτε καὶ εἰς Δελφοὺς ἐλθὼν ἐτόλμησε τοῦτο μαντεύσασθαι· καί, ὅπερ λέγω, μὴ θορυβεῖτε, ὦ ἄνδρες· ἤρετο γὰρ δή, εἴ τις ἐμοῦ εἴη σοφώτερος· ἀνεῖλεν οὖν ἡ Πυθία μηδένα σοφώτερον εἶναι.

(2) Οὐκοῦν εἴπερ δαίμονας ἡγοῦμαι, ὡς σὺ φής, εἰ μὲν θεοί τινές εἰσιν οἱ δαίμονες, τοῦτ᾽ ἂν εἴη ὃ ἐγώ φημί σε αἰνίττεσθαι καὶ χαριεντίζεσθαι, θεοὺς οὐχ ἡγούμενον φάναι ἐμὲ θεοὺς αὖ ἡγεῖσθαι πάλιν, ἐπειδήπερ γε δαίμονας ἡγοῦμαι· εἰ δ᾽ αὖ οἱ δαίμονες θεῶν παῖδές εἰσι νόθοι τινὲς ἢ ἐκ νυμφῶν ἢ ἔκ τινων ἄλλων, ὧν δὴ καὶ λέγονται, τίς ἂν ἀνθρώπων θεῶν μὲν παῖδας ἡγοῖτο εἶναι, θεοὺς δὲ μή ;

(3) καὶ ταῦτα μὲν ἦν ἔτι δημοκρατουμένης τῆς πόλεως· ἐπειδὴ δὲ ὀλιγαρχία ἐγένετο, οἱ τριάκοντα αὖ μεταπεμψάμενοί με πέμπτον αὐτὸν εἰς τὴν θόλον προσέταξαν ἀγαγεῖν ἐκ Σαλαμῖνος Λέοντα τὸν Σαλαμίνιον, ἵνα ἀποθάνοι· οἷα δὴ καὶ ἄλλοις ἐκεῖνοι πολλοῖς πολλὰ προσέταττον, βουλόμενοι ὡς πλείστους ἀναπλῆσαι αἰτιῶν· τότε μέντοι ἐγὼ οὐ λόγῳ ἀλλ᾽ ἔργῳ αὖ ἐνεδειξάμην, ὅτι ἐμοὶ θανάτου μὲν μέλει, εἰ μὴ ἀγροικότερον ἦν εἰπεῖν, οὐδ᾽ ὁτιοῦν, τοῦ δὲ μηδὲν ἄδικον μηδ᾽ ἀνόσιον ἐργάζεσθαι, τούτου δὲ τὸ μᾶν μέλει.

(4) ἀλλὰ μὴ οὐ τοῦτ᾽ ᾖ χαλεπόν, ὦ ἄνδρες, θάνατον
ἐκφυγεῖν, ἀλλὰ πολὺ χαλεπώτερον πονηρίαν· θᾶττον γὰρ
θανάτου θεῖ. καὶ νῦν ἐγὼ μὲν ἅτε βραδὺς ὢν καὶ πρεσ-
βύτης ὑπὸ τοῦ βραδυτέρου ἑάλων,· οἱ δ᾽ ἐμοὶ κατήγοροι ἅτε
δεινοὶ καὶ ὀξεῖς ὄντες ὑπὸ τοῦ θάττονος, τῆς κακίας. καὶ
νῦν ἐγὼ μὲν ἄπειμι ὑφ᾽ ὑμῶν· θανάτου δίκην ὄφλων, οὗτοι
δ᾽ ὑπὸ τῆς ἀληθείας ὠφληκότες μοχθηρίαν καὶ ἀδικίαν.

C. Xenophon, Memorabilia.

(1) Ὅσα μὲν οὖν μὴ φανερὸς ἦν ὅπως ἐγίγνωσκεν, οὐδὲν
θαυμαστὸν ὑπὲρ τούτων περὶ αὐτοῦ παραγνῶναι τοὺς
δικαστάς· ὅσα δὲ πάντες ᾔδεσαν, οὐ θαυμαστὸν, εἰ μὴ
τούτων ἐνεθυμήθησαν; βουλεύσας γάρ ποτε καὶ τὸν βου-
λευτικὸν ὅρκον ὀμόσας, ἐν ᾧ ἦν κατὰ τοὺς νόμους βουλεύ-
σειν, ἐπιστάτης ἐν τῷ δήμῳ γενόμενος, ἐπιθυμήσαντος τοῦ
δήμου παρὰ τοὺς νόμους, ἐννέα στρατηγοὺς μιᾷ ψήφῳ τοὺς
ἀμφὶ Θράσυλλον καὶ Ἐρασινίδην ἀποκτεῖναι πάντας, οὐκ
ἠθέλησεν ἐπιψηφίσαι.

(2) Πῶς οὖν ἔνοχος ἂν εἴη τῇ γραφῇ; ὃς ἀντὶ μὲν τοῦ
μὴ νομίζειν θεοὺς, ὡς ἐν τῇ γραφῇ γέγραπτο, φανερὸς ἦν
θεραπεύων τοὺς θεοὺς μάλιστα τῶν ἄλλων ἀνθρώπων· ἀντὶ
δὲ τοῦ διαφθείρειν τοὺς νέους, ὃ δὴ ὁ γραψάμενος αὐτὸν
ᾐτιᾶτο, φανερὸς ἦν τῶν συνόντων τοὺς πονηρὰς ἐπιθυμίας
ἔχοντας τούτων μὲν παύων, τῆς δὲ καλλίστης καὶ μεγα-
λοπρεπεστάτης ἀρετῆς, ᾗ πόλεις τε καὶ οἴκους εὖ οἰκοῦσι,
προτρέπων ἐπιθυμεῖν· ταῦτα δὲ πράττων πῶς οὐ μεγάλης
ἄξιος ἦν τιμῆς τῇ πόλει;

(3) Δοκεῖς δέ μοι καὶ αὐτὸς τοῦτο γιγνώσκειν· οὐδένα
γοῦν τῆς συνουσίας ἀργύριον πράττῃ· καίτοι τό γε ἱμάτιον
ἢ τὴν οἰκίαν ἢ ἄλλο τι ὧν κέκτησαι, νομίζων ἀργύριου
ἄξιον εἶναι, οὐδενὶ ἂν μὴ ὅτι προῖκα δοίης, ἀλλ᾽ οὐδ᾽ ἐλατ-
τον τῆς ἀξίας λαβών. Δῆλον δὴ ὅτι, εἰ καὶ τὴν συνουσίαν
ᾤου τινὸς ἀξίαν εἶναι, καὶ ταύτης ἂν οὐκ ἔλαττον τῆς ἀξίας
ἀργύριον ἐπράττου.

D. Thucydides VI.

(1) καὶ οἴεσθε ἴσως τὰς γενομένας ὑμῖν σπονδὰς ἔχειν
τι βέβαιον· αἳ ἡσυχαζόντων μὲν ὑμῶν ὀνόματι σπονδαὶ
ἔσονται (οὕτω γὰρ ἐνθένδε τε ἄνδρες ἔπραξαν αὐτὰ καὶ ἐκ
τῶν ἐναντίων), σφαλέντων δέ που ἀξιόχρεῳ δυνάμει ταχεῖαν
τὴν ἐπιχείρησιη ἡμῖν οἱ ἐχθροὶ ποιήσονται, οἷς πρῶτον
μὲν διὰ ξυμφορῶν ἡ ξύμβασις καὶ ἐκ τοῦ αἰσχίονος ἢ ἡμῖν
κατ' ἀνάγκην ἐγένετο, ἔπειτα ἐν αὐτῇ ταύτῃ πολλὰ τὰ
ἀμφισβητούμενα ἔχομεν. εἰσὶ δ' οἳ οὐδὲ ταύτην πω τὴν
ὁμολογίαν ἐδέξαντο, καὶ οὐχ οἱ ἀσθενέστατοι· ἀλλ' οἱ μὲν
ἄντικρυς πολεμοῦσιν, οἱ δὲ καὶ διὰ τὸ Λακεδαιμονίους ἔτι
ἡσυχάζειν δεχημέροις σπονδαῖς καὶ αὐτοὶ κατέχονται.

(2) ξυνέβη δὲ πρός τε σφᾶς αὐτοὺς ἅμα ἔριν γενέσθαι,
ᾧ τις ἕκαστος προσετάχθη, καὶ ἐς τοὺς ἄλλους Ἕλληνας
ἐπίδειξιν μᾶλλον εἰκασθῆναι τῆς δυνάμεως καὶ ἐξουσίας ἢ
ἐπὶ πολεμίους παρασκευήν.

(3) Οὐδὲ γὰρ τὴν ἄλλην ἀρχὴν ἐπαχθὴς ἦν ἐς τοὺς
πολλούς, ἀλλ' ἀνεπιφθόνως κατεστήσατο· καὶ ἐπετήδευσαν
ἐπὶ πλεῖστον δὴ τύραννοι οὗτοι ἀρετὴν καὶ ξύνεσιν, καὶ
Ἀθηναίους εἰκοστὴν μόνον πρασσόμενοι τῶν γιγνομένων
τήν τε πόλιν αὐτῶν καλῶς διεκόσμησαν καὶ τοὺς πολέμους
διέφερον καὶ ἐς τὰ ἱερὰ ἔθυον. τὰ δὲ ἄλλα αὐτὴ ἡ πόλις
τοῖς πρὶν κειμένοις νόμοις ἐχρῆτο, πλὴν καθ' ὅσον ἀεί τινα
ἐπεμέλοντο σφῶν αὐτῶν ἐν ταῖς ἀρχαῖς εἶναι.

(4) παραστήτω δέ τινι καὶ τόδε, πολύ τε ἀπὸ τῆς ἡμετέρας αὐτῶν εἶναι καὶ πρὸς γῇ οὐδεμιᾷ φιλίᾳ ἥντινα μὴ αὐτοὶ
μαχόμενοι κτήσεσθε. καὶ τοὐναντίον ὑπομιμνήσκω ὑμᾶς
ἢ οἱ πολέμιοι σφίσιν αὐτοῖς εὖ οἶδ' ὅτι παρακελεύονται·
οἱ μὲν γὰρ ὅτι περὶ πατρίδος ἔσται ὁ ἀγών, ἐγὼ δὲ ὅτι οὐκ
ἐν πατρίδι, ἐξ ἧς κρατεῖν δεῖ ἢ μὴ ῥᾳδίως ἀποχωρεῖν· οἱ
γὰρ ἱππῆς πολλοὶ ἐπικείσονται.

(5) καὶ ὑμεῖς μήθ' ὡς δικασταὶ γενόμοι τῶν ἡμῖν ποιου-
μένων μήθ' ὡς σωφρονισταί, ὃ χαλεπὸν ἤδη, ἀποτρέπειν
πειρᾶσθε, καθ' ὅσον δέ τι ὑμῖν τῆς ἡμετέρας πολυπραγ-
μοσύνης καὶ τρόπου τὸ αὐτὸ ξυμφέρει, τούτῳ ἀπολαβόντες
χρήσασθε. καὶ νομίσατε μὴ πάντας ἐν ἴσῳ βλάπτειν αὐτά,
πολὺ δὲ πλείους τῶν Ἑλλήνων καὶ ὠφελεῖν.

(6) φυγάς τε γάρ εἰμι τῆς τῶν ἐξελασάντων πονηρίας
καὶ οὐ τῆς ὑμετέρας ἣν πείθησθέ μοι, ὠφελίας· καὶ πολε-
μιώτεροι οὐχ οἱ τοὺς πολεμίους που βλάψαντες ὑμεῖς ἢ οἱ
τοὺς φίλους ἀναγκάσαντες πολεμίους γενέσθαι. τό τε φιλό-
πολι οὐκ ἐν ᾧ ἀδικοῦμαι ἔχω, ἀλλ' ἐν ᾧ ἀσφαλῶς ἐπολι-
τεύθην.

CLASSICAL SCHOLARSHIPS.

GREEK.

TRANSLATIONS AT SIGHT.

1. Πολλαχῆ δ' ἄν τις λογιζόμενος εὕροι ταύτας τὰς
πράξεις μάλιστα λυσιτελούσας ἡμῖν. φέρε γάρ, πρὸς τίνας
χρὴ πολεμεῖν τοὺς μηδεμιᾶς πλεονεξίας ἐπιθυμοῦντας ἀλλ
αὐτὸ τὸ δίκαιον σκοποῦντας; οὐ πρὸς τοὺς καὶ πρότερον
κακῶς τὴν Ἑλλάδα ποιήσαντας καὶ νῦν ἐπιβουλεύοντας
καὶ πάντα τὸν χρόνον οὕτω πρὸς ἡμᾶς διακειμένους; τίσι
δὲ φθονεῖν εἰκός ἐστι τοὺς μὴ παντάπασιν ἀνάνδρως διακειμένους ἀλλὰ μετρίως τούτῳ τῷ πράγματι χρωμένους; οὐ
τοῖς μείζους μὲν τὰς δυναστείας ἢ κατ' ἀνθρώπους περιβε-
βλημένοις, ἐλάττονος δ' ἀξίοις τῶν παρ' ἡμῖν δυστυχούν-
των;

2. ΠΥ. καλῶς ἔλεξας τῶν θεῶν ἐμοῦ θ' ὕπερ.
σήμαινε, δ' ᾧ χρὴ τάσδ' ἐπιστολὰς φέρειν
πρὸς Ἄργος, ὅ τι τε χρὴ κλύοντά σου λέγειν.
ΙΦ. ἄγγελλ' Ὀρέστῃ, παιδὶ τἀγαμέμνονος·

ἡ 'ν Αὐλίδι σφαγεῖσ' ἐπιστελλει τάδε
ζῶσ' Ἰφιγένεια, τοῖς ἐκεῖ δ' οὐ ζῶσ' ἔτι.
ποῦ δ' ἔστ' ἐκείνη ; κατθανοῦσ' ἥκει πάλιν ;
ἥδ' ἦν ὁρᾷς σύ· μὴ λόγοις ἔκπλησσέ με.
κόμισαί μ' ἐς Ἄργος, ὦ σύναιμε, πρὶν θανεῖν,
ἐκ βαρβάρου γῆς καὶ μετάστησον θεᾶς
σφαγίων, ἐφ' οἷσι ξενοφόνους τιμὰς ἔχω.
ΟΡ. Πυλάδη, τί λέξω ; ποῦ ποτ' ὄνθ' εὑρήμεθα ;
ἢ σοῖς ἀραία δώμασιν γενήσομαι,
Ὀρέσθ'. ἵν' αὖθις ὄνομα δὶς κλύων μάθης.

CLASSICAL SCHOLARSHIPS.

LATIN TRANSLATION:—Three Hours Paper.

1. Translate :—

Me vero primum dulces ante omnia Musae, ,
Quarum sacra fero ingenti percussus amore,
Accipiant, caelique vias et sidera monstrent,
Defectus solis varios lunaeque labores;
Unde tremor terris, qua vi maria alta tumescant
Obicibus ruptis rursusque in se ipsa residant,
Quid tantum Oceano properent se tinguere soles
Hiberni, vel quae tardis mora noctibus obstet.
Sin, has ne possim naturae accedere partes,
Frigidus obstiterit circum praecordia sanguis,
Rura mihi et rigui placeant in vallibus amnes,
Flumina amem silvasque inglorius. O ubi campi
Spercheosque et virginibus bacchata Lacaenis
Taygeta, o qui me gelidis convallibus Haemi
Sistat et ingenti ramorum protegat umbra?
Felix, qui potuit rerum cognoscere causas,
Atque metus omnes et inexorabile fatum
Subiecit pedibus strepitumque Acherontis avari.
Who is supposed to be alluded to in the last three lines?

2. Translate, adding a short note where necessary :—

   (a) Silvarumque aliae pressos propaginis arcus
      Exspectant et viva sua plantaria terra.

   (b) Plantis et durae coryli nascuntur et ingens
      Fraxinus Herculeaeque arbos umbrosa coronae.

What is the last tree alluded to ?

   (c) Argitisque minor, cui non certaverit ulla
      Aut tantum fluere aut totidem durare per annos.

   (d)   Te, Lari maxime, teque
      Fluctibus et fremitu adsurgens, Benace, marino.

What are the modern names of these lakes?

   (e) Cui super indignas hiemes solemque potentem
      Silvestres uri adsidue capreaeque sequ ces
      Inludent.

3. Translate :—Sed, per deos immortales quam ob rem in sententiam non addidisti, uti prius verberibus in eos anima-duorteretur? an quia lex Porcia vetat? at aliae leges item condemnatis civibus non animam eripi sed exilium permitti iubent. An quia gravius est verberari quam necari? quid autem acerbum aut nimis grave est in homines tanti facinoris convictos? Sin quia levius est, qui convenit in minore negotio legem timere, cum eam in maiore neglegeris?

What do you notice irregular in the Grammar here?

What is the lex Porcia here alluded to?

4. Translate :—Sed tamen, qui semel verecundiae fines transierit, eum bene et naviter oportet esse impudentem. Itaque te plane etiam atque etiam rogo, ut et ornes ea vehe-mentius etiam, quam fortasse sentis, et in eo leges historiae neglegas gratiamque illam, de qua suavissume quodam in pro-oemio scripsisti, a qua te flecti non magis potuisse demons-tras quam Herculem Xenophontium illum a Voluptate, eam, si me tibi vehementius commendabit, ne aspernere amorique nostro plusculum etiam, quam concedet veritas, largiare.

To whom is this letter addressed?

5. (a) Translate :—

   It, redit et narrat, Volteium nomine Menam,
   Praeconem, tenui censu, sine crimine, notum
   Et properare loco et cessare et quaerere et uti,
   Gaudentem parvisque sodalibus et lare certo
   Et ludis et post decisa negotia campo.

'Scitari libet ex ipso quodcunque refers; dic
Ad cenam veniat. Non sane credere Mena,
Mirari secum tacitus. Quid multa? 'Benigne'
Respondet. 'Neget ille mihi?' Negat improbus et te·
Neglegit aut horret?' Volteium mane Philippus
Vilia vendentem tunicato scruta popello
Occupat et salvere iubet prior. Ille Philippo
Excusare laborem et mercennaria vincla,
Quod non mane domum venisset, denique quod non
Providisset eum. 'Sic ignovisse putato
Me tibi, si cenas hodie mecum? 'Ut libet?' 'Ergo
Post nonam venies: nunc i, rem strenuus auge.'
(b) Comment on the various views taken of the lines :—
Zmyrna quid et Colophon? Maiora minorave fama,
Cunctane prae campo et Tiberino flumine sordent?

6. Translate :—

Romae ad primum nuntium cladis eius cum in genti terrore
ac tumultu concursus in forum populi est factus. Matronae
vagae per vias, quae repens clades allata quaeve fortuna
exercitus esset, obvios percontantur: et quum frequentis con-
tionis modo turba in comitium et curiam versa magistratus
vocaret, tandem haud multo ante solis occasum M. Pompo-
nius praetor 'Pugna' inquit 'magna victi sumus.' Et quan-
quam nihil certius ex eo auditum est, tamen alius ab alio im-
pleti rumoribus domos referunt, consulem cum magna parte
copiarum caesum; superesse paucos aut fuga passim per
Etruriam sparsos aut captos ab hoste. Quot casus exercitus
victi fuerant, tot in curas dispertiti animi eorum erant, quorum propinqui sub C. Flaminio consule meruerant, ignoran-
tium, quae cuiusque suorum fortuna esset; nec quisquam
satis certum habet, quid aut speret aut timeat. Postero ac
deinceps aliquot diebus ad portas maior prope mulierum quam
virorum multitudo stetit, aut suorum aliquem aut nuntios
de iis opperiens; circumfundebanturque obviis sciscitantes,
neque avelli, utique ab notis, priusquam ordine omnia in·
quisissent, poterant.'

What different views have been held about Hannibal's route
over the Alps?

LATIN PROSE COMPOSITION AND UNSEEN.

CLASSICAL SCHOLARSHIPS.

FOR LATIN PROSE.

The yoke of Ariovistus had now become more intolerable than Roman supremacy, and at a diet of the tribes of central Gaul the Roman general was asked to come to the aid of the Celts against the Germans. Caesar consented; at his suggestion the Haedui refused the customary tribute, and demanded the restoration of the hostages. When Ariovistus proceeded to attack the Roman clients, Caesar sent to demand from him the hostages of the Haedui, and a promise to leave the latter tribe at peace, and to bring no more Germans over the Rhine. Ariovistus replied in terms which asserted a claim to equal right and equal power with the Romans. Northern Gaul, he said, had become subject to himself as southern Gaul to the Romans; he did not hinder the Romans from levying tribute on the Allobroges and the Romans had no right to prevent him from taxing his own subjects. He also showed that he was acquainted with the political condition of Italy and offered to help Caesar to make himself ruler of Italy, if only Caesar would leave him alone in Gaul.

FOR UNSEEN TRANSLATION.

1. Tempore ruricolae patiens fit taurus aratri,
   Praebet et incurvo colla premenda iugo,
   Tempore paret equus lentis animosus habenis,
   Et placido duros accipit ore lupos,
   Tempore Poenorum compescitur ira leonum,
   Nec feritas animo, quae fuit ante, manet,
   Quaeque sui monitis obtemperat Inda magistri
   Belua, servitium tempore uicta subit.
   Tempus ut extensis tumeat facit uva racemis
   Uixque merum capiant grana, quod intus habent;
   Tempus et in canas semen producit aristas,
   Et ne sint tristi poma sapore cavet.
   Hoc tenuat dentem terras scindentis aratri,
   Hoc rigidas silices, hoc adamanta terit.
   Hoc etiam saeuas paulatim mitigat iras,
   Hoc minuit luctus maestaque corda levat.

Cuncta potest igitur tacito pede lapsa vetustas
Praeterquam curas attenuare meas.
Ut patria careo, bis frugibus area trita est,
Dissiluit nudo pressa bis uva pede.
Nec quaesita tamen spatio patientia longo est,
Mensque mali sensum nostra recentis habet.

2. Domi maius certamen consulibus cum plebe ac tribunis erat. Fidei iam suae non solum virtutis ducebant esse, ut accepissent duo patricii consulatum, ita ambobus patriciis mandare: quin aut toto cedendum esse, ut plebeius iam magistratus consulatus fiat, aut totum possidendum, quam possessionem integram a patribus accepissent. Plebes contra fremit: quid se vivere, quid in parte civium censeri, si, quod duorum hominum virtute. L. Sextii ac C. Licinii, partum sit, id obtinere universi non possint? Vel reges vel decemviros vel si quod tristius sit imperii nomen, patiendum esse potius, quam ambos patricios consules videant nec in vicem pareatur atque imperetur, sed pars altera in aeterno imperio locata plebem nusquam alio natam quam ad serviendum putet.

CLASSICAL SCHOLARSHIPS.

ROMAN HISTORY.

1. Distinguish the terms *populus* and *plebes, comitia* and *concilium, centuria* and *tribus, lex* and *Plebiscitum.*

2. State briefly the functions of *consules* and *praetores;* mention some facts about the development of courts of judicial procedure and the selection of iudices in the 2nd and 1st centuries B.C.

3. What do you know of Sertorius, Sp. Maelius, M. Aemilius Scaurus, P. Lentulus Spinther, L. Plancus, M' Curius Dentatus, Deiotarus, Cato the Elder, Philopoemen, Saturninus, Spartacus ?

4. What events are connected with the following places:—
Zama, Aquae Sextiae, Saguntum, Civita, Gergovia, Nola, Chaeronea, Trasumene, Caudine Forks.

5. State briefly the history of events *either* (a) between Caesar's invasion of Italy and his assassination or (b) in the years 53 and 52 B.C.

6. Criticise from a political point of view either (a) the establishment of an empire on the ruins of the republic or (b) the policy of Cicero.

***

CLASSICAL SCHOLARSHIPS.

September.

FOR GREEK PROSE.

By the providence of the Gods we Britons rule the sea and possess a great empire over many lands and cities far distant from each other. And we shall think rightly, and piously too, if we give thanks to the gods for these things, nor ought we to imagine that accident gave us what we possess. For in the first place the fact that we inhabit an island gives us training in nautical skill; in the second place, it is inborn in us to travel to many lands, either for trade or to hunt animals, so that it is said that the Britons leave their dead everywhere on earth. And we gladly make our homes away from our native land. And in courage we are not inferior to others, so that we are able to hold what we have won. Again, through our commerce we gain wealth, and wealth gives the means of war. And sometimes, though at first we settled merely for the sake of gain, we have won at last, as it were, by chance, lands and wealth and empire and honor.

***

SCHOLARSHIP EXAMINATION.
GREEK HISTORY.

1. Give, in as much detail as you can, the methods employed at Athens for raising revenue.

2. What is meant by the age of the Tyrants' in Greece ? Give examples and dates.

3. Indicate the events connected with the following names :—Mycalé, Melos, Egesta, Chaeronea, Arginusae, Amphipolis, Cirrha.

4. Indicate the historical importance of :—Cleisthenes, Brasidas, Nicias, Æschines, Pelopidas, Hermocrates.

5. What do you know of :—Alcaeus, Tyrtaeus, Hecataeus, Menander, Eupolis, Zeno, Anaximander?

6. What are the technical meanings of :—ἀντίδοσις τριηραρχία, ὑπωμοσία, προεδρία, ἑστίασις, εὔθυνα?

MATHEMATICAL SCHOLARSHIPS.

WEDNESDAY, SEPT. 15TH :—MORNING, 9 TO 12.

Examiner,.. ......ALEXANDER JOHNSON, M.A., LL.D.

1. Describe the *Elliptic Compasses*, and prove the principle on which the mechanical description of the ellipse therewith depends.

2. If φ and φ' be the eccentric angles corresponding to two points on an ellipse, find the equation of the chord joining them, and *thence* show that the equation at the point corresponding to φ is

$$\frac{x}{a} \cos + \phi + \frac{y}{b} \sin \varphi = 1 .$$

(*a*) Prove the truth of this equation in any other way.

3. Show that the locus of the intersection of tangents to a parabola which cut at a given angle (*θ*) is

$$y^2 + (x - m)^2 = (x + m)^2 \sec^2 \theta,$$

and hence that it is an hyperbola having the same focus and directrix as the parabola.

4. Prove that the locus of the intersection of the perpendicular from the centre of an ellipse on any tangent with the radius vector from a focus to the point of contact is a circle.

5. The angle between any two tangents to a parabola is half the angle between the focal radii vectores to their points of contact.

6. Any focal chord of an ellipse is a third proportional to the transverse axis and the parallel diameter.

7. Prove that the conics

$$\frac{x^2}{a^2} + \frac{y^2}{a^2-h^2} = 1 \text{ and } \frac{x^2}{a'^2} + \frac{y^2}{a'^2-h^2} = 1$$

cut one another at right angles.

8. Investigate the figure of the hyperbola from its equation, and show its relation to its asymptotes.

9. Taking the general equation of a conic, determine the condition whether it is an ellipse, a parabola, or an hyperbola.

10. Through the intersection of two circles a right line is drawn, find the locus of the middle point of the portion intercepted between the circles.

11. Find the angle between the straight lines represented by

$$x^2 + x y - 6 y^2 = 0.$$

12. Prove analytically that the perpendiculars erected at the middle points of the sides of a triangle are concurrent.

MATHEMATICAL SCHOLARSHIPS.

ANALYTIC GEOMETRY—(Second Paper.)

THURSDAY, SEPT. 16TH:—MORNING, 9 TO 12.

Examiner.................... ....ALEXANDER JOHNSON, M.A., LL.D.

1. Taking $L M = R^2$ as the equation of a conic referred to two tangents and their chord of contact, find the locus of the vertex of a triangle circumscribed to a conic which has two of its vertices moving on two fixed right lines.

2. Prove that two conics similar and similarly placed can cut each other only in two finite points.

3. Prove by trilinear co-ordinates that the three bisectors of a triangle meet in a point.

4. If three conic sections have one chord common to all, their three other common chords will pass through the same point.

5. Prove that if through a given point in a conic any two lines at right angles to each other be drawn to meet the curve, the line joining their extremities will pass through a fixed point on the normal.

6. Find the equation of the pair of tangents drawn from a given point to a given circle.

5

7. Taking the general equation of a conic, find the condition that the pole of the axis of x should be on the axis of y and *vice versa*.

8. The lines joining the corresponding vertices of a triangle and its conjugate with regard to a circle meet in a point.

9. Find the Anharmonic ratio of the pencil given by $a = o$, $\beta = o$; $a \sim k \beta = o$ $a \cdot \cdot k' \beta = o$.

10. Given vertex and vertical angle of a triangle and rectangle under sides, if one base angle describe a right line or a circle find locus described by the other base angle.

11. Given base and difference of base angle of a triangle, find locus of vertex.

12. Interpret the equation $xy = 16$.
   Plot the Curve.

MATHEMATICAL SCHOLARSHIPS.

CALCULUS.

MONDAY, SEPTEMBER 20TH.

Examiner..................................AELXANDER JOHNSON, M.A., L.L.D.

1. Find a value for the radius of curvature in terms of the radius vector from the origin (r), and the perpendicular (p) on the tangent; and apply it to prove that in an ellipse.

$$\rho = \frac{a^2 b^2}{p^3}.$$

2. Prove that in any curve

$$ds = \sqrt{1 + \frac{r^2 \, d\theta'^2}{dr^2}} \, dr.$$

3. Find six terms of the development of $\dfrac{e^x}{\cos x}$ in ascending powers of x.

4. Find the equation of the normal at any point on the curve $y^m = ax^n$.

5. Given one angle of a right-angled spherical triangle, find when the difference between the sides which contain it is a maximum.

6. Find the value, when $x = 0$, of

$$\frac{\tan x - \sin x}{\sin^3 x}$$

7. Being given that $y = (x + \sqrt{x^4 - 1})^m$,

prove that $(x^2 - 1)\dfrac{d^2y}{dx^2} + x\,\dfrac{dy}{dx} - m^2y = 0$.

8. In the cardioid $r = a(1 + \cos \theta)$, prove that $s = 4a \sin \dfrac{\theta}{2}$.

9. Find the length of an arc of the parabola.

10. Find the area of the curve

$$y = \frac{2a}{x}\sqrt{2ax - x^2}.$$

11. Integrate

$$\int \frac{dx}{a + b \sin x}\;;\;\int^x \epsilon \sin k^x\,dx\;;\;\int \frac{\sin \theta\,d\theta}{\theta^n}\;.$$

12. Find the formula of reduction for

$$\int \frac{x^m\,dx}{(1 + x^2)^n}.$$

13. An arc of a circle revolves round a diameter passing through one extremity, show that the volume of the *spherical cap* thus generated is

$$\pi\,h^2\left(a - \frac{h}{3}\right).$$

14. Integrate

$$\int \cos^3 x \sin 2x\,dx\;;\;\int \cos^4 x \sin 4x\,dx\;;\;\int x^3\,(\log x)^2\,dx.$$

MATHEMATICAL SCHOLARSHIPS.

HIGHER ALGEBRA—THEORY OF EQUATIONS—TRIGONOMETRY.

TUESDAY, SEPT. 21ST:—MORNING, 9 TO 12.

Examiner ....ALEXANDER JOHNSON, M.A., LL.D.

1. Prove that the determinant

$$\begin{vmatrix} \cos \tfrac{1}{2}(A - B), & \cos \tfrac{1}{2}(B - C), & \cos \tfrac{1}{2}(C - A) \\ \cos \tfrac{1}{2}(A + B), & \cos \tfrac{1}{2}(B + C), & \cos \tfrac{1}{2}(C + A) \\ \sin \tfrac{1}{2}(A + B), & \sin \tfrac{1}{2}(B + C), & \sin \tfrac{1}{2}(C + A) \end{vmatrix} = \begin{matrix} 2 \sin \tfrac{1}{2}(A - B) \\ \sin \tfrac{1}{2}(B - C) \\ \sin \tfrac{1}{2}(A - C) \end{matrix}$$

2. If a system of equations

$$a_1 X + b_1 Y + c_1 Z = 0, \quad a_2 X + b_2 Y + c_2 Z = 0, \quad a_3 X + b_3 Y + c_3 Z = 0,$$

be transformed by the substitutions,

$$X = a_1 x + a_2 y + a_3 z, \quad Y = \beta_1 x + \beta_2 y + \beta_3 z, \quad Z = \gamma_1 x + \gamma_2 y + \gamma_3 z,$$

prove that the determinant of the transformed system will be equal to $(a_1 \, b_2 \, c_3)$, the determinant of the original system, multiplied by $(a_1 \, \beta_2 \, \gamma_3)$

3. Define the reciprocal of a given determinant, and prove that

$$(A_1 \, B_2 \, C_3) = (a_1 \, b_2 \, c_3)^2.$$

4. Calculate the determinant

$$\begin{vmatrix} 7, & -2, & 0, & 5 \\ -2, & 6, & -2, & 2 \\ 0, & -2, & 5, & 3 \\ 5, & 2, & 3, & 4 \end{vmatrix}$$

5. Calculate by Horner's method the real roots of the equations

$$x^3 + x - 3 = 0.$$

6. Explain Newton's method of approximations to the numerical value of a root of an equation.

7. Solve the equation

$$2x^4 - 5x^3 + 6x^2 - 5x + 2 = 0.$$

8. Resolve $2x^2 - 21xy - 11 \, y^2 - x + 34y - 3$ into two factors of the first degree.

9. Calculate the Napierian logarithm of 2 to 6 places of decimals.

10. Investigate the expression for the area of a spherical triangle in terms of two sides and the contained angle.

$$\cot \tfrac{1}{2} E = \frac{\cot \tfrac{1}{2} a \cot \tfrac{1}{2} b + \cos C}{\sin C}.$$

11. The three angles of a spherical triangle are respectively 70° 39′, 48° 36′, 119° 15′, find the side opposite the last angle.

12. In any spherical triangle prove

$$\cos a = \frac{\cos A + \cos B \cos C}{\sin B \sin C}.$$

THIRD YEAR SCHOLARSHIPS.

ENGLISH LITERATURE.

SHAKSPERE AND MILTON.

FRIDAY, SEPT. 17TH : —MORNING, 9 TO 12.

(Write the answers to Sets A and B in different books).

A.

1. Relate the events contained in either Bk. I or Bk. II of Paradise Lost.

2. Select six peculiarly Miltonic words or phrases, and explain them carefully.

3. Shew, with the help of quotations : (*a*) Milton's varied range of knowledge, (*b*) his familiarity with classical literature, (*c*) his originality in allusion and in the invention of poetical figures.

B.

1. On what grounds may it be assumed that the date of the writing of The Tempest lies between the years 1603 and 1613 ?

2. Estimate Prospero's character.

3. Trace Ariel through the play.

4. Give the meaning of the following words and phrases, and say in what part of the play each occurs : two glasses, foison, pied ninny, still-vexed Bermoothes, urchins.

5. Mention two or three passages that show (*a*) extreme compression of language, and (*b*) " run-on " lines. Scan :—

  (*a*) Then meet and join. Jove's lightnings the precursors

  (*b*) Without a parallel, these being all my study

  (*c*) He thinks me now incapable ; confederates

  (*d*) With all my honours on my brother : whereon

  (*e*) The most opportune place, the strong'st suggestion

What peculiarities of Elizabethan as compared with modern English do the following extracts illustrate ?

  (*a*)   . For my good will is to't
  And yours it is against.

  (*b*) For you, most wicked sir, whom to call brother
  Would even infect my mouth, I do forgive
  Thy rankest fault.

  (*c*) The very rats instinctively have quit it.

THIRD YEAR SCHOLARSHIP EXAMINATIONS.

MYERS' MEDIAEVAL AND MODERN HISTORY, Part I.

Friday, September 17th :—2 to 5 p.m.

1. Trace the rise of papal power.

2. Enumerate the causes of the Crusades, and estimate their results.

3. Write a short essay on Chivalry.

4. What do you understand by Scholasticism? Indicate its connection with the rise of universities. Mention four of the great schoolmen.

5. Outline the most conspicuous features of German history under the Franconian and Hohenstaufen emperors.

6. Make brief notes on: Romance Languages; Wager of Battle; Heraclius; Abbassides; Hanseatic League.

THIRD YEAR SCHOLARSHIPS.

CHARLES LAMB: ESSAYS OF ELIA.

ENGLISH COMPOSITION.

Monday, Sept. 20th :—2 to 5 p.m.

(Write the answers to A and B in different books.)

A.

1. What qualities would you expect to find in the Essay. State and illustrate characteristics, other than Wit and Humour, of Lamb as an essayist.

2. Give the substance of the portions of " Elia " suggested by any *two* of the following extracts :

(*a*) I counsel thee, shut not thy heart nor thy library against S. T. C.

(*b*) In one of my daily jaunts between Bishopsgate and Shacklewell the coach stopped to take up a staid-looking gentleman.

(*c*) The swine-herd Ho-ti.

3. Give in your own words some idea of the contents of *one* of the following essays :

(*a*) Mrs. Battle's Opinions on Whist.

(*b*) Dream Children.

(*c*) Witches and other Night Fears.

B.

Write an essay of not less than *two* pages on *one* of the following subjects :

(a) The Humour and Wit of Charles Lamb.

(b) The Revival of Learning.

(c) The contrast between Ariel and Caliban in The Tempest.

BOURSES ET PRIX,

TROISIÈME ANNÉE—LETTRES.

Lundi, 20 Septembre.

Examinateurs,..... .... { M. Ingres.
{ J. L. Morin.

I. GRAMMAIRE.

Dans les phrases suivantes remplacer les tirets par des mots qui conviennent au sens.

Nous croyons que tout change quand ce —— nous qui changeons.

Nous croyons conduire les chose et ce —— elles qui nous conduisent.

Une foule de gens —— à l'influence des astres.

Le bonheur ou le malheur des hommes —— toujours de leur conduite.

Le malheur comme la prospérité —— la mesure d'un homme.

La vie de l'avare est une comédie ——'on n'applaudit que la dernière scène.

L'Espagne donna une prison à Colomb, —— —— avait donné un monde.

Les bouteilles se font avec du sable marin et de la potasse —— on ajoute un peu de chaux.

La paresse amollit le corps, le travail le fortifie : —— avance la vieillesse, —— prolonge la jeunesse.

L'Anglais porte partout sa patrie avec ——.

On doit rarement parler de ——.

Le choix d'une profession est important : pensez ——.

Les bons vins fortifient, mais il ne faut pas —— abuser.

Si quelqu'un vous rend un service, payez —— —— par la reconnaissance.

Jeanne d'Arc méritait une —— autre destinée.

Tous les hommes ont —— défauts ; leur devoir consiste à —— —— corriger.

Il faut qu'une porte —— ouverte ou fermée.

Questions orales.

II. LITTÉRATURE.

1. *Les Femmes Savantes.* Faire une comparaison entre Armande et Henriette et en dégager l'enseignement de la pièce. (500 mots environ).

2. *Britannicus.* Esquisser un portrait de Britannicus, de Junie et de Burrhus. (150 à 200 mots sur chacun).

3. Essai sur le théâtre en France depuis les origines jusqu'à Beaumarchais.

4. Questions orales.

THIRD YEAR SCHOLARSHIP EXAMINATION.

GERMAN.

Tuesday, Sept. 21st:—Afternoon, 2 to 5.

*Examiner,.....................................*L. R. Gregor, B.A., Ph.D.

1. Translate in *Egmont's Leben und Tod* the last paragraph of Chapter VIII.

2. Translate the following extract from *Schiller's Lied von der Glocke.*

> Dem dunkeln Schooß der heil'gen Erde
> Vertrauen wir der Hände That,
> Vertraut der Sämann seine Saat
> Und hofft, daß sie entkeimen werde
> Zum Segen, nach des Himmels Rat.
> Noch köstlicheren Samen bergen
> Wir trauernd in der Erde Schooß
> Und hoffen, daß er aus den Särgen
> Erblühen soll zu schönerm Los.

3. Translate the first paragraph of *Iphigenie,* Act. II, Scene I.

4. Translate *Immermann, Der Oberhof*, Ch. V, Parag. I.

5. What are the main points of difference between Goethe's *Iphigenie* and that of Euripides? Comment on the metre of Goethe's.

6. Comment briefly on the following expressions, etc. (*a*) Theſeus' Stadt. (*b*) Und hoffte mit der Fichte Kranz. des Sängers Schläfe zu umwinden. (*c*) Erinyen. (*d*) Eumeniden. (*e*) Reichs-fürsten. (*f*) Rat der Unruhen. (*g*) Genſenbund.

7. State as fully as possible in what circumstances the subjunctive mood is employed in German.

8. Translate into German (Horning) :—

A. Good morning; I was just going to knock. Is your husband at home?

B. I am sorry, but he is not. He went to town this morning about 9.45.

A. When do you expect him back?

B. He intends coming by train to-morrow afternoon. He will, I fancy, be here between 5 and 6 if the train is not late.

A. Well, that is often the case you know in summer. There are so many travellers and so much luggage.

B. Yes, and in winter the snow is the hindrance. How are the children?

A. Quite well, thank you. They were very glad to see their mother again.

B. Why, I didn't know she was home! When did she come?

A. Just this morning. We expected her the day before yesterday, but that very morning I got a letter saying that her mother was sick and she could not get away.

B. Surely her mother is not well already!

A. No, not exactly, but she is better. She had caught a slight cold.

B. With elderly people that often means a good deal.

A. Yes, indeed. Well, good-bye. I will try and see you the day after to-morrow.

SCIENCE SCHOLARSHIP.

CHEMISTRY.

FRIDAY, SEPT. 17TH :—MORNING, 9 TO 12.

Examin ....B. J. HARRINGTON, M.A., Ph. D.

1. Distinguish between empirical and constitutional formulæ, giving examples of each.

2. Explain the action of Phosphorus Pentachloride upon concentrated Sulphuric Acid, and draw conclusions as to the constitution of the Acid.

3. The gas in a cudiometer measures 68 c.c., the level of the Mercury in the tube and trough being the same. The barometer indicates an atmospheric pressure of 739 mm. The temperature is 20 ° C. What would be the volume of the gas at 0 ° C. and under 760 mm. pressure ?

4. What weight of green Vitriol could be obtained, theoretically, by the slow oxidation of 20 Kilograms of Iron Pyrites containing 37.5 per cent. of Sulphur ?

5. State briefly how you would prepare any form of the following compounds :—(1) Chlorine Monoxide, (2) Boric Acid, (3) Hydrocyanic Acid, (4) Carbon Disulphide, (5) Chromium Trioxide.

6. Explain the distinction between Mercurous and Mercuric compounds, and describe the preparation and properties of one member of each class.

7. How may the exact composition of Hydrochloric Acid gas be determined?

8. How would you estimate the proportions of Carbon, Hydrogen, Nitrogen and Oxygen in an organic body composed of these elements ?

9. Give briefly the preparation and properties of any three of the following bodies :— (1) Acetic Acid, (2) Vrea, (3) Nitro-benzine, (4) Aniline.

10. What are compound Alcoholic Ammonias, and what the more important ways in which they are formed ?

11. State what you know with regard to the chemistry of the natural fats and oils.

12. Explain the constitution of each of the following bodies :—(1) Ether, (2) Glycol, (3) Phenol, (4) Napthalene.

FACULTY OF APPLIED SCIENCE.

ENTRANCE EXAMINATIONS.
1897.

MATRICULATION EXAMINATION.

MATHEMATICS (*First Paper.*)

THURSDAY, SEPTEMBER 16TH :—MORNING, 9 TO 12.

ARITHMETIC.

1. A cubical vessel of which each edge is 3 ft. is filled with water from which 10 gallons are drawn ; what is the resulting depth of water, a gallon of water weighing 10 lbs. and a cubic foot 1,000 oz. ?

2. Find the present value of $780 due 3 months hence, interes being at 6 per cent. per annum.

3. Find, to 4 decimal places, the square root of 625.25.

4. The adjacent sides of a rectangle are $8\frac{1}{4}$ and $13\frac{1}{4}$ inches. Find in centimetres one side of a square of the same area as the rectangle.

ALGEBRA.

5. Find the factors of $a^3 - a^2x - 6 ax^2$, $x^6 - 2a^2 x^2 + a^4 x^2$, $x^4 + 4y^4$

6. Reduce to their lowest terms the fractions

$$\frac{x^2 + x - 12}{x^3 - 5 x^2 + 7x - 3} \quad \text{and} \quad \frac{x^4 + a^2 x^2 + a^4}{x^4 + a x^3 - a^3 x - a^4}$$

7. Find the continued product of $\sqrt{8}$, $\sqrt[3]{6}$, $\sqrt[4]{54}$, and rationalize the denominator of $\dfrac{y^2}{x + \sqrt{x^2 - y^2}}$.

8. Solve the equations :—

(1) $\dfrac{x + 22}{3} - \dfrac{4}{x} = \dfrac{9x - 6}{2}$,

(2) $a + x - \sqrt{a^2 + x^2} = b$,

(3) $\begin{cases} x^2 - y^2 = 25, \\ x - y = 1, \end{cases}$

(4) $\begin{cases} x^2 + y^2 = 25, \\ x + y = 1. \end{cases}$

9. Two rectangles contain the same area, 480 sq. ft. The difference of their lengths is 10 ft. and of their breadths 4 ft. ; find their sides.

MATRICULATION EXAMINATION.

MATHEMATICS (*Second Paper*).

THURSDAY, SEPTEMBER 16TH:—AFTERNOON, 2 TO 5.

GEOMETRY.

1. Prove that the diagonals of a parallelogram bisect each other.

a. Show that any straight line which passes through the middle point of the diagonal of a parallelogram and is terminated by either pair of opposite sides, bisects the parallelogram.

2. If a straight line be divided into any two parts, the squares on the whole line and one part shall be together equal to twice the rectangle contained by the whole line and that part, together with the square on the other part.

a. Show that the sum of the squares on any two lines can never be less than twice their rectangle.

3. From a given circle to cut off a segment containing an angle equal to a given angle.

4. To inscribe a regular pentagon in a given circle.

5. Similar polygons may be divided into the same number of similar triangles which have the same ratio as the polygons, and the polygons are to one another in the duplicate ratio of their homologous sides.

TRIGONOMETRY.

6. The sine of an angle is $\frac{4}{5}$, calculate the cosine. The cosine is $+$ or $-$, when $+$ and when $-$?

7. Which of the trigonometrical ratios can never lie between $+1$ and -1 ? Which may range from $+\infty$ to $-\infty$?

8. If $\sin A = \frac{4}{5}$, calculate $\sin 2A$ and $\cos 2A$.

9. Show that:

 (1) $\cos^2 A + \sin^2 A = 1$

 · (2) $\sec^4 A - \sec^2 A = \tan^4 A + \tan^2 A$.

 ·(3) $\cos(180^\circ - A) = -\cos A$.

(4) $\cos (A - B) = \cos A \cos B + \sin A \sin B$.

(5) $\dfrac{\sin A - \sin B}{\cos A + \cos B} = \tan \frac{1}{2} (A - B)$.

10. Solve the equation $3 \tan^2 \phi + 8 \cos^2 \phi = 7$, for ϕ.

SECOND YEAR EXHIBITION AND PRIZE EXAMINATION.

September 16th :—Morning, 9 to 12.

Examiners,.. $\begin{cases} \text{G. H. Chandler, M. A.} \\ \text{R. S. Lea, Ma.E.} \end{cases}$

1. Divide a given straight line internally and externally in a given ratio.

2. Show that the sum of the squares on any two lines is never less than twice the rectangle contained by the lines.

3. Find the locus of the centre of a circle which touches two given circles.

4. The diameter of a parabola bisects all chords parallel to the tangent at its extremity.

5. Prove that there cannot be more than five regular polyhedra.

6. Show that the $(r + 1)$th term of the expansion of $(1 - x)^{-3}$ is $\frac{1}{2} (r + 1) (r + 2) x r$.

7. Determine a formula for the number of ways in which any number of things may be arranged, taking them all at a time, it being understood that the things are not all different.

8. Solve the equations :—

(1) $\sqrt{x + 4ab} = 2a + \sqrt{x}$

(2) $\dfrac{4}{x - 1} - \dfrac{5}{x + 2} = \dfrac{3}{x}$,

(3) $\begin{cases} \dfrac{x}{y} + \dfrac{y}{x} = \dfrac{7}{2}, \\ x + y = 6. \end{cases}$

9. Show that

(1) $\tan (A + B) = \dfrac{\tan A + \tan B}{1 - \tan A \tan B}$,

(2) $\cot A - \tan A = 2 \cot 2A$,

(3) $2 \sin \dfrac{A}{2} \quad \sqrt{1 + \sin A} - \sqrt{1 - \sin A}$.

10. In any plane triangle

(1) $\sin^2 A - \sin^2 B + \sin^2 C = 2 \sin A \cos \sin C$,

(2) $\dfrac{\sin A}{a} = \dfrac{\sin B}{b} = \dfrac{\sin C}{c}$.

11. In any spherical triangle

(1) $\dfrac{\sin A}{\sin a} = \dfrac{\sin B}{\sin b} = \dfrac{\sin C}{\sin c}$,

(2) The half sum of any two angles and the half sum of the opposite sides are of the same species.

12. Find an expression for the acceleration in uniform circular motion.

13. One pound of lead is tied to a piece of cork, and when they are put into water one-half of the cork is immersed ; how much does the cork weigh, the specific gravity of lead being 11 and that of the cork .22 ?

THIRD YEAR EXHIBITION.

MATHEMATICS.

FRIDAY, OCTOBER 1ST :—MORNING, 9 TO 12

Examiner,................ ....G. H. CHANDLER, M.A.

1. Find the moment of inertia (1) of a circle about a diameter, (2) of a sphere about a diameter.

2. Sketch the curve $y (1 + x^2) = 1$, and find the total area between the curve and the axis of x.

3. Integrate $e^x \sin x \, dx$ by parts.

4. Show that

(1) $\displaystyle\int_1^2 \sqrt{x - 1} \, dx = .667$,

(2) $\int_0^{\frac{1}{3}\pi} \dfrac{\sin \frac{1}{2}\theta}{\sin \theta}\, d\theta = \cdot549$,

(3) $\int_1^2 \dfrac{dx}{x^2 + 4\,x} = \cdot127$,

(4) $\int \dfrac{(1 + x)\, dx}{x\,(1 + x^2)} = \tan^{-1} x + \log \dfrac{x}{\sqrt{1 + x^2}}$

5 Show that the vertical angle of the cone of greatest volume which can be described by a right-angled triangle of given hypotenuse is $2 \tan^{-1} \sqrt{2}$.

6. Prove that the evolute of the common parabola $y^2 = 4\,ax$ is the cubical parabola $27\,ay^2 = 4\,(x - 2\,a)^3$.

7. Solve the equation $x^x = 28$.

8. Find the equation of the tangent at any given point of a parabola.

9. Find the equation of the polar of the circle $x^2 + y^2 - 2\,x - 6\,y = 4$ with respect to the point $(-2, 3)$.

10. Find the equation of a circle which passes through the origin and the intersections of the line $y = 2\,x + 1$ with the circle of question 9.

11. Prove that the time of sliding to the lowest point of a vertical circle along any chord is $2\sqrt{r\,/g}$.

12. A locomotive weighing 12 tons moves round a horizontal curve of 1000 feet radius at the rate of 3 miles per hour; what is the horizontal pressure on the rails?

EXHIBITION EXAMINATION.
FOURTH YEAR.
MATHEMATICS.

Thursday, September 16th:—Morning, 9 to 12.

Examiner, ...G. H. Chandler, M.A.

1. Given (1) $y = \dfrac{1}{x}$, (2) $y = 1 + x\,e^y$, (3) $u = \log\ x$,

show that

(1) $\dfrac{dx}{\sqrt{1 + x^4}} + \dfrac{d\,y}{\sqrt{1 + y^4}} = 0$, (2) $d\,x = (2 - y)\,d\,y\,/e^y$,

(3) $u\,x\,\dfrac{d\,u}{d\,x} + y\,\dfrac{d\,u}{d\,y} = 0$

6

2. For the curve $a^2 + y^2 = 2 x y$, show that

$$\frac{d^2 y}{d x^2} = \frac{a^2}{(x-y)^3}.$$

3. Show that the radius of curvature of the curve of question 2 is

$$\frac{1}{a^2} [(x-y)^2 + y^2]^{\frac{3}{2}}.$$

4. Show that the length of the evolute of the ellipse is $4 (a^3 - b^3) / a b$.

5. If a cone of the greatest possible volume were cut out of a given sphere, show that the height of the cone would be $\frac{2}{3}$ of the diameter of the sphere.

6. Integrate (1) $x e^{-x^2} dx$, (2) $\cos^2 \theta \, d\theta$, (3) $d x \sqrt{\frac{a-x}{a+x}}$

and show that (4) $\int \frac{2 x \, d x}{1 + x + x^2 + x^3} = \log \frac{\sqrt{1 + x'}}{1 + x} + \tan^{-1} x$

7. Show that

(1) $\int_0^\infty x e^{-x^2} \, d x = \frac{1}{2},$

(2) $\int_{\frac{1}{4}\pi}^{\frac{1}{2}\pi} \cot^3 \theta \, d \theta = \frac{1}{2} (1 - \log 2),$

(3) $\int_1^2 \frac{x \, dx}{x^4 + 4} = \frac{1}{4} \tan^{-1} \frac{3}{4}.$

8. Find the equation of a line which touches the parabola $y^2 = 8 x$ and makes an angle of 30° with the line $y = 2 x + 1$. Show that the slope of the required line is $-(8 + 5 \sqrt{3})$.

9. The angle between a pair of conjugate semi-diameters of the ellipse is $\sin^{-1} \left(\frac{a' b'}{a b} \right)$, where a' and b' are their lengths.

10. Reduce the conic $1 \div y^2 = 2 x y$ to its principal diameters as axes.

11. A rough plane rises 4 feet in 3 horizontal, the coefficient of friction is $\frac{1}{3}$, and a body is projected up the plane with a velocity $3 g$; find how far it moves along the plane and the time before it returns to the starting point.

12. Show that the energy stored up in a train of W lbs. going at the rate of V miles per hour is $\dfrac{W V^2}{30}$ foot-pounds, nearly.

FACULTY OF ARTS

SESSIONAL EXAMINATIONS,

1898

GREEK.

FIRST YEAR SESSIONAL EXAMINATION.

HOMER, ILIAD XXII; XENOPHON, SELECTIONS; EURI-
PIDES, MEDEA.

MONDAY, APRIL 4TH:—MORNING, 9 TO 12.

A. Homer, Iliad XXII.

1. Translate with notes on words and phrases underlined :—

(a) ὡς δὲ δράκων ἐπὶ χειῇ ὀρέστερος ἄνδρα μένῃσιν,
βεβρωκὼς κακὰ φάρμακ'· ἔδυ δέ τέ μιν χόλος αἰνός,
σμερδαλέον δὲ δέδορκεν ἑλισσόμενος περὶ χειῇ·
ὡς Ἕκτωρ ἄσβεστον ἔχων μένος οὐχ' ὑπεχώρει,
πύργῳ ἔπι προὔχοντι φαεινὴν ἀσπίδ' ἐρείσας.

(b) οἱ δὲ παρὰ σκοπιὴν καὶ ἐρινεὸν ἠνεμόεντα
τείχεος αἰὲν ὑπὲκ κατ' ἀμαξιτὸν ἐσσεύοντο,
κρουνὼ δ' ἵκανον καλλιρρόω· ἔνθα δὲ πηγαὶ
δοιαὶ ἀναΐσσουσι Σκαμάνδρου δινήεντος.
ἡ μὲν γάρ θ' ὕδατι λιαρῷ ῥέει, ἀμφὶ δὲ καπνὸς
γίγνεται ἐξ αὐτῆς ὡς εἰ πυρὸς αἰθομένοιο·
ἡ δ' ἑτέρη θέρεϊ προρέει ἐϊκυῖα χαλάζῃ
ἢ χιόνι ψυχρῇ ἢ ἐξ ὕδατος κρυστάλλῳ.

How far does this description correspond with the
actual typography ?

(c) τῆλε δ' ἀπὸ κρατὸς βάλε δέσματα σιγαλόεντα,
ἄμπυκα κεκρύφαλόν τε ἰδὲ πλεκτὴν ἀναδέσμην
κρήδεμνόν θ', ὅ ῥά οἱ δῶκε χρυσέη Ἀφροδίτη,
ἤματι τῷ ὅτε μιν κορυθαίολος ἠγάγεθ' Ἕκτωρ
ἐκ δόμου Ἠετίωνος, ἐπεὶ πόρε μυρία ἕδνα.

2. Write notes on :—

(a) ἀπὸ δρυὸς οὐδ' ἀπὸ πέτρης ὀαριζέμεναι.

(b) γλαυκῶπις 'Αθήνη.

(c) τριτογένεια.

(d) θεοὺς ἐπιδώμεθα..

(e) τετραφάλῳ.

(f) λιποῦσ' ἀδρότητα καὶ ἥβην.

(g) οὐδ' ἄρα οἵ τις ἀνουνητί γε παρέστη.

(h) εἰ δ' ἄγετε.

(i) νήπιος αὔτως.

(k) ἀπουρίσσοισιν ἀρούρας.

(l) ἀμφιθαλὴς.

(m) 'Αστυάναξ.

3. What do you know of the forms :—μεμανῖαν, τεθ νᾶσι, εἴδομεν (subj.), ἤμβροτες, ἔσταν, κέονται.

B. Euripides, Medea and Xenophon, Selections.

1. Translate :—

πατὴρ δ' ὁ τλήμων ξυμφορᾶς ἀγνωσίᾳ
ἄφνω προσελθὼν δῶμα προσπίτνει νεκρῷ·
ᾤμωξε δ' εὐθύς, καὶ περιπτύξας δέμας
κυνεῖ προσαυδῶν τοιάδ'· ' ὦ δύστηνε παῖ,
' τίς σ' ὧδ' ἀτίμως δαιμόνων ἀπώλεσεν ;
' τίς τὸν γέροντα τύμβον ὀρφανὸν σέθεν
' τίθησιν ; οἴμοι, ξυνθάνοιμί σοι, τέκνον.'
ἐπεὶ δὲ θρήνων καὶ γόων ἐπαύσατο,
χρῄζων γεραιὸν ἐξαναστῆσαι δέμας,
προσείχεθ' ὥστε κισσὸς ἔρνεσιν δάφνης
λεπτοῖσι πέπλοις, δεινὰ δ' ἦν παλαίσματα·
ὁ μὲν γὰρ ἤθελ' ἐξαναστῆσαι γόνυ,

ἡ δ' ἀντελάζυτ'· εἰ δὲ πρὸς βίαν ἄγοι,
σάρκας γεραιὰς ἐσπάρασσ' ἀπ' ὀστέων,
χρόνῳ δ' ἀπέσβη καὶ μεθῆχ' ὁ δύσμορος
ψυχήν· κακοῦ γὰρ οὐκέτ' ἦν ὑπέρτερος.

2. Parse the following verbs, adding the principal
parts:—ἧκε, φράσουσα, ἐκτύπει, ἀπέρρεον, κτενοῦμεν,
ἐφθέγξω, ἴψει, ἐγγελῶν, προσθείς, αἰτιῶ.

3. Translate :—

Σωτηρίδης δέ τις εἶπεν· "Οὐκ ἐξ ἴσου, ὦ Ξενοφῶν,
ἐσμεν· σὺ μὲν γὰρ ὀχεῖ ἐφ' ἵππου, ἐγὼ δὲ χαλεπῶς κάμνω
φέρων τὴν ἀσπίδα." ὁ δὲ Ξενοφῶν ἀκούσας ταῦτα, κατα-
πηδήσας ἀπὸ τοῦ ἵππου, ὠθεῖται τὸν Σωτηρίδην ἐκ τῆς
τάξεως· καὶ ἀφ-ελόμενος τὴν ἀσπίδα ἐπορεύετο ὡς ἐδύνατο
τάχιστα, ἔχων αὐτήν. ἐτύγχανε δὲ καὶ ἔχων θώρακα τὸν
ἱππικόν· ὥστε ἐπιέζετο. καὶ παρ-εκελεύετο τοῖς μὲν ἔμπ-
ροσθεν ὑπ-άγειν, τοῖς δὲ ὄπισθεν παρ-ιέναι. οἱ δ' ἄλλοι
στρατιῶται ἔπαιον καὶ ἐλοιδόρουν τὸν Σωτηρίδην, ἔστε
ἠνάγκασαν αὐτὸν λαβόντα τὴν ἀσπίδα πορεύεσθαι. ὁ δὲ
Ξενοφῶν ἀνα-βὰς, ἕως μὲν τὰ χωρία βάσιμα ἦν τῷ ἵππῳ,
ἦγεν ἐπὶ τοῦ ἵππου· ἐπεὶ δὲ ἄβατα ἦν, κατα-λιπὼν τὸν
ἵππον ἔσπευδε πεζῇ. καὶ οἱ Ἕλληνες φθάνουσι τοὺς πολεμίους γενόμενοι ἐπὶ τῷ ἄκρῳ.

4. Translate adding a note if necessary :—

(α) Κράτιστα τὴν εὐθεῖαν, ᾗ πεφύκαμεν
σοφαὶ μάλιστα, φαρμάκοις αὐτοὺς ἑλεῖν.

(β)   Πρὸς δὲ καὶ πεφύκαμεν
γυναῖκες.

(γ) Δεῖ μ' ὥστε ναὸς κεδνὸν οἰακοστρόφον
ἄκροισι λαίφους κρασπέδοις ὑπεκδραμεῖν
τὴν σὴν στόμαργον, ὦ γύναι, γλωσσαλγίαν.

(δ) Οὔτ' ἄν τι δεξαίμεσθα μηδ' ἡμῖν δίδου.

(ε) 'Ω δυστάλαινα τῆς ἐμῆς αὐθαδίας.

(ζ) Εὐδαιμονοῖτον ἀλλ' ἐκεῖ.

(η) Εἶτ' ἀντίμολπον ἧκεν ὀλολυγῆς μέγαν κωκυτόν.

(θ) 'Επεὶ εἶδον ὑμᾶς εἰς πολλὰ κακὰ πεπτωκότας, ἠτούμην βασιλέα δοῦναι ἐμοὶ ἀποσῶσαι ὑμᾶς εἰς τὴν 'Ελλάδα. οἴομαι γὰρ καὶ ὑμᾶς καὶ πάντας τοὺς "Ελληνας ἕξειν μοι χάριν διὰ ταῦτα. Account for the difference of breathing in ἔχω, ἔξω.

(ι) "Ωσπερ ἐξὸν ἡμῖν ἡσυχίαν ἄγειν.

(κ) 'Ησαν δὲ καὶ πυροὶ καὶ κριθαὶ καὶ ὄσπρια καὶ οἶνος κρίθινος ἐν κρατῆρσιν.

FIRST YEAR SESSIONAL EXAMINATION.

GREEK COMPOSITION, TRANSLATION AT SIGHT, AND HISTORY.

MONDAY, APRIL 4TH :—AFTERNOON, 2 TO 4.

A. Translate into Greek :—

(1) If any one has beautiful hands, all men admire her.

(2) He thought that Cyrus was not leading his army thither.

(3) I said that one ought to praise the beauty of virtue.

(4) We ought to take measures that we may manage well the affairs of the city.

(5) Whenever anyone injured his parents, they used to punish him.

(6) How are we to announce what happened there ?

(7) Let us accustom ourselves to do well to those who spend their lives justly.

(8) He said that he had been present in order to save his own property.

(9) You know that anyone is foolish who does not benefit the good.

(10) They said that, if he had not sailed out then, he would have greatly injured our city.

B. Translate into English —:

περὶ τοῦ Βουσίριδος λέγουσιν οἱ ἐκεῖθεν πλέοντες, ὡς βασιλεὺς ἐγένετο τῆς Αἰγύπτου, ἔθυε δὲ ἐπὶ τῷ Διὸς βωμῷ καθ᾽ ἕκαστον ἔτος ἄνδρα ξένον. ἐννέα γὰρ ἔτη λιμός τις ἰσχυρὸς κάτεσχε τὴν Αἴγυπτον, οἱ δὲ ἐπιχώριοι ὑπ᾽ αὐτοῦ δεινότατα ἔπασχον. ἐλθὼν οὖν ἐκ Κύπρου μάντις τις ὀνόματι Θράσιος, ἔφη τὸν λιμὸν παύσεσθαι, ἐὰν θύσωσι τῷ Διὶ ξένον ἄνδρα κατ᾽ ἔτος. ἀκούσας δὲ ταῦτα ὁ Βούσιρις αὐτὸν τὸν μάντιν ἀπέκτεινε πρῶτον, ἵνα αὐτὸς μὲν ἀξίαν δοίη δίκην, οἱ δὲ θεοὶ ἅμα ὡς μάλιστα ἥδοιντο. τέλος δὲ Ἡρακλέα ἐκεῖσε ἐλθόντα ἐπειρῶντο θύειν, ὁ δὲ τὰ δεσμὰ καταρρήξας καὶ τοὺς ἐκεῖ νικήσας οὕτως ἔπαυσε τὸ πρᾶγμα.

C. History—Persian Wars. 4·5.

    I. Write on *any three* of the following :—

        (1) The place of Peisistratus in Athenian history.

        (2) The Scythian Expedition of Darius.

        (3) The Battle of Marathon.

        (4) The services of Themistocles to Athens and to Greece.

    II. Contrast the political organization of Sparta with that of Athens.

    III. Add a very brief note on each of the following:—
'Ostracism,' 'Medism,' Mardonius, Miltiades, Thespiae, Aristides, Susa, Lade, Phrynichus, Aristagoras, Amasis, Harpagus, Mycale, Cambyses.

INTERMEDIATE EXAMINATION.

THUCYDIDES AND SOPHOCLES.

MONDAY, APRIL 4TH :—MORNING, 9 TO 12.

A.—MOORE'S SELECTIONS FROM THUCYDIDES.

(1) Translate with notes on words and phrases underlined :—

(*a*) οὕτω δὴ τούς τε Λακεδαιμονίους μᾶλλον κατιδὼν
πλείους ὄντας, ὑπονοῶν πρότερον ἐλάσσοσι τὸν σῖτον
αὐτοὺς ἐσπέμπειν, τό τε ὡς ἐπ' ἀξιόχρεων τοὺς Ἀθηναίους
μᾶλλον σπουδὴν ποιεῖσθαι, τήν τε νῆσον εὐαποβατωτέραν
οὖσαν, τὴν ἐπιχείρησιν παρεσκευάζετο στρατίαν τε μετα-
πέμπων ἐκ τῶν ἐγγὺς ξυμμάχων καὶ τὰ ἄλλα ἑτοιμάζων.

(*b*) μάλιστα δὲ οἱ Ἀργίλιοι, ἐγγύς τε προσοικοῦντες καὶ
ἀεί ποτε τοῖς Ἀθηναίοις ὄντες ὕποπτοι καὶ ἐπιβουλεύοντες
τῷ χωρίῳ, ἐπειδὴ παρέτυχεν ὁ καιρὸς καὶ Βρασίδας ἦλθεν
ἔπραξάν τε ἐκ πλείονος πρὸς τοὺς ἐμπολιτεύοντας σφῶν
ἐκεῖ, ὅπως ἐνδοθήσεται ἡ πόλις, καὶ τότε δεξάμενοι αὐτὸν
τῇ πόλει καὶ ἀποστάντες τῶν Ἀθηναίων, ἐκείνῃ τῇ νυκτὶ
κατέστησαν τὸν στρατὸν πρόσω ἐπὶ τὴν γέφυραν τοῦ
ποταμοῦ. ἀπέχει δὲ τὸ πόλισμα πλέον τῆς διαβάσεως.

(*c*) Ἀργεῖοι δὲ καὶ αὐτοὶ ἔτι ἐν πολλᾷ πλείονι αἰτίᾳ
εἶχον τοὺς σπεισαμένους ἄνευ τοῦ πλήθους, νομίζοντες
κἀκεῖνοι μὴ ἂν σφίσι ποτὲ κάλλιον παρασχὸν Λακεδαιμονίους διαπεφευγέναι.

Explain the circumstances.

(*d*) ὡς δὲ ταύτῃ ἐνεδεδώκει τὸ τῶν Ἀργείων καὶ ξυμμάχων στράτευμα, παρερρήγνυντο ἤδη ἅμα καὶ ἐφ' ἑκάτερα,
καὶ ἅμα τὸ δεξιὸν τῶν Λακεδαιμονίων καὶ Τεγεατῶν ἐκυκ-

λοῦτο τῷ περιέχοντι σφῶν τοὺς Ἀθηναίους, καὶ ἀμφοτέρωθεν αὐτοὺς κίνδυνος περιειστήκει, τῇ μὲν κυκλουμένους,
τῇ δὲ ἤδη ἡσσημένους.

(e) παρασκευὴ γὰρ αὕτη πρώτη ἐκπλεύσασα μιᾶς
πόλεως δυνάμει Ἑλληνικῇ πολυτελεστάτη δὴ καὶ εὐπρε-
πεστάτη τῶν ἐς ἐκεῖνον τὸν χρόνον ἐγίγνετο.

2. Write a brief account of the campaigns of Brasidas
in the North East of Greece, giving a map. What was
their effect ?

3. Explain the terms πρόξενος, οἰκιστής, μέτοικος, πεν-
τηκοστύς, ἐνωμοτία, νεοδαμώδης.

B.—SOPHOCLES, ELECTRA.

1. Translate with notes on words and phrases underlined :—

(a) οὔτοι σοὶ μούνᾳ, τέκνον, ἄχος ἐφάνη βροτῶν,
πρὸς ὅτι σὺ τῶν ἔνδον εἶ περισσά,
οἷς ὁμόθεν εἶ καὶ γονᾷ ξύναιμος,
οἷα Χρυσόθεμις ζώει καὶ Ἰφιάνασσα,
κρυπτᾷ τ᾽ ἀχέων ἐν ἥβᾳ
ὄλβιος, ὃν ἁ κλεινὰ
γᾶ ποτε Μυκηναίων
δέξεται εὐπατρίδαν, Διὸς εὔφρονι
βήματι μολόντα τάνδε γᾶν Ὀρέσταν.

(b) ἀλλὰ ταῦτα μὲν μέθες· σὺ δὲ
τεμοῦσα κρατὸς βοστρύχων ἄκρας φόβας
κἀμοῦ ταλαίνης, σμικρὰ μὲν τάδ᾽, ἀλλ᾽ ὅμως
ἄχω, δὸς αὐτῷ, τήνδ᾽ ἀλιπαρῆ τρίχα
καὶ ζῶμα τοὐμὸν οὐ χλιδαῖς ἠσκημένον.

vv. ll. τήνδε λιπαρῇ· τήνδε τ᾽ ἀλίπαρον.

(c) ἐροῦ δὲ τὴν κυναγὸν Ἄρτεμιν, τίνος
ποινὰς τὰ πολλὰ πνεύματ' ἔσχ' ἐν Αὐλίδι.

(d) ἔπειτα λύων ἡνίαν ἀριστέραν   v.l. ἔπειτα δ' ἕλκων
κάμπτοντος ἵππου λανθάνει στήλην ἄκραν
παίσας· ἔθραυσε δ' ἄξονος μέσας χνόας
κἀξ ἀντύγων ὤλισθε.

(e) ΗΛ. ὁθούνεκ' εἰμὶ τοῖς φονεῦσι σύντροφος.
ΟΡ. τοῖς τοῦ; πόθεν τοῦτ' ἐξεσήμηνας κακόν;
ΗΛ. τοῖς πατρός· εἶτα τοῖσδε δουλεύω βίᾳ.
ΟΡ. τίς γὰρ σ' ἀνάγκη τῇδε προτρέπει βροτῶν;
ΗΛ. μήτηρ καλεῖται, μητρὶ δ' οὐδὲν ἐξισοῖ.

(f) παράγεται γὰρ ἐνέρων
δολιόπους ἀρωγὸς εἴσω στέγας,
ἀρχαιόπλουτα πατρὸς εἰς ἐδώλια,
νεακόνητον αἷμα χειροῖν ἔχων·   v.l. νεακόνητον αἰ
                                           μάχαιραν φέρων

2. Explain Πέλοπος ἁ πρόσθεν πολύπονος ἱππεία and
ὁ ποντισθεὶς Μυρτίλος ἐκοιμάθη and give an account of
the house of Pelops.

INTERMEDIATE EXAMINATION.

GREEK PROSE AND TRANSLATION AT SIGHT.

MONDAY, APRIL 4TH:—AFTERNOON, 3 TO 6.

Translate into Greek:—

Neotonios, who discovered for what reason apples and
other things fall to the ground, was the wisest man of his
time in regard to geometry, but sometimes appeared somewhat foolish in regard to other matters. For he had two

dogs, one large and the other small, which were accustomed
to sleep in his house and go out whenever they wished.
And he thought it would be a good thing if it were not
always necessary for him to rise from his seat and open
the door. So he contrived the following plan. Having
sent for a carpenter he ordered him to cut through the door
and make two holes, in order that the dogs might more
easily go out, the larger through the larger hole, and the
smaller through the smaller. And most people consider
that this was unworthy of such a man, since one hole
would have sufficed for both.

Geometry = γεωμετρία, *f.*   *Hole* = τρύπημα, *n.*

Translate into English :—

(1) διηγήσομαι δὲ καὶ τὴν μάχην· καὶ γὰρ ἐγένετο
οἵαπερ οὐκ ἄλλη τῶν ἐφ' ἡμῶν. συνῄεσαν μὲν γὰρ εἰς τὸ
κατὰ Κορώνειαν πεδίον οἱ μὲν σὺν Ἀγησιλάῳ ἀπὸ τοῦ
Κηφισοῦ, οἱ δὲ σὺν τοῖς Θηβαίοις ἀπὸ τοῦ Ἑλικῶνος.
ἑώρων δὲ τάς τε φάλαγγας ἀλλήλων μάλα ἰσομάχους,
σχεδὸν δὲ καὶ οἱ ἱππεῖς ἦσαν ἑκατέρων ἰσοπληθεῖς. εἶχε
δὲ ὁ Ἀγησίλαος μὲν τὸ δεξιὸν τοῦ μεθ' ἑαυτοῦ, Ὀρχομέ-
νιοι δὲ ἔσχατοι ἦσαν αὐτῷ τοῦ εὐωνύμου. οἱ δ' αὖ Θηβαῖοι
αὐτοὶ μὲν δεξιοὶ ἦσαν, Ἀργεῖοι δ' αὐτοῖς τὸ εὐώνυμον
εἶχον. συνιόντων δὲ τέως μὲν σιγὴ πολλὴ ἦν ἀπ' ἀμφο-
τέρων· ἡνίκα δὲ ἀπεῖχον ἀλλήλων ὅσον στάδιον, ἀλαλά-
ξαντες οἱ Θηβαῖοι δρόμῳ ἐφέροντο.

(2) ΘΕΡΑΠΑΙΝΑ. δέσποιν', ἐγώ τοι τοὔνομ' οὐ φεύγω
τόδε
καλεῖν σ', ἐπείπερ καὶ κατ' οἶκον ἠξίουν
τὸν σόν, τὸ Τροίας ἡνίκ' ᾠκοῦμεν πέδον,
εὔνους δὲ καὶ σοὶ ζῶντί τ' ἦ τῷ σῷ πόσει·
καὶ νῦν φέρουσά σοι νέους ἥκω λόγους,

φόβῳ μέν, εἴ τις δεσποτῶν αἰσθήσεται,
οἴκτῳ δὲ τῷ σῷ· δεινὰ γὰρ βουλεύεται
Μενέλαος εἰς σὲ παῖς θ', ἅ σοι φυλακτέα.

ΑΝΔΡΟΜΑΧΗ. ὦ φιλτάτη σύνδουλε, σύνδουλος
γὰρ εἶ
τῇ πρόσθ' ἀνάσσῃ τῇδε, νῦν δὲ δυστυχεῖ,
τί δρῶσι; ποίας μηχανὰς πλέκουσιν αὖ,
κτεῖναι θέλοντες τὴν παναθλίαν ἐμέ;

ΘΕΡΑΠΑΙΝΑ. τὸν παῖδά σου μέλλουσιν, ὦ δύστηνε σύ,
κτείνειν ὃν ἔξω δωμάτων ὑπεξέθου.

INTERMEDIATE EXAMINATION.

SUMMER READINGS.

THURSDAY, APRIL 7TH :—MORNING 9 TO 10.30.

A. Plato, Crito and Cebetis Tabula, (alternative with B).

Translate :—

(1) ἔτι δέ, ὦ Σώκρατες, οὐδὲ δίκαιόν μοι δοκεῖς ἐπιχειρεῖν πρᾶγμα, σαυτὸν προδοῦναι, ἐξὸν σωθῆναι· καὶ τοιαῦτα
σπεύδεις περὶ σεαυτὸν γενέσθαι, ἅπερ ἂν καὶ οἱ ἐχθροί
σου σπεύσαιέν τε καὶ ἔσπευσαν σε διαφθεῖραι βουλόμενοι.

(2) Οὐκ ἄρα, ὦ βέλτιστε, πάνυ ἡμῖν οὕτω φροντιστέον,
τί ἐροῦσιν οἱ πολλοὶ ἡμᾶς, ἀλλ' ὅ τι ὁ ἐπαΐων περὶ τῶν
δικαίων καὶ ἀδίκων, ὁ εἷς, καὶ αὐτὴ ἡ ἀλήθεια. ὥστε ταύτῃ
οὐκ ὀρθῶς εἰσηγεῖ εἰσηγούμενος τῆς τῶν πολλῶν δόξης
δεῖν ἡμᾶς φροντίζειν.

(3) Ἀλλ' ἐκ μὲν τούτων τῶν τόπων ἀπαρεῖς, ἥξεις δὲ
εἰς Θετταλίαν παρὰ τοὺς ξένους τοὺς Κρίτωνος· ἐκεῖ γὰρ
δὴ πλείστη ἀταξία καὶ ἀκολασία, καὶ ἴσως ἂν ἡδέως σου
ἀκούοιεν ὡς γελοίως ἐκ τοῦ δεσμωτηρίου ἀπεδίδρασκες,

σκευήν τέ τινα περιθέμενος, ἢ διφθέραν λαβὼν ἢ ἄλλα
οἷα δὴ εἰώθασιν ἐνσκευάζεσθαι οἱ ἀποδιδράσκοντες, καὶ τὸ
σχῆμα τὸ σαυτοῦ μεταλλάξας.

(4) διὸ καί, ὅταν ἀναλώσῃ πάντα ὅσα ἔλαβε παρὰ τῆς
Τύχης, ἀναγκάζεται ταύταις ταῖς γυναιξὶ δουλεύειν, καὶ
πάνθ᾽ ὑπομένειν, καὶ ἀσχημονεῖν, καὶ ποιεῖν ἕνεκεν τούτων πάνθ᾽ ὅσα ἐστὶ βλαβερά· οἷον ἀποστερεῖν, ἱεροσυλεῖν,
ἐπιορκεῖν, προδιδόναι, λῄζεσθαι, καὶ πάνθ᾽, ὅσα τούτοις
παραπλήσια.

(5) Οὐκοῦν παρὰ τὴν πύλην ὁρᾷς, ἔφη, ὅτι γυνή τις
ἐστί, καλὴ καὶ καθεστηκυῖα τὸ πρόσωπον, μέσῃ δὲ καὶ
κεκριμένη ἤδη τῇ ἡλικίᾳ, ἁπλῆν δ᾽ ἔχουσα στολὴν καὶ
καλλωπισμόν; ἔστηκε δὲ οὐκ ἐπὶ στρογγύλου λίθου, ἀλλ᾽
ἐπὶ τετραγώνου, ἀσφαλῶς κειμένου. καὶ μετὰ ταύτης ἄλλαι
δύο εἰσί, θυγατέρες τινὲς δοκοῦσαι εἶναι.

(6) ἔστι γὰρ καὶ ἄνευ τούτων βελτίους γενέσθαι. ὅμως
δὲ οὐκ ἄχρηστα κἀκεῖνά ἐστιν. ὡς γὰρ δι᾽ ἑρμηνέως συμ-
βάλλομεν τὰ λεγόμενά ποτε, ὅμως μέντοι γε οὐκ ἄχρη-
στον ἦν ἡμᾶς καὶ αὐτοὺς τὴν φωνὴν εἰδέναι (ἀκριβέστερον
γὰρ ἄν τι συνήκαμεν)· οὕτω καὶ ἄνευ τούτων τῶν μαθη-
μάτων οὐδὲν κωλύει γενέσθαι.

B. Euripides, Alcestis (alternative with A).

Translate:—

(1) ΘΑ. πόλλ᾽ ἂν σὺ λέξας οὐδὲν ἂν πλέον λάβοις·
ἡ δ᾽ οὖν γυνὴ κάτεισιν εἰς Ἅιδου δόμους.
στείχω δ᾽ ἐπ᾽ αὐτήν, ὡς κατάρξωμαι ξίφει·
ἱερὸς γὰρ οὗτος τῶν κατὰ χθονὸς θεῶν
ὅτου τόδ᾽ ἔγχος κρατὸς ἁγνίσῃ τρίχα.

(2) σὺ δ᾽ ἀντιδοῦσα τῆς ἐμῆς τὰ φίλτατα
ψυχῆς ἔσωσας. ἀρά μοι στένειν πάρα

τοιᾶσδ' ἁμαρτάνοντι συζύγον σέθεν;
παύσω δὲ κώμους ξυμποτῶν θ' ὁμιλίας
στεφάνους τε μοῦσάν θ', ἢ κατεῖχ' ἐμοὺς δόμους.
οὐ γάρ ποτ' οὔτ' ἂν βαρβίτου θίγοιμ' ἔτι
οὔτ' ἂν φρέν' ἐξαίροιμι πρὸς Λίβυν λακεῖν
αὐλόν· σὺ γάρ μου τέρψιν ἐξείλου βίου.

(3) ἴστω δ' Ἀΐδης ὁ μελαγχαίτας θεός, ὅς τ' ἐπὶ κώπᾳ
πηδαλίῳ τε γέρων.
νεκροπομπὸς ἵζει,
πολὺ δὴ πολὺ δὴ γυναῖκ' ἀρίσταν
λίμναν Ἀχεροντίαν πορεύσας ἐλάτᾳ διώπῳ.

(4) ποτῆρα δ' ἐν χείρεσσι κίσσινον λαβὼν
πίνει μελαίνης μητρὸς εὔζωρον μέθυ,
ἕως ἐθέρμην' αὐτὸν ἀμφιβᾶσα φλὸξ
οἴνου· στέφει δὲ κρᾶτα μυρκίνης κλάδοις,
ἄμουσ' ὑλακτῶν, δισσὰ δ' ἦν μέλη κλύειν.

(5) καὶ τὸν ἐν Χαλύβοις δαμάζεις σὺ βίᾳ σίδαρον,
οὐδέ τις ἀποτόμου λήματός ἐστιν αἰδώς·
καὶ σ' ἐν ἀφύκτοισι χερῶν εἷλε θεὰ δεσμοῖς·
τόλμα δ'· οὐ γὰρ ἀνάξεις ποτ' ἔνερθεν
κλαίων τοὺς φθιμένους ἄνω. καὶ θεῶν σκότιοι
φθίνουσι παῖδες ἐν θανάτῳ.

(6) ΑΔ. ὦ θεοί, τί λέξω; θαῦμ' ἀνέλπιστον τόδε·
γυναῖκα λεύσσω τήνδ' ἐμὴν ἐτητύμως,
ἢ κέρτομός με θεοῦ τις ἐκπλήσσει χαρά;
ΗΡ. οὐκ ἔστιν, ἀλλὰ τήνδ' ὁρᾷς δάμαρτα σήν.
ΑΔ. ὅρα γε μή τι φάσμα νερτέρων τόδ' ᾖ·
ΗΡ. οὐ ψυχαγωγὸν τόνδ' ἐποιήσω ξένον.

INTERMEDIATE GREEK.
HISTORY AND LITERATURE.

THURSDAY, 7TH APRIL, 1898.

One Hour and a Half allowed.

A.—HISTORY.

(*Not more than four questions to be attempted, of which* (6) *must be one.*)

(1) Describe the constitutional changes which took place between the Persian Wars and the Death of Pericles.

2. Compare the position of Athens as head of her allies, and Sparta as the leading power of the Peloponnese. Discuss the elements of insecurity in each,

3. Trace the causes of the Peloponnesian War.

4. Discuss (*a*) the influence on the results of the work of Cimon, Brasidas, Nicias, Phormio, Thrasybulus ; (*b*) the importance of the alliance with Megara.

5. Give some account of Athenian Finance.

6. Give some account of the following events (with dates), and discuss their historical importance :—(*a*) The Revolt of Naxos, (*b*) The Battle of Coronea, (*c*) The Annexation of Melos ; (*d*) The Capture of Ithomé ; (*e*) The Mutilation of the Hermae.

B.—LITERATURE.

(*Not more than five.*)

1. Briefly characterize the main periods into which the history of Greek Literature may be divided.

2. *Either* (*a*) State the "Homeric Question," as you understand it, *or alternatively* (*b*). Give a brief description of Life in the Homeric Age.

3. Distinguish between Aeolian Lyric Poetry and Dorian Lyric Poetry, naming the leading representatives of each.

4. Write briefly on Thucydides as a philosophic historian.

5. The place of Sophocles in the development of the Drama at Athens.

6. Write a brief note on each of the following : Cyclic Poets, Trilogy, Rhapsodists, Elegiac Metre, Choral Ode, Bacchylides, Theognis, Archilochus, Thespis, Hesiod.

THIRD YEAR SESSIONAL EXAMINATION.

WEDNESDAY, APRIL 13TH :—MORNING, 9 TO 12.

DEMOSTHENES, LEPTINES, AND ARISTOPHANES, EQUITES.

A.—DEMOSTHENES, LEPTINES.

1. Translate with notes :—

(a) τῇ μὲν γὰρ χρείᾳ τῇ τῶν εὑρισκομένων τὰς δωρειὰς οἱ τύραννοι καὶ οἱ τὰς ὀλιγαρχίας ἔχοντες μάλιστα δύνανται τιμᾶν· πλούσιον γὰρ ὃν ἂν βούλωνται παραχρῆμ' ἐποίησαν· τῇ δὲ τιμῇ καὶ τῇ βεβαιότητι τὰς παρὰ τῶν δήμων δωρειὰς εὑρήσετ' οὔσας βελτίους.

(b) τὰ μὲν οὖν ἄλλ' ὅσα χρησίμους ὑμῖν ἑαυτοὺς ἐκεῖνοι παρέσχον, ἐάσω· ἀλλ' ὅθ' ἡ μεγάλη μάχη πρὸς Λακεδαιμονίους ἐγένεθ', ἡ ἐν Κορίνθῳ, τῶν ἐν τῇ πόλει βουλευσαμένων μετὰ τὴν μάχην μὴ δέχεσθαι τῷ τείχει τοὺς στρατιώτας, ἀλλὰ πρὸς Λακεδαιμονίους ἐπικηρυκεύεσθαι, ὁρῶντες ἠτυχηκυῖαν τὴν πόλιν καὶ τῆς παρόδου κρατοῦντας Λακεδαιμονίους, οὐχὶ προὔδωκαν οὐδ' ἐβουλεύσαντ' ἰδίᾳ περὶ τῆς αὐτῶν σωτηρίας.

(c) φημὶ τοίνυν ἐγώ (καὶ πρὸς Διός, ἄνδρες Ἀθηναῖοι, μηδεὶς φθόνῳ τὸ μέλλον ἀκούσῃ, ἀλλ' ἂν ἀληθὲς ᾖ σκοπείτω), ὅσῳ τὸ φανερῶς τοῦ λάθρα κρεῖττον, καὶ τὸ νικῶντας τοῦ παρακρουσαμένους πράττειν ὁτιοῦν ἐντιμότερον, τοσούτῳ κάλλιον Κόνωνα τὰ τείχη στῆσαι Θεμιστοκλέους· ὁ μὲν γὰρ λαθών, ὁ δὲ νικήσας τοὺς κωλύσοντας αὔτ' ἐποίησεν. οὐ τοίνυν ἄξιον τὸν τοιοῦτον ὑφ' ὑμῶν ἀδικηθῆναι, οὐδ' ἔλαττον σχεῖν τῶν ῥητόρων τῶν διδαξόντων ὑμᾶς, ὡς ἀφελέσθαι τι χρὴ τῶν ἐκείνῳ δοθέντων.

(d) Ἔτι τοίνυν ἴσως ἐπισύροντες ἐροῦσιν, ὡς Μεγαρεῖς καὶ Μεσσήνιοί τινες εἶναι φάσκοντες, ἔπειτ' ἀτελεῖς εἰσιν ἀθρόοι παμπληθεῖς ἄνθρωποι, καί τινες ἄλλοι δοῦλοι καὶ μαστιγίαι, Λυκίδας καὶ Διονύσιος, καὶ τοιούτους τινὰς ἐξειλεγμένοι.

2. Write notes on :—

(a) λόγων δὲ γιγνομένων καὶ τῶν μὲν τοὺς δανεισαμένους ἀποδοῦναι κελευόντων, τοὺς ἐξ ἄστεως, τῶν δὲ τοῦτο πρῶτον ὑπάρξαι τῆς ὁμονοίας σημεῖον ἀξιούντων, κοινῇ διαλῦσαι τὰ χρήματα.

(b) τίν' οὖν ῥαστώνην τοῖς πολλοῖς ὁ σός, ὦ Λεπτίνη, ποιεῖ νόμος, εἰ μιᾶς ἢ δυοῖν φυλαῖν ἕνα χορηγὸν καθίστησιν, ὃς ἀνθ' ἑνὸς ἄλλου τοῦθ' ἅπαξ ποιήσας ἀπηλλάζεται.

(c) τούτων δ' ἁπάντων στήλας ἀντιγράφους ἐστήσαθ' ὑμεῖς κἀκεῖνος, τὴν μὲν ἐν Βοσπόρῳ, τὴν δ' ἐν Πειραιεῖ, τὴν δ' ἐφ' Ἱερῷ.

(d) φανήσεται γὰρ οὐδὲ πολλοῦ δεῖ τῆς γενησομένης ἄξιον αἰσχύνης.

(e) καὶ πρὸ τούτων γ' ἐπέταξεν ἐκθεῖναι πρόσθε τῶν ἐπωνύμων.

(f) ἐκεῖ μὲν γάρ ἐστι τῆς ἀρετῆς ἆθλον τῆς πολιτείας κυρίῳ γενέσθαι μετὰ τῶν ὁμοίων·

3. (a) Indicate the importance in the argument of the names of Leucon and Chabrias. (b) Explain fully the terms :—λῃτουργία, παρεισφέρειν, εἰσαγγέλλειν, εἰσφορά, νομοθέται, σιτοφύλακες, συντέλεια, γράφειν, γράφεσθαι.

B.—KNIGHTS OF ARISTOPHANES.

1. Translate :—

(a) ΔΗΜ. ἀλλ' οὐχ οἷόν τε τὸν Παφλαγόν' οὐδὲν λαθεῖν·
ἐφορᾷ γὰρ οὗτος πάντ'· ἔχει γὰρ τὸ σκέλος
τὸ μὲν ἐν Πύλῳ, τὸ δ' ἕτερον ἐν τἠκκλησίᾳ.
τοσόνδε δ' αὐτοῦ βῆμα διαβεβηκότος
ὁ πρωκτός ἐστιν αὐτόχρημ' ἐν Χάοσι,
τὼ χεῖρ' ἐν Αἰτωλοῖς, ὁ νοῦς δ' ἐν Κλωπιδῶν.

(b) ΧΟΡ. πάντα τοι πέπραγας οἷα χρὴ τὸν εὐτυχοῦντα·
　　　　 εὗρε δ᾽ ὁ πανοῦργος ἕτερον πολὺ πανουργίαις
　　　　 μείζοσι κεκασμένον,
　　　　 καὶ δόλοισι ποικίλοις,
　　　　 ῥήμασίν θ᾽ αἱμύλοις.
　　　　 ἀλλ᾽ ὅπως ἀγωνιεῖ φρόν-
　　　　 τιζε τἀπίλοιπ᾽ ἄριστα·
　　　　 συμμάχους δ᾽ ἡμᾶς ἔχων εὔ-
　　　　 νους ἐπίστασαι πάλαι.

(c) ΚΛ. ἄκουε δή νυν καὶ πρόσεχε τὸν νοῦν ἐμοί.
　　　　 Φράζευ, Ἐρεχθείδη, λογίων ὁδόν, ἥν σοι Ἀπόλ-
　　　　 λων.
　　　　 ἴαχεν ἐξ ἀδύτοιο διὰ τριπόδων ἐριτίμων.
　　　　 σώζεσθαί σ᾽ ἐκέλευσ᾽ ἱερὸν κύνα καρχαρόδοντα,
　　　　 ὃς πρὸ σέθεν λάσκων καὶ ὑπὲρ σοῦ δεινὰ κε-
　　　　 κραγὼς
　　　　 σοὶ μισθὸν ποριεῖ, κἂν μὴ δρᾷς ταῦτ᾽, ἀπολεῖ-
　　　　 ται.
　　　　 πολλοὶ γὰρ μίσει σφε κατακρώζουσι κολοιοί.

(d) ΑΓΟΡ. ἀλλ᾽ οὐ σὺ τούτων αἴτιος, μὴ φροντίσῃς,
　　　　 ἀλλ᾽ οἵ σε ταῦτ᾽ ἐξηπάτων. νυνδὶ φράσον·
　　　　 ἐάν τις εἴπῃ βωμολόχος ξυνήγορος·
　　　　 οὐκ ἔστιν ὑμῖν τοῖς δικασταῖς ἄλφιτα,
　　　　 εἰ μὴ καταγνώσεσθε ταύτην τὴν δίκην·
　　　　 τοῦτον τί δράσεις, εἰπέ, τὸν ξυνήγορον ;
　ΔΗ.　 ἄρας μετέωρον ἐς τὸ βάραθρον ἐμβαλῶ,
　　　　 ἐκ τοῦ λάρυγγος ἐκκρεμάσας Ὑπέρβολον.
　ΑΓΟΡ. τουτὶ μὲν ὀρθῶς καὶ φρονίμως ἤδη λέγεις·
　　　　 τὰ δ᾽ ἄλλα, φέρ᾽ ἴδω, πῶς πολιτεύσει φράσον.
　ΔΗ.　 πρῶτον μὲν ὁπόσοι ναῦς ἐλαύνουσιν μακράς,
　　　　 καταγομένοις τὸν μισθὸν ἀποδώσω ᾽ντελῆ.

2. Determine the metre of each of these passages, and
scan one line of each.

3. Translate and comment :—

(a) κάκιστα δῆθ' οὗτός γε πρῶτος Παφλαγόνων
αὐταῖς διαβολαῖς.

(b) νῦν οὖν ἀνύσαντε φροντίσωμεν ὦγαθέ,
ποίαν ὁδὸν νὼ τρεπτέον καὶ πρὸς τίνα.

(c) διώξομαί σε δειλίας.

(d) ἀπολῶ σε νὴ τὴν προεδρίαν τὴν ἐκ Πύλου.

(e) ἐγὼ δέ γε μυστίλας μεμυστιλημένας
ὑπὸ τῆς θεοῦ τῇ χειρὶ τηλεφαντίνῃ.

(f) ὦ μιαρέ, κλέπτων δή με ταῦτ' ἐξηπάτας ;
ἐγὼ δὲ τυ ἐστεφάνιξα κάδωρησάμαν.

(g) ἐγώ σε ποιήσω τριηραρχεῖν, ἀναλισκοντα τῶν
σαυτοῦ, παλαιὰν ναῦν ἔχοντ',
ε.ς ἣν ἀναλῶν οὐκ ἐφέ- . ..
ξεις οὐδὲ ναυπηγούμενος.

4. Writes brief notes on the following proper names, or terms :—

Cleon, Nicias, Demosthenes, Cratinus, Bacis; Δῆμος πυκνίτης, 'Εκβάτανα, Πυλαίμαχος, βυρσαίετος, γραφαί, Κεχηναῖοι, μουσική, ὀστρακίνδα βλέπειν, Τριτογένης, φράτερες τριωβόλου.

THIRD YEAR SESSIONAL EXAMINATION.

GREEK PROSE COMPOSITION AND TRANSLATION AT SIGHT.

WEDNESDAY, APRIL 13TH :—AFTERNOON, 2 TO 5.

1. Translate into Greek :—

The Iapanioi having made war on the Chinesioi and conquered them, demanded a large sum of money ; and it was agreed that they should occupy a certain sea-port in the territory of the Chinesioi named Iaeia until the money

was paid. And when some time had now passed it ·
became evident to all that the Empire of the Chinesioi
was weak. So the Russoi and Germanoi decided that it
would be well to seize for themselves as much territory as
they could, both that they might have forts in that region
and that their merchants might be able to carry on trade
exempt from all taxes. Now the Angloi being indignant
at this, Salisburius and those in power made a treaty with
both the Chinesioi and the Iapanioi to the effect that
they would lend the Chinesioi as much as was necessary
to pay what they owed, on condition that they themselves
should occupy Iaeia and their merchants import and export
freely by the river Angixanos, by which one can sail many
miles into the interior.

2. Translate into English :—

(a) Γενομένης δ' ἰσχυρᾶς τῆς ναυμαχίας, καὶ πολλῶν
νεῶν ἀμφοτέροις καὶ ἀνθρώπων ἀπολομένων, οἱ Συρακό-
σιοι καὶ οἱ ξύμμαχοι ἐπικρατήσαντες τά τε ναυάγια καὶ
τοὺς νεκροὺς ἀνείλοντο, καὶ ἀποπλεύσαντες πρὸς τὴν πόλιν
τροπαῖον ἔστησαν. οἱ δ' Ἀθηναῖοι, ὑπὸ μεγέθους· τῶν
παρόντων κακῶν, νεκρῶν μὲν πέρι ἢ ναυαγίων οὐδὲ ἐπε-
νόουν αἰτῆσαι ἀναίρεσιν, τῆς δὲ νυκτὸς ἐβουλεύοντο εὐθὺς
ἀναχωρεῖν.

(b) ἐγὼ δ' ἄκομψος εἰς ὄχλον δοῦναι λόγον,
ἐς ἥλικας δὲ κὠλίγους σοφώτερος.
ἔχει δὲ μοῖραν καὶ τόδ'· οἱ γὰρ ἐν σοφοῖς
φαῦλοι παρ' ὄχλῳ μουσικώτεροι λέγειν.
ὅμως δ' ἀνάγκη, συμφορᾶς ἀφιγμένης,
γλῶσσάν μ' ἀφεῖναι. πρῶτα δ' ἄρξομαι λέγειν
ὅθεν μ' ὑπῆλθες πρῶτον ὡς διαφθερῶν,
κοὐκ ἀντιλέξοντ'. εἰσορᾷς φάος τόδε
καὶ γαῖαν ; ἐν τοῖσδ' οὐκ ἔνεστ' ἀνὴρ ἐμοῦ,
οὐδ' ἢν σὺ μὴ φῇς, σωφρονέστερος γεγώς.

THIRD YEAR SESSIONAL EXAMINATION.

SUMMER READINGS—LUCIANI VERA HISTORIA.

Thursday, April 14th:—Afternoon, 2 to 3.30.

1. Translate :—

(a) τότε δὲ τὸν ποταμὸν διαπεράσαντες, ἧ διαβατὸς ἦν, εὕρομεν ἀμπέλων χρῆμα τεράστιον· τὸ μὲν γὰρ ἀπὸ τῆς γῆς, ὁ στέλεχος αὐτὸς εὐερνὴς καὶ παχύς· τὸ δ' ἄνω γυναῖκες ἦσαν, ὅσον ἐκ τῶν λαγόνων, ἅπαντ' ἔχουσαι τέλεια. τοιαύτην παρ' ἡμῖν τὴν Δάφνην γράφουσιν ἄρτι τοῦ Ἀπόλλωνος καταλαμβάνοντος ἀποδενδρουμένην. ἀπὸ δὲ τῶν δακτύλων ἄκρων ἐξεφύοντο αὐταῖς οἱ κλάδοι, καὶ μεστοὶ ἦσαν βοτρύων. καὶ μὴν καὶ τὰς κεφαλὰς ἐκόμων ἕλιξί τε καὶ φύλλοις καὶ βότρυσι.

(b) μέχρι μὲν οὖν Σικελίας εὐτυχῶς διεπλεύσαμεν· ἐκεῖθεν δὲ ἁρπασθέντες ἀνέμῳ σφοδρῷ τριταῖοι ἐς τὸν Ὠκεανὸν ἀπηνείχθημεν, ἔνθα τῷ κήτει περιτυχόντες καὶ αὐτανδροι καταποθέντες δύο ἡμεῖς, τῶν ἄλλων ἀποθανόντων, ἐσώθημεν. θάψαντες δὲ τοὺς ἑταίρους καὶ ναὸν τῷ Ποσειδῶνι δειμάμενοι τουτονὶ τὸν βίον ζῶμεν, λάχανα μὲν κηπεύοντες ἰχθῦς δὲ σιτούμενοι καὶ ἀκρόδρυα. πολλὴ δὲ ὡς ὁρᾶτε ἡ ὕλη, καὶ μὴν καὶ ἀμπέλους ἔχει πολλὰς, ἀφ' ὧν ἥδιστος οἶνος γίγνεται· καὶ τὴν πηγὴν δὲ ἴσως εἴδετε καλλίστου καὶ ψυχροτάτου ὕδατος. εὐνὴν δὲ ἀπὸ τῶν φύλλων ποιούμεθα καὶ πῦρ ἄφθονον καίομεν, καὶ ὄρνεα δὲ θηρεύομεν τὰ εἰσπετόμενα καὶ ζῶντας ἰχθῦς ἀγρεύομεν ἐξιόντες ἐπὶ τὰ βραγχία τοῦ θηρίου, ἔνθα καὶ λουόμεθα, ὁπόταν ἐπιθυμήσωμεν.

(c) ἔνθα δὴ καὶ καθεωρῶμεν λιμένας τε πολλοὺς περὶ πᾶσαν ἀκλύστους καὶ μεγάλους, ποταμούς τε διαυγεῖς ἐξιόντας ἠρέμα ἐς τὴν θάλατταν· ἔτι δὲ λειμῶνας καὶ ὕλας καὶ ὄρνεα μουσικὰ, τὰ μὲν ἐπὶ τῶν ἠϊόνων ᾄδοντα πολλὰ δὲ καὶ ἐπὶ τῶν κλάδων. ἀὴρ δὲ κοῦφος καὶ εὔπνους πέριε-κέχυτο τὴν χώραν· καὶ αὖραι δέ τινες ἡδεῖαι διαπνέουσαι ἠρέμα τὴν ὕλην διεσάλευον· ὥστε καὶ ἀπὸ τῶν κλάδων κινουμένων τερπνὰ καὶ συνεχῆ μέλη ἀπεσυρίζετο, ἐοικότα τοῖς ἐπ' ἐρημίας αὐλήμασι τῶν πλαγίων αὐλῶν.

(d) ἐπεὶ δὲ τὸν εὐώδη ἀέρα προϊόντες παρεληλύθειμεν, αὐτίκα ἡμᾶς ὀσμή τε δεινὴ διεδέχετο, οἷον ἀσφάλτου καὶ θείου καὶ πίσσης ἅμα καιομένων· καὶ κνίσσα δὲ πονηρὰ καὶ ἀφόρητος, ὥσπερ ἀπ' ἀνθρώπων ὀπτωμένων· καὶ ὁ ἀὴρ ζοφερὸς καὶ ὀμιχλώδης, καὶ κατέσταζεν ἐξ αὐτοῦ δρόσος πιττίνη. καὶ μέντοι καὶ μαστίγων ψόφος ἠκούετο καὶ οἰμωγὴ ἀνθρώπων πολλῶν. ταῖς μὲν οὖν ἄλλαις οὐ προ-σέσχομεν· ἧς δ' ἐπέβημεν τοιάδε ἦν· κύκλῳ μὲν πᾶσα κρημνώδης καὶ ἀπόξυρος, πέτραις καὶ τράχωσι κατεσκλη-κυῖα, δένδρον δὲ οὐδὲν οὐδὲ ὕδωρ ἐνῆν· ἀνερπύσαντες δὲ ὅμως κατὰ τοὺς κρημνοὺς προῄειμεν διά τινος ἀκανθώδους καὶ σκολόπων μεστῆς ἀτραποῦ, πολλὴν ἀμορφίαν τῆς χώρας ἐχούσης·

(e) τὰ λύτρα δ' ἦν τυροὶ πολλοὶ καὶ ἰχθῦς ξηροὶ καὶ κρόμμυα καὶ ἔλαφοι τέτταρες, τρεῖς ἑκάστη πόδας ἔχουσα, δύο μὲν τοὺς ὄπισθεν οἱ δὲ πρόσω ἐς ἕνα συμπεφύκεσαν. ἐπὶ τούτοις ἀποδύντες τοὺς συνειλημμένους καὶ μίαν ἡμέ-ραν ἐπιμείναντες ἀνήχθημεν.

THIRD YEAR SESSIONAL EXAMINATIONS.

GREEK HISTORY AND LITERATURE.

THURSDAY, APRIL 14TH :—3.30 TO 5 P. M.

(*Show up A and B in separate books.*)

A. History :—

1. What events do you associate with the following places :—Delium, Pylos, Leuctra, Coronea, Cuidos, Munychia, Salamis in Cyprus, Cu_ naxa, Potidaea, Elatea, Megalopolis, Amphissa. State where the above places are, and add dates where you can.

2. State briefly what you know of the following :—Phocion, Demades, Lamachus. Thrasybulus, Theramenes, Clearchus, Iphicrates,
Pharnabazus, Antiphon, Phayllus.

3. Trace the course of events from the Revolution of the 400 to the
end of the Peloponnesian War.

B. Literature :—

1. Describe the arrangements in connection with the Great Dionysia,
giving the date of the Festival, distinguishing the tribal from the non-
tribal contests, and indicating the machinery employed for arriving at a
verdict.

2. Indicate the chief changes in the character of the Tragic Drama
during the years from 480 B. C. to 408 B. C., contrasting, if possible, two
plays with which you are acquainted. How far is the later Euripidean
Drama a forerunner of subsequent developments?

3. What do you know of Isaeus, Hecataeus, Arion,
Phrynichus, Antiphon? Explain the terms αἰτεῖν χόρον;
παραχορήγημα, ἐκκύκλημα, ὑπόρχημα, διθύραμβος. State
(without discussing) any disputed points in connection
with the structure of the Greek Theatre.

B.A. EXAMINATION.

PLATO, PROTAGORAS; AND EURIPIDES, ORESTES.

MONDAY, APRIL 18TH :—MORNING, 9 TO 12.

A.—PLATO, PROTAGORAS.

1. Translate with notes :—

(a) ἐπειδὰν δὲ ἐκ διδασκάλων ἀπαλλαγῶσιν, ἡ πόλις
αὖ τούς τε νόμους ἀναγκάζει μανθάνειν καὶ κατὰ τούτους
ζῆν, ἵνα μὴ αὐτοὶ ἐφ᾽ αὑτῶν εἰκῇ πράττωσιν, ἀλλ᾽ ἀτεχνῶς
ὥσπερ οἱ γραμματισταὶ τοῖς μήπω δεινοῖς γράφειν τῶν
παίδων ὑπογράψαντες γραμμὰς τῇ γραφίδι οὕτω τὸ γραμ-
ματεῖον διδόασιν καὶ ἀναγκάζουσι γράφειν κατὰ τὴν ὑφή-
γησιν τῶν γραμμῶν, ὣς δὲ καὶ ἡ πόλις νόμους ὑπογράψασα,

ἀγαθῶν καὶ παλαιῶν νομοθετῶν εὑρήματα, κατὰ τούτους ἀναγκάζει καὶ ἄρχειν καὶ ἄρχεσθαι· ὃς δ᾽ ἂν ἐκτὸς βαίνῃ τούτων, κολάζει, καὶ ὄνομα τῇ κολάσει ταύτῃ καὶ παρ᾽ ὑμῖν καὶ ἄλλοθι πολλαχοῦ, ὡς εὐθυνούσης τῆς δίκης, εὐθῦναι.

(b) εἰ δὲ ἐπανέροιτό τινά τι, ὥσπερ βιβλία οὐδὲν ἔχουσιν οὔτε ἀποκρίνασθαι οὔτε αὐτοὶ ἐρέσθαι, ἀλλ᾽ ἐάν τις καὶ σμικρὸν ἐπερωτήσῃ τι τῶν ῥηθέντων, ὥσπερ τὰ χαλκία πληγέντα μακρὸν ἠχεῖ καὶ ἀποτείνει ἐὰν μὴ ἐπιλάβηταί τις, καὶ οἱ ῥήτορες οὕτω σμικρὰ ἐρωτηθέντες δόλιχον κατατείνουσι τοῦ λόγου.

(c) ἐγὼ μὲν οὖν καὶ δέομαι καὶ συμβουλεύω, ὦ Πρωταγόρα τε καὶ Σώκρατες, συμβῆναι ὑμᾶς ὥσπερ ὑπὸ διαιτητῶν ἡμῶν συμβιβαζόντων εἰς τὸ μέσον, καὶ μήτε σὲ τὸ ἀκριβὲς τοῦτο εἶδος τῶν διαλόγων ζητεῖν τὸ κατὰ βραχὺ λίαν, εἰ μὴ ἡδὺ Πρωταγόρᾳ ἀλλ᾽ ἐφεῖναι καὶ χαλάσαι τὰς ἡνίας τοῖς λόγοις, ἵνα μεγαλοπρεπέστεροι καὶ εὐσχημονέστεροι ἡμῖν φαίνωνται, μήτ᾽ αὖ Πρωταγόραν πάντα κάλων ἐκτείναντα, οὐρίᾳ ἐφέντα, φεύγειν εἰς τὸ πέλαγος τῶν λόγων, ἀποκρύψαντα γῆν, ἀλλὰ μέσον τι ἀμφοτέρους τεμεῖν.

(d) ταῦτα δὴ καὶ τῷ Πιττακῷ λέγει ὅτι ἐγώ, ὦ Πιττακέ, οὐ διὰ ταῦτά σε ψέγω· ὅτι εἰμὶ φιλόψογος, ἐπεὶ ἔμοιγ᾽ ἐξαρκεῖ

ὃς ἂν μὴ κακὸς ᾖ μηδ᾽ ἄγαν ἀπάλαμνος.
εἰδώς γ᾽ ὀνησίπολιν δίκαν
ὑγιὴς ἀνήρ· οὐ μὴν ἐγὼ
μωμήσομαι
(οὐ γάρ εἰμι φιλόμωμος)·
τῶν γὰρ ἠλιθίων
ἀπείρων γενέθλα·
ὥστ᾽ εἴ τις χαίρει ψέγων, ἐμπλησθείη ἂν ἐκείνους μεμφόμενος.

2. Write notes on :—

(*a*) ποίας ἐργασίας ἐπιστάτης ;

(*b*) ταῦτ' οὖν ἤδη σὺ σκόπει, πότερον περὶ αὐτῶν μόνος οἴει δεῖν διαλέγεσθαι πρὸς μόνους, ἢ μετ' ἄλλων.

(*c*) ὅθεν δὲ αὐτὸ ἡγοῦμαι οὐ διδακτὸν εἶναι μηδ' ὑπ ἀνθρώπων παρασκευαστὸν ἀνθρώποις, δίκαιός εἰμι εἰπεῖν.

(*d*) καὶ πολλάκις μὲν ἀγαθοῦ αὐλητοῦ φαῦλος ἂν ἀπέβη.

(*e*) οὐ γὰρ τοῦτο ὁ Πιττακὸς ἔλεγε τὸ γενέσθαι ἐσθλόν, ὥσπερ ὁ Σιμωνίδης, ἀλλὰ τὸ ἔμμεναι.

(*f*) ἐὰν μὲν γὰρ ἡδέα πρὸς ἡδέα ἱστῆς, τὰ μείζω ἀεὶ καὶ πλείω ληπτέα.

(*g*) καὶ οἱ μὲν ὦτά τε κατάγνυνται μιμούμενοι αὐτούς, καὶ ἱμάντας περιειλίττονται καὶ φιλογυμναστοῦσιν καὶ βραχείας ἀναβολὰς φοροῦσιν.

3. Indicate briefly the general purpose of the Dialogue with an analysis of its contents.

B.—EURIPIDES, ORESTES.

1½ HOURS.

1. Translate :—

(*a*)   τίνα γὰρ ἔτι πάρος οἶκον ἄλλον
    ἕτερον ἢ τὸν ἀπὸ θεογόνων ·γάμων
    τὸν ἀπὸ Ταντάλου σέβεσθαί με χρή ;
    καὶ μὴν βασιλεὺς ὅδε δὴ στείχει,
    Μενέλαος ἄναξ, πολὺ δ' ἀβροσύνῃ
    δῆλος ὁρᾶσθαι
    τῶν Τανταλιδῶν ἐξ αἵματος ὤν.
    ὦ χιλιόναυν στρατὸν ὁρμήσας
    εἰς γῆν Ἀσίαν,
    χαῖρ', εὐτυχίᾳ δ' αὐτὸς ὁμιλεῖς,
    θεόθεν πράξας ἅπερ ηὔχου.

(*b*) ΗΛ. οἴμοι· προσῆλθεν ἐλπίς, ἣν φοβουμένη
πάλαι τὸ μέλλον ἐξετηκόμην γόοις.
ἀτὰρ τίς ἀγών, τίνες ἐν Ἀργείοις λόγοι
καθεῖλον ἡμᾶς κἀπεκύρωσαν θανεῖν ;
λέγ', ὦ γεραιέ· πότερα λευσίμῳ χερὶ
ἢ διὰ σιδήρου πνεῦμ' ἀπορρῆξαί με δεῖ,
κοινὰς ἀδελφῷ συμφορὰς κεκτημένην ;

(*c*) ΗΜΙΧ. χωρεῖτ', ἐπειγώμεσθ'· ἐγὼ μὲν οὖν τρίβον
τόνδ' ἐκφυλάξω, τὸν πρὸς ἡλίου βολάς.
ΗΜΙΧ. καὶ μὴν ἐγὼ τόνδ', ὃς πρὸς ἑσπέραν φέρει.
ΗΛ.   δόχμιά νυν κόρας διάφερ' ὀμμάτων
ἐκεῖθεν ἐνθάδ', εἶτα παλινσκοπιάν.
ΗΜΙΧ. ἔχομεν ὡς θροεῖς.

(*d*) ΜΕ. ὦ Ζηνὸς Ἑλένη χαῖρε παῖ· ζηλῶ δέ σε
θεῶν κατοικήσασαν ὄλβιον δόμον.
Ὀρέστα, σοὶ δὲ παῖδ' ἐγὼ κατέγγυω,
Φοίβου λέγοντος· εὐγενὴς δ' ἀπ' εὐγενοῦς
γήμας ὄναιο καὶ σὺ χὠ διδοὺς ἐγώ.

2. Explain the metre of each of these passages, scanning the first line of each.

3. Translate and comment on the following passages :—

(*a*) βούλει θίγω σου κἀνακουφίσω δέμας ;

(*b*) ἐκκλῄομαι γὰρ δωμάτων ὅπη μόλω.

(*c*) δουλεύομεν θεοῖς, ὅτι ποτ' εἰσὶν οἱ θεοί.

(*d*) οὐχὶ Μενέλεω τρόποισι χρώμεθ'· οἰστέον τάδε

(*e*) εἰ μὲν γὰρ ἐς γυναῖκα σωφρονεστέραν
ξίφος μεθεῖμεν, δυσκλεὴς ἂν ἦν φόνος.

(*f*) οὐ γάρ, ἥτις Ἑλλάδ' αὐτοῖς Φρυξὶ διελυμήνατο ;

(*g*)   εἰ δὲ δὴ κατακτενεῖτέ με,
ὁ νόμος ἀνεῖται, κοὐ φθάνοι θνῄσκων τις ἄν,
ὡς τῆς γε τόλμης οὐ σπάνις γενήσεται.

4. Give a brief outline of the plot of the play.

B.A. EXAMINATION.

GREEK PROSE COMPOSITION AND TRANSLATION AT SIGHT.

MONDAY, APRIL 18TH :—AFTERNOON, 2 TO 5.

1. Translate into Greek :—

This Xenophon at that time was very young, and never had seen the wars before; neither had any command in the army, but only followed the war as a volunteer, for the love and conversation of Proxenus his friend. He was present when Falinus came in message from the great king to the Grecians, after that Cyrus was slain in the field, and they a handful of men left to themselves in the midst of the king's territories, cut off from their country by many navigable rivers, and many hundred miles. The message imported that they should deliver up their arms and submit themselves to the king's mercy. To which message before answer was made, divers of the army conferred familiarly with Falinus, and amongst the rest Xenophon happened to say : " Why, Falinus, we have now but these two things left, our arms and our virtue ; and if we yield up our arms, how shall we make use of our virtue ?

LORD BACON.

2. Translate into English :—

(a) Αἰσχυνθέντες οὖν τάς τε τῶν Ἑλλήνων ἐς ὑμᾶς ἐλπίδας καὶ Δία τὸν Ὀλύμπιον, ἐν οὗ τῷ ἱερῷ ἴσα καὶ ἱκέται ἐσμέν· ἐπαμύνατε Μυτιληναίοις ξύμμαχοι γενόμενοι, καὶ μὴ πρόησθε ἡμᾶς, ἴδιον μὲν τὸν κίνδυνον τῶν σωμάτων παραβαλλομένους, κοινὴν δὲ τὴν ἐκ τοῦ κατορθῶσαι ὠφελίαν ἅπασι δώσοντας, ἔτι δὲ κοινοτέραν τὴν βλάβην, εἰ μὴ πεισθέντων ὑμῶν σφαλησόμεθα. γίγνεσθε

δὲ ἄνδρες οἵουσπερ ὑμᾶς οἵ τε ῞Ελληνες ἀξιοῦσι καὶ τὸ
ἡμέτερον δέος βούλεται.

(b) Τὴν δ᾽ ἀπαμειβόμενος προσέφη πολύμητις ᾽Οδυσ-
　　σεύς·

πότνα θεά, μή μοι τόδε χώεο· οἶδα καὶ αὐτὸς
πάντα μάλ᾽ οὕνεκα σεῖο περίφρων Πηνελόπεια
εἶδος ἀκιδνοτέρη μέγεθός τ᾽ εἰσάντα ἰδέσθαι·
ἡ μὲν γὰρ βροτός ἐστι, σὺ δ᾽ ἀθάνατος καὶ ἀγήρως.
ἀλλὰ καὶ ὣς ἐθέλω καὶ ἐέλδομαι ἤματα πάντα
οἴκαδέ τ᾽ ἐλθέμεναι καὶ νόστιμον ἦμαρ ἰδέσθαι.
εἰ δ᾽ αὖ τις ῥαίῃσι θεῶν ἐπὶ οἴνοπι πόντῳ,
τλήσομαι ἐν στήθεσσιν ἔχων ταλαπενθέα θυμόν·
ἤδη γὰρ μάλα πόλλ᾽ ἔπαθον καὶ πόλλ᾽ ἐμόγησα
κύμασι καὶ πολέμῳ· μετὰ καὶ τόδε τοῖσι γενέσθω.

B.A. EXAMINATION.

SUMMER READINGS—HOMER: THE STORY OF ACHILLES.

THURSDAY, APRIL 21ST :—MORNING, 10.30 TO 12.

1. Translate :—

(a) ἄρᾱται δὲ τάχιστα φανήμεναι ᾽Ηῶ δῖαν·
στεῦται γὰρ νηῶν ἀποκόψειν ἄκρα κόρυμβα
αὐτάς τ᾽ ἐμπρήσειν μαλεροῦ πυρός, αὐτὰρ ᾽Αχαιοὺς
δηώσειν παρὰ τῆσιν, ὀρινομένους ὑπὸ καπνοῦ.
ταῦτ᾽ αἰνῶς δείδοικα κατὰ φρένα, μή οἱ ἀπειλὰς
ἐκτελέσωσι θεοί, ἡμῖν δὲ δὴ αἴσιμον εἴη
φθίσθαι ἐνὶ Τροίῃ, ἑκὰς ῎Αργεος ἱπποβότοιο.

(b) τοὺς ἄρ᾽ ὅ γ᾽ ἡγεμόνας Δαναῶν ἕλεν, αὐτὰρ ἔπειτα
πληθύν, ὡς ὁπότε νέφεα Ζέφυρος στυφελίξῃ
ἀργεστᾶο Νότοιο, βαθείῃ λαίλαπι τύπτων·
πολλὸν δὲ τρόφι κῦμα κυλίνδεται, ὑψόσε δ᾽ ἄχνη
σκίδναται ἐξ ἀνέμοιο πολυπλάγκτοιο ἰωῆς·
ὣς ἄρα πυκνὰ καρήαθ᾽ ὑφ᾽ ῞Εστορι δάμνατο λαῶν.

(c)   αὐτὰρ Ἀχιλλεὺς
βῆ ῥ᾽ ἴμεν ἐς κλισίην, χηλοῦ δ᾽ ἀπὸ πῶμ᾽ ἀνέῳγε
καλῆς δαιδαλέης, τήν οἱ Θέτις ἀργυρόπεζα
θῆκ᾽ ἐπὶ νηὸς ἄγεσθαι, ἐὺ πλήσασα χιτώνων
χλαινάων τ᾽ ἀνεμοσκεπέων οὔλων τε ταπήτων.
ἔνθα δέ οἱ δέπας ἔσκε τετυγμένον, οὐδέ τις ἄλλος
οὔτ᾽ ἀνδρῶν πίνεσκεν ἀπ᾽ αὐτοῦ αἴθοπα οἶνον,
οὔτε τεῳ σπένδεσκε θεῶν, ὅτι μὴ Διὶ πατρί.
τό ῥα τότ᾽ ἐκ χηλοῖο λαβὼν ἐκάθηρε θεείῳ
πρῶτον, ἔπειτα δὲ νίψ᾽ ὕδατος καλῇσι ῥοῇσι,
νίψατο δ᾽ αὐτὸς χεῖρας, ἀφύσσατο δ᾽ αἴθοπα οἶνον.

(d)   οἱ δὲ λοετροχόον τρίποδ᾽ ἵστασαν ἐν πυρὶ κηλέῳ,·
ἐν δ᾽ ἄρ᾽ ὕδωρ ἔχεαν, ὑπὸ δὲ ξύλα δαῖον ἑλόντες·
γάστρην μὲν τρίποδος πῦρ ἄμφεπε, θέρμετο δ ὕδωρ
αὐτὰρ ἐπειδὴ ζέσσεν ὕδωρ ἐνὶ ἤνοπι χαλκῷ,
καὶ τότε δὴ λοῦσάν τε καὶ ἤλειψαν λίπ᾽ ἐλαίῳ,
ἐν δ᾽ ὠτειλὰς πλῆσαν ἀλείφατος ἐννεώροιο·
ἐν λεχέεσσι δὲ θέντες ἑανῷ λιτὶ κάλυψαν
ἐς πόδας ἐκ κεφαλῆς, καθύπερθε δὲ φάρεϊ λευκῷ.

(e)   ἠΰτε πάρδαλις εἶσι βαθείης ἐκ ξυλόχοιο
ἀνδρὸς θηρητῆρος ἐναντίον, οὐδέ τι θυμῷ
ταρβεῖ οὐδὲ φοβεῖται, ἐπεί κεν ὑλαγμὸν ἀκούσῃ·
εἴπερ γὰρ φθάμενός μιν ἢ οὐτάσῃ ἠὲ βάλῃσιν,
ἀλλά τε καὶ περὶ δουρὶ πεπαρμένη οὐκ ἀπολήγει
ἀλκῆς, πρίν γ᾽ ἠὲ ξυμβλήμεναι, ἠὲ δαμῆναι·
ὣς Ἀντήνορος υἱὸς ἀγαυοῦ, δῖος Ἀγήνωρ,
οὐκ ἔθελεν φεύγειν, πρὶν πειρήσαιτ᾽ Ἀχιλῆος.

(f)   ζωσαμένω δ᾽ ἄρα τώ γε βάτην ἐς μέσσον ἀγῶνα,
ἀγκὰς δ᾽ ἀλλήλων λαβέτην χερσὶ στιβαρῇσιν
ὡς ὅτ᾽ ἀμείβοντες, τούς τε κλυτὸς ἤραρε τέκτων,
δώματος ὑψηλοῖο, βίας ἀνέμων ἀλεείνων.
τετρίγει δ᾽ ἄρα νῶτα θρασειάων ἀπὸ χειρῶν

ἑλκόμενα στερεῶς· κατὰ δὲ νότιος ῥέεν ἱδρώς·
πυκναὶ δὲ σμώδιγγες ἀνὰ πλευράς τε καὶ ὤμους
αἵματι φοινικόεσσαι ἀνέδραμον· οἱ δὲ μάλ᾽ αἰεὶ
νίκης ἱέσθην τρίποδος πέρι ποιητοῖο.

FOURTH YEAR.
GREEK LITERATURE AND ANTIQUITIES.
THURSDAY, APRIL 21ST:—10.30 TO 12 A. M.

N.B.—All questions to be answered very briefly.

1. Discuss the four old Attic tribes, adding their names.

2. Mention any of the reforms of Cleisthenes.

3. An outline of the Spartan Constitution.

4. Traces of the Phenicians in Greece.

5. Explain briefly the following terms, the Four Hundred, the Eleven, the Thirty, Ephetae, Neodamodeis, Seisachtheia, psephisma, probou-leuma.

6. The position of slaves and metics at Athens.

7. What do you know of Theognis, Mimnermus, Bacchylides, Theocritus, Agathon, Demades, Hellanicus, Parmenides, Agathias, Plotinus, Apollonius Rhodius ?

8. The religious and moral ideas of Aeschylus.

9. Criticise the mind and art of Sophocles, and quote the lines in which he is spoken of by (*a*) M. Arnold, (*b*) E. B. Browning, (*c*) Aristophanes, (*d*) the Anthologist.

THIRD AND FOURTH YEAR HONOURS.

EURIPIDES, Electra; PLATO, Republic I.-IV.

TUESDAY, APRIL 12TH :—AFTERNOON, 2 TO 5.

1. Translate:—

Κἄσφαξ᾽ ἐπ᾽ ὤμων μόσχον ὡς ἦραν χεροῖν
δμῶες, λέγει. δὲ σῷ κασιγνήτῳ τάδε·
ἐκ τῶν καλῶν κομποῦσι τοῖσι Θεσσαλοῖς
εἶναι τόδ᾽, ὅστις ταῦρον ἀρταμεῖ καλῶς
ἵππους τ᾽ ὀχμάζει. λαβὲ σίδηρον, ὦ ξένε,
δεῖξόν τε φήμην ἔτυμον ἀμφὶ Θεσσαλῶν.
ὃ δ᾽ εὐκρότητον Δωρίδ᾽ ἁρπάσας χεροῖν,
ῥίψας ἀπ᾽ ὤμων εὐπρεπῆ πορπάματα,
Πυλάδην μὲν εἵλετ᾽ ἐν πόνοις ὑπηρέτην,
δμῶας δ᾽ ἀπωθεῖ· καὶ λαβὼν μόσχου πόδα,
λευκὰς ἐγύμνου σάρκας ἐκτείνων χέρα.
θᾶσσον δὲ βύρσαν ἐξέδειρεν ἢ δρομεὺς
δίσσους διαύλους ἱππίους διήνυσε,
κἀνεῖτο λαγόνας. ἱερὰ δ᾽ εἰς χεῖρας λαβὼν
Αἴγισθος ἤθρει καὶ λοβὸς μὲν οὐ προσῆν
σπλάγχνοις, πύλαι δὲ καὶ δοχαὶ χολῆς πέλας
κακὰς ἔφαινον τῷ σκοποῦντι προσβολάς.

2. Translate, adding a short note whese necessary :—

(*a*) Καὶ τειχέων μὲν ἐντὸς οὐ βαίνω πόδα.

(*b*) χρύσεά τε χάρισι προθήματ᾽ ἀγλαΐας.

(*c*) ᾤμωξ᾽ ἀδελφὸν σόν. Μυκηναίων τινί ;

(*d*) μέθῃ δὲ βρεχθεὶς τῆς ἐμῆς μητρὸς πόσις
ὁ κλεινός, ὡς λέγουσιν, ἐνθρώσκει τάφῳ
πέτροις τε λεύει μνῆμα λάινον πατρός.

(*e*) ὃς, ἀμφὶ ποταμὸν Τάναον Ἀργείας ὅρους
τέμνοντα γαίας Σπαρτιάτιδός τε γῆς
ποίμναις ὁμαρτεῖ πόλεος ἐκβεβλημένος.

(*f*) θ μὲν παλαίστραις ἀνδρὸς εὐγενοῦς τραφείς,
δ δὲ κτενισμοῖς θῆλυς.

(*g*) τοὐνθένδε πρὸς τὸ πῖπτον αὐτὸς ἐννόει.

(*h*) δύστηνός ἐστιν, εἰ δοκεῖ τὸ σωφρονεῖν
ἐκεῖ μὲν αὐτὴν οὐκ ἔχειν, παρ' οἷ δ' ἔχειν.

(*i*) λέκτροις ἐπεισέφρησε.

(*k*) ὀργάδων δρύοχα νεμομένα.

(*l*) σοφὸς δ' ὢν οὐκ ἔχρησέ σοι σοφά.

(*m*) τοῖς μὲν μυσαροῖς οὐκ ἐπαρήγομεν.

(*n*)   αἷμα δ' αἵματος
πικρὸς δανεισμὸς ἦλθε τῷ θανόντι νῦν.

3. Translate:

(*a*) Ἀλλ' ἄρα τὸν μὲν σκυτοτόμον διεκωλύομεν μήτε
γεωργὸν ἐπιχειρεῖν εἶναι ἅμα μήτε ὑφάντην μήτε οἰκοδό-
μον, ἵνα δὴ ἡμῖν τὲ τῆς σκυτικῆς ἔργον καλῶς γίγνοιτο,
καὶ τῶν ἄλλων ἑνὶ ἑκάστῳ ὡσαύτως ἐν ἀπεδίδομεν, πρὸς ὃ
πεφύκει ἕκαστος καὶ ἐφ' ᾧ ἔμελλε τῶν ἄλλων σχολὴν
ἄγων διὰ βίου αὐτὸ ἐργαζόμενος οὐ παριεὶς τοὺς καιροὺς
καλῶς ἀπεργάζεσθαι· τὰ δὲ δὴ περὶ τὸν πόλεμον πότερον
οὐ περὶ πλείστου ἐστὶν εὖ ἀπεργασθέντα; ἢ οὕτω ῥᾴδιον,
ὥστε καὶ γεωργῶν τις ἅμα πολεμικὸς ἔσται καὶ σκυτοτο-
μῶν καὶ ἄλλην τέχνην ἡντινοῦν ἐργαζόμενος, πεττευτικὸς
δὲ ἢ κυβευτικὸς ἱκανῶς οὐδ' ἂν εἰς γένοιτο μὴ αὐτὸ τοῦτο
ἐκ παιδὸς ἐπιτηδεύων, ἀλλὰ παρέργῳ χρώμενος; καὶ ἀσπίδα μὲν λαβὼν ἤ τι ἄλλο τῶν πολεμικῶν ὅπλων τε καὶ
ὀργάνων αὐθημερὸν ὁπλιτικῆς ἤ τινος ἄλλης μάχης τῶν
κατὰ πόλεμον ἱκανὸς ἔσται ἀγωνιστής, τῶν δὲ ἄλλων
ὀργάνων οὐδὲν οὐδένα δημιουργὸν οὐδὲ ἀθλητὴν ληφθὲν
ποιήσει οὐδ' ἔσται χρήσιμον τῷ μήτε τὴν ἐπιστήμην ἑκάσ-
του λαβόντι μήτε τὴν μελέτην ἱκανὴν παρασχομένῳ;
Πολλοῦ γὰρ ἄν, ἦ δ' ὅς, τὰ ὄργανα ἦν ἄξια.

(β) Ἦ δοκεῖ σοι, ἦν δ᾽ ἐγώ, τούτου αἴσχιον εἶναι τοῦτο, ὅταν τις μὴ μόνον τὸ πολὺ τοῦ βίου ἐν δικαστηρίοις φεύγων τε καὶ διώκων κατατρίβηται, ἀλλὰ καὶ ὑπὸ ἀπειροκαλίας ἐπ᾽ αὐτῷ δὴ τούτῳ πεισθῇ καλλωπίζεσθαι, ὡς δεινὸς ὢν περὶ τὸ ἀδικεῖν καὶ ἱκανὸς πάσας μὲν στροφὰς στρέφεσθαι, πάσας δὲ διεξόδους διεξελθὼν ἀποστραφῆναι λυγιζόμενος, ὥστε μὴ παρασχεῖν δίκην, καὶ ταῦτα σμικρῶν τε καὶ οὐδενὸς ἀξίων ἕνεκα, ἀγνοῶν ὅσῳ κάλλιον καὶ ἄμεινον τὸ παρασκευάζειν τὸν βίον αὐτῷ μηδὲν δεῖσθαι νυστάζοντος δικαστοῦ; Οὐκ, ἀλλὰ τοῦτ᾽, ἔφη, ἐκείνου ἔτι αἴσχιον. Τὸ δὲ ἰατρικῆς, ἦν δ᾽ ἐγώ, δεῖσθαι ὅ τι μὴ τραυμάτων ἕνεκα ἤ τινων ἐπετείων ἐπιπεσόντων, ἀλλὰ δι᾽ ἀργίαν τε καὶ δίαιταν οἵαν διήλθομεν, ῥευμάτων τε καὶ πνευμάτων ὥσπερ λίμνας ἐμπιπλαμένους φύσας τε καὶ κατάρρους νοσήμασιν ὀνόματα τίθεσθαι ἀναγκάζειν τοὺς κομψοὺς Ἀσκληπιάδας, οὐκ αἰσχρὸν δοκεῖ;

4. Translate, with notes (where necessary), grammatical or explanatory:

(a) ἐπειδὴ οὖν ἡμεῖς οὐ δεινοί, δοκεῖ μοι, ἦν δ᾽ ἐγώ, τοιαύτην ποιήσασθαι ζήτησιν αὐτοῦ, οἵανπερ ἂν εἰ προσέταξέ τις γράμματα σμικρὰ πόρρωθέν ἀναγνῶναι μὴ πάνυ ὀξὺ βλέπουσιν, ἔπειτά τις ἐνενόησεν, ὅτι τὰ αὐτὰ γράμματα ἔστι που καὶ ἄλλοθι μείζω τε καὶ ἐν μείζονι, ἕρμαιον ἂν ἐφάνη, οἶμαι, ἐκεῖνα πρῶτον ἀναγνόντας οὕτως ἐπισκοπεῖν τὰ ἐλάττω, εἰ τὰ αὐτὰ ὄντα τυγχάνει.

(β) Εἰπέ μοι, ἔφη, ὦ Σώκρατες, τίτθη σοι ἔστιν; Τί δέ; ἦν δ᾽ ἐγώ. οὐκ ἀποκρίνεσθαι χρῆν μᾶλλον ἢ τοιαῦτα ἐρωτᾶν; Ὅτι τοί σε, ἔφη, κορυζῶντα περιορᾷ καὶ οὐκ ἀπομύττει δεόμενον, ὅς γε αὐτῇ οὐδὲ πρόβατα οὐδὲ ποιμένα γιγνώσκεις.

9

(γ) οὐκοῦν, ἐπειδὴ τὸ δοκεῖν, ὡς δηλοῦσί μοι οἱ σοφοί, καὶ τὰν ἀλάθειαν βιᾶται κοὶ κύριον εὐδαιμονίος, ἐπὶ τοῦτο δὴ τρεπτέον ὅλως· πρόθυρα μὲν καὶ σχῆμα κύκλῳ περὶ ἐμαυτὸν σκιαγραφίαν ἀρετῆς περιγραπτέον, τὴν δὲ τοῦ σοφωτάτου Ἀρχιλόχου ἀλώπεκα ἑλκτέον ἐξόπισθεν κερδαλέαν καὶ ποικίλην.

(δ) τὰ γὰρ δὴ τοιαῦτα οὔτ' ἐπιστάμεθα ἡμεῖς οἰκίζοντέ τε πόλιν οὐδενὶ ἄλλῳ πεισόμεθα, ἐὰν νοῦν ἔχωμεν, οὐδὲ χρησόμεθα ἐξηγητῇ ἀλλ' ἢ τῷ πατρίῳ.

6. Explain very briefly the following words and phrases : ἐπεισαγώγιμα, σαρδάνιον, εἰρωνεία, τελεταί, πλεονεξία, παρανομία, βίου διαγωγή, ὑῶν πόλις, ἐν παρέργου μέρει, αὐτάρκης πρὸς τὸ εὖ ζῆν, ξυρεῖν ἐπιχειρεῖν λέοντα, ἀδελφὸς ἀνδρὶ παρείη.

(1) State the reasoning of Book I., so as to show how far it brings to light ethical truth, and how far it is a mere quibble.

(2) Sophistic traits as illustrated in Plato's sketch of Thrasymachus.

(3) Anticipations of Political Economy in the Republic.

B.A. CLASSICAL HONOURS.

PINDAR, Selections ; LYRIC POETS, Selections ; HERODOTUS VII.

WEDNESDAY, APRIL 13TH :—2 TO 5 P.M.

A. PINDAR.

1. Translate, with notes :—

(a) ἄλλοτε δ' ἄλλον ἐποπτεύει χάρις ζωθάλμιος ἀδυμελε
θάμα μὲν φόρμιγγι παμφώνοισί τ' ἐν ἔντεσιν αὐλῶν.
καὶ νῦν ὑπ' ἀμφοτέρων σὺν Διαγόρᾳ κατέβαν τὰν
ποντίαν

ὑμνέων παῖδ' 'Αφροδίτας, 'Αελίοιό τε νύμφαν, 'Ρόδον-
εὐθυμάχαν ὄφρα πελώριον ἄνδρα παρ' 'Αλφειῷ στεφα-
νωσάμενον
αἰνέσω πυγμᾶς ἄποινα
καὶ παρὰ Κασταλίᾳ, πατέρα τε Δαμάγητον ἀδόντα
Δίκᾳ,
'Ασίας εὐρυχόρου τρίπολιν νᾶσον πέλας
ἐμβόλῳ ναίοντας 'Αργείᾳ σὺν αἰχμᾷ.

(b) ἀλλ' ὅτ' Αἰήτας ἀδαμάντινον ἐν μέσσοις ἄροτρον σκίμ-
ψατο
καὶ βόας, οἳ φλόγ' ἀπὸ ξανθᾶν γενύων πνέον καιομέ
νοιο πυρός,
χαλκέαις δ' ὁπλαῖς ἀράσσεσκον χθόν' ἀμειβόμενοι·
τοὺς ἀγαγὼν ζεύγλᾳ πέλασσεν μοῦνος. ὀρθὰς δ' αὔ-
λακας ἐντανύσαις
ἤλαυν', ἀνὰ βωλακίας δ' ὀρόγυιαν σχίζε νῶτον
γᾶς. ἔειπεν δ' ὧδε· Τοῦτ' ἔργον, βασιλεύς,
ὅστις ἄρχει ναός, ἐμοὶ τελέσαις ἄφθιτον στρωμνὰν
ἀγέσθω,
κῶας αἰγλᾶεν χρυσέῳ θυσάνῳ;

(c) μισθὸς βὰρ ἄλλοις ἄλλος ἐφ' ἔργμασιν ἀνθρώποις
γλυκύς,
μηλοβότᾳ τ' ἀρότᾳ τ' ὀρνιχολόχῳ τε καὶ ὃν πόντος
τράφει.
γαστρὶ δὲ πᾶς τις ἀμύνων λιμὸν αἰανῆ τέταται·
ὃς δ' ἀέθλοις ἢ πολεμίζων ἄρηται κῦδος ἀβρόν,
εὐαγορηθεὶς κέρδος ὕψιστον δέκεται, πολιατᾶν καὶ
ξένων γλώσσας ἄωτον.

2. Give, as accurately as you can, the dates of foundation of the Great Games of Greece, the locality in which
each took place, and the time of year at which it was held.

3. Write briefly on the religious aspect of Pindar's poetry.

B. Lyric Poets.

1. Translate, with notes:—

(a) Ὄρνιθος φωνήν, Πολυπαΐδη, ὀξὺ βοώσης
ἤκουσ', ἥτε βροτοῖς ἄγγελος ἦλθ' ἀρότου
ὡραίου· καὶ μοι κραδίην ἐπάταξε μέλαιναν,
ὅττι μοι εὐανθεῖς ἄλλοι ἔχουσιν ἀγροός
οὐδέ μοι ἡμίονοι κύφων' ἕλκουσιν ἀρότρον,
τῆς μάλα μισητῆς εἵνεκα ναυτιλίης.

(b) Μαρμαίρει δὲ μέγας δόμος χάλκῳ· πᾶσα δ' Ἄρῃ κε-
κόσμηται στέγα
λάμπραισιν κυνίαισι, καττὰν λεῦκοι καθύπερθεν ἵπ-
πιοι λόφοι
νεύοισιν, κεφάλαισιν ἄνδρων ἀγάλματα, χάλκιαι δὲ
πασσάλοις
κρύπτοισιν περικείμεναι κνάμιδες, ἄρκος ἰσχύρω βέ-
λευς.
θώρακές τε νέοι λίνω κοΐλαί τε κατ' ἄσπιδες βεβλή-
μεναι·
παρ δὲ Χαλκίδικαι σπάθαι, παρ δὲ ζώματα πολλὰ
καὶ κυπάττιδες·
τῶν οὐκ ἔστι λάθεσθ', ἐπειδὴ πρώτισθ' ὑπὸ ἔργον
ἔστμενα τόδε.

(c) Ἔστι τις λόγος
τὰν ἀρετὰν ναίειν δυσαμβάτοις ἐπὶ πέτραις,
ἁγνὰν δέ μιν θεὰν χῶρον ἁγνὸν ἀμφέπειν.
οὐδὲ παντων βλεφάροις θνατῶν ἔσοπτος,
ᾧ μὴ δακέθυμος ἱδρὼς
ἔνδοθεν μόλῃ, ἵκηταί τ' ἐς ἄκρον
ἀνδρείας.

2. Ascribe the above passages to their respective authors, indicating the place each bears in the development of Greek Lyric Poetry. Give dates.

3. Give some of the chief peculiarities of the Æolic Dialect.

C. Herodotus.

1. Translate with notes :—

(*a*) Ἀράβιοι δὲ ζειρὰς ὑπεζωμένοι ἦσαν, τόξα δὲ παλίντονα εἶχον πρὸς δεξιά, μακρά. Αἰθίοπες δὲ παρδαλέας τε καὶ λεοντέας ἐναμμένοι, τόξα δὲ εἶχον ἐκ φοίνικος σπάθης πεποιημένα, μακρά, τετραπηχέων οὐκ ἐλάσσω, ἐπὶ δὲ καλαμίνους ὀϊστοὺς σμικρούς, ἀντὶ δὲ σιδήρου ἐπῆν λίθος ὀξὺς πεποιημένος, τῷ καὶ τὰς σφρηγῖδας γλύφουσι· πρὸς δὲ αἰχμὰς εἶχον, ἐπὶ δὲ κέρας δορκάδος ἐπῆν ὀξὺ πεποιημέ. νον τρόπον λόγχης· εἶχον δὲ καὶ ῥόπαλα τυλωτά.

(*b*) ἐπεὰν δὲ συμμιχθέωσι τάχιστα, ἐνθεῦτεν ἤδη ὁ Πηνειὸς τῷ οὐνόματι κατακρατέων ἀνωνύμους τοὺς ἄλλους εἶναι ποιέει.

(*c*) ἑτέρη τε Θεμιστοκλέϊ γνώμη ἔμπροσθε ταύτης ἐς καιρὸν ἠρίστευσε, ὅτε Ἀθηναίοισι γενομένων χρημάτων μεγάλων ἐν τῷ κοινῷ, τὰ ἐκ τῶν μετάλλων σφι προσῆλθε τῶν ἀπὸ Λαυρείου, ἔμελλον λάξεσθαι ὀρχηδὸν ἕκαστος δέκα δραχμάς.

(*d*) ὡς δὲ πεσὼν οὐκ ἀπέθανε ἀλλ᾽ ἦν ἔμπνοος, οἱ Πέρσαι, οἵ περ ἐπεβάτευον ἐπὶ τῶν νεῶν, δι᾽ ἀρετὴν τὴν ἐκείνου περιποιῆσαί μιν περὶ πλείστου ἐποιήσαντο, σμύρνῃσί τε ἰώμενοι τὰ ἕλκεα καὶ σινδόνος βυσσίνης τελαμῶσι κατειλίσσοντες· καί μιν, ὡς ὀπίσω ἀπίκοντο ἐς τὸ ἑωυτῶν στρατόπεδον, ἐπεδείκνυσαν ἐκπαγλεόμενοι πάσῃ τῇ στρατιῇ, περιέποντες εὖ· τοὺς δὲ ἄλλούς τοὺς ἔλαβον ἐν τῇ νηὶ ταύτῃ περιεῖπον ὡς ἀνδράποδα.

(e) ἐκ ταύτης τῆς νήσου ὁρμώμενοι φοβεόντων τοὺς Λακεδαιμονίους. παροίκου δὲ πολέμου σφι ἐόντος οἰκηίου οὐδὲν δεινοὶ ἔσονταί τοι μὴ τῆς ἄλλης Ἑλλάδος ἁλισκομένης ὑπὸ τοῦ πεζοῦ βοηθέωσι ταύτῃ.

2. Illustrate from the above extracts some of the main differences between Ionic and Attic forms.

B.A. HONOURS.

DEMOSTHENES DE CORONA AND JEBB'S ATTIC ORATORS.

FRIDAY, APRIL 15TH :—MORNING, 9 TO 12.

1. Translate :—

'Ανὴρ δὲ γενόμενος τῇ μητρὶ τελούσῃ τὰς βίβλους ἀνεγίγνωσκες καὶ τἆλλα συνεσκευωροῦ, τὴν μὲν νύκτα νεβρίζων καὶ κρατηρίζων καὶ καθαίρων τοὺς τελουμένους καὶ ἀπομάττων τῷ πηλῷ καὶ τοῖς πιτύροις καὶ ἀνιστὰς ἀπὸ τοῦ καθαρμοῦ κελεύων λέγειν " ἔφυγον κακόν, εὗρον ἄμεινον," ἐπὶ τῷ μηδένα πώποτε τηλικοῦτ᾿ ὀλολύξαι σεμνυνόμενος (καὶ ἔγωγε νομίζω· μὴ γὰρ οἴεσθ᾿ αὐτὸν φθέγγεσθαι μὲν οὕτω μέγα, ὀλολύζειν δ᾿ οὐχ ὑπέρλαμπρον), ἐν δὲ ταῖς ἡμέραις τοὺς καλοὺς θιάσους ἄγων διὰ τῶν ὁδῶν, τοὺς ἐστεφανωμένους τῷ μαράθῳ καὶ τῇ λεύκῃ, τοὺς ὄφεις τοὺς παρείας θλίβων καὶ ὑπὲρ τῆς κεφαλῆς αἰωρῶν, καὶ βοῶν εὐοῖ σαβοῖ, καὶ ἐπορχούμενος ὑῆς ἄττης ἄττης ὑῆς, ἔξαρχος καὶ προηγεμὼν καὶ κιστοφόρος καὶ λικνοφόρος καὶ τοιαῦτα ὑπὸ τῶν γραδίων προσαγορευόμενος, μισθὸν λαμβάνων τούτων ἔνθρυπτα καὶ στρεπτοὺς καὶ νεήλατα, ἐφ᾿ οἷς τίς οὐκ ἂν ὡς ἀληθῶς αὐτὸν εὐδαιμονίσειε καὶ τὴν αὐτοῦ τύχην ;

2. Translate :—

(a) Οὐ γὰρ τὰ ῥήματα τὰς οἰκειότητας ἔφη βεβαιοῦν, μάλα σεμνῶς ὀνομάζων, ἀλλὰ τὸ ταῦτα συμφέρειν.

(b) Ἀλλ' ἐπειδὰν τῶν πραγμάτων ἐγκρατὴς ὁ ζητῶν ἄρχειν καταστῇ, καὶ τῶν ταῦτα ἀποδομένων δεσπότης ἐστί, τὴν δὲ πονηρίαν εἰδὼς τότε δὴ, τότε καὶ μισεῖ καὶ ἀπιστεῖ καὶ προπηλακίζει.

(c) καίτοι σύ γ' ἔφησθά με ταῦτα λέγοντα εἰς ἔχθραν ἐμβαλεῖν τουτουσὶ, Εὐβούλου καὶ Ἀριστοφῶντος καὶ Διοπείθους τῶν περὶ τούτων ψηφισμάτων ὄντων, οὐκ ἐμῶν, ὦ λέγων εὐχερῶς ὅ τι ἂν βουληθῇς.

(d) Τῶν δ' ἀδικουμένων τοῖς μὲν ὑμῖν τότε πεισθεῖσιν ἡ σωτηρία περιεγένετο, τοῖς δ' ὀλιγωρήσασι τὸ πολλάκις ὧν ὑμεῖς προείπατε μεμνῆσθαι.

(e) Ἦν γὰρ αὐτοῖς ἐκ τοῦ ἐμοῦ νόμου τὸ γιγνόμενον κατὰ τὴν οὐσίαν ἕκαστον τιθέναι.

(f) Τί οὖν ; ἐπιχειρεῖ, θεάσασθ' ὡς εὖ, πόλεμον ποιῆσαι τοῖς Ἀμφικτύοσι καὶ περὶ τὴν Πυλαίαν ταραχήν.

3. Translate —

Ὅσοι δ' ἐκ Πειραιῶς ἔστε, πρῶτον μὲν τῶν ὅπλων ἀναμνήσθητε, ὅτι πολλὰς μάχας ἐν τῇ ἀλλοτρίᾳ μαχεσάμενοι οὐχ ὑπὸ τῶν πολεμίων ἀλλ' ὑπὸ τούτων εἰρήνης οὔσης ἀφηρέθητε τὰ ὅπλα, ἔπειθ' ὅτι ἐξεκηρύχθητε μὲν ἐκ τῆς πόλεως ἣν ὑμῖν οἱ πατέρες παρέδοσαν, φεύγοντας δὲ ὑμᾶς ἐκ τῶν πόλεων ἐξητοῦντο· ἀνθ' ὧν ὀργισθῆτε μὲν ὥσπερ ὅτ' ἐφεύγετε, ἀναμνήσθητε δὲ καὶ τῶν ἄλλων κακῶν ἃ πεπόνθατε ὑπ' αὐτῶν, οἳ τοὺς μὲν ἐκ τῆς ἀγορᾶς τοὺς τ' ἐκ τῶν ἱερῶν συναρπάζοντες βιαίως ἀπέκτειναν, τοὺς δὲ ἀπὸ τέκνων καὶ γονέων καὶ γυναικῶν ἀφέλκοντες φονέας αὐτῶν ἠνάγκασαν γενέσθαι καὶ οὐδὲ ταφῆς τῆς νομιζομένης εἴασαν τυχεῖν, ἡγούμενοι τὴν αὐτῶν ἀρχὴν βεβαιοτέραν εἶναι τῆς παρὰ τῶν θεῶν τιμωρίας.

4. Translate :—

(a) Οὕτως εἴς γε ταύτην τὴν ἀπαγωγὴν νομιμωτάτην καὶ δικαιοτάτην πεποιήκασιν ὑμῖν τὴν ἀποψήφισίν μου.

(b) Ἀπειληφέναι δὲ παρὰ τοῦδε προσεποιεῖτο, παρ᾿ ἐμοῦ δὲ οὐκέτι ἤθελεν ἀπολαβεῖν, ὑποπαρωθών, ὅπως ἐκεῖνος δοκοίη θάπτειν ἀλλὰ μὴ ἐγὼ τὸν πάππον.

(c) Τοσούτου γὰρ ἔδεον αὐτοὺς λανθάνειν οἱ κακόν τι δεδρακότες, ὥστε καὶ τοὺς ἐπιδόξους ἁμαρτήσεσθαί τι προῃσθάνοντο. Τοιγαροῦν οὐκ ἐν τοῖς σκιραφείοις οἱ νεώτεροι διέτριβον, οὐδὲ ἐν ταῖς αὐλητρίσιν οὐδ᾿ ἐν τοῖς τοιούτοις συλλόγοις ἐν οἷς νῦν διημερεύουσιν.

5. Characterise the style of (a) Lysias or (b) Antiphon, adding in each case a short life.

B.A. CLASSICAL HONOURS.

THUCYDIDES IV.

SATURDAY, APRIL 16TH:—AFTERNOON, 2 TO 5.

1. Translate with notes :—

(a) Ἔπεμψαν ἡμᾶς Λακεδαιμόνιοι, ὦ Ἀθηναῖοι, περὶ τῶν ἐν τῇ νήσῳ ἀνδρῶν πράξοντας ὅ τι ἂν ὑμῖν τε ὠφέλιμον ὂν τὸ αὐτὸ πείθωμεν καὶ ἡμῖν ἐς τὴν ξυμφορὰν ὡς ἐκ τῶν παρόντων κόσμον μάλιστα μέλλῃ οἴσειν. τοὺς δὲ λόγους μακροτέρους οὐ παρὰ τὸ εἰωθὸς μηκυνοῦμεν, ἀλλ᾿ ἐπιχώριον ὂν ἡμῖν οὗ μὲν βραχεῖς ἀρκῶσι μὴ πολλοῖς χρῆσθαι, πλείοσι δὲ ἐν ᾧ ἂν καιρὸς ᾖ διδάσκοντάς τι τῶν προὔργου λόγοις τὸ δέον πράσσειν.

(b) ἔστι δὲ ὁ πορθμὸς ἡ μεταξὺ Ῥηγίου θάλασσα καὶ
Μεσσήνης, ἦπερ βραχύτατον Σικελία τῆς ἠπείρου ἀπέχει·
καὶ ἔστιν ἡ Χάρυβδις κληθεῖσα τοῦτο, ᾗ Ὀδυσσεὺς λέγε-
ται διαπλεῦσαι· διὰ στενότητα δὲ καὶ ἐκ μεγάλων πελα-
γῶν, τοῦ τε Τυρσηνικοῦ καὶ τοῦ Σικελικοῦ, ἐσπίπτουσα ἡ
θάλασσα ἐς αὐτὸ καὶ ῥοώδης οὖσα εἰκότως χαλεπὴ ἐνομί-
σθη.

(c) ξυνελάβοντο δὲ τοῦ τοιούτου οὐχ ἥκιστα, ὥστε
ἀκριβῆ τὴν πρόφασιν γενέσθαι καὶ τοὺς τεχνησαμένους
ἀδεέστερον ἐγχειρῆσαι, οἱ στρατηγοὶ τῶν Ἀθηναίων, κατά-
δηλοι ὄντες τοὺς ἄνδρας μὴ ἂν βούλεσθαι ὑπ᾽ ἄλλων κομι-
σθέντας, διότι αὐτοὶ ἐς Σικελίαν ἔπλεον, τὴν τιμὴν τοῖς
ἄγουσι προσποιῆσαι.

(d) καὶ μετὰ τοῦτο ἐπὶ Ἄντανδρον στρατεύσαντες· προ-
δοσίας γενομένης λαμβάνουσι τὴν πόλιν. καὶ ἦν αὐτῶν ἡ
διάνοια τάς τε ἄλλας πόλεις τὰς Ἀκταίας καλουμένας, ἃς
πρότερον Μυτιληναίων νεμομένων Ἀθηναῖοι εἶχον, ἐλευθε-
ροῦν, καὶ πάντων μάλιστα τὴν Ἄντανδρον, καὶ κρατυνά-
μενοι αὐτὴν (ναῦς τε γὰρ εὐπορία ἦν ποιεῖσθαι αὐτόθεν
ξύλων ὑπαρχόντων καὶ τῆς Ἴδης ἐπικειμένης,) καὶ τῇ ἄλλῃ
παρασκευῇ ῥᾳδίως ἀπ᾽ αὐτῆς ὁρμωμενοι τήν τε Λέσβον
ἐγγὺς οὖσαν κακώσειν καὶ τὰ ἐν τῇ ἠπείρῳ Αἰολικὰ πο-
λίσματα χειρώσασθαι.

(e) οὐ γὰρ τοῖς ἔθνεσιν, ὅτι δίχα πέφυκε, τοῦ ἑτέρου
ἔχθει ἐπίασιν, ἀλλὰ τῶν ἐν τῇ Σικελίᾳ ἀγαθῶν ἐφιέμενοι,
ἃ κοινῇ κεκτήμεθα. ἐδήλωσαν δὲ νῦν ἐν τῇ τοῦ Χαλκιδι-
κοῦ γένους παρακλήσει· τοῖς γὰρ οὐδεπώποτε σφίσι κατὰ
τὸ ξυμμαχικὸν προσβοηθήσασιν αὐτοὶ τὸ δίκαιον μᾶλλον
τῆς ξυνθήκης προθύμως παρέσχοντο.

(f) ἀπάτῃ γὰρ εὐπρεπεῖ αἴσχιον τοῖς γε ἐν ἀξιώματι
πλεονεκτῆσαι ἢ βίᾳ ἐμφανεῖ· τὸ μὲν γὰρ ἰσχύος δικαιώσει,
ἣν ἡ τύχη ἔδωκεν, ἐπέρχεται, τὸ δὲ γνώμης ἀδίκου ἐπιβου-

λῆ. οὕτω πολλὴν περιωπὴν τῶν ἡμῖν ἐς τὰ μέγιστα διαφόρων ποιούμεθα· καὶ οὐκ ἂν μείζω πρὸς τοῖς ὅρκοις βεβαίωσιν λάβοιτε ἢ οἷς τὰ ἔργα ἐκ τῶν λόγων ἀναθρούμενα δόκησιν ἀναγκαίαν παρέχεται ὡς καὶ ξυμφέρει ὁμοίως ὡς εἶπον.

(g) οἱ δὲ Βοιωτοὶ ἀπεκρίναντο, εἰ μὲν ἐν τῇ Βοιωτίᾳ εἰσὶν, ἀπιόντας ἐκ τῆς ἑαυτῶν ἀποφέρεσθαι τὰ σφέτερα, εἰ δὲ ἐν τῇ ἐκείνων, αὐτοὺς γιγνώσκειν τὸ ποιητέον, νομίζοντες τὴν μὲν Ὠρωπίαν, ἐν ᾗ τοὺς νεκροὺς (ἐν μεθορίοις τῆς μάχης γενομένης) κεῖσθαι ξυνέβη, Ἀθηναίων κατὰ τὸ ὑπήκοον εἶναι, καὶ οὐκ ἂν αὐτοὺς βίᾳ σφῶν κρατῆσαι αὐτῶν· οὐδ' αὖ ἐσπένδοντο δῆθεν ὑπὲρ τῆς ἐκείνων· τὸ δὲ " ἐκ τῆς ἑαυτῶν" εὐπρεπὲς εἶναι ἀποκρίνασθαι " ἀπιόντας καὶ ἀπολαβεῖν ἃ ἀπαιτοῦσιν."

(h) τοὺς γὰρ δὴ ἄνδρας περὶ πλείονος ἐποιοῦντο κομίσασθαι, ὡς ἔτι Βρασίδας ηὐτύχει· καὶ ἔμελλον ἐπὶ μεῖζον χωρήσαντος αὐτοῦ καὶ ἀντίπαλα καταστήσαντος τῶν μὲν στέρεσθαι, τοῖς δ' ἐκ τοῦ ἴσου ἀμυνόμενοι κινδυνεύειν καὶ κρατήσειν.

2. Annotate fully :—

(a) ἢν βούληται καταλαμβάνων τὴν πύλιν δαπανᾶν.

(b) καὶ αἱ μὲν νῆες κατὰ τάχος ἔπλεον κατὰ τὰ ἐπεσταλμένα ὑπὸ Δημοσθένους.

(c) σωφρόνων δὲ ἀνδρῶν οἵτινες τἀγαθὰ ἐς ἀμφίβολον ἀσφαλῶς ἔθεντο.

(d) πυνθανόμενοι περὶ τῆς στρατιᾶς ὅτι ταλαιπωρεῖται καὶ σῖτος τοῖς ἐν τῇ νήσῳ ὅτι ἐσπλεῖ.

(e) ἢν γὰρ αὐτοῖς τῶν τε ἀπ' Αἰγύπτου καὶ Λιβύης ὁλκάδων προσβολή, καὶ λῃσταὶ ἅμα τὴν Λακωνικὴν ἧσσον ἐλύπουν ἐκ θαλάσσης ἧπερ μόνον οἷον τ' ἦν κακουργεῖσθαι· πᾶσα γὰρ ἀνέχει πρὸς τὸ Σικελικὸν καὶ Κρητικὸν πέλαγος.

(f) τῷ παρ' ἐλπίδα μὴ χαλεπῶς σφαλλέσθω.

(g) καὶ οὕτω σφίσιν ἀσφαλεστέρως ἔχειν.

(h) λογιζόμενοι...... τοῖς δὲ ξυμπάσης τῆς δυνάμεως καὶ τῶν παρόντων μέρος ἑκάστων κινδυνεύειν εἰκότως ἐθέλειν τολμᾶν.

MSS. ἕκαστον.

(i) δεῖξαι ὅτι ὧν μὲν ἐφίενται πρὸς τοὺς μὴ ἀμυνομένους ἐπίοντες κτάσθωσαν.

(k) ἐς χωρίον καθίσας ὅθεν λόφου ὄντος μεταξὺ οὐκ ἐθεώρουν ἀλλήλους.

(l) ἀπέχει δὲ τὸ πόλισμα πλέον τῆς διαβάσεως, καὶ οὐ καθεῖτο τείχη ὥσπερ νῦν.

(m) πόλεως τε ἐν τῷ ἴσῳ οὐ στερισκόμενοι καὶ κινδύνου παρὰ δόξαν ἀφιέμενοι.

(n) ἐταινίουν τε καὶ προσήρχοντο ὥσπερ ἀθλητῇ.

B.A. HONOURS.

CONSTITUTIONAL HISTORY, LITERATURE AND ANTIQUITIES.

WEDNESDAY, APRIL 20TH :—MORNING, 9 TO 12.

(*Ten questions will be sufficient to obtain full marks.*)

1. To what extent does the epoch of Aristocracy differ from that of Oligarchy? Discuss the connexion of these with the founding of colonies and the genesis of Tyranny. Illustrate with all the instances you know, with dates.

2. Indicate (a) the evidence which leads us to believe that the population of Greece was not strictly " Hellenic; " (b) the Asiatic influences on Greek religion and early Greek history.

3. Compare the constitutional history of Sparta with that of Rome, showing the influence of environment in each case. Quote any modern parallels. Indicate the main differences and resemblances between the constitutions of Sparta and those of the Cretan cities.

4. Discuss the early divisions of the Athenian people *tribal, social and political, local, administrative.* In what ways were these modified under the constitution of Cleisthenes? Into what main epochs does Aristotle divide the constitutional history of Athens?

5. Discuss *one* of the following statements :—

(*a*) The best democrat is usually an aristocrat.

(*b*) A mob cannot govern an Empire.

6. Give the meanings of the following terms, quoting historical instances where possible :—αἰσυμνήτης, γεωμό-ροι, μόθακες, κρυπτεία, τριώβολον, φράτορες, δωδεκάπο-λις, εἰσφορά, ἐπιφορά, συμμορία, μετοίκιον.

7. Explain the terms φάσις, ἔνδειξις, ἀπαγωγή, εὔθυνα, εἰσαγγελία, δοκιμασία, εἰσαγωγεύς, διαιτήτης, κάκωσις, ὑπωμοσία.

8. Give a short account of the rise of Philosopinhy in Greece down to the time of Socrates.

9. State what you know of the writings of :—Tyrtaeus, Solon, Callimachus, Polybius, Zenodotus, Bion, Babrius.

10. Give a list of the Attic months, indicating also the method of dating employed. Mention any festivals asso-eiated with particular months. Explain the principle of the Metonic circle.

11. Explain the general principles governing the use of

the negatives οὐ, μή, in Greek. Under what circumstances
are οὐ μή and μὴ οὐ used?

Discuss the following passages :—

(a) οὔτ᾽ ἂν δυναίμην μήτ᾽ ἐπισταίμην λέγειν.

(b) ὅτ᾽ οὐδὲν ὢν τοῦ μηδὲν ἀντέστης ὕπερ.

(c) οὗτος σύ, ποῖ|θεῖς; ἐπεὶ καδίσκους. Μηδαμῶς.

(d) εἰ . . . οὐκ ἀρκέσει.

(e) διὰ τὴν . . . οὐ περιτείχισιν.

(f) κρύψω τόδ᾽ ἔγχος, ἔνθα μήτις ὄψεται.

(g) μὴ παρῇ τὸ μὴ οὐ φράσαι.

(h) οὐ μή σοι μεθέψομαί ποτε.

12. Compare the origin and development of the Greek
and English Drama, taking the drama of Sophocles and
that of Shakespeare as the highest developments of their
respective types. What are meant by the Dramatic Unities?

13. Compare Attic and Homeric syntax in regard to (a)
case-constructions, (b) mood-constructions.

14. Illustrate the main differences between Tragedy and
Attic Prose in regard to vocabulary and syntax.

15. Discuss the orthography of the following :—εχω,
τημ πολιν, δραχμησι, φερσιφονη, θαλασσα, σωω, πωω,
ποησω, οικτειρω, ετισα, ωον, ιππεις

B.A. CLASSICAL HONOURS.

SOPHOCLES, ANTIGONE; ARISTOPHANES, THE FROGS; |
ARISTOTLE, ETHICS I, H, X AND POETICS.

FRIDAY, APRIL 22ND:—MORNING, 9 TO 12.

A.—SOPHOCLES.

1. Translate with notes :—

(a) καὶ φθέγμα καὶ ἀνεμόεν
 φρόνημα καὶ ἀστυνόμους ὀργὰς ἐδιδάξατο καὶ δυσ- |
 αύλων
 πάγων ἐναίθρεια καὶ δύσομβρα φεύγειν βέλη,
 παντοπόρος· ἄπορος ἐπ' οὐδὲν ἔρχεται
 τὸ μέλλον· "Αιδα μόνον φεῦξιν οὐκ ἐπάξεται·
 νόσων δ' ἀμηχάνων φυγὰς ξυμπέφρασται.

(b) παρὰ δὲ Κυανεᾶν πελάγει διδύμας ἁλὸς
 ἀκταὶ Βοσπόριαι ἰδ' ὁ Θρηκῶν ἄξενος
 Σαλμυδησσός, ἵν' ἀγχίπολις "Αρης
 δισσοῖσι Φινείδαις
 εἶδεν ἀρατὸν ἕλκος
 τυφλωθὲν ἐξ ἀγρίας δάμαρτος,
 ἀλαὸν ἀλαστόροισιν ὀμμάτων κύκλοις,
 ἀραχθέντων ὑφ' αἱματηραῖς
 χείρεσσι καὶ κερκίδων ἀκμαῖσιν.

(c) εὐθὺς δὲ δείσας ἐμπύρων ἐγευόμην
 βωμοῖσι παμφλέκτοισιν. ἐκ δὲ θυμάτων
 "Ηφαιστος οὐκ ἔλαμπεν, ἀλλ' ἐπὶ σποδῷ
 μυδῶσα κηκὶς μηρίων ἐτήκετο
 κἄτυφε κἀνέπτυε, καὶ μετάρσιοι
 χολαὶ διεσπείροντο, καὶ καταρρυεῖς
 μηροὶ καλυπτῆς ἐξέκειντο πιμελῆς·

2. Comment on the following Mss. readings :—

(a) Ἐτεοκλέα μέν, ὡς λέγουσι, σὺν δίκης | χρησθεὶς
δικαίᾳ καὶ νόμῳ, κατὰ χθονὸς | ἔκρυψε.

(b) τὰ δεινὰ κέρδη πημονὰς ἐργάζεται.

(c) εἰ τὸν ἐξ ἐμῆς | μητρὸς θανόντ' ἄθαπτον ἠσχόμην
κύνες.

(d) τάδ' ἐξ ἀθύμου δεσπότου κελεύσμασιν ἠθροῦμεν.

(e) κατ' αὖ νιν φοινία θεῶν τῶν νερτέρων ἀμᾷ κόνις.

B.—ARISTOPHANES.

1. Translate and explain :—

(a)   δοῦλον οὐκ ἄγω
εἰ μὴ νεναυμάχηκε τὴν περὶ τῶν κρεῶν.

(b) ἔξεστι θ' ὥσπερ Ἡγέλοχος ἡμῖν λέγειν
ἐκ κυμάτων γὰρ αὖθις αὖ γαλῆν ὁρῶ.

(c)   ἢ τἀπόρρητ' ἀποπέμπει
ἐξ Αἰγίνης Θωρυκίων ὤν, εἰκοστολόγος κακοδαίμων,
ἀσκώματα καὶ λίνα καὶ πίτταν διαπέμπων εἰς
Ἐπίδαυρον.

(d) βούλεσθε δῆτα κοινῇ
σκώψωμεν Ἀρχέδημον ;
ὃς ἑπτέτης ὢν οὐκ ἔφυσε φράτερας,
νυνὶ δὲ δημαγωγεῖ
ἐν τοῖς ἄνω νεκροῖσι.

(e)   πλὴν πράσῳ
μὴ τύπτε τοῦτον μηδὲ γητείῳ νέῳ.

(f) ῥύζει δ' ἐπίκλαυτον ἀηδόνιον νόμον, ὡς ἀπολεῖται,
κἂν ἴσαι γένωνται.

(g) ΕΤ. γνώσει δὲ τοὺς τούτου τε κἀμοῦ γ' ἑκατέρου
μαθητάς.
τουτουμενὶ Φορμίσιος Μεγαίνετός θ' ὁ Μανῆς,
σαλπιγγολογχυπηνάδαι, σαρκασμοπιτυοκάμπται,
οὑμοὶ δὲ Κλειτοφῶν τε καὶ Θηραμένης ὁ κομψός.

ΔI. Θηραμένης; σοφός γ' ἀνὴρ καὶ δεινὸς ἐς τὰ πάντα,
ὃς ἦν κακοῖς που περιπέσῃ καὶ πλησίον παραστῇ,
πέπτωκεν ἔξω τῶν κακῶν, οὐ Χῖος, ἀλλὰ Κεῖος.

(h) αἵ θ' ὑπωρόφιοι κατὰ γωνίας
εἱειειειειειλίσσετε δακτύλοις φάλαγγες
ἱστότονα πηνίσματα,
κερκίδος ἀοιδοῦ μελέτας,
ἵν' ὁ φίλαυλος ἔπαλλε δελ-
φὶς πρῴραις κυανεμβόλοις
μαντεῖα καὶ σταδίους.

2. (a) ὁ δὲ χόρος γ' ἤρειδεν ὁρμαθοὺς ἂν μελῶν ἐφεξῆς
τέτταρας ξυνεχῶς ἂν.

Compare the functions of the Chorus in Æschylus
and Euripides.

(b) Ἑρμῆ χθόνιε, πατρῷ' ἐποπτεύων κράτη,
σωτὴρ γενοῦ μοι σύμμαχός τ' αἰτουμένῳ.
ἥκω γὰρ ἐς γῆν τήνδε καὶ κατέρχομαι.

Summarize the criticisms of Euripides and Dionysus
on these lines.   What do these indicate?

C.—ARISTOTLE.

1. Translate and comment on :—

(a) καὶ γὰρ τέκτων καὶ γεωμέτρης διαφερόντως ἐπιζη-
τοῦσι τὴν ὀρθήν· ὁ μὲν γὰρ ἐφ' ὅσον χρησίμη πρὸς τὸ
ἔργον, ὁ δὲ τί ἐστιν ἢ ποῖόν τι· θεατὴς γὰρ τἀληθοῦς.

(b) ἐν παντὶ δὴ συνεχεῖ καὶ διαιρετῷ ἔστι λαβεῖν τὸ μὲν
πλεῖον τὸ δ' ἔλαττον τὸ δ' ἴσον, καὶ ταῦτα ἢ κατ' αὐτὸ τὸ
πρᾶγμα ἢ πρὸς ἡμᾶς· τὸ δ' ἴσον μέσον τι ὑπερβολῆς καὶ
ἐλλείψεως. λέγω δὲ τοῦ μὲν πράγματος μέσον τὸ ἴσον
ἀπέχον ἀφ' ἑκατέρου τῶν ἄκρων, ὅπερ ἐστὶν ἓν καὶ τὸ αὐτὸ
πᾶσιν, πρὸς ἡμᾶς δὲ ὃ μήτε πλεονάζει μήτε ἐλλείπει·
τοῦτο δ' οὐχ ἕν, οὐδὲ ταὐτὸν πᾶσιν.

(c) διὸ χαίροντες ὁτῳοῦν σφόδρα οὐ πάνυ δρῶμεν ἕτερον, καὶ ἄλλα ποιοῦμεν ἄλλοις ἠρέμα ἀρεσκόμενοι, οἷον
καὶ ἐν τοῖς θεάτροις οἱ τραγηματίζοντες, ὅταν φαῦλοι οἱ
ἀγωνιζόμενοι ὦσι, τότε μάλιστ᾽ αὐτὸ δρῶσιν.

(d) ἐν τρισὶ δὴ ταύταις διαφοραῖς ἡ μίμητίς ἐστιν. ὡς
εἴπομεν κατ᾽ ἀρχάς, ἐν οἷς τε καὶ ἃ καὶ ὥ:.

(e) τρίτον δὲ τὸ ὅμοιον. τοῦτο γὰρ ἕτερον τοῦ χρηστὸν
τὸ ἦθος καὶ ἁρμόττον ποιῆσαι ὥσπερ εἴρηται. τέταρτον
δὲ τὸ ὁμαλόν. κἂν γὰρ ἀνώμαλός τις ᾖ ὁ τὴν μίμησιν
παρέχων καὶ τοιοῦτον ἦθος ὑποτιθείς, ὅμως ὁμαλῶς ἀνώ-
μαλον δεῖ εἶναι.

(f) ἔτι δὲ ᾽Αριφράδης τοὺς τραγῳδοὺς ἐκωμῴδει, ὅτι ἃ
οὐδεὶς ἂν εἴποι ἐν τῇ διαλέκτῳ τούτοις χρῶνται, οἷον τὸ
δωμάτων ἄπο ἀλλὰ μὴ ἀπὸ δωμάτων, καὶ τὸ σέθεν καὶ τὸ
ἐγὼ δέ νιν, καὶ τὸ ᾽Αχιλλέως πέρι ἀλλὰ μὴ περὶ ᾽Αχιλ-
λέως, καὶ ὅσα ἄλλα τοιαῦτα. διὰ γὰρ τὸ μὴ εἶναι ἐν τοῖς
κυρίοις ποιεῖ τὸ μὴ ἰδιωτικὸν ἐν τῇ λέξει ἅπαντα τὰ τοιαῦ-
τα· ἐκεῖνος δὲ τοῦτο ἠγνόει.

2. Write *very* briefly on the following :—

(a) Aristotle's views on life after death, and the connexion of the subject with εὐδαιμονία.

(b) The reasons for considering θεωρητική the highest
form of happiness. .

(c) The evidence of the names of different forms of
drama as indicating their origin.

(d) The circumstance under which actions affect us as
tragic and the poet's duty in regard to legendary material.

B.A. CLASSICAL HONOURS.

HOMER, ODYSSEY IX, X, XII; AESCHYLUS, AGAMEMNON.

Saturday, April 23rd:—Afternoon, 2 to 5.

A.—HOMER.

1. Translate with notes :—

(a) αὐτή δὲ χθαμαλὴ πανυπερτάτη εἰν ἁλὶ κεῖται
πρὸς ζόφον, αἱ δέ τ' ἄνευθε πρὸς ἠῶ τ' ἠελιόν τε,
τρηχεῖ. ἀλλ' ἀγαθὴ κουροτρόφος· οὔ τοι ἐγώ γε
ἧς γαίης δύναμαι γλυκερώτερον ἄλλο ἰδέσθαι.

(b) ταρσοὶ μὲν τυρῶν βρῖθον, στείνοντο δὲ σηκοὶ
ἀρνῶν ἠδ' ἐρίφων· διακεκριμέναι δὲ σηκοὶ
ἔρχατο, χωρὶς μὲν πρόγονοι, χωρὶς δὲ μέτασσαι,
χωρὶς δ' αὖθ' ἔρσαι· ναῖον δ' ὀρῷ ἄγγεα πάντα,
γαυλοί τε σκαφίδες τε, τετυγμένα, τοῖς ἐνάμελγεν.

(c) ἡ δὲ μάλ' αὐτίκα πατρὸς ἐπέφραδεν ὑψερεφὲς δῶ.
οἱ δ' ἐπεὶ εἰσῆλθον κλυτὰ δώματα, τὴν δὲ γυναῖκα
εὗρον ὅσην τ' ὄρεος κορυφήν, κατὰ δ' ἔστυγοⲛ αὐτήν.

(d)   αὐτὰρ ἐγὼ σπασάμην ῥῶπάς τε λύγους τε,
πεῖσμα δ', ὅσον τ' ὄργυιαν, ἐυστρεφὲς ἀμφοτέρωθεν
πλεξάμενος συνέδησα πόδας δεινοῖο πελώρου,
βῆν δὲ καταλοφάδεια φέρων ἐπὶ νῆα μέλαιναν,
ἔγχει ἐρειδόμενος, ἐπεὶ οὔ πως ἦεν ἐπ' ὤμου
χειρὶ φέρειν ἑτέρῃ· μάλα γὰρ μέγα θηρίον ἦεν.

(e) ὡς δ' ὅτ' ἐπὶ προβόλῳ ἁλιεὺς περιμήκεῖ ῥάβδῳ
ἰχθύσι τοῖς ὀλίγοισι δόλον κατὰ εἴδατα βάλλων
ἐς πόντον προΐησι βοὸς κέρας ἀγραύλοιο,
ἀσπαίροντα δ' ἔπειτα λαβὼν ἔρριψε θύραζε.

(*f*) αὐτὰρ ἐγὼ ποτὶ μακρὸν ἐρινεὸν ὑψόσ' ἀερθεὶς
τῷ προσφὺς ἐχόμην ὡς νυκτερίς· οὐδέ πῃ εἶχον
οὔτε στηρίξαι ποσὶν ἔμπεδον οὔτ' ἐπιβῆναι·
ῥίζαι γὰρ ἑκὰς εἶχον, ἀπήωροι δ' ἔσαν ὄζοι,
μακροί τε μεγάλοι τε, κατεσκίαον δὲ Χάρυβδιν.
νωλεμέως δ' ἐχόμην, ὄφρ' ἐξεμέσειεν ὀπίσσω
ἱστὸν καὶ τρόπιν αὖτις.

2. Annotate fully :—

(*a*) ἐπεὶ μάλα πῖαρ ὑπ' οὖδας.

(*b*)   τὰ δ' ἄρσενα λεῖπε θύρηφιν
ἀρνείους τε τράγους τε βαθείης ἔντοθεν αὐλῆς.
Mss. ἔκτοθεν ;

(*c*) οἱ δ' ἔλαχον τοὺς ἄν κε καὶ ἤθελον αὐτὸς ἑλέσθαι,
τέσσαρες, αὐτὰρ ἐγὼ πέμπτος μετὰ τοῖσιν ἐλέγμην.

(*d*) δῶκε δέ μ' ἐκδείρας ἀσκὸν βοὸς ἐννεώροιο.

(*e*) μερμήριξα | ἠὲ πεσὼν ἐκ νηὸς ἀποφθίμην ἐνὶ πόντῳ.

(*f*) ὡς δ' ὅτ' ἂν ἀμφὶ ἄνακτα κύνες δαίτηθεν ἰόντα
σαίνωσι.

(*g*) μακάρων μέγαν ὅρκον.

(*h*) ἑτάρους προΐειν ἐς δώματα Κίρκης | οἰσέμεναι
νεκρὸν Ἐλπήνορα τεθνηῶτα.

(*i*) κλαιόντεσσι δὲ τοῖσιν ἐπήλυθε νήδυμος ὕπνος.

3. Discuss the following words and phrases:—ἐγχείη,
βουλυτόνδε, θέμιστες, δειδίμεν, ἔχραε, κατεβήσετο, ὀρέστε-
ροι, βεβολημένος, πεποίθομεν, πέποσθε, κεκληγῶτας (v. l.
κεκλήγοντας), ἀριζήλως.

B.—AESCHYLUS, AGAMEMNON.

1. Translate and comment on :—

(*a*) οὔθ' ὑποκαίων οὔθ' ὑπολείβων
οὔτε δακρύων ἀπύρων ἱερῶν

ὀργὰς ἀτενεῖς παραθέλξει.
ἡμεῖς δ' ἀτίται σαρκὶ παλαιᾷ
τῆς τότ' ἀρωγῆς ὑπολειφθέντες
μίμνομεν ἰσχὺν
ἰσόπαιδα νέμοντες ἐπὶ σκήπτροις.
ὅ τε γὰρ νεαρὸς μυελὸς στέρνων
ἐντὸς ἀνάσσων
ἰσόπρεσβυς, Ἄρης δ' οὐκ ἔνι χώρᾳ,
τό θ' ὑπεργήρων φυλλάδος ἤδη
κατακαρφομένης τρίποδας μὲν ὁδοὺς
στείχει, παιδὸς δ' οὐδὲν ἀρείων
ὄναρ ἡμερόφαντον ἀλαίνει.

Mss. ὑποκλαίων, ἀνάσσων, τιθιπεργήρως.

(b) τόσον περ εὔφρων, καλά,
δρόσοισι λέπτοις μαλερῶν λεόντων,
πάντων τ' ἀγρονόμων φιλομάστοις
θηρῶν ὀβρικάλοισι τερπνά,
τούτων αἴνει ξύμβολα κρᾶναι,
δεξιὰ μέν, κατάμομφα δὲ φάσματα στρουθῶν.

Mss, τόσσων, δρόσοισιν ἀέλπτοις, ὄντων, αἰτεῖ.

(c) λίμνην δ' ὑπὲρ Γοργῶπιν ἔσκηψεν φάος·
ὄρος τ' ἐπ' Αἰγίπλαγκτον ἐξικνούμενον
ὤτρυνε θεσμὸν μὴ χατίζεσθαι πυρός.
πέμπουσι δ' ἀνδαίοντες ἀφθόνῳ μένει
φλογὸς μέγαν πώγωνα, καὶ Σαρωνικοῦ
πορθμοῦ κάτοπτον πρῶν' ὑπερβάλλειν πρόσω
φλέγουσαν.

Mss. χαρίζεσθαι, κάτοπτρον.

(d) Πάρις γὰρ οὔτε συντελὴς πόλις
ἐξεύχεται τὸ δρᾶμα τοῦ πάθους πλέον.

ὀφλὼν γὰρ ἁρπαγῆς τε καὶ κλοπῆς δίκην
τοῦ ῥυσίου θ' ἥμαρτε καὶ πανώλεθρον
αὐτόχθονον πατρῷον ἔθρισεν δόμον.
διπλᾶ δ' ἔτισαν Πριαμίδαι θἀμάρτια.

ΧΟ. κῆρυξ Ἀχαιῶν χαῖρε τῶν ἀπὸ στρατοῦ.

ΚΗ. χαίρω γε· τεθνάναι δ' οὐκ ἔτ' ἀντερῶ θεοῖς.

Mss. χαίρω τεθνᾶναι δ' οὐκ ἀντερῶ θεοῖς.

(ε) φιλεῖ δὲ τίκτειν ὕβρις
μὲν παλαιὰ νέα-
ζουσαν ἐν κακοῖς βροτῶν
ὕβριν τότ' ἢ τόθ', ὅτε τὸ κύριον μόλῃ
φάος τόκου,
δαίμονά τε τὰν ἄμαχον, ἀπόλεμον,
ἀνίερον θράσος, μελαίνας μελάθροισιν ἄτας,
εἰδομένας τοκεῦσιν.

Mss. ὅταν· νεαρὰ φάους κότον, νέα δ' ἔφυσεν κόρον·
τὸν (for τὰν), εἰδομέναν

2; Annotate fully :—

(a) λήμασι δισσούς.

(b) προβουλόπαις ἄφερτος ἄτας.

(c) ἀλλ' ἦ σ' ἐπίανέν τις ἄπτερος φάτις ;

(d) καὶ πολλὰ χαίρειν ξυμφοραῖς καταξιῶ.

(e) κικλήσκουσα Πάριν τὸν αἰι∙λεκτρον.

(f) ἐμῶν τε καὶ σῶν κύριος πιστευμάτων.

(g) δαιμόνων δέ που χάρις βίαιος (Mss.—ως) σέλμα
σεμνὸν ἡμένων.

(h) πόθῳ δ' ὑπερποντίας φάσμα δόξει δόμων ἀνάσσειν.

3. Translate, without notes :—

(a) ἰδοὺ δ' Ἀπόλλων αὐτὸς ἐκδύων ἐμὲ
χρηστηρίαν ἐσθῆτ', ἐποπτεύσας δέ με

κἀν τοῖσδε κόσμοις καταγελωμένην μέγα
φίλων ὑπ᾽ ἐχθρῶν οὐ διχορρόπως μάτην—
καλουμένη δὲ φοιτὰς ὡς ἀγύρτρια
πτωχὸς τάλαινα λιμοθνὴς ἠνεσχόμην—
καὶ νῦν ὁ μάντις μάντιν ἐκπράξας ἐμὲ
ἀπήγαγ᾽ ἐς τοιάσδε θανασίμους τύχας.
βωμοῦ πατρῴου δ᾽ · ντ᾽ ἐπίξηνον μένει
θερμῷ κοπείσης φοινίῳ προσφάγματι.

(b) δέδοικα δ᾽ ὄμβρου κτύπον δομοσφαλῆ
τὸν αἱματηρόν· ψακὰς δὲ λήγει.
δίκην δ᾽ ἐπ᾽ ἄλλο πρᾶγμα θηγάνει βλάβης
πρὸς ἄλλαις θηγάναισι Μοῖρα.
ἰὼ γᾶ γᾶ, εἴθ᾽ ἔμ᾽ ἐδέξω,
πρὶν τόνδ᾽ ἐπιδεῖν ἀργυροτοίχου
δροίτας κατέχοντα χαμεύναν.

B.A. CLASSICAL HONOURS.

TRANSLATION AT SIGHT.

1. τῆλε δ᾽ ἀπὸ σχεδίης αὐτὸς πέσε, πηδάλιον δὲ
ἐκ χειρῶν προέηκε· μέσον δέ οἱ ἱστὸν ἔαξε
δεινὴ μισγομένων ἀνέμων ἐλθοῦσα θύελλα,
τηλοῦ δὲ σπεῖρον καὶ ἐπίκριον ἔμπεσε πόντῳ
τὸν δ᾽ ἄρ᾽ ὑπόβρυχα θῆκε πολὺν χρόνον, οὐδ᾽. ἐδυ-
νάσθη
αἶψα μάλ᾽ ἀνσχεθέειν μεγάλου ὑπὸ κύματος ὁρμῆς.
εἵματα γὰρ ῥ᾽ ἐβάρυνε, τά οἱ πόρε δῖα Καλύψ
ὀψὲ δὲ δή ῥ᾽ ἀνέδυ, στόματος δ᾽ ἐξέπτυσεν ἅλμην
πικρὴν, ἥ οἱ πολλὴ ἀπὸ κρατὸς κελάρυζεν.
ἀλλ᾽ οὐδ᾽ ὣς σχεδίης ἐπελήθετο, τειρόμενός περ,
ἀλλὰ μεθορμηθεὶς ἐνὶ κύμασιν ἐλλάβετ᾽ αὐτῆς,
ἐν μέσσῃ δὲ καθῖζε τέλος θανάτου ἀλεείνων.

2. ποθουμένᾳ γὰρ φρενὶ πυνθάνομαι
τὰν ἀμφινεικῇ Δηιάνειραν ἀεί,
οἷά τιν' ἄθλιον ὄρνιν,
οὔποτ' εὐνάζειν ἀδακρύτων βλεφάρων πόθον, ἀλλ'
εὔμναστον ἀνδρὸς δεῖμα τρέφουσαν ὁδο͡
ἐνθυμίοις εὐναῖς ἀνανδρώτοισι τρύχεσθαι, κακὰν
δύστανον ἐλπίζουσαν αἶσαν.

3. ΑΘ. Τῆς μὲν τοίνυν πρὸς τὸ θεῖον εὐμενείας οὐδ' ἡμεῖς
οἰόμεθα λελείψεσθαι. οὐδὲν γὰρ ἔξω τῆς ἀνθρωπείας τῶν
μὲν ἐς τὸ θεῖον νομίσεως τῶν δ' ἐς σφᾶς αὐτοὺς βουλήσεως
δικαιοῦμεν ἢ πράσσομεν. ἡγούμεθα γὰρ τό τε θεῖον δόξῃ,
τὸ ἀνθρώπειόν τε σαφῶς διὰ παντὸς ὑπὸ φύσεως ἀναγκαίας,
οὗ ἂν κρατῇ, ἄρχειν. καὶ ἡμεῖς οὔτε θέντες τὸν νόμον οὔτε
κειμένῳ πρῶτοι χρησάμενοι, ὄντα δὲ παραλαβόντες καὶ
ἐσόμενον ἐς ἀεὶ καταλείψοντες, χρώμεθα αὐτᾷ, εἰδότες
καὶ ὑμᾶς ἂν καὶ ἄλλους ἐν τῇ αὐτῇ δυνάμει ἡμῖν γενομέ-
νους δρῶντας ἂν αὐτό. καὶ πρὸς μὲν τὸ θεῖον οὕτως ἐκ τοῦ
εἰκότος οὐ φοβούμεθα ἐλασσώσεσθαι· τῆς δὲ ἐς Λακεδαιμονίους δόξης, ἣν διὰ τὸ αἰσχρὸν δὴ βοηθήσειν ὑμῖν πισ-
τεύετε αὐτούς, μακαρίσαντες ὑμῶν τὸ ἀπειρόκακον οὐ
ζηλοῦμεν τὸ ἄφρον.

4. κάλλος δὲ τότ' ἦν ἰδεῖν λαμπρόν, ὅτε σὺν εὐδαίμονι
χορῷ μακαρίαν ὄψιν τε καὶ θέαν, ἑπόμενοι μετὰ μὲν Διὸς
ἡμεῖς, ἄλλοι δὲ μέτ' ἄλλου θεῶν, εἶδόν τε καὶ ἐτελοῦντο
τῶν τελετῶν ἣν θέμις λέγειν μακαριωτάτην, ἣν ὠργιάζο-
μεν ὁλόκληροι μὲν αὐτοὶ ὄντες καὶ ἀπαθεῖς κακῶν, ὅσα
ἡμᾶς ἐν ὑστέρῳ χρόνῳ ὑπέμενεν, ὁλόκληρα δὲ καὶ ἁπλᾶ
καὶ ἀτρεμῆ καὶ εὐδαίμονα φάσματα μυούμενοί τε καὶ
ἐποπτεύοντες ἐν αὐγῇ καθαρᾷ, καθαροὶ ὄντες καὶ ἀσήμαν-
τοι τούτου, ὃ νῦν σῶμα περιφέροντες ὀνομάζουσιν, ὀστρέου
τρόπον δεδεσμευμένοι.

5. ἔχει γὰρ οὕτως. ἂν μὲν ἀπογνῶτε τὴν γραφὴν ταύτην, ἅπαντές εἰσιν ἀπηλλαγμένοι καὶ δίκην οὐδεὶς οὐδεμίαν
μὴ δῷ· τίς γὰρ ἔτ' ἂν καταψηφίσαι τ' ἐκείνων, τὴν βουλὴν
ὑμῶν ἐστεφανωκότων, ἧς οὗτοι προέστασαν; ἐὰν δὲ καταγ-
νῶτε, πρῶτον μὲν τὰ εὔορκ' ἔσεσθ' ἐψηφισμένοι, εἶτ' ἐπὶ
ταῖς εὐθύναις ἕκαστον τούτων λαμβάνοντες, ὃς μὲν ἂν ὑμῖν
ἀδικεῖν δοκῇ, κολάσετε, ὃς δ' ἂν μὴ, τότ' ἀφήσετε. μὴ
οὖν ὡς ὑπὲρ τῆς βουλῆς λεγόντων καὶ τῶν πολλῶν ἀκούετε,
ἀλλ' ὡς ὑπὲρ αὐτῶν παρακρουομένοις ὀργίζεσθε.

6. Δύσμορος ἐκρύφθην πόντῳ νέκυς, ὃν παρὰ κῦμα
    ἔκλαυσεν μήτηρ μύρια Λυσιδίκη,
  ψεύστην αὐγάζουσα κενὸν τάφον· ἀλλά με δαίμων
    ἄπνουν αἰθυίαις θῆκεν ὁμορρόθιον
  Πυνταγόρην· ἔσχον δὲ κατ' Αἰγαίην ἅλα πότμον
    πρυμνούχους στέλλων ἐκ Βορέαο κάλους.
  ἀλλ' οὐδ' ὣς ναύτην ἔλιπον δρόμον, ἀλλ' ἀπὸ νηὸς
    ἄλλην πὰρ φθιμένοις εἰσενέβην ἄκατον.

B. A. AND THIRD YEAR CLASSICAL HONOURS.

GREEK PROSE.

MONDAY, APRIL 25TH :—MORNING, 9 TO 12.

1. *B. A. Honours.*

OF FALSEHOOD.

Lying supplies those who are addicted to it with a plausible apology
for every crime and with a supposed shelter from every punishment. It
tempts them to rush into danger from the mere expectation of impunity,
and when practised with frequent success, it teaches them to confound
the gradations of guilt, from the effects of which there is, in their im-
aginations at least, one sure and common protection. It corrupts the
early simplicity of youth ; it blasts the fairest blossoms of genius ; and
will most assuredly counteract every effort by which we may hope to
improve the talents and mature the virtues of those whom it infects.

S. PARR.

2. *Third Year Honours.*

PERKIN WARBECK, AS RICHARD THE FOURTH, BESIEGING EXETER.

When therefore they were come before Exeter, they forbare to use any force at the first, but made continual shouts and outcries to terrify the inhabitants. They did likewise in divers places call and talk to them from under the walls to join with them and be of their party : telling them that the king would make them another London, if they would be the first town that should acknowledge him. But they had not the wit to send to them in any orderly fashion agents or chosen men to tempt them and to treat with them. The citizens on their part showed themselves stout and loyal subjects. Neither was there so much as any tumult or division amongst them ; but all prepared themselves for a valiant defence and making good the town. For well they saw, that the rebels were of no such number or power, that they needed to fear them as yet, and well they hoped, that before their numbers increased the king's succours would come in. LORD BACON.

LATIN.

SESSIONAL EXAMINATIONS.

FIRST YEAR.

Tuesday, April 5th :—Morning, 9 to 12.

A. OVID, METAMORPHOSES XIII. VIRGIL. GEORGICS I.

1. Translate :—

> Iuppiter huc specie mortali, cumque parente
> Venit Atlantiades positis caducifer alis.
> Mille domos adiere, locum requiemque petentes :
> Mille domos clausere serac. Tamen una recepit,
> Parva quidem, stipulis et canna tecta palustri :
> Sed pia Baucis anus parilique aetate Philemon
> Illa sunt annis iuncti iuvenalibus, illa
> Consenuere casa ; paupertatemque fatendo
> Effecere levem nec iniqua mente ferendo.
> Nec refert, dominos illic, famulosne requiras :
> Tota domus duo sunt, idem parentque iubentque.

2. Translate, adding where necessary a brief explanatory note :—

(a) Palladios latices.

(b) Et adhuc a coniuge tutus
Oeclides.

(c) Truncoque dedit leuc volnus acerno.

(d) At gemini, nondum caelestia sidera, fratres.

(e) Seruatusque tuos, iuvenis, servaverat anuos.

(f) Planguntur matres Calydonides Eveninae.

(g) Erectheas Tritonidos ibat ad arces.

(h)   Nec fortibus illic
profuit armentis nec equis uelocibus esse.

(i) Interea medias fallunt sermonibus horas.

(j) Testa parem fecit.

(k) Vota fides sequitur.

(l) Ut tibi, complexi terram maris incola, Proteu.

(m) Haud aliter fluxit discusso cortice sanguis,
quam solet, ante aras ingens ubi uictima taurus
concidit, abrupta cruor e cernice profundi.

(n) Dominum generosa recusat.

3. Translate :

> Continuo, ventis surgentibus, aut freta ponti
> Incipiunt agitata tumescere, et aridus altis
> Montibus audiri fragor; aut resonantia longe
> Litora misceri, et nemorum increbrescere murmur.
> Iam sibi tum curvis male temperat unda carinis,
> Quum medio celeres redolant ex aequore mergi,
> Clamoremque fernut ad litora, quumque marinae
> In sicco ludunt fulicae, notasque paludes
> Deserit atque altam supra volat ardea nubem.
> Saepe etiam stellas, vento inpendente, videbis
> Praecipites coelo labi, noctisque per umbram
> Flammarum longos a tergo albescere tractus ;
> Saepe levem palcam et frondes volitare caducas,
> Aut summa nantis in aqua coaludere plumas.

4. What do you observe irregular about the scansion of the following lines :—

(1) Lappaeque tribolique interque nitentia culta.

(2) Ante tibi Eoae Atlantides abscondantur.

(3) Illic, ut perhibent aut intempesta silet nox.

(4) Coeumque Iapetumque creat, saeuumque Typhoea.

(5) Ter sunt conati imponere Pelio Ossam.

(6) Tenuia nec lanae per caelum vellera ferri.

(7) Glauco et Panopeae et Inoo Melicertae.

5. Translate, adding a brief explanatory note where necessary :—

(a) Poculaque inventis Acheloia miscuit unis.

(b) Urunt Lethaeo perfusa papauera somno.

(c) Quid dicam, iacto qui semine comminus arua
insequitur.

(d) Huic ab stirpe pedes temo protentus in octo.

(e) Contemplator item cum se nux plurima siluis
induct in florem.

(f) Vere fabis satio.

(g) Nona fugae melior, contraria furtis.

(h)   Aut illum surgentem nallibus imis
aeriae fugere grues.

i Neque insidiis noctis capiere serenae.

' B. PRO LEGE MANILIA.

1. Translate, and write a brief note on the words or phrases printed in italics:

(*a*) Quare, si propter socios, nulla ipsi ˌiniuria lacessiti, maiores nostri cum *Antioho*, cum *Philippo*, cum *Aetolis*, cum *Po⁻nis* bella gesserunt, quanto vos studio convenit, iniuriis provocatos, sociorum salutem una cum imperii vestri dignitate defendere, praesertim cum de maximis vestris vectigalibus agatur ?

(*b*) Ego enim sic existimo, *Maximo*, *Marcello*, *Scipioni*, *Mario* et ceteris magnis imperatoribus non solum propter virtutem, sed etiam propter fortunam saepius imperia mandata atque exercitus esse commissos.

(*c*) Quae civitas antea unquam fuit—non dico *Atheniensium*, quae satis late quondam mare tenuisse dicitur, non *Karthaginiensium*, qui permultum classe ac maritimis rebus valuerunt, non *Rhodiorum*, quorum usque ad nostram memoriam disciplina navalis et gloria remansit, —quae [civitas] umquam antea tam tenuis, tam parva insula fuit, quae non portus suos et agros et aliquam partem regionis atque orae maritimae per se ipsa defenderet ?

2. Translate, and remark on the grammatical construction of italicised words :—

(*a*) Nunc vero cum *sit* unus Cn. Pompeius, qui non modo eorum hcminum, qui nunc sunt, gloriam, sed etiam antiquitatis memoriam virtute *superarit,* quae res est quae cuiusquam animum in hac causa dubium facere *possit ?*

(*b*) *Hiemis* enim, non *avaritiae* perfugium maiores nostri in sociorum atque amicorum tectis esse voluerunt.

(*c*) Utrum ille, qui postulat ad tantum bellum legatum quem velit, *idoneus non est qui impetret,* cum ceteri ad expilandos socios diripiendasque provincias quos voluerunt legatos eduxerint, an ipse, cuius lege salus, ac dignitas populo Romano atque omnibus gentibus constituta est, expers esse debet *gloriae* eius imperatoris atque eius exercitus, qui consilio ipsius ac periculo est constitutus ?

––––––––––

FIRST YEAR.

LATIN PROSE.

1. Translate into Latin :

(1) Do not wait for me ; start alone.

(2) Do you love me and despise my money ?

(3) The consul led the middle of the line.

(4) Where is the boy I gave my horse to ?

(5) Do not believe all men.

(6) Why does he not spare those he loves ?

(7) Claudius fought boldly that he might not be taken alive.

(8) I fear I shall not see you.

(9) I got this horse for 300 sesterces.

(10) When Pyrrhus reigned at Epirus there was no King at Rome.

(11) We believe that Cæsar with his army was four miles off.

(12) They said he was absent.

(13) I think he was followed by a slave.

(14) I think that Pompeius will capture the city.

(15) I think that the city will be captured by Pompeius.

(16) Tell us which brother is the elder.

(17) They have been persuaded to try again.

(18) He wrote the letter and started.

(19) He promises to lend me the largest ship he possesses.

(20) I repent of my anger.

(21) It is to the advantage of the Romans to fight in Italy.

TRANSLATION AT SIGHT.

I.

Xerxes, in proelio apud Salamina commisso devictus, in Asiam mare transmittebat. Tum, cum magis fureret tempestas et nimis onerata esset navis, magno Persarum numero invecto, rex timore perculsus e gubernatore quaesivit, ecqua salutis esset spes. Cui gubernator respondit non aliam esse spem, nisi de numero multorum hominum in nave vectorum pars amoveretur. " Viri Persae," inquit Xerxes, "ecquis regem esse sibi curae ostendere vult? namque in vobis mea salus posita esse videtur." Quibus auditis, illi, cum regem adorassent, in mare prosiluere e nave, quae, hoc modo levata, salva in Asiam pervenit. Xerxes vero simul atque in terram erat expositus, aurea corona gubernatorem donavit, quod regis ipsius vitam conservasset, deinde, quod magnum Persarum numerum perdidisset, caput ei praecidi iussit.

FIRST YEAR LATIN.

ROMAN HISTORY—THE CARTHAGINIAN WARS.

TUESDAY, APRIL 5th :—AFTERNOON, 4 to 5.

1. Estimate briefly the comparative resources of Rome and Carthage as evidenced in the course of the long struggle between the two powers.

2. Trace the extension of the Roman provincial system in connection with the Carthaginian Wars.

3. How was Rome mainly occupied (*a*) in the interval between the first and second of the wars with Carthage, and (*b*) in that between the second and third?

4. Add a very brief note to each of the following :—Corinth, Capua, Metaurus, Achaean League, Magnesia, Saguntum, Aegates Insulae, Agrigentum, Regulus, Zama.

INTERMEDIATE EXAMINATION.

TUESDAY, APRIL 5TH :—MORNING, 9 TO 12.

(A) LIVY, Book I.—*2 hours.*

1. Translate :—

(*a*) Nec iam publicis magis Servius quam privatis munire opes, et ne, qualis Anci liberum animus adversus Tarquinium fuerat, talis adversus se Tarquini liberum esset, duas filias iuvenibus regiis Lucio atque Arrunti Tarquiniis iungit. nec rupit tamen fati necessitatem humanis consiliis, quin invidia regni etiam inter domesticos infida omnia atque infesta faceret· peropportune ad praesentis quietem status bellum cum eientibus—iam enim indutiae exierant—aliisque Etruscis sumptum, in eo bello et virtus et fortuna enituit Tulli ; fusoque ingenti hostium exercitu baud dubius rex, seu patrum seu plebis animos periclitaretur, Romam rediit.

(*b*) Numitor inter primum tumultum hostis invasisse urbem atque adortos regiam dictitans, cum pubem Albanam iu arcem praesidio armisque obtinendam avocasset, postquam iuvenes perpetrata caede pergere ad se gratulantes vidit, extemplo advocato concilio scelera in se fratris, originem nepotum, ut geniti, ut educati, ut cogniti essent, caedem deinceps tyranni seque eius auctorem ostendit.

Remark on the use of the present participle *gratulantes*, and the general structure of this sentence.

(*c*) Tum interrex contione advocata "quod bonum faustum felixque sit ' inquit, " Quirites, regem create : ita patribus visum est. patres deinde, si dignum qui. secundus ab Romulo numeretur crearitis, auctores fient." adeo id gratum plebi tuit, ut, ne vieti beneficio viderentur, id modo sciscerent iuberentque, ut senatus decerneret qui Romae regnaret.

Account for the use ot all the subjunctives in this passage.

(*d*) Roma est ad id potissimum visa : in novo populo, ubi omnis repentina atque ex virtute nobilitas sit, futurum locum forti ac strenuo viro ; regnasse Tatium Sabinum, arcessitum in regnum Numam a Curibus, et Ancum Sabina matre ortum nobilemque una imagine Numae esse. facile persuadet ut cupido honorum, et cui Tarquinii materna tantum patria, esset.

Give the geographical position of *Cures* and *Tarquinii*. Remark on the phrase *una imagine*. Account for the construction of *cupido* and *esset*.

(*e*) Ubi id parum processit, obsidione munitionibusque coepti premi hostes. in his stativis, ut fit longo magis quam acri bello, satis liberi commeatus erant, primoribus tamen magis quam militibus ; regii quidem iu, venes interdum otium conviviis comissationibusque inter se terebant.

2. Define the terms : pater patratus, fetialis, flamen, velamen, duellum-contio, concilium, comissatio, convivium. Give the derivation, where known.

3. Translate, and write brief comments on :

(*a*) Remus Aventinum ad inaugurandum templa capit.

(*b*) Herculem in ea loca Geryone interempto boves mira specie abegisse memorant.

(*c*) pergit ad proximam speluncam, si forte eo vestigia ferrent.

(*d*) accedebant blanditiae virorum, factum purgantium amore.

(*e*) multa alia sacrificia locaque sacris faciendis, quae Argeos pontifices vocant, dedicavit.

(*f*) id inaugurato Romulus fecerat.

(*g*) hac fiducia virium Tullus bellum indicit.

(*h*) Inde puerum liberum loco coeptum haberi erudirique artibus quibus ingenia ad magnae fortunae cultum excitantur. Evenit facile quod dlis cordi esset.

(B) VIRGIL, AENEID VII.—1 *hour.*

1. Translate :

(*a*) Quem capta cupidine coniunx
aurea percussum uirga uersumque uenenis
fecit auem Circe, sparsitque coloribus alas.

(*b*) Saturni gentem haud uinclo nec legibus aequam.

(*c*) Nec sidus regione uiae litusve fefellit.

(*d*) Quanta per Idaeos saeuis effusa Mycenis
tempestas ierit campos, quibus actus uterque
Europae atque Asiae fatis concurrerit orbis,
audiit, et si quem tellus extrema refuso
submouet Oceano, et si quem extenta plagarum
quattuor in medio dirimit plaga solis iniqui.

(*e*) Moliri iam tecta uidet iam fidere terrae.

(*f*) Ille inter uestes et leuia pectora lapsus
uoluitur attactu nullo, fallitque furentem.

(*g*) I nunc, ingratis offer te, inrise, periclis.

(*h*)   lubet arma parari
     tutari Italiam, detrudere finibus bostem.

(*i*)   Vocat agmina Tyrrheus
     quadrifidam quercum cuneis ut forte coactis
     scindebat, rapta spirans immane securi.

(*j*) Turnus adest, medioque in crimine caedis et igni
     terrorem ingeminat.

(*k*) Nam mihi parta quies, omnisque in limine portus
     funere felici spolior. Add a brief note.

(*l*) Quinque adeo magnae positis incudibus urbes
     tela nouant, Atina potens, Tiburque superbum,
     Ardea Crustumerique et turrigerae Antemnae.

(*m*)   Dignus patriis qui laetior esset
     imperiis et cui pater haud Mezentius esset.

Who is referred to here?

(*n*) Hi Fescenninas acies Aequosque Faliscos
     hi Soractis habent arces Flauiniaque arua.

(*o*) Et pastoralem, praefixa cuspide myrtum.

2. Translate :
     Namque ferunt fama Hippolytum postquam arte nouercae
     occiderit patriosque explerit sanguine poenas
     turbatis distractus equis, ad sidera rursus
     aetheria et superas caeli uenisse sub auras,
     Pæoniis reuocatum herbis et amore Dianae.

Scan these five lines.

INTERMEDIATE EXAMINATION.

LATIN COMPOSITION AND TRANSLATION AT SIGHT.

TUESDAY, APRIL 5TH :—2 TO 5.

I. Translate into Latin prose :—

A. It is related that five years after his capture the Carthaginians, being anxious to arrange terms of peace, despatched an embassy to Rome, and with it they sent Regulus, whom they bound on *parole* to return to Carthage if their offers were rejected. The senate, it is said, was well inclined to accept the proposed terms, but to the surprise and admiration of all, Regulus exhorted them not to do so. Resisting the entreaties of his friends, he refused even to enter the city, and stood firmly by his resolution to go back into captivity.

B. 1. Unhappy that I am in not having seen this!

2. He said that the city would have been taken, if Cæsar had not come to its aid.

3. You have come here manifestly[1] with reluctance, and you say that you will not wait any longer for the arrival of your friends, who will, you think, be far from[2] secure in our camp.

For myself I have promised you again and again to say nothing about the past[3] and I have resolved both to pardon you and to spare them.

1. Employ "manifestum est."
2. parum ("but little.")
3. praeterita.

II. Translate :—

A. Hannibali victori cum ceteri circumfusi gratularentur suaderentque, ut, tanto perfunctus bello, diei quod reliquum esset, noctisque insequentis quietem et ipse sibi sumeret et fessis daret militibus, Maharbal, praefectus equitum, minime cessandum ratus, " immo, ut, quid hac pugna sit actum, scias, die quinto," inquit " victor in capitolio epulaberis. Sequere ; cum equite, ut prius venisse quam venturum sciant, praecedam." Hannibali nimis lacta res est visa, majorque quam ut eam statim capere animo posset ; itaque voluntatem se laudare Maharbalis ait, ad consilium pensandum temporis opus esse.

PLUTO TO PROSERPINE.

B.   Desine funestis animum, Proserpina, curis
Et vano vexare metu. Maiora dabuntur
Sceptra, nec indigni taedas patiere mariti.
Ille ego Saturni proles, cui machina rerum
Servit, et immensum tendit per inane potestas.
Amissum ne crede diem. Sunt altera nobis
Sidera, sunt orbes alii : lumenque videbis
Purins, Elysiumque magis mirabere solem.

INTERMEDIATE LATIN.
SUMMER READINGS.

HORACE : *Selected Odes.* CAESAR : *Bell. Gall. III.* VIRGIL : *Georgics,* Book I.

WEDNESDAY, 6TH APRIL, 1898.

Two Hours allowed.

I. Translate :—

Nequicquam deus abscidit
Prudens Oceano dissociabili
Terras, si tamen impiae
Non tangenda rates transiliunt vada.
Audax omnia perpeti

11

Gens humana ruit per vetitum nefas.
Audax Iäpeti genus
Ignem fraude mala gentibus intulit.
Post ignem aetheria domo
Subductum macies et nova febrium
Terris incubuit cohors,
Semotique prius tarda necessitas
Leti corripuit gradum.

(2)   Quo nos cunque feret melior fortuna parente,
Ibimus, o socii comitesque.
Nil desperandum, Teucro duce, et auspice Teucro ;
Certus enim promisit Apollo,
Ambiguam tellure nova Salamina futuram.
O fortes peioraque passi
Mecum saepe viri, nunc vino pellite curas ;
Cras ingens iterabimus aequor.

II. (a) Translate the following, scanning the lines in each case, and naming the metre :—

(1)   Quod si me lyricis vatibus inseres
Sublimi feriam sidera vertice.

(2)   Sive neglectum genus et nepotes
Respicis auctor.

(3)   Undique decerptam fronti praeponere olivam.

(b) Explain the following : *domus Albuneae resonantis, bimaris Corinthi moenia, Catonis nobile letum, spatio brevi spem longam reseces.*

Candidates will choose between III. and IV., and must not attempt both.

III. Translate :—

(a) Erant eiusmodi fere situs oppidorum, ut posita in extremis lingulis promunturiisque neque pedibus aditum haberent, cum ex alto se aestus incitavisset, quod his accidit semper horarum duodecim spatio, neque navibus, quod rursus minuente aestu naves in vadis afflictarentur. Ita utraque re oppidorum oppugnatio impediebatur ; ac si quando magnitudine operis forte superati, extruso mari aggere ac molibus atque his oppidi moenibus adaequatis, suis fortunis desperare coeperant, magno numero navium appulso, cuius rei summam facultatem habebant, sua deportabant omnia seque in proxima oppida recipiebant : ibi se rursus isdem opportunitatibus loci defendebant. Haec eo facilius magnam partem aestatis faciebant, quod nostrae naves tempestatibus detinebantur, summaque erat vasto atque aperto mari, magnis aestibus, raris ac prope nullis portibus, difficultas navigandi.

(*b*) Una erat magno usui res praeparata a nostris falces praeacutae insertae adfixaeque longuriis non absimili forma muralium falcium. His cum funes, qui antemnas ad malos destinabant, comprehensi adductique erant, navigio remis incitato praerumpebantur.

(*c*) Itaque se suaque omnia Caesari dediderunt. In quos eo gravius Caesar vindicandum statuit, quo diligentius in reliquum tempus a barbaris ius legatorum conservaretur. Itaque omni senatu necato reliquos sub corona vendidit.

(*d*) Quibus fortiter resistentibus vineas turresque egit. Illi alias eruptione tentata, alias cuniculis ad aggerem vineasque actis (cuius rei sunt longe peritissimi Aquitani, propterea quod multis locis apud eos aerariae structuraeqve sunt), ubi diligentia nostrorum nihil his rebus profici posse intellexerunt, legatos ad Crassum mittunt seque in deditionem ut recipiat, petunt·

IV. Translate :—

(*a*)　　　　　　　Numquam imprudentibus imber
　　　Obfuit : aut illum surgentem vallibus imis
　　　Aeriae fugere grues, aut bucula caelum
　　　Suspiciens patulis captavit naribus auras,
　　　Aut arguta lacus circumvolitavit hirundo,
　　　Et veterem in limo ranae cecinere querelam.
　　　Saepius et tectis penetralibus extulit ova
　　　Angustum formica terens iter, et bibit ingens
　　　Arcus, et e pastu decedens agmine magno
　　　Corvorum increpuit densis exercitus alis.
　　　Iam varias pelagi volucres, et quae Asia circum
　　　Dulcibus in stagnis rimantur prata Caystri,
　　　Certatim largos humeris infundere rores,
　　　Nunc caput obiectare fretis, nunc currere in undas,
　　　Et studio incassum videas gestire lavandi.
　　　Tum cornix plena pluviam vocat improba voce
　　　Et sola in sicca secum spatiatur arena.

(*b*)　　Illa seges demum votis respondet avari
　　　Agricolae, bis quae solem, bis frigora sensit ;
　　　Illius immensae ruperunt horrea messes.

(*c*)　　　　　Frigidus agricolam si quando continet imber,
　　　Multa, forent quae mox caelo properanda sereno,
　　　Maturare datur : durum procudit arator
　　　Vomeris obtunsi dentem, cavat arbore lintres,
　　　Aut pecori signum aut numeros impressit acervis.

(*d*)　　Ergo inter sese paribus concurrere telis
　　　Romanas acies iterum videre Philippi ;
　　　Nec fuit indignum superis, bis sanguine nostro
　　　Emathiam et latos Haemi pinguescere campos.

Scan the last four lines.

INTERMEDIATE EXAMINATIONS.
ROMAN HISTORY AND LITERATURE.
WEDNESDAY, 6TH APRIL, 1898.
One and a Half Hours allowed.

A.—HISTORY.

Write on *any four* of the following topics, adding dates where you can :—

(*a*) *Gaius Gracchus.* His legislation for (*a*) improving the condition of the people, (*b*) diminishing the power of the Senate.

(*b*) *The War with Iugurtha.*

(*c*) Battles of *Aquae Sextiae, Dyrrachium, Pharsalus.*

(*d*) The *Gabinian Law* and its results.

(*e*) *Sulla's Dictatorship.* His proscriptions ; his legislative reforms.

(*f*) The Banishment of *Cicero.*

(*g*) The *Second Triumvirate.*

(*d*) *Julius Caesar.* The conspiracy against him and its causes.

B.—LITERATURE.

(*a*) Give a short account of the origin and growth of the Roman Drama.

(*b*) Trace the growth of Greek influence on Roman literature.

(*c*) Give a short life of Livy, and describe his great work.

(*d*) Write brief notes on each of the following : Livius Andronicus, Lucretius, Seneca, Catullus, Ovid, Martial, Tibullus, Juvenal, Ovid.

APRIL, 1898.
LATIN PROSE AND UNSEEN TRANSLATION.
THIRD YEAR.
MONDAY, APRIL 4TH :—2 TO 5 P. M.
FOR LATIN PROSE.

Before he left the Palatine, a soldier ran up to him with a bloody sword, crying that he had killed Otho. ' Fellow soldier,' said Galba, 'Who ordered you ? ' But there in the meantime, Otho had been saluted imperator by the praetorians and the regiment of marine soldiers had also joined him. Otho armed the troops and led them from the camp into the city to suppress the opposition of the populace and senators. Galba and Piso had halted in the Forum, uncertain whether to advance or to return to the palace. When the cohort which surrounded Galba perceived the advance of Otho s forces, the standard bearer dashed the image to the ground, thus showing that the soldiers sympathised with Otho. The people fled from the Forum. The litter in which Galba was borne was overturned near the Pool of Curtius and the Emperor was hewn in pieces.

FOR UNSEEN TRANSLATION.
THE BATTLE OF ARBELA.

1. Ceterum, sive ludibrium oculorum, sine uera species fuit, qui circa Alexandrum erant, uidisse se crediderunt paululum super caput regis placide uolantem aquilam, non sono armorum, non gemitu morientium territam ; diuque circa equum Alexandri pendenti magis quam uolanti similis apparuit. Certe nates Aristander, alba neste indutus, et dextra praeferens lauream, militibus iu pugnam intentis anem monstrabat, haud dubium uictoriae auspicium. Iugens ergo alacritas et fiducia paulo ante territos accendit ad pugnam, utique postquam auriga Darei qui ante ipsum sedens equos regebat hasta transfixus est. Nec aut Persae aut Macedones dubitauere, quin ipse rex esset occisus.

Epitaph Upon a Dog.

Amphitheatrales inter nutrita magistros
uenatrix, siluis aspera, blanda domi,
Lydia dicebar, domino fidissima Dextro,
qui non Erigones mallet habere canem :
Non me longa dies nec inutilis abstulit aetas,
qualia Dulichio fata fuere cani.
Fulmineo spumantis apri sum dente peremta,
quantus erat, Calydon, aut Erymanthe, tuus.
Nee queror, infernas quamuis cito rapta sub umbras :
non potni fato nobiliore mori.

THIRD YEAR.
TACITUS, HORACE AND LUCAN
TUESDAY, APRIL 5TH:—9 TO 12.

1. Translate :—

Multi in utroque exercitu sicut modesti quietique, ita mali et strenui. Sed profusa cupidine et insigni temeritate legati legionum Alienus Caecina et Fabius Valens ; e quibus Valens infensus Galbae, tanquam detectam a se Verginii cunctationem, oppressa Capitonis consilia ingrate tulisset, instigare Vitellium ardorem militum ostentans ; ipsum celebri ubique fama, nullam in Flacco Hordeonio moram ; adfore Britanniam, secutura Germanorum auxilia ; male fidas prouincias, precarium seni imperium et breni transiturum. Panderet modo sinum et uenienti Fortunae occurreret. Merito dubitasse Verginium equestri tamilia, ignoto patre, imparem si recepisset imperium, tutum, si recusasset. Vitellio tres patris consulatus, censuram, collegium Caesaris et imponere iam pridem imperatoris dignationem et auferre priuati securitatem.

2. Translate :—

(a) Seu uctito patrias ultra tibi cernere sedes.
sic Romam Fortuna dedit.

(*b*) Crastina dira quies et imagine mæsta diurna.

(*c*) Adfusi uinci socerum patiare rogamus.

(*d*)   Sanguine mundi
   fuso, Magne, semel totos consume triumphos.

(*e*) Hæc acies uictum factura nocentem est.

(*f*) Cinis qui fugerit esto.

(*g*) At plures tantum clamore cateruæ
   Bella gerent.

(*h*)   Nulloque frequentem
   Ciue suo Romam sed mundi faece repletam
   cladis eo dedimus ne tanto in corpore bellum
   iam posset cinile geri.

(*i*) Bella pares superis facient ciuilia dinos.

3. Translate and explain :—

   (*a*)   . Leviter curare uidetur
      quo promissa cadant et somnia Pythagorea.

   (*b*)   Memini quæ plagosum mihi paruo
      Orbilium dictare.

   (*c*)   Viuit siliquis et pane secundo.

   (*d*)   Valeat res ludicra si me
      palma negata macrum, donata reducit opimum.

   (*e*)   Sed quod non desit habentem
      quæ poterunt unquam satis expurgare cicutæ,
      ni melius dormire putem quam scribere uersus?

   (*f*) Discedo Alcæus puncto illins.

   (*g*) Tempus abire tibi est, ne potum largius æquo
         rideat et pulset lasciua decentius ætas.

4. Translate :—

   (*a*)   Fuit haud ignobilis Argis,
      qui se credebat miros audire tragœdos,
      in uacuo lætus sessor plausorque theatro ;
      cetera qui uitæ seruaret munia recto
      more, bonus sane uicinus, amabilis hospes,
      comis in uxorem, posset qui ignoscere sernis
      et signo læso non insanire lagenæ,
      posset qui rupem et puteum uitare patentem.

   (*b*) Hæc et apud seras gentes populosque nepotum,
      sine sua tantum veulent in sæcula fama,
      siue aliquid magnis nostri quoque cura laboris

nominibus prodesse potest, cum bella legentur,
spesque metusque simul perituraque uota mouebunt,
attonitique omnes ueluti uenientia fata,
non transmissa, legent et adhuc tibi, Magne, fauebunt.

5. Translate :—

(a) Secundæ res acrioribus stimulis animos explorant, quia miseriæ tolerantur, felicitate corrumpimur.

(b) Neque illis indicium aut veritas, quippe eodem die diversa pari certamine postulatuiis.

(c) Exacto per scelera die nouissimum malorum fuit lætitia.

(d) Is diu sordidus, repente dines mutationem fortunæ male tegebat, accensis egestate longa cupidinibus immoderatus et inopi inventa senex prodigus.

(e) Placuit ignoscentibus verso nomine, quod auaritia fuerat, nideri maiestatem, cuius tum odio etiam bonæ leges peribant.

6. What mention is made in this book of Tacitus, of Licinius Mucianus, Tigellinus, Plotius Firmus, Marcellus, Icelus, Clodius Macer, Nymphidius Sabinus, Scribonia, Caluia Crispinilla.
This question is to be answered very briefly.

THIRD YEAR.

SUMMER READINGS.—CICERO, PRO ROSCIO AMERINO. AND ROMAN LITERATURE.

TUESDAY, APRIL 5TH :—2 TO 5.

1. Translate :—

(a) Quadriduo quo haec gesta suut.

(b) Bona ueneunt hominis studiosissimi nobilitatis.

(c) Insutus in culleum.

(d) Aiunt hominem, ut erat furiosus, respondisse, quod non totum telum corpore recepisset.

(e) Ne tu, Eruci, accusator esses ridiculus, si illis temporibus natus esses, cum ab aratro arcessebantur qui consules fierent.

(f) Quaero qui scias.

(g) Sapienter fecisse dicitur, cum de eo nihil sanxerit, quod antea commissum non erat, ne non tam prohibere quam admonere uideretur.

(h) Noluerunt feris corpus obicere, ne bestiis quoque, quae tantum scelus attigissent, immanoribus uteremur.

(i) Spectatissima femina, quae cum patrem clarissimum amplissimos patruos, ornatissimum fratrem haberet, tamen cum esset mulier, uirtute perfecit, ut quanto honore ipsa ex illorum dignitate adficeretur, non minora illis ornamenta ex sua laude redderet.

2. Translate :—

Nolite enim putare, quem ad modum in fabulis saepenumero uidetis eos, qui aliquid impie scelerateque commiserunt, agitari et perterreri Furiarum taedis ardentibus ; sua quemque frans et suus terror maxime uexat, snum quemque scelus agitat amentiaque adficit, suae malae cogitationes conscientiaeque animi terrent : hae sunt impiis assiduae domesticaeque Furiae, quae dies noctesque parentium poenas a consceleratissimis filiis repetunt.

3. Enumerate any of the works of Plautus *or* Ovid.

4. What does Horace say of the characteristics of the ancient Roman dramatists Caecilius, Terentius, etc. Quote his words if possible.

5. State briefly what you know of the place in Roman literature of :— Suetonius, Seneca, Propertius, Cassiodorus, Claudian, Ennius, Phaedrus, Fronto, Cyprian.

6. Into what periods would you divide the history of Roman Literature in tracing its development.

7. Who are the authors of the following works :—De Consolatione Philosophiae, the Golden Ass, De Re Rustica, Noctes Atticae, Carmen Seculare, Dialogus de claris Oratoribus, the Nuptials of Peleus and Thetis, Thebais ?

THIRD YEAR.

ROMAN HISTORY.

THE MAKING OF ROME.

1. Give a brief account of the early inhabitants of Italy.

2. Describe (a) the early government of Rome ; and (b) the reforms in the constitution introduced by Servius Tullius.

3. Name the laws passed to establish political equality between the patricians and plebeians, giving the leading provisions of each.

4. Write brief notes on the following topics : (a) the Etruscans and their civilisation ; (b) Roma quadrata ; (c) origin of the plebeians ; (d) the traditional history of Rome ; (e) the war with Porsenna.

B.A. LATIN.

(A) JUVENAL.

1. Translate and comment on words or phrases italicised :

(a) Ex quo *Deucalion* nimbis tollentibus aequor
Navigio *montem* ascendit *sortesque poposcit*,
Paulatimque anima caluerunt mollia saxa,
Quidquid agunt homines, votum, timor, ira, voluptas,
Gaudia, discursus, nostri *farrago* libelli est.

(b) Et quoniam coepit Graecorum mentio, transi
Gymnasia atque audi facinus *maioris abollae :*
Stoicus occidit Baream delator, amicum
Discipulumque senex ripa nutritus in illa,
Ad quam *Gorgonei* delapsa est pinna *caballi !*

(c) Hic *novus Arpinas*, ignobilis et modo Romae
Municipalis eques, galeatum ponit ubique
Praesidium attonitis et in omni moute laborat.
Tantum igitur muros intra toga contulit *illi*
Nominis ac tituli, *quantum vix Leucade* quantum
Thessaliae campis Octavius abstulit udo
Caedibus assiduis gladio.

(d) Unus *Pellaeo iuveni* non sufficit orbis :
Aestuat infelix angusto limite mundi,
Ut *Gyari* clausus scopulis parvaque Seripho :
Cum tamen a *figulis* munitam intraverit urbem,
Sarcophago contentus erit.

(e) Nempe hoc indocti, quorum praecordia nullis
Interdum aut levibus videas flagrantia causis :
Quantulacumque adeo est occasio, sufficit irae.
Chrysippus non dicet idem nec mite *Thaletis*
Ingenium dulcique *senex* vicinus Hymetto,
Qui partem acceptae saeva inter vincla cicutae
Accusatori *nollet* dare.

2. Translate and write brief notes on the following :

(a) assiduo ruptae lectore columnae.

(b) haec ego non credam Venusina digna lucerna.

(c)   Quippe ille Deis auctoribus ultor
patris erat caesi media inter pocula.

(d)   Creditur olim
velificatus Athos, et quidquid Graecia mendax
audet in historia.

(*e*) quando maior avaritiae patuit sinus ?

(*f*) Libera si dentur populo suffragia, quis tam
perditus, ut dubitet Senecam praeferre Neroni.

(*g*) Et tamen, ut longe repetas longeque revolvas
nomen, ab infami gentem deducis asylo.

(*h*) Ennosigaeum: magnus auruncae alumnus:
stemmata: tunica molesta:. bulla.

(B) CICERO, TUSCULAN DISPUTATIONS.

3. Translate and comment on :

(*a*) Dicaearchum vero cum Aristoxeno aequali et condiscipulo suo
doctos sane homines, omittamus, quorum alter ne condoluisse quidem
umquam videtur, qui animum se habere non sentiat. alter ita delectatur
suis cantibus, ut eos etiam ad haec transferre conetur.   Harmoniam autem ex intervallis sonorum nosse possumus, quorum varia conpositio etiam
harmonias efficit plures, membrorum vero situs et figura corporis vacans
animo quam possit harmoniam efficere non video.   Sed hic quidem, quamvis eruditus sit, sicut est, haec magistro concedat Aristoteli, canere ipse
doceat ; bene enim illo Graecorum proverbio praecipitur :

quam quisque norit artem, in hoc se exerceat.

(*b*) Quid ? illa tandem num leviora censes, quae declarant inesse
in animis hominum divina quaedam ? quae si cernerem quem ad modum
nasci possent, etiam quem ad modum interirent viderem.   Nam sanguinem
bilem pituitam, ossa nervos venas, omnem denique membrorum et totius
corporis figuram videor posse dicere unde concreta et quo modo facta sint :
animum ipsum—si nihil esset in eo nisi id, ut per eum viveremus, tam natura putarem hominis vitam sustentari quam vitis, quam arboris . haec
enim etiam dicimus vivere. Item, si nihil haberet animus hominis, nisi
ut adpeteret aut fugeret, id quoque esset ei commune cum bestiis.

(*c*) Vetat enim dominans ille in nobis deus iniussu hinc non suo
demigrare ; cum vero causam iustam deus ipse dederit, ut tunc Socrati
nunc Catoni, saepe multis, ne ille medius fidius vir sapiens laetus ex his
tenebris in lucem illam excesserit, nec tamen illa vincla carceris ruperit—
leges enim vetant—, sed tanquam a magistratu aut ab aliqua potestate
legitima, sic a deo evocatus atque emissus exierit.   Tota enim philosopho-
rum vita, ut ait idem, commentatio mortis est.

(*d*) Sed plena errorum sunt omnia.   Trahit Hectorem ad currum reli-
gatum Achilles : lacerari eum et sentire, credo, putat.   Ergo hic ulciscitur,
ut quidem sibi videtur ; at illa sicut acerbissimam rem maeret :

Vidi, videre quod me passa aegerrume,

Hectorem curru quadriiugo raptarier.

Quem Hectorem, aut quam diu ille erit Hector? Melius Accius ec
aliquando sapiens Achilles :

Immo enimvero corpus Priamo reddidi Hectorem abstuli.
Non igitur Hectora traxisti, sed corpus, quod fuerat Hectoris.

4. Scan the following lines :

    (*a*) Di faciles nocitura toga nocitura petuntur.

    (*b*) Eloquio sed uterque perit orator utrumque.

    (*c*) Brachia Vulcanus Liparaea nigra taberna.

    (*d*) Quam quisque norit artem in hac se exerceat.

    (*e*) Haec omnia vidi inflammari.

FOURTH YEAR.

LATIN COMPOSITION AND TRANSLATION AT SIGHT

Tuesday, April 5th :—Afternoon, 2 to 5.

I.

I had barely seen our friend Furnius, and was not able to talk to him
or hear his news without inconvenience to myself, being, as I am, in a great
hurry, indeed actually on the march, and with troops already gone on in
advance, but I could not let the opportunity pass of writing you a letter
and getting him to convey it, and with it my thanks : though I have
done this already many times, and it seems to me I shall have to do so
many times more, so well do you deserve this from me. I must particularly request that since I trust shortly to come to the neighbourhood of
Rome, I may see you there to avail myself of your judgment, your influence, your position, and your assistance in all that concerns me. To return
to the point : excuse this hurry and the shortness of my letter : anything
further you will be able to hear from Furnius.

II.

Cyrenaici non omni malo aegritudinem effici censent, sed insperato et
necopinato malo. Est id quidem non mediocre ad aegritudinem augen-
dam ; videntur enim omnia repentina graviora. ex hoc et illa inre laudantur :   •

    Ego cum genui, tum morituros scivi et ei rei sustuli.

    Praeterea ad Troiam cum misi ob defendendam Graeciam,

    Scibam me in mortiferum bellum, non in epulas mittere.

Haec igitur praemeditatio futurorum malorom lenit corum adventum,
quae venientia longe ante videris. Itaque apud Euripidem a Theseo dicta
laudantur ; licet enim. ut saepe facimus, in Latinum illa convertere :

    Nam qui haec audita a docto meminissem viro,

    futuras mecum commentabar miserias :

    aut mortem acerbam aut exsili maestam fugam

aut semper aliquam molem meditabar mali,
ut, si qua invecta diritas casu foret,
ne me inparatum cura laceraret repens.

Quod autem Theseus a docto se audisse dicit, id de se ipso loquitur
Euripides ; nerat enim auditor Anaxagorae, quem ferunt nuntiata morte
filii dixisse sciębam me genuisse mortalem.   Quae vox declarat iis esse
haec acerba, quibus non fuerint cogitata.   Ergo id quidem non dubium
quin omnia, quae mala putentur, sint inprovisa graviora.

FOURTH YEAR LATIN.

Summer Readings.

Virgil : *Aeneid* I.-III.

Thursday, April 7th :—2 to 4 p.m.

I. Translate :—

(1) his commota fugam Dido sociosque parabat.
conveniunt, quibus aut odium crudele tyranni
aut metus acer erat ; naves, quae forte paratae,
corripiunt onerantque auro. portantur avari
Pygmalionis opes pelago ; dux femina facti.
devenere locos, ubi nunc ingentia cernis
moenia surgentemque novae Karthaginis arcem,
mercatique solum, facti de nomine Byrsam,
taurino quantum possent circumdare tergo.

(2)   Heu nihil invitis fas quemquam fidere divis !
ecce trahebatur passis Priameia virgo
crinibus a templo Cassandra adytisque Minervae,
ad caelum tendens ardentia lumina frustra,
lumina, nam teneras arcebant vincula palmas.
non tulit hanc speciem furiata mente Coroebus,
et sese medium iniecit periturus in agmen.
consequimur cuncti et densis incurrimus armis.
hic primum ex alto delubri culmine telis
nostrorum obruimur, oriturque miserrima caedes
armorum facie et Graiarum errore iubarum.

(3)   Postquam altum tennere rates, nec iam amplius ullae
adparent terrae, caelum undique et undique pontus,
tum mihi caeruleus supra caput adstitit imber,
noctem hiememque ferens, et inhorruit unda tenebris.
continuo venti volvunt mare magnaque surgunt
aequora ; dispersi iactamur gurgite vasto ;
involvere diem nimbi et nox humida caelum
abstulit : ingeminant abruptis nubibus ignes.

excutimur cursu et caecis erramus in undis.
ipse diem noctemque negat discernere caelo,
nec meminisse viae media Palinurus in unda.
tris adeo incertos caeca caligine soles
erramus pelago, totidem sine sidere noctes.
quarto terra die primum se attollere tandem
visa, aperire procul montes ac volvere fumum.
vela cadunt, remis insurgimus; haud mora, nautae
adnixi torquent spumas et caerula verrunt.

II. Translate and comment upon :—

(1) His ego nec metas rerum nec tempora pono,
Imperium sine fine dedi.

(2) O fortunati quorum iam moenia surgunt !

3) Urbem quam statuo vestra est; subducite naves;
Tros Tyriusque mihi nullo discrimine agetur.

(4)　　　　　timeo Danaos et dona ferentes.

(5) sacra suosque tibi commendat Troia Penates ;
hos cape fatorum comites, his moenia quaere
magna, pererrato statues quae denique ponto.

(6)　　　　　Fuimus Tioes, fuit Ilium et ingens
Gloria Teucrorum.

(7)　　　　　Sensit medios delapsus in hostes.

(8) Non tali auxilio nec defensoribus istis
Tempus eget.

(9)　　Ergo insperata tandem tellure potiti
lustramurque Iovi votisque incendimus aras,
Actiaque Iliacis celebramus litora Indis.

(10) Aeneadasque meo nomen de nomine fingo.

HISTORY OF THE ROMAN EMPIRE.

4 TO 5 P.M.

(Not more than four questions to be attempted.)

1. To what main causes do you attribute the transformation of the Republic into the Empire ?

2. Indicate the various steps by which Augustus secured his position as Emperor at Rome.

3. Characterize the main features of the Reign of Tiberius.

4. Describe the career and character of Seneca

5. Give a brief account of the events of the year A.D. 69, and estimate their significance.

HONOURS LATIN.

———

THIRD AND FOURTH YEARS—HONOURS LATIN.

CICERO *Pro Cluentio.*

FRIDAY, 1ST APRIL, 1898.

Three hours allowed.

I. Translate :

(a) Iam vero quod iter Romam eius mulieris fuisse existimatia ? quod ego propter vicinitatem Aquinatium et Fabraternorum ex multis audivi et comperi : quos concursus in his oppidis ? quantos et virorum et mulierum gemitus esse factos ? mulierem quamdam Larino atque illam usque a mari supero Romam proficisci cum magno comitatu et pecunia, quo facilius circumvenire iudicio capitis atque opprimere filium posset. Nemo erat illorum, paene dicam, quin expiandum illum locum esse arbitraretur, quacumque illa iter fecisset : nemo quin terram ipsam violari, quae mater est omnium, vestigiis consceleratae matris putaret. Itaque nullo in oppido consistendi potestas ei fuit : nemo ex tot hospitibus inventus est qui non contagionem aspectus fugeret. Nocti se potins ac solitudini quam ulli aut urbi aut hospiti committebat. Nunc vero quid agat, quid moliatur, quid denique cotidie cogitet quem ignorare nostrorum putat ? Quos appellarit, quibus pecuniam promiserit, quorum fidem pretio labefactare conata sit tenemus. Quin etiam nocturna sacrificia, quae putat occultiora esse, sceleratasque eius preces et nefaria vota cognovimus : quibus illa etiam deos immortalcs de suo scelere testatur neque intellegit pietate et religione et iustis precibus deorum mentes, non contaminata superstitione neque ad scelus perficiendum caesis hostiis poss? placari. Cuius ego furorem atque crudelitatem deos immortales a suis aris atque templis aspernatos esse confido.

Add a critical note on the sentence beginning *mulierem quamdam Larino.*

(b) Hic profertur id, quod iudicinm appellari non oportet, P. Septimio Scaevolae litem eo nomine esse aestimatam. Cuius rei quae consuetudo sit, quoniam apud homines peritissimos dico, pluribus verbis docere non debeo. Numquam enim ea diligentia, quae solet adhiberi in ceteris iudiciis, eadem reo damnato adhibita est. In litibus aestimandis fere indices aut, quod sibi eum, quem semel condemnarunt, inimicum putant esse, si quae in eum lis capitis illata est, non admittunt, aut, quod se perfunctos iam esse arbitrantur, cum de reo iudicarunt, negligentius attendunt cetera. Itaque et maiestatis absoluti sunt permulti, quibus damnatis de pecuniis

repetundis lites maiestatis essent aestimatae, et hoc cotidie fieri videmus, ut
reo damnato de pecuniis repetundis, ad quos pervenisso pecunias in litibus
aestimandis statutum sit, eos iidem indices absolvant : quod cum fit, non
indicia rescinduntur, sed hoc statuitur, aestimationem litium non esse
iudicium. Scaevola condemnatus est aliis criminibus, frequentissimis
Apuliae testibus. Omni contentione pugnatum est, uti lis haec capitis
aestimaretur. Quae res si rei iudicatae pondus habuisset, ille postea vel
iisdem vel aliis inimicis reus hac lege ipsa factus esset.

2. Translate and comment on :—

(1) Per illam L. Sullae vim atque victoriam Larinum in summo timore
omnium cum armatis advolavit.

(2) Id cum Oppianicus sciret—neque enim erat obscurum,—intellige-
bat Habito mortuo bona eius omnia ad matrem esse ventura : quae ab sese
postea aneta pecunia maiore praemio, orbata filio minore periculo necare-
tur.

(3) Adducti indices sunt non modo potuisse honeste ab eo reum con-
demnari, qui non perpetuo sedisset, sed, aliud si is iudex nihil scisset, nis
quae praeiudicia de eo facta esse constarent, audire praeterea nihil de-
buisse.

(4) Quid ? Albiana pecunia vestigiisne nobis odoranda est an ad ipsum enhile vobis ducibus venire possumus ?

(5) Hic indices ridere, stomachari atque acerbe ferre patronus, causam
sibi eripi et se cetera de illo loco *Respicite, iudices*, non posse dicere : nec
quidquam propius est factum, quam ut illum persequeretur et collo obtorto
ad subsellia reduceret, ut reliqua posset perorare.

(6) In omnibus legibus, quibus exceptum est, de quibus causis au
magistratum capere non liceat aut iudicem legi aut alterum accusare,
haec ignominiae causa praetermissa est. Timoris enim causam, non vitae
poenam in illa potestate esse voluerunt.

(7) Illi non hoc recusabant, ne ea lege accusarentur, qua nunc Habitus
accusatur, quae tunc erat Sempronia, nunc est Cornelia : intelligebant
enim ea lege equestrem ordinem non teneri, sed ne nova lege adligarentur
laborabant. Habitus ne hoc quidem umquam recusavit, quo minus vel ea
lege rationem vitae suae redderet, qua non teneretur.

(8) Tum est condemnatus, cum essex iudex quaestionis. Non modo
causae, sed ne legi quidem quidquam per tribunum plebis laxamenti datum est.

(9) Sed errat vehementer, si quis in orationibus nostris, quas in iudiciis
habuimus, auctoritates nostras consignatas se habere arbitratur. Omnes
enim illae causarum ac temporum sunt, non hominum ipsorum aut patro-
norum.

(10) Nam ut haec a i me causa delata est, qui leges eas, ad quas adhibemur et in quibus versamur, nosse deberem, dixi Habito statim eo capite : qui coisset quo quis condemnaretur, illum esse liberum : teneri autem nostrum oidinem. Atque ille me orare atque obsecrare coepit, ut ne sese lege defenderem.

3. Give the meaning ot each of the following words and phrases :—*ludec quaestionis, heredes secundi, sequester, scelus Oppianici, harenariae, rumusculos aucupari, de statu suo declinare, verbis conceptis peierare, circumscriptiones adulescentium, mittere in consilium, praevaricari accusationi, offensiones iudiciorum, subscriptio, prima octio, sedulo facere, in aerarios referre, decuriones, obsignatores, importunus, ambitus, contio, caput, salus, communia invidiae pericula*.

4. Criticise Cicero's account of the Scamander incident, and state what you consider to be the true version of what occurred.

5. *Longum est de singulorum virtute ita dicere ; quae quia cognita sunt vb omnibus verborum ornamenta non quaerunt.* How may this sentence be emended? Refer to and, if possible, illustrate any of the common sources of corruption in our MSS.

B.A. HONOURS—LATIN.

TACITUS, *Dialogus;* QUINTILIAN, Book X ; CICERO, *de Oratore,* Book I.

MONDAY, 4TH APRIL, 1898.

Three hours allowed.

1. Translate :

(*a*) Ego vero omnem eloquentiam omnesque eius partes sacras et venerabiles puto, nec solum cothurnum vestrum aut heroici carminis sonum, sed lyricorum quoque iucunditatem et clegorum lascivias et iamborum amaritudinem et epigrammatum lusus et quamcumque aliam speciem eloquentia habeat, anteponendam ceteris aliarum artium studiis credo. Sed tecum mihi, Materne, res est, quod, cum natura tua in ipsam arcem eloquentiae ferat, errare mavis et summa adepturus in levioribus subsistis. Ut, si in Graecia natus esses, ubi ludicras quoque artes exercere honestum est, ac tibi Nicostrati robur ac vires dii dedissent, non paterer immanes illos et ad pugnam natos lacertos levitate iaculi aut iactu disci vanescere, sic nunc te ab auditoriis et theatris in forum et ad causas et ad vera proelia voco, cum praesertim ne ad illud quidem confugere possis, quod plerisque patrocinatur, tamquam minus obnoxium sit offendere poetarum quam oratorum studium : effervescit enim vis pulcherrimae naturae uae, nec pro amico aliquo, sed, quod periculosius est, pro Catone offendis.

(b) Sed silentium et secessus et undique liber animus ut sunt maxime optanda, ita non semper possuut contingere, ideoque non statim, si quid obstrepet, abiciendi codices erunt et deplorandus dies ; ve rum incommodis repugnandum et hic faciendus usus, ut omnia quae impedient vincat intentio ; quam si tota mente in opus ipsum direxeris, nihil eorum, quae oculis vel auribus incursant, ad animum perveniet. An vero frequenter etiam fortuita hoc cogitatio praestat, ut obvios non videamus et itinere deerremus : non consequemur idem, si et voluerimus? Non est indulgen· dum causis desidiae. Nam si nonnisi refecti, nonnisi hilares, nonnisi omnibus aliis curis vacantes studendum existimarimus, semper erit propter quod nobis ignoscamus. Quare in turba, itinere, conviviis etiam faciat sibi cogitatio ipsa secretum. Quid alioqui fiet, cum in medio foro, tot circumstantibus iudiciis, iurgiis, fortuitis etiam clamoribus, erit subito continua oratione dicendum, si particulas, quas ceris mandamus, nisi in solitudine reperire non possumus ?

(c) ' Dicam equidem, quoniam institui, petamque a vobis,' inquit ' ne has meas ineptias efferatis ; quamquam moderabor ipse, ne ut quidam magister atque artifex, sed quasi unus e togatorum numero atque ex forensi usu homo mediocris neque omnino rudis videar non ipse a me aliquid promisisse, sed fortuito in sermonem vestrum incidisse. equidem cum peterem magistratum, solebam in prensando dimittere a me Scaevolam, cum ita ei dicerem, me velle esse ineptum, id erat, petere blandius, quod, nisi inepte fieret, bene non posset fieri ;—hunc autem hominem esse unum ex omnibus, quo praesente ego ineptum esse me minime vellem—quem quidem nunc mearum ineptiarum testem et spectatorem fortuna constituit : nam quid est ineptius, quam de dicendo dicere, cum ipsum dicere numquam sit non ineptum, nisi cum est necessarium ? ' ' perge vero, Crasse,' inquit Mucins ; ' istam enim culpam, quam vereris, ego praestabo.'

2. Translate and comment very briefly on :—

(1) Nam et Secundo purus et pressus et, in quantum satis erat, pro_ fluens sermo non defuit et Aper omni eruditione imbutus contemnebat potins literas quam nesciebat, tamquam maiorem industriae et laboris gloriam habiturus, si ingenium eius nullis alienarum artium adminiculis inniti videretur.

(2) Licet haec ipsa et quae deinceps dicturus sum, aures tuae, Materne, respuant : cui bono est, si apud te Agamemnon aut Iason diserte loquitur? quis ideo domum defensus et tibi obligatus redit? quis Saleium nostrum, egregium poetam vel, si hoc honorificentius est, praeclarissimum vatem, deducit aut salutat aut prosequitur ?

(3) In paucissimos sensus et augustas sententias detrudunt eloqucntiam velut expulsam regno suo, ut quae olim omnium artium domina pulcherrimo comitatu pectora implebat, nunc circumcisa et amputata, sine apparatu, sine honore, paene dixerim sine ingenuitate, quasi una ex sordidissimis artificiis discatur.

12

(4) Licet tamen nobis in digressionibus uti vel historico nonnumquam nitore, dum in his, de quibus erit quaestio, meminerimus, non athletarum toris sed militum lacertis *opus* esse ; nec versicolorem illam, qua Demetrius Phalereus dicebatur uti, vestem bene ad forensem pulverem facere.

(5) Simonides, tenuis alioqui, sermone proprio et iucunditate quadam, commendari potest ; praecipua tamen eius in commovenda miseratione virtus, ut quidam in hac eum parte omnibus eius operis auctoribus praeferant.

(6) Tractavit etiam omnem fere studiorum materiam. Nam et orationes eius et poemata et epistulae et dialogi feruntur. In philosophia parum diligens, egregius tamen vitiorum insectator fuit. Multae in eo claraeque sententiae, multa etiam morum gratia legenda ; sed in eloquendo corrupta pleraque atque eo perniciossisma, quod abundant dulcibus vitiis Velles eum suo ingenio dixisse, alieno iudicio.

(7) Ideoque qui horride atque incomposite quidlibet illud frigidum et inane extulerunt, antiquis se pares credunt ; qui carent cultu atque sententiis, Attici sunt scilicet ; qui praecisis conclusionibus obscuri, Sallustium atque Thucydidem superant ; tristes ac ieiuni Pollionem aemulantur ; otiosi et supini, si quid modo longius circumduxerunt, iurant ita Ciceronem locuturum fuisse.

(8) Quod vero in extrema oratione quasi tuo iure sumpsisti, oratorem in omnis sermonis disputatione copiosissime versari posse, id, nisi hic in tuo regno essemus, non tulissem multisque praeissem, qui aut interdicto tecum contenderent aut te ex iure manum consertum vocarent, quod in alienas possessiones tam temere inruisses.

(9) Est enim finitimus oratori poëta, numeris astrictior paulo, verborum autem licentia liberior, multis vero ornandi generibus socius ac paene par ; in hoc quidem certe prope idem, nullis ut terminis circumscribat aut definiat ius suum, quo minus ei liceat eadem illa facultate et copia vagari qua velit.

(10) Tum Cotta ' quoniam id, quod difficillimum nobis videbatur, ut omnino de his rebus, Crasse, loquerere, adsecuti sumus, de reliquo iam nostra culpa fuerit, si te, nisi omnia, quae percontati erimus, explicaris, dimiserimus.' ' de eis, credo, rebus,' inquit Crassus ' ut in cretionibus scribi solet : QUIBUS SCIAM POTEROQUE.'

3. Write briefly on the following topics :

(1) Quintilian as a literary critic.

(2) The question of the authorship and date of the Dialogus.

(3) The prose of the Silver Age as compared with the Latinity of Cicero.

B. A. HONOURS.

PLAUTUS AND CATULLUS.

SATURDAY, APRIL 9TH :—AFTERNOON, 2 TO 5.

1. Translate Catullus LXVI, 39-58 :

Invita, o regina, tuo de vertice cessi,
    Invita : adiuro teque tuomque caput,
Digna ferat quod siquis inaniter adiurarit :
    Sed qui se ferro postulet esse parem ?
Ille quoque eversus mons est, quem maximum in orbi
    Progenies Thiæ clara supervehitur,
Cum Medi peperere novom mare, cumque iuventus
    Per medium classi barbara navit Athon.
Quid facient crines, cum ferro talia cedant ?
    Iuppiter, ut Chalybon omne genus pereat,
Et qui principio sub terra quaerere venas
    Institit ac ferri frangere duritiem !
Abiunctae paulo ante comae mea fata sorores
    Lugebant, cum se Memnonis Aethiopis
Vnigena (inpellens nictantibus aera pennis)
    Obtulit Arsinoes Locridos ales equos,
Isque per aetherias me tollens avolat umbras
    Et Veneris casto collocat in gremio.
Ipsa suum Zephyritis eo famulum legarat,
    Graia Canopieis incola litoribus.

2. Plautus Rudens 1153-1170 :

DAE. Loquere nunciam, puella. Gripe, animum aduorte ac tace.
PA.   Sunt crepundia. DAE. Ecca uideo. GR. Perii in primo proelio :
    Mane : ne ostenderis. DAE. Qua facie sunt ? responde ex ordine.
PA.   Ensiculust aureolus primum litteratus. DAE. Dicedum,
    In eo ensiculo litterarum quid est ? PA. Mei nomen patris.
    Post altrinsecust securicula ancipes, itidem aurea,
    Litterata : ibi matris nomen in securiculast. DAE. Mane :
    Dic in ensiculo quid nomen est paternum ? PA. Daemones.
DAE. Di inmortales, ubi loci sunt spes meae ? GR. Immo edepol meae ?
TR.   Pergite, opsecro, continuo. GR. Placide, aut in malam crucem.
DAE. Loquere matris nomen hic quid in securicula siet.
PA.   Daedalis. DAE. Di me seruatum cupiunt. GR. At me perditum.

Dae. Filiam meam esse hanc oportet, Gripe.   Gr. Sit per me quidem.
     Qui te di omnes perdant, qui me hodie oculis uidisti tuis,
     Meque adeo scelestum, qui non circumspexi centiens
     Prius, me nequis inspectaret, quam rete extraxi ex aqua.
Pa. Post sicilicula argenteola et duae conexae maniculae et
     Sucula.   Gr. Quin tu i dierecta cum sucula et cum porculis.

    3. What rules does Plautus observe with regard to the feet in Iambic senarii? Under what conditions does he allow hiatus?

    4. Name the metre of the following lines in the Rudens :
     Nec prope usquam hic quiden cultum agrum conspicor
     Nam hoc mihi nil laborist laborem hunc potiri
     Nec mani adseruntur neque illinc partem quisquam postulat
     Iam ubi liber ero igitur demum mi instruam agrum atque aedis,
         mancipia,
     Ille qui uocauit nullus uenit.   Admodum.
     Scan the above lines.

    5. What do you observe about the quantity of the following words in Plautus, comparing them with classical usage: es, fierent, aedibus, auctior, habet, ego, morte, frustra.

    6. Translate, adding a note where desirable :—

    (a) Rutilam ferox torosa ceruice quate iuham.

    (b) Saepe pater diuum templo]in fulgente reuisens.

    (c) Ubi iste post phaselus antea fuit
       Comata silua.

    (d) Sed tu insulsa male et¯molesta uiuis,
       per quam non licet esse neglegentem.

    (e)   Sed uereris inepta
       crura ponticuli axulis stantis in redivivis.

    (f) Sed non uidemus manticae quod in tergo est.

    (g) Cinge tempora floribus
       suaue olentis amaraci,
       flammeum cape laetus, huc
       huc ueni, nineo gercus
       luteum pede soccum.

    (h) Nil mihi tam ualde placeat, Rhamnusia urigo,
       quod temere inuitis suscipiatur eris.

    (i) Nil nimium studeo, Caesar, tibi uelle placere,
       nec scire utrum sis albus an ater homo.

7. Quote any parts you may remember of the poem beginning "vivamus, mea Lesbia" *or* the lament of Ariadne, beginning "sicine me patriis."

B.A. HONOURS.

TACITUS AND CICERO.

MONDAY, APRIL 11TH:—2 TO 5.

1. Translate:—

Inter quae nulla palam causa delapsum Camuloduni simulacrum Victoriae ac retro conuersum, quasi cederet hostibus. et feminae in furorem turbatae adesse exitium canebant, externosque fremitus in curia eorum auditos; consonuisse ululatibus theatrum visamque speciem in aestuario Tamesae subuersae coloniae: iam Oceanus cruento aspectu, dilabente aestu humanorum corporum effigies relictae, ut Britannis ad spem, ita ueteranis ad metum trahebantur. sed quia procul Suetonius aberat, petiuere a Cato Deciano procuratore auxilium. ille haud amplius quam ducentos sine iustis armis misit; et inerat modica militum manus. tutela templi freti et impedientibus qui occulti rebellionis conscii consilia turbabant, neque fossam aut uallum praeduxerunt, neque motis senibus et feminis iuuentus sola restitit; quasi media pace incauti multitudine barbarorum circumveniuntur, et cetera quidem impetu direpta aut incensa sunt: templum in quo se miles conglobaverat, biduo obsessum expugnatumque.

2. Translate:—

Sed quoniam tauta faex est in urbe, ut nihil tam'sit ἀκύθηρον quod non alieni venustum esse videatur, pugna, si me amas, nisi acuta ἀμφιβολία, nisi elegans ὑπερβολή, nisi παράγραμμα bellum, nisi ridiculum παρὰ, προσδοκίαν, nisi cetera, quae sunt a me in secundo libro DE ORATORE per Antonii personam disputata de ridiculis, ἔντεχνα et arguta apparebunt, ut sacramento contendas mea non esse. Nam de indiciis quod quereris, multo laboro minus. Trahantur per me pedibus omnes rei, sit vel Selins tam eloquens, ut possit probare se liberum: non laboro. Urbanitatis possessionem, amabo, quibusvis interdictis defendamus: in qua te unum metuo, contemno ceteros. Derideri te putas? Nunc demum intellego te sapere.

3. Translate, adding a brief note where necessary:—

(*a*) Melius fuit perisse illo interfecto (quod nunquam accidisset) quam haec videre.

(*b*) Parhedrum excita, ut hortum ipse conducat; sic holitorem ipsum commovebis. Helico nequissimus H S M dabat, nullo aprico horto, nullo emissario, nulla maceria, nulla casa. Iste nos tanta impensa derideat? Calface hominem, ut ego Mothonem ; itaque ut ab utro coronas.

(c) De diplomate, admiraris, quasi nescio cuius te flagitii insimularim.

(d) Num inepti nos fuerimus, si nos quoque Academiæ fecerimus.

(e) Id autem ex eo, ut opinor, quod antecesserat Statius, ut prandium nobis videret.

(f) Lucretii poemata ut scribis ita sunt, multis luminibus ingenii, multae tamen artis.

(g) Neque autem ego ita demens, ut me sempiternae gloriae per eum commendari velim, qui non ipse quoque in me commendando propriam ingenii gloriam consequatur.

4. Translate :—

(a) Quae oblitterari non sinebat Capito Cossutianus, praeter animum ad flagitia praecipitem iniquus Thraseae, quod auctoritate eius concidisset, iuvantis Cilicum legatos, dum Capitonem repetundarum interrogant.

(b) Habitu et ore ad exprimendam imaginem honesti exercitus.

(c) Nihil metuens an dissimulando metu.

(d) Iam Spartacum et vetera mala rumoribus ferente populo.

(e) Et cum Ostorius nihil audivisse pro testimonio dixisset, adversis testibus creditum.

(f) Senecam adoriuntur tanquam ingentes et privatum modum evectas opes adhuc augeret.

5. State very briefly what mention is made in these books of Tacitus, of Memmius Regulus, Torquatus Silanus, Lucan, Cocceius Nerva, C. Cassius, Ostorius Scapula, P. Egnatius, Pedonius Secundus, Pallas, Polyclitus, L. Mummius, Rubellius Plautus, Faenius Rufus.

6. Enumerate the villas of Cicero, showing in a rough map the position of each.

B.A. HONOURS.

FOR LATIN PROSE.

The sarcasms of the King soon galled the sensitive temper of the poet. D'Arnaud and D'Argens might, for the sake of a morsel of bread, be willing to bear the insolence of a master ; but Voltaire was of another order. He knew that he was a potentate as well as Frederic, that his European reputation, and his incomparable power of covering whatever he hated with ridicule, made him an object of dread even to the leaders of armies and the rulers of nations. In truth, of all the intellectual weapons which have ever been wielded by man, the most terrible was the mockery of Voltaire. Bigots and tyrants, who had never been moved by the wailing and cursing of millions, turned pale at his name. Principles unassailable by reason, principles which had withstood the fiercest attacks of power, the most valuable truths, the most generous sentiments, the noblest and most graceful images, the purest reputations, the most august institutions, began to look mean and loathsome as soon as that withering smile was turned upon them. To every opponent however strong in his cause and his talents, in his station and his character, who ventured to encounter the great scoffer, might be addressed the caution which was given of old to the Archangel :—

> I forewarn thee, shun
> his deadly arrow, neither vainly hope
> to be invulnerable in those bright arms,
> though temper'd heavenly ; for that fatal dint,
> save Him who reigns above, none can resist.

HONOURS IN CLASSICS.

PROPERTIUS AND HORACE.

1. Translate :—

    (*a*) Quicunque ille fuit, puerum qui pinxit Amorem,
        nonne putas miras hunc habuisse manus ?
    Hic primum vidit, sine sensu vivere amantes,
        et levibus curis magna perire bona.
    Idem non frustra ventosas addidit alas,
        fecit et humano corde volare deum :
    scilicet alterna quoniam iactamur in unda,
        nostraque non ullis permanet aura locis.

    (*b*) Clausus ab umbroso qua ludit Pontus Averno,
        fumida Baiarum stagna tepentis aquae,
    qua iacet et Troiae tubicen Misenus arena,
        et sonat Herculeo structa labore via:
    hic, ubi, mortales dextra cum quaereret urbes,
        cymbala Thebano concrepuere deo :
    (at nunc, invisae magno cum crimine Baiae,
        quis deus in vestra constitit hostis aqua ?)
    his pressus Stygias vultum demersit in undas ;
        errat et in vestro spiritus ille lacu.

(c) Vincit Roma fide Phoebi, dat femina poenas :
   sceptra per Ionias fracta vehuntur aquas.
At pater Idalio miratus Caesar ab astro,
   "Sum deus : en nostri sanguinis ista fides."
Prosequitur cantu Triton, omnesque marinae
   plauserunt circa libera signa deae.
Illa petit Nilum cymba male nixa fugaci,
   hoc unum, iusso non moritura die.
Di melius ! Quantus mulier foret una triumphus.
   ductus erat per quas ante Iugurtha vias !
Actins hinc traxit Phoebus monumenta, quod eius
   una decem vicit missa sagitta rates.

2. (a) Give the various interpretations of *sine sensu*, and *humano corde* ?

(b) What is Hertzburg's reading and interpretation of the first two line lines of the second extract ? Remark on the topography of the place here mentioned. Comment further on the different readings and interpretations of the last four lines.

3. Translate and write explanatory notes on the following lines :

(a) Callimachi Manes et Coi sacra Philetae,
   In vestrum, quaeso, me sinite ire nemus.

(b) O prima infelix fingenti terra Prometheo !
   Ille parum cauti pectoris egit opus :
   Corpora disponens mentem non vidit in arte.

(c) In alis, et unde genus, qui sint mihi, Tulle, Penates,
   Quaeris pro nostra semper amicitia,

(d) Surge, anima, ex humili iam carmine sumite vires,
   Pirides : magni nunc erit oris opus.
   Iam negat Euphrates equitem post terga tueri
   Parthorum, et Crassos se tenuisse dolet ;
   India quin, Auguste, tuo dat colla triumpho,
   Et domus intactae te tremit Arabiae.

(e) Paete, quid aetatem numeras ? quid cara natanti
   Mater in ore tibi est ? non habet unda deos.
   Nam tibi nocturnis ad saxa ligata procellis
   Omnia detrito vincula fune cadunt.

(f) Nunc spolia in templo tria condita : causa Feretri,
   Omine quod certo dux ferit ense ducem.
   Seu quia victa suis humeris haec arma ferebant,
   Hinc Feretri dicta est ara superba Jovis.

4. Translate and comment on words italicised :—

(a) *Martiis* caelebs quid agam *Kalendis,*
quid velint flores et acerra turis
plena miraris, positusque carbo in,
caespite vivo,

docte sermones utriusque linguae !
Voveram dulces epulas et *album*
Libero caprum, prope funeratus
arboris ietu.

Hic dies, anno redeunte, festus
corticem adstrictum pice demovebit
amphorae, fumum bibere institutae
consule Tullo.

Sume, Maecenas, *cyathos amici*
sospitis centum ; et vigiles lucernas
perfer in lucem. Procul omnis esto
clamor et ira.

(b) Quantum distet ab *Inacho*
Codrus, pro patria non timidus mori,)
narras, et genus *Aeaci*
et pugnata sacro bella sub Ilio ;
quo Chium pretio cadum
mercemur, quis aquam temperet ignibus,
quo praebente domum, et quota
Pelignis caream frigoribus, taces.

(c) Non incisa notis marmora publicis,
per quae spiritus et vita redis bonis
post mortem ducibus, non *celeres fugae*
reiectaeque retrorsum Hannibalis minae,
non incendia Carthaginis impiae,
eius, *qui* domita nomen ab Africa
lucratus rediit, clarius indicant
laudes, quam *Calabrae* Pierides. Neque,
si chartae *sileant,* quod bene feceris,
mercedem tuleris.

HONOURS IN CLASSICS.

TERENCE, *Phormio*, and VIRGIL, *Aeneid*, IV.-VI.

I.

1. Translate:

DEMIPHO. GETA. HEGIO. CRATINUS. CRITO.

DE. Quanta me cura et sollicitudine adficit
gnatus, qui me et se hisce inpedivit nuptiis?
neque mi in conspectum prodit ; ut saltem sciam,
quid de hac re dicat, quidve sit sententiae.
Abi, vise redieritne iam an nondum domum.
GE. Eo. DE. Videtis quo in loco res haec siet.
Quid ago? dic, Hegio. HE. Ego? Cratinum censeo,
si tibi videtur. DE. Dic, Cratine. CRA. Méne vis?
DE Te. CRA. Ego quae in rem tuam sint, éa velim facias : mihi
sic hoc videtur. Quod te absente hic filius
egit, restitui in integrum aequom est ac bonum :
et id impetrabis. Dixi. DE. Dic, nunc, Hégio.
HE. Ego sédulo hunc dixisse credo : vérum ita est,
quot homines tot senténtiae : suus cuique mos.
Mihi non videtur, quod sit factum légibus,
rescindi posse : et turpe inceptu est. DE. Dic, Crito.
CRI. Ego amplius deliberandum cénseo :
res magna est. HE. Nunquid nos vis ? DE. Fecistis probe :
incértior sum multo quam dudum. GE. Negant
redisse. DE. Frater ést exspectandus mihi :
is quod mihi dederit de hac re consilium, id sequar :
percontatum ibo ad portum, quoad se récipiat.
GE. At ego Antiphonem quaéram, ut quae acta hic sint sciat.
Sed eccum ipsum video in témpore huc se récipere.

2. Translate and comment on :

(*a*) Antipho me excruciat animi.

(*b*) Meditata mihi sunt omnia mea incommoda,
          erus si redierit.

(*c*) Di tibi omnes id quod es dignus duint.

(*d*) 'Quod res postilla monstra evenerunt mihi !
Intro iit in aedis ater alienus canis :
Anguis per inpluvium decidit de tegulis ;
Gallina cecinit ; interdixit hariolus ;
Haruspex vetuit; ante brumam autem novi
Negoti incipere.'

(*e*)   CH. Cedo quid postulat?
GE. Quid ? nimium quantum. CH. Quantum? dic.
                          GE. Si quis daret
Talentum magnum. DE. Immo malum hercle : ut nil pudet.

f) Quid fiat? est parasitus quidam Phormio,
    Homo confidens: qui illum di omnes perduint.

(*g*) Adeon rem redisse, ut qui mi consultum optima velit esse,
    Phaedria, patrem ut extimescam, ubi in mentem eius advent
        veniat!
    Quod ni fuissem incogitans, ita cum exspectarem, ut par fuit.

(*h*)   .   DE. Quid tua malum id re fert?
                            CH. Magni, Demipho.
    Non satis est tuom te officium fecisse, id si non fama adprobat:
    Volo ipsius quoque voluntate haec fieri, ne se erectam praedicet.

(*i*) Suasum: repudium: scibit: edepol: volup: extrarius: extranius:
faxit: eccum: hisce: scribam dicam: parasitus.

3. Determine the metre of passages in 1 and 2, (*b*), (*c*), (*d*), (*f*), (*g*)
and (*h*). Scan all the lines of (*g*), the third line of (*d*), and the last line of
(*h*).

II.

4. Translate and comment on:

(*a*) Principio delubra adeunt, pacemque per aras
    Exquirunt: mactant leotas de more bidentes
    Legiferae Cereri, Phoeboque, patrique Lyaeo;
    Iunoni ante omnes, cui vincla iugalia curae.
    Ipsa, tenens dextra pateram, pulcherrima Dido
    Candentis vaccae media inter cornua fundit;
    Aut ante ora deum pingues spatiatur ad aras,
    Instauratque diem donis, pecudumque reclusis
    Pectoribus inhians spirantia consulit exta.

(*b*) Iamque dies, ni fallor, adest, quem semper acerbum,
    Semper honoratum (sic di voluistis), habebo.
    Hunc ego, Gaetulis agerem si Syrtibus exsul,
    Argolicove mari deprensus, et urbe Mycenae,
    Annua vota tamen solemnesque ordine pompas
    Exsequerer, strueremque suis altaria donis.

(*c*) "Infelix, quae tanta animum dementia cepit?
    Non vires alias conversaque numina sentis?
    Cede deo." Dixitque et, proelia voce diremit.
    Ast illum fidi aequales, genua aegra trahentem,
    Iactantemque utroque caput, crassumque cruorem
    Ore eiectantem, mixtosque in sanguine dentes,
    Ducunt ad naves; galeamque ensemque vocati
    Accipiunt: palmam Entello taurumque relinquunt.

(d) Idem ter socios pura circumtulit unda,
 Spargens rore levi et ramo felicis olivae,
 Lustravitque viros, dixitque novissima verba.
 At pius Aeneas ingenti mole sepulcrum
 Imponit, suaque arma viro, remumque tubamque
 . Monte sub aerio ; qui nunc Misenus ab illo
 Dicitur, aeternumque tenet per saecula nomen.

(e) Pars in gramineis exercent membra palaestris,
 Contendunt ludo, et fulva luctantur arena ;
 Pars pedibus plaudunt choreas, et carmina dicunt :
 Nec non Threicius longa cum veste sacerdos
 Obloquitur numeris septem discrimina vocum ;
 Iamque eadem digitis, iam pectine pulsat eburno.
 Hic genus antiquum Teucri, pulcherrima proles,
 Magnanimi heroes, nati melioribus annis,
 Ilusque, Assaracusque, et Troiae Dardanus auctor.
 Arma procul currusque virum miratur inanes.

5. Write brief notes on the following :

(a)   pendent opera interrupta, minaeque
   Murorum ingentes, aequataque machina eaelo.

(b) Ille dies primus leti primusque malorum
   Causa fuit.

(c) Dat somnos adimitque et lumina morte resignat.

(d)   Sic deinde locutus,
   Colligere arma inhet, validisque incumbere remis,
   Obliquatque sinus in ventum, ac talia fatur.

(e) Excisum Euboicae latus ingens rupis in antrum,
   Quo lati ducunt aditus centum, ostia centum ;
   Unde ruunt totidem voces, responsa Sibyllae.

(f) Gnosius haec Rhadamanthus habit durissima regna,
   Castigatque auditque dolos ; subigitque fateri,
   Quae quis apud superos, furto laetatus inani,
   Distulit in seram commissa piacula mortem.

B. A. HONOURS.

COMPARATIVE PHILOLOGY AND LATIN

GENERAL PAPER.

SATURDAY, APRIL 9TH :—MORNING, 9 TO 12.

1. What are the two main divisions of the Indo-Germanic language, and what is the essential mark of distinction between the two groups ? What are the essential differences between this and the other great families of speech.

2. (a) Show by diagram the relation of the vowel sounds, and explain. (b) Give a table of the consonantal sounds of the Indo-Germanic language. (c) When both in Latin and Greek, do two successive vowels form a diphthong?

3. (a) Connect etymologically the following words with any corresponding Latin words : ἕπομαι, χειμών, θήρ, ἐλαχύς, ὀχέομαι, ἕζομαι, βαίνω, χήν, σπαίρω. (b) Compare and explain the following forms : mare, maria : sero, ἵημι : ῥῖγος, frigus : ἰός, virus : dico, δείκνυμι : iugum, ζυγόν : θυμός, fumus : libet, lubet; γένους, generis : ἄγετε, agite : novos, νέος : moenia, munire : ἵπποι, equi : κτείνω, κτέννω : ἄλλος, alius : πέντε, quinque : ἡδύς, suavis : centum, ἕκατον : τίθημι, facio : aurora, ἕως. Give the probable Indo-Germanic form when you can.

4. Explain the terms (giving examples), anaptyxis, compensation-lengthening, contraction, vowel-absorption, ablaut, rhotacismus.

5. Write briefly on (a) the early laws of accentuation of the Indo-Germanic, Greek and Latin languages; (b) Verner's Law : (c) Sonant vowels.

6. How do you account for the changes in the character of Roman Literature after the Augustan age ?

7. State briefly what you know of any six the following Roman writers:—Venantius Fortunatus,Valerius Maximus, Quintus Curtius, Spartianus, Sidonius Apollinaris, Sedulius, Petronius Arbiter, Prudentius, Orosius, Manilius, Lampridius, Lactantius, Ammianus Marcellinus, Avianus, Ausonius.

8. Describe in outline the division of the Empire into provinces under (a) Nero and (b) Diocletian.

9. Enumerate any of the measures of Pompey during his sole consulship.

10. Write a note on the following words and expressions : medius fidius, macte, assidui, heres ex dennce, familiam erciscere, quadruplator, tribus praerogativa, confarreatio, victoriatus, iustitium, digitis micare, cisium, endromis, harpe, myoparo, pergula, saliarem in modum coenare, sambuca, tensa, cacabus, caduceus, capsa, instaurare.

11. Write down the ancient names of Belgrade, Coblenz, Cologne, Gibraltar, Monaco, Saragossa, Seville, Strasbourg, Turin, Varnay, Vienna, Paris, Orleans.

12. Trace briefly the history of Judaea from the time of Pompey to that of the Emperor Hadrian.

MATHEMATICS AND NATURAL PHILOSOPHY.

SESSIONAL EXAMINATIONS.

FIRST YEAR.

GEOMETRY AND ARITHMETIC.

WEDNESDAY, APRIL 13TH :—MORNING, 9 TO 12.

1. Divide a straight line into two parts, so that the rectangle contained by the whole line and one part shall be equal to the square of the other.

   (a) If the length of the line be denoted by M, prove that one part is equal to $\dfrac{M(\sqrt{5}-1)}{2}$ and the other part to $\dfrac{M(3-\sqrt{5})}{2}$

2. If two chords of a circle intersect, the rectangle contained by the segments of the one shall be equal to the rectangle contained by the segments of the other.

3. If four straight lines be proportionals, the rectangle contained by the first and fourth shall be equal to that contained by the second and third.

4. Extract the square roots of .5, .05, .005 to three places of decimals.

5. In any circle, angles at the centre have the same ratio as the arcs on which they stand.

6. If two circles touch one another, the line which joins the centre of one circle to the point of contact must pass through the centre of the other.

7. If a gallon of water weigh 10 lbs. find the number of cubic centimetres it contains, assuming that a cubic inch of water weighs 252.5 grs.

8. Find the interest and discount on $1639 for $4\frac{3}{4}$ months at 6 3·19 per cent.

9. Inscribe an equilateral triangle in a given circle.

   (a) Tangents are drawn at the vertices of the equilateral triangle inscribed in a circle ; prove that the resulting figure is an equilateral triangle.

10. Divide a given straight line in a given ratio.

11. Describe a rectilineal figure which shall be equal to one and similar to another rectilineal figure.

12. Reduce 4 miles, 7 furlongs, 39 rods, 5 yards, 1 foot, 8 inches to inches, and show that the work is correct by changing it to miles, etc.

SESSIONAL EXAMINATIONS.

FIRST YEAR.

TRIGONOMETRY—ALGEBRA.

THURSDAY, APRIL 14TH :—MORNING, 9 TO 12.

(*Write the answers in books marked A, B and C respectively, to correspond to the questions.*)

A.

1. Prove the following relations :

(a) $\sin A \div 2 \sin B = \sin \dfrac{A + B}{2} \cos \dfrac{A - B}{2}$

(b) $\sin 2A = 2 \sin \dfrac{A}{8} \cos \dfrac{A}{8}$.

(c) $\dfrac{\sin \theta + \sin 2\theta + \sin 3\theta}{\cos \theta + \cos 2\theta + \cos 3\theta} = \tan 2\theta$.

(d) $\sin 40° + \cos 60° = 2 \sin 35° \cos 5°$.

2. (a) Derive and explain the formula :

$$A \qquad \frac{a}{r}$$

(b) Show that the unit of circular measure is equal to 57 ·2598°.

3. Given $a = 53$, $b = 49$, and $c = 98$. Find the area of the triangle.

4. Solve the equations :—
$$\begin{cases} x^2 - xy = 66 \\ x^2 + y^2 = 11 \end{cases}$$

B.

5. Prove

(a) $\cos A + \cos B = 2 \cos \dfrac{A + B}{2} \cos \dfrac{A - B}{2}$

(b) $\cos\left(\dfrac{\pi}{3} + \theta\right) + \cos\left(\dfrac{\pi}{3} - \theta\right) = \cos\theta$

(c) $\operatorname{Tan}(A + B) = \dfrac{\tan A + \tan B}{1 - \tan A \tan B}$

6 Show that in any triangle

(a) $\cos A = \dfrac{b^2 + c^2 - a^2}{2\,bc}$

(b) $\sin\dfrac{A}{2} = \sqrt{\dfrac{(s-b)\,s-c)}{bc}}$

7. Solve the equations :

(1) $4x^2 + 9\,xy = 190,\ 4 + -5y = 10$

(2) $x - \dfrac{y-2}{7}\quad 5,\ 4y - \dfrac{x+10}{3} = 3$

(3) $\dfrac{3x+2}{x-1} + \dfrac{2x-4}{x+2} = 5$

8. Simplify $7\sqrt[3]{54} + 3\sqrt[3]{16} + \sqrt[3]{432}$ and

$$\dfrac{1+x}{1+x+x^2}\quad \dfrac{1-x}{1-x+x^2} - \dfrac{2}{1+x^2+x^4}$$

C.

9. The sine of an angle changes in sign with the angle itself. The cosine remains the same.

(a) Prove that $\cos A = - \cos(\pi - A)$.

10. In a plane triangle the sum of the sides is to their difference in the same ratio as the tangent of half the sum of the base angles is to the tangent of half their difference. •

11. Solve the equations :

(a) $x^2 + \dfrac{1}{32} = - \dfrac{9}{16}\,x.$

(b) $\left.\begin{array}{l}\dfrac{x}{b} + \dfrac{y}{c} = 1 \\[2mm] \dfrac{ax}{c} - \dfrac{by}{a} = 0\end{array}\right\}$

11. The differences between the hypotenuse and two sides of a right angled triangle are 3 and 6 respectively : find the sides.

13

INTERMEDIATE EXAMINATION.

GEOMETRY—ARITHMETIC.

WEDNESDAY, APRIL 13TH :—MORNING, 9 TO 12.

*Write the answers on separate papers marked A, B, C, respectively
to correspond to the questions.*

A.

1. If two triangles have one angle of the one equal to one angle of the other, and the sides about the equal angles proportional, the triangles shall be equiangular to one another, and shall have those angles equal which are opposite the homologous sides.

2. If from any point without a circle two straight lines be drawn, one of which cuts the circle, and the other meets it, and if the rectangle contained by the whole line which cuts the circle and the part of it without the circle be equal to the square on the line which meets the circle, the line which meets the circle will touch it.

3. Describe through two given points a circle that will touch a given unlimited straight line.

4. A tunnel is to be 5 miles long and the vertical sides are crowned by a semicircular arch. The internal breadth is to be 20 feet, and the height to the top of the ·arch 22 feet. The brick work is to be 2 feet thick. Find (*a*) the number of cubic yards of earth to be excavated, (*b*) the number of cubic ·yards of brickwork required. (Area of a circle = $3\cdot1416 \times r^2$.)

B

5. Triangles which have the same altitude are to one another as their bases.

6. If two triangles, which have an angle in one equal to an angle in the other be equal in area, their sides about the equal angles are reciprocally proportional.

7. Describe a circle about a given triangle.

8. If a river, 25 feet deep, 150 feet wide, flow at the rate of four miles an hour, how many tons of water will pass a given point on the bank in one minute, assuming a cubic yard to weigh $\frac{3}{4}$ of a ton? Reduce your answer to kilograms.

C

9. Equal chords in a circle are equidistant from the centre ; and, conversely, chords which are equidistant from the centre are equal.

(*ı*) Find the locus of the middle points of equal chords in a circle.

10. If a straight line be divided equally, and also unequally, the rectangle contained by the unequal parts, and the square on the line between the points of section, are together equal to the square on half the line.

(*a*) Hence show how to describe a rectangle equal to the difference between two squares. ·

11. Inscribe a regular quindecagon in a given circle.

12. A log of timber is 18 feet long, 1 foot 4 inches wide, and 15 inches thick. If a piece containing $2\frac{1}{2}$ solid feet be cut off the end of it, what length will be left ?

INTERMEDIATE EXAMINATIONS.

TRIGONOMETRY—ALGEBRA.

THURSDAY, APRIL 14TH:—MORNING, 9 TO 12.

(*Write the answers in separate books marked A, B and C, respectively, to correspond to the questions.*)

A.

1. Prove that in any triangle
$$\frac{\cos 2A}{a^2} - \frac{\cos 2B}{b^2} = \frac{1}{a^2} - \frac{1}{b^2} \quad \dots \ (1).$$
$$(b^2 - c^2) \cot A + (c^2 - a^2) \cot B + (a^2 - b^2) \cot C = 0 \quad (2).$$

2. Having given two angles and a side, show how to solve the triangle. Find the longest side of the triangle ABC, where $AB = 1,000$ yards, $CAB = 35°, 10'$, $CBA = 83°, 15'$.

3. Solve the equations
$$\frac{2x}{15} + \frac{3x - 50}{3(10 + x)} = \frac{12x + 70}{390}.$$

$$\sqrt{2x + 9} + \sqrt{3x - 15} = \sqrt{7x + 8}$$

$$\left.\begin{array}{l} x^2 + y^2 = \dfrac{5}{2}\, xy \\[2mm] x - y = \dfrac{1}{2}\, xy \end{array}\right\}$$

4. A game is played twice by the same two parties. One side makes 20 p. ct. more, and the other 20 p. ct. less, on the second occasion than they did on the first. The former wins on the whole by 20 points, but would have lost by 20 points on the first occasion taken alone. How many points were made by each side on the whole ?

B.

5. Deduce the formula, $\tan \dfrac{A}{2} \quad \sqrt{\dfrac{(s-b)\ (s-c)}{s\ (s-a)}}$.

6. Prove that the area of a triangle divided by its semiperimeter gives the radius of the circle inscribed in the triangle, or show that
$\tan \dfrac{A}{2} = \dfrac{r}{s-a}$.

7. From the top of a house 40 ft. high, it is observed that a tower 180 ft. high subtends an angle of 36°; what is the horizontal distance of the tower ?

8. A person observes the elevation of the top of a mountain to be 15° and after walking a mile directly towards it on level ground the elevation is 75° : find the height of the mountain in feet.

C.

9. Define logarithm. Enunciate the rules for the employment of logarithms in arithmetical calculations. Prove one of those rules.
Given $\log. 3 = 0.4771213$; find $\log. 75$.

10. (a) If $\sin A = \frac{3}{5}$, find $\sin 3A$.
(b) If $A = 36^\circ$, $a = 4$ and the perpendicular from C upon $AB = (\sqrt{5} - 1)$; find the other angles.

11. Solve the equations:
(a) $mx^2 - \dfrac{m^3 - n^2}{mn}\ x = 1$
(b) $\begin{array}{l} xy = a^2 \\ x - y = b \end{array} \Big\}$

12. A draper bought a piece of silk for £16 4s., and the number of shillings which he paid per yard was $\frac{4}{9}$ the number of yards. How much did he buy ?

THIRD YEAR.

MECHANICS.

MONDAY, APRIL 4TH :—MORNING, 9 TO 12.

1. Find the resultant of two like parallel forces acting on a rigid body.

2. A body starting from rest with uniform acceleration travels 63 feet in a straight line while gaining a velocity of 81 feet per second. Find the acceleration.

3. Find the specific gravity of a stone which when placed in the upper pan of a Nicholson's Hydrometer needs the addition of a weight of 70 grains to sink the instrument to the marked point, and when placed in the lower pan needs 130 grains; the weight in the upper pan required to sink the Hydrometer (without the stone) to the marked point being 220 grains.

4. If a cubic foot of water weigh 1,000 ounces, what is the pressure per square inch at the depth of a mile below the surface?

5. A body of given weight rests on a smooth inclined plane; show how to determine the relation between the power, the weight, and the reaction of the plane, whatever be the direction in which the power acts.

(a) Hence prove that, if a body be supported on a plane inclined at an angle of 60° to the horizon, by a force whose direction makes an angle of 30° with the horizon, the force and the reaction of the plane are each equal to the weight of the body.

6. Enunciate Newton's Laws of Motion and assign a meaning to the expression $P = mf$.

(a) A 30 ton mass is moving on smooth horizontal rails at the rate of 20 miles an hour; what force would stop it in (1) half a minute, and (2) half a mile?

7. The arms of a false balance, whose weight is neglected, are in the ratio of 10 : 9. If goods be alternately weighed from each arm, show that the seller loses 5/9 per cent.

8. Describe the specific gravity bottle and explain how it is used.

A sp. gr. bottle completely full of water weighs 38.4 grms., and when 22.3 grms. of a certain solid have been introduced it weighs 49 8 grms. Find the sp. gr. of the solid.

9. An air-bubble at the bottom of a pond 10 ft. deep has a volume of .00006 of a cubic inch. Find what its volume becomes when it just reaches the surface, the barometer standing at 30 ins. and mercury being 13.6 times as heavy as water.

10. Six forces act at the centre of a regular hexagon towards the angular points. Their magnitudes taken in order are 6, 5, 4, 3, 2, 1 pounds respectively. Find the direction and magnitude of their resultant.

11. A shot is fired at an elevation of 30° with a velocity of 2,000 feet per second. Find the range and time of flight.

12. A diving bell 10 feet high is lowered till the top is 6 inches below the surface, when it is found that the water has risen 2 feet inside the bell. What is the height of the water barometer?

ORDINARY EXAMINATION.

THIRD YEAR.

ASTRONOMY AND OPTICS.

THURSDAY, APRIL 14TH:—MORNING, 9 TO 12.

1. Explain the principle of Foucault's pendulum experiment showing the rotation of the earth.

2. Define the *equation of time*. How is the time a clock ought to show found from observation of the sun?

3. What is the explanation of the November star-showers, and of their extraordinary display about every thirty-three years?

4. Find the curvature of a plano-convex lens of water ($\mu = 1.336$) of 4 inches focal length.

5. Account for the succession of day and night, and also of the seasons.

6. Show (by diagram where necessary) how eclipses of the moon are caused, noting the different kinds.

7. Explain as fully as you can the nebular hypothesis.

8. A bright ball 4 inches in diameter is suspended in front of a convex mirror of 11 inches radius, at a distance of 14 inches; find the apparent size of the image, and its position.

9. Enunciate the laws of reflection and refraction of light. Explain what is meant by total reflection, and the " critical angle."

10. Prove that after reflection at two plane mirrors a ray is deviated through twice the angle between mirrors.
Describe the sextant, showing the use made of the above principle.

11. *Either* (*a*) prove that the focal length of a concave spherical mirror is a mean proportional between the distances of the conjugate foci from the principal focus; *or* (*b*) prove the formula :

$$\frac{1}{d} + \frac{1}{D} = \frac{1}{f}$$

A pencil of light diverges from a point 11 inches in front of a con-. cave mirror of 6 inches focal length; find its conjugate focus.

12. Determine the nature and focal length of glasses which will enable a person whose distance of distinct vision is 4 inches to read with the book at 10 inches distance.   Will the type be magnified or diminished ?

B. A. ORDINARY EXAMINATIONS.

MECHANICS AND HYDROSTATICS.

WEDNESDAY, APRIL 13TH :—MORNING, 9 TO 12.

1. A uniform rod, 12 feet long and weighing 17 lbs., can turn freely about a point in it, and the rod is in equilibrium when a weight of 7 lbs. is hung at one end ; calculate how far from the end is the point about which it can turn.

2. A particle is projected vertically upwards with a velocity of 80 feet per second.   Find what time elapses before it is at a height of 64 feet.

3. A particle is projected in a vacuum with a velocity u in a direction making an angle e with the horizon, show that the horizontal range is $\dfrac{2 \, u^2 \sin e \cos e}{g}$

4. A Nicholson's hydrometer weighs 8 ozs.   The addition of 2 ozs. to the upper pan causes it to sink in one liquid to the marked point, while 5 ozs. are required to produce the same result in another liquid.   Compare the sp. grs. of the liquids ; explaining the action of the instrument fully.

5. Describe the suction pump and explain its action.

6. A cylindrical test-tube is held in a vertical position and immersed mouth downwards in water.   When the middle of the tube is at a depth of 32.75 feet it is found that the water has risen halfway up the tube. Find the height of the water barometer.

7. If a litre of air weighs 1.293 gramme at $0°$ centigrade when the barometer is at 760^{mm}, find the weight of air in a litre flask at $60°C$ and 820^{mm} pressure.

8. Find the conditions of equilibrium of any number of forces acting at a point.

9. A sphere of diameter 1 foot, hangs against a smooth vertical wall by a string 6 inches long fastened to its circumference and to the wall ; find the tension of the string, if the sphere weighs 3 lbs.

10. Draw a diagram of a set of weightless pulleys in which 3 lbs. balances 96 lbs. ; how much would the 3 lbs. support if each pulley weighed 1 lb ?

11. A uniform force equal to the weight of 20 lbs. acts upon a body which is initially at rest, and causes it to move through 24 feet in the first second. Find the mass of the body.

12. Find in foot pounds the work done on a 2oz. bullet which leaves the muzzle of a gun with a velocity of 1000 feet per second'; if the gun barrel is 3 feet long, what was the average pressure on the bullet ?

B. A. ORDINARY EXAMINATIONS.

ASTRONOMY—OPTICS.

THURSDAY, APRIL 14TH :—MORNING, 9 TO 12.

1. Explain the periodic display of the November Star showers every 33 years. When did the last display occur ? What reason is there for supposing a connection between them and comets ?

2. Define *horizontal parallax.* How is this used to find the distance of a planet ? Why does it fail in the case of Jupiter?

(*a*) Explain the method of finding the distance of Jupiter by its annual parallax.

3. Define horizon, meridian, altitude, azimuth, zenith, nadir, equator, ecliptic, right ascension, declination, vertical circles, obliquity of the ecliptic, tropics, solstices, latitude and longitude on the celestial sphere.

4. Define *precession of the equinoxes.* Explain its physical cause. How does it affect the length of the year ? What indication of it have we in the names of the signs of the Zodiac ?

5. Prove that the altitude of the Pole is equal to the latitude of the place. How is the fact used in finding the latitude?

6. Prove that the refraction is proportional to the tangent of the zenith distance. What limitation is there to the truth of this statement?

7. Prove that by reflection at two plane mirrors a ray of light is deflected through twice the angle between the mirrors.

Describe the sextant, and explain how the above principle is applied in its use.

8. Write down formulæ for the course of a ray through a prism; if D be the deviation and i the angle of the prism, prove that (1) $D = (\mu - 1)\, i$, if i be small; (2) $\sin \dfrac{D + i}{2} = \mu \sin \dfrac{i'}{2}$, for any value of i, if the ray goes through symmetrically.

9. Prove that when an object is placed midway between a concave mirror and its principal focus, the image is twice as large as the object.

10. Distinguish *Deviation, Dispersion, Dispersive power.* How is an achromatic object glass constructed? Explain carefully the effects of its lenses upon a pencil of white light.

11. The focal lengths of the objective and eye-piece of a microscope are $\frac{1}{4}$th of an inch and 1 inch respectively, and they are exactly 10 inches apart. The object is placed $\frac{100}{389}$ths of an inch in front of the objective. Prove that the image will be 10 inches from the eye and magnified 789 times.

12. State the law by which the index of refraction from one substance to another may be calculated if those from air to both substances are known. Taking the indices for glass and water to be $\frac{3}{2}$ and $\frac{4}{3}$ respectively, prove that the focal length of a glass lens immersed in water is four times its focal length in air.

SESSIONAL EXAMINATIONS.

THIRD YEAR ARTS, SECOND YEAR SCIENCE.

EXPERIMENTAL PHYSICS—HEAT, LIGHT AND SOUND.

WEDNESDAY, APRIL 6TH :—MORNING, 9 TO 12.

(Not more than nine questions to be attempted.)

1. Describe the process of making and graduating a mercury thermometer, and explain the origin of the Centigrade and Fahrenheit scales.

Find the temperature at which the number of degrees on the Fahrenheit scale is double that on the Centigrade scale, and also that at which the two scales agree.

2. Give some applications of the differences of expansion between different metals. Define the term Coefficient of Expansion, and show how to calculate the allowance to be made for expansion in the case of the Victoria Bridge.

3. Describe one form of air thermometer, and explain the method of using it to verify the laws of gases. What are the principal difficulties attending its use?

4. State the two principal laws of change of state. Define the boiling point of a liquid. Distinguish between a saturated and unsaturated vapour, and explain how their behaviour differs from that of a gas.

5. Describe experiments to illustrate the different conducting powers of different materials. State the Law of Conduction, and describe some form of apparatus for measuring the conductivity of a metal.

6. How is the velocity of sound in the air affected by changes in pressure and temperature? How may the velocity in other gases and materials be compared with it?

7. A lump of ice weighing 80 grammes, and at a temperature of —10°, is dropped into water at 0°. 5 grammes of water freeze on to the lump and the temperature of the ice rises to 0°. Calculate the specific heat of ice.

8. Describe the Sonometer, and explain how to use it in determining the vibration number of a given tuning-fork, quoting the formula.

A string is stretched in such a way that a wave runs along it at a rate of 64 feet per second. Two points on the string, 4 feet apart, are now clamped without altering the tension. How many vibrations per second will this length of the string make when disturbed?

9. Explain the principle of Resonance.

A tuning fork is held over a resonance tube, and the maximum effect is found when the air column is 64 8 cm. long. The vibration number of the fork is 128. What is the velocity of sound ?

10. Describe the Spectrometer and its adjustments. Explain how to use it to find (1) the angle of a given prism; (2) the index of refraction of the prism for a given ray.

11. Describe the experimental arrangements for producing Newton's rings upon the screen. Give a general explanation of the rings. Why is the centre black instead of white?

12. Describe the optical arrangements in some form of Polariscope, explaining the functions of the polarizer and analyzer.

B.A. ORDINARY EXAMINATIONS.

FOURTH YEAR ARTS, THIRD YEAR SCIENCE.

EXPERIMENTAL PHYSICS—ELECTRICITY AND MAGNETISM.

WEDNESDAY, APRIL 6TH :—MORNING, 9 TO 12.

(Not more than nine questions to be attempted.)

1. Sketch the lines of force in a horizontal plane in the neighbourhood of a bar magnet suspended freely with its axis in the meridian. Explain the terms used, and show how to calculate the moment of the magnet by finding the point of the field at which the magnetic intensity vanishes.

2. Describe and contrast the magnetic properties of iron and steel. Explain the phenomena of induction, saturation, and retention, and give the relation between the permeability and susceptibility.

3. Give the essential points of the construction of a tangent galvanometer. If the coil has 30 turns of 10 cm. radius, what will be the moment of the couple acting on a magnet 1 cm. long, strength of pole 10 units, at the centre, due to a current of 1 ampere flowing in the wire.

4. Describe the construction and use of the mirror galvanometer. What are the comparative advantages of the movable coil and movable magnet types? Give the elementary formula for either, and explain the term "figure of merit."

5. Assuming the law of force acting on a conductor carrying a current in a magnetic field, find an expression for the work done in moving the conductor so as to cut N lines of force. Apply the principle of the con·

servation of energy to deduce Faraday's law of the induction of electric currents.'

6. State the laws of the chemical action of an electric current. Describe experiments by which they may be verified. Explain why a single Daniel cell is unable to send a current through a water voltameter.

7. Describe and explain the action of the Water-dropping Accumulator, and compare it with a Wimshurst Machine.

8. Explain the principle of a Wheatstone's Bridge, proving the formula. Explain Carey Foster's method of using the bridge, pointing out its advantages.

9. Two equal cells when connected in series through a given wire produce a current of .28 ampere ; when connected in parallel they give through the same wire .2 ampere ; prove that the resistance of the wire is 3 times that of either cell.

10. Explain clearly why a high voltage is required for economically transmitting power to a great distance.

A dynamo gives 123.6 amperes through an external resistance of 1.224 ohm ; the power absorbed is 28 H. P. Shew that its commercial efficiency is 89.5.

11. A coil of 50 turns of wire in the form of a circle 30 cm. in diameter rotates 20 times a second about a vertical axis. Find the average E. M. F. produced (in volts) if $H = .18$ C. G. S. units.

12. Explain (1) the construction of the Blake transmitter, (2) a method of duplexing a telegraph line.

HONOUR EXAMINATIONS IN MATHEMATICS.

HONOUR EXAMINATIONS.

FIRST YEAR.

GEOMETRY (*First Paper.*)

WEDNESDAY, APRIL 20TH :—MORNING, 9 TO 12.

1. If two circles touch each other at any point P, and any line cut the circles in the points A, B, C, D, then the angle $A P B = C B D$.

2. Given the vertical angle of a triangle, and the segments into which the line bisecting it divides the base, construct it.

3. Define the *centre of mean position*. Prove that the sum of the perpendicular let fall from n given points, on any line, is equal to n times the perpendicular from the centre of mean position on the same line.

4. Describe a triangle of given species, whose sides shall pass through three given points, and whose area shall be a maximum.

5. Describe a circle having its centre at a given point, and cutting a given circle orthogonally.

6. Given, in magnitude and position, the base of a triangle and the ratios of the sides, find the locus of the vertex.

7. The sum of the squares of the four sides of a quadrilateral is equal to the sum of the squares of its diagonals plus four times the square of the line joining the middle points of the diagonals.

8. The rectangle contained by the perpendiculars from any point O in the circumference of a circle on two tangents AC, BC, is equal to the square of the perpendicular from the same point on their chord of contact AB.

9. If from any point perpendiculars be let fall on the sides of a regular polygon of n sides, their sum is equal to n times the radius of the inscribed circle.

10. If through O, the intersection of the diagonals of a quadrilateral $ABCD$, a line OH be drawn parallel to one of the sides AB, meeting the opposite side CD in G, and the third diagonal in H, OH is bisected in G.

11. If O be the centre of the inscribed circle of the triangle ABC, then $\overline{AO}^2 : AB . AC :: s-a : s$.

12. Given the base of a triangle, the perpendicular, and the sum of the sides, to construct it.

FACULTY OF ARTS.

HONOUR EXAMINATION.

FIRST YEAR.

GEOMETRY (*Second Paper.*)

WEDNESDAY, APRIL 20TH:—AFTERNOON, 2 TO 5.

1. If through any point O two lines be drawn cutting a circle in four points, then joining these points, both directly and transversely; if the direct lines meet in P and the transverse lines in Q, the line PQ will be the polar of the point O.

2. Define the inverse of a circle, and prove that if two circles touch each other, their inverses will also touch each other.

3. If from any point two tangents be drawn to a circle, the points of contact and the points of intersection of any secant from the same point form a harmonic system of points. (Define.)

4. Describe a circle touching three given circles.

5. If two circles touch two others, the radical axis of either pair passes through a centre of similitude of the other pair.

6. The locus of the intersection of tangents to a circle at the extremities of a chord which passes through a given point is the polar o the point.

7. State and prove Pascal's Theorem.

8. If two equal pencils have a common ray, the intersections of the remaining three homologous pairs of rays are collinear.

9. The six centres of similitude of three circles lie three by three on four lines, called axes of similitude of the circles.

10. Any line cutting the circle and passing through a fixed point is cut harmonically by the circle, the point and the polar of the point.

11. Any two circles can be inverted into themselves.

12. Any quadrilateral is divided by a straight line into two others; prove that the intersection of the diagonals of the three lie in a straight line.

HONOUR EXAMINATIONS.

FIRST YEAR.

THEORY OF EQUATIONS—ALGEBRA.

FRIDAY, APRIL 22ND :—MORNING, 9 TO 12.

1. Solve the equation
$$2 x^6 - 5 x^5 + 4 x^4 - 4 x^2 + 5 x - 2 = 0$$

2. Solve the equation $x^6 - 1 = 0$

3. Show that the equation $x^5 - 4 x^2 + 3 = 0$ has at least two imaginary roots.

4. Apply Sturm's Theorem to the equation
$$x^3 + x^2 - 2 x - 1 = 0$$

5. Prove that in the Napierean system
$$\log (1 + y) = y - \tfrac{1}{2} y^2 + \tfrac{1}{3} y^3 - \text{etc.}$$

6. Divide $\dfrac{3 x^2 + 7 x - 5}{(x - 3) (x - 2)^2}$ into partial fractions.

7. If an equation $f(x) = 0$, whose coefficients are all real quantities, have for a root the imaginary expression $a + \beta \sqrt{-1}$, it must also have for a root the conjugate imaginary expression $a - \beta \sqrt{-1}$.

8. (a) Transform the equation
$$x^4 - 5 x^3 + 7 x^2 - 17 x + 11 = 0$$ into an equation whose roots are less by 4 than the roots of the given equation.

(b.) Transform the equation $x^4 + 8 x^3 + x - 5 = 0$ into one which shall want the second term.

9. Solve the equation
$$x^3 + qx + r = 0$$

10. Find the superior limit of the positive roots of $x^7 + 4 x^6 - 3 x^5 + 5 x^4 - 9 x^3 - 11 x^2 + 6 x - 8 = 0.$

Prove your method.

11. Prove that every equation of an odd degree has at least one real root.

12. Prove the Binomial theorem when the index is negative.

FACULTY OF ARTS.

HONOUR EXAMINATIONS.

SECOND YEAR.

ANALYTIC GEOMETRY (*First Paper*).

WEDNESDAY, APRIL 20TH :—MORNING, 9 TO 12.

1. Given the vertical angle of a triangle and the sum of the reciprocals of the sides ; the base will always pass through a fixed point.

2. Prove analytically that angles in the same segment of a circle are equal.

3. Given the base of a triangle and m times the square of one side $+ n$ times the square of the other, find the locus of the vertex.

4. Find the polar equation of a right line, and verify it by transformation of co-ordinates.

5. Find the equation of a right line passing through a given point perpendicular to a given right line.

6. Transform the equation $2x^2 - 5xy + 2y^2 = 4$ from axes inclined to each other at an angle of 60° to the straight lines which bisect the angles between the given axes.

7. Find the area of the triangle formed by three given points. Write the result in the form of a determinant.

8. How are the lines $a = \kappa\beta$, $\beta = \kappa a$, related to each other ?

If through the vertices of a triangle there be drawn any three lines meeting in a point, the three lines drawn through the same angles equally inclined to the bisectors of the angles will also meet in a point.

9. Find the polar of the point $(5, 2)$ with respect to the circle $x^2 + y^2 - 4x + 6y = 3$.

10. Find the polar equation of a circle, and from it the locus of the middle point of a chord which always passes through a fixed point.

11. Find the length of the perpendicular from (h, k) on the straight line $ax + by + c = 0$.

Show that the area of the triangle whose vertices are $(1, 2)$, $(2, 3)$, $(3, 1)$, is $\frac{3}{2}$.

12. If ABC is the triangle of reference in trilinear co-ordinates, show that the equation to the line joining the middle points of AC, BC, is $aa + b\beta - c\gamma = 0$.

13. Investigate the equation to the tangent at the point $x^1\ y^1$ to the circle $x^2 + y^2 = a^2$.

Find the equation to the pair of tangents from an external point $x^1\ y^1$ to the same circle.

. 14. The polar equation to a circle being $r = 2c \cos \theta$, show that the equation $2c \cos \beta \cos \alpha = r \cos (\beta + \alpha - \theta)$ represents the chord joining the points in which it is cut by two lines drawn from the pole making angles $\alpha,\ \beta$ with the initial line.

_____

HONOUR EXAMINATIONS.

SECOND YEAR.

ANALYTIC GEOMETRY (*Second Paper*).

WEDNESDAY, APRIL 20TH :—AFTERNOON, 2 TO 5.

1. Taking the general equation of conics, prove that in general a chord can be drawn through any given point which will be bisected at that point.

2. If two diameters of a conic be such that one of them bisects all chords parallel to the other, then, conversely, the second will bisect all chords parallel to the first.

3. In the parabola the sub-normal is constant.

4. The harmonic mean between the segments of a focal chord of an ellipse is constant, and equal to the semi-parameter.

5. Find the condition that the general equation of the second degree should represent (1) an ellipse, (2) an hyperbola, (3) a parabola.

6. The angle θ which the principal axes of a conic make with the co-ordinate rectangular axes is given by the equation

$$\tan 2\theta = \frac{2h}{a-b} .$$

7. Define the conjugate diameters of an ellipse, and show that the sum of the squares of a pair of conjugate diameters is constant.

8. What kind of a conic is represented by the equation

$$\left(\frac{x}{a}\right)^{\frac{1}{2}} + \left(\frac{y}{b}\right)^{\frac{1}{2}} = 1,$$

and what is the equation of the polar of the origin?

9. Show how to determine the centre of the conic

$$ax^2 + 2\ hxy + by^2 + 2\ gx + 2\ fy + c = 0.$$

14

10. Find the equation of the polar of $(x^1 \, y^1)$ with reference to the ellipse

$$\frac{x^2}{a^2} + \frac{y^2}{b^2} = 1$$

and prove that the locus of intersection of tangents drawn at the extremities of chords passing through a fixed point is a straight line.

11. Obtain the equation to the tangent to a parabola, $y^2 = 4\,ax$, in the form

$$y = \underline{mx} + \frac{a}{m} \cdot$$

(a) If θ, θ' are the inclinations to the axis of the parabola of the two tangents through $(h \; k)$, shew that

$$\tan \theta + \tan \theta' = \frac{k}{h}; \quad \tan \theta \tan \theta = \frac{a}{h} \cdot$$

12. Transform the equation of the hyperbola

$$\frac{x^2}{a^2} - \frac{y^2}{b^2} = 1$$

to the asymptotes as axes.

HONOUR EXAMINATIONS.

SECOND YEAR.

CALCULUS.

FRIDAY, APRIL 22ND :—MORNING, 9 TO 12.

1. Find the conditions that a given $f(x)$ should have a maximum value.

    a. Find the value of x which makes

$$\frac{\sin x \, . \, \cos x \, . }{\cos^2 (60^0 - x)}$$

a maximum.

2. Differentiate $y = \sin^{-1} \dfrac{1 - x^2}{1 + x^2}$; $y = \dfrac{1 - \tan x}{\sec x} \cdot$

3. Prove that the equation of the tangent at x', y' to any curve $y = f(x)$ is

$$y - y^1 = \left(\frac{dy}{dx} \right)^1 (x - x^1)$$

4. Integrate $\displaystyle\int \frac{d\theta}{\sin^3 \theta}$ $\displaystyle\int \frac{d\theta}{\sin^{\frac{3}{2}} \theta \cos^{\frac{5}{2}} \theta}$; $\displaystyle\int \frac{d\theta}{\sin \theta} \cdot$

5. If $y = a \cos (\log x) + b \sin (\log x)$, prove that

$$x^2 \frac{d^2y}{dx^2} + x \frac{dy}{dx} + y = 0.$$

6. Show by Maclaurin's Theorem that

$$\log \sec x = \frac{x^2}{2} + \frac{x^4}{12} + \frac{x^6}{45} + \dots$$

7. Explain why $\frac{f^1(x)}{\varphi^1(x)}$ gives the limiting value of $\frac{f(x)}{\phi(x)}$ when the latter approaches the form $\frac{0}{0}$.

Find the value of $\frac{\log \sec x}{x^2}$ and of $x^{\frac{a+x}{\log x}}$ when $x = 0$.

8. Integrate the following

(1) $\int \frac{d\theta}{\cos \theta}$, (2) $\int \frac{d\theta}{1 + \cos \theta}$, (3) $\int \frac{x \, dx}{a^4 + x^4}$, (4) $\int \frac{dx}{x^4 (1 + x^2)}$

9. Differentiate

(a) $y = \log (\log x)$;

(b) $y = \tan^{-1} \frac{x}{\sqrt{1-x^2}}$ and prove that

if $y = x^3 \log x$ $\dfrac{d^4 y}{dx^4} = \dfrac{6}{x}$

10. Prove Taylor's Theorem

$$f(x + y) = f(x) + \frac{y}{1} f'(x) + \frac{y^2}{1.2} f''(x) +$$

$$\frac{y^n f^{(n)} x}{\lfloor n}$$

11. Integrate

$$\int \sin^2 x \, dx \; ; \quad \int \frac{dy}{x^2 - 3} \; ; \quad \int \frac{dx}{\sqrt{x^2 \pm a^2}}$$

12. Integrate

$$\int \frac{(x + 1) \, dx}{(x + 3)(x + 2)} \; ; \quad \int \frac{\sin^5 \theta \, d\theta}{\cos^2 \theta} \; ; \quad \int \frac{d\theta}{\sin \theta}$$

HONOUR EXAMINATIONS.

SECOND YEAR.

PLANE AND SPHERICAL TRIGONOMETRY.

FRIDAY, APRIL 22ND:—AFTERNOON, 2 TO 5.

1. Any two sides of a spherical triangle are greater than the third.

2. The sum of the three angles of a spherical triangle is greater than two and less than six right angles.

3. In a right-angled spherical triangle given
$$c = 81° \ 29' \ 32'' \quad A = 32° \ 28' \ 17'' \text{ find } B.$$

4. If $A + B + C = 180°$ prove
$$\sin 2A + \sin 2B + \sin 2C = 4 \sin A \sin B \sin C.$$

5. State DeMoivre's Theorem, and prove it when the index is a positive integer.
Hence also find $\sin 3\theta$ and $\cos 3\theta$ in terms of $\sin \theta$ and $\cos \theta$.

6. Prove that
$$\frac{\pi}{8} = \frac{1}{1.3} + \frac{1}{5.7} + \frac{1}{9.11} + \dots,$$

7. In any right-angled spherical triangle
$$(1) \ \cos A = \frac{\tan b}{\tan c},$$
$$(2) \ \tan^2 \frac{A}{2} = \frac{\sin (c-b)}{\sin (c+b)},$$

(3) either side and the opposite angle are of the same affection.

8. One side of a spherical regular polygon of n sides is a, and A is one the angles ; show that
$$\sin \frac{A}{2} = \sec \frac{a}{2} \ \cos \left(\frac{180°}{n}\right).$$

9. In a spherical triangle
$$(a) \ \cos A = \frac{\cos a - \cos b \cos c}{\sin b \sin c}$$
$$(b) \ \cos \frac{A}{2} . \sqrt{\frac{\sin s \ \sin (s-a)}{\sin b \sin c}}$$

10. The arcs drawn from the vertices of a spherical triangle perpendicular to the opposite sides are concurrent.

11. Find the sum of the series

$$\sin a + \sin (a + \delta) + \sin (a + 2 \delta) +$$
$$+ + \quad \sin \{a + (n-1) \delta \}$$

12. Prove that

$$\cos \theta = 1 - \frac{\theta^2}{\lfloor 2} + \frac{\theta^4}{\lfloor 4} - \frac{\theta^6}{\lfloor 6} + \text{etc.}$$

B.A. HONOUR EXAMINATIONS.

MATHEMATICS AND NATURAL PHILOSOPHY.

DIFFERENTIAL EQUATIONS.

WEDNESDAY, APRIL 13TH:—MORNING, 9 TO 12.

1. Apply the symbolical method of solution to the equation

$$\frac{d^2 u}{dx^2} - 3 \frac{du}{dx} + 2 u = x e^{mx}$$

2. Integrate by Monge's method the differential equation

$$x^2 r + 2 xys + y^2 t = 0.$$

3. Integrate $(y^2 + z^2 - x^2) p - 2 xyq + 2 xz = 0.$

4. Solve the equations :—

(a) $\frac{dx}{dt} + 7 x - y = 0; \quad \frac{dy}{dt} + 2 x + 5 y = 0.$

(b) $\frac{d^2 x}{dt^2} = ax + by; \quad \frac{d^2 y}{dt^2} = a' x + b' y.$

5. Prove that $\dfrac{1}{(x + y + z)^2}$ is an integrating factor of

$$(y + z) dx + (z + x) dy + (x + y) dz = 0$$

and find a general expression for such factors.

6. Prove that the curve in which the radius of curvature varies as the cube of the normal is a conic section.

7. Solve the equations :—

$$\frac{d^2 y}{dx^2} = \frac{2 y}{x^2}; \quad y \frac{d^2 y}{dx^2} + \left(\frac{dy}{dx} \right)^2 = 1$$

$$a^2 \frac{d^4 y}{dx^4} = \frac{dy^2}{dx^2} .$$

8. Integrate

$$\frac{d^4 y}{dx^4} - 4 \frac{d^3 y}{dx^3} + 6 \frac{d^2 y}{dx^2} - 4 \frac{dy}{dx} + y = 0.$$

9. Integrate

$$x = a \frac{dy}{dx} + b \left(\frac{dy}{dx} \right)^2$$

10. Show that the equation

$$x \frac{dy}{dx} - ay + by^2 = cx^n$$

is solvable when $n = 2 a$.

11. Determine an integrating factor for

$$(x^2 + y^2 + 2 x) \, dx + 2y \, dy = 0$$

and integrate the equation.

12. Integrate

$$\frac{2 x \, dx}{y^3} + \left(\frac{1}{y^2} - \frac{3 x^2}{y^4} \right) \, dy = 0.$$

B. A. HONOUR EXAMINATIONS.

MATHEMATICS AND NATURAL PHILOSOPHY.

CALCULUS, ETC.

FRIDAY, APRIL 15TH : —MORNING, 9 TO 12.

1. If the equation to a curve of a third degree be of the form

$$u_3 + u_1 + u_0 = 0$$

the lines represented by $u_3 = 0$ are its asymptotes.

2. Discuss the character of the origin on the curve

$$(y - x^2)^2 = x^5$$

3. Show that the origin is a conjugate point on the curve

$$y^2 (x^2 - a^2) = x^4$$

4. Find the envelope of a right line, when the rectangle under the perpendiculars from two given points is constant.

5. From a point of inflexion on a cubic only three tangents can be drawn to the curve, and their three points of contact lie on a right line.

6. Find the length of the radius of curvature at the origin in the curve.

$$y^4 + x^3 + a \, (x^2 + y^2) = a \, ^2y$$

7. Trace the curve $y^3 - 3 \, axy + x^3 = 0$, drawing its asymptotes.

8. Prove that the evolute of an epicycloid is a similar epicycloid.

9. Eliminate A and $\dot{B}$, by differentiation, from

$$y = x \sin nx + A \cos nx + B \sin nx$$

10. Find the volume of the portion of the elliptic paraboloid

$$px^2 + qy^2 = 2 \, pq_, \, z$$

cut off by a plane perpendicular to the axis of the surface.

11. A sphere is cut by a right cylinder, the radius of whose base is half that of the sphere and one of whose edges passes through the centre of the sphere ; find the volume common to both surfaces.

12 Find the moment of inertia with regard to the axis c of the ellipsoid.

$$\frac{x^2}{a^2} + \frac{3^2}{b^2} + \frac{z^2}{c^2} = 1$$

13. Prove that the value of $\displaystyle\int_{0}^{\infty} e^{-x} x^n \, dx$ is $1.2.3\ldots n$

B.A. HONOURS IN MATHEMATICS AND NATURAL PHILOSOPHY.

LUNAR THEORY—NEWTON'S PRINCIPIA.

Monday, April 18th :—Morning, 9 to 12.

1. Define the true ecliptic· Define the plane of reference in the Lunar Theory, and prove that the Sun will have a latitude always of the same name as that of the moon.

2. Investigate the equation

$$\frac{d^2u}{d\,\theta^2} + u = \frac{\dfrac{P}{h^2 u^2} - \dfrac{T}{h^2 u^3} \dfrac{du}{d\theta}}{1 + 2 \displaystyle\int \frac{T}{h^2 u^3} \, d\,\theta}.$$

3. Prove that the disturbing force of the sun on the moon is of the second order·

4. Assuming

$$\frac{T}{h^2\, u^3} = -\tfrac{3}{2}\, m^2 \left\{ \sin (2 - 2\, m)\, \theta - 2\, \beta \right\}$$

$$- 2\, e \left\{ \sin\ (2 - 2\, m - c)\ \theta - 2\, \beta + a \right\}$$

$$+ \tfrac{5}{2}\, e^2 \sin \left\{ \left(2 - 2\ m - 2c \right) \theta - 2\, \beta + 2\, a \right\}$$

and supposing that T is the only disturbing force that acts, show that the integral of the differential equation in question 2 is

$$u = a \{ 1 + e \cos (c\ \theta - a) + \tfrac{1}{2}\ m^2 \cos \{ (2 - 2\ m)\ \theta - 2\, \beta \}$$

$$+ \tfrac{21}{16}\ me \cos (2 - 2\ m - c)\ \theta - 2\, \beta + 2\ a]$$

5. Show that the evection in longitude, viz.,

$$\tfrac{15}{4}\ m\, e \sin \{ (2 - 2\, m - c)\ pt - 2\beta + a \}$$

may be represented as the combined effect of periodic changes in the eccentricity of the lunar orbit, and in the mean longitude of its apse.

6. A body describes the arc PQ round a fixed centre of force S, QR is a subtense parallel to SP; QT is a perpendicular on SP; prove that the force is equal to

$$\frac{2\ h^2}{SP}\ \text{limit}\ \frac{QR}{QT^2}$$

where $h =$ twice the area described in the unit of time.

7. If the body revolves in an ellipse with one of the foci as a centre of force, find the law of force.

(a) In the same case, find the periodic time.

8. If a central orbit revolves with an angular velocity proportional at each instant to that of the radius vector in the orbit, prove in Newton's manner that the new orbit is also a central orbit.

9. Show that the difference of the forces by which the bodies are retained in the fixed orbit and in the revolving orbit varies inversely as the cube of the distance from the centre of force.

10. Assuming the geometrical representation of the disturbing force of the sun on the moon, show that the velocity of the moon is greatest in syzygies and least in quadratures.

B. A. AND THIRD YEAR HONOUR EXAMINATIONS.

MATHEMATICS AND NATURAL PHILOSOPHY.

GEOMETRY OF THREE DIMENSIONS.

WEDNESDAY, APRIL 20TH :—MORNING, 9 TO 12.

1. If the equation of a surface be given in the form $z = \phi\ (x,\ y)$, prove that the principal radii of curvature at any point are given by the equation

$$R^2(rt - s^2) - R\ \{ (1 + q^2)\ r - 2\ pqs + (1 + p^2)\ t \}\ \sqrt{1 + p^2 + q^2} + (1 + p^2 + q^2)^2 = 0$$

2. The cuspidal edge of the developable generated by the normals along a line of curvature is the locus of one of the systems of centres of curvature corresponding to all the points of that line.

3. The sum of the reciprocals of the radii of curvature of two normal sections at right angles to each other is constant.

4. Find the partial differential equation of surfaces of revolution.

5. Find the equation of the helix.

(a) Find the equation of a surface generated by a right line which moves parallel to the base of the cylinder on which a helix is traced, while intersecting the axis of the cylinder, and the helix. Draw the section of this surface made by any plane parallel to the axis.

6. Find the equation of a cone whose vertex is the point $0\ 0\ h$, and which stands on the circle $z = 0,\ x^2 + y^2 = a^2$

7. Find the locus of the middle points of all lines parallel to a fixed plane and terminated by two non-intersecting lines.

8. From the equation of the hyperboloid of one sheet prove that there are two systems of right lines lying on the surface.

(a) Prove that any two lines of opposite systems lie in one plane.

9. Find the planes of the circular sections of an ellipsoid.

(a) Find the co ordinates of the umbilics.

10. If $a,\ \beta,\ \gamma;\ a',\ \beta',\ \gamma'$, are the direction angles of two conjugate diameters of an ellipsoid, prove the following equation :

$$\frac{\cos a \; \cos a'}{a^2} + \frac{\cos \beta \cos \beta'}{b} + \frac{\cos \gamma \; \cos \gamma'}{c^4} = 0$$

11. Prove that the condition that the plane $a_1 x + b_1 y + c_1 z + d_1 = 0$ should be a tangent to the surface

$$\frac{x^2}{a^2} + \frac{y^2}{b^2} + \frac{z^2}{c^2} = 1$$

is $a^2 a_1^2 + b^2 b_1^2 + c^2 c_1^2 = d_1^2$

12. Prove that a quadric has in general three principal diametral planes.

13. Find the equation of a plane drawn through a given point perpendicular to a given plane.

14. Find the direction cosines of the line

$$x = m z + a ; y = n z + b$$

15. Find the equation of a plane through the origin perpendicular to the two planes $a_1 x + b_1 y + c_1 z = 0$

$$\text{and } a_2 x + b_2 y + c_2 z = 0$$

B. A. AND THIRD YEAR HONOUR EXAMINATIONS.

ASTRONOMY.

FRIDAY, APRIL 22ND :—MORNING, 9 TO 12.

1. Investigate a formula for determining the parallax of the moon, being given her true zenith distance and horizontal parallax.

2. Given the latitude of a place, explain a method for finding the time of year when a star rises at a given hour.

3. Given the latitudes of two places on the earth's surface, one of which is N. E. of the other, find the difference of their longitudes and their distance from each other, considering the earth a sphere.

4. Show how to determine the latitude of a place from the times of rising of two known stars.

5. Show that the equation of time vanishes four times in the year.

6. Explain the cause of aberration, and prove that for a fixed star Aberration $= k \times$ sine of the earth's way.

a. Calculate the value of k approximately.

β. Show that in consequence of aberration the apparent place of a fixed star describes an ellipse annually about the true place.

7. If t be the hour-angle of the sun at rising or setting at a place whose latitude is l, and if δ be the declination of the sun, prove

$$\cos 15^\circ \; t = - \tan l \tan \delta$$

a. Hence compare the lengths of the day at a given place at different times of the year.

8. Investigate a method for finding the time, magnitude and duration of a lunar eclipse.

9. The sun was observed to pass the meridian at 11h. 59m. 18.7s. by chronometer, the equation of time being + 13m. 22.5s. ; find the error of the chronometer.

10. The true altitude of the sun at 1h. 14m. 11.6s. apparent time was 33° 40′ 35″.5 ; his declination was 5° 15′ 28″·08, find the latitude of the place.

11. On the 22nd September, the sun's declination was 17′ 2″.8 N. and on the 23rd it was 6′ 21″.56 S. ; the sidereal interval of the transits was 24h. 3m. 35.5s.   Find the sun's right ascension at the second observation, explaining the method.

12. If the obliquity of the ecliptic be 23° 27′ 30″.69 and the sun's longitude be 214° 14′ 45″.2, find his R. A.

B A. AND THIRD YEAR HONOURS.

DYNAMICS.

FRIDAY, APRIL 1ST :—MORNING, 9 TO 12.

(Eight questions to be attempted.)

1. Find expressions for the accelerations of a point along and perpendicular to the radius vector.

If the angular velocity of a particle about the origin be constant, prove that its acceleration perpendicular to the radius vector is proportional to the radial component of its velocity.

2. A point moves in a plane in such a manner that its tangential and normal accelerations are always (equal, and its velocity is $e^{\tan-1\frac{s}{c}}$, s being the arc measured from a fixed point. Prove that $s = c\frac{dy}{dx}$, and hence that the path is a catenary.

3. Particles slide from a fixed point vertically above the vertex of a cone (axis vertical, angle $= 2\tan^{-1}\frac{1}{\mu}$) down rough planes (co-efficient of friction μ). Prove that they will all have the same velocity on reaching the cone.

4. Shew how to determine the velocities of two elastic balls after direct impact, explaining the principles involved.

A ball A strikes directly a ball B at rest; B strikes directly C at rest, and is then again struck by A. If A is brought to rest, and B and C move with equal velocities, prove that

$$A : B : C :: 3 : 1 : 2,$$

all the balls being perfectly elastic.

5. A particle, initially at rest, is attracted to a fixed point with a force proportional to the distance. Determine its position and velocity at any time, and prove that the time of oscillation is independent of the amplitude.

6. A particle of mass m initially at rest at distance a from the origin is acted on by a force $m\mu\left(r + \frac{a^4}{r^3}\right)$ to the origin, r being the distance: Find the time in which it arrives at the origin.

7. Prove the formulae for central orbits

$$\frac{d^2u}{d\theta^2} + u - \frac{P}{h^2 u^2} = 0,$$

$$P = \frac{h^2}{p^3}\frac{dp}{dr}$$

8. Find the law of force to the pole when the path is the cardioid, $r = a(1 - \cos\theta)$; and prove that if F be the force at the apse and v the velocity

$$3 v^2 = 4 a F.$$

9. Shew that the velocity of a projectile is that due to a fall from the directrix of the parabola it is describing.

Particles fall down chords of a verticle circle to the lowest point. Prove that the tangents to the circle at the upper ends of the chords pass through the foci of the parabolas described after leaving the lowest point.

10. A particle moves under a force

$\mu\{3\ a\ u^4 - 2\ (a^2 - b^2)\ u^5\}$, a being $> b$, and is projected from

an apse at distance $a + b$ with velocity $\dfrac{\sqrt{\mu}}{a + b}$; shew that the orbit is

$$r = a + b \cos \theta.$$

11. Find the moment of inertia of a cube (1) about an edge, (2) about a diagonal.

A cube is rotating with angular velocity ω about a diagonal when one of its edges, which does not need that diagonal, becomes fixed ; shew that the angular velocity about this axis will be $\dfrac{\omega}{4\sqrt{3}}$

12. A uniform rod of length l is suspended by a point distant h from one end. Find the length of the equivalent pendulum. What is the *centre of oscillation*, and where is it ?

Explain the use of Kater's pendulum for determining gravity, and point out its advantages.

B.A. HONOUR EXAMINATIONS.

ATTRACTIONS AND ELECTRICITY.

MONDAY, APRIL 11TH :—MORNING, 9 TO 12.

1. Prove that the total normal electric induction over any closed surface drawn in the electric field is 4π times the total charge of electricity inside the closed surface.

Show that the electric intensity at a point distant r from the axis of an infinitely long cylinder charged with E units per unit length of axis is

$$\frac{2E}{r}.$$

2. A condenser consists of two infinitely long co-axial cylinders, a being the radius of the inner, and b of the outer cylinder. Prove that its capacity per unit length is $1/2 \log \dfrac{b}{a}$.

3. Two parallel plates, distant d from each other, are charged up to a difference of potential V. Prove that the force per unit area between them is $\dfrac{V^2}{8\,\pi\,d^2}$, in air.

4. Employ the method of electrical images to show that the distribution of electricity on an infinite plane maintained at zero potential in the presence of a charged point varies inversely as the cube of the distance from the point.

5. Define the *strength* of a uniform magnetic shell, and prove that the potential of a shell of strength I in a magnetic field is — IN, where N is the number of lines of force threading its contour.

6. A periodic E. M. F. given by $E \cos pt$ is applied to a circuit of resistance R and self-induction L. Write down the equation determining the flow of current and integrate it, shewing that the phase of the current lags behind that of the E. M. F. by $\tan^{-1} \dfrac{Lp}{R}$.

7. Obtain the equation :

$$4\pi\mu \; \frac{du}{dt} \; = \; \sigma \; \left(\frac{d^2 u}{dx^2} \; + \; \frac{d^2 u}{dy^2} \; + \; \frac{d^2 u}{dz^2}\right)$$

(and two similar equations) where u, v, w are components of current, μ the permeability and σ the specific resistance of the metal in which the currents are flowing.

8. Find the potential of a spherical attracting shell at a point outside it distant c from the centre.

9. Find the resultant attraction of a straight rod on a point outside it, and show that it bisects the angle subtended by the rod at the point.

THIRD YEAR HONOURS.

STATICS.

MONDAY, APRIL 18TH :—MORNING, 9 TO 12.

1. A weight of 10 lbs. is suspended by two strings, 7 and 24 inches long, their other ends being fastened to the extremities of a rod whose length is 25 inches. If the rod be held so that the weight hangs vertically below its middle point, find the tensions of the strings.

2. A pole 12 feet long, weighing 25 lbs., rests with one end against the foot of a wall, and from a point 2 feet from the other end a cord runs horizontally to a point in the wall 8 feet from the ground ; find the tension of the cord, and the pressure on the lower end of the pole.

3. State the principle of Virtual Work, and prove its truth for any number of forces acting on a *particle*.

A heavy elastic ring whose radius, when unstretched, is a, surrounds a smooth vertical cone of angle 90 °. Prove, by the principle of Work, that it will rest at a depth $\dfrac{2\pi+1}{2\pi}$ a below the vertex of the cone, if the tension of the ring is equal to its own weight when it is stretched to double the radius.

4. Define a Couple, and prove that the effect of a Couple is not altered if the arm be turned through any angle round one extremity.

5. Show how to reduce a system of forces acting on a rigid body in one plane to a single force and a couple; and hence deduce the conditions of equilibrium for any system of forces acting on a rigid body in one plane.

6. (a) Find the Centre of Gravity of a segment of a circle.

(b) Show that the centre of gravity of a hemisphere, whose density varies as the square of the distance from the centre, is distant 5/12 of the radius from the centre.

7. Explain what is meant by the "angle" and "cone" of friction.

A uniform beam rests with one end on a rough horizontal plane and the other against an equally rough vertical wall, and when inclined 30 ° to the horizon is on the point of slipping down. Find μ

8. Determine the equation of equilibrium of a weightless string stretched over a rough curved surface (in one plane.)

If $\mu = \dfrac{1}{2\pi}$ find roughly the force which could be sustained by a pull of 10 lbs. at the other end of a rope coiled twice round a post.

9. Investigate the equation to the Common Catenary.

LIGHT AND OPTICS.

1. How does the illumination of a surface depend on the angles of incidence and emission from the source ?

Shew how to calculate the illumination at any point of a surface by a given surface of uniform brightness.

2. Obtain the formula for a lens

$$\frac{1}{v} - \frac{1}{u} = \frac{1}{f}$$

by the principles of the undulatory theory or otherwise.

3. A lens (ot index μ') is placed so as just not to touch the plane surface of a liquid (index μ) : light diverges from a point in the medium and forms an image at a distance v from the lens ; if the lens be now just immersed, and v^1 be the new value of v, and f the local length of the lens, shew that

$$\frac{1}{v} - \frac{1}{v^1} = \frac{\mu - 1}{\mu^1 - 1} \cdot \frac{1}{f} \cdot$$

4. Obtain formulae for the passage of a ray through a prism, and shew that the deviation ot a ray is a minimum when it passes through the prism symmetrically.

5. Find a formula for the aberration of a given ray, when a pencil is incident directly on a spherical mirror

6, Find the position of the primary focal line when a small pencil is incident obliquely on a spherical mirror.

What is the meaning of " circle of least confusion," and how is it connected with the definition of an image ?

7. Describe a Ramsden's Eyepiece, and determine its focal length in terms of that of its lenses.

8. Calculate the breadth of the field ot view by whole pencils in the Astronomical telescope.

9. Find the orbit of a particle subject to two simultaneous simple harmonic vibrations, the period of one being double that of the other, and the epochs different.

10. Describe and investigate the theory of a Rowland Concave Grating and its mounting.

11. State the hypotheses on which Fresnel proceeded in his theory of double refraction, and obtain in any manner the equation to the wave surface.

ENGLISH LANGUAGE AND LITERATURE.

SESSIONAL EXAMINATIONS.

FIRST YEAR.

ENGLISH COMPOSITION.

WEDNESDAY, 6TH APRIL:—AFTERNOON, 2 TO 5.

1. A contemporary critic declares that "the right test to apply to a group of words purporting to be a sentence, is not whether it is good grammar, but whether it makes good sense." Comment upon this assertion.

2. Explain and illustrate, with original examples, if possible: Conciseness, prolixity, periodic sentence, explicit reference, inversion for purposes of emphasis, balance in sentences.

3. Under what circumstances is the use of the parenthesis deemed advisable? What reasonable restrictions may be placed upon its employment? Give examples.

4. Contrast coherence with incoherence, in relation to the simple sentence; and give *original* illustrations in support.

5. To what leading conditions does a well constructed paragraph conform? Illustrate with an *original* paragraph consisting of at least six sentences.

6. What is meant by the application of principles of division to a subject, before beginning to write upon it? Show how this applies to the cases submitted in question (7).

7. Write an essay of at least two pages (more, if possible) on any *one* of the following topics:

    (*a*) International Exhibitions.

    (*b*) Great Explorers.

    (*c*) The Spirit of Independence.

15

SESSIONAL EXAMINATIONS.

FIRST YEAR.

ENGLISH COMPOSITION.

(For Affiliated Colleges.)

WEDNESDAY, APRIL 6TH :—2 HOURS.

1. Correct the following if necessary, giving reasons for so doing :
   (a) If you leave the window open you will be apt to take cold.
   (b) He sat down to a bountiful repast.
   (c) His views are wrong.

2. Illustrate, by means of quotations, violation against purity of style.

3. Define (a) Archaism, (b) Provincialism, with examples.

4. Define Balanced and Periodic sentences.   Give examples.

5. Explain Hyperbole, Antithesis, Epigram.   Give examples.

6. Mention the properties of sentences.

7. Discuss the Paragraph.

8. Write a short essay on one of the following subjects :—Klondike,
The Discovery of Canada, Victoria's Reign.

SESSIONAL EXAMINATIONS.

FIRST YEAR.

ENGLISH LITERATURE.

WEDNESDAY, APRIL 6TH :—MORNING, 9 TO 12.

1. Discuss carefully *two* conditions, connected with the intellectual life
of England in the early part of the 18th century, which favoured the production of prose essays.

2. Give some account of :—The Tatler, The Spectator, The Rambler,
The Citizen of the World.

3. Describe briefly and characterise :—The Shortest Way with Dissenters,
The Idea of a Patriot King, A Tale of a Tub.

4. Make notes on : The character of Swift's satire, Steele's attitude towards women, Addison's judgment of Milton, the diction and style of
Samuel Johnson.   Give direct references, or quotations, in support of
your answer.

5. The following short quotations are judgments or opinions of famous critics; explain precisely what they mean, and confirm or reject them as you think fit, giving your own reasons for your conclusion :

Thackeray.—" The Dean (Swift) was no Irishman."

Taine.—" Addison's essays are in reality sermons."

Bentham.—Johnson is a pompous preacher of melancholy moralities."

Carlyle.—" The last of the Tories was Johnson."

6. What is meant by the term *Humourist?* Does it apply in the same sense to Swift, to Addison, and to Goldsmith ? "

Give illustrative quotations.

7. Discuss the literary style of Swift, *or* of Goldsmith.

<hr>

SESSIONAL EXAMINATIONS.
FIRST YEAR.
ENGLISH HISTORY.
(For Affiliated Colleges.)

SEEBOHM : *Era of the Protestant Revolution.*

WEDNESDAY, APRIL 6TH :—1½ HOURS.

1. What do you know about the feudal system, and the forces which at the beginning of the 16th century were undermining it ?

2. Sketch the reign of Henry VII of England.

3. Describe the main events of the Reformation at Zurich.

4. What causes tended to retard the course of the Protestant Revolution ?

<hr>

SESSIONAL EXAMINATIONS.
FIRST YEAR.
ENGLISH LITERATURE.

DAWSON : *Makers of Modern English.*

(For Wesleyan College, Stanstead.)

WEDNESDAY, APRIL 6TH :—2 HOURS.

[Statements may be illustrated by *brief* quotations.]

1. Why has Byron been called a " cosmopolitan poet ?

2. Give some idea of Wordsworth's attitude towards external nature.

3. Make short notes on :—The Prelude, Maud, The Idylls of the King, Endymion, Adonais,

4. Mention and discuss with some fulness any two marked characteristics of Browning's poetry.

SESSIONAL EXAMINATIONS.

FIRST YEAR.

ENGLISH AND HISTORY.

MORLEY : *First Sketch of English Literature.*

(*For St. Francis College, Richmond.*)

WEDNESDAY, APRIL 6TH : —2½ HOURS.

1. Discuss the influence of Italian Literature on English. Name the writers of the 1st Italian Triumvirate, with the chief work of each.

2. Write short notes on : (*a*) Gododin, (*b*) Merlin, (*c*) Judith, (*d*) Columba, (*e*) Orosius, (*f*) A. S. Chronicle, (*g*) Brunellus.

3. Write a brief description of the first great Anglo-Saxon poem.

4. Describe the origin and development of the "Arthur Story."

5 Give a brief sketch of Chaucer's life, name his works and outline the plan of the last one.

6. Give the authors' names and a brief description of the following works :

(*a*) Golden Terge, (*b*) Pricke of Conscience, (*c*) Topography of Ireland, (*d*) King's Quair, (*e*) Piers Plowman.

INTERMEDIATE EXAMINATIONS.

MODERN HISTORY.

WEDNESDAY, APRIL 6TH :—9 TO 12 A.M.

1. Take any one from among the French politicians of 1789-95 and, after describing his career, estimate his public character and influence.

2. Give an outline of French military operations during the Directory period.

3. In what main respects do the institutions of modern France differ from those of 1789 ? Give special instances and trace them, wherever possible, to the regime of Napoleon I.

4. Sketch the European situation at the end of 1806 with a view to explaining the relations which then existed between France and the other States.

5. Show how lines of political development (on both sides of the Rhine) converge to the Franco-German war. Begin your survey with 1851.

6. The progress of the Italian National movement was affected by non-Italian influences and consiaerations. Illustrate this statement, taking your cases in chronological order and from as wide an area as you can. Period, 1815-70.

7. Make brief notes on:—Lotharingia, Frederick Barbarossa, Peace of Westphalia, The Crisis at Marengo, The End of the Holy Roman Empire Carlsbad Decrees, Casimir-Perier, The Possessions of Charles Albert, "The Moral and Civil Headship of the Italians," Belfort.

INTERMEDIATE EXAMINATIONS.
MODERN HISTORY (AFFILIATED COLLEGES).

WEDNESDAY, APRIL 6TH :—9 TO 12 A.M.

1. What were the main conditions (a) Political, (b) Social, (c) Religious, which led to the French Revolution of 1789?

2. Write notes on any *three* of the following :—*Oath of the Tennis Court, Reign of Terror, Character of Louis XVI., Code Napoléon, Bulgarian Atrocities.*

3. State clearly the *causes* and *results* of the French Revolution of 1848.

4. Give leading incidents in the growth of a national spirit in Italy, and show briefly the tendency of each.

5. What phase of the Eastern Question led to the Crimean War? What were the main provisions of the treaty at the close of that war? What effects have these had on the subsequent history of the question?

6. Write on any *two* of the following wars :—Austro-Sardinian 1859, Austro-Prussian 1866, Franco-Prussian 1870, Russo-Turkish 1877-78, giving (a) the causes, (b) the results.

7. Discuss the character and work of any *two* of the following : Stein, Bismarck, Cavour, Mazzini, Guizot.

8. What difficulties are met with in the attempt to establish a nation in Austro-Hungary?

SESSIONAL EXAMINATIONS.

THIRD YEAR.

CHAUCER, *Prologue to Canterbury Tales;* RHETORIC.

WEDNESDAY, APRIL 6TH :—2 TO 5 P.M.

(Write the answers to A and B in separate books.)

A. CHAUCER.

1. Refer each of the following lines to its place in the Prologue and give its context :

(*a*) ' Cometh neer,' quod he, my lady prioresse.

(*b*) For he had geten him yet no benefice.

(*()* And in his hand he bar a mighty bowe.

(*d*) A limitour, a ful solempne man.

(*e*) God loved he best with al his hole herte.

(*f*) Ful big he was of braun and eek of bones.

(*g*) Short was his goune, with sleves longe and wyde.

(*h*) Of double worsted was his semi-cope.

(*i*) His resouns he spak ful solempnely.

(*j*) Hir frendscipe was nat newe to biginne.

2. Describe the Wyf of Bathe and the Pardoner.

3. Explain i-ronre, for to seeken, atte, chivachye, tappestere, him was levere.

4. (*a*) Give the meaning (and nothing else) of the following words : gobet, stot, cop, streite, laas, mewe, ceint, rote, for-pyned, raughte.

(*b*) Choose any five of the words just given, and over against each write the name of the pilgrim in whose description it occurs.

5. Give some account of the social condition of Chaucer's Engand, noticing, preferably, such matters as were touched on and illustrated in the "demonstration."

B. RHETORIC.

(N.B.—Excellence of method and style will be taken into account in determining the respective merits of candidates.)

1. Explain fully, with original examples if you can, the various meanings of the word *style ;* and state clearly in how far the study of Rhetoric bears upon each of them.

2. Discuss, from your own or from any point of view, the question as to the admissibility of rhythmical effects in prose.

3. In how far is Description amenable to rules, if at all? Support your views by reference to, or quotation from, examples of indisputable merit.

4. What are the conventional divisions of the Oration, or spoken discourse? Illustrate their application, in outline, with the help of an example of your own selection.

5. Explain why Poetry has been said not to admit of precise definition.

B. A. ORDINARY EXAMINATION.

ENGLISH LITERATURE.

MODERN POETS.

WEDNESDAY, APRIL 6TH :—2 TO 5 P. M.

A

1. Mention the heads under which Tennyson's early poems were noticed. Name a poem belonging to each.

2. Indicate, with brevity and precision, two striking and wholly disconnected passages in *Maud* of which the burden is Mammonism. Deal similarly with (*a*) Patriotism and (*b*) Nature as an interpretative medium. Treat one of the two under (*b*) in some detail.

3. Notice *very* briefly and pointedly : —

    (*a*) The mythical Arthur.

    (*b*) The historical Arthur.

    (*c*) The geographical limits of the Arthurian land.

    (*d*) The depression of Gawain and the exaltation of Arthur.

    (*e*) Barendou.

    (*f*) Wolfram von Eschenbach.

4. Write on (*a*) the coronation of Arthur.

    (*b*) Camelot as described in the *Idylls;* contrast Pellam's castle.

    (*c*) The experience of Percivale in the *Holy Grail.*

5. State the main views expressed in the Prologue to *In Memoriam*. By a single reference in each case, show that they point to important places in the poem itself, and by brief reference to *Christmas Eve and Easter Day* show that they are visible there. Justify the Epilogue.

6. Give, in a page, some idea of literature which treated the education of women previous to the *Princess*.

7. Name two poets whose influence is clearly seen in *Pauline.* Unfold in not more than a page, the inner meaning and course of thought of *Pauline.*

8. State very briefly the views of Paracelsus regarding (*a*) the physical body, (*b*) Flagæ, (*c*) magic, (*d*) the healing power of Christ, (*e*) the four pillars of medicine, (*f*) Naturales and Specifici.

In Browning's *Paracelsus* contrast Paracelsus, Aprile, Festus. What is the view of Paracelsus regarding the origin of truth ?

B

Name the works in which the following extracts are found, and the author of each :—(Use simply the prefixed letters to save space.)

 (*a*) I bind the sun's throne with a burning zone

 (*b*) Creus was one; his ponderous iron mace
   Lay by him

 (*c*) There shall they rot—Ambition's honour'd fools

 (*d*) God help the husband then !

 (*e*) Silent, upon a peak in Darien

 (*f*) My old fat woman purred with pleasure

 (*g*) The boatmen rest their oars and say
   Miserere Domine.

 (*h*) His marrow grew cold at the touch of death

 (*i*) He saw thro' life and death, thro' good and ill

 (*j*) Oh ! lift me as a wave, a leaf, a cloud !
   I fall upon the thorns of life !

 (*k*) 'Twill murmur on a thousand years
   And flow as now it flows

 (*l*) Like a glow-worm golden
   In a dell of dew

 (*m*) E'en the slight hare-bell raised its head
   Elastic from her airy tread

 (*n*) Heard melodies are sweet, but those unheard
   Are sweeter

 (*o*) Life went a-maying
   With Nature, Hope and Poesy,
    When I was young

 (*p*) Little we see in nature that is ours

 (*q*) She gave me eyes, she gave me ears

(r) And those thin clouds above in flakes and bars,
    That give away their motion to the stars
(s) The trees which grew along the broken arches
    Waved dark in the blue midnight
(t) The scourge is wight, the spur is bright

2. Give pointedly, in connected prose and within the limit of one page, an outline of Childe Harold, canto I.

3. Deal similarly with the Lady of the Lake.

4. Deal similarly with Adonais.

5. Bring out the leading points in *Johannes Agricola*, and in one of the longer sketches in *Men and Women*.

FINAL EXAMINATIONS.

HISTORY (MORRIN COLLEGE).

BRYCE :—" *The Holy Roman Empire.*"

MYERS : "*Mediæval and Modern History.*"

APRIL 6TH :—9 TO 12 A.M.

Examiner, ... C. W. COLBY, M.A., PH.D.

1. Under what circumstances did the Roman Empire of the West come to an end, and what theory was held at the time with regard to its extinction?

2. Illustrate the international position of the Mediæval Empire.

3. Indicate the main results of the Reformation upon the Holy Roman Empire.

4. Estimate the part of William the Silent in founding the Dutch Republic.

5. What do you know of the contest between Frederick the Great and Marie Theresa?

6. Examine Napoleon's campaigns from 1805 to the outbreak of the Peninsular War.

7. Make brief notes on : Edict of Caracalla ; *Patricius Romanorum ;* Frederick Barbarossa and Hadrian IV. ; The Electoral College ; Rudolf of Hapsburg ; St. Benedict ; Council of Clermont ; Hanseatic League ; Conspiracy of Amboise ; September Massacres.

THIRD YEAR EXAMINATION FOR HONOURS IN ENGLISH.

THURSDAY, MARCH 31ST :—9 TO 12 A.M.

MILTON : *Minor Poems.*

1. Name the poems from which the following extracts are taken :

(a) The labour of an age in piled stones.

(b) Not Typhon huge, ending in snaky twine.

(c) Or Trent, who like some earth-born giant spreads
His thirty arms along the indented meads.

(d) Soft silken primrose fading timelessly.

(e) Both them I serve and of their train am I.

Indicate, with illustrative references, the character of the English poems which precede *l'Allegro.*

2. Straight mine eye hath caught new pleasures,
Whilst the landscape round it measures —*L'Allegro.*
Describe them. Is the landscape real or ideal ?

3. State in what connection and in what divisions of *Il Penseroso* reference is made to—storied windows, Pelops' line, th'accustomed oak, thrice-great Hermes, Sylvan, Canace, forests and enchantments drear. Write explanatory notes.

4. Milton is distinguished from the Spenserians generally, by (a) solemnity of tone joined to sensuous beauty, (b) a careful style, (c) marked artistic taste. Illustrate from *Comus.*

5. Contrast *Arcades* and *Comus.*

6. Define the character of the three songs in *Arcades*, and explain the allusions they contain. Give some account of the Ptolemaic system, and refer to Arcades in this connection.

7. Refer the following to their speakers, and say in what portion of *Comus* each is found.

(a) Love Virtue, she alone is free.

(b) What hath night to do with sleep ?

(c)   beckoning shadows dire
And airy tongues.

(d) Summer drouth or singed air
Never scorch thy tresses fair.

(e) Their port was more than human as they stood.

(f) Sabrina is her name.

(g) Himself is his own dungeon.

(h) He called it hæmony.

(i) How charming is divine philosophy !

8. Within the navel of this hideous wood,
Immured in cypress shades, a sorcerer dwells.
Give the substance of the subsequent part of the speech.

EXAMINATIONS FOR HONOURS IN ENGLISH.

THIRD YEAR.

SPENSER :—*Shepheards Calender ; Faerie Queene*, BK. I.

FRIDAY, APRIL 1ST :—9 to 12 A. M.

1. Exhibit the contemporaneousness of *Mother Hubberds Tale* and *Colin Clouts Come Home Againe* ?

2. Mention the Æglogues in the *Shepheards Calender* which are distinctly Elizabethan in tone, and state in a line or two the subject of each.

3. Indicate the varieties of pastoral exhibited by Theocritus, Mantuan, Sannazaro.

4. "This noble and pregnant piece (*October Eglogue*) is the very core of the Shepheards Calender." What is its subject and how does Spenser treat it?

5. Where are " fables " found in the *Shepheards Calender?* Give an outline of them.

6. Write a page on the language of the *Shepheards Calender*, paying more attention to details than to general principles.

7. Notice in Spenser's Prefatory Letter to the *Faerie Queene*

(a) the difference between Ariosto and Tasso

(b) the aim of the poem

(c) the superiority of Xenophon to Plato.

8. Name, in order, the combats in which the Red Cross Knight takes part. State the result of each, and point out the allegory when necessary.

9. Make a list of names corresponding to the following references, and say where the references occur :

(a) And in his hand his portesse still he bare

(b) For seven great heads out of his body grew

(c) His three deformed heads

(d) His haughtie helmet, horrid all with gold

(e) his weake steps governing
And aged limbs on cypresse stadle stout,
And with anyvie twyne his wast is girt about.

(f) His flaggy wings——— were like two sayles.

(g) His garment nought but many ragged clouts.

10. Where do the following appear, and what is the office of each—Ignaro, Slowth, Humiltù, Malvenu? Add a word or two describing the first.

11. Describe Heavenly Contemplation, and give an account of what passed between him and the Red Cross Knight.

12. Describe the structure of the Spenserian stanza, and say something about its origin. Quote a stanza other than the first of the poem. Give the meaning of the following words : nil, recreaunt, sam, tire, warrayd, avale, bowrs, fere, gobbet, owch. Place four of them in the poem.

EXAMINATION FOR HONOURS IN ENGLISH.

THIRD YEAR.

WORDSWORTH : *Prelude.* CAMPBELL : *Pleasures of Hope.*

FRIDAY, APRIL 8TH :—9 TO 12 A.M.

1. State in what general connection each of the following extracts occurs explain each extract :

(a) By a bequest sufficient for my needs
Enabled me to pause for choice

(b)   the name
Of Wallace to be found, like a wild flower

(c) It is the sacrificial altar, fed
With living men

(d)   a huge peak, black and huge

(e)   there I heard—
The sunset cannon

(f)   that single wren
Which one day sang so sweetly in the nave

(g) And pocketed the relic

(h) I travelled round our little lake, five miles
Of pleasant wandering

(i)   thy most eloquent tongue—
Now mute, for ever mute, in the cold grave

(j) A feeling that I was not for that hour
Nor for that place

(k) Half-rural Sadler's Wells

(l) Sweet Spenser

(m) Its dumb cataracts and streams of ice

(n) I saw the snow-white church upon her hill

(o)   the very eve
Of that great federal day

(p)   I made no vows, but vows
Were then made for me.

2. What feature of Wordsworth's poetry is seen in (f) of question 1 ? Give two other examples from the Prelude.

3. Give the substance of Wordsworth's description of (a) the London preacher, (b) the life and character of Beaupuis, (c) Cambridge and his haunts there.

4. In one place (Bk. IV) Wordsworth, touching a vital centre of his doctrine, writes :

How gracious, how benign is Solitude ;
How potent a mere image of her sway ;
Most potent when impressed upon the mind
With an appropriate human centre.

Give the outline of a set of striking passages elsewhere which present the same theme filled out with details.

5. Write a short paragraph on (a) Campbell's practical interest in Poland, (b) *Gertrude of Wyoming.* To what is the poetic force of *Hohenlinden* due ?

6. What is commonly said to have suggested the Pleasures of Hope ?

7. Indicate or quote the context of (a) 'Tis distance lends enchantment to the view, (b) *Iona's saint,* (c) the dread Indian chants a dismal song, (d) *The robber Moor,* (e) Thy woes. *Arion,* (f) " my bleeding country save," (g) Eden's rosy bower, (h) Faint, weeping, bound, he weeps the night away. Make notes on the italicized extracts.

8. State the leading thought with which each of the extracts in the previous question is connected.

9. Give an outline (a) of the portion of Pt. I where Hope appears " with Genius hand in hand," (b) of any division of equal importance in Pt. II.

10. Quote any ten consecutive lines other than the first ten of Pt. I.

EXAMINATION FOR HONOURS IN ENGLISH.

THIRD YEAR.

ADDISON, *Papers on the Imagination and Paradise Lost;* DRYDEN, *Annus Mirabilis, Absalom and Achitophel, Preface to Fables.*

SATURDAY, APRIL 9TH:—9 TO 12 A. M.

1. State briefly how Addison treats the following matters :

(*a*) " I divide these pleasures into two kinds."

(*b*) the pleasures of the fancy are more conducive to health than those of the understanding.

(*c*) the pleasure derived from looking at a waterfall.

(*d*) the final cause of our feeling pleasure in what is (*a*) new, (*b*) great.

(*e*) the accidental landscapes of trees, clouds and cities that are sometimes found in the veins of marble.

(*f*) the inside of a dome as contrasted with a square pillar.

(*g*) description gives us more lively ideas than sight.

(*h*) a poet is born, not made.

(*i*) pleasure derived from the description of what is terrible.

(*j*) Spenser.

(*k*) the enlargement, by degrees, of the fancy when contemplating.

2. Elucidate briefly :

(*a*) Homer, Virgil and Milton hasten " into the midst of things "

(*b*) Milton has introduced all the variety of characters possible

(*c*) the only piece of pleasantry in Paradise Lost. Justify Milton.

(*d*) the elision of a final *y*

(*e*) technical language

(*f*) Satan and the Sun

(*g*) Raphael's behaviour ; contrast Michael

(*h*) the golden compasses

(*i*) the account of the Deluge

(*k*) the moral of Paradise Lost

3. Give an outline of Addison's paper on any *one* of books IV., VIII., X.

4. Give, in a page, an outline of the course of events in Paradise Lost.

5. What remark is made about the Preface to Gondibert in the prose introduction to Annus Mirabilis? Give Dryden's views concerning the general subject.

6. Tabulate the chief events described in Annus Mirabilis, giving dates. Give the details of one which Dryden treats at considerable length.

What was said in the lecture concerning the imagery of Annus Mirabilis?

7. Briefly indicate the political aspect of things when Absalom and Achitophel was written. Why has the poem a scriptural basis?

8. Sketch an important character belonging to each party. Give the Drydenic names and the real names of any other six, and say to what party they belong.

9. Refer the following lines to their places in the poem:

(a) Oh, that my power to saving were confined !

(b) Behold a banished man.

(c) The joyful people thronged to see him land.

10. In the preface to the Fables notice Dryden's observations regarding (a) the Fables and his previous writings; (b) the literary age, studies and originality of Ovid and Chaucer ; (c) the religion of Chaucer.

EXAMINATION FOR HONOURS IN ENGLISH.

THIRD YEAR.

ANGLO-SAXON.

WEDNESDAY, APRIL 13TH :—9 TO 12 A.M.

A

1. He sæde thæt Northmanna land wære swythe lang and swythe smæl. Eall thæt his man ather oththe ettan oththe erian mæg, thæt lith with that sæ ; and thæt is theah on sumum stowum swythe cludig ; and licgath wilde moras with eastan and with uppon emnlange thæm bynum lande.

Give reason for the long quantity of saede and swythe.

2. Alecgath hit thonne for·hwæga on anre mile thone mæstan dæl fram thæm tune, thonne otherne, thonne thæne thriddan, oth the hyt eall aled bith on thære anre mile; and sceall beon se læsta dæl nyhst thæm tune he se deada mann on lith.

Account for the long quantity of led in aled; other; and for the y in nyhst. Give the exact meaning of tun. What is the corresponding verb?

3. Tha hie tha fela wucena sæton on twa healfe thære e, ond se cyng wæs west on Defnum with thone sciphere, tha wæron hie mid metelieste gewægde, ond hæfdon micelne dæl thara horsa freten, ond tha othre wæron hungre acwolen.

4. Næfde se here, Godes thonces, Angelcynn ealles for swithe gebrocod ac hie wæron micle swithor gebrocede on thæm thrim gearum mid ceapes cwilde ond monna; ealles swithost mid thæm thæt manige thara selestena cynges thena the thær on londe wæron forthferdon on thæm thrym gearum.

B

1. With ymbe. Nim eorthan, oferweorp mid thinre swithran handa under thinum swithran fet, and cweth :

' Fo ic under fot; funde ic hit.
Hwæt, eorthe mæg with ealra wihta gehwilce,
and with andan, and with aeminde,
and with tha micelan mannes tungan.
Forweorp oter greot, thonne hi swirman, and cweth :

2. Stod under linder leohtum scylde,
thær tha mihtgan wif byra maegen beraeddon
and hy gyllende garas sacudan ;
ic him otherne eft wille sacudan
fleogende flan forane togeanes ;
ut, lytel spere, gif hit her-inne sy !

3 Warigeath wulfbleothu, windige naessas,
frecne fenngelad, thaer fyrgenstream
under naessa genipu nither gewiteth,
f lod under flodan. Nis thaet feorr heonon
milgemearces, thaet se mere standeth,
ofer thaem hongiath hrimge bearwas,
wudu wyrtum faest, waeter oferhelmath.
Thaer maeg nihta gehwaem nihwundor seon,
fyr on flode. No thaes frod leofath
gumena bearna, thaet thone grund wite.
theah the haethstapa hundum geswenced,

*h*eorot *h*ornum trum *h*oltwudu sece,
*f*eorran ge*f*lymed, aer he *f*eorh seleth,
*a*ldor on *o*fre, aer he *i*nn wille
*h*afelan [*h*ydan]   Nis thaet *h*eoru stow :
thonon *y*thgeblond *u*p astigeth
*w*on*n* to *w*olcnum, thonne *w*ind styreth
*l*ath gewidru, oth thaet *l*yft drysmath,
*r*oderas *r*eotath.

Scan the first four full lines of the extract.   Make a few notes on the
" schwellvers.

4. ' Nu eow is ge*r*ymed, gath *r*icene to us,
   *g*uman to *g*uthe ; *G*od ana wat,
   hwa thaere *w*aelstowe *w*ealdan mote.'
   Wodon tha *w*aelwulfas, for *w*aetere ne murnon,
   *w*icinga *w*erod, *w*est ofer Pantan,
   ofer *s*cir w*a*eter *s*cyldas waegon,
   *l*idmen*n* to *l*ande *l*inda baeron.
   Thaer ongean *g*ramum *g*earowe stodon
   *B*yrhtnoth mid *b*eornum : he mid *b*ordum het
   wyrcan thone *w*ihaga*n*, and thaet *w*or*o*d healdan
   *f*aeste with *f*eondum.   Tha waes *f*eohte neh
   *t*ir aet getohte ; waes seo *t*id cumen
   thaet thaer *f*aege men*n f*eallan sceoldon.

5. ' Is thes *a*eng*a* s*t*yde *u*ngelic s*w*ithe
   tham othrum the we *a*er cuthon,
   *h*ean on *h*eofonrice, the me min *h*earra onlag,
   theah we hine for tham *All*waldan *a*gan ne moston,
   *r*omigan ures *r*ices.   Naefth he theah riht gedon
   thaet he us haelth be*f*aelled *f*yre to botme,
   *h*elle thaere *h*atan, *h*eofonrice benumen,
   hafath hit ge*m*earcod mid *m*oncynne
   to gesettanne.
   Make a few notes on the source of the poem.

6. ' Her ge magon *s*weoto*l*e *s*igerofe haeleth,
   *l*eoda raeswan, on thaes *l*athestan
   *h*aethenes *h*eathorinces *h*eafod starian,
   *O*iofernus unly*f*igendes.
   The us *m*onna *m*aest morthra gefremede,
   *s*arra *s*orga, and thaet *s*wythor gyt
   *y*can wolde ; ac him ne *u*the God
   *l*engran *l*ifes, thaet I e mid *l*aeththum us
   eglan moste : ic him *e*aldor oththrong
   thurh *G*o*d*es fultum.

16

7. Feala ic on tham *b*eorge ge*b*iden bachho
*wr*athra *w*yrda : geseah ic *w*aruda God
*t*hearle *t*henian : *t*hystro haefdon
b*aw*rigen mid *w*olcnum *W*ealdendes hraew,
*s*cirne *s*ciman *s*ceadu fortheode
wann under *w*olcnum. *W*eop eal*l* ge*s*ceaft,
cwith*l*on cyninges *t*yll : *C*rist waes on rode.

8. Stondeth nu on *l*aste *l*eofre duguthe
*w*eal*l* *w*undrum heah, *w*yrmlicum fah :
*e*orlas fornomon *ae*sca thrythe,
*w*aepen *w*telgifru, *w*yrd seo maere,
and th*is* *s*tanhleothu *t*orma*s* cnyssath :
*h*rith *h*reosende *h*rusan bindeth,
*w*intres *w*oma, thonne *w*onn cymeth,
nipeth ni*h*tsc*i*a, *n*orthan onsendeth
*h*reo *h*aeg*l*fare *h*aelethum on andan.

9.   *H*eard mec siththan
snath *s*eaxes ecg *s*in*l*rum begrunden,
*f*ingra*s* *f*eoldan, and mec *f*ugles wyn*n*
geond [sprengde] *s*peddropum, *s*pyrede geneahhe
ofer *b*runne *b*rerd, *b*eamtelg*e* swealg,
*t*reames daele, *s*top eft on m*ec*,
ithade *s*weartlast.

C

1. Give the principal parts of laetan, gripan, beodan, helpan, feallan, flowan, beran, cwethan, faran, weorpan. Underline the verbs which are of reduplicative origin.

2. Write out the past tense (indic. and subj.) of gripan.

3. Decline til, god, se goda, thu.

4. Decline and give gender of ende, mann, modor, sawol, faet.

Translate—

Tha waes on thaere byrig on tham ylcan timan
an aenlie wimman on wudewanhade,
Judith gehaten, thaera beahfaedera cynnes ;
swithe gelyfed mann on thone lyfigendan God,
hlisfull on theawum, ribtlice lybbende
aefter Moyses ae, Manases laf :
se waes hire wer ache wearth ofslagen
thurb thaere sunnan haetan on haerfestlicrc tide.

EXAMINATION FOR HONOURS IN ENGLISH.

THIRD YEAR.

BURKE, *Reflections on the French Revolution:* LESLIE STEPHEN, *English Thought in the Eighteenth Century.*

TUESDAY, APRIL 19TH :—2 TO 5 P. M.

A.

1. What knowledge have you gained from Burke concerning the circumstances under which the Declaration of Right was enacted, and concerning the scope of that measure ?

2. How does Burke discuss the basis of government, bearing in mind natural rights on the one hand, and convenience on the other ?

3. What has Burke to say on :—

    (a) French men of letters who have fomented the Revolution ;

    (b) The division of France into departments ;

    (c) His own attitude towards the Revolution,—
               (concluding passage of the work) ?

4. Make notes on : the Rev. Hugh Peters ; Burke's attitude towards Bolingbroke ; Henry IV, of France ; the Areopagus of Athens ; the " fraudulent exhibitions of Mr. Law."

B.

1. Contrast Montesquieu and Rousseau.

2. What main points does Stephen make in dealing with :

    (a) Junius ;

    (b) Dr. Johnson ;

    (c) De Lolme ?

3. Consider the question of Burke's political consistency.

EXAMINATION FOR HONOURS IN ENGLISH.

THIRD YEAR.

Early English, MORRIS and SKEAT, Specimens, Part II., Extt. I.-IX.;
CHAUCER: *Parlement of Foules.*

SATURDAY, APRIL 23RD :—9 TO 12 A.M.

1. Translate :—

(*a*) *G*if he sede, that he nadde · none ri*g*te th*er*-to,
that vpe the popes lokinge · of Rome he ssolde it do,
& he wolde ther-to stonde · al withoute fi*g*te,
Wer Seint E*d*ward hit him *g*af · & wer he adde the*i*-to ri*g*te.

Willam bitho*g*te an quointise · & bi-*g*an to fie uaste,
& is folc uorth mid him · as hii were agaste,
& flowe ou*er* an longe dale ·· & so vp anhey.
The Engliss ost was prout ynou · tho he this isey,
& bigonne him to sprede · & *after* then wey nome.
The Normans wer*e* abcue the hul · the oth*er*e vpward come,
& bi-turnde home aboue al eseliche · as it wolde be donward,
& the oth*er*e binethe ne mi*g*te nc*g*t · so quicliche vpward.

So that al at one tyme · he was at threo stedes,
His honden th*er*, his hurte at God · his mouth to bidde his
    bedes ;
Therfore the deuel l adde ot him · g*r*et enuye & onde.
O tyme he cam to his smyththe · alone him to fonde,
Ri*g*t as the sonne wende adoun · ri*g*t as he w*o*mman were,
& spac with him of his worc · with [a] la*g*inge chere·

(*b*) To noght es led*e* lither in his sight ;
And dredand Laue*r*d he glades right.
He that to his neghburgh sweres,
And noght biswikes him ne deres.
Ne his siluer til okir noght es giuand ;
Ne giftes toke ou*er* vnderand.
That does these night and da*i*,
Noght sal he be stired in a*i*.
With hali halgh bes of the ;
With man vnderand, vnderand be.
With chosen, and be chosen thou sal ;
With il-torned, and il-tornest al.
For thou meke folk sauf make sal nou ;
And egben of pronde meke sal-tou.
And Lauerdes m*er*ci eure dwelland,
And til ai our him dreadeand ;

And in sones of sones his rightwisenes,
To thas that yhemes witeword his ;
And mined sal thai be, night and dai
Of his bodes to do tham ai.
Lauerd in heuen graithed sete his,
And his rike til alle sal Lauerd in blis
Blisses to Lanerd with alle your might
Alle his aungels, that ere bright:
Mightand of thew, doand his worle swa.
To here stenen of his saghs ma.

(c) Alle whyle ich wes on erthe,
Neuer lykede me my werthe,
    For none wynes fylle ;
Bote myn & myn owen won,
Wyn & water, stoke & ston,
    Al goth to my wille.
'Este bueth oune brondes ;'
                    Quoth Hendyng

Gef the lacketh mete other cloth,
Ne make the nout for-thy to wroth,
    Thah thou byde borewe ;
For he that haueth is god ploh,
Ant of worldes wele ynoh,
    Ne wot he of no sorewe.
'Gredy is the godles ;'
                    Q[u]oth Hendyng.

(d) Leuedy of alle londe,
    Les me out of bonde,
        Broht icham in wo;
    Haue resting on honde,
    & sent thou me thi sonde,
        Sone, er thou me slo ;
    My reste is with the ro :
    Thah men to me han onde,
    To loue nuly noht wonde,
    Ne lete for non of tho.

(e) In water ich wel the cristny her
    As Gode him-self hyt digte ;
    For mide to wessche nis nothynge
    That man cometh to so ligte,
                    In londe ;

Nis non that habben hit ne may
That habbe hit wile founde.
Ac *g*et ther beth cristnynges mo,
Ac no man ne may di*g*tti;
For hi beth Godes grace self,
Men of gode wil to ri*g*ti
     And wynne,
Wanne hi wolde i*cr*istned be,
And mo*g*e mid none ginne.

That on his cleped cristning of h:ode,
Wanne suche bledeth for Criste;
That other of the Holi Gost,
That mo*g*e mid none liste
     Be icristned;
And deyeth so, wanne hi beth deede,
In heuene hi beth igistned.

(*f*) ' Maria, me thine ferli o the
That se the gret heght o this tre;
The frut hu suld man reche vnto,
That man his hand mai to nan do?
Bot I site for an other thing,
That we o water has nu wanting;
Vr water purueance es gan,
And in this wildernes es nan,
Nather for vs, ne for vr fee,
Ne for nan of vr meiné.'
I*esu*s satt on his moder kne,
Wit a ful blith cher said he,
' Bogh thou til vs snith, thou tre,
And of thi frut thou giue vs plenté.'

(*g*) Tho*g*tes. and his besteriinge. wyt. and dedes / ase wel wyth-oute : ase wyth-inne. Thet is to zigge / huych mayné / to moche slae / and wylles-uol ssel by : bote yef the ilke uaderes stefhede hise strayny / and ordayny. Vor zothe yef he hym a lyte of his bysyhede wyth-dra*g*th : huo may zigge / hou tho*g*tes. e*g*en. earen. tonge. and alle othre wyttes : becometh wylde. Hous. is inwyt / in huychen the uader of house woneth. the hord of uirtues gadereth. Vor huych hord : thet ilke zelue hous ne by Y-dolue / he*g*lyche he waketh.   ..

(*h*) Theruore by ziker / uor eurych beth aseuele blyssen : ase he beth uela*g*es. and aseuele blissen to echen : ase his o*g*ene of alle. and theruore eureich more loueth wythoute comparisoun god : thet hym and othre made / thanne him zelue / and alle othre. More by b*j*eth glede wyth-oute ges-synge of godes holynesse : thanne of his c*g*ene / and of alle othre myd hym. Yef thanne on onneathe nymth al his blisse. hou ssel he nyme zuo uele and zuo mauye blyssen ? And theruore hit is yzed. guo into the blysse of thyne lhorde. na*g*t the blisse of thine lhorde / guo in to the. uor hy ne may.

2. Give an outline of the tale of the Usurer (Homilies in Verse).

B.

1. State the chief sources to which Chaucer was indebted and where he has made use of them.

2. Follow Chaucer in his account of what took place in the assembly of birds after the tercels had spoken.

3. Where do the following lines occur ?

(*a*) The carter dremeth how his cartes goon

(*b*) With face pale upon an hille of sond

(*c*) The note, I trowe, maked was in Fraunce

(*d*) Right with a subtil kerebef of Valence

(*e*) But God save swich a lord ! I can no more

4. Give the meaning (and nothing else) of the following words, and refer any five of them to their places in the poem : slit, tonne, sheter, orloge, heysugge, to-torn, gan misse.

B.A. EXAMINATION FOR HONOURS IN ENGLISH.

TENNYSON : *In Memoriam.*

THURSDAY, MARCH 31ST :—9 TO 12 A.M.

1. Use In Memoriam to illustrate identity of views between Tennyson and Wordsworth.

2. Indicate, sufficiently for identification, the sections in which (*a*) lovers or (*b*) husband and wife, illustrate the feelings cr relation of the poet in regard to Hallam.

3. "Are God and Nature then at strife ? " (LV.) State in a short paragraph the logical course of the poet's thought to this point. Give in your own words the substance of the section and of that which immediately follows it.

4. Give in your own words or otherwise :

(*a*) The contrast between the religion of reason and the religion of form.

(*b*) The picture of the third Christmas-eve.

5. Explain the following extracts, and briefly state the subject with which each of the first four is connected.

(*a*) Sick for thy stubborn hardihood

(*b*) And hushes half the babbling Wye

(c) And orb into the perfect star

(*d*) Or ruin'd chrysalis of one

(*e*) Before the crimson-circled star

Had fall'n into his father's grave

(*f*) Flits by the sea-blue bird of March.

6. Indicate Hallam's character and attainments from the poem, quoting briefly when you can.

7. Write an essay of not more than three pages in length on Nature in In Memoriam, giving identifiable references of a general kind, and also minute touches. Avoid using, except where you deem it wise, Tennyson's exact language, and in any case use it as sparingly as you can.

B.A. EXAMINATION FOR HONOURS IN ENGLISH.

ANGLO-SAXON.

Friday, April 1st:--9 to 12 a.m.

(A) Beowulf.

Translate :

(*a*) Oft Scyld Scefing   sceathena threatum,
monegum mægthum   meodo-setla ofteah.
Egsode eorl,   syththan ærest wearth
fea-sceaft funden :   he thas frofre gebad,
weox under wolcnum,   weorth-myndum thah,
oth that him æghwylc   thara ymb-sittendra
ofer bron-rade   byran scolde,
gomban gyldan :   that was god cyning !

(*b*) Tha sc ellen-gæst   earfothlice
thrage getholode,   se the in thystrum bad,
that he dogora gehwam   dream gehyrde

hludne in bealle ;   thær was hearpan sweg,
swutol sang scopes.   Sagde se the cuthe
frum-sceaft fira   feorran reccan,
cwath that se almihtiga   eorthan worhte,
wlite-beorhtne wang,   swa water bebugeth,
gesette sige-hrethig   sunnan and monan
leoman to leohte   land-buendum,
and gefratwade   foldan sceatas
leomum and leafum ;   lif eac gesceop
cynna gehwylcum,   thara the cwice hwyrfath.

(c)   Monig-oft gesat
rice to rune ;   ræd eahtedon,
hwat swith-ferhthum   selest wære
with fær-gryrum   to gefremmanne.
Hwilum hie gehetou   at harg-trafum
wig-weorthunga,   wordum bædon,
that him gast-bona   geoce gefremede
with theod-threaum.

(d) " Her syndon geferede   feorran cumene
" ofer geofenes begang   Geata leode :
" thone yldestan   oret-mecgas
" Beowulf nemnath.   Hy benan synt,
" that hie, theoden min,   with the moton
" wordum wrixlan ;   no thu him wearne geteoh,
" thinra gegn-cwida   gladnian, Hrothgar !
" Hy on wig-geatwum   wyrthe thinceath
" eorla geæhtlan ;   huru se aldor deah,
" se thæm heatho-rincum   hider wisade."

(e) " Habbe ic eac geahsod,   that se aglæca
" for his won-hydum   wæpna ne receth ;
" ic that thonne forhicge,   swa me Higelac sie,
" min mon-drihten,   modes blithe,
" that ic sweord bere   oththe sidne scyld
" geolo-rand to guthe ;   ac ic mid grape sceal
" fon with feonde   and ymb feorh sacan,
" lath with lathum;   thær gelyfan sceal
" dryhtnes dome   se the hine death nimeth.

(f)   Ne inc ænig mon
" ne leof ne lath,   belean mihte
" sorh-fullne sith ;   tha git on sund reon,
" thær git eagor-stream   earmum thehton,
" mæton mere-stræta,   mundum brugdon,

"glidon ofer gar-seeg ;　　geofon ythum weol,
" wintres wylme.　Git on wateres æht
" seofon niht swuncon ;　　he the at sunde oferflat,
" hafde mare magen.

(*g*) "Swa mec gelome　　　lath-geteonan
" threatedon thearle.　　Ic him thenode
" deoran sweorde,　　swa hit gedefe was ;
" nas hie thære fylle　gefean hafdon,
" man-fordædlan,　　that hie me thegon,
"symbel ymb-sæton　　sæ-grunde neah,
" ac on mergenne　　mecum wunde
" be yth-lafe uppe lægon,
" sweordum aswefede,　　that syththan na
" ymb brontne ford　　brim-lithende
"lade ne letton.　　Leoht eastan com,
"beorht heacen godes ; brimu swathredon,
" that ic sæ-næssas　　geseon mihte,
" windige weallas.

(*h*) " No ic me an here-wæsmum　　hnagran talige
" guth-geweorca,　　thonne Grendel hine ;
" forthan ic hine sweorde　　swebban nelle,
" aldre beneotan,　　theah ic eal mæge.
" Nat he thara goda,　　that he me on-gean slea,
" rand geheawe,　　theah the he rof sie
" nith-geweorca ;　　ac wit on niht sculon
" secge ofersittan,　　git he gesecean dear
" wig ofer wæpen,　　and siththan witig god
" on swa hwathere hond　　halig dryhten
"mærtho deme,　　swa him gemet thince."

B) TRANSLATION AT SIGHT.

1. Swa he his weorc weorthath, bi thon se witga cwæth,
thæt ahæfen wæren halge gimmas
bædre beofontungol heahlice upp,
sunne ond mona.　Hwæt sindan tha
gimmas swa seyne buton god sylfa ?
He is se sothfæsta sunnan leoma,
englum ond eorthwarum æthele scima !
Ofer middangeard mona lixeth,
gastlic tungol, swa seo godes circe
thurh gesomninga sothes ond ryhtes
beorhte bliceth, swa hit on bocum cwith,
siththan of grundum godbearn astag,
cyning heora gehwæs.

2. Wer sæt æt wine mid his witum twam
ond his twegen suno and his twa dohtor,
swnse gesweostor ond hyra suno twegen,
freolico lrumbearn : fæder wæs thær inne
thara æthelinga ægbwætbres mid,
eam ond nefa. Ealra wæron fife
eorla ond idesa insittendra.

3. Tha hit geberdon ealle tha untruman, the wæron thær on lande, ealle
hi hire lic gesohton and heora hæle ther gefetton. Sume hi wæron blinde
and deafa and sume crypeles and sume dumbe and sume ungewitfulle,
Ealle hi heora hæle æt thære halgan fæmnan onfenge, and mycel mancyn,
ealle tha the unhale wære, thære fæmnen lic gesohton, ealle hi hale and
gesunde on heora wege ham gewænton. And ures drihtnes ængles thider
comon and tha sawla underfengon and heo on heofone rice gebrohton.

4. Hwylc is hæletha thæs horse ond thæs hygecraftig,
thæt thæt mæge asecgan, hwa mec on sith wræce.
thonne ic astige strong, stundum rethe
thrymful thunie, thragum wræce
fere geond foldan, tolesalo bærne,
ræced reafige? recas stigath
haswe ofer brofum, hlin bith on eorthan,
wælcwealm wera.

C.

1. Make notes ou the following (Ext. (a) Scyld Scefing, otteah, egsode.

2. Beowulf. (1.19) *Scedelandum in* what is the other form of the name ;
what is the region meant and what may the name mean? (1.29) *swæse
gesithas* the exact meaning of *swæse?* (1.36, *heals-gebedde* what is the
reading ot the Ms? justify it. (1.101) *feond on helle* give translations and
emendations (1.112) *orcneas* refer to Latin and Italian-how are the *n* and
the termination *eas* explained? (1.168) *gifstol* how does Wülcker explain
the phrase? (1.215) *guthsearo geatolic* notice the various meanings of
geatolic (1.219) *antid* how is a common translation of this word supported ?
it is warranted? (1.366) *glædnian* (Ext. *d.*) emend. (1.403) *thæt he on
heothe gestod* how is this generally translated, and how may the line be
improved?

3. Write briefly on Runes.

B. A. EXAMINATION FOR HONOURS IN ENGLISH.

SHAKESPERE: *Love's Labour's Lost, A Midsummer Night's Dream, Hamlet, The Tempest.*

FRIDAY, APRIL 8TH :—9 TO 12 A. M.

1. Write on the sources of the four plays, noticing any important departure from them.

2. Apart from the course of the plot, contrast L. L. L. and the Tempest as an early and a late play, arranging your heads in tabular form, and giving, when necessary, brief references in illustration.

3. Write on the Fairies of the Dream.

4. Refer the following lines to their speakers, and say in what part of the play each is found :

(a) Suit the action to the word

(b) To lose an oath, to win a paradise

c) Cupid's butt shaft is too hard for Hercules' club

(d) No use of metal, corn or oil

(e) The glass of fashion and the mould of form

(f) Methought the billows spoke and told me of it

(g)   that made gape
    The pine, and let thee out

(h) We must speak by the card

(i) The course of true love never did run smooth

(j) Crook-kneed and dew-lapped like Thessalian bulls

(k) Misery acquaints a man with strange bed-fellows

(l) I do not set my life at a pin's fee

(m) Hence, you long-legg'd spinners, hence.

5. Devoting a few lines to each, indicate the character of three leading persons in Hamlet. Designate the scenes from which you have formed your opinion, but do not quote. Sketch the character of Caliban. Notice *Caliban upon Setebos.*

6. (a) Tone-relief in Shakspere is effected by the alternation of blank verse and prose.
Illustrate from the Tempest.

(b) L. L. L is the play in which Shakspere's metrical repertoire is most varied. " We may erect a metrical scale, at the bottom of which is prose ; next in order comes blank verse ; rhymed couplets are a degree more elevated ; and at the top come measures more lyrical than the couplet such as alternate rhyming or even trochaic and anapæstic rhythms. *Moulton.* Examine the scene (IV. 3) where the perjured celibates discover one another.

B. A. EXAMINATION FOR HONOURS IN ENGLISH.

Lycidas, Adonais, Thyrsis, Christmas-Eve and Easter-Day.

WEDNESDAY, APRIL 13TH :—9 TO 12 A.M.

1. *Lycidas* and *Thyrsis* :—contrast and compare.

2. Write on the construction of Adonais, and add a paragraph on the characteristics of its poetry.

3. Give an outline of the Professor's lecture, and of Browning's subsequent comments.

4.   " glut
                   Thy sense upon the world."
Trace the thought of the poem to the moment of renunciation.

5. Refer to their places in the poems, and explain :

   (*a*) His branded and ensanguined brow

   (*b*) But ah, of our poor Thames she never heard

   (*c*) Like Taylor's the immortal Jeremy

   (*d*) Smooth-sliding Mincius, crown'd with vocal reeds

   (*e*)   while it stood, we said,
        Our friend the Gipsy-Scholar was not dead

   (*f*) His Titan's arch-device

   (*g*) One keen pyramid with wedge sublime

   (*h*) The kingcraft of the Lucumons
        Or Fourier's scheme, its pros and cons

   (*i*) Like to that sanguine flower, inscrib'd with woe

   (*j*) The halt and maimed " Iketides."

B. A. EXAMINATION FOR HONOURS IN ENGLISH.

LECTURES ON THE HISTORY OF ENGLISH LITERATURE.

POPE : *Essay on Criticism.*

THURSDAY, APRIL 14TH :—2 TO 5 P. M.

A.

1. Name the authors of the following works :—(*a*) Ecclesiastical History of England and Normandy, (*b*) Brunellus, (c) Gemma Ecclesiastica, (*d*) Ormulum, (*e*) Romaunt of the Rose. Giving two or three lines to each, state the importance of (*a*), (*b*), (*d*), (*c*).

2. Give a brief outline of the Vision of Piers the Plowman.

3. Name the works of Dunbar and Douglas, and give an outline of such works of Lyndsay as were discussed.

4. Mention two distinct facts of literary importance in connection with Tottel's Miscellany, Carmina Burana, Colin Clout's Come Home Again, Steel Glas, The Shepherd's Play, Bartholomew Fair, The Misfortunes of Arthur, Confessio Amautis, Défense et Illustration de la Langue françoise, Microcosmographie, Christ's Victorie and Triumph, New Atlantis.

(*Do not fall back on authorship or date.*)

5. Give an outline of Lusty Juventus.

6. Mention plays which you would class with the Duchess of Malfi. Give an outline of the plot of Webster's drama.

7. Distinguish briefly between an Entertainment, a Masque, and "Barriers." Who introduced the antimasque ? What is its general character ? How would you reduce Comus to regular masque form ? What was said about Inigo Jones ?

8. Notice: William Drummond of Hawthornden's library : Ben Jonson's visit to him ; Drummond and Drayton ; Polemo-Middinia.

9. Present in tabular form four contrasts between Bacon and Montaigne. Classify the theological and amatory poets of the reign of Charles I. and make a few notes on one of each set.

B

1. From the *Essay on Criticism* answer, in a word or two, each of the following questions :

    (a) Is true criticism the result of training simply ?

    (b) Are rules the product of art ?

    (c) Why are faults pardonable ?

    (d) On what grounds should works command praise ?

    (e) Is ancient literature preferable to modern ?

    (f) What fault is beyond pardon ?

    (g) In what work do we find the justest rules?

    (h) What two deluges did Rome experience ?

2. Give the outline of the section that touches (a) on the critic partial to *Language*, (b) on the leading critics of "Athens and Rome."

3. Write a paragraph, within the limits of a page, giving your impressions of the *Essay*.

B.A. EXAMINATION FOR HONOURS IN ENGLISH.

MORE, *Utopia;* MATTHEW ARNOLD, *Essays in Criticism* (Second Series).

SATURDAY, APRIL 16TH :—MORNING, 9 TO 12.

A.

1. Describe Hythlodaye's appearance, attainments and career.

2. Answer the following points briefly :

(a) Legislation against theft being ineffective, what course should be pursued ? What is the main argument against that course, and how may it be met ?

(b) The nature of the country of the Polylerites. The marks by which the Polylerites distinguish their felons.

(c) The means for enriching the royal coffers. What oath does the king of the Macariens take ?

3. Make notes on : (a) Abraxa, Philarche, Anyder, Tranibore.

(b) " Now, sir, in their apparel mark (I pray you) how few workmen they need."

(c) The care of the sick.

(d) gold.

(e) Aldus his print.

4. State the views of the Utopians regarding (a) God, (b) liberty of religious thought. How do the Utopians dispose of their dead and arrange themselves in their churches ? Describe the Church service.

B.

5. What is meant by the historic and the personal estimate of poetry ? Enter into some detail regarding one illustration of each.

6. What is Matthew Arnold's cardinal doctrine regarding Milton ? Is it absolutely true ? How does Shakspere stand ?

7. What is the essential point in Gray's reply to West regarding the style fit for the stage ? What is Matthew Arnold's view of the difference between genuine poetry and the poetry of Dryden and Pope ?

8. Indicate the chief views advanced in the treatment of

(a) Wordsworth's classification of his poems ?

(b) Théophile Gautier.

(c) Wordsworth on Goethe.

9. " There we have, I think, Byron complete." Figure him.

10. Comment on these two extracts :

(a) " The Russian is my best race."

(b) " But there are two things in which the Russian novel is very advantageously distinguished from the type of novel now so much in request in France."

Touch on Tolstoi's religious views as given at the end of the Essay, and on Matthew Arnold's comments thereon.

11. Write a short paragraph on excellence and defect as seen in Amiel.

B.A. EXAMINATION FOR HONOURS IN ENGLISH.

TENNYSON : *Idylls of the King.*

MONDAY, APRIL 18TH :—MORNING, 9 TO 12.30.

1. State succinctly what an examination into the sources of *The Coming of Arthur* reveals.

2. Sketch, within the limits of a page, Tennyson's peculiar treatment of the story of Gareth and Lynette, and show in a short paragraph how it heightens the sense of unity in the Idylls.

3. How has Tennyson exalted the character of Geraint and of Yniol ? Mention, without detail, two important adventures of Geraint which find no reflection at all in Tennyson. What passage characteristic of Tennyson was alluded to in the discussion of the Idyll ?

4. State the exact source of *Balin and Balan*, and the source of that source. Mention three important incidents of Tennyson's invention, and show, briefly, how they serve an important purpose. Explain Vivien's song, and outline the part she plays in the poem.

5. What was said concerning the account of Ambrosius as given by Nennius ? From whom, in this connection, did the name Merlin come ? Mention two other Merlins. "His book came down to me :" sketch Merlin's story in a few lines.

6. Deal with *Lancelot and Elaine* in the manner required by question 2.

7. State without going into detail what the application of the Grail story to the Aryan-expulsion-and-Return Formula is held to prove.

8. State the exact source of Tennyson's poem and the source of that source. State in general terms how Tennyson's version differs from the earlier romance-type. Mention a few facts regarding that type. Show

succinctly that the experience of the knights harmonizes with their characters.

9. Treat the last four Idylls as illustrative of

(a) the decline of Arthur's realm.

(b) Nature as an interpretative medium.

10. State in general terms in what way the Idylls show a gradual change of conception during the period in which they were written. How would you reply to the criticism that Tennyson's treatment of the Arthur story is the " debased preachments of the modern muse ?"

11. State in what Idylls, and as definitely as possible in what places, the following lines occur :

(a) More things are wrough by prayer
    Than this world dreams of

(b) And o'er his head the Holy Vessel hung
    Redder than any rose

(c) Call and I follow, I follow ! let me die

(d) Let chance what will, I trust thee to the death

(e)   Lot beside the hearth
    Lies like a log

(f) My malice is no deeper than a moat,
    No stronger than a wall

(g) The blind wave feeling round his long sea-hall
    In silence

(h)   one side had sea
    And ship and sail and angels blowing on it

(i) Down in the cellars merry bloated things
    Shoulder'd the spigot

(j)   our slowly-grown
    And crown d Republic's crowning common sense

HONOUR EXAMINATIONS IN ENGLISH AND HISTORY.

THIRD AND FOURTH YEARS..

LECTURES ON GREEK AND MEDIÆVAL DEMOCRACY.

WEDNESDAY, APRIL 20TH :—9 TO 12 A.M.

1. Contrast heroic kingship in Greece with the despotisms of the Nile and the Euphrates.

17

2. Describe :

(*a*) the scope of the constitutional changes which were introduced at Athens by Pericles ;

(*b*) the judicial functions of the Athenian people when the democracy was at its height ;

(*c*) the evils of the restored democracy from the Peace of Antalcidas to the Battle of Mantinea.

3. Sketch the rise of Macedonia with a view to explaining Philip's encroachments upon Greece.

4. In what principal respects do classical and Teutonic democracy differ

5. Illustrate the character of feudal society in Northern France from your knowledge of communal revolution and the terms of town charters.

6. Outline the constitutional progress of Florence from the year in which the florin was first minted to the innovations of Gian della Bella.

7. Write brief but pointed notes on : Aristotle's definition of democracy ; sudra ; timocracy ; ochlocracy ; *epistates ; sabini ;* " Le Roi d'Yvetot " ; *firma burgi ;* the reason why Bordeaux looked to Rouen as a municipal model ; *Ciompi.*

THIRD AND FOURTH YEAR HONOURS IN ENGLISH AND HISTORY.

LECTURES ON THE FOURTEENTH CENTURY AND THE ITALIAN RENASCENCE.

MONDAY, APRIL 11TH :—9 TO 12 A.M.

1. What main ideas are suggested to you by a contrast between :

(*a*) Boniface VIII and Alexander VI ;

(*b*) Ambrogio Traversari and Francesco Filelfo ;

(*c*) Leon Battista Alberti and Benvenuto Cellini ;

(*d*) Pico della Mirandola and Baldassare Castiglione ?

2. Discuss Dante's attitude towards :

(*a*) Classical Rome ;

(*b*) The Empire and the Papacy ;

(*c*) Florence.

Illustrate your points by explicit reference to Dante's own writings.

3. Investigate the difficulties which Lewis of Bavaria had with Avignon. Pay particular heed in framing your answer to the views defended both by Marsilio of Padua and Occam.

4. Write (with some regard to style) an estimate of Petrarch's general character as a man of letters.

5. War was among the agencies which served to carry Italian culture beyond the Alps. Follow out the course of hostilities in which non-Italian states were engaged upon Italian soil, 1494-1508. Indicate causes and results wherever you can.

6. Write clearly, though not at great length, on the following subjects :

(a) The transition from xylography to modern printing ;

(b) the influence of local conditions in determining the part which Italy took in discovery and colonization during the Renascence.

(c) the light thrown by architectural change on 15th century tendencies.

HONOUR EXAMINATIONS IN ENGLISH AND HISTORY.

THIRD AND FOURTH YEARS.

LECTURES ON THE REFORMATION.

FRIDAY, APRIL 22ND :—9 TO 12 A.M.

1. Between 1517 and 1570 the basis of religious authority was debated with little intermission. Discuss what you consider to be the most distinctive and typical views then advanced on this subject. In cases where leaders of different Protestant sects appealed to the Bible, make clear the individual attitude of each one towards it.

2. (a) Examine the relations, both personal and polemical, which existed between Luther and Erasmus.

(b) Contrast their sentiments on the general question of revolt from Rome.

3. Emphasize main literary and academic features of the Renascence in Germany. Refer especially to towns which became centres of culture, and among scholars touch upon Reuchlin, Peutinger and Pirkheimer.

4. (a) Analyze the political situation at the Diet of Worms.

(b) What bearing had the Turkish question upon the Lutheran movement?·

5. (a) Dividing the Council of Trent into an earlier and a later period,

show how changes of great magnitude had taken place in Germany between the opening sessions of the first and the opening sessions of the second period.

(*b*) In what ways was the Council affected, during the final phase of its existence, by these changes ?

6. Make brief notes on : the Paulician heresy ; the order of procedure at the Council of Constance ; the *Kreis* system ; Zwingli at Einsiedeln ; Contarini ; Budæus ; Capuchins ; Borromean League ; Edict of Restitution ; League of Heilbronn.

EXAMINATION FOR HONOURS IN ENGLISH.
THIRD YEAR.
SATURDAY, APRIL 2ND :—9 TO 12 A.M.
SIDNEY : *Apologie for Poetrie.* MILTON : *Areopagitica.*

(*The citation of proper names with a brief explanatory note in the margin, when necessary, will obtain credit.*)

1. What occasioned the writing of Sidney's *Apologie?*

2. Give, in tabular form and in proper order, the chief divisions and sub-divisions of Sidney's matter. (Limit yourself to two pages at most.)

3. Give the substance of Sidney's remarks on
   (*a*) The Three Unities,
   (*b*) Diction.
   (*c*) Lyric poetry.

4. State in a word or two the views illustrated by the following extracts :—
   (*a*) So in the Italian language were the poets Dante, Boccace, Petrarch—so in our English were Gower and Chaucer.
   (*b*) so Herodotus entituled his history
   (*c*) wherein he painteth not Lucrecia whom he never saw
   (*d*) let but Sophocles bring you Ajax on a stage
   (*e*) Thebes written in great letters on a door
   (*f*) of such mind were certain Goths
   (*g*) Plato found fault that the poets of his time
   (*h*) *Orator fit : Poeta nascitur*
   (*i*) and, therefore, gracelessly may they use dactyls

5. Compare and contrast Milton with Isocrates.

6. Sketch the history of licensing to the time of the Council of Trent.

7. Notice references (*a*) to the state of England at the time when Milton wrote and (*b*) to English writers, stating in what part of the argument the latter occur.

8. Give the substance of Milton's statements regarding

(*a*) the religion of the wealthy man addicted to his pleasure and to his profits,

(*b*) the books that must be removed by licensing.

—————

B. A. EXAMINATION FOR HONOURS IN ENGLISH.

MOESO-GOTHIC AND EARLY ENGLISH.

SATURDAY, APRIL 2ND:—9 TO 12 A. M.

A.

1. Translate literally:—

(*a*) Jah kwath du im : gaggam du thaim bisunjane haimom jah baurgim ei jah jainar merjau, unte duthe kwam. Jah was merjands in synagogim ize and alla Galeilaian jah unhulthons uswairpands.

(*b*) Jah gahausjands Iesus kwath du im: ni thaurbun swinthai lekeis, ak thai ubilaba habandans; ni kwam lathon uswaurhtans, ak fra-waurhtans.

(*c*) Jah urreisands gasok winda jah kwath du marein : gaslawai, afdumbn!

(*d*) Ith is kwath du izai; dauhtar, galaubeins theina ganasida thuk; gagg in gawairthi, jah sijais haila at thamma slaha theinamma.

2. (*a*) Tabulate the ablaut-system in Gothic ; also the reduplicating verbs.

(*b*) Arrange the verbs of question 1 correspondingly.

(*c*) Arrange the nouns of the same question under stems. Decline one of each stem.

(*d*) Conjugate the past tense, indicative and subjunctive of any ablaut-verb, the full subjunctive of wisan, the past tense of haldan.

3. Translate literally :—Kwath than im Iesus thatei nist praufetus unswers, niba in gabaurthai seinai jah in ganithjam jah in garda seinam-ma. Jah ni mahta jainar ainohun mahte gataujan niba fawaim siukam handuns galagjands gahǎilida. Jah sildaleikada in ungalaubeinais ize. jah bitauh weihsa bisunjane, laisjands. Jah athaihait thans twalif jah dugann ins insandjan twans hwanzub, jah gaf in waldufni ahmane unhrainjaize. Jah faurbauth im ei waiht ni nemeina in wig, niba brugga aina, nih matibalg nih hlaif nih in gairdos aiz, Ak gaskohai suljom : jah ni wasjaith twaim paidom.

B.

Translate:

(1.) Whanne this werwolf was come · to his wlonk denne
     & hade bronzt bilfoder · for the barnes mete,
     that he hade wonne with wo · wide wher a-boute,
     than fond he nest & no neiz · for nouzt nas ther leued.
     & whan the best the barn missed · so balfully he g[r]inneth,
     that alle men vpon molde · no mizt telle his sorwe.
     For reuliche gan he rore· & rente al his hide,
     & fret oft of the erthe . & fel doun on swowe,
     & made the most dool · that man mizt diuise.
     & as the best in his bale · ther a-boute wente,
     he fond the feute al fresh · where forth the herde
     badde bore than barn · beter it to zeme.
     wiztly the werwolf· than went bi nose
     euene to the berdes house· & hastely was thare.
     there walked he a-boute the walles · in winne in sizt;
     & at the last lelly · a litel hole he findes.

(2.) & gode sire, for godes loue · also greteth wel oft
     alle my freyliche felawes · that to this forest longes,
     han pertilyche in many places ·· pleide with (me) ofte,
     hugonet, & huet · that hende litel dwerth,
     & abelot, & martynet· bugones gaie sone ;
     & the cristen akarin · that was mi kyn fere,
     & the trewe kinnesman · the payenes sone,
     & alle other frely felawes · that thou faire knowes,
     that god mak hem gode men · for his mochel grace.'

(3.) Bot quen the lorde of the lyfte ·lyked hymseluen
     For to mynne on his mon · his meth that abydez,
     Then he wakened a wynde · on watterez to blowe ;
     Thenne lasned the llak · that large watz are,
     Then he stac vp the stangez · stoped the wellez,
     Bed blynne of the rayn · hit batede as fast,
     Thenne lasned the loz : lowkande to-geder.

(4.) Clowdez clustered bytwene · kesten vp torres,
     That the thik thunder-thrast · thirled hem ofte.
     The rayn rueled adoun · ridlande thikke,
     Of felle flaunkes of fyr · & flakes of soufre,
     Al in smolderande smóke ' smachande ful ille,
     Swe about sodamas · & hit sydez alle,
     Gorde to gomorra · that the grounde lansed ;
     Ahdama and sybojm · thise ceteis alle faure,

Al birolled wyth the rayn · rostted & bren̄ned, .
& ferly flayed that folk · tnat in those fees lenged·
For when that the helle herde · the houndez of heuen,
He watz ferlyly fayu · vnfolded bylyue ;
The grete barrez of the abyme · he barst vp at onez,
That alle the regioun to-rof · in riftes ful grete,
& clonen alle in lyttel cloutes · the clyffez aywhere,
As lance leuez of the boke · that lepes in twyn̄ne.

(5·) For hit is brode & bothemlez · & bitter as the galle,
& nozt may lenge in that lake · that any lyf berez,
& alle the costez of kynde · hit combrez vchone :
For lay ther-on a lump of led · & hit on loft fletez.
& folde ther-on a lyzt fyther · & hit to founs synkkez.
& ther [that] water may walter · to wete any erthe,
Schal neuer grene ther-on growe · gresse ne wod nawther,
If any schalke to be schent · wer schowued ther-inne,
Thaz he bode in that bothem · brothely a monyth,
He most ay lyne in that loze · in losyng euer-more
& neuer dryze no dethe · to dayes of ende.
&, as hit is corsed of kynde · & hit coostez als,
The clay that clenges ther-by · arn corsyes strong,
As alum & alkaran · that angré arn bothe,
Soufre sour, & saundyuer · & other such mony ;
& ther waltez of that water · in waxlokes grete,
The spuniande aspaltoun · .that spyserez sellen ;
& suche is alle the soyle · by that se halues,
That fel fretes the flesch · and festred bones.

(6.) Ther houeth an Hundret · In Houues of selk,
Seriauns hit semeth ·' to seruen atte Barre ;
Pleden for pons · and poundes the lawe,
Not for loue of vr lord · vn-loseth beore lippes ones.
Thow mihtest beter meten the Myst · on Maluerne hulles,
Then geten a Mom of heore Mouth · til moneye weore schewed.
    I sauh ther Bisschops Bolde · and Bachilers of diuyn
Bi-coome Clerkes of A-Counte · the kynge for to seruen ;
Erchedekenes · that Dignite hauen,
To preche the peple · and pore men to feede,
Beon lopen to londun · bi leve of beore Bisschopes,
To ben Clerkes öf the kynges Benche · the Cuntre to schende.

6. Give in a page an outline of Chaucer's Tale of the Man of Lawe or of
Gower's Tale of the Coffers.

7. What do you learn concerning the English language from the extract
De incolarum linguis (John of Trevisa.)

MENTAL AND MORAL PHILOSOPHY.

INTERMEDIATE EXAMINATIONS.

FORMAL LOGIC.

MONDAY, 18TH APRIL :—MORNING, 9 TO 12.

1. Explain clearly the nature and function of Formal, or Deductive Logic.

2. Arrange the following terms, according as they are respectively, (*a*) singular or general, (*b*) positive or negative, (*c*) connotative or non-connotative : amorphous, the Fire-worshippers, indelible, vicious, The World's Fair, eccentric.

3. What do you understand by the Denotation and the Connotation of terms? In what way does the distinction between Denotation and Connotation bear on logical Division and Definition?

4. Make notes on :—The law of excluded middle, basis of division, property, figurative definition.

5. Convert the following propositions ; and give the contradictory of each :—

> Every able-bodied citizen is a possible soldier.
> The practice has been discontinued for years.
> Sensible people are united on this point.
> No fallacies are irrefutable.

If any of these propositions admit of contraposition, give the contrapositive.

6. Explain the principle of syllogistic reasoning ; show the applicability of the diagrammatic circles to the process ; and supply an *original* valid example of syllogism.

7. State the moods of the Third Figure ; and construct a syllogism (with terms, *not* with symbols) in any mood of that figure, reducing it afterwards to the first.

8. Explain and illustrate (preferably with original examples):—
Reasoning in a circle, Argumentum ad Hominem, Modus Ponens and
the corresponding fallacy.

9. Examine the following specimens of logical processes, and give
reasons for conclusions concerning their value :—

(*a*) The man who devised the deed is equally guilty with the one
who executed it ; for had he not devised it, the other could not have
executed it.

(*b*) A man cannot lose either the past or the future ; for what a
man has not, how can any man take this from him ?

Marcus Aurelius.

(*c*) Every idea that we have is conditioned by being an idea of what
exists, either as a whole or in parts ; and, therefore, an idea of the
existence of God proves that existence.

Joseph de Maistre.

(*d*) Natural right of sovereignty rests in the people alone ; the
suffrage is the external manifestation of this sovereignty, and is therefore also a natural right. All citizens have an equal share in this right,
and are consequently electors in precisely the same sense and degree.
Since, then, the right of sovereignty rests in the people who are the
electors, the representative is nothing more than a delegate, mandatary
or agent. He must speak not his own mind, but that of his constituents.

Charles Benoist.

(*e*) The fall of the Roman Empire is understood when it is regarded
as an instance of the law, that as nations adopt luxurious and vicious
habits, they lose their pristine vigour, become effeminate, and fall an
easy prey to more hardy barbarians.

———

B.A. EXAMINATIONS.

MURRAY'S INTRODUCTION TO ETHICS, BOOK II.

MONDAY, APRIL 4TH:—MORNING, 9 TO 12.

Answer only eight questions.

1. Show that the Law, the End and the Good of life are but different
forms of stating the same principle.

2. State the fundamental principle of Epicurean systems of Ethics, and its various modifications.

3. State the questions raised in the critique of Utilitarianism, and discuss one of them.

4. Sketch one of the modern systems of Stoical Ethics.

5. Distinguish Justice and Benevolence.

6. Discuss the application of the term *organism* to Society, *or* explain the duties which the individual owes to the State.

7. Explain the Law of Supply and Demand, and discuss its moral aspect.

8. Distinguish Sin, Wrong and Crime; and discuss the rival theories of Punishment.

9. Explain the Socratic definition of Virtue, and Aristotle's correction of it.

10. Explain the interdependence of the moral consciousness and the religious consciousness.

11. Explain how a virtuous habit of emotion may be trained both directly and indirectly.

12. Explain the rational principle involved in moral disciplines like fasting.

THIRD YEAR EXAMINATIONS.

HONOURS IN MENTAL AND MORAL PHILOSOPHY, GREEK PHILOSOPHY, AND PLATO'S THEÆTETUS.

SATURDAY, APRIL 9TH:—MORNING, 9 TO 12.

(Answer the last question and only five of the others.)

1. Who was the first evolutionist among the Early Greeks? Give some account of his philosophy.

2. Give an account of Herakleitos, *or* of Zeno the Eleatic, *or* of Demokritos.

3. Explain the historical significance of Anaxagoras.

4. Give an account of the teaching of Sokrates, both in its method and in its results.

5. Sketch the Dialectic *or* the Ethics of Plato.

6. Sketch the Physics *or* the Ethics of Aristotle.

7. Give an outline of the Ethics of the Epicureans, *or* of the Stoics.

8. Write a note on Arkesilaos, *or* on Karneades.

9. Give a brief account of the *rapprohement* of Hellenism and Orientalism in Alexandria.

10. Give a brief outline of the Theætetus, and a more detailed outline of the first part.

_____

THIRD YEAR EXAMINATION.

MURRAY'S HANDBOOK OF PSYCHOLOGY, BOOK II, PART I.

FRIDAY, APRIL 15TH :—MORNING, 9 TO 12.

(Answer only eight questions.)

1. Explain fully the nature of the two processes by which our knowledge is evolved.

2. Illustrate these processes *either* in the perceptions of taste *or* in those of smell.

3. Describe briefly the two classes of tactile perceptions, showing how both are aided by muscular sensibility.

4. Explain the auditory perceptions of space, *or* how far speech depends on the musical sensibility of the ear.

5. Explain the illusion in regard to distance and magnitude of objects seen through a fog.

6. Explain the nature of abstraction.

7. Does knowledge begin with classes or with individuals ?

8. Discuss the controversy between Nominalism and Conceptualism.

9. Define idealisation, and distinguish its different forms.

10. Write a note *either* on the visual arts *or* on literary art.

11. Explain the nature of illusions as distinguished from hallucinations and from fallacies.

12. Give a brief account of the rival theories on the general nature of Knowledge.

THIRD YEAR HONOURS IN MENTAL AND MORAL PHILOSOPHY.

LOGIC.

WEDNESDAY, APRIL 20TH :—MORNING, 9 TO 12.

1. Make short and summary notes on Mill's views in regard to Colligation, Abstraction, and Classification, as subsidiary to Induction.

2. Explain clearly, with original examples if possible: Fallacy of Simple Inspection (any *one* form), Fallacy of Mal-observation, Fallacy of False Analogy, Petitio Principii

3. What, according to Thomson, are the four functions of language? In what sense and measure does he connect Logic with language ?

4. How does Jevons discriminate between Certainty and Probability ?

5. Express some opinion as to the value of Hypotheses in assisting investigation; point out the difficulties and dangers connected therewith ; and bear out the assertions with original examples.

6. State the views of Jevons and Venn concerning the nature and justifiable use of Analogy.

7. What does Venn mean by saying that the position of the Empirical logician implies a dualistic conception of the universe ?

8. Summarise the views of Venn in regard to the importance of verification, and the care demanded for its correct performance.

THIRD YEAR EXAMINATIONS.

HONOURS IN MENTAL AND MORAL PHILOSOPHY.

JAMES' PRINCIPLES OF PSYCHOLOGY, CHAPTERS 10—16,

AND

FRASER'S SELECTIONS FROM BERKELEY.

FRIDAY, APRIL 22ND :—MORNING, 9 TO 12.

Answer four questions from A, and three from B.

A

1. Describe the rivalry and conflict between our different selves, *or* state and examine the Associationist theory of self-consciousness.

2. Describe the effects of attention on sensation, on discrimination, on recollection, on reaction-time; or discuss the question whether voluntary attention is a resultant or a force.

3. "Nothing can be conceived twice over without being conceived in entirely different states of mind." Explain.

4. State the conditions of discrimination, or show that all differences are not differences of composition.

5. What, according to James, is the elementary law of association?

6. Show that we have no perception of empty time any more than of empty space.

7. What are the conditions of goodness in memory? or wherein does all improvement of memory consist?

B

1. What is the doctrine attacked in the " Principles of Human Knowledge," and what is the doctrine defended?

2. How does Berkeley meet the objections, (a) that there is a great difference between real fire and the idea of fire, (b) that, as we see things at a distance from us, these must be without our minds?

3. Explain the general drift of the "New Theory of Vision."

4. Explain Berkeley's theory of visual language.

5. Give some account of " Siris."

B.A. HONOURS IN MENTAL AND MORAL PHILOSOPHY.
SPENCER AND MILL.

THURSDAY, 31ST MARCH :—MORNING, 9 TO 12.

1. How does Spencer establish the unknowable character of the absolute, in any one department of thought? On what grounds does he still continue to assert its existence? In what way does his system differ from strict Pyrrhonism?

2. Express some independent opinion as to the philo ophical value of the Spencerian fundamental position.

3. Explain:—Segregation, equilibration, dissolution as the correlate of evolution.

4. Apply Spencer's formula of the Law of Evolution to an example of your own selection. Treat it with some elaboration of detail.

5. Give the substance of Mill's view of the moral problem of liberty and necessity.

6. Explain the relation of Psychology with Ethics, as understood by Mill.

7. What is Mill's conception of the Historical Method? Offer any criticism or addition of your own.

B. A. EXAMINATIONS.
HONOURS IN MENTAL AND MORAL PHILOSOPHY.
ZELLER'S STOICS, EPICUREANS AND SCEPTICS.
FRIDAY, APRIL 1ST :—MORNING, 9 TO 12.

1. Sketch the history of the Stoical School.

2. Give an outline *either* of the Stoical Theory of Nature *or* of the Stoical Theology.

3. Explain, in its leading features, the Ethics of Stoicism.

4. Give an outline of the Epicurean Science of Nature.

5. Explain the Epicurean Ethics, both in its general principles and in its application to particular moral relations.

6. Sketch the teaching of one of the representatives of the New Academy.

B. A. EXAMINATIONS.
HONOURS IN MENTAL AND MORAL PHILOSOPHY.
THE PHILOSOPHY OP KANT.
THURSDAY, APRIL 7th :—AFTERNOON, 2 TO 5.
(*Answer only Six Questions.*)

1. Explain the terms *pure, a priori, transcendental, transcendent,* as used by Kant.

2. Give an outline of the metaphysical and transcendental expositions of Space.

3. What is the " guiding thread " for the discovery of the Categories? Give the table of Categories.

4. Explain the procedure by which the Principles of Pure Understanding are derived from the Categories

5. State the Analogies of Experience, and explain their general principle.

6. What are the Ideas of Pure Reason, and how are they formed ?

7. Give the system of Cosmological Ideas, and indicate the general drift of the antinomy founded on each, as well as of the solution of the several antinomies.

8. Sketch Kant's classification and criticism of theistic arguments·

9. Give a brief outline of the Critique of Pure Practical Reason.

B. A. EXAMINATIONS.

HONOURS IN MENTAL AND MORAL PHILOSOPHY.

MAINE'S ANCIENT LAW.

TUESDAY, APRIL 12TH . :—MORNING, 9 TO 12.

1. Explain the Conception of Law in the Homeric poems.

2. In what school of philosophy did the conception of a Law of Nature originate? How was the conception modified when adopted by the Roman jurists?

3. Trace the history of the conception in modern times.

4. What was the historical origin of the Patria Potestas?

5. Explain the primitive ideas of property as connected with the state of primitive society.

6. Sketch the early history *either* of contract *or* of criminal law.

B.A. EXAMINATIONS.
HONOURS IN MENTAL AND MORAL PHILOSOPHY.
ARISTOTLE'S NICOMACHEAN ETHICS.
THURSDAY, APRIL 14TH:—AFTERNOON, 2 TO 5.

(Answer only eight questions.)

1. Give Aristotle's definition of the supreme good or end of life, and his critique of Plato's definition.

2. Why are certain virtues called moral (ethical), others intellectual (dianoetic) ?

3. State and explain fully Aristotle's definition of the former class of virtues.

4. Explain the nature of deliberate preference ($\pi\rho o\alpha i\rho\varepsilon\sigma\iota\varsigma$), distinguishing it from other mental states with which it is apt to be confounded.

5. Give an outline of the exposition of courage, distinguishing it from the vices between which it is the mean.

6. In what sense is justice identical with virtue in general; in what sense is it merely a particular virtue ?

7. Distinguish distributive and corrective justice.

8. Distinguish justice and equity ($\dot{\varepsilon}\pi\iota\varepsilon i\kappa\varepsilon\iota\alpha$).

9. Define each of the dianoetic virtues.

10. On what grounds does Aristotle make intemperance in appetite a worse vice than intemperance in anger ?

11. What are the different objects of friendship ? Which is highest ?

12. What is Aristotle's final theory of the nature of happiness ?

B.A. EXAMINATIONS.
HONOURS IN MENTAL AND MORAL PHILOSOPHY.
WATSON'S OUTLINE.
MONDAY, APRIL 18TH:—MORNING, 9 TO 12.

Answer only six Questions.

1. Explain fully and discuss Mill's theory of causation.

2. Examine Comte's theory of the limitation of knowledge.

3. State and discuss Mill's theory of numbers.

4. Show that Darwinism does not exclude, but rather implies, purpose.

5. Explain the Monadology of Leibnitz, pointing out how far it anticipates the view of Tyndall & Haeckel.

6. Compare Scientific Evolutionism and Philosophical Idealism.

7. Examine Darwin's theory of selfish and social impulses.

8. Explain fully what is meant by motive.

9. Examine Kant's doctrine of original sin.

B. A. EXAMINATIONS.

HONOURS IN MENTAL AND MORAL PHILOSOPHY.

SPINOZA'S ETHICS.

WEDNESDAY, 20TH APRIL :—MORNING, 9 TO 12.

Answer only eight questions.

1. How does Spinoza prove the unity of substance ?

2. How do you reconcile the proposition that God is a free cause (I. 17, coroll. 2) with the proposition that things cannot be produced by God in any other manner or order than that in which they are produced (I. 33) ?

3. What are the body and mind of man on Spinoza's theory ?

4. Distinguish the three kinds of cognition.

5. Define cause, and distinguish adequate and inadequate causes.

6. Explain the proposition, that the impulse (*conatus*), by which everything endeavours to continue its existence, is nothing but the actual essence of the thing (III. 7). When is this impulse called *voluntas*, when *appetitus*, when *cupiditas?*

7. Define pleasure (*laetitia*) and pain (*tristitia*).

8. When is man active ; when passive ?

18

9. What makes one *affectus* stronger than another ? '

10. Explain the proposition, that the impulse to self conservation is the primary and sole foundation of virtue (IV. 22, coroll.)

11. Explain the proposition, that the highest impulse of the mind and the highest virtue is to understand things by the third kind of knowledge.

12. Show that this begets the "amor Dei intellectualis."

B. A. EXAMINATIONS.

HONOURS IN MENTAL AND MORAL PHILOSOPHY.

JAMES' PRINCIPLES OF PSYCHOLOGY, VOL. II.

FRIDAY, APRIL 22ND :—MORNING, 9 TO 12.

(Answer only six questions.

1. "Pure sensation can be realized only in the earliest days of life." Explain.

2. Explain Galton's researches on different types of imagination.

3. Sketch James' theory of the perception of space.

4. Explain the nature of belief and its opposites.

5. What is the fundamental distinction between the human and the brute mind ?

6. How does James explain avarice ?

7. Show that voluntary movement presupposes involuntary.

8. What does James regard as the fundamental phenomenon in willing ?

9. Write a note on hypnotism.

10. State James' theory on the genesis of the elementary categories of science.

FRENCH.

EXAMENS DE FIN D'ANNÉE

LETTRES—1ère ANNÉE.

Vendredi, 15 Avril :—De 9 heures à midi.

I. Faire l'analyse logique de la poésie suivante :

Le matin toute la nature.
Vocalise, fredonne, rit
Je songe. L'aurore est si pure
Et les oiseaux ont tant d'esprit !
Tout chante, geai, pinson, linotte,
Bouvreuil, alouette au zénith,
Et la source ajoute sa note
Et le vent parle, et Dieu bénit.

Victor Hugo.

II. Dire la valeur et la disposition des rimes de la poésie précédente.

III. Remplacer les infinitifs par les formes qui conviennent au sens de la phrase :

Tous les peuples ont cru qu'il y *avoir* un Dieu. Quintillien a dit que la conscience *valoir* mille témoins. Nous *travailler* aujourd'hui aux devoirs que le professeur nous *donner* hier. Les anciens croyaient que le sang *n'avoir* qu'un mouvement très lent du cœur vers les extrémités du corps. Il faut que tu *acquérir* de l'instruction. Ma mère craint que je ne *courir* trop et que je ne *être* malade. L'avare voudrait que tout l'or de la Californie lui *appartenir*. Fais aux autres ce que tu voudrais qu'on te *faire*.

IV. Le gendre de M. Poirier.

A. (*a*) Notice biographique de l'auteur.

(*b*) Quel travers de la société cette comédie a-t-elle pour but de combattre ?

(*c*) Esquisser brièvement les caractères suivants : *M. Poirier, Verdelet* et *Le Duc*.

B. Ecrire sous forme d'analyse, de résumé ou de critique, environ 300 mots sur un des ouvrages suivants :

Le Curé de Tours, Le Conscrit, Colomba, Cinq-Mars, La Question d'Argent.

V. Reproduire par écrit l'anecdote suivante :

(Au lieu de cette reproduction MM. les examinateurs des collèges affiliés voudront bien faire une dictée d'environ cent mots prise dans Cinq-Mars.)

Dater en toutes lettres.

_____

EXAMENS DE FIN D'ANNÉE.

LETTRES-DEUXIÈME ANNÉE.

(INTERMÉDIAIRE).

VENDREDI, 15 AVRIL :—DE 9 HEURES A MIDI.

I. Traduire les passages suivants :

A. What is the voice I hear,
On the wind of the western seas ?
Sentinel, listen from out Cape Clear,
And say what the voice may be.
'Tis a proud free people calling,
Calling loud to a people proud and free.

And it says to them, Kinsmen, hail,
We severed have been too long,
Now let us have done with a worn-out tale,
The tale of an ancient wrong ;
And our friendship last long as love doth last,
And be stronger than death is strong.

AUSTIN.

B. Ainsi, pour résumer les points que nous venons d'indiquer, trois sortes de ravages défigurent aujourd'hui l'architecture gothique. Rides et verrues à l'épiderme c'est l'œuvre du temps. Voies de fait, brutalités contusions, fractures ; c'est l'œuvre des révolutions depuis Luther jusqu'à Mirabeau. Mutilations, amputations, dislocation de la membrure, _restaurations;_ c'est le ravail grec, romain et barbare des professeurs selon Vitruve et Vignole. Cet art magnifique que les Vandales avaient produit les académies l'ont tué. Aux siècles, aux révolutions, qui dévastent du moins avec impartialité et grandeur, est venue s'adjoindre la nuée de, architectes d'école, patentés, jurés et assermentés, dégradant avec le discernement et le choix du mauvais goût, substituant les chicorées de Louis XV aux dentelles gothiques, pour la plus grande gloire du Parthénon. C'est le coup de pied de l'âne au lion mourant. C'est le vieux chêne qui se couronne, et qui, pour comble, est piqué, mordu, déchiqueté par les chenilles.

N. D. DE PARIS.

II   Tracer brièvement l'origine du théâtre en France.

III. (*a*) Donner à toutes les formes du mot *tout* (adj. pronom et adv.) avec la prononciation.

(*b*) L'origine du futur et du conditionnel.

IV. (*a*) Écrire environ 200 mots sur la vie et l'œuvre de deux des écrivains suivants : Victor Hugo, Mme de Staél, Th. Gautier, Lecontc de Lisle, A. Chénier, Barbier, Ronsard.

(*b*) Écrire sous forme d'analyse, de résumé, ou de critique, environ 300 mots sur un des ouvrages suivants :
Notre-Dame de Paris, Le Roman de la Momie, Corinne, Jack, Les Misérables, Les Martyrs, L'Abbé Constantin.

(*c*) Résumer le chapitre de N. D. de Paris ayant pour titre : Ceci tuera Cela, ou bien faire un portrait de Quasimodo et d'Esmeralda.

V. Reproduire par écrit l'anecdote suivante :

(Au lieu de cette reproduction MM. les examinateurs des collèges affiliés voudront bien faire une dictée d'environ cent mots prise dans Le Roman de la Momie.)
Dater en toutes lettres.

EXAMENS DE FIN D'ANNÉE,

LETTRES, 3ème. ANNÉE.

Mardi, 19 Avril :—De 9 heures a midi.

1. Faire un état de la littérature française à la fin du XVII. Siècle. (Pas plus de 1,000 mots.)

2. Ecrire environ 500 mots sur un des ouvrages suivants : Horace, Le Misanthrope, Athalie, Emile, Paul et Virginie, Lettres de Mme. de Sévigné.

3. Ecrire environ 500 mots sur la vie et l'œuvre de deux des écrivains suivants : Vaugelas, Maleherbe, Pascal, Bossuet, Voltaire.

4. Reproduire par écrit l'anecdote suivante.

BACCALAURÉAT ÈS-LETTRES.

Mardi, 18 Avril :— De 9 heures a midi.

1. Donner un aperçu de la situation politique, religieuse et sociale en France à l'époque où parut la Satire Ménippée.

2. Faire une analyse de cet ouvrage.

3. Montrer à grands traits le fond et l'intention de l'œuvre de Rabelais.

4. Donner un aperçu général des Essais de Montaigne.

5. Apprécier l'œuvre des principaux chroniqueurs.

Autres jours.

6. Thèse.

7. Composition d'une heure sur l'esprit de répartie de Jeanne d'Arc.

EXAMENS DE FIN D'ANNÉE.

HONNEURS, 3ème ANNÉE.

EXAMEN ORAL.

Vendredi, 1er Avril : —De 9 Heures à Midi.

1. Indiquer la provenance de l'article français et de l'S comme marque du pluriel.

2. Qu'appelle-t-on *doublets?* Exemples.

3. Comment les langues romanes ont-elles modifié la conjugaison latine ?

4. Citer les pronoms indéfinis et en tracer l'origine.

5. Résumer et apprécier la préface de Cromwell.

6. Etablir les différences de fond et de forme entre une tragédie classique et un drame moderne.

7. Traduire le passage suivant en français moderne avec explications des constructions et des termes vieillis.

> Guillaume, nous t'avons prié
> Moult doucement, et supplié
> Quant de ce que touche la paix
> De l'Eglise ; mais tu ne fais
> Fors nous refuser et despire.
> Vezcy ton Dieu, vezcy ton Sire
> Qui se voult tout a Dieu offrir
> Et pour toy mort en croix souffrir,
> Et qui te jugera, n'en doubtes ;
> Devant qui touz genoux, tous coutes
> Et toute puissance s'incline ;
> C'est cilz qui par vertu divine
> A fait le monde et toutes gens,

Qui cy vient après ses sergents
Pour toy prier et supplier
Se pourra ton dur cuer plier.
Di moi se tu le despiras,
Ne se tu le refuseras
Com fait as nous.

EXAMENS DE FIN D'ANNÉE.

HONNEURS, 4ème ANNÉE.

EXAMEN ORAL.

Vendredi, 1er Avril :—De 9 Heures a Midi.

1. Établir l'état de la langue et de la littérature au commencement de notre siècle.

2. Tracer le développement du genre historique depuis la chanson de geste jusqu'à nos jours.

3. Indiquer l'origine, le fond général, la valeur littéraire et philologique des fabliaux.

3. Montrer comment le Romantisme se rapporte aux idées politiques et religieuses de l'époque.

4. Apprécier l'influence de Flaubert sur la littérature française.

5. Traduire le passage suivant en français moderne avec explications des constructions et des termes vieillis.

Li Emperere est repairiez d'Espaigne,
E vient ad Ais, a l'meillur sied de France,
Muntet el palais, est venuz en la sale,
As li venue Alde, une bele dame.
Ço dist a l'rei : " U est Rollanz l'catanies
Ki me jurat cume sa per a prendre ? "
Carles en ad e dulur e pesance,
Pluret des oilz, tiret sa barbe blanche :
" Soer, chere amie, d'hume mort me demandes.
Jo t'en durrai mult esforciet escange :
C'est Loewis, mielz ne sai jo qu'en parle.
Il est mis filz et si tiendrat mes marches."
Alde respunt : " Cist moz mei est estranges.
Ne placet Deu ne ses seinz ne ses angles
Apres Rollant que jo vive remaigne !"
Pert la culur, chiet as piez Carlemagne.
Sempres est morte. Deus ait mercl de l'anme !
Franceis barun en plurent ; si la plaignent.

GERMAN.

FIRST YEAR DONALDAS.

Friday, April 15th :—Afternoon, 2 to 5.

1. Translate into English :—

(a) Ihr wart durch blutige Beleidigung
 Gereizt und)urch des Mannes Übermut,
 Den eure Liebe aus der Dunkelheit
 Wie eine Götterhand hervorgezogen,
 Den Ihr durch Euer Brautgemach zum Throne
 Geführt, mit Eurer blühenden Person
 Beglückt und Eurer angestammten Krone.
 Konnte er vergessen, daß sein prangend Los
 Der Liebe großmutsvolle Schöpfung war?
 Und doch vergaß er's, der Unwürdige!
 Beleidigte mit niedrigem Verdacht,
 Mit ro)en Sitten Eure Zärtlichkeit.
 Und widerwärtig wurd'er Euren Augen.

(b) O. Dank, Dank diesen freundlich grünen Bäumen,
 Die meines Kerkers Mauern mir verstecken!
 Ich w ll mich frei und glücklich träumen,
 Warum aus meinem süßen Wahn mich wecken?
 Umfängt mich nicht der weite Himmelsschoß?
 Die Blicke, frei und fessellos,
 Ergehen sich in ungemess'nen Räumen.
 Dort, wo die grauen Nebelberge ragen,
 Fängt meines Reiches Grenze an,
 Und diese Wolken, die nach Mittag jagen
 Sie suchen Frankreich's fernen Ocean.

(c) For students of Stanstead College only. Translate into
English the paragraph in the Third Act of *Die Journalisten*
beginning with the words *Solche Resignation.*

2. Translation at sight.

Translate into English :—

Mit dem Reisen in einem Eisenbahnzug ist es eine ganz wunder-
liche Sache, und man muß es in der That erst lernen, ehe man es
ordentlich kann. Manche Leute werden mir das nicht glauben und
sagen: „Was ist aber dabei zu lernen? Ich löse mir eben ein Billet,
gebe meine Sachen auf, setze mich ein und fahre dann mit fort —
das kann ein jeder."— Das allerdings und er reist dann ebenso
rasch als die Übrigen — aber wie? Zehn gegen eins, daß er in ein
dichtgefülltes Coupé kommt, wo er nicht einmal die Füße ausstrecken
kann; möglicherweise hat er auch eine Dame, mit einem schreienden
Kind auf dem Schoß, gegenüber, während ein kleiner, ihr ebenfalls
gehörender Bursche von fünf oder sechs Jahren ununterbrochen
über seine Füße fort nach dem Fenster klettert und ihm dabei ein
angebissenes Butterbrot mit der gestrichenen Seite auf die Knice
drückt. Er möchte rauchen, aber es geht nicht — eine Dame an
seiner Seite erklärt, daß sie keinen Tabaksdampf ebensowenig aber
auch Zug vertragen könne; und er darf deshalb das Fenster nicht
herunter lassen, obgleich im Coupé eine drückende Schwüle herrscht.

3. Translate into German.

(a) My dear parents.

To-day is the beginning of the new year and I am still in this
interesting old town. Leipsic lies in a broad plain ; in the
whole neighbourhood one sees no mountain, no high hills. The
town is famous on account of its great university and its rich
trade, it is the centre of the book-trade for all Germany. The
Leipsic theatres are especially good ; almost every evening I
visit the old or the new theatre, and gain in this way daily in
knowledge of the German language and in insight into German
life.

(*b*) Do you know how late it is? I must go home at once.

It is pretty dark outside; do you think you will be able to find your way to your house?

I hadn't thought of that. In case of necessity I could ask a policeman.

You must not rely on the police. Shall I not go with you? I know the streets better than you.

(*c*) You ask where I shall be next week, and whether I intend to continue my studies in Germany. Well, both questions are hard to answer, for everything depends on the wishes of my parents.

(*d*) Please take a seat. That chair is not comfortable—take this one.

That one by the window is better still, I will get it.

Well, how do you find yourself since that week in the country?

Oh, don't speak of that. The contrast between that time and this gives me a headache.

4. (*a*) Tell what you know about the declension of proper names of persons. (*b*) What is peculiar in the declension of *hoch*, of adjective formed from names of towns, of *ganz* and *halb*? (*c*) Give all possible meanings of *sich*. (*d*) *Describe* the declension of the following pronouns : *meiner, derselbe, etwas*. (*e*) Give a half dozen prepositional adverbs which may occupy the place of the dative of *was* (wanting). (*f*) Give the distinguishing characteristics of strong verbs in general. (*g*) Give the principal parts of the German equivalents of the following verbs : *lock, shine, go, do, begin, forget, translate, prophesy*.

5. (*a*) Tell what you know about Freytag's relations to his *Alma Mater*. (*b*) Mention Schiller's masterpieces of his last period. (*c*) Give a brief account of the Schiller-Goethe friendship.

6. Reading aloud.

7. Translation into English of a German passage read aloud by examiner.

SESSIONAL EXAMINATION IN GERMAN.

FIRST YEAR (Men).

Friday, April 15th :—Afternoon, 2 to 5.

1. Translate into English :—

(a) Oldendorf. Sei jetzt wenigstens kein Hanswurst. —
Du kannst dir denken, wie peinlich meine Stellung im Hause des
Obersten geworden ist. Der würdige alte Herr entweder kalt oder
heftig, die Unterhaltung mit beißenden Anspielungen gewürzt, Ida
leidend, ich sehe oft, daß Sie geweint hat. Siegt unsere Partei,
werde ich Abgeordneter der Stadt, so fürchte ich, ist mir jede Hoff-
nung auf eine Verbindung mit Ida benommen.

Bolz (eifrig). Und trittst du zurück, so erleidet unsere Partei
einen empfindlichen Verlust. (schnell und nachdrücklich) Die bevor-
stehende Sitzung der Kammern wird verhängnißvoll für den Staat.
Die Parteien sind einander fast gleich. Jeder Verlust einer Stimme ist für unsere Sache ein Unglück. In dieser Stadt haben wir
außer dir keinen Candidaten, dessen Popularität groß genug ist,
seine Wahl wahrscheinlich zu machen. Entziehst du dich aus irgend
einem Grunde der Wahl, so siegen unsere Gegner.

(b) Senden. Einer nach dem andern aus der Gesellschaft trat
vor, gab seine Stimme, und „Professor Eduard Oldendorf" kam
aus jedem Munde.— Der letzte war dieser Piepenbrink. Bevor er
die Stimme abgab, frug er seinen Nachbar: Hat's der Professor
sicher?—Ja, war die Antwort. Und ich wähle als letzter Wahl-
mann zum Deputirten —(hält inne).

Adelheid. Den Professor?

Senden. Nein. Einen sehr gescheiten und pfiffigen Politi-
kus, wie er sagte: den Doctor Konrad Bolz — und damit drehte er
sich um, und ihm folgten seine Spießgesellen.

Adelheid (bei Seite, lächelnd). Ah!

Senden. Oldendorf ist Abgeordneter durch ein Mehr von
zwei Stimmen.

Oberſt. Ei!

Senden. Es iſt ſchändlich! Niemand iſt an dieſem Ausfall Schuld, als dieſe Journaliſten von der Union. Das war ein Laufen, ein Intriguiren, ein Händeſchütteln mit allen Wahlmännern, ein Lobpreiſen dieſes Oldendorf und ein Achſelzucken über uns und über Sie, verehrter Herr!

(c) Das Geſpräch nahm eine andere Wendung; man unterhielt ſich wieder vom illuſtrierten Wochenblatt, und die Kanzleirätin ließ die Gelegenheit, ſich als Frau von Bildung zu zeigen, nicht vorübergehen. Der Doktor wurde warm und erzählte von Pompeji und Herkulanum; er ſchilderte das häusliche Leben der Bewohner jener Städte ſo lebendig, als ob er ſelber pompejaniſcher Hausbeſitzer geweſen wäre, und veranlaßte die Kanzleirätin zu der Frage, ob er in Italien geweſen ſei. Er verneinte, teilte aber mit, daß er beabſichtige, in den nächſten Ferien eine Römerfahrt zu machen, worauf die Kanzleirätin ſeufzend ſagte, dies ſei in früheren Jahren ihr ſehnlichſter Wunſch geweſen, ſie habe eine Zeitlang keine Zitrone in die Hand nehmen können, ohne von Verlangen ergriffen zu werden nach dem Land, wo „im dunklen Laub die Goldorangen glühen".

2. Retranslation.

Translate into German.

Sir, I must beg you to find my expressions less amusing. I do not know Mr. P., but I have the pleasure of knowing his wine, and therefore I repeat the assertion that P. has better wine in his cellar than this is. Why do you find that ridiculous? You do not know Mr. P's wines and have no right to express an opinion.

3. Translate into German.

(a) When shall we have the longest day and the shortest night? (b) In the summer the days are longest and the nights shortest. (c) We should have had a great deal of pleasure if we had had more time. (d) This gentleman says that he has bought a gold watch for his little son. (e) To whom did you show the castle of the count? (*f*) The king sat on the throne and his ministers came before him. (*g*) I beg your pardon, sir; I was mistaken. (*h*) The sick man would like to speak with the physician. (*i*) They have been obliged to work the whole day. (*j*) The author of this book will be rewarded by the king. (*k*) A German monk invented gunpowder. (*l*) The king has accepted the work which a celebrated writer had offered him. (*m*) We are sorry that you have not succeeded. (*n*) The train will arrive in three hours and a half.

4. (*a*) Give the nominative plural of the German for *fossil, study, bed, son, sister, bird, painter, grammar*. (*b*) Compare the German equivalents of the following adjectives *old, short, good, high*. (*c*) Give a half-dozen German verbs which take the auxiliary *sein*. (*d*) Give a careful analysis of the position of the words in the following sentence. *Gestern habe ich nicht früh genug nach Hause kommen können*. (*e*) State the different moods by which commands may be expressed. Compose a short sentence exemplifying each. (*f*) State in detail peculiarities in the conjugation and use of separable verbs.

5. (*a*) Describe with some detail Freytag's relation to the question of Prussian supremacy in Germany. (*b*) Criticise his *Verlorene Handschrift*.

6. Reading aloud a passage from *Der Schwiegersohn*.

SESSIONAL EXAMINATIONS IN GERMAN.

SECOND YEAR DONALDAS.

FRIDAY, APRIL 15TH :—AFTERNOON, 2 TO 5.

1. Translate into English :—

(*a*) Das Fräulein. Nein, ich)rauch)' es auch nicht einmal zu hören. Es versteht sich von selbst. Sie könnten eines so häßlichen Streiches fähig sein, daß Sie mich nun nicht wollten? Wissen Sie, daß ich auf Zeit meines Lebens beschimpft wäre? Meine Landsmänninnen würden mit Fingern auf mich weisen.— „Das ist sie," würde es heißen, „das ist das Fräulein von Barnhelm, die sich einbildete, weil sie reich sei, den wackern Tellheim zu bekommen: als ob die wackern Männer für Geld zu haben wären!" So würde es heißen, denn meine Landsmänninnen sind alle neidisch auf mich. Daß ich reich bin, können sie nicht leugnen; aber davon wollen sie nichts wissen, daß ich auch sonst noch ein ziemlich gutes Mädchen bin, das seines Mannes wert ist. Nicht wahr, Tellheim?

(*b*) J u st. Wir lassen anschreiben, und wenn man nicht mehr anschreiben will und uns zum Hause hinauswirft, so versetzen wir, was wir noch haben, und ziehen weiter.— Höre nur, Paul, dem Wirte)ier müssen wir einen Possen spielen.

W e r n e r. Hat er dem Major was in den Weg gelegt?— Ich bin da)ei!—

„Just Wie wär's, wenn wir ihm des Abends, wenn er aus der Tabagie kommt, aufpaßten und ihn brav durchprügelten? —

W e r n e r. Des Abends?— aufpaßten?—ihrer zwei einem? — Das ist nichts.—

(*c*) Und es begab sich an einem der nächsten Sonntage, daß Frau Eckart, als sie aus der Kirche kam, ganz zufällig mit der Kanzleirätin auf dem Markt zusammentraf. Die beiden Damen)atten sich seit der Zeit, da sie zusammen in der Mädchenschule gesessen, nicht mehr gesprochen, nichtsdestoweniger aber war die Begrüßung über die Maßen herzlich. Sie erkundigten sich nach dem gegenseitigen Befinden, gedachten seufzend der schönen Jugendzeit und trösteten einander mit dem Hinweis auf die Freude, welche wohlgeratene Kinder ihren Eltern bereiten.

(*d*) Wie der wandernde Mann, der vor dem Sinken der Sonne
    Sie noch einmal ins Auge, die schnellverschwindende, faßte,
Dann im dunkeln Gebüsch und an der Seite des Felsens
Schweben siehet ihr Bild; wo)in er die Blicke nur wendet,
Eilet es vor und glänzt und schwankt in herrlichen Farben:
    So)ewegte vor Hermann die lie)liche Bildung des Mäd-
        chens
    Sanft sich vorbei, und schien dem Pfad' ins Getreide zu
folgen.

(e) Aber es fiel sogleich die gute Mutter behend ein :
Sohn, fürwahr! du hast Recht; Wir Eltern gaben das
Beispiel.
Denn wir haben uns nicht an fröhlichen Tagen erwählet.
Und uns knüpfte vielmehr die traurigste Stunde zusammen.
Montag Morgens — ich weiß es genau ; denn Tages
vorher war
Jener schreckliche Brand, der unser Städtchen verzehrte —
Zwanzig Jahre sind's nun ; es war ein Sonntag wie heute,
Heiß und trocken die Luft und wenig Wasser im Orte.
Alle Leute waren, spazierend in festlichen Kleidern,
Auf den Dörfern verteilt und in den Schenken und Mühlen.

2. Translation at sight.

Translate into English :—

Der erste Bonaparte, der bekanntlich Fatalist war, glaubte mit
Zuversicht an seinen Stern. Er glaubte aber auch an seinen Ring.
Woher dieses Kleinod stammte, hat man niemals erfahren können.
Thatsache aber ist, daß Napoleon in ihm einen Talisman erblickte,
von dem er sich niemals trennte. Als er im Jahre 1814 in Fon-
tainebleau im Moment seiner Abdankung einen vergeblichen Ver-
such gemacht hatte, sich zu vergiften, sagte er zum Doktor Corvisart,
der ihn pflegte : „Ich sollte nicht sterben ; ich hatte nicht an meinen
Talisman gedacht." Bei diesen Worten wies er auf seinen Ring
hin. Nach seinem Tode sollte das Kleinod auf seinen Sohn, den
König von Rom, übergehen, aber der Übermittlung nach Wien stell-
ten sich Schwierigkeiten entgegen. So übergab man den Ring
einstweilen der Königin Hortense zur Aufbewahrung und diese
schenkte ihn später dem Prinzen Louis. Napoleon III. trug nur
diesen Ring, den man in seiner Umgebung als den Ring des Kaisers
bezeichnete, und einen andern, den er von seiner Mutter geerbt.

Retranslation.

3. Translate into German.

Mrs. Eckart sat at the window and cast occasionally a glance on the wintry street ; but her thoughts were elsewhere. She had become perceptibly older, and although, for the sake of her son and her husband, she sometimes showed a pleasant face, yet she had to force herself to it. The same was true of (galt) the master. He was no longer the life-lusty man, whose acquaintance we had made the previous summer. The sorrow of the son grieved both parents very much, all the more that (by so much more as) he endeavoured to hide it.

Retranslation.

4. Translate into German.

"The necessary steps on my side are taken already," continued the count. "It required great sacrifices to obtain the consent of my family ; but for the prize of your charming daughter no sacrifice is too great."

"Your family consents?" exclaimed Mrs. Englemann in joyous surprise.

The count nodded his head in confirmation.

5. Reading aloud a passage from *Hermann und Dorothea.*

6. (*a*) Where did Goethe get the story of *Hermann und Dorothea?* (*b*) To what class of poetical composition does *H. and D.* belong? Give reasons for your statement. (*c*) Compare Goethe's words about *Luise* with Voss' reception of *H. and D.* (*d*) Mention other examples of the metre of *H. and D.* in the Greek, Latin and German languages.

7. (*a*) What sort of reception did *Minna von Barnhelm* receive from the German public ? (*b*) Criticise the action of the same. (*c*) What did Goethe say about the exposition of *M. v. B.*? (*d*) Mention Lessing's greatest critical works. (*e*) Discuss Lessing's relations to the French and the Shakesperian stage.

(*f*) —— to Frederick the Great.

INTERMEDIATE EXAMINATION (Men).
GERMAN.
Friday, April 15th : Afternoon 2 to 5.

1. Translate into English :—

(a) Hier unter diesen Felsen lasset uns
Halt machen und ein festes Lager schlagen,
Ob wir vielleicht die flücht'gen Völker wieder sammeln,
Die in den ersten Schrecken sich zerstreut.
Stellt gute Wachen aus,)esetzt die Höhn!
Zwar sichert uns die Nacht vor der Verfolgung,
Und wenn der Gegner nicht auch Flügel hat,
So fürcht' ich keinen Überfall — Dennoch
Bedarf's der Vorsicht, denn wir haben es
Mit einem kecken Feind und sind geschlagen.

(b) Wer ward nicht irr' an ihr und)ätte nicht
Gewankt an diesem unglücksel'gen Tage,
Da alle Zeichen gegen sie)ewiesen!
Wir waren überrascht, betäubt; der Schlag
Traf zu erschütternd unser Herz — Wer konnte
In dieser Schreckensstunde prüfend wägen?
Jetzt kehrt uns die Besonnenheit zurück;
Wir sehn sie, wie sie unter uns gewandelt,
Und keinen Tadel finden wir an ihr.

(c) Während solcherlei Gespräche hin und her flogen, verlor man
doch das Nützliche nicht aus den Augen, und den großen Schüsseln,
die mit Fleisch, Kartoffeln u. s. w. ehrlich angefüllt waren, wurde
fleißig zugesprochen. Je)och war das Essen schlecht. Dies erwähnte
ich leichthin gegen meinen Nachbar, der aber mit einem Accente,
woran ich den Schweizer erkannte, gar unhöflich antwortete, daß
wir Deutschen, wie mit der wahren Freiheit, so auch mit der wahren
Genügsamkeit unbekannt seien. Ich zuckte die Achseln und bemerkte,
daß die eigentlichen Fürstenknechte und Leckerkramverfertiger überall

19

Schweizer sind und vorzugsweise so genannt werden, und das überhaupt die jetzigen schweizerischen Freiheitshelden, die so viel Politisch-Kühnes ins Publikum hineinschwatzen, mir immer vorkommen wie Hasen, die auf öffentlichen Jahrmärkten Pistolen abschießen, alle Kinder und Bauern durch ihre Kühnheit in Erstaunen setzen, und dennoch Hasen sind.

(d) Es waren lauter Verse, die meisten füllten höchstens eine Seite. Elisabeth wandte ein Blatt nach dem andern um; sie schien nur die Überschriften zu lesen. „Als sie vom Schulmeister gescholten war." „Als sie sich im Walde verirrt hatten." „Mit dem Ostermärchen." „Als sie mir zum ersten Mal geschrieben hatte;" in der Weise lauteten fast alle. Reinhardt blickte forschend zu ihr hin, und indem sie immer weiter blätterte, sah er, wie zuletzt auf ihrem klaren Antlitz ein zartes Rot hervorbrach und es allmählich ganz überzog. Er wollte ihre Augen sehen; aber Elisabeth sah nicht auf und legte das Buch am Ende schweigend vor ihn hin.

(e) For women students of Morrin College only.

Es war keiner außer ihm in den zwei Kammern, durch die er nun hin und her ging. Zu den offenen Fensterchen, die nur mit hölzernen Läden verschlossen wurden, strich die Luft etwas erfrischender herein, als über das ruhige Meer; und in der Einsamkeit war ihm wohl. Er stand auch lange vor dem kleinen Bilde der Mutter Gottes und sah die aus Silberpapier daraufgeklebte Sternenglorie andächtig an. Doch zu beten fiel ihm nicht ein. Um was hätte er bitten sollen, da er nichts mehr hoffte.

Und der Tag schien heute still zu stehn. Er sehnte sich nach der Dunkelheit, denn er war müde, und der Blutverlust hatte ihn auch mehr angegriffen, als er sich gestand. Er fühlte heftige Schmerzen an der Hand, setzte sich auf einen Schemel und löste den Verband. Das zurückgedrängte Blut schoß wieder hervor, und die Hand war stark um die Wunde angeschwollen. Er wusch sie sorgfältig und kühlte sie lange.

2. Translate into German :—

I met the two young men again in the inn at N. One was eating his breakfast and the other was talking to the maid. In

order to lighten my knapsack I took out my blue breeches and
gave them to the little waiter. Meanwhile the old landlady
brought me' a slice of bread and butter and complained that I
visited her so seldom, for she is very fond of me.

3. (*a*) This exercise is very easy ; we shall have finished it in
half an hour. (*b*) My friend, of whom I thought so highly,
died in his nineteenth year. (*c*) The soldiers ran blindly into
the battle and fought like lions. (*d*) These two ships set sail at
the same time, but the smaller arrived first. (*e*) He will be
obliged to study another year, if he does not pass his examination. (*f*) Lazy boys learn only because they are obliged to
learn. (*g*) I am learning a poem by heart ; I have already
repeated it ten times. (*h*) Have you decided to leave the town
and pass the summer in the country ?

4. (*a*) Give the first person singular and plural of the present
tense of all the model auxiliaries. (*b*) Give the various meanings
of mögen ; give an example of each in a well constructed German
sentence. (*c*) Explain the meanings of *oben, ober, über, drüben,
hinüber, herüber, übrig.* (*d*) Explain the treatment of the
prefix in verbs compounded with *durch, hinter, über, unter, um.*

5. (*a*) Give a brief account of the employment of the iambic
pentameter in the German and English languages. (*b*) What
are the chief deviations of Schiller's *Jungfrau* from the facts of
history ? (*c*) Give a somewhat detailed account of Schiller's
connection with Goethe ?

6. (*a*) Describe Heine's student days. (*b*) Give some examples of his satirical wit in the Harzreise.

7. Reading aloud.

8. Translation at sight.

Translate into English :—

Wenn das Wort : „Die besten Frauen sind die, von denen man
am wenigsten spricht," auch von Fürstinnen gilt, so gehört die
Prinzessin von Wales zu den besten Frauen. Die Welt weiß von -

ihr nicht viel mehr, als daß sie im Alter von neunzehn Jahren mit
dem zweiundzwanzigjährigen Prinzen von Wales vermählt wurde,
und daß sie heute eine ebenso liebvolle Mutter ihrer Kinder ist, als
sie eine zärtliche Tochter war.   Und doch lassen die ernsten Augen
der hohen Frau vermuten, daß die Sonne des Glücks ihr Leben
nicht immer bestrahlte.

Prinzessin Alexandra ist eine ernste Natur mit stark entwickelten
Pflichtgefühl.   Ihre hohe Gestalt, die Grazie und Vornehmheit
ihrer Bewegungen, die edle Form, ihres Gesichtes, in welchem sich
Güte mit stolzer Zurückhaltung paart, lassen die Fürstin erkennen.
In ihren Augen liegt etwas Fragendes und zugleich Träumerisches ;
sie scheint die Dinge auf ihren innern Wert hin zu prüfen, scheint
Herz und Phantasie zu besitzen.   Wäre sie auch nicht)azu bestimmt,
dereinst die Königskrone von England und die Kaiserkrone von
Indien zu tragen, sie bliebe doch eine höchst interessante Frau.

SESSIONAL EXAMINATIONS IN GERMAN.

THIRD AND FOURTH YEARS.

Tuesday, April 19th :—Afternoon, 2 to 5.

1. Translate into English :—

> (a) Armsel' ge Gleiszner, wie veracht' ich euch,
> Die ihr euch selbst, so wie die Welt, belügt !
> Ihr Engelländer streckt die Räuberhände
> Nach diesem Frankreich aus, wo ihr nicht Recht
> Noch gült' gen Anspruch habt auf so viel Erde,
> Als eines Pferdes Huf bedeckt.—Und dieser Herzog,
> Der sich den *Guten* schelten läszt, verkauft
> Sein Vaterland, das Erbreich seiner Ahnen,
> Dem Reichsfeind und dem fremden Herrn.—Gleichwohl
> Ist euch das dritte Wort Gerechtigkeit.

> (b) Und *einer* Freude Hochgefühl entbrennet,
> Und *ein* Gedanke schlägt in jeder Brust,
> Was sich noch jüngst in blut' gem Hasz getrennet,
> Das teilt entzückt die allgemeine Lust.

Wer nur zum Stamm der Franken sich bekennet,
Der ist des Namens stolzer sich bewuszt;
Erneuert ist der Glanz der alten Krone,
Und Frankreich huldigt seinem Königssohne.

(c) Von Goslar ging ich den andern Morgen weiter,)al) auf Geratewohl,)al) in der Absicht, den Bruder des Klausthaler Bergmanns aufzusuchen. Wieder schönes, liebes Sonntagswetter. Ich bestieg Hügel und Berge, betrachtete, wie die Sonne den Nebel zu verscheuchen suchte, wanderte freudig durch die schauernden Wälder, und um mein träumendes Haupt klingelten die Glockenblümchen von Goslar. In ihren weißen Nachtmänteln standen die Berge, die Tannen rüttelten sich den Schlaf aus den Gliedern, der frische Morgenwind frisierte ihnen die herabhängenden, grünen Haare, die Vöglein hielten Betstunde, das Wiesenthal blitzte wie eine diamantbesäete Golddecke, und der Hirt schritt darüber hin mit seiner läutenden Heerde.

TRANSLATION AT SIGHT.

2. Translate into English :

Die erste Begrüßung der Kaiser von Österreich und Frankreich in Salzburg)atte stattgefunden, und alle Zeitungen waren voll von der Beschreibung des Empfangsceremoniells und des Diners am Abend des ersten Tages, bei welchem der Kaiser Franz Joseph persönlich dem Fürsten Richard Metternich den Orden des goldenen Vließes überreicht)atte, wo er ihm seine Anerkennung ausgedrückt für die Verdienste, die er um die guten Beziehungen der beiden Höfe sich erworben.

Der Kaiser Napoleon)atte, den Sinn dieser Auszeichnung in ostensiblem Verständnis erfassend, dem Kaiser von Österreich dafür, als für eine ihm selbst erwiesene Artigkeit, gedankt, und damit der ganzen Begegnung noch um einen Grad mehr den politischen Stempel aufgedrückt. Daneben berichtete man ausführlich von der Begegnung der Kaiserinnen, über die Toiletten der)o)en Damen, über den Spazierstock der Kaiserin Eugenie, über den Hund der Kaiserin von Österreich und über alle jene tausend kleinen Details.

Kurz, das Schauspiel, welches sie) vor den Augen Europas voll-
zog, war in vollem Gang. In der alten Bergstadt, umragt von
den mächtigen Alpen, entwickelte sich das ganze bunte und geschäf-
tige Treiben zweier großen Höfe, welches den eigentlichen Kern des
Lebens der Souveräne wie mit einer glänzenden Wolfe verhüllt,
die profanen Blicke ablenkend auf kleine und unscheinbare Äußer
lichkeiten.

3. Translate into German :—

Let us go out into the country together. I know no greater pleasure
than a walk through the woods in fine weather. It is a joy to live,
when the birds are twittering and chirping above your head, and the
sun shines through the leaves. I have always loved nature. I cannot look on a spring blossom without emotion. What a pity that
botany was not better taught in our school days. We hated the name
of it, and yet there is no science which would contribute so much to
the enjoyment of life, if we only studied it in the right way. What a
pleasure to understand the various parts of the flowers which you
meet in your walks. Yes, that is true, but do not forget that botany
cannot teach you the everlasting mystery of flowers ; God reserves
that for himself.

TRANSLATION AT SIGHT.

4. Translate into German :

The house in which I was born is very old; it was built in the
eighteenth century. Most of the rooms are large and the walls are
covered with beautiful pictures. I can never forget the happy days
I spent in that dear old house. We used to get up at six o'clock. We
began to work immediately after breakfast. Our lessons were finished
when the clock struck twelve. I had a pony of my own. Every
afternoon I paid a visit to an elderly aunt who lived in the village
six miles away. She always gave me something good. Otherwise I
suppose I should not have been so regular with my visits.

5. (a) Explain briefly the Old German metrical system. (b) What
are the chief metrical differences between a line of the *Jungfrau* and
an Old German line of poetry? (c) Analyse the " Romantic " features
of the *Jungfrau*. (d) What was Heine's attitude towards Paris,
French poetry, German sovereigns, Napoleon the First, his Göttin-
gen professors, the Christian religion, the English people ?

GERMAN.

B.A. AND THIRD YEAR HONOURS.

WEDNESDAY, APRIL 6TH :—MORNING, 9 TO 12.

N.B.—*Questions expressed in German are to be answered in German.*

1. Translate into English :

(*a*) Die Braut von Messina, first paragraph spoken by *Erster Chor* (Cajetan).

 (*b*) Die Braut von Messina, Die Säulenhalle, Isabella's speech beginning with the words : Ich seh' auch, dasz......

(*c*) Faust, Vor dem Thor, first half of paragraph beginning with the words : O glücklich, wer noch hoffen kann (line 1064 in Thomas).

2. Make brief comments on the following : (*a*) Fliegengott, (*b*) Spruch der Viere, (*c*) Drudenfusz, (*d*) mit eigensinnigem Krittel, (*e*) Doctorschmaus, (*f*) Spanische Stiefeln, (*g*) Ihr seid von Rippach, (*h*) Junker Satan.

3. Welches ist das durchgängige Masz der Chorlieder in der B. v. M ?

4. Geben Sie einige heidnische Züge der B. v. M. an.

5. Wie sollten nach Schiller's Brief an Iffland die Reden des Chors vorgetragen werden ?

6. Nennen Sie andere bedeutende moderne Werke, worin Chöre vorkommen.

7. Geben Sie eine kurze Geschichte der Entstehung und der Entwickelung des Chors bei den Griechen.

8. Erläutern Sie die verschiedenen möglichen Erklärungsarten des Goethe' schen Faust.

oder.

Erklären Sie den Unterschied zwischen der teuflischen und der kirchlichen Magie.

9. In welchem Jahre erschien das frankfurter Volksbuch ? Geben Sie den Inhalt desselben an. Wie heiszen die anderen Faustbücher ?

10. Inwiefern ist Faust ein historischer Charakter? In welchem Verhältnis steht Leipzig zu der Faustsage.

oder.

Geben Sie den Inhalt der Lessing' schen Faustscenen nach Blankenberg's oder Engel's Bericht an.

11. Beschreiben Sie Goethe's Straszburger Tage, besonders sein damaliges Verhältnis zu Herder.

12. Welche Scenen waren in dem " Fragment " enthalten? Zu welcher Zeit wurden die drei einleitenden Stücke geschrieben? Wo wurde die " Hexenküche " geschrieben?

13. Erläutern Sie folgende Worte aus der Zueignung: " Wie ihr aus Dunst und Nebel um mich steigt."

oder.

Warum konnte Goethe zur Zeit der italienischen Reise seinen Faust nicht vollenden? Was schrieb er zu dieser Zeit über den Plan des Faust?

GERMAN.

B.A. AND THIRD YEAR HONOURS.

WEDNESDAY, APRIL 13TH :—MORNING, 9 TO 12.

N.B.—*Questions expressed in German are to be answered in German.*

1. Translate into English. Emilia Galotti, Act I, Scene 4., Conti, paragraph beginning with words: Gleichwohl hat mich...

2. Translate into English Goethe's Egmont, Act II., first fifteen lines.

3. Welches sind die Hauptcharakteristika der vierten Periode der deutschen Litteratur (1300-1500)?

4. Führen Sie spanische, italienische und französische Muster des deutschen Schäferromans an.

5. (a) Von wem wurde die Insel Felsenburg geschrieben. (b) Erwähnen Sie andere Werke, welche zu derselben Gattung gehören.

oder,

(a) Wie heiszen die bedeutendsten deutschen sogenannten "moralischen Wochenschriften"? (b) In welchem Verhältnis stehen sie zu dem Familienroman von Richardson?

6. Geben Sie eine Biographie Gellert's.

oder,

Beschreiben Sie den Kampf zwischen Gottsched und den Schweizern.

7. (a) Was sagt Lessing von Gottsched's Einflusz auf die deutsche Bühne? (b) Wie verhält sich Lessing zu der Nachahmung der französischen klassischen Poesie? (c) In welchen Werken behandelt er diese Frage? (d) In welchen Hinsichten gleicht Lessing Friedrich dem Groszen?

8. (a) Wie entstand der Name "Bremer. Beiträger"? (b) Wie heiszen die bedeutendsten derselben?

oder,

9. (a) Citieren Sie aus Goethe's "Dichtung und Wahrheit" einen Beweis der Beliebtheit des "Messias." (b) Warum hat der Messias seine hohe Stellung nicht behalten, wie z. B. Dante's Divina Commedia? (c) Was ist ein "Bardiet"?

10. (a) Unterscheiden Sie die grozen Geistesrichtungen Wielands und charakterisieren Sie dieselben. (b) Erwähnen Sie sämmtliche gröszere Werke Wielands.

oder,

Beschreiben Sie Goethe's italienische Reise.

11. (a) In welchem Aufsatz vergleicht Schiller die antike mit der modernen Dichtung? (b) Geben Sie den Inhalt der "Räuber" an. (c) Welches ist das sogenannte Balladenjahr? (d) Welches sind Schiller's schönste Balladen?

12. (a) Wo stammt der Name "romantisch" her? (b) Welche schönen Übersetzungen verdanken wir der romantischen Schule? (c) Beschreiben Sie Heine's Verhältnis zu A. W. v. Schlegel. (d) Geben Sie eine kurze Biographie von A.W. v. Schlegel. (e) Wie heiszt ein gewisser berüchtigter Roman von Friedrich Schlegel? (f) Welcher Theolog hat eine günstige Kritik darüber geschrieben? (g) Wie heiszt das bekannteste Werk dieses Theologen?

HEBREW.

1. Translate literally :—

וַיִּקַּח יְהוָה אֱלֹהִים אֶת־הָאָדָם וַיַּנִּחֵהוּ בְגַן־עֵדֶן לְעָבְדָהּ
וּלְשָׁמְרָהּ׃ וַיְצַו יְהוָה אֱלֹהִים עַל־הָאָדָם לֵאמֹר מִכֹּל
עֵץ־הַגָּן אָכֹל תֹּאכֵל׃ וּמֵעֵץ הַדַּעַת טוֹב וָרָע לֹא
תֹאכַל מִמֶּנּוּ כִּי בְּיוֹם אֲכָלְךָ מִמֶּנּוּ מוֹת תָּמוּת׃

(a) What is the peculiarity of ל in לָקַח?

(b) Explain the pointing of יְהוָה.

(c) Why is אֱלֹהִים in the plural?

(d) Nature of the vowels in הָאָדָם.

(e) Explain the tsere in לֵאמֹר.

(f) Explain the formation of (1) מִמֶּנּוּ (2) דַּעַת.

(g) Translate and parse :—(1) אֲכָלְךָ (2) לְשָׁמְרָה.

(h) Render into Hebrew :—Thou mayest eat from all the fruit which God has given.

2. Translate literally :—

וַתֵּרֶא הָאִשָּׁה כִּי טוֹב הָעֵץ לְמַאֲכָל וְכִי תַאֲוָה־הוּא
לָעֵינַיִם וְנֶחְמָד הָעֵץ לְהַשְׂכִּיל וַתִּקַּח מִפִּרְיוֹ וַתֹּאכַל
וַתִּתֵּן גַּם־לְאִישָׁהּ עִמָּהּ וַיֹּאכַל׃ וַתִּפָּקַחְנָה עֵינֵי שְׁנֵיהֶם
וַיֵּדְעוּ כִּי עֵירֻמִּם הֵם וַיִּתְפְּרוּ עֲלֵה תְאֵנָה וַיַּעֲשׂוּ לָהֶם

חֲגֹרת ׃ וַיִּשְׁמְעוּ אֶת־קוֹל יְהֹוָה אֱלֹהִים מִתְהַלֵּךְ בַּגָּן
לְרוּחַ הַיּוֹם וַיִּתְחַבֵּא הָאָדָם וְאִשְׁתּוֹ מִפְּנֵי יְהֹוָה אֱלֹהִים
בְּתוֹךְ עֵץ הַגָּן ׃

(a) Name the main accents in the first sentence, and state their use.

(b) Parse fully וַתֵּרֶא. Write out the full form.

(c) Account for the dagesh in (1) הָאִשָׁה. (2) נֶחְמָד.

(d) Parse fully לָעֵינַיִם.

(e) Inflect the Hiphil perfect of שָׂכַל.

(f) What is the root of פְּרִי ?

(g) Parse וַתִּפָּקַחְנָה.—To what class does that verb belong ?

(h) Characteristics of Niphal imperfect.

(i) Parse וַיַּעֲשׂוּ.—What would be the vowels of the preformative and of the first radical in the strong verb ?

(j) Render into Hebrew :—Let us make for ourselves large girdles.

3. Point, translate and parse :—יקרש אלהים את היום הזה

4. Tabular view of פָּקַד in Piel and Hiphil.

5. Inflect the Niphal perfect of שָׁמַר.

6. Oral examination.

HEBREW.

SECOND YEAR.

FRIDAY, APRIL 1ST :—MORNING, 9 TO 12.

1. Translate literally :

וְלֹא־מָצְאָה הַיּוֹנָה מָנוֹחַ לְכַף־רַגְלָהּ וַתָּשָׁב אֵלָיו
אֶל־הַתֵּבָה כִּי מַיִם עַל־פְּנֵי כָל־הָאָרֶץ וַיִּשְׁלַח יָדוֹ וַיִּקָּחֶהָ

וַיָּבֹא אֵלָיו אֶל־הַתֵּבָה : וַיָּחֶל עוֹד שִׁבְעַת יָמִים
אֲחֵרִים וַיֹּסֶף שַׁלַּח אֶת־הַיּוֹנָה מִן־הַתֵּבָה : וַתָּבֹא אֵלָיו
הַיּוֹנָה לְעֵת עֶרֶב וְהִנֵּה עֲלֵה־זַיִת טָרָף בְּפִיהָ וַיֵּדַע נֹחַ כִּי־
קַלּוּ הַמַּיִם מֵעַל הָאָרֶץ : וַיִּיָּחֶל עוֹד שִׁבְעַת יָמִים אֲחֵרִים
וַיְשַׁלַּח אֶת־הַיּוֹנָה וְלֹא־יָסְפָה שׁוּב־אֵלָיו עוֹד :

(a) Inflect מָצָא in the Kal perfect.

(b) Iuflect רֶגֶל

(c) Explain the formation of (1) מָנוֹחַ.   (2) כַּף.

(d) Parse (1) וַתֵּשֶׁב.   (2) וַיִּקָּחֶהָ   (3) וַיָּחֶל.   (4) וַיִּיָּחֶל.

(e) State the principle of Syntax involved in שִׁבְעַת יָמִים.

2. Translate literally :—

זָכוֹר אֶת־יוֹם הַשַּׁבָּת לְקַדְּשׁוֹ : שֵׁשֶׁת יָמִים תַּעֲבֹד וְעָשִׂיתָ
כָל־מְלַאכְתֶּךָ : וְיוֹם הַשְּׁבִיעִי שַׁבָּת ׀ לַיהֹוָה אֱלֹהֶיךָ
לֹא־תַעֲשֶׂה כָל־מְלָאכָה אַתָּה ׀ וּבִנְךָ־וּבִתֶּךָ עַבְדְּךָ
וַאֲמָתְךָ וּבְהֶמְתֶּךָ וְגֵרְךָ אֲשֶׁר בִּשְׁעָרֶיךָ : כִּי שֵׁשֶׁת־יָמִים
עָשָׂה יְהֹוָה אֶת־הַשָּׁמַיִם וְאֶת־הָאָרֶץ אֶת־הַיָּם וְאֶת־כָּל־
אֲשֶׁר־בָּם וַיָּנַח בַּיּוֹם הַשְּׁבִיעִי עַל־כֵּן בֵּרַךְ יְהֹוָה אֶת־יוֹם
הַשַּׁבָּת וַיְקַדְּשֵׁהוּ :

(a) Parse (1) זָכוֹר.   (2) לְקַדְּשׁוֹ.

(b) Explain the sign over כָּל־.

(c) Name the accent over ךָ in the next word, and state its peculiarity.

(d) Inflect עָשָׂה in the Kal imperfect.

(e) Root of גֵּר.

(f) Synopsis of בָּרַךְ in Pual.

(*g*) Point out the differences between Exodus X X and Deuterono-
my V as to the fourth Commandment·

3. Translate literally :—

וַתֹּאמְרוּ הֵן הֶרְאָנוּ יְהוָה אֱלֹהֵינוּ אֶת־כְּבֹדוֹ וְאֶת־גׇּדְלוֹ
וְאֶת־קֹלוֹ שָׁמַעְנוּ מִתּוֹךְ הָאֵשׁ הַיּוֹם הַזֶּה רָאִינוּ כִּי־יְדַבֵּר
אֱלֹהִים אֶת־הָאָדָם וָחָי : וְעַתָּה לָמָּה נָמוּת כִּי תֹאכְלֵנוּ
הָאֵשׁ הַגְּדֹלָה הַזֹּאת אִם־יֹסְפִים ׀ אֲנַחְנוּ לִשְׁמֹעַ אֶת־קוֹל
יְהוָה אֱלֹהֵינוּ עוֹד וָמָתְנוּ : כִּי מִי כָל־בָּשָׂר אֲשֶׁר שָׁמַע
קוֹל אֱלֹהִים חַיִּים מְדַבֵּר מִתּוֹךְ־הָאֵשׁ כָּמֹנוּ וַיֶּחִי :

(*a*) Parse (1) הֶרְאָנוּ· (2) גׇּדְלוֹ· (3) וָחָי·

(*b*) Inflect רָאָה in the Niphal imperfect.

(*c*) Inflect בָּשָׂר in singular and plural.

(*d*) Give the Greek and the Latin of that word.

4. Render into Hebrew :—(1) Our Father who art in heaven. (2)
Take with thee in the ark thy father and thy sons and thy daugh-
ters. (3) This is my word which I have spoken to you·

5. Point, translate and parse :—דספר ואלה סכום פסוקי
שמות אלה ומאתים ותשעה. ופרשיותיו י"א.

6. Make a note on the work of the Masoreths.

7. Explain what is meant by פרשה and הפטרה.

HEBREW.

B.A. ORDINARY.

Examiner,...D. Coussirat, B.A., B.D., D.D., Officier d'Académie.

1. Translate literally—Isaiah 1, 2, 3.

(*a*) Make philological and historical notes on (1) יְשַׁעְיָהוּ· (2)
יְרוּשָׁלַ͏ִם· (3) אָחָז. (4) יְהוּדָה·

(b) Inflect the Hiphil perfect of יָדַע.

(c) Give the various renderings of עַל־מֶה תְכוּ, and parse the verb.

2. Tŕanslate literally—Isaiah 2, 12, 13, 14, 15.

(a) Whó are the persons designated as אַרְזֵי הַלְּבָנוֹן ?

(b) Name and point out the use of the accents in the second, verse.

3. Translate literally—Isaiah 5, 21, 22.

(a) Inflect the plural of חָכָם.

(b) Inflect the Hiphil imperfect of סוּר.

(c) Render into Hebrew: They put darkness for light.

4. Translate literally—Isaiah 10, 28, 29, 30, 31, 32.

(a) To what invasion does that passage refer?

(b) Make geographical notes on the places mentioned here.

(c) Parse כֵּלָיו. Give its various meanings.

(d) Parse לָנוּ.

(e) Comment on the style of these verses.

5. Translate literally—Psalm 46, 1. 2, 3.

(a) Write a note on Al-alamoth.

(b) Is it possible to determine the date of Psalm 46 from its contents?

(c) How is that psalm divided as to its form?

6. Point and translate :— סכום הפסוקים של ישעיהו
אלף ומאתים ותשעים וחמשה.

7. What may the participle be in respect to government?

8. How many Targums are extant? What are the most useful ones, and in what respect?

9. (a) How was the Talmud formed? (b) Describe the treatises of its fourth order. (c) Give one or two examples of its contents.

B.A. AND THIRD YEAR HONOURS.

ARAMAIC.

THURSDAY, APRIL 7TH :—MORNING, 9 TO 12.

*Examiner,.....*D. COUSSIRAT, B.A., B.D., D.D., OFFICIER D'ACADÉMIE.

1. Translate literally Daniel VII, 1-8 inclusive : —

(a) Write a full note on בֵּלְאשַׁצַּר.

(b) Parse the verbs of verse 8.

(c) Inflect חֵיוָא (singular and plural).

(d) Translate the Masoretic note of verse 7.

(e) Discuss the traditional and the modern explanations of this vision.

(f) Render into Chaldee: (1) His sons were eating and drinking. (2) The day of the month. (3) The basest of men.

2. Translate literally Jonathan's Targum on Ruth II, 11-14 inclusive :—

(a) Inflect the Aphel imperfect of הוּב.

(b) Make a note on דְּחַלְתִּיךְ.

(c) Parse (1) דְּאָתִי. (2) תְּשֵׁיזִיב.

(d) Explain the nature of שְׁכִינָא and מֵימְרָא.

(e) Inflect זְכוּ.

(f) Make a note on the proper names found in verse 12.

(g) How is the suffix added in נְחַמְתַּנִי ?

(h) Analyze רִית.

(i) How is טְמָשׁ rendered into Hebrew ?

(j) Compare the Hebrew text and this passage.

3. State what is known of Onkelos and Jonathan Ben Uzziel.

HONOUR EXAMINATIONS.

THIRD YEAR.

HEBREW.

SATURDAY, APRIL 9TH:—MORNING, 9 TO 12.

1. Translate literally Genesis 49, 8. 9. 10. 11. 12. 18.

(a) Inflect יָדָה in the Hiphil perfect.

(b) Parse יִשְׁתַּחֲווּ. Give its meaning in Greek.

(c) Distinguish between אַרְיֵה and לָבִיא.

(d) Plural of לָבִיא.

(e) Write an explanatory note on שִׁלֹה.

(f) What kind of יְשׁוּעָה did Jacob wait for ?

(g) Inflect עַיִן.

(h) Root and fundamental signification of עֵין.

2. Translate literally Isaiah 61, 1 to 9 inclusive.

(a) Give the Greek equivalents of בֵּשֵׂר and עֲנָוִים.

(b) How is the pronominal suffix joined to the perfect of strong verbs in the 3rd pers. sing. masc.?

(c) Describe the functions of the כֹהֵן.

(d) Inflect קָרָא in the Niphal imperfect.

(e) How is the word גּוֹיִם rendered in the Greek of the N. T.?

(f) Write an explanatory note on פְּקַח־קוֹחַ.

(g) Discuss the root and meaning of תִתְיַמָּרוּ.

3. Point, translate and parse the Masoretic note at the end of Isaiah.

HEBREW PROSE AND TRANSLATION AT SIGHT.

SATURDAY, APRIL 9TH:—AFTERNOON, 2 TO 5.

1. Translate at sight 2 Kings 5, 8 to 14 inclusive.

2. Translate into Hebrew :—

(1) He judged the people six years.

(2) And he died and was buried in one of the cities of Judah.

(3) And they did evil again in the sight of the Lord.

(4) The Angel of the Lord appeared unto him.

(5) God hearkened to our voice.

(6) I will not eat of thy bread.

(7) They anointed him King over Israel.

(8) What is thy name ?

(9) Who is as the wise man ?

(10) He lived one hundred and forty and five years, and saw his sons, even four generations.

B. A. HONOURS.

SEMITIC LANGUAGES.

COMPARATIVE GRAMMAR.

THURSDAY, APRIL 14TH :—MORNING, 9 TO 12.

Write on any four of the following subjects :—

1. The Semitic alphabets :—(a) Origin—(b) Oldest monuments of Semitic writings—(c) Alphabet of the Siloam inscription—(d) Square character—(e) Aramaic Alphabet—(f) Alphabet of the Southern Semites—(g) Inadequacy of the Semitic alphabets.

2. The vowels :—(a) Original vowel-system—(b) Modifications of the vowels in Arabic—(c) The influence of the tone in Hebrew—(d) The diphthongs —(e) Prosthetic vowels.

3. The noun :—(a) Cases in Arabic and Ethiopic—(b) Origin of the case-endings—(c) Nunation— (d) Mimation— (e) The emphatic state in Aramaic—(f) Pronominal suffixes to the noun.

20

4. The verb :—(a) Forms with characteristic *a, i, u* in the perfect—(b) The preformatives in the Imperfect—(c) Moods of the Imperfect in Arabic.

5. Derived stems :—(a) The intensive stem—(b) The Conative stem —(c) The Nithpael.

———

B. A. HONORS.

HISTORY OF THE SEMITIC LANGUAGES.

Friday, April 15th :—Morning, 9 to 12.

Write on any eight of the following subjects :—

1. A table of the Semitic languages.

2. Original seat of the Semites.

3. Characteristics of the Semitic mind.

4. Main features of the Arabic language.

5. Peculiarities of the Rabbinical dialect.

6. Short notice on the Peshito.

7. General contents of the Koran.

8. Comparison between Semitic, Hamitic and Aryan families of languages.

9. How and by whom were deciphered the Assyrian characters.

10. Describe two Semitic inscriptions.

11. What are the Semitic languages still living ? Where and by whom are they spoken ?

———

THIRD YEAR HONOURS,

LENORMANTS BEGINNINGS OF HISTORY.

Thursday, April 20th :—Morning, 9 to 12.

Write on any eight of the following subjects :

1. The creation of man according to Plœnician traditions.

2. Idea of the primordial androgyn.

3. Conception of the Edenic felicity of the first men among the Aryan nations.

4. Aryan theory of the four ages of humanity.

5. The trees of life of the Indians.

6. The serpent in the religious symbolism of antiquity.

7. The serpent of the storms in the Vedas.

8. The Aryanist school in Biblical exegesis.

9. The Assyriologist school's interpretation of the Kerubim.

10. The word *lachat* in Hebrew.

11. Symbolic nomenclature of the months in Babylonia and Assyria.

12. Diluvian traditions of *Irân*.

B.A. HONOURS.

HEBREW.

THURSDAY, APRIL 21ST :—MORNING, 9 TO 12.

1. Translate literally with notes Malachi III, 7, 8, 9, 10.

2. Describe the circumstances of the Jews in the time of Malachi.

3. Characterize the style of the book of that prophet.

4. Translate literally with notes Psalm LXVII.

5. The collection and arrangement of the Psalms.

6. Translate literally with notes Job XIX, 25.

7. Translate literally with notes Job XXIX, 18 to 20.

8. Translate literally with notes Job XXXVIII, 31 to 36.

9. Discuss briefly the various views of the book of Job.

N.B.—Notes include the parsing of unusual verbs and nouns.

NATURAL SCIENCE.

SECOND YEAR.

BOTANY.

FIRST PAPER.

1897-98.

1. Give a concise history of classification, and outline a scheme for the principal divisions of the vegetable kingdom in conformity with our present knowledge of relationships.

2. Discuss the occurrence of heterospory in its bearing upon development.

3. Give a short account of the reproductive process in *Zamia*.

4. Discuss the term *Alternation of Phases* (Generations) as applied to the life-history of a plant, and indicate the limitations of such phases.

5. Give a full account of the structure and life history of *Pleurococcus vulgaris*.

6. Describe the structure and function of the prothallus, and discuss its gradual obliteration as an evidence of development.

7. Give a brief description of the general morphology and the reproduction of *Equisetum arvense*.

8. Describe the chief characteristics of the Phæophyceæ as illustrated by a specific case.

9. Discuss the relationship of the Angiosperms and Gymnosperms on the basis of the reproductive process.

10. Discuss the principal modifications of the floral organs of seed-plants, arising through cohesion and adhesion. Apply these modifications to classification.

SECOND YEAR.

BOTANY.

SECOND PAPER.

1. Describe fully the process of photosynthesis in plants.

2. Explain the mechanism of root action.

3. Discuss the conditions which regulate the movement of sap, indicating the direction of the flow.

4. Explain the function of respiration and the chemical changes involved.

5. Give a full description of the structure of the root-tip of a Monocotyledon.

6. Describe the structure and mode of development of an exogenous stem.

7. Explain the structure of the epidermal tissue of a leaf and its functional adaptations.

8. State what you know of the influence of ocean-currents in promoting distribution of species.

9. Give an account of the chemical and physical properties of protoplasm.

10. Describe the structure of the nucleus and the various steps in its mitosis.

THIRD YEAR.

BOTANY.

1897-98.

1. Given, two eye-pieces of 2 and 1 inch focus, and two objectives of 1½ and ⅕ inch focal length. Determine the theoretical amplification of each possible combination—eye-piece and objective—for a tube length of 10 inches.

2. Describe the use of (a) the stage micrometer and (b) the eye-piece micrometer, and show how the latter may be standardised.

3. Indicate a distinctive color test for albuminoids. Enumerate the principal representatives of this group, and give a concise statement of their distinctive features.

4. Discuss the movements of protoplasm as to (a) characteristics, (b) occurrence, (c) general conditions under which they are promoted.

5. Give a concise account of the occurrence and special tests for the recognition of mucilage.

6. Give a full account of the structure and relations of parts in a vascular bundle of the open collateral type.

7. Describe the structure of a Dicotyledonous stem of the woody type of one year's growth, and show what changes take place through secondary development.

8. Give a full account of primary and secondary growth in an endogenous stem.

9. Give an account of the structure and distribution of stomata, and indicate some of their principal variations as special adaptations.

10. Describe the structure of the growing extremity of a root, as in *Monstera deliciosa*.

———

FOURTH YEAR.
BOTANY.
1897-98.

1. Discuss fully the relationships of the *Cyanophyceæ* and *Schizomycetes*.
　　Describe the structure and reproduction of *Stigonema minutem.*

2. Give a full account of the structure and mode of reproduction of *Vaucheria sessilis*.

3. Write a full account of the life-history of *Fucus vesiculosus*.

4. Discuss reproduction and alternation of generations in the *Rhodophyceæ*.

5. Give a description oi *Cystopus bliti*.

6. Compare the reproductive processes of the *Ascomycetes* and *Basidiomycetes*.

7. Describe the structure and development of the pores of the gametophyte of the *Marchantiaceæ*, and compare them with the stomata of the sporophyte of higher forms.

8. Give a full description of the gametophyte of *Adiantum cuneatum*.

9. Compare the structure of the stem of *Pteris, Equisetum, Lycopodium* and *Selaginella*.

10. Discuss the relationships of the Archegoniatæ.

FIRST YEAR.

CHEMISTRY.

MONDAY, APRIL 18TH :—MORNING, 9 TO 12.

1. How does Fluorine occur in nature ? How may it be isolated ? What are its properties ?

2. Explain the distinction between (a) a normal and an acid salt, (b) a Sulphide and a Sulphate, (c) a Chloride and a Chlorate.

3. Explain the cause of the slow drying of freshly plastered rooms.

4. A solution contains a salt of either; Barium, Strontium or Calcium. How would you ascertain which is really present ?

5. Explain the distinction between acid-forming and base-forming elements.

6. How would you separate the metals Copper, Iron and Calcium, if present together in solution ?

7. Give the names and formulæ of the principal compounds of Boron, and state what you know with regard to the uses of these compounds.

8. Give the names and composition of the ores of Iron, and explain their reduction in the blast furnace.

9. What volume of gases at 760 mm. and 0° C. would be produced on burning 100 grams of gunpowder if the constituents and chemical changes were as indicated in the following equation ?—

$$2KNO_3 + 3C + S = 3CO_2\ 2N + K_2S.$$

10. Explain the chemical changes that take place in the manufacture of Sulphuric Acid. What are properties of the acid ?

B.A. HONOURS IN NATURAL SCIENCE AND
B.A.Sc. (*Chemistry and Mining Courses*).

(FIRST PAPER)—MINERALOGY.

MONDAY, DEC. 20TH :—MORNING, 9 TO 12.

1. Explain the constitution of Metasilicates, Orthosilicates and Polysilicates, giving examples of minerals belonging to each class.

2. Describe the different methods of twinning observable in the Feldspars.

3. Give the chemical formula of each of the following species, and the crystallographic characters as observable in Canadian specimens :—Zircon Apatite, Pyroxene, Titanite, Garnet.

4. Briefly describe each of the following species :—Aragonite, Azurite, Cassiterite, Chrysolite, Leucite.

5. Give the general characters of the Zeolites, and describe any two members of the group.

6. How would you distinguish Göthite from Limonite, Marcasite from Arsenopyrite, Mimetite from Pyromorphite, Phlogopite from Muscovite, Albite from Orthoclase ?

7. State what you know with regard to the mode of occurrence and economic applications of the following species :—Talc, Serpentine, Tetrabedrite, Chromite, Molybdenite, Pyrolusite.

8. Explain hemihedry as occurring in the tetragonal and hexagonal systems of crystallography.

9. Define any fine of the following terms: Percussion Figure, Parameter, Pseudomorph, Hemitrope, Asterism, Crystal Form.

10. Deduce a formula for each of the minerals represented by the following analyses :

	I.		II.
Lead,	56.61	Silver,	36.70
Arsenic,	20.87	Antimony,	41.00
Iron,	.32	Arsenic,	.21
Copper,	.22	Sulphur,	22.03
Sulphur,	22.30		

AFTERNOON, 2 TO 4.

Describe carefully any 20 of the 24 mineral specimens exhibited.

SCIENCE SCHOLARSHIP, 1897.

CHEMISTRY.

FRIDAY, SEPT. 17TH :—MORNING, 9 TO 12.

1. Distinguish between empirical and constitutional formulæ, giving examples of each.

2. Explain the action of Phosphorous Pentachloride upon concentrated Sulphuric Acid, and draw conclusions as to the constitution of the Acid.

3. The gas in a eudiometer measures 68 c. c., the level of the Mercury in the tube and trough being the same. The barometer indicates an atmospheric pressure of 739 mm. The temperature is $20°$ C. What would be the volume of the gas at $0°$ C. and under 760 mm. pressure?

4. What weight of Green Vitriol could be obtained, theoretically, by the slow oxidation of 20 Kilograms of Iron Pyrites containing 37.5 per cent· of Sulphur?

5. State briefly how you would prepare any four of the following compounds :—(1) Chlorine Monoxide, (2) Boric Acid, (3) Hydrocyanic Acid, (4) Carbon Disulphide, (5) Chromium Trioxide.

6. Explain the distinction between Mercurous and Mercuric compounds, and describe the preparation and properties of one member of each class. ·

7. How may the exact composition of Hydrochloric Acid gas be determined?

8. How would you estimate the proportions of Carbon, Hydrogen, Nitrogen and Oxygen in an organic body composed of these elements?

9. Give briefly the preparation and properties of any three of the following bodies :—(1) Acetic Acid, (2) Urea, (3) Nitro-benzene, (4) Aniline.

10. What are compound Alcoholic Ammonias, and what the more important ways in which they are formed?

11. State what you know with regard to the chemistry of the natural fats and oils.

12. Explain the constitution of each of the following bodies :—(1) Ether, (2) Glycol, (3) Phenol, (4) Napthalene.

- SECOND YEAR.

FACULTY OF ARTS (*Additional*), FACULTY OF APPLIED SCIENCE (*Practical Chemistry Course.*)

TUESDAY, 12TH APRIL :—MORNING, 9 TO 12.

1. How is potassium nitrate obtained? What are its uses?

2. Describe carefully the Solvay or Ammonia-Soda process.

3. Tell what you know with regard to Calcium and its compounds.

4. Describe the preparation of Aluminium, and give its properties.

5. What is meant by such a statement as the following :—" Aluminium oxide is weakly basic, and somewhat acidic " ?

6. Describe the metallurgy of copper *or* of silver.

7. Describe one of the methods by which "white lead" ·is manufactured.

8. What is the principal source of the compounds of chromium, and how are they obtained from it ?

9. Gold—occurrence and preparation.

———

THIRD YEAR—*(Chemistry Course.)*

ORGANIC CHEMISTRY.

TUESDAY, APRIL 12TH :—MORNING, 9 TO 12.

1. Explain Fittig's synthesis of the Aromatic Hydrocarbons.

2. What are the products of the reduction of Nitro-benzene ?

3. What do you understand by Diazo-compounds ? Explain their con-·stitution.

4. What are Sulphonic Acids, and how are they generally obtained ?

5. What is the relation (*a*) of Quinone to Benzol, (*b*) of Anthra quinone to Anthracene, (*c*) of Alizarine to Anthraquinone ?

6. Explain the constitution of Aniline Yellow, Bismarck Brown and Methyl Orange.

7. Explain the relation of Racemic to Dextro and Lævo·tartaric acids, or of the members of the Cane-sugar to those of the Grape-sugar group.

8. State what you know with regard to the chemistry of the Ferro· and Ferri-cyanides.

9. Explain the constitution of Pyridine and Quinoline.

10. How would you prepare (*n*) pure Dextrine, and (*b*) Glycogen ? Give the properties of each of these bodies.

FACULTY OF APPLIED SCIENCE.—(*Mining Course*).

THIRD YEAR.

PRACTICAL CHEMISTRY.

TUESDAY, APRIL 5TH:—MORNING, 9 TO 12.

1. How may pure sodium chloride be prepared from table-salt?

2. What special precautions, if any, are to be taken in the ignition of the following precipitates: (*a*) calcium oxalate, (*b*) silver chloride, (*c*) antimony sulphide?

3. Describe carefully the quantitative determination of SO_4 in a sample of copper sulphate.

4. How may the percentages of aluminium and calcium in a mixture of the chlorides of these metals be determined?

5. An alloy contains copper, lead, tin, zinc, and iron : describe how the percentage of each may be determined.

6. One gram of an iron ore is dissolved in HCl, and the iron is precipitated by ammonia; the precipitate, after ignition, is found to weigh 0.8572 gr. What was the percentage of iron in the ore?

7. How much iron sulphide and how much sulphuric acid would be required to produce enough sulphuretted hydrogen to precipitate the copper in 1 gram of cupric chloride?

———

THIRD YEAR HONOURS IN NATURAL SCIENCE AND THIRD YEAR IN APPLIED SCIENCE (*Chemistry and Mining Courses*).

MINERALOGY.

WEDNESDAY, APRIL 20TH:—MORNING, 9 TO 12.

1. Explain symmetry as occurring in surfaces and solids. How are crystals classified according to degree of symmetry?

2. Explain the principles of spherical projection as applied to crystals, and give a projection of an isometric crystal composed of the cube, octahedron and rhombic dodecahedron.

3. What form is produced (1) by truncating the edges of a cube, (2) by truncating the edges of a rhombic dodecahedron, (3) by bevelling the

edges of a cube, (4) by bevelling the edges of a rhombic dodecahedron ? Give the symbols in each case.

4. Distinguish between hemihedrism and tetartohedrism, and describe hemihedrism as occurring in the Tetragonal system.

5. Explain the origin and significance of fluid cavities in crystals.

6. Explain the methods of Naumann and Miller for distinguishing the different faces of Triclinic pyramids.

7. Give examples of isomorphous groups of minerals and of isomorphous replacement

8. How would you determine the specific gravity of a mineral (a) with the Jolly balance, (b) with the pycnometer, (c) with Walker's balance ? Mention any special precautions to be taken.

9. Discuss the constitution of the Spinels, and give the characters of the species.

10. Describe briefly each of the following minerals: Argentite, Pyrargyrite, Millerite, Cuprite, Menaccanite.

11. Describe carefully the specimens and models exhibited.

————

THIRD YEAR HONOURS IN NATURAL SCIENCE, AND THIRD YEAR APPLIED SCIENCE (*Chemistry and Mining Courses*).

DETERMINATIVE MINERALOGY.

FRIDAY, APRIL 22ND :—MORNING, 9 TO 11.

1. Describe the use of the following substances in determinative mineralogy, giving examples : carbonate of soda, copper oxide, magnesium, cobalt nitrate, fluor-spar.

2. What phenomena are to be observed when heating a fragment of mineral in the platinum forceps ?

3. Describe carefully the operation of roasting, telling what chemical reactions are involved.

4. Give the principal reactions of the following elements : antimony, fluorine, manganese, phosphorus, zinc.

5. Heating in the open tube.—Describe the process, and the principal phenomena that may be observed.

6. Mention the principal phenomena observed in the treatment of minerals with hydrochloric acid. In cases where the action is doubtful, how is one to proceed ?

7. What is the " scale of fusibility ?' How is the fusibility of a mineral determined, and what special treatment is required in the case of decrepitating minerals ?

8. Give the blowpipe characters of the following minerals : almandite, barite, cassiterite, franklinite, stibnite, zircon.

9. How may gold be distinguished from pyrite, chromite and menaccanite from magnetite, apatite from pyroxene, arsenopyrite from nicolite, epidote from malachite, molybdenite from graphite?

B.A. ORDINARY EXAMINATION AND THIRD YEAR APPLIED SCIENCE.

GEOLOGY.

Friday, April 15th :—Morning, 9 to 12 and 2 p.m.

1. What do you understand by Historical Geology? How did Dante account for the elevation of the land into mountain masses? State what you know concerning Nicolaus Steno and William Smith.

2. Of what minerals are the following rocks composed :—Syenite, Gabbro, Peridotite, Diorite? What are their volcanic equivalents?

3. Explain the following terms as applied to Mineral Veins : Gangue, Horse, Foot Wall, Country Rock.

.4. What evidences have we of life on our planet in Eozoic times?

5. The Laurentian system. Its distribution in Canada. Its origin. What are the chief minerals of economic importance which it contains ?.

6. Draw a geological section showing the succession and relation of the strata between Lachute and St. Lambert.

7. State what you know concerning the character and affinities of the Trilobites. What is their range in geological time? Give an account of Mr. Beecher's recent discoveries concerning them.

.8. State what you know concerning the origin of earthquakes. Explain their connection with volcanoes and mountain chains. What is meant by the terms *Centrum, Epicentrum, Meizoseismic Area ?* De-

scribe the method proposed by Mallet for determining the point from
which the shock originates. What are the objections to it?

9. Distribution and subdivision of the Lower Silurian System in
Canada. Name and describe a few of its characteristic fossils.

10. Describe the succession of strata which would be passed through
by a shaft 100 feet deep sunk on the College campus. Enumerate a few
of the principal fossils contained in each formation, and point out the
climatal conditions indicated.

2 O'CLOCK P. M.

11. Name the fossils exhibited, and state the geological formation to
which they belong.

12. Name and describe the rock specimens.

B.A. HONOURS EXAMINATIONS IN GEOLOGY AND NATURAL HISTORY.

(SECOND PAPER) PETROGRAPHY.

FRIDAY, APRIL 1ST :—MORNING, 9 TO 1.

1. What well known rocks occur at the following localities :—Baveno,
Biella, Vesuvius, Oberstein, Volpersdorf, Mount Royal, Arran.

2. Name and describe the chief products of differentiation in the case of
the Gabbro Magma.

3. Describe the following structures :—Poikilitic, Cataclastic, Porphyr-
itic, Scoriaceous.

4. Describe in detail the changes which take place in the several con-
stituent minerals of a Biotite Granite under the influence of decay. Explain the changes which take place in the microscopic appearance of the
several minerals, and state the final results attained.

5. Draw out a scheme showing Rosenbusch's classification of the Plu-
tonic rocks with their Volcanic equivalents.

6. Nepheline Syenite and Basanite—their essential and commonly occurring accessory constituents, their structures and subdivisions. Are
they acid or basic ?

7. Describe briefly the following :—Liparite, Pegmatite, Diabase, Basalt,
Phonolite.

8. Describe the characters of the following minerals as seen under the microscope, illustrating your descriptions by sketches : Apatite, Sillimanite, Quartz, Ilmenite, Muscovite.

9. Name the ten hand specimens. What structures are exhibited by Nos. 8, 9 and 10.

10. Examine the six thin sections under the microscope. State in each case what minerals are present, as well as the name and structure of the rock.

B. A. HONOUR EXAMINATIONS IN GEOLOGY AND NATURAL HISTORY. •

(THIRD PAPER) ADVANCED GEOLOGY.

THURSDAY, APRIL 7TH:—AFTERNOON, 2 TO 5.

1. Classify mountain ranges according to their structure and origin. Explain briefly the origin in each case. Give one example of each class, taken from the Dominion of Canada if possible.

2. Select any area, and explain how in it geological structure has determined the character of the country and has influenced its inhabitants.

3. State what you know concerning the origin and development of the great lakes of the St. Lawrence drainage basin. Illustrate your remarks by sketches of the country at successive stages of the development of the drainage system.

4. State what you know concerning the geology of the Dakotas, and show how the geological structure nas influenced the supply of Artesian water.

5. Describe clearly Posepny's theory of the origin of ore deposits, and give the chief lines of evidence in favor of it. State what you know of the " Sea Mills of Cephalonia," and their bearing upon this theory.

6. Into what great physical divisions does Canada naturally fall when considered geologically ? Define the limits of these, and state briefly the systems which underlie them.

7. State what you know of the distribution and petrographical character of the Triassic rocks of the Dominion.

8. Draw a line of section from the Laurentian axis across Ontario to the west end of Lake Erie.

9. Describe the petrographical character and mode of occurrence of the Eozoic rocks of the Lake of the Woods area, and compare the sequence there with that found in the area north of Lake Huron.

10. Describe the physical features of the Labrador Peninsula, and state what you know concerning its geology. Describe the condition of Labra-. dor during the glacial period, and indicate the direction of the ice movement there at that time.

B.A. HONOUR EXAMINATIONS IN GEOLOGY AND NATURAL HISTORY.

(FOURTH PAPER) PALÆONTOLOGY.

SATURDAY, APRIL 9TH :—MORNING, 9 TO 12.30.

1. What do you understand by the terms "Vertical Range" and "Persistent Type?" Give examples.

2. Describe the parts of a typical crinoid, illustrating your description by sketches.

3. Describe any six fossils found in the Potsdam Sandstone.

4. Describe any four fossils found in the Acadian Series.

.5. State the zoological relations and geological age of the following :— *Saccamina, Astylospongia, Petraia, Tetradium, Crania, Melonites, Strophomena, Calceola, Toxaster, Dictyophyton, Olenellus, Dikellocephalus.*

6. Describe any three genera of foraminifera which have built up great limestone formations. State the age of the limestones in each case.

7. State what you know of the fossil remains of Medusae.

8. Describe in detail any three monoprionidian Graptolites, stating in each case the range of the form.

9. Refer the specimens exhibited to their geological formations and to their places in the zoological classification.

B.A. HONOUR EXAMINATIONS IN GEOLOGY AND NATURAL HISTORY.

(FIFTH PAPER) PRACTICAL GEOLOGY.

MONDAY, APRIL 18TH : -MORNING, 9 TO 12.30.

1. Define the terms *Ore, Gangue, Horse, Chute, Flucan, Selvage, Comb,* as used in connection with mineral veins.

2. State what you know concerning *Gossan,* treating of its character, value, origin and mode of occurrence.

3. Describe Daubree's experiments on the development of fissures under strain, and show their bearing on the study of mineral veins.

4. Give a classification of Ore Deposits.

5. State what you know concerning the Iron Ores of the Clinton.

6. Describe the Witwatersrand gold deposits.

7. Explain the terms :—*Strike, Overthrust, Slickenside, Breccia, Stockwork.*

8. Explain the mode of constructing a detailed horizontal section along any line of country from one point to another.

9. A model of a portion of the earth's crust is submitted. Describe in detail the stratigraphical relations of the several formations represented, and enumerate the successive geological changes which the district has experienced as indicated by the features of the district.

10. State what you know concerning the nature and origin of the specimens exhibited.

11. Two maps are exhibited lettered A and B. Describe in detail in each case the attitude and relations of the strata along the line of section crossing the map.

B.A. HONOUR EXAMINATIONS IN GEOLOGY AND NATURAL HISTORY.

(SIXTH PAPER) ADVANCED GEOLOGY (*Part Two*).

WEDNESDAY, APRIL 20TH :—MORNING, 9 TO 12.30.

1. Describe in its main outlines the structure of the Continent of Europe.

2. Explain the terms *Table Horst* and *Folded Horst.* Give an example of each.

3. Write a short account of the chief theories which have been put forward to account for the movements of glaciers.

4. What do you understand by the doctrine of Uniformatarianism as taught by Lyell? Explain the services rendered to geology by its establishment.

5. State and explain Wallace's classification of islands with reference to the distribution of organisms. Give examples. Give also a summary

21

of the evidence which he adduces in favour of the permanency of ocean beds.

6. Explain the relations of the Fauna and Flora of the following islands to their geological history :—St. Helena, Java and Borneo.

7. Give a sketch of the geology of the Scotch Highlands, and explain the character and origin of the table land.

8. Define Merrill's term *Regolith*, and give his classification of the various deposits composing it. Describe Loess and Adobe, explaining their origin and their place in the classification.

9. State what you know concerning the relative rapidity and the difference in character of rock weathering in warm and cold climates.

10. What do you understand by a *Plain of Marine Denudation*. Give an example.

11. Write an account of the life of Jean Étienne Guettard, pointing out the chief services which he rendered to the science of Geology.

THIRD YEAR.

SESSIONAL EXAMINATION IN ZOOLOGY.

MONDAY, APRIL 18TH :—MORNING, 9 TO 12.

Not more than seven questions are to be attempted, of which ONE is to be selected from questions 8 to 11 inclusive.

1. Define the term " cell " as used in zoology. Are Polystomella and the Myxomycetes to be regarded as multicellular or unicellular? Give reasons for your answer in each case.

2. Describe carefully the structure of a Medusa belonging to the group Hydrozoa, including in your description the various kinds of cells of which it is made up and the functions which they respectively perform.

In what relation does the medusoid form stand to other phases in the life-history of a Hydrozoan? Can you suggest any explanation of how these various phases came into existence?

3. Write a short clear statement embodying the main outline of Darwin's theory of the origin of species.

Point out what are the unexplained presuppositions of this theory.

4. What is meant by the term "cœlom"? How is a cœlom to be discriminated from other forms of body-cavity?

In what relation does the pericardium in Unio, Cambarus (the crayfish) and Mustelus stand to the cœlom in each of the three animals mentioned? Do we know any facts tending to throw light on the evolution of the cœlom?

5. Write a short essay on the development of connective tissue in the animals which you have studied, tracing it from its first appearance up to the modifications under which it appears in the higher Vertebrata.

Can you state in what relation connective tissue stands to the circulatory system?

6. Give a classification of the group Mollusca, describing those organs and their principal modifications which are relied on as a basis for the .classification.

Can you point out which forms amongst living Mollusca retain the most primitive habits, and indicate the probable changes in habits which have led to the differentiation of the various groups of Mollusca?

7. Describe the water vascular system of the starfish, giving the structure of the different parts and their respective functions.

Supposing that a Brittle star has been developed from a primitive starfish, point out the modifications which the water vascular system has undergone, and correlate these with changes in the habits of the animal.

8. Give a description of the structure and arrangement of the genital .organs and kidneys in the dogfish. Compare their disposition with that of the corresponding organs in Amphioxus and Lumbricus.

Can you suggest an explanation of the different relations which the ovary on the one hand and the testis on the other sustain to the kidney in the Vertebrata?

9. Compare the circulatory systems of the Amphioxus, the Dog-fish and the Frog, giving a description of the essential points in each.

Can you suggest any of the causes which led to the development of the differences in this respect between Amphioxus and the Dog-fish on one hand, and the Dog-fish and the Frog on the other.?

10. Give a comparative description of the various kinds of eyes met with in the animal kingdom.

Sketch the evolutionary history of *either*

 (*a*) the Cephalopod eye,

or (*b*) the Vertebrate eye.

11. Give an account of the fundamental characters which distinguish the Amniota from the lower groups.

Compare the relative amounts of sacrifice made by the mother on behalf of the young in the case of

    (*a*) The Swallow,

    (*b*) The Cat.

In which case do you think that the sacrifice made is likely to have the most direct effect on mental and moral development ?

THIRD YEAR.

PRACTICAL EXAMINATION IN ZOOLOGY.

Monday, April 18th :—2 to 5 p.m.

1. Make a dissection of the dog-fish provided so as to display as much as possible of the Brain and Cranial nerves, marking the positions of the principal parts with flag labels.

2. Make a permanent preparation of the specimen A. Sketch your preparation, indicating the principal parts, and refer the specimen as accurately as you can to its place in a system of classification.

3. Make a permanent preparation of the specimen B. Sketch it, indicating the principal parts, and identify it.

4. Sketch specimen X sufficiently to indicate the principal features which you can recognize. Identify the specimen.

N.B.—Students belonging to the **Faculty of Applied Science** will omit (4) and substitute for (1) the following question, viz. :—Make a dissection of the dog-fish provided, so as to display as much as possible of the *heart* and ventral arterial system, indicating the principal parts by flag labels.

(A. Polyp of Pennaria. B Parapodium of Nereis. X. Transverse section of hinder part of Lumbricus.)

FACULTY OF APPLIED SCIENCE.

SESSIONAL EXAMINATIONS,

1898.

FACULTY OF APPLIED SCIENCE.

SECOND YEAR.
BOTANY.
FIRST PAPER.

1. Give a concise history of classification, and outline a scheme for the principal divisions of the vegetable kingdom in conformity with our present knowledge of relationships.

2. Discuss the occurrence of heterospory in its bearing upon development.

3. Give a short account of the reproductive process in *Zamia*.

4. Discuss the term *Alternation of Phases* (Generations) as applied to the life-history of a plant, and indicate the limitations of such phases.

5. Give a full account of the structure and life history of *Pleurococcus vulgaris*.

6. Describe the structure and function of the prothallus, and discuss its gradual obliteration as an evidence of development.

7. Give a brief description of the general morphology and the reproduction of *Equisetum arvense*.

8. Describe the chief characteristics of the Phæophyceæ as illustrated by a specific case.

9. Discuss the relationship of the Angiosperms and Gymnosperms on the basis of the reproductive process.

10. Discuss the principal modifications of the floral organs of seed-plants, arising through cohesion and adhesion. Apply these modifications to classification.

SECOND YEAR.
BOTANY.
SECOND PAPER.

1. Describe fully the process of photosynthesis in plants.

2. Explain the mechanism of root action.

3. Discuss the conditions which regulate the movement of sap, indicating the direction of the flow.

4. Explain the function of respiration and the chemical changes involved.

5. Give a full description of the structure of the root-tip of a Monocotyeldon.

6. Describe the structure and mode of development of an exogenous-stem.

7. Explain the structure of the epidermal tissue of a leaf and its functional adaptations.

8. State what you know of the influence of ocean-currents in promoting distribution of species.

9. Give an account of the chemical and physical properties of protoplasm.

10. Describe the structure of the nucleus and the various steps in its mitosis.

B.A. ORDINARY EXAMINATION AND THIRD YEAR APPLIED SCIENCE.

GEOLOGY.

FRIDAY, APRIL 15TH :—MORNING, 9 TO 12 AND 2 P. M.

1. What do you understand by Historical Geology? How did Dante account for the elevation of the land into mountain masses? State what you know concerning Nicolaus Steno and William Smith.

2. Of what minerals are the following rocks composed:—Syenite, Gabbro, Peridotite, Diorite? What are their volcanic equivalents?

3. Explain the following terms as applied to Mineral Veins : Gangue, Horse, Foot Wall, Country Rock.

4. What evidences have we of life on our planet in Eozoic times?

5. The Laurentian system. Its distribution in Canada. Its origin. What are the chief minerals of economic importance which it contains ?

6. Draw a geological section showing the succession and relation of the strata between Lachute and St. Lambert.

7. State what you know concerning the character and affinities of the Trilobites. What is their range in geological time? Give an account of Mr. Beecher's recent discoveries concerning them.

8. State what you know concerning the origin of earthquakes. Explain their connection with volcanoes and mountain chains. What is meant by the terms *Centrum*, *Epicentrum*, *Meizoseismic Area*? Describe the method proposed by Mallet for determining the point from which the shock originates. What are the objections to it?

9. Distribution and subdivision of the Lower Silurian System in Canada. Name and describe a few of its characteristic fossils.

10. Describe the succession of strata which would be passed through by a shaft 100 feet deep sunk on the College campus. Enumerate a few of the principal fossils contained in each formation, and point out the climatal conditions indicated.

2 O'CLOCK P. M.

11. Name the fossils exhibited, and state the geological formation to which they belong.

12. Name and describe the rock specimens.

—— —

THIRD YEAR HONOURS IN NATURAL SCIENCE, AND THIRD YEAR APPLIED SCIENCE (*Chemistry and Mining Courses*).

DETERMINATIVE MINERALOGY.

FRIDAY, APRIL 22ND :—MORNING, 9 TO 11.

Examiners, ... { B. J. HARRINGTON, M.A., PH.D.
{ NEVIL NORTON EVANS, M.A.Sc.

1. Describe the use of the following substances in determinative mineralogy, giving examples : carbonate of soda, copper oxide, magnesium, cobalt nitrate, fluor-spar.

2. What phenomena are to be observed when heating a fragment of mineral in the platinum forceps?

3. Describe carefully the operation of roasting, telling what chemical reactions are involved.

4. Give the principal reactions of the following elements: antimony, fluorine, manganese, phosphorus, zinc.

5. Heating in the open tube.—Describe the process, and the principal phenomena that may be observed.

6. Mention the principal phenomena observed in the treatment of minerals with hydrochloric acid. In cases where the action is doubtful, how is one to proceed?

7. What is the "scale of fusibility?" How is the fusibility of a mineral determined, and what special treatment is required in the case of decrepitating minerals?

8. Give the blowpipe characters of the following minerals : almandite, barite, cassiterite, franklinite, stibnite, zircon.

9. How may gold be distinguished from pyrite, chromite and menaccanite from magnetite, apatite from pyroxene, arsenopyrite from niccolite, epidote from malachite, molybdenite from graphite?

FIRST YEAR.

CHEMISTRY.

FRIDAY, APRIL 15TH :—MORNING, 9 TO 12.

Examiners,.. .... { B. J. HARRINGTON, M A., PH.D.
                                         { ALEXANDER BRODIE, B.A.Sc.

1. How would you obtain a soluble salt of Barium, such as the Chloride or Nitrate, from the insoluble Sulphate?

2. Explain by means of equations the chemical changes involved in the Leblanc process for the manufacture of Sodium Carbonate.

3. In the change of 100 lbs. of slaked Lime in mortar into Calcium Carbonate, how many pounds of water are produced?

4. State briefly how you would prepare each of the following :—Caustic Potash, Lime Water, Hydrogen Sulphide, Phosphine.

5. State what you know with regard to the properties and uses of Potassium Nitrate, Calcium Sulphate, Calcium Sulphide, Strontium Hydroxide.

6. How is Iodine obtained from sea-weeds? What are its properties? How may it be detected (*a*) when free, and (*b*) when in combination?

7. How are the following substances used in elementary inorganic analysis : (1) Borax. (2) Sodium Carbonate. (3) Potassium Cyanide. (4) Potassium Nitrate?

8. How would you detect Lead, Silver, and Mercurous Mercury, in a mixture of their Nitrates?

9. How would you distinguish between (*a*) a Tartrate and a Citrate, (*b*) salts of Bismuth and Lead, (*c*) salts of Cadmium and Tin, (*d*) compounds of Arsenic and Antimony?

10. What weight of Iron Pyrites (FeS_2) would be required to make a ton of Sulphuric Acid? Give the properties of the Acid.

SECOND YEAR.

CHEMISTRY.

FACULTY OF ARTS (*Additional*), FACULTY OF APPLIED SCIENCE (*Practical Chemistry Course.*)

TUESDAY, 12TH APRIL :—MORNING, 9 TO 12.

Examiners, ... { B. J. HARRINGTON, M.A., PH.D.
{ NEVIL NORTON EVANS, M.A.Sc.

1. How is potassium nitrate obtained? What are its uses?

2. Describe carefully the Solvay or Ammonia-Soda process.

3. Tell what you know with regard to Calcium and its compounds.

4. Describe the preparation of Aluminium, and give its properties.

5. What is meant by such a statement as the following :—" Aluminium oxide is weakly basic, and somewhat acidic "?

6. Describe the metallurgy of copper *or* of silver.

7. Describe one of the methods by which "white lead" is manufactured.

8. What is the principal source of the compounds of chromium, and how are they obtained from it?

9. Gold—occurrence and preparation.

THIRD YEAR.—(*Mining Course.*)

PRACTICAL CHEMISTRY.

TUESDAY, APRIL 5TH:—MORNING, 9 TO 12.

Examiners,... { B. J. HARRINGTON, M.A., PH.D.
{ NEVIL NORTON EVANS, M.A.Sc.

1. How may pure sodium chloride be prepared from table-salt?

2. What special precautions, if any, are to be taken in the ignition of the following precipitates: (*a*) calcium oxalate (*b*) silver chloride, (*c*) antimony sulphide ?

3. Describe carefully the quantitative determination of SO_4 in a sample of copper sulphate.

4. How may the percentages of aluminium and calcium in a mixture of the chlorides of these metals be determined ?

5. An alloy contains copper, lead, tin, zinc, and iron : describe how the percentage of each may be determined.

6. One gram of an iron ore is dissolved in HCl, and the iron is precipitated by ammonia; the precipitate, after ignition, is found to weigh 0.8572 gr. What was the percentage of iron in the ore?

7. How much iron sulphide and how much sulphuric acid would be required to produce enough sulphuretted hydrogen to precipitate the copper in 1 gram of cupric chloride ?

———

THIRD YEAR (*Chemistry Course.*)

PRACTICAL CHEMISTRY.

TUESDAY, APRIL 5TH :—MORNING, 9 TO 12.

Examiner,..B. J. HARRINGTON, M.A., PH.D.

1. One gram of Marble was dissolved in 25 cc. of normal Hydrochloric Acid, and 5.8 cc. of normal Alkali solution were required to neutralise the remaining free acid. What was the percentage of Lime in the Marble?

2. Suggest a method for the analysis of a sample of Gypsum.

3. How would you calibrate (*a*) a litre-flask, (*b*) a burette ?

4. Taking 1.82 as the specific gravity of Sulphuric Acid (at 15° c.), if you wished to employ 200 grams for a chemical experiment how many cubic centimetres would you measure out ?

5. Explain the use of a standard solution of Iodine in the estimation, (a) of Antimony in Tartar Emetic, and (b) of Hydrogen Sulphide in aqueous solution.

6. In the analysis of a sample of Chrome Iron Ore by the Sodium Peroxide method 0.25 gram of the ore was employed and the solution, prepared in the usual way, made up to half a litre. Of this solution 51 cc. were required to oxydise the Iron in 0.20 gram of Ferrous Ammonium Sulphate. Calculate the proportion of Chromium Sesquioxide in the ore Gr. = 52).

7. How would you determine the proportions of Tin and Lead in a sample of Solder?

8. Describe the Adams' method for the estimation of Fat in Milk.

9. In the analysis of a sample of Apatite 0.25 gram of the mineral was taken and the precipitate of Ammonium Magnesium Phosphate, after ignition, weighed 0.1429 gram. What was the percentage of Tricalcium Phosphate in the sample?

10. How would you determine the value of a sample of Bleaching Powder?

11. Explain the principles of electrolytic analysis, and briefly describe the electrolytic determination of Copper in an ore of that metal.

———

B. A. SC. (*Chemistry Course*).

PRACTICAL CHEMISTRY.

MONDAY, APRIL 4TH :—MORNING, 9 TO 12.

Examiner,... B. J. HARRINGTON, M.A., PH.D.

1. The Silver salt of an organic acid was found to contain 62.44 per cent. of metallic Silver. It also contained 17.34 per cent. of Carbon and 1.73 per cent. of Hydrogen. From these data deduce a formula for the acid.

2. How would you estimate the proportions of Cane Sugar and Glucose in a sample of Sugar?

3. 10.55 grams of an organic body were dissolved in 77.14 grams of water, causing a depression in the freezing-point of the water of 1.45° C. *T* being 19, deduce the molecular weight of the body.

4. How would you estimate the Nitrogen in a sample of Coal?

5. 5 grams of an Iron ore gave 6 milligrams of Magnesium Pyrophosphate. What percentage of Phosphorus Pentoxide did the ore contain?

6. Describe briefly the chemical analysis of a drinking Water, discussing the interpretation of the results.

7. In the combustion of an organic body containing Carbon, Hydrogen and Oxygen, 0 4739 gram of the substance was burnt. The Calcium Chloride tube gained 0.2727 gram in weight, the Soda-lime tube 0.728 gram. Calculate the percentage composition of the body. Taking 342 as the molecular weight, deduce its formula.

8. Describe the estimation of Zinc with standard solution of Potassium Ferrocyanide.

9. State what you know with regard to the interference of other metals in the estimation of Copper by the Cyanide or the battery method.

10. How would you determine the Silver and Gold in a specimen of Tetrahedrite containing these metals?

11. State how you would estimate the Phosphorus in a sample of steel.

SECOND YEAR (*Chemistry Course*).

ORGANIC CHEMISTRY.

WEDNESDAY, APRIL 13TH :—MORNING, 9 TO 12.

Examiner, ...B. J. HARRINGTON, M.A., PH.D.

1. Point out some of the principal analogies existing between classes of organic and inorganic bodies.

2. The Silver salt of an Organic Acid was found to contain 47.1 per cent, of Metallic Silver. Deduce its molecular weight.

3. What do you understand by Aldehydic derivatives of the Glycols? Give examples.

4. How many Butyl Alcohols are theoretically possible? How many have been prepared? Explain the constitution of each, giving formulæ.

5. By what reactions may Oxalic Acid be obtained? Give its properties Why is the formula written $C_2H_2O_4$, and not CHO_2? .

6. How is Glycocoll prepared? Give its properties and explain its constitution.

7. Explain the relationship of Fumaric and Maleic Acids

8. What are Amines, and how may they be classified?

9. Explain briefly the constitution of each of the following bodies:—Aldehyde, Glycerin, Succinic Acid, Lactamide.

10. Explain the determination of molecular weights by depression of freezing point.

THIRD YEAR—(*Chemistry Course.*)

ORGANIC CHEMISTRY.

TUESDAY, APRIL 12TH :—MORNING, 9 TO 12.

Examiner,...B. J. HARRINGTON, M.A., PH.D.

1. Explain Fittig's synthesis of the Aromatic Hydrocarbons.

2. What are the products of the reduction of Nitro-benzene?

3. What do you understand by Diazo-compounds? Explain their constitution.

4. What are Sulphonic Acids, and how are they generally obtained?

5. What is the relation (*a*) of Quinone to Benzol, (*b*) of Anthra quinone to Anthracene, (*c*) of Alizarine to Anthraquinone?

6 Explain the constitution of Aniline Yellow, Bismarck Brown and Methyl Orange.

7. Explain the relation of Racemic to Dextro and Lævo-tartaric acids, or of the members of the Cane-sugar to those of the Grape-sugar group.

8. State what you know with regard to the chemistry of the Ferro- and Ferri-cyanides.

9. Explain the constitution of Pyridine and Quinoline.

10. How would you prepare (*a*) pure Dextrine, and (*b*) Glycogen? Give the properties of each of these bodies.

B.A. Sc. (*Chemistry Course.*)

ORGANIC CHEMISTRY.

TUESDAY, APRIL 12TH:—MORNING, 9 TO 12.

Examiner,...B. J. HARRINGTON, M.A., PH.D.

1. What are the principal reactions by which primary Aliphatic Amines may be obtained ? Give equations.

2. In what ways may an Alcoholic Hydroxyl group be replaced by a Halogen atom ?

3. What reactions take place (*a*) when Acetic Acid is treated with Phosphorus Trichloride, and (*b*) when Nitro-benzene is treated with Tin and Hydrochloric Acid ?

4. Explain Skraup's synthesis of Quinoline.

5. Describe the preparation of Diphenyl Thiourea. How are the Mustard Oils obtained from the Thioureas ? Give equations.

6. Explain Emil Fischer's method for the reduction of Diazo-compounds to Hydrazines. Point out also the importance of Phenyl-hydrazine in the recognition and separation of the Sugars.

7. Explain the constitution and relationship of Mannite, Mannose and Mannonic Acid.

8. Compare the Phenols with the true Alcohols of the Aromatic series.

9. What are Anilides ? Describe one of them and its preparation.

10. Compare Borneol, Cineol and Camphor as to constitution.

11. State what you know with regard to Ptomaines and their composition.

12. Explain the use of the microscope in distinguishing Starches, giving sketches.

13. State briefly how you would prepare each of the following bodies :— Iodoform, Dinitro-benzene, Aniline, Picric Acid.

14. An organic base yielded on analysis
$$\left.\begin{array}{ll} \text{Carbon,} & 77.4 \\ \text{Hydrogen,} & 7.5 \\ \text{Nitrogen,} & 15.0 \end{array}\right\} \text{per cent.}$$
Its Platino-chloride contained 32.9 per cent. of Platinum (195). Deduce the molecular weight and formula of the base.

15. How would you prove that the formula of Marsh Gas is CH_4 ?

B. A. Sc. (*Chemistry Course.*)

INORGANIC CHEMISTRY.

SATURDAY, APRIL 9TH :—MORNING, 9 TO 12.

Examiner,...... ....B. J. HARRINGTON, M.A., PH.D.

1. When a soluble base acts upon a salt there are four possible kinds of action. What are they ?

2. How may the constitution of the Oxyacids of Chlorine be explained ?

3. Describe the preparation and properties of the two Chlorides of Phosphorus.

4. Give a brief account of the acids of Silicon and their constitution.

5. What are the relative intrinsic values of crystallised Aluminium Sulphate ($18H_2O$), Potassium Alum and Ammonium Alum, if the quantity of Aluminium Hydroxide obtainable from each be taken as the standard ?

6. What takes place (*a*) when dry Ammonia Gas and dry Carbon Dioxide are brought together, (*b*) when Red Lead is treated with dilute Nitric Acid, (*c*) when an aqueous solution of Mercuric Chloride is treated with Sulphurous Acid?

7. When a solution of Copper Sulphate is decomposed by an electrical current, what chemical changes take place ?

8. What are the principal exceptions to the law of specific heats ?

9. Discuss briefly (*a*) the products of the oxidation of Ammonia, or (*b*) the relations between Chromates and Dichromates.

10. State what you know with regard to Thiocarbonic Acid and its salts, or concerning Beryllium and its compounds.

B.A. Sc. (*Mining Course.*)

ANALYTICAL CHEMISTRY AND ASSAYING.

TUESDAY, APRIL 5TH :—MORNING, 9 TO 12.

Examiner, ...B. J. HARRINGTON, M.A., PH.D.

1. What are the principal methods for reducing solutions of Ferric to Ferrous compounds, and the conditions regulating their applicability ?

2. In the titration of Iron with Potassium Permanganate, what precautions should be taken if the solution contain Hydrochloric Acid ?

22

3. Distinguish between a proximate and an ultimate analysis of Coal. How should the results of a proximate analysis be stated ? What inferences would you draw from the colour of the ash ?

4. What do you understand by the Basic Acetate separation of Iron ? Mention any cases in which its employment is advisable.

5. Describe the Eggertz method for the estimation of combined Carbon in Steel, or Emmerton's method for the estimation of Phosphorus.

6. State briefly how you would estimate (*a*) the proportion of Magnesia in a Limestone, and (*b*) the Sulphur in a sample of Iron Pyrites.

7. Explain the principle of the scorification assay for Gold and Silver. What precautions would you take in the scorification assay of ores containing (*a*) much Zinc Blende, (*b*) much Heavy Spar, (*c*) Tellurides?

8. If in a crucible assay for Gold and Silver you obtained a button of matte or speiss, how would you treat it ?

9. Describe the crucible assay for Lead ores, pointing out briefly any advantages or disadvantages which it possesses as compared with other methods.

10. State how you would ascertain the value of the ores, etc,. represented by the samples shown.

SECOND YEAR.—(*Mining and Practical Chemistry Courses.*)

QUALITATIVE ANALYSIS.

SATURDAY, APRIL 9TH :—MORNING, 9 TO 12.

Examiners,. .... { B. J. HARRINGTON, M.A., PH.D.
{ NEVIL NORTON EVANS, M.A.Sc.

1. A solution contains metals of the copper and tin groups; how may the metals of the one group be separated from those of the other?

2. How are tin, antimony, and arsenic recognized in a mixture of their sulphides ?

3. Describe the methods of recognizing cadmium in presence of copper.

4. Define the terms oxidation and reduction as employed in analytical chemistry, illustrating what you mean by examples. .

5. What preliminary tests are applied before precipitating the metals of the iron group? Why is it necessary to obtain, at this point in the process, the information supplied by these tests?

6. A solution containing metals of the iron and calcium groups, and phosphoric acid, is boiled with nitric acid, and a certain quantity of ferric chloride is added, the solution is nearly neutralized, and barium carbonate is added in excess. Why is the solution boiled with nitric acid? How much ferric chloride is to be added? and why? Why is barium carbonate added?

7. A mixture contains barium, strontium, and calcium as carbonates; how may the metals be separated from one another?

8. In the scheme of analysis employed, ammonium sulphate and ammonium oxalate are sometimes added to the filtrate from the precipitate produced by ammonium carbonate in presence of ammonium hydrate and ammonium chloride. When is this done? and why?

9. In testing for acids, strong sulphuric acid is added to the original substance, and the mixture heated. Mention the most important effects that may be produced, and what they signify.

10. Give tests for any five of the following acids: Sulphuric, boric, hydrofluoric, hydrobromic, silicic, hydriodic, nitric.

11. Describe the preparation of the solution for analysis in the case of alloys.

12. In the case of salts and industrial products, how is a solution obtained for the determination of the acids present?

FIRST YEAR.

MATHEMATICS, I.

TUESDAY, DECEMBER 15TH :—MORNING, 9 TO 12.30.

Examiner,......... .... R. S. LEA, MA.E.

1. Bisect a given triangle by a straight line drawn from a given point in one of its sides.

2. If any chord is drawn through a fixed point within a circle, the product of its segments is constant in whatever direction the cord is drawn. What is the locus of its middle point?

3. Prove that the distance between the points of contact of the inscribed and escribed circles on any side of a triangle is equal to the difference of the other two sides.

4. The rectangle contained by the diagonals of a quadrilateral inscribed in a circle is equal to the sum of the rectangles contained by its opposite sides.

5. Equal triangles which have one angle of the one equal to one angle ot the other have their sides about the equal angles reciprocally proportional.

6. Prove that the bisectors of the angles of a triangle all pass through one point.

7. The sum of the faces of any convex polyhedral angle is less than four right angles.

8. Pyramids on equal bases and of the same altitude are equal. Also, find the volume of a triangular pyramid.

9. Find the volume of a sphere.
The diameter of one sphere is one-sixth that of another ; what are the ratios of their surfaces and volumes?

10. Given the focus and directrix of a parabola ; show how to determine :—

　　(a) Any number of points on the curve.

　　(b) The tangents at those points.

11. In a parabola :—

　　(a) Tangents from any point subtend equal angles at the focus.

　　(b) The subnormal is constant.

12. Find the locus of the vertex of a triangle if the base is constant and

　　(a) the area constant,

　　(b) the sum of the sides constant,

　　(c) the sum of the squares on the sides constant.

———

FIRST YEAR.

MATHEMATICS, II.

TUESDAY, APRIL 5TH :—MORNING, 9 TO 12.30.

Examiner,..R. S. LEA, MA.E.

1. Factor (1) $a (b^2 - c^2) + b (c^2 - a^2) + c (a^2 - b^2)$,

　　(2) $m^4 - 18 m^2 n^2 + n^4$,

　　(3) $\dfrac{xy^4}{72} - \dfrac{x^3 y^3}{32} - \dfrac{1}{9 x^2} + \dfrac{y^2}{4}$.

2. Show that

$$(1) \quad \frac{(1-x^2)(1-x^3)}{x(1+x)(1-x)^2} - \frac{x^3 + \dfrac{1}{x^3}}{x^2 + \dfrac{1}{x^2} - 1} = 1,$$

$$(2) \quad \left\{ \frac{\sqrt{x+a}}{\sqrt{x-a}} - \frac{\sqrt{x-a}}{\sqrt{x+a}} \right\} \times \frac{\sqrt{x^3-a^3}}{\sqrt{(x+a)^2-ax}} = \frac{2a}{\sqrt{x+a}} .$$

$$(3) \quad \frac{\left\{ 9^n \times 3_2 \times \dfrac{1}{3^{-n}} \right\} -27^n}{3^{3n} \times 9} = \frac{8}{9} .$$

3. Solve

$$(1) \quad \left. \begin{array}{l} \dfrac{x^2}{y^2} + \dfrac{4x}{y} = \dfrac{85}{9} \\ x - y = 2 \end{array} \right\},$$

$$(2) \quad \left. \begin{array}{l} 2x + 4y-3z = 22 \\ 4x-2y + 5z = 18 \\ 6x + 7y- z = 63 \end{array} \right\},$$

$$(3) \quad 2x^{\frac{2}{3}} + 3x^{\frac{1}{3}} = 2,$$

$$(4) \quad \sqrt{x+2} + \sqrt{4x+1} - \sqrt{9x+7} = 0,$$

$$(5) \quad {}^x C_3 = 1\,\frac{3}{5} \times {}^{x-1} C_4 .$$

4. State and prove the relations between the roots and coefficients of a quadratic.

5. Deduce formulae for finding the sum of n terms of

(1) An Arithmetical Progression,

(2) A Geometrical Progression.

6. An $A.\ P.$ and a $G.\ P.$ have each a and b for their first and second terms. Find their r^{th} terms.

7. There are three numbers in geometrical progression, which if increased respectively by 4, 8 and 8, will be in geometrical progression with a common ratio less by 1 than that of the original. Find them.

8. Find the total number of combinations that can be made of n dissimilar things.

9. How many permutations can be made of the letters of the word *Canadian*,

(1) Without any restriction as to order,

(2) With the vowels and consonants occurring alternately.

10. State the Binomial Theorem.

11. Find the coefficient of x in $\left(x^2 - \dfrac{a}{2x}\right)^{14}$

12. Assuming the Binomial Theorem true for fractional indices, find the value to 4 places of decimals of $\sqrt[7]{132}$.

FIRST YEAR.

MATHEMATICS, III.

TUESDAY, APRIL 12TH:—MORNING, 9 TO 1.

Examiner,...R. S. LEA, MA.E.

1. Prove geometrically that $\frac{1}{2}\tan A > \tan \frac{1}{2} A$.

2. In making a degree protractor with a diameter of 20 inches, what will be the length of arc between the graduations?

3. Prove that:

(1) $(\operatorname{cosec} \theta - \cot \theta)^2 = \dfrac{1 - \cos \theta}{1 + \cos \theta}$

(2) $\tan^{-1}\frac{1}{3} + \tan^{-1}\frac{1}{4} + \tan^{-1}\frac{1}{5} + \tan^{-1}\frac{1}{47} = \dfrac{\pi}{4}$

(3) $\cot A = \operatorname{cosec} 2A + \cot 2A$.

(4) $\dfrac{1 - 2\sin^2 A}{1 + \sin 2A} = \dfrac{1 - \tan A}{1 + \tan A}$.

4. Given $\cos \theta = \frac{1}{2}$, write down an expression which will include all possible values of θ.

5. Solve the equations:

(1) $\tan \theta + \sec \theta = 2$.

(2) $\sin 2\theta - \cos 2\theta = \cos \theta - \sin \theta$.

6. Prove the sine and cosine formulae for plane triangles. Make use of the latter to obtain a formula adapted to the use of logarithms.

7. A, B and C are the angles of a plane triangle. Show that

(1) $4 \sin A \sin B \sin C = \sin 2A + \sin 2B + \sin 2C$.

(2) $\tan \dfrac{A - B}{2} = \dfrac{a - b}{a + b} \cot \dfrac{C}{2}$.

8. Which are the ambiguous cases in the solution of (a) plane triangles, (b) spherical triangles?

Explain in what the ambiguity consists, and how its existence may be known by inspection.

9. State Napier's rules for the solution of right-angled spherical triangles. Verify them when one side is the middle part.

10. In a spherical triangle show that

(a) $\sin \dfrac{A}{2} = \sqrt{\dfrac{\sin (s - b) \sin (s - c)}{\sin b \sin c}}$

(b) $\cos \dfrac{a}{2} = \sqrt{\dfrac{\cos (S - B) \cos (S - C)}{\sin B \sin C}}$

(c) $\tan \tfrac{1}{2} (A + B) = \dfrac{\cos \tfrac{1}{2} (a - b)}{\cos \tfrac{1}{2} (a + b)} \cot \dfrac{C}{2}$

11. Solve the plane triangle in which $A = 33°$ $35'$, $B = 320$, $C = 128°$ $4'$.

12. In the spherical triangle in which $a = 84°$ $14'$ $29''$, $b = 44°$ $13'$ $45''$, $C = 36°$ $45'$ $28''$, show that
$A = 130°$ $5'$ $22.4''$, $B = 32°$ $26'$ $6.4''$, $c = 51°$ $6'$ $11.6''$.

FIRST YEAR.

MATHEMATICS, IV.

Monday, April 18th :—Morning, 9 to 12.

Examiner,..G. H. Chandler, M.A.

1. Find the resultant of velocities 4, 4 and 5 in the directions of the sides of an equilateral triangle taken in order.

2. An acceleration is 32 when the units of distance and time are a foot and a second. Express the same acceleration in terms of yards and minutes.

3. Masses of 3 and 4 lbs. are arranged as in an Atwood machine. How far will they move from rest in two seconds?

4. A stone is let fall, and another is, at the same instant, projected upward from a point 500 feet lower in the same vertical line. With what speed must it be projected so that the two may meet half way?

5. From a square a triangle is cut off by a line passing through the middle points of two adjacent sides. Show that the distance of the centre of gravity of the remaining part from the centre of the square is $\frac{1}{3}$r of the diagonal.

6. What is meant by " coefficient of friction " and " angle of repose," and what is the relation connecting them?

7. The arms of a balance are unequal. If the apparent weights of a body when weighed successively in the two pans be W_1 and W_2, show that the true weight is $\sqrt{W_1 \, W_2}$.

8. Sketch two systems of pulleys in each of which the weight is four times the power.

9. A piece of cork (sp. gr. $\frac{1}{4}$) floats in water with $40\frac{1}{2}$ cu. in. above the surface; find

(1) the whole volume of the cork,

(2) how many cubic inches would be above the surface if the cork were floating in mercury (sp. gr. $13\frac{1}{2}$).

10. A mercurial barometer is sunk in water until the cistern is 27 feet below the surface of the water. What is the reading of the barometer if the reading at the surface is 29 inches?

SECOND YEAR.

MATHEMATICS, I.

MONDAY, DEC. 20TH:—AFTERNOON, 2 TO 5.30.

Examiner, ...G. H. CHANDLER, M A.

1. Draw with the same axes the curves $y = x^2$, $y = -\frac{1}{x}$, $y = x^2 - \frac{1}{x}$, from $x = -3$ to $x = 3$.

2. The angular points of a triangle are (2, —1), (1,6), (—4,2), find (1) the centre of gravity, (2) the orthocentre, (3) the area.

3. Find the equation of a circle passing through the points (4,0), (0,4) (6,4).

4. Find the equation of a circle touching the line $3x + 2y = 10$, and having for centre the point $(5,3)$.

5. Find the equation of a circle which passes through the point $(1,1)$ and meets the circle $x^2 + y^2 - 2x + 6y - 3 = 0$ in the chord $x + 2y - 2 = 0$.

6. The axes of the curve $4 x^2 + 15 xy - 4 y^2 + 8x + 15y = 0$ are transferred to parallel positions through the point $(-1,0)$, and are afterwards turned round through an angle whose tangent is $\frac{3}{5}$; show that the equation becomes $x^2 - y^2 = \frac{8}{17}$.

7. Show that $y = mx + \frac{p}{m}$ is a tangent to the parabola $y^2 = 4 px$.

8. Find the equation of a line which touches $y^2 = 8x$ and makes an angle $45°$ with the line $y = 2x + 3$.

9. Define the ellipse, and from the definition deduce the ordinary equation.

10. The distance from the centre of an ellipse to a tangent making an angle φ with the major axis is $a \sqrt{1 - e^2 \cos^2\varphi}$.

11. Show that in an equilateral hyperbola the subnormal is equal to the abscissa of the point of contact.

12. Find the locus of a point in a line which moves with its extremities on two straight lines which are perpendicular to each other.

SECOND YEAR.

MATHEMATICS, II.

Tuesday, April 12th:—Morning, 9 to 12.30.

Examiner, ...,...... G. H. Chandler, M.A.

1. Tangents are drawn at the extremities of an arc of a circle. Show that the difference between the chord of the arc and the sum of the tangents is an infinitesimal of the third order, when the arc is regarded as of the first order. ·

2. Prove the fundamental formulae

(1) $d (a_x) = A a^x dx$,

(2) $d \tan \theta = \sec^2 \theta d\theta$,

(3) $d \tan^{-1} \frac{x}{a} = \frac{a dx}{a^2 + x^2}$.

3. Show that if

(1) $y = \log \tan \frac{1}{2}\theta$, then $dy = \operatorname{cosec}\theta \, d\theta$,

(2) $y = \log \sqrt{\dfrac{x - a}{x + a}} + \tan^{-1}\dfrac{x}{a}$, then $dy = \dfrac{2a\,x^2\,dx}{x^4 - a^4}$,

(3) $y = e^{-x}\cos x$, then $d^4 y \,/\, dx^4 + 4y = 0$.

4. Distinguish between total and partial differentials, and explain why $du = d_x u + d_y u$.

5. Find to two decimal places one root of
$$x^5 - 12\,x = 200.$$

6. Integrate (1) $\cos^2\theta\,d\theta$, (2) $\cos^3\theta\,d\theta$, (3) $\dfrac{x\,dx}{\sqrt{a^4 + x^4}}$.

7. Show that

(1) $\displaystyle\int_0^{2} \frac{dx}{x^2 + 4} = \frac{\pi}{8}$,

(2) $\displaystyle\int_0^{\frac{1}{4}\pi} \cos^3\theta \sin\theta \, d\theta = \frac{3}{16}$,

(3) $\displaystyle\int x^2\,e^x\,dx = (x^2 - 2x + 2)\,e^x$.

4) $\displaystyle\int \frac{dx}{x^4 - 1} = \frac{1}{4}\log\left(\frac{x-1}{x+1}\right) - \frac{1}{2}\tan^{-1} x.$

8. In a given right segment of a parabola is described the rectangle of greatest area. Show that the length of the latter is $\frac{2}{3}$ of that of the former.

9. Find the minimum value of $\dfrac{x}{\log x}$.

10. In the common parabola $y^2 = 4\,ax$, show that

(1) the radius of curvature at (x, y) is $2\sqrt{\dfrac{(a + x)^3}{a}}$,

(2) the centre of curvature is $\left(2a + 3x, -\dfrac{y^3}{4\,a^2}\right)$,

(3) the area of a right segment is $\frac{2}{3}$ of the area of the circumscribed rectangle,

(4) the volume of the solid of revolution about the axis of x is $\frac{1}{2}$ of the volume of the circumscribed cylinder.

11. Find the asymptote of the curve $y (1 + x^2) = 1$, and show that the area between the curve and the asymptote $= \pi$.

12. Find the moment of inertia (1) of a right-angled triangle about a normal axis through the centre of gravity, (2) of a sphere about a diameter.

SECOND YEAR.

MATHEMATICS, III.

TUESDAY, APRIL 19TH :—MORNING, 9 TO 12.30.

Examiner,....................................... .... R. S. LEA, MA.E.

1. Define acceleration, poundal, couple, moment, equilibrium.

2. Find the acceleration of a body moving uniformly in a circle.
If the mass of the body is 10 lbs., the radius of the circle 10 feet, and the constraining force 10 pounds, what is the velocity of the body ?

3. Explain simple harmonic motion. Show that the motion of a pendulum is approximately simple harmonic.

4. A body of mass 4 lbs. starts from rest with an acceleration of 10 feet per second. After 5 seconds it is acted upon by a retarding force of $\frac{1}{4}$ of a pound.
In what time will it come to rest ?
When will it have a velocity of 1 foot per second ?
How far will it have travelled in each case ?

5. Find the time of flight, range and greatest height of a projectile.

6. A body is projected up a plane inclined at an angle of $30°$ to the horizontal and 50 feet long, with a velocity of 50 feet per second.
In what time and with what velocity will it reach the top of the plane '
How much higher will it rise, and when will it again be at the same elevation ?

7. Prove the method for finding graphically the resultant of a number of forces in one plane acting upon a body.

8. Two masses of 3 and 4 lbs rest on the outside of a smooth vertical hoop and are connected by a string which subtends a right angle at the centre of the hoop. Find the inclination of the string to the horizontal when in the position of equilibrium.

9. In the given figure find the stresses in the different members due to the action of the forces indicated.

THIRD YEAR.

MATHEMATICS. I.

Monday, Dec. 20th :—Afternoon, 2 to 5.30.

Examiner, ...G. H. Chandler, M.A.

1. Given the conic $4 x^2 - 24\ xy - 3y^2 + 24y - 4 = 0$, find

    (1) the co-ordinates of the centre,

    (2) the angle which the principal diameters make with the co-ordinate axes,

    (3) the equation when referred to these diameters, and hence make a rough sketch of the curve.

2. When will the general equation of the second degree represent a parabola? How may the term containing xy be made to disappear from the equation of a parabola?

3. The parallelogram formed by tangents at the extremities of a pair of conjugate diameters of an ellipse is of constant area.

4. Show that the normal of the ellipse at the point $(x_1,\ y\ )$ is

$$\frac{a^2 x}{x_1} - \frac{b^2 y}{y_1} = a^2 - b^2.$$

5. Find the angle between the lines joining the origin to the points $(1,2,3),\ (5,-4,1)$.

6. Show that

    (1) $\displaystyle\int \frac{(x^3 + 1)\ dx}{x\ (x^3 - 1)} = \tfrac{2}{3} \log (x^3 - 1) - \log x,$

    (2) $\displaystyle\int \frac{dx}{x^3 \sqrt{x^2 - 1)}} = \tfrac{1}{2} \sec^{-1} x + \frac{\sqrt{x^2 - 1}}{2\ x^2},$

the latter by the substitution of $\sec \theta$ for x.

7. By integrating by parts, or otherwise, show that

$$\int \sqrt{x^2 - a^2}\ dx = \tfrac{1}{2}\ x \sqrt{x^2 - a^2} - \tfrac{1}{2} a^2 \log (x + \sqrt{x^2 - a^2}).$$

8. Expand $\cos x$ into a series.

9. Find the limits of the values of

$$(1) \quad \frac{e^x - e^{-x}}{\log (1+x),} \quad (2) \ x^{\frac{x}{x}},$$

as x approaches 0.

10. Of the curve $xy = x^3 - 1$, find

(1) the point of inflexion,

(2) the radius of curvature at the point where $x = 2$,

(3) the length of the normal at the same point.

11. Show that the area bounded by the hyperbola

$\dfrac{x^2}{a^2} - \dfrac{y^2}{b^2} = 1$, the axis of x, and the ordinate at the point (x_1, y_1) is

$$\tfrac{1}{2} x_1 \ y_1 - \tfrac{1}{2} \ ab \ \log\!\left(\frac{x_1}{a} + \frac{y_1}{b}\right).$$

12. How could you cut out four equal squares from the corners of a given square so the remaining area (the edges being turned up) would form a rectangular box of greatest volume.

13. Find the moment of inertia of a uniform sphere with respect to a diameter.

THIRD YEAR.

MATHEMATICS, II.

Tuesday, April 19th :—Morning, 9 to 12.30.

Examiner .... G. H. Chandler. M.A.

1. The distance of the centre of gravity of a quadrantal circular arc from the centre is $r . 2\sqrt{2} / \pi$

2. A body is projected with a speed v on a horizontal plane and comes to rest after travelling a distance s. Show that the coefficient of friction $= v^2 / 2gs$.

3. Find the horizontal force necessary to push a body weighing W lbs. up a rough incline, the angle of inclination of the plane being θ and the angle of friction φ.

4. A steamer running at 15 miles per hour begins to turn on a curve of 125 ft. radius. Show that objects on the deck (which is assumed to remain horizontal) will slide unless the coefficient of friction exceeds .121.

5. In a single pulley of radius a and axle radius r, a vertical force P raises a weight W. Show that $\frac{P}{W} = 1 + 2\,\mu\,\frac{r}{a}$, nearly.

6. A train of 100 tons mass runs at 42 miles per hour on a level track, the resistance being 8 pounds per ton. Show that its speed up a one per cent. grade, the engine power being unchanged, would be only 12 miles per hour.

7. Show that to give a train a velocity of 20 miles per hour requires the same energy as to lift it vertically through a height of 13.4 feet.

8. Prove that in the motion of a rigid body about an axis, moment of inertia × angular acceleration = sum of moments of external forces about the axis.

9. A circular disk 10 in. in diameter makes small oscillations about a horizontal tangent. Find the centre of oscillation.

10. Explain what is meant by centre of percussion, and state how it is found.

A triangle is held vertically by one angle. Where may the triangle be struck by a normal blow, which will not be felt at the point of support?

11. A hammer weighing 1 lb. strikes a nail weighing 1 oz. with a velocity of 34 feet per second, and drives the nail 1 in. into a block of wood. Show that the mean resistance of the wood is 204 pounds.

12. Explain the meaning of centre of pressure, and find an expression for the determination of the centre of pressure of any plane area.

THIRD YEAR ARTS, SECOND YEAR SCIENCE.

EXPERIMENTAL PHYSICS—HEAT, LIGHT AND SOUND.

WEDNESDAY, APRIL 6TH :—MORNING, 9 TO 12.

(*Not more than nine questions to be attempted.*)

1. Describe the process of making and graduating a mercury thermometer, and explain the origin of the Centigrade and Fahrenheit scales.

Find the temperature at which the number of degrees on the Fahrenheit scale is double that on the Centigrade scale, and also that at which the two scales agree.

2. Give some applications of the differences of expansion between different metals. Define the term Coefficient of Expansion, and show how to calculate the allowance to be made for expansion in the case of the Victoria Bridge.

3. Describe one form of air thermometer, and explain the method of using it to verify the laws of gases. What are the principal difficulties attending its use?

4. State the two principal laws of change of state. Define the boiling point of a liquid. Distinguish between a saturated and unsaturated vapour, and explain how their behaviour differs from that of a gas.

5. Describe experiments to illustrate the different conducting powers of different materials. State the Law of Conduction, and describe some form of apparatus for measuring the conductivity of a metal.

6. How is the velocity of sound in the air affected by changes in pressure and temperature? How may the velocity in other gases and materials be compared with it?

7. A lump of ice weighing 80 grammes, and at a temperature of —10°, is dropped into water at 0°. 5 grammes of water freeze on to the lump and the temperature of the ice rises to 0°. Calculate the specific heat of ice.

8. Describe the Sonometer, and explain how to use it in determining the vibration number of a given tuning-fork, quoting the formula.
A string is stretched in such a way that a wave runs along it at a rate of 64 feet per second. Two points on the string, 4 feet apart, are now clamped without altering the tension. How many vibrations per second will this length of the string make when disturbed?

9. Explain the principle of Resonance.
A tuning fork is held over a resonance tube, and the maximum effect is found when the air column is 64·8 cm. long. The vibration number of the fork is 128. What is the velocity of sound?

10. Describe the Spectrometer and its adjustments. Explain how to use it to find (1) the angle of a given prism ; (2) the index of refraction of the prism for a given ray.

11. Describe the **experimental** arrangements for producing Newton's rings upon the screen. Give a general explanation of the rings. Whyi the centre black instead of white?

12. Describe the optical arrangements in some form of Polariscope. explaining the functions of the polarizer and analyzer.

B.A. ORDINARY EXAMINATIONS AND THIRD YEAR APPLIED SCIENCE.

EXPERIMENTAL PHYSICS—ELECTRICITY AND MAGNETISM.

WEDNESDAY, APRIL 6TH :—MORNING, 9 TO 12.

(Not more than nine questions to be attempted.)

1. Sketch the lines of force in a horizontal plane in the neighbourhood of a bar magnet suspended freely with its axis in the meridian. Explain the terms used, and show how to calculate the moment of the magnet by finding the point of the field at which the magnetic intensity vanishes.

2. Describe and contrast the magnetic properties of iron and steel. Explain the phenomena of induction, saturation, and retention, and give the relation between the permeability and susceptibility.

3. Give the essential points of the construction of a tangent galvanometer. If the coil has 30 turns of 10 cm. radius, what will be the moment of the couple acting on a magnet 1 cm. long, strength of pole 10 units, at the centre, due to a current of 1 ampere flowing in the wire.

4. Describe the construction and use of the mirror galvanometer. What are the comparative advantages of the movable coil and movable magnet types? Give the elementary formula for either, and explain the term " figure of merit."

5. Assuming the law of force acting on a conductor carrying a current in a magnetic field, find an expression for the work done in moving the conductor so as to cut N lines of force. Apply the principle of the conservation of energy to deduce Faraday's law of the induction of electric currents.

6. State the laws of the chemical action of an electric current. Describe experiments by which they may be verified. Explain why a single Daniel cell is unable to send a current through a water voltameter.

7. Describe and explain the action of the Water-dropping Accumulator, and compare it with a Wimshurst Machine.

8. Explain the principle of a Wheatstone's Bridge, proving the formula. Explain Carey Foster's method of using the bridge, pointing out its advantages.

9. Two equal cells when connected in series through a given wire produce a current of .28 ampere ; when connected in parallel they give through the same wire .2 ampere ; prove that the resistance of the wire is 3 times that of either cell.

10. Explain clearly why a high voltage is required for economically transmitting power to a great distance.
A dynamo gives 123.6 amperes through an external resistance of 1.224 ohm ; the power absorbed is 28 H. P. Shew that its commercial efficiency is 89.5.

11. A coil of 50 turns of wire in the form of a circle 30 cm. in diameter rotates 20 times a second about a vertical axis. Find the average E. M. F. produced (in volts) if $H = .18$ C. G. S. units.

12. Explain (1) the construction of the Blake transmitter, (2) a method of duplexing a telegraph line.

THIRD YEAR.
ELECTRICAL ENGINEERING.
PHYSICAL LABORATORY WORK.

FRIDAY, APRIL 15TH :—AFTERNOON, 2 TO 5.

Examiner ....H. L. CALLENDAR, M.A., F.R.S.

(*Not more than six questions to be attempted.*)

1. Give the elementary theory of Gauss's method of finding the horizontal intensity of the earth's magnetic force, and describe its application.

2. Describe the adjustment of the Compass Box Variometer. If the north pole of the needle turns through an angle of 175° when $H = .1,500$ and the stops of the control magnet are set 60° apart, find the value of H for which the stops were set to make the needle turn through 180°.

3. Explain how to use a sine galvanometer, and how to correct it for torsion of the fibre if the angle is measured by allowing the needle to swing back to the meridian. How may the torsion coefficient be determined ?

23

4. A tangent galvanometer gives a deflection of 60° with a resistance of 1,000 ohms in circuit with it. When it is shunted with 100 ohms, the deflection falls to 30°. Find the resistance of the galvanometer.

5. Describe and explain the method of calibrating a bridge wire.

6. How may the resistance and E. M. F. of a cell be measured with the aid of a standard cell, a suitable resistance and a condenser?

7. A current is passed through an insulated coil of wire immersed in a copper calorimeter weighing 80 grammes and containing 150 grammes of water, and through a copper voltameter, for ten minutes. If it deposits one decigramme of copper, and raises the temperature of the calorimeter 10° C, find the resistance of the coil. (Electro-chemical equivalent of copper .000329 per ampere second.)

8. Explain the potentiometer method of comparing potential differences. Describe the method of calibrating a low-range voltmeter.

9. The resistance of a copper wire one millimetre in diameter is 1 ohm at 20° C., and 1.32 ohms at 100° C. Find its temperature coefficient, and its resistance at 0° C. If the specific resistance of copper is 1.60 microhms at 0° C., find the length of the wire in question.

·

———

B. A. Sc. EXAMINATION.

ELECTRICAL ENGINEERING.

FOURTH YEAR.

PHYSICAL LABORATORY WORK.

FRIDAY, APRIL 15TH:—AFTERNOON, 2 TO 5.

Examiner...H. L. CALLENDAR, M.A., F.R.S.

(*Not more than six questions to be attempted.*)

1. Give the theory of Gauss's method of determining the horizontal intensity of the earth's magnetic field, explaining the corrections for temperature, torsion, induction, and for the lengths of the magnets.

2. Describe the Ballistic method of determining the form of the reversal curve of B and H, and of the hysteresis loop for an iron ring.

3. Describe the method of determining the E M.F. of a Clark cell in absolute measure by means of the Weber Electrodynamometer, explaining the method of calculating the constants of the coils, and of finding the directive force.

4. Explain the principal steps in the testing and adjustment of a 5,000 range Weston ammeter. What errors would be caused by the heating of the shunt and of the indicator respectively?

5. Describe the commutator bridge method of comparing standard resistances, and of determining their temperature-coefficients. What precautions are necessary to avoid errors from thermo-electric effects?

6. How would you proceed to find the relation between voltage and candle-power in the case of an incandescent lamp? What is the nature of the curve, and how may it be best represented by an empirical formula?

7. What apparatus would you require to determine the puncturing point and the insulation resistance of a specimen of rubber covered wire? In what manner should the two tests be conducted?

8. Describe the principal phenomena in the charge and discharge of a storage cell. Give an example of the characteristic curves, and explain how to find the watt-efficiency.

9. Describe the construction and graduation of an electrical resistance pyrometer. Explain how to find the delta-coefficient, and how to plot the difference curve in terms of platinum-temperature scale as abscissa.

SECOND YEAR.

THEORY OF ARCHITECTURE.

Wednesday, April 13th :—2 to 5.30 p.m.

Examiner, ...S. Henbest Capper, M.A.

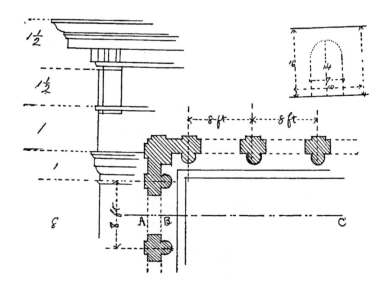

A. Above is sketch plan of angle of courtyard, treated as a one storey open arcade with engaged columns of the Roman Doric Order, which are 8 feet from centre to centre. Upon this is to be added a second storey, forming an open gallery or arcade, after the fashion of an Italian loggia. This, while necessarily classical or renaissance in character, is left free to candidates to design in detail.

Required, elevation to half inch scale along line A.B.C., showing two complete bays and section (at A. B.)

B. Answer not more than two of the following questions :—

1. Criticize the statement that "architecture is merely construction beautified."

2. Sketch a Greek Doric Capital in perspective looking up to angle of abacus. Criticize briefly its design and add a note as to its suggested derivation from an earlier architecture.

3. Draw a section (not less than $2\frac{1}{2}$ inches in depth) of an Attic base, naming the mouldings; and a similar section of the enriched Attic base usually given to Corinthian columns.

4. Name the Order (or Orders) used in the following buildings:—The Parthenon ; the Erectheum ; the Pantheon ; the Coliseum ; St. Peter's, Rome (entrance front) ; Library of St. Mark's, Venice ; or, alternatively,

Name *five* buildings of Ancient Greek and Roman Architecture in which the Corinthian (or Composite) Order is used, and *five* in which the Ionic Order is used.

SECOND YEAR.

HISTORY OF ARCHITECTURE.

THURSDAY, APRIL 14TH :—9 TO 12 A.M.

Examiner, ...S. HENBEST CAPPER, M.A.

(N.B.—The number of marks assigned is given in brackets ; candidates are only expected to answer questions corresponding to a total of 200 ; all are expected to attempt Question *A ;* marks will be given for clear and good sketching.)

A. Give a full written description of not less than *two* and not more than *four* of the following buildings (in so far as illustrated in the photographs herewith supplied) ; adding your criticism of the architectural forms and features, and indicating, as far as possible, the probable dates or periods of the work.

1. " Maison Carrée," Nîmes (France).   (30)

2. Interior of the Church of St. Martin de Boscherville, Normandy (France).   (30)

3. West front of Amiens Cathedral (France).   (35)

4. Southwest view of the Monastery of Batalha (Portugal).   (35)

5. The Library of St. Mark's, Venice.   (25)

B. 2. Give a sketch plan and some account, both historical and architectural, of the Parthenon, with any additional sketches in illustration that may be necessary.   (45)

3. Outline the development of vaulting from Roman, through Roman-esque, to and including Gothic times. (40)

4. Give a brief account of the great Monastic Orders and their influence on the progress of architecture. (40)

5. Note briefly the development and successive characteristic forms of Gothic window tracery. (30)

6. Selecting any period or phase of architecture, or any special architectural form or feature, or any important building, that has seemed to you noteworthy in connection with the lectures (and is not otherwise included among the questions here set), write a note upon it, giving weight to any characteristics that have made it interesting to you. (10 to 35)

THIRD YEAR.

HISTORY OF ARCHITECTURE :—*ITALIAN RENAISSANCE.*

THURSDAY, APRIL 14TH :—9 TO 12 A. M.

Examiner,............... ....S. HENBEST CAPPER, M.A.

Note.—Candidates are not required to answer more than *five* questions.

1. Write a note on the rise of the Renaissance movement in Italy, giving a short account of the position of Florence, politically and artistically, in the 15th century, and contrasting it briefly with Venice and Rome.

2. Criticize the following statement :—" With the advent of the Renaissance all continuity in architecture is immediately lost; the principles and practice of Gothic architecture are abandoned in toto and at once, inspiration being sought directly from Ancient Rome."

3. Give some account of Filippo Brunelleschi, enumerating his principal works, with brief notes and sketches in illustration, and estimate his influence on the Architecture of the Renaissance.

4. Sketch in elevation any *two* of the following, adding brief notes as to date, architect, etc :—

(1) Palazzo Strozzi (Florence) ; (2) Palazzo Vendramini *or* Spinelli, ' Venice '; (3) Certosa (Pavia) ; (4) Farnese Palace (Rome), exterior *or* court ; (5) any important Italian Renaissance building not otherwise included in your answers.

5. What architects were chiefly employed in the building of St. Peter's, Rome, and what were their respective shares in the work ?

5. Criticize Michael Angelo's influence on architecture.

7. What would you regard as the principal points in which Sixteenth Century Architecture differs from Fifteenth Century in Italy ? and what would you note as the chief differences between Florentine, Venetian and Roman Architecture?

8. Enumerate with brief notes the principal works of any *two* of the following architects :—

(1) Baldassare Peruzzi ; (2) Bramante ; (3) Sanmicheli ; (4) Palladio ; (5) Sansovino ; (6) Vignola.

9. Sketch a capital and *one* other example of ornament which you would consider typical of Italian Renaissance work.

THIRD YEAR.

HISTORY OF ARCHITECTURE: RENAISSANCE (*Second Paper*).

THURSDAY, APRIL 14TH :—2 TO 4.30 P.M.

Examiner, ...S. HENBEST CAPPER, M.A.

A. Taking a single bay of the front elevation of a large residence two storeys in height, sketch out a design such as you would consider typical of (*a*) an Italian Palazzo (either Florentine *or* Venetian *or* " Palladian ") ; (*b*) French Renaissance ; (*c*) English Renaissance. *Two only of the three are required.*

NOTE.—All candidates are expected to attempt Question *A.* The sketches are not intended to be finished drawings, but must be large enough to be clear.

B. Answer any *three* of the following questions :—

1. Mention some of the characteristic features of Early Renaissance work in *either* France *or* England *or* Spain.

2. Write a note on the French Renaissance Château, commenting on its relation to the Gothic feudal castle.

3. Describe briefly any *one* of the following buildings, giving its approximate date and the name of the architect where known : (*a*) the château of Blois ; (*b*) the Palace of Versailles ; (*c*) the Escorial ;

or,

· Mention, with a note as to his principal works, one important architect of the 17th century in France and one in England ; and one in each country of the 18th century.

4. Give a slight survey of English architecture in the 16th century, contrasting it with contemporary Italian work.

5. Describe briefly any *three* important domed buildings erected subsequently to St. Peter's, either in Italy or elsewhere.

BUILDING CONSTRUCTION.

SECOND YEAR.

SATURDAY, APRIL 2ND : —MORNING, 9 TO 12.

Examiner,...CECIL B. SMITH, MA.E

1. Describe different methods of taking soundings for foundations either on land or in water.

2. Comment on the bearing power of clay soils.

3. What are the ordinary methods of driving piles ? Describe one of them.

What load will a pile safely carry that has been driven by a drop hammer weighing 1,800 lbs. falling 22 feet, and driving it $1\frac{1}{2}$ inches per blow ?

4. Sketch different systems of foundations on land.

5. Mention two methods of securing deep foundations. Describe one of them in detail.

6. Describe methods of ·driving tunnels through soft ground, illustrating by sketches.

7. Mention explosives in general use.
Describe one of them in detail.

8. Give various methods of preventing moisture from entering through brick masonry walls. (Sketches, if necessary.)
Also sketch English and Flemish bond in brick masonry.

9. How would you calculate the load which a lintel over an opening should be designed to carry ? Make the calculation.

10. Give general rules for laying stone masonry walls.

11. Mention various classes of stone masonry, with approximate cost per cubic yard.

12. To what various forms of construction may concrete be applied, describing one application in detail ?

13. What is porous terra cotta? How is it made and used, and what are its special applications ?

THEORY OF STRUCTURES. 47

THIRD AND FOURTH YEAR EXAMINATIONS.

THEORY OF STRUCTURES. (*Paper I.*)

MONDAY, APRIL 4TH :—9 A M.

Examiner,.................................HENRY T. BOVEY, LL.D., M.INST. C.E.

1. Explain what is meant by a funicular polygon. Show that the bending moment at any point of a horizontal girder carrying a number of concentrated loads may be represented by the intercept on the vertical through that point, cut off by the closing line and the opposite bounding line of the funicular polygon.

2 Explain graphically the relation between a shearing force and a bending moment, and illustrate your answer in the shearing force and bending moment diagrams for a horizontal beam $ABCD$, resting upon three supports at A, B and D, and hinged at C. $AB = 24$ ft.; $BC = 8$ ft.; $CD = 32$ ft.; uniformly distributed loads upon AB, BC and CD are 24 tons, 32 tons and 32 tons respectively.

3. Two wheels, 8 ft. apart and each carrying a load of 4 tons, travel over a beam of 16 ft. span. Draw curves of maximum *S.F.* and *B.M.*
What uniformly distributed load will give the same bending moment diagram ?

4. In the 4 ton crane shown in diagram, the chain has 4 falls and passes from A to E. Determine the stresses in every member, with a brace from (1) B to D, (2) from C to E.

5. Draw a stress diagram for the 5 ton crane shown by Fig.

6. Draw the stress diagram for roof shown by Fig., and loaded as indicated.

7. Determine stresses in all members of roof truss shown by Fig., and loaded as indicated.

8. One side of the truss shown by Fig. is fixed at the lower end, and is acted upon by two loads each of 200 lbs. The truss also carries vertical loads of 100, 200 and 300 lbs., as shown. Determine the stresses in all the members.

9. Determine the anchorage forces in the truss shown by Fig. when loaded as indicated.

10. The Fig. represents a swing-bridge truss. The weight of the truss is equivalent to a load of 2 tons at H and C and a load of 4 tons at each of the points G and F. If C is the counter-weight concentrated at C,

find *C*, and determine the stresses in all the members, assuming that the reaction at *E* is equal to the reaction at *D*.

11. The Fig. represents a Pratt truss. Draw the stress diagram, (1) when a load of 5 tons is concentrated at each of the panel points, (2) when a load of 5 tons is concentrated at the first 3 panel points only.

12. Determine the stresses in all the members of the 80 ft. roof truss shown by Fig. The end *B* is absolutely fixed. A normal wind pressure of 200 lbs. is concentrated at *B*, of 400 lbs. at *D*, of 600 lbs. at *F*, and of 500 lbs. at *A*. The dead weight consists of a load of 200 lbs. at *D* and *L*, 400 lbs. at *F* and *H*, and 1,000 lbs. at *A*. Determine the stresses in all the members.

THIRD AND FOURTH YEAR EXAMINATIONS.

THEORY OF STRUCTURES. (*Paper II.*)

SATURDAY, APRIL 9TH:—9 A.M.

Examiner, ...HENRY T. BOVEY, LL.D., M.INST. C.E.

1. Find the work expended in raising the materials (112 lbs. per cubic foot) for a brick tower, 125 ft. high, the external and internal diameters being 24 ft. and 16 ft., respectively.

In what time could the materials be raised by a $2\frac{1}{2}$ H P. engine?

2. A 6 ft. plank *A B,* hinged at *B,* has its middle point supported on a 24 in. grindstone and carries a weight of 100 lbs at the end *A.* The grindstone weighs 600 lbs. and makes 175 revolutions per minute on a 1 in. axle. Taking the co-efficient of plank friction and rolling friction to be .3 and .05, respectively, find in how many turns the grindstone will come to rest when the motive power ceases to act.

3. Give the formulæ usually adopted in calculating the sectional area of structural members subjected to repeated stresses.

A steel diagonal is subjected to stresses which vary from a maximum compression of 10,000 lbs. to a maximum tension of 10,000 lbs. Find its sectional area, taking 3 as the factor of safety and $u = 2s = 60,000$ lbs.

4. Prove that at any point in a strained body the shearing intensities on any two planes at right angles to each other are equal.

At a point in a strained solid the intensity of shear on two planes at right angles is 24 lbs.; the obliquity of the resultant stresses on one plane is sin -1 .8 and of the resultant forces on the other plane is $\sin^{-1}$.6. Find the magnitudes of the two forces.

Also find (1) the stresses upon a plane bisecting the two planes in question, (2) the principal stresses at the point.

5. The ground surface at the rear of a retaining wall rises at an angle of θ to the horizontal, the angle of repose being ϕ. Show that the total pressure upon the back of the wall, which is vertical and of height h, is $\dfrac{w h^2}{2} \cos \theta \tan \dfrac{\beta}{2}$ where $\cos \phi = \sin \beta \cos \theta$, and w is the specific weight of the wall. What are the assumptions made in your proof?

A wall of rectangular section, 20 ft. high and 8 ft. thick, weighs 125 lbs. per cubic foot. Find the maximum intensity of pressure at the base when the wall retains (a) water level with the top, (b) earth level with the top ; the angle of repose in the latter case being 30° and the earth weighing 100 lbs. per cubic foot

6. An endless belt weighing $\frac{1}{2}$ lb. per lineal foot connects two 35 in. pulleys and transmits 5 H P., a pulley making 300 revolutions per minute. Find the tight and slack tensions, μ being .28.

7. Write down the relations which are usually assumed in the determination of the transverse strength of a beam, stating all the assumptions made.

The weight of 200 lbs. per sq ft. upon a platform 60 ft. long and 10 ft. wide is equally borne by six cast iron girders of rectangular section triangular in profile, 10 ft. long and 3 ins. wide. Find the depth at the fixed end, taking 2 tons per square inch as the coefficient of safety.

If $E = 17,000,000$ lbs., find the deflection at the free end.

8. A cast-iron girder has a $4'' \times 1''$ upper flange, a $25'' \times 1''$ lower flange and a $20'' \times 1''$ web. Determine the moment of resistance of the section, 2,000 and 5,000 lbs. being the coefficients of tensile and compressive strength, respectively.

9. Explain how to design a cantilever of uniform strength when carrying any given transverse load.

10. Deduce the relation $q\, w\, I = S\, A\, \bar{y}$.

A built up beam is composed of two equal flanges, each consisting of a $6\frac{1}{4}'' \times \frac{1}{2}''$ plate connected by a $24'' \times \frac{1}{2}''$ web, being open 6'' in the middle, by means of 4 equal angle irons, each $3'' \times 3'' \times \frac{1}{4}''$. Determine the moment of resistance, the maximum shearing strength, the ratio of the maximum to the average intensity of longitudinal shear and the intensity of longitudinal shear 12'' from the neutral axis, 6 tons per sq. in. being coefficient of strength.

11. Find the least diameter of a shaft which will transmit 1,000 H.P. at a surface velocity of 10 ft. per second and a maximum working stress of 10,000 lbs. per square inch.

12. Explain how to determine the strength of a long thin pillar.

———

13. A horizontal girder of length l is absolutely fixed at one end and rests upon a support at the other. Find the reactions at each end and the maximum deflection (1) when the girder carries a uniformly distributed load, (2) when it carries a single weight at the centre.

14. Deduce an expression giving the work done in bending a horizontal beam under a transverse load. Find the work done in bending the beam in the preceding example.

———

THIRD AND FOURTH YEAR EXAMINATIONS.

THEORY OF STRUCTURES. (*Paper III.*)

Examiner........ ....HENRY T. BOVEY LL.D., M.INST. C.E.

1. The Fig. represents a Pauli truss for a single track deck bridge of 80 ft. span. Find the lengths of the verticals, the length being governed by the condition that the stress in every member of the bow is the same and equal to 48,000 lbs., for a load of 6,000 lbs. at each panel point. Find the corresponding stresses in each of the horizontal members.

Also, taking the panel live load per truss to be 5,000 lbs. and the panel dead load to be 1,000 lbs., determine the maximum and minimum stresses in each member of the truss.

2. The diagram represents a 16 panel Petit (Baltimore) deck truss for a bridge of 400 ft. span and 30 ft. deep. The panel live load per truss = 45,000 lbs., the panel dead load per truss = 37,500 lbs. Determine the stresses of the 6th and 7th verticals from one end and in all the members of the 7th panel.

3. A horizontal platform, carrying a uniformly distributed load, is suspended from a cable. Show that the curve of the cable is a parabola.

Show how to determine the stresses in the back stays. If the lengths of the back stays vary under a change of temperature, determine the corresponding change in the dip of the cable and find the stresses thus produced in the flange of a stiffening truss.

4. Determine the transformed catenary for an arch of 52.738 ft. span and 12 ft. rise. The depth of masonry (120 lbs. per cubic foot) over the crown being 18 ft.

Find the curvature at the rise and at the springing and also the direction and magnitude of the thrust at the latter point.

5 An arched rib of span $2l$ and rise k, carries a weight P at a horizontal distance a from the middle point. Show that the horizontal thrust at any point of rib $= \dfrac{15}{32}\ P\ \dfrac{(l^2 - a^2)^2}{k\ l^3}$ and the reaction at a support

$$= \tfrac{1}{4}\ P\ \frac{(_2l \mp a)\ (l \pm a)^2}{l^3}$$

6. A parabolic arched rib, of 80 ft. span and $13\frac{1}{2}$ ft. rise, with both ends fixed, carries three weights of 2 tons, 4 tons and 6 tons at 10, 20 and 30 ft. from one end. Draw the equilibrium polygon and determine the thrust and shear on each side of the point at which the 6 ton load is concentrated.

7. The Fig. represents one of two braced arches for a deck bridge of 80 ft. span, hinged at the ends and hinged also at the centre. The panel live load is 6 tons ; the panel dead load is 2 tons. Determine the maximum stresses in the 3rd and 4th verticals from one end and in all the members of the third panel.

If the lower boom instead of being horizontal be curved, as shown by the dotted line which represents a parabola of the same rise as the arch, determine the stresses in the horizontal chord and explain the result.

8. Enunciate and prove the general Theorem of Three Moments and apply to the following case : The Fig. represents a swing bridge resting upon four supports. Find the reactions and draw the stress diagram for the given loading.

TESTING LABORATORY AND MATERIALS.

THIRD YEAR.

Saturday, April 2nd :—Morning, 9 to 1.

Examiners, ... $\begin{cases} \text{Henry T Bovey, M.A., LL.D.} \\ \text{C. B. Smith, Ma.E.} \end{cases}$

1. Describe the Wicksteed testing machine with sketches. Also describe in detail the process of making a transverse test of a timber beam and notes to be taken.

2. Describe the Emery testing machine with sketches, and give a detailed description of a compression test.

3. A pine floor beam, 15 feet c. to c., 18 inches deep and 8 inches wide, is not to deflect more than $\frac{1}{2}$ inch at the centre. Taking $E = 1,000,000$ what uniformly distributed load will it carry ? Find value also of skin stress f.

4. What safe load will an oak pillar, 10 feet long and 8 inches square, carry when $f = 6000$ and $a = \frac{1}{3000}$ in the Gordon-Rankine formula. How much will it carry by Johnson's straight line formula when $K = 6000$ and $C = 28$?

5. What is the effect on the compressive, tensile, shearing and transverse strengths of timber when the moisture is driven out?

6. At what age and at what times of year should trees be preferably felled ? Why?
State the characteristics of a good quality of timber.

7. Describe minutely the method of seasoning by direct extraction of sap ; mention other methods of seasoning.

8. Write a short account of the Teredo Navalis.

9. Describe the creosoting process of preserving wood, and mention other processes for the same purpose.

10. To what different tests may timber be subjected in a testing machine ? What are the average tensile and shearing strengths of white and red pine, white oak, spruce, Douglas fir, and hemlock, per square inch.

11. Design a tension joint consisting of a white pine stick 4 inches deep, connected by an oak key projecting 1 inch above the surface of the pine.

12. Describe spathic iron ore, and name other well-known varieties of iron ore.

13. Describe the complete process of reducing ore into pig iron.

14. State the effect of combined and of graphitic carbon on cast iron. How does silicon affect the distribution?

15. What is the effect of Manganese, Phosphorus, Sulphur and Carbon on steel and iron ?

16. Describe the Bessemer process, and distinguish between acid and basic Bessemer methods.

17. Enumerate workshop tests on different forms of iron.

18. Describe the data sought for in a tensile test of iron.

19. State and show by sketches the method of obtaining equivalent extensions when a test specimen breaks near one end.

20. Draw typical stress strain diagrams of cast iron, wrought iron, mild steel and cast steel, in tension and compression.

B.A.Sc. EXAMINATIONS.

HYDRAULICS. (*Paper I.*)

Examiners,.............................. $\begin{cases} \text{HENRY T. BOVEY, LL.D., M.INST. C.E.} \\ \text{RICHARD S. LEA, MA.E.} \end{cases}$

1. Show that in a frictionless pipe of gradually changing section the energy in ft. lbs. per cubic foot of water is distributed uniformly throughout the pipe.

In a frictionless pipe the diameter gradually changes from 6″ at a point *A* 20 ft. above datum to 3″ at *B* 15 ft. above datum. The pressure at *A* is 20 lbs. per square inch; find the pressure at *B*; the delivery of the pipe being 2¾ cubic feet per second.

2. A cylindrical vessel, 10 ft. high and 1 ft. in diameter, is half full of water. Find the number of revolutions per minute which the vessel must make so that the water may just reach the top, the axis of revolution being (1) co-incident with the axis of the vessel, (2) a generating line of the vessel.

3. Explain what is meant by "loss in shock," and obtain an expression for the loss in shock at the point where a pipe suddenly enlarges.

The water flowing at 2 ft. per second in a 12″ pipe, discharges into a 24″ pipe and again into a 12″ pipe. Determine the loss of head at the junctions.

How will this loss be affected if the flow is doubled?

4. A pipe is fitted with a ring nozzle. Show that, very approximately, the sectional area of the mouthpiece is an harmonic mean between the sectional areas of the contracted area and the sectional area of the pipe.

5. Deduce an expression for the discharge through a triangular notch, and point out the advantage of such a notch.

A reservoir, rectangular in plan and 10,000 sq. ft. in area, has in one side a 90° triangular notch 2 ft. deep. If the reservoir is full, in what time will the level sink to the bottom of the notch?

6. A stream of rectangular section 24 ft. wide, delivers 145 cubic feet per second. The edge of a drowned weir is 15 ins. below the surface of the water on the down-stream side. Determine the difference of level between the surfaces of the water on the up and down stream sides, the velocity of approach being 2 ft. per second.

7. The pressure from an accumulator at the entrance of a 6″ pipe *L* ft. long is 750 lbs. per sq. in. If H.P. is the total H.P. entering the pipe, show that the number of H.P. absorbed by frictional resistance

$$= L \left(\frac{H.P.}{147} \right)^3$$

taking $f = .0064$ and $w = 62.5$ lbs. per cub. ft.

8. A pipe of length l and diameter d is fitted with a·nozzle having an outlet of diameter D. Deduce an expression giving the height to which the water on issuing from the nozzle is capable of rising.

Water enters a 3 in. hose under a head of 100 ft. The length of the hose is 400 ft. and the hose terminates in a ⅝ in. nozzle. Find the velocity of efflux and the height to which the jet is capable of rising, disregarding the frictional resistance in the nozzle. Also find the pressure head at the entrance to the nozzle.

Taking $f = .00625$, what is the force required to hold the nozzle?

9. Find the H.P. required to pump 1,000,000 gallons of water per day of 24 hours to a height of 300 ft. through a line of straight piping 3,000 feet long, the diameter of the pipe being 8 in. for the first 1,000 ft., 6 in. for the second 1,000 ft., and 4 in. for the third 1,000 ft., making allowance for the loss of head at entrance and at abrupt changes of section. Also take 4 as the co-efficient of resistance for pump valves

What should be the diameter of an equivalent uniform pipe?

10. A pipe 800 ft. long with a fall of 2½ ft. discharges into two branches, the one 200 ft. long with a fall of 5 ft., the other 600 ft. long with a fall of 10 ft. The total quantity of water passing through the pipe per minute is 94 2/7 cub. ft., ⅔ of which passes into the 600 ft. branch. The velocity of flow in the main is 2 ft. per second; determine the diameters of the main and branches.

11. Deduce the formula giving the velocity of steady flow in a channel of constant section, and explain how you determine the dimensions of a water-way of given sectional area, which would make this velocity a maximum.

12. A pipe of radius r connects two reservoirs. If Q is the total discharge from the upper reservoir and the quantity Q_2 is drawn away through a branch of radius r at a junction dividing the main into two segments of lengths $l_{\overline{3}}$ and $l_{\overline{2}}$ respectively, show that $(Q - (Q_3)\, l_1 + l_{\overline{2}}) = Q_2\, l_1$, Q_3 being the end discharge.

13. In an open channel v_s is the surface of velocity. Show that, adopting Navier's hypothesis as to viscous resistance, the velocity at a depth y is given by

$$v = -\ \frac{wi}{2k}\ y^2 + ay + vs$$

and hence, if v_m be the mean velocity for the whole depth of the channel and $v_{\frac{1}{2}}$ be the mid-depth velocity, shew that

$$24\, k\, (v_{\frac{1}{2}} - vm) = w\, i\, h_2.$$

14. In a stream of rectangular section and of great width as compared with the depth, discuss the flow when

$$a\, u^2 > gh \text{ and } H < h.$$

B.A Sc. EXAMINATIONS.

HYDRAULICS (*Paper 11.*)

Examiners, ... $\begin{cases} \text{HENRY T. BOVEY, LL D., M.Inst.C.E.} \\ \text{R. S. LEA, M\u1.E.} \end{cases}$

1. A stream of water 1 in. thick and 8 ins. wide, moving with a velocity of 18 ft. per second, strikes without shock a circular vane, of a length subtending an angle of 90° at the centre, The vane is driven in the direction of the stream with a velocity of 6 ft. per second. Find the pressure on the vane, the work done and the efficiency.

2. A stream of sectional area A impinges upon a vane in the form of a surface of revolution, in the direction of the axis, with a velocity v_1 and drives the vane in the same direction with a velocity u. If the tangent at the edge of the vane make an angle β with the axis, show that the useful work done per second

$$= \frac{w}{g} A u \, (v_1 - u)^2 \, (1 + \cos \beta)$$

A Pelton wheel of 2 ft. diameter makes 822 revolutions per minute under a pressure head of 200 lbs. per sq. inch, the delivery of water being 100 cub. ft. per minute. Find the total H.P., assuming that the buckets are so formed that the water is returned parallel to its original direction. If the actual H.P. is 70.3, what is the efficiency ?

3. 24 cub. ft. of water enter the buckets of a 36 ft breast wheel, the total fall being 11¼ ft. At the point of entrance the direction of the water makes an angle of 30° with the periphery and also $2v_1 = 5u24$ f/s. Find the mechanical effect of the wheel and the position of the lip of the sluice through which the water passes to the wheel.

Also, if the depth of the shrouding is 1 ft. and the buckets are only half-filled, find the width of the wheel.

The axle bearings are 6 ins. in diameter. Taking the co-efficient of friction to be .008, how much power is absorbed by frictional resistance, assuming the weight of the wheel and contents to be 30,000 lbs ?

4. Show how to determine the mechanical effect of an over-shot wheel.

5. An over-shot wheel of 32 ft. diameter, revolves with an angular velocity ω. Show that the angle between the horizontal and the water surface in a bucket at 90° from the summit of the wheel is equal to

$$\tan^{-1} \frac{\omega^2}{2}$$

6. Write down the equations which govern the design of a reaction turbine, and show how these equations are modified in the case of an impulse turbine.

24

7. A radial impulse flow turbine, of 3½ ft. external diameter, and 3 ft. internal diameter, passes 100 cub. ft. of water per second, under an effective head of 625 ft. At entrance the direction of the water makes an angle of 30° with the periphery. If $u_2 = V_2$, find the efficiency, the number of revolutions per minute, the direction and magnitude of the velocity of the water when it leaves the turbine, (1) if the depths of the inlet and outlet surfaces are equal, (2) if the inlet and outlet areas are equal.

8. An axial flow reaction turbine of 7 ft. mean diameter, passes 198 cub. ft. of water per second under a total head of 13.5 ft., the depth of the wheel being 1 ft. At the inlet surface the vane lip is vertical and the water leaves the wheel vertically. If the inlet width of the wheel is 1 ft. and the outlet width 1¼ ft., find the direction in which the water enters the wheel, the direction of the lip at outlet, the revolutions per minute, the H.P. of the turbine and its efficiency.

9. A centrifugal pump with a 21 in. fan, pumps $110\sqrt{3}$ cub. ft. per second to a height of 31¼ ft. The outlet lip makes an angle of 60° with the periphery. The depth of the fan is 6 ins. Find the peripheral speed, the H.P. and the velocity of the pump.
Also find the loss of head due to frictional resistance.

10. Show that if the water in a stream is flowing steadily at a point with a velocity v along a path which, at the point, has a radius of curvature r, the variation of pressure in the direction of r is given by

$$\frac{dp}{dr} = \frac{w\,v^2}{gr}$$

and find the law of variation of pressure in a free vortex. Explain how the existence of a free spiral vortex affects the efficiency of a centrifugal pump.

B.A. Sc. EXAMINATIONS.
HYDRAULIC LABORATORY WORK.
Thursday, March 24th :—

Examiners, ... { Henry T. Bovey, LL.D. M. Inst. C.E.
{ Richard S. Lea, M.A.E.

(N.B.) It is most important that the answers to the following questions should be illustrated by sketches neatly and accurately drawn.

Describe the apparatus required, the mode of procedure and the results obtained in the determination of

1. The co-efficient of discharge for a sharp-edged orifice.

2. The resistance due to angles and bends in a pipe.

3 The efficiency of a turbine or a Pelton wheel.

SECOND YEAR.

SURVEYING (*First Paper.*)

THURSDAY, APRIL 7TH :— 9 TO 12 A. M.

Examiners, ... $\left\{ \begin{array}{l} \text{C. H. McLeod, MaE.} \\ \text{J. G. G. Kerry, MaE.} \end{array} \right.$

1. Describe briefly the Locke and Wrede hand levels, mentioning the principles upon which they depend for their operation, and explain how they can be adjusted.

2. Discuss the variations and changes in the pointing of a compass needle, mentioning the precautions taken in ordinary practice to prevent any discrepancy arising from these changes, and explain the use of the declination arc ?

3. Work out formulæ for calculating the horizontal distance from a transit to a rod much below it, vertical angles being measured to two points on the rod ?

4. Write out in the long form the set of level notes from which the cross sections on the board were taken. The elevation of the B. M. at starting is 109.40. The grade height at Station 1 is 105.00 and the grade is falling at a rate of 1.30 per 100. The rod used was 14.0 ft. long.

5. Examine the adjustments of the Y level, and state in what direction, if at all, the adjustable parts must be moved to put the instrument into adjustment?

6. Reduce the following set of stadia notes and plot the survey to a scale of 100 ft. = 1 in., marking the elevation of the ground on each plotted point. Do not omit the small factor in calculating the horizontal and vertical distances. The plotting must be done without a protractor. Bearings increasing from right to left. Stadia constant 117.0. $f + c = 1.4$. Sights taken on 8.0 on rod. Elevation of station = 92.4. Height of instrument = 3.90

Upper Wire.	Lower Wire.	Horizontal Angle	Vertical. Angle.
8.28	7.72	212° 48′	— 16° 52′
8.95	7.05	197° 29′	— 4° 42′
9.01	7.00	180° 30′	+ 4° 14′
8.38	7.63	129° 30′	— 13° 57′
8.60	7.40	105° 43′	— 2° 00′
11.34	4.66	188° 12′	+ 0° 40′

SECOND YEAR.

SURVEYING. (*Second Paper*).

THURSDAY, APRIL 7 :—2 TO 5 P.M.

Examiners...... .... { C. H McLEOD, MA.E.
{ J. G. G. KERRY, MA.E.

1. Correct the following notes for local attraction, and calculate the area enclosed by the survey :

	Back sight.	Foresight.	Distance.
A.		N. 35 E.	
			649 links.
B.	S. 37 W	S. 54¼ E.	
			1415 "
C.	N. 57¼ W	S. 33 W	
			510 '
D.	N. 35½ E.	N. 54½ W	
			584 '
E.	S. 57 E.	S. 28½ W	
			252 '
F.	N. 28 E.	N. 49¾ W	
			873 "
A.	S. 48¼ E.		

2. Find the distance of point on the black board from A and B.

3. Determine the constants of the telescope for stadia work by 3 measurements.

4. Explain the principle of the slide rule, and state how you would determine the position of the decimal point in results obtained by its use. As examples calculate $643 \times \tan 15° 15'$, $7.03 \times \sin 20° 30'$, $.0045 \times \cos 87° 20'$, $\dfrac{765 \times 8.69}{48.3}$

5. Describe the telescope of a transit or level, mentioning at least 5 principal parts, and the exact utility of each in the operation of the instrument.

6. Describe briefly the plane table and its attachments, and explain how you would plot the position of your instrument when commencing a survey to fill in the details of a triangulation survey, the points of which are already plotted on the plane table sheet.

7. How does the method of balancing latitudes and departures for a compass survey differ from the method for a transit survey, and what is the reason for this difference ?

THIRD YEAR.

SURVEYING.

MONDAY, APRIL 11TH :—2 TO 5 P.M.

Examiners, ... { C. H. McLEOD, MA.E.
{ J. G. G. KERRY, MA.E.

1. Mention three methods of connecting underground and surface surveys.

2. Describe the adjustments of the sextant.

3. Explain how to reduce an inclined angle measured with the sextant to the horizontal.

4. It is proposed to connect two points A and B, in a mine by a slope. The following survey was run between them. Calculate the bearing, length and inclination of the proposed slope.

Line.	Bearing.	Vert. Angle.	Distance.
A — I	11°39	+ 4 57	42.27
I — II	267°25	+ 7 41	70.59
II — B	13°52	0 00	23.55

5. Examine the adjustments of the dumpy level, and state what movements, if any, are necessary to bring it into adjustment. Determine the scale value of the level, and calculate what would be the error in a sight 350 ft. long due to lack of adjustment and to the fact that the bubble had moved two divisions from the centre towards the eye end.

· 6. A pole is put in a river, and is so weighted that it floats with the mean velocity of the river. The position of the triangulation points is sketched on the board, and the following observations were taken by two sextants at the pole upon them.

Position.	A B.	B C.
1	88°40'	25°50'
2	81 40	52 00
3	54 10	72 45
4	40 10	73 10

Calculate the mean velocity of the river.

7. Describe three methods of fixing the position of soundings.

8. Write out the notes for a 8° degree with transition ends between two tangents intersecting at an angle of 40°, the instrument to be set up at the beginning of the transition curve, at 150 ft. along it and at the beginning, centre and end of the circular curve.

PRACTICAL ASTRONOMY.

THIRD YEAR.

MONDAY, APRIL 11TH :—9 TO 12 A. M.

Examiners.. { C. H. McLEOD, MA E.
{ J. G. G. KERRY, MA.E.

· 1. Define sidereal, mean solar, apparent solar and standard time, and give the time corresponding to noon standard time in Montreal to-day in each of the three first mentioned.·

2. Describe three methods of determining the astronomical meridian, mentioning all the instruments used and outlining the several methods of reduction.

3. The following observation was made on the sun on February 5th, 1898, in latitude 45° 30′: At 3h 13m 14s standard time the altitude was 17° 14′ 00″. Calculate the error of the watch.

4. On March 17, 1898, μ Ursa Majoris (p. 398) crossed the prime vertical at 8h 22m 50s sidereal time. Calculate the latitude of the place, neglecting the effect of refraction.

5. α Bootis (p. 414) was observed in latitude 48° 56′ to-day at an altitude of 42° 0′. Calculate the azimuth of the star at the time of observation.

6. α Andromeda (p. 356) was observed on the meridian at an altitude of 75° 30′ on Jan. 1st, 1898. Find the latitude of the place of observation.

7. Explain the effect of small errors in (a) azimuth, (b) level, (c) collimation in the astronomical transit in the meridian. Suppose the error in each case to be 1s, what will be the effect upon the time of passage of a star in declination 65° in latitude 45° N ?

8. What are the equatorial intervals of an astronomical transit, and how are they determined ?

NOTE.—Architectural students will omit questions 7 and 8.

B.A. Sc. EXAMINATIONS.

GEODESY AND PRACTICAL ASTRONOMY (*First Paper*).

JANUARY 14TH.

Examiner,.. C. H. McLEOD , MA.E.

1. Obtain the necessary formulæ and show how to measure eccentricity in a circle having two microscopes.

2. Show by a sketch, marking the directions of the rays, the arrangement of a repeating reflecting circle to measure angles of more than 140° and explain its use.

3. Show that, $a = T' + \Delta\ T' + m + n\ \tan\delta + c\ \sec\delta$, in the use of a transit instrument in the meridian where $m = b\ \cos\phi + a\ \sin\phi$, and $n = b\ \sin\varphi - a\ \cos\varphi$.

4. Explain fully three methods of measuring the collimation error of an astronomical transit.

B.A. Sc. EXAMINATIONS

GEODESY AND PRACTICAL ASTRONOMY (Second Paper.) ·

WEDNESDAY, APRIL 6TH :—9 TO 12 A. M.

Examiners .... { C. H. McLEOD, MA.E.
{ J. G. G. KERRY, MA.E.

1. Determine (*a*) the wire intervals, (*b*) the error in collimation of the middle wire of the alt-azimuth.

2. Explain fully the adjustment of a quadrilateral in a triangulation survey.

3. The difference of longitude between stations A and B was determined with a probable error of 0.012 sec., and between B and C with a probable error of 0.020 sec. What is the probable error of the difference A C ?

4. Describe briefly the Colby base line apparatus. (*a*) Describe a base measuring apparatus in use at the present time.

5. Obtain a formula for the determination of differences of elevation from simultaneous reciprocal observations of angles of altitude. (*a*) How are such observations applied to the determination of the value of refraction ?

6. Compare the methods of precise levelling with those of ordinary engineering levelling, and point out the methods adopted in the former to obviate errors and improve the accuracy of the work.

7. The following observations for time were made with an astronomical transit. Find the clock-error. Inclination of axis $+0s$ .20.

	LAMP WEST.			LAMP EAST.		
A	0.71	0.06	2.34	0 95	0.48	0.63
B	0.70	1.36	2.80	2.40	0.94	0.78
C	1.00	1.36	4.46	2 57	1.05	1 00
T	23.*m* 41*s* .49	09*s* .70	22*s* .30	08*s* .31	18*s* .06	04*s* .13
a	21.43 30	09.13	12 84	03.61	19.01	05.60

THIRD YEAR.

MAP CONSTRUCTION AND PERSPECTIVE.

THURSDAY, APRIL 7TH:—9 TO 12 A.M.

Examiners,............... .... { C. H. McLEOD, Ma.E.
{ J. G. G. KERRY, MA.E.

1. Determine the bearings and vertical angles to the points in the perspective shown on the black board. The distance of the eye from the picture plane was 10 inches and the bearing of the centre line of sight N. 60 E.

2. The points in Ques. 1 are on the edge of a lake whose elevation is 553.0. The elevation of the instrument is 733.0. Draw a plan of the lake on a scale of 100 ft. to 1 in. by direct inverse perspective methods.

3. Draw the perspective of a pyramid with an isosceles triangle of 2″ side and 1″ base for base, and with its apex 4′ above the centre of gravity of the base. Place the base horizontal, and 1″ above the ground plane and with the intersection of its equal sides 3″ to the right of the principal plane and ½″ behind the picture plane ; one side of the base makes an angle of 60° with the picture plane. The eye is 10″ away from the picture plane and 3″ above the ground plane.

4. Draw the perspective of the shadow cast by the above object on the horizontal plane when the projections of the rays make angles of 60 and 30 with xy.

5. The sun was observed in lat. 45.30, when its altitude was 15°00′ and its declination 21°50′; determine its azimuth.

6. Describe the draughting of meridians and parallels on maps by Bonne and Polyconic projections, and show how co-ordinates may be calculated for these projections taking the earth as a sphere.

7. Identify and mention the merits and fault of the projections by which the maps on the desk are drawn.

NOTE :—Architectural students will omit questions 6 and 7.

THIRD YEAR.

ELECTRICAL ENGINEERING.

TUESDAY, APRIL 5TH :—MORNING, 9 TO 12.

Examiner......... ....C. A. CARUS-WILSON, M. A., M..INST. E. E.

1. Given a calibrating coil 8 inches mean diameter, 1 square inch section, with 700 magnetizing turns, and 400 turns on the search coil. Also a

galvanometer which gives one degree of deflection when 1,080 lines are reversed through one turn. Find the deflection when 3 amperes is reversed ' in the calibrating coil.

2. An iron rod, 1.32 square cms. section, is tested in a yoke which has 960 magnetizing turns and 10 search turns. The clear length of the rod inside is 30 cms. Find the permeability when 0.7 amperes reversed gives 198 degrees deflection in the galvanometer of question 1.

3. A rod of magnetic quality represented in the B. & H. diagram supplied to you is tested in the yoke of question 2. Find the deflection on the galvanometer of question 1 when 0.5 ampere is reversed in the main coil.

4. An iron ring, quality as in question 3, has a mean diameter of 7 nches, a section of 0.75 square inches, with 500 magnetizing turns. Find the current required to give 72,600 lines.

5. Same ring as in question 4. Find how many lines will be produced by a current of 4.2 amperes.

· 6· Same ring as in question 4. If a single gap of 0.15 cms. is cut in the ring, find how many lines will be produced by a current of 6 amperes.

7. Same ring as in question 4. If a single gap of 0.1 cms. is cut in the ring, find the current required to produce 68,700 lines.

8. Same ring as in question 4. Two search turns are wound round the ring and connected to the galvanometer of question 1. A certain current reversed gave 135 degrees deflection, but when a single gap was cut in the ring, the same current reversed gave only 81 degrees. Find the width of the gap in centimetres.

9. Same ring as in question 4. The ring is cut in two parts across a diameter but closed up so that there is no air gap. Find the current required to hold the two halves together with a force of 146 pounds.

B.A.Sc. EXAMINATIONS.

ELECTRICAL ENGINEERING.

SATURDAY, APRIL 9TH:—MORNING, 9 TO 12.

Examiner,..............................C. A. CARUS-WILSON, M.A., M. INST. E.E.

·1· Find the self-induction in milhenries of a single ring of copper wire 18 inches mean diameter and 0.5 inches thick.

2. A non-inductive load is supplied through one mile of double leads 18 inches apart, 0.32 inches thick, the resistance of the complete length of leads being 2.62 ohms. Find the drop in the leads for a current of 12.2 amperes and a frequency of 92.

3. The magnets of a dynamo are wound with 4,200 turns. When connected to a line of 125 volts tension, 0.632 of the final current is reached in 6.3 seconds. Find the number of lines through the cores, assuming the self-induction to r main constant.

4. What must be the self-induction of a circuit having a resistance of 4 ohms so that when placed on a line of 100 volts tension and frequency 120, the current shall be 9 amperes ?

5. A load with self-induction of 0.0015 henries is supplied through a line of self-induction of 0.0036 henries and resistance 0.46 ohms. Find the tension at the generator end required to give 50 volts at the load when the current is 32 amperes and the frequency 60.

6. A circular wooden ring, 6 inches mean diameter, 1 sq. inch in section is wound with 900 primary and 800 secondary turns. An alternating current of 4.2 amperes, frequency 90, is passed through the primary. Find the reading on a voltmeter connected to the secondary.

7. The open secondary loss on a transformer is 64 watts. The resistance of the primary and secondary windings are 14 and 0 2 ohms respectively. The ratio of the windings is ten to one. Find the total loss for 20 amperes in the secondary.

8. A wattmeter being tested on a transformer reads 42 watts. The true watts is 39, and the product of the amperes and the volts is 61. The shunt resistance of the wattmeter is 400 ohms, find its self-induction. The frequency is 89.

9. The iron circuit of a transformer is 75 sq. cms in section and 42 cms long. There are 960 turns on the primary. If the permeability is 1900, the frequency 60, and the primary volts 1000, find the measured current required to make up the hysteresis loss.

B.A.Sc. EXAMINATIONS.

ELECTRICAL ENGINEERING.

WEDNESDAY, APRIL 6TH : —MORNING, 9 TO 12.

Examiner, ... C. A. CARUS-WILSON, M.A., M.INST.E.E.

1. A motor generator runs at 550 revolutions per minute on a tension of 588 volts The current in the motor is 64 amperes, and in the generator 280. The motor has $R = 0.175$ ohms, and M five times that of the generator. Find the total torque losses in the two machines.

2. A motor is being tested by Hopkinson's method. The total mechanical out-put is 45 horse-power when running at 900 revolutions per minute on a tension of 125 volts. The resistances of the motor and of the generator used in the test are each equal to 0.015 ohms. The torque in-put measured on the belt is 600 inch-pounds. What is the torque loss in the motor ?

3. A car weighing 40,000 pounds is driven by two bipolar motors in parallel at 14 miles an hour up a grade of 1 in 15 The total frictional resistance is 10 pounds per 1,000. E = 500 volts. R = 1.0 ohm per motor. v = 5. d = 33 inches. There are 520 surface conductors, and the area of each polar gap is 967 sq. cms. Find the magnetisation in the gap in lines per sq. cm.

4. A crane has to lift a weight of 5 tons through 22 feet from rest. M is constant and equal to 16.4. R = 1.3 ohms. d = 36 inches. v = 65. The friction amounts to 380 inch-pounds of torque on the motor shaft. E = 225 volts. Find the time required to cover the given distance if the maximum current is limited to 160 amperes. •

5. An elevator is driven by a motor which is continually running, and whose motion is communicated to the chain drum by means of a clutch coupling. Find the weight of a fly-wheel of radius of gyration 6 inches that must be placed on the motor shaft, so that on connecting the clutch the current may not exceed 50 amperes, when a weight of 2 tons is being started from rest. M = 18 and is constant. R = 0.15 ohms. v = 95 d = 24 inches. E = 120 volts. The torque due to friction is 254 inch-pounds on the motor shaft and may be taken as constant throughout.

6. A train weighing 120 tons has to be started from rest and cover 2,500 feet in 90 seconds. E = 500 volts. v = 1. d'= 42 inches. The drop at full speed is to be 10 volts. The whole frictional resistance is 10 pounds per 1,000. The locomotive has four motors, started 2 in parallel and thrown over to 4 in parallel for full-speed. Find the maximum current from the line required to start if M remains constant.

7. The armature of a motor with an attached fly-wheel weighs 1,500 pounds, the radius of gyration being 9.2 inches. If the motor is switched on to a line of 100 volts tension and left to run by itself, how many revolutions will it make in two minutes ? M = 8.1, and is constant. R = 2.4 ohms. The frictional resistance is 280 inch-pounds.

8. A train weighing 40 tons is to be hauled by two motors with constant M, series-parallel control. E = 500 volts. v = 3. d = 33 inches. The drop at full speed is to be 5 volts. The total frictional resistance is 700 pounds per motor. The mechanical efficiency is 87 per cent. The train has to cover 3,000 feet in 85 seconds. Find the watt-hours per ton-mile.

9 The opening span of the Tower Bridge consists of two leaves rotating in a vertical plane. Each leaf weighs 1,070 tons, is perfectly balanced, and has a radius of gyration of 40 feet. The complete arc of rotation is 82 degrees, and has to be made in 90 seconds. The brakes can stop the motion in 12 degrees and 20 seconds. The frictional resistance is 200 inch-pounds of torque per ton on the main bearings. Motion is derived from a motor with a velocity ratio of 360. The drop at full speed is to be 4 volts. $E = 100$ volts. Find the induction factor of the motor, which is to be constant, and the maximum current.

B.A.Sc. EXAMINATIONS.

ELECTRICAL ENGINEERING.

WEDNESDAY, APRIL 13TH :—MORNING, 9 TO 1.

Examiner, ...L. A. HERDT, B.A.Sc., E.E.

1. Define the terms : Ampere, Volt, Ohm. Explain the relation existing between them.

2. Describe briefly the fundamental principles underlying the working of dynamo electric machines.
   Sketch the magnetic circuit of a two-pole dynamo.

3. What is meant by Self-Exciting dynamos ?
   Describe two ways in which machines are made to self-excite.

4. Give and describe the two distinct systems for the distribution of electrical energy, their respective use, advantages and disadvantages.

5. An electrical road, 24 miles in length, single track, is divided up in three sections. There is to be a 10-minute service, average speed of cars 12 miles per hour, average current per car 25 amperes, line volts 550, with a total drop in trolley wire and feeders of 15 per cent.
   Ascertain size of trolley wire and feeders ; station situated in the middle of the road.

6. A generator has to feed 400 lights of 16 c.p. at a pressure of 110 volts, the centre of distribution of the system is 475 ft. distant from the station, find the size of the feeders. Maximum drop allowed 5 per cent. Lamps rated at 3 watts per candle power.

7. Suppose the same number of lamps were placed on the three wire system, the middle wire being made half the size of the other. All conditions being the same as in question 6, compare the actual weights of copper in the two installations.

8. 500 H. P. of electrical energy is to be transmitted a distance of 5 miles and utilized for lighting purposes. The generators are wound for 2,000 volts, the pressure on the line is to be raised to 12,000 volts, the pressure at the lamps 100 volts. Show how this can be done, and calculate the difference in the size of the feeders used if the 2,000 volts pressure had been utilized. 10 per cent. drop allowed.

9. A drum wound alternator has 24 poles alternately N. and S., the machine runs at 900 revs. per min. What is the frequency? Show on the polar ring the waves of E. M. F.

10. The network of a direct current system is to be tested for insulation, the negative side of the mains is known to be grounded.

(a) Measure the resistance of the fault, a voltmeter and resistance box being given.

(b) Localize the fault approximately.

11. How would you protect the motors in a car from a lightning discharge, and explain the working of such a device?

All candidates are expected to answer the first 8 questions.

Electrical students are at liberty to select 6 questions of the first 8, but must answer questions 9, 10 and 11.

B.A.Sc. EXAMINATIONS.

ELECTRICAL ENGINEERING.

THURSDAY, APRIL 14TH :—MORNING, 9 TO 1.

Examiner, ... C. A. CARUS-WILSON, M A., M.INST.E.E.

A train weighing 145 tons (2240 lbs.) is driven by a locomotive equipped with 4 motors started 2 in parallel and 2 in series. The tension on the line is 500 volts. The maximum current which is to be kept constant as long as possible is 300 amperes per motor. The resistance of the motors is .0565 ohms each. The car wheels are 42 inches in diameter, no gearing used. The friction is equal to 15 lbs. per 2000 lbs. horizontally. Mechanical efficiency = 95 p.c. Construct a curve of acceleration from the given Induction Curve and find the distance covered in 70 seconds. Scale one inch = 5 feet per second and 10 seconds.

B.A.Sc. EXAMINATIONS.

MECHANICAL ENGINEERING. LABORATORY WORK.

MONDAY, APRIL 11TH :—MORNING, 9 TO 12.

Examiners, ... { J. T. NICOLSON, B.Sc.
R. J. DURLEY, B.Sc.
H. M. JAQUAYS, B.A.Sc.

(Not more than eight.)

1. Give an account of the experiments you made and the results you obtained with regard to the slipping of a belt on a fixed pulley.

2. Describe how you would calibrate a Thurston oil-tester.

3. Explain how you would allow for loss by radiation in a calorimetric experiment to determine the heat value of a sample of coal.

4. In the experiment of last question (made with a Bryan Donkin calorimeter), you use 0.003 lb. of coal and 7 lbs. of water. Let it be assumed that you are liable to make an error in the weighing of the coal of ± 0.00005 lb., and of the water of ± 0.002 lb. In the thermometer readings you may make an error of $\frac{1}{40}°$ F. In a coal whose heat value works out 14,000 T.U.F., what is the greatest possible error you could have in the result?

Find the proportion of weight of water to coal which will give a result least liable to error.

5. Make out a list of headings of sheets and of columns for observations to be taken on the trial of either

(a) Such an engine as the large one at the M. S. Ry. Co.'s Power-house.

(b) A steam boiler of any type.

6. Sketch and dimension an apparatus for weighing the jacket drain from the L. P. cylinder of a 3,000 H.P. engine which uses 16.5 lbs. of steam per I.H.P. per hour. The L.P. jacket uses 5 p.c. of the whole feed ; the pressure being 120 lbs. by gauge. You may take it that 5 thermal units can be transmitted across each square foot of pipe surface per minute per degree difference of temperature of warm water on one side and cold water on the other.

7. On the indicator card supplied, show dotted the cards and atmos-pheric lines you would get :—

(a) If the pencil pressure were too heavy.

(b) If there were a sixteenth of an inch of slack in the ball joint between spring and piston in a Crosby indicator (due to slacking back of the piston rod after altering the height of the atmospheric line).

(c) If the barrel spring had very little tension, and the cord were rather long.

8. An engine uses 32,000 lbs. of steam per hour, which all passes through the main separator. The drip from this is weighed and found to be 170 lbs. an hour. The throttling calorimeter fitted between separator and cylinder gives the following average readings :

Pressure in steam pipe,   122 lbs.
Pressure in calorimeter,   39 lbs.
Temperature   "   290 ° F.

What was the quality of steam supplied by the boiler ?

9. Describe the preparations you would make for testing either a gas engine or a hot air engine. Make out the sheets and fill them in (partially) with such results as you would expect to get.
Show how to work out the results.

10. Describe how you would test an indicator spring.

THIRD YEAR.

MACHINE DESIGN.

TUESDAY, APRIL 12TH :—MORNING, 9 TO 12.

Examiners,...... .... { JOHN T. NICOLSON, B·Sc.
{ HOMER M. JAQUAYS, B.A., B.A,Sc.

1. What size would you make the screwed portion of a wrought-iron eyebolt to lift a cylinder cover weighing one ton ?

2. Calculate the diameter of a square-threaded screw for a copying press in which a couple of 3,600 lbs.-ins. gives a load of 32,000 lbs. on the plate·

3. Find the proper thickness of plate for a boiler shell 40 inches in dia., which is to stand a working pressure of 150 lbs. per sq. in. The joint is to be double riveted lap, the rivet diameter being twice the plate thickness. Determine the pitch of the rivets $f_t = 10,000$, $f_s = 8,000$.

4. A wrought iron stay to carry 65,000 lbs. is to be cottered into a casting by means of a steel cotter whose thickness is one quarter of its depth. Take $f_t = 10,000$ for W. I., 13,000 for steel. $f_s = 8,000$ and 10,000 resp. Calculate the dimensions of stay and cotter. Give figured sketch.

5. Design an ordinary flange coupling for a three inch W. I. shaft. You may make the boss of the coupling 7 ins. dia. and put in 5 bolts, whose sate shearing strength is the same as that of the shaft. Sketch the coupling carefully, and put in as many dimensions as you can·

6. Find the size of the journals of a fly-wheel shaft, if the bearing pressure allowable is 250 lbs. The wheel weighs 20 tons ; and the bearings are 10 feet apart. Find the size of the shaft near the fly-wheel, which is two ft. nearer one bearing than the other· $f_t = 11,000$.

7. Give Poncelet's geometrical proof that, when an isotropic material is subjected simultaneously to a tensile strain ε and to a shear strain γ, the greatest tensional strain in the body is

$$E_{\max} = \frac{3'}{8\varepsilon} + \sqrt{\left(\frac{5'}{8\varepsilon}\right)^2 + \left(\frac{1'}{2\gamma}\right)^2}$$

8. Apply the formula of last question to find the stress due to the maximum strain in a rivet which is subjected to a tensile stress of 9,000 and a shear stress of 8,000 lbs. per sq. in., at one and the same time.

B.A.Sc. EXAMINATIONS.

MACHINE DESIGN. I.

SATURDAY, APRIL 16TH :—MORNING, 9 TO 12.

Examiner,.................................R. J. DURLEY, B.Sc., Assoc. M.INST. C.E

(Not more than six questions are to be attempted. Show all calculations for determining dimensions. Sketches should be freehand and in fair proportion. Figures after the questions give the proportional marks assigned to each.)

1. A travelling crane is to lift a load of 50,000 lbs. at 14 feet per minute, the load being attached to a hook block weighing 900 lbs. The hoisting gear is driven by an electric motor, on whose shaft is a worm, gearing with a worm-wheel secured to the hoisting drum. What must be the electrical H.P. of the motor, assuming the following efficiencies :—

Hoisting gear,	0.85
Worm gear (including thrust bearing),	0.60
Motor,	0.91 (15)

2. Sketch and describe a form of fly wheel governor which will alter the throw and angular advance of the eccentric. (15)

3. Sketch a sluice valve suitable for a large water main, naming the materials of which the various parts should be made. (15)

4. Two mild steel rods of rectangular section $7' \times 1'$ are to be connected by a butt joint having a cover plate on each side. Design and sketch the joint, and estimate its efficiency. (20)

5. A wrought iron shaft transmits 80 H.P. at 100 revolutions per minute. Design and sketch one half of a cast iron flange coupling for the shaft. (20)

6. Design a helical spring of round steel to satisfy the following conditions :—

Load to compress spring 1 inch = 400 lbs.
Mean diameter of coil = 3 inches.
Length uncompressed = 8 inches.

Allow a working stress of 20,000 lbs. per square inch, and take G = 12,000,000. Find the size of steel, the number of free coils, and the capable length. (20)

7. Find an expression for the tension at the end of a stretched wire or rope in terms of the sag, weight of unit length, and span; the ends of span being at the same level. (20)

8. Show that the relative displacement of the main and expansion valves in a Meyer gear may be represented by a pair of Zeuner valve circles. (25)

9. Deduce Kirsch's expression

$$n = 188 \ \sqrt{\frac{P}{W}}$$

for the critical number of revolutions per minute of a long vertical shaft having a bearing at each end. (30)

B.A Sc. EXAMINATIONS.

MACHINE DESIGN. II.

TUESDAY, APRIL 19TH :—MORNING, 9 TO 2.

Examiner,...... ....R. J. DURLEY, B.Sc., Assoc. M. Inst. C.E.

Instructions.—All necessary calculations are to be made in full on the foolscap paper provided, and must be handed in with the drawings, which are to be in pencil, and fully dimensioned. Mathematical tables, slide rules, note-books and books of reference may be used. Ten per cent. marks will be given for neatness and accuracy of drawing.

Design a worm and worm-wheel from the following data .
H.P. transmitted, 20.
Revolutions of worm shaft, 1,000 per minute.
    "   of worm-wheel, 66.6   "
Diameter of pitch circle of } 14¾ inches.
    worm wheel,   }

25

Diameter of worm outside
    thread,   5 inches.
Diameter of worm shaft at
    bearings.   ·   1⅜ inches.
Thickness of thread at root,   0.66 pitch of teeth of wheel.
    "   "   tip   0.33   "   "
Depth _   "   0.66   "   "
The efficiency of the gear may be taken as 0.6.

The worm is cast steel, and the profile of its thread is bounded by straight lines. The thread is double, and right handed. The worm wheel is phosphor bronze, the teeth being cast to shape as nearly as possible, and trimmed up by a hob or cutter.

The worm shaft and wheel shaft are each of mild steel :

Find (1) Number of teeth in worm wheel.

(2) Pitch   "   "   "

(3)   "   thread of worm.

(4) Thrust on worm shaft.

(5) Width of face of worm wheel (allow 6,500 lbs. per square inch working stress in metal of teeth).

(6) Diameter of worm wheel shaft.

Draw (full size) :—

(1) A section showing the profile of the worm and wheel on the me_dian plane of the latter.

(2) A section of the worm and half the wheel by a plane normal to the worm axis and passing through the wheel axis.

(3) Two sections of the wheel teeth by planes parallel to the median plane but at distances of ½ ″ and 1″ from it respectively.

(4) A detail showing how the worm is secured to its shaft.

Calculate the T. M. on the worm-shaft and the stress in it due (1) to thrust, (2) to T. M.

B. A. Sc. EXAMINATIONS.

MACHINE DESIGN.

Electrical Engineering Students only.

SATURDAY, DECEMBER 18TH :—9 TO 12.

Examiner,........... .... .R. J. DURLEY, B. Sc., A.M. INST. C.E.

Sketches should be freehand, clear, and in fair proportion, but need not be to scale. Figures after the questions give the proportional marks assigned to each. Any eight questions may be attempted.

1. Design a sunk key for securing a steel pulley (length of boss 4") to a steel shaft $2\frac{1}{4}$" diameter. The allowable shearing stress may be taken as $\frac{3}{4}$, and the crushing stress twice the tensile stress. (10)

2. A bolt of 1" diameter has a head of square cross section through which a cotter passes. Determine the dimensions of the head and cotter-hole, taking stresses as in question (1). (15)

3. The coupling flange on a steel shaft 14" diameter has eight steel bolts, the diameter of pitch circle being 23". Find the diameter of the bolts, assuming the stress to be equally distributed among them. (10)

4. Sketch and describe the construction of either (*a*) the bearing used in Parson's steam turbine or (*b*) a self-lubricating bearing. (20)

5. Sketch the form of pulley rim adopted for transmitting power by means of (*a*) hemp ropes and (*b*) wire ropes. State the circumstances under which each method of transmission is generally employed. (20)

6. With involute wheel teeth show how the least possible number of teeth in a wheel is fixed by the obliquity of the path of contact. The obliquity being $14\frac{1}{2}$°, find the least number of teeth, given that cos 75° 30' = 0.251. What are the advantages and disadvantages of involute teeth? (20)

7. Find an expression for the work wasted in overcoming the stiffness of a pitch chain, and hence show how the efficiency is affected by an increase in the diameter of the sprocket wheels, other conditions remaining the same. (25)

8. A dynamo is driven by a belt transmitting 800 H. P. from an engine flywheel 22 feet diameter running at 72 revolutions per minute. The belt is 48" wide and $\frac{1}{4}$" thick, and embraces an angle of 150° on the dynamo pulley. Neglecting the effect of centrifugal force, find the working stress on the leather. Take $\mu = 0.3$ and $\iota = 2.718$. (25)

9. A hard copper telephone wire weighing 200 lbs. per mile (diameter 0.1105 inch) has a sag of 2 feet on a span of 240 feet. Find the maximum stress on the copper (1) before and (2) during the application of a horizontal wind pressure of 10 lbs. per square foot of projected surface of wire.   (30)

10. The conductors of an armature are 132 copper bars, 0.2″ deep, 0.1″ thick, and 15″ long, the diameter (outside) of armature being 12″, and the revolutions 680 per minute. Find the number of turns of binding wire (.025 inch diameter) required, if it is wound on with an initial tension of 3 lbs., allowing a stress of 12,000 lbs. per square inch, and neglecting the weight of the insulation of the conductors. Copper weighs 0.31 lbs. per cubic inch.   (30)

11. The crankshaft of a direct driven generator of 4,000 H.P. is 22 feet long over all and is carried by two bearings 16′—4″ apart centre to centre. At 4′—4″ from the centre of one bearing is a flywheel weighing 200,000 lbs. and at 8′—2″ from the same point is an armature weighing 70,000 lbs. The twisting moment on the shaft is 4,500,000 inch—lbs., the maximum stress 6,000 lbs. per square inch, and the pressure on the bearings 150 lbs. per square inch of projected area. Find the diameter of the shaft (supposing it uniform), neglecting the stress due to its own weight. Also find the length of bearings if the journals are $22\frac{1}{2}$″ diameter. The material of the shaft weighs 0.29 lbs. per cubic inch.   (35)

THIRD YEAR.

THERMODYNAMICS.

Examiner. ....JOHN T. NICOLSON. B.Sc.

(*Not more than eight.*)

1. Prove that $K_v = K_p - c$.

2. Show that the equation to the curve of adiabatic expansion of a perfeet gas is PV^γ = constant.

3. Find the ratio of the final (r_2) to the initial temperature (r_1) when air is compressed adiabatically from pressure P_1 to pressure P_2.

Air at 60° F is compressed from a pressure of 14.7 lbs. to 100 lbs. absolute per square inch. The equation to the compression curve being $PV^{1.2}$ = constant; find the final temperature.

4. What are the three conditions of reversibility in a heat engine ?

5. Describe the cycle of a Stirling's regenerative air-engine ; and deduce the efficiency.

Sketch any form of the engine with explanations.

6. Make a tabular statement of the various quantities of heat usually distinguished in the heating and evaporating of water. Give an approximate formula for each.

7. The volume of one pound of dry saturated steam at 230 lbs. pressure absolute is two cubic feet, find the volume of one pound of wet steam (dryness fraction 0.75) at the same pressure (a) exactly, (b) approximately.

8. Enumerate the improvements effected on the steam engine by Watt.

9. An engine uses steam of pressure P_1, volume per pound V, non-expansively, and rejects it at a pressure P_2. Find the efficiency. What is its numerical value when P_1 is 70 ; P_2 is 18 ; and V_1 is 6.11.

10 How nearly may the cycle of a steam engine be made to approach reversibility ? Calculate the efficiency of such an (ideal) engine.

B. A. Sc. EXAMINATIONS.

THERMODYNAMICS.

Thursday, April 21st :—Morning, 9 to 12.

Examiner,.................. ....J. T. Nicolson, B., Sc.

(*Not more than eight in all.*)

[*Mechanical students may not attempt questions* (2), (5), (6) *or* (10).]

1. Find the work done when fluid expands from the state p, and v, to the state p_2 and v_2, the law of expansion being $pv^n =$ a constant. When $n=1$ the formula is indeterminate ; find a determinate solution for this case ; and give a physical example in which this case is met with.

2. What is a Saturation Curve ? Show how it may be used on an indicator diagram to indicate the dryness during expansion.

3. How nearly may the cycle of a steam engine be made to approach reversibility? Calculate the efficiency of such an ideal engine.

4. "Of a given quantity of heat, at a given temperature, only a certain portion, depending on the available fall of temperature, can be

converted into work." State generally the course of reasoning on which this statement depends.

5. Sketch any form of steam boiler you are acquainted with.

6. Define the following terms as applied to steam, and give formulæ for them: Total heat, latent heat, external work of evaporation, total internal heat, heat of formation.

7. What happens when saturated steam is compressed at constant temperature ?

8. Describe, with a sketch and indicator diagram, the action of a refrigerating machine using the vapour of a liquid.

9. In what respects do actual cards from steam engines differ from those indicated in question (3) ? Give the causes of the variations.

10. Find the size of cylinder required in a double acting steam engine working at 75 revolutions with 5 ft. stroke to develop 1200 horse power. The boiler pressure is 125 lbs ; the back pressure 10 lbs (both by gauge) ; the cut off is at one-third of the stroke.

11. Given a gas engine card, show how to calculate the temperatures at the various points of the cycle.

12. The volume of one pound of dry steam at 230 lbs. abs. is 2 cub. ft.; find the volume of one pound of wet steam, dryness 0.8.

(Mechanical Engineering and Honours students not less than three.)

13. Calculate the temperature which we ought to get upon the ignition of one cubic foot of coal gas in eight of air, if the calorific value of the gas is 650 thermal units Fahr. per cubic foot. Take the density of coal gas 0.44 that of air, and the specific heat of the products equal to 0.18. Initial temperature 200° F.

Why does the actual temperature of ignition in a gas engine fall so far below this value ?

14. Find the change of entropy when one pound of steam is heated from 338° F to 398° F at the constant pressure of 115 lbs. absolute.

15. Evaluate the equation giving the dryness of steam expanding adiabatically :

$$\frac{q\,L}{\tau} = \frac{q_1\,L_1}{\tau_1} + \log \varepsilon \frac{\tau_1}{\tau}$$

16. Calculate the efficiency of Joule's air engine, or of a refrigerating machine.

B. A. Sc. EXAMINATIONS.

THERMODYNAMICS.

HONOURS.

THURSDAY, APRIL 21ST :—AFTERNOON, 2 TO 5.

Examiners, ... | H. L. CALLENDAR, M.A., F.R.S.
| J. T. NICOLSON, B. Sc.

(*Not more than six.*)

1. Describe the construction of a temperature entropy chart. Show how curves of constant volume are plotted ; and how, with the assistance of a pressure-temperature curve, the external work of evaporation may be represented.

2. Justify the assumption that the temperature v at any depth x, in a cylinder wall whose surface is exposed to a simple harmonic variation of temperature of semi-range D is :

$$v = De - ^{mx} \cos (\theta - mx)$$

when the crank makes the angle θ with its position at maximum surface temperature

Find the value of m.

3. Find the range at depth $0'' .04$, if the range at surface is $10°$; the speed being 60 revs. per min. Thermal conductivity of cast iron is 3.4 ; density 440 lbs. per cubic foot ; specific heat 0.124.

4. Prove that the heat absorbed per sq. ft. per cycle, in question (2) is $\dfrac{6.36 D}{m}$, where D is the semi-range at the surface.

5. One pound of wet steam, dryness x, latent heat L', is condensed at temperature t' and re-evaporated at t'', in a steam engine cylinder.

Prove that the heat abstracted by the steam from the walls is ·

$$L' (1 - x) - \cdot 3 (t' - t'')$$

Find the values when $x = 0.95$, $L' = 900$,

for $t' - t'' = 100°, 150°, 200°$.

6. Explain how the amount of condensation in a steam engine cylinder attains a limiting value, which it is difficult to exceed, when the wall temperature is the mean of the temperature cycle diagram.

7. Show how you would calculate the weight of steam condensed. per hour on the clearance surfaces of a steam engine from an indicator card and the wall temperatures.

8. State what you know about the law of leakage of steam in slide valves.

9. Describe an experiment to ascertain the rate of condensation of steam on a metal surface, by the use of a thick hollow metal cylinder.

Deduce the law of the distribution of temperature in the metal.

THIRD YEAR.

DYNAMICS OF MACHINERY.

TUESDAY, APRIL 12TH :—MORNING, 9 TO 12.

Examiner,............... ....J T. NICOLSON, B.Sc.

(Not more than eight.)

1. In the direct acting steam engine, find an expression for the crank-effort in terms of the piston load for any angle of the crank.

2. In any form of quick return shaping-machine, find the relation between the force acting on the tool and the force acting tangentially to the crank pin path.

3. Find the ratio of the tractive force to the weight of a train which must cover one mile on the level from start to stop in three minutes. The train resistance is 21 lbs. per ton (independent of speed), and the brake resistance 450 lbs per ton. Find where the brakes must be put on, and the average and maximum speeds.

4. Give Mohr's construction for finding the piston acceleration in the direct acting engine. Prove its correctness.

5. The coefficient of friction of the wheel-tires of a cart upon ice is 0.01. The wheels are 4 ft. in diameter and the axles 3″. Find whether the wheels will turn or slide over the ice, if the coefficient of axle-friction is 0.1. Calculate the tractive force (horizontal) if the cart weighs 1 ton.

6. Enumerate the laws of friction; and state by whom they were respectively determined.

· 7. Find the efficiency of a screw press. The diameter of the screw is $1\frac{1}{4}$″, the pitch of the thread $\frac{3}{8}$″ (square thread); and the coefficient of friction of both screw thread and pivot is 0.1. Neglect guide friction.

8. Find the tension on the high speed belt of a thickness planer, if its velocity is 70 feet per second, and its weight per foot of length is $\frac{1}{4}$ lb. The belt embraces 150° of the smaller pulley, and the coefficient of friction is 0:4. The standing tension was 25 lbs.

9. The initial loads (W_0 and w_0) of a rope-brake are 800 lbs. and 20 lbs. The rope is $\frac{7}{8}''$ dia. and the wheel 5 ft. dia. When the engine runs at 275 revs. under steam the weighing machine balances at 400 lbs. and the spring balance reads 32 lbs. What brake horse power is the engine developing ?

10. In the last question find the weight of cooling water that must be supplied per minute at 60° F, if it is allowed to rise to 120° F. If the thermal conductivity of cast iron is 5.4, and the rim of the brake wheel is 1 ft. wide and $1\frac{1}{2}''$ thick, find the temperature of the rope surface touching the wheel, if the inside of the rim is at 150° F.

B.A.Sc. EXAMINATIONS.

DYNAMICS OF MACHINERY.

TUESDAY, APRIL 5TH:—MORNING, 9 TO 12.

*Examiner..*J. T. NICOLSON, B.Sc.

(*Not more than* 10.)

1. In a Porter governor, each ball weighs 9 lbs. and the load is 80 lbs. The angle which all four arms make with the vertical has its tangent equal to $\frac{1}{2}$ in the lowest, and 1 in the highest position of the balls. Find the controlling forces and the speeds of equilibrium for these two positions, the ball-path radii being then 9 inches and $12\frac{1}{2}$ inches respectively.

2. Show how to draw curves of controlling force in governors after the manner of Hartnell. By their means illustrate *stability, sensitiveness* and *isochronism.* Exhibit also the effect of *friction* and how *powerfulness* is represented.

3. Obtain from first principles the expression $\dfrac{Mr\omega^2}{g}\left(1 \pm \cdot\dfrac{1}{n}\right)$ for the alternating force at the ends of the stroke of a direct acting engine.

4. Give expressions for the alternating force and couple in a Willans engine for any angle of the cranks ; and find where they are a maximum.

5. A horizontal sieve weighing 400 lbs. when full, is shaken by a crank, making 100 turns a minute whose half travel is 3". Balance weights in the form of eccentric discs can only be put on at distances 15" and 12" on each

side of the crank pin centre line. They must clear a wall distant 10′ from the shaft centre. Specify the diameter and thickness of suitable discs

6. In a von Hefner Alteneck transmission dynamometer, you are given W, the weight in the scale pan, α and β the angles the belt makes with the horizontal line of pulley centres ; find the horse-power transmitted if one pulley has a diameter D feet and makes N turns per minute.

7. In the dynamometer of last question, if the roller-frame has a length four times the distance between centres of rollers ; if $\alpha = \beta = 30°$; and the weight in the scale pan is 50 lbs., of which 4 lbs is due to friction of rollers and stiffness of belt over them. Find the percentage error made in estimating the horse-power received by the driven pulley on the assumption that the whole scale pan weight is the measure of the power.

8. An elevator weighs 8,000 lbs. and its balance weight 7,000 lbs. The attached rope drums are equivalent to one of 4 feet diameter, 1,500 lbs. weight, and radius of gyration 2 feet. It free to descend, find the speed it will have attained after five seconds. How would you allow for friction ?

9. How would you find experimentally the radius of gyration of an engine connecting rod.

10. A rocking lever for the valve motion of a Corliss engine has its fixed bearing at its bottom end, and it is actuated by attachment at its middle point to a long eccentric rod driven by an eccentric of half travel r feet rotating with angular velocity ω. The lever is kinetically equivalent to uniform bar of mass m and length l. Prove that Q, the force on the journal due to inertia of the bar at either end of the travel, is

$$ Q = \frac{m \, r \, \omega^2}{6 \, g \, \sqrt{\left(\frac{1}{4} - \frac{r}{l}\right)}}. $$

11. A street car running 10 miles an hour starts down a 10 per cent. gradient under maximum brake resistance, the wheels being just on the point of skidding (coefficient of adhesion $\frac{1}{4}$). How far will it run ?

12. In the last question the car weighs 10 tons ; the length of its wheel base is 7 feet ; and its centre of mass is 5 feet above rail level. Find the loads on the front and back wheels under the conditions specified.

13. A man holds the front wheel of his bicycle in the air (front fork horizontal, say), and spins it at 4 turns per second. He then applies a clockwise couple of 20 foot lbs. to the handle-bar, how will the fork tend to move? The mass of the wheel is 10 lbs., its radius of gyratus 1 ft. If he prevents the axis of the fork from changing its position. find the magnitude and direction of the forces on the bearings, 5″ centre to centre.

B.A.Sc. EXAMINATIONS.

DYNAMICS OF MACHINERY.

HONOURS

AFTERNOON, 2 TO 5.

1. Find the pressure on the inside of the drum of a centrifugal separator, 3 ft. diameter, 2 ft. high, running at 1,000 revolutions per minute. It was two-thirds full of water when at rest.

2. Investigate the cause of " knocking " of the connecting rod on the crank pin in a direct acting steam engine. How does the intensity of the blow vary with the mass of the parts. the amount of the slack, the ratio of connecting rod to crank length, and the effective pressure curve on the piston.

3. Show how to draw speed and distance curves on a time base representing the motion of a train, the law of the variation of the tractive force with speed being given.

Explain carefully how the proper scales are obtained.

Or : Obtain an analytical solution for the case of the resistance varying as the square of the speed.

4. Investigate the magnitude and direction of the forces required to accelerate an engine connecting rod.

5. A street car travelling v ft. per sec. takes a curve of radius r ft. The length of the wheel base being l ft. and the moment of inertia of the car about a vertical axis through its centre of mass being mk^2; find the forces between wheel and rail, neglecting centrifugal force.

B. A. Sc. EXAMINATIONS.

MECHANICAL ENGINEERING.

WEDNESDAY, APRIL 6TH :—MORNING, 9 TO 12.

Examiners................ .... { J. T. NICOLSON, B. Sc.
{ R. J. DURLEY, B. Sc.

(*Not more than six.*)

1. Find the diameter of cylinders and stroke of a condensing compound engine of 3,000 1 H. P. with the following data :—

Revolutions per minute........ 75
Cut off in H. P. cylinder........ .... 0.5 stroke
Referred mean pressure........... .... 40 lbs per sq. in.
Piston speed....... .... 750 ft. per min.
Total rate of expansion...... .... 6.25

2. Explain clearly (with a sketch) how you would draw the ideal combined indicator diagrams for a tandem compound engine, showing how you would calculate the pressures for the different points of the stroke in each cylinder.

3. A Babcock & Wilcox boiler burning 20 lbs. of coal per sq. ft. of grate per hour is to evaporate 2,500 lbs. of water per hour from and at 212°. What must be its grate surface and total heating surface, assuming the following data : —

Heat transmitted to water per sq. ft. of total heating surface
    per hour.... ....   3,500 T. U.
Thermal efficiency of boiler.. ....   0.55
Thermal value of 1 lb. of coal to be used......... ....   13,600 T. U.
Latent heat of steam at 212°........................ ....   966 T. U.

4. Draw carefully the indicator diagrams you would expect from :—
    a. A good air pump on a surface condenser.
    b. A water pump which does not draw in or discharge air, but has an air pocket in the pump chamber.
    c. A water pump with leaky suction valves.
    d. A water pump with leaky discharge valves.

5. Calculate and plot curves of the losses of head between suction well and pump chamber for a pump with the following particulars :—
Plunger 7″ dia. 18″ stroke, making 150 strokes per minute.

Difference of height between plunger bottom and suction well 8 feet ; length of 12″ pipe between well and vacuum vessel, 13 feet ; length of 12″ pipe between vacuum vessel and pump chamber, 3 feet ; clearance coefficient 0.3 ; two square bends between vacuum vessel and pump chamber, one between well and vacuum vessel. The coefficient of resistance through suction valve is to be 3 and for bends 0.2.

Assume an available vacuum of 28 ft. of water below plunger. Suction pipe bell-mouthed, no foot valve.

6. In a single-acting pump : if A is the area of the plunger and S its stroke ; O the area of the water surface in the vacuum vessel ; prove that the fluctuation of level in the vacuum vessel is

$$0.55 \ S \frac{A}{O} \text{ ft.}$$

If the pressure in the vessel is not to vary more than 10 %, what must be its volume relatively to the plunger displacement.

7. Justify the form of Bach's expression for the minimum force which must act on a valve in order to secure prompt closure :.

$$P = 62.4 \ a \frac{u^2}{2g} \left[\left(\frac{d}{4 \, r h} \right)^2 + f \right]$$

8. Make a sketch showing clearly the various plates of which a locomotive boiler is constructed, and describe the ways in which the flat-surfaces are stayed. (Stays need not be shown on the sketch.)

.9. Discuss briefly the causes of internal corrosion in boilers, mentioning the precautions that should be adopted in each case.

10. What are the conditions necessary to ensure smokeless combustion in a boiler furnace?

FIRST YEAR.

DESCRIPTIVE MECHANISM.

WEDNESDAY, APRIL 13TH :—MORNING, 9 TO 12.

Examiner,......... .... R. J. DURLEY, B.Sc., ASSOC.M.INST.C.E.

(Not more than ten questions are to be attempted. Sketches should be freehand, clear, and in good proportion. Figures after the questions denote the proportional marks awarded for each.)

1. Sketch a section through the mouth of a jack plane. What is the purpose of the top iron? (15)

2. In a cutting tool, what is meant by the terms tool-angle, top rake, bottom rake. Why is the tool-angle so much greater in a tool for cutting metal than in one for cutting wood? (12)

3. Describe the action of a milling tool. In machining a metallic surface, what are the advantages or disadvantages of milling as opposed to shaping or planing? (15)

4. Sketch a punch and die for punching iron or steel plates, and explain exactly what occurs in the process of punching. (15)

5. Under what circumstances would you use (a) bolts, (b) studs, (c) screws (d) rivets for fastenings. (12)

6. Sketch a method of jointing together lengths of wrought iron steam or gas pipes. (10)

7. Sketch and describe some arrangement for allowing for expansion in a length of steam pipe. (10)

8. Make a diagrammatic sketch showing the arrangement of either (a) a locomotive boiler or (b) some form of water tube boiler. (20)

9. Name, and describe the uses of, the necessary fittings on a steam boiler. (20)

10. Sketch a form of adjustable bearing for a shaft.   (15)

11. Sketch a longitudinal section througn the cylinder of a steam engine, naming the various parts.   (25)

12. Give a diagrammatic sketch of the arrangement of a surface con-denser for a steam engine.   (20)

13. Explain the mechanism on a locomotive by means of which the direction of motion is reversed.   (25)

14. Give a general explanation of the action of a gas or oil engine. (25)

SECOND YEAR.

KINEMATICS OF MACHINES.

Monday, April 11th:—Morning, 9 to 12.

Examiner,.................R. J. Durley, B.Sc., Assoc.M.Inst.C.E.

(Not more than ten questions may be attempted. Figures after the questions give the proportional marks awarded for each.)

1. Distinguish between a Mechanism and a Structure. Define: Element, Link, Compound Chain, Inversion of a Chain.   (12)

2. Show that any plane motion of a rigid figure is at any instant equivalent to a simple rotation about some axis perpendicular to the plane of motion.   (15)

3. What is a centrode? Show how to draw the centrode of the connecting rod in a direct-acting steam engine relatively to the engine frame.   (15)

4. A stone is thrown vertically upwards with a velocity of 128.8 feet per second. Draw its diagrams of position, velocity and acceleration (to any convenient scales) on a time base.   (15)

5. Show how to find graphically the acceleration of the piston of a direct-acting engine and prove your construction.   (20)

6. Make a sketch showing the arrangement of the common pantagraph, and prove that it copies proportionally.   (15)

7. Sketch the Tchebicheff straight line motion. Is it exact or approximate?   (10)

8 Sketch the ball bearing of a bicycle crank axle. Explain how to find the rate of spinning of the balls.   (20)

9. The end of a slot drill has the form of an equilateral curve triangle. Find by construction what motion must be given to the work in order to drill an approximately square hole. (20)

10. In a pair of spur wheels, having given the profile of the tooth of one wheel, show how to find the shape of tooth of another wheel to work with the given form with uniform velocity ratio, and prove the correctness of your method. (20)

11. The leading screw of a lathe has 3 threads per inch, right handed. Calculate the numbers of teeth of wheels necessary to cut (1) a right hand thread 14 per inch, (2) a left hand thread 5 per inch, and sketch the way in which they are arranged. The change wheels are in a set, rising by five, from 20 to 125 teeth. (15)

12. In an epicyclic reverted train, the fixed wheel (a) has 98 teeth, (b) and (c) have 100 and 101 teeth, and are rigidly connected together, (d) is on the same axis as (a) and has 100 teeth. How many revolutions does (d) make for each revolution of the arm? (15)

13. Make a diagrammatic sketch of the working parts of the "Dake" engine. To what class of mechanisms does it belong kinematically? (15)

14. Distinguish between a click and a ratchet, and give an example of the use of each in some simple mechanism. (10)

B.A.Sc. EXAMINATIONS—(*Civil Engineering.*)

STRUCTURAL DESIGNING.

Examiners, ... { HENRY T. BOVEY, M.A., LL. D.
{ CECIL B. SMITH, MA. E.

Strain Sheets, Calculations, Detail Designs, Bills of Material and Estimates of Cost for

(*a*) Fifty foot Semi-Elliptical Stone Railway and Highway Arches.

(*b*) Wing, "T" and "U" Abutments.

(*c*) Fifty foot Deck Plate Railway Girder.

(*d*) Steel Tower details for Railway Viaduct.

(*e*) Roof Truss for one hundred and ten foot span for train shed.

(*f*) Wooden Trestle.

(*g*) Wooden Home Truss fifty foot Span.

(*h*) Through Pratt Pin-connected Railway Span one hundred and fifty-five feet centres.

SECOND YEAR.

MINING.

WEDNESDAY, APRIL 13TH:—9 A.M.

Examiners...................... · .... { J. B. PORTER, PH.D.
{ J. W. BELL, B.A.Sc

1. Give a classification of ore deposits.

2. Describe a fissure vein, and tell what ores are most likely to be found in one.

3. What is a placer deposit, and what valuable minerals are found in such deposits?

4. How does coal occur, and what is the theory of its formation?

5. What are the six most important minerals or ores which are obtained by mining operations?

6. Where does the gold in a river gravel come from, and what is the common method of getting it?

7. For what purposes are explosives required in mining, and what is the method of their use?

8. How are the minerals obtained by mining removed from the working places to the surface?

9. What are the three most serious kinds of accidents in mines?

10. What are the most common causes of fires in mines, and what means are taken to prevent them and to put them out when they do take place?

11. How is water removed from mines?

12. When ores consist of small particles of valuable mineral dissemina-ted through a comparatively large amount of worthless rock, how are they treated for the extraction of the valuable portion?

THIRD AND FOURTH YEARS.

ORE DRESSING AND METALLURGY.

SATURDAY, APRIL 16TH :—9 A.M.

Examiners, ...   { J. B. PORTER, PH.D.
                                                       { J. W. BELL, B.A.Sc.

ORE DRESSING.

1. What are the purposes of Ore Dressing, and what are the chief phenomena on which its operations are based ?

2. Why is rock sized before separation ; and what are the conditions calling for greater or less care and accuracy in this sizing ?

3. What are (*a*) sizers, (*b*) classifiers, (*c*) separators, (*d*) tables, (*e*) amalgamators, (*f*) crushers ; and name one or more well-known examples of each.

METALLURGY.

4. Define carefully calorific power and calorific intensity.

(*b*) State the calorific powers of several fuels.

(*c*) Deduce the calorific intensity (theoretical) of carbon burning in air, and explain why this theoretical intensity is not realized in practice.

5. Define carefully Elasticity, Malleability and Ductility of Metals.

(*b*) What are Alloys ? Why are some alloys stable and others unstable ?

(*c*) Name some well-known alloys and give their characteristics and approximate composition.

6. What is the usual effect of adding to a metal small quantities of one or more other metals or elements, and give examples.

(*b*) What relation do these effects bear to the proportions of added elements ?

(*c*) What theory or theories are advanced in explanation of these phenomena ?

7. Give a classification of fuels with brief comments stating their origin, use and comparative importance.

8. Describe briefly the manufacture of coke.

9. What is pig iron, and how is it manufactured ?

10. What is regeneration ?

(*b*) Describe briefly the use of regenerators in some metallurgical operation.

11. Name the chief methods of making steel.

(b) Describe briefly one of these methods.

· 12. Under what conditions do ores of copper or lead require roasting, and how is the operation conducted ?

13. What is Matte ? (b) How is it made, and what is done with it ?

14. Describe briefly (from ore to metal) some commercial wet method for extracting copper and silver from an ore containing Quartz, Calcite, Chalcopyrite, Bornite, Pyrite and Silver Sulphides.

15. Describe briefly (from ore to metal) the operations of extracting gold from a quartz ore carrying free gold and gold-bearing sulphides by means of first milling and then tailings treatment by either chlorination or cyaniding.

Assume that the ore runs $\frac{1}{2}$ ounce free gold and $\frac{1}{2}$ oz combined gold, the sulphides being mixed Pyrrhotite and Chalcopyrite.

THIRD YEAR MEN.

Answer 1, 2, 3, 7, 8, 9, 10, 11, and 2 out of 4, 5, and 6.

FOURTH YEAR MEN.

Answer 1, 2, 3, 14 and 15.
      Any 2 of 4, 5 and 6.
      Any 4 of 7, 8, 9, 10 and 11.
      Any 1 of 12 and 13.

———

THIRD YEAR.—(Civil and Mining.)

RAILWAY ENGINEERING.

MONDAY, APRIL 18TH :—Morning, 9 TO 1.

Examiner, ...CECIL B. SMITH, MA.E.

1. Point out distinctive features of the railways of America, as compared with English ones, showing in what ways this has favoured the rapid extension of the former.

2. Discuss the effect which the character and density of population have on the traffic receipts of a railway.

3. Mention leading considerations in the location of Trunk and Branch lines.

4. What are the causes of curve resistance, and about how much does it amount to per degree of curve? What is, therefore, the theoretical equi-

valence of grades and curves, and how much is a grade reduced in prae-
tice on curves ? Why ?

5. Two routes of practically the same length (125 miles) and number of
.feet rise and fall and traffic are being compared, one will cost less than the
other by $300,000, but has 3,000 degrees of curvature more than the
other, and such heavier grades that one more freight train per day each·
way is necessary to handle the traffic. Which route will be the better investment, there being an expected traffic of five trains per day each way.

6 At what points should vertical curves be introduced, and to what
extent ?
Will this become more or less important in the future ?

7. In a circular curve what is the formula for offsetting intermediate
stakes from chords. What is such an offset from the middle of a 50 feet
chord on an 8 ° curve ?

8. Outline the general idea and necessity for transitions at the ends of·
circular curves.

9. Obtain the offsets from tangent and transit deflections from B. T. C.
for a transition cubic parabola that sharpens at the rate of 1˙ degree each
30 feet of its length.

10. In reconnaissance, point out some general guiding principles in
studying a route.

11. Detail the duties of Transitman and Leveller on preliminary and
location surveys.

12. Describe various ways of prolonging a straight line past obstacles.

FOURTH YEAR.—(Civil and Mining).

RAILWAY ENGINEERING.

(PAPER I.)

MONDAY, APRIL 18TH :—9 TO 12 A.M.

Examiner,...CECIL B. SMITH, M.A.E.

1. What circumstances affect the maximum flow of water from a given
watershed past a given point on the outlet stream. Give a formula con·
neeting acreage drained and square feet of waterway required ; to what
extent is a formula satisfactory ?

2. Design a structure to carry 4 square feet of waterway through a bank 4 feet deep, also design a stone structure to accommodate at least 12 feet of waterway with the same depth of bank.

3. Sketch different styles of headwalls for box or arch culverts, commenting on their merits.

4. Comment on the conditions under which various forms of Bridge abutments would be most suitable.

5. Write a specification for 1st class Bridge masonry.

6. A drop hammer weighing 1800 lbs. falling 22 feet drives a pile 1½ inches per blow with an unbroomed head, calculate the probable safe load by any formula familiar to you.

7 Sketch two forms of floating cofferdams and two forms of fixed ones, commenting on their use in different situations.

8. Make such sketches as will illustrate the principles involved in sinking foundations by compressed air (with necessary narrative).

9. Give sketches of various timber trestle joints, commenting on their merits or demerits. When are split caps and sills or cluster bent trestles justifiably used.

10. Give a cross-section, sketched to scale with all dimensions, of a good form of trestle deck for Canadian Railways.

11. State Eckel's formula for calculating cross-section areas, giving an application to illustrate it.

12. Transform the prismoidal formula into a shape that will enable it to be used without determining the middle area.

FOURTH YEAR.—(Civil and Mining).

RAILWAY ENGINEERING.

PAPER II.

Monday, April 18th:—2 to 5 p.m.

Examiner,...... ....Cecil B. Smith, Ma.E.

1. Mention various kinds of ballast used, and draw cross-sections of road beds, including formation level, ditches and shape of ballasting for various kinds of ballast.

2. What are the usual dimensions and spacing apart centre to centre of wooden cross-ties?

What are some of the deficiences of wooden ties? Describe the creosot - ing process of treating ties.

What is the cost of treatment and effect on the use of ties in track, what other processes are also in use ?

3. Draw detail sketches of the Post metal tie, show dimensions and method of connecting the rail. Comment on this and other metal ties, as to advantages and disadvantages of their use as compared with wooden ones.

4. Draw a section, with dimensions, for a 70 lb. rail, either (a) American Standard, (b) or C. P. Railway, (c) or a rail suitable for use on tie base plates. What are the objections to use of flanged rails, and how can they. be met ? Give chemical and drop tests for rails.

5. Sketch, with general dimensions and descriptions, three .forms of joint fastenings for flanged rails.

๑ 6. Draw skeleton outlines of Stub, Lorenz and Wharton Switches, describing their special features and methods of use.

7. Calculate the "lead" and length of slide rails for a No. 9 frog (a) with stub switch, (b) with split switch.

8. Mention various methods of line block signalling, and describe one method minutely in detail.

9. Give some general principles of applying brakes to trains.

10. Mention various methods of braking trains, and describe, in detail, the plain vacuum brake method, giving its defects and advantages.

11. Describe the procedure necessary to obtain right of way lands for a railway company by arbitration.

12. What are the Canadian regulations governing under and over highway crossings of a railway.

(Any 10 questions a full paper.)

FOURTH YEAR.—(Architectural, Civil and Mining).

MUNICIPAL ENGINEERING.

ROADS AND PAVEMENTS.

TUESDAY, APRIL 19TH :—MORNING 9 to 1.

Examiner,.................... ....CECIL B. SMITH, MA.E.

(1.) Enumerate the different resistances to hauling waggons. Under hwat condition are the various ones of any importance ?

(2.) Give a general idea of the rate and manner of variation of different resistances under different conditions?

(3.) What is resistance per ton for

(a) Good macadam?

(b) Granite block?

(c) Asphalt?

(4.) Draw up an ordinance regulating the tire widths of wheels of waggons.

(5.) Institute a comparison of routes as to ultimate economy, using symbols.

(6.) Comment on grades for different kinds of traffic and on different wearing materials.

(7.) Give details of treatment necessary to obtain best possible

(a) Clay roads

(b) Sand roads.

(c) Loam roads.

Both as regards construction and maintenance.

(8.) Draw to scale the cross section of a macadam or telford road, thirty feet wide with gutters, berme, footwalk and one main ditch.

(9.) Describe the best methods of constructing such roads as No. (8), including a general specification.

(10.) Give a detailed account of the manufacture of the material used for asphalt pavements in America, beginning at the raw state. Point out some of the advantages and disadvantages of asphalt pavements.

(11.) Write a short thesis on Stone Block Pavements.

(12.) Write a thesis on Brick Pavements.

Faculty of Law.

FACULTY OF LAW.

FINAL EXAMINATIONS FOR DEGREE CF B.C.L.

ROMAN LAW— *First Paper.*

FRIDAY, APRIL 15TH :— 10 TO 12 A.M.

Examiner,.. PROF. WALTON.

1. Explain the terms *jus, leges, fas, fides, rescriptum,* novel.

2. What do you know of Alaric's Breviary ? Of what parts is the *Corpus Juris* composed ?

3. Explain *mancipatio.* For what purposes was it employed ? What theories have been advanced to account for certain things being called *res mancipi ?*

4. Trace the history of the praetorian edict, and shew its importance in shaping the law.

5. Explain the growth of the law as to the rights of a *filius familias* to acquire and own property.

6. What were the modes of constituting marriage in the earlier and in the later law ?

7. In marriage without *manus* what was the position of the property of the wife ?

8. To what extent could a pupil enter into a valid contract without his tutor's *auctoritas ?* Could a debtor who had paid a pupil his debt be compelled in every case to pay it again to the tutor ?

9. Explain *capitis deminutio.*

10. Give a sketch of the formulary procedure.

ROMAN LAW (*Second Paper.*)

SATURDAY, 16TH APRIL :—3 TO 6.

Examiner,... PROF. WALTON.

I: Explain the nature of legal Possession. .

II. State the Roman Law as to *specificatio.*

III. Define *traditio* and explain *nunquam nuda traditio transfert dominium, sed ita si venditio aut aliqua justa causa praecesserit propter quam traditio sequeretur.*

IV. *Servitus in faciendo consistere nequit.* Why not? Was there any exception?

V. Explain shortly the right of *usus.*

VI. Distinguish *fiducia, pignus, hypotheca.*

VII. What kind of error was a ground of nullity of a contract?

VIII. What are the essential characteristics of a condition?

IX. In the law of suretyship what was meant by the *beneficium divisionis* and the *beneficium ordinis* or *excussionis?* Do they still exist in our law?

X. What are the rules as to imputation of payments when several debts are due by the same debtor?

XI. What were the innominate real contracts? By what action were they enforced?

XII. What is the main difference between the contract of sale in the Roman Law and in our law?

HISTORY OF THE LAW OF THE PROVINCE AND MUNICIPAL. LAW.

THURSDAY, 14TH APRIL :--10 A.M. TO 1 P.M.

Examiner,..PROF. McGOUN.

1. By what ordinance was the reduction to writing of the customs of France ordered? Mention their publication and the dates of certain of the principal customs.

2. How was the custom of Paris introduced into this country?

3. What relation existed between Roman and customary Law in France before the Code Napoleon?

4. What were the provisions of the proclamation of October, 1763?

5. Give the provisions of the Quebec Act relating to Civil Law, to Criminal Law, and to the rights of the clergy to the collection of tithes?

6. What were the recommendations of Lord Durham's report as to municipal institutions, and as to the general Government of British North America?

7. What was the effect of the Seigniorial Act of 1854?

8. By the British North America Act 1867, what body has the power of passing laws relating to (*a*) Bankruptcy, (*b*) Municipal Institutions, (*c*) Organisation of the Courts?

MUNICIPAL LAW.

1. What is a municipal corporation? How many kinds are there? What persons compose a local council? A county council?

2. Describe the proceedings of a municipal election from the opening of the meeting to the holding of a poll?

3. Upon what grounds can the election of a councillor be contested? Describe the proceedings of such contestation?

4. What grounds of defence can be urged against the candidate for whom the seat is claimed?

CIVIL LAW. (1st *Paper*.)

FRIDAY, 15TH APRIL :—3 P. M. TO 6 P. M.

Examiners, ... { PROF. FORTIN. PROF. LAFLEUR.

1. What laws regulate the acquisition and loss of the quality of British subject, and the status of aliens in the Province of Quebec.

2. Discuss the legality of a marriage celebrated in this Province between two Roman Catholics by a Protestant minister, and cite the leading cases on the subject.

3. (*a*) Can a tutor be compelled to account during the pendency of his administration ?

(*b*) What is the value of a settlement between the ward who has attained his majority and his tutor, before the latter has rendered an account of his administration ?

4. What constitute the assets of the community? What things do not enter into the community ?

5. What are the liabilities of the community? *Quid* of the debts contracted by the wife before marriage? During marriage ?

6. What is the liability of the community and of each consort, with regard to debts of successions falling to either of them during the existence of the community ?

7. What are the rights of the husband upon the property of the community ? Upon that of the wife ?

8. Explain and illustrate the effect of a sale of moveables by weight, number or measure, as regards the passing of the property and the risk of the things sold.

9. Against what defects is the seller obliged by law to warrant the buyer? What remedies has the buyer resulting from this obligation?

10. Does any implied warranty exist in the sale of a chattel with a trade mark thereon, or of a patent right?

11. If an immoveable be sold with a statement of its superficial contents, and the seller is unable to deliver the exact quantity mentioned in the contract, what are the rights of the buyer in case of excess or deficiency in such quantity?

12. What is the order of preference,

(a) between two titles creating hypothec entered for registration at the same moment ?

(b) between a deed of purchase and a deed creating a hypothec entered at the same time ?

13. Can want of registration be invoked against minors? Does registration interrupt prescription ?

CIVIL LAW. (*2nd Paper*)

THURSDAY, 14TH APRIL :—3 TO 6 P. M.

Examiner, ...PROF. MR. JUSTICE DOHERTY.

[N. B —The First and Second Years to answer Questions 1, 2, 3, save Sub-Divisions (c) and (d), 4 and 5.]

1. In what order are the relatives of a person dying intestate called to his succession? To what extent does proximity in degree of relationship to the deceased regulate the rights to come to his succession of persons related to him in the same line, or in different lines?

2. What is the position as regards the rights and obligations of the *de cujus*, of the heir who has as yet neither accepted nor renounced ? How is that position affected (a) by his acceptance, (b) by his renunciation? Do you make any distinction in this regard between the testamentary heir and the heir ab intestate?

3. What capacity is required in order to receive

(*a*) By testamentary succession ?
(*b*) By abintestate succession ?
(*c*) By gift inter vivos ?
(*d*) As substitute under a substitution ?
When must the capacity exist in each case ?

4. What is the effect of the partition as regards the transmission of ownership of the things comprised in the share of each co-partitioner ? How is the hypothec created by one of several co-owners upon his share of an undivided property affected by the result of the partition ?

5. What do you understand by the obligation to make returns ? Of what property, by whom and to whom are returns due, and how are they effected ?

6. What is the fiduciary substitution ? By what acts can it be created ?

7. By whom can the non-registration of a deed of gift inter vivos be invoked ?
By whom can the non-registration of a substitution be invoked ?

8. What obligation of warranty is incumbent upon the lessor as regards defects in the thing leased ? To what extent is any such obligation affected by the lessor's knowledge of such defects—either as regards the existence of such obligation, or the rights therefrom resulting to the lessee ?

9. To what extent, if any, is the lessor bound to warrant the lessee against disturbance in his enjoyment of the thing leased, caused by the acts of third parties ?

10. What is the effect upon the obligations of the lessee of a farm, of the loss of his crop caused by a fortuitous event or irresistible force ?

11. What are the privileged rights of the unpaid vendor of moveable property ?

12. When can the holder of a property hypothecated who is not personally liable for the debt, plead an exception of warranty to the hypothecary action ?

CIVIL LAW. (*3rd Paper.*)

MONDAY, APRIL 18TH :—10 A. M. TO 1 P. M.

Examiners,.. Prof. FORTIN and Mr. A. GEOFFRION.

1. Enumerate and explain fully the different kinds of immoveables and of moveables, giving examples. What are the fruits ? Give their division. Give the rule of accretion as to them in the case of ownership and of mere possession.

2. Define usufruct. Distinguish it from use and habitation. Define servitudes. Give their division, and examples of each kind. Define emphyteutic lease.

3. Explain the difference between real and personal rights. What sort of rights do the following contracts give a creditor before payment of the price, and delivery : (a) A sale of a particular house. (b) A sale of 10 tons of coal generally ? Define an obligation. What are the causes from which obligations arise? Define them.

4. Are all the nullities which may affect contracts similar ? If not, explain their differences, giving examples. Is there any difference between the nullity of a contract resulting from the immorality of its consideration and its nullity resulting from error of one of its parties ? What is the difference, it any ?

5. Give and explain the essential elements of an offence and of a quasi-offence. When and under what conditions can a person be held responsible for offences or quasi-offences committed by another?

6. When is a debtor liable in damages for the inexecution of his obligation? Is there a condition precedent to the existence of that liability? What is the measure of damages generally ? What is it when the debtor was in good faith ?

7. What is a condition? Give the principal division of conditions. What is the effect of their happening in an obligation to give a determinate thing when that thing is lost without the debtor's fault, before he was in default ?

8. What is subrogation? What are its effects? How many kinds of subrogation are there? Give the cases in which it takes place, the conditions required for its validity.

9. Define suretyship. Enumerate and explain the different exceptions or benefits that belong to the surety. Define pledge.

10. What is possession? How is it acquired? How is it retained and lost?

11. Describe the different characters possession must have, in order to avail for prescription.

12. What is interversion of title, and how is it effected? What is the meaning and effect of the rule that no one can prescribe against his title? *Quid* in the case of negative prescription?

COMMERCIAL LAW.

MONDAY, APRIL 18TH :—3 TO 6 P.M.

AGENCY AND PARTNERSHIP.

Examiner,...PROF. McGOUN.

1. What circumstances change the gratuitous nature of mandate?

2. In what cases is an agent personally liable to third persons contracting with him?

3. Distinguish a partnership from joint ownership and from a joint stock company.

4. What is an anonymous partnership? What is the liability of promoters of a company?

5. What is the effect upon a limited partnership of failure to contribute the capital promised?

JOINT STOCK COMPANIES.

6. Explain the terms: preferential shares, provisional directors.

7. How may a person become shareholder in a company, and what is the extent of his liability in ordinary commercial companies?

BILLS AND NOTES.

8. How is a bill of exchange accepted, and what is the difference between general and qualified, especially conditional acceptance?

9. What is an accommodation note?.

10. What are the rights of the holder of a bill of exchange transferred to him (a) before maturity; (b) after maturity?

11. What is the effect on the maker, and on the endorser of a promissory note, of failure to protest the same at maturity? Give the reason of the distinction.

INSURANCE.

12. Define the following terms: Representation, concealment, warranty, general average, jettison.

13. What is provided by our law as to insurance for the benefit of wife and children?

MERCHANT SHIPPING.

14. What authority has the master of a ship to raise loans of money on the security of the ship?

15. What is the port of registry of a ship?

16. How is a mortgage upon a ship created, and in what order do different claims rank?

CRIMINAL LAW.

WEDNESDAY, APRIL 20TH:—3 TO 6.

Examiner,........................... PROF. MR. JUSTICE DAVIDSON.

1. What is criminal law? What is a crime?

2. Over what places and offences has the criminal law of Canada jurisdiction?

3. Detail the principal incidents in a criminal prosecution up to verdict.

4. What are the different parts of an indictment?

5. What are the pleas which may be pleaded to an indictment?

6. When are confessions admissible in evidence?
Give some examples of causes for their exclusion.

7. Distinguish between "a speedy trial," "a summary trial," and "a summary conviction."

8. In R. *v.* Lafrance *et al,* what was the decision of the Court of Queen's Bench, (Crown side) as to defendants, who were charged with keeping a common gaming house, being subject to a summary trial, and on what principle did the judgment rest?

9. When can a person be guilty of the theft of his own property?

10. What special plea may be made to an indictment for libel?
By what English statute was this plea allowed?
By what English statute was the right given to the jury to find a general verdict of guilty or not guilty to an indictment for libel?
What is an innuendo?
From what prosecutions for libel is the right of " stand aside " taken away?

11. What is the purpose and effect of the writ of *Habeas Corpus ad subjiciendum?* Give a brief account of the laws, statutory or otherwise, which govern it in England and in this Province.

THIRD YEAR ONLY.

12. Mention and define some of the offences against the Queen's authority and person.
What is homicide?
What is murder?
What is the distinction between murder and manslaughter?

CONSTITUTIONAL LAW AND INTERNATIONAL LAW.

WEDNESDAY, APRIL 13TH :—3 TO 6 P.M.

Examiners, ...PROFESSORS McGOUN AND LAFLEUR.

1. Explain the doctrine of the Sovereignty of Parliament.

2. What connection is there in the British Constitution between the executive and legislative functions of Parliament.

3. To what extent is a member of parliament legally responsible to his constituents?

4. What are some of the chief differences between the powers of the Parliament of Canada and the powers of the Congress of the United States?

5. In what authority is vested the right of holding Crown lands in Canada?

6. What are the differences as to power of taxation between the Parliament of Canada and the Legislatures of the Provinces?

7. How are members of the Senate of Canada appointed, and what remedy does the Constitution provide for a case of disagreement between the Senate and the House of Commons?

8. What are the powers of the Senate as regard money bills?

INTERNATIONAL LAW.

PUBLIC.

1. What is the basis of the international rule of non-intervention? In what cases, if any, is interference in the internal affairs of a foreign state regarded as justifiable?

2. What are the characteristics of occupation as a mode of international territorial acquisition, and what is the area affected by an act of occupation?

3. Discuss the definition of "Contraband of War," with special reference to the Anglo-American doctrine of "contraband by circumstances.

27

1. To what extent have our courts recognized the validity, both as to substance and as to form, of the so-called " Indian marriages " contracted in the North-West Territory between white men and Indian women ?

2. A minor domiciled in Ontario is sued in this province upon a promissory note signed and made payable here by a commercial firm of which he is a member. Under the laws of Ontario the incapacity of minors is absolute even when they are engaged in trade. Can the action against such minor be maintained ?

3. Consorts were married without antenuptial contract in the State of Vermont, where they were domiciled then, and for some years after the marriage. By the laws of that State, consorts so married are separate as to property and may confer benefits on each other *inter vivos* during the marriage. Some years after the marriage the consorts left Vermont and acquired a domicile in the Province of Quebec, which they preserved until the wife's death. After the change of domicile the husband conferred divers benefits on his wife, by paying the price of immoveables which had been purchased here in her name, and by gifts of moveable property. After the wife's death, an action was brought by the husband against his daughter, who was the universal legatee of the wife, to recover these gifts as made in violation of the prohibition contained in article 1265 C. C. Discuss the validity of these donations and the matrimonial *régime* of the consorts in the Province of Quebec.

CIVIL PROCEDURE.

TUESDAY, 19TH APRIL :—3 TO 6.

THIRD YEAR.

Examiner,..MR. PERCY C. RYAN.

1. What are the conditions precedent to an action-at-law ?
Explain the general requisites of each.

2. Have the Courts of this Province jurisdiction over a suit in which the cause of action arose entirely in the United States, between two persons resident in England, both of whom have property in the Province of Quebec ?
If so, in what district should the action be brought ?
How should the alleged want of jurisdiction be pleaded ?
Draft the appropriate pleading in a case in which an action arising under the above circumstances would be brought before a Court not having jurisdiction.

3. A sues B for $500, upon a promissory note made to the order of A, and alleges that the note is lost. C holds the note, and claims to have obtained it for a valid consideration, before maturity, from A.

What remedy has C ? Draft the appropriate pleading, and state how C should proceed to enforce his rights.

4. State the rules for calling in warrantors.

5. When can a deposition given at a former trial of the same action be given in evidence ?

6. State the rules as to joinder of causes of action.
Also the rules as to joinder of actions.

7. In what cases does Mandamus lie ?
How is it obtained, contested and executed ?

8. Before what Court must actions for separation from bed and board be brought ?

What are the special and exceptional requirements to which such actions are subject ?

9. In what cases does Capias lie ?
What persons are exempt from Capias ?

10. In what cases can a pleading be amended.
(a) Without leave,
(b) With leave ?
What rules must be observed by the party making the amendment ?

11. In what cases can a new trial of an action be obtained, and under what conditions ?

12. In what cases has the Court of Review an original jurisdiction ?

FIRST YEAR.

SESSIONAL EXAMINATION.

OBLIGATIONS.

MONDAY, APRIL 18 :—PROM 10 A.M. TO 12 A.M.

Examiner, ...MR. A. GEOFFRION

1. Define a *contract*, a quasi-contract, an offence, a quasi–offence. Give the essential elements of each, and show their principal differences.

2. What is required to annul a contract for error, fraud, violence or fear ? What sort of nullities result from those causes ?

3. What may be the effects of a contract between the parties to it ? What are the two actions which creditors have to protect themselves against acts or omissions of their debtors, which cause them prejudice ? Give the conditions required for the exercise of those actions.

4. What is a natural obligation ? When, if ever, can repetition be made of what has been paid in discharge of it ?

5. Can an omission constitute an offence or quasi-offence ? When is a person responsible for damage caused to third parties, (1) by an animal, (2) by an inanimate thing ?

6. What can be the object of an obligation ? Has the creditor ever any other remedy than an action in damages when the debtor fails to execute his obligation ? If so, what remedy or remedies, and under what conditions?

7. Give the rules of putting in default ? For what purpose is it neces. sary ? When is it dispensed with ? How is it made ?

8. In an obligation to give a thing certain, what is the effect of the loss of the object without the debtor's fault, and before he is in default ? What is the reason of the rule ?

9. What is a conditional obligation ? A joint and several obligation ? An indivisible obligation ? An alternative obligation ? How many sorts of conditions are there ? How many sorts of solidarities ? What are the effects of solidarity and indivisibility ? What are the differences between them ?

LAW OF PERSONS.

FRIDAY, 15TH APRIL—4 TO 6.

Examiner, ...PROF. LAFLEUR.

1. What laws regulate the acquisition and loss of the quality of British subject and the status of aliens in the Province of Quebec ?

2. What is the domicile of

(a) a married woman not separated from bed and board ?

(b) an unemancipated minor ?

(c) a person of the age of majority interdicted for insanity ?

3. Under what circumstances and to whom is provisional possession given of the estate of an absentee ?

4. Within what degrees of relationship or alliance is marriage prohibited ?

5. Discuss the legality of a marriage celebrated in this Province between two Roman Catholics by a Protestant minister, and cite the leading cases on the subject.

6. For what causes can separation from bed and board be obtained.

(a) by the husband ?

(b) by the wife ?

7. In what cases and under what restrictions is verbal testimony admitted as proof of filiation ?

8. (a) Can a tutor be compelled to account during the pendency of his administration ?

(b) What is the value of a settlement between the ward who has attained his majority and his tutor, before the latter has rendered an account of his administration ?

9. In what cases are curators to property appointed ?

REAL RIGHTS.

THURSDAY, 14TH APRIL :—10 TO 12.

Examiner, ...PROFESSOR MARLER, B.A., D.C.L.

1. Give examples of moveable things becoming immoveable by destination.

2. Do they ever resume their moveable character, and under what circumstances?

3. Of incorporeal property, what is moveable and what immoveable

4. Give the distinctions between real and personal rights.

5. When is a possessor in good faith? When does it cease ?

6. What are the obligations of the possessor as to fruits : (*a*) when in good faith, (*b*) when otherwise?

7. A proprietor has erected buildings with materials of another ; can the owner of the materials regain them ?

8. What are the distinctions between natural, civil and industrial fruits ?

9. What obligations are incumbent on the usufructuary before entering upon his usufruct?

10. What is a servitude ? How do they arise ? What persons can establish them ?

11. A common wall is insufficient to support my proposed buildings, what are my rights and what are my duties towards my neighbour and his tenants?

12. What are the essential characteristics of emphyteusis

SECOND YEAR.

PRIVATE INTERNATIONAL LAW.

WEDNESDAY, APRIL 13TH :—4 TO 6 P. M.

Examiner,................................ ....PROF. LAFLEUR.

1. Distinguish between the *a priori* and the positive method of dealing with conflicts of laws.

2. What, according to the doctrine laid down by the Judicial Committee of the Privy Council, is the true test of the international competency of a court to pronounce a decree of divorce, so as to entitle such decree to extra-territorial authority ? Have our courts recognized the authority of foreign decrees of divorce upon other principles ?

3. To wnat extent have our courts recognized the validity, both as to substance and as to form, of the so-called " Indian marriages " contracted in the North-West Territory between white men and Indian women ?

4. A minor domiciled in Ontario is sued in this province upon a pro. missory note signed and made payable here by a commercial firm of which he is a member. Under the laws of Ontario the incapacity of minors is absolute, even when they are engaged in trade. Can the action against such minor be maintained ?

5. Consorts were married without ante-nuptial contract in the State of Vermont, where they were domiciled then and for some years after the marriage. By the laws of that State, consorts so married are separate as to property, and may confer benefits on each other *inter vivos* during the marriage. Some years after the marriage the consorts left Vermont and acquired a domicile in the Province of Quebec, which they preserved until the wife's death. After the change of domicile the husband conferred divers benefits on his wife, by paying the price of immoveables which had been purchased here in her name, and by gifts of moveable property. After the wife's death an action was brought by the husband against his daughter, who was the universal legatee of the wife, to recover these gifts

as made in violation of the prohibition contained in art. 1265 C. C Discuss the validity of these donations and the matrimonial *régime* of the consorts in the Province of Quebec.

6. What theories have been advanced as to the law which should govern the devolution of an abintestate succession, and which of these would probably be adopted by our courts

7. A bill of exchange is drawn by the master of a ship in Buenos Ayres on a firm in New York for disbursements necessary to enable the ship to proceed on her voyage, and is endorsed by the mortgagee in Buenos Ayres. The bill is subsequently transferred to a bank in Quebec, where action is brought against the endorser upon the bill after it has been dishonoured. By the law of the Argentine Republic, where the bill was drawn, the holder is obliged to use diligence to collect the amount of such a bill out of the freight, hull and cargo of the vessel before applying to the endorser in default of which the endorser is discharged. By the law of New York, where the bill was made payable, this defence could not avail the endorser. Should this plea be maintained upon proof that the bank has made no efforts to levy out of freight, hull or cargo?

8. Discuss the permissive or imperative nature of the rule *Locus regit actum* in its application to wills, gifts *inter vivos* and contracts.

CONSTITUTIONAL LAW.

Examiner, ... PROF. WALTON

1. " The King can do no wrong." Explain.

2. Sketch briefly the history and powers of the Privy Council.

3. Define " Colony." What are the chief classes of Colonies, and why are the distinctions important ?

4. " It is a fundamental principle of English lawyers that Parliament can do everything but make a woman a man, and a man a woman." Discuss.

5. What peculiarities are there as to money bills ?

6. What points of constitutional law were raised in the case of Ship money and the case of the Seven Bishops ?

FACULTY OF LAW.

MARRIAGE COVENANTS.

FRIDAY, APRIL 15TH :—AFTERNOON, 4 TO 6.

Examiner,..PROF. FORTIN.

1. What agreements may lawfully be made in a marriage contract ? In what form must the marriage contract be made ?
   Quid if the parties marry without marriage contract ?
2. What constitute the assets of the community ? What things do not enter into the community ?

3. What are the liabilities of the community ?
   Quid of the debts contracted by the wife before marriage ? During marriage ?

4. What is the liability of the community and of each consort, with regard to debts of successions falling to either of them during the existence of the community ?

5. What are the rights of the husband upon the property of the community ? Upon that of the wife ?

6. How is community dissolved ? What is the effect of dissolution when consorts are living ? Can it be re-established ?

7. What option has the wife or her heirs at the dissolution of community ? Has the husband or his heirs the same option ?

8. What are the clauses of realization and mobilization ? What are their effects ?

9. What is the difference betweeen exclusion of community and separation of property ?

AGENCY AND PARTNERSHIP.

MONDAY, 18TH APRIL :—4 TO 6.

Examiner,..PROF. McGOUN.

1. Define the contract of mandate, and state what circumstances change its gratuitous nature.

2. For what acts is express authority required by an agent ?

3. In what cases is an agent personally liable to third persons contracting with him ?

4. What agents have power to sell or to pledge goods belonging to their principals ?

5. What exceptions are there to the rule that participation in profit constitutes partnership?

6. If an intending partner agrees to contribute a cargo of grain and the use of a ship to the firm, on whom does the loss (*a*) of the grain, (*b*) of the ship, (*c*) of the profits from the use of the ship, fall, if the ship and cargo are lost before delivery to the firm, and on whom if lost after delivery?

7. Distinguish a partnership from joint ownership, and from membership in a joint stock company.

8. (*a*) What is an anonymous partnership? (*b*) Are promoters of a company partners?

9. (*a*) What is the effect upon a limited partnership of failure to contribute the capital promised? (*b*) What if the capital be paid in after the date mentioned in the certificate filed?

10. What are the rights of creditors of an individual partner and of the firm, upon the property of the firm, and on the property of the individual partner?

11. When a partner receives a sum of money from a person indebted to himself individually, and also to his firm, how is the money received to be applied?

12. If a partnership is formed under a firm name and afterwards renewed under the same name, but with different partners, what is the effect of failure to register notice of the dissolution of the firm as at first composed?

CIVIL PROCEDURE.

FIRST AND SECOND YEARS.

Tuesday, 19th April :—3 to 6 p. m.

Examiner, ...PERCY C. RYAN.

1. Define Procedure, and explain its relationship to Substantive Law.

2. What are the conditions precedent to an action-at-law? Explain the general requisites of each.

3. State the elements of a complete action-at-law.

4. Are laws of procedure retroactive?

5. Describe the jurisdiction of the Superior Court and of the Circuit Court.

6. Draw defences of:

(a) Payment ;

(b) Novation ;

(c) Compensation ;

(d) Lesion.

7. A contracts with B for the supply of 100,000 bricks for a house which B is building. A neglects to deliver the bricks at the time agreed upon. In consequence B is obliged to purchase other bricks at a price which is $1,500.00 higher than that at which A had contracted to supply them. Draft an action by B against A.

8. How are issues of law pleaded to a declaration ? To a defence ?

9. What are the rules governing Discovery and Inspection of Documents ? On what general grounds can discovery be resisted ?

10. State how want of jurisdiction *ratione personae* is pleaded, and give the proper conclusions.

UNIVERSITY SCHOOL EXAMINATIONS, 1898.

ORDINARY A. A.

AND

PRELIMINARY SUBJECTS,

(In order of date of Examination.)

UNIVERSITY SCHOOL EXAMINATIONS.

ORDINARY A. A.

PRELIMINARY SUBJECTS.

ENGLISH GRAMMAR.

MONDAY, MAY 30TH :—MORNING, 9 TO 10.30.

(N.B.—Answer *two* questions *only* from each group).

1. Distinguish between a sentence and a clause. How many kinds are there (*a*) of sentences, (*b*) of clauses ?

2. Parse the words in italics :

   " As *his* eye *falls* on the comfortable home in which he dwells, or wanders from the *well* trimmed orchard, already glorious with the promise of autumn, to the distant hills, *where* the fragrant hay imparts its sweetness to the air and the flocks roam in well fed *content*, it is difficult for him to realize *that* a few short years *ago these* hills on which he gazes with proprietary complacency reechoed the shouts of *fierce* men engaged in sanguinary conflict."

III.

3. Analyze :

   > " It lies among a thousand hills
   > Where no man ever trod,
   > And only nature's stillness fills
   > The silences of God."

4. Mention four classes of pronouns, giving examples of each class. Give the inflection of one class.

5. Give the second person singular of
   (1) the Present Perfect Indicative of *be*,
   (2) the Present Perfect Subjunctive of *be*,
   (3) the Present Perfect Subjunctive Passive of *strike*.

III.

6. Correct the following where necessary :
   (1) Refuse to obey tyrants and reverence them.
   (2) The ebb and flow of the tide have been explained.

(3) He asked to be made captain or mate or purser, for either of which places he considered himself adapted.

(4) Nothing could exceed the enormity of his pretences.

(5) He confessed the mistake they accused him of.

7. Classify and give the inflections of the following words : each, nigh, far, rapid, tenth, forth, several, much, who.

8. Construct a complex sentence of not less than twenty-five words. *This sentence must not be compound.*

PRELIMINARY SUBJECTS.

DICTATION.

MONDAY, 30TH MAY :—MORNING, 10:30 TO 11.15.

As to the comforts and luxuries which were to be found in the interior of the houses by the fashionable visitors who resorted thither in search of health or amusement, we possess information more complete and minute than can generally be obtained on such subjects. A writer who published an account of the city about sixty years after the Revolution has accurately described the changes which had taken place within his own recollection. He assures us that, in his younger days, the gentlemen who visited the springs slept in rooms hardly as good as the garrets which he lived to see occupied by footmen. The floors of the dining-room were uncarpeted, and were coloured brown with a wash made of soot and small beer in order to hide the dirt. Not a wainscot was painted. Not a hearth or a chimney-piece was of marble. A slab of common freestone and fire irons which had cost from three to four shillings were thought sufficient for any fireplace. The best apartments were hung with coarse woollen stuff, and were furnished with rush-bottomed chairs. Readers who take an interest in the progress of civilization and of the useful arts will be grateful to the humble topographer who has recorded these facts, and will perhaps wish that historians of far higher pretensions had sometimes spared a few pages from military evolutions and political intrigues for the purpose of letting us know how the parlours and bedchambers of our ancestors looked.

Macaulay.

N. B.—Instructions for the local examiner.

I. The extract shall be read *three* times :—

(a) Fluently, in order to convey to the candidates the general sense of the passage. During this reading, pens must be laid on the desks.

(b) Slowly, for dictation.

(c) For punctuation and candidates' private correction.

II. Any word may be repeated by the examiner at the request of any candidate.

III. No re-writing of the extract is permitted.

PRELIMINARY SUBJECTS.

ESSAY.

MONDAY, MAY 30TH:—MORNING, 11.15 TO 12.

Write an essay of not less than *one* page on any *one* of the following subjects:—

(a) The Spirit of Adventure.

(b) The New Gold Fields of Canada.

(c) A Modern Invention.

ALGEBRA.

MONDAY, MAY 30TH:—AFTERNOON, 2 TO 3.30.

1. Resolve into elementary factors the following expressions :

(a) $x^2 - 3x - 28$.

(b) $x^6 - y^6$.

(c) $ab - bc + 2ad - 2cd$.

and find the Highest Common Factor of

$6x^3 - 22x^2 - x + 35$ and $3x^3 + 10x^2 - 25x$.

2. Find the value of

$$\frac{a - b + \dfrac{(a+b)^2}{a - b}}{a + b - \dfrac{(a - b)^2}{a + b}} \times \frac{2ab}{a^4 - b^4}.$$

Extract the square root of

$$x^6 - 6ax^5 + 15a^2x^4 - 20a^3x^3 + 15a^4x^2 - 6a^5x + a^6.$$

4. (a) Reduce $\dfrac{3 \sqrt{2} + 2 \sqrt{3}}{3 \sqrt{2} - 2 \sqrt{3}}$ to a whole number and a surd.

(b) Divide $x^{-3} - 4x^{-\frac{3}{4}} \dfrac{\cdot}{y} - \dfrac{3}{2} + 3y^2$

by $x^{-\frac{3}{2}} - 2x^{-\frac{3}{4}} y^{\frac{1}{2}} + y$.

5. A person lent a sum of money at $5\frac{1}{2}$ per cent., simple interest ; in twelve years the interest amounted to $51 less than the sum lent; what was the sum lent?

6. Solve the equations:

(a) $\dfrac{4x + 5}{6} + \dfrac{x + 7}{2x + 4} = \dfrac{2x + 5}{3}$

(b) $\sqrt{x} + \sqrt{x - 16} = 8$.

(c) $2 x^2 + 3x - 35 = 0$.

(d) $\begin{cases} 5z - 4y = 7. \\ \frac{y}{2} + \frac{z}{3} - x = 1. \\ 2x + 3y - z = 5. \end{cases}$

7. Divide n into two such parts that their product may be equal to twice their difference.

FRENCH.

LUNDI, 21 MAI:—DE 3.30 À 5.30.

A.

1. Indiquer (a) la différence entre chaque et chacun, (b) quelles peuvent être les fonctions des mots *qui* et *que*. *Exemples.*

2. Comment se forme le pluriel des substantifs composés? Exemples.

3. Quel est l'emploi de *y* pronom? Exemples.

4. Donner les temps primitifs des verbes suivants: avoir, battre, courir, dire, falloir, haïr, joindre, mettre, naître, prendre, suivre, savoir.

5. Faire l'analyse grammaticale de la phrase suivante :
On ne se sent à son aise que là où l'on se sait à sa place (Daudet)

B.

Traduire les deux passages suivants :

LE SOLDAT DE MARATHON.

Ce n'était qu'un soldat obscur entre dix mille,
Quand on eut la victoire, il voulut, le premier
En porter la nouvelle à sa lointaine ville,
Et partit, fier coureur agitant un laurier.
Épuisé par sa course effrayante et sans trêve
Il mourut dès qu'il fut au terme du chemin.
Heureux qui peut de même, ayant atteint son rêve
Mourir la flamme au cœur et la palme à la main.

A. RENAUD.

SOLITUDE.

Do you seek solitude ? Go not to fields
    Or pathless woods, or to the lonely shore,
    Nor court the privacy seclusion yields
    In some old house whose very ancient door
Proclaims the absence of intrusive guests.
    Think not of desert waste, nor mountain height,
    Nor tropic isle, nor where the eider nests
    In arctic silence, nor the sea-gull's flight
In voiceless azure. But for solitude
    Perfect, unparalleled, abiding, deep,
    When next you feel the solitary mood
Insistent, trust not even dreamless sleep—
    When for true loneliness your soul entreats,
    Come to New York, and walk these crowded streets.

JOHN H. BONER.

C.

Rédiger une lettre d'environ 100 mots sur le canevas suivant :—

René a terminé ses études primaires et va entrer au collège. Il remercie son instituteur des bonnes leçons et des excellents préceptes que celui-ci lui a donnés ; il ne les oubliera pas, etc.

28

D.

1. Remplacer les tirets par des mots qui conviennent au sens.

Soyons justes —— tout le monde.

La terre est fécondée —— le soleil.

Il n'est jamais —— tard pour bien faire.

L'agriculture et le commerce —— un peuple.

Le chameau reste plusieurs jours —— boire —— manger.

Les rivières sont —— —— qui marchent.

L'ivrognerie est un abîme si profond qu'on ne peut —— sortir ——
on —— est tombé.

Esaü —— —— droit d'aînesse —— ——.

2. Mettre les Infinitifs à un temps de l'Indicatif.

On *déclarer* la guerre. Aussistôt un souffle embrasé *parcourir*
le pays. Tous se *croire* en état de combattre, tous *vouloir* s'engager ;
on les *recevoir*, on les *enrôler*, ils *partir* pour la frontière. Les
vieillards se *souvenir* de leurs exploits passés et les *redire* volontiers.

Les jeunes gens s'en *aller* et les mères *faire* des vœux pour eux.
Elles mêmes *s'employer* et se *rendre* utiles de leur mieux.

E.

1. Reproduire en français ce qui suit :

(*L'examinateur délégué voudra bien lire ou dire en anglais une
anecdocte quelconque pouvant se reproduire dans une centaine de
mots*).

OU

2. Ecrire sous forme de résumé ou de critique environ 250 mots sur un
des ouvrages suivants : Le Chien du Capitaine (Enault). La Fée (Feuil-
let).

Dater en toutes lettres.

———

PRELIMINARY ARITHMETIC.

TUESDAY, MAY 31ST :—MORNING, 9 TO 10.30.

*Answer two questions from each division. All work must be shown ;
results alone will not be considered.*

SECTION I.

1. How much will it cost to dig a canal 1 mi. 3 fur. 10 per. long
18 ft. wide ; and 6 ft. deep, at 48 cents per cub. yard ?

2. Simplify

(a) $\dfrac{\frac{5}{14} - \frac{1}{7} \text{ of } \frac{1}{2}}{1\frac{9}{21} - (\frac{7}{8} \text{ of } 2\frac{2}{21} - 1\frac{7}{12})} \div \dfrac{\frac{1}{3} \text{ of } \frac{1}{2} + \frac{3}{2} \text{ of } 5}{9\frac{1}{3} - 1\frac{2}{3}}$.

(b) $\dfrac{2.8 \text{ of } 2.\overset{..}{2}\overset{.}{7}}{1.1\overset{..}{3}\overset{.}{6}} - \dfrac{2.49 - 1.1\overset{.}{9}\overset{.}{9}}{4.8 + .3\overset{.}{9}}$.

3. A vessel leaves port with provisions sufficient for her crew of 18 men for 10 weeks. Twenty-two days after leaving port she picks up 14 ship-wrecked sailors. How long will the provisions then last?

SECTION II.

4. A merchant sends 4,000 bushels of barley to an agent with instructions to sell at 5·1 cents per bush. and to invest the proceeds in tea. The agent charges 1½ per cent. commission for selling and 2 per cent. for buying; what was the total amount of his commission, and what the value of tea bought?

5. A house is rented for $60 a month. The owner sells the house for $12,000 which he invests in 6 per cent. stock at 124⅝. Find the alteration in his income. Brokerage ⅜ per cent.

6. Two persons start from the same place and go, one due north at the rate of 8 miles an hour, and the other due west at 6 miles an hour. How far apart will they be at the end of 4 hours ?
Find the square root of .00056169.

SECTION III.

7. A labourer agreed to work for a farmer on condition that he was to receive $1.25 and his board every day he worked, while he must pay 50 cents for his board every day he was idle. At the end of 64 days he received $52. How many days did he work?

8. Find the value of a nugget of gold 6.4 cm. long, 2.5 cm. wide, and 1.75 cm. thick at 60 cents a gram, gold being 19.3 times as heavy as water.
Name the principal units of the metric system and give the table of measures of capacity.

9. A gentleman wishes to make a gravel walk 2 metres wide around the outside of his lawn which is 250 m. long by 120 m. wide. A offers to make the walk for 21 cents per sq. m., and B offers to do the work for 18 cents per sq. yd. Which is the better offer and by how much?

PRELIMINARY HISTORY.

TUESDAY, MAY 31ST :—MORNING, 10 30 TO 12.

A.

ENGLISH HISTORY.

Answer any three parts of question 1 ; question 2 or 3 ; and question 4.

1. (*a*) Give an account of Christianity in Britain prior to the reign of Alfred the Great.

(*b*) Describe William the Conqueror's rule of England.

(*c*) Sketch the reign of Henry VI.

(*d*) Follow out the relations of England and Spain during the sixteenth century.

(*e*) Explain the nature of Charles I's rule from 1625-41.

2. Write a careful synopsis of the events of the Seven Years' War.

3. Describe England's opposition to Napoleon Bonaparte from 1803-12.

4. Make brief but precise notes on :—the Treaty of Chippenham (or Wedmore); Dunstan; England under interdict; the Black Death; John Wyclif; the Pilgrimage of Grace; the Fight of the Revenge; Walpole's Excise Bill; the Clare Election; the Chartists in 1848.

B.

CANADIAN HISTORY.

Answer any two of the first three questions and question 4.

1. Write as long a list as you can of the settlements or forts which were founded by the French in Canada prior to 1700, and make a brief historical note about each.

2. Explain how Canada was affected by the war of the English colonies with the mother country. Pay regard to the whole period 1774-84 ; and bear in mind new laws, invasion and immigration.

3. Sketch the history of Upper Canada to 1837.

4. Write a fact and a date about each of the following subjects : John Cabot, Brébeuf, Lachine Massacre, Braddock's expedition, Ticonderoga, Conspiracy of Pontiac, Constitutional Act, Berlin Decree, Lundy's Lane Charlottetown Conference.

GEOMETRY.

TUESDAY, MAY 31ST :—AFTERNOON, 2 TO 4.

A.

[Answer No. (3) and any other three from this group.]

1. The greater side of every triangle has the greater angle opposite to it.

2. If the square on one side of a triangle is equal to the sum of the squares on the other two sides, the angle opposite the first side is a right angle.

3. (a) If AB be divided at C, the sum of the squares on AB, BC, equal twice the rectangle AB, BC, together with the square on AC.

(b) Prove this, and express it algebraically.

(c) Express this proposition as the square of the difference of two straight lines.

4. From an external point it is required to draw a straight line to touch a circle.

5. On a straight line construct a segment of a circle containing a given angle.

6. Prove that the opposite angles of a quadrilateral with its angles on a circle are together equal to two right angles.

GROUP.

B.

(a) Define plane, rectilineal angle, circle, rhombus.

(b) What are the two requisites of parallel straight lines ?

(c) If two straight lines are parallel, and a third straight line crosses, then it shall make the alternate angles equal.

(d) Define "angle in a segment," "angle of a segment," "similar segments."

8. (a) If the three sides of a triangle be bisected by perpendiculars, these three perpendiculars shall meet in one and the same point, which point shall be equidistant from the angular points.

(b) The three bisectors of the angles of a triangle meet in one point, which shall be perpendicularly equidistant from each of the sides.

(c) Bisect a quadrilateral area by a straight line drawn from an angular point.

TRIGONOMETRY.

TUESDAY, MAY 31ST :—AFTERNOON, 4 TO 5.30.

1. Define the unit of circular measure, and prove that it is equal to 57.2958°.

2. Trace the changes of sign in the tangent of an angle as the angle increases from 0° to 360°.

3. Prove the following relations :—

(1) $\sin^2 \theta + \cos^2 \theta = 1$.

(2) $\sin \theta = \dfrac{1}{\sqrt{1 + \cot^2 \theta}}$

(3) $\sin \theta = \dfrac{\sqrt{\sec^2 \theta - 1}}{\sec \theta}$

(4) $\sec^2 \theta + \operatorname{cosec}^2 \theta . = \sec^2 \theta . \operatorname{cosec}^2 \theta$

4. Prove :—(1) $\sin A = \cos (90 - A)$,

(2) $\cos A = - \cos (180 - A)$.

5. Prove :—(1) $\sin (A + B) = \sin A \cos B + \cos A \sin B$

(2) $\cos (A + B) = \cos A \cos B - \sin A \sin B$

(3) $\tan (A + B) = \dfrac{\tan A + \tan B}{1 - \tan A \tan B}$

6. Prove the following relations :—

(1) $\dfrac{\sin A + \sin B}{\cos A + \cos B} = \tan \dfrac{A + B}{2}$

(2) $\cos (30 - \theta) - \cos (30 + \theta) = \sin \theta$

(3) $\cos (A + B) . \cos (A - B) = \cos^2 A - \sin^2 B$.

ENGLISH LITERATURE.

WEDNESDAY, 1ST JUNE :—MORNING, 9 TO 10.30.

1. Make short notes on :—The Anglo-Saxon Chronicle, The Canterbury Tales, The Faerie Queen, Hudibras, Decline and Fall of the Roman Empire, In Memoriam. Give the name of the author and the date (or dates) of each work.

2. Give, with dates, some account of the literary life and labours of any *one* of the following: Francis Bacon, John Milton, Samuel Johnson, William Wordsworth,

3. Name (*a*) one great dramatist prior to Shakspere ; (*b*) one great dramatist contemporary with Shakspere ; (*c*) two famous novelists of the eighteenth century ; (*d*) two leading historians of the nineteenth century Give in each case the principal work of the writer selected.

4. Give, in outline, the events contained in any *one* act of King Richard II.

5. Explain the meaning of the italicised words in the following quotations:

(*a*) Away, *fond* woman !
(*b*) And thy abundant goodness shall excuse
This deadly blot in thy *digressing* son.
(*c*) The *chopping*-French we do not understand.
(*d* It is so hard to come as for a camel
To thread the *postern* of a needle's eye.
(*e*) *Spur.gall'd* and tired by *jauncing* Bolingbroke.

6. Write a short account (from the Lady of the Lake) of the preparing and despatching of the Fiery Cross, *or* of the Scottish sports described in the poem. Of the narratives chosen quote from live to ten lines deserving of notice on account of their poetical vigour , and give grounds for your selection.

7. Illustrate from The Lady of the Lake :—(*a*) Scottish superstitions, (*b*) Scottish national feeling, (*c*) Scott's power in describing persons or scenes.

BOTANY.

WEDNESDAY, JUNE 1ST :—MORNING, 10.30 TO 12.

1. Describe pollination and fertilization in a typical angiosperm.

2. Describe the chief modifications of stamens and pistils due to cohesion and adhesion.

3. Give a full account of the structure and development of an exogenous stem, and compare it with an endogenous stem.

4. Give a description of the structure and mode of reproduction of an Equisetum.

5. What are the chief plant foods ? Whence are they obtained ? What products are derived from them ?

6. Classify and-describe the accompanying specimen.

Examiners will please supply each candidate with a common wild-flower, taking pains that all parts of the plant are present.

OPTIONAL EXAMINATIONS.

WEDNESDAY, JUNE 1ST :—AFTERNOON, 3.30 TO 5.

I. LATIN GRAMMAR.

1. Write out the declension of *hostis noster, omnis fructus, acies triplex nnum iter, hoc ipsum tempus.*

2. Divide into syllables the following words: *deles, inutilis, dixit, iniquus, magnus,* marking the quantity of each vowel.

Distinguish veni, vēni; refert, rēfert; voces, vŏces.

3. Compare *facilis, multus, celer, prudens, felix.* Form adverbs from the preceding adjectives, and compare them.

4. Form and translate the present and future participles of *cogo, do, habeo.* Parse fully, adding principal, parts: *norint, sinas, edat, nolito, eamus, iussus, franget, ibimus, recti erunt.*

5. State and illustrate the construction used with *obliviscor, interest, potior, libet, coram, tenus, oportet, iubeo, cum* (temporal), *quamvis.*

6. Give three ways of expressing negative commands or prohibitions, and illustrate. Frame a rule for imperative expressions in indirect discourse.

II. LATIN PROSE COMPOSITION.

1. He strengthens the place with walls and trenches.

2. He will winter in Gaul with the rest of the legion and the cavalry.

3 There is no doubt they were influenced by this speech.

4. They did this to take away the hope of returning home.

5. On that day they all assembled on the bank of the Rhine.

6. If you wish anything, return on the Ides of April.

7. Was not Dumnorix friendly to the Helvetians?

8. When he had made a trial to see what his men could do in a cavalry skirmish, he found that they were not inferior to the enemy.

LATIN.

I. Caesar, Bks. I. and II. Virgil, Bk. I.

Wednesday, June 1st :—Afternoon, 2 to 3 30.

1. Translate :

(*a*) *Bello* Helvetiorum confecto totius fere Galliae legati, principes civitatum, ad Caesarem *gratulatum* convenerunt ; Intelligere sese, tametsi pro veteribus Helvetiorum iniuriis populi Romani ab his poenas bello *repetisset*, tamen eam rem non minus ex usu terrae Galliae quam populi Romani accidisse, propterea quod eo consilio florentissimis rebus domos suas Helvetii reliquissent, uti toti Galliae bellum inferrent imperioque potirentur locumque domicilio ex magna copia deligerent, quem ex omni Gallia opportunissimum ac fructuosissimum *iudicassent*, reliquasque civitates stipendiarias *haberent*.   Caesar, Bk. I.

(*b*) Ac primo adventu exercitus nostri crebras ex oppido excursiones faciebant parvulisque proeliis cum nostris contendebant: postea vallo pedum duodecim, in circuitu quindecim millium, crebrisque *castellis* circummuniti oppido sese continebant. Ubi vincis actis, aggere exstructo, turrim procul constitui viderunt, primum *irridere* ex muro atque increpitare vocibus, quod tanta machinatio ab tanto spatio instrueretur: Quibusnam manibus aut quibus viribus, praesertim homines *tantulae staturae* (nam plerumque omnibus Gallis prae magnitudine corporum snorum, brevitas nostra *contemptui* est), tanti oneris turrim in muros sese collocare confiderent?   Caesar, Bk. II.

(*c*)   Talia flammato secum dea corde volutans,
Nimborum in patriam, loca feta furentibus *Austris*,
Aeoliam venit. Hic vasto rex Aeolus antro
Luctantes ventos tempestatesque sonoras
Imperio premit, ac vinclis et carcere frenat.
Illi indignantes magno cum murmure montis
Circum claustra fremunt; celsa sedet Aeolus *arce*
Sceptra tenens, mollitque animos, et temperat iras,
Ni *faciat*, maria ac terras caelumque profundum
Quippe ferant rapidi secum verrantque per auras.

(*d*)   Hic regina gravem gemmis auroque poposcit
Implevitque mero pateram, quam Belus et omnes
A Belo soliti ; tum facta silentia tectis :
" Jupiter, hospitibus nam te dare iura loquuntur,
Hunc laetum Tyriisque diem Troiaque profectis
Esse velis, nostrosque huius meminisse minores.
Adsit laetitiae Bacchus dator, et bona Juno.
Et voc, o, coetum, Tyrii, celebrate faventes."

2. Explain (a) the case of *bello, castellis, staturae, contemptui, Austris, arce*: (b) the mood and tense of *repetisset, iudicassent, haberent, irridere faciat, adsit ;* (c) the construction of *gratulatum.*

3. Write a brief note on the meaning or construction of the following words and phrases : vinea ; a. d. V. Kal. Apr. ; equo admisso ; pro Helvetiorum iniuriis populi Romani ; civitate donatus erat ; hominum milia expedita ; adverso colle ; urbem Patavi ; Mavortia moenia ; belli portae ; nimbosus Orion.

II. TRANSLATION AT SIGHT.

(a) Capella (*she-goat*), stans in tecto domus, lupum vidit praetereuntem et ludificavit. Sed lupus, "Non tu," inquit, "sed locus tuns, me ludificat."

Saepe locus et tempus homines timidos audaces reddit.

(b) Apud Xenophontem moriens Cyrus maior haec dicit: "Nolite arbitrari, o mei carissimi filii, me cum a vobis discessero, nusquam aut nullum fore. Nec enim, oum eram vobiscum, animum meum videbatis, sed eum esse in hoc corpore ex iis rebus quas gerebam intellegebatis. Eundem igitur esse creditote, etiam si nullum videbitis.

CHEMISTRY.

THURSDAY, JUNE 2ND .—MORNING, 9 TO 10.30.

Answer two questions from each group.

I.

1. Explain the distinction between elements and compounds. What is meant by the statement that the elements combine in definite weights?

2. How may Nitrogen be obtained from the air ? What are its properties ?

3. What takes place (a) when a piece of Sodium is thrown upon water, and (b) when steam is passed over heated iron ?

II.

1. What gas is evolved when Sal Ammoniac and Quicklime are mixed together ? Describe its properties.

2. How would you determine the proportions by weight of Oxygen and Hydrogen in Water ? Give a sketch of the apparatus that you would employ.

3. What takes place when an acid and a base are brought together? Illustrate by means of two equations.

III.

1. What solvents would you employ if you wished to dissolve (1) Silver, (2) Gold, (3) Iodine, (4) Sulphur?

2. How is Crude Petroleum treated in order to obtain from it an oil fit for household use?

3. Express by means of equations the chemical changes that take place (a) when Copper and Sulphuric Acid are heated together, (b) when Iron Sulphide is treated with dilute Sulphuric Acid.

PHYSICS.

THURSDAY, JUNE 2ND :—MORNING, 10.30 TO 12.

1. Explain carefully how a mercury barometer is made, and how it measures the atmospheric pressure.

If mercury and sulphuric acid are 13.6 and 1.84 times as heavy as water respectively, what height would a sulphuric acid barometer stand at, when the mercury barometer indicated 30 inches?

2. How would you proceed to find the specific gravity of a piece of platinum? Give reasons where necessary.

A piece of platinum, specific gravity 22.069, is dropped into a measuring glass containing water, and causes the water to rise from 24.3 to 28.7 cubic centimetres. What does the platinum weigh?

3. Describe and explain the action of an air pump.

4. How would you find experimentally the centre of gravity of an irregular flat board?

5. A steam crane lifts a weight of 10 tons through 3 feet vertically in 7 seconds. How many foot pounds of work does it perform? At what Horse Power is it working?

6. Illustrate the following terms by a brief description of *one ex-*periment for each : *conduction, convection, radiation* of heat.

7. Shew by a drawing, with brief explanation, the principle of the steam-engine.

GERMAN.

THURSDAY, JUNE 2ND :—AFTERNOON, 2 TO 3.30.

N.B.—Candidates from Ontario Schools may substitute No. 9 for No. 1 (a) and (b). Other candidates will omit No. 9.

1. Translate into English :—

(a) Das waren die Söjue zufrieden; der älteste wollte ein Huffschmied, der zweite ein Barbier, der dritte aber ein Fechtmeister werden. Darauf bestimmten sie eine Zeit, wann sie wieder nach Hanse kommen wollten, und zogen fort. Es traf sich auch, daß jeder einen tüchtigen Meister fand. Der Schmied mußte des Königs Pferde beschlagen. Der Barbier rasierte lauter vornehme Herren und meinte auch, das Haus wäre schon sein. Der Fecht-meister bekam manchen Hieb, biß aber die Zähne zusammen und ließ sich's nicht verdrießen, denn er dachte bei sich : „Fürchtest du dich vor einem Hiebe, so bekommst du das Haus nimmermehr."

(b) Auf dem seltsamsten Umweg kam ein deutscher Handwerksburfche in Amsterdam durch den Irrtum zur Wahrheit, und zu ihrer Erkenntnis. Denn als er in diese große und reiche Handelsstadt, voll prächtiger Häuser, und geschäftiger Menschen, gekommen war, fiel ihm sogleich ein großes und schönes Haus in die Augen, wie er auf seiner ganzen Wanderschaft von Düttlingen bis nach Amsterdam noch keines gesehen Jatte. Lange betrachtete er mit Verwunderung dies kostbare Gebäude, und die sechs Kamine auf dem Dach.

TRANSLATION AT SIGHT.

2. Translate into English :—

Ein Mann im Reiseanzug stand an der Schwelle und fragte, ob es hier das Wirtshaus zum Goldenen Adler sei. Auf das kurze Ja des Mädchens trat er ein, warf sein Plaid auf den Tisch, die Reisetasche daneben und ließ sich auf der Bank nieder, ohne den regenschweren Hut abzunehmen oder den Stuck aus den Händen zu lassen, als wolle er nach kurzer Raft wieder weg-gehen. Die Magd war vor ihm stehen geblieben und wartete, was er zu befehlen hätte. Er schien es aber ganz zu vergessen, daß noch jemand außer ihm im Zimmer war, lehnte den Kopf zurück gegen die Mauer und schloß die Augen So schwieg wieder alles in der Stube, und nur das Summen der Fliegen unterbrach dann und wann die Stille.

Endlich kam die Wirtin mit dem Essen herein; ein kleiner Bube trug ihr ein Licht nach, der Wirt erhob sich von der Ofenbank, gähnte und trat an den Tisch herun.

3. Translate into German :—

(a) Shall we be allowed to burn our exercises when we have done with them ? (b) What would you do with your money if you were rich ? (c) I like to hear the singer who sang in the concert yesterday. (d) The ship has sunk and the people who were on board have been drowned. (e) When our neighbours were at church, a thief entered the house and stole several hundred dollars. (f) The sick man lay seven weeks in the hospital, but he has now recovered. (g) This tree grows quickly ; it is at least four times as high as it was three years ago. (h) I wrote to my cousin a month ago, but the letter has not yet been answered. (i) The train for Montreal leaves at twelve o'clock at night. (j) My father could have sold his house last year, but now it is impossible.

4. Give the prepositions which govern, (a) the genitive only, (b) the dative and accusative, (c) the dative only, (d) the accusative only.

5. Decline in the singular and plural the German equivalent of *your good sister*.

6. Decline the following pronouns in the singular *etwas*, *Niemand, was, der* (relative).

7. The lake is broader than the river, but the sea is *broadest*. In the preceding sentence what form of the superlative do you employ ? Give reasons for your opinion.

8. Give the other two principal parts of the following verbs *fliehen, ziehen, zwingen, gehen, kommen, sehen, finden, gieszen werfen, nehmen, treffen, vergessen.*

9. Translate the accompanying passage from *Das kalte Herz.*

Translate into English :—

(a) So sprach der arglistige Michel, und die andern waren es zufrieden ; die einen, weil sie gerne nach Holland gezogen wären, es zu sehen, die andern des Geldes wegen. Nur ein einziger war redlich und mahnte sie ab, das Gut ihres Herrn der Gefahr auszusetzen oder ihn um den höheren Preis zu betrügen ; aber sie hörten nicht auf ihn und vergaßen seine Worte, aber der Holländer-Michel vergaß sie nicht. Sie fuhren auch mit dem Holz den Rhein hinab,

Michel leitete den Floß und brachte sie schnell bis nach Rotterdam. Dort bot man ihnen das Vierfache von dem früheren Preis; und besonders die ungeheueren Balken des Michel wurden mit schwerem Geld gezahlt.

(*b*) „Du dauerst mich, so schlecht Du auch bist," sprach das Männlein nach einigem Nachdenken. „Aber weil Dein Wunsch nicht töricht ist, so kann ich Dir wenigstens meine Hülfe nicht versagen. So höre. Dein Herz kannst Du mit keiner Gewalt mehr bekommen, wohl aber mit List, und es wird vielleicht nicht schwer halten; denn Michel bleibt doch nur der dumme Michel obgleich er sich ungemein klug dünkt. So gehe denn geraden, Weges zu ihm hin und thue, wie ich Dir heiße!"

PHYSICAL GEOGRAPHY.

THURSDAY, 2ND JUNE:—AFTERNOON, 3.30 TO 5.

1. Explain the following terms and the way in which they are used in this subject :—Meridian, Equator, Ecliptic, Isothermal, Halo.

2. Describe concisely the physical features and mineral wealth of the African continent.

3. Point out any special features of the South American continent especially those in which it resembles, and those in which it differs from the Northern half of the continent.

4. Explain the phenomena of the Trade Winds and of the Gulf Stream.

5. (*a*) Draw a map showing any two areas of shallow depression in the water system of the world, where a comparatively small upheaval would produce a land surface.

(*b*) Draw a rough section of the bed on which an Atlantic cable might be laid from Ireland to Nova Scotia.

6. Describe what is meant by the following terms : Archipelago, Coral Islands, Volcanoes, Geysers, Glaciers. Give an example of each.

7. (*a*) Describe with a map the basin of the St. Lawrence point out its unique features; and on a map of North America draw approximately a watershed line between that basin and that of the Mississippi.

(*b*) Note the chief physical features and properties of the Yukon basin.

GREEK.

GRAMMAR, SENTENCES, AND TRANSLATION AT SIGHT.

THURSDAY, JUNE 2ND :—MORNING, 9 TO 10.30.

1. Translate into Greek :—

(a) He spoke thus to the same soldiers.

(b) Many great cities are in that country.

(c) Cyrus, having marched ten parasangs, remained there three days.

(d) He led away all the Greeks into another country.

(e) Why do you not trust our general?

(f) Cyrus had a far more beautiful chariot than the Queen herself.

2. Give the aor. ind. mid. 2nd pers. sing. ; aor. imp. pass. 2nd pers. sing.; perf. inf. pass.; gen. sing. fem. perf. part. act. ; dat. plur. fem. aor. part. pass. ; dat. sing. mas. pres. part. act. of φιλέω, πλέκω, λαμβάνω, αἱρέω.

3. Give acc. and dat., sing. and plur., of βασιλεὺς, ναῦς, εὔθυνα, χώρα, λέων, νοῦς.

4. Give comparative and superlative of μέγας, μικρός πολύς, αἰσχρός, ταχύς.

5. With what cases are the following prepositions used, and with what meanings :—ἐπί, ὑπό, πρός, παρά.

6. Translate into English :—

ὁ δὲ Δημοσθένης, στρατηγὸς ὤν, παρεκάλεσε τοὺς λοχα- γοὺς καὶ ἐκέλευσε μηκέτι μένειν ἀλλὰ εὐθὺς τοὺς ἄνδρας εἰς τὴν τῶν πολεμίων ἄγειν. οἱ δὲ εἶπον ὅτι οὐ δέοι ἐκεῖ- θεν πορεύεσθαι πρὶν παραγένοιντο καὶ οἱ ἱππῆς. πολλῶν δὲ λόγων γιγνομένων, ἦλθέ τις ἀγγέλλων ὅτι τὰς πύλας καλουμένας, δι' ὧν ἐστιν ἡ ὁδὸς, καταλάβοιεν ἤδη οἱ πολέμιοι, ὥστε οὐκέτι ἂν δύναιντο διελθεῖν.

XENOPHON, ANABASIS, BOOK 1.

THURSDAY, JUNE 2ND :—MORNING, 10.30 TO 12.

1. Give the derivation and exact meaning of the word ἀνάβασις, also the date of the events related in this book.

2. Translate with notes on the construction of the words underlined :—

(a) ʽΩς μὲν στρατηγήσοντα ἐμὲ ταύτην τὴν στρατηγίαν μηδεὶς ὑμῶν λεγέτω· πολλὰ γὰρ ἐνορῶ δι' ἃ ἐμοὶ τοῦτο οὐ ποιητέον· ὡς δὲ τῷ ἀνδρὶ ὃν ἂν ἕλησθε πείσομαι ᾗ δυνατὸν μάλιστα, ἵνα εἰδῆτε ὅτι καὶ ἄρχεσθαι ἐπίσταμαι ὥς τις καὶ ἄλλος μάλιστα ἀνθρώπων.

(b) ῥίψαντες γὰρ τοὺς πορφυροῦς κάνδυς ὅπου ἔτυχεν ἕκαστος ἑστηκώς, ἵεντο ὥσπερ ἂν δράμοι τις περὶ νίκης καὶ μάλα κατὰ πρανοῦς γηλόφου, ἔχοντες τούτους τε τοὺς πολυτελεῖς χιτῶνας καὶ τὰς ποικίλας ἀναξυρίδας, ἔνιοι δὲ καὶ στρεπτοὺς περὶ τοῖς τραχήλοις καὶ ψέλια περὶ ταῖς χερσίν· εὐθὺς δὲ σὺν τούτοις εἰσπηδήσαντες εἰς τὸν πηλὸν θᾶττον ἢ ὥς τις ἂν ᾤετο μετεώρους ἐξεκόμισαν τὰς ἁμάξας.

(c) Κῦρος γὰρ ἔπεμπε βίκους οἴνου ἡμιδεεῖς πολλάκις ὁπότε πάνυ ἡδὺν λάβοι, λέγων ὅτι οὔπω δὴ πολλοῦ χρόνου τούτου ἡδίονι οἴνῳ ἐπιτύχοι· τοῦτον οὖν σοὶ ἔπεμψε καὶ δεῖταί σου τήμερον τοῦτον ἐκπιεῖν σὺν οἷς μάλιστα φιλεῖς.

3. In the above extracts parse fully λεγέτω, εἰδῆτε, ἕλησθε, χερσίν, θᾶττον, ᾤετο, ἡδίονι, ἐκπιεῖν, ἐπιτύχοι.

4. Explain the terms ἀγορὰ πλήθουσα, παρασάγγης, φάλαγξ, τάλαντον, ἅρματα δρεπανηφόρα, παιανίζειν.

5. Write brief notes on the following names :—Tissaphernes, Syennesis, Orontes, Miletus, Maeander, Thapsakos.

(N.B.—The answers to this paper are to be sent in separately from the answers to the Greek Grammar Paper.)

PRELIMINARY SUBJECTS.

GEOGRAPHY,

FRIDAY, 3RD JUNE :—AFTERNOON, 2 TO 3.

(N.B.—*Answer two questions only from each group.*)

I.

1. Draw a map of Cuba, showing the adjacent coasts and important islands.

2. What and where are : Manilla, Key West, Berber, Matanzas, Klondyke, Suez, Hong Kong, Dry Tortugas, Puget?

3. Explain: isthmus, isotherm, moraine, estuary, delta, geyser, plateau, meridian, tropic.

II.

4. Locate : Malta, Vancouver, Havanna, Khartoum, Carthagena, Bristol, Sunda, Nicaragua, Port Arthur.

5. Name the chief ocean currents, indicating the direction of each by drawing or otherwise.

6. Draw a map of Africa.

III.

7. Describe the motions of the earth. Which of these cause the seasons of the year.

8. Draw a map of Europe.
Show (1) the seas,
(2) the countries,
(3) ten rivers,
(5) ten important cities.

29

PRELIMINARY SUBJECTS.

NEW TESTAMENT HISTORY.

FRIDAY, JUNE 3RD :—AFTERNOON, 3 TO 4.

(N.B.—*Answer any two questions from each group.*)

I.

1. Describe (*a*) The visit of Mary to Elizabeth :
  (*b*) The visit of the Magi.

2. How often (*a*) was Our Saviour brought to the Temple ?
  (*b*) Did He go of His own accord ?
  (*c*) Relate briefly the circumstances connected with each of these visits.

3. (*a*) What do you understand by a Miracle ?
  (*b*) Why did our Lord use Parables ?
  (*c*) Name six parables peculiar to St. Matthew, six to St. Luke, and four miracles mentioned only by St. John.

II.

4. Describe as concisely as you can :
  (*a*) The Night Storm on the Lake ;
  (*b*) The Feeding of the 5,000.

5. Connect each of the following quotations with its context :
  "Receipt of custom," "My Father worketh hitherto, and I work," "I am the Resurrection and the Life," "Another Comforter," "That they all may be one," "What, could ye not watch with me one hour !" "Behold the Man," "I Thirst," "Lovest thou Me?" "Behold he prayeth."

6. Give all the New Testament proofs you can of Our Lord's Resurrection.

III.

7. Account for the appointment of
  (*a*) Matthias to the Apostolate ;
  (*b*) The Seven Deacons.
  (*c*) Sum up the acts of Philip the Deacon.

8. (*a*) Trace briefly the events leading up to St. Paul's visit to Athens.
  (*b*) What did he do there?
  (*c*) What success attended his efforts?

9. (*a*) Who were : Jairus, Timon, Dorcas, Sergius Paulus, Demetrius, Agabus, Lysias, Publius.
  (*b*) What happened at : Troas, Melita, Miletus, Syracuse, Myra.

WRITING.

FRIDAY, JUNE 3RD :—AFTERNOON. 4 TO 4.15.

1. Write your name in full, the name of your school, your age, and if you employ the vertical style of writing state how long you have done so.

2. Write all the letters of the alphabet in capitals, and the numerals from 1 to 20.

3. Write the following :—

Energy is never lost, but only changed in form, and whatever transformations take place, the sum total of kinetic energy and potential energy remains the same.

PHYSIOLOGY AND HYGIENE.

1. Name the principal organs of the thorax, state their relative positions and their functions.

2. State the situation of the following and name two functions connected with each :

Thyroid gland, Medulla oblongata, Liver, Parotid Gland, Pancreas.

3. Describe the structure of the eye, and briefly state the functions of the different parts.

4. Briefly name the functions of Skin, Tympanum, Synovial membrane, Mitral valve, Stomach, Cerebrum, Diaphragm, Spinal cord, Thoracic duct, Tongue.

5. "Plenty of fresh air," " Plenty of exercise," "Plenty of sunlight." Why are these essential in youth to perfect health ?

6. State the principal impurities likely to be met with in milk, meat water and vegetables respectively.

ORDINARY A. A.

OPTIONAL ARITHMETIC.

MONDAY, JUNE 6TH :—MORNING, 10.30 TO 12.

1 If 1 kilometre of ⅔ of a mile, how many turns will a wheel make in 20 miles.—The circumference of the wheel being 4 metres, 5 millimetres.

(a) Write down the table of weights in the metric system.

(b) State rules for finding the area of a circle, the volume of a sphere of the cylinder and of a cone.

2. What will be the cost of carpeting a room 48 ft long and 33 ft. 9 in. wide with carpet ·75 yds. wide, at 4s 6d a yard?

3. A rectangular plantation, whose width is 88 yards, contains 2½ acres, find the distance from corner to corner.

4. A rectangular cistern, 9 feet long, 5 ft. 4 in. wide, and 2 ft. 3 in. deep, is filled with liquid which weighs 2,520 pounds. How deep must a rectangular cistern be which will hold 3,850 pounds of the same liquid, its length being 8 feet and width 5 feet 6 inches?

5. Find the cube root of 28 to 4 places of decimals, without using logarithms.

6. Find the difference between : —

   (a) The Simple Interest,
   (b) The Banker's Discount,
   (c) The Compound Interest,
   (d) The True Discount,
on $1,000 for 2 years at 5 per cent.

   (e) A banker in discounting a bill due in 3 months at 4 per cent. charges $1,225 more than the true discount. Find the amount of the bill.

7. Given log 2 = ·301030.
         log 3 = ·477121.
   Find logarithms of 6, · ·6 , 5 , · 625.
         also log of 3808.

GEOMETRICAL AND FREEHAND DRAWING.

MONDAY, JUNE 6TH:—AFTERNOON, 2 TO 5.

1. Construct an equilateral triangle having an altitude of 1.5 in.

2. Find the straight line representing the cube of a line A, 0.75 in. in length, to the unit length 0.5 in.

3. From a point A one inch without the circumference of a circle of 0.75 in. radius, draw a tangent to the circle.

4. Describe a circle of one inch radius, touching a given circle of 2 in. radius externally, and also being tangent to a line which being produced passes 0.75 in. from the centre of the given circle.

5. C D, having a length of 2.5 in., is the axis of a parabola, and the ordinate at the point D is 1 in., construct the parabola.

6. Draw the internal epicycloid generated by a point in the circumference of a circle of 1 in. diameter, which rolls on a circumference of 3 in. diameter.

7. What do you understand by (*a*) Epitrochoidal curves; (*b*) an evolute?

8. Sketch freehand an example of Greek ornament.

9. Make a freehand drawing of the Early Gothic ornament before you. Enlarge it somewhat.

10. Make a freehand drawing of the base of a Roman Doric pillar, as it appears from your point of view.

N.B.—Question 7 is not compulsory but marks will be given for it. The first six questions cannot be answered without instruments (compasses and straight edge). Marks will not be given for the *freehand* questions 8, 9 and 10 if instruments are used in drawing them.

The object in question 10 is to be placed at a distance of four feet from the eye resting upon a surface 1.5 ft below the eye. The vertical face of the plinth, which is to the right of the candidate, is to make an angle of 06 ° with the line joining the eye to the centre of the object.

HISTORY.

A.

1. Sketch the Peloponnesian War.

2. Make brief but precise notes on : Sparta and Messenia, Hippias and Hipparchus, Artemisium, Mantinea, Egypt under the Ptolemies.

B.

3. Trace the struggle of patricians and plebeians down to 366 B.C.

4. Make brief but precise notes on : the Etruscans, the battle of the Metaurus, Caius Gracchus, the first Triumvirate, Actium.

C.

5. Write on (*a*) Early persecutions of the Christian Church.
 (*b*) The first three Crusades.
 (*c*) Frederick the Great.

6. Make brief but precise notes on : Theodosius, the Lombard Kingdom in Italy, the Treaty of Verdun, the Medici, Cortez, William the Silent Gustavus Adolphus, the Edict of Nantes, the Reign of Terror, Garibaldi

ENGLISH LANGUAGE.

TUESDAY, 7TH JUNE :—MORNING, 10.30 TO 12.30.

1. (a) Distinguish strong from weak verbs, and say whether the following are strong or weak : teach, chide, fight, sleep, feed, seek.

(b) Distinguish the gerund from the verbal noun, the present participle, and the infinitive with " to."

(c) Give the plurals of brother, cloth, die, fish, shot, genius, and distinguish the meanings of these plurals.

2. (a) What preposition does each of the following words take after it? Affinity, adapted change, convenient, dependent, differ.

(b) English prefixes are divided into separable and inseparable prefixes. Explain this and illustrate from both classes.

(c) What meaning does each of the following suffixes give to a word to which it is attached? Ard, croft, dom, en, hood, kin.

3. (a) Give the origin of the words : gospel, drench, domineer, vulgar, idiot, cicerone.

(b) What is a figure of speech? What is an allegory? Give examplee of metonymy, personification, synecdoche.

(c) What are Caesura, Spenserian Stanza, Sonnet?

4. (a) Into what periods would you divide the English language? Chacterize briefly each period.

(b) Give a brief account of the Latin contributions to our language at different times.

(c) Explain the presence of the double guttural ' gh ' in so many of our words.

Give three distinctive marks of Early English.

(d) Refer the following words to their period of introduction into the language : castra, candle, assize, beast, alligator, prow, realm, captive.

5. " Language then is fossil poetry," and " fossil history." Illustrate this from the following words:

Tribulation, daisy, Frank.

6. Write on " Degeneration " in the meaning of words, and illustrate your answer.

7. (a) Show, by our present language, what the relative positions of the Normans and the Saxons must have been after the conquest.

(b) During what periods of French history did the following words arise? Dragonnade, roué, lanterner, razzia, pétroleuse.

(c) Make a short note on the danger of etymologising on the strength of mere surface similarities of sound, and give an example of this.

8. (a) What are synonyms? how do they arise, and why is their study important ?

(b) Distinguish : Palliate and cloak, illegible and unreadable, boyish and puerile, " to blanch," and to " whiten," genuine and authentic.

ADVANCED A. A.

ADVANCED A. A.

1. Simplify :

$$\frac{x^3 - y^3}{x^2 - y^2 + \dfrac{2\,y_2}{1 + \dfrac{x+y}{x-y}}} \div \frac{4\,x^3 - 5\,x^2\,y + y^2\,x}{6\,x^3 - 6\,x^2\,y + 2\,x\,y^2 - 2\,y^3}.$$

2. Prove that $\dfrac{3\sqrt{2} - \sqrt{3}}{\sqrt{3} - \sqrt{\frac{1}{2}}} = \sqrt{6}.$

3. Divide $8\,x^{\frac{3}{2}} + y^{-\frac{3}{2}} - z + 6\,x^{\frac{1}{2}}\,y^{-\frac{1}{2}}\,z^{\frac{1}{3}}$ by $2\,x^{\frac{1}{2}} + y^{-\frac{1}{2}} - z^{\frac{1}{3}}.$

4. Resolve the following expressions into elementary factors :

   (a) $a^3\,x^2\,y + 27\,x^2\,y\,4.$

   (b) $6\,b^2 - 7\,b\,x - 3\,x^2.$

   (c) $x^4 + x^2\,y^2 + y^4.$

   (d) $x^9 + y^9.$

5. There are two bars of metal, the first containing 14 oz. of silver and 6 of tin, and the second containing 8 of silver and 12 of tin ; how much must be taken from each to form a bar of 20 oz. containing equal weights of silver and tin.

6. Find the last terms and the sum of (a) $7 + 5.\frac{4}{5} + 4\frac{3}{5}. + $ etc., to eleven terms and (b) $3 - 6 + 12 - $ etc., to nine terms.

7. Insert 4 harmonical means between 2 and 12.

8. In a " potato " race, 50 potatoes are placed in line on the track two and one half feet apart. How far will a runner travel who brings them one by one to a basket placed 4 feet from the first potato ?

9. Solve the following equations :

   (a) $\dfrac{x^2 + 3\,x + 2}{x + 1} - \dfrac{x^2 - x - 6}{x + 2} = \dfrac{5\,x}{2}.$

   (b) $\dfrac{1}{x} - \dfrac{1}{x - 3} = \dfrac{1}{6}.$

(c) $\begin{cases} \sqrt{x+y} + \sqrt[3]{x-y} = \sqrt{c}; \\ b\,(x--a) + a\,(b-y) = 0. \end{cases}$

(d). $x^2 + 3\,x + 3\,\sqrt{(x^2 + 3\,x - 2)} = 6.$

10. A number consists of two digits: the sum of the squares of the digits is equal to the number increased by the product of its digits, and if 36 be added to the number, the digits are reversed. Find the number.

FRENCH.

Lundi, 21 Mai:—De 3.30 à 5.30.

A.

1. Indiquer (a) la différence entre chaque et chacun. (b) quelles peuvent être les fonctions des mots *qui* et *que*. *Exemples.*

2. Comment se forme le pluriel des substantifs composés? Exemples.

3. Quel est l'emploi de *y* pronom? Exemples.

4. Donner les temps primitifs des verbes suivants: avoir, battre, courir, dire, falloir, haïr, joindre, mettre, naître, prendre, suivre, savoir.

5. Faire l'analyse grammaticale de la phrase suivante :
On ne se sent à son aise que là où l'on se sait à sa place (Daudet)

B.

Traduire les deux passages suivants :

LE SOLDAT DE MARATHON.

Ce n'était qu'un soldat obscur entre dix mille,
Quand on eut la victoire, il voulut, le premier
En porter la nouvelle à sa lointaine ville,
Et partit, fier coureur agitant un laurier.
Épuisé par sa course effrayante et sans trêve
Il mourut dès qu'il fut au terme du chemin.
Heureux qui peut de même, ayant atteint son rêve
Mourir la flamme au cœur et la palme à la main.

A. Renaud.

SOLITUDE.

Do you seek solitude ?   Go not to fields
Or pathless woods, or to the lonely shore,
Nor court the privacy seclusion yields
In some old house whose very ancient door
Proclaims the absence of intrusive guests.
Think not of desert waste, nor mountain height,
Nor tropic isle, nor where the eider ne-ts
In arctic silence, nor the sea-gull's flight
In voiceless azure. But for solitude
Perfect, unparalleled, abiding, deep,
When next you feel the solitary mood
Insistent, trust not even dreamless sleep—   •
When for true loneliness your soul entreats,
Come to New York, and walk these crowded streets.

JOHN H. BONER.

C.

Rédiger une lettre d'environ 100 mots sur le canevas suivant :—

René a terminé ses études primaires et va entrer au collège. Il
remercie son instituteur des bonnes leçons et des excellents préceptes
que celui-ci lui a donnés ; il ne les oubliera pas, etc.

D.

1. Remplacer les tirets par des mots qui conviennent au sens.

Soyons justes —— tout le monde.
La terre est fécondée —— le soleil.
Il n'est jamais —— tard pour bien faire.
L'agriculture et le commerce —— un peuple.
Le chameau reste plusieurs jours —— boire —— manger.
Les rivières sont —— —— qui marchent.

L'ivrognerie est un abîme si profond qu'on ne pent —— sortir ——
on —— est tombé.

Esaü —— —— droit d'aînesse —— ——.

2. Mettre les Infinitifs à un temps de l'Indicatif.

On déclarer la guerre. Aussistôt un souffle embrasé parcourir
le pays. Tons se croire en état de combattre, tous vouloir s'engager ;

on les *recevoir*, on les *enrôler*, ils *partir* pour la frontière. Les vieillards se *souvenir* de leurs exploits passés et les *redire* volontiers.

Les jeunes gens s'en *aller* et les mères *faire* des vœux pour eux. Elles mêmes *s'employer* et se *rendre* utiles de leur mieux.

E.

1. Traduire les expressions suivantes tirées du *Bourgeois Gentilhomme*.

Ce nous est une douce rente que ce monsieur. Jourdain avec les visions de noblesse et de galanterie qu'il est allé se mettre en tête. Des louanges toutes pures. Se trémousser. Tout beau ! Je le donne en six coups aux tailleurs les plus éclairés. Voilà ce que c'est que de se mettre en personne de qualité. Je te baillerai sur le nez. Tout à l'heure. On dirait qu'il est céans carême-prenant tous les jours. Ce maître d'armes vous tient bien au cœur. Notre accueil de ce matin t'a fait prendre la chèvre. Il n'y faut pas chercher tant de façons.

2. Quel travers de la société Molière critique-t-il dans le *Bourgeois Gentilhomme* ?

3. Faire un portrait de M. Jourdain et de Dorante (100 mots environ.

4. Faire une courte notice biographique de Lamartine.

5. Pourquoi Jeanne d'Arc fut-elle portée à prendre les armes en faveur de son roi ?

6. Décrire la mort de Jeanne d'Arc ; en indiquer les causes (150 mots environ).

Dater en toutes lettres.

GEOMETRY.

TUESDAY, MAY 31ST :—MORNING, 9 TO 12.

1. To bisect :
(a) A finite straight line.
(b) An arc of a circle.
(c) A triangle from the vertex.
(d) A triangle from any non-central point in a side.
(e) Any quadrilateral from an angular point.
(f) The area of a triangle by a parallel to the base.

2. Two triangles A, B, C and D, E, F, have the angles A and D equal, and the sides about angles B and E equal, prove that remaining angles C and F are either equal or supplementary.

3. To a given straight line to apply a parallelogram with a given angle and equal in area to given triangle.

4. To find a point H in the straight line AB,—

(a) So that rectangle AB, BH = square on AH.

(b) Find an external solution as well as the usual internal solution given in II. 11.

5. Prove universally that the angle in the same segment is the same.

6. Define the " angle of a segment " and " the angle in a segment," and granting that the angle a curve makes with another line is given by the tangent line of the curve at the point of crossing, prove that the angle in a segment added to the angle of the segment always makes a total of 2 right angles.

7. Describe a regular pentagon with its corners on a circle.

8. (a) Prove that the three perpendiculars drawn from angular points A, B, C of a triangle to the opposite sides respectively meet in one and the same point.

(b) Calling this point O (orthocentre). Prove that the circle bisecting OA, OB, OC also bisects the sides of the triangle and passes through the feet of the perpendiculars AD, BE, CF drawn from angular points. A, B, C to meet sides BC, CA, AB respectively.

9. AB, BC being two straight lines, find a 3rd proportional to them, also a mean proportional between them.

10. Equal equiangular parallelograms have the sides about the equal angles reciprocally proportional.

———

ENGLISH LITERATURE

FRIDAY, 3RD JUNE :—AFTERNOON, 2 TO 5.

1. Give some account of :—Beowulf, The Vision of Piers Plowman, The Hind and the Panther, An Essay on the Human Understanding, The Campaign, The Task, The Earthly Paradise.

2. What specially literary qualities are noticeable in the style of each of the following writers :—Edmund Spenser, Francis Bacon, Joseph Addison Alexander Pope, Robert Burns, Percy Bysshe Shelley ?

3. Write an outline account of the production of dramatic literature in England during the reign of Queen Elizabeth ; and state clearly the principal causes to which the rise and growth of this form of literature is usually ascribed.

4. State briefly what you know of the life and labours of William Shakspere; classify his dramatic works, with two leading examples in each kind; and explain why among English playwrights Shakspere indisputably holds the foremost place.

5. For what are the following writers remarkable? John Knox, Bishop Jewel, Roger Ascham, Philip Sidney, George Chapman.

6. Write an outline narrative of the events told in *either* Book I. *or* Book II. of Paradise Lost.

7. Illustrate fully, from the two books mentioned in Question (6), the following Miltonic characteristics·:

(*a*) Milton's power of discovering original and eminently poetic comparisons.

(*b*) The variety of Milton's learning.

(*c*) Peculiar use of words and constructions by Milton, with a view to definiteness or precision of meaning.

(*d*) The magnificence of sonorous effects, and the suggestiveness of sound in Milton's blank verse.

8. Quote ten successive verses from either book, descriptive of a personage or a place; and note carefully any peculiarities of scansion.

HISTORY.

FRIDAY, JUNE 3RD :—MORNING, 9 TO 12.

1. Give a list of all the Greek communities which played a part in the wars against Persia, and estimate the value of the service rendered by each.

2. State the causes and describe the events of the Syracusan Expedition.

3. Trace the downfall of the Roman Senate as an independent body.

4. How was the Roman world governed during the reigns of the first two emperors ? Write with a view to explaining the powers vested in the emperor, and the administration of the provinces.

5. Make brief but precise notes on : Histiaens, the policy of Aristides, the siege of Plataea, 429-27, the victories of Phormio, Melos, Cinnna, the Gladiators' War, resistance to Caesar after Pompey's death, Cicero's attack on Antony, Sejanus

6. Write what you know about the relations between Elizabeth and Mary Stuart.

7. By what means did Charles I. manage to rule without the help of parliament ?

8. Make brief but precise notes on : Latimer, the "Protestant Terror," Elizabeth and Ireland, Puritanism and Culture, Arminian, Bacou's Fall, the Spanish Marriage, the Grand Remonstrance, the Self-Denying Ordinance, Barebones Parliament.

BOTANY.

WEDNESDAY, JUNE 1ST :—MORNING, 9 TO 12.

1. Describe fully the structure of the seeds and the development of the embryos of Monocotyledons and Dicotyledons.

2. Give a description of the structure and mode of development of an exogenous stem.

3. State what you know of phyllocladia, cladophylla and phyllodia.

4. What are the chief modifications of the flower, arising through cohesion and adhesion ?

5. Describe the chief varieties of dichogamous flowers. What purpose are such modifications intended to serve ?

6. Give an account of those modifications of fruits and seeds which ensure wide distribution.

7. State what you know of reversion. Of what truth is reversion a proof?

8. Distinguish between the great groups of the vegetable kingdom.

9. Describe and classify specimen (1).

10. Describe and classify specimen (2).

Examiners will please supply each candidate with two specimens, the one belonging to the Pteridophytes, the other to the Spermaphytes. All parts of each plant must be present.